COST
ACCOUNTING

IRWIN SERIES IN UNDERGRADUATE ACCOUNTING

Anthony and Reece
Accounting Principles
Seventh Edition

Anthony and Reece
Accounting: Texts and Cases
Ninth Edition

Anthony and Young
Management Control in Nonprofit
Organizations
Fifth Edition

Barr and Morris
Short Audit Case
Sixth Edition

Bernstein
Financial Statement Analysis:
Theory, Application and
Interpretation
Fifth Edition

Bernstein and Maksy
Cases and Financial Statement
Analysis
Second Edition

**Boatsman, Griffin, Vickrey and
Williams**
Advanced Accounting
Seventh Edition

Boockholdt
Accounting Information Systems
Third Edition

Brownlee
Corporate Financial Reporting
Text and Cases
Second Edition

Dalton
1993 Individual Tax Return
Eighth Edition

Dalton
1993 Corporate Tax Return
Eighth Edition

Danos and Imhoff
Financial Accounting
Second Edition

Dyckman, Dukes and Davis
Intermediate Accounting
Revised Edition

Dyckman, Dukes and Davis
Intermediate Accounting
Standard Edition

Edwards, Hermanson and Maher
Principles of Financial and
Managerial Accounting
Revised Edition

Engler
Managerial Accounting
Third Edition

Engler and Bernstein
Advanced Accounting
Second Edition

Epstein and Spalding
The Accountant's Guide to Legal
Liability and Ethics

FASB 1993–1994 Edition
Current Text: General Standards
Current Text: Industry Standards
Original Pronouncements,
Volume I
Original Pronouncements,
Volume II
Financial Accounting Concepts

Ferris
Financial Accounting and Corporate
Reporting: A Casebook
Third Edition

Garrison and Noreen
Managerial Accounting
Seventh Edition

Hay and Engstrom
Governmental Accounting
Third Edition

Hay and Wilson
Accounting for Governmental and
Nonprofit Entities
Ninth Edition

Henriksen and Van Breda
Accounting Theory
Fifth Edition

Hermanson and Edwards
Financial Accounting
Fifth Edition

Hermanson, Edwards and Maher
Accounting Principles
Fifth Edition

**Hermanson, Turner, Plunkett
and Walker**
Computerized Accounting with
Peachtree

Hermanson, Strawser, and Strawser
Auditing Theory and Practice
Sixth Edition

Holt, Grinnaker and Broome
Principles Disk

Hopson and Meyer
Income Tax Fundamentals for
1993 Tax Returns,
1994 Edition

Hoyle
Advanced Accounting
Fourth Edition

Jesser
Integrated Accounting for
Microcomputers

Koerber
College Accounting
Revised Edition

Larson and Miller
Fundamental Accounting Principles
Thirteenth Edition

Larson and Miller
Financial Accounting
Fifth Edition

Larson, Spoede and Miller
Principles of Financial and
Managerial Accounting

Maher and Deakin
Cost Accounting
Fourth Edition

Marshall
A Survey of Accounting: What the
Numbers Mean
Second Edition

Miller and Redding
The FASB: The People, the
Process and the Politics
Third Edition

Mueller, Gernon and Meek
International Accounting
Third Edition

Pany and Whittington
Auditing

Pratt and Kulsrud
Individual Taxation
1995 Edition

Pratt and Kulsrud
Corporate, Partnership, Estate and
Gift Taxation
1995 Edition

Pratt and Kulsrud
Federal Taxation
1995 Edition

Rayburn
Cost Accounting: Using a Cost
Management Approach
Fifth Edition

Robertson
Auditing
Seventh Edition

Schroeder and Zlatkovich
Survey of Accounting

Short
Fundamentals of Financial
Accounting
Seventh Edition

Smith and Wiggins
Readings and Problems in
Accounting Information Systems

Whittington, Pany, Meigs and Meigs
Principles of Auditing
Tenth Edition

COST ACCOUNTING

Fourth Edition

Michael W. Maher
The University of California at Davis

Edward B. Deakin
The University of Texas at Austin

IRWIN
Burr Ridge, Illinois
Boston, Massachusetts
Sydney, Australia

The previous editions of this text were published under the authorship of Deakin and Maher.

Cover photograph: © Jeff Goldberg/Esto

Senior sponsoring editor: Ron M. Regis
Developmental editor: Cheryl D. Wilson
Marketing manager: Cindy L. Ledwith
Project editor: Waivah Clement
Production manager: Ann Cassady
Cover/Interior designer: · Maureen McCutcheon
Art coordinator: Mark Malloy
Art studio: ElectroGraphics, Inc.
Compositor: Better Graphics, Inc.
Typeface: 10/12 Times Roman
Printer: Von Hoffmann Press, Inc.

Library of Congress Cataloging-in-Publication Data

Maher, Michael, date
    Cost accounting / Michael W. Maher, Edward B. Deakin.—4th ed.
        p.   cm.
    Deakin's name appears first on the earlier editions.
    Includes bibliographical references and index.
    ISBN 0-256-11657-1
    1. Cost accounting.   I. Deakin, Edward B.   II. Title.
HF5686.C8D24   1994
    658.15′52—dc20   93–9616

Printed in the United States of America
1 2 3 4 5 6 7 8 9 0 VH 0 9 8 7 6 5 4 3

Dedicated to Edward B. Deakin, who passed away during the revision of the fourth edition of Cost Accounting. *His tremendous energy and valuable contributions are reflected in this and prior editions. He will be missed by his family, friends, and colleagues.*

According to the noted management guru Peter Drucker, "Accounting has become the most intellectually challenging area in the field of management, and the most turbulent one."[1] The competitive challenges facing businesses are changing rapidly. Cost accounting methods must respond accordingly. Our students face a world that requires not only a sound understanding of cost accounting concepts, but also innovative and responsive applications of those concepts. As teachers, we dedicate this book to helping students learn how to make cost accounting work for them.

This 4th edition of *Cost Accounting* has been thoroughly revised and updated to reflect changes in the field. It includes new chapters reflecting innovative changes in cost accounting and a unique chapter on ethical issues facing accountants and managers. These two topics are completely integrated throughout the book. These changes not only bring this book up to date in coverage of activity-based costing, accounting for quality, "lean" production, and other characteristics of the new production environment, but they also make this book a leader in discussing ethical issues facing managers and accountants.

BUILDING ON TRADITIONAL STRENGTHS

Reviewers of this edition and users of previous editions have consistently noted the following as strengths of this book:

- Presents the material in a way that's interesting and clear to students.
- Provides a logical sequence of chapters with flexibility that allows instructors to rearrange chapters to suit their needs.
- Focuses students' attention on the big picture.

- Emphasizes critical thinking and "learning to learn."
- Emphasizes use of cost accounting as a managerial tool.
- Provides excellent pedagogical aids, including exercises keyed to learning objectives, definitions of key terms in the margins, and self-study questions with fully worked out solutions.
- Provides a variety of assignment materials, including simple exercises, more challenging problems, and thought-provoking cases.

Using numerous reviews and extensive class testing, we have thoroughly revised this edition to enhance these strengths and improve the text. We have rewritten chapters to improve the exposition and worked and reworked assignment materials to make them more clear. We have made additional improvements in the organization of the book by rearranging topics within chapters and by rearranging certain chapters in the first part of the book as described in detail in the next section. By adding more real company references and illustrations, we have placed cost accounting problems into a broader business context and made the material more relevant for students.

We have given this edition a stronger managerial focus by increasing our emphasis on product costing for managerial decision making and decreasing our emphasis on product costing for inventory valuation. Users of the previous edition commented that this book helps students develop "learning to learn" skills. We hope so, and we have continued that theme in this edition. To help students learn how to think about cost accounting problems, we have added more "critical thought" assignments and more opportunities for students to write reports to management explaining their analyses.

---

[1] P. Drucker, "Be Data Literate—Know What to Know," *The Wall Street Journal,* December 1, 1992, p. A16.

ORGANIZATION AND USE OF THE BOOK

This book is intended to be used in a cost or managerial accounting course in which students have had a course in accounting principles or financial accounting. This prerequisite assures that students understand basic accounting terminology and the financial reporting system. *It is not necessary that students had a previous course in managerial or cost accounting.*

Users of the book should have a knowledge of elementary algebra. Although previous coursework in statistics, operations research, computer sciences, and other similar disciplines is not required, such work can enrich the students' experience with this book.

There is ample material in the text to challenge students who have had a previous course in managerial accounting. Chapters 4–9, 13–16, and 20–26 cover topics that are only introduced or not covered at all in managerial accounting courses. The material in chapter appendixes and the longer problems and integrative cases in the book are designed to challenge students who have had at least one course in managerial accounting.

This book can be used in either undergraduate or graduate courses. Most instructors emphasize exercises and short problems in undergraduate courses; MBA instructors generally use longer problems and cases.

Cost accounting covers three major topic areas: (1) product costing and cost accounting systems (e.g., process costing, job costing), (2) costing for nonroutine decision making (e.g., pricing decisions, capital investment decisions), and (3) the use of cost data in planning and performance evaluation (e.g., budgeting, variance analysis). The chapters in this book are grouped into these three major topic modules as follows:

Part One of the text, Chapters 1–9, contains a comprehensive discussion of *cost accounting systems and product costing,* including the flow of costs, job and process costing, just-in-time, activity-based costing, cost allocation, and variable costing.

Part Two of the text, Chapters 10–16, addresses the use of *differential costs for decision making.* Here, the focus is on the role of the accountant as a supplier of cost data for use in making decisions. This part includes cost estimation, cost-volume-profit analysis, differential costing for short- and long-run decisions, and capital investment analysis. This approach shows why differential cost concepts are important, how to identify costs that are differential, and how to use those differential costs in decisions.

Part Three, Chapters 17–23, addresses the use of *cost data for performance evaluation and control.* In this section, the budget as the operating plan is presented. We also analyze budget versus actual results, flexible budgets, variance analysis, and standard costs. Performance evaluation in decentralized organizations is also discussed in this part of the text.

Chapters 24–26, Part Four, deal with special topics. Chapter 24 covers management ethics and financial fraud and can be covered anywhere in the book as long as students have some basic accounting background (e.g., principles of accounting). Chapter 25 covers variance investigation for quality control, and Chapter 26 deals with uncertainty.

An advantage of grouping topics into these categories is that it overcomes students' negative reactions to the lack of cohesion if similar topics are scattered throughout the book. It also allows instructors to cover topics in a logical sequence without skipping around the book.

At the same time, it is important that instructors have the flexibility to adapt the text to their particular curriculum, students, and personal preferences. We have built flexibility into this text in two ways. First, some instructors prefer to cover major topic areas in a different sequence than presented in this book. For example, some instructors prefer to cover decision-making topics or planning and control topics before covering cost accounting systems. This book is designed so that any major part, or "module," can be covered after Chapter 2, which presents all of the background concepts necessary for continuing to any of the three major topic modules. Adopters have used the book in class with each of the following sequences of the three major parts:

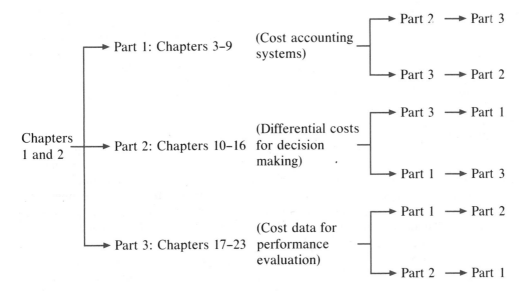

Second, chapters are self-contained. Therefore, instructors can skip chapters or rearrange the sequence of chapters. Adopters of previous editions were able to skip chapters or change the sequence as appropriate. We have put special emphasis on making this easier in the present edition. End-of-chapter materials that cover topics from more than one chapter (e.g., integrative cases) are clearly labeled to facilitate flexibility.

IMPORTANT CHANGES IN THIS EDITION

In keeping with the many changes in cost accounting in the past several years, we have revised this edition more extensively than any other since this book was first written.

Substantially Increased Coverage of Recent Developments in the Field

Throughout the book, we emphasize the importance of quality management, activity management, and a lean production environment using just-in-time.

New chapter on activity-based costing. This new chapter on activity-based costing (Chapter 7) takes a management orientation to activity management and product costing using ABC. Topics include the cost-benefit implications of ABC versus other costing methods, implementing ABC, strategic opportunities provided by ABC, impact of ABC on product costs and cost flows through accounts, use

of ABC to eliminate non-value-added costs, use of ABC in marketing, and opportunities to improve ABC in practice.

New chapter on operations costing, just-in-time methods/backflush costing, and spoilage. This new chapter (Chapter 5) features operations costing as a method with characteristics of both job and process costing, giving it a logical placement just after the job and process costing chapters. It also covers backflush costing in a just-in-time setting, and how alternative methods of accounting for spoilage affect management's attempts to improve quality. The assignment materials in this chapter have been organized and labeled so instructors can easily assign portions of this chapter while skipping other parts if they wish.

Integrated materials on activity-based costing throughout the book. Chapter 10 discusses the use of regression to develop cost drivers and Chapter 19 explains the use of activity-based costing in standard costing and variance analysis, for example.

Integrated discussions of the new production environment throughout the book. This edition has increased coverage of quality, starting with Chapter 1 and including use of activity-based costing to identify costs of quality (Chapter 7), a substantial coverage of the cost advantages of quality (Chapter 12), and a discussion of nonfinancial performance measures to assess quality (Chapter 19). We discuss the use of just-in-time methods in standard costing and variance analysis (Chapter 20), and we put variance investigation into a total quality context (Chapter 25).

Additional Real World Illustrations

Students are more highly motivated to learn the material if they see its application to real world problems, particularly ones they believe they will face. An earlier edition of this book pioneered the use of "Real World Applications" as short illustrations of actual company experiences. These applications are like sidebars in news magazines; they allow the student to explore company practices that illustrate concepts discussed in the text without disrupting its flow. Students often remember these real company illustrations long after classes are over.

This edition better incorporates these illustrations. For example, in Chapter 1, we tie our discussion of ethical issues in accounting into the Real World Application that discusses Johnson & Johnson's corporate code of conduct. The Real World Application in Chapter 3 describes how a company executive used the basic cost flow model (described in that chapter) to detect the fraudulent activities of a division manager. And Chapter 4's discussion of process costing ties to the Real World Application that discusses the production canning process for Coca–Cola®. Nearly all chapters have one or more assignment questions that require students to evaluate the practices described in the Real World Applications.

In addition, we have substantially increased the number of references to real companies and descriptions of their practices. Chapter 3 uses the Nissan plant near Memphis, Tennessee, to demonstrate the nature of an operation for example. Several chapters describe the impact of the new production environment on Hewlett-Packard, including the impact of just-in-time methods and HP's development of activity-based costing in several chapters. Chapter 12 includes the Texas Instruments cost of quality program in our discussion of quality.

The Company Index at the end of this book lists the names of the organizations discussed in this book. Looking at this list, you will see a broad range of organizations including retail, service, university and professional athletic programs, the U.S. Army, airlines, and numerous others. In addition, many chapters use examples drawn from real companies that prefer to remain anonymous but have provided us with interesting examples. The Unique Denims example in Chapter 2, which is based on a real jeans manufacturer, is one such example.

Increased Managerial Orientation

Many of our colleagues among accounting faculty and the Accounting Education Change Commission and many in the business community and the accounting profession believe that accounting students should approach problems more as business problems and less as pure accounting problems. To this end, we have strengthened the managerial orientation in both the text and assignment materials.

We have added a managerial decision context to many assignment items that were purely computational in previous editions. In Chapters 1–9, we have increased the emphasis on product costing and cost management for decision making and reduced the emphasis on costing for inventory values in external financial statements. The new chapter on activity-based costing (Chapter 7) focuses on managers' problems in managing activities and includes a discussion of strategic uses of ABC. We have increased the critical thought requirements that require students to explain their analyses to management.

New Material on Ethical Issues in Accounting That Affect Managers and Accountants

Reviewers of our previous edition would like to have seen greater coverage of ethical issues. Our students are facing a future of increasing concern about accountability of accountants and managers for their actions. While we do not believe we can "teach" people to be ethical, we can present examples of situations faced by people who have careers like those our students aspire to. These discussions primarily focus on cost accounting issues, but inevitably, they also include discussions about organizational and managerial issues, corporate accountability, the role of internal and external auditors, and societal expectations for accountability. Our approach is not "preachy"; instead, we point out the difficult situations our students are likely to encounter and the hard choices they will probably have to make during their careers.

Here is a sample of the new items on ethics in this edition:

New chapter on management ethics and financial fraud. This new chapter (Chapter 24) is a stand-alone chapter that can be assigned anywhere in the book. It discusses actual financial fraud situations and discusses ways to prevent and detect fraud. We take the students through these situations, making it clear that ordinary people like our students themselves can become entangled in ethical dilemmas involving managerial and cost accounting. This chapter also provides students with a conceptual framework for evaluating situations conducive to fraud, including concepts drawn from work by the Treadway Commission. The assignment material has been thoroughly class-tested and found to be very interesting to all levels of students.

Ethics integrated into chapters throughout the book. Starting with a discussion of the ethical choices faced by managers, Chapter 1 includes a discussion of the Johnson & Johnson approach to ethical issues and discusses the Institute of Management Accountants code of ethical conduct. Some examples of chapter-by-chapter discussions include improperly assigning costs to jobs in Chapter 3, whether it's ethical to increase production solely to increase profits using full-absorption costing in Chapter 9, overstating the benefits of capital investment projects in Chapter 15, providing incorrect information in budgeting in Chapter 17, and using questionable revenue recording practices to meet performance targets in Chapter 18. We include assignment materials on ethics, including material from the CMA examination.

Reorganization

We have substantially reorganized Chapters 2–8, which discuss product costing and cost systems. The new organization has Chapters 3, 4, and 5 on product costing in alternative production environments (i.e., jobs, processes, operations, and just-in-time). Placing three chapters dealing with product costing in different production environments together enables instructors to compare and contrast production settings and the impact of different production methods on costing. Instructors also are able to demonstrate the common principles of product costing in all production environments. Chapters 6, 7, and 8 cover cost allocation and activity-based costing (ABC). These three chapters provide more detailed costing and activity management concepts. By placing these chapters together, instructors can show similarities of cost allocation methods and demonstrate important differences, such as the activity-based management concept that underlies ABC versus the more traditional thinking in allocating department costs.

Flexibility. The three chapters on product costing precede the three chapters on cost allocation and ABC, so students first see the "big picture" of product costing before going into the more detailed cost allocation and ABC. Instructors who prefer to cover cost allocation first can easily do so by covering one or all of Chapters 6, 7, and 8 before covering Chapters 3, 4, and 5. Instructors can skip job and process costing (Chapters 3 and 4) before covering operations costing and the effect of just-in-time (Chapter 5) if the students have some familiarity with jobs and processes from a previous course, or if the instructor assigns the first few pages of Chapter 3, which provides an overview of jobs, processes, and operations.

This new organization combines chapters that duplicated materials from the previous edition. Chapters 3 and 7 in the previous edition were repetitive and have been combined into one chapter on job costing, Chapter 3. By carefully editing and rewriting, we have made the new Chapter 3 a little simpler than the job costing chapter in the previous edition. We simplified the chapter on process costing, which is now Chapter 4, by eliminating some superfluous materials at the beginning of the chapter, rearranging topics so the easier average-costing method precedes the FIFO method, and moving the discussion of spoilage out of this chapter into Chapter 5. The text of this revised chapter is about 40 percent shorter than the text of the process costing chapter in the previous edition. Even so, we have expanded our discussion of process costing issues, particularly of spoilage, by moving spoilage to a separate chapter. By rewriting and eliminating repetitive materials, we combined the two chapters on department cost allocation (one of which was quite short) into one chapter in this edition.

If students have had a principles or managerial accounting course that covered job costing and process costing, then those chapters can be skipped (or only the FIFO portion of the process costing chapter assigned). If students have had basic cost allocation but not ABC, then Chapter 6 on cost allocation to departments can be skipped. Instructors may wish to assign certain sections of Chapter 5, because it covers three topics: operations costing, just-in-time/backflush costing, and spoilage/quality issues. The assignment material is organized by topic to make it easy to assign any one of the three sections without assigning the others.

Special topics. The previous edition of this book had two chapters on decision making under uncertainty (Chapters 24 and 26), which overlapped. We have eliminated some of the material and combined the other discussions in these two chapters to create one chapter on decision making under uncertainty, which is the last chapter in this edition (Chapter 26). We have added a new chapter on managerial ethics and financial fraud (Chapter 24), which is a stand-alone chapter that could be assigned at any time in the course.

Improved Pedagogy

Revised assignment materials. We have thoroughly revised the assignment materials and prepared a lot of new material. Virtually all of the exercises are new or substantially revised from the previous edition. We have written new problems and revised others as needed to improve them.

Self-study questions. We want this book to be as user-friendly and interactive as possible. To that end, we have changed our approach to self-study questions by placing them throughout the chapter instead of at the end. As in previous editions, we provide fully worked out solutions to the self-study questions. In this edition, these solutions are at the end of each chapter after the assignment material.

In our experience, students often do not work the self-study questions when they are placed at the end of the chapter. By making these questions shorter and placing them immediately after the topic in the text, students get immediate feedback about their understanding, and they find it less intimidating to work one short self-study question right after they have covered the material than to work several at the end of the chapter. We encourage instructors to recommend or even require their students to answer the self-study questions as they read the chapter.

Expanded learning objectives. We have expanded the learning objectives in each chapter. As in the previous edition, exercises in the assignment materials are keyed to learning objectives so instructors can assign exercises based on the learning objectives they want to emphasize.

Relevance to students. We have increased the use of real world examples and references to real companies in the chapter introductions to capture the student's interest in the material at the outset. Our fellow teachers tell us they agree with our experiences in the classroom—if we start with an example that is relevant to students, then we have a good opportunity to help them learn. The same holds for textbooks. We have endeavored to refer to companies that students will recognize because of their products or frequent appearance in the media. We recognize that most students understand the workings of bicycle shops, pizza restaurants, landscaping, and other small businesses better than Fortune 500 companies, so we orient our assignment materials to these smaller organizations.

Definitions of key concepts in margins. Key concepts are defined both in the text and in chapter margins. This enables students to easily identify and review key concepts. The book also has a complete glossary.

Rewriting and editing. The reviewers provided particularly good feedback on the previous edition and early drafts of this edition. In addition, we extensively class-tested this book at both of our universities. This book has had a good reputation for readability, but we believe this edition is considerably better because of the quality of the reviews and the extensive class-testing. We have eliminated long sentences and paragraphs, simplified difficult concepts, improved the clarity of assignment materials, and actively engaged the student more in the discussion of concepts and examples.

Chapter by Chapter Changes

We have made extensive changes in this edition. Many of these changes involve the new material on the new production environment and on ethical issues, but that is not all. Every chapter has been rewritten to eliminate long passages, to clarify difficult concepts, and to improve the quality of the assignment materials. The following list highlights major changes in each chapter.

Chapter 1, "Cost Accounting: Its Nature and Usefulness"

- Added a section that stresses the importance of interactive learning, such as that provided by the self-study and assignment materials.
- Added new sections on the new production environment, including the emphasis on quality, lean production, and activity-based costing.
- Expanded discussion of ethical issues, including a new Real World Application about the Johnson & Johnson approach to corporate conduct.

Chapter 2, "Cost Concepts and Behavior"

- Added discussion of cost drivers.
- Moved discussion of activity-based costing to Chapter 7.
- Added mixed and semifixed costs to the cost behavior discussion.
- Made the discussion of product cost buildup consistent with an income statement format with variable manufacturing costs at the top and fixed marketing and administrative costs at the bottom.

Chapter 3, "Job Costing"

- Combined Chapters 3 and 7 in the previous edition to simplify presentation.
- Expanded coverage of the effect of alternative production methods on cost accounting to include operations.
- Incorporated predetermined overhead rates as part of the job costing example and discussed normal costing before actual costing.
- Increased coverage of perpetual versus periodic inventory, including a new Real World Application about a company using the basic cost flow model to detect financial fraud.
- Added a Real World Application of job costing problems for movies.
- Eliminated discussion of cost flows in merchandising, which was redundant with coverage in financial accounting and the financial accounting portion of principles courses.
- Added ethical issues involving cost overruns in job costing.

Chapter 4, "Process Costing"

- Moved process costing from Chapter 8 to follow job costing.
- Considerably shortened and simplified the discussion of equivalent units.
- Rearranged the chapter so the simpler weighted-average method precedes the FIFO method.
- Added a Real World Application describing the canning production cycle for Coca-Cola®[2] and related the material to the discussion of process costing.
- Completely rewrote "Accounting for Process Costs" for both weighted-average and FIFO methods to simplify and clarify the ideas.
- Moved the discussion of spoilage to Chapter 5 where it has been expanded and put in the context of initiatives for quality improvement.

Chapter 5, "Accounting for Operations, Just-in-Time Production, and Spoilage"

- Added operations costing, using an example from a motorcycle plant.
- Moved just-in-time coverage from Chapter 14 to Chapter 5 to emphasize its importance.
- Expanded coverage of backflush costing in a just-in-time setting, using Hewlett-Packard's experience to illustrate key issues in applications.
- Added Real World Application illustrating problems with just-in-time for helicopter parts in the Persian Gulf War and at Saturn Corporation when a strike shut down the Lordstown plant.
- Moved discussion of spoilage from the process costing chapter and expanded coverage.
- Added section on reworked products and discussed two methods of accounting for rework.
- Added discussion about how accounting for spoilage affects attempts to improve quality.

Chapter 6, "Allocating Costs to Departments"

- Introduced the chapter with a classic discussion between a small business owner and his consultant to demonstrate inherently controversial aspects of cost allocation.
- Combined material from Chapters 4 and 5 in the previous edition into this chapter by moving the discussion of basic cost allocation concepts and

---

[2] Registered trademark of the Coca-Cola Company.

choice of allocation bases (cost drivers) from Chapter 4 in the previous edition and the discussion of direct, step, and reciprocal methods from Chapter 5 in the previous edition.

- Added discussion of ethical issues arising from the inherent arbitrariness of cost allocation.

Chapter 7, "Cost Allocation to Products; Activity-Based Costing"

- New chapter reflects authors' views that activity-based costing provides an important new *concept* of management; however, many of the accounting applications in practice are simply more detailed extensions of traditional methods.
- Major features include:
  + Introduction has company managers discussing how the company's accounting system is not providing the information needed for the company to remain competitive.
  + Comparison of plantwide and department allocation to ABC, including cost-benefit considerations.
  + Description of the steps involved, including identifying activity centers and cost drivers and assigning costs to products.
  + Demonstration of cost flows through accounts.
  + Use of ABC to eliminate non-value-added costs.
  + Use of ABC in analyzing marketing costs.
  + Strategic opportunities with ABC.
  + Real World Application discussing new ways to use ABC in managing health care costs.
  + Discussion of opportunities to improve ABC in practice, including the hierarchy of costs approach proposed by Cooper and Kaplan.

Chapter 8, "Allocating Joint Costs"

- Moved joint costing from Chapter 6 in the previous edition to Chapter 8 in this edition so joint costing would follow process and operation costing, and so it would follow department allocation and ABC which discuss basic cost allocation concepts.
- Expanded discussion of by-product costing.
- Added Real World Application dealing with Union Pacific's use of ABC in joint costing.

Chapter 9, "Variable Costing"

- Expanded discussion of the contribution margin format and compared it to the traditional format of the income statement.
- Added discussion of ethical issues involving an actual situation in which a division manager in-

creased production to increase profits, using full-absorption costing.

Chapter 10, "Cost Estimation"

- Simplified and clarified discussion of regression.
- Added section on the use of regression to identify cost drivers for ABC.
- Added Real World Application discussing empirical research, using regression to identify overhead cost drivers.

Chapter 11, "Cost-Volume-Profit Analysis"

- Simplified and clarified discussion, particularly simplifying the formulas.
- Added illustration summarizing target volume and break-even formulas.
- Demonstrated how computer spreadsheets are used in cost-volume-profit analysis.
- Added Real World Application analyzing the use of break-even analysis for a management education seminar.

Chapter 12, "Differential Cost Analysis"

- Added section on using differential cost analysis for quality improvements.
- Included discussion of the Texas Instruments cost of quality program and the limitations of accounting in measuring the cost of poor quality products purchased by customers.

Chapter 14, "Inventory Management Costs"

- Moved backflush costing discussion to Chapter 5, where it has been expanded. Kept a short discussion of just-in-time methods in this chapter.
- Added Real World Application describing how the use of just-in-time by a Japanese parent company placed considerable financial hardship on its U.S. distribution subsidiary.

Chapter 15, "Capital Investment Cash Flows"

- Added discussion on problems with applications of discounted cash flow models when investing in improved technology.
- Added discussion of ethical issues in overstating the benefits of proposed projects based on an actual situation.

Chapter 17, "The Master Budget"

- Added illustrations of the production budget, direct materials budget, direct labor budget, cash collections and cash disbursements budgets, and purchases budget.

- Added discussion of ethical issues in budgeting and Real World Application analyzing the way General Electric deals with employee problems arising from the company's expectations for both high performance and ethical behavior.
- Added discussion of the use of spreadsheets in budgeting.

Chapter 18, "Using the Budget for Performance Evaluation and Control"

- Simplified discussion of the case when units produced do not equal units sold.
- Expanded discussion of responsibility centers, particularly profit and cost centers. Assignment exercises demonstrate difficulties in assigning responsibility for joint actions.
- Added discussion of the conflict between pressure to perform and ethical behavior, using actual events at Comserv and Ronson Corporation and included Real World Application of the financial fraud at MiniScribe.

Chapter 19, "Production Cost Variances"

- Demonstrated how the use of ABC affects the way variances are calculated and analyzed.
- Added section on nonfinancial performance measures emphasizing nonfinancial quality and non-value-added costs.
- Added Real World Application comparing the way the NUMMI plant developed standards using top-down methods in the past compared to the worker-determined standards under the new GM-Toyota joint venture.

Chapter 22, "Decentralization and Performance Evaluation"

- Simplified the discussion of organizational relationships and added real company examples of organizational relationships.
- Simplified discussion of ROI computations using inflation adjusted measures of investments.

Chapter 23, "Transfer Pricing"

- Simplified discussion of the general rule of transfer pricing.
- Added illustration of transfer pricing practices in the United States, Canada, and Japan.
- Added discussion of multinational transfer pricing, including a Real World Application of a transfer pricing dispute between U.S. tax authorities and a Japanese company.
- Simplified discussion of segment reporting.

Chapter 24, "Management Ethics and Financial Fraud"

- New chapter describes actual financial fraud situations and discusses ways to prevent and detect fraud. This stand-alone chapter can be assigned anywhere in the book.
- Major features of this chapter include:
  + Discussing common types of fraud, such as early revenue recognition and inventory overstatement.
  + Identifying motives and opportunities to commit fraud.
  + Explaining the importance of the "tone at the top."
  + Identifying difficulties in controlling employee behavior in countries with different ideas about what is ethical.
  + Analyzing actual case studies of financial fraud.
  + Emphasizing throughout the chapter that it is often ordinary people, like our students, who find themselves entangled in fraudulent activities.

Chapter 25, "Quality Control and Variance Investigation"

- Rewritten to place variance investigation in the context of efforts to achieve total quality.
- Simplified discussion of the relation between in-control and out-of-control processes.

Chapter 26, "Decision Making under Uncertainty and Information Economics"

- Combined materials from Chapters 24 and 26 into one chapter in this edition.
- Eliminated discussion of loss-minimization criteria, because it was peripheral to the chapter's topic.
- Simplified discussion of information economics.
- Simplified discussion of cost of prediction error.

ASSIGNMENT MATERIALS

The need for accurate and interesting assignment materials is self-evident to cost accounting instructors. The assignment material has been class-tested at both of our universities. In addition, we have had students work and rework every assignment item. Most important, as authors, we have worked every question, exercise, problem, and case at least twice in preparing this book.

The variety and quality of assignment materials allow the book to be used in various levels of courses. To help the instructor assign homework and select items for class presentation, we have divided the assignment materials into four categories.

- *Questions* include straightforward questions about key concepts, questions about ethical and real world company discussions in the chapter, and thought-provoking questions about the challenging issues managers and accountants face in dealing with an imperfect world. Questions are particularly good for written essays and class discussions.

- *Exercises* reinforce key concepts in the chapter, often referring the student to a particular illustration. Exercises are keyed to the chapter's learning objectives to enable instructors to assign exercises that emphasize particular points. Exercises typically deal with a single topic and are particularly useful for classroom demonstration.

- *Problems* challenge the student to apply and interpret the material in the chapter. Many problems have thought-provoking discussion or essay questions. (Instructors can also easily add additional essay and critical thought questions.) Problems generally require students to think about the managerial problem, not just the cost accounting problems.

- *Integrative cases* encourage students to apply concepts from multiple chapters and their other courses to deal with complex managerial issues. These are particularly good for advanced students and graduate students with some previous background in managerial accounting.

COMPLETE LEARNING PACKAGE

The text and related materials are integrated into a complete, accurate, and clear learning package. The total learning package contains numerous items to help the student and instructor.

1. The text uses examples and illustrations to make the concepts understandable. Each chapter has learning objectives, a summary of important concepts, key terms, and extensive end-of-chapter materials. Several chapters have appendixes to facilitate flexibility in covering topics in more detail or at a more advanced level.

The glossary at the end of the book has definitions for all key terms and concepts. Recommended additional Readings, also at the end of the text, provide listings of articles from the contemporary accounting literature. They may be used to enhance the chapter discussions.

2. The *Solutions Manual* presents solutions in large, easy-to-read type to facilitate the use of quality overhead transparencies for classroom use.

3. The *Instructor's Lecture Guide*, prepared by Professor Mark Nigrini (Saint Mary's University, Halifax), provides extensive materials for the instructor, including the following:

   - Sample course outlines.
   - Assignment charts showing topic coverage and degree of difficulty for exercises and problems.
   - Chapter-by-chapter discussions of chapter objectives, overview, and topic outlines.
   - Lecture transparency masters, more than 200 in all, for each chapter with detailed lecture notes.
   - Self-tests with solutions.

4. The *Test Bank* has more than 2,000 true-false, multiple-choice, and short problem items with detailed solutions and was prepared by Professor Robert Gruber (University of Wisconsin—Whitewater).

5. *CompuTest 3* is an advanced-featured test generator that allows the instructor to add and edit questions, save and reload tests, create up to 99 different versions of each test, attach graphics to questions, import and export ASCII files, and select questions based on type, level of difficulty, or key word. The program allows password protection of saved tests and question databases and is networkable.

6. Written by Michael Maher, the *Study Guide* is designed to help students learn the material in the text. Each chapter contains:
   - Chapter overview and outline to review major points in the chapter. The outline encourages students to "get back into the text" with frequent references to illustrations and examples.
   - A set of questions that matches key terms and concepts with definitions and tests student's basic knowledge of the concepts discussed in the chapter.
   - Numerical exercises and problems with fully worked out solutions. These help the student see how to work exercises and problems in the text.

7. *Solution Transparencies* for all exercises, problems, and cases.

8. *Computer-assisted student learning.* Software for more than 70 selected exercises and problems from the text prepared by Minta Berry (Berry Publication Services). These problems and exercises are identified in the text by SPATS (Spreadsheet Application Template Software).

9. A *check list of key figures* is available free in quantity to adopting instructors.

VIDEOS

Richard D. Irwin Managerial/Cost Accounting Video Library—This video library was prepared by Bright Light Productions, Inc., Cincinnati, Ohio, and Pacific Lutheran University, Tacoma, Washington. This video series is designed to strengthen your classroom presentations, grab your students' interest, and add variety to your students' learning process. The fifteen video segments provide 10–15 minutes each of important coverage of various topics:

Volume I contains:

- Behind the Bill—Illustrates how service industry costs are allocated at Good Samaritan Hospital.
- How Many Bucks in a Bag—Follows the production of potato chips and shows how standard costs are determined.
- The Vancouver Door Company—Features the manufacturing of wooden doors in a job plant and examines the company's cost accounting system.

Volume II contains:

- Moving the Merchandise—Features the operation of a small warehouse food distributor and follows a customer purchase order through the revenue and expenditure systems.
- Ogre Mills, After the Curtain Fell—Involves a large textile plant in Latvia and its move from the command economy of the former Soviet Union to free market. The video follows the production process from raw wool to yarn, fabric, and completed garments with some discussion of product costs and the problem facing the company.

Volume III contains:

- Lean Production—Shows and discusses how Lean Production is used at Caterpillar, Cummins Engine, and Navistar. Interviews with upper management at the three companies bring out the importance of customer-driven "pull" systems and how the companies employ JIT, Kanban, Jidoka, and MRP II to perform better.
- Quality—George Bush at the Baldrige Award ceremony opens this segment, which goes on to list the seven basic tools. Then Zytec, Motorola, and Hewlett-Packard are used as examples.
- The Manufacturing Process—Presents the Hayes-Wheelright continuum, from customized, low-volume to mechanized, high-volume manufacturing. Most of the segment is on-site footage from a tool and die shop, Caterpillar, Ford, and Nucor Steel.

Volume IV contains:

- Computer-Integrated Manufacturing—Presents an on-site tour of the Nucor Steel minimill, focusing on the automation system. Included are interviews with the plant manager, controller, and caster foreman.
- Inventory Management—Contrasts Navistar's high turnover-low inventory heavy truck manufacturing system with the high inventory-service parts business at Caterpillar. Interviews bring out Navistar's reduction efforts as well as Caterpillar's responsiveness and corresponding efforts on inventory and costs.
- Service—Features First National Bank of Chicago and particularly the operations aspect of its check-clearing system. Interviews are included, which help reiterate the point that service businesses use "operations" principles to deliver quality "products."

Volume V contains:

- Accounting Careers—Individuals from different backgrounds describe employment opportunities for business and accounting graduates in their industries. Ernst & Young, Arthur Andersen, FASB, Ben & Jerry's, the University of Cincinnati, and the IRS are just a few of the private, public, and governmental examples featured.
- Supplier Development Outreach Program (Flex-N-Gate Project)—Illustrates how Toyota changed over to a just-in-time inventory system with the help of Japanese consultants.
- Manufacturing—This video addresses accounting for a manufacturing concern. It examines in detail the three elements of manufacturing costs —direct materials, direct labor, and factory overhead—and the two systems designed to accurately reflect those costs—general accounting system, and process cost accounting system.

Volume VI contains:

- Atlas Foundry and Machine Company—This video describes job costing as a process where products are designed to customer specifications. The cost accounting system must be capable of identifying the cost of each batch of products.
- Management Accounting and Concepts—This tape describes how continuous improvement is related to the production management concepts of customer orientation, total quality management, just-in-time inventory management, and the theory of constraints. This tape also defines management accounting and describes how it differs from financial accounting.
- International Accounting—This tape describes accounting techniques used to account for imports and exports, especially the foreign exchange gains and losses that occur as currency rates change. Also, the need for international accounting and standards and the workings of the International Accounting Standards are described.

ACKNOWLEDGMENTS

We are indebted to many people for their assistance and ideas. Robert N. Anthony was instrumental in developing this book. He and Professor James S. Reece graciously permitted us to use several of their cases copyrighted by Osceola Institute. Special thanks go to Professors Mark Nigrini and Robert Gruber for their excellent suggestions. They have prepared two outstanding supplements to accompany the text: the *Instructor's Lecture Guide* and the *Test Bank*.

We wish to thank the following reviewers for their valuable comments and insightful recommendations. They have made a tremendous contribution to the fourth edition.

Wayne G. Bremser
Villanova University

Gail Lynn Cook
Syracuse University

Kenneth Danko
San Francisco State University

Lee Dexter
Moorhead State University

Al Hartgraves
Emory University

Cynthia D. Heagy
University of Houston–Clear Lake

David E. Keys
Northern Illinois University

Ronald A. Milne
University of Nevada–Las Vegas

Fred Nordhauser
University of Texas–San Antonio

Arnold Schneider
Georgia Institute of Technology

Bonnie P. Stivers
Kennesaw State College

Igor Vaysman
University of California–Berkeley

We are grateful to numerous colleagues for their comments and reviews of this and earlier editions.

Rick Antle
Yale University

David Brecht
California State University–Sacramento

Ray Brown
California State University–Sacramento

Stephen Butler
University of Oklahoma

Robert Colson
Daemen College

Eugene Comiskey
Georgia Institute of Technology

Ted Compton
Ohio University

Harold B. Cook
Central Michigan University

Frank Daroca
Loyola Marymount University

Andrew Demotses
Fairfield University

Joel Demski
Yale University

Ron Dye
Northwestern University

James Emig
Villanova University

John Fellingham
University of Illinois–Urbana

James M. Fremgen
Naval Postgraduate School

Robert A. Gruber
University of Wisconsin–Whitewater

Thomas Hrubec
Northern Illinois University

Robert Kaplan
Harvard University

Lawrence Klein
Bentley College

Eugene Laughlin
Kansas State University

James Mackey
California State University–Sacramento

M. Laurentius Marais
University of Chicago

Patrick McKenzie
Arizona State University

Frances McNair
Mississippi State University

Richard J. Murdock
Ohio State University

Alfred Nanni
Boston University

Harry Newman
University of Illinois–Chicago

C. Douglas Poe
University of Kentucky

Kasi Ramanathan
University of Washington

Lynn Rans
California State University–Los Angeles

Joseph Razek
University of New Orleans

James Reece
University of Michigan

Leo Ruggle
Mankato State University

Avi Rushinek
University of Miami

Donald R. Simons
University of Wisconsin-Oshkosh

Arnold Schneider
Georgia Institute of Technology

Melkote Shivaswamy
Ball State University

Kenneth Sinclair
Lehigh University

Carl S. Smith
West Chester University

Curtis Stanley
California State University–Sacramento

Thomas Stober
Indiana University

Peter Tiessen
University of Alberta

John Tracy
University of Colorado

Jacob Wambsganss
University of North Dakota

Neil Wilner
University of North Texas

Harry Wolk
Drake University

Rick Young
Ohio State University

Numerous students and associates have read the manuscript, worked problems, checked solutions, and otherwise helped us to write a teachable, error-free manuscript. We are grateful to Laura Tapper, Christian Belz, Matthew Dudman, David Patch, Barak Kassar, Greg Schweider, Eben Johnson, Vanetta Van Cleave, Krista Maher, and numerous students who class-tested this material. We acknowledge the helpful feedback from users of the previous editions.

We wish to express our appreciation to the many people and organizations who allowed us to use their problems and cases. These include the Certificate in Management Accounting Examinations by the Institute of Management Accountants; the Uniform CPA Examinations by the American Institute of Certified Public Accountants; the President and Fellows of Harvard College; the Osceola Institute; Professor David Solomons; and l'Institute pour l'Etude des Methodes de Direction de l'Enterprise (IMEDE).

We are grateful to all the people at Irwin for their outstanding support. In particular we thank Ron Regis, senior sponsoring editor; Cheryl Wilson, developmental editor; Cindy Ledwith, marketing manager; Waivah Clement, project editor; Maureen McCutcheon, designer; Ann Cassady, production manager, and Diane Van Bakel for lots of creative help.

Writing and rewriting this book has been challenging, but it also has been satisfying and fun(!). Thanks to the people who have helped us with this endeavor. We extend special thanks to our families and colleagues who have been so supportive.

Ideas from users for text revision and problem materials have been particularly helpful in making this the best possible textbook for teaching cost accounting. We welcome ideas from the people who face the day-to-day challenge of teaching, and we look forward to receiving more.

Michael W. Maher
Edward B. Deakin

CONTENTS IN BRIEF

CONTENTS

CHAPTER 20

STANDARD COSTING
747

CHAPTER 21

MIX, YIELD, AND REVENUE VARIANCES
783

CHAPTER 22

*DECENTRALIZATION AND PERFORMANCE
EVALUATION*
808

C H A P T E R   23

TRANSFER PRICING
841

P A R T   IV

SPECIAL TOPICS
869

C H A P T E R   24

MANAGEMENT ETHICS AND FINANCIAL FRAUD
870

CHAPTER 25

QUALITY CONTROL AND VARIANCE INVESTIGATION
907

CHAPTER 26

DECISION MAKING UNDER UNCERTAINTY AND INFORMATION ECONOMICS
930

COST ACCOUNTING: AN OVERVIEW

OUTLINE

Cost Accounting: Its Nature and Usefulness

LEARNING OBJECTIVES

After reading this chapter, you should be able to:

1. Explain how accounting is used for decision making and performance evaluation in organizations.
2. Explain how important developments in the economy and in industry have affected cost accounting in recent years.
3. Identify the roles and functions of accountants in organizations.
4. Identify accounting's professional organizations.
5. Understand ethical issues faced by accountants and ways of dealing with ethical problems that you may face in your career.
6. Explain why accounting systems are subject to cost-benefit tests.

You are beginning the study of a subject that is critical to the success of organizations and the people who work in them. Information is often called the fuel of organizations; information makes organizations go. This first chapter presents an overview of cost accounting and previews the rest of the book.

WHAT IS COST ACCOUNTING?

Cost Accounting The field of accounting that records, measures, and reports information about costs.

This book deals with the use of accounting to help people manage organizations. **Cost accounting** is the field of accounting that records, measures, and reports information about how much things cost. It is a much broader field than you might think because managers use cost accounting information in many different ways. Here are some examples:

Marketing people need to know how much products cost to help them set prices.

Department managers need to know the costs of running their departments to determine how to control costs.

A hospital's top management needs to know how much a new hospital wing will cost to determine whether the benefits of the new wing will exceed its costs.

People from all over the organization need to predict the costs of running the organization for budgeting purposes.

Cost accounting is used in all organizations: manufacturing, merchandising, and service companies; governments; universities; and not-for-profit and profit-making enterprises. Further, most organizations are facing an increasing need for cost information. If you follow the ongoing problems in the airline industry, for example, you know that several airlines are facing bankruptcy. These problems generally occur because companies do not have a good understanding of their costs. Observers of the health care industry note that health care takes more than 10 percent of the U.S. gross national product, and the costs keep growing. Hospitals and other health care providers need better cost information to control their costs and prevent a national catastrophe. Many industries that were dominated by U.S. firms, such as automobile, electronics, and steel, are struggling to compete with foreign producers because the U.S. companies are not able to control their costs as well as their foreign competitors.

If you have been in a situation where you did not have much money to spend, then you know what it means to be concerned about the cost of items you buy. Companies operate in a similar way. When companies face stiff competition and cannot pass cost increases on to consumers in the form of higher prices, management becomes very concerned about how much things cost. For example, managers in a Hewlett-Packard plant that we visited told us, "In the early 1980s, we sold a particular calculator for $120 each. Although we did not know the exact cost of the calculator, it didn't matter much to us because we knew we were selling the product at a profit. Later, when competition forced the price down to $35, we had to be much more precise in our cost measurement because what certainly made money at $120 may or may not make money at $35."

Many U.S. companies, such as steel and automobile companies, were less concerned about costs in the past, when their profit margins were high, than they are today. As one of the few industrial powers with its economy intact after World War II, and with pent-up demand for consumer products like automobiles that were unavailable during the war, U.S. industry was in a unique position to make high profits without much competition. That situation has changed. U.S. producers now face stiff competition and need to survive with small profit margins. Consequently, management's interest in controlling costs is very high.

With increased interest in cost control comes increased emphasis on cost accounting. Managers need to know how their decisions affect costs. Auditors need to improve their audits of cost methods and control systems. Consultants are looking for ways to improve cost systems. Tax people are finding that many tax disputes occur over disputed measures of costs.[1] In short, the need for good cost accounting information has increased job opportunities in numerous fields. We assume that most of you will not specialize in cost accounting throughout your career; however, we are sure that virtually all of you will need to understand how to get the information you want from cost accounting systems. This book is dedicated to helping you learn how to make cost accounting work for you.

LEARNING COST ACCOUNTING

We are believers in interactive learning. A few of you may learn cost accounting just by reading the book or by listening to lectures. Most of you will learn cost accounting as we did—with a lot of trial and error, questions and answers, and problem solving. You will learn the subject by interacting with your teachers, fellow students, and even the textbook. We will facilitate this interactive learning process in several ways. First, we place self-study questions and problems throughout each chapter. We strongly recommend that you write out your answers to these and then check your answers with the solutions to the self-study questions that we have placed at the end of each chapter. Each chapter has a variety of questions, exercises, and problems to test your knowledge of the subject.

We have also prepared a study guide, available from your bookstore, that includes numerous questions and exercises with solutions—*Study Guide for Use with Cost Accounting*. Many students have told us the study guide helps them review the material in the text both in preparation to work homework problems and in preparation for examinations. However you learn the subject, we wish you good luck in your study of cost accounting. We hope this book makes a substantial contribution to your education.

USES OF COST ACCOUNTING

Cost accounting is used by many different people in an organization. Illustration 1–1 shows the four types of uses. The top two pictures show managerial uses. In the top left picture, the woman reviews the accounting reports to evaluate performance. In the top right picture, the marketing manager is calling the accounting department for cost estimates of motorized skateboards.

Cost accounting is also used in preparing financial reports to investors and in preparing tax returns, as shown in the bottom pictures in Illustration 1–1. These four uses of cost accounting information—performance evaluation, decision making, financial reporting, and tax reporting—are found in practically all businesses. Cost information is also used for setting prices based on cost-plus-a-profit contracts, such as those sometimes found in the defense industry, and for other special contract and regulatory purposes.

---

[1] For example, the Internal Revenue Service has claimed that some Japanese manufacturers have overstated the cost of products made in Japan and shipped to the United States. This alleged practice reduces the profits earned in the United States by the U.S. distributor of the Japanese products. Resolving this dispute over the cost of products made in Japan and sold in the United States could increase U.S. tax revenues and reduce the deficit, according to arguments in political circles.

I L L U S T R A T I O N   *How Cost Accounting Information Is Used*

Managerial Accounting The preparation of cost and related data for managers to use in performance evaluation or decision making.

Financial Accounting The preparation of financial statements and data for outsiders.

When costs are used inside the organization by managers to evaluate the performance of operations or personnel, or as a basis for decision making, we say the costs are used for **managerial accounting** purposes. When costs are used by outsiders, such as shareholders or creditors, to evaluate the performance of top management and make decisions about the organization, we say the costs are used for **financial accounting** purposes. This book focuses on cost accounting systems and on managerial uses of cost data for decision making and performance evaluation.

COST DATA FOR MANAGERIAL PURPOSES

Managers must often choose between two or more alternatives. Their decision is usually based on each action's financial consequences. Choosing among alternative actions is an important management activity in all organizations—large and small; profit making and not for profit; traditional and high tech; manufacturing, merchandising, and service. Managers' calculations range from simple "back-of-the-envelope" figuring to complex computer simulation. Regardless of the complexity, calculating the financial consequences of alternative actions is an important part of managing every organization. Managers also use cost data to help evaluate performance and control operations. Because these activities are so important for the success of a venture, we want you to understand how costs can be used (and misused).

Costs for Decision Making

One of the most difficult tasks in calculating the financial consequences of alternatives is to estimate how costs (or revenues or assets) will *differ* among the alternatives. Suppose the management of a department store is considering expanding its operations and store size to include several new product lines. As an alternative, the store could open a new outlet in a different location. The key is to determine which would be most profitable: remain the same size, expand operations in the current location, or open a new outlet. Using cost accounting techniques, the store can estimate **differential costs,** that is, how costs will differ for each alternative.

Differential Costs Costs that change in response to a particular course of action.

For example, suppose Jennifer's Sandwiche Shoppe has been open for lunch only, Monday through Friday, from 11 A.M. to 2 P.M. The owner-manager, Jennifer, is considering expanding her hours by opening Monday through Friday evenings from 5 P.M. to 8 P.M. Jennifer figures her revenues, food costs, labor, and utilities would increase 50 percent, rent would remain the same, and other costs would increase by 25 percent if she opens in the evening. Jennifer's present and estimated future costs, revenues, and profits are shown in columns 1 and 2 of Illustration 1–2. The differential costs, revenues, and profits, shown in column 3, are the differences between the amounts in columns 1 and 2.

ILLUSTRATION

1–2

Differential Costs, Revenues, and Profits for One Week

JENNIFER'S SANDWICHE SHOPPE
Projected Income Statements
For One Week

	(1) Baseline Open 11 A.M.–2 P.M.	(2) Alternative Open 11 A.M.–2 P.M. and 5 P.M.–8 P.M.	(3) Difference (2) − (1)
Sales revenue	$1,100	$1,650[a]	$550
Costs:			
Food	500	750[a]	250
Labor	200	300[a]	100
Utilities	80	120[a]	40
Rent	250	250	—
Other	60	75[b]	15
Total costs	1,090	1,495	405
Operating profits	$ 10	$ 155	$145

[a] Fifty percent higher than baseline.
[b] Twenty-five percent higher than baseline.

The analysis shows an increase in operating profits of $145 if the shop is opened in the evening. All other things being equal, Jennifer would therefore probably expand her hours. Note that only differential costs and revenues figure in the decision. For example, rent does not change, so it is irrelevant to the decision.

Costs for Planning and Performance Evaluation

An organization usually divides responsibility for specific functions among its employees. A maintenance group, for example, is responsible for maintaining a particular area of an office building, a Kmart store manager is responsible for most operations of a particular store, while the president of a company is responsible for the entire company. A **responsibility center** is a specific unit of an organization assigned to a manager who is held accountable for its operations and resources.

Responsibility Center A specific unit of an organization assigned to a manager who is held accountable for its operations and resources.

Consider the case of Jennifer's Sandwiche Shoppe. When Jennifer first opened her shop, she managed the entire operation herself. As the enterprise became more successful, she added a catering service. She then hired two managers: Sam to manage the shop and Carol to manage the catering service. Jennifer, as general manager, oversaw the entire operation.

Each manager is responsible for the revenues and costs of his or her department. Jennifer's salary, rent, utilities, and other costs are shared by both departments. Jennifer is directly responsible for these shared costs; the department managers are not.

Jennifer's organization has three responsibility centers as follows:

Responsibility Center	Manager Responsible	Responsible for
Entire organization	Jennifer, general manager	All of the organization's operations and resources, revenues, and costs
Sandwich Department	Sam, manager	Sandwich Department operations and resources (see Illustration 1–3 for revenues and costs)
Catering	Carol, manager	Catering operations and resources (see Illustration 1–3 for revenues and costs)

Departmental income statements are shown in Illustration 1–3. Note that some costs—utilities, rent, other, and general manager's salary—are administrative and general costs of running the entire organization.

Budgeting

Managers in all organizations set goals to achieve return on investment, cash balances, costs, earnings, and other performance indicators. Each responsibility center usually has a **budget,** which is a financial plan of the resources needed to carry out the center's tasks and meet financial goals. Estimates, as stated in budgets, help managers decide if their goals can be achieved and, if not, what modifications will be necessary.

Budget A financial plan of resources needed to carry out tasks and meet financial goals.

At regular intervals of time, resources actually used are compared with the amount budgeted to assess the center's and the manager's performance. By comparing actual results with the budget plans, it is possible to identify the probable causes of variances from planned costs, profits, cash flows, and other financial targets. Managers can then take action to change their activities or revise their goals and plans. This process of planning and performance evaluation for responsibility centers is sometimes called *responsibility accounting.*

ILLUSTRATION

*Responsibility Centers,
Departmental Costs, and
Revenues*

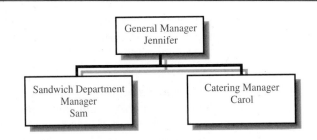

JENNIFER'S SANDWICHE SHOPPE
Income Statement
Month Ending October 31

	Sandwich Department	Catering	Total
Sales revenue	$17,000	$11,000	$28,000
Department costs:			
Food	7,000	3,000	10,000
Labor[a]	3,000	5,000	8,000
Total department costs	10,000	8,000	18,000
Department margin[b]	$ 7,000	$ 3,000	$10,000
General and administrative costs:			
Utilities			$ 1,500
Rent			2,500
Other			900
General manager's salary (Jennifer)			4,000
Total general and administrative costs			8,900
Operating profit			$ 1,100

[a] Includes department managers' salaries but excludes Jennifer's salary.

[b] The difference between revenues and costs attributable to a department.

As part of the planning and control process, managers prepare budgets containing expectations about revenues and costs for the coming period. At the end of the period, managers compare actual results with the budget to see whether changes can be made to improve operations in the future. Illustration 1–4 illustrates the type of statement that might be used to compare actual results with the planning budget for Jennifer's Sandwich Department.

By analyzing the figures in Illustration 1–4, Sam, the department manager, can immediately see which, if any, costs need to be controlled and how the budget may need to be revised to assist in planning for future months.

For instance, Sam observes that the Sandwich Department sold 4,100 sandwiches as budgeted, but actual costs were higher than budgeted. Costs that appear to need follow up are the cost of fish and meat and the cost of counter labor. Should Sam inquire whether there was waste in using fish or

Department Costs

JENNIFER'S: SANDWICH DEPARTMENT
Department Budget versus Actual
Month Ending October 31

Department	Budget	Actual
Food:		
Bakery	$1,100	$ 1,050
Meat	2,500	2,700
Fish	1,500	1,750
Dairy	1,500	1,500
Total food	6,600	7,000
Labor:		
Manager and chef	2,000	2,000
Counter	800	1,000
Total labor	2,800	3,000
Total sandwich costs	$9,400	$10,000
Number of sandwiches sold	4,100	4,100

meat? Did the cost per pound rise unexpectedly? Were customers given larger portions than expected? Was there unexpected overtime for the counter staff? These are just a few of the questions that would be prompted by the information in Illustration 1–4.

We should also note that budgeting is difficult, and differences between actual costs and budget could also be due to budgets set too low or too high. Finally, differences between budget and actual costs are information signals that things are not as we expected; they do not necessarily imply that something is wrong.

*Different Needs Require
Different Data*

Each time you are faced with an accounting problem, you should first ascertain whether the data will be used for managerial or financial purposes. Is the goal to value inventories in financial reports to shareholders? Is it to provide data for performance evaluation? Or are the data to be used for decision making? The answers to these questions will guide your selection of the most appropriate accounting data.

Management Accounting and GAAP

In contrast to cost data for financial reporting to shareholders, cost data for managerial use (that is, within the organization) need not comply with **generally accepted accounting principles (GAAP).** Management is quite free to set its own definitions for cost information. Indeed, the accounting data used for external reporting may need to be modified to provide appropriate information for managerial decision making. For example, managerial decisions deal with the future, so estimates of future costs may be more valuable for decision making than the historical and current costs that are reported externally.

Generally Accepted Accounting Principles (GAAP) The rules, standards, and conventions that guide the preparation of financial accounting statements.

TRENDS IN COST ACCOUNTING

Although even the early Babylonians and Egyptians practiced cost accounting, the roots of modern cost accounting developed in the 1800s.[2] During this period, companies began integrating production cost records with financial accounts.

Budgets became important tools for planning, cost control, and performance evaluation. Estimating and measuring costs for managerial decisions about alternative actions also became increasingly common. In his 1923 book, *The Economics of Overhead Costs,* J. M. Clark established the principle of different costs for different purposes, which is widely recognized and implemented by managerial accountants today.

The content of cost accounting textbooks has reflected accounting changes over the years. In the early 1950s, cost accounting textbooks focused on procedures for measuring, recording, and reporting actual product costs for external purposes. The scope of cost accounting has broadened to consider how accounting affects managerial decision models used in behavioral sciences, finance, economics, and operations management.

In most organizations, people who are called cost accountants, managerial accountants, and/or financial analysts have the responsibility of operating the accounting system for the benefit of the organization's managers. Cost accountants must work with management to provide the best possible information for managerial purposes. As noted in the first Real World Application for this chapter, "The Accountant As a Communicator," your ability to communicate financial issues and concepts to nonfinancial people will be valuable both to you and to them.

THE REVOLUTION IN COST ACCOUNTING

Cost accounting is experiencing dramatic changes. Developments in computer systems have nearly eliminated manual bookkeeping. There is an increasing emphasis on cost control in hospitals, in industries like computers and automobiles where companies face stiff competition, and in airlines and many other organizations that have traditionally not focused on cost control. Cost accounting has become a necessity in virtually every organization, including banks, fast-food outlets, professional organizations, and government agencies.

---

[2] See David Solomons, "The Historical Development of Costing," in *Studies in Cost Analysis,* ed. David Solomons (Homewood, Ill.: Richard D. Irwin, 1968); and Robert Kaplan and Thomas Johnson, *Relevance Lost: The Rise and Fall of Management Accounting* (Boston: Harvard Business School Press, 1987).

REAL WORLD APPLICATION

Note to readers: We have included "real world applications" of cost accounting throughout the book. Our purpose is to describe some of the many cost accounting issues that occur in the real world.

These brief applications are based on articles by practitioners who describe their experiences, or on research into real world problems. We hope you will find these applications enjoyable and informative.

The Accountant As a Communicator*

Although accounting is often called the *language of business*, it is a *foreign* language to most people in business. According to Joseph Barra, a division controller at Lever Brothers Co., the solution may lie with accountants. "I have encountered many very good accountants who were excellent technical people and who really knew their field but could not communicate with management and get the message across. They could not present basic accounting information in a simplified way."

Communication with nonaccountants is particularly important because of the interaction that takes place between accountants and users of information. According to Mr. Barra, marketing people at Lever Brothers look to the accountants for information about distribution costs for established products. If management decides to change a product, the accountants work with people in purchasing to obtain new materials and packaging cost information. If the company is considering a new product, "the analysis and estimation of the cost is controlled by the controller right from the beginning. . . . Ideally, this process results in a combination of the disciplines. The marketing people make the estimates of what they think sales will be and also calculate what happens if the estimates are missed."

What is required for effective communication with nonfinancial people? Mr. Barra lists four basic ground rules:

1. Keep examples simple.
2. Avoid technical jargon.
3. Show an understanding of marketing and production issues.
4. Avoid lessons in bookkeeping.

Good communication is self-serving. By making managers aware of financial issues, accountants will find their services in greater demand.

* Source: Joseph A. Barra, "Marketing the Financial Facts of Life," *Management Accounting*, March 1983, p. 29.

Cost Accounting in High-Tech Companies

Recently, many companies have installed computer assisted methods of manufacturing products, merchandising products, or providing services. These new technologies have had a major impact on cost accounting. We discuss the impact of these new developments throughout this book.

For example, robots and computer assisted manufacturing methods have replaced humans for some jobs. Labor costs have shrunk from 20–40 percent of product costs in traditional manufacturing settings to less than 5 percent in many highly automated settings. Cost accounting in traditional settings required much more work to keep track of labor costs than is necessary in current systems. On the other hand, in highly automated environments, cost accountants have had to become more sophisticated at determining the causes of manufacturing costs because those costs are no longer driven by labor.

Just-in-Time Methods

Just-in-Time Method In production or purchasing, each unit is purchased or produced just in time for its use.

The development of **just-in-time (JIT)** production and purchasing methods also affects cost accounting systems. Using just-in-time methods, units are produced or purchased just in time for use and inventories are kept to a minimum. If inventories are low, accountants can spend less time on inventory valuation for external reporting and more time on managerial activities.

For example, a Hewlett-Packard plant eliminated 100,000 journal entries per month after installing just-in-time production methods and adapting the cost accounting system to the new production methods. Just-in-time inventory freed up two additional staff people to assist managers in running the business.[3]

Emphasis on Quality

Total quality management A method of management such that the organization is managed to excel on all dimensions and the customer ultimately defines quality.

Many companies have adopted the concept of total quality management (TQM). **Total quality management** means the organization is managed to excel on all dimensions and quality is ultimately defined by the customer. This means that you, as customer, determine the company's performance standards according to what is important to *you* as the customer (which is not necessarily what is important to product engineers, accountants, or marketing people). This exciting and sensible idea affects accountants who measure and report on people's performance. Under total quality management, performance measures are likely to include things like product reliability and service delivery, as well as traditional measures like product cost. We discuss these issues further in later chapters.

Lean Production

Just-in-time production is part of a "lean production" philosophy that has been credited for the success of many Japanese companies and such U.S. companies as Lincoln Electric. Using lean production, Lincoln Electric is eliminating inventories between production departments, making the quality and efficiency of production the highest priority, providing the flexibility to change quickly from one product to another, and emphasizing training and worker skills. Companies that do not have these characteristics find it difficult to implement just-in-time production methods.

Activity-Based Costing

Activity-Based Costing A costing method that assigns indirect costs to those activities needed to make products, then sums the cost of those activities needed to make a particular product to determine the product's cost.

Activity-based costing is a product costing method that is becoming more widely used, particularly in industries like computers where competition is keen and direct labor costs are low. **Activity-based costing** is a costing method that assigns the indirect costs of making a product, such as quality testing, machine repairs, and product engineering, to the activities that are needed to make a product, then sums the cost of those activities to determine the cost of making the product. This costing method is more detailed and complicated than conventional costing methods, but it can provide more accurate cost numbers. We devote an entire chapter to activity-based costing later in the book, and we discuss the topic in several other chapters. Those of you who plan careers in consulting and industry will likely have an opportunity to use the material on activity-based costing in this book to help companies develop and install activity-based costing systems.

ORGANIZATIONAL ENVIRONMENT

In most corporations, the controller is the chief accounting officer and a senior member of the management team. In some firms, the controller has the rank of corporate vice president and reports directly to the company president. In others, the controller and the treasurer both report to a financial vice president who is responsible for both accounting and financial

---

[3] Rick Hunt, Linda Garrett, and C. Mike Merz, "Direct Labor Cost Not Always Relevant at H-P," *Management Accounting*, February 1985, pp. 58–62.

ILLUSTRATION   *Partial Organization Chart, E. I. du Pont de Nemours & Company*

1–5

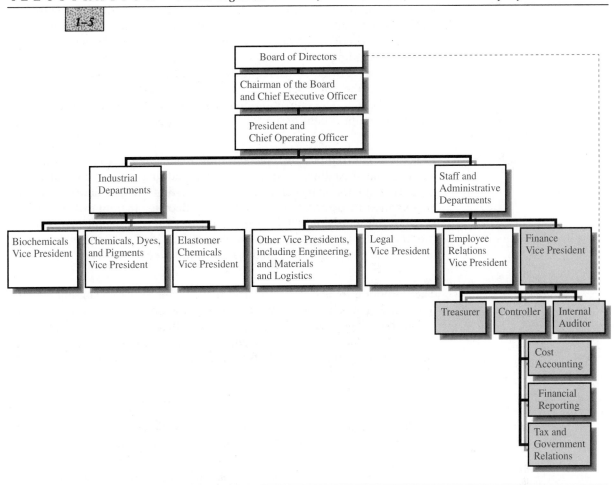

affairs. The highest level financial officer is generally called the chief financial officer (CFO). The cost accounting function is typically the responsibility of the controller.

Illustration 1–5 shows an abbreviated version of the Du Pont Company's organization chart. The board of directors establishes policy. Officers of the company carry out that policy. Either the board chairman or the president is designated chief executive officer. The *chief executive officer* (CEO) is responsible for supervising all officers of the corporation and thus is the top-ranking manager. Vice presidents are assigned responsibility over individual divisions. They will usually appoint managers to supervise specified activities within their divisions.

Controller

As the chief accounting officer, the controller is responsible for both external and internal accounting reports. External reports include published financial statements and reports to taxing authorities like the Internal Revenue Service and regulatory bodies like the Securities and Exchange Commission (SEC).

Internally, the controller is responsible for budgeting and for supplying management with accounting data for planning, performance evaluation, and decision making and for overseeing the company's internal control system. In addition, the controller maintains all cost and other accounting records, including inventories, receivables, payables, and fixed asset accounts. Most of these duties require the use of electronic data processing. In some cases, the controller supervises data processing operations, but frequently, data processing is an independent department reporting to the financial vice president or another staff vice president.

Internal Auditor

In many organizations, the *internal audit department* provides a variety of auditing and consulting services, including auditing internal controls, auditing cost data for managerial use, and assisting outside auditors in their examination of external financial reports. Because the controller's record-keeping role may conflict with the audit function, the audit manager may report directly to the controller's superior (as at Du Pont), and is often given authority to communicate with the audit committee of the board of directors.

Treasurer

The corporate treasurer is primarily responsible for managing liquid assets (cash and short-term investments), handling credit reviews, and collecting receivables. The treasurer usually conducts business with banks and other financial sources and oversees public issues of stock and debt. In most cases, the treasurer focuses on financial issues, while the controller concentrates on operating issues.

 *Self-Study Questions*

3   What are the major causes of changes in cost accounting systems in recent years?

4   What are the major financial offices or departments in organizations?

The solutions to these questions are at the end of this chapter on page 29.

PROFESSIONAL ENVIRONMENT

The accounting profession includes many kinds of accountants—external auditors, consultants, controllers, internal auditors, tax experts, and so forth. Because accounting positions carry great responsibility, accountants must be highly trained and well informed about new developments in their field. As a result, special organizations and certification programs have been established to serve accountants' needs and the public interest.

Organizations

Numerous organizations have arisen to keep accounting professionals aware of current issues. Most of these organizations have journals that help keep professional accountants up to date. Some of these organizations are listed below.

The *Financial Executives Institute* is an organization of financial executives such as controllers, treasurers, and financial vice presidents. It publishes a monthly periodical, *Financial Executive,* and a number of studies on accounting issues.

The *Institute of Management Accountants* has thousands of members who work in management accounting. It publishes the journal *Management Accounting,* numerous policy statements, and research studies on accounting issues. It also sponsors the Certified Management Accountant (CMA) program.

The *Institute of Internal Auditors* is an organization of internal auditors. It publishes a periodical called the *Internal Auditor* and numerous research studies on internal auditing. It also sponsors the Certificate in Internal Auditing program.

The *Association of Government Accountants* is an organization of federal, state, and local government accountants. It publishes the *Government Accountant's Journal.*

Certifications

Anyone who wishes to be licensed as a certified public accountant (CPA) must pass an examination that includes questions on cost accounting as well as other questions on accounting practice, theory, law, and auditing. We have included samples of CPA examination cost accounting questions in this book.

Certified Management Accountant Program A program established to recognize educational achievement and professional competence in management accounting.

The **Certified Management Accountant (CMA)** program recognizes educational achievement and professional accomplishment in the field of managerial accounting. The examination, education, and experience requirements for the CMA are similar to those for CPA certification, but they are primarily for professionals in management and cost accounting. We have included a large number of problems from CMA examinations in this book.

In Canada, the Society of Management Accountants gives the professional examination and certification for the certified management accountant (CMA) certificate.

Cost Accounting Standards Board

The **Cost Accounting Standards Board (CASB)** was set up by the U.S. Congress in 1970 to establish cost accounting standards for U.S. defense contractors. The CASB's primary purpose is to avert disputes between the U.S. government and defense contractors about the allocation of costs in cost-based government contracts.

CHOICES: ETHICAL ISSUES FOR ACCOUNTANTS

Accountants report information that can have a substantial impact on the careers of managers. Managers are generally held accountable for achieving financial performance targets. Failure to achieve these targets can have serious negative consequences for these managers, including being fired. If a division or company is having trouble achieving financial performance targets, accountants may find themselves under pressure by management to make accounting choices that will improve performance reports.

For example, companies have been known to record sales before the revenue was earned.[4] This early revenue recognition would occur just before

---

[4] For example, see M. Maher, "Divisional Performance Incentives and Financial Fraud" (working paper, Graduate School of Management. University of California, Davis. August, 1993).

the end of the reporting period, say, in late December for a company using a December 31 year-end. Management might rationalize the early revenue recognition on the grounds that the sale would probably be made in January anyway; this practice just moved next year's sale (and profits) into this year.

Despite such rationalization, this practice is wrong and has resulted in many legal actions by the Securities and Exchange Commission and others against accountants and business executives.

As a professional accountant or businessperson, you will be facing ethical situations on an everyday basis. Therefore, it stands to reason that you, as students, should be provided with some preparation to face these upcoming predicaments. The following discussion, a Real World Application, and an appendix are meant to help prepare you for the decisions you will face.

Your personal ethical choices can affect not only your own self-image, but others' perception of you. Ultimately, the ethical decisions you make directly influence the type of life you are likely to lead. You should confront ethical dilemmas bearing in mind the type of life that you would *like* to lead.

In an attempt to influence the accounting profession, many of its professional organizations such as the Institute of Management Accountants (IMA) and the American Institute of Certified Public Accountants (AICPA) have developed codes of ethics to which their members are expected to adhere. Similarly, businesses such as Johnson & Johnson generally use these codes as a public statement of their commitment to certain business practices with respect to their customers and also as a guide for their employees.

Throughout this book, we have included discussions of ethical issues. Our aim is to make you aware of potential problems that you and your colleagues will face in your careers. Many accountants and business people have found themselves in serious trouble because they did many small things, none of which appeared seriously wrong, only to find these small things added up to big trouble. If you know the warning signs of potential ethical problems, you will have a chance to protect yourself and set the proper moral tone for your company and your profession at the same time.

Most large organizations have a corporate code of conduct. We think the code developed by Johnson & Johnson is particularly impressive, so we have reproduced it in the Real World Application "A Company that Takes Its Conduct Seriously."

The Institute of Management Accountants (IMA) has also developed a code of conduct, which we have reproduced in the appendix to this chapter. In its code of conduct, "Standards of Ethical Conduct for Management Accountants," the IMA states management accountants have a responsibility to maintain the highest levels of ethical conduct. Management accountants have a responsibility to maintain professional competency, refrain from disclosing confidential information, and maintain integrity and objectivity in their work. These standards recommend that accountants faced with ethical conflicts follow the established policies that deal with such conflicts. If the policies do not resolve the conflict, accountants should consider discussing the matter with superiors, potentially as high as the audit committee of the board of directors. In extreme cases, the accountant may have no alternative but to resign.

*A Company that Takes Its Conduct Seriously**

Johnson & Johnson has a corporate code of conduct and believes in it! Management's belief in the company's code of conduct may explain why this pharmaceutical and household products company is so highly regarded, and why it has done well despite such threats as the Tylenol tampering problem in the 1980s.

Johnson & Johnson's code emphasizes the company's responsibility to its community, employees, customers, and society as a whole, as well as to its stockholders. Many companies publish a corporate code of conduct. When you look at the way executives are rewarded, however, you find considerable emphasis on short-term profits at the expense of the ideals in the corporate code of conduct. At Johnson & Johnson, the way executives are rewarded is consistent with the ideals in the code of conduct.

The Johnson & Johnson code of conduct, called "Our Credo," is reproduced below.

Most large organizations have a corporate code of conduct. We think the code developed by Johnson & Johnson is particularly impressive, so we have reproduced it in the Real World Application "A Company that Takes Its Conduct Seriously."

The Institute of Management Accountants (IMA) has also developed a code of conduct, which we have reproduced in the appendix to this chapter. In its code of conduct, "Standards of Ethical Conduct for Management Accountants," the IMA states management accountants have a responsibility to maintain the highest levels of ethical conduct. Management accountants have a responsibility to maintain professional competency, refrain from disclosing confidential information, and maintain integrity and objectivity in their work. These standards recommend that accountants faced with ethical conflicts follow the established policies that deal with such conflicts. If the policies do not resolve the conflict, accountants should consider discussing the matter with superiors, potentially as high as the audit committee of the board of directors. In extreme cases, the accountant may have no alternative but to resign.

* Source: Authors' research and the Johnson & Johnson credo.

Our Credo

We believe our first responsibility is to
the doctors, nurses and patients,
to mothers and all others who use
our products and services.
In meeting their needs everything we
do must be of high quality.
We must constantly strive to reduce our costs
in order to maintain reasonable prices.
Customers' orders must be serviced
promptly and accurately.
Our suppliers and distributors must have
an opportunity to make a fair profit.

We are responsible to our employees,
the men and women who work with us
throughout the world.
Everyone must be considered as an individual.
We must respect their dignity and
recognize their merit.
They must have a sense of security in their jobs.
Compensation must be fair and adequate,
and working conditions clean, orderly and safe.
Employees must feel free to make
suggestions and complaints.
There must be equal opportunity
for employment, development
and advancement for those qualified.

We must provide competent management,
and their actions must be just and ethical.

We are responsible to the communities
in which we live and work
and to the world community as well.
We must be good citizens—support
good works and charities
and bear our fair share of taxes.
We must encourage civic improvements
and better health and education.
We must maintain in good order
the property we are privileged to use,
protecting the environment and natural resources.

Our final responsibility is to our stockholders.
Business must make a sound profit.
We must experiment with new ideas.
Research must be carried on, innovative programs
developed and mistakes paid for.
New equipment must be purchased, new facilities
provided and new products launched.
Reserves must be created to provide
for adverse times.
When we operate according to these principles,
the stockholders should realize a fair return.

Many people believe that the appropriate way to deal with ethical issues is not by requiring employees to read and sign codes of ethics but to rely on more fundamental concepts of right and wrong. Codes of conduct look good on paper, but ultimately much of ethical behavior comes from an individual's personal beliefs. We are certain you will be faced with important ethical choices during your career, and we wish you well in making the right choices.

COSTS AND BENEFITS OF ACCOUNTING

How much accounting information is enough? Managers often complain that they never have all the facts they need. More data could usually be provided to decision makers, but at a cost. For example, a company recently installed a cost system for several million dollars. Management could justify the expenditure because it believed the system would help control costs and increase the efficiency of operations, thereby saving the company much more than it cost.

The question of how much accounting information is enough can be resolved by evaluating costs and benefits of accounting information. In practice, it is especially difficult to measure the benefits of accounting systems. Future benefits and costs can never be known with certainty. Nonetheless, accounting for managerial uses must, in principle, meet the **cost-benefit requirement.**

Cost-Benefit Requirement The criterion that an alternative will be chosen if and only if the benefits from it exceed the costs. This criterion is one basis for evaluating cost systems.

The analysis of costs and benefits requires considerable cooperation between the users of accounting information and accountants. Users are more familiar with the benefits of the data, and accountants are more familiar with the costs. Such cooperation is shown in Illustration 1–6, where users identify their decision-making needs and request data from accountants, who develop information systems to supply the data when it is cost-benefit justified. In practice, the process sometimes works in reverse. Accountants sometimes report data that users do not use. But if accountants

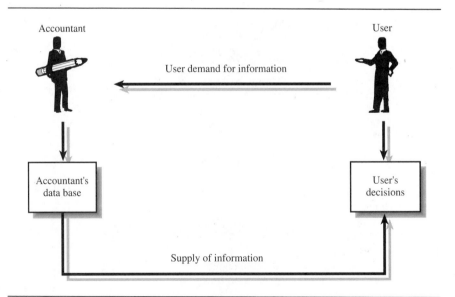

ILLUSTRATION

1-6

Interaction between Users and Accountants

Accountant

User

User demand for information

Accountant's data base

User's decisions

Supply of information

and users interact, they eventually settle on a cost-benefit-justified supply of accounting data that meets users' needs.

Accounting theoreticians are working on solutions to the difficult problem of determining the optimal cost-benefit-justified accounting data system. We present some of these developments in Chapter 26. Throughout this book, we assume that both users and accountants assess the costs and benefits of information in deciding whether to change an accounting system, whether to prepare a special report, and so forth.

ORGANIZATION OF THE BOOK

Chapter 2 describes fundamental concepts on which the rest of the book is based. The remaining chapters are organized around the four major subject areas in the book: (1) cost accounting systems, (2) costs for managerial decision making, (3) costs for managerial performance evaluation, and (4) special topics.

1. Cost Accounting Systems

Chapters 3 through 9 describe how various organizations design and use cost systems. This information will help you understand how organizations function financially.

2. Costs for Managerial Decision Making

Chapters 10 through 14 are concerned with specific ways managers use cost information for decisions. We focus on short-term operating decisions. For example, how will costs (as well as revenues and profits) be affected by an increase in volume? By closing a store? By developing a new product line?

Chapters 15 and 16 cover the use of cost information in long-term capital investment decisions. We discuss cashflow estimation and include tax effects of capital investment decisions.

3. Costs for Managerial Performance Evaluation

Chapters 17 through 21 discuss how managers use cost accounting to plan and budget their activities and to evaluate the performance of people who work for them. Chapters 22 and 23 discuss the use of cost accounting in decentralized organizations that have multiple divisions.

4. Special Topics

Chapters 24 through 26 cover special topics, including cases in financial fraud, quality control and variance investigation, and decision making under uncertainty.

SUMMARY

This chapter provides an overview of cost accounting, which is the field of accounting that records, measures, and reports information about costs.

This book discusses cost accounting systems and the use of cost accounting in its two primary managerial uses: decision making and performance evaluation. In decision making, cost accounting is used by managers to assess financial consequences of alternative actions. In performance evaluation, accounting is used by managers to assign responsibility for costs and to measure employee performance.

In recent years, cost accounting has changed from an emphasis on inventory and cost of goods sold valuation for external financial reporting to an emphasis on cost uses for managerial purposes.

Like any other service, product, or system in an organization, cost accounting is subject to economic cost-benefit evaluation. Perfectly accurate and complete accounting information, even if possible to obtain, would almost certainly be too costly to justify. The benefits of cost accounting information are usually determined by the managers who use it. An effective cost accounting system requires cooperation between the managers who use the information and the accountants who provide it.

TERMS AND CONCEPTS

The following terms and concepts should be familiar to you after reading this chapter (the numbers are page references):

Activity-Based Costing, *12*	**Differential Costs,** *6*
Budget, *7*	**Financial Accounting,** *5*
Certified Management Accountant (CMA) Program, *15*	**Generally Accepted Accounting Principles (GAAP),** *9*
Cost Accounting, *3*	**Just-in-Time (JIT) Method,** *11*
Cost Accounting Standards Board (CASB), *15*	**Managerial Accounting,** *5*
	Responsibility Center, *7*
Cost-Benefit Requirement, *18*	**Total Quality Management,** *12*

APPENDIX

Institute of Management Accountants: Standards of Ethical Conduct for Management Accountants

Management accountants have an obligation to the organizations they serve, their profession, the public and themselves to maintain the highest standards of ethical conduct. In recognition of this obligation, the Institute of Management Accountants has promulgated the following standards of ethical conduct for management accountants. Adherence to these standards is integral to achieving the *Objectives of Management Accounting.*[5] Management accountants shall not commit acts contrary to these standards nor shall they condone the commission of such acts by others within their organizations.

Competence
Management accountants have a responsibility to:

- Maintain an appropriate level of professional competence by ongoing development of their knowledge and skills.
- Perform their professional duties in accordance with relevant laws, regulations, and technical standards.

---

[5] National Association of Accountants, *Statements on Management Accounting: Objectives of Management Accounting,* Statement No. 1B, New York, N.Y., June 17, 1982. These standards are reprinted with the permission of the Institute of Management Accountants.

- Prepare complete and clear reports and recommendations after appropriate analyses of relevant and reliable information.

Confidentiality

Management accountants have a responsibility to:

- Refrain from disclosing confidential information acquired in the course of their work except when authorized, unless legally obligated to do so.
- Inform subordinates as appropriate regarding the confidentiality of information acquired in the course of their work and monitor their activities to assure the maintenance of that confidentiality.
- Refrain from using or appearing to use confidential information acquired in the course of their work for unethical or illegal advantage either personally or through third parties.

Integrity

Management accountants have a responsibility to:

- Avoid actual or apparent conflicts of interest and advise all appropriate parties of any potential conflict.
- Refrain from engaging in any activity that would prejudice their ability to carry out their duties ethically.
- Refuse any gift, favor, or hospitality that would influence or would appear to influence their actions.
- Refrain from either actively or passively subverting the attainment of the organization's legitimate and ethical objectives.
- Recognize and communicate professional limitations or other constraints that would preclude responsible judgment or successful performance of an activity.
- Communicate unfavorable as well as favorable information and professional judgments or opinions.
- Refrain from engaging in or supporting any activity that would discredit the profession.

Objectivity

Management accountants have a responsibility to:

- Communicate information fairly and objectively.
- Disclose fully all relevant information that could reasonably be expected to influence an intended user's understanding of the reports, comments, and recommendations presented.

Resolution of Ethical Conflict

In applying the standards of ethical conduct, management accountants may encounter problems in identifying unethical behavior or in resolving an ethical conflict. When faced with significant ethical issues, management accountants should follow the established policies of the organization bearing on the resolution of such conflict. If these policies do not resolve the ethical conflict, management accountants should consider the following courses of action:

- Discuss such problems with the immediate superior except when it appears that the superior is involved, in which case the problem should be presented initially to the next higher managerial level. If satisfactory resolution cannot be achieved when the problem is initially presented, submit the issues to the next higher managerial level.

    If the immediate superior is the chief executive officer, or equivalent, the acceptable reviewing authority may be a group such as the audit committee, executive committee, board of directors, board of trustees, or owners. Contact with levels above the immediate superior should be initiated only with the superior's knowledge, assuming the superior is not involved.

- Clarify relevant concepts by confidential discussion with an objective advisor to obtain an understanding of possible courses of action.

- If the ethical conflict still exists after exhausting all levels of internal review, the management accountant may have no other recourse on significant matters than to resign from the organization and to submit an informative memorandum to an appropriate representative of the organization.

Except where legally prescribed, communication of such problems to authorities or individuals not employed or engaged by the organization is not considered appropriate.

QUESTIONS

1-1 Column 1 lists three decision categories. Column 2 lists three accounting costs and a corresponding letter. Place the letter of the appropriate accounting cost in the blank next to each decision category.

Column 1

_____ Analysis of divisional performance
_____ Costing for income tax purposes
_____ Determining how many units to produce in the coming weeks

Column 2

A. Costs for inventory valuation
B. Costs for decision making
C. Costs for performance evaluation

1-2 A manager once remarked, "All I need are the differential costs for decision making—don't bother me with information about any other costs. They aren't relevant." Give examples of other costs useful to management. Comment on this remark.

1-3 You are considering sharing your living quarters with another person. What costs would you include if you decide to split costs. What costs would differ if another person were to move in with you? Discuss the agreement options available to you.

1-4 Would you support a proposal to develop a set of "generally accepted" accounting standards for performance evaluation? Why or why not?

1-5 A telephone company established discounts for off-peak use of telephone services. A discount of 35 percent is offered for calls placed in the evenings during the week, and a discount of 60 percent is offered for late-night and weekend calls. Since the telephone company would probably not be profitable if these discounts were offered all the time, explain what cost considerations may have entered into management's decision to offer the discounts.

1-6 A critic of the expansion of the role of the accountant has stated, "The controller should have enough work filling out tax forms and the paperwork required by the bureaucracy without trying to interfere with management decision making. Leave that role to those more familiar with management decisions.'' Comment.

1-7   You are considering whether to purchase a new car for personal use to replace your present car. Being strictly rational in an economic sense, which of the following cost data would you include in making your decision?

    a. Original cost of the present car.

    b. Trade-in value of your present car.

    c. Maintenance costs on the present car.

    d. Maintenance costs on the new car.

    e. Fuel consumption on the present car.

    f. Fuel consumption on the new car.

    g. Cost of parking permits, garage rental, and similar storage costs.

    h. Liability insurance on the present car.

    i. Liability insurance on the new car.

    j. Property and collision insurance on the present car.

    k. Property and collision insurance on the new car.

    l. Changes in the relative frequency of your friends saying, ''Let's use your car since it's newer,'' and the related costs of using the new car.

You should be able to give reasons why each element should or should not be included in your analysis. (Hint: Which costs will be differential, that is, will be different if the new car is purchased?)

1-8   Why would the controller have an interest in the structure of an organization?

1-9   Sometimes the internal auditor reports to the person who is responsible for preparation of the accounting reports and the maintenance of accounting records. What are some advantages of such a supervisory relationship? What conflicts might exist, and what procedures might be installed to minimize the extent of conflict?

1-10   For a corporation organized according to the organization chart in Illustration 1-5, what potential conflicts might arise between production managers and the controller's staff? How might these potential conflicts be resolved with a minimum of interference from the chief executive officer?

1-11   What certifications are available to a person in an accounting career?

1-12   Refer to the Real World Application, ''The Accountant as a Communicator.'' Why is it important for accountants at Lever Brothers Co. to communicate effectively with marketing people?

1-13   Refer to the Real World Application about Johnson & Johnson's code of conduct. Why does the company list its responsibility to stockholders last instead of first?

EXERCISES

1-14   Cost Data for Managerial Purposes
(L.O.1)[6]

In your first day as a member of the controller's staff, you are asked to report on a contemplated change in the use of a new type of material in production. The new material is expected to result in a 10 percent reduction in materials costs but no

---

[6] Each exercise in this book is keyed to one or more learning objectives. The key L.O.1 refers to the first learning objective on the title page of the chapter.

changes in any other costs. Last year, materials costs were $6 per unit produced. Other costs were $8 per unit produced. The company can sell as many units as it can manufacture. The materials vendor has informed the company that it will increase the materials prices by 5 percent in the coming year. In addition, analysis of other costs indicates that these costs may be expected to increase by 4 percent in the coming year.

Required:

a. Identify the differential costs for the decision to use the new material. What would the cost savings per unit be if the company were to use the new material instead of the old material?

b. Describe how management would use the information in (*a*), and any other appropriate information, to proceed with the contemplated use of the new material.

1–15   Cost Data for Managerial Purposes
(L.O.1)

Management of the Microwave Division of Technology, Inc., wants to know whether to continue operations in the division. The division has been operating at a loss for the past several years as indicated in the accompanying divisional income statement. If the division is eliminated, corporate administration is not expected to change, nor are any other changes expected in the operations or costs of other divisions.

Required:

What costs are probably differential for the decision to discontinue this division's operations?

TECHNOLOGY, INC., MICROWAVE DIVISION
Divisional Income Statement
For the Year Ending December 31

Sales revenue	$860,000
Costs:	
Advertising	35,000
Cost of goods sold	430,000
Divisional administrative salaries	58,000
Selling costs	82,000
Rent	181,000
Share of corporate administration	95,000
Total costs	881,000
Net loss before income tax benefit	(21,000)
Tax benefit at 40% rate	8,400
Net loss	$(12,600)

1–16   The Role of Accounting in Organizations
(L.O.3)

Lorraine DuVere has just been named chief executive officer of a high-technology company. Lorraine started in the budgeting section of the controller's office and has risen rapidly through the ranks of the organization. She has been so impressed with the importance of budgeting that she proposed creating a new vice president for budgeting since, as Lorraine noted, it was often difficult for a mere "supervisor" to obtain the complete cooperation of other division managers in the budgeting function.

Required:

Comment on the proposed new position and suggest other ways that Lorraine might accomplish her objectives.

1–17   The Role of Accounting in Organizations
(L.O.3)

Carmen Lorenzo was recently appointed chief executive officer of a diversified corporate organization. The company has been organized along functional lines similar to Illustration 1–5. This company has three separate manufacturing divisions, each dealing with different products and markets. Each manufacturing division is headed by an assistant vice president, with a vice president for manufacturing heading up all manufacturing operations. One vice president proposed that the organization would be more efficient if the company set up each manufacturing division as a decentralized unit. As the vice president pointed out, "Each of these manufacturing divisions is sufficiently dissimilar that they would operate better on their own. If each division had its own marketing and accounting staffs, there would be less need to cross division lines each time a marketing study or an accounting report is required. Moreover, the accounting sections could adapt their decision-making and performance-evaluation functions to the needs of the specific manufacturing divisions rather than treat them all alike."

Required: Prepare comments on the advantages and disadvantages of the proposal. Your supervisor is the controller, who coordinates accounting activities for all three divisions.

1–18 The Role of Accounting in Organizations
(L.O.3)

Barbara Scott has just been hired as the new controller for Physical Therapy Equipment, Inc., a manufacturer of physical therapy equipment. The vice president of finance reports directly to the president of the company. The finance area has three offices—controller, treasurer, and internal auditor. Other departments who have vice presidents reporting directly to the president are Marketing and Production.

The controller's office consists of three departmental supervisors who each supervises three employees. The three departments are Cost Accounting, Financial Reporting, and Tax.

Required: *a.* Construct an organizational chart for Physical Therapy Equipment, Inc.

b. What duties would you expect the controller and her staff to perform?

1–19 The Role of Accounting in Organizations
(L.O.3)

Reginald Langley, corporate vice president for UniProduct, a large multinational corporation, made a request for a review of the corporation's recycling management system. The review was assigned to Fiona Brooks, a senior internal auditor.

The recycling management system was introduced eight years ago and has been modified and enhanced periodically. James Dunley, director of resource management, designed the original system and currently manages it.

Required: Suggest ways that Brooks can clearly communicate the results of her audit to Langley and Dunley.

(CMA adapted)

1–20 Ethics and Altering the Books
(L.O.5)

Alert, a closely held investment services group, has been very successful over the past three years. Bonuses for top management have ranged from 50 percent to 100 percent of base salary. Top management, however, only holds 35 percent of the common stock, and recent industry news indicates that a major corporation may try to acquire Alert. Top management fears that they might lose their bonuses, not to mention their employment, if the takeover occurs. Management has told Roger Deerling, Alert's controller, to make a few changes to several accounting policies and practices, thus making Alert a much less attractive acquisition. Roger knows that these "changes" are not in accordance with generally accepted accounting principles. Roger has also been informed not to mention these changes to anyone outside the top-management group.

Required: *a.* From the viewpoint of the "Standards of Ethical Conduct for Management Accountants," what are Roger Deerling's responsibilities?

b. What steps should he take to resolve this problem?

(CMA adapted)

PROBLEMS

1–21 Responsibility for Ethical Action

Jorge Martinez recently joined GroChem, Inc., as assistant controller. GroChem processes chemicals for use in fertilizers. During his first month on the job, Jorge spent most of his time getting better acquainted with those responsible for plant operations. Jorge asked the plant supervisor what the procedure was for the disposal of chemicals. The response was that he (the plant supervisor) was not involved in the disposal of waste and that Jorge would be wise to ignore the issue. Of course, this just drove Jorge to investigate the matter further. Jorge soon discovered that GroChem was dumping toxic waste in a nearby public landfill late at night. Further, he discovered that it appeared that several members of management were involved in arranging for this dumping. Jorge was, however, unable to determine whether his superior, the controller, was involved. Jorge considered three possible courses of action. He could discuss the matter with his controller, anonymously release the information to the local newspaper, or discuss the situation with an outside member of the board of directors whom he knows personally.

Required:

a. Does Jorge have an ethical responsibility to take a course of action?

b. Of the three possible courses of action, which are appropriate and which are inappropriate?

(CMA adapted)

1-22 Ethics and Inventory Obsolescence

The external auditors of HHP (Heart Health Procedures) are currently performing their annual audit of the company with the help of assistant controller Linda Joyner. Several years ago Heart Health Procedures developed a unique balloon technique for opening obstructed arteries in the heart. The technique utilizes an expensive component that HHP purchases from a sole supplier. Until last year, HHP maintained a monopoly in this field.

During the past year, however, a major competitor developed a technically superior product that uses an innovative, less costly component. The competitor was granted FDA approval, and it is expected that HHP will lose market share as a result. HHP currently has several years' worth of expensive components essential for the manufacturing of its balloon product. Linda Joyner knows that these components will decrease in price due to the introduction of the competitor's product. She also knows that her boss, the controller, is aware of the situation. The controller, however, has informed the chief financial officer that there is no obsolete inventory, nor any need for reductions of inventories to net realizable values. Linda is aware that the chief financial officer's bonus plan is tied directly to corporate profits.

In signing the auditor's representation letter, the chief financial officer acknowledges that all relevant information has been disclosed to the auditors and that all accounting procedures have been followed according to generally accepted accounting principles. Linda knows that the external auditors are unaware of the inventory problem, and is unsure what to do.

Required:

a. Has the controller behaved unethically?

b. How should Linda Joyner resolve this problem? Should she report this inventory overvaluation to the external auditors?

(CMA adapted)

1-23 Cost Data for Managerial Purposes

Florida Fruits, Inc., agreed to sell 20,000 cases of a dehydrated fruit drink called "Fang" to NASA for use on space flights at "cost plus 20 percent."

Florida Fruits operates a manufacturing plant that can produce 60,000 cases per year. The company normally produces 40,000 cases per year. The costs to produce 40,000 cases are as follows:

	Total	Per Case
Materials	$ 480,000	$12
Labor	760,000	19
Supplies and other indirect costs that will vary with production	320,000	8
Indirect costs that will not vary with production	440,000	11
Variable marketing costs	80,000	2
Administrative costs (all fixed)	160,000	4
Totals	$2,240,000	$56

Based on the above data, company management expects to receive $67.20 (that is, $56 × 120 percent) per case for the cases sold on this contract. After completing

5,000 cases, the company sent a bill (invoice) to the government for $336,000 (that is, 5,000 cases at $67.20 per case).

The president of the company received a call from NASA, who stated that the per case cost should be:

Materials	$12
Labor	19
Supplies, etc.	8
Total	$39

Therefore, the price per case should be $46.80 (that is, $39 × 120 percent). NASA ignored marketing costs because the contract bypassed the usual selling channels.

Required:

What price would you recommend? Why? (Note: You need not limit yourself to the costs selected by the company or by the government agent.)

1–24 Cost Data for Managerial Purposes

Amos Division is a division of a large corporation. It normally sells to outside customers but, on occasion, will sell to another division of the corporation. When it does, corporate policy states that the price will be cost plus 10 percent. Amos received an order from the Field Division, which is also a division of the corporation, for 10,000 units. Amos Division's planned output for the year had been 50,000 units before the order from Field. Amos's capacity is 75,000 units per year. The costs for producing those 50,000 units are:

	Total	Per Unit
Materials	$ 20,000	$ .40
Direct labor	100,000	2.00
Other costs varying with output	10,000	.20
Fixed costs	90,000	1.80
Total costs	$220,000	$4.40

Based on these data, the Amos Division controller, who was new to the corporation, calculated that the unit price for the Field Division order should be $4.84 ($4.40 × 110 percent). After producing and shipping the 10,000 units, Amos Division sent an invoice for $48,400. Shortly thereafter, Amos received a note from the buyer at Field Division that stated this invoice was not in accordance with company policy. The unit cost should have been:

	Per Unit
Materials	$ .40
Direct labor	2.00
Other costs varying with output	.20
Total	$2.60

The price would be $2.86 ($2.60 × 110 percent) per unit.

Required:

If the corporation asked you to review this intercompany policy, what policy would you recommend? Why? (Note: You need not limit yourself to the Field Division calculation or current policy.)

1–25 Cost Data for Managerial Purposes

Pete's Coffee, Inc., operates a small coffee shop in the downtown area. Profits have been declining, and management is planning to expand and add ice cream to the menu. The annual ice cream sales are expected to increase revenue by $40,000. The cost of purchasing ice cream from the manufacturer is $20,000. The coffee shop and ice cream shop will be supervised by the present manager. However, due to expansion, the labor costs and utilities would increase by 50 percent. Rent and other costs will increase by 20 percent.

PETE'S COFFEE, INC.
Annual Income Statement
Before Expansion

Sales revenue	$38,000
Costs:	
Food	15,000
Labor	12,000
Utilities	2,000
Rent	4,000
Other costs	2,000
Manager's salary	6,000
Total costs	41,000
Operating profit (loss)	$ (3,000)

Required:

a. Prepare a report of the differential costs and revenues if ice cream is added. (Hint: Use format of Illustration 1–2.)

b. Should management open the ice cream shop?

1–26   Cost Data for Managerial Purposes

Denver Data Corp. writes software for computer applications. Recently, one of the company's officers was approached by a representative of a scientific research firm who offered a contract to Denver Data Corp. for some specialized programs. Denver Data Corp. reported the following costs and revenues during the past year.

DENVER DATA CORP.
Annual Income Statement

Sales revenue	$600,000
Costs:	
Programmer labor	285,000
Equipment lease	42,000
Rent	36,000
Supplies	27,000
Officers' salaries	175,000
Other costs	19,000
Total costs	584,000
Operating profit	$ 16,000

If the company decides to take the contract to produce scientific programs, it will need to hire a full-time programmer at $60,000. Equipment lease would increase by 20 percent because of the need to buy certain computer equipment. Supplies would increase by an estimated 10 percent, and other costs would increase by 20 persent. The existing building has space for the new programmer. In addition, management believes that no new officers will be necessary for this work.

Required:

a. What are the differential costs that would be incurred as a result of taking the contract?

b. If the contract will pay $75,000 in the first year, should Denver Data take the contract?

c. What considerations, other than costs, would be necessary before making this decision?

SOLUTIONS TO

Self-Study
Questions

1   Managerial accounting is the preparation and use of accounting information for *managers inside organizations* in making decisions and evaluating performance. Financial accounting is the preparation and use of accounting information for *outsiders,* such as investors and creditors.

2   All costs in Illustration 1–2 would have increased 50 percent. Total costs would increase from $1,090 in the baseline to $1,635 (150% × $1,090). Profits would increase from $10 in the baseline to $15 ($1,650 revenues − $1,635 costs). Jennifer's profits increase compared to the baseline, but not as much as in Illustration 1–2 because some of the costs in Illustration 1–2 do not increase proportionately with sales revenue.

3   Causes of changes include the following:

Accounting has become more computerized, thus reducing manual book-keeping.

Increased competition in many industries, including automobiles and electronic equipment, has increased management's interest in managing costs.

Deregulation in industries like banks, airlines, and health care has increased management's interest in managing costs.

Developments of more highly technical production processes has reduced emphasis on labor and increased emphasis on overhead cost control.

Developments in new management techniques have affected accounting. For example, by reducing inventory levels, just-in-time (JIT) methods have reduced the need to compute costs of inventory.

4   Major financial offices or departments in organizations are:

Controller

Treasurer

Internal Auditor

Also, many organizations have a vice president of finance who is in charge of all financial activities. The highest level financial official is generally called the chief financial officer.

Cost Concepts and Behavior

After reading this chapter, you should be able to:

1. Explain the basic concept of cost.
2. Explain how costs are presented in financial statements.
3. Understand how materials, labor, and overhead costs are added to a product at each stage of the production process.
4. Define basic cost concepts for decision making, such as differential costs, and fixed versus variable costs.
5. Identify the components of full cost.

*T*his chapter provides the foundation for your study of cost accounting. We present and discuss fundamental concepts in cost accounting that you will encounter whatever your accounting career. For many of you, this will be the chapter that you most often refer to in your work. As we stated in Chapter 1, many companies are getting "back to basics" in understanding and managing their costs. The Real World Application for this chapter gives an example of a company that failed to manage its costs effectively. To be competitive, we must understand fundamental cost concepts and manage companies and governmental units so that costs are kept under control and resources are used wisely.

We begin this chapter with a discussion of general concepts of costs. We then discuss how costs appear on financial statements. Next we show how costs are added to a product at each stage of production using a jeans manufacturer as our example. We define and apply cost ideas that managers use in making decisions, using a particular decision for the jeans manufacturer as our case study. Finally, we present several diagrams that will help you keep track of the different components of a product's cost. Illustration 2–13 at the end of the chapter summarizes the most important cost concepts in this chapter.

*Costs and Competitiveness**

A classic example of the problems that arise from failure to monitor costs properly is the case of Bethlehem Steel Corp. The company operated in a market characterized by government import restrictions and few domestic producers. The net effect was limited competition and an environment where prices could be set to cover costs.

Like other domestic steelmakers, Bethlehem failed to invest in more efficient basic oxygen furnaces because to do so would increase initial cash outlays even though long-run costs would be reduced. As a result, Bethlehem lost its ability to produce steel at as low a cost as foreign producers. Export markets for U.S. steel dried up. Imports rose as fast as possible under control regulations. Moreover, because Bethlehem and other U.S. steel pro-

ducers charged high prices to compensate for their high costs, substitute materials like fiberglass, prestressed concrete, aluminum, and plastics took over a substantial portion of the market for steel products.

The U.S. steel industry declined from near total domination of world steel markets in the 1950s to being a marginally profitable minor presence in world steel by 1990. Steel was not the first nor will it probably be the last industry to ignore costs at its own peril. With increased world competition, the steel industry has begun to pay closer attention to costs. Whether the industry can stage a comeback is an open question.

* Based on the authors' research.

THE CONCEPT OF COST

Outlay Cost A past, present, or future cash outflow.

Opportunity Cost The lost benefit an alternative course of action could provide.

A cost is a sacrifice of resources. In going about our daily affairs, we buy many different things—clothing, food, books, perhaps an automobile, a desk lamp, and so on. Each item has a price that measures the sacrifice we must make to acquire it. Whether we pay immediately or agree to pay at some later date, the cost is actually established by that price.

There are two major categories of costs: outlay costs and opportunity costs. An **outlay cost** is a past, present, or future cash outflow. Consider the cost of a college education. Clearly, the cash outflows for tuition, books, and fees are outlay costs for college. For many college students, cash is not all that is sacrificed. Students also sacrifice their time to get a college education.

While there is no cash outlay because of this time sacrifice, there is an opportunity cost. **Opportunity cost** is the *benefit* that could be realized from the *best forgone alternative use* of a resource. For example, many students give up other jobs to earn a college degree. Their forgone income is part of the cost of getting a college degree. This forgone income is the benefit that could be realized from an alternative use of the scarce resource—time.

Similarly, the opportunity cost of funds invested in a government bond is the forgone interest that could be earned on a bank certificate of deposit, assuming both securities were equal in risk and liquidity. The opportunity cost of using a factory to produce a particular product is the sacrifice of profits that could be made by producing other products or by renting the factory to someone else. In each case, we assume that the forgone alternative use was the *best* comparable use of the resource given up.

Of course, no one can ever know all the possible opportunities available at any moment. Hence, some opportunity costs will undoubtedly not be considered. Accounting systems typically record outlay costs but not opportunity costs. Unfortunately, managers sometimes incorrectly ignore opportunity costs in making decisions.

Cost and Expenses

Expense A cost that is charged against revenue in an accounting period.

It is important to distinguish *cost* from *expense*. As previously discussed, a cost is a sacrifice of resources. An **expense** is a cost that is charged against revenue in an accounting period; hence, expenses are deducted from revenue in that accounting period. We use the term *expense* only when speaking of external financial reports.

The focus of cost accounting is on *costs*, not expenses. Generally accepted accounting principles (GAAP) and regulations such as the income tax laws specify when costs are to be treated as expenses. In practice, the terms *costs* and *expenses* are sometimes used synonymously. We use the term *cost* in this book unless we are dealing with expense as an income measurement issue under GAAP.

Operating Profit The excess of operating revenues over the operating costs necessary to generate those revenues.

We shall relate much of our analysis and discussion to income statements. This makes it easier to see where the specific object of our analysis fits into an organization's total performance. Unless otherwise stated, we assume these income statements are prepared for *internal* management use, not for external reporting. We focus on **operating profit,** which for internal reporting purposes is the excess of operating revenues over the operating costs incurred to generate those revenues. This figure differs from **net income,** which is operating profit adjusted for interest, income taxes, extraordinary items, and other adjustments required to comply with GAAP and other regulations.

Cost accounting provides cost data for external reporting, and also provides data for managerial accounting. To distinguish the amounts that might be reported internally from those reported externally, we reserve the term *net income* for external reporting.

Period Costs versus Product Costs

Product Costs Those costs that can be attributed to a product; costs that are part of inventory.

Period Costs Costs that can be attributed to time intervals.

Cost accountants divide costs into product or period categories. **Product costs** are costs more easily attributed to products, while **period costs** are more easily attributed to time intervals. The annual rent of an office building and the salary of a company executive are period costs. The costs of merchandise purchased for resale or related transportation-in costs are examples of product costs.

As shown in Illustration 2–1, marketing and administrative costs are not product costs in either merchandising or manufacturing companies. Merchandising companies inventory merchandise purchases and their related costs while manufacturing companies inventory the materials, labor, and overhead that go into making a product.

COSTS IN FINANCIAL STATEMENTS

We now discuss product costing for measuring the value of inventory. The product costs assigned to inventory are carried in the accounts as assets. When the goods are sold, the costs flow from inventory to cost of goods sold. At that time, these previously inventoried costs become period costs or expenses.

Cost of a Product Sold in Merchandising

Consider the cost of items offered for sale in a merchandising organization like a supermarket, clothing store, or furniture store. In such companies, no manufacturing activity takes place; the items purchased are sold in the same condition they are received. Merchants do not incur additional costs to alter the form or nature of the products they acquire.

Even in such a basic cost accounting situation, the cost of the merchandise acquired for sale may include a number of individual costs. Besides the

*Comparison of Product
and Period Cost*

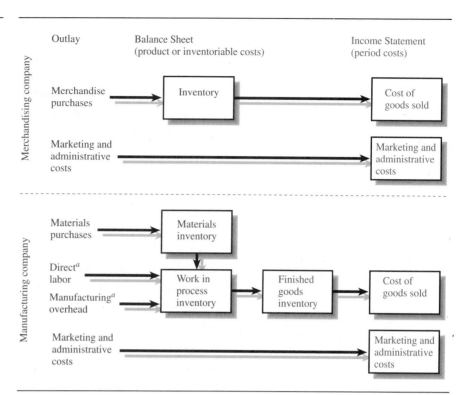

^a These costs are part of product costs under *full-absorption costing.*

cost of the merchandise itself, the buyer may pay to transport the merchandise to the selling outlet, and insure it while it is in route.

For example, Masthead Clothing Stores had a beginning inventory of $125,000 on January 1. They purchased $687,000 during the year and had transportation-in costs of $26,000. During the year, they sold goods costing $662,000, which included transportation-in costs. Sales revenue for the year was $1 million; marketing and administrative costs were $200,000. Masthead had an ending inventory of $176,000 on December 31.

An income statement and a cost of goods sold statement are shown in Illustration 2–2. The term **cost of goods sold** is self-descriptive. It includes only the actual costs of the goods that were sold. It does not include the costs of selling the goods, such as the salaries of sales and delivery people. Nor does it include the cost of the facilities in which the sales are made. These are other costs of doing business. They are deducted from sales revenue as a period cost when they are incurred.

Cost of Goods Sold The cost assigned to products sold during a period.

*Cost of a
Manufactured Product*

Now consider a manufacturing operation. The cost of a manufactured product includes all the costs of making it. The manufacturer purchases materials (for example, unassembled parts), hires workers to work on the material to convert it to a finished good, then offers the product for sale. For cost accounting purposes, three cateogries of manufacturing costs receive attention:

Direct Materials Those materials that can feasibly be identified directly with the product.

1. **Direct materials** from which the product is made. (To the manufacturer, purchased parts, including transportation-in, are included in direct materials.) Direct materials are also called *raw materials*.

MASTHEAD CLOTHING STORES
Income Statement
For the Year Ended December 31

Sales revenue	$1,000,000
Cost of goods sold (see statement below)	662,000 ◄
Gross margin	338,000
Marketing and administrative costs	200,000
Operating profit	$ 138,000

Cost of Goods Sold Statement
For the Year Ended December 31

Beginning inventory	$ 125,000
Cost of goods purchased:	
Merchandise cost	687,000
Transportation-in costs	26,000
Total cost of goods purchased	713,000
Cost of goods available for sale	838,000
Less cost of goods in ending inventory	176,000
Cost of goods sold	$ 662,000 ◄

Direct Labor The cost of workers who actually transform materials into finished products during the production process.

Manufacturing Overhead All production costs except direct labor and direct materials.

2. **Direct labor** of workers who transform the materials into a finished product.
3. All other costs of transforming the materials to a finished product, often referred to in total as **manufacturing overhead.** Some examples of manufacturing overhead are:
   a. *Indirect labor,* the cost of workers who do not work directly on the product yet are required for the factory to operate, such as supervisors, maintenance workers, and inventory storekeepers.
   b. *Indirect materials,* such as lubricants for the machinery, polishing and cleaning materials, repair parts, and light bulbs, which are not a part of the finished product but are necessary to manufacture the product.
   c. *Other manufacturing costs,* such as depreciation of the factory building and equipment, taxes on the factory assets, insurance on the factory building and equipment, heat, light, power, and similar expenses incurred to keep the factory operating.

Although we use the term *manufacturing overhead* in this book, other common synonyms used in practice are *factory burden, factory overhead, burden, factory expense,* and the unmodified word *overhead.*

STAGES OF PRODUCTION

Work in Process Product in the production process, not yet complete.

There are three stages in which materials might exist in a manufacturing company at any time. The company may have *direct materials* that have not yet been put into production. There is also likely to be uncompleted work on the production line, which accountants refer to as **work in process.** And there may be **finished goods** that have been completely processed and are ready for sale. Because material in each of these stages has incurred costs, a cost accounting system will include three different inventory accounts: Direct

ILLUSTRATION   *Unique Denims—Departmental Responsibilities*

Work in Process Departments

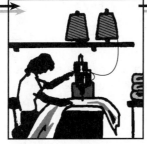

Direct Materials Receiving	**Cut, Make, and Trim (CMT)**	**Wash and Inspect (WI)**	**Finished Goods**
Receive raw materials. Ensure that correct amount is received. Inspect materials. Release materials to manufacturing as needed.	Make pattern to conform with customer specifications for fit and size distribution. Cut denim into individual parts for sewing. Sew garments. Apply buttons, zippers, and labels.	Wash garments to customer specifications. Inspect garments for fabric or sewing flaws.	Pack finished garments to customer specifications for size and style, and ship garments.

Finished Goods Product fully completed, not yet sold.

Inventoriable Costs Costs of a product regarded as an asset (inventory).

Materials Inventory, Work in Process Inventory, and Finished Goods Inventory.

Each inventory account is likely to have a beginning inventory amount, additions (debits) and withdrawals (credits) during the period, and an ending inventory based on the units still on hand. Those costs that are initially charged to inventory accounts are called **inventoriable costs.**

We now present a simplified version of the actual production process of a company that manufactures jeans, a company we call Unique Denims. Illustration 2–3 shows the stages of production from receipt of materials through manufacturing to the finished goods warehouse. Unique Denims receives denim at its Direct Materials Receiving Department. The people in this department are responsible for checking each order to be sure it meets quality specifications and the goods received are what was ordered.

If Unique Denims uses just-in-time (JIT) purchasing, people in Direct Materials Receiving will send the materials—denim—to the manufacturing departments immediately. If Unique does not use JIT purchasing, people in this department would send the denim to a materials warehouse until needed for production. Any product that has been purchased but not yet transferred to manufacturing departments will be part of Direct Materials Inventory on the balance sheet at the end of the accounting period.

When the production process begins, the production department cuts the denim to size. Next, the denim is sent to sewing stations where it is sewn into jeans and trim is added. These first two steps are shown in Illustration 2–3 as taking place in the Cut, Make, and Trim (CMT) Department. From there, the jeans are sent to the Wash and Inspect (WI) Department where they are washed to meet customer specifications for hand feel and appearance, and inspected for fabric or sewing flaws. Note that both the CMT and

WI Departments are part of work in process. Any product still in these departments at the end of an accounting period is part of Work in Process Inventory on the balance sheet.

After the goods are inspected, they are shipped immediately to customers under a just-in-time system; otherwise they are shipped to a warehouse that holds finished goods until they are shipped to customers. Any product that is finished but not yet sold to customers is included in Finished Goods Inventory on the balance sheet at the end of an accounting period.

To demonstrate how costs would appear on the financial statements, assume the company's direct materials inventory on hand January 1 was $200,000, purchases of denim during the year were $800,000, ending inventory on December 31 was $150,000. The cost of direct materials put into production during the year was $850,000, computed as follows:

Beginning direct materials inventory, January 1	$ 200,000
Add purchases during the year	800,000
Direct materials available during the year	1,000,000
Less ending direct materials inventory, December 31	150,000
Cost of direct materials put into production	$ 850,000

The Work in Process Inventory account had a beginning balance on January 1 of $350,000, as shown in the schedule below. Costs incurred during the year were $850,000 in direct materials from the schedule of direct materials costs above; $700,000 in direct labor costs; and $1,850,000 in manufacturing overhead. The sum of materials, labor, and manufacturing overhead costs incurred, $3,400,000, is the total manufacturing costs incurred during the year, as shown in the schedule below.

Adding the beginning work in process inventory, $350,000, to the $3,400,000 gives $3,750,000, the total cost of work in process for the year. At year-end, the inventory is found to have a cost of $400,000. This $400,000 is subtracted to arrive at $3,350,000, the cost of goods manufactured. These events are summarized in the following cost of goods manufactured schedule, which is part of the comprehensive statement appearing in Illustration 2–4.

Beginning work in process inventory, January 1		$ 350,000
Manufacturing costs during the year:		
Direct materials	$ 850,000	
Direct labor	700,000	
Manufacturing overhead	1,850,000	
Total manufacturing costs incurred during the year		3,400,000
Total cost of work in process during the year		3,750,000
Less ending work in process inventory, December 31		400,000
Cost of goods manufactured during the year		$3,350,000

Finished Goods Inventory   The work finished during the period is transferred from the production department to the finished goods storage area and is added to the inventory of finished goods as items available for sale. The beginning (January 1) and ending (December 31) finished goods inventory balances were $920,000 and $1,460,000, respectively. Cost of goods manufactured, or finished, by pro-

ILLUSTRATION

2-4

*Cost of Goods Manufactured
and Sold Statement*

UNIQUE DENIMS
Cost of Goods Manufactured and Sold Statement
For the Year Ending December 31

Beginning work in process inventory, January 1 . . .			$ 350,000
Manufacturing costs during the year:			
Direct materials:			
Beginning inventory, January 1	$ 200,000		
Add purchases	800,000		
Direct materials available	1,000,000		
Less ending inventory	150,000		
Direct materials put into production		$ 850,000	
Direct labor		700,000	
Manufacturing overhead		1,850,000	
Total manufacturing costs incurred during the year			3,400,000
Total cost of work in process during the year			3,750,000
Less ending work in process inventory, December 31			400,000
Cost of goods manufactured during the year			3,350,000
Beginning finished goods inventory, January 1 . . .			920,000
Finished goods inventory available for sale			4,270,000
Less ending finished goods inventory, December 31			1,460,000
Cost of goods manufactured and sold			$2,810,000

duction and transferred out of work in process inventory was $3,350,000. Cost of goods sold was $2,810,000, as computed in the following schedule:

Beginning finished goods inventory, January 1	$ 920,000
Cost of goods manufactured (finished) during the year	3,350,000
Cost of goods available for sale during the year	4,270,000
Less ending finished goods inventory, December 31	1,460,000
Cost of goods sold	$2,810,000

Cost of Goods Manufactured and Sold Statement

As part of its internal reporting system, Unique Denims prepares a **cost of goods manufactured and sold statement.** This statement is shown in Illustration 2–4. It incorporates and summarizes information from the discussion above.

If you compare Illustration 2–2 with Illustration 2–4 and the income statement in Illustration 2–5, you will see that product costing in a manufacturing setting is more complex than product costing in merchandising. As a result, we devote a substantial amount of discussion to cost flows and product costing in a manufacturing setting in later chapters. Many of the product costing concepts used in manufacturing can be applied to merchandising and service organizations, too.

ILLUSTRATION

2-5

UNIQUE DENIMS
Income Statement
For the Year Ending December 31

Sales revenue	$4,500,000
Cost of goods sold (see Illustration 2–4)	2,810,000
Gross margin	1,690,000
Less: marketing and administrative costs	1,440,000
Operating profit before taxes	$ 250,000

The cost of goods manufactured and sold statement in Illustration 2–4 is composed of three building blocks. The gray shaded area is the schedule of the cost of direct materials. Direct materials costs are combined with direct labor and manufacturing overhead which collectively form the charges to work in process. The shaded light purple area of Illustration 2–4 reflects the Work in Process account with its beginning balance, charges, and ending balance. The last item in the light purple shaded area is the credit to work in process, which reflects the transfer to finished goods. The unshaded area of the statement is the adjustment to reflect differences between the beginning and ending finished goods inventory. The final line item is, of course, cost of goods manufactured and sold.

Income Statement

In addition to the manufacturing costs noted above, Unique Denims incurred marketing and administrative costs of $1,440,000 and generated sales revenue of $4,500,000. These period costs, together with revenues and the cost of goods manufactured and sold, are presented in the income statement shown in Illustration 2–5.

Self-Study Question

1 This self-study question reviews the financial statement presentation of the costs of making and selling products. The following items appeared in the records of Shoreline Products, Inc., for the current year:

Administrative costs	$ 304,000
Depreciation—manufacturing	103,000
Direct labor	482,000
Finished goods inventory, January 1	160,000
Finished goods inventory, December 31	147,000
Heat, light, and power—plant	87,000
Marketing costs	272,000
Miscellaneous manufacturing costs	12,000
Plant maintenance and repairs	74,000
Direct materials purchases	313,000
Direct materials inventory, January 1	102,000
Direct materials inventory, December 31	81,000

Sales revenue	2,036,000
Supervisory and indirect labor	127,000
Supplies and indirect materials	14,000
Work in process inventory, January 1	135,000
Work in process inventory, December 31	142,000

Prepare an income statement with a supporting cost of goods manufactured and sold statement. (Refer to Illustrations 2–4 and 2–5).

The solution to this question is at the end of this chapter on page 61.

COMPONENTS OF A PRODUCT'S COST

Prime Costs and Conversion Costs

Prime Cost The sum of direct materials and direct labor.

Conversion Costs The sum of direct labor and manufacturing overhead.

The sum of direct materials and direct labor is called **prime cost**. We think of manufacturing as the conversion of raw materials into a finished product. Direct labor and manufacturing overhead are required to accomplish this conversion. Therefore, the total of direct labor and manufacturing overhead is called **conversion cost**.

Illustration 2–6 summarizes the relationship between conversion costs and the three elements of manufactured product cost—direct materials, direct labor, and manufacturing overhead.

ILLUSTRATION

Components of Manufactured Product Cost

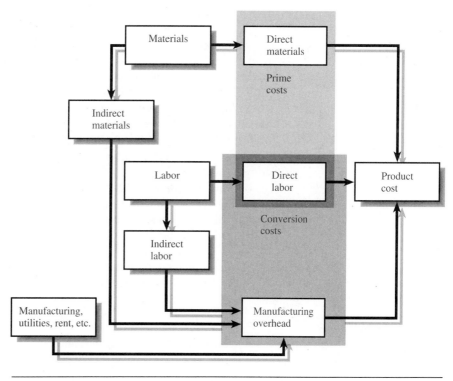

Nonmanufacturing Costs

Nonmanufacturing costs are composed of two elements: marketing costs and administrative costs. **Marketing costs** are the costs required to obtain customer orders and provide customers with finished products. These include advertising, sales commissions, shipping, and marketing departments' building occupancy costs, among others. **Administrative costs** are the costs required to manage the organization and provide staff support. They include executive and clerical salaries; costs such as legal, finance, data processing, and accounting services; and building occupancy for administrative personnel.

Nonmanufacturing costs are expensed in the period incurred for financial accounting, so they are considered *period* expenses for *financial* accounting purposes.

It is sometimes difficult to distinguish between manufacturing costs and nonmanufacturing costs. For example, are the salaries of accountants who handle factory payrolls manufacturing or nonmanufacturing costs? What about the rent for offices for the manufacturing vice president? There are no clear-cut classifications, so companies usually set their own guidelines and follow them consistently.

Direct versus Indirect Costs

Earlier we distinguished between *direct* and *indirect* labor costs. *Direct* labor costs are the costs of the workers who transform direct materials into finished products, while *indirect* labor costs are the costs of workers who are needed to operate the factory but do not work directly on a product.

Cost Object Any end to which a cost is assigned. Examples include a product, a department, or a product line.

Any cost that can be directly related to a **cost object** is a direct cost of that cost object. Those that cannot are indirect costs. A cost object is any end to which a cost is assigned—for example, a unit of inventory, a department or a product line.

Accountants use the terms *direct cost* and *indirect cost* much as a nonaccountant might expect. The only difficulty is that a cost may be direct to one cost object and indirect to another. For example, the salary of a supervisor in a manufacturing department is a direct cost of the department but an indirect cost of the individual items produced by the department. So whenever someone refers to a cost as either direct or indirect, you should immediately ask, "Direct or indirect with respect to what cost object? Units produced? A department? A division?" (When we use the terms *direct* and *indirect* to describe *direct labor, direct materials, indirect materials,* and *indirect labor,* the cost object is the unit being produced.)

Indirect costs are sometimes referred to as *common costs*. When indirect costs result from the sharing of facilities (buildings, equipment) or services (data processing, maintenance staff) by several departments, some method must frequently be devised for assigning a share of those costs to each user. The process of assignment is referred to as **cost allocation.** The allocation of costs pervades cost accounting. We discuss implications of allocating costs throughout this book.

Cost Allocation The process of assigning indirect costs to cost objects.

Self-Study Question

2 Using the data from self-study question 1 (Shoreline Products, Inc.), place dollar amounts in each of the boxes in Illustration 2–6.

The solution to this question is at the end of this chapter on page 62.

*COSTS FOR
MANAGERIAL
DECISION MAKING*

Differential Costs

Differential Costs Costs that change in response to a particular course of action.

Sunk Costs ◆

Sunk Cost An expenditure made in the past that cannot be changed by present or future decisions.

Decision making involves estimating costs of alternative actions. **Differential costs** are costs that change in response to a particular course of action. To estimate differential costs, the accountant determines which costs will be affected by an action and how much they will change.

In contrast to a differential cost, a **sunk cost** is an expenditure made in the past that *cannot be changed.* Sunk costs in and of themselves are not differential costs even though people sometimes act as if the sunk costs were relevant. For example, a clothing store has 15 pairs of slacks that cost the retailer $20. No slacks have been sold at the regular price of $39.95, and they cannot be returned to the manufacturer. The manager of the store knows that he can sell the slacks at $15 per pair, but he refuses to take a loss on them. The manager states, ''I've got $20 apiece in these slacks. How can I afford the loss?'' The $20 expenditure per pair of slacks is a sunk cost. It is not affected by the sale of the product. Consequently, the $20 is not relevant to the pricing decision. The store manager should ignore the sunk cost. The ''loss'' occurred when the market value of the slacks fell below the cost. The manager must act in the best way possible given the present and expected future conditions. If the expected future price is less than $15, the best the manager can do is take the loss now.

Most past expenditures are sunk costs. However, this does not mean that information about past expenditures is irrelevant. The store manager should ignore the cost of the slacks *now owned,* but information about the difficulty of selling the slacks for more than their cost is necessary for future decisions about buying that kind of merchandise. Also, the past cost is relevant for deriving the tax and book gain or loss on the eventual sale of the slacks.

Cost Behavior

Cost Driver A factor that causes, or "drives," an activity's costs.

Cost behavior deals with the way costs respond to changes in activity levels. Throughout this book we refer to the idea of a cost driver. A **cost driver** is a factor that causes, or "drives," an activity's costs. For example, suppose the activity is building a house. The cost driver for the cost of lumber could be the number of board feet of lumber used, and the cost driver for direct labor costs could be the number of labor hours worked.

Managers need to know how costs behave to make informed decisions about products, to plan, and to evaluate performance. Fundamentally, managers need to know cost behavior for four basic categories: fixed, variable, mixed, and step costs as discussed next.

*Fixed versus
Variable Costs*

Suppose management contemplates a change in the volume of activity. Management might ask questions like:

- How much will our costs decrease if the volume of production is cut by 1,000 automobiles per month?
- How much will our costs increase if we serve 200 more meals per day?
- How much will costs increase if the number of students enrolled in the university increases by 10 percent?

Variable Costs Costs that change with a change in volume of activity.

Fixed Costs Costs that are unchanged as volume changes within the relevant range of activity.

Mixed Cost A cost that has both fixed and variable components. Also called a semivariable cost.

Step Cost A cost that increases with volume in steps. Also called a semifixed cost.

To answer questions like these, we need to know which costs are **variable costs** that will change proportionally with the volume of activity and which costs are **fixed costs** that will not change. Estimating the behavior of costs—which are fixed and which are variable—is very important for managerial purposes.

Variable manufacturing costs typically include direct materials, direct labor, and some manufacturing overhead (for example, indirect materials, materials-handling labor, energy costs). Also, such nonmanufacturing costs as distribution costs and sales commissions are variable. Much of manufacturing overhead and many nonmanufacturing costs are usually fixed costs.

Direct labor has traditionally been considered a variable cost. Today at many firms, the production process is very capital intensive. In a setting where a fixed amount of labor is needed only to keep machines operating, direct labor is probably best considered to be a fixed cost.

In merchandising, variable costs include the cost of the product and some marketing and administrative costs. In merchandising, all of a merchant's product costs are variable; in manufacturing, a portion of the product cost is fixed.

In service organizations (for example, consulting and auto repair), variable costs typically include direct labor, materials used to perform the service, and some overhead costs.

Three aspects of cost behavior complicate the task of classifying costs into fixed and variable categories. First, not all costs are strictly fixed or strictly variable. For example, electric utility costs may be based on a fixed minimum monthly charge plus a variable cost for each kilowatt-hour in excess of the specified minimum usage. Such a **mixed cost** has both fixed and variable components. Mixed costs are also called semivariable costs. Illustration 2–7 compares mixed costs, variable costs, fixed costs, and step costs.

Second, some costs increase with volume in "steps." **Step costs,** also called semifixed costs, increase in steps as shown in Illustration 2–7. For example, one supervisor might be needed for up to four firefighters in a fire station, two supervisors for five to eight firefighters, and so forth as the number of firefighters increased. The supervisors' salaries would be a step cost.

Third, the distinction between fixed and variable costs is only valid within a certain range of activity. For example, the manager of a Bakers Square restaurant increased the capacity from 150 to 250 seats, requiring an increase in rent costs, utilities, and many other costs.

ILLUSTRATION

Four Cost Patterns

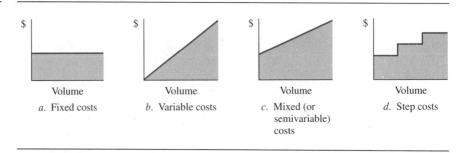

| a. Fixed costs | b. Variable costs | c. Mixed (or semivariable) costs | d. Step costs |

Although these costs are usually thought of as fixed, they change when activity moves beyond a certain range. This range within which the fixed costs do not change is referred to as the **relevant range.**

Relevant Range. The activity levels within which a given fixed cost will be unchanged even though volume changes.

We now return to the Unique Denims example. After reviewing the previous year's results the marketing vice president told the other members of the team that the jeans market was experiencing a major slowdown. Sales could not be increased without lowering prices substantially, and there were no apparent additional efficiencies that could be derived to lower costs further.

The marketing VP noted that there was additional room in the factory to make another product and presented a plan to manufacture a new product, imitation leather jackets. The marketing VP estimated annual sales of 10,000 jackets to be sold wholesale for $40 each. The necessary manufacturing equipment could be leased.

The controller suggested that the team develop an estimate of product costs. Fixed costs per year would be divided by 10,000 units to obtain a unit cost. However, it would be understood that the unit fixed cost number would be correct only at a volume of 10,000 units. The controller developed the numbers that appear in Illustration 2–8. The following conversation took place among officers of the company concerning the plan to manufacture and sell imitation leather jackets.

ILLUSTRATION

2–8

Unique Denims—Unit Costs for New Jacket

	Cost per Unit
Variable manufacturing costs:	
Direct materials	$ 9
Direct labor	6
Variable manufacturing overhead	5
Total variable manufacturing cost per unit	20
Variable marketing and administrative costs:	
Commission (5% of selling price)	2
Distribution costs	1
Total variable marketing and administrative cost per unit	3
Fixed manufacturing costs:	
Manager ($30,000 ÷ 10,000 units)	3
Equipment ($20,000 ÷ 10,000 units)	2
Total fixed manufacturing cost per unit	5
Fixed marketing and administrative costs	2
Total costs	$30

Summary Based on 10,000 Units per Year

	Per Unit		Per Year	
Variable costs	$23	($20 + $3)	$230,000	($23 × 10,000)
Fixed costs	7	($5 + $2)	70,000	($7 × 10,000)
Total costs	$30		$300,000	

VP Production: I first determined how much materials and labor time would be required to make these jackets. I used the labor time figure and multiplied it by our regular wage rate, including benefits, to determine our direct labor cost per unit. Direct materials cost is based on quotes from our suppliers. Variable overhead is based on my estimate of energy costs, supplies, and other variable manufacturing overhead costs.

Controller: Whether we produce one jacket or 10,000, we have to hire a manager and lease additional equipment.

VP Production: That's right. My estimate is $30,000 per year for the manager and $20,000 per year for the equipment.

VP Marketing: I estimate that we'll need to hire additional marketing and administrative staff and incur other fixed costs amounting to $20,000.

Controller: That gives a total cost per unit of $30. [See Illustration 2–8.] Next we use differential analysis to see what impact adding the jacket line would have on profits. I used last year's results as the baseline and added the jacket numbers to the baseline to see what the new profit numbers would be. [See columns 1 and 2 of Illustration 2–9.] As shown in column 3, we anticipate a $100,000 increase in operating profits. Now I think it's time to make a recommendation to the president.

Unit Fixed Costs Can Be Misleading for Decision Making

When fixed costs are allocated to each unit, accounting records often make the cost appear as though it is a variable cost. For example, allocating some of factory rent to each unit of product would result in including the rent as part of the "unit cost" even though the total rent does not change with the manufacture of another unit of product. Cost data that include allocated common costs may, therefore, be misleading if used incorrectly. The following example demonstrates the problem.

Superstar, Inc., manufactures ski boots that have a unit manufacturing cost of $80, made up of $50 per unit variable manufacturing cost and $30 per unit fixed manufacturing cost computed as follows (each pair of boots is one unit):

Variable manufacturing costs per unit $50

Fixed manufacturing costs:

$$\text{Unit cost} = \frac{\text{Fixed manufacturing cost per month}}{\text{Units produced per month}}$$

$$= \frac{\$600,000}{20,000 \text{ units}} = \underline{30}$$

Total unit cost used as the inventory value for external financial reporting $\underline{\underline{\$80}}$

ILLUSTRATION

2–9

Unique Denims—Differential Cost Analysis for Year One

	(1) Baseline[a]	(2) Alternative[b]	(3) Difference (2) − (1)
Sales revenue	$4,500,000	$4,900,000	$400,000
Total costs	4,250,000	4,550,000	300,000
Operating profit	$ 250,000	$ 350,000	$100,000

[a] Amounts based on Illustration 2–5.
[b] Column 1 amounts plus $400,000 revenue ($40 × 10,000 jackets) and $300,000 costs from Illustration 2–8.

Superstar received a special order for 1,000 pairs of ski boots at $75 each. These units can be produced with capacity that is currently idle. Marketing, administrative costs, and the total fixed manufacturing costs of $600,000 would not be affected by accepting the order. Accepting this special order would not affect the regular market for this product.

Marketing managers believed the special order should be accepted as long as the unit price of $75 exceeded the cost of manufacturing each unit. When the marketing managers learned from accounting reports that the inventory value was $80 per unit, their initial reaction was to reject the order because, as one manager stated, "We are not going to be very profitable if our selling price is less than our production cost!"

Fortunately, some additional investigation revealed the variable manufacturing cost to be only $50 per unit. Marketing management accepted the special order, which had the following impact on the company's operating profit:

Revenue from special order (1,000 units × $75)	$75,000
Variable costs of making special order (1,000 units × $50)	50,000
Contribution of special order to operating profit	$25,000

The moral of this example is that it is easy to interpret unit costs incorrectly and make incorrect decisions. In the example above, fixed manufacturing overhead costs had been allocated to units, most likely to value inventory for external financial reporting and tax purposes. The resulting unit cost of $80 appeared to be the cost of producing a unit. Of course, only $50 was a variable cost of producing a unit, while the fixed costs of $600,000 per month would not be affected by the decision to accept the special order.

COMPARISON OF COST AND MARGIN CONCEPTS

Full Cost The sum of fixed and variable costs of manufacturing and selling a unit of product.

Full Absorption Cost The cost used to compute a product's inventory value under generally accepted accounting principles.

By now you realize there are various concepts of costs. The diagrams in this section have been used in practice to explain cost concepts. Starting with Illustration 2–10, assume Unique Denims uses the data for the imitation leather jackets. The **full cost** to manufacture and sell one jacket is estimated to be $30, as shown on the left side of Illustration 2–10. The unit cost of *manufacturing* the jacket is $25, also shown on the left side of the illustration. This full cost of manufacturing the jacket is known as the **full absorption cost**; it is the amount of inventoriable cost for external financial reporting according to generally accepted accounting principles. The full absorption cost "fully absorbs" the variable and fixed costs of manufacturing a product.

The full absorption cost excludes nonmanufacturing costs, however, so marketing and administrative costs are not inventoriable costs. These nonmanufacturing costs equal $5 per unit, which is the sum of the two blocks at the bottom of Illustration 2–10.

Each of the unit costs stated above includes a unit fixed cost. As noted earlier, the unit fixed cost is valid only at one volume. For Unique Denims, that volume is 10,000 units per year. By definition, *total* fixed costs do not change as volume changes (within the relevant range, of course). Therefore, a change in volume results in a change in the unit fixed cost, as demonstrated by the self-study question that follows shortly.

I L L U S T R A T I O N   *Unique Denims—Product Cost Components*

2–10

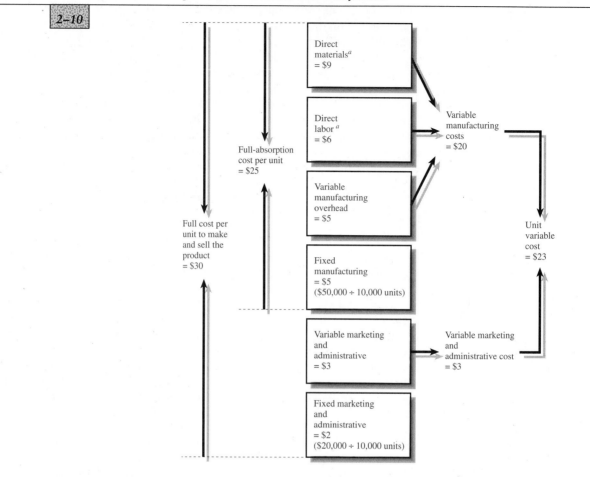

ᵃ Direct labor and direct materials are assumed to be variable costs for this illustration. Direct labor is classified as a fixed manufacturing cost in many cases—particularly in highly automated companies.

The variable costs of making the product are made up of variable manufacturing costs, totaling $20 per unit, and variable nonmanufacturing costs, $3 per unit. Variable nonmanufacturing costs could, in general, be either administrative or marketing costs. For Unique Denims, variable nonmanufacturing costs are selling costs and the costs of distributing products. In other cases, variable administrative costs could include costs of data processing, accounting, or any administrative activity that is affected by volume.

Self-Study
Question

3   Refer to the Unique Denims example in Illustration 2–10. That illustration is based on a volume of 10,000 units per year. Assume the same total fixed costs and unit variable costs, but a volume of only 8,000 units. What is the fixed manufacturing cost per unit and the fixed marketing and administrative cost per unit?

The solution to this question is at the end of this chapter on page 62.

2-11

Unique Denims—Gross Margin per Unit

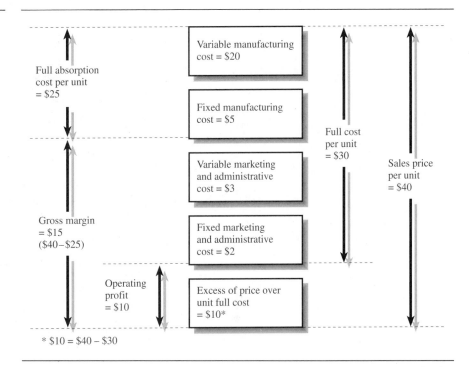

* $10 = $40 − $30

Illustrations 2–11 and 2–12 are designed to clarify distinctions between gross margin, contribution margin, and operating profit. You recall from your financial accounting courses that the gross margin appears on external financial statements as the difference between revenue and cost of goods sold. Cost of goods sold is simply the full absorption cost per unit times the number of units sold. Illustration 2–11 presents the gross margin per unit for Unique Denims' new product—imitation leather jackets that sell for $40 each. Recall from Illustration 2–10 that each jacket is estimated to have a full absorption cost of $25, which is shown on the left side of Illustration 2–11. Therefore, the gross margin per unit is $15 ($40 − $25). The operating profit per unit is the difference between the sales price and the full cost of making and selling the product. For Unique Denims, Illustration 2–11 shows the operating profit per unit to be $10 ($40 sales price − $30 full cost).

Illustration 2–12 shows another margin that is generally not reported on external financial statements, but is useful for managers. That margin is the **contribution margin**, which is the difference between revenues and total variable costs. On a per unit basis, the contribution margin is the difference between the sales price and the variable cost per unit. Illustration 2–12 shows the contribution margin per unit for Unique Denims' new jacket to be $17 ($40 sales price − $23 variable cost per unit). Note the difference between contribution margin and gross margin in Illustrations 2–11 and 2–12.

Contribution Margin The difference between revenues and variable costs.

Gross margin = Sales price − *Full absorption cost*
Contribution margin = Sales price − *Variable costs*

Unique Denims—
Contribution Margin
per Unit

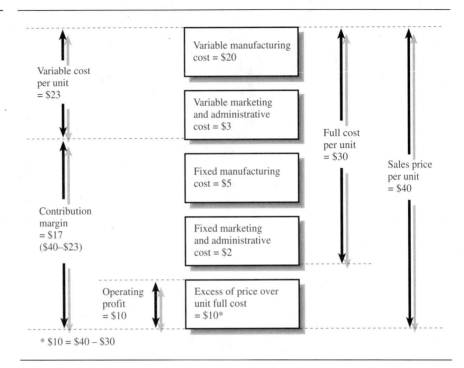

* $10 = $40 – $30

Q *Self-Study*
uestion

4 Refer to the Unique Denims example in Illustrations 2–11 and 2–12.

   a. Assume the variable marketing and administrative cost is $6 per unit; all other cost numbers remain the same. What are the new gross margin, contribution margin, and operating profit amounts?
   b. Assume the fixed manufacturing cost dropped from $50,000 to $40,000 in total, or from $5 to $4 per unit. All other cost numbers remain the same as in Illustrations 2–11 and 2–12. What are the new gross margin, contribution margin, and operating profit amounts?

The solution to this question is at the end of this chapter on page 62.

SUMMARY

The term *cost* is ambiguous when used alone; it has meaning only in a specific context. The adjectives used to modify the term *cost* constitute that context. Illustration 2–13 summarizes alternative uses of the term. Each cost concept can be applied to specific managerial problems. For example, most managerial economic decisions rely on the concept of differential costs. Product costing and inventory valuation use concepts related to full manufacturing costs.

It is important to consider how use of these terms in cost accounting differs from common usage. For example, in common usage, a variable cost

ILLUSTRATION

2–13

Summary of Definitions

Concept	Definition
Nature of Cost	
Cost	A *sacrifice* of resources.
Opportunity cost	The benefit that could be realized from the best forgone alternative use of a resource.
Outlay cost	Past, present, or near-future cash outflow.
Expense	The cost charged against revenue in a particular accounting period. We use the term *expense* only when speaking of external financial reports.
Cost Concepts for Cost Accounting Systems	
Product costs	Costs that can be more easily attributed to products; costs that are part of inventory.
Period costs	Costs that can be more easily attributed to time intervals.
Full absorption costs	Costs used to compute a product's inventory value for external reporting according to generally accepted accounting principles.
Direct costs	Costs that can be directly related to a cost object.
Indirect costs	Costs that cannot be directly related to a cost object.
Additional Cost Concepts Used in Decision Making	
Variable costs	Costs that vary, in total, with the volume of activity.
Fixed costs	Costs that do not vary, in total, with the volume of activity.
Differential costs	Costs that change in response to a particular course of action.
Sunk costs	Costs that result from an expenditure made in the past and cannot be changed by present or future decisions.

may vary with anything (geography, temperature, and so forth); in cost accounting, variable cost depends solely on volume.

*TERMS
AND CONCEPTS*

The following terms and concepts should be familiar to you after reading this chapter:

QUESTIONS

2–1   Contrast the meanings of the terms *cost* and *expense.*

2–2   Identify the difference between product costs and period costs.

2–3   Is cost of goods manufactured and sold an expense?

2–4   Identify the similarities between the Direct Materials Inventory account of the manufacturer and the Merchandise Inventory account of the merchandiser. Are there any differences between the two accounts? If so, what are they?

2–5   What are the three categories of product cost in a manufacturing operation? Describe each element briefly.

2–6   ''Prime costs are always direct costs, and overhead costs are always indirect.'' Comment on this statement.

2–7   Unit costs represent the average cost of all units produced. If you want to know the cost to produce an extra quantity of product, why not just multiply the unit average cost by the extra quantity you want?

2–8   Compare the accounting for marketing and administrative costs in a manufacturing organization with the way those costs are treated in a merchandising organization.

2–9   Define step and mixed costs.

2–10 Since historical costs are sunk (and, hence, not directly useful for decision-making purposes), why are accounting systems and reports based on historical costs?

2–11 In this chapter's Real World Application why did Bethlehem Steel Corp. need to monitor costs more closely?

2–12 Will the steel industry stage a comeback? How can managerial accounting methods be used to help see that it does?

EXERCISES

2–13 Basic Concepts
(L.O.1)

For each of the following costs incurred in a manufacturing operation, indicate whether the costs would be fixed or variable (F or V) and whether they would be period costs or product costs (P or R, respectively) under full absorption costing.

a.   Transportation-in costs on materials purchased.

b.   Assembly-line workers' wages.

c.   Property taxes on office buildings for administrative staff.

d.   Salaries of top executives in the company.

e.   Overtime pay for assembly workers.

f.   Sales commissions.

g. Sales personnel office rent.

h. Sales supervisory salaries.

i. Controller's office rental.

j. Administrative office heat and air conditioning.

2–14 Basic Concepts
(L.O. 1)

For each of the following costs incurred in a manufacturing operation, indicate whether the costs would be included in prime costs (P), conversion costs (C), or both (B).

a. Factory heating and air conditioning.

b. Production supervisor's salary.

c. Transportation-in costs on materials purchased.

d. Assembly-line worker's salary.

e. Raw materials used in production process.

f. Indirect materials.

2–15 Basic Concepts
(L.O.1)

Place the number of the appropriate definition in the blank next to each concept.

Concept	Definition
_____ Period costs	1. Costs that vary with the volume of activity.
_____ Sunk costs	2. A sacrifice of resources.
_____ Indirect costs	3. The cost charged against revenue in a particular accounting period.
_____ Fixed costs	4. Costs that are part of inventory.
_____ Opportunity costs	5. Costs that can be more easily attributed to time intervals.
_____ Outlay costs	6. Costs that change in response to a particular course of action.
_____ Differential costs	7. Past, present, or near-future cash flow.
_____ Direct costs	8. The lost benefit from the best forgone alternative.
_____ Expense	9. Costs used to compute inventory value according to GAAP.
_____ Cost	10. Costs that cannot be directly related to a cost object.
_____ Variable costs	11. Costs that can be directly related to a cost object.
_____ Full-absorption cost	12. Costs that do not vary with the volume of activity.
_____ Product costs	13. Costs that result from an expenditure made in the past and cannot be changed by present or future decisions.

2–16 Basic Concepts
(L.O.1)

For each of the following costs incurred in a manufacturing operation, indicate whether the costs would be fixed or variable (F or V) and whether they would be period costs or product costs (P or R, respectively) under full absorption costing.

a. Factory security personnel.

b. Utilities in controller's office.

c. Factory heat and air conditioning.

d. Power to operate factory equipment.

e. Depreciation on furniture for company executives.

2–17 Prepare Statements for a Merchandising Company
(L.O.2)

Laptop Computers, Inc., sells laptop computers. On January 1 last year, it had a beginning merchandise inventory of $250,000 including transportation-in costs. It purchased $1,300,000 of merchandise, had $130,000 of transportation-in costs, and had marketing and administrative costs of $800,000 during the year. The ending inventory of merchandise on December 31 was $150,000, including transportation-in costs. Revenue was $2,500,000 for the year.

Required:

Prepare an income statement with a supporting cost of goods sold statement.

2–18 Prepare Statements for a Manufacturing Company
(L.O.2)

The following balances appeared in the accounts of Nishimoto Machine Tools Company during the current year.

	January 1	December 31
Direct materials inventory	$24,500	$27,200
Work in process inventory	32,300	29,000
Finished goods inventory	4,500	6,500
Direct materials used	–0–	47,700
Cost of goods sold	–0–	56,000

Required:

Reconstruct a cost of goods manufactured and sold statement and fill in the following missing data:

a. Direct materials purchased during the year.

b. Cost of goods manufactured during the year.

c. Total manufacturing costs incurred during the year.

2–19 Prepare Statements for a Manufacturing Company
(L.O.2)

The following balances appeared in the accounts of Alexis Manufacturing during a current year.

	January 1	December 31
Direct materials inventory	$16,400	$ 18,300
Work in process inventory	18,100	17,700
Finished goods inventory	7,300	7,500
Direct materials used	–0–	86,600
Cost of goods sold	–0–	300,000

Required:

Reconstruct a cost of goods manufactured and sold statement and fill in the following missing data:

a. Cost of goods manufactured during the year.

b. Total manufacturing costs incurred during the year.

c. Direct materials purchased during the year.

2–20 Prepare Statements for a Manufacturing Company
(L.O.3)

The following information appears in Sebastian's Company's records for last year:

Administrative costs	$ 44,300
Manufacturing building depreciation	27,000
Indirect materials and supplies	6,300
Sales commissions	15,200
Direct materials inventory, January 1	18,400
Direct labor	35,600
Direct materials inventory, December 31	19,000
Finished goods inventory, January 1	10,900
Finished goods inventory, December 31	9,000
Direct materials purchases	22,300
Work in process inventory, December 31	13,100
Supervisory and indirect labor	14,400
Property taxes, manufacturing plant	8,400
Plant utilities and power	23,500
Work in process inventory, January 1	15,400
Sales revenue	210,400

Required:

Prepare an income statement with a supporting cost of goods manufactured and sold statement.

2–21 Prepare Statements for a Manufacturing Company
(L.O.3)

The following information appears in Cary's Cakes' records for last year:

Administrative costs	$ 43,100
Manufacturing building depreciation	25,000
Indirect materials and supplies	4,300
Sales commissions	14,200
Direct materials inventory, January 1	16,400
Direct labor	32,600
Direct materials inventory, December 31	18,000
Finished goods inventory, January 1	8,900
Finished goods inventory, December 31	8,100
Direct materials purchases	20,300
Work in process inventory, December 31	11,100
Supervisory and indirect labor	12,400
Property taxes, manufacturing plant	7,400
Plant utilities and power	21,500
Work in process inventory, January 1	13,200
Sales revenue	194,400

Required:

Prepare an income statement with a supporting cost of goods manufactured and sold statement.

2–22 Prepare Statements for a Manufacturing Company
(L.O.3)

The following information appears in Tots' Toy Factory records for last year:

Sales revenue	$262,300
Work in process, January 1	15,400
Work in process, December 31	12,420
Direct materials inventory, January 1	17,200
Direct materials inventory, December 31	16,100
Finished goods inventory, January 1	7,100
Finished goods inventory, December 31	9,900
Direct materials transportation-in	2,300
Direct materials purchased	23,120
Direct labor	38,700
Supervisory and indirect labor—plant	21,900
Administrative salaries	36,000
Supplies and indirect materials—plant	2,900
Heat, light, and power (77.6 percent for plant)	25,000
Depreciation (80 percent for plant)	30,000
Property taxes (75 percent for plant)	8,400
Cost of goods manufactured during the year	142,700
Other administrative costs	8,700
Marketing costs	32,700

Required:

Prepare an income statement with a supporting cost of goods manufactured and sold statement.

---

[1] This logo indicates the exercise or problem is part of the SPATS software package available for this book.

2–23 Cost Behavior for Decision Making (L.O.4)

Cytotech Company manufactured 1,000 units of product last year and identified the following costs associated with the manufacturing activity (variable costs are indicated with V; fixed costs, with F):

Direct materials used (V)	$35,200
Direct labor (V)	66,500
Supervisory salaries (F)	31,100
Indirect materials and supplies (V)	8,000
Plant utilities (other than power to run plant equipment) (F)	9,600
Power to run plant equipment (V)	7,100
Depreciation on plant and equipment (straight-line, time basis) (F)	4,800
Property taxes on building (F)	6,500

Required:

Unit variable costs and total fixed costs are expected to remain unchanged next year. Calculate the unit cost and the total cost if 1,200 units are produced next year.

2–24 Cost Behavior (L.O.4)

Refer to the information in exercise 2–23 and assume the unit sales price is $200 per unit.

Required:

Construct graphs of fixed and variable costs. (See Illustration 2–7.)

2–25 Differential Costing (L.O.4)

Assume you had invested $168 in supplies to set up a window washing business for the summer. During the first week, you are presented with two opportunities. You can wash the windows at a housing development for $320, or you can help paint an apartment for $300. The additional costs you will incur are $60 and $25, respectively. These costs include $4.50 under each alternative for transportation to the job.

Required:

Which alternative should you choose?

2–26 Differential Costing (L.O.4)

Excalabur Enterprises converted an old train station into a warehouse space, an office space, restaurants, and specialty shops. If the whole train station was used for warehouse space, the estimated revenue and variable costs per year to Excalabur would be $980,000 and $44,000, respectively. If the train station was used for office space only the estimated revenue and variable costs per year would be $1,060,800 and $70,000, respectively. If all of the space was used for restaurants and specialty shops, the estimated revenue and variable costs would be $1,200,100 and $145,000, respectively. Fixed costs per year would be $600,000 regardless of the alternative chosen.

Required:

What should Excalabur Enterprises do? Give supporting computations.

2–27 Components of Full Costs (L.O.5)

Illustration 2–10 in the text shows basic relationships among costs. Given the following facts, complete the requirements below:

Sales price	$ 200	per unit
Fixed costs:		
Marketing and administrative	24,000	per period
Manufacturing overhead	36,000	per period
Variable costs:		
Marketing and administrative	8	per unit
Manufacturing overhead	9	per unit
Direct labor	35	per unit
Direct materials	60	per unit
Units produced and sold	1,200	per period

Required:

Determine each of the following unit costs (see Illustration 2–10):

a. Variable manufacturing cost.

b. Variable cost.

c. Full absorption cost.

d. Full cost.

2-28 Components of Full Costs
(L.O.5)

For external financial reporting, all costs of manufacturing the product are product costs (that is, they are inventoriable). (See Illustration 2-1.)

Required:

Using the data from exercise 2-27, what are the following:

a. Product costs per *unit*.

b. Period costs for the *period*.

2-29 Components of Full Costs
(L.O. 5)

The following cost, price, and volume data apply to Dabelles Company for a particular month:

Sales price per unit . . . . $	1,300 per unit
Fixed costs:	
Marketing and administrative	130,000 per period
Manufacturing overhead	150,000 per period
Variable costs:	
Marketing and administrative	80 per unit
Manufacturing overhead	200 per unit
Direct labor	300 per unit
Direct materials	350 per unit
Units produced and sold	1,000 per period

Required:

a. Determine each of the following *unit* costs (see Illustration 2-10):
   (1) Variable manufacturing cost.
   (2) Variable cost.
   (3) Full absorption cost.
   (4) Full cost.

b. Determine each of the following unit margins (see Illustrations 2-11 and 2-12):
   (1) Profit margin.
   (2) Gross margin.
   (3) Contribution margin.

2-30 Components of Full Costs
(L.O.5)

Georgina's Gardening Service provides gardening services to various organizations. For a particular month, it had the following costs and revenues:

Hours worked and billed to customers	10,000 hours
Price charged per hour	$35
Variable costs per hour	$20
Fixed costs for the month	$55,000

Required:

a. What is the full cost *per unit* of providing the service?

b. Determine the following *unit* margins:
   (1) Profit margin.
   (2) Contribution margin.

PROBLEMS

2-31 Cost Concepts: Multiple Choice

Items (*a*) through (*e*) are based on the following data pertaining to Cheung Company's manufacturing operations:

Inventories	April 1	April 30
Direct materials	$18,000	$15,000
Work in process	9,000	6,000
Finished goods	27,000	36,000

Additional information for the month of April:

Direct materials purchased $42,000

Direct labor costs   30,000

Manufacturing overhead   40,000

a. For the month of April, prime cost was:
    (1) $75,000.
    (2) $69,000.
    (3) $45,000.
    (4) $39,000.

b. For the month of April, conversion cost was:
    (1) $30,000.
    (2) $40,000.
    (3) $70,000.
    (4) $72,000.

c. For the month of April, total manufacturing costs were:
    (1) $118,000.
    (2) $115,000.
    (3) $112,000.
    (4) $109,000.

d. For the month of April, cost of goods manufactured was:
    (1) $118,000.
    (2) $115,000.
    (3) $112,000.
    (4) $109,000.

e. For the month of April, cost of goods sold was:
    (1) $118,000.
    (2) $115,000.
    (3) $112,000.
    (4) $109,000.

(CPA adapted)

2–32 Find the Unknown Account Balances

Each column below is independent and for a different company. The data refer to one year for each company. Use the data given to find the unknown balances.

Account	Company 1	Company 2	Company 3
Direct materials inventory, January 1	$ 12,300	$ 4,000	$ 22,500
Direct materials inventory, December 31	10,000	6,200	(d)
Work in process inventory, January 1	5,800	6,280	(e)
Work in process inventory, December 31	6,000	6,280	42,600
Finished goods inventory, January 1	127,100	1,400	167,240
Finished goods inventory, December 31	(a)	2,300	183,700
Purchases of direct materials	131,000	(c)	124,200
Cost of goods manufactured during this year	339,600	29,000	759,110
Total manufacturing costs	339,800	829,000	763,400
Cost of goods sold	380,000	28,100	(f)
Gross margin	164,000	6,700	937,300
Direct labor	86,500	11,600	(g)
Direct materials used	(b)	7,500	117,100
Manufacturing overhead	120,000	9,900	215,300
Sales revenue	544,000	34,800	1,679,950

2-33   Find the Unknown Account Balances

Each column below is independent and for a different company. The data refer to one year for each example. Use the data given to find the unknown account balances.

	Company		
Account	1	2	3
Direct materials inventory, January 1	(a)	$ 3,500	$ 16,000
Direct materials inventory, December 31 . . . . $	3,600	2,900	14,100
Work in process inventory, January 1	2,700	6,720	82,400
Work in process inventory, December 31	3,800	3,100	76,730
Finished goods inventory, January 1	1,900	(d)	17,200
Finished goods inventory, December 31	300	4,400	28,400
Purchases of direct materials	16,100	12,000	64,200
Cost of goods manufactured during this year	(b)	27,220	313,770
Total manufacturing costs	55,550	23,600	308,100
Cost of goods sold	56,050	27,200	302,570
Gross margin	(c)	16,400	641,280
Direct labor	26,450	3,800	124,700
Direct materials used	15,300	(e)	66,100
Manufacturing overhead	13,800	7,200	(g)
Sales revenue	103,300	(f)	943,850

2-34   Differential Cost Analysis for Decision Making

Rob Roberts has been working a summer job that pays $1,100 a month. His employer has offered to convert the job into a full-time position at $1,500 per month. Take-home pay is 70 percent of these amounts. In view of this offer, Rob is tempted not to return to school for the coming year. His friend Alice is trying to convince him to return to school.

Rob remarks, "I've been talking to other friends, and no matter how you figure it, school is extremely expensive. Tuition is about $2,200 per year net of scholarship assistance. Books and supplies are another $800. Room and board will cost $6,000 a year even if I share a room. It costs $2,400 a year to keep up my car. Clothing and other incidentals amount to about $3,000 per year. I figure school will cost me the total of all these costs, which is $14,400 plus my lost salary of $18,000 per year. At $32,200 a year, who can justify higher education?"

Required:

If you were Alice, how would you respond to Rob's remarks? The costs of room, board, car, clothing, and other incidentals will be the same whether or not Rob returns to school.

2-35   Cost Analysis in a Service Organization

Pat MacDonald, an independent engineer, has been invited to bid on a contract engineering project. Pat is not the only bidder on the project and wants the bid only if it will return an adequate profit for the time and effort involved. The contract calls for 250 hours of Pat's time. The following cost data have been extracted from Pat's records and are not expected to change for the contract period.

	Per Hour
Normal consulting rate	$100
Office costs, secretary, etc.	(38)
Travel, other variable costs	(22)
Normal "profit" per hour	$ 40
Billable hours (typical week)	30

The hourly rate for the office costs, secretary, etc., is based on a fixed cost of $1,140 per week divided by the 30 billable hours per typical week. Billable hours represent the time that Pat can charge to clients. However, these costs are fixed regardless of the number of hours Pat works per week. Under the contract, the travel and other expenses will be the same as for normal consulting.

Required:

What kind of costs should Pat consider under each of the following independent situations? Support your chosen cost basis.

a. Pat will work on the contract during hours that would otherwise not be billable to other clients.

b. Pat will give up work for other clients to meet the time requirements under the contract. No ill will would be generated as a result of accepting the contract.

c. Pat believes that the contract would be the start of a long-term business relationship that could take up most of Pat's time. The initial bid would have to be close to the amount charged on subsequent projects. While Pat has the time now to take the project without giving up clients, eventually Pat would have to give up some other clients.

2–36 Reconstruct Financial Statements

The following data appeared in Pacific Northwest's records on December 31 of last year:

Direct materials inventory, December 31	$ 85,000
Direct materials purchased during the year	360,000
Finished goods inventory, December 31	90,000
Indirect labor	32,000
Direct labor	400,000
Plant heat, light, and power	37,200
Building depreciation ($7/9$ is for manufacturing)	81,000
Administrative salaries	51,400
Miscellaneous factory cost	31,900
Marketing costs	37,000
Maintenance on factory machines	12,100
Insurance on factory equipment	19,000
Distribution costs	1,600
Taxes on manufacturing property	13,100
Legal fees on customer complaint	8,200
Direct materials used	382,100
Work in process inventory, December 31	24,600

On January 1, at the beginning of last year, the Finished Goods Inventory account had a balance of $80,000, and the Work in Process Inventory account had a balance of $25,900. Sales revenue during the year was $1,625,000.

Required:

Prepare a cost of goods manufactured and sold statement and an income statement.

2–37 Cost Behavior: Estimate Most Profitable Operating Level[2]

The following production and sales data are for a company division with a capacity of 13,000 units and an unchangeable unit sales price of $4.50. The company is required by a sales contract to keep the division operating and wants to operate at the optimal level given these conditions. The manufacturing vice president suggested: "We should operate at 13,000 units since that gives us the lowest unit cost."

[2] Adapted from W. J. Vatter, "Tailor-Making Cost Data for Specific Uses," *National Association of (Cost) Accountants Bulletin (1954 Conference Proceedings).*

	Production Volume			
	10,000	11,000	12,000	13,000
Variable manufacturing cost	$37,000	$40,800	$44,600	$48,400
Fixed manufacturing cost	9,000	9,000	9,000	9,000
Marketing costs	6,000	6,600	7,200	7,800
Administrative costs	6,000	6,000	6,200	6,400
Total costs	$58,000	$62,400	$67,000	$71,600
Unit cost	$5.80	$5.67	$5.58	$5.51

Required:

What is the optimal level of output if production must take place at one of the levels indicated in this schedule?

2–38   Analyze the Costs at Different Demand Levels[3]

To increase production beyond the current level of 10,000 units, Melville Corporation must lease additional equipment and pay overtime premiums to its employees. At the present level of operations of 10,000 units, fixed costs total $50,000 and variable costs are $3 per unit. If Melville incurs an additional $20,000 in fixed costs, they can produce and sell an additional 10,000 units at a variable cost of $5 each. Management policy forbids expanding capacity unless unit average cost remains constant.

Required:

How many units must Melville produce and sell to maintain the same average cost as at 10,000 units?

INTEGRATIVE CASES

2–39.   Analyze the Impact of a Decision on Income Statements

You have been appointed manager of an operating division of HI-TECH, Inc., a manufacturer of products using the latest developments in microprocessor technology. Your division manufactures the chip assembly, ZP-1. On January 1 of this year, you invested $1 million in automated processing equipment for chip assembly. At that time, your expected income statement for this year was as follows:

Sales revenues	$3,200,000
Operating costs:	
Variable (cash expenditures)	400,000
Fixed (cash expenditures)	1,500,000
Equipment depreciation	300,000
Other depreciation	250,000
Total operating costs	2,450,000
Operating profits (before taxes)	$ 750,000

On October 25 of this year, you are approached by a sales representative for the Mammoth Machine Company. Mammoth wants to rent to your division a new assembly machine, which would be installed on December 31. The new equipment has an annual rental charge of $460,000. The new equipment would enable you to increase your division annual revenue by 10 percent. Fixed cash expenditures would decrease by 5 percent per year due to the more efficient machine. You will have to

[3] Adapted from C. Purdy, R. K. Zimmer, and J. H. Grenell, "Costs in Relation to Pricing Products and Services," in *The Managerial and Cost Accountant's Handbook,* eds. Homer A. Black and James Don Edwards (Homewood, Ill.: Dow Jones-Irwin, 1979).

write off the cost of the automated processing equipment this year because it has no salvage value. Equipment depreciation in the income statement above is for the automated processing equipment.

Your bonus is determined as a percentage of your division's operating profits before taxes. Equipment losses are included in the bonus and operating profit computation.

Ignore taxes and any effects on operations on the day of installation of the new machine. Assume the data given in your expected income statement are the actual amounts for this year and next year if the current equipment is kept.

Required:

a. What is the difference in this year's divisional operating profit if the new machine is rented and installed on December 31 of this year?

b. What would be the effect on next year's divisional operating profit if the new machine is rented and installed on December 31 of this year?

c. Would you rent the new equipment? Why or why not?

2–40. Chris Collins's Use of Costs in Decision Making[4]

Chris Collins supervised an assembly department in Dexter Electronics Company. Recently, Collins became convinced that a certain component, number S-36, could be produced more efficiently by changing assembly methods. Collins described this proposal to Dexter's industrial engineer, who quickly dismissed Collins's idea—mainly, Collins thought, because the engineer had not thought of the idea first.

Collins felt that producing the S-36 component at a lower cost might provide the opportunity to start a new business. Dexter's purchasing agent assured Collins that Dexter would buy S-36s from Collins if the price were 10 to 15 percent below Dexter's current cost of $1.65 per unit. Working at home, Collins experimented with the new assembly method. This experimentation seemed successful, so Collins prepared estimates for large-scale S-36 production. Collins determined the following:

1. A local toolmaker would make the required assembly workstations for $800 each. One workstation would be needed for each assembly worker.

2. Assembly workers were readily available, on either a full-time or part-time basis, at a wage of $6.00 per hour. Another 20 percent of wages would be necessary for fringe benefits. Collins estimated that on average (including rest breaks), a worker could assemble, test, and pack 15 S-36s per hour.

3. Purchased components for the S-36 would cost $.85 per unit. Shipping materials and delivery costs would cost $.05 per unit.

4. Suitable space was available for assembly operations at a rental of $600 per month.

5. Collins would receive a salary of $2,000 per month.

6. An office manager was required and would cost $1,500 per month in salary.

7. Miscellaneous costs, including maintenance, supplies, and utilities, will average about $325 per month (all fixed costs).

8. Dexter Electronics would purchase between 400,000 and 525,000 units of S-36 a year, with 450,000 being Dexter's purchasing agent's "best guess." Collins would have to commit to a price of $1.50 per unit for the next 12 months even though the exact volume would not be known.

Collins showed these estimates to a cost analyst in another electronics firm. This analyst said that the estimates appeared reasonable, but the analyst advised buying enough workstations to enable producing the maximum estimated volume (525,000 units per year) on a one-shift basis (assuming 2,000 labor-hours per assembler per year). Collins thought this was good advice.

Required:

a. What are Collins's expected variable costs per unit? Fixed costs per month? What would be the total costs per year of Collins's business if volume was

---

[4] Copyright © Osceola Institute, 1979, with the permission of Professors Robert N. Anthony and James S. Reece.

400,000 units? 450,000 units? 525,000 units? (Limit yourself to cash costs; ignore depreciation of workstation equipment. Also, disregard any interest costs Collins might incur on borrowed funds.)

b.   What is the average cost per unit of S-36 at each of these three volumes (400,000, 450,000, and 525,000 units)?

c.   Would you encourage Chris Collins to resign from Dexter Electronics and form the proposed enterprise? Assume Chris would need to invest $70,000 for working capital plus whatever is needed for the assembly workstations. Support your answer.

SOLUTIONS TO

Self-Study
Questions

1

SHORELINE PRODUCTS, INC.
Income Statement
For the Year Ended December 31

Sales revenue	$2,036,000
Cost of goods sold (see statement below)	1,239,000
Gross margin	797,000
Less:	
Marketing costs	272,000
Administrative costs	304,000
Operating profit	$ 221,000

Cost of Goods Manufactured and Sold Statement
For the Year Ended December 31

Beginning work in process inventory, January 1			$ 135,000
Manufacturing costs during the year:			
Direct materials:			
Beginning inventory, January 1	$102,000		
Add purchases	313,000		
Direct materials available	415,000		
Less ending inventory, December 31	81,000		
Direct materials put into production		$334,000	
Direct labor		482,000	
Manufacturing overhead:			
Supervisory and indirect labor	127,000		
Supplies and indirect materials	14,000		
Heat, light, and power—plant	87,000		
Plant maintenance and repairs	74,000		
Depreciation—manufacturing	103,000		
Miscellaneous manufacturing costs	12,000		
Total manufacturing overhead		417,000	
Total manufacturing costs incurred during the year			1,233,000
Total cost of work in process during the year			1,368,000
Less ending work in process inventory, December 31			142,000
Cost of goods manufactured during the year			1,226,000
Beginning finished goods inventory, January 1			160,000
Finished goods inventory available for sale			1,386,000
Less ending finished goods inventory, December 31 . .			147,000
Cost of goods manufactured and sold			$1,239,000

2

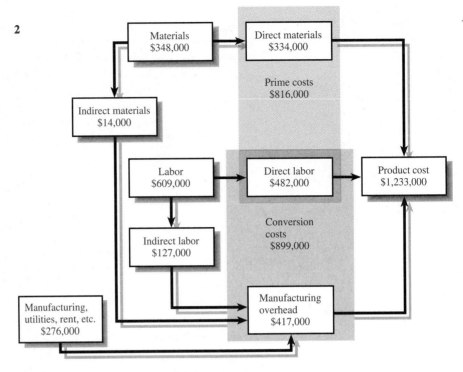

3   Fixed mfg. = $6.25 (= $50,000 ÷ 8,000);
Fixed mktg. and admin. = $2.50 (= $20,000 ÷ 8,000).

4   *a.*   Gross margin = Sales price − Full-absorption cost
= Sales price − (Variable manufacturing + Fixed
manufacturing)
= $40 − ($20 + $5)
= $15

Contribution margin = Sales price − Variable costs
= Sales price − (Variable manufacturing + Variable
marketing and administrative)
= $40 − ($20 + $6)
= $14

Operating profit = Sales price − Full cost to make and sell product
= Sales price − (Variable manufacturing + Fixed manufacturing + Variable marketing and administrative +
Fixed marketing and administrative)
= $40 − ($20 + $5 + $6 + $2)
= $7

Note the gross margin does not change from Illustration 2–11 because
marketing and administrative costs are subtracted *after* gross margin.

   b.   Gross margin = $40 − ($20 + $4)
= $16

Contribution margin = $40 − ($20 + $3)
= $17

Operating profit = $40 − ($20 + $4 + $3 + $2)
= $11

Note the contribution margin does not change from Illustration 2–12; however, the gross margin changes from Illustration 2–11.

CHAPTER

3

Job Costing

LEARNING OBJECTIVES

After reading this chapter, you should be able to:

1. Explain how different accounting systems are designed for different production systems.
2. Explain the basic cost flow model.
3. Assign costs in a job cost system.
4. Account for overhead using predetermined rates.
5. Apply job costing methods in service organizations.
6. Identify the causes of and accounting treatment for differences between actual and applied overhead (Appendix).

Jobs Units that are easily distinguishable from other units.

When you see construction sites where people are constructing new homes, repairing highways, remodeling office buildings, or building rapid transit systems, you are seeing job costing at work. **Jobs** are units of a product that can be easily distinguished from other units. If you or your family remodel or build a home, the construction work is called a *job* because it can be easily distinguished from other construction "jobs."

ALTERNATIVE PRODUCTION AND COSTING SYSTEMS

Job Costing An accounting system that traces costs to individual units or to specific jobs, contracts, or batches of goods.

Process Costing An accounting system used when identical units are produced through a series of uniform production steps.

Project A complex job that often takes months or years to complete and requires the work of many different departments, divisions, or subcontractors.

Continuous Flow Processing Systems that generally mass-produce a single, homogeneous output in a continuing process.

A **job costing** system records costs and revenues for each individual job. By contrast, process costing (discussed in Chapter 4) does not separate and record costs for each unit. The next time you have a soft drink, consider whether the manufacturer kept track of the cost of the liquid you are drinking. Not likely! Soft drink manufacturers, and other companies that produce in continuous flow processes, use process costing. **Process costing** is an accounting system used when identical units are produced through uniform production steps.

During your career, you may audit, consult for, or be employed by some companies that produce jobs, others that produce using continuous process production methods, and still others that use a combination of jobs and processes. It will be important that you first understand the company's production methods before you can understand how to account for costs.

Illustration 3–1 shows a continuum of production methods ranging from those requiring job costing to those needing process costing. Companies using job costing include construction companies like Morrison-Knudsen, defense contractors like Lockheed and Northrop, hospitals like the Mayo Clinic (where the jobs would be called *cases*), moviemakers like Universal Studios, public accounting firms like Arthur Andersen & Co and Price Waterhouse (where the jobs are often called *clients*), and Richard D. Irwin, the publisher of this textbook. These companies produce customized products, as indicated in Illustration 3–1.

Some jobs are called *projects*. A **project** is a complex job that often takes months or years to complete and requires the work of many different departments, divisions, or subcontractors (for example, bridges, shopping centers, complex lawsuits).

Continuous flow processing is at the opposite end of the spectrum from job shops. Process systems generally mass-produce a single, homogeneous product in a continuing process. Process systems are used in manufacturing chemicals, grinding flour, and refining oil. Companies with continuous flow processing use process costing methods.

ILLUSTRATION 3–1

Alternative Production Methods and Accounting Sytems

Accounting system	Job costing (Chapter 3)	Operation costing[a] (Chapter 5)	Process costing (Chapter 4)
Type of production	Jobs shops • Construction • Movie studios • Hospitals	Batch production • Clothing • Automoblies • Computer terminals	Continuous flow processing • Oil refinery • Paper • Paint
Type of product	Customized product	Different batches of products, but standardized within a batch	Standardized product

a Operation costing is a hybrid of job and process costing.

Many organizations use job systems for some work and process systems for others. A home builder might use process costing for standardized homes with a particular floor plan. The same builder might use job costing when building a custom-designed home for a single customer. Honeywell, Inc., a high-tech company, uses process costing for most of their furnace thermostats, but job costing for specialized defense and space contracting work.

Many companies use a hybrid of job and process costing, called *operation costing*. An **operation** is a standardized method of making a product that is performed repeatedly in production. Companies using **operation costing** produce products using standardized production methods, like companies using process costing, but materials can be different for each product or batch of products as indicated in Illustration 3–1.

For example, Nissan manufactures a variety of models of cars and trucks on one assembly line in its manufacturing plant near Nashville, Tennessee. Each car or truck goes through the same work stations; for example, every car and truck goes through the same painting work station where it is painted. Each vehicle type has a different set of materials, however. (This difference in materials is quite obvious when we compare cars to trucks!)

Operation costing is discussed in Chapter 5, after you have learned more about the two methods at the extremes of the continuum—job and process costing.

Operation A standardized method or technique that is repetitively performed.

Operation Costing A hybrid-costing system often used in manufacturing of goods that have some common characteristics plus some individual characteristics.

THE BASIC COST FLOW MODEL

The fundamental framework for recording costs is the basic cost flow model. You have applied this model in your previous accounting classes; we repeat it here because it is so important and helpful in assigning costs to jobs. The model is:

$$\begin{array}{ccccccc} \text{Beginning} & & \text{Transfers-} & & \text{Transfers-} & & \text{Ending} \\ \text{balance} & + & \text{in} & = & \text{out} & + & \text{balance} \\ (BB) & & (TI) & & (TO) & & (EB) \end{array}$$

Application

This model helps you solve for unknown amounts in accounts, which is very useful for both accountants and managers who frequently find they are missing key accounting information. For example, suppose Hurricane George has just wiped out your Uncle Chuck's store's inventory of fine clothes. The insurance company will pay for the cost of the destroyed inventory, but you have to prove the cost of the inventory, which is nowhere to be found. Unfortunately, nobody bothered to count the inventory before the storm hit.

The basic accounting model comes to your rescue. Based on the model,

$$BB + TI = TO + EB,$$

we rearrange terms to solve for the missing inventory, which was the ending balance in the inventory account just before the storm hit:

$$EB = BB + TI - TO$$

Now you find from last year's financial statements that the ending inventory at the end of last year was $500,000, which was also the beginning inventory this year. From your uncle's suppliers you find he purchased $1,200,000 of clothes so far this year, and you find from sales records he has sold clothes that cost $1,400,000. Therefore, you know the beginning balance to be $500,000, the amount transferred in to inventory to be $1,200,000 and the amount transferred out of inventory to be $1,400,000. Using the basic cost flow model,

$$EB = BB + TI - TO$$
$$EB = \$500,000 + \$1,200,000 - \$1,400,000$$
$$= \$300,000$$

Your uncle can report inventory costing $300,000 was lost in the storm.

In practice, we do not need a disaster to find the cost flow model useful. Auditors use it frequently to perform reasonableness checks on the data they receive from clients. For example, a client may report that ending inventory is $500,000 based on a count of the inventory. If you know from the basic cost flow model that the inventory should be $400,000, then you know something is wrong.

Many financial frauds are discovered when an auditor finds the amounts based on the basic cost flow model are different from those reported by the client. The first Real World Application in this chapter, "Using the Basic Cost Flow Model to Detect Fraud," describes a case in which the basic cost flow model helped management discover fraudulent inventory reporting in one of its divisions.

REAL WORLD APPLICATION

Using the Basic Cost Flow Model to Detect Fraud*

A senior official at Doughties Foods became curious about the high levels of inventory reported on the divisional financial statements of the Gravins Division. Based on Gravins' purchases (transfers-in) and cost of goods sold (transfers-out), the amount of ending inventory seemed high compared to other divisions in the company. When asked about the high inventory levels, the division manager confessed that he had overstated the inventory numbers to make his divisional profits look better than they really were.

Overstating the ending balance in the inventory understates cost of goods sold, which overstates gross margin and profits. In equation form:

$$BB + TI - (EB + F) = TO - F$$

where F is the amount of overstatement from the financial fraud, EB is the correct ending inventory amount, and TO is the correct transfer out of inventory, which is also Cost of Goods Sold. As the manager of the Gravins Division discovered to his dismay, the ending inventory for Period 1 is the beginning inventory for Period 2. Thus, the beginning inventory on the books carried an overstated amount, which had to be matched by an equal amount of overstatement at the end of Period 2.

As time passed, the manager of the Gravins Division continued to make increasing overstatements of ending inventory to continue to look good to his superiors. He must have felt considerable personal pressure because, when the official from corporate headquarters arrived, the division manager confessed, handed over a notebook where he had kept track of the overstatement, and resigned. The Securities and Exchange Commission subsequently filed a formal complaint charging the division manager and the auditors with committing financial fraud.

* Based on the authors' research.

*Application to
Manufacturing and
Service Organizations*

Service and manufacturing organizations have both Work in Process and Finished Goods Inventory accounts. The basic cost flow model ties these accounts together as shown below:

Work in Process Inventory Account	Finished Goods Inventory Account	
BB		Beginning **Work in Process Inventory**
+		plus
TI		**Manufacturing Costs** incurred during the period
–		minus
EB		Ending **Work in Process Inventory**
=		equals
TO ⟶	TI	**Cost of Goods Manufactured** during the period
	+	plus
	BB	Beginning **Finished Goods Inventory**
	–	minus
	EB	Ending **Finished Goods Inventory**
	=	equals
	TO	**Cost of Goods Sold** during the period

Note the *transfer-out (TO)* of Work in Process Inventory is the *transfer-in (TI)* to Finished Goods Inventory. The transfer-out *(TO)* of Finished Goods Inventory is Cost of Goods Sold.

 *Self-Study
Questions*

1 Classify each of the following products as either a job or the output of a process:
   a. Work for a client on a lawsuit by lawyers in a law firm.
   b. Diet cola.
   c. Patient care in an emergency room for a college basketball player.
   d. House painting by a company called Student Painters.
   e. The paint used by Student Painters.

2 Fill in the missing item for each of the following inventory accounts:

	A	B	C
Beginning balance	$40,000	——	$35,000
Ending balance	32,000	$16,000	27,000
Transfers-in	——	8,000	8,000
Transfers-out	61,000	11,000	——

The solutions to these questions are at the end of this chapter on page 109.

*Perpetual versus Periodic
Inventories*

Perpetual Inventory Method
Method of accounting for inventory that keeps a continuous record of inventory additions and reductions.

Periodic Inventory Method
Method of accounting for inventory that does not require a continuous record.

The **perpetual inventory** method requires an ongoing record of transfers-in and transfers-out of inventory accounts. Using the perpetual inventory method, inventory levels are updated continuously. For example, using the perpetual inventory method, Macy's Department Store records the reduction in inventory for each item of merchandise it sells. Management knows the level of inventory for each item without taking a physical inventory count.

In contrast to the perpetual inventory method, the **periodic inventory** method does not update inventory levels. Instead of maintaining continuous records of transfers in or out of inventory accounts, people must take a physical inventory. Then they derive the amount sold or transferred from one inventory account to another using the basic cost flow model.

For example, consider the sale of Super Sweet tennis rackets at Martha's Sport Shop in March. Beginning inventory was 10 rackets. Management counted the ending inventory on March 31 and found there were 15 rackets. Based on records of purchases, management knew they had purchased 40 rackets during March. All rackets cost $10 each, so the cost amounts are:

Beginning inventory (10 rackets at $10) $100
Ending inventory (15 rackets at $10) 150
Purchases (40 rackets at $10) 400

Using the basic cost flow model,

$$BB + TI = TO + EB$$

management solves for the unknown cost of goods sold, or *TO*, as follows:

$$TO = BB + TI - EB$$
$$TO = \$100 + \$400 - \$150$$
$$TO = \underline{\underline{\$350}}$$

A perpetual inventory provides more data than a periodic inventory. For example, with a perpetual system, up-to-date inventory balances and cost of goods sold are always available. But with a periodic system, these data are only available after making a physical inventory count. Perpetual inventory is useful for control purposes, too, because the clerical record of transfers-out can be compared with a physical count to check for theft, spoilage, and other problems. However, the perpetual method requires more expensive data maintenance systems.

With the expanded use of bar codes and other computerized inventory systems, nearly all large organizations use perpetual inventories. Periodically—say, every six months—they may take a physical inventory to check for shortages, theft, and clerical accuracy and to satisfy internal or external auditors. They often use the periodic method for office supplies and small merchandise.

BENEFITS OF JOB COSTING

Having provided an overview of alternative production methods and costing systems, we now begin discussing how to account for costs in organizations that use job costing.

Job costing is important for pricing and cost control. Prospective customers always ask for estimates in advance, and they frequently award jobs on a competitive basis. Consequently, suppliers must be able to estimate costs accurately if they are to compete and make a profit.

For example, management of Public Consultants, a firm that customizes accounting systems for government agencies, recently completed jobs for two municipalities. The job for Gotham City, a large metropolis, required 7,000 hours of staff time and several sophisticated computer applications. The job for Smallville, a modest farming community, required 70 hours of staff time and one very simple computer application. To charge each municipality the same price by averaging the estimated total costs for the two jobs would obviously be incorrect. Job costing allowed Public Consultants to accurately estimate the costs for each job separately. Thus, they were able to submit a competitive bid and still make a reasonable profit on each job.

ASSIGNING COSTS TO JOBS

Source Document A basic record in accounting that initiates the entry of an activity into the accounting system.

In job operations, managers estimate and control costs by keeping separate records of costs for each job. The **source document** is a job cost record, called a *job cost sheet, card,* or *file.* Open job files are used when accounting data are collected and stored by computer. Job cost sheets or cards are used when data are collected manually.

Illustration 3–2 (p. 70) presents a printout of a job cost record for Job No. 102 for New Abilities Manufacturing Company, a company that makes customized health-care equipment for people with physical limitations. Note that this record shows detailed calculations for the direct materials, direct labor, and manufacturing overhead charged to the job.

As noted on the job cost record, the actual costs accumulated for the job are compared with estimated costs to evaluate employee performance in controlling costs and to provide information for negotiating for a price increase with the customer. The comparison of actual and estimated job costs also provides feedback on the accuracy of the cost estimation, which is important for pricing.

Recording Job Costs in the Accounts

Job Cost Record The source document for entering costs under job costing. This is sometimes referred to as a *job cost sheet, job cost file,* or *job card.*

Most companies with jobs follow the basic steps presented in this section. We show the journal entries to record cost flows using New Abilities Manufacturing Company as an example. The account, Work in Process Inventory, is a control account. Each individual job cost record is a subaccount with Work in Process Inventory.

New Abilities Manufacturing had one job in process on January 1—Job No. 101. After some minor work on Job No. 101, it was completed and shipped to a customer in January. The costs for the second job of New Abilities Manufacturing, Job No. 102, were presented on the **job cost record** in Illustration 3–2. Job No. 102 was started in January and moved to finished goods inventory on January 26. At January 31, it awaited shipment to a customer. The third job, Job No. 103, was started in January and is still in process on January 31.

Beginning Inventories

Materials Inventory on hand January 1 was $10,000. Beginning Work in Process Inventory on January 1 was Job No. 101, which was in process on January 1. The following costs had been incurred for Job No. 101 as of January 1:

Direct materials	$14,000
Direct labor	22,000
Manufacturing overhead	25,000
Total	$61,000

Hence, the Work in Process Inventory balance on January 1 was $61,000.

Note the difference between Materials Inventory, $10,000, that has not yet been sent to production departments, and the materials component of

I L L U S T R A T I O N   Job Cost Record

New Abilities Manufacturing

Job number:	102	Customer:	D. Bell
Date started:	Jan 8	Date finished:	Jan 26
Description:	Manufacture custom equipment		
	according to customer specifications		

- -

Assembly Department

- -

Direct materials			Direct labor			Manufacturing overhead	
Date	Requistion number	Cost	Date	Employee number	Cost	Date	Cost
Jan 8	102-A1	$23,000	Jan 8–14	88	$980	Jan 31	$52,000
Jan 13	102-A2	4,000	Jan 12–18	67	720		
Jan 24	(return to storeroom)	(3,000)					

(Many more employees were added to this list. In total, $40,000 direct labor cost was incurred).

Total costs

Direct materials	$24,000	
Direct labor	40,000	
Manufacturing overhead	52,000	$116,000

Transferred to finished goods inventory on   Jan 26

Total job costs:	Actual	Estimate
Direct materials	$24,000	$26,000
Direct labor	40,000	36,000
Manufacturing overhead	52,000	46,800
Total	$116,000	$108,800

Explain any unusual items below:

None

Note: Data and comments are assumed for purposes of this illustration.

ILLUSTRATION   *Cost Flows through T-Accounts—Materials*

3–3

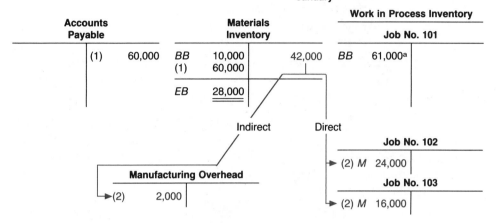

NEW ABILITIES MANUFACTURING COMPANY
January

Note: *BB* = Beginning balance; *EB* = Ending balance; and *M* = Materials. Numbers in parentheses correspond to journal entries presented in text.

ᵃ Beginning inventory is composed of:

Direct material	$14,000
Direct labor	22,000
Manufacturing overhead	25,000
Total	$61,000

beginning Work in Process Inventory, $14,000. The latter has already been sent to production.

These beginning balances are shown in Illustration 3–3. There was no beginning Finished Goods Inventory.

Assume that in January, New Abilities Manufacturing purchased $60,000 of direct and indirect materials and accumulated the costs in one account. This purchase was recorded as follows:

(1) Materials Inventory 60,000
        Accounts Payable   60,000

When the supplier sends an invoice or bill for the shipment, the payable is recorded as shown earlier. Payment is recorded with a debit to Accounts Payable and a credit to Cash.

A job supervisor or other authority requisitions the materials needed for a job using a **materials requisition** form. The materials requisition form is the source document for the entry transferring materials from Materials Inventory to the job.

No materials were requisitioned for Job No. 101 in January. Job No. 102 had requisitions for materials totaling $27,000 and a return of $3,000 excess materials to materials inventory (see Illustration 3–2). The entries to record these transfers of direct materials are as follows:

Materials Requisition A form used to obtain materials from a storeroom.

(2a)	Work in Process Inventory—Job No. 102 27,000	
	Materials Inventory	27,000
	Per requisitions 102-A1 and 102-A2 (see Illustration 3–2).	
	Materials Inventory 3,000	
	Work in Process Inventory—Job No. 102	3,000
	Return of materials to materials inventory (see Illustration 3–2).	

Direct materials of $16,000 were requisitioned for Job No. 103, and recorded in entry (2b) below. The flow of costs is shown in Illustration 3–3. Each job is a subaccount for Work in Process Inventory.

Indirect materials   Materials inventory is also used for indirect materials and supplies that are not assigned to specific jobs but are charged to the Manufacturing Overhead account. For New Abilities Manufacturing, indirect materials requisitioned amounted to $2,000 in January and were recorded in entry (2b) below.

(2b)	Work in Process Inventory—Job No. 103 16,000	
	Manufacturing Overhead 2,000	
	Materials Inventory	18,000
	To record direct materials costs of $16,000 assigned to Job No. 103 and indirect materials costs of $2,000 charged to Manufacturing Overhead.	

Note that Illustration 3–3 presents the ending materials inventory balance, which can be found from the facts given above by solving the basic cost flow equation:

$$\begin{array}{ccccccc} \text{Beginning} & + & \text{Transfers-} & = & \text{Transfers-} & + & \text{Ending} \\ \text{balance} & & \text{in} & & \text{out} & & \text{balance} \\ BB & + & TI & = & TO & + & EB \\ \$10{,}000 & + & \$60{,}000 & = & \$42{,}000 & + & EB \\ \$10{,}000 & + & \$60{,}000 & - & \$42{,}000 & = & EB \\ & & EB & = & \$28{,}000 \end{array}$$

Accounting for Labor

Production workers are usually paid an hourly rate and account for their time each day on time cards, time sheets, or other records. The time record provides space for them to account for the hours spent on the job during the day. This time record is the basis for the company's payroll.

The total cost to the company includes gross pay plus the employer's share of social security taxes and employment taxes, employer's contribution to pension and insurance plans, and any other benefits that are paid for the employee by the company. In general, these costs range from about 15 percent to about 70 percent of the wage rate, depending on the fringe-benefit plans in effect at a company. Companies commonly add their fringe-benefit costs to the wage rate to assign costs to jobs, although fringe benefits may be part of overhead, too.

The payroll department of New Abilities Manufacturing Company recorded accumulated costs of $110,000 for manufacturing employees. Of the $110,000 total, $80,000 was attributed to direct labor costs, including employee benefits and taxes. The $80,000 is charged (that is, debited) to Work in Process Inventory and assigned to the specific jobs worked on during the period. Based on time cards, Job No. 101 was charged with $10,000 in January, Job No. 102 was charged with $40,000 as presented in the job cost record in Illustration 3–2, and Job No. 103 with $30,000.

The remaining $30,000 is *indirect labor* and charged to Manufacturing Overhead. This indirect labor includes the costs of supervisory, janitorial, maintenance, security, and timekeeping personnel, as well as idle time by direct labor employees and overtime premiums paid to direct laborers.

The following entry was made to record labor costs in January.

```
(3) Work in Process Inventory—Job No. 101 . . . . . . . . . . . . . .  10,000
    Work in Process Inventory—Job No. 102 . . . . . . . . . . . . . .  40,000
    Work in Process Inventory—Job No. 103 . . . . . . . . . . . . . .  30,000
    Manufacturing Overhead  . . . . . . . . . . . . . . . . . . . . . .  30,000
        Wages Payable (or Accrued Factory Payroll)  . . . . . . . .           110,000
```

To record direct labor costs of $80,000 assigned to jobs and indirect labor costs of $30,000 charged to Manufacturing Overhead.

The flow of labor costs through the T-accounts is shown in Illustration 3–4.

Accounting for Manufacturing Overhead
Indirect manufacturing costs, including indirect materials and indirect labor, are usually accumulated in the Manufacturing Overhead account. Each department usually has its own Manufacturing Overhead Summary account

I L L U S T R A T I O N   *Cost Flows through T-Accounts—Labor Costs*

3–4

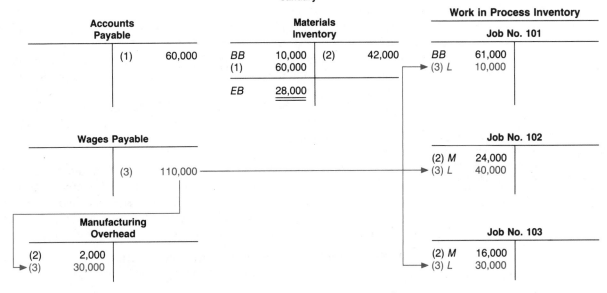

NEW ABILITIES MANUFACTURING COMPANY
January

Note: *M* = Materials; *L* = Labor.

so each department manager can be held accountable for departmental overhead costs. This helps top management evaluate how well department managers control costs. This first stage of cost allocation is to allocate costs from the accounts in which they were initially entered to responsibility centers. In this case, the responsibility centers are departments.

For example, in January, New Abilities Manufacturing has indirect materials costs of $2,000 and indirect labor costs of $30,000 charged to the Manufacturing Overhead account as described above in entries (2) and (3). Utilities and other costs credited to Accounts Payable were $46,000. The portion of prepaid taxes and insurance applicable to the period, $7,000, is included in the actual overhead, as is depreciation of $19,000. These items total $104,000 and represent the actual overhead incurred during the period.

The journal entry to record manufacturing overhead was:

(4)	Manufacturing Overhead	72,000	
	Accounts Payable		46,000
	Prepaid Expenses		7,000
	Accumulated Depreciation		19,000

To record actual manufacturing overhead costs other than indirect labor and indirect materials.

This entry is labeled (4) in the T-account diagram in Illustration 3–5.

USE OF PREDETERMINED OVERHEAD RATES

Companies generally use predetermined overhead rates to allocate manufacturing overhead to jobs. The **predetermined overhead rate** is usually established before the year in which it is to be used, and is used for the entire year.

Predetermined Overhead Rate An amount obtained by dividing total estimated overhead for the coming period by the total estimated overhead allocation base for the coming period.

By using a predetermined overhead rate, a company normalizes overhead applied to jobs. Over the course of time, manufacturing overhead costs can be quite erratic. Preventive maintenance costs are often higher in months when activity is low. Utility costs in cold climates are higher in winter than in summer, and the opposite is true in warm climates. A job in some months would be assigned more overhead than the same job in other months if actual overhead costs were assigned to jobs. In addition, a company might not know its actual overhead costs until the close of an accounting period. Management can prepare financial statements and use product-cost data for managerial purposes based on a good estimate of product costs by using predetermined overhead rates.

Predetermined overhead rates "normalize" the application of manufacturing overhead to jobs; hence, the resulting product costs are called *normal costs,* and the accounting method is called **normal costing**.

Normal Costing A system of accounting whereby direct materials and direct labor are charged to objects at actual costs, and manufacturing overhead is applied using predetermined rates.

Example Assume New Abilities Manufacturing used an annual predetermined rate to apply manufacturing overhead to jobs. Predetermined rates are based on the estimated volume of activity, sometimes called the *normal volume* of activity. The activity is usually estimated for one year. However, cyclical businesses may use estimates for periods longer than one year.

$$\text{Predetermined rate} = \frac{\text{Estimated manufacturing overhead for the year}}{\text{Estimated machine-hours for the year}}$$

$$= \frac{\$1,200,000}{10,000 \text{ mh}}$$

$$= \$120 \text{ per machine-hour}$$

ILLUSTRATION   *Cost Flows through T-Accounts—Manufacturing Overhead Costs*

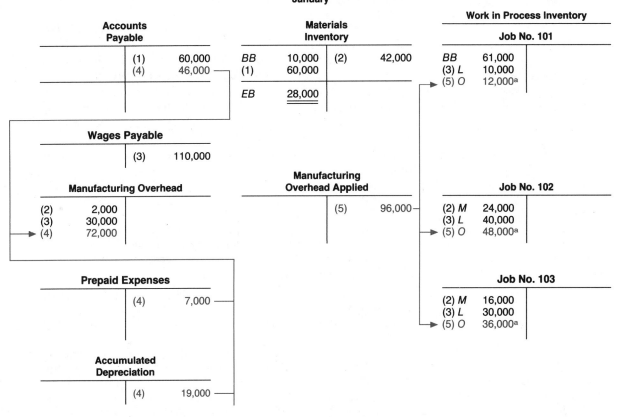

NEW ABILITIES MANUFACTURING COMPANY
January

a Overhead application rate = \$120 per machine-hour = $\dfrac{\text{Estimated manufacturing overhead for year}}{\text{Estimated machine-hours for year}}$ = $\dfrac{\$1,200,000}{10,000 \text{ machine-hours}}$

Note: M = Direct materials; L = Direct labor; O = Manufacturing overhead.

Here is how New Abilities used its predetermined rate to charge manufacturing overhead to individual jobs.

	Actual Machine-Hours Used		Predetermined Overhead Rate		Manufacturing Overhead Applied
Job No. 101	100	×	\$120 per mh	=	\$12,000
Job No. 102	400	×	120	=	48,000
Job No. 103	300	×	120	=	36,000
Total	800	×	120	=	\$96,000

The entry to record the allocation of manufacturing overhead to jobs using a predetermined overhead rate is:

(5)	Work in Process Inventory—Job No. 101	12,000	
	Work in Process Inventory—Job No. 102	48,000	
	Work in Process Inventory—Job No. 103	36,000	
	Manufacturing Overhead Applied		96,000
	To record application of manufacturing overhead to jobs.		

Illustration 3–5 shows a separate account for Manufacturing Overhead Applied. Two overhead accounts may be used to separate actual and applied overhead so that all entries in one account refer to *actual* overhead, while all those in the other account refer to **applied overhead.** We title the account that records actual overhead ''Manufacturing Overhead'' and call the new account that records applied overhead ''Manufacturing Overhead Applied.''[1] These accounts are closed at the end of the period, as described later in this chapter.

Applied Overhead Overhead applied to a cost object using a predetermined overhead rate.

The flow of these costs through T-accounts is illustrated in Illustration 3–5.

Self-Study Question

3 Soweto Manufacturing Company worked on three jobs during November. Job 1 was in process on November 1 with total charges coming to $11,000. During the month, the following additional transactions occurred.

  a. Purchased $20,000 worth of new materials.

  b. Charged materials to jobs as follows: $2,000 to job 1; $8,000 to job 2; $6,000 to job 3; and $4,000 as indirect materials.

  c. Charged labor to jobs as follows: $2,000 to job 1; $6,000 to job 2; $4,000 to job 3; and $2,000 as indirect labor.

  d. Incurred indirect expenses including depreciation totaling $20,000. Utilities and other expenses credited to Accounts Payable were $12,000. Depreciation was $8,000.

  e. Allocated manufacturing overhead for the month of November to work in process based on materials used in each job. The predetermined rate was based on expected materials of $160,000 and expected overhead of $240,000 for this year.

Show the journal entries to record these transactions. Show the flow of costs using T-accounts as in Illustration 3–5.

The solution to this question is at the end of this chapter on page 109.

COMPLETING THE OPERATING CYCLE

Transfers to Finished Goods Inventory

When jobs are transferred out of production to the finished goods storage area, an entry is made transferring the costs of the jobs from the various work in process inventory accounts to the Finished Goods Inventory account. For example, New Abilities Manufacturing Company completed Job Nos. 101 and 102 in January and transferred them to the Finished Goods Inventory account. The journal entry is:

---
[1] Companies can combine the overhead into one account. In such a setting, the left side of the account is basically overhead ''incurred'' and the right side is overhead ''applied.''

(6) Finished Goods Inventory 195,000

Work in Process Inventory—Job No. 101   83,000

Work in Process Inventory—Job No. 102   112,000

To transfer completed jobs to the finished goods
storage area.

Note that the amount transferred includes costs incurred in both the current period and previous periods. For example, the transfer for Job No. 101 includes both $61,000 from beginning work in process inventory and $22,000 of costs incurred in January to complete the job.

Transfers to Cost of
Goods Sold

When the goods are sold, they are transferred from the Finished Goods Inventory account to the Cost of Goods Sold account. For example, New Abilities Manufacturing Company sold Job No. 101 in January for $120,000 on account. When the job was sold, the journal entry to record the cost of goods sold was:

(7) Cost of Goods Sold   83,000

Finished Goods Inventory   83,000

Accounts Receivable 120,000

Sales Revenue   120,000

Closing the
Overhead Accounts

Manufacturing overhead accounts are temporary accounts. At the end of an accounting period, the actual and applied overhead accounts are closed. Usually this is not done until the end of the year when the books are closed. For illustrative purposes, however, we assume that New Abilities Manufacturing Company closes its books for the month of January.

Under normal costing, the amount debited to the Manufacturing Overhead account (the actual manufacturing overhead) is unlikely to equal the amount applied. The difference between the actual and the applied manufacturing overhead is called the **overhead variance** and is debited or credited to Work in Process, Finished Goods, and/or Cost of Goods Sold through the proration procedure discussed below. We use a *Manufacturing Overhead Variance* account.

Overhead Variance The difference between actual and applied overhead.

Assume $96,000 was credited to Manufacturing Overhead Applied and $104,000 was debited to Manufacturing Overhead during January, as shown in Illustration 3–6. In that case, the entry to close the actual against applied overhead for New Abilities is:

(8) Manufacturing Overhead Applied   96,000

Manufacturing Overhead Variance   8,000

Manufacturing Overhead   104,000

Underapplied Overhead The excess of actual overhead over applied overhead in a period.

Overapplied Overhead The excess of applied overhead over actual overhead incurred during a period.

This entry is shown in Illustration 3–6 with the original entry during the month in regular typeface and the closing entries in italics. **Underapplied overhead** occurs when actual overhead exceeds applied overhead as for New Abilities Manufacturing. Underapplied overhead is shown as a *debit* to the Manufacturing Overhead Variance account. **Overapplied overhead** *occurs when actual overhead is less than applied overhead.* Overapplied overhead is shown as a *credit* to the Manufacturing Overhead Variance account. We discuss methods of "disposing" of the manufacturing overhead variance later in this chapter.

ILLUSTRATION   *Closing Entries for Manufacturing Overhead*

3–6

Overhead: Normal Costing

Manufacturing Overhead			Manufacturing Overhead Applied			Work in Process Inventory	
104,000	(8)	104,000*a*	(8)	96,000*a*	96,000 ——————▶	96,000	

Manufacturing Overhead Variance	
(8) 8,000*a*	

a Refers to closing entry.

SUMMARY OF MANUFACTURING COST FLOWS

The flow of all manufacturing costs from the acquisition of materials to the sale of product appears in Illustration 3–7.

Self-Study Question

4 Refer to the data for Soweto Manufacturing Company in self-study question 3. Suppose the following additional transactions occurred:

  a. Completed and charged the following jobs to Finished Goods: job 1 for $18,000; job 2 for $26,000.

  b. Sold job 1 for $24,000 and job 2 for $30,000.

  c. Closed actual and applied manufacturing overhead. Recall that actual manufacturing overhead for the month was $26,000.

Show journal entries and T-accounts for the above transactions. Include the entry to close the manufacturing overhead accounts to Manufacturing Overhead Variance for the month of November.

The solution to this question is at the end of this chapter on page 110.

Marketing and Administrative Costs

Marketing and administrative costs do not flow through inventory accounts. Marketing and administrative costs are period costs that are recorded in accounts to be closed at the end of the accounting period. For example, New Abilities Manufacturing's marketing and administrative costs (all on account) were $10,000 in January. The entry to record these costs is:

Marketing and Administrative Costs	10,000	
Accounts Payable		10,000
To record marketing and administrative costs incurred in January.		

We do not show T-accounts for this entry, but note that the costs appear on the income statement in Illustration 3–8.

Note the Cost of Goods Manufactured and Sold statement in Illustration 3–8 presents the data from T-accounts in Illustration 3–7. You should cross-reference each item in the statement in Illustration 3–8 back to the

3–7

NEW ABILITIES MANUFACTURING COMPANY
January

Work in Process Inventory

Job No. 101

BB	61,000	(6)	83,000
(3) L	10,000		
(5) O	12,000		
	–0–		

Job No. 102

(2) M	24,000	(6)	112,000
(3) L	40,000		
(5) O	48,000		
	–0–		

Job No. 103

(2) M	16,000	
(3) L	30,000	
(5) O	36,000	
EB	82,000	

Finished Goods Inventory

BB	–0–	(7)	83,000
(6)	195,000		
EB	112,000		

Cost of Goods Sold

(7)	83,000

Manufacturing Overhead Variance

(8)	8,000

Accounts Payable

(1)	60,000
(4)	46,000

Materials Inventory

BB	10,000	(2)	42,000
(1)	60,000		
EB	28,000		

Manufacturing Overhead Applied

(8)	96,000	(5)	96,000

Wages Payable

(3)	110,000

Manufacturing Overhead

(2)	2,000	(8)	104,000
(3)	30,000		
(4)	72,000		

Prepaid Expenses

(4)	7,000

Accumulated Depreciation

(4)	19,000

ILLUSTRATION

Income Statement

NEW ABILITIES MANUFACTURING COMPANY
Income Statement
For the Month Ended January 31

Sales revenue	$120,000
Costs of goods sold (see statement below)	83,000
Underapplied manufacturing overhead	8,000[a]
Gross margin	29,000
Less marketing and administrative costs	10,000
Operating profit	$ 19,000

Cost of Goods Manufactured and Sold Statement
For the Month Ended January 31

Beginning work in process inventory, January 1			$ 61,000
Manufacturing costs during the month:			
Direct materials:			
Beginning inventory, January 1	$10,000		
Add purchases:	60,000		
Materials available	70,000		
Less ending inventory, January 31	28,000		
Total materials used	42,000		
Less: Indirect materials used	2,000		
Direct materials put into process		$ 40,000	
Direct labor		80,000	
Manufacturing overhead		96,000	
Total manufacturing costs incurred during the month			216,000[b]
Total costs of work in process during the month			277,000
Less work in process inventory, January 31			82,000
Cost of goods manufactured during the period			195,000[c]
Beginning finished goods inventory, January 1			–0–
Less ending finished goods inventory, January 31			112,000
Cost of goods sold			$ 83,000[d]

[a] This amount is the amount of manufacturing overhead underapplied during the month.
[b] This amount equals the total debits made to Work in Process Inventory during January (not counting the beginning balance).
[c] This amount equals the total debits to Finished Goods Inventory during January.
[d] This amount equals the total credits to Finished Goods Inventory during January.

T-accounts in 3–7. The $8,000 amount in the Manufacturing Overhead Variance account in Illustration 3–7 appears in the income statement in Illustration 3–8 as underapplied manufacturing overhead.

Disposition
of the Manufacturing
Overhead Variance

At year-end, the manufacturing overhead variance is either (1) prorated to Work in Process Inventory, Finished Goods Inventory, and Costs of Goods Sold; or (2) assigned in total to Cost of Goods Sold. Illustration 3–9 recaps the costs of jobs before proration at New Abilities Manufacturing.

ILLUSTRATION

3–9

NEW ABILITIES MANUFACTURING COMPANY
Costs of Jobs before Prorating the Manufacturing Overhead Variance

Job No.	Beginning Inventory	Direct Materials	Direct Labor	Manufacturing Overhead Applied in January	Total Costs Charged to Jobs	Status of Job at End of Month
101	$61,000	–0–	$10,000	$12,000	$ 83,000	Cost of Goods Sold
102	–0–	$24,000	40,000	48,000	112,000	Finished Goods Inventory
103	–0–	16,000	30,000	36,000	82,000	Work in Process Inventory
	$61,000	$40,000	$80,000	$96,000	$277,000	

Method 1: Prorate the Overhead Variance

If the variance is prorated to Work in Process Inventory, Finished Goods Inventory, and Cost of Goods Sold, then the cost of each job is adjusted to approximate actual cost. For New Abilities Manufacturing, the status and cost of each job before prorating the overhead variance are shown in Illustration 3–9. The variance will be prorated so that each account and job bears a share of the $8,000 manufacturing overhead variance. For our example, this share will be proportional to the overhead applied to the account during the month as shown in Illustration 3–10. Other methods for allocating the overhead variance are used also, including the total cost of jobs before the allocation.

The following entry is made to prorate the variance:

Cost of Goods Sold	1,000	
Finished Goods Inventory	4,000	
Work in Process Inventory	3,000	
Manufacturing Overhead Variance		8,000

Method 2: Assign the Adjustment to Cost of Goods Sold

Many companies do not prorate the manufacturing overhead variance to inventories and Cost of Goods Sold; instead they transfer the entire variance to Cost of Goods Sold for both internal and external reporting using the following journal entry:

Cost of Goods Sold	8,000	
Manufacturing Overhead Variance		8,000

In a company with many kinds of products and inventories, proration can be complicated. If the amounts to be prorated are immaterial relative to net income for external reporting, or do not affect managerial decisions, it may not be necessary to prorate. The difference in net income between prorating the variance and assigning it to Cost of Goods Sold is a matter of timing. Any difference between actual and applied overhead will eventually be expenses (or credited to expense), even if a company prorates. Prorating

ILLUSTRATION   *Prorating Variances*

3–10

NEW ABILITIES MANUFACTURING COMPANY
Prorating Variances

		(1)	*(2)*	*(3)*		*(4)*		*(5)*
Job		Account	Manufacturing Overhead Applied in January[a]	Percent of Total Overhead Applied in January[b]		Overhead to Be Prorated		Prorated Variance
101	Cost of Goods Sold		$12,000	12.5	×	$8,000	=	$1,000
102	Finished Goods Inventory		48,000	50.0	×	8,000	=	4,000
103	Work in Process Inventory		36,000	37.5	×	8,000	=	3,000
			$96,000	100.0				$8,000

a $120 per machine-hour.
b 12.5% = $12,000 ÷ $96,000; 50.0% = $48,000 ÷ $96,000; 37.5% = $36,000 ÷ $96,000.

the overhead variance merely defers expensing the portion allocated to inventories until those inventories are sold. For managerial purposes, one must ask how useful it is to revalue work in process and finished goods inventories to actual cost. A large overhead variance may affect some cost control, performance evaluation, pricing, and other decisions, but if the variance is small, proration is probably not worthwhile.

However the variance is disposed of, the key managerial issue is to understand causes of the difference between actual and applied overhead. Management may need to revise overhead rates, impose new cost control procedures, or take other action.

 *Self-Study Question*

5   Refer to the information regarding Soweto Manufacturing Company in self-study questions 3 and 4. Dispose of the manufacturing overhead variance by (1) prorating the variance to Work in Process Inventory and Cost of Goods Sold based on the applied overhead in jobs, and (2) charging the entire variance to Cost of Goods Sold.

Show journal entries for the above transactions.

The solution to this question is at the end of this chapter on page 111.

Interim Reporting

When normal costing is used and the overhead accounts are not closed monthly, there are two ways of reporting the balance in the Manufacturing Overhead Variance account on financial statements. It can either be (1) reported on the income statement, for example, as an adjustment to Cost of Goods Sold or (2) carried on the balance sheet as an adjustment to inventory or as a deferred debit or credit. The first option treats the adjustment as a period cost; the second, as a product cost. Management and accountants select the option they prefer and use it continuously for interim reporting consistency. When the accounts are formally closed, the Manufacturing Overhead Variance account is prorated (Method 1, above) or closed to Cost of Goods Sold (Method 2, above).

Normal versus Actual Costing

Suppose New Abilities Manufacturing had not used a predetermined overhead rate but had used only actual costs to compute job costs. Then management would have waited until the actual overhead costs were known and allocated the costs to jobs based on the actual machine-hours worked. Sometime in February, management would know the actual overhead costs for January were $104,000. These would be allocated to jobs based on the actual machine-hours worked on each job, as follows:

$$\frac{\text{Actual manufacturing overhead costs}}{\text{Actual machine-hours used}} = \frac{\$104,000}{800 \text{ mh}} = \$130 \text{ per mh}$$

The actual manufacturing overhead applied to each job in January would be:

	Machine-Hours Used		Actual Overhead Rate		Manufacturing Overhead Applied
Job No. 101	100	×	$130	=	$ 13,000
Job No. 102	400	×	$130	=	52,000
Job No. 103	300	×	$130	=	39,000
Total	800				$104,000

Actual Costing A system of accounting whereby overhead is assigned based on actual overhead costs incurred.

Actual costing is the method of assigning only actual costs to the products. Following is a comparison of actual and normal costing:

	Product Costing Method	
	Actual	Normal
Direct materials	Actual cost	Actual Cost
Direct labor	Actual Cost	Actual Cost
Manufacturing overhead	**Actual** rate times actual allocation base	**Predetermined** rate times actual allocation base

Note that actual costing requires that management wait until actual costs are known before determining product costs. This wait is usually short for direct materials and direct labor, but is considerably longer for manufacturing overhead. Managers generally prefer normal costing because it provides product cost data sooner and it normalizes fluctuations in overhead.

JOB COSTING IN SERVICE ORGANIZATIONS

Job operations are also found in service organizations, such as architectural, consulting, and accounting firms. The job costing procedure is basically the same in both service and manufacturing organizations, except that service firms use no direct materials.

Example Creative Designs is a consulting firm specializing in interior design work. Assume Creative Designs has the same cost data for January as New Abilities Manufacturing, but Creative Designs has no direct materials. In addition, Creative Designs has $2,000 in supplies in place of the $2,000 in

ILLUSTRATION Cost Flows through T-Accounts—Service Organization

3-11

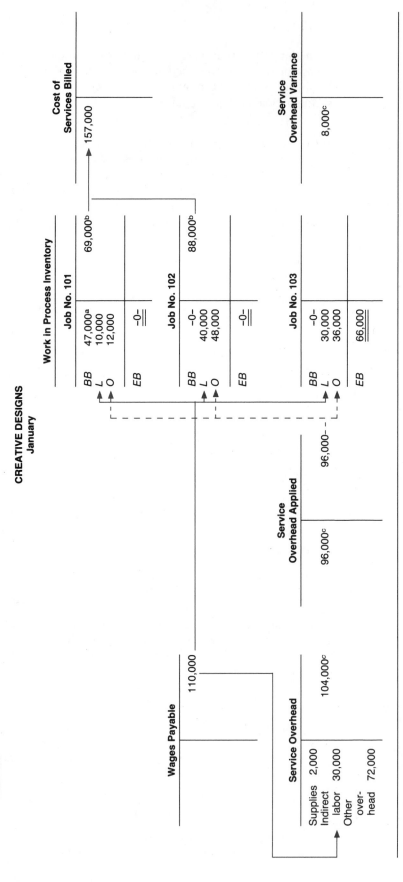

CREATIVE DESIGNS
January

Work in Process Inventory

Job No. 101 | **Cost of Services Billed**

BB	47,000ª	69,000ᵇ	→ 157,000
L	10,000		
O	12,000		
EB	–0–		

Job No. 102

BB	–0–	88,000ᵇ	
L	40,000		
O	48,000		
EB	–0–		

Job No. 103 | **Service Overhead Variance**

BB	–0–		8,000ᶜ
L	30,000		
O	36,000		
EB	66,000		

Wages Payable

	110,000

Service Overhead Applied

	96,000ᶜ
96,000--	

Service Overhead

Supplies	2,000	104,000ᶜ
Indirect labor	30,000	
Other overhead	72,000	

ª Beginning balance represents contract work in process but not billed. It is composed of $22,000 for direct labor and $25,000 for service overhead incurred in previous periods on Job No. 101.

ᵇ Job Nos. 101 and 102 were completed and billed in January.

ᶜ Closing entry.

indirect materials that New Abilities Manufacturing had. These supplies are purchased on account and shown on the debit side of the Service Overhead account.

Illustration 3–11 illustrates job costing in a service organization. You will find it parallels Illustration 3–7, which shows cost flows for a manufacturing organization, except that direct materials costs have been deleted, there is no finished goods inventory, and some minor changes have been made in account titles. Service overhead is allocated to jobs using a predetermined rate of 120 percent of the direct labor cost. We assume that the January 1 cost balance for Job No. 101 was $22,000 in direct labor and $25,000 in service overhead, for a total of $47,000. Job No. 102, which was completed in January, is assumed to have been billed in January. Illustration 3–12 shows an income statement for Creative Designs, assuming $200,000 in sales and $20,000 in marketing and administrative expenses.

CHOICE OF OVERHEAD APPLICATION BASE

Our example of applying overhead to jobs used machine-hours to apply overhead to jobs for New Abilities Manufacturing and direct labor costs as a basis for applying overhead at Creative Designs. For now, make a mental note that organizations use a variety of bases to apply overhead to products, including the number of machine-hours worked on each job, the number of direct labor hours worked on each job, the amount of direct labor costs on each job, and many others. The choice of allocation base for applying overhead is an important and complex topic; we devote much of Chapters 6 and 7 to this topic.

ETHICAL ISSUES IN JOB COSTING

There are several ethical issues in job costing. Many organizations have been called to task for improprieties in the way they assign costs to jobs. For example, major defense contractors have come under fire for overstating the cost of jobs. Numerous universities have been accused of overstating the cost of research projects. Improprieties in job costing generally are caused by one or more of the following actions: misstating the stage of completion of jobs, charging costs to the wrong jobs or categories (for example, charging the cost of university yachts to research projects), or simply misrepresenting the cost of jobs.

ILLUSTRATION

3–12

Income Statement—Service Organization

CREATIVE DESIGNS
Income Statement
For the Month Ended January 31

Sales revenue	$200,000
Cost of services billed	157,000
Underapplied service overhead	8,000
Gross margin	35,000
Marketing and administrative costs	20,000
Operating profit	$ 15,000

REAL WORLD APPLICATION

*Job Costing for Movies**

Movies and television shows are jobs. Some are successful, some are not. Studios must decide what to do with the cost of unsuccessful shows—flops. Some studios have been criticized for assigning the cost of flops to successful shows, which in turn reduces profits available under profit-sharing agreements with actors, actresses, directors, and others associated with the successful show.

Studios point out that flops have to be paid for out of the profits from successful shows. For example, Orion Pictures, maker of Academy Award winner *Dances with Wolves*, was recently criticized for carrying the cost of flops in inventory, thereby over-

stating assets and overstating profits. "While Orion recorded profits every year but 1986, it was also showing rising assets, a growing proportion of which were actually failed films that hadn't been written down."† By the early 1990s, people realized that many of Orion's assets were worthless shows, and Orion faced a plummeting stock price, debt restructuring, and possible bankruptcy.

* Based on Jane Mayer, "Hollywood Mystery: Woes at Orion Stayed Invisible for Years," *The Wall Street Journal,* October 16, 1991, p. A8.
† Ibid.

Management needs to know the stage of completion of projects to evaluate performance and control costs. If the expenditures on a job are 90 percent of the amount estimated to be spent on the project, but the job is only 70 percent complete, management needs to know as soon as possible the job will require more costs than estimated to complete. Job supervisors who report the stage of completion of their jobs may be tempted to overstate the stage of completion of jobs.

To avoid the appearance of cost overruns on jobs, job supervisors sometimes ask employees to charge costs to the wrong jobs. If you work in consulting or auditing, you may encounter cases where superiors ask you to allocate your time spent on old jobs that are in danger of exceeding cost estimates to other jobs that are in less danger of cost overruns. At minimum, this practice misleads managers who rely on accurate cost information for pricing, cost control, and other decisions. At worst, it also cheats people who may be paying for a job on a cost-plus-a-fee basis when that job has not really cost as much as the producer claims.

The above issues are part of the problem of misrepresenting the cost of jobs. Job costs can be misrepresented in other ways, too. Sometimes managers know the correct cost of a job, but they intentionally deceive a customer to obtain a larger payment. Sometimes they deceive a banker to obtain a larger loan for the job, or for other reasons. Many people insist on audits of financial records to avoid such deception. Government auditors generally work on-site at defense contractors, universities, and other organizations that have contracts with the government for large jobs.

SUMMARY

Most methods of producing goods and services can be classified into two general categories: job and process. Each requires a different costing system. Job costing concepts are used when products are easily identifiable as individual units or batches of identical units. In job costing, costs are traced to each unit or job. Construction contractors, print shops, and consulting firms are likely to use job costing methods. Job costing data can be used in bidding and pricing, controlling costs, and evaluating performance.

Our discussion of cost flows in the chapter is summarized by the flow of cost diagrams in Illustrations 3–7 and 3–11.

The source document for job costing is the job cost record (also called a *job cost sheet* or *card*). Each job has a separate record on which its costs are accumulated. These records are used to place value on inventory for external financial reporting, for the accuracy of job costing estimations, and for evaluating how well costs were controlled on each job.

Manufacturing overhead is often applied to jobs by using a predetermined overhead rate. When predetermined overhead rates are used, actual overhead rarely equals applied overhead. The difference is a variance. This manufacturing overhead variance may be debited or credited in total to Cost of Goods Sold or prorated between Finished Goods in Inventory and Cost of Goods Sold.

TERMS AND CONCEPTS

The following terms and concepts should be familiar to you after reading this chapter. Terms followed by an asterisk are found in this chapter's appendix.

Actual Costing, *83*	Overapplied Overhead, *77*
Applied Overhead, *76*	Overhead Variance, *77*
Continuous Flow Processing, *64*	Periodic Inventory, *67*
Denominator Reason*, *88*	Perpetual Inventory, *67*
Job Costing, *64*	Predetermined Overhead Rate, *74*
Job Cost Record, *69*	Process Costing, *64*
Jobs, *63*	Production Volume Variance*, *88*
Materials Requisition, *71*	Project, *64*
Normal Costing, *74*	Source Document, *69*
Numerator Reason*, *87*	Spending Variance*, *88*
Operation, *65*	Underapplied Overhead, *77*
Operation Costing, *65*	

APPENDIX

Spending and Production Volume Variances

Numerator Reason The overhead variance caused by differences between estimated and actual overhead costs for the period.

Actual and applied manufacturing overhead are usually unequal when the normal costing method is used because normal costing uses *predetermined* instead of actual overhead rates. There are two basic reasons why actual and applied rates may not be equal: the **numerator reason,** which causes the **spending variance;** and the **denominator reason,** which causes the **production volume variance.** These two variances combine to make up the total manufacturing overhead variance.

Spending Variance A variance caused by a difference between actual and estimated manufacturing costs.

Denominator Reason Overhead variance caused by differences between actual activity and the estimated activity used to compute the predetermined rate.

Production Volume Variance A variance caused by a difference between actual and estimated volume.

The *production volume variance* is caused by the difference between estimated and actual volumes of activity. The actual volume of activity may turn out to be higher or lower than originally estimated. The *spending variance* is the difference between the actual manufacturing overhead cost and the amount estimated to be spent at the actual activity level. The following example demonstrates how to derive these variances. It is helpful to separate what happens before the period when the estimates are made from what happens during and after the period.

Before the Period
Assume the predetermined overhead rate for a company was based on the assumption that manufacturing overhead would be $6,000 + ($.40 per machine-hour × Machine-hours).

		Then Manufacturing Overhead Is Expected to Be:	
If Activity Level Is:	Fixed	Variable	Total
(1) 3,000 machine-hours	$6,000	$.40 × 3,000 = $1,200	$7,200
(2) 5,000 machine-hours	6,000	.40 × 5,000 = 2,000	8,000
(3) 7,000 machine-hours	6,000	.40 × 7,000 = 2,800	8,800

Now, assume that the company *expects* machine-hours to be 5,000. It would compute the predetermined overhead *rate* as follows:

$$
\begin{aligned}
\text{Predetermined rate} &= \frac{\text{Estimated manufacturing overhead}}{\text{Estimated machine-hours}} \\
&= \frac{\$6,000 + (\$.40 \times \text{Machine-hours})}{\text{Machine-hours}} \\
&= \frac{\$6,000 + (\$.40 \times 5,000)}{5,000} \\
&= \frac{\$8,000}{5,000} \\
&= \$1.60 \text{ per machine-hour}
\end{aligned}
$$

Note that this is the predetermined rate for activity level (2): 5,000 machine-hours. The predetermined rate would be different than $1.60 per machine-hour if some other activity level had been estimated.

During and after the Period
Assume the *actual* machine-hours worked are 3,000 [that is, activity level (1)] and the *actual* manufacturing overhead costs are $7,900. Now the amount applied equals the predetermined rate ($1.60) times the actual volume of activity (3,000 machine-hours); that is, $4,800 ($1.60 × 3,000 hours). The actual and applied amounts are shown below:

Manufacturing Overhead		Manufacturing Overhead Applied	
(Actual) 7,900			(Applied) 4,800

Comparing the amount applied to the actual cost shows the amount underapplied = \$3,100 (\$7,900 − \$4,800). How much of this \$3,100 is due to the lower-than-expected activity level? Did the company spend more than it expected for manufacturing overhead at this level of activity?

Compute Spending and Production Volume Variances

To answer these questions, we compute the *spending* and *production volume variances* as follows:

$$\begin{array}{c} \text{Spending} \\ \text{variance} \end{array} = \begin{array}{c} \text{Actual} \\ \text{manufacturing} \\ \text{overhead} \end{array} - \begin{array}{c} \text{Manufacturing overhead} \\ \text{expected to be incurred} \\ \text{at the actual activity level} \end{array}$$

For this example:

$$\begin{array}{c} \text{Spending variance} = \text{Actual} - \begin{array}{c} \text{Budgeted overhead} \\ \text{at activity level (1)} \end{array} \\ \$700 \; = \; \$7,900 \; - \; \$7,200 \end{array}$$

Note that the manufacturing overhead expected to be incurred is based on *the level of activity that actually occurred,* not on the estimated activity level. The company spent less on overhead than the \$8,000 originally estimated, but then they *should* have spent less because activity was lower than originally estimated. *The variable overhead is expected to be lower if activity levels are lower,* so the actual overhead is compared with the "revised estimate" for activity level (1), not the original estimate for activity level (2).

The predetermined rate was based on the original estimate, of course, because it was derived before the period—before the actual activity became known.

The *production volume variance* is computed as follows:

$$\begin{array}{c} \text{Production} \\ \text{volume} \\ \text{variance} \end{array} = \begin{array}{c} \text{Manufacturing overhead} \\ \text{expected to be incurred} \\ \text{at the actual activity level} \end{array} - \begin{array}{c} \text{Manufacturing} \\ \text{overhead} \\ \text{applied} \end{array}$$

$$\begin{array}{c} \text{Production volume} \\ \text{variance} \\ \$2,400 \end{array} \begin{array}{c} \\ = \\ = \end{array} \begin{array}{c} \text{Overhead amount expected} \\ \text{at activity level (1)} \\ \$7,200 \end{array} \begin{array}{c} \text{Amount} \\ - \;\text{applied} \\ - \;\$4,800 \end{array}$$

The amount of the underapplied overhead attributable to a lower-than-expected activity level is \$2,400. The breakdown of the total underapplied manufacturing overhead into *spending* and *production volume* components is shown in Illustrations 3–13 and 3–14.

Favorable and Unfavorable Variance

The terms **favorable** and **unfavorable** are often used in practice to indicate whether these amounts are underapplied or overapplied, where *unfavorable means overhead was underapplied* and *favorable means overhead was overapplied*. The terms *favorable* and *unfavorable* are *not* intended to indicate whether a variance is good or bad.

In later chapters we shall see how these variances between actual and applied overhead may provide information useful for evaluating how well an organization and its people are performing.

ILLUSTRATION

Components of Over- or Underapplied Overhead: Spending Variance and Production Volume Variance

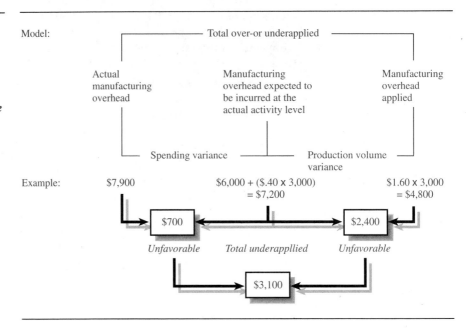

ILLUSTRATION

Graphic Presentation of Spending and Production Volume Variances

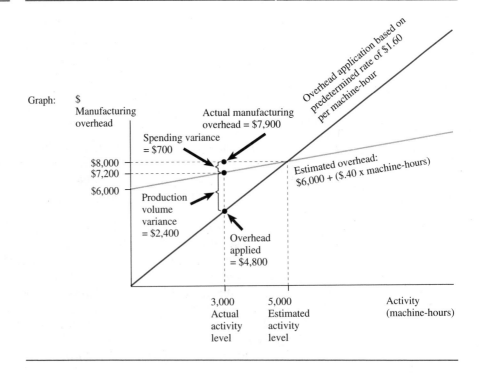

*Q**Self-Study**uestion**(Appendix)*

6 Assume the following facts:

$$\text{Estimated manufacturing overhead for Year 1} = \$20{,}000 + (\$5 \times \text{Direct labor-hours})$$

Manufacturing overhead is applied on a direct labor-hour basis.
Estimated direct labor-hours for Year 1 = 1,000 hours.

a. Compute the predetermined overhead rate for each of the following possible levels of activity:
   (1) 800 direct labor-hours.
   (2) 1,000 direct labor-hours.
   (3) 1,200 direct labor-hours.

b. During Year 1, the company works 700 direct labor-hours on job A-01 and 500 direct labor-hours on job B-01. The actual manufacturing overhead was $27,000. What is the amount of overhead applied to each job if the predetermined rate was $25 because the company had estimated 1,000 hours would be worked?

c. Refer to the facts in *b.* What is the:
   (1) Total under- or overapplied overhead?
   (2) Spending variance?
   (3) Production volume variance?

d. Graph the relationship between overhead costs and direct labor-hours like the graph shown in Illustration 3–14

The solution to his question is at the end of this chapter on page 111.

QUESTIONS

3–1 What are the characteristics of companies that are likely to be using a job order cost system?

3–2 What is the function of the *job cost record?*

3–3 What is the difference between the *Manufacturing Overhead* account and the *Manufacturing Overhead Applied* account?

3–4 On the first day of the job, a member of the management training program remarked: "The whole procedure of applying overhead and then spending a lot of time adjusting the Inventory and Cost of Goods Sold accounts back to the actual numbers looks like a complex solution to a simple problem. Why not simply charge the actual overhead to production and be done with it?" How would you reply to this comment?

3–5 What methods, documents, and approvals are used to control materials inventories?

3–6 Why is control of materials important from a *managerial-planning* perspective?

3–7 Refer to the Real World Aplication about Orion Prictures on page 86. What did Orion do with the cost of "flops"? How did this practice overstate assets and profits?

3–8 How is job costing in service organizations (for example, consulting firms) different from job costing in manufacturing organizations?

3–9   What are the costs of a product using normal costing?

3–10 Refer to the Real World Application about Doughties Foods on page 66. How did the senior company official detect fraud?

EXERCISES

3–11 Basic Cost Flow Model
(L.O.2)

Power Records, Inc., experienced the following events during the current year:

1. Incurred marketing costs of $250,000.
2. Purchased $800,000 of merchandise.
3. Paid $20,000 for transportation-in costs.
4. Incurred $400,000 of administrative costs.
5. Took a periodic inventory at year-end and learned that goods with a cost of $250,000 were on hand. This compared with a beginning inventory of $300,000 on January 1.
6. Sales revenue during the year was $2,000,000.

All costs incurred were debited to the appropriate account and credited to Accounts Payable. All sales were for cash.

Required:

Identify the following:

a. Beginning Balance (BB), Merchandise Inventory account.
b. Transfers-in (TI), Merchandise Inventory account.
c. Ending Balance (EB), Merchandise Inventory account.
d. Transfers-out (TO), Merchandise Inventory account.

3–12 Basic Cost Flow Model
(L.O.2)

The following events took place at the Bridal Wear Corp. for the current year.

1. Purchased $90,000 in direct materials.
2. Incurred direct labor costs of $52,000.
3. Manufacturing overhead was $82,000.
4. Transferred 70 percent of the materials purchased to work in process.
5. Completed work on 60 percent of the work in process. Costs are assigned equally across all work in process.

There were no beginning balances in the inventory accounts. All costs incurred were debited to the appropriate account and credited to Accounts Payable.

Required:

Identify the following:

a. Transfers-in (TI) to Work in Process account.
b. Transfers-out (TO) of Work in Process account.
c. Ending balance (EB) in Work in Process account.

3–13 Basic Cost Flow Model
(L.O.2)

Fill in the missing item for the following inventories:

	(A)	(B)	(C)
Beginning balance	$17,000	$ 7,100	$39,000
Ending balance	——	6,200	32,000
Transferred in	16,000	——	70,000
Transferred out	19,000	22,000	——

3–14 Basic Cost Flow Model
(L.O.2)

Assume the following T-accounts represent data from a division of Boeing Co.'s accounting records. Find the missing items represented by the letters. (Hint: Rearrange accounts to conform with flow of costs.)

Costs of Goods Sold	
82,000	

Direct Materials Inventory		
BB	(a)	
Purchases	18,000	Transferred out 21,000
EB	7,500	

Finished Goods Inventory		
BB	46,400	(d)
	(c)	
EB	(f)	

Work in Process Inventory		
BB	6,000	
Materials	(b)	
Labor	17,000	58,600
Overhead	(e)	
EB	9,700	

3–15 Basic Cost Flow Model
(L.O.2)

Singh Co. manufactures tools to customers' specifications. The following data pertain to job 1501 for February:

Direct materials used	$4,200
Direct labor-hours worked	300
Direct labor rate per hour	$8
Machine-hours used	200
Applied factory overhead rate per machine-hour	$15

Required:

What is the total manufacturing cost recorded on job 1501 for February?

(1) $ 8,800.
(2) $ 9,600.
(3) $10,300.
(4) $11,100.

(CPA adapted)

3–16 Assigning Costs to Jobs
(L.O.3)

The following transactions occurred in January at Kustom-Kraft, Inc., a job order custom manufacturer of cabinets:

1. Purchased $40,000 in materials.
2. Issued $2,000 in supplies from the materials inventory.
3. Purchased materials costing $28,000.
4. Paid for the materials purchased in transaction 1.
5. Issued $34,000 in direct materials to the production department.
6. Incurred direct labor costs of $50,000, which were credited to Payroll Payable.
7. Paid $53,000 cash for utilities, power, equipment maintenance, and other miscellaneous items for the manufacturing plant.
8. Applied overhead on the basis of 125 percent of $50,000 direct labor costs.
9. Recognized depreciation on manufacturing property, plant, and equipment of $25,000.

Required:

Prepare journal entries to record the above transactions.

3–17 Assigning Costs to Jobs
(L.O.3)

Refer to the data in exercise 3–16. The following balances appeared in the accounts of Kustom-Kraft, Inc., for January:

	Beginning	Ending
Materials Inventory	$74,100	
Work in Process Inventory	16,500	
Finished Goods Inventory	83,000	$ 71,600
Cost of Goods Sold		131,700

Required:

Prepare T-accounts to show the flow of costs during the period from materials inventory purchases through cost of goods sold.

3–18 Assigning Costs to Jobs
(L.O.3)

Partially completed T-accounts and additional information for the Xavier Company for the month of March are presented below:

Materials Inventory	
BB 3/1 1,000	
4,000	3,200

Work in Process Inventory	
BB 3/1 2,000	
Direct labor 3,000	

Finished Goods Inventory	
BB 3/1 3,000	
6,000	4,000

Cost of Goods Sold	

Manufacturing Overhead	
2,600	

Manufacturing Overhead Applied	

Additional information:

1. Labor wage rate was $12 per hour.
2. Manufacturing overhead is applied at $10 per direct labor-hour.
3. During the month, sales revenue was $9,000, and selling and administrative costs were $1,600.

Required:

a. What was the amount of direct materials issued to production during March?
b. What was the amount of manufacturing overhead applied to products during March?
c. What was the cost of products completed during March?
d. What was the balance of the Work in Process Inventory account at the end of March?
e. What was the manufacturing overhead variance during March?
f. What was the operating profit for March?

3–19 Predetermined Overhead Rates
(L.O.3, L.O.4)

Owings Corporation manufactures one product and accounts for costs by a job order cost system. You have obtained the following information for the year ended December 31 of last year from the corporation's books and records:

1. Total manufacturing cost during last year (called *cost to manufacture*) was $1 million based on actual direct material, actual direct labor, and applied manufacturing overhead on the basis of actual direct labor-dollars.
2. Manufacturing overhead was applied to work in process at 75 percent of direct labor-dollars. Applied manufacturing overhead for the year was 33 percent of the total manufacturing cost during last year.

Required:

Compute actual direct material used, actual direct labor, and applied manufacturing overhead.

3–20 Predetermined Overhead Rates
(L.O.4)

Apex Products estimates its manufacturing overhead to be $22,000 and its direct labor costs to be $40,000 for Year 1. The actual direct labor costs were $10,000 for job 1, $15,000 for job 2, and $20,000 for job 3 during Year 1. The actual manufacturing overhead was $26,000 during Year 1. Manufacturing overhead is applied to jobs on the basis of direct labor costs using predetermined rates.

Required:

a. How much overhead was assigned to each job during Year 1?
b. What was the manufacturing overhead variance for Year 1?

3–21 Applying Overhead Using a Predetermined Rate
(L.O.4)

Havesham Co. has a job order cost system. The following debits (credits) appeared in the Work-in-Process account for the month of May:

	Description	Amount
May 1	Balance . . . . $	10,000
Entire month	Direct materials	60,000
Entire month	Direct labor	40,000
Entire month	Factory overhead	32,000
Entire month	To finished goods	(120,000)

Havesham applies overhead to production at a predetermined rate of 80 percent based on direct labor cost. Job No. 23, the only job still in process at the end of May, has been charged with direct labor of $5,000.

Required:

What was the amount of direct materials charged to Job No. 23?

(1) $6,250.

(2) $7,500.

(3) $13,000.

(4) $17,000.

(CPA adapted)

3–22 Calculating Overhead Variance
(L.O.4)

Avian Co. uses a predetermined factory overhead rate based on direct labor-hours. For the month of October, Avian's budgeted overhead was $300,000 based on a budgeted volume of 100,000 direct labor-hours. Actual overhead amounted to $325,000 with actual direct labor-hours totaling 110,000.

Required:

How much was overhead overapplied or underapplied?

(1) $30,000 overapplied.

(2) $30,000 underapplied.

(3) $5,000 overapplied.

(4) $5,000 underapplied.

(CPA adapted)

3–23 Prorate Under- or Overapplied Overhead
(L.O.4)

Refer to the information in exercise 3–20. Prepare an entry to prorate the overhead variance as follows:

Work in Process Inventory 10%

Finished Goods Inventory 25%

Cost of Goods Sold 65%

3–24 Compute Job Costs for a Service Organization

At the beginning of the month, Paige Printing had two jobs in process that had the following costs assigned from previous months:

Job No.	Direct Labor	Applied Overhead
X-10	$640	?
Y-12	420	?

During the month, jobs X-10 and Y-12 were completed but were not billed to customers. The completion costs for X-10 required $700 in direct labor. For Y-12, $2,000 in labor was used.

During the month, a new job, Z-14, was started but not finished. No other new jobs were started. Total direct labor costs for all jobs amounted to $4,120 for the month. Overhead in this company refers to the cost of work that is not directly traced to particular jobs. Examples of such costs are copying, printing, and travel costs for meetings with clients. Overhead is applied at a rate of 50 percent of direct labor costs for this and previous periods. Actual overhead for the month was $2,000.

Required:

a. What are the costs of jobs X-10 and Y-12 at the beginning and the end of the month?

b. What is the cost of job Z-14 at the end of the month?

c. How much was the manufacturing overhead variance for the month?

3–25 Job Costing in a Service Organization (L.O.5)

For the month of September, Touche Andersen & Company worked 300 hours for client A and 700 hours for client B. Touche Andersen bills clients at the rate of $140 per hour, whereas the labor cost for its audit staff is $70 per hour. The total number of hours worked in September was 1,000, and overhead costs were $10,000. Overhead is applied at $12 per labor hour. Overhead is assigned to clients. In addition, Touche Andersen & Company had $42,000 in marketing and administrative costs. All transactions are on account. All services were billed.

Required:

a. Show labor and overhead cost flows through T-accounts.

b. Prepare an income statement for the company for September.

3–26 Analyze the Over- or Underapplied Overhead (Appendix) (L.O.6)

Refer to the data for exercise 3–20. Assume all manufacturing overhead costs were fixed costs.

How much of the under- or overapplied overhead was a spending variance, and how much was a production volume variance?

3–27 Analyze the Overhead Variance (Appendix) (L.O.6)

Grault Company estimates manufacturing overhead to be $80,000 + (.65 × Direct labor costs). Direct labor costs are estimated to be $100,000 for Year 1. The actual manufacturing overhead costs for Year 1 were $160,000. The actual direct labor costs were $120,000.

Required:

a. What is the expected total overhead for each of the following direct labor cost amounts:
   (1) $80,000?
   (2) $100,000?
   (3) $120,000?

b. How much is the under- or overapplied overhead for Year 1?

c. How much is the spending variance? The production volume variance?

3–28 Analyze the Over- or Underapplied Overhead (Appendix) (L.O.6)

Assume the following facts:

$$\frac{\text{Estimated manufacturing}}{\text{overhead for Year 1}} = \$30,000 + (\$10 \times \text{Direct labor-hours})$$

Estimated direct labor-hours for Year 1 = 1,000 hours

Required:

a. Compute the predetermined overhead rate per direct labor hour.

b. What is the expected manufacturing overhead for each of the following levels of activity:
   (1) 800 direct labor-hours?
   (2) 1,000 direct labor-hours?
   (3) 1,200 direct labor-hours?

c. During Year 1, the company works 800 direct labor-hours on job 21 and 400 direct labor-hours on job 22. The actual manufacturing overhead was $37,000. What is the amount of overhead applied to each job?

d. What is the:
   (1) Total under- or overapplied overhead?
   (2) Spending variance?
   (3) Production volume variance?

PROBLEMS

3–29 Estimate Hours Worked from Overhead Data

Terne Corporation had projected its fixed overhead costs to be $240,000. Direct labor was estimated to total 30,000 hours during the year, and the direct labor-hours would be used as a basis for the application of overhead. During the year, all overhead costs were exactly as planned ($240,000). There was $8,000 in overapplied overhead.

Required:

How many direct labor-hours were worked during the period? Show computations.

3–30 Assigning Costs— Missing Data

Materials Inventory

BB 10/1	8,000		
	(a)	4,300	
EB 10/31	9,700	(b)	

Finished Goods Inventory

BB 10/1	14,200		
	(e)		(f)
EB 10/31	(g)		

Work in Process Inventory

BB 10/1	22,300		
	180,500		
	121,000		
	94,000		
EB 10/31	17,700	(e)	

Cost of Goods Sold

402,800	

Manufacturing Overhead Applied

	(d)

Wages Payable

		BB 10/1	124,300
162,000			(c)
			36,200
		EB 10/31	119,500

Manufacturing Overhead

121,000	
4,300	
36,200	
31,600	
3,200	

Accounts Payable—Materials Suppliers

	100,000

Accumulated Depreciation— Manufacturing Property, Plant, and Equipment

	BB 10/1	204,100
		(h)
	EB 10/31	235,700

Prepaid Insurance

BB 10/1	24,300		
EB 10/31	21,100		(i)

Required:

Compute the missing amounts indicated by the letters (a) through (i).

3–31 Assigning Costs— Missing Data

The following T-accounts are to be completed with the missing information. Additional data appear after the accounts.

Materials Inventory

EB 9/30	28,200	

Work in Process Inventory

BB 9/1	16,300	
Direct materials	43,100	

Finished Goods Inventory

EB 9/30	50,500	

Cost of Goods Sold

Manufacturing Overhead		Manufacturing Overhead Applied	
(Actual)			132,000

Wages Payable		Sales Revenue	
			362,700

1. Materials of $56,800 were purchased during the month, and the balance in the inventory account increased by $5,500.

2. Overhead is applied at the rate of 150 percent of direct labor cost.

3. Sales are billed at 180 percent of Cost of Goods Sold before overhead variance is prorated.

4. The balance in Finished Goods Inventory decreased by $14,300 during the month.

5. Total credits to the Wages Payable account amounted to $101,000 for direct and indirect labor.

6. Factory depreciation totaled $24,100.

7. Overhead was underapplied by $12,540. Overhead other than indirect labor and depreciation was $99,240, which required payment in cash. Underapplied overhead is to be prorated.

8. The company has decided to allocate 25 percent of underapplied overhead to Work in Process Inventory, 15 percent to Finished Goods Inventory, and the balance to Cost of Goods Sold. Balances shown in T-accounts are before proration.

Required:

Complete the T-accounts.

3–32 Analysis of Overhead Using a Predetermined Rate: Multiple Choice

Czech Corporation uses a job order accounting system for its production costs. A predetermined overhead rate based on direct labor-hours is used to apply overhead to individual jobs. An estimate of overhead costs at different volumes was prepared for the current year as follows:

Direct labor-hours	100,000	120,000	140,000
Variable overhead costs	$350,000	$420,000	$490,000
Fixed overhead costs	216,000	216,000	216,000
Total overhead	$566,000	$636,000	$706,000

The expected volume is 120,000 direct labor-hours for the entire year. The following information is for November. Jobs 50 and 51 were completed during November.

Inventories, November 1:	
Raw materials and supplies	$ 10,500
Work in process (Job 50)	54,000
Finished goods	112,500
Purchases of raw materials and supplies:	
Raw materials	135,000
Supplies	15,000
Materials and supplies requisitioned for production:	
Job 50	45,000
Job 51	37,500
Job 52	25,500
Supplies	6,000
	$114,000

Factory direct labor-hours:

Job 50	3,500 DLH
Job 51	3,000 DLH
Job 52	2,000 DLH

Labor costs:

Direct labor wages	$ 68,000
Indirect labor wages (4,000 hours)	17,000
Supervisory salaries	6,000

Building occupancy costs
(heat, light, depreciation, etc.):

Factory facilities	6,500
Sales and administrative offices	2,500
	$ 9,000

Factory equipment costs:

Power	$ 4,000
Repairs and maintenance	1,500
Other	2,500
	$ 8,000

Required: Answer the following multiple-choice questions.

a. The predetermined overhead rate (combined fixed and variable) to be used to apply overhead to individual jobs during the year is:
   (1) $3.50 per DLH.
   (2) $4.69 per DLH.
   (3) $5.05 per DLH.
   (4) $5.30 per DLH.
   (5) None of these.

   Note: Without prejudice to your answer to requirement a, assume that the predetermined overhead rate is $4.50 per direct labor-hour. Use this amount in answering requirements b through e.

b. The total cost of Job 50 when it is finished is:
   (1) $88,750.
   (2) $135,750.
   (3) $142,750.
   (4) $145,550.
   (5) None of these.

c. The factory overhead costs applied to Job 52 during November were:
   (1) $9,000.
   (2) $47,500.
   (3) $46,500.
   (4) $8,000.
   (5) None of these.

d. The total amount of overhead applied to jobs during November was:
   (1) $29,250.
   (2) $38,250.
   (3) $47,250.
   (4) $56,250.
   (5) None of these.

e. Actual factory overhead incurred during November was:
   (1) $37,500.
   (2) $43,500.

(3) $46,000.
(4) $47,500.
(5) None of these.

f. At the end of the year, Czech Corporation had the following account balances:

Overapplied Overhead	$ 1,000
Cost of Goods Sold	980,000
Work in Process Inventory	38,000
Finished Goods Inventory	82,000

What would be the most common treatment of the overapplied overhead, assuming it is not material?

(1) Prorate it between Work in Process Inventory and Finished Goods Inventory.
(2) Prorate it between Work in Process Inventory, Finished Goods Inventory, and Cost of Goods Sold.
(3) Carry it as a credit on the balance sheet.
(4) Carry it as miscellaneous operating revenue on the income statement.
(5) Credit it to Cost of Goods Sold.

(CMA adapted)

3–33 Basic Cost Flow Model

A hysterical I. M. Dunce corners you in the hallway 30 minutes before accounting class. "Help me, help me!" I. M. pleads. "I woke up this morning and discovered that Fifo and Lifo (two pet German Shepherds) ate my homework, and these shredded pieces are all that I have left!" Being a kind and generous soul, you willingly declare, "There is no need to fear! I am a real whiz at accounting and will be glad to help you." A relieved I. M. Dunce hands you the following torn homework remnants.

Page 1

Direct labor-hours used	375
Direct labor rate - $5 per hour	
Direct materials purchased	$5,250
Direct materials beginning inventory	$1,400

Page 2

Actual manufacturing overhead.................................	$ 750
Beginning work in process inventory................................	1,500
Cost of goods manufactured........	8,000
Ending finished goods inventory.................................	3,000

Page 3

Job remaining in ending work in process inventory:	
Labor	$ 500
Direct materials	1,300
Overhead	200
Ending work in process inventory.....................................	$ 2,000
Total revenue..............................	$13,500
Gross margin..............................	4,000
Marketing and administrative costs...................	
Operating profit...........................	1,000

Required:

a. Prepare T-accounts to show the flow of costs and determine each of the following:

(1) Marketing and administrative costs.
(2) Cost of goods sold.
(3) Beginning finished goods inventory.
(4) Direct materials used.
(5) Ending direct materials inventory.

b. Prepare an income statement.

3–34 Basic Cost Flow Model

After a dispute concerning wages, Steve W. Ozniak contaminated the computerized accounting system at Sparkle Company with a virus that destroyed most of the company records. The computer experts at the company could only recover a few fragments of the company's factory ledger, as shown below:

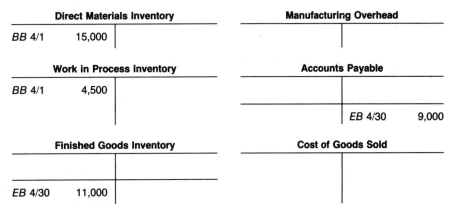

Direct Materials Inventory		Manufacturing Overhead	
BB 4/1 15,000			

Work in Process Inventory		Accounts Payable	
BB 4/1 4,500			
		EB 4/30 9,000	

Finished Goods Inventory		Cost of Goods Sold	
EB 4/30 11,000			

Further investigation and reconstruction from other sources yielded the following additional information.

1. The controller remembers clearly that actual manufacturing overhead costs are recorded at $3 per direct labor-hour.

2. The production superintendent's cost sheets showed only one job in work in process inventory on April 30. Materials of $2,600 had been added to the job, and 300 direct labor-hours had been expended at $6 per hour.

3. The Accounts Payable are for direct materials purchases only, according to the accounts payable clerk. He clearly remembers that the balance in the account was $6,000 on April 1. An analysis of canceled checks (kept in the treasurer's office) shows that payments of $42,000 were made to suppliers during the month.

4. The payroll ledger shows that 5,200 direct labor-hours were recorded for the month. The employment department has verified that there are no variations in pay rates among employees (this infuriated Steve, who felt his services were underpaid).

5. Records maintained in the finished goods warehouse indicate that the finished goods inventory totaled $18,000 on April 1.

6. The cost of goods manufactured for April was $89,000.

Required:

Determine the following amounts:

a. Work in process inventory, April 30.

b. Direct materials purchased during April.

c. Actual manufacturing overhead incurred during April.

d. Cost of goods sold for April.

3–35 Cost Accumulation: Service

White and Brite Dry Cleaners has five employees and a president, Hexter Strength. Hexter and one of the five employees manage all the marketing and administrative duties. The remaining four employees work directly on operations. White and Brite has four service departments: dry cleaning, coin washing and drying, special cleaning, and repairs. A time card is marked, and records are kept to monitor the time each employee spends working in each department. When business is slow, there is idle time, which is marked on the time card. (It is necessary to have some idle time because White and Brite promises 60-minute service, and it is necessary to have direct labor-hours available to accommodate fluctuating peak-demand periods throughout the day and the week.)

Some of the November operating data are as follows:

	Idle Time	Dry Cleaning	Coin Washing and Drying	Special Cleaning	Repairs
Sales revenue		$4,625	$5,250	$2,000	$625
Direct labor (in hours)	25	320	80	125	90
Direct overhead traceable to departments:					
Cleaning compounds		$ 500	$ 250	$ 400	$-0-
Supplies		125	200	175	140
Electric usage		250	625	100	25
Rent		200	500	90	10

Other data:

1. The four employees working in the operating departments all make $8 per hour.
2. The fifth employee, who helps manage marketing and administrative duties, earns $1,500 per month; and Hexter earns $2,000 per month.
3. Indirect overhead amounted to $512 and is assigned to departments based on direct labor-hours used. Since there are idle hours, some overhead will not be assigned to a department.
4. In addition to salaries paid, marketing costs for such items as advertising and special promotions totaled $400.
5. In addition to salaries, other administrative costs were $150.
6. All revenue transactions are cash, and all others are on account.

Required:

Management wants to know if each department is contributing toward the company's profit. Prepare an income statement for November that shows the revenue and cost of services for each department. Write a short report to management about departmental profitability. No inventories were kept.

3–36 Job Costs: Service

For the month of May, Correctall Accountants worked 500 hours for Misfit Manufacturing, 150 hours for Hang Ten Surf Shop, and 250 hours for Mandarin Restaurants. Correctall bills clients at $80 an hour, and labor costs are $30 an hour. A total of 1,000 hours were worked in May with 100 hours not billable to clients. Overhead costs of $15,000 were incurred. Overhead was assigned to clients on the basis of direct labor-hours. Since 100 hours were not billable, some overhead was not assigned to jobs. Correctall had $10,000 in marketing and administrative costs. All transactions were on account.

Required:

a. What is the revenue and cost per client?
b. Prepare an income statement for the month of May.

3–37 Job Costs in a Service Company

On June 1, two jobs were in process at the Springer Landscaping Company. Details of the jobs are as follows:

Job No.	Direct Materials	Direct Labor
A-15	$87	$32
A-38	16	42

Materials inventory (for example, plants and shrubs) on June 1 totaled $460, and $58 in materials were purchased during the month. Indirect materials of $8 were withdrawn from materials inventory. On June 1, finished goods inventory consisted of two jobs, Job No. A-07, costing $196, and Job No. A-21, with a cost of $79. Both of these jobs were transferred to Cost of Goods Sold during the month.

Also during June, Jobs No. A-15 and A-38 were completed. To complete Job No. A-15 required an additional $34 in direct labor. The completion costs for Job No. A-38 included $54 in direct materials and $100 in direct labor.

Job No. A-40 was started during the period but was not finished. A total of $157 of direct materials was used (excluding the $8 indirect materials) during the period, and total direct labor costs during the month amounted to $204. Overhead has been estimated at 150 percent of direct labor costs, and this relation has been the same for the past few years.

Required:

Compute costs of Jobs No. A-15 and A-38 and balances in the June 30 inventory accounts.

3–38 Tracing Costs in a Job Company

The following transactions occurred at Super Dynamics, Inc., a defense contractor that uses job costing:

1. Purchased $71,600 in materials on account.
2. Issued $2,000 in supplies from the materials inventory to the production department.
3. Paid for the materials purchased in (1).
4. Issued $34,000 in direct materials to the production department.
5. Incurred wage costs of $56,000, which were debited to a temporary account called Payroll. Of this amount, $18,000 was withheld for payroll taxes payable. The remainder was paid in cash to the employees. [See transactions (6) and (7) for additional information about Payroll.]
6. Recognized $28,000 in fringe benefit costs, which were incurred as a result of the wages paid in (5). This $28,000 was debited to the temporary account called Payroll.
7. Analyzed the Payroll account and determined that 60 percent was direct labor, 30 percent was indirect manufacturing labor, and 10 percent represented administrative and marketing costs.
8. Paid for utilities, power, equipment maintenance, and other miscellaneous items for the manufacturing plant. The total amount waas $43,200.
9. Paid $53,500 for new equipment.
10. Applied overhead on the basis of 175 percent of *direct* labor costs, including fringe benefits recorded in (5) and (6) above.
11. Recognized depreciation on manufacturing property, plant, and equipment of $21,000.

Required:

a. Prepare journal entries to record these transactions.

b. The following balances appeared in the accounts of Super Dynamics, Inc.:

	Beginning	Ending
Materials Inventory	$74,100	—
Work in Process Inventory	16,500	—
Finished Goods Inventory	83,000	$ 66,400
Cost of Goods Sold	—	131,700

Required:

Prepare T-accounts to show the flow of costs during the period.

3–39 Cost Flows through Accounts

Donegal Woolens employed 20 full-time knitters at $5 per hour. Since beginning operations last year, they had priced the various jobs by applying a markup of 20 percent on direct labor and direct material costs. However, despite operating at capacity, last year's performance was a great disappointment to the managers. In total, 10 jobs were taken and completed, incurring the following total costs:

Direct materials	$ 51,770
Direct labor	200,000
Manufacturing overhead	52,000

Thirty percent of the $52,000 manufacturing overhead was variable overhead; 70 percent was fixed.

This year Donegal Woolens expected to operate at the same activity level as last year, and overhead costs and the wage rate were not expected to change.

For the first quarter of this year, Donegal Woolens had just completed two jobs and was beginning on the third. The costs incurred were as follows:

Jobs	Direct Materials	Direct Labor Costs
111	$6,860	$24,500
112	4,650	15,620
113	4,700	9,880
Total factory overhead		13,560
Total marketing and administrative costs		5,600

You are a consultant associated with Vesting Concerns Management Consultants, a firm Donegal Woolens has asked for help. The senior partner of your firm has examined Donegal Woolens' books and has decided to divide actual factory overhead by job into fixed and variable portions as follows:

	Actual Factory Overhead	
Jobs	Variable	Fixed
111	$1,495	$ 5,200
112	1,375	4,410
113	230	850
	$3,100	$10,460

In the first quarter of this year, 40 percent of marketing and administrative costs were variable and 60 percent were fixed. You are told that jobs 111 and 112 were sold for $42,500 and $27,500, respectively. All over- or underapplied overhead for the quarter is expensed on the income statement.

Required:

a. Present in T-accounts the full absorption, actual manufacturing cost flows for the three jobs in the first quarter of this year.

b. Using last year's overhead costs and direct labor-hours as the estimate for this year, calculate predetermined overhead rates per direct labor-hour for variable and fixed overhead.

c. Present in T-accounts the full absorption, normal manufacturing cost flows for the three jobs in the first quarter of this year. Use the overhead rates derived in part (b).

d. Prepare income statements for the first quarter of this year under the following costing systems:
   (1) Full absorption, actual.
   (2) Full absorption, normal.

3–40 Show Flow of Costs to Jobs

Pulsar Light Equipment Company assembles light and sound equipment for installation in various entertainment facilities. An inventory of materials and equipment is on hand at all times so that installation may be started as quickly as possible. Special equipment is ordered as required. On September 1, the Materials and Equipment Inventory account had a balance of $48,000. A Work in Process Inventory account is maintained to record costs of installation work not yet complete. There were two such jobs on September 1, with the following costs:

	Job No. 46 Wheels and Spokes Country Music Hall	Job No. 51 Stars Theater
Materials and equipment	$32,000	$95,000
Technician labor	6,500	9,700
Overhead (applied)	4,800	14,250

Overhead has been applied at 15 percent of the costs of materials and equipment installed.

During September, two new installations were begun. Additional work was carried out on Job Nos. 46 and 51, with the latter job completed and billed to the Stars Theater. Details on the costs incurred on jobs during September are as follows:

	Job No. 46	Job No. 51	Job No. 55	Job No. 56
Materials and equipment	$3,200	$14,200	$17,000	$6,200
Technician labor (on account)	1,800	1,200	3,100	900

In addition to these costs, other events of the period included:

1. $25,000 payment received on Job No. 55 delivered to customer.

2. Purchased materials and equipment for $18,700.

3. Billed Stars Theater $175,000 and received payment for $100,000 of that amount.

4. Payroll for indirect labor personnel totaled $1,300.

5. Issued supplies and incidental installation materials for current jobs. The cost of these items was $310.

6. Recorded overhead and advertising costs for the installation operation as follows (all cash except equipment depreciation):

Property taxes	$1,100
Showroom and storage area rental	1,350
Truck and delivery cost	640
Advertising and promotion campaign	1,200
Electrical inspections	400
Telephone and other miscellaneous	650
Equipment depreciation	900

Required:

a. Prepare journal entries to record the flow of costs for the installation operation during September.

b. Calculate the amount of over- or underapplied overhead for the month. This amount is debited or credited to Cost of Goods Sold.

c. Determine inventory balances for Materials and Equipment Inventory and Work in Process Inventory.

3–41 Reconstruct Missing Data

Disaster struck the only manufacturing plant of the Complete Transaction Equipment Corporation on December 1. All the work in process inventory was destroyed. A few records were salvaged from the wreckage and from the company's headquarters. The insurance company has stated that it will pay the cost of the lost inventory if adequate documentation can be supplied. The insurable value of work in process inventory is made up of direct materials, direct labor, and applied overhead.

The following information about the plant appears on the October financial statements at the company's headquarters:

Materials inventory, October 31 .... $ 49,000
Work in process inventory, October 31 86,200
Finished goods inventory, October 31 32,000
Cost of goods sold through October 31 348,600
Accounts payable (materials suppliers) on October 31 21,600
Manufacturing overhead through October 31 184,900
Payroll payable on October 31 .... –0–
Withholding and other payroll liabilities on October 31 9,700
Overhead applied through October 31 179,600

A count of the inventories on hand November 30 shows:

Materials inventory $43,000
Work in process inventory .... ?
Finished goods inventory 37,500

The accounts payable clerk tells you that there are outstanding bills to suppliers of $50,100 and that cash payments of $37,900 have been made during the month to these suppliers.

The payroll clerk informs you that the payroll costs last month included $82,400 for the manufacturing section and that $14,700 of this was indirect labor.

At the end of November, the following balances were available from the main office.

Manufacturing overhead through November 30 .... $217,000
Cost of goods sold through November 30 396,600

You recall that each month there is only one requisition for indirect materials. Among the fragments of paper, you located the following pieces:

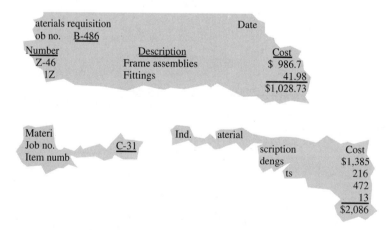

You also learn that the overhead during the month was overapplied by $1,200.

Required: Determine the cost of the work in process inventory lost in the disaster.

INTEGRATIVE CASES

3–42 Deriving Overhead Rates

Tastee-Treat Company prepares, packages, and distributes six frozen vegetables in two different sized containers. The different vegetables and different sizes are prepared in large batches. The company uses a normal costing job order costing system. Manufacturing overhead is assigned to batches by a predetermined rate on the basis of machine-hours. The manufacturing overhead costs incurred by the company during two recent years (adjusted for changes using current prices and wage rates) are as follows:

	Year 1	Year 2
Machine-hours worked	2,760,000	2,160,000
Manufacturing overhead costs incurred:		
Indirect labor	$11,040,000	$ 8,640,000
Employee benefits	4,140,000	3,240,000
Supplies	2,760,000	2,160,000
Power	2,208,000	1,728,000
Heat and light	552,000	552,000
Supervision	2,865,000	2,625,000
Depreciation	7,930,000	7,930,000
Property taxes and insurance	3,005,000	3,005,000
Total overhead costs	$34,500,000	$29,880,000

Required:

Tastee-Treat Company expects to operate at a 2.3 million machine-hour level of activity in Year 4. Using the data from the two recent years, calculate fixed and variable overhead rates to assign manufacturing overhead to its products. (Hint: The variable rate can be found by comparing the change in costs to the change in hours.)

(CMA adapted)

3–43 Incomplete Data—Job Costing

The Quik Copy Publishing Company is a rapidly growing company that has not been profitable despite its increases in sales. You have been called in as a consultant to find ways of improving the situation. You believe the problem results from poor cost control and inaccurate cost estimation on jobs. To gather data for your investigation, you turn to the accounting system, and find it almost nonexistent. However, you piece together the following information for April:

1. Production:
   a. Completed Job No. 101.
   b. Started and completed Job No. 102.
   c. Started Job No. 103.

2. Inventory values:
   a. Work in process inventory:

   March 31: Job No. 101—direct materials $1,000
             —labor   480 hours @ $10 = $4,800
   April 30: Job No. 103—direct materials $800
             —labor   520 hours @ $10 = $5,200

   b. Each job in work in process inventory was exactly one half done in labor-hours; however, *all* of the direct materials necessary to do the entire job were charged to each job as soon as the job was started.

c.   There were no direct materials inventories or finished goods inventories at either March 31 or April 30.

3.   Actual manufacturing overhead, $10,000.

4.   Cost of goods sold (before adjustment for over- or underapplied overhead):

Job No. 101:

Materials	$ 1,000
Labor	?
Overhead	?
Total	$15,400

Job No. 102:

Materials	?
Labor	?
Overhead	?
Total	?

5.   Overhead was applied to jobs using a predetermined rate per labor-dollar. The same rate had been used since the company began operations.

6.   All direct materials were purchased for cash and charged directly to Work in Process Inventory when purchased. Direct materials purchased in April amounted to $2,300.

7.   Direct labor costs charged to jobs in April were $16,000. All labor costs were the same per hour for April for all laborers.

Required: Trace the flow of costs through the system, highlighting the following figures:

a.   The cost elements (that is, material, labor, and overhead) of cost of goods sold *before* adjustment for over- or underapplied overhead, for *each job sold.*

b.   The value of each cost element (that is, material, labor, and overhead) for each job in work in process inventory at April 30.

c.   Over- or underapplied overhead for April.

3–44   Job Costing and Ethics   Maria Peters, an accountant for a consulting firm, has just received the monthly cost reports for the two jobs she supervises: one for General Dynamics and one for the U.S. government. She immediately called her boss after reading the figures for the General Dynamics job.

"We're going to be way over budget on the General Dynamics contract," she informed her boss. "The job is only about three-fourths complete, but we've spent all the money that we had budgeted for the entire job."

"You had better watch these job costs more carefully in the future," her boss advised. "Meanwhile, charge the rest of the costs needed to complete the General Dynamics job to your U.S. government job. The government won't notice the extra costs. Besides, we get reimbursed for costs on the government job, so we won't lose any money on this problem you have with the General Dynamics contract."

Required: a.   What should Maria do?

b.   Does it matter that Maria's company is reimbursed for costs on the U.S. government contract? Explain.

SOLUTIONS TO

Q *Self-Study*
   uestions

1 *a.* Lawsuit—job.
   b. Diet cola—process.
   c. Emergency room care—job.
   d. House painting—job.
   e. Paint—process.

2 For each case, start with the formula:

$$BB + TI = TO + EB$$

   a. $TI = TO + EB - BB$
         $= \$61{,}000 + \$32{,}000 - \$40{,}000$
         $= \$53{,}000$
   b. $BB = TO + EB - TI$
         $= \$11{,}000 + \$16{,}000 - \$8{,}000$
         $= \$19{,}000$
   c. $TO = BB + TI - EB$
         $= \$35{,}000 + \$8{,}000 - \$27{,}000$
         $= \$16{,}000$

3 (1) Materials Inventory 20,000

            Accounts Payable   20,000

   (2) Work in Process Inventory—Job 1   2,000

        Work in Process Inventory—Job 2   8,000

        Work in Process Inventory—Job 3   6,000

        Manufacturing Overhead   4,000

            Materials Inventory   20,000

   (3) Work in Process Inventory—Job 1   2,000

        Work in Process Inventory—Job 2   6,000

        Work in Process Inventory—Job 3   4,000

        Manufacturing Overhead   2,000

            Wages Payable   14,000

   (4) Manufacturing Overhead 20,000

            Accounts Payable   12,000

            Accumulated Depreciation   8,000

   (5) $\dfrac{\text{Predetermined overhead}}{\text{application rate}} = \dfrac{\text{Estimated manufacturing overhead costs}}{\text{Estimated direct materials used}}$

        $= \dfrac{\$240{,}000}{\$160{,}000}$

        $= \$1.50$ per dollar of direct material

   The amount of overhead applied to each job is:
       Job 1: $\$2{,}000 \times \$1.50 = \$\ 3{,}000$
       Job 2: $\$8{,}000 \times \$1.50 = \ 12{,}000$
       Job 3: $\$6{,}000 \times \$1.50 = \ \underline{\ 9{,}000}$
                                      $\underline{\underline{\$24{,}000}}$

The journal entry to record this is:

Work in Process Inventory—Job 1	3,000
Work in Process Inventory—Job 2	12,000
Work in Process Inventory—Job 3	9,000
Manufacturing Overhead Applied	24,000

Accounts Payable

	(1) 20,000
	(4) 12,000

Materials Inventory

(1) 20,000	(2) 20,000

Work in Process Inventory

Job 1

BB 11,000	
(2) 2,000	
(3) 2,000	
(5) 3,000	

Wages Payable

	(3) 14,000

Job 2

(2) 8,000	
(3) 6,000	
(5) 12,000	

Manufacturing Overhead

(2) 4,000	
(3) 2,000	
(4) 20,000	

Manufacturing Overhead Applied

	(5) 24,000

Job 3

(2) 6,000	
(3) 4,000	
(5) 9,000	

Accumulated Depreciation

	(4) 8,000

4

(1)

Finished Goods Inventory 44,000	
Work in Process Inventory—Job 1	18,000
Work in Process Inventory—Job 2	26,000

(2)

Cost of Goods Sold 44,000	
Finished Goods Inventory	44,000
Accounts Receivable 54,000	
Sales	54,000

(3)

Manufacturing Overhead Applied 24,000	
Manufacturing Overhead Variance 2,000	
Manufacturing Overhead	26,000

Work in Process—Job 1

(1) 18,000	

Work in Process—Job 2

(1) 26,000	

Finished Goods

(1) 44,000	(2) 44,000

Accounts Receivable

(2) 54,000	

Cost of Goods Sold

(2) 44,000	

Manufacturing Overhead		Manufacturing Overhead Applied		Sales	
(3) 26,000		(3) 24,000			(2) 54,000

Manufacturing Overhead Variance	
(3) 2,000	

5 (1) Overhead is prorated according to the amount of manufacturing overhead applied during the month. The amount can be calculated as follows:

Job	Manufacturing Overhead Applied in November	Percent of Total[a]		Manufacturing Overhead Variance		Prorated Overhead
1	$ 3,000	12.5	×	$2,000	=	$ 250
2	12,000	50.0	×	2,000	=	1,000
3	9,000	37.5	×	2,000	=	750
	$24,000	100.0%				$2,000

[a] 12.5% = $3,000 ÷ $24,000, etc.

Jobs 1 and 2 were sold during the month. Only job 3 remained in work in process inventory at the end of the month. The journal entry to prorate the overhead variance is:

Cost of Goods Sold 1,250
Work in Process Inventory—Job 3 750
    Manufacturing Overhead Variance 2,000

(2) If the entire variance is charged to Cost of Goods Sold, the journal entry is:

Cost of Goods Sold 2,000
    Manufacturing Overhead Variance 2,000

6 (Appendix) *a*.

Level	Estimated Hours	Expected Total Manufacturing Overhead Costs	Predetermined Rate per Hour
(1)	800	$20,000 + ($5 × 800) = $24,000	$24,000 ÷ 800 = $30
(2)	1,000	$20,000 + ($5 × 1,000) = $25,000	$25,000 ÷ 1,000 = $25
(3)	1,200	$20,000 + ($5 × 1,200) = $26,000	$26,000 ÷ 1,200 = $21.67

b.

Manufacturing Overhead Applied		
Job A = 01	Job B = 01	Total
$25 × 700 hours = $17,500	$25 × 500 hours = $12,500	$30,000

c.

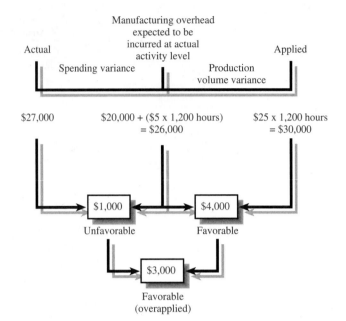

Manufacturing overhead
expected to be
incurred at actual
activity level

Actual   Applied

Spending variance   Production
volume variance

$27,000 $20,000 + ($5 x 1,200 hours) $25 x 1,200 hours
                  = $26,000   = $30,000

$1,000 $4,000

Unfavorable   Favorable

$3,000

Favorable
(overapplied)

d.

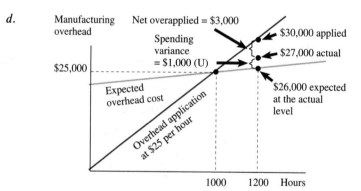

Manufacturing   Net overapplied = $3,000
overhead
                 Spending $30,000 applied
                 variance
                 = $1,000 (U) $27,000 actual
$25,000

Expected $26,000 expected
overhead cost   at the actual
                 Overhead application   level
                 at $25 per hour

                                1000   1200   Hours

Production volume variance is the difference between
$30,000 applied and $26,000 expected at the
actual activity level = $4,000 F.

U = Unfavorable variances.
F = Favorable variances.

Process Costing

LEARNING OBJECTIVES

After reading this chapter, you should be able to:

1. Explain the purpose of process costing.
2. Compute equivalent units.
3. Assign costs to products using weighted-average costing.
4. Assign costs to products using first-in, first-out costing.
5. Prepare and analyze a production cost report.
6. Analyze the accounting choice between first-in, first-out and weighted-average costing.
7. Assign costs to products when costs are introduced to the process at different stages.
8. Identify the characteristics of production that make process costing appropriate and those that make job costing appropriate.

Process Costing A costing method that assigns costs equally to homogeneous units within a particular time period. Used in continuous flow production settings.

Chapter 3 presented a continuum of production methods and accounting systems (see Illustration 3–1 in Chapter 3) and focused on organizations that produce jobs. In this chapter, we focus on **process costing** methods. Process costing is used in companies having continuous flow production, like Sherwin-Williams (paint), Shell (petroleum), and Dow Chemical. One such company, The Coca-Cola Company, produces cola concentrate where the unit of measure is a gallon.

In job shops, costs are recorded for specific jobs. In continuous flow production, costs are first recorded for each department and then assigned to the units (for example, gallons of cola concentrate) passing through the department. We show this distinction between job costing and process costing in Illustration 4–1. Note that for process costing, at the bottom of Illustration 4–1, costs are added to the product as it passes through each department. (Although we show the product passing through each department sequentially, in practice, some products might skip departments; in other cases, products could recycle back through departments.)

ILLUSTRATION   *Comparison of Job and Process Costing*

4–1

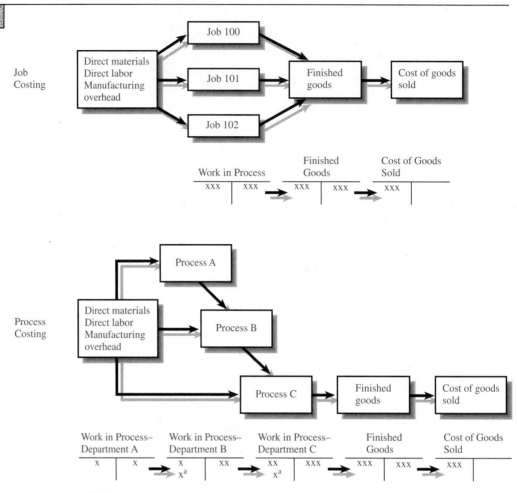

a Direct materials, labor, and manufacturing overhead added in production in the department.

ACCOUNTING FOR PROCESS COSTS

The purpose of process costing is to assign production costs to units produced in a department. These costs are used for managerial decision making, such as pricing, and for cost control. If a department has no beginning or ending inventory for a period, then all of the costs recorded in the department for the period are assigned to the units transferred out of the department. One example of this situation is when a company uses just-in-time production methods and has no beginning or ending work in process inventory.

The problem we address in this chapter occurs when companies have inventory in Work in Process Inventory accounts at the beginning and/or end of the period. Inventory in Work in Process Inventory accounts at the beginning or end of a period is generally incomplete. For costing purposes, accountants need to convert the partially completed product into equivalent units of completed product, as discussed next.

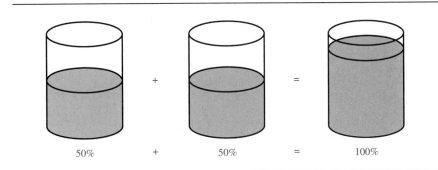

50%   +   50%   =   100%

THE EQUIVALENT UNIT CONCEPT

Equivalent Unit The amount of work actually performed on products with varying degrees of completion, translated to that work required to complete an equal number of whole units.

The **equivalent unit** concept is one of the keys to process costing. Under this concept, if two units were started at the beginning of a month and each was 50 percent finished at the end of the month, the cumulative work done on the two partial units would be considered as equivalent to the work done on one whole unit. Thus, for process costing purposes, the two half-finished units would be one equivalent unit. The equivalent unit concept is shown in Illustration 4–2, where two glasses of water one-half full are equivalent to one glass that is full.

The equivalent unit concept is not limited to manufacturing. For example, university administrators often count the number of students in a department in terms of "full-time equivalents." Two half-time students are considered to be one full-time equivalent.

ASSIGNING COSTS USING WEIGHTED-AVERAGE COSTING

Weighted-Average Costing The inventory method that combines costs and equivalent units of a period with the costs and the equivalent units in beginning inventory for product costing purposes.

Companies generally use one of two alternative methods of assigning costs to inventories in process costing: first-in, first-out (FIFO) or weighted-average. **Weighted-average costing** combines the costs in beginning inventory with costs incurred during the period to compute how much cost is assigned to units transferred out and how much to ending inventory. Many regard the weighted-average method as easier to learn and to apply in practice, so we discuss it first. We discuss the FIFO method later in this chapter. If you have learned the weighted-average method from a previous class in managerial accounting or accounting principles, you may want to skip ahead to the section titled "Assigning Costs Using First-In, First-Out Costing."

To illustrate accounting for process costing using weighted-average costing, assume Spirit Beverages is a soft drink company that produces a soft drink syrup that can be sold to bottlers or in the fountain market (for example, to restaurants or convenience stores). The top panel of Illustration 4–3 shows a diagram of unit flows for the Blending Department for the month of December. The department had 2,000 units in beginning inventory, which it finished during the month. Of the 12,000 units that were started in December, 8,000 were finished while the remaining 4,000 units were left in ending inventory, partially completed.

For weighted-average costing, we do not have to know which of the finished units were from beginning inventory and which were started and finished in the current period. This saves considerable time and effort both

Panel A

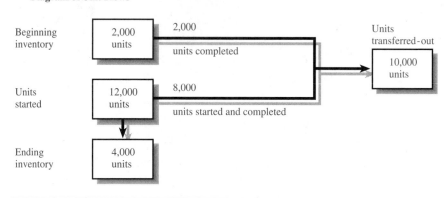

SPIRIT BEVERAGES
Blending Department
Month Ending December 31

Diagram of Unit Flows

Panel B

Cost and Unit Data	Units	Percent Complete	Costs
Beginning work in process inventory, December 1	2,000	80%	$ 2,580
Costs incurred in December			21,600
Transfers out of blending	10,000	100	?
Ending work in process, inventory, December 31	4,000	60	?

in textbook problems and in real world applications. As we discuss later, weighted-average costing does not provide as much information about current period product costs because it mixes current period costs with costs of products in beginning inventory. Costs of products in beginning inventory were not incurred in the current period; they were incurred in a previous period.

Panel B of Illustration 4–3 shows the costs of beginning inventory to be $2,580 and the costs incurred in December to be $21,600. That is, the Blending Department has $24,180 to account for in December ($24,180 = $2,580 in beginning inventory plus $21,600 in costs incurred during December). Our problem is indicated by the question marks in Panel B of Illustration 4–3. How much of the $24,180 should be assigned to the 10,000 units transferred out and how much to the partially complete 4,000 units in the Blending Department's ending inventory on December 31?

Conceptual Basis: The
Basic Cost Flow Model

Note the problem we are trying to solve comes from the basic cost flow model. From the model

$$\underset{(BB)}{\text{Beginning balance}} + \underset{(TI)}{\text{Transfers-in}} = \underset{(TO)}{\text{Transfers-out}} + \underset{(EB)}{\text{Ending balance}}$$

REAL WORLD APPLICATION

Canning Production Cycle for Coca-Cola*,†

The direct materials required for canning Coca-Cola† are: syrup, carbonated water, and cans. The bottler purchases syrup, or a concentrate that it converts to syrup, from The Coca-Cola Company. Carbonated water and syrup are combined in the first stage of production to make the liquid that is to be canned. At this point, materials costs are the costs of carbonated water and syrup.

In a separate process, empty cans are delivered to the plant where they are inspected and rinsed. Cans are filled with Coke† in the second stage,

which requires only conversion costs. Tops are placed on the cans in the third stage. Next the filled cans are formed into cases of cans and packaged. This completes their journey through work in process. The product enters finished goods inventory when it is shipped to a warehouse. Cases of Coke† become cost of goods sold when they are distributed to retail outlets.

* Based on the authors' research and information provided by The Coca-Cola Company.
† Registered trademarks of The Coca-Cola Company.

---

we know $BB = \$2{,}580$ and $TI = \$21{,}600$. We are trying to determine how much of these costs should be assigned to units transferred out (TO) and how much to units in ending inventory (EB). Next we discuss the five steps required to assign costs to TO and EB.

Five Steps in Assigning Costs

We assign costs to ending inventory and to units transferred out in five steps. These steps are:

1. Summarize the flow of physical units.
2. Compute the equivalent units produced.
3. Summarize the total costs to be accounted for. These costs are the sum of the costs in beginning inventory and the costs incurred in the department during the period.
4. Compute costs per equivalent unit.
5. Assign costs to goods transferred out and to ending inventory.

Step 1: Summarize the Flow of Physical Units

This step identifies the flow of physical units regardless of their stage of completion. This step has two parts: (1) units to be accounted for and (2) units accounted for. We identify these units for Spirit Beverages, as follows:

(1) Units to account for:

Units in beginning work-in process inventory	2,000
Units started this period	12,000
Total units to account for	14,000

(2) Units accounted for:

Units transferred out	10,000
Units in ending work in process inventory	4,000
Total units accounted for	14,000

This step indicates that we must account for the costs of 14,000 units, of which 2,000 were in beginning inventory and 12,000 units were started during December. Of those 14,000 units, 10,000 were transferred out and 4,000 remained in ending inventory at December 31.

Step 2: Compute the Equivalent Units Produced

This is an important step that some people find to be the most difficult part of process costing to understand. We intend to make it as straightforward as possible.

The formula to compute weighted-average equivalent units produced during a period is:

$$\text{Weighted-average equivalent units produced} = \text{Total units transferred out} + \text{Equivalent units in ending inventory}$$

We use this formula to compute the equivalent units produced during December in the Blending Department. We know from Illustration 4–3 that 10,000 units were transferred out of the department in December, and 4,000 units were still in ending inventory at the end of the month. Illustration 4–3 also indicates that these 4,000 units in ending inventory were 60 percent complete at the end of the month. From these facts we compute the equivalent units in ending inventory to be 2,400 equivalent units (60% complete × 4,000 units). That is, the 4,000 units that are 60 percent finished are equivalent to 2,400 units that are 100 percent complete.

Applying the formula for computing equivalent units using the weighted-average method, we get:

$$\text{Weighted-average equivalent units produced} = \text{Total units transferred out} + \text{Equivalent units in ending inventory}$$
$$= 10,000 + (60\% \times 4,000 \text{ units})$$
$$= 12,400 \text{ equivalent units}$$

Step 3: Summarize the Total Costs to Be Accounted for

The total costs to be accounted for are those in beginning inventory plus those incurred during the period. These costs are the costs of the units to be accounted for in step 1 above, namely, the 2,000 units in beginning inventory and 12,000 units transferred out. For Spirit Beverages, assume these costs are:

Costs to be accounted for:

Costs in beginning work in process inventory	$ 2,580
Current period costs	21,600
Total costs to be accounted for	$24,180

This information says we have $24,180 to assign either to products transferred out of the department or to ending inventory.

Step 4: Compute Costs per Equivalent Unit

Note that we have $24,180 in costs to be assigned, and we have computed the equivalent units in step 2 to be 12,400 equivalent units. The cost per equivalent unit is simply the costs to be accounted for divided by the equivalent units for the period. In formula form this is:

$$\text{Cost per equivalent unit} = \frac{\text{Costs to be accounted for}}{\text{Equivalent units (weighted-average)}}$$

For Spirit Beverages, the cost per equivalent unit is:

$$\begin{aligned}\text{Cost per equivalent unit} &= \$24,180/12,400 \text{ equivalent units} \\ &= \$1.95 \text{ per equivalent unit}\end{aligned}$$

Step 5: Assign Costs to Goods Transferred Out and to Ending Inventory
Now we have the data and computations needed to perform our task, which is to divide costs between goods transferred out and those in ending inventory. To perform step 5, we multiply the cost per equivalent unit computed in step 4 by the number of equivalent units in ending inventory to obtain the cost of ending inventory:

$$\begin{aligned}\text{Costs in ending inventory} &= \text{Cost per equivalent unit} \times \text{Equivalent units in ending inventory} \\ &= \$1.95 \times 2,400 \text{ equivalent units} \\ &= \$4,680\end{aligned}$$

Also, we multiply the cost per equivalent unit by the number of (equivalent) units transferred out to obtain the cost of goods transferred out. (Note the equivalent units transferred out equal units transferred out in every case because units are only transferred out if they are complete with respect to the particular department being analyzed.)

$$\begin{aligned}\text{Cost of goods transferred out} &= \text{Cost per equivalent unit} \times \text{Equivalent units transferred out} \\ &= \$1.95 \times 10,000 \text{ equivalent units transferred out} \\ &= \$19,500\end{aligned}$$

To summarize this final step:

Costs accounted for:

Costs assigned to units transferred out	$19,500
Cost of ending work in process inventory	4,680
Total costs accounted for	$24,180

Note the total costs accounted for equal the total costs to be accounted for summarized in step 3. *This equality must hold in every case, whatever costing method you are using.* Why must costs accounted for equal costs to be accounted for? Recall the principle of the basic cost flow model: *BB + TI = TO + EB.* Costs to be accounted for represent the left side of the equation, *BB + TI;* while the costs accounted for represent the right side of the equation, *TO + EB.* Now we have accomplished our objective by accounting for the costs in step 5 that we set out to account for in step 3.

Cost Flows through T-Accounts

Illustration 4–4 shows the flow of costs through the Work-in-Process Inventory T-account for the Blending Department. The top panel shows the T-account as it would look at the end of December after the costs incurred during the month were known, but before completing the five steps above to assign costs to ending inventory and transfers out. The bottom panel shows the T-account after completing step 5 above.

ILLUSTRATION

Cost Flows—
Weighted-Average

SPIRIT BEVERAGES
Blending Department
Month Ending December 31

Work in Process Inventory—Blending			Finished Goods Inventory or Next Department in Work in Process
Beginning inventory	2,580	Costs transferred out ? ⟶	?
Current period costs	21,600		
Ending inventory	**?**		

Work in Process Inventory—Blending			Finished Goods Inventory or Next Department in Work in Process
Beginning inventory	2,580	Costs transferred out **19,500** ⟶	**19,500**
Current period costs	21,600		
Ending inventory	**4,680**		

Production Cost Report

Production Cost Report A report that summarizes production and cost results for a period. This report is generally used by managers to monitor production and cost flows.

The **production cost report** summarizes the production and cost results for a period. The production cost report is important for managers to monitor the flow of production and costs. Using this report, managers can determine whether inventory levels are getting too high, costs are not low enough, or the number of units produced is too low.

Illustration 4–5 presents a production cost report for the Blending Department of Spirit Beverages for the month of December. Although it may look complex, you will soon see that this report simply reports on the five steps for assigning costs to goods tranferred out and to ending inventory that we described above. To help relate the production cost report to those five steps, we present the report in five sections, each section corresponding to a step.

Sections 1 and 2: Managing the Physical Flow of Units

Sections 1 and 2 of the production cost report correspond to steps 1 and 2 above. Section 1 summarizes the flow of physical units and shows 14,000 units to be accounted for and accounts for 10,000 as transfers out and 4,000 in ending inventory. Section 2 shows the equivalent units of the units accounted for: 10,000 units transferred out and 2,400 equivalent units (60% complete × 4,000 units) in ending inventory, for a total of 12,400 equivalent units accounted for.

ILLUSTRATION

Production Cost Report—
Weighted-Average

SPIRIT BEVERAGES
Blending Department
Month Ending December 31

	(Section 1) Physical Units	(Section 2) Equivalent Units
Flow of units:		
Units to be accounted for:		
Beginning work in process inventory	2,000	
Units started this period	12,000	
Total units to account for	**14,000**	
Units accounted for:		
Completed and transferred out	10,000	10,000
In ending work in process inventory	4,000	2,400ª
Total units accounted for	**14,000**	**12,400**

	Costs
Flow of costs:	
Costs to be accounted for (Section 3):	
Costs in beginning work in process inventory	$ 2,580
Current period costs	21,600
Total costs to be accounted for	**$24,180**
Costs per equivalent unit (Section 4):	**$ 1.95**
	($24,180 ÷ 12,400 E.U)
Costs accounted for (Section 5):	
Costs assigned to units transferred out	$19,500
Cost of ending inventory	4,680
Total costs accounted for	**$24,180**

ª Ending inventory is 60 percent complete. 2,400 equivalent units = 60% × 4,000 units.

Sections 3, 4, and 5: Managing Costs

Sections 3, 4, and 5 provide information about costs. Corresponding to step 3, section 3 shows the costs to be accounted for, $2,580 in beginning inventory and $21,600 incurred during the month of December. Section 4 shows how we computed the cost per equivalent unit of $1.95, which equals the total costs to be accounted for in section 3 divided by the total equivalent units in section 2.

Finally, section 5 shows the cost assignment that we did above in step 5. Costs assigned to the 10,000 units transferred out equal the number of units transferred out times the cost per equivalent unit from section 4. Costs assigned to the 2,400 equivalent units in ending inventory equal the number of equivalent units in ending inventory times the cost per equivalent unit.

We now have completed assigning costs to units, showing cost flows through T-accounts, and reporting the steps performed on the production cost report. Having followed the five-step procedure in the text, you now have an opportunity to assign costs in the self-study question.

Self-Study Question

1 Green Earth Cleaners makes an environmentally sound household cleaner. The following data are available for the month of April:

Physical flow of units:

Beginning inventory	1,000 units
Started in April	6,000 units
Ending inventory	2,700 units, 80% complete

Cost data:

Beginning inventory	$ 730
Costs incurred in April	2,500

Using weighted-average process costing:

a. Derive the number of units transferred out.
b. Compute the amounts needed for each of the five steps described in the text.
c. Show the flow of costs through a T-account.
d. Prepare a production cost report.

The solution to this self-study question is at the end of this chapter on page 148.

ASSIGNING COSTS USING FIRST-IN, FIRST-OUT COSTING

First-In, First-Out Costing The inventory method whereby the first goods received are the first charged out when sold or transferred.

First-in, first-out (FIFO) costing assumes the first units worked on are the first units transferred out of a production department. Whereas weighted-average costing mixes current period costs and costs from prior periods that are in beginning inventory, FIFO keeps current period costs separate from those in beginning inventory. In FIFO costing, the costs in beginning inventory are transferred out in a lump sum (assuming the units in beginning inventory were completed during the current period) and not mingled with current period costs.

Under FIFO costing, current period costs are accounted for separately from costs in beginning inventory. Current period costs are first assigned to complete beginning inventory, then assigned to units started and completed in the current period, and finally assigned to units still in the department's ending inventory. Managers benefit from this separation of current period costs from costs in beginning inventory because they can identify and manage current period costs. If the production process is a FIFO process, the inventory numbers are more likely to reflect reality under FIFO costing than under weighted-average costing. This is because the units in ending inventory are likely to have been produced in the current period. FIFO costing assigns current period costs to those units, but weighted-average costing mixes current and prior period costs in assigning a value to ending inventory.

To illustrate accounting for process costing using FIFO, we use the data from the Spirit Beverages example. This enables you to compare FIFO and weighted-average costing and to see how the results are different. Recall the following facts:

	Units	**Costs**
Beginning inventory	2,000 (80% complete)	$ 2,580
Current period	12,000 started	21,600
Transferred out	10,000 (100% complete)	?
Ending inventory	4,000 (60% complete)	?

We combine the five-step procedure with the five sections of the production cost report to reduce redundancy in the presentation.

Step 1: Summarize the Flow of Physical Units
This step identifies the flow of physical units regardless of their stage of completion, and is the same for both FIFO and weighted-average costing. Section 1 of the production cost report in Illustration 4–6 summarizes the flow of physical units, showing 14,000 units to be accounted for and accounting for 10,000 as transfers out of the Blending Department and 4,000 units remaining in ending inventory.

Step 2: Compute the Equivalent Units Produced
Computing equivalent units is different in FIFO costing than in weighted-average costing. Recall that FIFO costing separates what was in beginning inventory from what occurs this period. The FIFO equivalent unit computation is confined only to what was produced this period. Under FIFO, we compute equivalent units in three parts:

1. Equivalent units to complete beginning inventory.
2. Equivalent units of goods started and completed during the current period.
3. Equivalent units of goods still in ending inventory.

For Spirit Beverages, 2,000 units in beginning inventory were 80 percent complete at the beginning of the period. Completing beginning inventory required 400 equivalent units, that is, 20 percent (100% − 80%) times 2,000 units equals 400 equivalent units.

The units started and completed can be derived by examining the physical flow of units. Since 12,000 units were started and 4,000 of those 12,000 remain in ending inventory, according to the FIFO method, the remaining 8,000 were completed. Thus, 8,000 units were started and completed. Another way to get the same result is to observe that of the 10,000 units completed during December, 2,000 came from beginning inventory (according to the FIFO method), so the remaining 8,000 units completed must have been started during December.

Either way you view the physical flow, 8,000 units were started and completed. Since these 8,000 units are 100 percent complete when transferred out of the department, the units started and completed represent 8,000 equivalent units produced during the current period.

Finally, we have the equivalent units of production in ending inventory.[1]

---

[1] For our examples, units in ending inventory come from the current period's production. Although unlikely, you may encounter cases in practice where the inventory levels are so high relative to current period production that some of the beginning inventory is still in ending inventory. In that case, you should keep separate the costs and units in ending inventory that come from beginning inventory. Having separated those costs and units, you can perform the computations described in the text for the current period costs.

ILLUSTRATION

*Production Cost
Report—FIFO*

SPIRIT BEVERAGES
Blending Department
Month Ending December 31

	(Section 1) Physical Units	(Section 2) Equivalent Units
Flow of units:		
Units to be accounted for:		
Beginning work in process inventory	2,000	
Units started this period	12,000	
Total units to account for	**14,000**	
Units accounted for:		
Units completed and transferred out:		
From beginning inventory	2,000	400[a]
Started and completed currently	8,000	8,000
Total	10,000	8,400
Units in ending work in process inventory	4,000	2,400[b]
Total units accounted for	**14,000**	**10,800**

	Costs
Flow of costs:	
Costs to be accounted for (Section 3):	
Costs in beginning work in process inventory	$ 2,580
Current period costs	21,600
Total costs to be accounted for	**$24,180**
Costs per equivalent unit (Section 4):	**$ 2.00**
	($21,600 ÷ 10,800 E.U)
Costs accounted for (Section 5):	
Costs assigned to units transferred out:	
Costs from beginning WIP inventory	$ 2,580
Current costs added to complete beginning WIP inventory	800
Total costs from beginning inventory	3,380
Current costs of units started and completed	16,000
Total costs transferred out	19,380
Cost of ending WIP inventory	4,800
Total costs accounted for	**$24,180**

[a] 20 percent of costs must be added to complete beginning inventory.
[b] Ending inventory is 60 percent complete.

Ending inventory of 4,000 units is 60 percent complete, so 2,400 equivalent units (60% × 4,000 units) produced this period are in ending inventory. In total 10,800 equivalent units were produced this period (10,800 = 400 + 8,000 + 2,400). These equivalent unit results appear in section 2 of the production cost report in Illustration 4–6.

You will note that the equivalent units under FIFO are less than or equal to those under weighted-average because the FIFO computations refer to this period's production only. Weighted-average equivalent units consider all units in the department, whether produced this period or in a previous period. (If the department has no beginning inventory, the weighted-average and FIFO equivalent units are equal.)

Step 3: Summarize the Total Costs to Be Accounted for
The total costs to be accounted for under FIFO costing are the same as in weighted-average costing. Whatever our assumption about cost flows, we have to account for all of the costs in the department, comprised of those in beginning inventory plus those incurred during the period. For Spirit Beverages, these costs are:

Costs to be accounted for:

Costs in beginning work in process inventory	$ 2,580
Current period costs	21,600
Total costs to be accounted for	$24,180

These costs are shown in section 3 of the production cost report in Illustration 4–6.

Step 4: Compute Costs per Equivalent Unit
Under FIFO, the costs per equivalent unit are confined to *the costs incurred this period,* $21,600, and the equivalent units *produced this period,* which were computed in step 2 to be 10,800 equivalent units. In formula form:

$$\text{Cost per equivalent unit} = \frac{\text{Current period costs}}{\text{Equivalent units of production this period}}$$
$$\text{(FIFO method)}$$

For Spirit Beverages, the cost per equivalent unit under FIFO is:

$$\text{Cost per equivalent unit} = \$21{,}600/10{,}800 \text{ equivalent units}$$
$$= \$2.00 \text{ per equivalent unit}$$

The cost per equivalent unit appears in section 4 of the production cost report.

Step 5: Assign Costs to Goods Transferred Out and to Ending Inventory
The cost of goods transferred out is comprised of the following components:

Costs in beginning inventory (at beginning of period)	$ 2,580
Costs to complete beginning inventory, 400 equivalent units required to complete beginning inventory at $2.00 per equivalent unit	800
Cost of the 8,000 units started and completed this period at $2.00 per equivalent unit	16,000
Total	$19,380

The cost of ending inventory equals $4,800, which is the 2,400 equivalent units in ending inventory at $2.00 per equivalent unit.

Cost Flows—FIFO

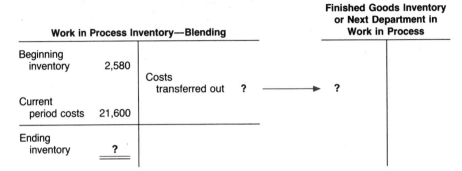

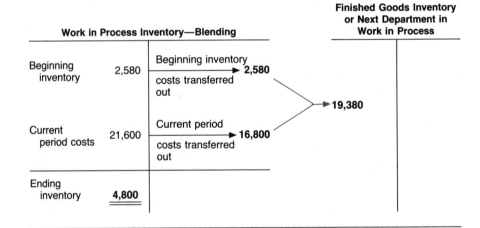

These results appear in section 5 of the production cost report. Note that the costs to be accounted for in section 3, $24,180, equal the costs accounted for in section 5, $24,180.

Cost Flows through T-Accounts

Illustration 4–7 shows the flow of costs through the Work in Process Inventory T-account for the Blending Department using FIFO. The top panel shows the T-accounts as they would appear before computing cost of goods transferred out and ending inventory amounts. (Note the question marks, which indicate the amounts unknown.) After the computations shown in the production cost report in Illustration 4–6, we complete the T-accounts as shown in the bottom panel of Illustration 4–7. We find it helpful to use T-accounts to keep the big picture in mind when working on detailed computations like those reported in Illustration 4–6.

Q Self-Study uestion

2 We continue the example from Green Earth Cleaners. The data for the month of April are repeated below. We have added the stage of completion of beginning inventory, which is needed to compute equivalent units using the FIFO method.

Physical flow of units:

Beginning inventory . . . . 1,000 units, 60% complete

Started in April . . . . 6,000 units

Ending inventory . . . . 2,700 units, 80% complete

Cost data:

Beginning inventory . . . . $ 730

Costs incurred in April 2,500

Using FIFO costing:

a. Derive the number of units transferred out.

b. Compute the amounts needed for each of the five steps described in the text.

c. Show the flow of costs through a T-account.

d. Prepare a production cost report.

The solution to this self-study question is at the end of this chapter on page 149.

COMPARISON OF WEIGHTED-AVERAGE AND FIFO COSTING

Weighted-average costing does not separate beginning inventory from current period activity. Unit costs are a weighted average of the two, whereas under FIFO costing, unit costs are based on current period activity only.

Illustration 4–8 compares the unit costs, costs transferred out, and ending inventory values under the two methods for Spirit Beverages. In this example, costs per unit are lower under weighted-average than under FIFO because the unit costs in beginning inventory are lower than current period unit costs. Thus, the lower unit costs in beginning inventory decrease the weighted-average unit cost.

While either weighted-average or FIFO costing is acceptable for assigning costs to inventories and cost of goods sold for external reporting, the weighted-average method has been criticized for masking current period costs. Thus, using weighted-average costing, the unit costs reported for December are based not only on December's costs but also on previous periods' costs that were in December's beginning inventory. For a company like Phillips Petroleum, which faces changing crude oil prices, managers' decisions require knowledge of current period costs. If computational and recordkeeping costs are about the same under both FIFO and weighted-average, then FIFO costing is generally preferred.

I L L U S T R A T I O N

4–8

Comparison of Weighted-Average and FIFO Costing

	Weighted-Average (from Illustration 4–5)	FIFO (from Illustration 4–6)
Equivalent unit costs	$ 1.95	$ 2.00
Cost of goods transferred out	$19,500	$19,380
Ending inventory	4,680	4,800

ILLUSTRATION

Summary of Steps for Assigning Process Costs to Units

Step 1: Summarize the flow of physical units.

Step 2: Compute the equivalent units produced.

Weighted-average: Equivalent units (E.U.) produced = Units transferred out + E.U. in ending inventory

FIFO: E.U. produced = E.U. to complete beginning inventory + Units started and finished during the period + E.U. in ending inventory

Step 3: Summarize the total costs to be accounted for.

Total costs to be accounted for = Costs in beginning inventory + Costs incurred this period

Step 4: Compute costs per equivalent unit.

Weighted-average:

$$\frac{\text{Weighted-average}}{\text{unit cost}} = \frac{\text{Costs in beginning inventory + Current period costs}}{\text{Units transferred out + E.U. in ending inventory}}$$

FIFO: $\frac{\text{Unit cost of}}{\text{current period work}} = \frac{\text{Current period costs}}{\text{E.U. of current work done}}$

Step 5: Assign costs to goods transferred out and to ending inventory.

Weighted-average: Using weighted-average, the cost of goods transferred out equals the total units transferred out times the weighted-average unit cost computed in step 4.

Using weighted-average, the cost of goods in ending inventory equals the equivalent units in ending inventory times the weighted-average unit cost computed in step 4.

FIFO: Using FIFO, the cost of goods transferred out equals the sum of the following three items:

a. The costs already in beginning inventory at the beginning of the period.

b. The current period cost to complete beginning inventory, which equals the equivalent units to complete beginning inventory from step 2 times the current period unit cost computed for FIFO in step 4.

c. The costs to start and complete units, calculated by multiplying the number of units started and finished from step 2 times the cost per equivalent unit computed for FIFO in step 4.

Using FIFO, the cost of goods in ending inventory equals the equivalent units in ending inventory from step 2 times the cost per equivalent unit computed for FIFO in step 4.

SUMMARY OF THE STEPS FOR ASSIGNING COSTS TO UNITS

Illustration 4–9 summarizes the steps for assigning costs to units in process costing using FIFO and weighted-average costing. Notice how the steps correspond to the production cost report used by management to monitor production unit and cost flows.

DIRECT MATERIALS AND CONVERSION COSTS

In some processes, direct materials are not introduced into the product at the same rate as the work performed on the product. For example, all the direct materials may be introduced at the beginning of the production process and conversion costs (Direct labor + Manufacturing overhead) may occur throughout the production process, as illustrated in the diagram on page 129. The conversion costs would be allocated like the illustrated Blending Department costs.

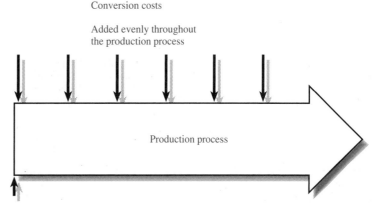

Conversion costs

Added evenly throughout
the production process

Production process

Direct materials

Added entirely at the
beginning of the
production process

To illustrate this situation, we look at Cures-R-Us, a pharmaceutical company with a production department called pharmacology. The relevant data for April are shown in Illustration 4–10.

On April 1, there were 3,000 units in beginning work in process. All direct materials are added at the beginning of the production process, so materials for units in work in process are 100 percent complete. Direct materials costs in beginning inventory were $3,000. The beginning inventory was 30 percent complete with respect to conversion costs. Conversion costs in the beginning inventory were $7,400.

Twenty-seven thousand units were started and completed during the period, and 9,000 units were in ending work in process inventory on April 30. Direct materials costs for the current period were $45,000. Current period conversion costs were $256,470. The units in ending inventory were 100 percent complete with respect to direct materials and 20 percent complete with respect to conversion costs.

The computations for calculating equivalent units and cost flows using FIFO are shown in Illustration 4–10. Equivalent units to complete beginning inventory are 0, since the beginning inventory is 100 percent complete with respect to direct materials. Since units started and completed and units in ending inventory are both 100 percent complete, total materials equivalent units for the current period are 36,000 (27,000 + 9,000).

The materials cost per equivalent unit is shown in section 4 of Illustration 4–10 to be $1.25 per unit, computed as follows:

$$\begin{aligned}
\text{Materials cost per} \atop \text{equivalent unit} &= \text{Current period} \atop \text{materials costs} \div \text{Current period equivalent} \atop \text{units for materials} \\
&= \$45,000 \quad\div\; 36,000 \\
&= \$1.25
\end{aligned}$$

$$\begin{aligned}
\text{Materials costs} \atop \text{transferred out} &= \text{Materials costs} \atop \text{from beginning} + \text{Current materials} \atop \text{costs added to} + \text{Materials costs} \atop \text{of units started} \\
& \quad\; \text{WIP inventory} \quad\;\; \text{completed WIP} \quad\;\; \text{and completed} \\
&= \$\,3,000 \qquad\;\; + \$0 \qquad\quad + (27,000 \times \$1.25) \\
&= \$\,3,000 \qquad\;\; + \$0 \qquad\quad + \$33,750 \\
&= \$36,750
\end{aligned}$$

ILLUSTRATION *Cures-R-Us Production Cost Report*

4–10

CURES-R-US
Pharmacology Department
Production Cost Report—FIFO
Month Ending April 30

	(Section 1) Physical Units	(Section 2) Equivalent Units for Current Period For Direct Materials	For Conversion
Flow of Units:			
Units to be accounted for:			
Beginning work in process inventory	3,000		
Units started this period	36,000		
Total units to account for	39,000		
Units accounted for:			
Completed and transferred out from beginning inventory	3,000	–0–	2,100
Started and completed currently	27,000	27,000	27,000
Total	30,000	27,000	29,100
In ending work in process inventory	9,000	9,000	1,800
Total units accounted for	39,000	36,000	30,900

	Total Costs	Direct Materials Costs	Conversion Costs
Flow of Costs:			
Costs to be accounted for (Section 3):			
Costs in beginning WIP	$ 10,400	$ 3,000	$ 7,400
Current period costs	301,470	45,000	256,470
Total costs to be accounted for	$311,870	$48,000	$263,870
Cost per equivalent unit (Section 4):		$1.25	$8.30
		($45,000 ÷ 36,000)	($256,470 ÷ 30,900)
Costs accounted for (Section 5):			
Costs assigned to units transferred out:			
Costs from beginning inventory	$ 10,400	$ 3,000	$ 7,400
Current costs added to complete beginning inventory	17,430	–0–	17,430[a]
Current costs of units started and completed	257,850	33,750[b]	224,100[c]
Total costs transferred out	285,680	36,750	248,930
Cost of ending inventory	26,190	11,250[d]	14,940[e]
Total costs accounted for	$311,870	$48,000	$263,870

[a] $17,430 = $8.30 × 2,100.

[b] $33,750 = $1.25 × 27,000.

[c] $224,100 = $8.30 × 27,000.

[d] $11,250 = $1.25 × 9,000.

[e] $14,940 = $8.30 × 1,800.

Total cost of ending work in process inventory with regards to direct materials equals equivalent units of direct materials in ending work in process inventory times the current period direct materials unit cost—$11,250 (9,000 × $1.25). Note that costs to be accounted for, $48,000, are the same as costs accounted for.

The ending inventory could also be derived using the basic cost flow model:

$$\begin{array}{lll} \text{Ending materials} \\ \text{balance} \end{array} = \begin{array}{l} \text{Beginning materials} \\ \text{balance} \end{array} + \text{Transfers-in} - \text{Transfers-out}$$

$$= \$\ 3,000 \quad + \$45,000 \quad - \$36,750$$

$$= \$11,250$$

Similar calculations are made for conversion costs. For Cures-R-Us, equivalent units with respect to conversion costs are different from the equivalent units with respect to direct materials. The equivalent units are shown in Illustration 4–10 based on the following calculations:

Needed to complete beginning inventory . . . . 3,000 × 70% = 2,100
Started and completed 27,000
Started for ending inventory . . . . 9,000 × 20% = 1,800

This yields a total of 30,900 equivalent units with respect to conversion costs.

The conversion costs per equivalent unit are calculated based on the current period conversion costs and the equivalent units for conversion costs as follows:

$$\text{Cost per equivalent unit} = \text{Current period costs} \div \begin{array}{l} \text{Current period} \\ \text{equivalent units} \end{array}$$

$$= \$256,470 \div 30,900$$

$$= \$8.30 \text{ per equivalent unit}$$

Once the cost per equivalent unit is obtained, it is possible to calculate the costs transferred out and the costs assigned to ending inventory. Remember, under FIFO, all beginning inventory costs are assumed transferred out as long as current period production exceeds the number of units in beginning inventory. The beginning inventory costs of $7,400 are transferred out.

Current period costs are apportioned between transferred out and ending inventory. This period, 2,100 equivalent units of work were required to complete the beginning inventory, so 2,100 times $8.30, which equals $17,430, is transferred out. Likewise, the cost of the 27,000 units at $8.30 (= $224,100) is transferred out. The total conversion costs transferred out, then, are $248,930, which is the sum of $7,400 plus $17,430 plus $224,100. All of these figures are shown in Illustration 4–10, Section 5.

Next, we determine the conversion costs in the ending inventory. Conversion costs in ending inventory equals $14,940, which is the 1,800 equivalent units with respect to conversion costs in the ending inventory times $8.30. The total of the costs transferred out ($248,930) and the ending inventory costs ($14,940) is $263,870. Note the total costs *to be* accounted for equals total costs accounted for, $263,870.

ACCOUNTING FOR PRIOR DEPARTMENT COSTS

Prior Department Costs Manufacturing costs incurred in some other department and charged to a subsequent department in the manufacturing process.

Our discussion so far has assumed a single department. Usually products pass through a series of departments, however. As the product passes from one department to another, its costs must follow.

In principle, the units transferred out of one department and into another are essentially the same as any other direct material for the receiving department. The costs of those units, which are called **prior department costs,** or transferred-in costs, are similar to the costs of direct materials put into process at the start of production in that department. The costs of processing cereal at Kellogg would be a prior department cost to the Packaging Department. Equivalent whole units are 100 percent complete in terms of prior department costs, so cost computations for prior department costs are relatively easy.

Assume that on April 1, the Biologicals Department of Cures-R-Us had 4,100 physical units in its beginning inventory with prior department costs of $36,900 attributable to the beginning inventory. Moreover, the units were 40 percent complete with respect to conversion and materials costs. Conversion and direct materials costs totaled $10,168 for the beginning inventory. Materials and conversion costs occur evenly throughout the process in the Biologicals Department.

During the month of April, the units that had been completed in the Pharmacology Department were transferred to the Biologicals Department. The cost of $285,680 for the 30,000 units transferred is a *prior department cost* for the Biologicals Department.

During the month, 24,500 units are started and completed with 5,500 units remaining in ending inventory. The ending inventory is 65 percent complete with respect to conversion costs. The Biologicals Department incurred $183,210 in direct materials and conversion costs.

A FIFO cost of production report that summarizes these data is given in Illustration 4–11. As you review this report, you should notice that the prior department costs are treated exactly as direct materials added at the beginning of a production process. Illustration 4–12 shows the flow of costs through the Biologicals Department of Cures-R-Us using FIFO. You should be able to relate the costs in the production cost report to the T-accounts.

Responsibility for Prior Department Costs

An important issue for performance evaluation is: Should a department manager be held accountable for *all* costs charged to the department? The answer is usually no. A department and its people are usually evaluated on the basis of costs *added by* the department relative to the good output from the department. Prior department costs are often excluded when comparing actual department costs with a standard or budget. We discuss this point more extensively in later chapters on performance evaluation, but we raise it here to emphasize that different information is needed for different purposes. Assigning costs to units for inventory valuation requires that prior department costs be *included* in department product cost calculations. However, assigning costs to departments for performance evaluation usually requires that prior department costs be *excluded* from departmental costs.

SYSTEMS CHOICE: JOB COSTING VERSUS PROCESS COSTING

In job costing, costs are collected for each unit produced, as discussed in Chapter 3. For example, a print shop collects costs for each order, a defense contractor collects costs for each contract, and a custom home builder collects costs for each house. In process costing, costs are accumulated in a

CURES-R-US
Biologicals Department
Production Cost Report—FIFO
Month Ending April 30

	(Section 1) Physical Units	(Section 2) Equivalent Units for Current Period	
		For Prior Department	For Materials and Conversion
Flow of Production Units:			
Units to account for:			
Beginning work in process inventory	4,100		
Units started this period	30,000		
Total units to account for	34,100		
Units accounted for:			
Completed and transferred out from beginning inventory	4,100	–0–	2,460[a]
Started and completed currently	24,500	24,500	24,500
Total	28,600	24,500	26,960
In ending inventory	5,500	5,500	3,575[b]
Total units accounted for.....................	34,100	30,000	30,535

	Total Costs	Prior Department Costs	Materials and Conversion Costs
Flow of Costs:			
Costs to be accounted for (Section 3):			
Costs in beginning WIP	$ 47,068	$ 36,900	$ 10,168
Current period costs	468,890	285,680	183,210
Total costs to be accounted for	**$515,958**	**$322,580**	**$193,378**
Cost per equivalent unit (Section 4):		**$9.5227 (rounded)**	**$6.00**
		($285,680 ÷ 30,000); ($183,210 ÷ 30,535)	
Costs accounted for (Section 5):			
Costs assigned to units transferred out:			
Costs from beginning inventory	$ 47,068	$ 36,900	$ 10,168
Current costs added to complete beginning inventory	14,760	–0–	14,760[c]
Units started and completed	380,305	233,305[d]	147,000[e]
Total costs transferred out	442,133	270,205	171,928
Cost of ending inventory	73,825	52,375[f]	21,450[g]
Total costs accounted for	**$515,958**	**$322,580**	**$193,378**

[a] 2,460 = (1.0 − .4 complete) × 4,100 units.
[b] 3,575 = .65 complete × 5,500 units.
[c] $14,760 = $6.00 × 2,460.
[d] $233,305 = $9.5227 (rounded) × 24,500.
[e] $147,000 = $6.00 × 24,500.
[f] $52,375 = $9.5227 × 5,500.
[g] $21,450 = $6.00 × 3,575.

ILLUSTRATION   *Cost Flows with Prior Department Costs—FIFO Method*

4–12

Work in Process		Finished Goods	
Beginning inventory: Prior department costs	36,900		
Materials and conversion	10,168		
		Transferred out from beginning inventory 47,068[a]	
Current costs: Prior department costs	285,680	Current costs: Prior department 233,305	From WIP: Biologicals 442,133
Materials and conversion	183,210	Materials and conversion 161,760[b]	
Ending inventory: Prior department costs	52,375		
Materials and conversion	21,450		

[a] $47,068 = $36,900 + $10,168.

[b] $161,760 = $14,760 + $147,000.

department for an accounting period (for example, a month), then spread evenly, or averaged, over all units produced that month. Process costing assumes each unit produced is relatively uniform. A comparison of cost flows under each method is demonstrated by the following example.

Assume Marmaduke Manufacturing Company makes a customized product. In June, three jobs were started and completed (there were no beginning inventories). The manufacturing cost of each job was:

Job No. 10	$16,000
Job No. 11	12,000
Job No. 12	14,000
Total	$42,000

Job No. 10 was sold; hence, the cost of goods sold in June would be the cost of Job No. 10—$16,000. This flow of costs is shown in the top part of Illustration 4–13.

Suppose Marmaduke Manufacturing Company had used process costing. For convenience, assume each job is defined to be a single unit of product. Total manufacturing costs were $42,000, so each unit would be assigned a cost of $14,000. One unit was sold; hence, the cost of goods sold under process costing would be the *average cost* of all three jobs—$14,000. This flow of costs is shown in the bottom part of Illustration 4–13.

Note that with process costing, Marmaduke Manufacturing Company does not maintain a record of the cost of each unit produced. Process costing has less detailed recordkeeping; hence, if a company was choosing between job and process costing, it would generally find that recordkeeping costs are lower under process costing. Of course, process costing does not provide as

ILLUSTRATION   *Comparative Flow of Costs: Job and Process Costing*

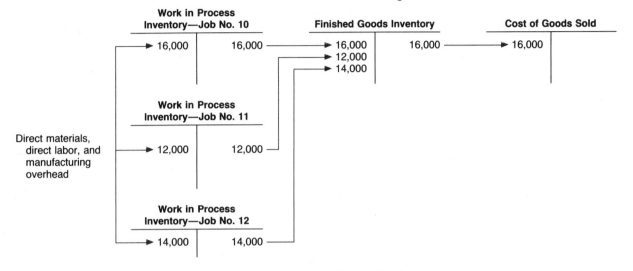

MARMADUKE MANUFACTURING COMPANY
June
Job Costing

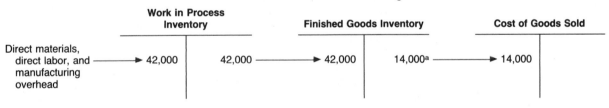

a $14,000 = \dfrac{\text{1 job}}{\text{3 jobs}} \times \$42,000.

much information as job costing because records of the cost of each unit produced are not kept using process costing. The choice of process versus job costing systems involves a comparison of the costs and benefits of each system.

A Cost-Benefit Comparison of Job and Process Costing

Consider a house builder. Under job costing, the costs must be accumulated for each house. If lumber is sent on a truck for delivery to several houses, it is not sufficient to record the total lumber issued—records must be kept of the amount delivered to, and subsequently returned from, each house. If laborers work on several houses, they must keep track of the time spent on *each* house. Process costing, however, simply requires recording the total costs incurred on all jobs. For the home builder, process costing records the average cost of all houses built. A custom home builder would probably use job costing. A developer might consider each development a job, but use process costing for houses within each development.

Under process costing, the actual cost incurred for a particular unit is not reported. If all units are homogeneous, this loss of information is probably minimal. Is it important for Intel to know whether the cost of the 10,001st microprocessor chip is different from the 10,002nd? Probably not—particularly if the unit cost is calculated primarily to value inventory for external financial reporting. Cost control and performance evaluation will take place by department, not by unit produced, in process systems. For companies like Intel making homogeneous units, the additional benefits of job costing would not justify the additional recordkeeping costs.

What if recordkeeping costs were equal under job and process systems for the units in a product line? Then we would say that job systems are better because they provide all of the data that process systems do, plus more. As a general rule, job systems are usually more costly than process systems, however. Thus, managers and accountants must decide whether there are enough additional benefits (for example, from better decisions) from knowing the actual cost of each unit, which is available in a job costing system, to justify additional recordkeeping costs. For companies producing relatively large, heterogeneous items, the additional benefits of job costing usually justify the additional recordkeeping costs.

Self-Study Question

3 FlyingFast, Inc., manufactures tennis rackets in two departments: frames and strings. Rackets are formed in the frames department. The completed frames are sent to the strings department where the rackets are strung and packaged for shipment to sporting goods stores. Six thousand frames were transferred to the strings department this month.

Because the rackets are homogeneous and manufactured in a continuous process, the company uses a process costing accounting system to assign costs to rackets. The following information is available for the strings department during October:

STRINGS DEPARTMENT
October

	Units	Prior Department Costs	Direct Materials	Conversion Costs
Physical flow:				
Beginning inventory . . 1,000		100% complete	60% complete	75% complete
Ending inventory 2,700		100% complete	80% complete	45% complete
Transferred in 6,000				
Costs incurred:				
Beginning inventory . .		$ 7,100	$ 600	$ 420
Current costs		43,200	2,500	6,475

a. Prepare a production cost report for the strings department using FIFO.

b. Use a T-account to show the cost flows in the strings department using FIFO.

The solution to this self-study question is at the end of this chapter on page 152.

SUMMARY

Process costing is used when it is not possible or practical to identify costs with specific lots or batches of product. The two most common methods of process costing are first-in, first-out (FIFO) costing and weighted-average costing. FIFO costing separates current period costs from the beginning inventory costs. The weighted-average method makes no distinction between beginning inventory and current period costs. As a result, weighted-average computations are simpler. However, the FIFO method is potentially more informative because it keeps separate track of current and previous period costs.

Illustration 4–9 is a summary of the steps required to assign costs to units. In comparing the weighted-average and FIFO methods, note the importance of matching costs with units. Weighted-average costing includes beginning inventory (that is, work done in a previous period) in computing both equivalent units and unit costs, while FIFO costing *excludes* beginning inventory in computing equivalent units and unit costs.

Costs are usually applied to products at different times in the production process. Costs applied at the same time are usually grouped together for computational purposes. For example, if direct labor and manufacturing overhead are applied at the same time, they are combined into one category—conversion costs. Companies typically have three distinct categories of costs: direct materials, conversion costs, and prior department costs. Prior department costs are transferred in from previous departments (which, conceptually, are a type of direct materials to the receiving department).

Sometimes inputs and outputs are measured differently. When this is the case, the input units are typically redefined into the way output units are measured.

Process costing systems accumulate costs for each production department, but do not maintain separate records of costs for each unit produced. When comparing job and process costing, companies generally find that job costing provides more data but has greater recordkeeping costs. Managers and accountants must decide whether the additional data available under job costing justify the higher recordkeeping costs. For companies in which relatively homogeneous units are produced in a continuous process, cost-benefit analysis generally favors process costing.

TERMS AND CONCEPTS

The following terms and concepts should be familiar to you after reading this chapter.

Equivalent Unit, *115*	**Process Costing,** *113*
First-In, First-Out (FIFO) Costing, *122*	**Production Cost Report,** *120*
Prior Department Costs, *132*	**Weighted-Average Costing,** *115*

QUESTIONS

4–1   Why are equivalent units computed for process costing?

4–2   A manufacturing company has records of its current activity in work in process inventory and of its ending work in process inventory. However, the record of its beginning inventory has been lost. Express in equation form the data that would be needed to compute the beginning inventory.

4–3   If costs change from one period to another, costs that are transferred out of one department under FIFO costing will include units with two different costs. Why?

4–4   Management of a company that manufactures cereal is trying to decide whether to install a job or process costing system. The manufacturing vice president has stated that job costing gives them the best control because it is possible to assign costs to specific lots of goods. The controller, however, has stated that job costing would require too much recordkeeping. Would a process costing system meet the manufacturing vice president's control objectives? Explain.

4–5   What is the distinction between equivalent units under the FIFO method and equivalent units under the weighted-average method?

4–6   Farleigh O. Tuvit is a new member of the controller's staff in the same company as you. Farleigh has just completed a report that urges the company to adopt the Last-in, First-out (LIFO) method for inventory accounting. The controller is concerned about the recommendation because the cost records are maintained on a FIFO basis. Indeed, the controller has not even heard of using LIFO for process cost accounting. Can you suggest how the controller might resolve the problem?

4–7   It has been said that prior department costs behave similarly to direct materials costs. Under what conditions are the costs similar? Why account for them separately?

4–8   Assume the number of units transferred out of a department is unknown. Using the basic cost flow model, write a formula to solve for units transferred out.

4–9   Refer to the Real World Application on page 117. Describe the materials and the conversion process at each stage of production for canning such soft drinks.

4–10 Select the best answer:

Under which of the following conditions will the first-in, first-out method of process costing produce the same cost of goods manufactured as the weighted-average method?
(1)   When goods produced are homogeneous.
(2)   When there is no beginning inventory.
(3)   When there is no ending inventory.
(4)   When beginning and ending inventories are each 50 percent complete.
(CPA adapted)

4–11 Select the best answer:

An error was made in the computation of the percentage of completion of the current year's ending work in process inventory. The error resulted in assigning a lower percentage of completion to each component of the inventory than actually was the case. Assume there was no beginning inventory. What is the effect of this error upon:

a.   The computation of total equivalent units?

b.   The computation of costs per equivalent unit?

c.   Costs assigned to cost of goods transferred out for the period?

Choose one of the four options in the following table:

	a	b	c
(1)	Understate	Overstate	Overstate
(2)	Understate	Understate	Overstate
(3)	Overstate	Understate	Understate
(4)	Overstate	Overstate	Understate

(CPA adapted)

4–12   Select the best answer:

In computing the cost per equivalent unit, the weighted-average method considers:
(1)   Current costs only.
(2)   Current costs plus costs in beginning work in process inventory.
(3)   Current costs plus cost of ending work in process inventory.
(4)   Current costs less costs in beginning work in process inventory.

(CPA adapted)

4–13   Select the best answer:

When using the FIFO method of process costing, total equivalent units produced for a given period are equal to the number of units:
(1)   Started and completed during the period, plus the number of units in beginning WIP, plus the number of units in ending WIP.
(2)   In beginning WIP plus the number of units started during the period, plus the number of units remaining in ending WIP times the percent of work necessary to complete the items.
(3)   In beginning WIP times the percent of work necessary to complete the items, plus the number of units started and completed during the period, plus the number of units started this period and remaining in ending WIP times the percent of work necessary to complete the items.
(4)   Transferred out during the period plus the number of units remaining in ending WIP times the percent of work necessary to complete the items.
(5)   None of these.

(CPA adapted)

EXERCISES

4–14   Compute Equivalent Units—Weighted-Average Method
(L.O.2)

A company's records show the following information concerning the work in process in a chemical plant:

1.   Beginning inventory—7,000 partially complete units.
2.   Transferred out—18,000 units.
3.   Ending inventory—(materials are 10 percent complete; conversion costs are 15 percent complete).
4.   Started this month—24,000 units.

Required:

a.   Compute the equivalent units for materials using weighted-average.
b.   Compute the equivalent units for conversion costs using weighted-average.

4–15   Compute Equivalent Units—FIFO Method
(L.O.2)

Refer to the data in exercise 4–14. Assume beginning inventory is 20 percent complete with respect to materials and 15 percent complete with respect to conversion costs.

Required:

a.   Compute the equivalent units for materials using FIFO.
b.   Compute the equivalent units for conversion costs using FIFO.

4–16 Compute Equivalent Units—Weighted-Average Method
(L.O.2)

Mesozoic Company shows the following information concerning the work in process at an assembly plant:

1. Beginning inventory was partially complete.
2. Transferred out—30,000 units.
3. Ending inventory—10,000 units (materials are 50 percent complete; conversion costs are 30 percent complete).
4. Started this month—35,000 units.

Required:

a. Compute the equivalent units for materials using weighted-average.

b. Compute the equivalent units for conversion costs using weighted-average.

4–17 Compute Equivalent Units—FIFO Method
(L.O.2)

Refer to the data in exercise 4–16. Assume beginning inventory is 45 percent complete with respect to materials and 60 percent complete with respect to conversion costs.

Required:

a. Compute the equivalent units for materials using FIFO.

b. Compute the equivalent units for conversion costs using FIFO.

4–18 Compute Equivalent Units—Weighted-Average Method
(L.O.2)

Baka Co. adds materials at the beginning of the process in Department M. The following information pertains to Department M's work in process during April:

	Units
Work in process, April 1 (60% complete as to conversion costs)	3,000
Started in April	25,000
Completed	20,000
Work in process, April 30 (75% complete as to conversion costs)	8,000

Required:

Under the weighted-average method, the equivalent units for conversion costs are:

(1) 26,000.
(2) 25,000.
(3) 24,200.
(4) 21,800.

(CPA adapted)

4–19 Compute Equivalent Units—FIFO Method
(L.O.2)

Thoreau Co. has a process costing system using the FIFO cost flow method. All materials are introduced at the beginning of the process in Department One. The following information is available for the month of January.

	Units
Work in process, January 1 (40% complete as to conversion costs)	500
Started in January	2,000
Transferred to Department Two during January	2,100
Work in process, January 31 (25% complete as to conversion costs)	400

Required:

What are the equivalent units of production for the month of January?

	Materials	Conversion
(1)	2,500	2,200
(2)	2,500	1,900
(3)	2,000	2,200
(4)	2,000	2,000

(CPA adapted)

4–20 Compute Costs per Equivalent Unit— Weighted-Average Method

(L.O.3)

The following information pertains to Top Co.'s Division D for the month of May:

	Number of Units	Cost of Materials
Beginning work in process	30,000	$11,000
Started in May	80,000	36,000
Units completed	85,000	
Ending work in process	25,000	

All materials are added at the beginning of the process.

Required:

Using the weighted-average method, the cost per equivalent unit for materials is:
(1) $0.43.
(2) $0.45.
(3) $0.55.
(4) $0.59.

(CPA adapted)

4–21 Compute Equivalent Units—FIFO Method

(L.O.2)

Department A is the first stage of Lublu Co.'s production cycle. The following information is available for conversion costs for the month of April:

	Units
Beginning work in process (60% complete)	20,000
Started in April	340,000
Completed in April and transferred to Department B	320,000
Ending work in process (40% complete)	40,000

Required:

Using the FIFO method, the equivalent units for the conversion cost calculation are:
(1) 320,000.
(2) 324,000.
(3) 336,000.
(4) 360,000.

(CPA adapted)

4–22 Compute Costs per Equivalent Unit— Weighted-Average Method

(L.O.3)

A company uses the weighted-average method to account for its work in process inventories. The accounting records show the following information:

Beginning work in process inventory:
Direct materials	$ 488
Conversion costs	136
	$ 624

Current period costs in work in process:
Direct materials	$5,720
Conversion costs	3,322

Quantity information is obtained from the manufacturing records and includes the following:

Beginning inventory	300 units (partially complete)
Current period units started	2,000 units
Ending inventory	600 units
Percent of completion:	
Direct materials	40%
Conversion costs	20%

Required:

Compute the cost per equivalent unit for direct materials and conversion costs.

4–23 Assign Costs to Goods Transferred Out and Ending Inventory— Weighted-Average Method
(L.O.3)

Refer to the data in exercise 4–22. Compute the cost of goods transferred out and the ending inventory, using the weighted-average method.

4–24 Compute Costs per Equivalent Unit— FIFO Method
(L.O.4)

Using the data in exercise 4–22, compute the cost per equivalent unit for direct materials and for conversion costs using the FIFO method. Assume that beginning inventory is 60 percent complete with respect to materials and 30 percent complete with respect to conversion costs.

4–25 Assign Costs to Goods Transferred Out and Ending Inventory— FIFO Method
(L.O.4)

Refer to the data in exercise 4–22 and 4–24. Compute the cost of goods transferred out and the ending inventory using the FIFO method.

4–26 Compute Costs per Equivalent Unit— Weighted-Average Method
(L.O.3)

The beginning work in process inventory showed a balance of $62,080. Of this amount, $25,410 is the cost of direct materials, and $36,670 are conversion costs. There were 8,000 units in the beginning inventory that were 30 percent complete with respect to both direct materials and conversion costs.

During the period, 17,000 units were transferred out and 5,000 remained in the ending inventory. The units in the ending inventory were 80 percent complete with respect to direct materials and 40 percent complete with respect to conversion costs.

Costs incurred during the period amounted to $195,300 for direct materials and $252,320 for conversion.

Required:

Compute the cost per equivalent unit for direct materials and for conversion costs using the weighted-average method.

4–27 Assign Costs to Goods Transferred Out and Ending Inventory— Weighted-Average Method
(L.O.3)

Refer to the data in exercise 4–26. Compute the costs of goods transferred out and the ending inventory using the weighted-average method.

4–28 Compute Costs per Equivalent Unit— FIFO Method
(L.O.4)

Refer to the data in exercise 4–26. Compute the cost per equivalent unit for direct materials and for conversion costs using the FIFO method. Are these unit costs higher or lower under weighted-average compared to FIFO? Why?

4–29 Assign Costs to Goods Transferred Out and Ending Inventory— FIFO Method
(L.O.4)

Refer to the data in exercise 4–26. Compute the cost of goods transferred out and the cost of ending inventory using the FIFO method. Is the ending inventory higher or lower under weighted-average compared to FIFO? Why?

4–30 Prepare a Production Cost Report—FIFO Method
(L.O.5, L.O.6)

The following information appears in the records of the Spinelli Production Company:

Work in process inventory—Department No. 2:

Beginning inventory:		
Prior department costs	$ 7,250	3,000 units (100% complete)
Department No. 2 costs	1,953	20% complete
Current work:		
Prior department costs	16,450	7,000 units (100% complete)
Department No. 2 costs	37,170	

The ending inventory has 1,000 units, which are 45 percent complete with respect to Department No. 2 costs and 100 percent complete for prior department costs.

Required:

Prepare a production cost report, using FIFO.

4–31 Prepare a Production Cost Report— Weighted-Average Method
(L.O.5, L.O.6)

Refer to the information in exercise 4–30.

a. Prepare a production cost report using the weighted-average method.

b. Is the ending inventory higher using FIFO or weighted-average? Why?

PROBLEMS

4–32 Compute Equivalent Units

Each of the following multiple-choice questions is independent. Select the best answer.

a. Overland Corporation's production cycle starts in the First Department. The following information is available for April:

	Units
Work in process, April 1 (30% complete)	50,000
Started in April	240,000
Work in process, April 30 (40% complete)	25,000

Materials are added at the beginning of the process in the First Department. Using the weighted-average method, what are the equivalent units of production for the month of April?

	Materials	**Conversion**
(1)	240,000	260,000
(2)	265,000	265,000
(3)	290,000	275,000
(4)	280,000	270,000
(5)	None of the above.	

b. The Second Department is the second stage of Dressler Company's production cycle. On May 1, the beginning work in process contained 25,000 units, which were 80 percent complete as to conversion costs. During May, 160,000 units were transferred in from the first stage of the production cycle. On May 31, ending work in process contained 20,000 units, which were 90 percent complete as to conversion costs. Materials are added at the end of the process. Using the weighted-average method, the equivalent units produced on May 31 were:

	Prior Department Costs	**Materials**	**Conversion Costs**
(1)	160,000	165,000	183,000
(2)	185,000	165,000	163,000
(3)	185,000	165,000	185,000
(4)	185,000	165,000	183,000
(5)	None of the above		

c. Department A is the first stage of Hurley Corporation's production cycle. The following information is available for conversion costs for the month of April:

	Units
Beginning WIP (60% complete)	8,000
Started in April	136,000
Completed in April and transferred to Department B	128,000
Ending WIP (40% complete)	16,000

Using the FIFO method, the equivalent units for the conversion cost calculation are:
(1) 128,000.
(2) 129,600.
(3) 134,400.
(4) 144,000.

d. Drax Corporation computed the physical flow of units for Department A for the month of April as follows:

Units completed:

From WIP on April 1	10,000
From April production	35,000
Total	45,000

Materials are added at the beginning of the process. Units of WIP at April 30 were 8,000. The WIP at April 1 was 70 percent complete as to conversion costs, and the WIP at April 30 was 50 percent complete as to conversion costs. What are the E.U. produced for the month of April using the FIFO method?

	Materials	Conversion Costs
(1)	43,000	42,000
(2)	43,000	43,000
(3)	53,000	50,000
(4)	53,000	51,000
(5)	None of the above	

(CPA adapted)

4–33 Multiple-Choice–FIFO Method

The following questions are based on the Refining Department of the Baja Petroleum Corporation. Conversion costs for this department were 80 percent complete as to beginning WIP and 50 percent complete as to ending WIP. Information about conversion costs for January is as follows:

	Units	Conversion Costs
WIP at January 1 (80% complete)	25,000	$ 86,000
Units started and costs incurred during January	135,000	$484,000
Units completed and transferred to next department during January	100,000	—

The company uses FIFO in the Refining Department.

Required:

a. What was the conversion cost of WIP in the Refining Department at January 31?
(1) $121,000.
(2) $130,000.
(3) $132,000.
(4) $155,000.

b. What were the conversion costs per equivalent unit produced last period and this period, respectively?

   (1) $4.30 and $5.18.
   (2) $4.30 and $4.40.
   (3) $4.40 and $4.40.
   (4) $4.40 and $5.18.

(CPA adapted)

4–34   Prepare a Production Cost Report— Weighted-Average Method

Lakeview Corporation is a manufacturer that uses the weighted-average process costing method to account for costs of production. Lakeview manufactures a product that is produced in three separate departments: Molding, Assembling, and Finishing. The following information was obtained for the Assembling Department for the month of June.

Work in process, June 1—2,000 units made up of the following:

	Amount	Degree of Completion
Prior department costs transferred in from the Molding Department	$32,000	100%
Costs added by the Assembling Department:		
Direct materials	$20,000	100
Direct labor	7,200	60
Manufacturing overhead	5,500	50
	32,700	
Work in process, June 1	$64,700	

The following activity occurred during the month of June: 10,000 units were transferred in from the Molding Department at a prior department cost of $160,000. The Assembling Department added the following $150,000 of costs.

Direct materials	$ 96,000
Direct labor	36,000
Manufacturing overhead	18,000
	$150,000

Eight thousand units were completed and transferred to the Finishing Department.

At June 30, 4,000 units were still in work in process. The degree of completion of work in process at June 30 was as follows:

Direct materials	90%
Direct labor	70
Manufacturing overhead	35

Required:

Prepare a production cost report using the weighted-average method.

(CPA adapted)

4–35   Prepare a Production Cost Report—FIFO Method

Refer to the facts in problem 4–34. Prepare a production cost report, using FIFO.

4–36   Prepare a Production Cost Report and Adjust Inventory Balances—Weighted-Average Method

Spirit Processing Corporation's unaudited records show the following ending inventory balances, which must be adjusted to actual costs:

	Units	Unaudited Costs
Work in process inventory	300,000	$ 660,960
Finished goods inventory	200,000	1,009,800

As the auditor, you have learned the following information. Ending work in process inventory is 50 percent complete with respect to conversion costs. Materials are added at the beginning of the manufacturing process, and overhead is applied at the rate of 60 percent of the direct labor costs. There was no finished goods inventory at the start of the period. The following additional information is also available:

	Units	Costs	
		Direct Materials	Direct Labor
Beginning inventory (80% complete as to labor)	200,000	$ 200,000	$ 315,000
Units started	1,000,000		
Current costs		1,300,000	1,995,000
Units completed and transferred to finished goods inventory	900,000		

Required:

a. Prepare a production cost report for Spirit Processing Corporation using weighted-average.

b. Show the adjusting journal entry required to reconcile the difference between the unaudited records and actual ending balances of Work in Process Inventory and Finished Goods Inventory. Adjust Cost of Goods Sold for any difference.

c. If the adjustment in (b) above had not been made, would the company's income and inventories have been overstated or understated?

(CPA adapted)

4–37   Show Cost Flows— FIFO Method

Malcolm Company uses continuous processing of cereals and uses FIFO process costing to account for its manufacturing costs. FIFO is used because costs are quite volatile due to the price volatility of commodities. The cereals are processed through one department. Overhead is applied on the basis of direct labor costs. The application rate has not changed over the period covered by the problem. The Work in Process Inventory account showed the following balances at the start of the current period:

Direct materials	$32,750
Direct labor	65,000
Overhead applied	81,250

These costs were related to 26,000 units that were in the process at the start of the period.

During the period, 30,000 units were transferred to finished goods inventory. Of the units finished this period, 70 percent were sold. After units have been transferred to finished goods inventory, no distinction is made between the costs to complete beginning work in process inventory and the costs of goods started and completed in work in process this period.

The equivalent units this period for materials were 25,000 (using FIFO). Of these units, there were 5,000 equivalent units with respect to materials in the ending work in process inventory. Materials costs incurred during the period totaled $75,100.

Conversion costs of $321,750 were incurred this period, and there were 31,250 equivalent units for conversion costs (using FIFO). The ending inventory consisted of 11,000 equivalent units of conversion costs.

The actual manufacturing overhead for the period was $165,000.

Required:

Prepare T-accounts to show the flow of costs in the system. Any difference between actual and applied overhead of the period should be debited or credited to Cost of Goods Sold.

4–38 **Prepare a Production Cost Report and Show Cost Flows through Accounts—FIFO Method**

Mercantile Recovery Corporation has devised a process for converting garbage into liquid fuel. While the direct materials costs are zero, the operation requires the use of direct labor and overhead. The company uses a process costing system and keeps track of the production and costs of each period. At the start of the current period, there were 1,000 units in the work in process inventory. These units were 40 percent complete and were carried at a cost of $420.

During the month, costs of $18,000 were incurred. There were 9,000 units started during the period, and there were 500 units still in process at the end of the period. The ending units were 20 percent complete.

Required:

a.   Prepare a production cost report, using FIFO.

b.   Show the flow of costs through T-accounts. Assume current period conversion costs are credited to Various Payables.

4–39 **Solving for Unknowns—FIFO Method**

For each of the following independent cases, determine the information requested, using FIFO costing.

a.   Beginning inventory amounted to 1,000 units. There were 4,500 units started and completed this period. At the end of the period, there were 3,000 units in inventory that were 30 percent complete. Using FIFO costing, the equivalent production for the period was 5,600 units. What was the percentage of completion of the beginning inventory?

b.   The ending inventory included $8,700 for conversion costs. During the period, 4,200 equivalent units were required to complete the beginning inventory, and 6,000 units were started and completed. The ending inventory represented 1,000 equivalent units of work this period. FIFO costing is used. What was the total conversion costs incurred this period?

c.   There were 500 units in the beginning inventory that were 40 percent complete with respect to materials. During the period, 4,000 units were transferred out. Ending inventory consisted of 700 units that were 70 percent complete with respect to materials. How many units were started and completed during the period?

d.   At the start of the period, there were 4,000 units in the work in process inventory. There were 3,000 units in the ending inventory, and during the period, 9,500 units were transferred out to the next department. Materials and conversion costs are added evenly throughout the production process. FIFO costing is used. How many units were started this period?

4–40 **Solving for Unknowns— Weighted-Average Method**

For each of the following independent cases, determine the units or equivalent units requested, (assuming weighted-average costing):

a.   There were 8,200 units in the beginning inventory that were 40 percent complete with respect to conversion costs. During the period, 7,000 units were started. There were 6,500 units in the ending inventory that were 20 percent complete with respect to conversion costs. How many units were transferred out?

b.   The beginning inventory consisted of 2,000 units with a direct materials cost of $14,200. The equivalent work represented by all of the direct materials costs in the Work in Process Inventory account amounted to 9,000 units. There were 3,000 units in ending inventory that were 20 percent complete with respect to materials. The ending inventory had a direct materials cost assigned of $4,500. What was the total materials cost incurred this period?

c.   The Work in Process Inventory account had a beginning balance of $1,900 for conversion costs on items in process. During the period, $18,100 in conversion costs were charged to the account. Also during the period, $19,200 in costs were transferred out. There were 400 units in the beginning inventory, and 4,800 units were transferred out during the period. How many equivalent units are in the ending inventory?

d. There were 2,100 units transferred to the department during the period. The 3,200 units transferred out were charged to the next department at an amount that included $3,360 for direct materials costs. The ending inventory was 25 percent complete with respect to direct materials and had a cost of $630 assigned to it. How many units are in the ending inventory?

SOLUTIONS TO

Self-Study
uestions

1 *a.* From the basic cost flow model, $BB + TI = TO + EB$, solve for TO:

$$BB + TI = TO + EB$$
$$1,000 + 6,000 = TO + 2,700$$
$$TO = 7,000 - 2,700$$
$$TO = 4,300 \text{ units}$$

b. Step 1: Summarize the flow of physical units:

Units to account for:

Units in beginning inventory	1,000
Units started in April	6,000
Total units to be accounted for	7,000

Units accounted for:

Completed and transferred out	4,300
Units in ending WIP inventory	2,700
Total accounted for	7,000

Step 2: Compute the equivalent units produced:

Units transferred out (4,300 × 100%)	4,300
Units in ending inventory (2,700 × 80%)	2,160
Total equivalent units	6,460

Step 3: Summarize the total costs to be accounted for:

Cost in beginning WIP inventory	$ 730
Current period costs	2,500
Total costs to be accounted for	$3,230

Step 4: Cost per equivalent unit:

Costs to be accounted for (from step 3) divided by equivalent units (from step 2) ($3,230/6,460 equivalent units) . . . . $.50 per equivalent unit

Step 5: Assign costs to goods transferred out and to ending inventory:

Costs accounted for:

Costs assigned to units transferred out ($.50 × 4,300)	$2,150
Costs assigned to ending WIP inventory ($.50 × 2,160)	1,080
Total costs accounted for	$3,230

c.   Cost flows through T-account:

Work in Process Inventory

Beginning inventory	730		
Current period costs	2,500	Transfers-out 2,150 ─────▶ to Finished Goods Inventory	
Ending inventory	1,080		

d.   Production cost report—weighted-average:

	(Section 1) Physical Units	(Section 2) Compute Equivalent Units
Flow of Units:		
Units to account for:		
Beginning work in process inventory	1,000	
Units started this period	6,000	
Total units to account for	7,000	
Units accounted for:		
Units completed and transferred out	4,300	4,300
Units in ending WIP inventory	2,700	2,160 (80%ᵃ)
Total units accounted for	7,000	6,460

Flow of Costs:		
Costs to be accounted for (Section 3):		
Costs in beginning WIP inventory	$ 730	
Current period costs	2,500	
Total costs to be accounted for	$3,230	
Cost per equivalent unit (Section 4):	$.50	
	($3,230 ÷ 6,460)	
Costs accounted for (Section 5):		
Costs assigned to units transferred out: ($.50 × 4,300)	$2,150	
Costs assigned to ending WIP inventory: ($.50 × 2,160)	1,080	
Total costs accounted for	$3,230	

ᵃ Stage of completion.

2   a.   The physical flow of units is the same using either the weighted-average or FIFO method. The calculations are as follows. From the basic cost flow model, $BB + TI = TO + EB$, solve for TO:

$$BB + TI = TO + EB$$
$$1,000 + 6,000 = TO + 2,700$$
$$TO = 7,000 - 2,700$$
$$TO = 4,300 \text{ units}$$

b.   Step 1: Summarize the flow of physical units:
(Same as Step 1 in solution above for weighted average.)

Step 2: Compute the equivalent units produced this period:

Complete units in beginning inventory
(40% to complete × 1,000 units)   400

Units started and completed this period
(6,000 units started − 2,700 in ending inventory)   3,300

Units in ending inventory (80% complete × 2,700 units)   2,160

      Total equivalent units   5,860

Step 3: Summarize the total costs to be accounted for:

Cost in beginning WIP inventory . . . . $ 730

Current period costs   2,500

      Total costs to be accounted for $3,230

Step 4: Cost per equivalent unit:

Costs to be accounted for (current costs from step 3)
divided by equivalent units (from step 2)
($2,500/5,860 E.U. =) $0.4266

Step 5: Assign costs to goods transferred out and to ending inventory:

Costs accounted for:

   Costs in beginning inventory . . . . $ 730.00

   Current period cost incurred to complete
   beginning inventory ($0.4266 × 400 E.U.) 170.64

   Costs to start and complete units
   ($0.4266 × 3,300 units) 1,407.78

   Costs assigned to ending WIP inventory
   ($0.4266 × 2,160 E.U. =) 921.46

      Total costs accounted for . . . . $3,229.88[a]

---

[a] Rounding difference.

c. Cost flows through T-account (amounts rounded to whole dollars):

Work in Process Inventory

Beginning inventory	730	Transfers-out	2,308
Current period costs	2,500		
Ending inventory	922		

d.   Production cost report—FIFO:

GREEN EARTH CLEANERS
Month Ending April 30

	(Section 1) Physical Units	(Section 2) Equivalent Units
Flow of Units:		
Units to be accounted for:		
Beginning work in process inventory	1,000	
Units started this period	6,000	
Total units to be accounted for . . .	7,000	
Units accounted for:		
Units completed and transferred out:		
From beginning inventory	1,000	400
Started and completed currently	3,300	3,300
Total	4,300	3,700
In ending inventory	2,700	2,160
Total units accounted for	7,000	5,860

Flow of Costs:		
Costs to be accounted for (Section 3):		
Costs in beginning WIP	$	730
Current period costs		2,500
Total costs to be accounted for .	**$**	**3,230**
Costs per equivalent unit (Section 4):		**$ 0.4266**
Costs accounted for (Section 5):		
Costs assigned to units transferred out:		
Costs from beginning WIP inventory		$ 730.00
Current costs added to complete beginning WIP inventory		170.64
Total costs from beginning inventory . .		900.64
Current costs of units started and completed		1,407.78
Total costs transferred out		2,308.42
Cost of ending WIP inventory		921.46
Total costs accounted for		**$3,229.88**[a]

[a] Rounding difference.

3 *a*. Production cost report—FIFO:

FLYINGFAST, INC.
Strings Department
Month Ending October 31

	(Section 1) Physical Units	(Section 2) Equivalent Units		
		For Prior Department Costs	For Materials	For Conversion Costs
Flow of Production Units:				
Units to account for:				
Beginning work in process inventory	1,000			
Units started this period	6,000			
Total units to account for	7,000			
Units accounted for:				
Units completed and transferred out:				
From beginning inventory	1,000	–0–[a]	400[a](40%[b])	250[a](25%[b])
Started and completed, currently	3,300[c]	3,300	3,300	3,300
Units in ending WIP inventory	2,700	2,700	2,160 (80%[d])	1,215 (45%[d])
Total units accounted for	7,000	6,000	5,860	4,765

	Total Costs	Prior Department Costs	Materials	Conversion Costs
Flow of Costs:				
Costs to be accounted for (Section 3):				
Costs in beginning WIP inventory	$ 8,120	$ 7,100	$ 600	$ 420
Current period costs	52,175	43,200	2,500	$ 6,475
Total costs to be accounted for	**$60,295**	**$50,300**	**$3,100**	**$ 6,895**
Cost per equivalent unit (Section 4):				
Prior department costs ($43,200 ÷ 6,000)		$7.2000		
Materials ($2,500 ÷ 5,860)			$.4266	
Conversion costs ($6,475 ÷ 4,765)				$1.3589

[a] Equivalent units required to complete beginning inventory.

[b] Percent required to complete beginning inventory.

[c] Units in beginning inventory + Units started and completed + Units in ending inventory = Total units accounted for. So: 1,000 + X + 2,700 = 7,000; X = 7,000 − 2,700 − 1,000 = 3,300.

[d] Stage of completion.

	Total Costs	Prior Department Costs	Materials	Conversion Costs
Flow of Costs:				
Costs to be accounted for (Section 5):				
Costs assigned to units transferred out:				
Costs from beginning WIP inventory	$ 8,120	$ 7,100	$ 600	$ 420
Current costs added to complete beginning WIP inventory:				
Prior department costs	–0–	–0–		
Materials (400 × $.4266)	171		171	
Conversion costs (250 × $1.3589)	340			340
Total costs to complete beginning inventory	511			
Costs of units started and completed:				
Prior department costs (3,300 × $7.20)	23,760	23,760		
Materials (3,300 × $.4266)	1,408		1,408	
Conversion costs (3,300 × $1.3589)	4,484			4,484
Total costs of units started and completed	29,652			
Total costs transferred out	38,283			
Costs assigned to ending WIP inventory:				
Prior department costs (2,700 × $7.20)	19,440	19,440		
Materials (2,160 × $.4266)	921		921	
Conversion costs (1,215 × $1.3589)	1,651			1,651
Total cost of ending WIP inventory	22,012			
Total costs accounted for	**$60,295**	**$50,300**	**$3,100**	**$6,895**

b. Cost flows—FIFO:

Work in Process Inventory— Strings Department				Finished Goods Inventory	
Beginning inventory	8,120[a]	To Finished Goods Inventory:			
This period's costs:		From beginning			
Prior department		inventory			
costs included		costs	8,120[b] ⌉		
in units		From this			
transferred into		period's costs	30,163[e] ⌋	38,283[b]	
this department					
this period	43,200[a]				
Materials used					
this period	2,500[a]				
Conversion costs					
incurred this					
period	6,475[a]				
Ending inventory	$22,012[b]				

[a] See section 3 in the production cost report.

[b] See section 5 in the production cost report.

[c] Sum of total costs of units started and completed plus costs added to complete beginning WIP inventory.

Accounting for Operations, Just-in-Time Production, and Spoilage

---

LEARNING OBJECTIVES

After reading this chapter, you should be able to:

1. Explain how operation costing compares and contrasts with job costing and process costing.
2. Demonstrate and analyze cost flows through accounts in operations.
3. Explain how to account for product costs using backflush costing in a just-in-time (JIT) production environment.
4. Contrast cost flows through accounts using backflush costing versus traditional sequential costing.
5. Demonstrate two methods of accounting for "normal" spoilage.
6. Demonstrate how to account for "abnormal" spoilage.
7. Recognize potential cost distortions from assigning the cost of re-worked goods to products.
8. Explain the conflict between total quality management and assigning the cost of rework and spoilage to good units produced.

*T*his chapter expands our discussion of product costing systems in Chapters 3 and 4. Many of the topics in this chapter reflect new developments in production, such as just-in-time production and increased emphasis on quality lean production. We begin with a discussion of operation costing, which, as noted in Chapter 3, is a hybrid of job costing and process costing.

OPERATION COSTING

Operation Costing A hybrid costing system used in manufacturing goods that have some common characteristics plus some individual characteristics.

Operation A standardized method of making a product that is repeatedly performed.

Operation costing is a hybrid of job and process costing, as shown by the following continuum:

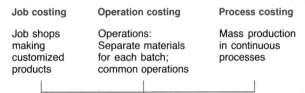

Job costing	Operation costing	Process costing
Job shops making customized products	Operations: Separate materials for each batch; common operations	Mass production in continuous processes

An **operation** is a standardized method of making a product that is repeatedly performed. For example, an automobile assembly plant will make several models on the same assembly line. Each model will have seat covers installed. Installing the seat covers is an operation.

A company using operation costing will typically use a variety of different materials for products that pass through the same operation. Some automobiles will have leather seats; others will have cloth seats. Whether the material is leather or cloth, the car will pass through the same seat cover installation operation. We define *operation costing* as a hybrid costing system used in manufacturing goods that have some common characteristics plus some individual characteristics.

Companies like Nike (shoes) and Volvo (automobiles) use operation costing. A shirtmaker like Van Heusen will have a cutting operation for each shirt and a stitching operation for each shirt, although the materials for each type of shirt may be different (for example, cotton, wool, polyester).

PRODUCT COSTING IN OPERATIONS

The key difference between operation costing and the two methods discussed in the previous two chapters, job and process costing, is that direct materials are different for each work order or batch but conversion costs (direct labor and manufacturing overhead) are the same for each work order or batch passing through a particular operation.

For example, assume the Yahonzi Motorcycle Company makes two models of motorcycles: Jets and Sharks. The Shark has a larger engine and generally more costly direct materials than the Jet. Both models pass through the first two operations of the company: Engine Assembly and Final Assembly. The Shark also passes through a third operation, called Special Finishing, which adds finishing touches to the Shark model.

Illustration 5–1 shows the flow of products through departments (assume each department has one operation). Note that Sharks pass through all three departments, but Jets pass through only the first two. Direct materials costs are added to both models in Engine Assembly and Final Assembly. No direct materials are added to Sharks in Special Finishing. Conversion costs are added to Jets in the first two departments and to Sharks in all three departments. In principal, direct materials costs could be added in any operation. In this example, the direct materials costs are higher for Sharks. The two operations, Engine Assembly and Final Assembly, are identical for both types of motorcycles.

ILLUSTRATION OF OPERATION COSTING

Assume Yahonzi Motorcycle Company management gave the following production work order for the month of March. Each work order is also called a batch.

ILLUSTRATION   *Overview of Operation Costing*

5–1

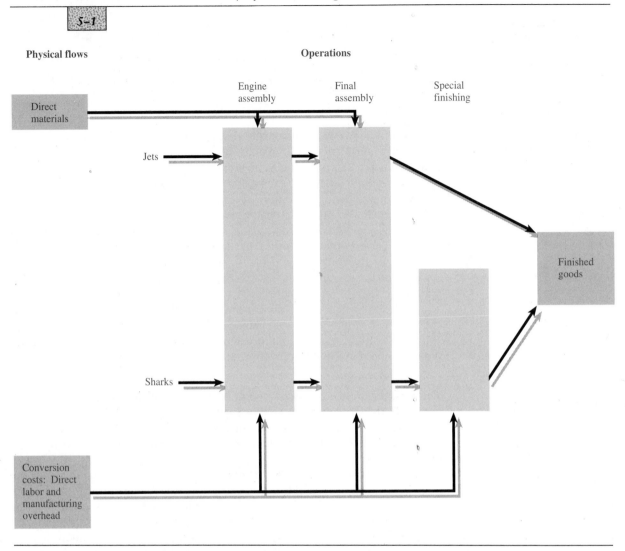

Yahonzi Motorcycle Company

	Work Order 101	Work Order 102
Number and model of motorcycles	1,000 Sharks	2,000 Jets
Work order costs		
Direct materials:		
Engine parts	$150,000	$200,000
Motorcycle parts, other than engines .	200,000	300,000
Conversion costs (direct labor and manufacturing overhead):		
Engine Assembly	50,000	100,000
Final Assembly	100,000	200,000
Special Finishing	50,000	—
Total costs	$550,000	$800,000

ILLUSTRATION   *Cost Flows through T-accounts for Operation Costing*

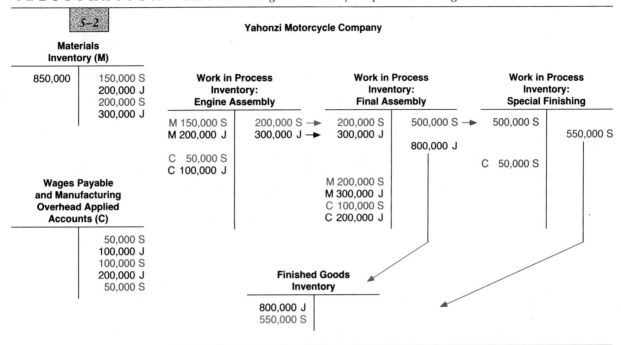

5–2

Yahonzi Motorcycle Company

S = Sharks.

J = Jets.

M = Direct materials, credited to Materials Inventory.

C = Conversion costs, credited to Wages Payable and Manufacturing Overhead Applied Accounts.

Note: Amounts for Sharks are in color.

Note that the materials costs *per unit* are more for Sharks than for Jets, but the conversion costs *per unit* are the same for the two operations that both models pass through. For example, engine assembly conversion costs are $50 per motorcycle for both models ($50 = $50,000/1,000 units for Sharks and $50 = $100,000/2,000 units for Jets).

Illustration 5–2 shows the flow of these costs through T-accounts to Finished Goods Inventory. In practice, direct labor and manufacturing overhead could be combined as in a Japanese motorcycle company that the authors studied. Direct labor and manufacturing overhead could be charged separately to production, as well. In many companies, direct labor is such a small portion of the total product cost that the accountants classify direct labor as part of manufacturing overhead. For example, in numerous high-tech companies, such as Hewlett-Packard, direct labor is less than five percent of total manufacturing costs in many operations.

Journal Entries

The journal entries for applying costs to the Sharks motorcycles follow. These entries are shown in color in Illustration 5–2. The same entries (with different numbers, of course) would be used for the Jets, except no entry would be made for Work in Process Inventory: Special Finishing because Jets skip that operation.

1. First, direct materials are requisitioned for engine assembly and shown by the following entry debiting Work in Process (WIP) Inventory:

Engine Assembly (the top amount on the debit side of the account in Illustration 5–2):

WIP Inventory: Engine Assembly	150,000	
Materials Inventory		150,000

2. Conversion costs for Engine Assembly are recorded as follows:

WIP Inventory: Engine Assembly	50,000	
Wages Payable and Manufacturing Overhead		
Applied Accounts		50,000

3. After the engines are assembled, they are sent to Final Assembly where they are combined with other motorcycle components to build the motorcycle. The costs transferred are the sum of entries 1 and 2 above. The transfer of the costs of assembled engines from Engine Assembly to Final Assembly is:

WIP Inventory: Final Assembly	200,000	
WIP Inventory: Engine Assembly		200,000

This entry is shown in Illustration 5–2 as the top numbers on the debit side of WIP Inventory: Final Assembly and the credit side of WIP Inventory: Engine Assembly.

4. The materials added in Final Assembly are recorded as follows:

WIP Inventory: Final Assembly	200,000	
Materials Inventory		200,000

5. The conversion costs incurred in Final Assembly to assemble motorcycles are recorded as follows:

WIP Inventory: Final Assembly	100,000	
Wages Payable and Manufacturing Overhead		
Applied Accounts		100,000

6. After the Shark model motorcycles are assembled, they are transferred to Special Finishing. A total of $500,000 costs would have been accumulated in Final Assembly for Work Order No. 101, which is the total of the costs recorded in entries 3, 4, and 5 above. The entry to reflect the transfer of the motorcycles in Work Order No. 101 in Special Finishing is:

WIP Inventory: Special Finishing	500,000	
WIP Inventory: Final Assembly		500,000

7. Work Order No. 101 requires $50,000 of conversion costs and no direct materials costs in Special Finishing. The entry to record these conversion costs is:

WIP Inventory: Special Finishing	50,000	
Wages Payable and Manufacturing Overhead		
Applied Accounts		50,000

8. Now the entire manufacturing cost of Work Order No. 101 has been incurred. The following entry transfers this cost to Finished Goods Inventory:

Finished Goods Inventory	550,000	
WIP Inventory: Special Finishing		550,000

Companies generally apply manufacturing overhead using predetermined overhead rates. As noted in previous chapters, when using predetermined rates, overhead can be overapplied or underapplied compared to actual manufacturing overhead. The over- or underapplied overhead is treated as an expense or allocated to inventories, if the goods are still in inventory, as explained in Chapter 3.

COMPARISON OF JOB COSTING, PROCESS COSTING, AND OPERATION COSTING

We have discussed how to account for product costs in three types of organizations: job shops, like construction companies, which use job costing; organizations with continuous flow processing, like soft drink syrup manufacturers, which use process costing; and companies with operations, like automobile manufacturers, which use operation costing. Operation costing combines the aspect of job costing that assigns materials separately to jobs (which are also called *work orders* or *batches* in operation costing) with the aspect of process costing that assigns conversion costs equally to each operation. Thus, in our motorcycle example, Sharks had different per unit materials costs, but the same operations costs per unit for the two operations that both models passed through.

In practice, you are likely to find elements of all three production methods, and thus you will find elements of all three costing methods. Also, you will find that every company has its own unique costing methods that do not precisely fit any textbook description. Having studied these three basic costing methods will enable you to figure out the variations on the methods presented here.

 *Self-Study Question*

1 Show the journal entries for the Jets motorcycles (Work Order No. 102) using the data given in the example in the text.

The solution to this question is at the end of this chapter on page 185.

JUST-IN-TIME INVENTORY

Just-in-Time Inventory An inventory system designed to obtain goods just in time for production (in manufacturing) or sale (in merchandising).

Recent innovations in inventory management and manufacturing methods have the potential to revolutionize both inventory management and the way accounting is done in manufacturing companies. One of these is the **just-in-time inventory** philosophy. The objective of just-in-time (JIT) inventory is to obtain materials just in time for production and to provide finished goods just in time for sale and other inventory items just when needed. This reduces, or potentially eliminates, inventory carrying costs. It also has been found to have another, perhaps more important, benefit.

Just-in-time inventory requires that processes or people making defective units be corrected immediately because there is no inventory where defective units can be sent to await reworking or scrapping. Manufacturing managers find that eliminating inventories can prevent production problems from being hidden. The principal feature of a JIT inventory system is that production does not begin on an item until an order is received. Upon receipt of an order, raw materials are ordered and the production cycle begins. As soon as the order is filled, production ends.

In theory, a JIT system eliminates the need for inventories because no production takes place until it is known that the item will be sold. As a practical matter, companies using this system will normally have a backlog of orders so they can keep their production operations going. The benefits of the JIT system would be lost if a company had to shut down its operations for lengthy periods of time while awaiting receipt of a new order.

Users of this system claim that it minimizes the need to carry inventories. Moreover, by producing only enough to fill orders, better control is initiated over goods lost or spoiled in production. This occurs because the entire production line is set up to produce just enough units to fill the order received. If there are spoiled or lost units, a supplemental order is required. Initiation of the supplemental order serves to notify management of the spoilage or lost goods.

Flexible Manufacturing A computer-based manufacturing system that allows companies to make a variety of products with minimal setup time.

To achieve just-in-time objectives, many companies install a flexible manufacturing system. A **flexible manufacturing system** is a computer-based manufacturing system that allows companies to make a variety of products with minimal setup time. A company using flexible manufacturing can minimize its inventories while making products with small production runs. For example, Ford Motor Company installed flexible manufacturing so it could produce numerous different types of valves for the various engines that go into its cars and trucks.

Lean Production Methods

Just-in-time production is part of a "lean production" philosophy that has been credited for the success of many Japanese companies and such U.S. companies as Lincoln Electric. Lean production is characterized by eliminating buffers, such as inventory, and by placing the quality and efficiency of production at the highest importance. Lean production requires the flexibility to change quickly from one product to another, it emphasizes training and worker skills, and it relates people's compensation to company and individual performance. Companies that do not have these characteristics find it difficult to implement just-in-time production methods.

Many Japanese companies are presently using just-in-time inventory, including automobile manufacturers such as Toyota and motorcycle manufacturers such as Yamaha. The Saturn Corporation uses just-in-time inventory (see the Real World Application for this chapter), as does Federal Express.

Illustration 5–3 compares the cost flow through T-accounts at a Hewlett-Packard division before and after just-in-time production was introduced. If inventories are low, accountants may prefer to charge all manufacturing costs directly to Cost of Goods Sold and bypass the usual inventory accounts. As shown in Illustration 5–3, Hewlett-Packard used a slightly different approach. Its direct materials costs flowed through inventory accounts, but its direct labor and manufacturing overhead bypassed the inventory accounts and flowed directly to Cost of Goods Sold. This approach enabled Hewlett-Packard to save the time and trouble of keeping track of direct labor and manufacturing overhead for each work order, but allowed the accountants to track materials costs through the production process.

Backflush Costing

Traditional costing systems use sequential tracking to record product costs. That is, as a product goes through its production steps, the costing system tracks the product and attaches costs at each step. This sequential tracking is time consuming and expensive, not only for accountants but also for

ILLUSTRATION

Comparing Cost Flows: Hewlett-Packard's Simplified System and a Conventional System

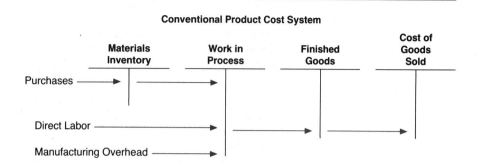

Source: R. Hunt, L. Garrett, and C. M. Merz, "Direct Labor Cost Not Always Relevant at H-P," *Management Accounting,* February 1985, pp. 58–62.

workers and managers who must keep records of labor time and other costs incurred at each step.

Just-in-time production provides an opportunity to reduce the cost of accounting and recordkeeping. If JIT production eliminates inventories, then there is no need to keep track of costs for inventory valuation. Managers would still want to know the cost of products for decision making, of course.

What if a company's accountants record all manufacturing costs directly in Cost of Goods Sold, but at the end of the accounting period, the accountants learn that the company has some inventory? (Despite using JIT production, companies often find they have some inventory levels.) Companies that record costs directly in Cost of Goods Sold, thus bypassing the inventory accounts, can use a method called **backflush costing** to transfer any costs back to the inventory accounts, if necessary.

Backflush Costing A costing method that works backward from output to assign costs to inventories.

Backflush costing is a method that works backward from the output to assign manufacturing costs to work in process inventories. The term *backflush* probably arose because costs are "flushed back" through the production process to the points at which inventories remain. Illustration 5–4 compares the traditional method of sequential costing with the backflush approach. Costs are initially recorded at the end of the production process, either in Finished Goods Inventory or in Cost of Goods Sold, on the grounds that there are little or no work in process inventories at the end of the period.

If there are no inventories at the end of the period, the company does not need to record the backflow of costs. (The backflow of costs is indicated by the arrows pointing to the left and up in the bottom of Illustration 5–4.) If there are inventories, the company must backflush costs from the end of the production process (for example, from Finished Goods Inventory or Cost of Goods Sold) to the inventories, as demonstrated by the following example.

Example Denton Biotechnics Corp., which uses the JIT system, sells diagnostic kits for medical use. Direct materials cost $5.00 per kit. The company received an order for 10,000 kits in January, which was its only business in January. It had no beginning inventory in January. Materials costs of $50,000 were incurred as were conversion costs of $94,000. Materials costs were credited to Accounts Payable as they were incurred. Of the conversion costs, $54,000 was credited to Manufacturing Overhead Applied and $40,000 to Wages Payable, as incurred. Using backflush costing and charging

ILLUSTRATION   *Comparison of Traditional Sequential Tracking of Costs with Backflush Costing*

5–4

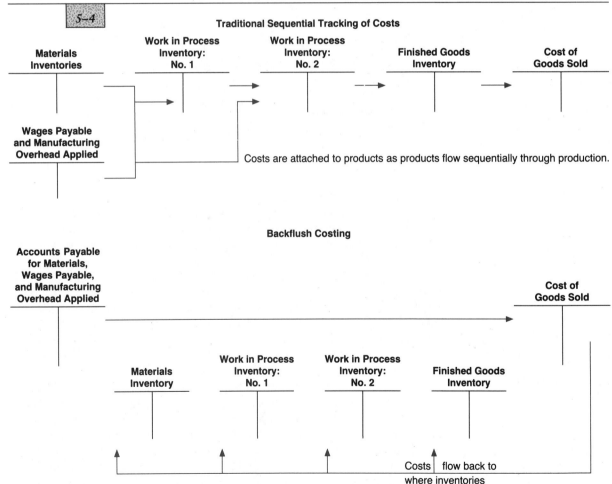

the costs directly to Cost of Goods Sold, the journal entries for January would be:

Cost of Goods Sold	50,000	
Accounts Payable		50,000
To record the use of materials.		
Cost of Goods Sold	94,000	
Wages Payable		40,000
Manufacturing Overhead Applied		54,000
To record conversion costs.		

This example presents the extreme version of JIT production by charging all manufacturing costs to Cost of Goods Sold as they were incurred. Other versions charge labor and overhead costs to an account called "Conversion Costs," then assign these conversion costs to Finished Goods Inventory or Cost of Goods Sold. Whatever peculiarity you encounter in practice, just remember the principle that accountants normally do not need to keep track of costs in work in process inventories for external reporting.

If Denton Biotechnics Corp. had sold all 10,000 kits and had no inventories at the end of January, there would be no need for additional entries. However, if the company had inventories at the end of January, it would need to assign costs to those inventories. To demonstrate, we assume the company had the following inventories at the end of January:

Work in process inventory: 1,000 units complete as to materials costs and 40 percent complete as to conversion costs.

Finished goods inventory: 1,000 units completed but not yet shipped or recorded in Cost of Goods Sold.

The company further computes its conversion costs to be $10.00 for each completed kit. In addition, direct materials of $5.00 per kit are incurred at the beginning of work in process. Based on this information, the cost of each ending inventory is computed as follows:

Work in process inventory: (1,000 units × $5 for materials) + (40% stage of completion × 1,000 units × $10 per unit for conversion costs) = $5,000 + $4,000 = $9,000

Finished goods inventory: 1,000 units × ($5 for materials + $10 for conversion costs) = $15,000.

The entries to backflush the costs of inventories out of Cost of Goods Sold would be:

Work in Process Inventory	9,000	
Finished Goods Inventory	15,000	
Cost of Goods Sold		24,000
To record inventories.		

If the costs of these kits had been charged to the accounts using traditional sequential costing, we would have recorded materials in Materials Inventory when purchased. As materials were used and conversion costs were incurred, these costs would have been recorded in Work in Process and Finished Goods, and finally in Cost of Goods Sold. Illustration 5–5 compares diagrams of the cost flows, first using the traditional method, then using backflush costing.

What happens to the beginning inventory next period? The company can

I L L U S T R A T I O N   *Comparison of Traditional Cost Flows to Backflush Costing*

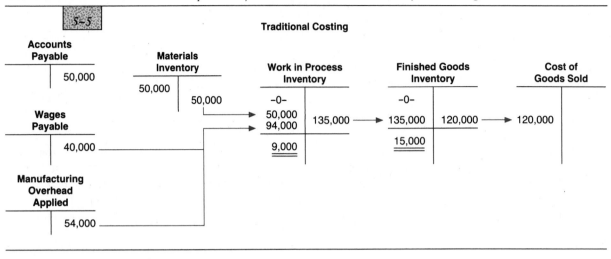

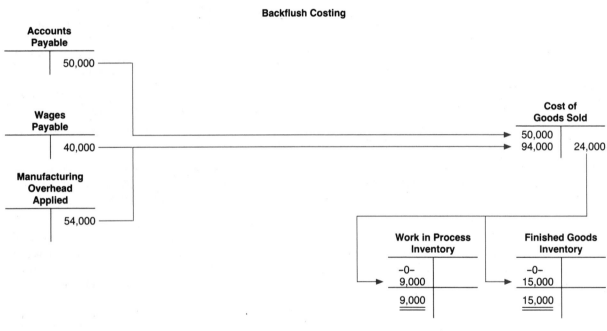

either use traditional sequential costing to record the movement of costs and products out of the inventory accounts, or the company can reverse the backflush entry. By reversing the backflush entry, the company credits the inventory accounts and debits Cost of Goods Sold, thus recreating the situation that appeared before making the backflush entry. (If you recall how adjusting and reversing entries work, the backflush entry can be treated as an adjusting entry at the end of a period that is reversed at the beginning of the next period.)

JIT: A Note of Caution   Although proponents of JIT systems claim significant cost savings, some cautions are necessary. Using a JIT approach means that goods will not be produced to stockpile in inventory. With seasonal products, companies must

---

REAL WORLD APPLICATION

When JIT May Not Be a Good Idea*

A United Auto Workers local strike against a General Motors parts plant resulted in a shutdown of the Saturn plant in Spring Hills, Tennessee. The Saturn plant was forced to close within a few hours of the strike against the Lordstown plant because Saturn used just-in-time inventory and had only enough inventory for one or two shifts. The Lordstown plant provided steel hoods, trunk lids, and roofs for the Saturn cars.

During the Persian Gulf War, the U.S. Army kept some of its Apache helicopters flying by grounding other helicopters to get parts. Prewar flight time was cut in half to preserve parts, and emergency unpriced contracts were issued to obtain spare parts. The army had spent about $12 billion on the Apache program but almost nothing for spare parts according to a General Accounting Office study. Apparently the army would need 6 to 12 months' lead time before the next war started to have enough time to acquire parts. Army officials argued that stockpiling parts would lead to criticisms that the army had excessive inventories.

*Based on articles in the *Washington Post*, September 6, 1992, and the *Sacramento Bee*, April 27, 1991.

---

build inventories in preparation for the heavy sales period or increase production substantially during the busy season. A company needs to have a backlog of orders and reliable suppliers so that it can keep the production line moving with a JIT system. If there is no backlog, production would stop when an order has been filled and remain idle until a new order is received. This could create chaos in the factory.

Finally, materials must be readily obtained from suppliers; otherwise, production would not begin upon receipt of an order but would be delayed until goods were received. This could create customer dissatisfaction if the delay were long. This chapter's Real World Application describes two cases in which there was insufficient support for JIT to work.

Many manufacturing companies have found that JIT can be used to varying degrees. If replacement goods could be obtained rapidly from reliable suppliers, inventory levels of one week's supply or less could be optimal. On the other hand, if replacement materials were difficult to obtain (for example, goods imported from overseas), companies require substantially greater inventory levels.

Self-Study Question

2 Metro Media uses JIT production in producing commercials. For the month of January, the company incurred costs of $100,000 in making commercials. Ten thousand dollars of those costs were tied up in one commercial for a real estate company that was not complete at the end of the month, and $20,000 had been assigned to one commercial for a clothing store that was finished but not recorded in Cost of Goods Sold yet. Show the flow of costs through T-accounts using (1) traditional costing and (2) backflush costing. The company has no Materials Inventory account, one Work in Process Inventory account, and one Finished Goods Inventory account. Assume the credit entries for these costs when they were recorded during the month were: 60 percent to Accounts Payable and 40 percent to Wages Payable. The company had no beginning inventories and no other business in January.

The solution to this question is at the end of this chapter on page 185.

ACCOUNTING FOR SPOILAGE

Spoilage Goods that are damaged, do not meet specifications, or are otherwise not suitable for further processing or sale as good output.

Good Output Units that are expected to be completed and suitable for further processing or for sale at the end of a production process.

If you have ever tried to make something that did not work out (for example, art projects in school), then you know the concept of spoilage. **Spoilage** refers to the loss of goods during production. There are two methods of accounting for normal spoilage. Method 1 spreads the cost of spoiled units over the remaining good units. Thus, units produced is expressed in terms of **good output.** The computation results in an increased cost per finished unit that has the effect of averaging the normal losses over the good units.

For example, suppose a department uses weighted-average costing. It has no beginning inventory and started 3,000 units. These units cost $24,000 for materials and conversion costs. It produced only 2,500 units of good output and lost 500 units. Using Method 1, the company would record 2,500 units produced at a cost of $9.60 per unit ($24,000 ÷ 2,500 good units = $9.60).

Method 2 accounts for the cost of spoiled units separately. Method 2 would record the 3,000 units at their cost of $8 per unit ($24,000 ÷ 3,000 units). At the end of the period, the $4,000 cost of the 500 lost units would be assigned to work in process inventory, finished goods inventory, or cost of goods sold, depending on the status of the good units. For example, if 1,000 of the good units are in ending finished goods inventory and the remaining 1,500 good units were sold, the entry would be:

Finished Goods Inventory—Lost Unit Costs .... 1,600 $\left(= \frac{1,000}{2,500} \times \$4,000 \right)$

Cost of Goods Sold—Lost Unit Costs .... 2,400 $\left(= \frac{1,500}{2,500} \times \$4,000 \right)$

Work in Process Inventory—Lost
   Unit Costs 4,000

Assuming there were no beginning inventories and these were the only costs incurred, both methods result in the same value of finished goods inventory and cost of goods sold. However, Method 2, which explicitly assigns costs to spoiled units, provides managers with data they would not get from Method 1; namely, the cost of spoilage. The flow of costs for both methods is diagrammed in Illustration 5–6. A summary of the computations for both methods is shown below:

Two Methods of Assigning Spoilage to Units

Method 1: Assign spoilage costs to good units:

Costs to be accounted for	$24,000
Equivalent units (E.U.)	÷2,500
Cost per E.U.	=$9.60
Cost assignment to units transferred out ($9.60 × 2,500 units)	$24,000

Method 2: Compute the cost of spoiled units:

Costs to be accounted for	$24,000
Equivalent units:	
Started and completed	2,500
Spoilage	500
Total equivalent units	3,000
Unit cost ($24,000 ÷ 3,000)	$ 8
Cost assignment:	
Transferred out (2,500 × $8)	$20,000
Spoiled units (500 × $8)	4,000
Total costs accounted for	$24,000

ILLUSTRATION *Cost Flows for Normal Lost Units*

5–6

Work in Process Inventory

Finished Goods Inventory

Cost of Goods Sold

Method 1:
Average spoiled unit costs over good units

(3,000 units started at $8 per unit) 24,000 | (2,500 good units completed at $9.60 per unit) 24,000

→ 24,000 → (1,500 units at $9.60 per unit) 14,400 → 14,400

9,600

Work in Process Inventory

Finished Goods Inventory

Cost of Goods Sold

Method 2:
Assign spoiled unit costs to ending inventories and the cost of goods sold

(3,000 units started at $8 per unit) 24,000 | (2,500 good units completed at $8 per unit) 20,000
Spoilage adjustment: (500 spoiled units at $8) 4,000

→ 20,000 → (1,500 units at $8 per unit) 12,000 → 12,000

Spoilage adjustment 1,600[a]

8,000

9,600

Spoilage adjustment 2,400[a]

[a] Allocate spoilage costs proportional to good units costs.

$1,600 = $8,000/$20,000 × $4,000 to Finished Goods Inventory.

$2,400 = $12,000/$20,000 × $4,000 to Cost of Goods Sold.

Spoilage Occurs during the Process

What if spoilage occurs and is detected during the process? Using Method 1, spoilage costs are automatically part of good units produced, wherever spoilage occurs. Method 2 discussed above would compute the spoilage based on the equivalent units of the goods produced. For example, starting with the facts from the previous example, assume the following additional facts:

Materials, all added at the beginning of the process . . . . $ 9,000
Conversion costs, added evenly throughout the process 15,000

Spoilage of 500 units occurs and is detected when the process is 40 percent complete (but after all materials have been added).

The cost of spoiled units would be derived as follows:

1. Compute the cost per unit for materials and conversion costs:

   Materials: $9,000 \div [2,500 + (1.0 \times 500)]$ equivalent units
     = $\underline{\underline{\$3}}$ per equivalent unit

   For materials, spoilage occurs *after* all materials have been added, so the stage of completion is "100 percent" for materials.

   Conversion costs: $15,000 \div [2,500 + (.4 \times 500)]$
     = $15,000 \div 2,700$ equivalent units
     = $\underline{\underline{\$5.556}}$ (rounded) per equivalent unit

2. Compute the cost of spoiled units by multiplying the cost per equivalent unit times the number of units spoiled:

Materials: 500 equivalent units $\times$ $3	=	$1,500
Conversion costs: 200 equivalent units $\times$ $5.556	=	$\underline{1,111}$
Total cost of units spoiled		$\underline{\underline{\$2,611}}$

The equivalent units of goods spoiled for *conversion costs* is only 200 (40 percent $\times$ 500 units spoiled) because spoilage occurred and was detected at the 40 percent stage. Consequently, the total equivalent units produced, incuding equivalent units of goods spoiled, equals 2,700, *not* 3,000.

Spoilage occurred after *all materials were added,* however, so the equivalent units spoiled for materials costs equal 500 units; the total equivalent units produced, including spoiled goods, equal 3,000.

Computing Equivalent Units and Spoilage Costs When Companies Have Beginning and Ending Inventories

The previous example assumed no beginning or ending work in process inventories. Adding work in process inventories complicates the calculations, but it does not affect the general principles.

For example, suppose a company uses weighted-average costing to compute product costs. At the beginning of the period, it had 200 units in beginning inventory that were 100 percent complete with respect to materials and 60 percent complete with respect to conversion costs. All units in beginning inventory were good units. During the period, the company started 2,800 units. It produced 2,500 good units and lost 500 units to spoilage. Management is concerned that so many units were spoiled and wants us to determine the cost of spoiled units.

To determine the cost of spoiled units, we have to compute the equivalent units produced. We learn that production people detect spoilage at the

30 percent stage of production, that is, after 30 percent of conversion costs and 100 percent of materials costs had been applied. Of the 2,500 good units, we learn that 2,100 were transferred out to Finished Goods Inventory. The remaining 400 units were in ending work in process inventory, 100 percent complete with respect to materials and 20 percent complete with respect to conversion costs.

Using weighted average costing, with spoilage, equivalent units are computed using the following formula:

$$\begin{matrix}\text{Equivalent} \\ \text{units produced}\end{matrix} = \begin{matrix}\text{Good units} \\ \text{transferred} \\ \text{out}\end{matrix} + \begin{matrix}\text{Equivalent units} \\ \text{in ending} \\ \text{inventory}\end{matrix} + \begin{matrix}\text{Equivalent units} \\ \text{spoiled}\end{matrix}$$

Assuming materials were added at the beginning of the production process, we compute the equivalent units produced for materials costs as follows:

Equivalent units = 2,100 units transferred out + 400 units in
       ending inventory + 500 units spoiled
   = 3,000 equivalent units for materials.

For conversion costs, assuming conversion costs were added evenly throughout the process, we compute the equivalent units produced as follows:

Equivalent units = 2,100 units transferred out
     + (400 × .20) equivalent units in ending inventory
     + (500 × .30) equivalent units spoiled
   = 2,100 units transferred out + 80 equivalent units in ending inventory + 150 equivalent units spoiled
   = 2,330 equivalent units produced with respect to conversion costs.

Note the equivalent units produced for conversion costs includes the equivalent units of spoiled goods. Thus, 150 equivalent units were spoiled, based on 500 units detected after 30 percent of the conversion costs had been applied.

From the accounting records, we find the following costs that will enable us to compute cost per equivalent unit and assign costs to units spoiled:

	Beginning Inventory	Current Period Costs	Total
Materials	$2,000	$28,000	$30,000
Conversion costs	2,400	44,200	46,600

To compute the cost per equivalent unit, we divide the total costs by the equivalent units produced:

Materials: $30,000/3,000 equivalent units = $10 per unit.
Conversion costs: $46,600/2,330 equivalent units = $20 per unit.

To compute the cost of spoilage, using Method 2:

Materials: 500 units spoiled × $10 = $5,000
Conversion costs: 150 equivalent units spoiled × $20 =   3,000
      Total cost of spoiled units $8,000

Note the 150 equivalent units spoiled reflect 500 units spoiled, detected after 30 percent of conversion costs had been applied.

Using Method 1, all costs would have been spread over the good units produced, computed as follows:

Materials: $30,000/2,500 good units produced = $12 per unit
Conversion costs: $46,000/2,180 good units produced = $21.10 (rounded).

Although Method 1 is simpler, it does not inform managers about the cost of spoilage.

In general, the earlier we can detect spoilage, the less costly to the company. If spoilage cannot be prevented, it should be detected as early as possible.

ABNORMAL SPOILAGE

Lost Units Goods that evaporate or otherwise disappear during a production process.

Normal Spoilage Spoiled goods that are a result of the regular operation of the production process.

Abnormal Spoilage Spoilage due to reasons other than the usual course of operations of a process.

If units are lost for unusual or abnormal reasons, as shown in the bottom panel of Illustration 5–7, the debit in the journal entry is made to an account such as Abnormal Spoilage Costs, which writes off the costs for the period. Whereas *normal* **lost units** or **normal spoilage** is usually treated as a product cost, abnormal lost units or **abnormal spoilage** is treated as a period expense. For example, referring back to Illustration 5–6, if the $4,000 spoilage was lost due to abnormal reasons, the journal entry to record the transfer of spoilage costs out of Work in Process Inventory would be:

Abnormal Spoilage	4,000	
Work in Process Inventory		4,000

The Abnormal Spoilage account would be a period expense and would appear in the income statement. Abnormal Spoilage requires us to use Method 2, described above, because we must explicitly compute the cost of spoiled units.

Companies that employ a production system based on the philosophy that there should be zero defects would treat all spoilage as abnormal. For these companies, the Abnormal Spoilage account is monitored closely with the intention of identifying the causes for the spoilage and finding ways to prevent such spoilage from occurring in the future. (These companies would probably *not* consider the top panel of Illustration 5–7 to be normal).

When abnormal spoilage is charged to expense, cost of goods sold is stated at the cost per unit excluding the abnormal lost unit costs. Thus, for this example, the cost of goods sold would be $12,000 or $8 per unit. T-accounts to represent this flow of costs are shown in Illustration 5–8.

REWORKED PRODUCTS

Reworked products are those that did not pass inspection and are subsequently reworked and sold. Many of us do a job, find it is not acceptable, and rework it. The accounting question is: How should we account for the additional costs of reworking the defective products?

If a job has gone through several stages of production before the defect is discovered, then considerable costs have already been assigned to that job. If the additional rework costs are added to that particular job's costs, then the job's costs will be considerably higher than the cost of similar jobs that did not have to go through rework.

Product Identification Method

There are two approaches to accounting for the cost of rework. First, using the *product identification* method, the cost can be assigned to the particular

ILLUSTRATION

5-7

*Normal versus Abnormal
Spoilage*

job, batch, or unit that is being reworked. Assigning rework costs to the
particular job has the advantage of sending a message to management that
the company has a problem. If a particular job is considerably more costly
than other similar jobs, or more costly than estimated, management can take
action to improve the problems that created the defects in the first place. By
measuring and reporting the costs of rework, accountants can show manage-

ILLUSTRATION   *Cost Flows with Abnormal Spoilage**

5-8

Work in Process Inventory				Finished Goods Inventory				Cost of Goods Sold	
(3,000 units at $8 per unit) 24,000	(2,500 units at $8 per unit) 20,000			20,000 8,000	(1,500 units at $8 per unit) 12,000			12,000	
	(500 units at $8 per unit) 4,000							**Abnormal Spoilage**	
								► 4,000	

* Based on data from Illustration 5–6.

ment there are benefits from employee training, new machinery, better materials, and other quality improvement methods.

Accounting for rework using the product identification approach is a simple concept, but it may be difficult to apply. In concept, if a job incurs $1,000 in costs from normal production plus $600 for additional rework, then the job costs $1,600. The total costs debited to Work in Process Inventory would amount to $1,600. Assume the original materials costs were $600, the direct labor costs were $100, and the manufacturing overhead costs were $300. Further, the rework required $150 additional materials and $150 additional direct labor, and $300 additional manufacturing overhead was applied. Then the journal entry would appear as follows:

Work in Process Inventory	1,600	
Materials Inventory		600
Wages Payable		100
Manufacturing Overhead Applied		300
Materials Inventory—Rework		150
Wages Payable—Rework		150
Manufacturing Overhead Applied—Rework		300

The amount transferred from Work in Process Inventory to Finished Goods Inventory and ultimately to Cost of Goods Sold for that job would be $1,600, with the $600 for rework accounted for separately in Finished Goods Inventory and Cost of Goods Sold.

Overhead Method

In practice, the product identification approach may be difficult to implement because it may be time consuming (and perhaps impossible) to tie the rework costs to a particular product. If the unit is a job, such as a building, accountants will likely find it feasible to tie rework costs to a particular job. In a process, however, the costs of rework are difficult to tie to particular units. Consequently, in practice, the costs of rework are often charged to manufacturing overhead. Using this method, which we call the *overhead method,* these rework costs are spread over all units produced whether good units or defective units. The journal entry to record the costs of rework using the overhead method with the same data as the example above is as follows:

First, to record the initial costs incurred in making the product:

Work in Process Inventory 1,000		
Materials Inventory	600	
Wages Payable	100	
Manufacturing Overhead Applied	300	

Second, to record the additional costs to rework the above units:

Manufacturing Overhead 600		
Materials Inventory	150	
Wages Payable	150	
Manufacturing Overhead Applied	300	

Applied manufacturing overhead rates are increased to take into account the costs of rework that are charged to Manufacturing Overhead. Thus, all products share in rework costs, whether they needed rework or not, because all products are charged with more applied overhead.

We believe the product identification method is preferred to the overhead method because it better informs managers. We recognize, however, that certain circumstances may preclude accountants from tying costs of rework to particular products.

ACCOUNTING FOR SPOILAGE AND TOTAL QUALITY MANAGEMENT

As you can see from the treatment of normal spoilage, when spoilage costs are assigned to good units, the cost of spoilage is buried. If managers want to identify the cost of spoilage, accountants should use Method 2 to account for spoilage, or they should account for all spoilage as abnormal. Advocates of total quality management would likely consider all spoilage to be abnormal.

A Comment

We believe it is important for companies to make a concerted effort to measure costs of spoilage and as many other costs *and benefits* related to quality as possible. In the case of spoilage, by measuring both the costs of spoilage and such costs of reducing spoilage as employee training and higher quality materials, managers have information enabling them to make informed decisions to improve quality.

Baldridge Quality Award winners like Ritz-Carlton Hotels and Motorola have emphasized the importance of providing quality services and goods to customers. Cost accounting systems are poorly equipped to measure the cost of poor quality resulting in lost customer goodwill and sales. When considering the cost of quality, it is crucial that managers recognize there is a substantial benefit from high-quality products that may appear as a cost today, but will have substantial future benefits in the form of increased customer satisfaction and revenues.[1]

Self-Study Question

3 A company using the weighted-average costing method maintains a Spoilage Expense account for spoiled goods. This account is charged with the cost of units spoiled in process. Each unit spoiled is considered 80 percent complete with

---

[1] Numerous articles in the accounting literature have dealt with quality. See, for example, T. L. Albright and H. P. Roth, "The Measurement of Quality Costs: An Alternative Paradigm," *Accounting Horizons* 6, no. 2, pp. 15–27.

respect to conversion costs and 100 percent complete with respect to materials at the time of spoilage.

The accounting records show the following information for the activities in the Work in Process Inventory account:

Beginning inventory:
　　Direct materials $10,000
　　Conversion costs $20,000
Current period:
　　Direct materials $40,000
　　Conversion costs $80,000
　　Units transferred out . . . .　20,000　units
　　Units spoiled . . . .　　2,000　units
Ending inventory:
　　Physical count . . . .　　6,000　units
　　Percent of completion:
　　　Direct materials　. . . . . . . 40%
　　　Conversion costs　. . . . . . . 25%

Compute the costs to be assigned to the spoiled units using Method 2 from the chapter. Recall that Method 2 explicitly identifies the cost of spoiled units.

The solution to this question is at the end of this chapter on page 185.

SUMMARY

This chapter deals with operation costing, backflush costing, and accounting for spoilage. Operation costing is a hybrid of job order and process costing. Each batch or work order has particular materials assigned to it, similar to job shops. Each batch or work order goes through similar operations, like continuous process production. We noted in Chapter 3 that custom-built houses or major remodels of buildings are examples of jobs. On the other hand, if those houses are built in factories, like mobile homes, then the houses are built in operations in which different models of mobile homes have different materials, but they pass through similar operations. Of course, some work orders or batches do not pass through the same operations as other work orders or batches. (Recall in the chapter example, the Jets motorcycles did not pass through the final operation.)

Just-in-time production is part of the lean production philosophy that emphasizes quality, high worker skills, and eliminating inventory buffers. With the just-in-time method, companies have an opportunity to simplify accounting for inventories by bypassing inventory accounts and charging production costs directly to Cost of Goods Sold. If there are no inventories at the end of the period, accounting has been considerably simplified. If there are inventories at the end of the period, companies use backflush costing to back costs out of Cost of Goods Sold and set up inventories by crediting Cost of Goods Sold and debiting inventory accounts (for example, Work in Process Inventory) for the amount of inventory balances at the end of the period. Companies *can* use backflush costing whether or not they use the just-in-time method. Companies that use the just-in-time method are likely to have simplified their accounting by initially charging production costs to Cost of Goods Sold. Such companies would have to use a backflush approach if they have significant ending inventory balances or changes in inventory levels during the period.

When units are spoiled in production, Method 1 spreads all costs, including costs incurred on the spoiled units, over the *good units* produced. Method 2 removes the spoiled units from work in process (that is, credits Work in Process Inventory) and charges them to ending inventories and cost of goods sold. If the spoilage or lost units are not a normal part of production, then they are typically written off as a period expense for external financial reporting purposes.

Advocates of total quality management might consider all spoilage to be abnormal. Accounting practices that ''bury'' spoilage in the cost of products reduce information about an important cost and can deter management's efforts to identify and eliminate spoilage.

TERMS AND CONCEPTS

The following terms and concepts should be familiar to you after reading this chapter:

Abnormal Spoilage, *170*	**Lost Units,** *170*
Backflush Costing, *161*	**Normal Spoilage,** *170*
Flexible Manufacturing, *160*	**Operation,** *155*
Good Output, *166*	**Operation Costing,** *155*
Just-in-Time Inventory, *159*	**Spoilage,** *166*

QUESTIONS

5–1 What is an operation?

5–2 Why is operation costing called a hybrid costing method?

5–3 How does operation costing compare and contrast with job costing and process costing?

5–4 Name three types of companies that are likely to use operation costing.

5–5 True or false? All products have to flow through the same operations in operation costing.

5–6 True or false? An operation could be an entire department or it could be part of a department.

5–7 What is the key difference between backflush costing and traditional sequential costing?

5–8 True or false? Backflush costing can only be used by companies that use just-in-time production methods.

5–9 What are important requirements for a company to use just-in-time production methods?

5–10 Traditional production methods are sometimes called *production push* while just-in-time production is sometimes called *demand pull*. Why do you think just-in-time is called *demand pull*?

5–11   What are key characteristics of lean production?

5–12   Refer to the Real World Application for this chapter. Why did a strike against General Motors' Lordstown plant affect the Saturn plant?

5–13   Refer to the Real World Application in this chapter. What was the effect of maintaining minimal inventories for the Apache helicopter during the Persian Gulf War?

5–14   What is the problem faced by a company that makes Christmas ornaments and wants to use just-in-time production? What would you recommend to the management of this company?

5–15   "We cannot successfully implement JIT without higher quality in production." Why might JIT require particularly high quality?

5–16   As a manager, would you prefer to see normal spoilage costs computed and presented using Method 1 or Method 2 in the text? Why? (Method 1 incorporates spoilage costs into good units.)

5–17   Which method of accounting for spoilage do you think would be simpler in practice: Method 1, which assigns spoilage costs to good units, or Method 2, which computes the cost of spoiled units?

5–18   Why might advocates of total quality management prefer to see all spoilage considered abnormal spoilage?

5–19   The chapter discusses the cost of spoilage when spoilage is detected during the production. What costs might a company incur if spoilage is not detected during production and defective goods are sold to customers?

EXERCISES

5–20   Operation Costing: Cost Flows
(L.O.2)

Sweatshirts, Inc., makes two types of sweatshirts: plain and deluxe. Both types of sweatshirts go through two operations, cutting and sewing. The deluxe sweatshirts go through a third operation that prints emblems and words on the sweatshirts. The deluxe sweatshirts use more expensive materials.

The following data are for work orders for these two products:

	Work Order 111	Work Order 112
Type	Deluxe	Plain
Quantity	10,000	12,000
Direct materials:		
Cloth added in the cutting operation	$50,000	$48,000
Conversion costs (direct labor and manufacturing overhead):		
Cutting	10,000	12,000
Sewing	10,000	12,000
Printing	5,000	—
Total costs	$75,000	$72,000

Required:

Prepare journal entries to show the flow of costs through accounts to Finished Goods Inventory. Keep the costs for each work order separate as you transfer costs from account to account.

**5–21 Operation Costing:
Cost Flows**
(L.O.2)

Refer to the data in exercise 5–20. Show the flow of costs through T-accounts.

**5–22 Operation Costing:
Decision Making**
(L.O.2)

Refer to the data in exercise 5–20. New operations have been discovered that will reduce the cost of sewing and cutting by 10 percent. This operation requires a new type of cloth that will increase materials costs by 6 percent. No other costs would be affected. Customers would not detect a difference in the quality of cloth. In any case, the company does not plan to increase the market price of its sweatshirts. Management wants your advice about purchasing this new type of cloth.

Required:

Should Sweatshirts, Inc., use the new operations that require the new type of cloth?

**5–23 Operation Costing:
Cost Flows**
(L.O.2)

Outdoors, Inc., makes two types of backpacks: book bags and hiking packs. Both types of backpacks go through Operations 1 and 3. The hiker backpacks also go through Operation 2, which adds compartments that are particularly useful for carrying hiking gear. Operation 2 requires additional materials to make these compartments.

The following data are for work orders for these two products:

	Work Order B21	Work Order H22
Type	Book bag	Hiker backpack
Quantity	20,000	4,000
Direct materials:		
Added in Operation 1	$ 60,000	$20,000
Added in Operation 2	—	8,000
Added in Operation 3	20,000	8,000
Conversion costs (direct labor and manufacturing overhead):		
Operation 1	20,000	4,000
Operation 2	—	10,000
Operation 3	10,000	2,000
Total costs	$110,000	$52,000

Required:

Prepare journal entries to show the flow of costs through accounts to Finished Goods Inventory. Keep the costs for each work order separate as you transfer costs from account to account.

**5–24 Operation Costing:
Cost Flows**
(L.O.2)

Refer to the data in exercise 5–23. Show the flow of costs through T-accounts.

**5–25 Operation Costing:
Decision Making**
(L.O.2)

Refer to the data in exercise 5–23. New operations have been discovered that will reduce the cost of Operations 1 and 3 by 10 percent. This operation requires a new type of cloth that will increase materials costs by 5 percent. No other costs would be affected. This change in materials and operations would have no effect on the sales price or quantity sold. Management wants your advice about the costs of these potential new operations and materials.

Required:

Should Outdoors, Inc., use the new operations that require the new materials?

5–26 Backflush Costing
(L.O.3)

Interplay Systems, Inc., manufactures networking devices for personal computer systems. The company uses a JIT system. An order for 600 devices was received. To fill this order, materials costing $7,000 were purchased on account. Manufacturing costs of $24,000 were incurred, of which $8,000 was paid in cash, $6,000 was credited to Wages Payable, and the balance was credited to Manufacturing Overhead Applied.

While production was in progress, it was necessary to compute an inventory value for this order for financial statement purposes. The company has only one production division. The work in process inventory cost was estimated at $1,580. There was no finished goods inventory.

Required: Prepare journal entries for these transactions using backflush costing.

5-27 Backflush Costing
(L.O.3)

Carson Biotech, Inc., manufactures surgical tools. An order was received for 500 autoclaves. Materials costing $12,500 were ordered on account. Additional manufacturing costs were $47,000, of which $25,000 were accounts payable and the balance was wages payable. At the end of the accounting period, $4,100 of goods were not yet completed and were in the company's sole processing area. There was no finished goods inventory.

Required: Prepare journal entries to show the flow of costs using backflush costing.

5-28 Backflush Costing
(L.O.3)

Artful Designs uses JIT production in producing designs for dresses. For the month of June, the company incurred costs of $500,000 in making designs. Assume the credit entries for these costs when they were recorded during the month were: 40 percent to Accounts Payable and 60 percent to Wages Payable. Ten percent of those costs were tied up in one design for an Italian dressmaker that was not complete at the end of the month, and 20 percent of the costs had been assigned to one design for a dressmaker in Japan that was finished but not yet sold. Artful Designs has no Materials Inventory account, one Work in Process Inventory account, and one Finished Goods Inventory account.

Required: Prepare journal entries to show the flow of costs using backflush costing.

5-29 Comparing Backflush and Traditional Costing
(L.O.4)

Refer to the data for exercise 5-26. Show the flow of costs through T-accounts using both traditional sequential costing and backflush costing.

5-30 Comparing Backflush and Traditional Costing
(L.O.4)

Refer to the data for exercise 5-27. Show the flow of costs through T-accounts using both traditional sequential costing and backflush costing.

5-31 Comparing Backflush and Traditional Costing
(L.O.4)

Refer to the data for exercise 5-28. Show the flow of costs through T-accounts using both traditional sequential costing and backflush costing.

5-32 Normal Spoilage
(L.O.5)

Management of Alta Company is concerned about the cost of spoilage. Alta Company provides the following facts:

	Units	Dollars
Beginning inventory	–0–	–0–
Units started; costs incurred	1,000	$10,000
Good units of output produced	800	
Spoiled units	200	

Required:

a. What is the cost of good units produced if spoilage costs are assigned to good units? (Method 1 in the chapter).

b. Assume 500 units were sold and 300 units remained in ending finished goods inventory. If spoilage costs are assigned to spoiled units, but not to good units (Method 2 discussed in the chapter), what is the cost of spoiled units assuming spoilage occurs at the end of the process? Using this method, show the flow of these costs through T-accounts from work-in-process to cost of goods sold.

5–33   Normal Spoilage
(L.O.5)

Park City Company has the following facts regarding spoilage:

	Units	Dollars
Beginning inventory	–0–	–0–
Units started; costs incurred	4,000	$21,600
Good units of output produced	3,600	
Spoiled units	400	

Management is concerned about the cost of spoilage.

Required:

a. What is the cost of good units produced if spoilage costs are assigned to good units (Method 1 in the chapter)?

b. Assume 3,000 units were sold and 600 good units remained in ending finished goods inventory. If spoilage costs are assigned to spoiled units, but not to good units (Method 2 discussed in the chapter), what is the cost of spoiled units assuming spoilage occurs at the end of the process? Using this method, show the flow of these costs through T-accounts.

5–34   Spoilage Occurs during the Process
(L.O.5)

Refer to the facts for exercise 5–32. Assume spoilage occurred when the process was 50 percent complete. Costs are added evenly throughout the process. The ending inventory is 100 percent complete.

Required:

a. What is the cost of good units when spoilage costs are assigned to good units (Method 1)?

b. What is the cost of spoiled units using Method 2 in the chapter?

5–35   Spoilage Occurs during the Process
(L.O.5)

Refer to the facts for exercise 5–33. Assume spoilage occurred when the process was 60 percent complete. Costs are added evenly throughout the process. The ending inventory is 100 percent complete.

Required:

a. What is the cost of good units when spoilage costs are assigned to good units (Method 1)?

b. What is the cost of spoiled units using Method 2 in the chapter?

5–36   Normal versus Abnormal Spoilage
(L.O.6)

In manufacturing its products for the month of March, Domingo Co. incurred abnormal spoilage of $12,000 that occurred during work in process. What is the journal entry to record Domingo Co.'s abnormal spoilage?

5–37   Normal versus Abnormal Spoilage— Multiple Choice
(L.O.6)

In its June production, Gorkei Co. incurred $30,000 normal spoilage and $40,000 abnormal spoilage. How would Gorkei Co. account for spoilage costs? (Choose one.)

(1)   Inventoriable cost of $30,000 and period expense of $40,000.
(2)   Period expense of $30,000 and inventoriable cost of $40,000.
(3)   Inventoriable cost of $70,000.
(4)   Period cost of $70,000.

PROBLEMS

5–38   Product Costing in Operations

Allterra Bicycles uses operation costing in its manufacturing plant. Allterra constructs a bicycle in the following operations: (1) the milling operation which produces kits of tubes, each kit containing enough tubes for one bicycle; (2) the welding operation which welds the tubes into frames; (3) the painting operation which paints the frames; and (4) the assembly operation which assembles the frames with sprockets, pedals, and other parts to make the completed bicycle. These other parts added to the frame in the assembly operation are purchased from outside suppliers.

Allterra sells three products. Allterra sells tube kits after the milling operation and frames after the painting operation to other bicycle manufacturers. It sells bicycles after the assembly operation to wholesalers.

Allterra's management needs to know the cost of each product it sells to help determine the appropriate selling prices. You are assigned the task of computing the cost of each product from the following information for February's production:

| | Operation | | | |
	Milling	Welding	Painting	Assembly
Direct materials	$325,000	$ 0	$ 0	$200,000
Direct labor	40,000	35,000	10,000	40,000
Manufacturing overhead	135,000	55,000	35,000	35,000

In February, Allterra Company produced 10,000 tube kits and sold 1,000 tube kits to other bicycle manufacturers after the milling operation. The remaining 9,000 tube kits were transferred to Allterra's welding operation. Nine thousand frames completed welding and painting. (Recall that one tube kit makes one frame.) Four thousand frames were sold after the painting operation to other bicycle manufacturers, and 5,000 frames were transferred to the assembly operation. All 5,000 frames were assembled into bicycles and sold. The company had no work-in-process or finished goods inventories at the beginning or end of February.

Required:

Compute the cost per unit for February for each of the three products: tube kits, frames, and bicycles. (Hint: Compute the costs incurred in each department first, then compute the cost per unit.)

5–39 Operation Costing and Decision to Buy Materials

Refer to the data in problem 5–38. Assume Allterra Company has an opportunity to purchase tube kits from Colorado Mountain Bikes for $40 per kit. Colorado Mountain Bikes could supply any or all of the tube kits that Allterra needs to produce frames. Colorado Mountain Bikes' products are high quality, at least as good as Allterra's quality. Colorado Mountain Bikes guarantees delivery of tube kits to meet Allterra's production schedule.

Required:

Allterra's management has asked for your opinion about the opportunity to buy tube kits from Colorado Mountain Bikes. Write a short report telling Allterra's management what things they should consider in deciding whether to purchase tubes from Colorado Mountain Bikes or make tubes themselves.

5–40 Operations Costing and Predetermined Rates for Conversion Costs

Herculean Company makes two types of exercise machines. Its regular model, the Tuffo machine, is made in two operations. Its deluxe model, the Buffo machine, is made in three operations. All direct materials are used for both machines in Operation 1. The following data have been made available for two work orders produced during the current year:

	Work Order Number 101 for 1,000 Units of the Tuffo Machine	Work Order Number 102 for 500 Units of the Buffo Machine
Direct materials	$100,000	$120,000
Conversion costs:		
In Operation 1	40,000	20,000
In Operation 2	?	?
In Operation 3	0	10,000

Operation 2 is highly automated. Manufacturing overhead and direct labor costs are combined and applied to units produced in Operation 2 using one combined predetermined conversion cost rate per machine hour. To compute this predetermined conversion cost rate per machine hour for the current year, Herculean's accountants had used budgeted labor costs of $200,000, budgeted manufacturing overhead of $880,000, and 18,000 estimated machine hours. Each exercise machine, whether Tuffo or Buffo, required 30 minutes of machining time in Operation 2.

Management believes a competitor can produce machines similar to the Tuffo for $200 per unit and machines similar to the Buffo for $350 per unit. Consequently, management wants you to compute the cost per unit for these two work orders.

Required:

a. Compute the unit cost for each machine for these two work orders. Is the cost of the Buffo and Tuffo lower or higher than the competition?

b. Suppose McDonald's Corporation offers to purchase 100 units of the Tuffo machine to place in their Ronald McDonald houses. McDonald's is willing to pay $125 per machine. Production of this special work order for McDonald's would not affect the production or sales of other Tuffo units or of the Buffo machine. Herculean has enough production capacity to produce the units for McDonald's without affecting other production. Write a brief report to Herculean's management indicating the things that should be considered in making this decision, and recommend whether to sell to McDonald's for $125 per unit. You should assume that the costs per unit that you computed in answering requirement a are typical of all units.

5–41 Compare Backflush and Traditional Cost Flows

Quad Cities Precision Instruments produces sensitive heat measurement devices. The units are produced in three manufacturing stages: (1) meter assembly, (2) case assembly, and (3) testing. The company has a large backlog of orders and had no beginning inventories because all units in production last year were sold by the end of the year. At the start of this year, an order was received for 4,000 meters. The company purchased $260,000 of materials on account. The Meter Assembly Division used $210,000 of the materials in production. The Case Assembly Division used $40,000, and the Testing Division used $10,000.

Direct labor costs of $640,000 were incurred. These costs were assigned as follows: Meter Assembly, $200,000; Case Assembly, $350,000; Testing, $90,000. Overhead costs of $1,040,000 were charged to departments based on materials used ($210,000/$260,000 × $1,040,000 to Meter Assembly, for example).

Ninety percent of the costs charged to Meter Assembly were transferred to Case Assembly during the period. Ninety-five percent of the costs charged to Case Assembly (including the costs transferred in from Meter Assembly) were transferred to Testing. All of the costs charged to Testing were transferred to finished goods, and all of the finished units were delivered to the buyer.

Required:

a. Use T-accounts to show the flow of costs under a traditional costing system.

b. Use T-accounts to show the flow of costs using a backflush system.

5–42 Compare Backflush and Traditional Cost Flows

Bio Agriproducts Corp. sells specialty hybrid seed packets for agricultural use. The packets are processed through two work in process departments: (1) Culturing and (2) Packaging. Direct materials cost $1.50 per packet ($1.30 in Culturing and $.20 in Packaging). Conversion costs are $.80 for Culturing and $.30 for Packaging. The company received an order for 10,000 packets. Materials costs of $14,800 were incurred as were conversion costs of $10,700.

Assume there are 1,000 units left at the end of the Culturing operation and 500 units at the end of Packaging when financial reports are prepared. The units are 100 percent complete within the respective operations.

Required:

a.   Use T-accounts to show the flow of costs using a backflush system.

b.   Use T-accounts to show the flow of costs under a traditional costing system.

5–43   Spoilage

Nishimoto Co. had the following production for the month of June:

Work in process at June 1 . . . . 10,000 units
Started during June 40,000
Completed and transferred to finished goods 33,000
Abnormal spoilage incurred 2,000
Work in process at June 30 15,000

Materials are added at the beginning of the process. As to conversion costs, the beginning work in process was 70 percent complete and the ending work in process was 60 percent complete. Spoilage is detected at the end of the process.

Required:

Using the weighted-average method, what were the equivalent units for June with respect to conversion costs?
(1)   42,000.
(2)   44,000.
(3)   45,000.
(4)   50,000.

(CPA adapted)

5–44   Spoilage—Rework

Simpson Co. manufactures electric drills to the exacting specifications of various customers. During April, Work Order No. 403 for the production of 1,100 drills was completed at the following costs per unit:

Direct materials $10
Direct labor 8
Applied factory overhead 12
Total $30

Final inspection of Work Order No. 403 disclosed 50 defective units and 100 spoiled units. The defective drills were reworked at an additional cost of $500, and the spoiled drills were sold to a parts manufacturer for $1,500.

Required:

Discuss alternative ways of accounting for the cost of rework and spoiled drills sold to the parts manufacturer.

5–45   Cost of Spoilage

Arizona Aspect, Inc., uses weighted-average costing to compute product costs. At the beginning of the period, it had 100 units in beginning inventory that were 100 percent complete with respect to materials and 40 percent complete with respect to conversion costs. All units in beginning inventory were good units. During the period, the company started 2,400 units. It produced 2,000 good units and lost 500 units to spoilage.

Arizona Aspect's production people detect spoilage after 20 percent of conversion costs had been applied and after 100 percent of materials costs had been applied. Of the 2,000 good units, 1,800 were transferred out to Finished Goods Inventory. The remaining 200 units were in ending work in process inventory, 100 percent complete with respect to materials and 50 percent complete with respect to conversion costs. From the accounting records, we find the following costs:

	Beginning Inventory	Current Period Costs	Total
Materials	$5,000	$95,000	$100,000
Conversion costs	2,000	98,000	100,000

Required:

Management is concerned that so many units were spoiled and has asked you to determine the cost of spoiled units. (Use Method 2 in the chapter.)

5-46   Spoilage

FlyingFast, Inc., manufactures racquetball racquets. The process requires two manufacturing departments: Frames and Strings. Racquets are formed in the Frames Department using aluminum tubing, handle materials, and frame decorations. The completed frames are sent to the Strings Department where the racquets are strung and packaged for shipment to sporting goods stores. Six thousand frames were transferred to the Strings Department this month.

Management is concerned about the cost of spoilage. The following information is available for FlyingFast manufacturing activities in the Strings Department during the past month. (Since there is no beginning inventory, it does not matter whether weighted-average or FIFO is used.)

STRINGS DEPARTMENT

	Units	Prior Department Costs	Direct Materials	Conversion Costs
Physical flow (No beginning inventory.):				
Transferred out	3,300			
Ending inventory	2,700	100% complete	80% complete	45% complete
Transferred in	6,000			
Current costs		$43,200	$2,500	$6,475

Spoilage occurred at the end of the stringing process. This was due to bending of the frames by tension produced at the end of the stringing process. Spoilage amounted to 100 units, and, consequently, the number of good units in ending inventory is 2,600. The good units are 80 percent complete for materials and 45 percent complete for conversion costs.

Required:

a. Compute the cost of spoiled units, using Method 2 in the chapter, for management.

b. Prepare a journal entry that removes the spoiled units from Work in Process Inventory and debits two thirds of their costs to Finished Goods Inventory and one third to Cost of Goods Sold.

c. Prepare a journal entry that treats all spoilage as abnormal spoilage.

d. Write a brief report to FlyingFast management discussing how alternative treatments of spoilage affects a company's attempts for total quality management.

INTEGRATIVE CASE

5-47   Process Costing with Spoilage

West Corporation makes a product called Aggregate in one department of the California Division.

Direct materials are added at the beginning of the process. Labor and overhead are added continuously throughout the process. Spoilage occurs at the beginning of the process just after materials have been added but before any conversion costs have been incurred. In the California Division, all departmental overhead is charged to the departments, and divisional overhead is allocated to the departments on the basis of direct labor-hours. The divisional overhead rate is $2 per direct labor-hour. The following information relates to production during November:

1. Work in process inventory, November 1 (4,000 pounds—75 percent complete):

Direct materials	$22,800
Direct labor at $5 per hour	24,650
Departmental overhead	12,000
Divisional overhead	9,860

2. Direct materials:

Inventory, November 1—2,000 pounds	$10,000
Purchases, November 3—10,000 pounds	51,000
Purchases, November 18—10,000 pounds	51,500
Sent to production during November—16,000 pounds	

3. Direct labor costs at $5 per hour, $103,350.

4. Departmental overhead costs, $52,000; divisional overhead to be computed.

5. Transferred out of work in process, 15,000 pounds.

6. Work in process inventory, November 30, 3,000 pounds, 33-1/3 percent complete.

The FIFO method is used for materials inventory valuation, and the weighted-average method is used for work in process inventories.

Required:

Prepare a production cost report for this department of the California Division for November. Include the costs assigned to spoiled units (Method 2 in the text).

(CMA adapted)

SOLUTIONS TO

Q *Self-Study Questions*

1 Entries for the Jets follow:

1. Direct materials requisitioned for engine assembly are recorded as follows:

WIP Inventory: Engine Assembly	200,000	
Materials Inventory		200,000

2. Conversion costs for Engine Assembly are recorded as follows:

WIP Inventory: Engine Assembly	100,000	
Wages Payable and Manufacturing Overhead Applied Accounts		100,000

3. The transfer of the costs from Engine Assembly to Final Assembly is:

WIP Inventory: Final Assembly	300,000	
WIP Inventory: Engine Assembly		300,000

4. The materials added in Final Assembly are accounted for in the following entry:

WIP Inventory: Final Assembly	300,000	
Materials Inventory		300,000

5. The conversion costs incurred in Final Assembly are recorded as follows:

WIP Inventory: Final Assembly 200,000
    Wages Payable and Manufacturing
      Overhead Applied Accounts   200,000

6. Now the entire manufacturing cost of Work Order No. 101 has been incurred. This cost is transferred to Finished Goods Inventory in the following entry:

Finished Goods Inventory 800,000
    WIP Inventory: Final Assembly   800,000

2

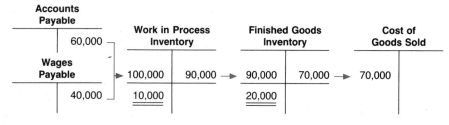

Traditional Costing

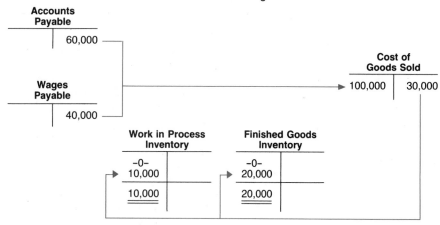

Backflush Costing

3 First, compute the equivalent units:

	Direct Materials		Conversion Costs	
Transferred out	20,000		20,000	
Spoiled 2,000 units	2,000	(100%)	1,600	(80%)
Ending inventory, 6,000 units	2,400	(40%)	1,500	(25%)
Totals	24,400	E.U.	23,100	E.U.

The total costs to be accounted for are:

Beginning inventory	$10,000	$ 20,000
Current costs	40,000	80,000
Totals	$50,000	$100,000

Next, compute costs per equivalent unit:

$50,000 \div 24,400$ E.U. $= \$2.049$ per E.U. (rounded)
$100,000 \div 23,100$ E.U. $= \$4.329$ per E.U. (rounded)

Then, multiply by the equivalent units spoiled:

Direct materials: $\$2.049 \times 2,000$ E.U. $= \$4,098$
Conversion costs: $\$4.329 \times 1,600$ E.U. $= \$6,926$

The total spoiled unit cost is $11,024 (= \$4,098 + \$6,926).

Allocating Costs to Departments

LEARNING OBJECTIVES

After reading this chapter, you should be able to:

1. Explain why costs are allocated.
2. Explain issues in selecting allocation bases.
3. Allocate service department costs using the direct method.
4. Allocate service department costs using the step method.
5. Allocate service department costs using the reciprocal method.
6. Analyze the effect of dual compared to single allocation bases.
7. Explain multiple-factor cost allocation.

---

*T*his chapter discusses cost allocation. Cost allocation is often controversial, as indicated by the following conversation between a small business manager, Joe, and his accountant/efficiency expert.[1]

Expert: Joe, you said you put in these peanuts because some people ask for them, but do you realize what this rack of peanuts is *costing* you?

Joe: It's not going to cost! It's going to be a profit. Sure, I had to pay $100 for a fancy rack to hold the bags, but the peanuts cost 24 cents a bag and I sell 'em for 40 cents. Suppose I sell 50 bags a week to start. It'll take 12½ weeks to cover the cost of the rack. After that I have a clear profit of 16 cents a bag. The more I sell, the more I make.

Expert: That is an antiquated and completely unrealistic approach, Joe. Fortunately, modern accounting procedures permit a more accurate picture, which reveals the complexities involved.

Joe: Huh?

---

[1] This piece appeared in a publication by Coopers & Lybrand as a reprint. The author is unknown to us.

Expert: To be precise, those peanuts must be integrated into your entire operation and be allocated their appropriate share of business overhead. They must share a proportionate part of your expenditures for rent, heat, light, equipment depreciation, decorating, salaries for your waitresses, cook, . . .

Joe: The *cook?* What's he got to do with the peanuts? He doesn't even know I have them.

Expert: Look, Joe, the cook is in the kitchen, the kitchen prepares the food, the food is what brings people in here, and the people ask to buy peanuts. *That's* why you must charge a portion of the cook's wages, as well as a part of your own salary, to peanut sales. This sheet contains a carefully calculated cost analysis, which indicates the peanut operation should pay exactly $2,278 per year toward these general overhead costs.

Joe: The peanuts? $2,278 a year for overhead? Nuts! The peanuts salesman said I'd make money—put 'em on the end of the counter, he said—and get 16 cents a bag profit.

Expert: [*With a sniff*] He's not an accountant. Do you actually know what the portion of the counter occupied by the peanut rack is worth to you?

Joe: Nothing. No stool there—just a dead spot at the end.

Expert: The modern cost picture permits no dead spots. Your counter contains 60 square feet, and your counter business grosses $60,000 a year. Consequently, the square foot of space occupied by the peanut rack is worth $1,000 per year. Since you have taken that area away from general counter use, you must charge the value of the space to the occupant.

Joe: [*Eagerly*] Look! I have a better idea. Why don't I just throw the nuts out—put them in a trash can?

Expert: Can you afford it?

Joe: Sure. All I have is about 50 bags of peanuts—cost about 12 bucks—so I lose $100 on the rack, but I'm out of this nutsy business and no more grief.

Expert: [*Shaking head*] Joe, it isn't quite that simple. You are *in* the peanut business! The minute you throw those peanuts out, you are adding $2,278 of annual overhead to the *rest* of your operation. Joe—be realistic—*can you afford to do that?*

Joe: [*Completely crushed*] It's unbelievable! Last week I was making money. Now I'm in trouble—just because I believe 50 bags of peanuts a week is easy.

Expert: [*With raised eyebrow*] That is the object of modern cost studies, Joe—to dispel those false illusions.

What should Joe do?

Joe should fire his accountant/efficiency expert. Joe has made a business decision that likely has little or no effect on overhead, yet the expert wants to allocate overhead to the otherwise unused counter space. During your career, you will have many encounters with other people about cost allocation. Don't be mislead by "experts." Use common sense.

WHAT IS COST ALLOCATION?

Cost Allocation The process of assigning indirect costs to cost objects.

Cost Object Any end to which a cost is assigned.

Common Costs Costs of shared facilities, products, or services.

Cost allocation is a proportional assignment of an indirect cost to **cost objects.** For example, if two divisions share a facility that costs $15,000, that shared cost is referred to as an indirect or **common cost.** If we decide that the cost should be shared based on, say, the number of employees in each department, then the number of employees is the allocation base and the departments are the cost objects. Carrying this one step further, if 40 percent of the employees are in the first department, then that department is charged with 40 percent of the $15,000 cost, or $6,000. This $6,000 is the cost allocated to the first department. The remaining 60 percent, or $9,000, is allocated to the second department. All of the common costs are allocated to the departments based on their proportional use of the allocation base. Hence, the full $15,000 has been allocated to the departments based on the relative number of employees in each department.

WHY ARE COSTS ALLOCATED?

There are numerous examples of cost allocation in organizations. Manufacturing overhead is a common cost that is usually allocated to each unit produced by a manufacturer. This allocation is required for financial reporting.

Large organizations often allocate headquarters costs to individual branches. For example, an executive of Kmart, a retail company with more than 2,500 stores, told us: ''Allocating corporate headquarters costs to stores makes each store manager aware that these costs exist and must be covered by the individual stores for the company as a whole to be profitable.'' This allocation was used as an attention-getting device by management.

Certain corporate overhead must also be allocated to inventories for tax purposes. The allocation method chosen can affect a company's tax liability.

Depreciation of long-term assets is another form of cost allocation required for financial reporting. The purpose of depreciation is to allocate the original cost of the asset over the time periods that the asset helps generate revenues.

In short, allocations are required for a variety of reasons. Because of the cash flow and behavioral effects of allocations, the approach taken must be carefully considered. The usual approach is to relate indirect costs to cost objects using an allocation method that reflects a cause-and-effect association.

THE ARBITRARY NATURE OF COST ALLOCATION

By definition, costs that are common to two or more cost *objects* are likely to be allocated to those cost objects on a somewhat arbitrary basis. This arbitrariness has led critics of cost allocation to claim that arbitrary cost allocations may result in misleading financial reports and poor decisions. Despite these asserted problems, a study of corporate cost allocation found 84 percent of companies participating in the survey reported allocating common headquarters costs to divisions.[2] The study indicated that the

---

[2] See J. M. Fremgren and S. S. Liao, *The Allocation of Corporate Indirect Costs* (New York: National Association of Accountants, now called Institute of Management Accountants, 1981).

primary managerial reason for cost allocation was to *remind responsibility center managers that common costs exist and had to be recovered by division profits*.

COST ALLOCATION METHODS: STAGE 1

The cost allocation process is composed of two stages. The first stage allocates costs to responsibility centers; the second stage allocates responsibility center costs to units. This chapter focuses on stage 1: allocating costs to responsibility centers. In particular, we are concerned with allocating costs of service departments to other departments that use those services.

Nature of Service Departments

Service Department A department that provides service to other subunits in the organization.

User Department A department that uses services of service departments.

Service departments are departments that provide services to other departments. **User departments** use the services of service departments. User departments could be other service departments or production or marketing departments that produce or market the organization's product, as shown in Illustration 6–1.

Illustration 6–2 shows an example of service departments and user departments in a hospital. In this case, the user departments are also production departments. Both the Emergency Room and the X-Ray departments are production departments that use the services of the two service departments: Information Services and Maintenance.

If you have ever been an emergency room patient, you used the hospital's products, which were the services provided by the Emergency Room and X-Ray departments. Maintenance cleaned up after you in those two departments, and Information Services kept track of your medical history and billing information. To the Emergency Room and X-Ray departments, you were the customer. To Maintenance and Information Services, the customers were X-Ray and the Emergency Room. Our task, in this chapter, is to determine how to allocate costs of service departments, such as Mainte-

---

ILLUSTRATION

6–1

Service and User Departments

Service Department provides service to the final user department

Service Department A provides service to Service Department B, which provides service to the final user department.

nance and Information Services, to the production departments, such as Emergency Room and X-Ray.

Service organizations, merchandising organizations, and manufacturing organizations all have production or marketing departments *and* service departments. Examples of production or marketing and service departments are:

Organization	Service Department	Production or Marketing Department
Manufacturing plant	Maintenance	Assembly
Marshall Fields	Data Processing	Sportswear
Massachusetts General Hosp.	Laundry	Emergency Room
City of Miami	Motor Pool	City parks

Manufacturing Term used to describe production departments in organizations that manufacture goods, such as an Assembly Department.

Intermediate Cost Center A cost center whose costs are charged to other departments in the organization.

Final Cost Center A cost center, such as a production or marketing department, from which costs are not allocated to another cost center.

The terms **manufacturing** and *production* are not synonymous—production is broader than manufacturing. In this book, when we refer to *manufacturing* departments, we specifically mean *production* departments in organizations that manufacture goods, such as an Assembly Department. An example of a production department in a service organization is the Tax Department of a public accounting firm like Deloitte and Touche.

Service departments are sometimes called **intermediate cost centers**, while production or marketing departments would be the **final cost centers**.

Next we discuss one of the most challenging tasks in cost allocation: selecting the base(s) for allocating costs to user departments.

ILLUSTRATION   *Examples of Service and User Departments*

6–2

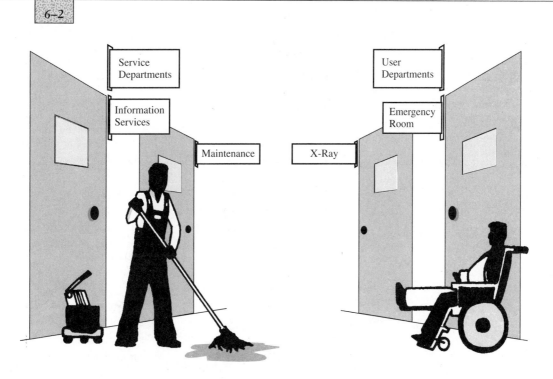

Choosing Allocation Bases

Allocation Base A measure related to two or more cost objects that is used to allocate indirect or common costs to those cost objects.

Cost Driver A factor that causes or drives an activity's costs.

Most common costs can be categorized into one of four groups. Certain bases of allocation are commonly associated with each. An **allocation base** is some measure related to cost objects that is used to allocate indirect or common costs shared by those cost objects. The allocation bases should reflect factors that cause the common costs to occur. For any common cost, one or more **cost drivers**, or allocation bases, may be used:

1. *Labor-related common costs.* Labor-related common costs are usually allocated on the basis of number of employees, labor-hours, wages paid, or similar labor-related criteria. (See items 1 and 2 in Illustration 6–3.)

2. *Machine-related common costs.* Machine-related common costs are usually allocated on the basis of machine-hours, current value of machinery and equipment, number of machines, or similar machine-related criteria. (See items 3 through 6 in Illustration 6–3.)

3. *Space-related common costs.* Space-related common costs are usually allocated on the basis of area occupied, volume occupied, or similar space-related criteria. (See items 7 through 11 in Illustration 6–3.)

4. *Service-related common costs.* Service-related common costs may be allocated on the basis of quantity, value, time, and similar service-related criteria. (See items 12 through 16 in Illustration 6–3.)

These allocation bases are examples only. Common costs should be analyzed case by case to determine the most suitable allocation base.

ILLUSTRATION

6–3

Typical Allocation Bases for Common Costs

		Common Cost	Typical Allocation Base
Labor Related	1.	Supervision	Number of employees Payroll dollars or labor-hours
	2.	Personnel services	Number of employees
Machine Related	3.	Insurance on equipment	Value of equipment
	4.	Taxes on equipment	Value of equipment
	5.	Equipment depreciation	Machine-hours, equipment value
	6.	Equipment maintenance	Number of machines, machine-hours
Space Related	7.	Building rental	Space occupied
	8.	Building insurance	Space occupied
	9.	Heat and air conditioning	Space occupied, volume occupied
	10.	Concession rental	Space occupied and desirability of location
	11.	Interior building maintenance	Space occupied
Service Related	12.	Materials handling	Quantity or value of materials
	13.	Laundry	Weight of laundry processed
	14.	Billing and accounting	Number of documents
	15.	Indirect materials	Value of direct materials
	16.	Dietary	Number of meals

Managers decide on the appropriate allocation base using the following three criteria:

1. *Causal relation.* If possible, find a cause-and-effect relation between the cost object and the cost. For example, if maintenance on an aircraft is scheduled based on the number of flight hours, then number of flight hours is a good basis for allocating maintenance costs to a particular route or flight.

2. *Benefits received.* If a causal relation cannot be found, it would be appropriate to select an allocation base that reflects benefits received. For example, the cost of employee training to improve quality would not necessarily be caused by a particular product, but the product might benefit from the training program.

3. *Reasonableness.* If managers cannot come up with an allocation base that reflects causality or benefits received, then they would select an allocation base that represents a "reasonable" cost allocation. For example, it is reasonable to allocate space-related costs, like housekeeping, on the basis of square feet cleaned.

The Real World Application about Bellcore shows the effect of inappropriate allocations on people's behavior.

REAL WORLD APPLICATION

Inappropriate Cost Allocations*

Bellcore is the central research and engineering organization for the seven regional holding companies that were previously part of the Bell system of companies. Bellcore charges its client companies for its services based on cost. In the 1980s, the company developed a system of internal cost allocations to determine the cost of each research or engineering job performed. Later, management noticed that its technical staff was typing its own letters and preparing its own graphics even though the company had word processing and graphics support available. Technical staff pay rates are way too high to justify their use as typists, yet this was happening at Bellcore.

Upon further investigation, Bellcore management learned that the Word Processing Department was charging $50 per page of document. Similar high costs were reported for other "people-intensive" service departments.

Management established a task force to investigate the situation and to consider options. A comparison with outside word processing companies showed that Bellcore was incurring excessively high building occupancy costs for its word processing group. Bellcore allocated building costs based on area occupied. Although this method is widely used, in Bellcore's case the allocation base did not recognize that a substantial amount of building space was specially constructed for laboratories. Lab space was three times as expensive as the type of office space used for word processing, yet all space was allocated on the same basis. The result was a substantial overcharge to Word Processing, which increased the costs that the Word Processing Department had to recover through page charges.

Costs of the library and travel support were allocated based on number of employees in departments. Further investigation revealed that only technical personnel used the library or took trips. Word Processing was being charged for a share of the library and travel support costs out of all proportion to their benefits from these costs. Again, these costs were passed through in the form of higher charges per page of output.

Bellcore carefully evaluated all of the cost centers and found that significant fine-tuning of its allocating system was in order. After implementing the task force's recommended revisions to the cost allocation system, word processing costs fell to the point where use increased and technical staff found it more economical to work on research and engineering projects rather than to type letters. By adjusting the cost allocation system, the company was able to improve productivity.

* Based on the authors' research.

METHODS OF ALLOCATING SERVICE DEPARTMENT COSTS

In this section, we describe three methods of allocating service department overhead costs: the direct method, the step method, and the reciprocal method. To make each method easier to understand, we use a comprehensive example. While our example is of a manufacturing company, keep in mind that the same methods can be used in nonmanufacturing organizations.

Assume All-Tech Manufacturing has three service departments: Product Engineering (S1), Building Occupancy (S2), and Factory Supervision (S3). Costs are recorded in these departments and allocated to two manufacturing departments and one marketing department: Networks (P1), Terminals (P2), and the Marketing Department (P3). All six departments share the same building.

All-Tech Manufacturing allocates costs to Networks and Terminals for two purposes: (1) to determine the cost of producing and marketing its goods and (2) to encourage department managers to monitor each other's costs; that is, *cross-department monitoring.*

Each service department is an *intermediate cost center* where costs are recorded as incurred and then distributed to other cost centers. At All-Tech Manufacturing, Product Engineering (S1) costs are distributed on the basis of engineering staff time required by the user department. Building Occupancy (S2) costs are distributed on the basis of area occupied by the user department. And Factory Supervision (S3) costs are distributed on the basis of the user department's payroll dollars.

Allocation Bases

Illustration 6–4 shows the basis of allocating costs for each service department and the proportions of costs allocated to user departments. For example, product engineering costs are allocated on the basis of engineering labor-hours worked for each user department. During the period, product engineering worked 14,000 hours for Networks and 56,000 hours for Terminals. Thus, 20 percent of product engineering costs are allocated to Networks

$$\left(20 \text{ percent} = \frac{14,000 \text{ hours}}{14,000 + 56,000 \text{ hours}}\right)$$

and 80 percent to Terminals. Identical methods are used to derive the percentages for allocating building occupancy and factory supervision costs. These percentages are shown in Illustration 6–4.

We use these percentages extensively in the examples that follow.

THE DIRECT METHOD

Direct Method A method of cost allocation that charges costs of service departments to user departments and ignores any services used by other service departments.

The **direct method** allocates costs directly to the final user of a service, ignoring intermediate users. Illustration 6–5 shows the flow of costs and the allocations to be recognized for the departments when the direct method is used. The direct costs of service departments are first recorded in those service departments. These costs are shown on the debit side of the service department accounts. Then, service department costs are allocated to the user departments.

Using the direct method, there are no allocations between service departments. Thus, the building occupancy costs and the factory supervision costs that are attributable to the Product Engineering Department are not allocated to Product Engineering. Likewise, the factory supervision costs that are related to the building occupancy function and the costs of the

ILLUSTRATION

*Bases for Service Department
Cost Allocations*

ALL-TECH MANUFACTURING

Product Engineering (S1)

Allocation base: Product engineering labor-hours worked in each
user department.

User Department	Product Engineering Labor-Hours Used	Proportion of Total
Networks (P1)	14,000	.20
Terminals (P2)	56,000	.80
Marketing (P3)	–0–	–0–
Totals	70,000	1.00

Building Occupancy (S2)

Allocation base: Area (square footage) in each user department.

User Department	Square Footage	Proportion of Total
Networks (P1)	80,000	.32
Terminals (P2)	60,000	.24
Marketing (P3)	60,000	.24
Product Engineering (S1)	20,000	.08
Factory Supervision (S3)	30,000	.12
Totals	250,000	1.00

Factory Supervision (S3)

Allocation base: Annual payroll dollars of user departments.

User Department	Payroll Dollars	Proportion of Total
Networks (P1)	$360,000	.45
Terminals (P2)	240,000	.30
Marketing (P3)	–0–	–0–
Product Engineering (S1)	120,000	.15
Building Occupancy (S2)	80,000	.10
Totals	$800,000	1.00

building space occupied by the factory supervision activity are not allocated
to their respective service departments.

The use of the direct method of cost allocation at All-Tech Manufacturing is discussed below and shown in Illustration 6–6. Assume the accounting records show that costs of $36,000, $84,000, and $25,000 are recorded in each service department, S1, S2, and S3, respectively. Costs are allocated *directly* to Networks (P1), Terminals (P2), and Marketing (P3)—hence the name *direct* method.

Note these are overhead costs only. Direct labor and direct materials are recorded in work in process accounts using the methods described in Chapters 3, 4, and 5. After service department manufacturing overhead has been allocated to each department's Manufacturing Overhead account, manage-

I L L U S T R A T I O N   *Flow of Cost Allocations—Direct Method*

ALL-TECH MANUFACTURING

Service Departments	User Departments

Product Engineering Department (S1)

Direct costs of product engineering 36,000	Allocated to: Manufacturing Overhead: Networks Terminals

Manufacturing Overhead—Networks (P1)

Direct overhead costs of Manufacturing Department 1 Allocated costs from service departments: Product Engineering Building Occupancy Factory Supervision	

Building Occupancy Department (S2)

Direct costs of building occupancy 84,000	Allocated to: Manufacturing Overhead: Networks Terminals Marketing

Manufacturing Overhead—Terminals (P2)

Direct overhead costs of Manufacturing Department 2 Allocated costs from service departments: Product Engineering Building Occupancy Factory Supervision	

Factory Supervision Department (S3)

Direct costs of factory supervision 25,000	Allocated to: Manufacturing Overhead: Networks Terminals

Marketing (P3)

Direct costs to the Marketing Department Allocated costs from service departments: Building Occupancy	

ment knows the actual manufacturing overhead for each manufacturing department.

Allocate Product Engineering Department Costs

Product Engineering Department costs of $36,000 are allocated to P1, P2, and P3 based on the product engineering labor-hours used by P1, P2, and P3. According to the facts given in Illustration 6–4, P1 (Networks) used 20 percent and P2 (Terminals) used 80 percent of the total product engineering labor-hours. The Marketing Department did not use any product engineering labor-hours. Hence, the allocation of Product Engineering Department costs is simply:

$$
\begin{array}{lrll}
\text{P1} & \dots\dots\dots & 20\% \times \$36,000 = & \$\ 7,200 \\
\text{P2} & \dots\dots\dots & \underline{80}\quad \times\ 36,000 = & \underline{28,800} \\
& \text{Total}\ \dots & \underline{\underline{100\%}} & \underline{\underline{\$36,000}}
\end{array}
$$

These proportions are used to allocate product engineering costs, as shown in Illustration 6–6. [Read across the Product Engineering (S1) row.]

*Cost Allocation
Computations—Direct
Method*

Panel A: Proportions

| | | Proportion Chargeable to: | | |
Service Department	Department's Direct Costs	Networks (P1)	Terminals (P2)	Marketing (P3)
Product Engineering (S1)	$36,000	.2	.8	–0–
Building Occupancy (S2)	84,000	.4	.3	.3
Factory Supervision (S3)	25,000	.6	.4	–0–

Panel B: Direct Method Cost Allocation

| From: | | To: | | |
Service Department	Amount	Networks (P1)	Terminals (P2)	Marketing (P3)
Product Engineering (S1)	$ 36,000	$ 7,200	$28,800	–0–
Building Occupancy (S2)	84,000	33,600	25,200	$25,200
Factory Supervision (S3)	25,000	15,000	10,000	–0–
Total allocated	$145,000	$55,800	$64,000	$25,200

Panel C: Selected Additional Computations	Amount Allocated	Proportions, from Panel A		Amount to Be Allocated
Product Engineering:	$ 7,200	= .2	×	$36,000
Building Occupancy:	$33,600	= .4	×	$84,000
	$25,200	= .3	×	$84,000
Factory Supervision:	$15,000	= .6	×	$25,000

Allocate Building Occupancy Department Costs

Building Occupancy Department costs are distributed to P1, P2, and P3 in
the same ratio as the proportions of the square footage occupied by those
departments alone. That is, the square footage proportions for P1, P2, and
P3, based on data given in Illustration 6–4, are:

$$
\begin{array}{ll}
\text{P1} \ldots \ldots \ldots & .32 \\
\text{P2} \ldots \ldots \ldots & .24 \\
\text{P3} \ldots \ldots \ldots & \underline{.24} \\
\text{Total} \ldots & \underline{.80}
\end{array}
$$

When these are scaled to 100 percent, we have:

$$
\begin{array}{lll}
\text{P1} \ldots \ldots \ldots & 40\% & = .32/.80 \\
\text{P2} \ldots \ldots \ldots & 30 & = .24/.80 \\
\text{P3} \ldots \ldots \ldots & \underline{30} & = .24/.80 \\
\text{Total} \ldots & \underline{100\%}
\end{array}
$$

These proportions are used to allocate Building Occupancy Department
costs as shown in Illustration 6–6. [Read across the Building Occupancy (S2)
row.]

Allocate Factory Supervision Department Costs

Similar calculations are made for Factory Supervision Department costs that are allocated on the basis of labor-dollars. The labor-dollars proportions for P1, P2, and P3 are (see Illustration 6–4):

$$
\begin{array}{lr}
\text{P1} & .45 \\
\text{P2} & .30 \\
\text{P3} & \underline{.00} \\
\text{Total} & \underline{\underline{.75}}
\end{array}
$$

When these are scaled to 100 percent, we have:

$$
\begin{array}{lrl}
\text{P1} & 60\% & = .45/.75 \\
\text{P2} & 40 & = .30/.75 \\
\text{P3} & \underline{\;\;0} & = 0/.75 \\
\text{Total} & \underline{\underline{100\%}}
\end{array}
$$

These proportions are used to allocate Factory Supervision Department costs, as shown in Illustration 6–6. [Read across the Factory Supervision (S3) row.]

Once these proportions are computed, the allocation proceeds with the cost distribution shown in Illustration 6–6. The Product Engineering costs of $36,000 are allocated $7,200 (or 20 percent) to Manufacturing Overhead—Networks, and $28,800 (or 80 percent) to Manufacturing Overhead—Terminals. The total allocated ($7,200 + $28,800) equals the total costs in the product engineering intermediate cost center ($36,000). (The step of scaling to 100 percent assures this result.)

Panels B and C explain allocations for the other two service centers. As a result of these allocations, the total service department costs charged are: to Networks, $55,800; to Terminals, $64,000; and to Marketing, $25,200.

Limitations of the Direct Method

Some people have criticized the direct method because it ignores services provided by one service department to another. If one purpose of cost allocation is to encourage cross-department monitoring, then the direct method falls short because it ignores the costs that service departments themselves incur when they use other service departments. An attempt to remedy this problem has resulted in the *step method* of allocating service department costs, discussed in the next section.

Self-Study Question

1 T. Schurt & Company manufactures and sells T-shirts for advertising and promotional purposes. The company has two manufacturing operations: shirtmaking and printing. When an order for T-shirts is received, the Shirtmaking Department obtains the materials and colors requested and has the shirts made in the desired mix of sizes. The completed shirts are then sent to the Printing Department where the custom labels or designs are prepared and embossed on the shirts.

To support the manufacturing activity, the company has a building that houses the two manufacturing departments as well as the Sales Department, a payroll department, and a design and patterns staff. To aid in cost control, the company accumulates the costs of these support functions in separate service cost centers: (1) building occupancy, (2) payroll accounting, and (3) design and patterns.

During the current period, the direct costs incurred in each of the departments are as follows:

Shirtmaking (P1)	$210,000
Printing (P2)	140,000
Sales (P3)	80,000
Building Occupancy (S1)	45,000
Payroll Accounting (S2)	20,000
Design and Patterns (S3) . . .	10,000

Building occupancy costs are allocated on the basis of the number of square feet of each user department. Payroll accounting costs are allocated on the basis of the number of employees. The design and pattern costs are charged to departments on the basis of the number of designs requested by each department. For the current period, the following table summarizes the usage of services by other service cost centers and other departments:

	S1	S2	S3	P1	P2	P3
Building Occupancy (S1) (square feet)	—	8,100	3,900	27,000	36,000	6,000
Payroll Accounting (S2) (employees)	3	—	6	30	15	6
Design and Patterns (S3) (designs)	—	—	—	15	40	5

Using the direct method for service cost allocations, what are the total costs in each of the three "producing" departments?

The solution to this question is at the end of this chapter on page 236.

THE STEP METHOD

Step Method The method of service department cost allocation that recognizes some interservice department services.

The **step method** recognizes services provided to other service departments. Allocations usually begin from the service department that has provided the greatest proportion of its total services to other service departments or that services the greatest *number* of other departments. Once an allocation is made *from* a service department, no further allocations are made back *to* that department. Hence, a service department that provides services to another service department and also receives services from that department will have only one of these two reciprocal relationships recognized. By choosing the allocation order suggested, we minimize the number of relationships that are ignored in the step allocation process. For example, when the step method is used at All-Tech, costs are allocated from the Factory Supervision Department to the Building Occupancy Department, but not vice versa as discussed below.

An analysis of service usage among service departments of All-Tech indicates that Factory Supervision supplies 25 percent of its services to other service departments, while Building Occupancy supplies 20 percent of its services to other service departments. (See Illustration 6–4.) Product

Engineering provides no services to other service departments. Based on services provided to other service departments, the rank ordering for step allocation is:

Order	Service Department
1	Factory Supervision (S3)
2	Building Occupancy (S2)
3	Product Engineering (S1)

Allocating Factory Supervision Department Costs
Factory supervision costs would be allocated to all service departments that made use of Factory Supervision's services, whereas Building Occupancy's costs would be allocated only to the service department that ranks below it in the allocation order. Recall that under the step method, once a service department's costs have been allocated to other departments, no costs can be allocated back to it. The computation of service department costs allocated to other service departments at All-Tech is shown in Illustration 6–7.

Factory Supervision Department costs are charged to user departments based on the total labor-dollars recorded for each. The distribution results in 15 percent of the $25,000 in Factory Supervision Department costs being charged to Product Engineering, 10 percent to Building Occupancy, 45 percent to Networks, and the remaining 30 percent to Terminals (based on Illustration 6–4). [See the Factory Supervision (S3) row in Panel A of Illustration 6–7.]

Allocating Building Occupancy Department Costs
In calculating the allocation of Building Occupancy Department costs (second in the allocation order), the step method ignores the area occupied by the Factory Supervision Department because costs have already been allocated from that department. As a result, the portion of Building Occupancy Department costs to be allocated to Product Engineering is determined by taking the 20,000 square feet used by Product Engineering (as shown in Illustration 6–4) and dividing by the 220,000 square-foot basis (250,000 total square feet less the 30,000 occupied by Factory Supervision). The result is approximately 9 percent.

The total cost to be allocated from Building Occupancy is $86,500, which equals the sum of the direct costs ($84,000) plus the allocated costs ($2,500 from Factory Supervision). Therefore, the transfer to Product Engineering is 9 percent of $86,500, which equals $7,785. Similar computations are made to allocate Building Occupancy's costs to the other departments as shown in Illustration 6–7.

Allocating Product Engineering Costs
Product Engineering was used 20 percent by Networks and 80 percent by Terminals, according to Illustration 6–4. These services are not used by any other service department, so they are allocated directly to the user departments (20 percent to P1 and 80 percent to P2).

The flow of costs under the step method is diagrammed in Illustration 6–8. Notice that Illustration 6–8 differs from Illustration 6–5, which showed cost flows using the direct method, because some costs flow from one service department to another. In addition, the costs allocated *from* service departments include not only the direct costs of the service departments but costs allocated *to* the service departments as well.

I L L U S T R A T I O N   *Cost Allocation Computations—Step Method*

6–7

ALL-TECH MANUFACTURING

Panel A: Proportions

		Proportion Chargeable to:					
Service Department	Department's Direct Costs	S3	S2	S1	P1	P2	P3
Factory Supervision (S3)	$ 25,000	–0–	.10[b]	.15[b]	.45[b]	.30[b]	–0–
Building Occupancy (S2)	84,000	–0–	–0–	.09[a]	.37[a]	.27[a]	.27[a]
Product Engineering (S1)	36,000	–0–	–0–	–0–	.20[b]	.80[b]	–0–
	$145,000						

Panel B: Step Method Allocation:

	Cost Allocation to:					
From:	S3	S2	S1	P1	P2	P3
Direct service department costs	$ 25,000	$ 84,000	$ 36,000			
Factory Supervision (S3)[c]	$(25,000)	2,500	3,750	$11,250	$ 7,500	–0–
Building Occupancy (S2)[d]		$(86,500)	7,785	32,005	23,355	$23,355
Product Engineering (S1)[e]			$(47,535)	9,507	38,028	–0–
Total costs allocated				$52,762	$68,883	$23,355

[a] Allocation of building occupancy to departments on a square footage basis. Total square feet are 220,000, which equals 250,000 total minus 30,000 used by Factory Supervision, according to Illustration 6–4:

.09 = 20,000 ÷ 220,000 square feet (rounded).

Similarly,

.37 = 80,000 ÷ 220,000 square feet (rounded)

and

.27 = 60,000 ÷ 220,000 square feet (rounded)

[b] Percentages from Illustration 6–4.
[c] Factory Supervision (S3):

$2,500 = .10 × $25,000; $3,750 = .15 × $25,000; etc.

[d] Building Occupancy (S2):

$86,500 = $84,000 + $2,500 (allocated costs from S3)
$7,785 = .09 × $86,500; $32,005 = .37 × $86,500; etc.

[e] Product Engineering (S1):

$47,535 = $36,000 + $3,750 + $7,785 (allocated costs from S2)
$9,507 = .20 × $47,535; $38,028 = .80 × $47,535

Proof:
Costs to be allocated = Costs allocated

$25,000 + $84,000 + $36,000 = $52,762 + $68,883 + $23,355

Limitations of the Step Method

The step method may result in more reasonable allocations than the direct method because it recognizes that some service departments are users of other service departments. However, it does not recognize reciprocal services—for example, that Building Occupancy and Factory Supervision both provide and use each other's services. The step method is *not necessarily* better than the direct method when both the costs and benefits of using cost

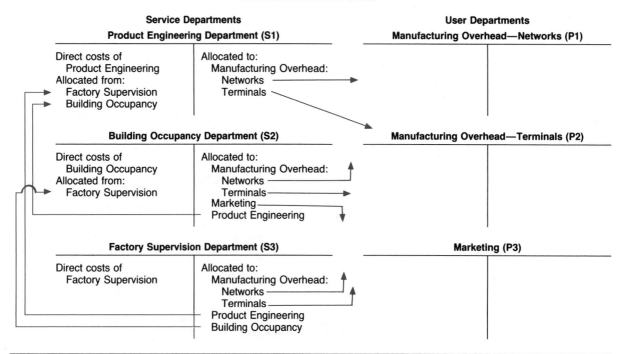

ALL-TECH MANUFACTURING

allocation are taken into account. A company that already uses the direct method may find it uneconomical to switch methods, especially if the only purpose of cost allocation is to value inventory for external financial reporting.

Self-Study Question (Appendix)

2 Refer to the facts for self-study question no. 1. Compute the cost allocations and total costs in each production department using the step method. Assume the order of allocation is S2, S1, S3.

The solution to this question is at the end of this chapter on page 237.

THE RECIPROCAL METHOD

Reciprocal Method The method of service department cost allocation that recognizes all services provided by any service department, including services provided to other service departments.

The reciprocal method addresses a limitation of the step method by making a reciprocal cost allocation when service departments provide reciprocal services (that is, they provide services to each other). The **reciprocal method** recognizes all services provided by any department, including services provided to other service departments.

With the reciprocal method, the costs of each production, marketing, and service department are written in equation form:

$$\text{Total costs} = \frac{\text{Direct costs of}}{\text{the service department}} + \frac{\text{Costs to be allocated}}{\text{to the service department}}$$

I L L U S T R A T I O N

Flow of Cost Allocations—
Reciprocal
Method

ALL-TECH MANUFACTURING

Service Departments

Product Engineering Department (S1)

Direct costs of	Allocated to:
Product Engineering	Manufacturing Overhead:
Allocated from:	Networks
Factory Supervision	Terminals
Building Occupancy	

Building Occupancy Department (S2)

Direct costs of	Allocated to:
Building Occupancy	Manufacturing Overhead:
Allocated from:	Networks
Factory Supervision	Terminals
	Marketing
	Product Engineering
	Factory Supervision

Factory Supervision Department (S3)

Direct costs of	Allocated to:
Factory Supervision	Manufacturing Overhead:
Allocated from:	Networks
Building Occupancy	Terminals
	Product Engineering
	Building Occupancy

The system of equations is then solved simultaneously using matrix algebra. By solving all of the equations simultaneously, we provide for all interservice department allocations. This method is called the *reciprocal method* because it accounts for cost flows in both directions among service departments that provide services to each other. It is also known as the *simultaneous solution method* because it solves a system of equations simultaneously.

The key difference between the step and reciprocal methods can be seen by comparing Illustrations 6–8 and 6–9. Note that the reciprocal method accounts for the reciprocal services between the Building Occupancy and Factory Supervision departments. The step method accounted for only one direction of services—from Factory Supervision to Building Occupancy, but not vice versa.

Both the step method and the direct method understate the cost of running service departments. These methods omit costs of certain services consumed by one service department that were provided by other service departments. For example, only the reciprocal method took into account services provided by Building Occupancy to Factory Supervision.

Reciprocal Method Using Matrix Algebra when There
Are Three or More Service Departments
The mathematical details of the reciprocal method when there are three (or more) service departments are presented in the appendix to this chapter.

ALL-TECH MANUFACTURING

Allocated Service Costs

Department	Direct Method	Step Method	Reciprocal Method[a]
Networks (P1)	$ 55,800	$ 52,762	$ 53,661
Terminals (P2)	64,000	68,883	70,328
Marketing (P3)	25,200	23,355	21,011
Totals	$145,000	$145,000	$145,000

[a] These costs are computed in the appendix to this chapter.

Generally, a computer is used to solve this allocation problem. Illustration 6–10 presents the costs allocated to the Production and Marketing departments using each of the three methods for All-Tech Manufacturing, so you can see the impact on the costs allocated to the user departments.

*Reciprocal Method Using Linear Algebra when There
Are Only Two Service Departments*

When there are only two service departments, linear algebra can be used to solve the allocation problem. To show how this works, we present a simpler example than the one previously used in this chapter.

Assume a company has two service departments, S1 and S2, and three production departments, P1, P2, and P3, with the following direct costs and allocation percentages:

Department	Direct Costs	Percent of Costs Allocated to:				
		S1	S2	P1	P2	P3
S1	$ 79,000	—	30%	30%	30%	10%
S2	26,000	10%	—	15	15	60
	$105,000					

The two service departments' costs may be expressed in equation form as:

$$\frac{\text{Total}}{\text{costs}} = \frac{\text{Direct costs of the}}{\text{service department}} + \frac{\text{Costs to be allocated}}{\text{to the service department}}$$

S1	= $79,000	+ .1 S2	Equation (1)
S2	= $26,000	+ .3 S1	Equation (2)

These yield two equations with two unknowns that can be solved by substitution.

Substituting Equation (2) into Equation (1) gives:

S1 = $79,000 + .1($26,000 + .3 S1)
S1 = $79,000 + $2,600 + .03 S1

Collecting terms and solving:

.97 S1 = $81,600
    S1 = $81,600/.97 = $84,124

Now substituting this value for S1 back into Equation (2) gives:

$$S2 = \$26,000 + .3(\$84,124)$$
$$S2 = \$26,000 + \$25,237$$
$$S2 = \$51,237$$

Thus, costs are simultaneously allocated between the two service departments. The values for S1 ($84,124) and S2 ($51,237) are then used as the total costs of the service departments that are to be allocated to the production departments. The allocations are:

| | | Allocated to: | | | | | |
| | | P1 | | P2 | | P3 | |
From:	Total Cost	Dollars	Percent	Dollars	Percent	Dollars	Percent
S1	$84,124	$25,237	30%	$25,237	30%	$ 8,412	10%
S2	51,237	7,686	15	7,686	15	30,742	60
Totals		$32,923		$32,923		$39,154	

Computations:

	For P1 and P2	For P3
S1:	$25,237 = .3 × $84,124	$ 8,412 = .1 × $84,124
S2:	$ 7,686 = .15 × $51,237	$30,742 = .6 × $51,237

The total cost allocated to the production departments amounts to $105,000 (= $32,923 + $32,923 + $39,154), which equals the costs to be allocated from the service departments ($79,000 + $26,000 = $105,000).

 Self-Study Question

3 Assume a company has two service departments, S1 and S2, and three production departments, P1, P2, and P3, with the following direct costs and allocation percentages:

| | | Percent of Costs Allocated to: | | | | |
Department	Direct Costs	S1	S2	P1	P2	P3
S1	$100,000	—	20%	30%	30%	20%
S2	200,000	10%	—	20	40	30
	$300,000					

What is the allocation of service department costs using the reciprocal method?

The solution to this question is at the end of this chapter on page 238.

COMPARISON OF METHODS

There are two ways to compare these three service department allocation methods. The first is to examine how each allocates costs to departments receiving services. Returning to the All-Tech example, as shown in Illustration 6–11, only the reciprocal method allocates costs to all departments receiving services from other departments.

The second way to compare these three methods is to examine the costs each ultimately allocates to manufacturing and marketing departments, as

*Comparison of Services
Provided with Departments
Receiving Costs for Each
Cost Allocation Method*

ALL-TECH MANUFACTURING

Service Department	Services Provided to:	Departments Receiving Costs under Each Method		
		Direct Method	Step Method	Reciprocal Method[a]
Product Engineering (S1)	P1	P1	P1	P1
	P2	P2	P2	P2
Building Occupancy (S2)	S1	None[b]	S1	S1
	S3	None[b]	None[b]	S3
	P1	P1	P1	P1
	P2	P2	P2	P2
	P3	P3	P3	P3
Factory Supervision (S3)	S1	None[b]	S1	S1
	S2	None[b]	S2	S2
	P1	P1	P1	P1
	P2	P2	P2	P2

[a] Cost computations appear in the appendix to this chapter.

[b] These are user departments receiving services, but costs are not allocated to them under the indicated method.

shown previously in Illustration 6–10. Each method allocates the same total cost for All-Tech—$145,000. The difference is in the amounts allocated to particular manufacturing and marketing departments.

The major factor affecting these allocations is the distribution of building occupancy costs. Under the direct method, the use of the building by other service departments is ignored. This results in a higher cost allocation to the Marketing Department (and less cost allocated to manufacturing) because that department makes no use of the other service departments. As the utilization of the building by other service departments is recognized, the allocation to Marketing decreases.

If these departments' managers' performance evaluations are based on their abilities to keep costs down, then which cost allocation method would they prefer? Answer: According to Illustration 6–10, Marketing would prefer the reciprocal method; Networks would prefer the step method; and Terminals would prefer the direct method!

As a general rule, when there are interservice department activities to which costs can be assigned, the allocations to manufacturing and marketing departments will differ under each method. If there are no interservice department activities, then all three methods will give identical results.

DUAL ALLOCATION RATES

Dual Rate Method A method of cost allocation that separates a common cost into fixed and variable components and then allocates each component using a different allocation base.

When different cost behavior relationships exist between a common cost and a cost object, two or more bases may be used to allocate common costs. When two bases are used, such an allocation is called a **dual rate method.**

For example, United Bank leased computer equipment based on projected demand for services. In addition to costs of leasing the computer, costs are incurred when the equipment is used. (These are mostly supplies and labor costs for computer operators.) Thus, there are two different relationships between the computer costs and the user departments: (1) capacity available to the user department and (2) current time usage.

Assume that the costs of renting the computer and other capacity costs are fixed costs, while the costs incurred for time usage are variable. The following equation could be used to allocate costs:

$$\frac{\text{Rate per unit}}{\text{of time charged}} = \frac{\text{Variable cost}}{\text{per unit of time}} + \frac{\text{Fixed capacity costs}}{\text{Units of time}}$$

Hence, user departments will be charged for an "average" use of both time and capacity. Further, user departments that use a lot of time but do not need much capacity subsidize user departments that need more capacity but do not use as much time.

An alternative method is to divide the computer costs into two separate components:

1. The fixed or capacity costs that are allocated on the basis of *capacity* demanded.
2. The variable costs that are allocated on the basis of *time* used.

With this alternative, the costs assigned to individual departments reflect as closely as possible the relationship between the cost allocated and the factors that caused the company to incur the cost.

For example, United Bank leased a specialty computer for $55,000 per month. This fee is based on the capacity of the equipment and has no relationship to actual usage. The computer costs $250 per hour to operate. Department A requested that it have access to 500 units of capacity, while Department B requested that it have access to 300 units of capacity. During the past month, Department A used 200 hours of computer time, while Department B used 400 hours. Assuming these are the only two departments using the computer, how should the computer costs be allocated?

The bank first considered allocating costs on the basis of *time usage* alone. The cost allocation on the basis of time usage was:

Department A: $\dfrac{200 \text{ department hours used}}{600 \text{ total hours used}} \times \$205{,}000^{a} = \$ 68{,}333$

Department B: $\dfrac{400 \text{ department hours used}}{600 \text{ total hours used}} \times \$205{,}000^{a} = \underline{136{,}667}$

Total cost of the computer center $\underline{\$205{,}000^{a}}$

a $205,000 = $55,000 + [(200 hours + 400 hours) × $250].

When this method was proposed, the manager of Department B argued, "My department is being charged for the monthly fixed rental fee on the basis of computer time used, but that monthly fee might have been lower if Department A had not demanded so much capacity!"

To deal with this argument, the firm next allocated solely on the basis of *capacity demanded*. The resulting allocation was:

Department A: $\dfrac{500 \text{ department units of capacity requested}}{800 \text{ total units of capacity requested}} \times \$205{,}000 = \$128{,}125$

Department B: $\dfrac{300 \text{ department units of capacity requested}}{800 \text{ total units of capacity requested}} \times \$205{,}000 = \underline{76{,}875}$

Total cost of the computer center $\underline{\$205{,}000}$

I L L U S T R A T I O N

Dual Rates for Cost Allocation

Department A:	Capacity: $\frac{5}{8}$ × $55,000		= $ 34,375
	Time:	200 hours × $250 per hour	= 50,000
	Total Department A		$ 84,375
Department B:	Capacity: $\frac{3}{8}$ × $55,000		= $ 20,625
	Time:	400 hours × $250 per hour	= 100,000
	Total Department B		$120,625
	Total cost of the computer center		$205,000

When this method was proposed, the Department B manager was happy, but the Department A manager argued, "My department is being penalized because of our demand for capacity. We believe more costs should be allocated to Department B because they used 400 hours of computer time while we only used 200 hours."

Instead of using either method alone, the firm used a dual rate based on both capacity demanded and time usage. The resulting allocation is shown in Illustration 6–12.

Self-Study Question

4 Dual Division Corporation allocates common costs to its Uno and Duo Divisions. During the past month, the following common costs were incurred:

Computer services (80% fixed) $254,000
Building occupancy   615,000
Personnel   104,000

The following information is available concerning various activity measures and service usages by each of the divisions:

	Uno	Duo
Area occupied	15,000 sq. ft.	40,000 sq. ft.
Payroll	$380,000	$170,000
Computer time	200 hrs.	140 hrs.
Computer storage	25 gbytes	35 gbytes
Equipment value	$175,000	$220,000
Operating profit—before allocations	$439,000	$522,000

a. Allocate the common costs to the two divisions using the most appropriate of the above allocation bases. For computer services, use computer time only.

b. Allocate the common costs to the two divisions using dual rates for the computer services.

The solution to this question is at the end of this chapter on page 238.

MULTIPLE-FACTOR METHOD

The dual method can be extended to multiple factors. The multiple-factor method is often used when there are many relationships between common costs and cost objects.

ILLUSTRATION

Multiple-Factor Method

Division	Fraction		Allocated Cost	
New York	$\dfrac{65\% + 75\% + 40\%}{3}$ = 60%		60% × $300,000	= $180,000
California	$\dfrac{35\% + 25\% + 60\%}{3}$ = 40%		40% × $300,000	= $\underline{120{,}000}$
	Total allocated costs			$300,000

Multiple-Factor Formula An allocation formula that uses multiple bases for allocating costs.

Suppose, for example, that Far Flung Co. wants to allocate corporate headquarters costs to each of its two divisions: New York and California. Some people might assert that headquarters costs are related to the size of the payroll; others might argue that headquarters costs are related to the volume of business. Still others might argue that headquarters costs are related to investment in assets. Actually, all three suggested bases may be valid.

In such cases, a company may use a **multiple-factor formula** that uses multiple bases for allocating costs. For Far Flung Co., the percentage of the common cost to be allocated to a plant may be the arithmetic average of the following three percentages:

1. Percentage of payroll dollars in each division to the total payroll dollars for all divisions.
2. Percentage of volume in each division to the total volume in all divisions.
3. Percentage of the average gross book value of tangible assets of each division to the total gross book value of tangible assets in all divisions.

Assume the company has $300,000 in corporate headquarters costs to apportion to the two divisions. An analysis of company records provides the following information:

Division	Payroll Dollars		Volume of Business		Gross Book Value of Tangible Assets	
	Amount	Percent	Amount	Percent	Amount	Percent
New York	$1,300	65%	$6,750	75%	$ 5,600	40%
California	700	35	2,250	25	8,400	60
Totals	$2,000	100%	$9,000	100%	$14,000	100%

The multiple-factor allocation to each division would be computed as shown in Illustration 6–13.

In recent years, many state taxing authorities have used this "three-factor" formula approach to assign the income of a multistate business to the individual state for state income tax purposes. For example, the State of Illinois Income Tax Return has the following section. (We have included handwritten amounts to make the form easier to follow.)

Business Income Apportionment Formula

		1 Total Everywhere	2 Inside Illinois	3 Column 2 ÷ Column 1		
1 Property factor	1	1,000,000	100,000	.10		
2 Payroll factor	2	200,000	30,000	.15		
3 Sales factor	3	800,000	160,000	.20		
4 Total—add lines 1 through 3					4	.45
5 Average					5	.15

The amount in line 5 is multiplied by total business taxable income to compute the amount of taxable income for the state of Illinois.

States that use these factors assume the measures of property or assets, sales, and payrolls reflect the income generated in the states where the company operates.

Self-Study Question

5 Merrill's Machine Tools Company has two plants and allocates the headquarters' costs to the plants based on a three-factor formula using plant payroll, plant volume, and gross book value of plant tangible assets. The allocation percentage is an arithmetic average of three percentages:

1. Percentage of payroll dollars in each plant to the total payroll dollars for both plants.
2. Percentage of volume, in dollars, in each plant to the total volume in both plants.
3. Percentage of the average gross book value of tangible assets of each plant to the total book value of tangible assets for both plants.

The company has $480,000 in headquarters costs to be allocated. The relevant factors for each plant are:

	Payroll	Volume	Assets
Michigan plant	$120,000	$ 600,000	$ 400,000
Texas plant	180,000	1,000,000	800,000
Total	$300,000	$1,600,000	$1,200,000

Determine the amount of headquarters costs to be allocated to each plant using the multiple-factor allocation method.

The solution to this question is at the end of this chapter on page 239.

INCENTIVE ISSUES IN ALLOCATING COSTS

It is usually advisable to allocate costs on a cause-and-effect basis. If this is not practical, the most reasonable basis possible should be found. By establishing a cause-and-effect relationship for the allocation of costs, service department managers can trace costs to their cause. Moreover, managers of user departments have an incentive to limit their use if the costs of the service center are allocated on a cause-and-effect basis. When the basis of cost allocation does not reflect cause and effect, cost control becomes difficult because departments tend to make excessive demands for underpriced services.

Determining how detailed and precise to make cost allocations is like other managerial decisions—it should be made on a cost-benefit basis. Cost allocation is, in itself, a costly procedure. If the benefits from increasing the detail of cost allocation are minimal, then more detailed cost allocations are probably not economically wise.

Allocating Fixed Service Department Costs

Although the allocation of variable service department costs can be useful for charging user departments, the allocation of fixed costs can have unintended effects. For example, the top administrators of a famous university observed that faculty and staff were using the university's WATS (Wide Area Telephone Service) so much that the lines were seldom free during the day.[3] WATS allowed the university unlimited toll-free service within the United States. The fixed cost of WATS was $10,000 per month; variable cost per call was zero.

University administrators learned that there was an average usage of 50,000 minutes per month on the WATS line, so they initially allocated the $10,000 monthly charge to callers (that is, departments) at a rate of 20 cents per minute ($10,000 ÷ 50,000 minutes). Now that they were being charged for the use of WATS, department heads discouraged their faculty and staff from using the telephone. Hence, the number of minutes used on WATS dropped to 25,000 per month, which increased the rate to 40 cents per minute ($10,000 ÷ 25,000). This continued until the internal cost allocation per minute exceeded the normal long-distance rates, and the use of WATS dropped almost to zero. The university's total telephone bill increased dramatically.[4]

University administrators subsequently compromised by charging a nominal fee of 10 cents per minute. According to the university's chief financial officer, "The 10 cents per minute charge made us aware that there was a cost to the WATS service, albeit a fixed cost. The charge was sufficiently low, however, so as not to discourage bona fide use of WATS."

Cost Allocations in Cost-Plus Contracts

Many organizations sell products on a "cost-plus" basis, where the "plus" is a profit. Defense contractors, for example, traditionally have sold products to national governments on a cost-plus basis. Hospitals and nursing homes traditionally provided medical services and were reimbursed on a cost-plus basis for their costs from government agencies for particular types of patients.

---

[3] This example is based on one given by Jerold L. Zimmerman, "The Costs and Benefits of Cost Allocations," *The Accounting Review,* vol. LIV, no. 354/(1979), pp. 510–11.

[4] The solution to this problem is not necessarily zero. According to Zimmerman (ibid.), the correct price to charge users is "the cost imposed by forcing others who want to use the WATS line to either wait or place a regular call . . . this cost varies between zero (if no one is delayed) to, at most, the cost of a regular toll call if a user cannot use the WATS line" (p. 510). The necessary procedure to implement such a pricing system is very difficult and costly. Zimmerman suggests that fixed allocations could be a simplified way of approximating the results of the more complicated, theoretically correct pricing systems.

Cost-plus contracts give incentives to the supplier of the good or service to seek as much reimbursement as possible and therefore to allocate as much cost as possible to the product for which reimbursement is possible. For example, suppose McBoheed Aircraft Co. is deciding how to allocate $120 million of overhead between two major lines of business: commercial and governmental. This overhead is common to the two lines of business and cannot be directly traced to either. Commercial products are sold at a price set in the market, but governmental products are sold for cost plus a fixed profit. Thus, every dollar of overhead that can be allocated to the governmental product line results in an additional dollar of revenue by way of cost reimbursement.

Suppose McBoheed is choosing between labor-hours and machine-hours as the two possible allocation bases. The relative use of labor- and machine-hours and the resulting allocation of overhead follows:

	Lines of Business	
	Commercial	Governmental
Percent of labor-hours used	30%	70%
Percent of machine-hours used	60	40

Naturally, McBoheed would prefer to allocate the $120 million using labor-hours because it could seek reimbursement from the government for $84 million (70 percent × $120 million), whereas it could seek reimbursement for only $48 million (40 percent × $120 million) using machine-hours.

McBoheed would be $36 million ($84 million − $48 million) better off if it could use labor-hours as the allocation base. Of course, the government could argue for machine-hours. Since the allocable costs cannot, by definition, be directly attributed to a contract, allocation debates abound in cost-plus contracting.

In cases like these, it is important to specify in the contract precisely how costs will be defined and how allocations will be made. Facing numerous disputes over cost reimbursements, the U.S. government established the Cost Accounting Standards Board to establish cost accounting standards that would serve to reduce disputes between defense contractors and government agencies.

Moral

The moral of the cost allocation story is as follows: Cost allocations are common in all types of organizations. Costs are allocated for a variety of reasons—for example, to satisfy regulatory and external financial reporting requirements; to meet contract requirements (for example, in cost-reimbursement defense contracts); to encourage cross-department monitoring of costs; to make user department personnel aware of costs incurred by service departments; and to compute product costs for decision making. Costs allocated for one purpose usually have unexpected side effects. Hence, cost allocations should be made much like doctors prescribe medicine—''with an eye on the side effects.''

ETHICAL ISSUES

The inherent arbitrariness of cost allocation implies there is often no clear-cut way to allocate costs. A lack of objective guidelines for allocating costs often leads to difficult ethical choices. An example that was touched on above is the allocation of costs in cost-plus contracts. We have seen cases in which the contracts specified "manufacturing cost plus a profit" where the producer hid advertising, general administrative, and similar costs in manufacturing overhead. Many legal actions involving contract disputes and tax disputes arise because people have allocated costs in inappropriate ways.

SUMMARY

Cost allocation is the process of assigning common costs to two or more cost objects. Manufacturing overhead is common to units produced, for example, and is allocated to provide product cost information for managers (and for inventory valuation). People sometimes make allocations in an arbitrary manner. Ideally, cost allocation reflects a cause-and-effect relation between costs and the objects to which they are allocated.

The first stage of cost allocation, which is the one discussed in this chapter, is to allocate costs to departments and other responsibility centers. This stage involves selecting a basis for allocation, such as the following:

1. Labor related—number of employees, labor-hours, labor costs.
2. Machine related—machine-hours, value of machinery.
3. Space related—area occupied.
4. Service related—computer usage, service personnel time.

A major reason for allocating costs to departments is to make the department manager and other personnel in the department accountable for costs. A service department is directly responsible for its own costs. But departments that use the services of service departments are also responsible for the service departments' costs.

Another reason to allocate service department costs to production departments is to figure out the costs of producing products. Also, in manufacturing companies, service department costs must be allocated to production departments to determine the value of any inventory the production department may have.

In the first stage of cost allocation, service department costs are allocated to user departments as follows:

1. Departments that provide and use each other's services are identified. At All-Tech Manufacturing, for example, Networks used the services of all three service departments.
2. Allocation bases are established. (Production Engineering's costs were allocated to user departments based on the engineering labor-hours worked in each user department.)
3. One of three methods of allocating service department costs is selected:
   a. Direct method.
   b. Step method.
   c. Reciprocal method.

The direct method allocates costs only to production and marketing departments. The step method recognizes some, but not all, service departments as user departments. Costs are allocated in steps, usually beginning with an allocation from the service department that provides the greatest portion of its services to other service departments. Once an allocation is made *from* a service department, no more costs can be allocated *to* it. The reciprocal method simultaneously allocates costs to all departments that receive services. Unlike the step and direct methods, all interservice department allocations are recognized.

Dual and multiple bases are often used for cost allocation when there is more than one relationship between a common cost and a cost object. Complexity measures may also be incorporated into allocation systems when a simple allocation base fails to satisfy the cause-and-effect criterion.

TERMS AND CONCEPTS

The following terms and concepts should be familiar to you after reading this chapter:

Allocation Base, *192*   **Intermediate Cost Center**, *191*

Common Costs, *189*   **Manufacturing**, *191*

Cost Allocation, *189*   **Multiple-Factor Formula**, *209*

Cost Drivers, *192*   **Reciprocal Method**, *202*

Cost Object, *189*   **Service Department**, *190*

Direct Method, *194*   **Step Method**, *199*

Dual Rate Method, *206*   **User Department**, *190*

Final Cost Center, *191*

APPENDIX

The Reciprocal Method Using Matrix Algebra

The reciprocal method requires that cost relationships be written in equation form. The method then solves the equations for the total costs to be allocated to each department. The direct costs of each department are typically included in the solution. Thus, for any department, we can state the equation:

Total costs = Direct costs + Allocated costs

The total costs are the unknowns that we attempt to derive.

For example, let's assume the direct overhead costs of the departments at All-Tech Manufacturing are:

Product Engineering (S1) . . . . $ 36,000
Building Occupancy (S2)   84,000
Factory Supervision (S3)   25,000
Networks (P1) 500,000
Terminals (P2) 270,000
Marketing (P3) 185,000

Using the information in Illustration 6–4, the total costs of Networks (P1) may be expressed as:

Total costs = Direct Costs + Allocated costs
P1 = $500,000 + 20% S1 + 32% S2 + 45% S3

Similar equations are constructed for each of the other production departments:

P2 = $270,000 + 80% S1 + 24% S2 + 30% S3
P3 = $185,000 + 0   S1 + 24% S2 + 0   S3

And for the service departments, the equations are:

S1 = $36,000 +   8% S2 + 15% S3
S2 = $84,000   + 10% S3
S3 = $25,000 + 12% S2

Now we have a set of equations that express the total cost of each department as a function of direct costs and allocated costs.

Setting the Equations in Matrix Form

To set the equations up in matrix form for solution, the terms are rearranged so that direct costs are on the right-hand side of the equation and all unknowns are on the left side. Each equation is expanded to include all the departments in the system.

For example, the cost equation of Networks (P1) is rearranged as:

1 P1 + 0 P2 + 0 P3 = .20 S1 + .32 S2 + .45 S3 + $500,000
1 P1 + 0 P2 + 0 P3 − .20 S1 − .32 S2 − .45 S3 = $500,000

This is repeated for all production and service departments. The results are:

1 P1 + 0 P2 + 0 P3 − .20 S1 − .32 S2 − .45 S3 = $500,000
0 P1 + 1 P2 + 0 P3 − .80 S1 − .24 S2 − .30 S3 =   270,000
0 P1 + 0 P2 + 1 P3 − 0   S1 − .24 S2 − 0   S3 =   185,000
0 P1 + 0 P2 + 0 P3 + 1   S1 − .08 S2 − .15 S3 =   36,000
0 P1 + 0 P2 + 0 P3 − 0   S1 + 1   S2 − .10 S3 =   84,000
0 P1 + 0 P2 + 0 P3 − 0   S1 − .12 S2 + 1   S3 =   25,000

Each equation may be interpreted as follows: The costs in any department before allocation (the right-hand side) equals the costs after allocation (the P terms) less the allocations that are to be charged to the service departments (the S terms with negative coefficients).

Reforming the system of equations in matrix notation saves repetition of all of the symbols for the unknowns and results in the following system of matrixes and vectors:

$$
\begin{bmatrix}
1 & 0 & 0 & -.20 & -.32 & -.45 \\
0 & 1 & 0 & -.80 & -.24 & -.30 \\
0 & 0 & 1 & 0 & -.24 & 0 \\
0 & 0 & 0 & 1 & -.08 & -.15 \\
0 & 0 & 0 & 0 & 1 & -.10 \\
0 & 0 & 0 & 0 & -.12 & 1
\end{bmatrix}
\times
\begin{bmatrix}
P1 \\ P2 \\ P3 \\ S1 \\ S2 \\ S3
\end{bmatrix}
=
\begin{bmatrix}
\$500,000 \\ 270,000 \\ 185,000 \\ 36,000 \\ 84,000 \\ 25,000
\end{bmatrix}
$$

To solve for the vector of unknowns (that is, the Ps and Ss), matrix algebra is used. If the matrix is labeled *A*, the vector of unknowns *X*, and the vector of direct costs *B*, the matrix form of the equation may be summarized as:

$AX = B$

To solve for X, we multiply both sides by the inverse of A, which is noted A^{-1}. This gives:

$$X = A^{-1}B$$

Computing the inverse of a matrix is tedious without the use of a computer.

Solving the Equations

Spreadsheet programs with built-in matrix capabilities may be used to solve this system of equations. One approach is to enter the coefficients matrix (A) beginning in the upper left corner of the spreadsheet.

Using Lotus 123™, these coefficients are entered in Cells A1 through F6 of the spreadsheet. Then use the /**DMI** (Data Matrix Invert) command to perform the matrix inversion. The data range is A1 through F6. The inverse may be output anywhere, but telling the program that the output range begins in Cell A9 allows the entire program and solution to appear on the screen. The computer then computes the matrix inverse and displays it in the range A9 through F14.

Next, enter the vector of direct costs (B) in Cells G9 through G14. To multiply A^{-1} by B, use the /**DMM** command. The first data range is the A matrix inverse, which is A9 through F14. The second data range is G9 through G14. The output range can be anywhere, but if you use H9, the results appear on the same screen. The output vector is the total cost assigned to each of the producing departments in the same order as included in the vector of unknowns (X).

The inverse of A as it appears on the screen is as follows:[5]

$$\begin{bmatrix} 1 & 0 & 0 & 0.20 & 0.3984 & 0.5198 \\ 0 & 1 & 0 & 0.80 & 0.3587 & 0.4559 \\ 0 & 0 & 1 & 0 & 0.2429 & 0.0243 \\ 0 & 0 & 0 & 1 & 0.0992 & 0.1599 \\ 0 & 0 & 0 & 0 & 1.0121 & 0.1012 \\ 0 & 0 & 0 & 0 & 0.1215 & 1.0121 \end{bmatrix}$$

The product of $A^{-1}B$, which is the solutions vector, is as follows:

$$\begin{bmatrix} 553,661 \\ 340,328 \\ 206,011 \\ 48,330 \\ 87,546 \\ 35,509 \end{bmatrix}$$

The amount $553,661 is the total of the direct and allocated costs for Department P1; $340,328 is the total direct and allocated cost for Department P2; and $206,011 (rounded down) is the total direct and allocated cost for Department P3.

The service costs allocated to Department P1 are $53,661, which is the solution vector element $553,661 minus the direct costs of Department P1 ($500,000). Likewise, for Department P2, the allocated costs are $70,328, which is $340,328 less $270,000. Similarly, for Department P3, the allocated

---

[5] Brackets have been added for ease of presentation.

costs are $21,011, which is the difference between the solution vector of $206,011 and the direct costs of $185,000.

Computational Hints

Let *NP* be the number of producing departments and *NS* the number of service departments. The coefficients matrix (*A*) should be square with *NP* + *NS* rows and *NP* + *NS* columns. All of the diagonal elements of the matrix should be 1s. In the first *NP* columns, the off-diagonal elements should all equal 0. In the rightmost *NS* columns, the off-diagonal elements are all negative. The sum of the rightmost *NS* columns should equal 0, within rounding.

You can check to see that the total of the costs charged to the producing departments equals the sum of the direct costs by using the @**SUM** command for H9 through H11 and comparing that total to the sum of G9 through G14. The check total is $1,100,000.

If these computational notes are followed, chances are quite high that the resulting cost allocation will be computationally correct.

These results may be tabled as follows:

Department	Allocated Cost		Total Cost		Direct Cost
Networks	$ 53,661	=	$553,661	–	$500,000
Terminals	70,328	=	340,328	–	270,000
Marketing	21,011	=	206,011	–	185,000
Total allocated cost	$145,000				

As a result of the allocation, a total of $145,000 has been allocated from the service departments to the operating departments. All of the interrelationships among service departments have been taken into account in this allocation.

Self-Study Question

6 Using the data provided in the T. Schurt & Company example in self-study question no. 1, compute the cost allocation and total costs for each producing department using the reciprocal method.

The solution to this question is at the end of this chapter on page 239.

QUESTIONS

6–1 If cost allocations are arbitrary and potentially misleading, should we assume that management is foolish for using information based on allocated costs?

6–2 What are some of the costs of cost allocation?

6–3 What are some of the benefits of cost allocation?

6–4 What principle is used to decide whether to allocate costs to cost objects?

6–5 One critic of cost allocation noted: "You can avoid the problem of arbitrary cost allocations by simply not allocating any common costs to other cost objects." What are your thoughts on this suggestion?

6–6   What are some management uses of information based on allocated costs?

6–7   Refer to the Real World Application about Bellcore on page 193. What effect did the initial cost allocations have? Why were the allocated costs so high?

6–8   List four broad categories of common costs and the usual basis for allocation of costs in each category.

6–9   A cost such as company headquarters cost does not fit into any one of the broad categories of common costs. A cost such as this may be a result of a number of different causal factors. Is there a way to allocate such a cost? Describe the approach.

6–10 Direct materials are considered direct with respect both to the manufacturing department using the materials and to the product. However, indirect materials cannot be associated directly with a specific job or product but may be related directly to the manufacturing department where the indirect materials are used. Explain the concepts *direct* and *indirect* in this setting.

6–11 What argument(s) could be given in support of the reciprocal method as the preferred method for distributing the costs of service departments?

6–12 Under what conditions would the results obtained from using the direct method of allocations be the same as the results from using either other method? Why?

6–13 Consider a company with two producing departments and one service department. The service department distributes its costs to the producing departments on the basis of number of employees in each department. If the costs in the service department are fixed, what effect would the addition of employees in one department have on the costs allocated to the other department? Comment on the reasonableness of the situation.

6–14 Compare and contrast the direct method, the step method, and the reciprocal method of allocating costs.

6–15 The manager of an operating department just received a cost report and has made the following comment with respect to the costs allocated from one of the service departments: "This charge to my division does not seem right. The service center installed equipment with more capacity than our division requires. Most of the service department costs are fixed, but we seem to be allocated more costs when other departments use less. We are paying for excess capacity of other departments when other departments cut their usage levels." How might this manager's problem be solved?

6–16 What criterion should be used to determine the order of allocation from service departments when the step method is used? Explain why.

EXERCISES

6–17 Why Costs Are Allocated
(L.O.1)

The Hatfields and the McCoys own two adjacent tracts of land. Each tract has a surface area of 4,000 acres. During a recent shoot-out, crude oil came bubbling to the surface where a bullet had entered the ground. A petroleum geologist determined that there was an underground rock formation that contained a substantial amount of oil and extended under both tracts of land. The formation was estimated at 800,000 acre feet of volume, of which 200,000 acre feet was under the McCoy's tract of land.

The Hatfields and the McCoys received an offer to buy the mineral rights for $8.5 million provided that they can agree on how much of the purchase price should be allocated to each family.

Required:

a. As a Hatfield, what basis would you recommend for allocating the purchase price? What arguments would you use to support your claim?

b. As a McCoy, what basis would you recommend for allocating the purchase price? What arguments would you use to support your claim?

6–18 Alternative Allocation Bases
(L.O.2)

For each of the types of common costs in the first column, select the most appropriate allocation base from the second column:

Common Cost	Allocation Base
Building utilities	Value of inventories
Payroll accounting	Number of units produced
Property taxes on inventories	Number of employees
Equipment repair	Space occupied
Quality control inspection	Number of service calls

6–19 Alternative Allocation Bases—Service
(L.O.2)

WARP Enterprises has a TV and a radio station that share the common costs of the company's AP wire service, which is $50,000 a year. You have the following information about the AP wire and the two stations:

Station	Wire Service—Hours Used This Period	Hours of News Broadcasts
TV	450	100
Radio	300	460

Required:

a. What is the AP wire service cost charged to each station if wire service–hours are used as an allocation basis?

b. What is the AP wire service cost charged to each station using hours of news broadcast as a basis for allocation?

c. Which method allocates more costs to TV? Which method allocates more costs to radio?

6–20 Alternative Allocation Bases
(L.O.2)

Acme Corporation operates a supermarket in Kennett Square, Pennsylvania. The store has 120,000 square feet. Each department in the store is charged with a share of the cost of the building. The following information is available concerning two of the departments in the store:

	Department	
	Meat	Dry Goods
Sales revenues	$500,000	$600,000
Cost of goods sold	170,000	180,000
Salaries and other direct expenses	110,000	140,000
Allocated administrative expenses	50,000	55,000
Operating profit before building occupancy costs	$170,000	$225,000
Area occupied	10,000 sq. ft.	30,000 sq. ft.

Other departments use the other 80,000 square feet. The total building occupancy costs are $800,000 per year.

Required:

a. If area occupied is the basis for allocation of building occupancy costs, what is the operating profit or loss for each of these two departments?

b. Would you allocate based on something other than square feet if you learned that the Dry Goods Department is located in a back corner of the store?

6–21 Alternative Allocation Bases (L.O.2)

The Leather Company produces two styles of leather jackets: standard and deluxe. The difference between the two is in the amount of handcrafting that is done. The deluxe jacket uses more skilled labor because additional cutting and trimming is done by hand, which is not done for the standard jacket. The relevant figures for the year just completed are given below.

Allocation Base	Standard	Deluxe
Materials used	$300,000	$ 200,000
Direct labor-hours	100,000	150,000
Machine-hours	40,000	10,000
Output	80,000	15,000

The company has $800,000 in manufacturing overhead costs to allocate to these two product lines.

Required:

For each of the four potential allocation bases, determine the amount of manufacturing overhead that would be allocated to each unit of output.

6–22 Alternative Allocation Bases (L.O.2)

Refer to your calculations for exercise 6–21. Your supervisor wants to know how much it costs to make a standard jacket and a deluxe jacket, including the cost of materials; labor, which costs $8 per hour; and manufacturing overhead.

Required:

a. Give your supervisor four different answers, for each type of jacket, to the question: "How much does it cost to make?"

b. Explain to your supervisor why there are four different cost numbers for each product. Also indicate whether total manufacturing costs are the same for The Leather Company regardless of the overhead allocation base used.

6–23 Cost Allocations— Direct Method (L.O.3)

Cytotech Corporation has two producing departments and two service departments labeled P1, P2, S1, and S2, respectively. Direct costs for each department and the proportion of service costs used by the various departments are as follows:

Department	Direct Costs	Proportion of Services Used by: S1	S2	P1	P2
P1	$80,000				
P2	70,000				
S1	40,000	—	.80	.10	.10
S2	50,000	.20	—	.50	.30

Required:

Compute the allocation of service department costs to producing departments using the direct method.

6–24 Allocating Service Department Costs First to Production Departments, Then to Jobs (L.O.3)

Refer to the facts in exercise 6–23. Assume P1 and P2 each work on two jobs: job 10 and job 11. Costs are allocated to jobs based on labor-hours in P1 and based on machine-hours in P2. The labor- and machine-hours worked in each department are as follows:

		P1	P2
Job 10:	Labor-hours	80	10
	Machine-hours	10	20
Job 11:	Labor-hours	10	10
	Machine-hours	10	90

Required:

How much of the service department costs allocated to P1 and P2 in the direct method would be allocated to job 10? How much to job 11?

6–25   Cost Allocations—Direct Method
(L.O.3)

Wear-with-All Fashions has two service departments (Maintenance and General Factory Administration) and two operating departments (Cutting and Assembly). Management has decided to allocate maintenance costs on the basis of the area in each department and general factory administration costs on the basis of labor-hours worked by the employees in each of their respective departments.

The following data appear in the company records for the current period:

	General Factory Administration	Maintenance	Cutting	Assembly
Area occupied (square feet)	1,000	—	1,000	3,000
Labor-hours	—	100	100	400
Direct labor costs (operating departments only)			$1,500	$4,000
Service department direct costs	$10,000	$24,000		

Required:

Use the direct method to allocate these service department costs to the operating departments.

6–26   Cost Allocations—Step Method
(L.O.4)

Refer to the data for the Cytotech Corporation (exercise 6–23). Use the step method to allocate the service costs, using:

a.   The order of allocation starting with S1.

b.   The allocations made in the reverse order (starting with S2).

6–27   Cost Allocation—Step Method
(L.O.4)

Refer to the data for Wear-with-All Fashions in exercise 6–25. Allocate the service department costs using the step method, starting with the Maintenance Department. What effect does using this method have on the allocation of costs?

6–28   Cost Allocations—Reciprocal Method
(L.O.5)

Refer to the data for the Cytotech Corporation (exercise 6–23). Use the reciprocal method to allocate the service costs. (Matrix algebra is not required.)

6–29   Cost Allocations—Reciprical Method—Two Service Departments
(L.O.5)

During the past month, the following costs were incurred in the three operating departments and two service departments in the company:

P1	$240,000
P2	625,000
P3	780,000
S1	134,000
S2	119,000

Use of services by other departments is as follows:

Service Cost Center	User Department				
	S1	S2	P1	P2	P3
S1	—	.40	.30	.20	.10
S2	.10	—	.20	.15	.55

Required:

Allocate service department costs to P1, P2, and P3 using the reciprocal method, and present the total costs of P1, P2, and P3.

6–30   Cost Allocation—Reciprocal Method
(L.O.5)

Refer to the data for Wear-with-All Fashions in exercise 6–25. Allocate the service department costs using the reciprocal method. (Matrix algebra is not required because there are only two service departments.)

6–31   **Evaluate Cost Allocation Methods** (L.O.3, L.O.4, L.O.5)

Refer to exercises 6–25, 6–27, and 6–30 (Wear-with-All Fashions). Which method do you think is best? How much would it be worth to the company to use the best method compared to the worst of the three methods? (Numbers not required in this answer.)

6–32   **Single versus Dual Rates** (L.O.6)

Refer to data for the company in exercise 6–19.

Determine the cost allocation if $26,000 of the wire service costs are fixed and allocated on the basis of hours of news; and the remaining costs, which are variable, are allocated on the basis of wire service–hours used.

6–33   **Single versus Dual Rates** (L.O.6)

A law firm has two departments, Bankruptcy and Personal Injury. Word processing is common to both departments. The cost of word processing is $400,000. The following information is given:

	Pages of Word Processing Used by Department	Payroll of Department
Bankruptcy	2,000	$500,000
Personal Injury	6,000	450,000

Required:

a. What is the cost charged to each department if pages of word processing is the allocation basis?

b. What is the cost charged to each department if departmental payroll is the allocation basis?

6–34   **Single versus Dual Rates** (L.O.6)

Using the data for the law firm in exercise 6–33, what is the cost allocation if there are fixed word processing costs of $200,000 that are allocated on the basis of department payroll, and the remaining costs (all variable) are allocated on the basis of pages of word processing used by the department?

6–35   **Multiple-Factor Allocations** (L.O.7)

Outback Clothing operates four clothing stores and allocates headquarters costs based on the arithmetical average of three factors:

1. Percentage of payroll dollars in each store to the total payroll dollars for all stores.

2. Percentage of sales dollars in each store to the total sales in all stores.

3. Percentage of the average gross book value of tangible assets of each store to the total book value of tangible assets for all stores.

The company has headquarters costs of $150,000. The relevant factors for the stores are:

	Stores				
	Anchorage	Boise	Columbus	Detroit	Total
Payroll	$ 85,000	$ 35,000	$ 60,000	$ 70,000	$ 250,000
Sales	1,000,000	1,200,000	1,100,000	700,000	4,000,000
Assets	240,000	250,000	210,000	200,000	900,000

Required:

Determine the amount of headquarters costs allocated to each store.

6–36   **Multiple-Factor Allocations** (L.O.7)

M.I.C., Inc., operates in three states: Missouri, Illinois, and California. The following information is available concerning the activities and taxing bases for each of the three states:

	Missouri	Illinois	California
Income tax rate	–0–	5%	7%
Basis for allocating income . .	—	Illinois sales, payroll, and property three-factor formula	California sales, payroll, and property three-factor formula
Company sales occurring by state	—	$2.4 million	$1.8 million
Company payrolls by state . .	$2.6 million	.8	.6
Company property by state . .	1.2	.3	.5

Company headquarters are located in Missouri. Total company profits were $800,000 before state taxes.

Required:

What would be the income tax liability due to each state using the multiple-factor formula?

PROBLEMS

6–37   Choosing an Appropriate Allocation Base in a High-Tech Environment

Silicon Valley Corp. manufactures two types of computer chips. The ROM-A chip is a commonly used chip for personal computer systems. The RAM-B chip is used for specialized scientific applications. Direct materials costs for the ROM-A chip are 25 cents per unit and for the RAM-B are 28 cents per unit. The company's annual output is 32 million chips. At this level of output, manufacturing overhead amounts to $2.4 million, and direct labor costs total $625,000.

The company's assembly process is highly automated. As a result, the primary function for direct labor is to set up a production run and to check equipment settings on a periodic basis.

Yesterday the equipment was set up to run 800 RAM-B units. When that run was completed, equipment settings were changed, and 100,000 ROM-A units were produced. Part of the daily cost report is as follows:

	ROM-A	RAM-B
Units Produced	100,000	800
Direct materials	$25,000	$224
Direct labor	$ 1,000	$600

Required:

a. For yesterday's production run, what is the total manufacturing cost per unit for ROM-A and RAM-B if direct labor costs are used to allocate manufacturing overhead?

b. For yesterday's production run, what is the total manufacturing cost per unit for ROM-A and RAM-B if units produced is the basis used to allocate manufacturing overhead?

6–38   Choosing an Appropriate Allocation Base in an Automated Environment

Birmingham Fabrication Corp. produces fence materials. One division manufactures fence rails and fence posts. As a general rule, more fence rails are produced than posts. For example, during the past week, 900 rails and 30 posts were manufactured. Direct materials costs are $3.10 per rail and $3.00 per post. Direct labor of $200 was attributed to the rail manufacturing operation, and $250 was attributed to posts during the past week. Most of the direct labor costs are incurred in setting up the automated equipment. In the manufacturing process, it takes about the same amount of time for the equipment to produce one rail as it does to produce one post.

This division has $550,000 in annual manufacturing overhead that is allocated based on direct labor costs. The annual direct labor costs are estimated at $44,000. The company produces 250,000 units per year.

Required:

a. Prepare a schedule to show the cost assigned to each rail and each post using direct labor as the basis for allocating overhead.

b. Prepare a schedule computing the unit costs of rails and posts using units of production as a basis for allocating overhead costs.

c. In light of the information provided, which method of overhead allocation appears more reasonable? Why?

6–39 Step Method with Three Service Departments

Oakland Corporation operates two producing departments—Painting and Polishing—in its automotive refinishing operations. The company has three service departments for its plant: Building Occupancy, Payroll Accounting, and Equipment Maintenance. The accumulated costs in the three service departments were $180,000, $250,000, and $132,000, respectively. The company decided that building occupancy costs should be distributed on the basis of square footage used by each production and service department. The payroll accounting costs are allocated on the basis of number of employees, while equipment maintenance costs are allocated on the basis of the dollar value of the equipment in each department. The use of each basis by all departments during the current period is as follows:

Allocation Base	Used by:				
	Building Occupancy	Payroll Accounting	Equipment Maintenance	Painting	Polishing
Building area	5,000	15,000	10,000	180,000	45,000
Employees	9	5	6	35	50
Equipment value (in thousands)	$12	$240	$35	$624	$324

Direct costs of the Painting Department included $475,000 in direct materials, $650,000 in direct labor, and $225,000 in overhead. In the Polishing Department, direct costs consisted of $820,000 in direct labor and $145,000 in overhead.

Required:

a. Using the step method, determine the allocated costs and the total costs in each of the two producing departments. Ignore self-usage (for example, ignore work done by Building Occupancy for itself). Rank-order the allocation as follows: (1) Equipment Maintenance, (2) Payroll Accounting, and (3) Building Occupancy.

b. Assume 1,000 units were processed through these two departments. What is the unit cost: For Painting? For Polishing? Total?

6–40 Solve for Unknowns

Pronto's Pizza has a commissary that supplies food and other products to its pizza restaurants. It has two service departments, Computer Services (S1) and Administration and Maintenance (S2), which support two operating departments, Food Products (P1) and Supplies (P2). As an internal auditor, you are checking the company's procedures for cost allocation. You find the following cost allocation results for June:

Costs allocated to P1:
$20,000 from S1
? from S2

Costs allocated to P2:
$11,250 from S2
? from S1

Total costs for the two service departments:
$50,000

S2's services are provided as follows:
20 percent to S1
50 percent to P1
30 percent to P2

The direct method of allocating costs is used.

Required:

a. What are the total service department costs (S1 + S2) allocated to P2?

b. Complete the following:

	To:	
From:	**P1**	**P2**
S1	$20,000	_____
S2	_____	$11,250

c. What were the proportions of S1's costs allocated to P1 and P2?

6–41 Cost Allocation: Step Method with Analysis and Decision Making

O-Hi-O Corporation is reviewing its operations to see what additional energy-saving projects might be carried out. The company's Intermac plant has its own electric generating facilities. The electric generating plant is powered by the production of some natural gas wells that the company owns and that are located on the same property as the plant. A summary of the use of service department service by other service departments as well as by the two producing departments at the plant is summarized as follows:

		Services Used by:				
		Electric Generating			**Production Department**	
Service Department	**Natural Gas Production**	**Fixed Costs**	**Variable Costs**	**Equipment Maintenance**	**No. 1**	**No. 2**
Natural Gas Production	—	—	.40	—	.10	.50
Electric Generating:						
Fixed costs	.10	—	—	.10	.30	.50
Variable costs	.10	—	—	.05	.55	.30
Equipment Maintenance . . .	.20	.10	.05	—	.50	.15

Direct costs (in thousands) in the various departments and the labels used to abbreviate the departments in the calculations are as follows:

Department	Direct Costs	Label
Natural Gas Production	$ 35	S1
Electric Generating:		
Fixed costs	15	S2
Variable costs	40	S3
Equipment Maintenance	24	S4
Production Maintenance:		
No. 1	300	P1
No. 2	220	P2

The company currently allocates costs of service departments to production departments using the step method. The local power company indicates that the power company would charge $80,000 per year for the electricity now being generated by the company internally. Management rejected switching to the public utility on the grounds that its rates would cost more than the $55,000 ($15,000 + $40,000) costs of the present company-owned system.

Required:

a. What costs of electric service did management use to prepare the basis for its decision to continue generating power internally?

b. Prepare an analysis for management to indicate the costs of the company's own electric generating operations. (Use the step method.) The rank order of allocation is: (1) S1, (2) S4, (3) S2, and (4) S3.

c. Would your answer in *(b)* change if the company could realize $29,000 per year from the sale of the natural gas now used for electric generating? (Assume no selling costs.)

6-42   (Appendix) Cost Allocations Reciprocal Method (computer required)

If O-Hi-O Corporation, problem 6–41, above, used the reciprocal method for cost allocation, what would the company's estimated cost savings (or loss) be if it were to acquire electricity from the outside and sell natural gas for a net realization from the gas sales of $29,000 per year? Use a computer to solve the system of simultaneous linear equations.

6-43   Cost Allocation and Decision Making

The Promotion Department of the Doxolby Company is reponsible for the design and development of all marketing campaign materials and related literature, pamphlets, and brochures. Management is reviewing the effectiveness of the Promotion Department to determine if the department's services could be acquired more economically from an outside promotion agency. Management has asked for a summary of the Promotion Department's costs for the most recent year. The following cost summary was supplied:

PROMOTION DEPARTMENT
Costs for the Year Ended November 30

Direct department costs	$257,500
Charges from other departments	44,700
Allocated share of general administrative overhead	22,250
Total costs	$324,450

Direct department costs are those that can be traced directly to the activities of the Promotion Department, such as staff and clerical salaries, including related employee benefits, supplies, etc. Charges from other departments represent the costs of services that are provided by other departments of Doxolby at the request of the Promotion Department. The company has developed a charging system for such interdepartmental uses of services. For instance, the in-house Printing Department charges the Promotion Department for the promotional literature printed. All such services provided to the Promotion Department by other departments of Doxolby are included in the "Charges from other departments." General administrative overhead is composed of such costs as executive salaries and benefits, depreciation, heat, insurance, and property taxes. These costs are allocated to all departments in proportion to the number of employees in each department.

Required:

Discuss the usefulness of the cost figures as presented for the Promotion Department of Doxolby as a basis for comparison with a bid from an outside agency to provide the same type of activities as Doxolby's own Promotion Department.

(CMA adapted)

6-44   Allocate Service Department Costs— Direct and Step Methods: Multiple Choice

Parker Manufacturing Company has three service departments (General Factory Administration, Factory Maintenance, and Factory Cafeteria), and two production departments (Fabrication and Assembly). A summary of costs and other data for each department prior to allocation of service department costs for the year ended June 30 are as follows:

	General Factory Administration	Factory Maintenance	Factory Cafeteria	Fabrication	Assembly
Direct material costs	–0–	$ 65,000	$ 91,000	$3,130,000	$ 950,000
Direct labor costs	$ 90,000	82,100	87,000	1,950,000	2,050,000
Manufacturing overhead costs	70,000	56,100	62,000	1,650,000	1,850,000
	$160,000	$203,200	$240,000	$6,730,000	$4,850,000
Direct labor-hours	31,000	27,000	42,000	562,500	437,500
Number of employees	12	8	20	280	200
Square footage occupied	1,750	2,000	4,800	88,000	72,000

The costs of the service departments are allocated on the following bases: General Factory Administration Department, direct labor-hours; Factory Maintenance Department, square footage occupied; and Factory Cafeteria, number of employees.

Required:

Round all final calculations to the nearest dollar.

a. Assume that Parker elects to distribute service department costs directly to production departments using the direct method. The amount of Factory Maintenance Department costs allocated to the Fabrication Department would be:
   (1) $0.
   (2) $111,760.
   (3) $106,091.
   (4) $91,440.
   (5) None of the above.

b. Assume the same method of allocation as in (a). The amount of General Factory Administration Department costs allocated to the Assembly Department would be:
   (1) $0.
   (2) $63,636.
   (3) $70,000.
   (4) $90,000.
   (5) None of the above.

c. Assume that Parker elects to distribute service department costs to other departments using the step method (starting with Factory Cafeteria, then Factory Maintenance), the amount of Factory Cafeteria Department costs allocated to the Factory Maintenance Department would be:
   (1) $0.
   (2) $96,000.
   (3) $3,840.
   (4) $6,124.
   (5) None of the above.

d. Assume the same method of allocation as in (c). The amount of Factory Maintenance Department costs allocated to the Factory Cafeteria would be:
   (1) $0.
   (2) $5,787.
   (3) $5,856.
   (4) $148,910.
   (5) None of the above.

(CPA adapted)

6–45   Allocate Service Department Costs Using Direct and Reciprocal Methods

(Note: Matrix algebra is not required for this problem. An algebraic equation can be set up for the costs of each of the two service departments and solved by substitution.)

Barrylou Corporation is developing departmental overhead rates based upon direct labor-hours for its two production departments—Molding and Assembly. The Molding Department employs 20 people, and the Assembly Department employs 80 people. Each person in these two departments works 2,000 hours per year. The production-related overhead costs for the Molding Department are budgeted at $200,000, and the Assembly Department costs are budgeted at $320,000. Two service departments—Repair and Power—directly support the two production departments and have budgeted costs of $48,000 and $250,000, respectively. The production departments' overhead rates cannot be determined until the service departments' costs are properly allocated. The following schedule reflects the use of the Repair Department's and Power Department's output by the various departments:

	Department			
	Repair	Power	Molding	Assembly
Repair hours	–0–	1,000	1,000	8,000
Kilowatt-hours	240,000	–0–	840,000	120,000

Required:

a.   Calculate the overhead rates per direct labor-hour for the Molding Department and the Assembly Department using the direct allocation method to charge the production departments for service department costs.

b.   Calculate the overhead rates per direct labor-hour for the Molding Department and the Assembly Department using the reciprocal method to charge service department costs to each other and to the production departments.

(CMA adapted)

6–46   Cost Allocations: Comparison of Dual and Single Rates

High Skies Airlines operates a centralized computer center for the data processing needs of its Reservation, Scheduling, Maintenance, and Accounting divisions. Costs associated with use of the computer are charged to the individual departments on the basis of time usage. Due to recent increased competition in the airline industry, the company has decided it is necessary to more accurately allocate its costs so it can price its services competitively and profitably. During the current period, the use of data processing services and the storage capacity required for each of the divisions were as follows (in thousands of seconds for time usage and in gigabytes for storage capacity):

Division	Time Usage	Storage Capacity
Reservations	2,500	1,500
Scheduling	1,700	600
Maintenance	6,300	210
Accounting	5,000	190

During this period, the costs of the computer center amounted to $3,525,000 for time usage and $2,500,000 for storage-related costs.

Required:

Determine the allocation to each of the divisions using:

a.   A single rate based on time used.

b.   Dual rates based on time used and capacity used.

You may round all decimals to three places.

6–47   Cost Allocation for Rate-Making Purposes

Failsafe Insurance, Inc., asked the regulatory board for an increase in the allowed premiums from its insurance operations. Insurance premium rates in the jurisdiction in which Failsafe operates are designed to cover the operating costs and insurance claims. As a part of Failsafe's expenses, its agents earn commissions based on premium revenues. Premium revenues are also used to pay claims and to invest in securities. Administrative expenses include costs to manage the company's investments. All administrative costs are charged against premium revenue. Failsafe claims that its insurance operations "just broke even" last year and that a rate increase is necessary. The following income statement (in millions) was submitted to support Failsafe's request:

Insurance income:	
Premium revenue	$400
Operating costs:	
Claims	250
Administrative	70
Sales commissions	80
Total operating costs	400
Insurance profit (loss)	–0–
Investment income	30
Profits after investment income	$ 30

Further investigation reveals that approximately 20 percent of the sales commissions may be considered related to investment activities. In addition, 10 percent of the administrative costs are incurred by the investment management division. The state insurance commission (which sets insurance rates) believes that Failsafe's insurance activities should earn about 5 percent on its premium revenues.

Required:

a. If you were a consumer group, how would you present Failsafe's income statement? (For example, how would you allocate administrative costs and sales commissions between the "insurance income" category and the "investment income" category?)

b. If you were Failsafe's management, what arguments would you present in support of the cost allocations included in the above income statement?

6–48 Cost Allocation for Travel Reimbursement

Your company has a travel policy that reimburses employees for the "ordinary and necessary" costs of business travel. Quite often employees will mix a business trip with pleasure either by extending the time at the destination or by traveling from the business destination to a nearby resort or other personal destination. When this happens, an allocation must be made between the business and personal portions of the trip. However, the travel policy is unclear on the allocation method to follow.

Consider the following example:

An employee obtained an excursion ticket for $1,320 and traveled the following itinerary:

From:	To:	Mileage	Regular Fare	Purpose
Washington, D.C.	Salt Lake City	1,839	$700	Business
Salt Lake City	Los Angeles	590	300	Personal
Los Angeles	Washington, D.C.	2,288	800	Return

Required:

Compute the business portion of the airfare and state the basis for the indicated allocation that would be appropriate according to each of the following independent scenarios:

a. Based on the maximum reimbursement for the employee.

b. Based on the minimum cost to the company.

c. Based on your recommendation.

| 6–49 | **Cost Allocations in Contracting** | Idiograms, Inc., entered into a contract to produce certain units on a cost-plus basis. During the contract period, Idiograms had 280 of its 520 employees working on the contract exclusively. Idiograms paid $340,000 in wages to the contract-related employees. During the same time, it paid $480,000 in wages to its noncontract-related employees. Its labor-related overhead costs amounted to $275,000. Idiograms submitted the following invoice to the purchaser: |

Materials costs	$ 645,306
Labor costs	340,000
Other overhead	260,000
Labor-related overhead (not included elsewhere)	148,077
Total costs	1,393,383
Agreed profit (20%)	278,677
Contract balance due	$1,672,060

Upon receipt of the invoice, the purchaser questioned the allocation of labor-related overhead, noting that the costs seemed out of line.

Required:

a. What basis did Idiograms use for the allocation of labor-related overhead costs?

b. What would be the effect on the contract balance due·if Idiograms used the alternative labor cost basis suggested in the problem?

c. Is it possible to conclude which basis is more appropriate?

| 6–50 | **Allocated Costs and Incentive Contracts** | Volume Sales Company has a highly competitive organization. Division managers (and division employees) receive a bonus if the division reports above-average returns for a year. Profits are determined using allocated common costs. Returns are measured by dividing profits by the book value of assets in each division. |

The following profit and performance reports were prepared for the managers of the Fashion and Style Divisions, two of many divisions in the company (dollar figures are in thousands):

	Fashion	Style
Sales revenue	$450	$600
Costs:		
Direct costs	200	300
Allocated costs	200	160
Division profit	$ 50	$140
Division assets	$200	$560
Division return (Profit ÷ Assets)	25%	25%

The average return for the company was also 25 percent.

The manager of the Fashion Division notes that allocated costs were distributed to each division on the basis of number of employees. She suggests that costs should be allocated on the basis of assets because the allocated costs are headquarters costs. In her view, the primary role of headquarters is to provide assets for the use of operating divisions. Had the costs been allocated on the basis of division assets, she calculated that the Fashion Division would have been allocated with costs of $140 and the Style Division with costs of $390.

The manager of the Style Division argues that central management is really concerned with maintaining employee relations. The advantage to a large organization such as this one is that employees identify with the company, not just with a division. He further asserts that the greater an employee's pay, the more the employee requires services of corporate headquarters. He therefore suggests that payroll costs be used as the basis for allocation of the common costs. If payroll costs were used, he calculated that the Fashion Division would be allocated with $220 of allocated costs and the Style Division with $135.

Required:

What would be each division's return using each manager's proposal? What suggestions do you have for the solution to the incentive compensation problem for Volume Sales Company?

**6–51 Cost Allocations
Using Multiple Factors**

The Cost Accounting Standards Board has concluded that certain indirect costs that cannot be related to a government contract by any other manner are to be charged to the contract based on a three-factor formula. The three factors are property, payrolls, and "all other costs" charged to the contract. These factors are entered into three fractions. The three fractions are summed and the sum divided by three. The result of this operation is the portion of these costs that are chargeable to the contract.

Stealthy Products, Inc., has a secret government contract. The company also engages in other activities. During the past year, it incurred $650,000 in costs chargeable to the government contract other than costs that must be allocated based on the three-factor formula. (The $650,000 represents "all other costs" charged to the government contract.) The company incurred a total of $812,500 in the "all other costs" category of costs.

In addition, Stealthy used $2 million of its $3 million in property for the government contract. Payrolls of employees engaged in the government contract amounted to $390,000 out of total payrolls of $468,000.

Stealthy's costs subject to the three-factor formula are $122,000.

Required:

How much of the $122,000 is chargeable to the government contract using the three-factor formula? (See Illustration 6–13 for an example.)

**6–52 Interaction of State
Taxes and Contract
Costs**

ArkFla, Inc., has two operating divisions. Fla Division operates entirely in Florida and is engaged exclusively in the manufacture and sale of commercial products. Ark Division operates exclusively in Arkansas and is engaged in the manufacture of military equipment. Prior to receiving a new defense contract, ArkFla, Inc., had the following distribution of property, payrolls, and sales between the two states:

	Arkansas	**Florida**
Property	$4.9 million	$ 5.6 million
Payrolls	1.2	1.6
Sales	7.4	11.7

Total income was $3 million. ArkFla received a government contract that required the addition of $1 million in property in Arkansas. Payroll in Arkansas was increased by $.9 million, and sales increased by $3.1 million. The contract added $300,000 to income.

Assume Florida levies its 6 percent state income tax using the property, payrolls, and sales factors. No other elements in the factors for either state changed.

Required:

What effect, if any, did the defense contract have on the Florida tax liability?

INTEGRATIVE CASES

**6–53 Job Costing with
Service Department
Cost Allocations**

WX Photography Company operates a job shop with two producing departments: Department A and Department B. Jobs are started in Department A and then moved to Department B. When the work is finished in Department B, the jobs are immediately sold. The company also has two service Departments, W and X, which perform support services for the producing departments. In addition, Departments W and X perform services for each other.

Overhead in Department A is applied to jobs on the basis of prime costs (that is, total direct materials and direct labor). Overhead in Department B is applied on the basis of machine-hours. For this period, the estimated overhead and estimated activity levels for applying overhead were as follows:

Department A:	Estimated overhead	$66,000
	Estimated prime costs	44,000
Department B:	Estimated overhead	$33,000
	Estimated machine-hours	30,000

During the month, direct materials and direct labor costs were incurred on jobs as follows:

	Job No. 22	Job No. 28	Job No. 36
Department A:			
Prime costs	$26,000	$13,200	$8,200
Department B:			
Direct materials	16,350	7,100	900
Direct labor	16,000	18,000	–0–
Machine-hours	12,000	18,000	–0–

The balances of other departmental costs in the accounts for the service and producing departments (before allocation of service department costs) are as follows:

Department W	$11,300
Department X	14,000
Department A	46,300
Department B	21,500

The use of services by other departments was as follows:

		Used by:		
Services of:	W	X	A	B
W	—	20%	30%	50%
X	40%	—	45	15

The company uses the step method for service cost allocation. Job Nos. 22 and 28 were completed during the period and were sold. Job No. 36 is in Department B.

Required:

a. What was the current period cost on Job Nos. 22 and 28 that was transferred to cost of goods sold?

b. If actual overhead had been charged to Job No. 28, what amount of current period costs would have been transferred to cost of goods sold for that job?

6–54 Impact of Using Machine-Hours versus Labor-Hours for Allocating Overhead

Herbert Manufacturing Company manufactures custom-designed restaurant furniture. Actual overhead costs incurred during the month are applied to the products on the basis of actual direct labor-hours required to produce the products. Overhead consists primarily of supervision, employee benefits, maintenance costs, property taxes, and depreciation.

Herbert Manufacturing recently won a contract to manufacture the furniture for a new fast-food chain. To produce this new line, Herbert Manufacturing must purchase more molded plastic parts for the furniture than for its current line. An efficient manufacturing process for this new furniture has been developed that requires only a minimum capital investment.

At the end of October, the start-up month for the new line, the controller prepared a separate income statement for the new product line. The profitability for the new line was less than expected. The president of the corporation is concerned that stockholders will criticize the decision to add this lower-quality product line at a time when profitability appeared to be increasing with the regular product line.

The results as published for the first nine months, for October, and for November are (in thousands):

	New Fast-Food Furniture	Regular Custom Furniture	Total
Nine months year to date:			
Gross sales	—	$8,100	$8,100
Direct material	—	2,025	2,025
Direct labor	—	2,630	2,630
Overhead	—	1,779	1,779
Cost of sales	—	6,434	6,434
Gross margin	—	$1,666	$1,666
Gross margin percentage	—	20.6%	20.6%
October:			
Gross sales	$400	$ 900	$1,300
Direct material	200	225	425
Direct labor	90	284	374
Overhead	60	180	240
Cost of sales	350	689	1,039
Gross margin	$ 50	$ 211	$ 261
Gross margin percentage	12.5%	23.4%	20.1%
November:			
Gross sales	$800	$ 800	$1,600
Direct material	400	200	600
Direct labor	159	250	409
Overhead	98	147	245
Cost of sales	657	597	1,254
Gross margin	$143	$ 203	$ 346
Gross margin percentage	17.9%	25.4%	21.6%

Ms. Jameson, cost accounting manager, stated that on the basis of a recently completed study of company overhead, she feels that only the supervision and employee benefits should be allocated on the basis of direct labor-hours. The balance of the overhead should be allocated on a machine-hour basis. In Jameson's judgment, the increase in the profitability of the custom-designed furniture is due to a misallocation of overhead.

Actual direct labor-hours and machine-hours for the past two months are shown below.

	Fast-Food Furniture	Custom Furniture
Machine-hours:		
October	1,320	18,480
November	2,560	17,040
Direct labor-hours:		
October	10,000	30,000
November	17,500	26,250

Actual overhead costs for the past two months were:

	October	November
Supervision	$ 13,000	$ 13,000
Employee benefits	95,000	109,500
Maintenance	50,000	48,000
Depreciation	42,000	42,000
Property taxes	8,000	8,000
All other	32,000	24,500
Total	$240,000	$245,000

Required:

a. Reallocate the overhead for October and November using direct labor-hours as the allocation base for supervision and employee benefits. Use machine-hours as the base for the remaining overhead costs.

b. Support or criticize the conclusion that the increase in custom-design profitability is due to a misallocation of overhead. Use the data developed in requirement (a) to support your analysis.

(CMA adapted)

6–55   Patient's Hospital— Cost Allocation, Step Method[6]

The annual costs of hospital care under the medicare program exceed $20 billion per year. In the medicare legislation, Congress mandated that reimbursement to hospitals be limited to the costs of treating medicare patients. Ideally, neither nonmedicare patients nor hospitals would bear the costs of medicare patients nor would the government bear costs of nonmedicare patients. Given the large sums involved, it is not surprising that cost reimbursement specialists, computer programs, publications, and other products and services have arisen to provide hospital administrators with the assistance needed to obtain an appropriate reimbursement for medicare patient services.

Hospital departments may be divided into two categories: (1) revenue-producing departments and (2) nonrevenue-producing departments. This classification is simple but useful. The traditional accounting concepts associated with "service department cost allocation," while appropriate to this context, lead to a great deal of confusion in terminology since all of the hospital's departments are considered to be rendering services.

Costs of revenue-producing departments are charged to medicare and nonmedicare patients on the basis of actual use of the departments. These costs are relatively simple to apportion. Costs of nonrevenue-producing departments are somewhat more difficult to apportion. The approach to finding the appropriate distribution of these costs begins with the establishment of a reasonable basis for allocating nonrevenue-producing department costs to revenue-producing departments. Statistical measures of the relationships between departments must be ascertained. The cost allocation bases listed in Exhibit A were established as acceptable for cost reimbursement purposes. The regulated order of allocation must be used for medicare reimbursement.

A hospital may then use either the reciprocal method to the cost allocation problem, or they may use the step method. If the step method is used, the order of departments for allocation is the same order as that by which the departments are listed in Exhibit A. Thus, Depreciation—Buildings is allocated before Depreciation—Movable Equipment. Cost centers must be established for each of these nonrevenue-producing costs that are relevant to a particular hospital's operations.

---

[6] © 1991 by CIPT Co.

Nonrevenue Cost Center	Basis for Allocation
Depreciation—Buildings	Square feet in each department
Depreciation—Movable Equipment	Dollar value of equipment in each department
Employee Health and Welfare	Gross salaries in each department
Administrative and General	Accumulated costs by department
Maintenance and Repairs	Square feet in each department
Operation of Plant	Square feet in each department
Laundry and Linen	Pounds used in each department
Housekeeping	Hours of service to each department
Dietary	Meals served in each department
Maintenance of Personnel	Number of departmental employees
Nursing Administration	Hours of supervision in each department
Central Supply	Costs of requisitions processed
Pharmacy	Costs of drug orders processed
Medical Records	Hours worked for each department
Social Service	Hours worked for each department
Nursing School	Assigned time by department
Intern/Resident Service	Assigned time by department

In the past year, the Patient's Hospital reported the following departmental costs:

Nonrevenue-producing:
Laundry and Linen	$ 250,000
Depreciation—Buildings	830,000
Employee Health and Welfare	375,000
Maintenance of Personnel	210,000
Central Supply	745,000

Revenue-Producing:
Operating Room	1,450,000
Radiology	160,000
Laboratory	125,000
Patient Rooms	2,800,000

Percentage usage of services by one department from another department were as follows:

From	Laundry and Linen	Depreciation—Buildings	Employee Health and Welfare	Maintenance of Personnel	Central Supply
Laundry and Linen	—	.05	.10	—	—
Depreciation—Buildings	.10	—	—	.10	—
Employee Health and Welfare	.15	—	—	.05	.03
Maintenance of Personnel	—	—	—	—	.12
Central Supply	.10	—	—	.08	—

	Operating Rooms	Radiology	Laboratory	Patient Rooms
Laundry and Linen	.30	.10	.05	.40
Depreciation—Buildings	.05	.02	.02	.71
Employee Health and Welfare	.25	.05	.04	.43
Maintenance of Personnel	.36	.10	.08	.34
Central Supply	.09	.04	.03	.66

The proportional use of revenue-producing department services by medicare and other patients was as follows:

	Medicare	Other
Operating Rooms	25%	75%
Radiology	20	80
Laboratory	28	72
Patient Rooms	36	64

Required:

What is the amount of the reimbursement claim for medicare services, using the step method of allocation? Use the following order of allocation: (1) depreciation—buildings, (2) employee health and welfare, (3) laundry and linen, (4) maintenance of personnel, and (5) central supply.

SOLUTIONS TO

 Self-Study Questions

1   To facilitate solving the problem, first express usage in percentage terms:

Service Center	Used by:					
	S1	S2	S3	P1	P2	P3
S1	—	.100[a]	.049	.333	.444	.074
S2	.050	—	.100	.500	.250	.100
S3	—	—	—	.250	.667	.083

[a] .100 = 8,100 ÷ (8,100 + 3,900 + 27,000 + 36,000 + 6,000). Other computations use the same approach.

Direct method:
Usage of services by producing departments only:

Service Center	Used by:		
	P1	P2	S3
S1	.391[a]	.522	.087
S2	.588[b]	.294	.118
S3	.250	.667	.083

[a] .391 = .333 ÷ (.333 + .444 + .074); .522 = .444 ÷ (.333 + .444 + .074); etc.
[b] .588 = .500 ÷ (.500 + .250 + .100); etc.

Allocation

| | | To: | | |
From:	Amount	P1	P2	P3
S1	$45,000	$ 17,595[a]	$ 23,490[a]	$ 3,915[a]
S2	$20,000	11,760[b]	5,880[b]	2,360[b]
S3	$10,000	2,500[c]	6,670[c]	830[c]
Allocated costs		31,855	36,040	7,105
Direct costs		210,000	140,000	80,000
Total costs		$241,855	$176,040	$87,105

Note: Allocations are rounded. Unrounded answers will be slightly different.

[a] $17,595 = $45,000 × .391; $23,490 = $45,000 × .522; $3,915 = $45,000 × .087.

[b] $11,760 = $20,000 × .588; $5,880 = $20,000 × .294; $2,360 = $20,000 × .118.

[c] $2,500 = $10,000 × .25; $6,670 = $10,000 × .667; $830 = $10,000 × .083.

2   Step method

Order of allocation: S2, S1, S3.

Usage of services by producing departments and service cost centers excluding reciprocal allocations:

Service Center	Used by:				
	S1	S3	P1	P2	P3
S2	.050	.100	.500	.250	.100
S1	—	.054[a]	.370[a]	.494[a]	.082[a]
S3	—	—	.250	.667	.083

[a] We use the numbers from the first display in the solution to self-study question 1 above.
.054 = .049 ÷ (.049 + .333 + .444 + .074) = .049 ÷ .900; .370 = .333 ÷ .900;
.494 = .444 ÷ .900 (rounded); .082 = .074 ÷ .90.

Allocation:

| | | | To: | | | |
From:	S2	S1	S3	P1	P2	P3
Direct department costs	$20,000	$ 45,000	$ 10,000			
S2	(20,000)	1,000[a]	2,000[a]	$ 10,000	$ 5,000	$ 2,000
S1		$(46,000)[b]	2,484[b]	17,020[b]	22,724	3,772
S3			$(14,484)[c]	3,621[c]	9,661	1,202
Total allocated costs				30,641	37,385	6,974
Direct costs of P1, P2, and P3				210,000	140,000	80,000
Total costs				$240,641	$177,385	$86,974

[a] $1,000 = $20,000 × .05; $2,000 = $20,000 × .10; etc.

[b] $46,000 = $45,000 direct costs + $1,000 allocated from S2; $2,484 = $46,000 × .054;
$17,020 = $46,000 × .37; etc.

[c] $14,484 = $10,000 direct costs + $4,484 allocated from S1 and S2; $3,621 = $14,484 × .25; etc.

3 Reciprocal method

$$\frac{\text{Total}}{\text{costs}} = \frac{\text{Direct}}{\text{costs}} + \begin{array}{l}\text{Costs to be}\\ \text{allocated to the}\\ \text{service department}\end{array}$$

S1 = $100,000 + .1 S2   Equation (1)
S2 = $200,000 + .2 S1   Equation (2)

Substituting:

S1 = $100,000 + .1($200,000 + .2 S1)
S1 = $120,000 + .02 S1
.98 S1 = $120,000
S1 = $\dfrac{\$120,000}{.98}$ = $122,449

S2 = $200,000 + .2($122,449)
S2 = $224,490

Allocation

	To:		
From:	P1	P2	P3
S1	.3($122,449) = $36,735	.3($122,449) = $36,735	.2($122,449) = $24,490
S2	.2($224,490) = $44,898	.4($224,490) = $89,796	.3($224,490) = $67,347

Total costs allocated to P1 + P2 + P3 = $300,001 (difference due to rounding).

4

a.

Cost	Allocation Base	Allocated to Uno	Allocated to Duo
Computer services	Computer time	$\dfrac{200}{200 + 140}$ × $254,000	$\dfrac{140}{200 + 140}$ × $254,000
		= $149,412	= $104,588
Building occupancy	Area occupied	$\dfrac{15,000}{15,000 + 40,000}$ × $615,000	$\dfrac{40,000}{15,000 + 40,000}$ × $615,000
		= $167,727	= $447,273
Personnel	Payroll	$\dfrac{\$380,000}{\$380,000 + \$170,000}$ × $104,000	$\dfrac{\$170,000}{\$380,000 + \$170,000}$ × $104,000
		= $ 71,855	= $ 32,145
Totals		$388,994	$584,006

Check: $254,000 + $615,000 + $104,000 = $388,994 + $584,006 = $973,000.

b.

Computer variable costs	Computer time	$\dfrac{200}{200 + 140}$ × $254,000 × 20%	$\dfrac{140}{200 + 140}$ × $254,000 × 20%
		= $ 29,882	= $ 20,918
Computer fixed costs	Computer storage	$\dfrac{25}{25 + 35}$ × $254,000 × 80%	$\dfrac{35}{25 + 35}$ × $254,000 × 80%
		= $ 84,667	= $118,533
Building occupancy—per *(a)*		$167,727	$447,273
Personnel—per *(a)*		$ 71,855	$ 32,145
Totals		$354,131	$618,869

Check: $254,000 + $615,000 + $104,000 = $354,131 + $618,869 = $973,000.

5

	Michigan Plant	Texas Plant	Total

Percentage factors:

Payroll $\dfrac{\$120{,}000}{\$300{,}000} = 40.0\%$ $\dfrac{\$180{,}000}{\$300{,}000} = 60.0\%$ 100%

Volume $\dfrac{\$600{,}000}{\$1{,}600{,}000} = 37.5\%$ $\dfrac{\$1{,}000{,}000}{\$1{,}600{,}000} = 62.5\%$ 100%

Assets $\dfrac{\$400{,}000}{\$1{,}200{,}000} = 33.3\%$ $\dfrac{\$800{,}000}{\$1{,}200{,}000} = 66.7\%$ 100%

Average:

Michigan $\dfrac{(40.0\% + 37.5\% + 33.3\%)}{3} = 36.9\%$

Texas $\dfrac{(60.0\% + 62.5\% + 66.7\%)}{3} = 63.1\%$

Allocation of headquarters costs:
Michigan $480,000 × 36.9% = $177,120
Texas $480,000 × 63.1% = $302,880
                              $480,000

6   (Appendix)
Reciprocal method:

Step 1.   Construct the cost equations.

$$P1 = \$210{,}000 + .333^{a}\ S1 + .500^{a}\ S2 + .250^{a}\ S3$$
$$P2 = \$140{,}000 + .444\ S1 + .250\ S2 + .667\ S3$$
$$P3 = \$ 80{,}000 + .074\ S1 + .100\ S2 + .083\ S3$$
$$S1 = \$ 45{,}000\qquad .074^{a}\ S1 + .050\ S2$$
$$S2 = \$ 20{,}000 + .100\ S1$$
$$S3 = \$ 10{,}000 + .049\ S1 + .100\ S2$$

---

[a] See top display in solution to self-study question 1, above.

Step 2.   Arrange the cost equations to place the coefficients in one section and the direct costs on the right-hand side of the equation.

$$1\ P1 + 0\ P2 + 0\ P3 - .333\ S1 - .500\ S2 - .250\ S3 = \$210{,}000$$
$$0\ P1 + 1\ P2 + 0\ P3 - .444\ S1 - .250\ S2 - .667\ S3 = 140{,}000$$
$$0\ P1 + 0\ P2 + 1\ P3 - .074\ S1 - .100\ S2 - .083\ S3 = 80{,}000$$
$$0\ P1 + 0\ P2 + 0\ P3 + 1.000\ S1 - .050\ S2 - .000\ S3 = 45{,}000$$
$$0\ P1 + 0\ P2 + 0\ P3 - .100\ S1 + 1.000\ S2 - .000\ S3 = 20{,}000$$
$$0\ P1 + 0\ P2 + 0\ P3 - .049\ S1 - .100\ S2 + 1.000\ S3 = 10{,}000$$

Step 3.   Use the information in step 2 to construct a matrix of coefficients, a vector of unknowns, and a vector of direct costs.

$$\begin{bmatrix} 1 & 0 & 0 & -.333 & -.500 & -.250 \\ 0 & 1 & 0 & -.444 & -.250 & -.667 \\ 0 & 0 & 1 & -.074 & -.100 & -.083 \\ 0 & 0 & 0 & 1 & -.050 & 0 \\ 0 & 0 & 0 & -.100 & 1 & 0 \\ 0 & 0 & 0 & -.049 & -.100 & 1 \end{bmatrix} \times \begin{bmatrix} P1 \\ P2 \\ P3 \\ S1 \\ S2 \\ S3 \end{bmatrix} = \begin{bmatrix} \$210{,}000 \\ 140{,}000 \\ 80{,}000 \\ 45{,}000 \\ 20{,}000 \\ 10{,}000 \end{bmatrix}$$

Step 4.   Invert the matrix *A* using a spreadsheet program such as Lotus™ beginning at the upper left of the spreadsheet. Use the **/DMI** command to invert the matrix. The data range should be Cells A1 through F6. Place the results in a range beginning with Cell A9. The inverse should appear on the screen as follows:

$$
\begin{bmatrix}
1 & 0 & 0 & .3997 & .5450 & .2500 \\
0 & 1 & 0 & .5109 & .3422 & .6670 \\
0 & 0 & 1 & .0894 & .1128 & .0830 \\
0 & 0 & 0 & 1.0050 & .0503 & 0 \\
0 & 0 & 0 & .1005 & 1.0050 & 0 \\
0 & 0 & 0 & .0593 & .1030 & 1
\end{bmatrix}
$$

Step 5.   Enter the direct costs in the range G9 to G14 and multiply the *A* matrix inverse by the direct costs vector using the /**DMM** command. The first data range is A9 through F14. The second data range is G9 through G14. Set the output range as H9. The results that appear in the output range should be as follows:

$$
\begin{bmatrix}
241,388 \\
176,506 \\
87,106 \\
46,231 \\
24,623 \\
14,728
\end{bmatrix}
$$

Check to see that the total of the costs charged to the producing departments equals the sum of the direct costs by using the @**SUM** command for H9 through H11 and comparing that total to the sum of G9 through G14. The check total is $505,000.

The costs allocated to P1 are obtained by taking the difference between the total costs from the solutions vector ($241,388) less the direct costs of $210,000. This difference is $31,388. For P2, the allocated costs are $36,506, which is the difference between the total costs of $176,506 and the direct costs of $140,000. Finally, for P3, the allocated costs are $7,106, which is the difference between the total costs of $87,106 and the direct costs of $80,000.

Cost Allocation to Products; Activity-Based Costing

LEARNING OBJECTIVES

After reading this chapter, you should be able to:

1. Describe cost allocation to products.
2. Compare and contrast plantwide and department allocation methods.
3. Explain advantages and disadvantages of activity-based costing.
4. Compute product costs using activity-based costing.
5. Compare activity-based product costing to traditional department product-costing methods.
6. Demonstrate the flow of costs through accounts using activity-based costing.
7. Identify problems to be addressed in implementing activity-based costing.

Assume the following discussion takes place in the offices of a company that makes jeans.

Pam (president of the company) [clearly frustrated]: Ten years ago, we were a highly profitable industry leader. In the last few years, our profits have shrunk to almost nothing. We can't even meet the competition on the prices of our basic jean pants, which have been our most important and highest volume product. We need to turn this situation around fast!

Lynn (vice president of marketing): I agree we aren't meeting the competition on jeans, but our prices are just barely above costs now. Surely you don't expect me to price below cost! I don't think the problem is in marketing; I think the problem is in production where the costs are too high.

Martha (vice president of production): I think we could reduce costs if we had a better cost system to tell us where to direct our efforts. To be frank, I don't trust the cost numbers we're getting now; I think they are way out of line with reality. Our overhead, which is about 50 percent of the cost of making the product, is allocated arbitrarily to our products. If you want us to reduce costs, we want a better cost system than the one we have now!

George (controller) [disturbed]: I hadn't realized the situation was quite this bad. This discussion prompts me to get started on a project that I have been planning for a long time. Could we meet tomorrow after I've had time to get some ideas together?

Pam: Fine. We'll meet at this time tomorrow.

Discussions like this one are taking place in many companies as you read this book. The exchange between the controller and his fellow managers emphasizes the importance of having accurate cost numbers for marketing and production decisions. Yet, cost numbers can differ considerably depending on how overhead costs are allocated to products. Dealing with overhead allocations is the most difficult task accountants face in computing accurate cost numbers.

Numerous companies, like Hewlett-Packard, Procter & Gamble, Boeing, Caterpillar, and IBM, have implemented new, more sophisticated cost methods to improve the way they allocate overhead costs. These new methods have revealed startling inaccuracies in the way product costs had previously been computed. For example, after installing new cost allocation methods, Tektronix, Inc., found that one of its products, a printed-circuit board, was generating negative margins of 46 percent.[1]

OVERVIEW OF COST METHODS

This chapter deals with allocating indirect costs to products. In this chapter, the cost object is a product. The product can be a good, such as an automobile, or a service, such as an X-ray examination in a hospital. Recall that indirect costs are those that cannot be traced directly to a product.

Indirect costs can be the overhead costs incurred in manufacturing a good or providing a service, or they can be indirect costs incurred in marketing the product or in administration. Some marketing costs, such as sales commissions, are direct, but many are indirect. Unlike direct materials and direct labor, which can be traced directly to a product, indirect costs must be *allocated* to products. Cost allocation is at least somewhat arbitrary in all cases; sometimes it is highly arbitrary.

Chapter 6 described how companies allocate costs to production departments, which is the first stage in the two-stage cost allocation process. This chapter describes how companies do the second stage—allocate from cost pools to products. **Cost pools** are simply groups of individual costs. In Chapter 6, the cost pools were departments. In this chapter, we expand our discussion to allow cost pools to be (1) plants, which are entire factories or stores, or (2) departments within plants, or (3) activities.

Cost Pools Groupings of individual costs.

We use predetermined overhead rates throughout this chapter. Recall from Chapter 3 that using predetermined rates normally results in over- or underapplied overhead. To keep the examples from becoming too complex, we will not use examples that involve over- or underapplied overhead in this chapter.

PLANTWIDE ALLOCATION

We start with the simplest allocation method, which is known as plantwide allocation. In the **plantwide allocation method,** the cost pool is the entire plant. This method uses one overhead allocation rate, or one set of rates, to

---

[1] "A Bean-Counter's Best Friend," *Business Week/Quality,* 1991, pp. 42–43.

Plantwide Allocation Method
This allocation method uses one cost pool for the entire plant. It uses one overhead allocation rate, or one set of rates, for all of the departments in a plant.

allocate overhead to products for *all* of the departments in a particular plant. We use the term *plant* to refer to an entire factory, store, hospital, or other multidepartment segment of a company. The key word in the definition is *all;* that is, a single rate or set of rates is used for all departments. We note that a company might use more than one rate, such as the dual rate method discussed in Chapter 6.

Although it is called *plant*wide allocation, this allocation concept can be used in both manufacturing and nonmanufacturing organizations. In a bank, for example, overhead could be applied to different customer accounts, to different types of loans, and to other products using just one overhead rate for the entire bank. Although we refer to the costs that are being allocated as *overhead* costs, the concepts apply to *any* indirect cost allocation.

The top of Illustration 7–1 (page 244) shows overhead allocation using plantwide allocation. Accounting for overhead is simple. All overhead costs are recorded in one cost pool in the Manufacturing Overhead (Actual) account for the plant without regard to the department or activity that caused them. A single overhead rate is used to apply overhead to products, crediting Manufacturing Overhead Applied. For example, if overhead is applied using a predetermined rate per machine-hour, then the amount of the credit to the Manufacturing Overhead Applied account and the debit to Work in Process for overhead costs equals the rate per machine-hour times the number of machine-hours worked on each product.

Companies using a single plantwide rate generally use a volume-based allocation base, such as direct labor-hours, machine-hours, volume of activity, or materials costs. Later in this chapter, we discuss other types of allocation bases with which companies are experimenting.

A single plantwide rate might be justified in simple organizations having only a few departments and not much variety in products. At Domino's Pizza, for example, using multiple overhead rates versus only one overhead rate for all of the products probably would not make much difference in the estimated costs of the regular or the large pizzas. Suppose Domino's Pizza becomes a more complex operation that includes extensive restaurant facilities, as well as home delivery and food service for schools and hospitals. In this case, using different overhead rates for different departments is appropriate because overhead costs are likely to be caused by different activities in different departments.

DEPARTMENT ALLOCATION

Department Allocation Method
Using this allocation method, companies have a separate cost pool for each department. Each department has its own overhead allocation rate, or set of rates.

Using **department allocation,** companies have a separate cost pool for each department. The company establishes a separate overhead allocation rate for each department. (Multiple rates could be set for each different department if the company uses dual or multiple-factor cost allocation, as discussed in Chapter 6.) Recall from Chapter 6 that service departments provide services to production departments, which produce goods and services. Each production department would be a separate cost pool. In contrast, using the plantwide allocation rate, the entire plant is one cost pool.

The middle and bottom of Illustration 7–1 shows department allocation. Each department is a cost pool; each department has an allocation rate. There are four overhead cost pools in the illustration, one each for Service Departments 1 and 2, and one each for Production Departments L and M. As each production department works on a product, overhead is applied based

I L L U S T R A T I O N   *Plantwide versus Department Allocation*

7–1

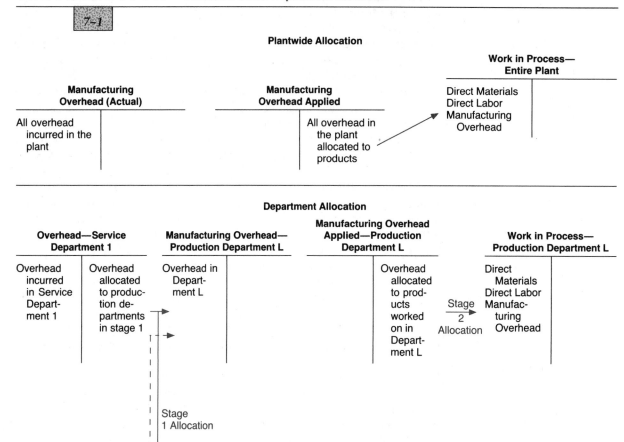

Note: Cost flows for direct materials and direct labor are omitted to simplify the presentation.

on the allocation rate for that department. The more departments the company has, the more overhead cost pools it has, and the more allocation rates there are to compute.

Choice of Cost Allocation Method: A Cost-Benefit Decision

The choice of a plantwide rate versus the more complex department rate versus the even more complex activity-based costing, discussed next, requires managers to make a cost-benefit decision. Selecting more complex allocation methods requires more time and skill to collect and process accounting information. Such incremental costs of additional information must be justified by an increase in benefits from improved decisions.

Note that companies using plantwide allocation, as in the top panel of Illustration 7–1, do not need to allocate service department costs to production departments. Although simpler, omitting the allocation of service department costs to production departments could have negative behavioral effects for the company. Allocating service department costs to production departments enables management to assign responsibility for service costs to the people in the production department who wanted the services.

A department rate provides more detailed cost measures and more accurate product cost numbers than a plantwide rate, particularly if the departments perform quite different activities. For example, if one department is labor intensive and another is machine intensive, it makes little sense to use a rate based on either machine-hours or labor-hours for both departments. Product costs will be more accurate if labor-hours are used for the labor-intensive department and machine-hours for the machine-intensive department.

The following self-study question demonstrates the differences between plantwide and department rates when computing product costs.

Self-Study Question

1 The Bank of Durango is considering either a bankwide overhead rate or a department rate. To get more information about these alternatives, management decided to test both rates for two departments: Commercial Loans and Mortgage Loans. The bankwide rate was based on a percent of direct labor time and was computed to be 50 percent of labor. The direct labor costs for the two departments for the test period were as follows:

> Commercial loans $100,000
> Mortgage loans   300,000

To develop department rates, the bank's accountants estimated overhead rates of 40 percent of direct labor for Mortgage Loans, and a dual rate for Commercial Loans of 20 percent of direct labor plus $40 per loan. Commercial Loans made 900 loans during the test period.

Compute the cost of labor and overhead for these two departments using (1) the bankwide rate and (2) the department rates. What are the advantages and disadvantages of the department rate compared to the bankwide rate?

The solution to this question is at the end of this chapter on page 285.

ACTIVITY-BASED COSTING

Activity-Based Costing A costing method that first assigns costs to activities, then assigns costs to products based on their consumption of activities.

Activity-based costing is a costing method that assigns costs first to activities, then to the products based on each product's use of activities. Activity-based costing is based on the concept: Products consume activities; activities consume resources.

If managers want their products to be competitive, they must know (1) the activities that go into making the good or providing the service, and (2) the cost of those activities. To reduce a product's costs, managers will likely have to change the activities consumed by the product. It is rarely sufficient for a manager to announce, " I want everyone to reduce costs by 10 percent," to effect a cost decrease. More likely, significant cost reduction requires managers, production and marketing people, accountants, engineers, and others to examine thoroughly the activities that a product consumes to determine how to rework those activities to make the product more efficiently.

For example, the Admissions Department of a university listed its activities: (1) receiving applications, (2) filing, (3) reviewing, checking, and completing files, (4) admitting students, and (5) notifying students. Management studied the activities of admitting students and found that certain activities could be made more efficient; others were eliminated for certain categories of students. By focusing on activities, the university was able to reduce costs.

Some people argue that activity-based costing is simply an extension of department allocation. Just as department allocation is more detailed than plantwide allocation, activity-based costing is generally more detailed than department allocation.

Many proponents of activity-based costing argue, however, that it is not just an extension of traditional department allocation. Rather it is an entirely new way of managing by focusing on activities. People manage activities, not costs, these proponents argue. Activity-based costing focuses attention on the things that matter, namely, those activities that are costly and should be made more efficient or otherwise changed.

To demonstrate important issues about the difficulty with traditional plantwide and department cost allocation methods and the advantages of activity-based costing, we continue the discussion at the jean clothing manufacturer from the beginning of this chapter. Recall that the participants had expressed concerns about the ability of the company to compete and the inadequate information provided by the company's cost accounting system. George, the controller, has returned the next day with new ideas about activity-based costing.

George: I have been reading numerous articles about companies like Ford, Deere & Company, and Hewlett-Packard that have discovered major problems with their cost systems. Their symptoms appear similar to our experience; namely, they can't lower prices to be competitive on high-volume products, and their profits are shrinking.

Pam (president): That sounds like us. What are they doing about it?

George: First, they're putting in a new type of cost system known as activity-based costing, or ABC for short. This system provides more detailed and better estimates of product costs, which helps our friends in marketing set prices. We may find, for example, that activity-based costing reveals that the cost of skirts is lower than we thought, meaning we could lower our prices.

Lynn (vice president of marketing): That would be good news, but I thought costs were pretty cut-and-dried. How can it be that a product would cost less under one cost system than under another system?

George: Lynn, the product doesn't cost less under one system or another. The problem is that no cost system can measure costs perfectly. We are able to trace some costs directly to the product. For example, we are pretty accurate in measuring the cost of denim, which is a direct material, in each of our products—shirts, pants, jackets, and so forth.

Overhead costs are another matter. Overhead, which includes such costs as electricity to run machines, and salaries of product designers, inspectors, and machine operators, is allocated to products using an allocation base like the number of hours that machines are used in cutting and stitching. Products that require more machine-hours will be allocated more overhead costs, even if the overhead isn't related to machine-hours. For example, the salaries of inspectors are related to the number of inspections, which is more related to how complicated the stitching is than to the number of machine-hours. If we change the allocation base, we change the product cost.

Pam: I understand that overhead allocation is somewhat arbitrary. How will activity-based costing help?

George: Activity-based costing provides more accurate information because we identify which activities cause costs, and we determine the costs of these activities. Activity-based costing more clearly identifies and measures costs of performing the activities that go into a product than traditional costing methods. For example, if a particular type of jacket requires 10 inspections for a production run of 1,000 jackets, we figure out the cost of those inspections and assign that cost to the production run for this particular jacket.

Martha (vice president of production): That makes sense to me. How would activity-based costing help us cut production costs?

George: By identifying activities that cause costs, we can eliminate or modify costly activities. For example, if we find that jackets require too many costly inspections, we could redesign the jacket to reduce the need for inspections. Our current cost system allocates all overhead costs, including inspection costs, to products based on machine-hours. We really don't know how much it costs to make an inspection and how much inspection cost is required by each product.

Pam: George, why haven't you used activity-based costing before?

George [somewhat defensive]: Activity-based costing provides more information, but it takes more time than traditional cost systems. New accounting methods sound great in theory, but there must be enough benefit from improved management decisions to justify the additional work required to provide numbers. Until now, I did not think activity-based costing would pass a cost-benefit test.

Pam: I see many benefits in better pricing, reducing costs of high-cost activities, and possibly dropping some products if we learn that their costs are too high. Our long-term strategy calls for new product lines in new markets where we are low-cost, low-price producers. We need the best cost information we can get to succeed in those markets. George, what do you need to get started developing an activity-based costing system for us?

George: I need a lot of support. Installing a new cost system requires teamwork between management, accounting, marketing, engineering, production, purchasing, and many other areas. This is not something to be done in an ivory tower. You need to educate us accountants about the activities that cause costs.

The preceding discussion made the following important points about activity-based costing:

1. Different cost allocation methods result in different estimates of how much it costs to make a product.
2. Activity-based costing provides more detailed measures of costs than plantwide or department allocation methods.
3. Activity-based costing can help marketing people by providing more accurate product cost numbers for decisions about pricing and which products to eliminate.
4. Production also benefits because activity-based costing provides better information about how much each activity costs. In fact, it helps identify cost drivers (that is, the activities that cause costs) that were previously unknown. To manage costs, production managers learn to manage the cost drivers.

5. Activity-based costing provides more information about product costs, but requires more recordkeeping. Managers must decide whether the benefits of improved decisions justify the additional cost of activity-based costing compared to department or plantwide allocation.

6. Installing activity-based costing requires teamwork between accounting, production, marketing, management, and other nonaccounting people.

We next discuss the methods used for activity-based costing, followed by an example.

Methods

Activity-based costing involves the following three steps:

1. Identify the activities that consume resources, and assign costs to those activities. Purchasing materials would be an activity, for example.

Cost Driver A factor that causes, or "drives," an activity's costs.

2. Compute a cost rate per cost driver unit or transaction. A **cost driver** is a factor that causes, or "drives," an activity's costs. For the purchasing materials activity, the cost driver could be number of orders. The cost driver rate could be the cost per purchase order, for example. Each activity could have multiple cost drivers.

3. Assign costs to products by multiplying the cost driver rate times the volume of cost driver units consumed by the product. For example, the cost per purchase order times the number of orders required for product A for the month of December would measure the cost of the purchasing activity for product A for December.

Identify the Activities that Consume Resources

This is often the most interesting and challenging part of the exercise because it requires people to understand all of the activities required to make the product. You can imagine the activities involved in making a simple product like a pizza—ordering, receiving, and inspecting materials; making the dough; putting on the ingredients; cooking; and so forth. Imagine the number of activities involved in making a complex product like an automobile or computer.

Using common sense and the principle that the benefits of more detailed costs should exceed the costs of getting the information, companies identify only the most important activities. A Deere & Company plant identified six major activities required to produce its products, for example. The company used one cost driver for each activity. Then it developed two cost rates, one for variable costs and one for fixed costs, for each cost driver.[2]

Complexity as an Activity that Consumes Resources

One of the lessons of activity-based costing has been that costs are a function not only of volume, but also of complexity.[3] While it might be obvious that a greater volume of production consumes resources, assuming

---

[2] See "John Deere Component Works," Harvard Business School case 187-107.

[3] R. D. Banker, G. Potter, and R. G. Schroeder, "An Empirical Analysis of Manufacturing Overhead Cost Drivers" (working paper, April 3, 1992), Carlson School of Management, University of Minnesota, Minneapolis, Minnesota; and G. Foster and M. Gupta, "Manufacturing Overhead Cost Driver Analysis," *Journal of Accounting and Economics,* January 1990.

the company has at least some variable costs, why does complexity consume resources?

To understand the answer to that question, imagine you produce 100,000 gallons of vanilla ice cream per month and your friend produces 100,000 gallons of 39 different flavors of ice cream per month. Further, assume your ice cream is sold only in one-liter containers, while your friend sells ice cream in various sizes of containers. Although both of you produce the same total volume of ice cream, it is not hard to imagine that your friend's overhead costs will be considerably higher. Your friend has more complicated ordering, storage, product testing (one of the more desirable jobs, nevertheless), and packing in containers. Your friend has more machine setups, too. Presumably, you can set the machinery to one setting to obtain the desired product quality and taste; your friend has to set the machines each time a new flavor is produced.

In general, the number of activities that consume resources is a function of the complexity of the company. The number of cost drivers has increased as companies have become more highly automated and more complex. Cost systems based on a simple direct labor base are generally inadequate in all but the simplest production or selling enterprise.

Department allocation rates based on volume, like direct labor-hours or machine-hours, have naturally allocated costs to products proportional to volume. High-volume products have been allocated a high proportion of overhead costs, and low-volume products have been allocated a low proportion of overhead costs. After installing activity-based costing, managers have frequently found that the low-volume products should be allocated more overhead. Low-volume products may be more specialized, requiring more drawings and specifications, and more inspections.

Low-volume products often require more machine setups for a given level of production output because they are produced in smaller batches. In the ice cream example above, one batch of 1,000 gallons of the low-volume 39th flavor might require as much overhead cost for machine setups, quality inspection, and purchase orders as one batch of 100,000 gallons of the highest-volume flavor. Further, the low-volume product adds complexity to the operation by disrupting the production flow of the high-volume items. You appreciate this fact every time you stand in line when someone ahead of you has a special and complex transaction.

When overhead is applied based on the volume of output, high-volume products are allocated relatively more overhead than low-volume products. High-volume products "subsidize" low-volume products in this case. The cost effects of keeping a large number of low-volume products are hidden by volume-based allocation methods. This has led many companies to continue producing or selling products without realizing how costly they are.

Choosing Cost Drivers   Illustration 7–2 presents several examples of the kinds of cost drivers that companies use. Most cost drivers are related either to the volume of production or to the complexity of the production or marketing process.

How do managers decide which cost driver to use? Chapter 6 discussed three criteria for selecting allocation bases that we can use to select cost drivers.

1. *Causal relation.* Choose a cost driver that causes the cost. This is ideal.

ILLUSTRATION

Examples of Cost Drivers

Machine-hours	Miles driven
Labor-hours or labor cost	Computer time
Pounds of materials handled	Items produced or sold
Pages typed	Customers served
Machine setups	Flight hours
Purchase orders	Number of surgeries
Quality inspections	Scrap/rework orders
Number of parts in a product	Hours of testing time
	Number of different customers

2. *Benefits received.* Choose a cost driver so costs are assigned in proportion to benefits received. For example, if the Physics Department in a university benefits more from the university's supercomputer than does the History Department, the university should select a cost driver that recognizes such differences in benefits (for example, the number of faculty and/or students in each department who use the computer).

3. *Reasonableness.* Some costs cannot be linked to products based on causality or benefits received, so they are assigned on the basis of fairness or reasonableness. We noted above that Deere & Company selected six cost drivers for a certain product. The cost of a seventh activity, general and administrative overhead, was allocated to the product using the reasonableness approach; namely, these costs were allocated to the product as a simple percentage of the costs of labor plus the other six activities that had been allocated to the product.

Compute a Cost Rate per Cost Driver

In general, predetermined rates for allocating indirect costs to products are computed as follows:

$$\text{Predetermined indirect cost rate} = \frac{\text{Estimated indirect cost}}{\text{Estimated volume of the allocation base}}$$

This formula applies to any indirect cost, whether manufacturing overhead, administrative cost, distribution costs, selling costs, or any other indirect cost.

Companies using department rates make the above computation for each department. Using activity-based costing, we first define the concept of activity center. An **activity center** is a unit of the organization that performs some activity. For example, the costs of setting up machines would be assigned to the activity center that sets up machines. Instead of a department rate, using activity-based costing, we have a cost driver rate that must be computed for each activity center. This means that each activity has an associated cost pool, as shown in Illustration 7–3. If the cost driver is the number of inspections, for example, then the company must be able to estimate the inspection costs before the period and, ideally, keep track of the actual cost of inspections as those costs are incurred during the period.

Activity Center A unit of the organization that performs some activity

ILLUSTRATION   *Cost Pools and Activities*

7–3

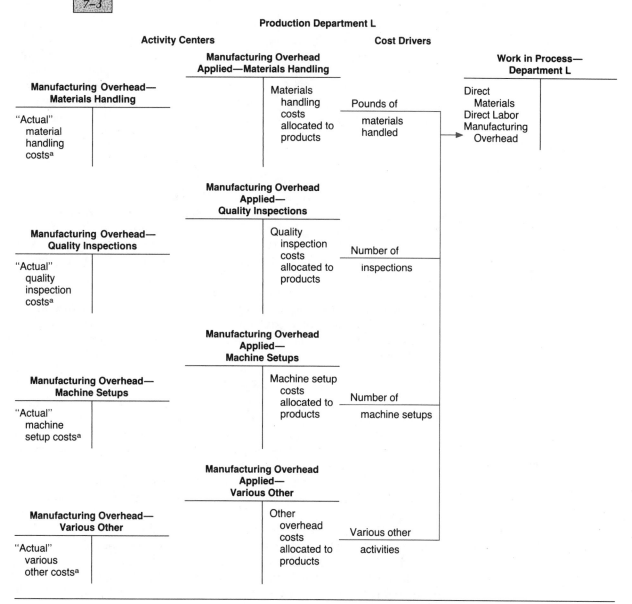

Production Department L

a "Actual" costs refers both to overhead costs directly traceable to the activity and to service department costs allocated to the activity in stage 1 cost allocation.

Assign Costs to Products   Workers and machines perform activities on each product as it is produced. Costs are allocated to products by multiplying each activity's indirect cost rate by the volume of activity used in making the product.

Assume in Illustration 7–3 that the service department overhead costs have already been allocated to the production department overhead accounts. That is, stage 1 allocation has been done and we are now looking at stage 2 allocation of overhead costs to products. Assume further that the illustration is for only one production department, say Department L. This reminds us that companies identify numerous activities, or cost drivers, for each department.

As a product is worked on in Department L, materials are moved to the work area. Materials handling overhead, such as the wages paid to the materials movers, is allocated to the product by multiplying the overhead allocation rate for materials handling times the number of pounds of materials moved. For quality inspections, the overhead is allocated based on the rate for inspections times the number of inspections made on the product. The same procedure is followed for all other activities. The procedure is repeated for each product worked on in Department L.

Circuit Board Illustration

Next, we present an example that shows how activity-based costing was developed for printed-circuit boards in a Hewlett-Packard plant.[4] (We have simplified some of the activities and rounded some of the numbers for presentation purposes.) The activities required to make the product, from materials purchasing to quality testing, are described in the top panel of Illustration 7–4. Examples of the overhead costs associated with each activity are shown next to the activity. The company must keep a separate overhead account to record the cost of each activity.

In the bottom panel of the illustration, these activities are shown in the first column, and the related cost drivers used to apply the activities, such as the number of parts for materials purchasing overhead, are presented in the second column.

The next step is to compute indirect cost rates using the formula presented above. These rates are shown in the third column of the bottom panel of Illustration 7–4. Managers have calculated the rates to be $.10 per part, $1.00 per board, and so forth. The fourth column shows the number of cost driver activities per circuit board required to make this particular product— PC Board Type 67A. Every other type of printed-circuit board would have different activities. The fifth column shows the overhead cost per circuit board of each activity required to make the product. When summed, the total overhead cost allocated to PC Board Type 67A is $43 per board.

We have just demonstrated how overhead is applied to the product. This particular Hewlett-Packard plant is sufficiently automated that there are virtually no direct labor costs traceable to a particular product. All labor cost is combined with overhead and is part of the indirect cost rates in Illustration 7–4. The cost of direct materials is traceable to the product and would be added to the overhead cost of $43 per unit to derive the total cost of manufacturing the product.

Armed with this information, Hewlett-Packard managers can investigate ways to change the product or production methods to manage costs. For example, if a way could be found to reduce test time from .20 hours to .10 hours, only six minutes shorter, the company could save $7 per circuit board, assuming these costs are variable. In fact, based on our interviews of managers and workers in this particular Hewlett-Packard plant, activity-

---

[4] Debbie Berlant, Reese Browning, and George Foster, "How Hewlett-Packard Gets Numbers It Can Trust," *Harvard Business Review,* January–February 1990, pp. 178–83.

ILLUSTRATION   *Activity-Based Costing of a Circuit Board*

7–4

Activities	Typical Overhead Costs
1. Purchasing materials	Costs of people involved in purchasing, inspecting, and storing materials.
2. Starting the product	Costs of people who prepare software for computer-driven machinery.
3. Inserting components	Costs of machines and people who insert components on the circuit boards.
4. Soldering	Cost of machines that solder components onto the board.
5. Quality testing	Costs of machines and people who check to see that components are properly inserted and the circuit board meets specifications.

(1) Activity	(2) Cost Driver Used to Allocate Overhead	(3) Rate per Cost Driver		(4) Number of Cost Driver Units in One Circuit Board		(5) Cost per Circuit Board for PC Board Type 67A
1. Purchasing materials	Number of parts in each circuit board	$.10 per part	×	90 parts	=	$ 9.00
2. Starting the product	Number of boards in the product	$1.00 per board	×	1 raw board	=	1.00
3. Inserting the components	Number of insertions per board	$.20 per insertion	×	80 insertions	=	16.00
4. Soldering	Number of boards soldered	$3.00 per board	×	1 board	=	3.00
5. Quality testing	Number of hours board is in testing	$70.00 per hour	×	.20 hours	=	14.00
Total overhead per printed-circuit board[a]						43.00
Cost of direct materials						75.00
Total cost of manufacturing the product						$118.00

[a] Direct labor is small and part of overhead in this plant.

Source: Adapted from Debbie Berlant, Reese Browning, and George Foster, "How Hewlett-Packard Gets Numbers It Can Trust," *Havard Business Review*, January–February 1990, pp. 178–83.

based costing revealed surprising information about the cost of activities, which caused a change in product design and different production methods. New cost accounting methods had a valuable impact on the company.

ACTIVITY-BASED COSTING ILLUSTRATED

The following example illustrates how unit costs are computed when companies use activity-based costing. We contrast the results using activity-based costing to those using a department-based rate.

Assume SU Company makes two products: Standard and Unique. The Standard product line is a high-volume line, and the Unique line is a low-volume, specialized product. Assume that the overhead costs from service departments have already been allocated to Department A's Manufacturing Overhead account in stage 1 of the cost allocation process (as discussed in Chapter 6).

Department Allocation

Using department allocation, SU Company used the following procedure to allocate manufacturing overhead costs to the two products for the month of January, Year 2.

1. Late in Year 1, managers and accountants developed a predetermined overhead rate based on the following estimates for Year 2:

Estimated annual overhead for Department A for Year 2 . . . . $2,000,000

Estimated machine-hours to be worked during Year 2 in
Department A . . . . 20,000 hours

Department A overhead rate ($2,000,000/20,000 hours) . . . . . . $100 per machine-hour

2. At the end of January, Year 2, the following information for the month of January was available:

Actual machine-hours used in January, Year 2:

Standard products 1,500

Unique products   500

Total actual machine-hours in January 2,000

3. Accountants then allocated overhead to the products worked on in January using the predetermined rate of $100 per hour times the actual machine-hours worked on each product in Department A during January:

Overhead allocated to products worked on in January:

Standard products ($100 × 1,500 hours) $150,000

Unique products ($100 × 500 hours)   50,000

Total overhead allocated to products $200,000

These calculations are summarized in Illustration 7–5.

ILLUSTRATION

SU Company: Department Allocation

Department Allocation

Late in Year 1, managers and accountants made the following estimates for Year 2:

Estimated annual overhead for the department $2,000,000

Estimated machine-hours to be worked during the year in
the department . . . . 20,000 hours

Department overhead rate ($2,000,000/20,000 hours) . . . . $100 per hour

At the end of January, Year 2, the following information is available:

Actual machine-hours in January:

Standard products 1,500

Unique products   500

Total actual machine-hours in January 2,000

Overhead is allocated to products worked on in January using the predetermined rate of $100 per hour times the actual machine-hours in January:

Standard products ($100 × 1,500 hours) $150,000

Unique products ($100 × 500 hours)   50,000

Total overhead allocated to products $200,000

Assigning Costs Using
Activity-Based Costing

When SU Company used activity-based costing, it first identified four activities that were important cost drivers and the cost drivers used to allocate overhead. These activities were (1) purchasing materials, (2) setting up machines when a new product was started, (3) inspecting products, and (4) operating machines.

The amount of overhead and the volume of activity events were estimated for each activity. For example, management estimated the company would purchase 100,000 pounds of materials that would require overhead costs of $200,000 for the year. Examples of these overhead costs would be salaries of people to purchase, inspect, and store materials. Consequently, each pound of materials used to make a product would be assigned an overhead cost of $2 ($200,000/100,000 pounds).

These estimates were made in Year 1 to be used during all of Year 2. (In practice, companies frequently set rates for the entire year; sometimes they set rates for shorter periods, such as a quarter.) Illustration 7–6 shows the predetermined annual rates computed for the four activities. The estimated overhead cost in column (3) is divided by the cost driver volume in column (4) to get the rate in column (5).

The total overhead estimated for Year 2 is $2,000,000 using activity-based costing, just as it was using department allocation. The estimate of total overhead should be the same whether using plantwide allocation, department allocation, or activity-based costing. The primary difference between activity-based costing and department allocation is the number of cost pools and activities used to allocate overhead costs. Department allocation uses just one cost pool per department. Activity-based costing uses four cost pools in this case. In practice, companies generally use more than four cost pools because more than four activities are important, but we want to keep the illustration as simple as possible.

By the end of January, Year 2, the SU Company has collected the information shown on the top of page 256 for January about the actual cost driver volume for each of the two products.

ILLUSTRATION   *Predetermined Annual Overhead Rates for Activity-Based Costing*

7–6

(1) Activity	(2) Cost Driver Used to Allocate Overhead	(3) Estimated Overhead Cost for the Activity	(4) Estimated Cost Driver Volume for Year 2	(5) Rate Col. (3)/Col. (4)
1. Purchasing materials	Number of pounds of materials in each unit of product	$200,000	100,000 pounds	$ 2 per pound
2. Machine setups	Number of machine setups	800,000	400 setups	$2,000 per setup
3. Inspections	Hours of inspections	400,000	4,000 hours	$ 100 per hour
4. Running machines	Machine-hours	600,000	20,000 hours	$ 30 per hour
Total estimated overhead		$2,000,000		

	Standard Product	Unique Product
1. Purchasing materials	6,000 pounds	4,000 pounds
2. Machine setups	10 setups	30 setups
3. Inspections	200 hours	200 hours
4. Running machines	1,500 hours	500 hours

Multiplying the actual activity events for each product times the predetermined rates computed above resulted in the overhead allocated to the two products shown in Illustration 7–7.

Unit Costs Compared

Assume SU Company produced 1,000 units of Standard and 200 units of Unique in January. Further, the direct materials cost is $100 per unit for Standard and $200 per unit for Unique. Direct labor cost is $20 per unit for Standard and $30 per unit for Unique. Comparing the overhead allocations of the department allocation and the activity-based costing allocation methods reveals the differences in unit costs shown in Illustration 7–8.

Analysis

More overhead is allocated per unit to the more specialized, lower-volume Unique product using activity-based costing. Unique is allocated more overhead primarily because activity-based costing recognizes the need for more setups for Unique and for as many inspection hours of Unique as for the higher-volume Standard. By failing to assign costs to all of the activities, Standard was subsidizing Unique. Many companies have found their situation to be similar to this example. Activity-based costing has revealed that low-volume, specialized products have been the cause of greater costs than managers had realized.

 **Self-Study Question**

2 It is now December of Year 2 for SU Company. Recall that the department overhead rate for Year 2 was $100 per machine-hour. At the end of December, Year 2, the following information is available:

ILLUSTRATION   *Overhead Costs Assigned to Products Using Activity-Based Costing*

7–7

		Standard Product		Unique Product	
Activity	Rate	Actual Cost Driver Units in January	Cost Allocated to Standard Product	Actual Cost Driver Units in January	Cost Allocated to Unique Product
1. Purchasing materials	$2 per pound	6,000 pounds	$12,000	4,000 pounds	$ 8,000
2. Machine setups	$2,000 per setup	10 setups	20,000	30 setups	60,000
3. Inspections	$100 per inspection hour	200 hours	20,000	200 hours	20,000
4. Running machines	$30 per hour	1,500 hours	45,000	500 hours	15,000
Total cost allocated to each product			$97,000		$103,000

	Machine-Hours	Units
Standard products	2,000 hours	1,300 units
Unique products	1,000 hours	400 units
Total	3,000 hours	

Activities	Standard Products	Unique Products
1. Purchasing materials	8,000 pounds	8,000 pounds
2. Machine setups	15 setups	50 setups
3. Inspections	220 hours	400 hours
4. Running machines	2,000 hours	1,000 hours

Compute the costs per unit for both the Standard product and the Unique product using both the department overhead rate and the activity-based costing rates. The actual activity levels for December are given in this self-study question. You should use the rates presented in the text. You should not assume that the total overhead assigned to products for December using activity-based costing equals the total overhead allocated using the department allocation rate. Assume the direct materials costs are $100 and $200 per unit for Standard and Unique, respectively; and direct labor costs are $20 and $30 per unit, respectively. Round unit costs to the nearest dollar.

The solution to this question is at the end of this chapter on page 286.

COST FLOWS THROUGH ACCOUNTS

Illustration 7–9 shows the flow of costs through accounts using activity-based costing. The amounts for direct labor and direct materials are based on the facts given above. The manufacturing overhead applied appeared in Illustration 7–7. The applied manufacturing overhead can be thought of as the stage 2 cost allocation or assignment to products, whereas the stage 1 allocation would have been to the Department A Manufacturing Overhead account, shown in the lower left of Illustration 7–9. We assume all costs

---

ILLUSTRATION

7–8

Comparison of Product Costs Using Department Allocation and Activity-Based Costing

	Department Allocation		Activity-Based Costing	
	Standard	Unique	Standard	Unique
Direct materials	$100	$200	$100	$200
Direct labor	20	30	20	30
Overhead	150[a]	250[b]	97[c]	515[d]
Total Unit Cost	$270	$480	$217	$745

[a] $150 = Overhead cost allocation to products using department rate from Illustration 7–5 ÷ Units produced = $150,000/1,000 units.

[b] $250 = Overhead cost allocation to products using department rate from Illustration 7–5 ÷ Units produced = $50,000/200 units.

[c] $97 = Overhead cost allocation to products using activity-based costing from Illustration 7–7 ÷ Units produced = $97,000/1,000 units.

[d] $515 = Overhead cost allocation to products using activity-based costing from Illustration 7–7 ÷ Units produced = $103,000/200 units.

I L L U S T R A T I O N   *Flow of Costs through Accounts Using Activity-Based Costing*

7–9

Material Inventory	
	100,000[a]
	40,000[b]

Wages Payable	
	20,000[c]
	6,000[e]

Work in Process—Department A

Standard:		
Direct Materials	100,000[a]	217,000 ⟶
Direct Labor	20,000[c]	
Manufacturing Overhead	97,000[d]	Costs transferred to subsequent departments
Unique:		
Direct Materials	40,000[b]	
Direct Labor	6,000[e]	149,000 ⟶
Manufacturing Overhead	103,000[d]	

Purchasing Materials

Manufacturing Overhead[f]		Manufacturing Overhead Applied[d]	
Actual costs			12,000 to Standard
			8,000 to Unique

Machine Setups

Manufacturing Overhead[f]		Manufacturing Overhead Applied[d]	
Actual costs			20,000 to Standard
			60,000 to Unique

Inspections

Manufacturing Overhead[f]		Manufacturing Overhead Applied[d]	
Actual costs			20,000 to Standard
			20,000 to Unique

Running Machines

Manufacturing Overhead[f]		Manufacturing Overhead Applied[d]	
Actual costs			45,000 to Standard
			15,000 to Unique

[a] $100,000 = 1,000 units × $100.
[b] $40,000 = 200 units × $200.
[c] $20,000 = 1,000 units × $20.
[d] Given as the overhead applied in Illustration 7–7.
[e] $6,000 = 200 units × $30.
[f] Actual manufacturing overhead for each activity center, or cost pool, in Department A is recorded here, including costs allocated to Department A in stage 1 cost allocation.

were transferred out of Work in Process Inventory—Department A to subsequent work in process departments.

IMPACT OF NEW PRODUCTION ENVIRONMENT ON ACTIVITY BASES

When cost systems were first being developed in industry, companies were far more labor intensive than today. Much of the overhead cost was related to the support of labor, so it made sense to allocate overhead to products based on the amount of labor in the products. Labor is still a major product cost in many companies, especially service organizations like public accounting firms. In those cases, overhead is often allocated to products (which are called *jobs*) on the basis of the amount of labor in the product.

As companies have become more automated, including companies in the service sector such as banks, direct labor has become less appropriate as a basis for allocating overhead. As direct labor has shrunk to less than 5 percent of product costs in many companies, and overhead increased, companies that stubbornly continue to allocate overhead to products based on direct labor are seeing rates increase as high as 500 percent or more. (We have seen cases where overhead rates are more than 1,000 percent of direct labor costs.)

When labor is such a small part of product costs, there is little, if any, relation between labor and overhead. Further, small errors in assigning labor to products are magnified many times when overhead rates are several hundred percent of labor costs, or more. Finally, allocating overhead on the basis of direct labor sends signals that direct labor is more expensive than it really is. This also creates tremendous incentives to reduce the labor content of products. While this may be desirable in particular circumstances, such decisions should be based on accurate cost numbers, not numbers that are heavily biased because of an arbitrary cost allocation method.

Japanese Allocation Methods

Managers in Japanese companies are known to prefer to allocate overhead to create particular incentive effects. Although a world leader in implementing new manufacturing technology, direct labor is still widely used as a basis for allocating overhead to products. For example, the Hitachi VCR plant is highly automated, yet continues to use direct labor as a basis for allocating overhead. "Hitachi, like many large Japanese manufacturers, is convinced that reducing direct labor is essential for ongoing cost improvement. The company is committed to aggressive automation to promote long-term competitiveness. Allocating overhead based on direct labor creates the strong proautomation incentives throughout the organization."[5]

In another Hitachi plant, overhead is allocated based on the number of parts in a product to create incentives to reduce the number of parts in the product. In a highly automated Japanese motorcycle plant studied by the authors, indirect costs are allocated to products based on the amount of direct materials and direct labor in each type of motorcycle in part to create incentives to reduce labor costs.

ACTIVITY-BASED COSTING IN MARKETING

Activity-based costing is not limited to the cost of producing goods and services, it can also be applied to marketing or administrative activities. The principles and methods are the same as discussed above: (1) Identify activities or cost drivers, (2) compute an indirect cost rate for each activity, and (3) allocate indirect costs by multiplying the indirect cost rate for each activity by the volume of activities.

Instead of computing the cost of a product, however, accountants compute a cost of performing an administrative or marketing service. For example, consider the activities of distributing tissue products through different distribution channels. Tissue products can be sold using several channels of

[5] Toshiro Hiromoto, "Another Hidden Edge—Japanese Management Accounting," *Harvard Business Review*, July–August 1988, p. 23.

distribution, such as grocery stores, convenience stores, and the industrial market. Each channel has different activities, such as:

- Convenience stores would require many shipments in small orders and considerable marketing support.
- Grocery stores would have relatively large shipments and a variety of products, and would require considerable marketing support.
- Industrial users would involve brokers, minimum marketing support, and larger orders.[6]

The cost of alternative channels of distribution is useful to marketing managers who make decisions about which channel to use. In this case, obvious cost drivers would include: number of shipments per period, size of shipments, number of products in a shipment, and measures of merchandising support.

STRATEGIC USE OF ACTIVITY-BASED COSTING

Many experts view activity-based costing as offering strategic opportunities for companies.[7] One of the key ways companies develop competitive advantages is to become a low-cost producer or seller. Companies such as Wal-Mart in retailing, United Parcel Service in delivery services, and Southwest Airlines in the airline industry have created a competitive advantage by reducing costs. Michael Porter, among others, has pointed out that certain companies have learned to use the information they have gained from their cost systems to make substantial price cuts to increase market share.[8]

Activity-based costing plays an important role in companies' strategies and long-range plans to develop a competitive cost advantage. Activity-based costing focuses attention on activities. Cost reduction generally requires a change in activities. Top management can send notices out to company employees to reduce costs, but the implementation will require a change in activities. If you have been in school during a period in which education costs are being cut, you know that achieving the cut required a change in activities such as canceled classes, larger class sizes, and reduced services. It is impossible to know the effect of a change in activities on costs without the type of cost information provided by activity-based costing.

USING ACTIVITY-BASED COSTING TO ELIMINATE NONVALUE ADDED COSTS

Activity-based costing can be used to identify and eliminate activities that add costs but not value to the product. Nonvalue added costs are costs of activities that could be eliminated without reducing product quality, performance, or value. For example, storing bicycle frames until needed for production does not add to the finished bicycle's value. Suppose management can find ways to eliminate storing bicycle frames, for example, by

---

[6] See J. M. Reeve, "Cost Management in Continuous-Process Environments," in *Emerging Practices in Cost Management,* ed. Barry J. Brinker (New York: Warren, Gorham & Lamont, 1992), pp. F3-1–F3-13.

[7] See J. Shank and V. Govindarajan, *Strategic Cost Analysis* (Homewood, Ill.: Richard D. Irwin, 1989), for an extensive discussion of the strategic use of cost analysis.

[8] M. E. Porter, *Competitive Advantage* (New York: Free Press, 1985).

using just-in-time purchasing. If so, the company could save money without reducing the quality of the finished product.

The following types of activities are candidates for elimination because they do not add value to the product:

1. *Storage*. Storage of materials, work-in-process, or finished goods inventories is an obvious nonvalue added activity. Many companies have applied the just-in-time philosophy to purchasing and production to reduce or even eliminate storage.

2. *Moving items*. Moving parts, materials, and other items around the factory floor is another activity that does not add value to the finished product. A steel mill in Michigan once had hundreds of miles of railroad tracks just to move materials and partially finished products from one part of the factory to another. Eliminating a hundred miles or so of track reduced both labor and overhead costs, and even eliminated some spoilage because products were sometimes damaged by train accidents.

3. *Waiting for work*. Idle time does not add value to products. Reducing the amount of time people wait to work on something reduces the cost of idle time.

4. *Production process*. Managers should investigate the entire production process from purchasing, to production, to inspection, to shipping, to identify activities that do not add value to the finished product. Managers should ascertain whether the company needs as many setups, whether the cost of higher quality materials and labor could be justified by a reduction in inspection time, whether the cost of ordering could be reduced, and so forth.

These are only a few examples of nonvalue added costs. We are certain that if you observe activities in healthcare organizations, fast food restaurants, construction sites, government agencies, and lots of other organizations, even in universities, you will see lots of examples of nonvalue added activities.

Activity-based costing helps measure the costs of nonvalue added activities. For example, referring to the case of Deere & Company discussed earlier, the company measured the variable cost of moving materials to be $293 per load, where a "load" was a movement of materials around the factory. If the company could have eliminated 1,000 loads per year, it would have saved $293,000, all things being equal, without any reduction in the value of the finished product.

OPPORTUNITIES TO IMPROVE ACTIVITY-BASED COSTING IN PRACTICE

The use of activity-based costing in industry is relatively new. Companies are continually encountering limitations and finding ways to improve activity-based costing. A philosopher once said that our knowledge is like a circle: The more we know, the larger the circle. But the larger the circle, the greater its boundary and the more we realize the limits of our knowledge. Activity-based costing has shown managers they have much to learn about the cost of the activities required to make their products. We next discuss several of the problems managers face in trying to improve on the basic activity-based costing model presented in this chapter.

Variable versus
Fixed Costs

A major area of difficulty encountered by companies is how to deal with variable versus fixed costs at the unit level.[9] If the cost of a quality inspection is estimated to be $100 per inspection, for example, does that mean that eliminating one inspection will save the company $100? The answer is no if the $100 inspection costs include some of the inspector's salary, because the inspector's salary will not likely be reduced if one inspection is eliminated. If any costs that are fixed in the short run are included in the activity's cost, then those costs would not be affected by short-run changes in the volume of activity.

Companies deal with this in several ways. First, they might consider only variable costs. Treat fixed costs as period costs and ignore them in computing product costs. This avoids unitizing fixed costs, but it leaves managers who are making long-term decisions about product pricing, profitability, and cost management in the dark.

Another approach is to compute separate activity rates for variable costs and for fixed costs. This approach was used successfully by Deere & Company.[10] Each activity, such as machine setup, had two rates—one for variable costs and one for fixed costs. Machine setup had a total rate of $34 per hour made up of $22 per hour for variable overhead items like maintenance and $12 per hour for fixed overhead items like salaries and depreciation.

Hierarchy of
Overhead Costs

Allocating all costs to units is misleading if some costs do not vary with the volume of units. For example, the costs of machine setups are generally batch-related costs. A machine setup is required for each new batch of products whether the batch contains 1 unit or 1,000 units. The setup cost is not affected by the number of *units,* but rather by the number of *batches.*

Management can establish a hierarchy of costs like that shown in Illustration 7–10.[11] Strictly variable costs, such as energy costs to run machines, are affected by the volume of units produced. These appear at the bottom of the illustration as unit-level costs. Naturally, any variable costs such as direct materials costs are unit-level costs.

At the other extreme, at the top of the illustration, are capacity-related costs. These costs are essentially fixed by management's decisions to have a particular size of store, factory, hospital, or other facility. Although they are fixed with respect to volume, it would be misleading to give the impression that these costs cannot be changed. Managers can make decisions that affect capacity costs; such decisions just require a longer time horizon to implement than do decisions to reduce unit-level costs.

[9] E. Noreen and N. Soderstrom, "Are Cost Drivers Strictly Proportional to Their Cost Drivers? Evidence from Hospital Service Departments," School of Business, University of Washington, Seattle, Wash., June 1991, provides empirical evidence from hospitals that indirect costs are not proportional to the volume of activities.

[10] "John Deere Component Works," Harvard Business School cases 187-107 and 187-108.

[11] R. Cooper and R. S. Kaplan, "Profit Priorities from Activity-Based Costing," *Harvard Business Review,* May–June 1991, pp. 130–35.

ILLUSTRATION

Hierarchy of Product Costs

Cost Category	Cost-Generating Activities
1. Capacity-related costs	Plant management Building depreciation and rent Heating and lighting
2. Product- and customer-level costs	Customer records and files Product specifications Customer service
3. Batch-related costs	Machine setups Quality inspections
4. Unit-level costs	Energy to run machines Direct materials

Adapted from R. Cooper and R. S. Kaplan, "Profit Priorities from Activity-Based Costing," *Harvard Business Review*, May–June 1991, p. 132.

The two middle categories of costs are affected by the way the company manages its activities. A company that makes products to order for a customer will have more product/customer-level costs than a company that provides limited choices. A company that schedules its work so that one product is made on Monday, a second product on Tuesday, and so on through Friday has lower batch-related costs than if it produced all five products on Monday, all five again on Tuesday, and so on through the week. In practice, many of the greatest opportunities for reducing costs are in these middle categories of product/customer-level and batch-related costs.

Using a hierarchy like this, if management makes decisions that affect units, but not batches, products, customers, or capacity, management would analyze costs in category 4—costs of unit-level activities. If management makes decisions that affect capacity, however, all activities in categories 1 through 4 would probably be affected, and costs in all four categories would be analyzed.

Cost of Activities when the Demand for Services Causes Congestion

Another opportunity to improve activity-based costing takes into account both the volume and the timing of the demand for an activity. If the demand for a product is uneven, then the demands on overhead activity are likely to increase. To see the point, imagine a local McDonald's restaurant could serve 1,000 meals per day spaced evenly at the rate of one meal per minute. At that rate, the company would probably need only a few people per day, each working an eight-hour shift. In reality, demand peaks at breakfast, again at lunch, and again at dinner. More than a few people have to be hired to serve the 1,000 meals scheduled according to these demands at peak times, although for shorter work shifts. Hiring additional people to meet these peak demands increases the overhead costs of hiring and training additional people, and of developing work schedules.

Work on this problem is in the early stages. Some academics and practitioners have worked to develop computer models of companies' activities, like the one discussed in the real world application for this chapter, that take into account both the volume of activity and the congestion that occurs when there are peaks and valleys in the demand for services.

Developing New Methods to Help Manage Healthcare Costs*

Healthcare costs are now nearly 15 percent of gross national product and promise to increase as baby boomers age. Yet many people go untreated under the current United States healthcare system. New medical technology will be required to improve the quality of health care while reducing costs.

Stuart Pharmaceuticals wanted to determine the impact of a new anesthesia on healthcare costs. This new drug had the potential to reduce the time that patients remained in recovery rooms after surgery because they would awaken sooner with fewer side effects. Reducing the time patients spent in the recovery room could reduce the amount of time nurses have to be present watching over patients, thereby reducing nursing costs.

In a study of two outpatient surgery centers, one at the Methodist Memorial Hospital in Peoria, Illinois, and the other at Emory University Hospital in Atlanta, Georgia, physicians and researchers attempted to determine the potential reduction in recovery room costs using activity-based costing as a tool. They found that using such cost drivers as patient minutes in the recovery room did not measure the potential cost savings. A reduction in patient minutes reduced the need for nursing time, but because nursing time is "purchased" in increments of several-hour shifts, not minutes, there was no simple relation between reduction in patient minutes and reduction in cost.

Further, although the number of patients in the recovery room varied during the day, enough nurses had to be on hand to deal with the times when the recovery room had the most patients. If the new drug reduced the number of patients in the recovery room at peak demand times, the cost savings would be greater than if the drug reduced demand in slack times.

To estimate the effects of the new drug on the need for nurses in the recovery room, the researchers and physicians collected data on two groups of patients, one group anesthetized with the new drug and one group with a traditional drug. Using these actual cases and a computer software package, the researchers simulated the running of the outpatient surgery centers as if patients had only the new drug and determined the number of nurses needed at each minute of the day. They did the same with the traditional drug. The research team found that the new anesthesia provided an opportunity to reduce nursing staff 10 to 25 percent without reducing the quality of patient care.

* Based on the paper by M. L. Marais and M. W. Maher, "Process-Oriented Activity-Based Costing," Graduate School of Management, University of California, Davis, Calif., March 1993.

3 Classify the following items as to whether they generate capacity-related costs, product- or customer-related costs, batch-related costs, or unit-level costs.

    a. Piecework labor.

    b. Long-term lease on a building.

    c. Energy to run machines.

    d. Engineering drawings for a product.

    e. Purchase order.

    f. Movement of materials for products in production.

    g. Change order to meet new customer specifications.

The solution to this question is at the end of this chapter on page 287.

BEHAVIORAL AND IMPLEMENTATION ISSUES

Accountants cannot implement activity-based costing without becoming familiar with the operations of the company. In identifying activities, accountants become part of a team with management and people from production, engineering, marketing, and other parts of the company who all work to identify the activities that drive the company's costs. This often creates discomfort at first as accountants are forced to deal with unfamiliar areas, but in the long-run, their familiarity with the company's operating activities can improve their contribution to the company. Also, nonaccounting personnel feel a greater sense of ownership of the numbers reported by the accounting system as accounting improves its credibility among nonaccountants.

One of the problems encountered when implementing activity-based costing is the failure to get influential people in the organization to buy into the process. Accounting methods in companies are like rules in sports; people become accustomed to playing by the rules and oppose change to something unknown.

For example, two analysts at one company spent several months of their time and hundreds of hours of computer time to develop an activity-based costing system. Their analysis revealed several hundred products that were clearly unprofitable and should be eliminated. However, the key managers to make product elimination decisions agreed to eliminate only about 20 products. Why? The analysts had failed to talk to these key managers early in the process. When presented with the final results, these managers raised numerous objections that the analysts had not anticipated. The moral is: If you are involved in trying to make a change, get all of the people who are important to that change involved in the process early.

SUMMARY

This chapter deals with the allocation of indirect costs to products. Product cost information helps managers make numerous decisions, including pricing, deciding whether to keep or drop a product, estimating the cost of making a similar product, and determining how to reduce the costs of making products.

Accounting for overhead is simple using plantwide allocation. All overhead costs are recorded in one cost pool for the plant without regard to the department or activity that caused them. An overhead rate, or set of rates, is used for the entire plant. A single plantwide rate might be justified in simple organizations having only a few departments and not much variety in products.

Using department allocation, each production department would be a separate cost pool. The company establishes a separate overhead allocation rate, or set of rates, for each department. In contrast, using the plantwide allocation rate, the entire plant is one cost pool.

Activity-based costing is a costing method that assigns costs first to activities, then to the products based on each product's use of activities. Activity-based costing is based on the premise: Products consume activities; activities consume resources. Activity-based costing involves the following three steps:

1. Identify the activities that consume resources, and assign costs to those activities. Purchasing materials would be an activity, for example.

2. Compute a cost rate per cost driver unit. A cost driver is a factor that causes, or "drives," an activity's costs. For the activity purchasing material, for example, the cost driver could be number of orders.

3. Assign costs to products by multiplying the cost driver rate times the volume of cost drivers consumed by the product.

The chapter discussion made the following important points about activity-based costing:

- Different cost allocation methods result in different estimates of how much it costs to make a product.
- Activity-based costing provides more detailed measures of costs than plantwide or department allocation methods.
- Activity-based costing can help marketing people by providing more accurate product cost numbers for decisions about pricing and which products to eliminate.
- Production also benefits because activity-based costing provides better information about how much activities cost. In fact, it helps identify cost drivers that were previously unknown. To manage costs, production managers learn to manage the cost drivers, that is, the activities that cause costs.
- Activity-based costing provides more information about product costs, but requires more recordkeeping. Managers must decide whether the benefits of improved decisions justify the additional cost of activity-based costing.
- Installing activity-based costing requires teamwork between accounting, production, marketing, management, and other nonaccounting people.

In thinking about what affects costs, management will likely improve decisions by categorizing costs according to major categories of activities. Using the example in the text, management could categorize costs according to the following hierarchy of costs:

1. Capacity-related costs, generated by activities such as building rent.
2. Product- and customer-level costs, generated by activities such as product and customer records.
3. Batch-related costs, generated by activities such as machine setups.
4. Unit-level costs, generated by activities such as energy to run machines.

Using a hierarchy like this, if management makes decisions that affect units, but not batches, products, customers, or capacity, management would analyze costs in category 4—costs of unit-level activities. If management makes decisions that affect capacity, however, all activities in categories 1 through 4 would probably be affected, and costs in all four categories would be analyzed.

TERMS
AND CONCEPTS

The following terms and concepts should be familiar to you after reading this chapter:

QUESTIONS

7–1   ''The problem of allocating direct costs to products is the primary subject of this chapter.'' True, false, or uncertain? Explain.

7–2   ''Activity-based costing is great for manufacturing plants, but it doesn't really address the needs of the service sector.'' Do you agree? Explain.

7–3   Stage 1 cost allocation is the allocation of costs to cost pools. What is stage 2 cost allocation?

7–4   Refer to the Real World Application on page 264. What was the problem with using patient minutes in the recovery room as a cost driver?

7–5   What activities do companies using a single plantwide rate usually select for the allocation of indirect costs?

7–6   ''A shortcut using department allocation is to ignore the allocation of service department costs to the production departments.'' True, false, or uncertain? Explain.

7–7   Explain the basic difference between plantwide and department allocation.

7–8   What exactly is a cost driver? Give at least three examples.

7–9   Lynn, the vice president of marketing, wonders how products can cost less under one cost system than under another: ''Aren't costs cut-and-dried?'' How would you respond?

7–10   ''Activity-based costing is the wave of the future. Everyone should drop their existing cost systems and adopt ABC!'' Do you agree? Explain.

7–11   A drawback to activity-based costing is that it requires more recordkeeping and extensive teamwork between all departments. What are the potential benefits of a more detailed product cost system?

7–12   What are the basic steps in computing costs using activity-based costing?

7–13   ''One of the lessons learned from activity-based costing is that all costs are really a function of volume of output.'' True, false, or uncertain? Explain.

7–14   Allocating overhead based on the volume of output, such as direct labor-hours or machine-hours, seems fair and equitable. Why then do many people claim that high-volume products subsidize low-volume products?

7–15   How do managers decide which activity bases to use? Give three criteria for choosing cost drivers.

7–16   ''Activity-based costing breaks down the indirect costs into several activities that cause costs (cost drivers). These should be the same for each department in an organization.'' True, false, or uncertain? Explain.

7–17   ''The total amount of estimated overhead used to determine allocation rates will differ depending on whether you use department allocation or activity-based costing.'' Do you agree? Explain.

7–18   What technological change has occurred in many companies that has resulted in great potential for erroneous product cost figures?

7–19   If the allocation of overhead based on direct labor can yield erroneous results, why then do highly automated plants such as Hitachi continue this practice?

7–20   "Activity-based costing is for accountants and production managers. I plan to be a marketing specialist so ABC won't help me." Do you agree with this statement? Explain.

7–21   What is the difference between a capacity-related cost and a unit-level cost? Why do we need a hierarchy of overhead costs?

EXERCISES

7–22 Plantwide versus Department Allocation
(L.O.2)

Hard & Soft Books, Inc., is a publisher of hardbacks, paperbacks, and other products. Department P produces the paperbacks and Department H produces the hardbacks. Hard & Soft Books, Inc., currently uses plantwide allocation to allocate its overhead to both types of books. The company uses machine-hours as their volume-based allocation base at a rate of $20 per machine-hour. Last year, revenue, materials, and direct labor were as follows:

	Paperbacks (P)	Hardbacks (H)
Revenue	$1,800,000	$1,250,000
Direct labor	300,000	200,000
Direct materials	800,000	400,000

Required:

a.   Compute the profit of both types of books, using plantwide allocation. Machine-hours totaled 10,000 for paperbacks and 15,000 for hardbacks.

b.   Harry, the manager of Department H, was convinced that hardbacks were really more profitable than paperbacks. He asked his good friend in accounting to break down the overhead costs into the two departments. Harry discovered that Department P would have had a rate of $18 per machine-hour while Department H would have had a rate of $25 per machine-hour if department rates had been used.

    Recompute the profits for each type of book and compute the department allocation rates for each department (use machine-hours as the allocation base).

c.   How do you explain the discrepancy between the two methods?

7–23 Plantwide versus Department Allocation
(L.O.2)

Smiley Chocolate Factory produces several different candy bars. The company currently uses a plantwide allocation method for allocating overhead. Overhead is allocated based on direct labor-hours, at a rate of $5 per labor-hour. Charlie is department manager of Department C, which manufactures the Chocco Bar and the Chewynutta Bar. Monica is department manager of Department M, which manufactures the Marsh Bar. The product costs (per case of 1,000) are as follows:

	Chocco Bar	Chewynutta Bar	Marsh Bar
Direct labor (per case)	$50	$55	$75
Raw materials (per case)	25	40	30

Required:

a.   If the Chocco Bar requires 10 hours of labor per case, the Chewynutta bar 11 hours of labor per case, and the Marsh Bar 15 hours of labor per case, compute the total cost of a case of each candy bar using plantwide allocation.

b. Monica's department uses older, outdated machines to produce the Marsh Bar. She believes that her department is being allocated some of the overhead of Department C, which recently bought state-of-the-art machines.

After requesting that overhead costs be broken down by department, the following information was discovered.

	Department C	Department M
Overhead	$8,820	$1,980
Machine-hours	1,260	1,800
Labor-hours	1,260	900

Use machine-hours as the department allocation base for Department C and labor-hours as the department allocation base for Department M, and compute the allocation rate for each.

c. Compute the cost of a case of each type of candy bar using the department allocation rates computed above if a case of Chocco Bars requires 10 machine-hours, a case of Chewynutta 11 machine-hours, and a case of Marsh Bar 15 labor-hours.

d. Was Monica correct in her belief? What happened to the cost of a case of the Marsh Bars? Which costing method provides more accurate product costs?

7–24 Activity-Based Costing
(L.O.4)

Assume that Bill Board, manager of the Engineering Department at Hewlett-Packard, has designed a new circuit board, the PC BB Special, which he believes can replace Type 67A described in the chapter. Bill Board is excited because he believes this new circuit board will save Hewlett-Packard money. The PC BB Special has 100 parts, but requires only 60 insertions, since some of the components can be easily joined together without an extra insertion into the board. Furthermore, this new board will require only .15 hours of quality testing. There is still one raw board, and one board for soldering. Despite the fact that the raw materials cost $85, Bill Board still believes that this board will be cheaper to produce than Type 67A.

Required:

a. Refer to Illustration 7–4 and compute the total cost of manufacturing the PC BB Special using the facts stated above.

b. Do you recommend that Hewlett-Packard start producing the PC BB Special?

7–25 Activity-Based Costing
(L.O.3, L.O.4)

Ned O. Williamson has just joined the SU Company (text example) as the new production manager. He was pleased to see that the SU Company uses activity-based costing. Williamson believes he can reduce production costs if he reduces the number of machine setups. He has spent the last month working with Purchasing and Sales to better coordinate raw material arrivals and the anticipated demand for the Standard and Unique products. In the month of March, he plans to produce 1,000 units of Standard and 200 units of Unique. Ned believes that with his efficient production scheduling he can reduce the number of setups for both the Standard and Unique products by 50 percent.

Required:

a. Refer to Illustration 7–7. Compute the amount of overhead allocated to the Standard and Unique products for the month of March using activity-based costing. (Assume all events are the same in March as in January except for the number of machine setups.)

b. Assume SU Company had used machine-hours and a department allocation method to allocate its overhead. Could Ned have made the cost reductions he did? What are the advantages of activity-based costing over the traditional volume-based allocation methods. What are the disadvantages?

7–26 Activity-Based Costing in a Nonmanufacturing Environment
(L.O.4)

The manager of Outdoor Adventures uses activity-based costing to compute the costs of her raft trips. Each raft holds six paying customers and a guide. She offers two types of raft trips, three-day float trips for beginners, and three-day white-water trips for seasoned rafters. The breakdown of the costs is as follows:

Activities (and cost drivers)	Float Trip Costs	White-Water Trip Costs
Advertising (trips)	$215 per trip	$215 per trip
Permit to use the river (trips)	30 per trip	50 per trip
Equipment use (trips, people)	20 per trip plus $5 per person	40 per trip plus $8 per person
Insurance (trips)	75 per trip	127 per trip
Paying guides (trips, guides)	300 per trip per guide	400 per trip per guide
Food (people)	60 per person	60 per person

Note: All per trip costs do not vary with the number of rafts or customers.

Required:

a. Compute the cost of a 28-person (including guides) float trip with four rafts and four guides.

b. Compute the cost of a 28-person (including guides) white-water trip with four rafts and four guides.

c. How much should the manager charge each customer if she wants to cover her costs?

7–27   ABC versus Traditional Costing (L.O.4, L.O.5)

Soundex Corporation produces two types of audio cassettes: standard and high-grade. The standard cassettes are used primarily in answering machines, and are designed for durability rather than accurate sound reproduction. The company only recently began producing the higher-quality high-grade model to enter the lucrative music recording market. Since the new product was introduced, profits have been steadily declining. Management believes the accounting system may not be accurately allocating costs to products, particularly since sales of the new product have been increasing.

Management has asked you to investigate the cost allocation problem. You find that manufacturing overhead is currently assigned to products based on the direct labor costs in the products. For your investigation, you have data from last year. Last year's manufacturing overhead was $440,000 based on production of 320,000 standard cassettes and 100,000 high-grade cassettes. Direct labor and direct materials costs were as follows:

	Standard	High-Grade	Total
Direct labor	$174,000	$ 66,000	$240,000
Materials	125,000	114,000	239,000

Management determined that overhead costs are caused by three cost drivers. The cost drivers and their costs for last year were as follows:

		Activity Level		
Cost Driver	Costs Assigned	Standard	High-Grade	Total
Number of production runs . . .	$200,000	40	10	50
Quality tests performed	180,000	12	18	30
Shipping orders processed . . .	60,000	100	50	150
Total overhead	$440,000			

Required:

a. How much of the overhead will be assigned to each product if the above three cost drivers are used to allocate overhead? What is the total cost per unit produced for each product?

b. How much of the overhead will be assigned to each product if direct labor cost had been used to allocate overhead? What would the total cost per unit produced be for each product?

c. How might the results explain Soundex's declining profits?

7–28 Activity-Based Costing in a Service Environment
(L.O.4, L.O.5)

Ms. Greenthumb, Inc., is a lawn and garden care service. The company originally specialized in serving small residential clients, but has recently started contracting for work on larger apartment and office building grounds. Since Ms. Greenthumb believes that commercial lawn care is more profitable, she is considering dropping residential services altogether.

Five field employees worked a total of 10,000 hours last year, 6,500 on residential jobs and 3,500 on commercial jobs. Wages amounted to $9.00 per hour for all work done. Direct materials used are included in overhead as "supplies." All overhead is allocated on the basis of labor-hours worked, which is also the basis for customer charges. Because of greater competition for commercial accounts, Ms. Greenthumb can charge $22 per hour for residential work but only $19 per hour for commercial work.

Required:

a. If overhead for the year was $62,000, what were the profits of commercial and residential service using labor-hours as the allocation base?

b. Overhead consists of transportation, equipment use costs and supplies. These costs can be traced to the following activities:

Activity	Cost Driver	Cost	Activity Level Commercial	Residential
Transportation	Number of clients serviced	$ 8,000	15	45
Equipment use	Equipment hours	18,000	3,500	2,100
Supplies	Area serviced in square yards	36,000	130,000	70,000
Total overhead		$62,000		

Recalculate profits for commercial and residential services based on these activity bases.

c. What recommendations do you have for management regarding the profitability of these two types of services?

7–29 ABC versus Traditional Costing
(L.O.3, L.O.4, L.O.5)

Timepiece Corporation manufactures travel clocks and watches. Overhead costs are currently allocated using direct labor-hours, but the controller has recommended using an activity-based costing system using the following data:

Activity	Cost Driver	Cost	Activity Level Travel Clocks	Watches
Production setup	Number of setups	$100,000	10	15
Material handling and requisition	Number of parts	30,000	18	36
Packaging and shipping	Number of units shipped	60,000	45,000	75,000
Total		$190,000		

Required:

a. Compute the amount of overhead to be allocated to each of the products under activity-based costing.

b. Compute the amount of overhead to be allocated to each product using labor-hours as the allocation base. Assume labor-hours required to assemble each unit is .5 per travel clock and 1.0 per watch, and that 60,000 travel clocks and 90,000 watches were produced.

c. Should the company follow the controller's recommendations?

7–30 ABC versus Traditional Costing in a Service Company (L.O.4, L.O.5)

John T. Bookmeister, CPA, provides consulting and tax preparation services to his clients. He charges a fee of $100.00 per hour for each service. His revenues and costs for the year are shown in the following income statement:

	Tax	Consulting	Total
Revenue	$65,000	$135,000	$200,000
Expenses:			
Secretary salary	———	———	40,000
Supplies	———	———	36,000
Computer equipment depreciation	———	———	20,000
Profit	———	———	$104,000

Being an accountant, John has kept good records of the following data for cost allocation purposes:

		Activity Level	
Overhead Cost	Cost Driver	Tax Preparation	Consulting
Secretary salary	Number of clients	72	48
Supplies	Number of requisitions	800	1,200
Computer costs	Computer hours	1,000	600

Required:

a. Complete the income statement using activity-based costing and using John's three cost drivers.

b. Recompute the income statement using direct labor-hours as the only allocation base (650 hours for Tax; 1,350 hours for consulting).

c. How might John's decisions be altered if he were to allocate all overhead costs using direct labor-hours?

d. Under what circumstances would the labor-based allocation and activity-based costing (using John's three cost drivers) result in similar profit results?

7–31 ABC: Cost Flows through T-Accounts (L.O.6)

Disks-To-Go, Inc., recently switched to activity-based costing from the department allocation method. The manager of Department F has estimated the following cost drivers and rates:

Activity Centers	Cost Drivers	Rate per Cost Driver Unit
Materials handling	Pounds of material handled	$ 6 per pound
Quality inspections	Number of inspections	$ 75 per inspection
Machine setups	Number of machine setups	$ 900 per setup
Running machines	Number of machine-hours	$7.50 per hour

Direct materials costs were $100,000, and direct labor costs were $50,000 during the month of March. During March, Department F handled 2,500 pounds of materials, made 500 inspections, had 25 setups, and ran the machines for 10,000 hours.

Required:

Use T-accounts to show the flow of materials, labor, and overhead costs from the four overhead activity centers through Work in Process Inventory, and out to Finished Goods Inventory. Use the following accounts: Materials Inventory, Wages

Payable, four Overhead Applied accounts, Work in Process Inventory, and Finished Goods Inventory.

7–32 ABC: Cost Flows through T-Accounts
(L.O.6)

Nykee, Inc., a shoe manufacturer, recently switched to activity-based costing from the department allocation method. The manager of Department B, which manufactures the shoes, has identified the following cost drivers and rates:

Activity Centers	Cost Drivers	Rate per Cost Driver Unit
Materials handling	Yards of material handled	$ 1 per yard
Quality inspections	Number of inspections	$100 per inspection
Machine setups	Number of machine setups	$800 per setup
Running machines	Number of machine-hours	$ 10 per hour

Direct materials costs were $200,000, and direct labor costs were $100,000 during July. During July, Department B handled 20,000 yards of materials, made 400 inspections, had 50 setups, and ran the machines for 10,000 hours.

Required:

Use T-accounts to show the flow of materials, labor, and the overhead costs from the four overhead activity centers through Work in Process Inventory and out to Finished Goods Inventory. Use the following accounts: Materials Inventory, Wages Payable, four Overhead Applied accounts, Work in Process Inventory, and Finished Goods Inventory.

PROBLEMS

7–33 Comparative Income Statements and Management Analysis

Fleetfoot, Inc., manufactures two types of shoes: B-Ball and Marathon. B-Ball has a complex design that uses gel-filled compartments to provide support. Marathon is simpler to manufacture and uses conventional foam padding. Last year, Fleetfoot had the following revenues and costs:

FLEETFOOT, INC.
Income Statement

	B-Ball	Marathon	Total
Revenue	$390,000	$368,000	$758,000
Direct materials	110,000	100,000	210,000
Direct labor	80,000	40,000	120,000
Indirect costs:			
Administration .... _____		_____	39,000
Production setup .... _____		_____	90,000
Quality control .... _____		_____	60,000
Sales and marketing .... _____		_____	120,000
Operating profit .... _____		_____	$119,000

Fleetfoot currently uses labor costs to allocate all overhead, but management is considering implementing an activity-based costing system. After interviewing the sales and production staff, management decides to allocate administrative costs on the basis of direct labor costs, but to use the following bases to allocate the remaining costs:

Activity	Cost Driver	Activity Level B-Ball	Activity Level Marathon
Production setup	Number of production runs	10	20
Quality control	Number of inspections	40	40
Sales and marketing	Number of advertisements	12	48

Required:

a. Complete the income statement using the activity bases above.

b. Write a brief report indicating how management could use activity-based costing to reduce costs?

c. Restate the income statement for Fleetfoot, Inc., using direct labor costs as the only overhead allocation base.

d. Write a report to management stating why product line profits differ using activity-based costing compared to the traditional approach. Indicate whether activity-based costing provides more accurate information and why (if you believe it does provide more accurate information). Indicate in your report how the use of labor-based overhead allocation could result in Fleetfoot management making suboptimal decisions.

7–34 Comparative Income Statements and Management Analysis

Magic Photography offers two types of services: Deluxe portraits and Standard portraits. Last year, Magic had the following costs and revenues:

MAGIC PHOTOGRAPHY
Income Statement

	Deluxe	Standard	Total
Revenue	$360,000	$400,000	$760,000
Direct materials	50,000	50,000	100,000
Direct labor	180,000	120,000	300,000
Indirect costs:			
Administration	————	————	50,000
Production setup	————	————	100,000
Quality control	————	————	50,000
Sales and marketing	————	————	40,000
Operating profit	————	————	$120,000

Magic Photography currently uses labor costs to allocate all overhead, but is considering implementing an activity-based costing system. After interviewing the sales and production staff, management decides to allocate administrative costs on the basis of direct labor costs, but to use the following bases to allocate the remaining overhead:

Overhead Cost	Allocation Base	Activity Level Deluxe	Activity Level Standard
Production setup	Number of photo sessions	150	250
Quality control	Number of customer inspections	300	200
Sales and marketing	Number of advertisements	60	40

Required:

a. Complete the income statement using the activity bases above.

b. Write a report indicating how management might use activity-based costing to reduce costs.

c. Restate the income statement for Magic Photography using direct labor costs as the only overhead allocation base.

d. Write a report to management stating why product line profits differ using activity-based costing compared to the traditional approach. Indicate whether activity-based costing provides more accurate information and why (if you believe it does provide more accurate information). Indicate in your report how the use of labor-based overhead allocation could result in Magic Photography management making suboptimal decisions.

7-35 ABC and Predetermined Overhead Allocation Rates

Bohemian Glass & Crystal Company manufactures three types of glassware: unleaded glass, low-lead crystal, and high-lead crystal. Glass quality increases with higher lead content, which allows for more detailed cutting and etching. Unleaded glass production is highly automated, whereas the cutting and etching of crystal products require a varying degree of labor, depending on the intricacy of the pattern. Bohemian applies all indirect costs according to a predetermined rate based on direct labor-hours. A consultant recently suggested that Bohemian switch to an activity-based costing system, and prepared the following cost estimates for Year 5 for the recommended cost drivers.

Activity	Recommended Cost Driver	Estimated Costs	Estimated Cost Driver Units
Order processing	Number of orders	$ 30,000	100 orders
Production setup	Number of production runs	120,000	50 runs
Materials handling	Pounds of materials used	200,000	80,000 pounds
Machine depreciation and maintenance	Machine-hours	160,000	8,000 hours
Quality control	Number of inspections	40,000	30 inspections
Packing	Number of units	80,000	320,000 units
Total estimated overhead		$630,000	

In addition, management estimated 5,000 direct labor-hours for Year 5.
Assume the following activities occurred in January of Year 5:

	Unleaded Glass	Low-Lead Crystal	High-Lead Crystal
Number of units produced	20,000	8,000	3,000
Direct materials costs	$13,000	$8,000	$5,000
Direct labor-hours	150	150	200
Number of orders	4	3	2
Number of production runs	1	1	2
Pounds of material	5,000	2,000	1,000
Machine-hours	580	140	80
Number of inspections	1	1	1
Units shipped	20,000	8,000	3,000

Actual labor costs were $15 per hour.

Required:

a. Compute a predetermined overhead rate for Year 5 for each of the cost drivers using the estimated costs and estimated cost driver units prepared by the consultant. Also compute a predetermined rate for Year 5 using direct labor-hours as the allocation base.

b. Compute the production costs for each product for January using direct labor-hours as the allocation base and the predetermined rate computed in a.

c. Compute the production costs for each product for January using the cost drivers recommended by the consultant and the predetermined rates computed in *a*. (Note: Do *not* assume total overhead applied to products in January will be the same for ABC as it was for the labor-hour–based allocation.)

d.   Management has seen your numbers and wants to know how you account for the discrepancy between the product costs using direct labor-hours as the allocation base and the product costs using activity-based costing. Write a brief response to management.

7–36   ABC and Predetermined Overhead Rates

Sparkle Company makes three types of sunglasses: Nerds, Stars, and Fashions. Sparkle presently applies overhead using a predetermined rate based on direct labor-hours. A group of company employees recommended that Sparkle switch to activity-based costing, and identified the following activities, cost drivers, estimated costs, and estimated cost driver units for Year 2 for each activity center.

Activity	Recommended Cost Driver	Estimated Costs	Estimated Cost Driver Units
Production setup	Number of production runs	$ 30,000	100 runs
Order processing	Number of orders	50,000	200 orders
Materials handling	Pounds of materials	20,000	8,000 pounds
Equipment depreciation and maintenance	Machine-hours	60,000	10,000 hours
Quality management	Number of inspections	50,000	40 inspections
Packing and shipping	Units shipped	40,000	20,000 units
		$250,000	

In addition, management estimated 2,000 direct labor-hours for Year 2.

Assume the following activities occurred in February of Year 2:

	Nerds	Stars	Fashions
Number of units produced	1,000	500	400
Direct materials costs	$4,000	$2,500	$2,000
Direct labor-hours	100	120	110
Number of orders	8	8	4
Number of production runs	2	4	8
Pounds of material	400	200	200
Machine-hours	500	300	300
Number of inspections	2	2	2
Units shipped	1,000	500	300

Direct labor costs were $20 per hour.

Required:

a.   Compute a predetermined overhead rate for Year 2 for each of the cost drivers recommended by the employees. Also compute a predetermined rate using direct labor-hours as the allocation base.

b.   Compute the production costs for each product for February using direct labor-hours as the allocation base and the predetermined rate computed in *a*.

c.   Compute the production costs for each product for February using the cost drivers recommended by the employees and the predetermined rates computed in *a*. (Note: Do *not* assume total overhead applied to products in February will be the same for ABC as it was for the labor-hour–based allocation.)

d.   Management has seen your numbers and wants to know how you account for the discrepancy between the product costs using direct labor-hours as the allocation base and the product costs using activity-based costing. Write a brief response to management.

7-37 Choosing an ABC System

Cyclaris Corporation manufactures three bicycle models: a racing bike, a mountain bike, and a children's model. The racing model is made of a titanium-aluminum alloy and is called the Aerolight. The mountain bike is called the Summit and is made of aluminum. The steel-framed children's bike is called the Spinner. Because of the different materials used, production processes differ significantly between models in terms of machine types and time requirements. However, once parts are produced, assembly time per unit required for each type of bike is similar. For this reason, Cyclaris has adopted the practice of allocating overhead on the basis of machine-hours. Last year, the company produced 1,000 Aerolights, 2,000 Summits, and 5,000 Spinners and had the following revenues and expenses.

CYCLARIS CORPORATION
Income Statement

	Aerolight	Summit	Spinner	Total
Sales	$380,000	$560,000	$475,000	$1,415,000
Direct costs:				
Direct materials	150,000	240,000	200,000	590,000
Direct labor	14,400	24,000	54,000	92,400
Variable overhead:				
Machine setup	_____	_____	_____	26,000
Order processing	_____	_____	_____	64,000
Warehousing costs	_____	_____	_____	93,000
Depreciation of machines	_____	_____	_____	42,000
Shipping	_____	_____	_____	36,000
Contribution margin	_____	_____	_____	471,600
Fixed overhead:				
Plant administration				88,000
Other fixed overhead				140,000
Gross profit				$ 243,600

The chief financial officer (CFO) of Cyclaris hired a consultant to recommend cost allocation bases. The consultant recommended the following:

		Activity Level		
Activity	Cost Driver	Aerolight	Summit	Spinner
1. Machine setup	Number of production runs	11	17	22
2. Sales order processing	Number of sales orders received	200	300	300
3. Warehousing costs	Number of units held in inventory	100	100	200
4. Depreciation	Machine-hours	5,000	8,000	12,000
5. Shipping	Number of units shipped	500	2,000	5,000

The consultant found no basis for allocating the plant administration and other fixed overhead costs, and recommended that these not be applied to products.

Required:

a. Using machine-hours to allocate production overhead, complete the income statement for Cyclaris Company. (See activity 4 above for machine-hours.) Do not attempt to allocate plant administration or other fixed overhead.

b. Complete the income statement using the bases recommended by the consultant.

c. How might activity-based costing result in better decisions by Cyclaris management?

d. After hearing the consultant's recommendations, the CFO decided to adopt activity-based costing, but expressed concern about not allocating some of the overhead to the products (plant administration and other fixed overhead). In the CFO's view, "Products have to bear a fair share of all overhead or we won't be covering all of our costs." How would you respond to this comment?

7–38   Benefits of Activity-Based Costing

Many companies recognize that their cost systems are inadequate for today's global market. Managers in companies selling multiple products are making important product decisions based on distorted cost information. Most systems of the past were designed to focus on inventory valuation.

Required:

If management should decide to implement an activity-based costing system, what benefits should they expect?

(CMA adapted)

7–39   Benefits of Activity-Based Costing

Moss Manufacturing has just completed a major change in the method it uses to inspect its product. Previously 10 inspectors examined the product after each major process. The salaries of these inspectors were charged as direct labor to the operation or job. In an effort to improve efficiency, the Moss production manager recently bought a computerized quality control system consisting of a microcomputer, 15 video cameras, peripheral hardware, and software. The cameras are placed at key points in the production process, taking pictures of the product and comparing these pictures with a known "good" image supplied by a quality control engineer. This new system allowed Moss to replace the 10 quality control inspectors with only two quality control engineers.

The president of the company is concerned. She was told that the production process was now more efficient, yet she notices a large increase in the factory overhead rate. The computation of the rate before and after automation is as follows:

	Before	After
Estimated overhead	$1,900,000	$2,100,000
Estimated direct labor	$1,000,000	$ 700,000
Predetermined overhead rate	190%	300%

Required:

How might an activity-based costing system benefit Moss Manufacturing and clear up the president's confusion?

(CMA adapted)

7–40   Choosing an Activity-Based Costing System

Roof-Over-Head, Inc. (ROH), makes three types of mobile homes: Basic, Homevalue, and Castle. In the past, ROH has allocated overhead to products using machine-hours. Last year, the company produced 100 units of Castle, 200 units of Homevalue, and 300 units of the Basic model, and had the following revenues and costs:

ROH, INC.
Income Statement

	Basic	Homevalue	Castle	Total
Sales	$3,000,000	$5,000,000	$4,500,000	$12,500,000
Direct costs:				
Direct materials	1,000,000	1,500,000	1,100,000	3,600,000
Direct labor	200,000	300,000	600,000	1,100,000
Variable overhead:				
Machine setup	———	———	———	800,000
Order processing	———	———	———	600,000
Warehousing costs	———	———	———	800,000
Machine operation	———	———	———	400,000
Shipping	———	———	———	300,000
Contribution margin	———	———	———	4,900,000
Plant administration				2,000,000
Gross profit				$ 2,900,000

The controller of ROH had heard about activity-based costing and put together an employee team to recommend cost allocation bases. The employee team recommended the following:

Activity	Cost Driver	Activity Level		
		Basic	Homevalue	Castle
Machine setup	Number of production runs	10	20	20
Sales order processing	Number of sales orders received	180	400	220
Warehousing costs	Number of units held in inventory	100	200	100
Machine operation	Machine-hours	6,000	9,000	10,000
Shipping	Number of units shipped	2,000	3,500	2,000

The employee team recommended that plant administration costs not be allocated to products.

Required:

a. Using machine-hours to allocate overhead, complete the income statement for ROH, Inc. Do not allocate plant administrative costs to products.

b. Complete the income statement using the activity-based costing method suggested by the employee team.

c. Write a brief report indicating how activity-based costing might result in better decisions by ROH, Inc.

d. After hearing the recommendations, the president expressed concern about failing to allocate plant administrative costs. If plant administrative costs were to be allocated to products, how would you allocate them?

INTEGRATIVE CASES

7–41 Plantwide versus Departmental Overhead Allocation for Step 1 and Step 2 Allocation

MumsDay Corporation manufactures a complete line of fiberglass attache cases and suitcases. MumsDay has three manufacturing departments—Molding, Component, and Assembly—and two service departments—Power and Maintenance.

The sides of the cases are manufactured in the Molding Department. The frames, hinges, locks, and so on are manufactured in the Component Department. The cases are completed in the Assembly Department. Varying amounts of materials, time, and effort are required for each of the various cases. The Power Department and Maintenance Department provide services to the three manufacturing departments.

MumsDay has always used a plantwide overhead rate. Direct labor-hours are used to assign the overhead to its product. The predetermined rate is calculated by dividing the company's total estimated overhead by the total estimated direct labor-hours to be worked in the three manufacturing departments.

Whit Portlock, manager of Cost Accounting, has recommended that MumsDay use departmental overhead rates. The planned operating costs and expected levels of activity for the coming year have been developed by Portlock and are presented by department in the following schedules (figures are in thousands):

	Manufacturing Departments		
	Molding	Component	Assembly
		(000)	
Departmental activity measures:			
Direct labor-hours	500	2,000	1,500
Machine-hours	875	125	–0–
Departmental costs:			
Raw materials	$12,400	$30,000	$ 1,250
Direct labor	3,500	20,000	12,000
Variable overhead	3,500	10,000	16,500
Fixed overhead	17,500	6,200	6,100
Total departmental costs	$36,900	$66,200	$35,850
Use of service departments:			
Maintenance:			
Estimated usage in			
labor-hours for			
coming year	90	25	10
Power (in kilowatt-hours):			
Estimated usage for			
coming year	360	320	120
Long-term			
capacity	500	350	150

	Service Departments	
	Power	Maintenance
	(000)	
Departmental activity measures:		
Maximum capacity	1,000 kwhr.	Adjustable
Estimated usage in coming		
year	800 kwhr.	125 hours
Departmental costs:		
Materials and supplies	$ 5,000	$1,500
Variable labor	1,400	2,250
Fixed overhead	12,000	250
Total service department		
costs	$18,400	$4,000

Required:

a. Calculate the plantwide overhead rate for MumsDay Corporation for the coming year, using the same method as used in the past.

b. Whit Portlock has been asked to develop departmental overhead rates for comparison with the plantwide rate. The following steps are to be followed in developing the departmental rates.
1. The Maintenance Department costs should be allocated to the three manufacturing departments, using the direct method.
2. The Power Department costs should be allocated to the three manufacturing departments as follows: the fixed costs allocated according to long-term capacity and the variable costs according to planned usage.

3. Calculate departmental overhead rates for the three manufacturing departments using a machine-hour base for the Molding Department and a direct labor-hour base for the Component and Assembly departments.

c. Should MumsDay Corporation use a plantwide rate or departmental rates to assign overhead to its products? Write a brief report explaining your answer.

(CMA adapted)

7-42 Distortions Caused by Inappropriate Overhead Allocation Base[12]

Steve Stanley, Inc. (SSI), manufactures creamy deluxe chocolate candy bars. The firm has developed three distinct products, Almond Dream, Krispy Krackle, and Creamy Crunch.

While SSI is profitable, Steve Stanley is quite concerned over the profitability of each product and the product costing methods currently employed. In particular, Steve questions whether the overhead allocation base of direct labor-hours accurately reflects the costs incurred during the production process of each product.

In reviewing cost reports with the marketing manager, Steve notices that Creamy Crunch appears exceptionally profitable, while Almond Dream appears to be produced at a loss. This surprises both Steve and the manager, and after much discussion, they are convinced the cost accounting system is at fault and that Almond Dream is performing very well at the current market price.

Steve Stanley decides to hire Jean Sharpe, a management consultant, to study the firm's cost system over the next month and present her findings and recommendations to senior management. Her objective is to identify and demonstrate how the cost accounting system might be distorting the firm's product costs.

Jean Sharpe begins her study by gathering information and documenting the existing cost accounting system. The system is rather simplistic, using a single overhead allocation base, direct labor-hours, to calculate and apply overhead rates to all products. The rate is calculated by summing variable and fixed overhead costs and then dividing the result by the number of direct labor-hours. The product cost is determined by multiplying the number of direct labor-hours required to manufacture the product by the overhead rate and adding this amount to the direct labor and direct material costs.

SSI engages in two distinct production processes for each product. Process 1 is labor intensive, using a high proportion of direct materials and labor. Process 2 uses special packing equipment that wraps each individual candy bar and then packs them into boxes of 24 bars. The boxes are then packaged into cases containing six boxes. The special packing equipment is used on all three products and has a monthly capacity of 3,000 boxes, each containing 144 candy bars.

To illustrate the source of the distortions to senior management, Sharpe collects the cost data for the three products—Almond Dream, Krispy Krackle, and Creamy Crunch (see Exhibit A).

SSI recently adopted a general policy of discontinuing all products whose gross profit margin [(Gross margin/Selling price) × 100] percentages were less than 10 percent. By comparing the selling prices to the firm's costs and then calculating the gross margin percentages, Sharpe could determine which products, under the current cost system, should be dropped. The current selling prices of Almond Dream, Krispy Krackle, and Creamy Crunch were $85, $55, and $35 per case, respectively.

Required:

a. Complete the following schedule (Exhibit A) under the current cost system and determine which product(s), if any, would be dropped.

b. What characteristic of the product that would be dropped makes it appear relatively unprofitable?

---

[12] Copyright © Michael W. Maher, 1993.

EXHIBIT

A

(7–42)

	Almond Dream	Krispy Krackle	Creamy Crunch
Product costs:			
Labor-hours per unit	7	3	1
Total units produced	1,000	1,000	1,000
Material cost per unit	$8.00	$2.00	$9.00
Direct labor cost per unit	$42.00	$18.00	$6.00
Labor-hours per product	7,000	3,000	1,000

Total overhead = $69,500

Total labor-hours = 11,000

Direct labor costs per hour = $6.00

Allocation rate per labor-hour =   (a)

Costs of products:			
Material cost per unit	$ 8.00	$ 2.00	$9.00
Direct labor cost per unit	42.00	18.00	6.00
Allocated overhead per unit (to be computed)	(b)	(c)	(d)
Product cost	(e)	(f)	(g)

c. Calculate the gross profit margin percentage for the remaining products. Assume SSI can sell all products it manufactures and that it will use the excess capacity from dropping a product to produce more of the most profitable product. If SSI maintains its current rule about dropping products, which additional products, if any, would SSI drop under the existing cost system? Overhead would remain $69,500 per month under all alternatives.

d. Recalculate the gross profit margin percentage for the remaining product(s) and ascertain whether any additional product(s) would be dropped.

e. Discuss the outcome and any recommendations you might make to management regarding the current cost system and decision policies.

7–43 Multiple Allocation Bases

Refer to integrative case 7–42.

Jean Sharpe decides to gather additional data to identify the cause of overhead costs and figure out which products are most profitable.

Jean Sharpe notices that $30,000 of the overhead originated from the equipment used. She decides to incorporate machine-hours into the overhead allocation base to see its effect on product profitability. Almond Dream requires two hours of machine time. Krispy Krackle requires seven hours, and Creamy Crunch requires six hours. Additionally, Jean notices that the $15,000 per month spent on the rental of 10,000 square feet of factory space accounts for almost 22 percent of the overhead. Almond Dream is assigned 1,000 square feet, Krispy Krackle is assigned 4,000 square feet, and Creamy Crunch is assigned 5,000 square feet. Jean decides to incorporate this into the allocation base for the rental costs.

Since labor-hours are still an important cost driver for overhead, Jean decides she should use labor-hours to allocate the remaining $24,500.

SSI still plans to produce 1,000 cases each of Almond Dream, Krispy Krackle, and Creamy Crunch. Assume SSI can sell all products it manufactures and that it will use excess capacity, if it drops any products, to produce additional units of the most profitable product. Overhead will remain $69,500 per month under all alternatives.

Required:

a. Based on the additional data, determine the product cost and gross profit margin percentages of each product using the three allocation bases to determine the allocation assigned to each product.

EXHIBIT

(7–44)

E-LABS, INC.
Income Statement
For the Year Ended December 31, 199X

	Adiamo	Bichlor	Cifloxo	Total
Revenues	$75,000,000	$81,000,000	$24,900,000	$180,900,000
Direct costs:				
Materials	15,000,000	12,480,000	3,276,000	30,756,000
Quality control	8,400,000	8,400,000	2,520,000	19,320,000
Labor	15,600,000	15,600,000	4,680,000	35,880,000
Utilities, power	2,400,000	2,520,000	684,000	5,604,000
Total direct costs	41,400,000	39,000,000	11,160,000	91,560,000
Overhead and Administrative:				
Setup and testing				2,013,750
Loading materials				439,020
Test runs				2,487,480
Detailing				10,081,500
Laboratory				1,529,000
Facilities				32,426,000
Research and development				19,321,000
Selling and administrative				14,720,000
Total overhead and administrative				83,017,750
Profit (loss)				$ 6,322,250

b. Would management recommend dropping any of the products based on the criterion of dropping products with less than 10 percent gross profit margin?

c. Based on the recommendation you make in (*b*), recalculate the allocations and profit margins to determine whether any of the remaining products should be dropped from the product line. If any additional products are dropped, substantiate the profitability of remaining products.

7–44   ABC Analysis: E-Labs (A)[13]

E-Labs, Inc., is a pharmaceutical manufacturer in San Juan. The company has a highly automated processing system that is used to manufacture three patented pharmaceuticals: Adiamo, Bichlor, and Cifloxo. Product prices are determined based on the prices for competitive pharmaceuticals. The company's market analysts determined that any price increases would be offset by reduced sales volume because of the competition. Similarly, price decreases would only generate sufficient additional volumes to overcome profits lost from the price cuts. Given these market constraints, the company launched a program to evaluate its costs in an effort to improve profitability.

For internal control and evaluation purposes, the company divides costs into two categories: (1) costs that can be directly associated with the units produced, and (2) overhead, which is defined as costs that cannot be associated directly with each unit produced. Revenue and direct cost data for each of the products have been developed in the comptroller's office. The income statement appears in Exhibit A for this case.

Production of the pharmaceuticals takes place in a common facility and uses common production equipment extensively. Setup and testing are required every time a different product is run through the system. These costs include cleaning out any of the previously run product, resetting equipment and computer programs, as well as the direct costs of a test run of the new product. Loading materials includes the costs associated with ordering and receiving goods under the company's just-in-time system as well as the labor costs needed to get the materials to the proper place in the processing unit.

Laboratory overhead includes costs of chemists, staff, equipment, computer time, and supplies used to support each product. This cost pool represents laboratory costs that are product specific.

Research and development (R&D) covers the company's research effort to develop new products as well as to improve the formulations of processing of existing products. In E-Lab's segment of the pharmaceutical industry, ongoing R&D is critical to the survival of the company. The selling and administrative cost pool includes all items related to the central operation of the company and sales. Management believes that products must "carry their weight" and cover an appropriate share of selling and administrative costs.

During a given year, the company produces and sells 1,200 units of Adiamo, 1,200 units of Bichlor, and 360 units of Cifloxo.

Charles Frishkoff, CEO of E-Labs, pointed out that current profit levels are insufficient to provide the cash flows necessary for the company to fund its ongoing research and development program. Before seeking additional external financing for R&D, Frishkoff wants an evaluation of each product line to see if there might be problem areas in any of the product lines. Identification of these problem areas would enable management to focus on them and seek ways to save costs, thus generating cash internally for R&D.

The comptroller, Amy Liu, and the head of Production Engineering, Bart Sampson, set out to identify these problem areas. Liu noted that overhead was currently being allocated to products on the basis of direct labor costs, and that activity-based costing might be considered as an alternative approach. However, the method would require gathering data that were not incorporated in the accounting system. Specifically, information would be needed to identify the cost drivers for each of the overhead costs. Sampson suggested that additional production and laboratory data were available in the engineering records and that the Marketing division might have more specifics on the detailing costs.

After reviewing the overhead cost schedule, Liu and Sampson agreed that the first three overhead costs were related to batches produced. Sampson reviewed the production scheduling records. He found that for Adiamo, a standard production run, or batch, consisted of 50 units and that 24 batches were run per year. Bichlor was produced in lots of 25 units and 48 batches were run each year. Cifloxo was manufactured in lots of 20 units with 18 batches run each year. These short production runs had been established to minimize inventories when each product was new and its marketability was highly uncertain.

Sampson developed the following schedule of costs related to setup activities for each product line:

	Adiamo	Bichlor	Cifloxo
Costs per batch:			
Setup and testing	$22,375	$22,375	$22,375
Loading materials	4,750	4,990	4,750
Test runs	25,920	31,760	18,940

Sampson studied the costs of the laboratory and identified $537,000 as related to Adiamo, $642,000 as related to Bichlor, and $350,000 as the laboratory costs of Cifloxo.

Detailing costs of $3,546,500 were attributable to Adiamo and $3,358,000 were found driven by Bichlor. The remaining $3,177,000 in detailing costs were attributable to Cifloxo. Detailing and laboratory costs were considered "product line costs."

Neither Liu nor Sampson could find an identifiable relationship between product lines and facilities, R&D, and selling and administrative costs. After reviewing the cost accounting literature, they concluded that allocation of these costs on the basis of revenue would be reasonable.

Required:

a. Prepare an income statement allocating overhead and administrative costs based on direct labor costs.

b. Using the additional information learned by Sampson and Liu, prepare the product-line income statement using activity-based costing.

c. Explain the differences in the product-line profits reported under each method.

7–45 ABC Analysis: E-Labs (B)[14]

Refer to integrative case 7–44.

After receiving the new product-line profit statement, and having received an explanation of the concept of cost drivers, Frishkoff, CEO of E-Labs, wanted to know the primary reasons for the differences in product-line profits under the two different approaches. He also asked if any of the staff had suggestions for improving cost efficiency.

Sampson noted that batch sizes had been developed at the early stage of the life of each product and had not changed since. He studied the problems of inventory levels, expiration dates, and similar issues. As a result, he suggested that the batch sizes be modified so that Adiamo was produced in batches of 100 units, Bichlor in batches of 50 units, and Cifloxo in batches of 60 units. Frishkoff asked Liu to prepare a proposed product-line profit statement using the proposed batch sizes.

Required:

a. Prepare a product-line income statement using Sampson's proposal for new batch sizes. What effect does the new batch-size proposal have on total company profits? (Assume that batch costs are variable costs.)

b. Discuss apparent reasons for the differences between the income statements before and after batch-size modification.

c. Liu and Sampson chose to allocate facilities, R&D, and administrative costs on the basis of revenue, despite finding no relationship between these costs and the product lines. How else might these costs have been handled?

SOLUTIONS TO

Self-Study Questions

1   (1) Using the bankwide rate:

	Commercial Loan Department	Mortgage Loan Department
Labor	$100,000	$300,000
Overhead	50,000[a]	150,000[a]
Total	$150,000	$450,000

[a] Overhead = 50 percent of direct labor.

---

(2) Using department rates:

	Commercial Loan Department	Mortgage Loan Department
Labor	$100,000	$300,000
Overhead	56,000[a]	120,000[b]
Total	$156,000	$420,000

[a] $56,000 = ($40 × 900 loans) + (20% × $100,000).
[b] $120,000 = 40% × $300,000

The department rate is likely to be more informative; but it is also likely to be more time consuming and difficult to compute. Department rates provide better identification of the activities that cause costs in each separate department. Department rates generally provide better estimates of product costs both because different departments may have different activities that cause costs and because the allocation rate is likely to be different across departments. (Note that different allocation methods using predetermined rates do not necessarily allocate the same *total* overhead.)

2   Using department allocation, overhead is allocated to products worked on in December using the predetermined rate of $100 per hour times the actual machine-hours in December:

Standard products ($100 × 2,000 hours)	$200,000
Unique products ($100 × 1,000 hours)	100,000
Total overhead allocated to products	$300,000

Assignment of overhead using activity-based costing:

Activity	Rate	Standard Product		Unique Product	
		Actual Activity Events	Costs Allocated	Actual Activity Events	Costs Allocated
1. Purchasing materials	$2 per pound	8,000 pounds	$ 16,000	8,000 pounds	$ 16,000
2. Machine setups	$2,000 per setup	15 setups	30,000	50 setups	100,000
3. Inspections	$100 per inspection hour	220 hours	22,000	400 hours	40,000
4. Running machines	$30 per hour	2,000 hours	60,000	1,000 hours	30,000
Total cost allocated to each product			$128,000		$186,000

Based on production of 1,300 units of Standard and 400 units of Unique, the per unit product costs (rounded to the nearest dollar) using the two costing methods are shown below:

	Department Allocation		Activity-Based Costing	
	Standard	Unique	Standard	Unique
Direct materials	$100	$200	$100	$200
Direct labor	20	30	20	30
Overhead	154[a]	250[b]	98[c]	465[d]
Total	$274	$480	$218	$695

[a] $154 = Allocation to products using department rate ÷ Units produced = $200,000/1,300 units.

[b] $250 = Allocation to products using department rate ÷ Units produced = $100,000/400 units.

[c] $98 = Allocation to products using activity-based costing ÷ Units produced = $128,000/1,300 units.

[d] $465 = Allocation to products using activity-based costing ÷ Units produced = $186,000/400 units.

3

Item	Cost Category
a. Piecework labor	Unit-level cost
b. Long-term lease on a building	Capacity-related cost
c. Energy to run machines	Unit-level cost
d. Engineering drawings for a product	Product-related cost
e. Purchase order	Batch-related cost
f. Movement of materials for products in production	Batch-related cost
g. Change order to meet new customer specifications	Customer-related cost

Allocating Joint Costs

LEARNING OBJECTIVES

After reading this chapter, you should be able to:

1. Allocate joint costs using the net realizable value method of joint cost allocation.
2. Allocate joint costs using the physical quantities method.
3. Account for by-products.
4. Explain how cost data are used in the sell-or-process-further decision.
5. Understand the replacement method of joint cost allocation. (Appendix)

Joint Cost A cost of a manufacturing process with two or more outputs.

Joint Products Outputs from a common input and common production process.

Split-Off Point Stage of processing where two or more products are separated.

A joint cost is a cost of a manufacturing process with several different outputs. For example, logs can be the input to lumber and chipboard. The cost of the logs is a joint cost of these two **joint products**. The problem in such cases is whether and how to allocate the joint cost of the input (for example the logs) to the joint products (for example, lumber and chipboard).

For example, Illustration 8–1 diagrams the flow of costs incurred to process logs by the Sacramento-Sierra Company. These costs include direct materials, direct labor, and manufacturing overhead. As the logs are processed, two products emerge: lumber and chipboard. The stage of processing where the two products are separated is called the **split-off point**. Processing costs incurred prior to the split-off point are called *joint costs*. This chapter shows how those joint costs can be allocated to products.

ILLUSTRATION

Diagram of Joint Cost Flows

SACRAMENTO-SIERRA COMPANY

April

Input: Logs
Direct materials cost = $125,000
Conversion cost[a]   = ___55,000
Total joint cost   = $180,000

Split-off point

Chipboard: Sales value = $252,000

Lumber: Sales value = $378,000

[a] Conversion costs are direct labor plus manufacturing overhead.

WHY ALLOCATE JOINT COSTS?

Joint costs are allocated for many reasons. A major reason in manufacturing companies is that joint costs must be allocated to value inventory and compute the costs of goods for external financial reporting under generally accepted accounting principles (GAAP). But there are many other reasons, too.

Joint cost allocations are useful in valuing inventory for insurance purposes. Should a casualty loss occur, the insurance company and the insured must agree on the value of the lost goods. One factor to be considered in arriving at a settlement is the cost of the material destroyed. If joint products are destroyed, material and conversion costs must be divided between the goods destroyed and those not destroyed.

Cost allocations can also be helpful in determining departmental or division costs for measuring executive performance. Many companies compensate executives and other employees, at least partly, on the basis of departmental or division earnings for the year. When a single raw material is converted into products sold by two or more departments, the cost of the raw material must be allocated to the products concerned.

When companies are subject to rate regulation, the allocation of joint costs can be a significant factor in determining the regulated rates. Crude oil and natural gas are usually produced out of a common well. In recent years, energy price policies and gas utility rates have been based in part on the allocation of the joint costs of crude oil and natural gas.

In each of these cases, opposing interests are involved. For example, neither the insurance company nor the insured wishes to pay more or receive less than is fair. Executives and employees will object to a cost of goods sold figure that they feel is overstated against them and understated for another department. Buyers and sellers of regulated products or services are both affected by pricing, and neither wishes to give the other an advantage. When the allocation of costs can impinge on the financial fortunes of opposing parties, both sides review the allocation method critically.

Any cost allocation method contains an element of arbitrariness. No allocation method can be beyond dispute. Consequently, methods of allocation must be clearly stated before they are implemented.

JOINT COST ALLOCATION METHODS

There are two major methods of allocating joint costs: (1) the net realizable value method and (2) the physical quantities method. A third method, the replacement method, is discussed in the appendix to the chapter.

Net Realizable Value Method

Net Realizable Value Method
Joint cost allocation based on the proportional values of the joint products at the split-off point.

Using the **net realizable value method** (also known as the *relative sales value method*), joint costs are allocated based on the net realizable value of each product at the split-off point. The net realizable value is the estimated sales value of each product at the split-off point. If the joint products can be sold at the split-off point, the market value or sales price may be used for this allocation.

If the products require further processing before they are marketable, then it is necessary to estimate the net realizable value at the split-off point. This approach is sometimes referred to as the *netback* or *workback method*. Normally, when a market value is available at the split-off point, it is preferable to use that value rather than the netback method. The *net realizable value* at the split-off point is estimated by taking the sales value after further processing and deducting those added processing costs. Joint costs are then allocated to the products in proportion to their net realizable values at the split-off point.

For example, the Sacramento-Sierra Company produces lumber and chipboard as shown in Illustration 8–2. Direct materials (that is, logs) cost $125,000, and conversion costs are $55,000, for a total of $180,000 in April. Lumber and chipboard have a total sales value of $630,000 at the split-off point. Chipboard has sales value of $252,000, or 40 percent of the total, while lumber's value is $378,000, or 60 percent of the total. We assume there is no additional processing required after the split-off point to make lumber and chipboard for purposes of this example.

The cost allocation would follow the proportional distribution of net realizable values:

To chipboard:
$$\left[\frac{\$252,000}{\$630,000}\right] \times \$180,000 = 40\% \times \$180,000 = \$\ 72,000$$

To lumber:
$$\left[\frac{\$378,000}{\$630,000}\right] \times \$180,000 = 60\% \times \$180,000 = \underline{\ \ 108,000}$$

$$\underline{\underline{\$180,000}}$$

ILLUSTRATION
8–2

Joint Products for Sacramento-Sierra Company

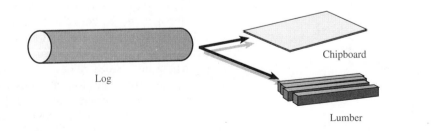

Log

Chipboard

Lumber

*Gross Margin Computations
Using Net Realizable
Value Method*

SACRAMENTO-SIERRA COMPANY
April

	Chipboard	Lumber	Total
Sales value	$252,000	$378,000	$630,000
Less allocated joint costs	72,000	108,000	180,000
Gross margin	$180,000	$270,000	$450,000
Gross margin as a percent of sales	71.43[a]	71.43[a]	71.43[a]

[a] 71.43 = $180,000 ÷ $252,000 = $270,000 ÷ $378,000 = $450,000 ÷ 630,000.

A condensed statement of margins at the split-off point is shown in Illustration 8–3.

Note that the margins as a percentage of sales are 71.43 percent for *both* products. This demonstrates an important concept of the net realizable value method—namely, that *revenue dollars from any joint product are assumed to make the same percentage contribution at the split-off point as the revenue dollars from any other joint product.* The net realizable value approach implies a matching of input costs with revenues generated by each output.

Illustration 8–4 shows the flow of these allocated costs through T-accounts. Note that logs are materials held in direct materials inventory until they are allocated to work in process inventory.

*Self-Study
Question*

1 Ferguson Confections Company purchases cocoa beans and processes them into cocoa butter, cocoa powder, and cocoa shells. The standard yield from each 100-pound sack of unprocessed cocoa beans is 20 pounds of butter, 45 pounds of powder, and 35 pounds of shells. The powder can be sold for $.90 per pound and the butter for $1.10 per pound at the split-off point. The shells are thrown away at no cost.

   The cost of the cocoa beans is $15 per hundred pounds. It costs $37 in labor and overhead to process each 100 pounds of beans up to the split-off point.

I L L U S T R A T I O N   *Flow of Costs Using Net Realizable Value Method*

ILLUSTRATION   *Sacramento-Sierra Processes Chipboard beyond Split-Off Point*

8-5

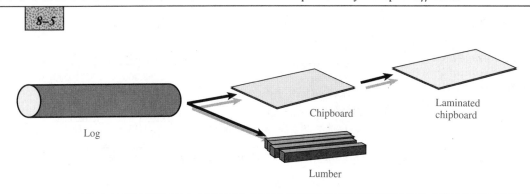

Compute the allocated joint cost of the butter and powder produced from 100 pounds of cocoa beans, using the net realizable value method.

The solution to this question is at the end of this chapter on page 313.

*Estimating Net
Realizable Value*

Estimated Net Realizable Value
Sales price of final product minus additional processing costs necessary to prepare a product for sale.

Not all joint products can be sold at the split-off point. Further processing may be required before the product is marketable. When no sales values exist for the outputs at the split-off point, the **estimated net realizable values** must be determined by taking the sales value of each product at the first point at which it can be marketed and deducting the processing costs that must be incurred to get there from the split-off point. This process is often referred to as "working back" to a value at a point in a process. The resulting estimated net realizable value is used for joint cost allocation in the same way as an actual market value at the split-off point.

Suppose management of Sacramento-Sierra finds the market for chipboard has changed such that it can no longer sell plain chipboard. However, the company could produce a new product known as laminated chipboard. Laminated chipboard requires additional processing, as shown in Illustration 8–5. This additional processing would cost $98,000 for the chipboard produced in April, after which the laminated chipboard could be sold for $260,000. The lumber could still be sold at the split-off point for $378,000. Illustration 8–6 diagrams the process.

Illustration 8–7 shows the allocation of the joint cost of $180,000 to laminated chipboard and lumber. First, we compute the estimated net realizable value at split-off for laminated chipboard and lumber, which are $162,000 and $378,000, respectively. (The amount for lumber is not really estimated because it is lumber's sales value at split-off.) Next, we multiply the ratio of each product's net realizable value to the total estimated net realizable value by the joint cost. To determine the portion of the joint cost allocated to lumber, for example, the computations are $378,000/$540,000 times the joint cost of $180,000 (= 70% × $180,000 = $126,000, as shown in Illustration 8–7).

ILLUSTRATION

Flow of Costs—
Further Processing beyond
Split-Off Point

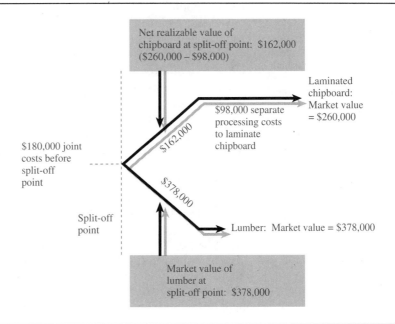

ILLUSTRATION

Net Realizable Value Method
Using Estimated Net
Realizable Value for
Laminated Chipboard

SACRAMENTO-SIERRA COMPANY

	Laminated Chipboard	Lumber	Total
Sales value	$260,000	$378,000	$638,000
Less additional process costs to point of marketability	98,000	–0–	98,000
Estimated net realizable value at split-off point	162,000	378,000	540,000
Allocation of joint costs:			
$\left[\dfrac{\$162,000}{\$540,000}\right] \times \$180,000 = 30\% \times \$180,000 =$	54,000		
$\left[\dfrac{\$378,000}{\$540,000}\right] \times \$180,000 = 70\% \times \$180,000 =$		126,000	180,000
Margin	$108,000	$252,000	$360,000
Margin as a percent of estimated net realizable value at split-off	66.67	66.67	66.67

Self-Study
Question

2   Refer to self-study question 1. Assume the cocoa butter cannot be sold at split-off, but requires additional processing. The additional processing costs $.15 per pound, at which point the butter can be sold for $1.20 per pound. Allocate the joint costs to the two products using the estimated net realizable value method.

The solution to this question is at the end of this chapter on page 313.

*Physical Quantities
Method*

Physical Quantities Method
Joint cost allocation based on
measurement of the volume,
weight, or other physical measure
of the joint products at the split-off
point.

The **physical quantities method** is often used when output product prices are highly volatile. This method is also used when much processing occurs between the split-off point and the first point of marketability, or when product prices are not available in the market. This latter situation may arise when regulators set prices in regulated pricing situations or in cost-based contract situations, for example.

Using the physical quantities method, joint costs are assigned to products based on a physical measure. This might be volume, weight, or any other common measure of physical characteristics.

Many companies allocate joint costs incurred in producing oil and gas on the basis of energy equivalent (BTU content). They use this method because, while oil and gas are often produced simultaneously from the same well, the products are typically measured in different physical units [gas by thousand cubic feet (mcf.), oil by barrel]. Moreover, the price of most gas is regulated so that relative market values are artificial. However, the common measure of quantity and the perceived value of the products are the relative energy content.

For example, assume that relative market values at the split-off point are not available at Sacramento-Sierra Company and that for every $180,000 of joint costs in processing logs we obtain 1,400 units of chipboard and 1,960 units of lumber. The allocation of joint costs using these physical quantity measures is shown in Illustration 8-8.

As long as the physical measures reflect economic values, this method of assigning costs may provide a reasonable basis for joint cost allocation. However, there are many cases where an allocation based on physical quantities would not accurately reflect economic values. For example, gold is often found in copper deposits. The physical quantity of gold may be small, yet its value may be significant. If the joint costs of mining the ore that contains the gold and copper were to be allocated to the output products on the basis of weight, the resulting product costs would not reflect a matching of costs with economic values.

*Comments on Joint Cost
Allocation Methods*

The "jointness" of joint production processes makes it impossible to separate the portion of joint costs attributable to one product from another on a cause-effect basis. As a result, if allocated joint costs are used for decision-making purposes, they should be used only with full recognition of their limitations, as in the Union Pacific example in the Real World Application. As long as the method used for allocation reasonably reflects the relative

ILLUSTRATION

Physical Quantities Method

SACRAMENTO-SIERRA COMPANY April			
	Chipboard	Lumber	Total
Output quantities	1,400 units	1,960 units	3,360 units
Joint allocation:			
$\left[\frac{1,400}{3,360}\right] \times \$180,000$ $75,000			
$\left[\frac{1,960}{3,360}\right] \times \$180,000$		$105,000	$180,000

economic benefits obtained from the jointly produced outputs, the method is usually considered acceptable for financial reporting purposes, for cost-based regulation, for tax purposes, and for contracts based on costs.

**Self-Study
Question**

3 Refer to self-study question 1. Use the physical quantities method to allocate joint costs.

The solution to this question is at the end of this chapter on page 313.

*SELL-OR-PROCESS-
FURTHER DECISIONS*

Many companies have opportunities to sell partly processed products at various stages of production. Management must decide whether it is more profitable to sell the output at an intermediate stage or to process it further. In such a sell-or-process-further decision, the relevant data to be considered are (1) the additional revenue after further processing and (2) the additional costs of processing further.

Suppose Sacramento-Sierra Company can sell chipboard for $252,000 at the split-off point, or process it further to make a new product, reinforced chipboard. The additional processing costs are $20,000, and the revenue from reinforced chipboard would be $290,000. Should the company sell chipboard or process it further? As indicated in earlier examples, the revenue from lumber is $378,000, and the joint cost of processing logs is $180,000.

As shown in Illustration 8–9, the profit will be greater by $18,000 if chipboard is processed further. It is important to note that the allocation of the joint costs between chipboard and lumber is irrelevant. The $38,000 additional revenue from processing beyond the split-off point justified the expenditure of $20,000 for additional processing, regardless of the way joint

ILLUSTRATION

8-9

*Income Statements for Sell-
or-Process-Further Decisions*

	Sell	Process Further	Additional Revenue and Costs from Processing Further
Revenues:			
From chipboard	$252,000	$290,000	$38,000
From lumber	378,000	378,000	—
Total revenues	630,000	668,000	38,000
Less costs:			
Joint costs	(180,000)	(180,000)	—
Separate processing of chipboard	–0–	(20,000)	(20,000)
Margin	$450,000	$468,000	$18,000 net gain from processing further

costs are allocated. *The only costs and revenues that are relevant to the decision are those that are changed by it*. These are examples of differential costs and revenues.

ACCOUNTING FOR BY-PRODUCTS

By-Products Outputs of joint production processes that are relatively minor in quantity or value.

By-products are outputs from a joint production process that are relatively minor in quantity and/or value when compared to the main products. For example, sawdust and wood chips are by-products of lumber production, and kerosene is a by-product of gasoline production. You may have seen advertisements for carpet and cloth mill ends at bargain prices. These are often by-products of textile production.

By-product accounting attempts to reflect the economic relationship between the by-products and the main products with a minimum of record-keeping for inventory valuation purposes. Two common methods of accounting for by-products are:

Method 1:   The net realizable value from sale of the by-products is deducted from the cost of the main product.

Method 2:   The proceeds from sale of the by-product are treated as other revenue.

Assume that By-Product Company has a production process that yields output C as the main product and output D as the by-product, all of which are sold this period. Sales of C total $200,000, while the sales of D total $1,100. Processing costs up to the split-off point are $80,000. These costs are like joint costs, but they are not allocated between output C and output D— they are *all* allocated to output C, the main product.

Also assume output D requires $300 additional costs of processing to make it salable; hence, output D's net realizable value is $800 ($1,100 − $300). The two methods of accounting for the by-product, output D, are shown in Illustration 8–10.

Column 1 of Illustration 8–10 shows the reduction in cost of sales for the net realizable value of the by-product when Method 1 is used. Illustration 8–11 shows the cost of revenue flows using Method 1. First, assume in entry 1 that the joint costs of production, amounting to $80,000, have been debited

ILLUSTRATION

8–10

Accounting for By-Products

BY-PRODUCT COMPANY

	Accounting Method[a]	
	(1)	*(2)*
Sales revenue from output C	$200,000	$200,000
Other revenue	–0–	800[b]
Total revenue	200,000	200,800
Cost of sales: Total production costs	80,000	80,000
Less by-product: Net realizable value	800[b]	–0–
Adjusted cost of sales	79,200	80,000
Gross margin	$120,800	$120,800

[a] Description of accounting methods:
    1. The net realizable value of the by-product is deducted from the cost of the main product.
    2. The net realizable value from the sale of the by-product is treated as other income.

[b] $800 is the net realizable value of the by-product ($1,100 selling price minus $300 separate costs to process the by-product).

to Work in Process Inventory. Second, assume the additional processing of by-products cost $100 in direct labor and $200 in manufacturing overhead. Entry 2 would appear as follows:

```
(2) Separable By-Product Costs  ..........................  300
        Wages Payable  ................................        100
        Manufacturing Overhead Applied  ...................        200
```

The debit part of entry 2 appears in the Separable By-Product Costs account in Illustration 8–11. Third, assume the by-product is sold for cash, $1,100:

```
(3) Cash  ..........................................  1,100
        By-Product Revenue  ...........................        1,100
```

The credit portion of entry 3 appears in the By-Product Revenue account in Illustration 8–11.

The next step depends on whether the joint product has been sold or is still in inventory. If the joint product has been sold, Cost of Goods Sold would be credited for $800. If the joint product is in Finished Goods Inventory, then Finished Goods Inventory would be credited for $800. Finally, as demonstrated by entry 4 in Illustration 8–11, if the joint product is still in Work-in-Process Inventory, then the following entry would be made:

```
(4) By-Product Revenue  ..............................  1,100
        Separable By-Product Costs  ....................        300
        Work in Process Inventory  .....................        800
```

Entries 5 and 6 in Illustration 8–11 show the transfer of the joint product, now at a cost of $79,200 instead of $80,000, through Finished Goods Inventory to Cost of Goods Sold.

ILLUSTRATION Accounting for By-Products

8–1

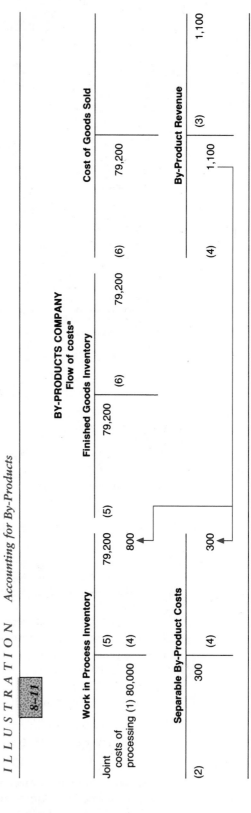

BY-PRODUCTS COMPANY
Flow of costs[a]

Work in Process Inventory

| Joint costs of processing (1) 80,000 | (5) 79,200 |
| | (4) 800 |

Finished Goods Inventory

| (5) 79,200 | (6) 79,200 |

Cost of Goods Sold

| (6) 79,200 | |

Separable By-Product Costs

| (2) 300 | (4) 300 |

By-Product Revenue

| (4) 1,100 | (3) 1,100 |

[a] Cost flows are shown using method 1 in the text. According to this method, the net realizable value of the by-product is deducted from the product costs of the main product.

Method 2, which appears in column 2 of Illustration 8–10, is generally simpler than Method 1. Using Method 2, the by-product's net realizable value is simply treated as other revenue at the point of sale. Assume By-Product Company had set up the accounts shown in Illustration 8–11, and had recorded the $300 of separable by-product costs in the Separable By-Product Costs account in Illustration 8–11. Now assume the by-product is sold for $1,100 cash. The following entry would record the transaction in accordance with Method 2:

Cash 1,100		
Separable By-Product Costs	300	
Other Revenue from Sale of By-Product	800	

A complication can arise, using Method 2, if the cost of processing by-products occurs in one period but the by-products are not sold until the next period. In such a case, companies may find it necessary to keep an inventory of the by-product processing costs in the Separable By-Product Cost account until the by-products are sold.

In our experience, some companies make by-product accounting as easy as possible by simply expensing the by-products' cost in the period the costs are incurred, then recording the total revenue from by-products when they are sold. Using this method, the accountants do not have to bother keeping an inventory of by-product processing costs, nor do they have to compute net realizable value of by-products. Although this simple approach technically violates the principle that revenues and expenses should be matched in the same accounting period, the amounts involved are often immaterial.

Whereas we have indicated two methods of accounting for by-products, there are many variations of these methods used in practice. By-products are relatively minor products, by definition; hence, alternative methods of accounting for by-products are not likely to have a material effect on the financial statements for either internal or external reporting.

Scrap

Our discussion so far has assumed that the secondary or by-product output has a positive net realizable value—that is, its sales value exceeds the costs of further processing and marketing. If an output's net realizable value is negative, it is usually considered *scrap,* and it is disposed of at minimum cost. The cost of scrapping an output is usually debited to manufacturing overhead.

Self-Study Question

4 Refer to self-study question 1. Assume the cocoa shells can be processed for $.10 per pound and sold for $.30 per pound to craftspeople who make them into jewelry. For this example, assume the joint costs to process 100 pounds of cocoa beans total $52, as in self-study question 1. The joint process produces 20 pounds of butter that can be sold for $1.10 per pound, 45 pounds of powder that can be sold for $.90 per pound, and 35 pounds of cocoa shells.

    a. Allocate the joint costs to the two main products using the net realizable value method in which the net realizable value of the by-product reduces the joint production costs.

    b. Prepare an income statement down to the gross margin in which the net realizable value of the by-product is treated as other revenue.

The solution to this question is at the end of this chapter on page 313.

SUMMARY

Joint cost allocations arise from the need to assign common costs to two or more products manufactured from a common input. The usual objective of joint cost allocation is to relate the economic sacrifice (costs) of the inputs to the economic benefits received. Since there is no direct way to do this for joint products, approximations are necessary. The two methods of joint cost allocation distribute joint costs based on net realizable value (or estimated net realizable value) or the physical quantities method. While these methods are acceptable for financial reporting purposes, care must be exercised before attempting to use the data for decision-making purposes because of the inherent arbitrariness in joint cost allocations.

The net realizable value method allocates joint costs to products in proportion to their relative sales values. If additional processing is required beyond the split-off point before the product can be sold, an estimate of the net realizable value can be derived at the split-off point by subtracting the additional processing costs from the sales value that is known.

The physical quantities method allocates joint costs to products in proportion to a physical measure (for example, volume or weight).

Management must often decide whether to sell products at split-off points or process them further. Joint cost allocations are usually irrelevant for these decisions.

By-products are relatively minor outputs from a joint production process. The two methods most commonly used to account for by-products are (1) to reduce the cost of the main product by the net realizable value (sales value minus by-product processing cost) of the by-product or (2) to treat the net realizable value of the by-product as other income.

TERMS AND CONCEPTS

The following terms and concepts should be familiar to you after reading this chapter:

By-Products, *296*	**Net Realizable Value Method,** *290*
Estimated Net Realizable Value, *292*	**Physical Quantities Method,** *294*
Joint Cost, *288*	**Replacement Method (Appendix),** *300*
Joint Products, *288*	**Split-Off Point,** *288*

APPENDIX

The Replacement Method

The replacement method for joint cost allocation is widely used in industries where management can change output proportions. In petroleum refining and chemical processing, for example, the same input can be converted into numerous mixes of output. The replacement method is used when an output proportion is changed from a previously established mix.

For example, assume that Sacramento-Sierra Company had used the physical quantities method to allocate the $180,000 joint cost of log processing as follows:

$$\text{Chipboard, 1,400 units: } \frac{1,400}{1,400 + 1,960} \times \$180,000 = \$ 75,000$$

$$\text{Lumber, 1,960 units: } \frac{1,960}{1,400 + 1,960} \times \$180,000 = \$105,000$$

One day, management decides to change this output mix to produce more chipboard. They find chipboard can be increased by 100 units if lumber is reduced by 80 units. They find it is also necessary to change the processing method in a way that adds $2,470 to the joint costs of processing logs.

Before the change in output mix, the unit cost of chipboard was $53.57 ($75,000 ÷ 1,400 units), and the unit cost of lumber was $53.57 ($105,000 ÷ 1,960). The cost of the 80 units of lumber that would be given up to produce the additional 100 units of chipboard would be $4,286 ($53.57 × 80 units). This amount would be added to the costs of chipboard together with the additional $2,470 processing costs. The costs of lumber would be credited with the $4,286. This would result in the cost allocation shown in Exhibit A. Exhibit B diagrams these cost flows in the accounts.

Note that the unit cost of lumber remains $53.57, but the unit cost of chipboard increases from $53.57 to $54.50. Thus, the product that increases in volume is charged with the additional cost. The unit cost is left unchanged, however, for the product whose volume is decreased.

In summary:

1. The replacement method is used *after* joint costs are allocated to output products using another method (for example, the physical quantities method or the relative sales value method).

2. The replacement method is used when management decides to change a previously determined product mix.

    a. For the output that is *decreased,* product costs are reduced (that is, credited to work in process inventory) by the number of units decreased times the unit cost of those units.

EXHIBIT

A

Replacement Method

SACRAMENTO-SIERRA COMPANY

	(1) Units	(2) Cost	(3) Cost per Unit[a]
Chipboard (initial allocation)	1,400	$ 75,000	$53.57
Replacement cost of lumber used to produce chipboard	100	4,286	
Additional processing costs		2,470	
Totals	1,500	$ 81,756	54.50
Lumber (initial allocation)	1,960	$105,000	53.57
Replacement cost of lumber used to produce chipboard	(80)	(4,286)	53.57
Totals	1,880	$100,714	53.57

[a] Rounded to two decimal places. Column 3 = Column 2 ÷ Column 1.

E X H I B I T   *Replacement Method*

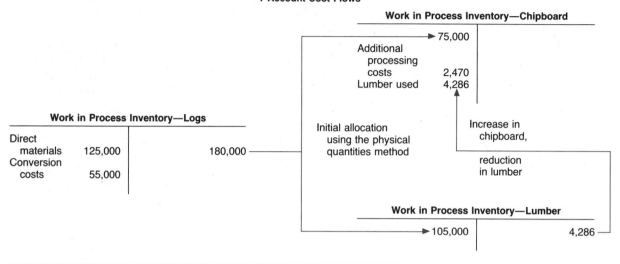

b. For the output that is *increased*, product costs are increased (debited to work in process inventory) by the sum of the amount of costs removed from the product that was decreased and additional processing costs that are required to change the output mix.

3. The replacement method is used only when a previously established product mix is changed so that one output is increased and another is decreased.

4. The cost of the input is assumed to be the same both before and after the change in product mix.

QUESTIONS

8-1   What is the objective of joint cost allocation?

8-2   Why would a number of accountants express a preference for the net realizable value method of joint cost allocation over the physical quantities method?

8-3   When would one prefer a physical quantities method for allocation?

8-4   Explain the basic difference between the allocation of joint costs to joint products and to by-products.

8-5   State the condition under which an item should be treated as a by-product rather than as a joint product.

8-6   Explain the two principal methods of assigning joint costs to joint products. State circumstances under which each would be appropriate.

8-7   Why are joint costs irrelevant in the sell-or-process-further decision?

8-8   The chapter indicated that joint costing is used mostly for financial reporting, inventory valuation, and regulatory purposes. Under what conditions might the method of joint cost allocation have an impact on other decisions?

8–9   What is the difference between joint products, by-products, and scrap?

8–10   How is joint cost allocation like service department cost allocation?

8–11   Name three industries that have joint products.

8–12   Refer to the chapter's Real World Application. Why was Union Pacific's old cost system inadequate?

EXERCISES

8–13   Net Realizable Value Method
(L.O.1)

A company processes Chemical DX-1 through a pressure treatment operation. After the process is complete, there are two outputs: L and T. The January costs of processing DX-1 are $100,000 for materials and $200,000 for conversion costs. This processing results in two outputs, L and T, that sell for a total of $500,000. The sales revenue from L amounts to $400,000 of the total.

Required:

Compute the costs to be assigned to L and T for January, using the net realizable value method.

8–14   Net Realizable Value Method

(L.O.1)

Crucible Corporation operates an ore processing plant. A typical batch of ore run through the plant will yield three refined products: lead, copper, and manganese. At the split-off point, the intermediate products cannot be sold without further processing. The lead from a typical batch will sell for $20,000 after incurring additional processing costs of $6,000. The copper is sold for $40,000 after additional processing costs of $5,000. The manganese yield sells for $30,000 but requires additional processing costs of $9,000. The costs of processing the raw ore, including the ore costs, amount to $50,000 per batch.

Required:

Use the net realizable value method to allocate the joint processing costs.

8–15   Net Realizable Value Method to Solve for Unknowns
(L.O.1)

Blarney Company manufactures leprechauns and shamrocks from a joint process on a product called Green. For leprechauns, 4,000 units were produced having a sales value at the split-off point of $21,000. For shamrocks, 2,000 units were produced having a sales value at split-off of $14,000. Using the net realizable value method, the portion of the total joint product costs allocated to leprechauns was $12,000.

Required:

Compute the total joint product costs before allocation.

(CPA adapted)

8–16   Net Realizable Value Method— Multiple Choice
(L.O.1)

a.   Net realizable value at split-off is used to:

    (1)   Allocate separable costs.

    (2)   Determine relevant costs.

    (3)   Determine break-even in sales dollars.

    (4)   Allocate joint costs.

b.   Net realizable value at split-off is used to allocate:

	Cost beyond Split-Off	Joint Costs
(1)	Yes	Yes
(2)	Yes	No
(3)	No	Yes
(4)	No	No

c.   For purposes of allocating joint costs to joint products, the net realizable value at split-off is equal to:

(1) Sales price less a normal profit margin at point of sale.

(2) Final sales price reduced by cost to complete after split-off.

(3) Total sales value less joint costs at point of split-off.

(4) Separable product cost plus a normal profit margin.

d. The method of accounting for joint product costs that will produce the same gross margin as a percentage of sales for all products is:

(1) The net realizable value method.

(2) The physical quantities method.

(3) Both methods.

(4) Neither method.

8-17 Net Realizable Value Method— Multiple Choice (L.O.1)

Each of the three multiple-choice exercises should be considered independent of each other.

a. The Rote Company manufactures products C and R from a joint process. The total joint costs are $60,000. The sales value at split-off was $70,000 for 8,000 units of product C and $30,000 for 2,000 units of product R. Assuming that total joint costs are allocated using the net realizable value at split-off approach, what were the joint costs allocated to product C?

(1) $18,000.

(2) $30,000.

(3) $42,000.

(4) $48,000.

b. Superior Company manufactures products A and B from a joint process, which also yields a by-product, X. Superior accounts for the revenues from its by-product sales as other income. Additional information is as follows:

	A	B	X	Total
Units produced	15,000	9,000	6,000	30,000
Joint costs	?	?	?	$234,000
Sales value at split-off	$250,000	$200,000	$50,000	$500,000

Assuming that joint product costs are allocated using the net realizable value at split-off approach, what was the joint cost allocated to product B?

(1) $70,200.

(2) $93,600.

(3) $104,000.

(4) $117,000.

c. Sesame Corp. manufactures products W, X, Y, and Z from a joint process. Additional information is as follows:

Product	Units Produced	Sales Value at Split-Off	If Processed Further Additional Costs	Sales Values
W	7,000	$ 70,000	$ 7,500	$ 90,000
X	5,000	60,000	6,000	70,000
Y	4,000	40,000	4,000	50,000
Z	4,000	30,000	2,500	30,000
	20,000	$200,000	$20,000	$240,000

Assuming that joint total costs of $160,000 were allocated using the sales value at split-off (net realizable value method), what joint costs were allocated to each product?

	W	X	Y	Z
(1)	$40,000	$40,000	$40,000	$40,000
(2)	$56,000	$40,000	$32,000	$32,000
(3)	$60,000	$46,667	$33,333	$20,000
(4)	$56,000	$48,000	$32,000	$24,000

(CPA adapted)

8–18 Physical Quantities Method
(L.O.2)

The following questions are based on Durango, Inc., which manufactures products X, Y, and Z from a joint process. Joint product costs were $63,000. Additional information is provided below.

Product	Units Produced	Sales Value at Split-Off	If Processed Further Sales Values	Additional Costs
X	7,000	$40,000	$55,000	$9,000
Y	5,000	35,000	45,000	7,000
Z	2,000	25,000	30,000	5,000

a. Assuming that joint product costs are allocated using the physical quantities (units produced) method, what were the total costs of product X (including $9,000 if processed further)?
  (1) $30,000.
  (2) $31,500.
  (3) $36,000.
  (4) $40,500.

b. Assuming that joint product costs are allocated using the sales value at split-off (net realizable value method), what were the total costs of product Y (including the $7,000 if processed further)?
  (1) $28,000.
  (2) $29,050.
  (3) $29,500.
  (4) $32,200.

(CPA adapted)

8–19 Physical Quantities Method with By-Product
(L.O.2)

Hi-Grow Corporation uses organic materials to produce fertilizers for home gardens. Through its production processes, the company manufactures a high-nitrogen fertilizer (with the trade name Hi-Nite) and a high-phosphorus fertilizer (with the trade name Hi-Bloom). A by-product of the process is methane, which is used to generate power for the company's operations. The fertilizers are sold either in bulk to nurseries or in individual packages for home consumers. The company chooses to allocate the costs on the basis of the physical quantities method.

Last month, 500,000 units of input were processed at a total cost of $90,000. The output of the process consisted of 100,000 units of Hi-Nite, 150,000 units of Hi-Bloom, and 300,000 cubic feet of methane. The by-product methane would have cost $2,000 had it been purchased from the local gas utility. This is considered to be its net realizable value, which is deducted from the processing costs of the main products.

Required:

What is the share of the joint costs to be assigned to each of the main products?

8–20 By-Products
(L.O.3)

Thin Skins Corporation engages in a manufacturing process that uses cowhide to produce three outputs (leather, suede, dog chews). Leather and suede are considered main products. Dog chews are a by-product. During a recent month, the following events occurred:

1. Produced and sold 200 units of leather and 100 units of suede. Produced 25 units of dog chews.

2. Recorded sales revenue of $35,000 from sales of leather and suede. The cost of sales before accounting for the by-product was $18,000.

3. Incurred $100 to process the 25 units of dog chews to completion. These costs are charged as they are incurred against any by-products' sales. (None of these by-product costs are kept in inventory at the end of the period.)

4. Received $550 in revenue from the sale of the 25 units of dog chews.

Required:

Prepare a statement showing, in parallel columns (as in Illustration 8–10), the sales revenue, other income, cost of goods sold, other relevant data, and gross margin that would be reported for each of the two methods of by-product accounting described in the text.

**8–21 By-Products—
Multiple Choice**
(L.O.3)

The following questions are based on Cramden Corporation, which manufactures a product that gives rise to a by-product called Norton. The only costs associated with Norton are additional processing costs of $1 for each unit. Cramden accounts for Norton sales first by deducting its separable costs from such sales and then by deducting this net amount from the cost of sales of the major product. (This is Method 1 discussed in the text. See Illustration 8–10, for example.) This year, 1,200 units of Norton were produced. They were all sold at $5 each.

Required:

a. Sales revenue and cost of goods sold from the main product were $400,000 and $200,000, respectively, for the year. What was the gross margin after considering the by-product sales and costs (that is, the "gross margin" in Illustration 8–10)?
  (1) $200,000.
  (2) $204,800.
  (3) $195,200.
  (4) $206,000.

b. If Cramden changes its method of accounting for Norton sales by showing the net amount as "other income," Cramden's *gross margin* would:
  (1) Be unaffected.
  (2) Increase by $4,800.
  (3) Decrease by $4,800.
  (4) Decrease by $6,000.

c. If Cramden changes its method of accounting as indicated in (b) above, what would be the effects of the change on the company's profits?
  (1) No effect.
  (2) Increase by $4,800.
  (3) Decrease by $4,800.
  (4) Decrease by $6,000.

(CPA adapted)

8–22 Sell or Process Further
(L.O.4)

Sierra Wood Products, Inc., operates a sawmill facility. The company accounts for the bark chips that result from the primary sawing operation as a by-product. The chips are sold to another company at a price of $6 per hundred cubic feet. Normally, sales revenue from this bark is $450,000 per month. There is no direct cost of processing bark chips.

As an alternative, the company can rent equipment that will process the chips and bag them for sale as horticultural bark. Approximately 30 percent of the bark will be graded "large" and will sell for $16 per hundred cubic feet. About 60 percent will be graded "medium" and will sell for $8 per hundred cubic feet. The remainder will be mulch and will sell for $2 per hundred cubic feet.

Costs of the equipment to process and bag chips and the personnel to operate the equipment are $260,000 per month and are fixed regardless of the quantities of bark processed.

Required:

Should the company sell the bark for $6 per hundred cubic feet or process it further (assuming a typical month)?

**8-23 (Appendix)
Replacement Method
(L.O.5)**

Mahalo Cane Company processes sugar cane into various output products. The outputs from the first stage of the process consist of two grades of sugar: refined and turbinado. In a typical month, $218,000 in sugar cane is processed and $322,000 in labor and overhead is incurred. A standard output mix consists of 40 percent refined sugar and 60 percent turbinado. Engineering studies assign 55 percent of the joint processing costs to the refined sugar.

If the processing temperature is increased, the yield of refined sugar can be increased by 20 percent (that is, from 40 percent of the initial output to an amount equal to 48 percent of the initial output). However, processing costs are increased by $43,200 when this is done, and 12 percent of the original yield of turbinado is lost.

Required: Compute the costs that would be assigned to the additional refined sugar, using the replacement method.

PROBLEMS

**8-24 Net Realizable Value
of Joint Products—
Multiple Choice**

Miller Manufacturing Company buys zeon for $.80 a gallon. At the end of distilling in Department 1, zeon splits off into three products: argon, xon, and neon. Argon is sold at the split-off point, with no further processing; xon and neon require further processing before they can be sold. Xon is fused in Department 2, and neon is solidified in Department 3. Following is a summary of costs and other related data for the year ended December 31.

	Department		
	(1) Distilling	**(2) Fusing**	**(3) Solidifying**
Cost of zeon	$96,000	—	—
Direct labor	24,000	$45,000	$65,000
Manufacturing overhead	20,000	21,000	54,000
	Products		
	Argon	**Xon**	**Neon**
Gallons sold	15,000	30,000	45,000
Gallons on hand at year-end	10,000	—	15,000
Sales in dollars	$30,000	$96,000	$141,750

There were no beginning inventories on hand at January 1, and there was no zeon on hand at the end of the year on December 31. All gallons on hand on December 31 were complete as to processing. Miller uses the net realizable value method of allocating joint costs.

Required: *a.* For allocating joint costs, the net realizable value of argon for the year ended December 31 would be:
   (1) $30,000.
   (2) $50,000.
   (3) $25,000.
   (4) $20,000.

b. The joint costs for the year ended December 31 to be allocated are:
(1) $325,000.
(2) $116,000.
(3) $140,000.
(4) $96,000.

c. The cost of xon sold for the year ended December 31 is:
(1) $94,000.
(2) $66,000.
(3) $88,857.
(4) Some other amount.

d. The value of the ending inventory for argon is:
(1) $28,000.
(2) $18,667.
(3) $20,000.
(4) Some other amount.

(CPA adapted)

8–25 Net Realizable Value and Effects of Processing Further

Bryce Industries, Inc., produces three products by a joint production process. Raw materials are put into production in Department A, and at the end of processing in this department, three products appear. Product X is immediately sold at the split-off point, with no further processing. Products Y and Z require further processing before they are sold. Product Y is processed in Department B, and product Z is processed in Department C. The company uses the net realizable value method of allocating joint production costs. Following is a summary of costs and other data for the quarter ended September 30.

There were no inventories on hand at the beginning of the quarter, or July 1. There was no raw material on hand at September 30. All the units on hand at the end of the quarter were fully complete as to processing.

	Products		
	X	Y	Z
Pounds sold	20,000	59,000	70,000
Pounds on hand at September 30	50,000	–0–	40,000
Sales revenues	$30,000	$177,000	$245,000

	Departments		
	A	B	C
Raw material cost	$112,000	–0–	–0–
Direct labor cost	48,000	$80,900	$191,750
Manufacturing overhead	20,000	21,100	73,250

Required:

a. Determine the following amounts for each product: (1) estimated net realizable value as used for allocating joint costs, (2) joint costs allocated to each of the three products, (3) cost of goods sold, and (4) finished goods inventory costs, September 30.

b. Assume that the entire output of product X could be processed further at an additional cost of $2.00 per pound and then sold at a price of $4.30 per pound. What is the effect on operating profits if all the product X output for the quarter had been processed further and sold, rather than all being sold at the split-off point?

8–26 Finding Missing Data—Net Realizable Value

Air Extracts, Inc., manufactures nitrogen, oxygen, and hydrogen from a joint process. Each gas can be liquified and sold for more. Data on the process are as follows:

	Product			
	Nitrogen	Oxygen	Hydrogen	Total
Units produced	8,000	4,000	2,000	14,000
Joint costs	$ 60,000ᵃ	(a)	(b)	$120,000
Sales value at split-off	(c)	(d)	$30,000	200,000
Additional costs to liquify	14,000	$10,000	6,000	30,000
Sales value if liquified	140,000	60,000	40,000	240,000

ᵃ This amount is the portion of the total joint cost of $120,000 that had been allocated to nitrogen.

Required: Determine the values for the lettered spaces.

(CPA adapted)

8–27 Joint Cost Allocations, with By-Product

The Roving Eye Cosmetics Company buys bulk flowers and processes them into perfumes in a two-stage process. Their highest-grade perfume, Seduction, and a residue that is processed into a medium-grade perfume called Romance come from a certain mix of petals. In July, the company used 25,000 pounds of petals. The first stage is a joint process known as Reduction, reducing the petals to Seduction and the residue. This first stage had the following costs:

- $200,000 direct materials.
- $110,000 direct labor.
- $90,000 overhead and other costs.

The additional costs of producing Romance in the second stage, known as the second pressing, were as follows:

- $22,000 direct materials.
- $50,000 direct labor.
- $40,000 overhead and other costs.

For the month of July, total production equaled 10,000 ounces of Seduction and 42,000 ounces of Romance. There was no beginning inventory on July 1. There were no uncompleted units.

Packaging costs incurred for each product as completed were $60,000 for Seduction and $154,000 for Romance. The sales price of Seduction is $90 an ounce; Romance sells for $31.50 per ounce.

Required:
a. Allocate joint costs using the estimated net realizable value method. (Packaging and additional processing costs must be subtracted from revenue to compute net realizable values.)

b. Allocate the joint costs using the physical quantities method. Round all percentages to one decimal place.

c. Are there any problems in using the physical quantities method in this case?

d. Assume that Roving Eye can sell the squeezed petals from the reduction process to greenhouses for use as fertilizer. In July, there were 12,000 pounds of squeezed petals left over that sold for $.75 per pound. The squeezed petals are a by-product of Reduction. Assume the net realizable value of by-products reduces joint costs of main products. With this new information, answer parts (a) and (b).

8–28 Cost Flows Through T-Accounts

Refer to problem 8–27. Show the flow of costs through T-accounts using the net realizable value method. Assume the net realizable value of by-products in part (d) was credited to Work in Process Inventory. Assume the joint products were sold.

8-29 Joint Costing in a Process Costing Context—Net Realizable Value Method

Harrison Corporation produces three products: alpha, beta, and gamma. Alpha and gamma are main products, while beta is a by-product of alpha. Information on the past month's production processes are given as follows:

1. In Department I, 110,000 units of raw material rho are processed at a total cost of $145,000. After processing in Department 1, 60 percent of the units are transferred to Department II, and 40 percent of the units (now un-processed gamma) are transferred to Department III.

2. In Department II, the materials received from Department I are processed at a total additional cost of $38,000. Seventy percent of the units become alpha and are transferred to Department IV. The remaining 30 percent emerge as beta and are sold at $2.10 per unit. The additional processing costs to make beta salable are $8,100.

3. In Department III, gamma is processed at an additional cost of $165,000. A normal loss of units of gamma occurs in this department. The loss is equal to 10 percent of the units of good output. The remaining good output is then sold for $12 per unit.

4. In Department IV, alpha is processed at an additional cost of $16,480. After this processing, the alpha can be sold for $5 per unit.

Required:

Prepare a schedule showing the allocation of the $145,000 joint cost between alpha and gamma, using the net realizable value approach. Revenue from sales of by-products should be credited to the manufacturing costs of the related main product (Method 1 in the text).

(CPA adapted)

8-30 Find Maximum Input Price—Net Realizable Value Method

Rambling Rose Corporation produces two joint products from its manufacturing operation. Product J sells for $41.50 per unit, while product M sells for $12 per unit at the split-off point. In a typical month, 19,000 units are processed. Fifteen thousand units become Product M. Four thousand units become product J after an additional $56,250 of processing costs are incurred.

The joint process has only variable costs; no fixed costs. In a typical month, the conversion costs amount to $114,075. Materials prices are volatile, and if prices are too high, the company will stop production.

Required:

What is the maximum price the company should pay for the materials?

8-31 Effect of By-Product versus Joint Cost Accounting

Ninja Turtle Company processes input Leonardo into three outputs: Michaelangelo, Raphael, and Donatello. Michaelangelo accounts for 60 percent of the net realizable value at the split-off point, while Raphael accounts for 30 percent. The balance is accounted for by Donatello. The joint costs total $182,750. If Donatello is accounted for as a by-product, its net realizable value at split-off of $18,800 would be credited to the joint manufacturing costs using Method 1 described in the text which credits the by-product's net realizable value against the joint costs. (See Illustration 8–10.)

Required:

What are the allocated joint costs for the three outputs?

a. If Donatello is accounted for as a joint product?

b. If Donatello is accounted for as a by-product?

8-32 Joint Cost Allocation and Product Profitability

Jasper Ridge Materials, Inc., receives silicon crystals that it processes into purified wafers and chips. Silicon crystals cost $30,000 per tank-car load. The process is such that the crystals are heated for 12 hours, at the end of which time there are 45,000 purified wafers, with a market value of $10,000, and 15,000 chips, with a market value of $70,000. The cost of the heat process is $12,800.

Required:

a. If the crystal costs and the heat process costs are to be allocated on the basis of units of output, what cost would be assigned to each product?

b. If the crystal costs and the heat process costs are allocated on the basis of the net realizable value, what cost would be assigned to each product?

    c. How much profit or loss does the purified wafers product provide using the data in this problem and your analysis in requirement (*a*)? Is it really possible to determine which product is more profitable? Explain why or why not.

INTEGRATIVE CASES

8–33 Effect of Cost Allocation on Pricing and Make versus Buy Decisions

Indio Agresearch is a large farm cooperative with a number of agriculture-related manufacturing and service divisions. As a cooperative, the company pays no federal income taxes. The company owns a fertilizer plant, which processes and mixes petrochemical compounds into three brands of agricultural fertilizer: Greenup, Maintane, and Winterizer. The three brands differ with respect to selling price and with respect to the proportional content of basic chemicals.

    The Fertilizer Manufacturing Division transfers the completed product to the cooperative's Retail Sales Division at a price based on the costs of each type of fertilizer plus a markup.

    The Manufacturing Division is completely automated so that the only costs incurred are costs of the petrochemical feedstocks plus overhead that is all considered fixed. The primary feedstock costs $1.50 per pound. Each 100 pounds of feedstock can produce either of the following mixtures of fertilizer.

	Output Schedules (in pounds)	
	A	**B**
Greenup	50	60
Maintane	30	10
Winterizer	20	30

    Production is limited to the 750,000 kilowatt-hours monthly capacity of the dehydrator. Due to different chemical makeup, each brand of fertilizer requires different dehydrator use. Dehydrator usage in kilowatt-hours per pound of product is:

Product	Kilowatt-Hour Usage per Pound
Greenup	32
Maintane	20
Winterizer	40

    Monthly fixed costs are $81,250. Now the company is producing according to output schedule A. Joint production costs including fixed overhead are allocated to each product on the basis of weight.

    The fertilizer is packed into 100-pound bags for sale in the cooperative's retail stores. The Manufacturing Division charges the retail stores the cost plus a markup. The sales price for each product charged by the cooperative's Retail Sales Division is as follows:

	Sales Price per Pound
Greenup	$10.50
Maintane	9.00
Winterizer	10.40

Selling expenses are 20 percent of the sales price.

The manager of the Retail Sales Division has complained that the prices charged are excessive and that he would prefer to purchase from another supplier.

The manager of the Manufacturing Division argues that the processing mix was determined based on a careful analysis of the costs of each product compared to the prices charged by the Retail Sales Division.

Required:

a. Assume joint production costs including fixed overhead are allocated to each product on the basis of weight. What is the cost per pound of each product including fixed overhead and the feedstock cost of $1.50 per pound, given the current production schedule?

b. Assume joint production costs including fixed overhead are allocated to each product on the basis of net realizable value if sold through the cooperative's Retail Sales Division. What is the allocated cost per pound of each product, given the current production schedule?

c. Assume joint production costs including fixed overhead are allocated to each product on the basis of weight. Which of the two production schedules, A or B, produces the higher operating profit to the firm as a whole?

d. Would your answer to part (c) be different if joint production costs including fixed overhead are allocated to each product on the basis of net realizable value? If so, by how much?

8–34   (Appendix) Joint Costing— Replacement Method

In refining crude oil, three primary classes of products are obtained: (1) gasolines; (2) distillates such as jet fuel, heating oil, and diesel fuel; and (3) residual fuel. Due to marketing considerations, a primary objective of the refining process is to obtain as much gasoline from the oil as possible. While some gasoline can be obtained with relatively little processing, obtaining greater yields of gasoline requires the use of catalytic processes under high pressures and temperatures. In addition to the characteristics of the refining process, a major determinant of the quantity of gasoline obtainable from a barrel of crude oil is the initial gravity of the oil. Certain heavy oils, while plentiful and relatively inexpensive, have yielded fairly low quantities of gasoline.

Great Lands Refining Company developed a new process for obtaining more gasoline from heavy crude oils. Without the new process, the typical yield from heavy crudes is 64 percent gasoline, 20 percent distillates, and 16 percent residual. With the new process, the yield of gasoline rises to 69 percent, distillates decrease to 18 percent, and residual decreases to 13 percent.

To obtain the increased yields, the variable costs of processing a barrel of crude oil increase by $1 from $2 to $3. The refinery that would process this crude has a daily capacity of 50,000 barrels. The capacity would be unchanged by the process, but the fixed costs of the refinery would increase from $200,000 per day to $230,000 per day. The cost of a barrel of heavy crude is $24.

Joint processing costs are first allocated using engineering estimates of the "refining effort" to obtain the standard mix of each product. Under the present system, 64 percent of the refining effort is considered applicable to gasoline, 20 percent to distillates, and 16 percent to residual fuels. Any change in the product output would be charged into the accounts using the replacement method.

All figures can be reported in terms of the cash and income flows from one day's operations. For simplicity, assume there is no loss of mass in refining and the refinery operates at 100 percent capacity.

Required:

Use the replacement method to determine the cost of the increased gasoline production on a per barrel basis.

SOLUTIONS TO

Q Self-Study
uestions

1   The joint costs to be allocated amount to $52—the total of the $15 in direct materials costs and the $37 in conversion costs. The total sales value for butter is $22, $1.10 per pound times 20 pounds. The net realizable value of the powder is $40.50, $.90 per pound times 45 pounds per hundred pounds of input. The allocation follows:

To cocoa butter:

$$\frac{\$22}{\$22 + \$40.50} \times \$52 = \$18.304$$

To cocoa powder:

$$\frac{\$40.50}{\$22 + \$40.50} \times \$52 = \$33.696$$

This results in an allocation of the total cost of $52 (which is $18.304 + $33.696) to the two products.

2   Using the estimated net realizable value (NRV) method, first compute the NRV of cocoa butter to be $21 [($1.20 − $.15) × 20 pounds]. Now the allocations are:

To cocoa butter:

$$\frac{\$21}{\$21 + \$40.50} \times \$52 = \$17.756$$

To cocoa powder:

$$\frac{\$40.50}{\$21 + \$40.50} \times \$52 = \$34.244$$

Compared to self-study question 1, the allocation to cocoa butter has gone down and the allocation to cocoa powder has gone up. Why did this happen? (Answer: The allocation to cocoa butter went down because its NRV went down.)

3   Since there is a total of 65 pounds of output of major products (20 pounds of butter and 45 pounds of powder) at the split-off point, the allocation is:

To cocoa butter:

$$\frac{20}{20 + 45} \times \$52 = \$16.00$$

To cocoa powder:

$$\frac{45}{20 + 45} \times \$52 = \$36.00$$

resulting in an allocation of the total $52 to the two products.

4   The by-product of 100 pounds of cocoa beans amounts to $7 [($.30 per pound selling price − $.10 per pound to process) × 35 pounds of cocoa shells produced].

   a.   The joint costs are now reduced to $45 ($52 − $7 for the net realizable value of the by-product). The new joint cost allocations are:

To cocoa butter:

$$\frac{\$22}{\$22 + \$40.50} \times \$45 = \$15.84$$

To cocoa powder:

$$\frac{\$40.50}{\$22 + \$40.50} \times \$45 = \$29.16$$

b.

FERGUSON CONFECTIONS COMPANY
Income Statement

Revenue from sale of cocoa butter and cocoa powder	$62.50
Other revenue from sale of shells	7.00
Total revenue	69.50
Joint production costs	52.00
Gross margin	$17.50

Variable Costing

LEARNING OBJECTIVES

After reading this chapter, you should be able to:

1. Compare and contrast the product costs computed under variable costing to those computed using full-absorption costing.
2. Explain the difference in operating profits under variable costing compared to full-absorption costing.
3. Compare cost flows through T-accounts using variable costing compared to full-absorption costing.
4. Explain how normal costing, with predetermined overhead rates, is used in variable costing.
5. See how additional information is provided using the contribution margin format income statement compared to the traditional format.
6. Explain how the difference in operating profits between variable costing and full-absorption costing can be derived using the algebraic approach. (Appendix)

Full-Absorption Costing A system of accounting for costs in which both fixed and variable manufacturing costs are considered product costs.

Our discussion of product costing methods has been consistent with the external reporting requirement that inventory in manufacturing companies be valued using *full-absorption costing* (also called *absorption costing*). In this chapter, we introduce an alternative method, *variable costing* (also called *direct costing*). Under **full-absorption costing,** all manufacturing costs—fixed and variable—are assigned to units produced. Under **variable costing,** only variable manufacturing costs are assigned to units produced. Fixed manufacturing costs are considered to be period expenses.[1]

---

[1] Recall from Chapter 2 that variable manufacturing costs vary with the volume of production, while fixed costs remain the same despite changes in production volume within a relevant range of activity. We explore the distinction between fixed and variable costs in more depth in Chapters 10 and 11.

Variable Costing (or Direct Costing) A system of cost accounting that only assigns the variable cost of manufacturing to products.

This chapter compares full-absorption and variable costing. We examine the differences between the two methods that arise in cost flows, income statements, and decision making. We also discuss the uses for which the two methods are appropriate.

VARIABLE COSTING FOR PRICING PURPOSES

Managers recognize the difference between variable costs and full-absorption costs in decision making. The Real World Application for this chapter tells how managers in a Chicago bank wisely knew this difference.

Have you ever wondered why airlines charge a fare from a few hundred dollars to more than a thousand dollars for a seat on one flight? How can the same product (an airplane seat between two cities) vary by such a substantial amount? The answer lies in the cost structure of the airlines and the way fixed and variable costs are treated for pricing purposes.

Once an air carrier decides to offer a flight between two cities, over 90 percent of the costs of that flight are fixed. Given a specific model of aircraft on the route, the flight will cost the airline almost the same amount to operate whether the plane is carrying 5 passengers or 300. Airlines can maximize revenues by setting a base fare that is high enough so that the revenues from travelers who need to take a specific flight will cover the fixed costs of that flight plus its variable costs. Lower fares can be used to induce others to take additional seats on that particular flight. These lower fares need only be slightly in excess of the variable costs of the flight for the airline to make a profit from the added discount passengers. As a practical matter, the discount fares add substantially to airline operating profits.

For example, suppose the costs of flying a 150-seat plane from Chicago to Boston are $20,000 fixed plus $15 per passenger variable. From past experience, an airline estimates that on the particular flight we are studying, approximately 80 passengers will take the flight regardless of cost. To cover the fixed and variable costs for those 80 passengers, the fare must amount to:

$$\frac{\$20,000}{80} + \$15 = \$265$$

If the airline sets its full fare at $300, its operating profits from the flight will be:

Revenues ($300 × 80)	$24,000
Costs:	
Fixed costs	20,000
Variable costs ($15 × 80)	1,200
Total costs	21,200
Operating profits	$ 2,800

However, there are 70 empty seats on that flight if only full-fare seats are sold. Suppose the airline offers a discount fare of 60 percent off the regular fare to fill up some of the empty seats. This fare adds 40 more passengers to the flight. Operating profits are now:

Revenues:	
Full fare ($300 × 80)	$24,000
Discount ($120 × 40)	4,800
Total revenues	28,800

Costs:	
Fixed costs	20,000
Variable costs ($15 × 120)	1,800
Total costs	21,800
Operating profits	$ 7,000

Profits from the flight have increased from $2,800 to $7,000 (250 percent) despite offering seats at a 60 percent discount.

Of course, this solution assumes that none of the full-fare passengers will buy discount tickets. Moreover, it assumes that larger planes will not be needed to accommodate the added passenger load. To avoid losing full-fare passengers to discounting, airlines put restrictions on the discount tickets. The other issues involved in fare setting to maximize profits for varying cost structures are complex.

Major airlines have revenue management departments charged with the responsibility of setting fares to maximize profits. Revenue managers need to know all the costs of operating a flight to set the full fares. They need to know the variable costs to set discount fares. In addition, they need to know what the competition is doing so that they are not priced out of the markets that they wish to serve. In this chapter, we look at full and variable costing principles, which form the foundation for this type of analysis. The analysis itself is called *differential costing* and is covered in Chapter 12.

VARIABLE VERSUS FULL-ABSORPTION COSTING

This section presents a numerical comparison of variable and full-absorption costing. Assume the facts for Stonewall Manufacturing for the months of January and February shown in the chart below.

	January	February
Units:		
Beginning inventory	–0–	100
Production	1,000	1,000
Sales	900	1,100
Ending inventory (all units are finished at the end of the period—there is no work in process inventory)	100	–0–
Costs:		
Variable manufacturing costs (per unit produced):		
Direct materials .... $	10	$ 10
Direct labor	5	5
Variable manufacturing overhead	3	3
Fixed manufacturing costs (per month)	8,000	8,000
Variable marketing costs (per unit sold)	2	2
Fixed marketing and administrative costs (per month)	12,000	12,000
Price per unit sold	45	45

Illustration 9–1 presents the flow of manufacturing costs through T-accounts in January for both full-absorption and variable costing. For now, we use **actual costing**; that is, actual direct materials, direct labor, and manufacturing overhead costs are debited to Work in Process Inventory. (Later in the chapter, we use **normal costing**, which is like actual costing except that manufacturing overhead is debited to Work in Process Inventory using a predetermined rate.)

Actual Costing A system of accounting whereby overhead is assigned based on actual overhead costs incurred.

I L L U S T R A T I O N   Variable and Full-Absorption Costing Comparison: Flow of Manufacturing Costs

9–1

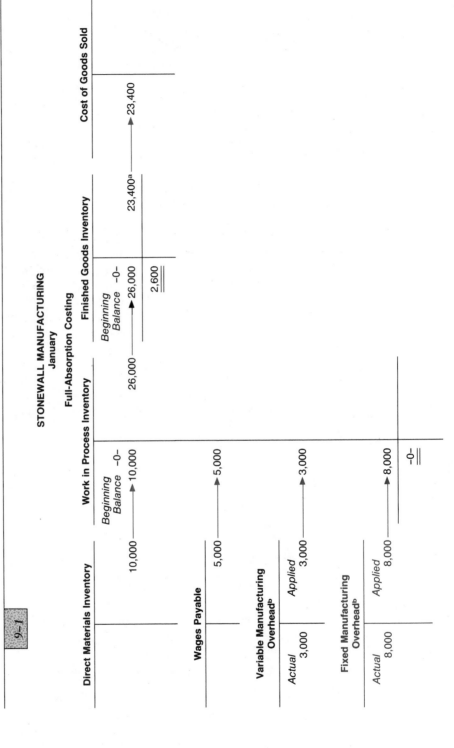

STONEWALL MANUFACTURING
January

Full-Absorption Costing

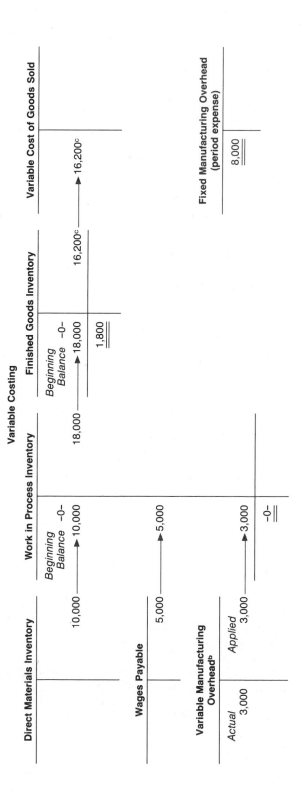

Variable Costing

| Direct Materials Inventory | Work in Process Inventory | Finished Goods Inventory | Variable Cost of Goods Sold |

Direct Materials Inventory

10,000 → 10,000

Work in Process Inventory

Beginning Balance –0–

10,000 →

5,000 →

3,000 →

18,000 → 18,000

–0–

Finished Goods Inventory

Beginning Balance –0–

18,000 → 16,200[c]

1,800

Variable Cost of Goods Sold

16,200[c]

Wages Payable

5,000

Variable Manufacturing Overhead[b]

Actual 3,000 | Applied 3,000

Fixed Manufacturing Overhead (period expense)

8,000

[a] $23,400 = $\left[\dfrac{900}{1,000}\right] \times \$26,000 = 900 \times (\$8 + 18) = 900 \times \$26.$

[b] We have placed actual and applied overhead in the same account with actual costs as debits and applied costs as credits. This was done for convenience in presentation. An alternative is to place actual overhead in one account and applied overhead in another account. Both methods are used in practice.

[c] Variable cost of goods sold = $18 per unit (direct materials, direct labor, and variable manufacturing overhead) times 900 units sold = $16,200.

319

Normal Costing A system of accounting whereby direct materials and direct labor are charged to objects at actual costs, and manufacturing overhead is applied using a predetermined overhead rate.

Note that while total actual costs incurred are the same under both full-absorption and variable costing, fixed manufacturing costs are debited to Work in Process Inventory under full-absorption costing but not under variable costing. As a consequence, the amounts in Work in Process Inventory and Finished Goods Inventory are higher under full-absorption costing.

Under full-absorption costing, the inventory value is:

$$\begin{array}{l} \dfrac{\text{Number}}{\text{of units}} \times \left(\dfrac{\text{Variable manufacturing}}{\text{cost per unit}} + \dfrac{\text{Fixed manufacturing}}{\text{cost per unit}} \right) \\[2ex] = 100 \text{ units} \times \left(\$18 + \dfrac{\$8,000 \text{ fixed manufacturing costs}}{1,000 \text{ units}} \right) \\[2ex] = 100 \times (\$18 + \$8) \\[1ex] = \underline{\underline{\$2,600}} \end{array}$$

Under variable costing, the inventory value is:

$$\dfrac{\text{Number}}{\text{of units}} \times \dfrac{\text{Variable manufacturing}}{\text{cost per unit}}$$

$$100 \text{ units} \times \$18 = \underline{\underline{\$1,800}}$$

Product Costs Costs that are attributed to a product; costs that are part of inventory.

Fixed manufacturing costs are treated as **product costs** and therefore assigned to each unit under full-absorption costing. Under variable costing, they are treated as **period costs** and thus are expensed in the period incurred.

Period Costs Costs that are attributed to time intervals.

Note that *all* manufacturing costs must be either expensed or inventoried for both methods. The fundamental concept is:

Cost incurred − Inventory increase + Inventory decrease = Cost expensed

Using full-absorption costing, finished goods and work in process inventory increases and decreases are more than they are using variable costing because these inventories include fixed manufacturing costs. For example, note the relation between manufacturing costs incurred and those expensed under the two systems shown in Illustration 9–2.

Note the source of difference between the two methods. *Variable* manufacturing costs are treated as product costs under both methods, and marketing and administrative costs are treated as period expenses under both methods. The source of the difference is the treatment of fixed manufacturing costs. *Fixed manufacturing costs are treated as product costs under full-absorption costing and as period expenses under variable costing.*

Effect on Profits

As shown in Illustration 9–3, the $800 higher profit in January under full-absorption costing is exactly the same as the difference in the amount of costs inventoried under the two methods. Full-absorption inventories $800 of fixed manufacturing costs that are expensed under variable costing. Hence, under full-absorption, costs expensed are $800 lower and operating profits are $800 higher than under variable costing. Under full-absorption,

ILLUSTRATION

9–2

Manufacturing Costs Incurred and Expensed when Production Volume Exceeds Sales Volume

STONEWALL MANUFACTURING
January

	Manufacturing Costs Incurred	Minus Increase in Inventory	Equals Manufacturing Costs Expensed
Full-Absorption Costing:			
Variable manufacturing costs	$18,000	$1,800[a]	$16,200[b]
Fixed manufacturing costs	8,000	800[c]	7,200[d]
Total	$26,000	$2,600	$23,400
Variable Costing:			
Variable manufacturing costs	$18,000	$1,800[a]	$16,200[b]
Fixed manufacturing costs	8,000	–0–	8,000
Total	$26,000	$1,800	$24,200

[a] $1,800 = 100 units inventoried × $18 per unit.
[b] $16,200 = 900 units sold × $18 variable cost per unit.
[c] $800 = 100 units inventoried × $8 per unit.
[d] $7,200 = 900 units sold × $\dfrac{\$8,000 \text{ fixed manufacturing cost}}{1,000 \text{ units produced}}$

= 900 units × $8.

ILLUSTRATION

*Variable and Full-Absorption
Costing Comparison:
Income Statements*

STONEWALL MANUFACTURING
January

Full-Absorption Costing

Sales revenue	$40,500[a]
Cost of goods sold	23,400
Gross margin	17,100
Marketing and administrative costs	13,800[b]
Operating profit	$ 3,300

Variable Costing

Sales revenue	$40,500[a]
Less:	
Variable cost of goods sold	16,200
Variable marketing and administrative costs	1,800[c]
Contribution margin	22,500
Less:	
Fixed manufacturing costs	8,000
Fixed marketing and administrative costs	12,000
Operating profit	$ 2,500

[a] $45 × 900 units sold = $40,500.
[b] Fixed costs + Variable costs = $12,000 + ($2 × 900 units sold) = $13,800.
[c] $2 × 900 units sold = $1,800.

the expensing of $800 of fixed manufacturing costs is deferred until the period when the units are sold.

As a general rule, under full-absorption costing, *when units produced exceed units sold* in a period, a portion of the period's fixed manufacturing costs is not expensed in that period. Under variable costing, however, all of the period's fixed manufacturing costs are expensed. Thus, when production exceeds sales, fewer fixed manufacturing costs are expensed, and *operating profits are higher* under full-absorption than under variable costing.

On the other hand, if units sold exceed units produced, then more fixed manufacturing costs are expensed under full-absorption costing, so operating profits are lower under full-absorption than under variable costing. We show this case in Illustration 9–4, which presents Stonewall Manufacturing's cost flows for February. The company produced 1,000 units in February and sold 1,100 units, including 100 units from inventory. In this case, full-absorption costing (FAC) expenses more fixed manufacturing costs than does variable costing (VC), because full-absorption now expenses the fixed manufacturing costs that were deferred from January.

A summary of our analysis of manufacturing costs is shown in Illustration 9–5. Note that manufacturing costs expensed equal costs incurred *plus the decrease in inventory*. In Illustration 9–2, note that in January, manufacturing costs expensed equaled costs incurred *minus the increase in inventory*.

Illustration 9–6 compares full-absorption costing (FAC) and variable costing (VC) at Stonewall Manufacturing for January and February. It presents some important results.

First, Illustration 9–6 shows that operating profit for the two-month period is the same under both methods—$10,000. This occurs because the company had no units in inventory at either the beginning or end of the period in question. Operating profits were higher under full-absorption costing in January, however, because units produced exceeded units sold. The reverse was true in February.

Second, Illustration 9–6 shows that the difference in operating profits between the two costing methods (FAC > VC by $800 in January, VC > FAC by $800 in February) equals the differences in the changes in the Finished Goods Inventory account. FAC inventory increased by $2,600, while VC inventory increased by $1,800 in January; FAC inventory decreased by $2,600, while VC inventory decreased by $1,800 in February.

Third, the difference in operating profits in each period equals the difference in fixed manufacturing costs expensed under the two systems.

In general, if there are no inventories, operating profits are the same under both methods. If production volume equals sales volume, the profit figures will differ only if the fixed manufacturing costs per unit differ in beginning and ending inventory.

Important Observations

There are four important observations to note before leaving this discussion. First, our example assumes that a portion of manufacturing overhead is the only cost that is fixed. In fact, some or all of direct labor might be fixed as well. This occurs when direct labor costs are neither reduced when production volume decreases nor increased when production volume increases. If direct labor is fixed, it is treated as a *product* cost under full-absorption costing and a *period* cost under variable costing, just like fixed manufacturing overhead in our example.

Second, while our example has assumed that finished goods are the only inventories, the results hold for work in process inventory, too. That is, fixed manufacturing costs would be part of work in process inventory under full-absorption costing, but they would not be under variable costing.

Third, this entire discussion refers only to manufacturing costs, which are the only costs inventoried. It does *not* refer to marketing and administrative costs, which are not part of inventory.

Fourth, we find the companies usually use FIFO for internal reporting purposes. Financial reports usually are based on an adjustment to FIFO data. All problems in this chapter assume FIFO to be consistent with practice.

ILLUSTRATION Variable and Full-Absorption Costing Comparison: Flow of Manufacturing Costs

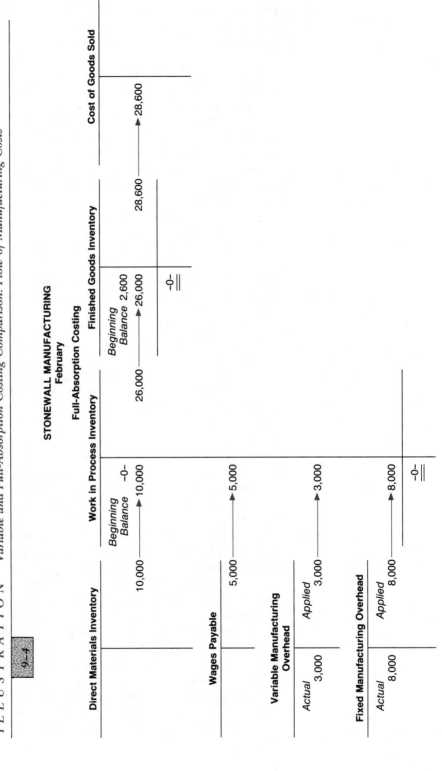

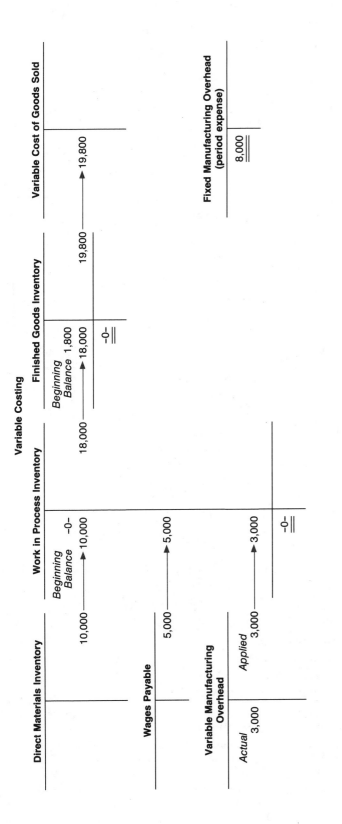

Variable Costing

Direct Materials Inventory

10,000 ──────→ 10,000

Work in Process Inventory

Beginning
Balance –0–
10,000 ──────→ 18,000

5,000 ──────→

3,000 ──────→

–0–

Wages Payable

5,000 ──────→ 5,000

Variable Manufacturing Overhead

Actual   Applied
3,000   3,000 ──────→

Finished Goods Inventory

Beginning
Balance 1,800
18,000 ──────→ 19,800

–0–

Variable Cost of Goods Sold

19,800 ──────→

Fixed Manufacturing Overhead (period expense)

8,000

ILLUSTRATION

Manufacturing Costs Incurred and Expensed when Sales Volume Exceeds Production Volume

STONEWALL MANUFACTURING
February

	Manufacturing Costs Incurred	Plus Decrease in Inventory	Equals Manufacturing Costs Expensed
Panel A:			
Full-Absorption Costing:			
Variable manufacturing costs	$18,000	$1,800[a]	$19,800[b]
Fixed manufacturing costs	8,000	800[c]	8,800[d]
Total	$26,000	$2,600	$28,600
Variable Costing:			
Variable manufacturing costs	$18,000	$1,800[a]	$19,800[b]
Fixed manufacturing costs	8,000	–0–	8,000
Total	$26,000	$1,800	$27,800

Panel B:
Calculations:

[a] $1,800 = 100 units from inventory × $18 variable cost per unit.

[b] $19,800 = 1,100 units sold × $18 variable cost per unit.

[c] $800 = 100 units from inventory × $8 fixed cost per unit.

[d] $8,800 = 1,100 units sold × $\dfrac{\$8,000}{1,000 \text{ units produced}}$

   = 1,100 units × $8.

 *Self-Study Question*

1 Mario Enterprises produced 84,000 units last year and sold 76,000 units. Costs incurred that year were:

Direct materials	$462,000
Direct labor	315,000
Variable manufacturing overhead	105,000
Fixed manufacturing overhead	399,000
Variable marketing and administrative costs	50,400
Fixed marketing and administrative costs	200,600

    a. Compute the product cost per unit (that is, the inventoriable amount per unit) using full-absorption costing and using variable costing.

    b. Prepare income statements. Assume Mario had no beginning or ending inventories except for the 8,000 units in finished goods ending inventory. Mario sold its product for $20 per unit.

    c. Explain why operating profits under full-absorption costing are higher (or lower) than under variable costing.

The solution to this question is at the end of this chapter on page 355.

ILLUSTRATION

9–6

Variable and Full-Absorption Costing Comparison: Comparative Income Statements

STONEWALL MANUFACTURING
January and February

Full-Absorption Costing

	January	February	Total
Sales revenue	$40,500	$49,500	$90,000
Cost of goods sold	23,400	28,600	52,000
Gross margin	17,100	20,900	38,000
Marketing and administrative costs	13,800[a]	14,200[b]	28,000
Operating profits	$ 3,300	$ 6,700	$10,000
Change in finished goods inventory	+$ 2,600[c]	−$ 2,600[d]	–0–

Variable Costing

	January	February	Total
Sales revenue	$40,500	$49,500	$90,000
Less:			
Variable cost of goods sold	16,200	19,800	36,000
Variable marketing and administrative costs	1,800	2,200	4,000
Contribution margin	22,500	27,500	50,000
Less:			
Fixed manufacturing costs	8,000	8,000	16,000
Fixed marketing and administrative costs	12,000	12,000	24,000
Operating profits	$ 2,500	$ 7,500	$10,000
Change in finished goods inventory	+$ 1,800[c]	−$ 1,800[d]	–0–

Calculations:

[a] $12,000 + ($2 × 900 units sold) = $13,800.

[b] $12,000 + ($2 × 1,100 units sold) = $14,200.

[c] From Illustration 9–2.

[d] From Illustration 9–5.

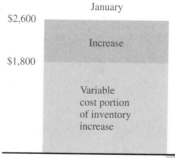

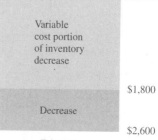

ILLUSTRATION

9–7

Variable and Full-Absorption Costing Comparison: Flow of Manufacturing Costs with Overhead Variances

STONEWALL MANUFACTURING
January
Full-Absorption Costing

Direct Materials Inventory

10,000

Work in Process Inventory

–0–
10,000 ⟶ 25,500

5,000

3,500

Finished Goods Inventory

–0–
25,500 ⟶ 22,950

2,550ᵃ

Cost of Goods Sold

22,950

Overhead Variance

1,000ᵇ   500ᶜ

Wages Payable

5,000

Variable Manufacturing Overhead

Actualᵉ	Applied
3,000	$1.75 × 2 hours per unit × 1,000 units = 3,500
500ᶜ	

Fixed Manufacturing Overhead

Actualᵉ	Applied
8,000	$3.50 × 2 hours per unit × 1,000 units = 7,000

1,000ᵇ   –0–

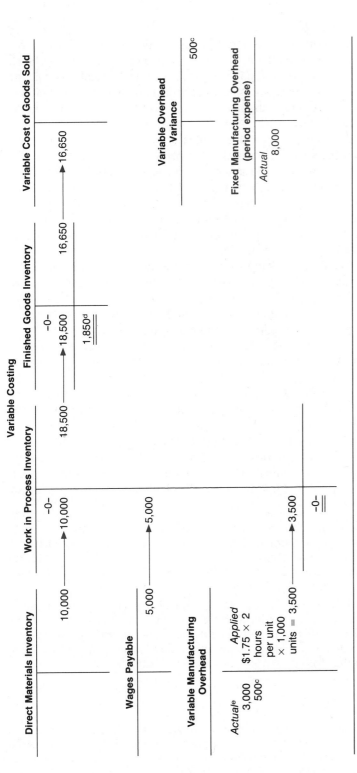

Variable Costing

a $2,550 = 100 units left in inventory × $\dfrac{\$25,500}{1{,}000\ \text{units produced}}$.

b This entry closes the Fixed Manufacturing Overhead account.

c This entry closes the Variable Manufacturing Overhead account.

d $1,850 = 100 units left in inventory × $\dfrac{\$18,500}{1{,}000\ \text{units produced}}$.

e To simplify the presentation, we have combined the actual and applied overhead into one account. In practice, you may find actual and applied overhead combined in one account or separated into two accounts—one for actual and one for applied.

EFFECT OF NORMAL COSTING AND MANUFACTURING OVERHEAD VARIANCES

In the previous example, we compared full-absorption costing with variable costing when there were no manufacturing overhead cost variances. When a manufacturing overhead cost variance exists, as under normal costing, the mechanics of comparison become a little more difficult. The essential effects of the different costing methods on calculated profits remain the same as previously discussed, however.

For example, assume Stonewall Manufacturing decided to use predetermined manufacturing overhead rates of $1.75 per actual direct labor-hour for variable manufacturing overhead and $3.50 per direct labor-hour for fixed manufacturing overhead. In both January and February, each unit required an average of two direct labor-hours to make. You can also think of overhead as applied at the rate of $3.50 per unit produced for *variable* manufacturing overhead and $7 per unit produced for *fixed* manufacturing overhead. These rates were used for both January and February.

Illustration 9–7 shows the flow of manufacturing costs for January under both variable and full-absorption costing. (Recall that 1,000 units were produced; 900 were sold in January.) By comparing Illustration 9–7 with Illustration 9–1, you will see that actual and applied manufacturing overhead are no longer equal; there is $500 overapplied variable overhead and $1,000 underapplied fixed overhead. We assume that the overhead variance is written off as a period cost, not prorated to inventories and cost of goods sold.

Illustration 9–8 compares full-absorption and variable costing when there is an overhead variance. Note the over- or under-applied overhead, which is shown in **color**.

The use of predetermined overhead rates instead of actual costs usually has little effect on the relationship between full-absorption and variable costing. For example, a comparison of Illustration 9–6 (no overhead variance) with Illustration 9–8 (with an overhead variance) shows two key similarities:

1. The conceptual difference between full-absorption costing and variable costing is the same whether or not there is an overhead variance. Differences in operating profits occur because fixed manufacturing costs are inventoried under full-absorption costing but not under variable costing.

2. When all inventory is sold at the end of a period, total operating profits are the same under all methods. For example, in Illustrations 9–6 and 9–8, operating profits for the entire period—January and February—are $10,000, whether or not there is an overhead variance and whether full-absorption or variable costing is used.

 *Self-Study Question*

2 Refer to the data in self-study question 1. Now assume Mario Enterprises uses normal costing, and applies variable manufacturing overhead at the rate of 40 percent of direct labor costs and fixed manufacturing overhead at the rate of 125 percent of direct labor costs. Note that applied overhead equals these predetermined rates times the actual direct labor cost.

   a. Compute the product cost per unit (that is, the inventoriable amount per unit) using full-absorption costing and using variable costing.

ILLUSTRATION

Variable and Full-Absorption Costing: Comparative Income Statements

STONEWALL MANUFACTURING
January and February

	January	February	Total
Full-Absorption Costing			
Sales revenue	$40,500	$49,500	$90,000
Less:			
Cost of goods sold	22,950[a]	28,050[b]	51,000
Underapplied overhead	500[c]	500[d]	1,000
Gross margin	17,050	20,950	38,000
Less: Marketing and administrative costs	13,800	14,200	28,000
Operating profits	$ 3,250	$ 6,750	$10,000
Change in finished goods inventory	+$ 2,550	−$ 2,550	−0−
Variable Costing			
Sales revenue	$40,500	$49,500	$90,000
Less: Variable cost of goods sold	16,650[e]	20,350[f]	37,000
Add: Overapplied variable overhead	500[g]	500[g]	1,000
Less: Variable marketing and administrative costs	1,800	2,200	4,000
Contribution margin	22,550	27,450	50,000
Less:			
Fixed manufacturing costs	8,000	8,000	16,000
Fixed marketing and administrative costs	12,000	12,000	24,000
Operating profits	$ 2,550	$ 7,450	$10,000
Change in finished goods inventory	+$ 1,850	−$ 1,850	−0−

Calculations:

[a] $22,950 = 900 units sold × $25.50 cost per unit.

[b] $28,050 = 1,100 units sold × $25.50 cost per unit. It also equals the cost of producing 1,000 units, or $25,500, plus the $2,550 cost of the 100 units sold from beginning finished goods inventory.

[c] The $500 underapplied overhead is the net result of $1,000 underapplied fixed manufacturing overhead and $500 overapplied variable manufacturing overhead. (See Illustration 9–7).

[d] The underapplied overhead is the same in February as in January because all production quantities and costs are the same in February as in January.

[e] $16,650 = 900 units sold × $18.50 cost per unit.

[f] $20,350 = 1,100 units sold × $18.50 cost per unit. It also equals the variable cost of producing 1,000 units, or $18,500, plus the $1,850 cost of the 100 units sold from beginning finished goods inventory.

[g] See Illustration 9–7. Overapplied variable overhead is the same in February as in January because all production quantities and costs are the same in both months.

b. Prepare income statements. Assume Mario had no beginning or ending inventories except for the 8,000 units in ending finished goods inventory. Mario sold its product for $20 per unit.

The solution to this question is at the end of the chapter on page 356.

DEBATE OVER
VARIABLE VERSUS
FULL-ABSORPTION
COSTING

Debates about the desirability of full-absorption costing versus variable costing have gone on for decades.[2] For the most part, differences of opinion stem from the search for a "conceptually superior" method of valuing inventory and measuring income in external financial statements. Our perspective is much different. *We are not as concerned about selecting a "true" measure of inventory value or net income as we are with selecting the cost measure that is most appropriate for decision making, after taking into account the costs and benefits of alternative costing methods.*

The most appropriate cost measure will usually be situation specific—it will depend on the nature of the decision, the nature of costs, the tastes of decision makers, and many other factors. As the airline industry and others have learned, full costs may be appropriate for some decisions and variable costs for others. The accountant's objective is to provide the information that is most useful in a given setting. The appropriate method will depend on the decision at hand. The following discussions present advantages of each costing method—variable costing and full-absorption costing—for different uses by decision makers.

Advantages of Variable Costing; Disadvantages of Full-Absorption Costing

Variable Costing Requires Breakdown of Manufacturing Costs into Fixed and Variable Components
Many managerial decisions require a breakdown of costs into variable and fixed components. The variable costing method is consistent with this breakdown. The full-absorption costing method is not; it treats fixed manufacturing costs as if they were unit (that is, variable) costs. Also, note that more data are presented under variable costing than under full-absorption in Illustration 9–6. Variable costing presents fixed and variable cost breakdowns and contribution margins.

Managers usually prefer to plan and control variable costs on a unit basis and fixed costs on a period basis. For example, managers plan and control the amount of direct materials and direct labor required to make a unit of output or the number of hours required to perform a job. Building rent, property taxes, and other fixed costs are planned and controlled per week, month, or year. It seldom makes much managerial sense to refer to rent costs as an amount per *unit* produced. Rather, rent would be referred to as an amount per *month*.

Criticism of Unit Fixed Cost under Full-Absorption Costing
Treating fixed costs as unit costs can be misleading. A unit fixed cost is a function of not only the amount of fixed costs but also the volume of activity. Any given unit fixed cost is only valid when production equals the number of units used to calculate the fixed cost per unit.

For example, a plant manager observed that maintenance costs, which were fixed, had decreased from $12 per unit of output in May to $10 per unit in August. She was on her way to congratulate the Maintenance Department manager for the cost reduction when she stopped in the plant controller's office. There she learned that maintenance costs had *increased* from $12,000

---

[2] For example, see C. Horngren and G. Sorter, "Direct Costing for External Reporting," *The Accounting Review*, January 1961; and J. Fremgen, "The Direct Costing Controversy—An Identification of Issues," *The Accounting Review*, January 1964.

in May to $18,000 in August. Meanwhile volume had increased from 1,000 units in May to 1,800 units in August. This explained the decrease in unit costs from $12 ($12,000 ÷ 1,000 units) to $10 ($18,000 ÷ 1,800 units).

The plant manager knew maintenance costs were supposed to be fixed. They should not have increased when volume increased. When she investigated further, she found that the Maintenance Department manager had hired several temporary employees to cover for a major absenteeism problem that occurred in August.

The moral of this story is that the conversion of fixed manufacturing costs to unit costs, which is done under full-absorption costing, can be misleading. Managers frequently find it necessary to convert the "unitized" fixed manufacturing cost (that is, the $12 and $10 per unit in the previous example) back to the original total for performance evaluation and decision-making purposes.

Variable Costing Removes the Effects of Inventory Changes from Income Measurement

Another advantage of variable costing is that it removes the effects of inventory changes from income measurement. For example, under full-absorption costing, a company could increase its reported profits by building up inventory or decrease them by reducing inventory.

For example, Full Products, Inc., uses full-absorption costing to value inventory. After seeing the Period 1 financial statements shown in the bottom part of Illustration 9–9, the board of directors fired the president and hired a new one, stating, "Whatever else you do, increase profits in Period 2."

The new president promptly stepped up production from 100,000 units to 200,000 units, as shown in column 2 of Illustration 9–9. Operating profits increased from $0 in Period 1 to $200,000 in Period 2, and the new president collected a generous bonus.

Was Full Products, Inc., more profitable in Period 2? No; in fact, the company had 100,000 additional units in inventory to carry and sell. The apparent increase in profits is solely due to the deferral of fixed manufacturing cost under full-absorption costing by increasing ending inventory. Variable costing would expense the entire $400,000 of fixed manufacturing costs in Period 2 despite the increase in inventory. Thus, the Period 2 operating profits would have been zero under variable costing—the same as in Period 1.

In short, variable costing tends to fit managerial decision models better than full-absorption costing does. In subsequent chapters in this book, when we discuss uses of accounting information for managerial decision making, planning, and performance evaluation, we assume the company uses variable costing for internal purposes unless otherwise stated.

Advantages of Full-Absorption Costing; Disadvantages of Variable Costing

Neither the Financial Accounting Standards Board (FASB) nor the Internal Revenue Service (IRS) has recognized variable costing as *generally acceptable* in valuing inventory for external reports and tax purposes. The Internal Revenue Service defines inventory cost to include: (1) direct materials and supplies entering into or consumed in connection with the product, (2) expenditures for direct labor, and (3) indirect expenses incident to and necessary for the production of the particular item. Indirect expenses neces-

ILLUSTRATION

Profit Improvement Program

FULL PRODUCTS, INC.

Facts

	(1) Period 1	(2) Period 2
Sales units	100,000	100,000
Production units	100,000	200,000
Selling price per unit . . . . $	10	$ 10
Variable manufacturing cost per unit .	5	5
Fixed manufacturing costs per period	400,000	400,000
Fixed manufacturing costs per unit produced	4	2
Marketing and administrative costs per period	100,000	100,000

Income Statements
(full-absorption costing methods)

Sales	$1,000,000	$1,000,000
Cost of goods sold	900,000[a]	700,000[b]
Gross margin	100,000	300,000
Marketing and administrative costs . . .	100,000	100,000
Operating profits	–0–	$ 200,000

[a] $900,000 = 100,000 units sold × ($5 + $4) manufacturing costs per unit.
[b] $700,000 = 100,000 units sold × ($5 + $2) manufacturing costs per unit.

sary for production would include fixed manufacturing costs. Thus, the most obvious advantage of full-absorption costing is that it complies with FASB pronouncements and tax laws.

Proponents of full-absorption costing contend that this method recognizes the importance of fixed manufacturing costs. They hold that all manufacturing costs are costs of the product. Further, they argue, companies that build up inventories in anticipation of further increases in sales are penalized under variable costing—they should be allowed to defer fixed manufacturing costs until the goods are sold, just as they defer variable manufacturing costs.

In practice, companies may prepare *both* variable and full-absorption costing income statements depending on how such information is used. Variable costing reports can be used for internal purposes, while full-absorption reports are prepared for external use. Preparation of many kinds of reports based on alternative accounting methods is possible at rapid speed and low cost with appropriately programmed computer equipment.

Another advantage of full-absorption costing is that it may be less costly to implement since it does not require a breakdown of manufacturing costs into fixed and variable components. While some manufacturing costs may fall neatly into fixed or variable categories, others do not. Supervision, indirect labor, and utilities, for example, are seldom either entirely fixed or entirely variable. Hence, variable costing may be more costly to implement than full-absorption costing. Like other accounting system choices, the costs and benefits of each method should dictate the best course of action in specific situations.

CONTRIBUTION MARGIN INCOME STATEMENT

Contribution Margin Format The outline of a financial statement that shows the contribution margin as an intermediate step in the computation of operating profits or income.

Traditional income statement formats do not lend themselves to variable costing because fixed and variable costs are not separated. The format used with variable costing is known as the **contribution margin format**. The variable costing income statements in this chapter use the contribution margin format. For comparative purposes, the two formats are shown in Illustration 9–10. These two statements are based on the January–February totals from Illustration 9–6.

If income statements are used to make decisions involving changes in volume, the contribution margin format can be very helpful. Managers can often understand relationships between prices, costs, and volume better with the contribution margin format than with the traditional approach. Further, the contribution margin format presents more information— namely, the breakdown of costs into fixed and variable portions.

Note the difference between the *contribution margin* and the *gross margin* in Illustration 9–10. The total contribution margin is $50,000 and represents the net revenue available to meet fixed costs and provide operating profits. The contribution margin ratio represents the fraction of each revenue dollar that is contributed toward fixed costs and profits. For the illustration, this amount would be 55.6 percent, which is $\frac{\$50,000}{\$90,000}$.

On the other hand, the gross margin is the difference between revenues and manufacturing costs, regardless of whether those manufacturing costs are fixed or variable.

The terms *contribution margin* and *gross margin* are often used interchangeably, but they are not the same. Virtually the only time they would be

---

ILLUSTRATION

9–10

Income Statement Comparison: Traditional and Contribution Margin Format

STONEWALL MANUFACTURING

Traditional Format	January–February Total	Contribution Margin Format	January–February Total
Sales revenue	$90,000	Sales revenue	$90,000
Cost of goods sold	52,000	Less:	
Gross margin	38,000	Variable cost of goods sold	36,000
Marketing and administrative costs	28,000	Variable marketing and administrative costs	4,000
Operating profit	$10,000	Contribution margin	50,000
		Less:	
		Fixed manufacturing costs	16,000
		Fixed marketing and administrative costs	24,000
		Operating profit	$10,000

mathematically equal is when all costs of goods sold are variable costs and marketing and administrative costs are fixed. There are very few such examples.

Self-Study Question

3 Barton Chemicals produces a line of extra-strength paint remover. The company produced 8,000 barrels and sold 7,500 barrels at a price of $60 per barrel. The costs incurred were as follows:

Direct materials	$ 24,000
Direct labor	80,000
Variable manufacturing overhead	19,200
Variable marketing and administrative costs	24,800
Fixed manufacturing overhead	120,000
Fixed marketing and administrative costs	110,000

There were no beginning inventories. Actual costing is used.

 a. Using T-accounts, trace the manufacturing cost flows under variable costing.

 b. Using T-accounts, trace the manufacturing cost flows under full-absorption costing.

 c. Prepare an income statement for this period, using the contribution margin format.

 d. Prepare an income statement for this period, using the traditional format.

The solution to this problem is at the end of this chapter on page 357.

IS IT ETHICAL TO INCREASE PRODUCTION TO INCREASE PROFITS?

Few nonaccountants understand that, using full-absorption costing, companies can increase profits just by increasing production. Consequently, nonaccountants can be misled by people who understand that fixed costs can be inventoried instead of expensed when full-absorption costing is used.

We encountered a case in a large Fortune 100 company in which a division manager decided to increase production so some of his division's fixed manufacturing costs would be inventoried instead of expensed. He knew the fixed manufacturing costs would be expensed in the future when the inventory was sold, but that would be someone else's problem because this manager expected to be transferred next year. Furthermore, if his division's profits were high enough this year, he would be promoted to a better position in the company.

Increasing production to defer recognizing fixed manufacturing costs as expenses did not conflict with the company's accounting policies. Nor would it conflict with generally accepted accounting practices. Nevertheless, this manager's actions were intended to deceive his superiors. Was this manager's action ethical?

We believe this manager's action was unethical if he intended to deceive his superiors and did not fully disclose how profits were increased. While his superiors *could* have discovered the increase in profit was correlated with an increase in ending inventory, it is unlikely they would have made that connection unless they had accounting expertise or advice.

SUMMARY

This chapter compares full-absorption costing with variable costing. Manufacturing companies use full-absorption costing for external reporting to comply with generally accepted accounting principles (GAAP) and income tax laws, both of which require that product costs include fixed and variable manufacturing costs. Our previous discussion of product costing in Chapters 3 through 8 assumed products were valued using full-absorption costing.

With variable costing, only variable manufacturing costs are inventoriable, while fixed manufacturing costs are treated as period costs. Many manufacturing companies use variable costing for internal reporting because it is consistent with the cost-behavior assumptions used in managerial decision making.

In the remaining chapters in this book, we focus on cost analysis for decision making. Hence, we assume variable costing is used for internal managerial purposes, while full-absorption costing is used for external financial reporting.

The key difference between the two methods is the treatment of fixed manufacturing costs—full-absorption costing "unitizes" them and treats them as product costs, while variable costing treats them as period costs. Thus, operating profits will differ under each method if units produced and sold are not the same, as shown in Illustration 9–11.

The use of predetermined manufacturing overhead rates (that is, *normal* costing) may give a different unit cost to inventory than does actual costing. But the *conceptual* differences between full-absorption costing and variable costing are the same regardless of the form of overhead rate—namely, fixed manufacturing costs are inventoried under full-absorption costing but not under variable costing. Illustration 9–12 reviews the conceptual differences

I L L U S T R A T I O N

9-11

Summary Comparison of Full-Absorption Costing (FAC) and Variable Costing (VC)

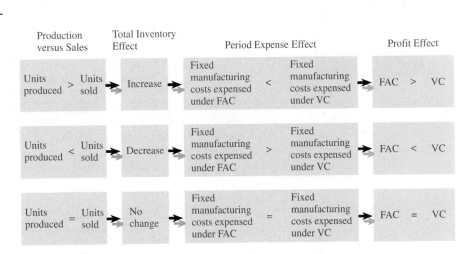

Note: These relationships assume the unit costs of inventory do not change from period to period.

Treatment of Overhead by Four Costing Methods: Full-Absorption, Variable, Actual, and Normal

	How Costs Are Measured	
	Actual Costing	**Normal Costing**
Variable Costing	Uses actual costs. Treats actual fixed manufacturing costs as period costs.	Uses predetermined overhead rates for variable overhead. Treats actual fixed manufacturing costs as period costs.
Full-Absorption Costing	Uses actual costs. Treats actual fixed manufacturing costs as product costs.	Uses predetermined overhead rates for both fixed and variable overhead. Treats fixed manufacturing costs (using predetermined rates) as product costs.

among the four methods: (1) actual, variable costing; (2) normal, variable costing; (3) actual, full-absorption costing; and (4) normal, full-absorption costing.

TERMS AND CONCEPTS

The following terms and concepts should be familiar to you after reading this chapter:

Actual Costing, *317*

Contribution Margin Format, *335*

Full-Absorption Costing, *315*

Normal Costing, *320*

Period Costs, *321*

Product Costs, *320*

Variable Costing (or Direct Costing), *316*

APPENDIX

Algebraic Comparison of Variable and Full-Absorption Costing[3]

This appendix presents an algebraic comparison of full-absorption and variable costing. The basic concepts are the same as those presented earlier in this chapter; but instead of comparing full-absorption and variable costing using income statements and T-accounts, we demonstrate the difference between the methods using algebra.

Basic Models

The algebraic definition of operating profit under full-absorption (actual) costing and variable (actual) costing follows the notation shown below. The

---

[3] This section was inspired by D. DeCoster and K. Ramanathan, "An Algebraic Aid in Teaching Differences between Direct Costing and Full-Absorption Costing Models," *The Accounting Review* 48, no. 4, pp. 800–801.

numbers for each equation are based on our previous example—Stonewall Manufacturing—for January.

Notation

X^s = Actual volume sold—superscript *s* designates *sales* volume (900 units for Stonewall Manufacturing in January)

X^p = Actual volume produced—superscript *p* designates *production* volume (1,000 units for Stonewall Manufacturing in January)

P = Actual unit selling price ($45)

VM = Actual *unit* variable *manufacturing* costs ($18 = $10 direct materials + $5 direct labor + $3 variable manufacturing overhead)

FM = Actual *total* fixed *manufacturing* costs per *month* ($8,000)

VK = Actual *unit* variable *marketing* costs ($2)

FK = Actual *total* fixed *marketing* and *administrative* costs per month ($12,000)

π_{fa} = Operating profit under full-absorption costing

π_v = Operating profit under variable costing

Recall that there is no beginning inventory in this example.

Variable costing profit equation

$$
\begin{aligned}
\pi_v &= PX^s - VMX^s - VKX^s \\
&\quad - FM - FK \\
&= (\$45 \times 900 \text{ units}) - (\$18 \times 900 \text{ units}) - (\$2 \times 900 \text{ units}) \\
&\quad - \$8,000 - \$12,000 \\
&= \$2,500
\end{aligned}
$$

which is the same as the variable costing operating profit for January shown in Illustration 9–6.

Full-absorption costing profit equation

$$
\begin{aligned}
\pi_{fa} &= PX^s - \left(VM + \frac{FM}{X^p} \right) X^s - VKX^s - FK \\
&= (\$45 \times 900 \text{ units}) - \left[\left(\$18 + \frac{\$8,000}{1,000 \text{ units}} \right) \times 900 \text{ units} \right] \\
&\quad - (\$2 \times 900 \text{ units}) - \$12,000 \\
&= \$3,300
\end{aligned}
$$

which is the same as the full-absorption costing operating profit for January shown in Illustration 9–6.

Source of the Difference in Operating Profits

Note that the only difference between the two equations above is the treatment of fixed manufacturing overhead. Under variable costing, FM is deducted to arrive at operating profit, while under full-absorption costing, $\left(\dfrac{FM}{X^p} \right) X^s$ is deducted. Hence, the difference in profits between the two methods is:

$$
\begin{aligned}
FM - \left(\frac{FM}{X^p} \right) X^s &= \$8,000 - \left(\frac{\$8,000}{1,000 \text{ units}} \times 900 \text{ units} \right) \\
&= \$8,000 - (\$8 \times 900 \text{ units}) = \$800
\end{aligned}
$$

That is, variable costing deducts $800 more in deriving operating profits; hence, its operating profits are $800 lower in January. It is important to note that if $X^p = X^s$, the fixed manufacturing costs deducted would be the same under both methods.

A similar analysis can be made in February. For variable costing:

$$\pi_v = PX^s - VMX^s - VKX^s - FM - FK$$
$$= (\$45 \times 1{,}100 \text{ units}) - (\$18 \times 1{,}100 \text{ units}) - (\$2 \times 1{,}100 \text{ units})$$
$$\quad - \$8{,}000 - \$12{,}000$$
$$= \$7{,}500$$

which is also shown in Illustration 9–6.

For full-absorption costing:

$$\pi_{fa} = \text{Sales revenue} - \text{Cost of goods sold for units produced in January} -$$
$$\text{Cost of goods sold for units produced in February} - \text{Marketing and administrative costs}$$

$$= (\$45)(1{,}100 \text{ units}) - \underbrace{\left(\$18 + \frac{\$8{,}000}{1{,}000}\right)100 \text{ units}}_{\substack{\text{Cost of goods sold for}\\\text{units produced in}\\\text{January}}}$$

$$- \underbrace{\left(\$18 + \frac{\$8{,}000}{1{,}000}\right)1{,}000 \text{ units}}_{\substack{\text{Cost of goods sold}\\\text{for units produced}\\\text{in February}}} - (\$2 \times 1{,}100 \text{ units}) - \$12{,}000$$

$$= \$6{,}700$$

which is also shown in Illustration 9–6.

QUESTIONS

9–1 Describe the key difference between full-absorption costing and variable costing.

9–2 How are marketing and administrative costs treated under variable costing? Under full-absorption costing?

9–3 Under what circumstances do you find operating profits under variable costing equal to full-absorption costing profits? When are variable costing profits smaller? When are they greater?

9–4 What are the advantages of variable costing? What are some of the criticisms advanced against it?

9–5 How can a company using full-absorption costing manipulate profits without changing sales volume?

9–6 Describe comparative inventory changes under both variable costing and full-absorption costing when

    a.   Sales volume exceeds production volume.

    b.   Production volume exceeds sales volume.

9–7 Multiple choice (assume direct materials and direct labor are variable costs):

    a.   The basic assumption made in a variable costing system with respect to fixed manufacturing costs is that fixed manufacturing costs are:

(1)   A sunk cost.
(2)   A product cost.
(3)   A part of inventory.
(4)   A period cost.

b.   Which costs are included in inventory under variable costing?
(1)   Only prime costs.
(2)   Only variable manufacturing costs.
(3)   All variable costs.
(4)   All variable and fixed manufacturing costs.

(CPA adapted)

9–8   Refer to the section of the chapter titled, ''Is It Ethical to Increase Production to Increase Profits?'' What is your view of the division manager's actions? How could increasing ending inventory hurt the company? How might increasing ending inventory help the company?

9–9   Refer to the section of the chapter titled, ''Is It Ethical to Increase Production to Increase Profits?'' Is full-absorption costing a less ethical accounting method than variable costing?

9–10   Refer to the real world application, ''Full versus Variable Costing in Banking,'' in this chapter. Why did American National Bank decide not to drop the check-processing service from its product line even though the service appeared to be unprofitable?

9–11   Multiple choice:

a.   Inventory under the variable costing method includes:
(1)   Direct materials cost and direct labor cost, but not factory overhead cost.
(2)   Direct materials cost, direct labor cost, and variable factory overhead cost.
(3)   Prime cost but not conversion cost.
(4)   Prime cost and total conversion cost.

b.   Which of the following must be known about a production process in order to institute a variable costing system?
(1)   The variable and fixed components of all costs related to production.
(2)   The controllable and noncontrollable components of all costs related to production.
(3)   Standard production rates and times for all elements of production.
(4)   Contribution margin and break-even point for all goods in production.

(CPA adapted)

EXERCISES

9–12   Variable Costing versus Full Absorption Costing: Comparison of Operating Profit
(L.O.1, L.O.2)[4]

Pratt, Inc., produces a single product, which sells for $21.50. Pratt produced 60,000 units and sold 52,000 units last year. There were no beginning inventories or ending work in process inventories last year.

Manufacturing costs and marketing and administrative costs for last year were as follows:

---

[4] L.O.1 and L.O.2 refer to ''Learning Objectives 1 and 2 from the title page of this chapter.

	Variable	Fixed
Direct materials	$390,000	—
Direct labor	225,000	—
Manufacturing overhead	90,000	$180,000
Marketing and administrative costs	69,120	120,000

Required:

a. Compute the unit product (manufacturing) cost using variable costing.

b. Compute Pratt's operating profit using variable costing.

c. Compute operating profit using full-absorption costing.

9–13   Comparison of Variable and Full-Absorption Costing— Multiple Choice
(L.O.1, L.O.2)

The following questions are based on Tustin Corporation, which produces a single product selling for $12 per unit. One hundred thousand units were produced, and 80,000 units were sold during year 1; all ending inventory was in finished goods inventory.

	Fixed Costs	Variable Costs
Direct materials	-0-	$2.40 per unit produced
Direct labor	-0-	1.60 per unit produced
Factory overhead	$240,000	.80 per unit produced
Marketing and administrative	128,000	.80 per unit sold

Tustin had no inventory at the beginning of the year.

Required:

a. In presenting inventory on the balance sheet at December 31, the unit cost under full-absorption costing is:
   (1) $4.00.
   (2) $4.80.
   (3) $5.60.
   (4) $7.20.

b. In presenting inventory on a variable costing balance sheet, the unit cost would be:
   (1) $4.00.
   (2) $4.80.
   (3) $5.60.
   (4) $7.20.

c. What is the operating profit using variable costing?
   (1) $80,000.
   (2) $144,000.
   (3) $192,000.
   (4) $208,000.

d. What is the operating profit using full-absorption costing?
   (1) $80,000.
   (2) $144,000.
   (3) $192,000.
   (4) $208,000.

e. What is the ending inventory using full-absorption costing?
   (1) $96,000.
   (2) $112,000.
   (3) $144,000.
   (4) $148,000.

f. What is the ending inventory under variable costing?
   (1) $96,000.
   (2) $112,000.
   (3) $144,000.
   (4) $148,000.

(CPA adapted)

9–14 Comparison of Variable and Full-Absorption Costing: Analyzing Profit Performance
(L.O.2)

Covina Enterprises released the following figures from its records for Year 1 and Year 2:

	Year 1	Year 2
Sales units	125,000	125,000
Production units	125,000	172,000
Selling price per unit	$20	$20
Variable manufacturing cost per unit	$12	$12
Annual fixed manufacturing cost	$430,000	$430,000
Variable marketing and administrative costs per unit sold	$1.20	$1.20
Fixed marketing and administrative costs	$420,000	$420,000
Beginning inventory	$0	?

Required:

a. Prepare income statements for both years, using the traditional method with full-absorption costing.

b. Prepare income statements for both years, using the contribution margin method with variable costing.

c. Comment on the different operating profit figures. Write a brief report explaining why the operating profits are different, if they are.

9–15 Comparison of Cost Flows under Full-Absorption and Variable Costing
(L.O.3)

Pool-Pro Products incurred the following costs for its line of swimming pool pumps:

	Variable	Fixed
Direct materials	$600,000	—
Labor	525,000	—
Supplies (mfg.)	80,000	—
Depreciation (mfg.)	—	$170,000
Repairs and maintenance (mfg.)	40,000	120,000
Other manufacturing	30,000	40,000
Marketing and administrative costs	40,000	110,000

100,000 units were produced, and 80,000 units were sold. There were no beginning inventories.

Required:

a. Using T-accounts, trace the manufacturing cost flows under variable costing.

b. Using T-accounts, trace the manufacturing cost flows under full-absorption costing.

9–16 Comparison of Full-Absorption and Variable Cost Flows Using Normal Costing
(L.O.3, L.O.4)

Okanagan Products manufactures Ogo Pogos, a line of stuffed toys. Variable manufacturing overhead is applied at the rate of $1.60 per labor-hour, and fixed manufacturing overhead at a rate of $2.00 per labor-hour. Actual costs were as follows:

Direct materials	$ 50,000
Direct labor (at $4.20 per hour)	126,000
Actual variable manufacturing overhead	52,000
Variable marketing and administrative costs	45,000
Actual fixed manufacturing overhead	58,000
Fixed marketing and administrative costs	28,000

During the period, 25,000 units were produced, and 23,800 units were sold at a selling price of $20 each. There were no beginning inventories.

Required:

a. Use T-accounts to trace the cost flows using variable costing.

b. Use T-accounts to trace the cost flows using full-absorption costing.

9–17   Comparison of Full-Absorption and Variable Costing Income Statements Using Normal Costing
(L.O.4, L.O.5)

Refer to exercise 9–16 and assume that Okanagan Products debits or credits under- or overapplied overhead to Cost of Goods Sold.

a.   Prepare an income statement for the period, using variable costing.

b.   Prepare an income statement for the period, using full-absorption costing.

9–18   Comparison of Full-Absorption and Variable Costing— Income Statement Formats
(L.O.5)

Consider the following facts:

	Year 1	Year 2
Sales volume	50,000 units	150,000 units
Production volume	100,000 units	100,000 units
Selling price	$12 per unit	$12 per unit
Variable manufacturing costs	$9 per unit	$9 per unit
Fixed manufacturing costs	$100,000	$100,000
Nonmanufacturing costs (all fixed)	$ 50,000	$ 50,000

Required:

Prepare comparative income statements, using the contribution margin format for variable costing and the traditional format for full-absorption costing. Show the total results for Years 1 and 2 combined in addition to the results for each year individually. There were no beginning inventories at the beginning of Year 1.

9–19   Compare Income Statement Amounts Using Actual Costing
(L.O.2, L.O.5)

Stonegate Products uses the following unit costs for one of the products it manufactures:

Direct materials	$82.00
Direct labor	35.40
Manufacturing overhead (based on 5,000 units):	
Variable	15.60
Fixed	14.00
Marketing and administrative costs (based on 6,500 units):	
Variable	10.40
Fixed	7.00

This year, there were 1,500 units in beginning finished goods inventory; 5,000 units were produced; and 6,500 units were sold at $200 per unit. The beginning inventory was valued at $133 per unit using variable costing and at $147 per unit using full-absorption costing. There was no beginning or ending work in process inventory.

Required:

a.   Prepare an income statement for the year, using the contribution margin format.

b.   Would reported operating profits be more, less, or the same if full-absorption costing was used? Support your conclusions with an income statement using full-absorption costing and the traditional format.

9–20   (Appendix) Comparison of Full-Absorption and Variable Costing, Using the Algebraic Method—Part I
(L.O.6)

Assume the following data about actual prices, costs, and volume for Bostick Company for the first quarter:

Selling price	$5 per unit
Variable manufacturing costs	$3 per unit
Fixed manufacturing costs	$100,000 for the quarter
Marketing and administrative costs (fixed and variable combined)	$30,000 for the quarter
Sales volume	110,000 units for the quarter
Production volume	125,000 units for the quarter

There were no beginning inventories.

Required:

a.   Using the algebraic method, derive the difference in operating profits between variable costing and full-absorption costing.

b. What is the inventory value at the end of the first quarter under (1) full-absorption costing and (2) variable costing?

9–21 (Appendix) Comparison of Full-Absorption and Variable Costing, Using the Algebraic Method—Part II
(L.O.6)

Refer to the information given in exercise 9–20. Assume it is now the second quarter of the same year. Volumes in the second quarter are as follows:

Sales volume . . . . 100,000 units
Production volume . . . . 100,000 units

Costs and prices remain the same in the second quarter as in the first quarter.

Required:

Using the algebraic method, show the difference, if any, in operating profit between variable costing and full-absorption costing. (Assume FIFO inventory flows.)

9–22 (Appendix) Comparison of Full-Absorption and Variable Costing, Using the Algebraic Method—Part III
(L.O.6)

Refer to the information given in exercise 9–20. Assume it is now the third quarter of the same year, and the volumes in the third quarter are as follows:

Sales volume . . . . 110,000 units
Production volume . . . . 95,000 units

Variable costs and selling price per unit remain the same in the third quarter as in the first quarter, as do quarterly fixed costs.

Required:

Using the algebraic method, show the difference in operating profits between variable costing and full-absorption costing. (Assume a FIFO inventory flow.)

PROBLEMS

9–23 Comprehensive Full-Absorption and Variable Costing Comparison

Kensington Company manufactures a single product with the following costs:

Selling price . . . . $ 5.00 per unit
Variable manufacturing costs (direct materials and direct labor) . . . .   3.00 per unit
Fixed manufacturing costs, based on a normal production volume of 100,000 units per month (all manufacturing overhead is fixed) . . . . . .   1.00 per unit
Marketing and administrative costs (all fixed) . . . .   50,000 per month

Estimated and actual fixed manufacturing costs equal $100,000 for the year. Beginning inventory of 30 units is valued at $4 per unit under full-absorption costing and at $3 per unit under variable costing. Assume units flow on a FIFO basis (if a product flow assumption is necessary). Any over- or underapplied fixed overhead appears on the income statement for this period.

The president of Kensington wants an analysis on the effect of variations in sales and production units. To help you he has included a chart (Exhibit 9–23A on the next page) for you to complete for nine situations (all numbers in thousands).

Required:

a. Complete the chart.

b. Write a short report to the president of Kensington that explains how the relation between units sold and units produced affects profits.

9–24 Conversion of Variable to Full-Absorption Costing

The S. T. Shire Company uses variable costing for internal management purposes and full-absorption costing for external reporting purposes. Thus, at the end of each year, financial information must be converted from variable costing to full-absorption costing for external reports.

At the end of last year, management anticipated that sales would rise 20 percent this year. Therefore, production was increased from 20,000 units to 24,000 units. However, economic conditions kept sales volume at 20,000 units for both years.

EXHIBIT

KENSINGTON COMPANY
(All numbers in thousands)

		Units Sold = Units Produced			Units Sold > Units Produced			Units Sold < Units Produced		
		(1)	(2)	(3)	(4)	(5)	(6)	(7)	(8)	(9)
Units	Beginning Inventory	30	30	30	30	30	30	30	30	30
	Production	100	80	110	80	60	80	100	80	110
	Sales	100	80	110	100	80	110	80	60	100
Full-Absorption Costing	Sales Revenue									
	Cost of Goods Sold:									
	Beginning Inventory									
	Cost of Goods Produced									
	Less: Ending Inventory									
	Cost of Goods Sold									
	Over-/Underapplied Overhead									
	Gross Margin									
	Marketing and Administration									
	Operating Profit									
Variable Costing	Sales Revenue									
	Variable Cost of Goods Sold:									
	Beginning Inventory									
	Variable Cost of Goods Produced									
	Less: Ending Inventory									
	Variable Cost of Goods Sold									
	Over-/Underapplied Variable Overhead									
	Contribution Margin									
	Fixed Manufacturing Costs									
	Marketing and Administration									
	Operating Profit									

(Problem 9–24 continued)

The following data pertain to the two years.

	Last Year	This Year
Selling price per unit	$ 60	$ 60
Sales (units)	20,000	20,000
Beginning inventory (units)	2,000	2,000
Production (units)	20,000	24,000
Ending inventory (units)	2,000	6,000
Underapplied variable overhead	$10,000	$ 8,000

(Problem 9–24 concluded) Variable cost per unit for both years was composed of:

Labor	$15.00
Materials	9.00
Variable overhead	6.00
	$30.00

Estimated and actual fixed costs for each year were:

Production	$180,000
Selling and administrative	200,000
	$380,000

The overhead rate under full-absorption costing is based on estimated volume of 30,000 units per year. Under- or overapplied overhead is debited or credited to Cost of Goods Sold.

Required:

Using these data:

a. Present the income statement based on variable costing for this year.

b. Present the income statement based on full-absorption costing for this year.

c. Explain the difference, if any, in the operating profit figures.

(CMA adapted)

9–25 Variable Costing Operating Profit and Reconciliation with Full-Absorption Costing

The Sierra Corporation employs a full-absorption costing system for its external reporting as well as for internal management purposes. The latest annual income statement appears as follows:

Sales revenue		$415,000
Cost of goods sold:		
Beginning finished goods inventory	$ 22,000[a]	
Cost of goods manufactured	315,000	
Ending finished goods inventory	(86,000)[b]	
Cost of goods sold		251,000
Gross margin		164,000
Marketing costs		83,000
Administrative costs		49,800
Operating profit before taxes		$ 31,200

[a] Includes $9,900 variable costs.
[b] Includes $60,200 variable costs.

Management is somewhat concerned that although they are showing adequate income, there has been a shortage of cash to meet operating costs. The following information has been provided to assist management with its evaluation of the situation:

Statement of Cost of Goods Manufactured

Direct materials:		
Beginning inventory	$ 16,000	
Purchases	62,000	
Ending inventory	(22,000)	$ 56,000
Direct labor		125,100
Manufacturing overhead:		
Variable		39,400
Fixed (including depreciation of $30,000)		94,500
Cost of goods manufactured		$315,000

There are no work in process inventories. Management reports it is pleased that this year's manufacturing costs are 70 percent variable compared to last year, when these costs were only 45 percent variable. While 80 percent of the marketing costs are variable, only 40 percent of the administrative costs are considered variable. The company uses FIFO.

Required:

a. Prepare a variable costing income statement for the year.

b. Reconcile the difference between the full-absorption costing operating profit given in the problem to the variable costing operating profit in part (*a*).

9–26 Full-Absorption versus Variable Costing

You have been given the following information concerning the All Fixed Company.

1. Sales: 10,000 units per year at a price of $46 per unit.

2. Production: 15,000 units in Year 1; 5,000 units in Year 2.

3. There was no beginning inventory in Year 1.

4. Annual production costs are all fixed and equal $225,000 per year.

5. Ending finished goods inventory in Year 1 was one third of that year's current production.

6. Annual marketing and administrative costs are $140,000 per year for each year.

Required:

a. Prepare full-absorption costing income statements for Year 1 and Year 2, and for the two years taken together.

b. Prepare variable costing income statements for Year 1 and Year 2, and for the two years taken together.

c. Prepare a reconciliation of full-absorption operating profit to variable costing operating profit for Year 1 and Year 2.

9–27 Effect of Changes in Production and Costing Method on Operating Profit ("I Enjoy Challenges")

(This is a classic problem based on an actual company's experience.) The X. B. Company uses an actual cost system to apply all production costs to units produced. While the plant has a maximum production capacity of 40 million units, only 10 million units were produced and sold during Year 1. There were no beginning or ending inventories.

The X. B. Company income statement for Year 1 is as follows:

X. B. COMPANY
Income Statement
For the Year Ending December 31, Year 1

Sales (10,000,000 units at $6)		$ 60,000,000
Cost of goods sold:		
Variable (10,000,000 at $2)	$ 20,000,000	
Fixed	48,000,000	68,000,000
Gross margin		(8,000,000)
Marketing and administrative costs		10,000,000
Operating profit (loss)		$(18,000,000)

The board of directors is concerned about the $18 million loss. A consultant approached the board with the following offer: "I agree to become president for no fixed salary. But I insist on a year-end bonus of 10 percent of operating profit (before considering the bonus)." The board of directors agreed to these terms, and the consultant was hired.

The new president promptly stepped up production to an annual rate of 30 million units. Sales for Year 2 remained at 10 million units.

The resulting X. B. Company income statement for Year 2 follows:

X. B. COMPANY
Income Statement
For the Year Ending December 31, Year 2

Sales (10,000,000 units at $6)		$60,000,000
Cost of goods sold:		
Cost of goods manufactured:		
Variable (30,000,000 at $2)	$ 60,000,000	
Fixed	48,000,000	
Total cost of goods manufactured	108,000,000	
Less ending inventory:		
Variable (20,000,000 at $2)	40,000,000	
Fixed $\left(\dfrac{20}{30} \times \$48,000,000\right)$	32,000,000	
Total inventory	72,000,000	
Cost of goods sold		36,000,000
Gross margin		24,000,000
Marketing and administrative costs		10,000,000
Operating profit before bonus		14,000,000
Bonus		1,400,000
Operating profit after bonus		$12,600,000

The day after the statement was verified, the president took his check for $1,400,000 and resigned to take a job with another corporation. He remarked, "I enjoy challenges. Now that X. B. Company is in the black, I'd prefer tackling another challenging situation." (His contract with his new employer is similar to the one he had with X. B. Company.)

Required:

a. What is your evaluation of the Year 2 performance?

b. Using variable costing, what would operating profit be for Year 1? For Year 2? What are the inventory values? (Assume all marketing and administrative costs are fixed.) Compare those results with the full-absorption statements shown above.

**9–28   "I Enjoy Challenges"
—Normal Costing**

Refer to the facts for problem 9–27. What would Year 2 operating profit (loss) be if X. B. Company used full-absorption normal costing with a fixed manufacturing overhead rate of $4.80 $\left(\dfrac{\$48,000,000 \text{ fixed manufacturing costs}}{10,000,000 \text{ estimated unit sales}}\right)$? Prepare an income statement and a T-account diagram of cost flows.

**9–29   Comparative Income
Statements, with
Overhead Variances**

A client requested your help to analyze the operations of one of her divisions, the Wheeler Division. "I don't understand this! I received this income statement yesterday from the Wheeler Division managers (see Exhibit 9–29A), but one of our internal auditors came across this other one (see Exhibit 9–29B). The second statement shows a lower net income! I think something strange is going on here. It looks like the division managers are sending me this first statement (Exhibit 9–29A), which makes them look good, while they're hiding the second statement (Exhibit 9–29B), which shows what's really going on. I want you to look into this for me." (Assume FIFO.)

Required:

a. How many units were sold in August?

b. What was the *actual* production (units) in August?

c. What was the *beginning* and *ending* inventory (units) in August?

EXHIBIT

9–29A

Wheeler Division
Income Statement
August

Sales revenue	$1,200,000
Cost of goods sold	800,000
Overapplied fixed overhead	50,000
Gross margin	450,000
Selling and administrative costs	200,000
Operating profit	$ 250,000

Notes:

1. Fixed manufacturing costs applied at predetermined rate of $2 per unit.
2. No under- or overapplied overhead is prorated to inventories.
3. Ending inventory is $640,000.

EXHIBIT

9–29B

Wheeler Division
Income Statement
August

Sales revenue	$1,200,000
Variable cost of goods sold	600,000
Fixed manufacturing costs	300,000
Gross margin	300,000
Selling and administrative costs	200,000
Operating profit	$ 100,000

d. (1) What were the actual total fixed manufacturing costs incurred in August?

(2) What were the total fixed manufacturing costs expensed on the income statement under full-absorption costing?

9–30 Comparison of Full-Absorption and Variable Normal Costing in a Process Operation

After a dispute with the company president, the controller of the Lance Company resigned. At that time, his office was converting the internal reporting system from full-absorption to variable costing. You have been called in to prepare financial reports for last year. A considerable amount of data are missing, but you piece together the following information.

1. The company manufactures valves, which pass through one department. All materials are added at the beginning of production, and processing is applied evenly throughout the department. There is no spoilage. FIFO costing is used.

2. From the Marketing Department, you learn that 90,000 units were sold at a price of $20 each during last year.

3. From various sources, you determine that actual variable manufacturing overhead was $330,000 and fixed manufacturing overhead was $210,000 for last year. Non-manufacturing costs (all fixed) were $580,000.

4. In one of the former controller's desk drawers, you discover the draft of a report with the following information:

a. "The present accounting system uses the normal costing approach for both internal and external reporting. We write off over- or underapplied overhead as part of cost of goods sold rather than allocate it to inventories."

b. "Equivalent unit costs during the year and in beginning inventories were: $4 per unit for materials costs and $2 per unit for direct labor. Variable overhead is applied at $3 per unit and fixed overhead at $2 per unit."

c. "110,000 units were transferred from work in process inventory to finished goods inventory. 120,000 units of materials were purchased, and 115,000 units were requisitioned to work in process inventory."

d. Inventory summary (in units):

	Beginning Inventories, January 1	Ending Inventories, December 31
Work in process inventory	10,000 (40% complete)	15,000 (20% complete)
Finished goods inventory	No records	30,000
Direct materials	No records	10,000

Required:

a. Show the flow of whole units, including units started in work in process inventory, transferred to finished goods, and sold. Be sure to include both beginning and ending inventories.

b. Show the flow of manufacturing costs during the year, including beginning and ending inventories, using full-absorption normal costing.

c. Prepare income statements using:
   (1) Full-absorption normal costing.
   (2) Variable normal costing.

9–31 Incomplete Records

On December 31 of last year, a fire destroyed the bulk of the accounting records of Malox Company, a small, one-product manufacturing firm. In addition, the chief accountant mysteriously disappeared. You have the task of reconstructing the records for last year. The general manager has said that the accountant had been experimenting with both full-absorption costing and variable costing on an actual costing basis.

The records are a mess, but you have gathered the following data for last year:

1. Sales $450,000
2. Actual fixed manufacturing costs incurred 66,000
3. Actual variable manufacturing costs per unit for last year and for units in beginning finished goods inventory on January 1 of last year 3
4. Operating profit, full-absorption costing basis 60,000
5. Notes receivable from chief accountant 14,000
6. Contribution margin 180,000
7. Direct material purchases 175,000
8. Actual marketing and administrative costs (all fixed) 21,000
9. Gross margin 81,000

The company had no beginning or ending work in process inventories. You also learn that full-absorption costs per unit in last year's beginning finished goods inventory is the same as the full-absorption cost per unit for units produced during the year.

<table>
<tr><td>Required:</td><td>

a. Prepare a comparative income statement on a full-absorption and variable costing basis.

b. At a meeting with the board of directors, the following questions were raised:
(1) "How many units did we sell last year?"
(2) "How many units did we produce last year?"
(3) "What were the unit production costs last year under both full-absorption and variable costing?"
How would you respond?

c. Reconcile the operating profit under variable costing with that under full-absorption costing, showing the exact source of the difference.

</td></tr>
</table>

9–32 Comparative Income Statements with Fixed Overhead Adjustment

Management of the Hillary Company uses the following unit costs for the one product it manufactures:

	Cost per Unit
Direct material (all variable)	$30.00
Direct labor (all variable)	19.00
Manufacturing overhead:	
Variable cost	6.00
Fixed cost (based on 10,000 estimated units per month)	5.00
Nonmanufacturing:	
Variable cost	4.00
Fixed cost (based on 10,000 estimated units per month)	2.80

The projected selling price is $80 per unit. The fixed costs remain fixed within the range of 4,000 to 16,000 units of production.

Management has also projected the following data for the month of June:

	Units
Beginning inventory	–0–
Production	9,000
Available	9,000
Sales	7,500
Ending inventory	1,500

Required:

Prepare a projected income statement for June for management purposes under *each* of the following product-cost methods.

a. Full-absorption costing. Under- or overapplied fixed overhead should be debited or credited to Cost of Goods Sold. There is no under-or overapplied variable overhead.

b. Variable costing.

(CPA adapted)

9–33 Evaluate Full-Absorption and Variable Costing; Normal Costing

The vice president for sales of Huber Corporation received the following income statement for November. The statement has been prepared using variable costing, which the firm has just adopted for internal reporting purposes.

HUBER CORPORATION
Income Statement
For the Month of November
(in thousands)

Sales revenue	$2,400
Less variable cost of goods sold	1,200
Contribution margin	1,200
Less fixed manufacturing costs	600
Gross margin	600
Less fixed nonmanufacturing costs	400
Operating profits before taxes	$ 200

The controller attached the following notes to the statements.

1. The unit sales price for November averaged $24.
2. The unit manufacturing costs for the month were:

Variable costs	$12
Fixed cost	4
Total cost	$16

The unit rate for fixed manufacturing costs is a predetermined rate based upon a normal monthly production of 150,000 units. Both actual and estimated fixed overhead was $600,000.

3. Production for November was 45,000 units in excess of sales.
4. The inventory at November 30 consisted of 45,000 units.

Required:

a. The vice president for sales is not comfortable with the variable cost basis and wonders what the operating profit would have been under the full-absorption cost basis, applying fixed overhead using a predetermined rate.

(1) Present the November income statement on a full-absorption cost basis.

(2) Reconcile and explain the difference between the variable costing and the full-absorption costing operating profit figures.

b. Explain the features associated with the variable costing approach to profit measurement that should be attractive to the vice president for sales.

(CMA adapted)

INTEGRATIVE CASES

9–34   Comprehensive Problem on Process Costing, Variable Costing, and Full-Absorption Costing

(This problem requires knowing how to compute equivalent units.) Whitaker Corporation manufactures Jink, which is sold for $20 per unit. Harsh (a direct material) is added before processing starts, and labor and overhead are added evenly during the manufacturing process. Actual costs per unit of Jink this year are:

Harsh, 2 pounds	$3.00
Labor	6.00
Variable manufacturing overhead	1.00
Fixed manufacturing overhead	1.10

These costs have remained the same for several periods. Inventory data for this year follow:

	Units	
	Beginning: January 1	Ending: December 31
Harsh (pounds)	50,000	40,000
Work in process inventory	10,000 (¹/₂ processed)	15,000 (¹/₃ processed)
Finished goods inventory	17,000	12,000

During the year, 220,000 pounds of Harsh were purchased, and 230,000 pounds were transferred to work in process inventory. Also, 110,000 units of Jink were transferred to finished goods inventory. Actual fixed manufacturing overhead during the year was $121,000. FIFO is used for inventory flows. Marketing and administrative costs were $145,000 for the year.

Required:

a. Determine the number of equivalent units produced for both materials (Harsh) and conversion costs.

b. Determine the work in process and finished goods inventories (in dollars) under (1) full-absorption costing and (2) variable costing on January 1 and December 31.

c. Prepare comparative income statements for the year, using full-absorption and variable costing.

d. Prepare a reconciliation of full-absorption to variable costing that compares the fixed manufacturing costs deducted from revenue (that is, expensed) under each method.

(CPA adapted)

9–35   Full-Absorption and Variable Costing Importing Decisions

Far Eastern Couture imports designer clothing that it has manufactured by subcontractors in Taiwan. Clothing is a seasonal product. The goods must be ready for sale prior to the start of the season. Any goods left over at the end of the season must usually be sold at steep discounts. The company prepares a dress design and selects fabrics approximately six months before a given season. These goods are received and distributed at the start of the season. Based on past experience, the company estimates that 60 percent of a particular lot of dresses will be unsold at the end of the season. These dresses are marked down to one half of the initial retail price. Even with the markdown, a substantial number of dresses remain unsold. These remaining dresses are returned to Far Eastern Couture and destroyed. Even though it is known that a large number of dresses must be discounted or destroyed, the company needs to place a minimum order of 1,000 dresses to have a sufficient selection of styles and sizes for marketing the design.

Recently, the company placed an order for 1,000 dresses of a particular design. The cost of the order was $25,000. In addition, the company pays import duties of $5,000. The company pays a commission of $7 for each dress that is actually sold at retail, regardless of whether it is sold at the regular price or at the markdown price. There is a cost of $3 for return mailing and disposing of each dress that is unsold after the end of the markdown period.

Required:

a. Use full-absorption costing to compute the inventoriable cost of each dress in this lot of dresses.

b. Suppose the company sells 30 percent of the dresses in this lot at a price of $75 each during the first accounting period. Using full-absorption costing, what is the value of the ending inventory and what is the operating profit or loss for the period assuming there are no other transactions and that the season has not ended so that the number of dresses subject to markdown or to be returned is unknown?

c. During the second period, 10 percent of the 1,000 dresses were sold at full price and 30 percent were sold at the half-price markdown. The remaining dresses were returned and disposed of. Using full-absorption costing, what is the operating profit or loss for the period assuming there are no other transactions?

d. Suggest a method of accounting for these dresses that would more closely relate revenues and costs.

SOLUTIONS TO

Self-Study Questions

1   a. Product costs are the actual costs given in the question divided by the 84,000 units *produced* (not the units *sold*).

	Full-Absorption Costing	Variable Costing
Direct materials	$ 5.50	$ 5.50
Direct labor	3.75	3.75
Variable manufacturing overhead . . .	1.25	1.25
Fixed manufacturing overhead	4.75	–0–
Total	$15.25	$10.50

b. *Income statements.* Note the cost of goods sold (full-absorption costing) and variable cost of goods sold (variable costing) are based on the 76,000 units sold, not the 84,000 units produced.

	Full-Absorption Costing
Sales revenue	$1,520,000[a]
Cost of goods sold	1,159,000[b]
Gross margin	361,000
Marketing and administrative	251,000[c]
Operating profits	$ 110,000

	Variable Costing
Sales revenue	$1,520,000[a]
Variable cost of goods sold	798,000[d]
Variable marketing and administrative	50,400
Contribution margin	671,600
Fixed manufacturing overhead	399,000
Fixed marketing and administrative	200,600
Operating profits	$ 72,000

Calculations:

[a] $1,520,000 = $20 × 76,000 units sold.

[b] $1,159,000 = $15.25 × 76,000 units sold.

[c] $251,000 = Sum of variable and fixed marketing and administrative costs. Fixed and variable marketing and administrative costs could be reported separately or combined as shown here.

[d] $798,000 = $10.50 × 76,000 units sold.

c. *Explanation*. Operating profits are $38,000 higher under full-absorption costing. The reason for the difference in operating profits is solely because of the way fixed manufacturing costs are treated. Under variable costing, *all* fixed manufacturing costs are expensed on the income statement in the period in which they occurred. If production exceeds sales, then a portion of fixed manufacturing costs are not expensed in the current period under full-absorption costing. In this case, 8,000 units remain in ending inventory. Under full-absorption costing, $38,000 of the fixed manufacturing cost, which equals 8,000 units × $4.75 fixed manufacturing cost per unit, remains in ending inventory. If the total units sold had exceeded the total units produced, then full-absorption costing would show lower operating profits than variable costing.

2 a. Product costs are the actual costs given in the question divided by the 84,000 units for materials and labor, but normal costs are used for overhead.

	Full-Absorption Costing	Variable Costing
Direct materials	$ 5.50	$ 5.50
Direct labor	3.75	3.75
Variable manufacturing overhead	1.50[a]	1.50[a]
Fixed manufacturing overhead	4.6875[b]	–0–
Total	$15.4375	$10.75

[a] $1.50 = 40% of direct labor.
[b] $4.6875 = 125% of direct labor.

b. *Income statements*. Note the cost of goods sold (full-absorption costing) and variable cost of goods sold (variable costing) are based on the 76,000 units sold, not the 84,000 units produced. To compute the over- or underapplied overhead, first compute the applied amounts based on the predetermined rates times the actual direct labor cost shown in self-study question 1 for the 84,000 units produced:

Variable overhead applied = 40% × $315,000 = $126,000
Fixed overhead applied = 125% × $315,000 = $393,750

Now find the difference between actual and applied:

	Actual Overhead per Self-Study Question 1	Applied Overhead	Difference
Variable manufacturing overhead . . .	$105,000	$126,000	$21,000 overapplied
Fixed manufacturing overhead	399,000	393,750	5,250 underapplied
Net overapplied manufacturing overhead			$15,750

	Full-Absorption Costing
Sales revenue	$1,520,000[a]
Cost of goods sold	1,173,250[b]
Overapplied overhead	15,750
Gross margin	362,500
Marketing and administrative costs	251,000[c]
Operating profits	$ 111,500

	Variable Costing
Sales revenue	$1,520,000[a]
Variable cost of goods sold	817,000[d]
Overapplied variable overhead	21,000
Variable marketing and administrative costs	50,400
Contribution margin	673,600
Fixed manufacturing overhead	399,000
Fixed marketing and administrative costs . . .	200,600
Operating profits	$ 74,000

Calculations:

[a] $1,520,000 = $20 × 76,000 units sold.

[b] $1,173,250 = $15.4375 × 76,000 units sold.

[c] $251,000 = Sum of variable and fixed marketing and administrative costs. Fixed marketing and administrative costs could be separated from variable marketing and administrative costs, or they could be combined as shown here.

[d] $817,000 = $10.75 × 76,000 units sold.

3   *a.*

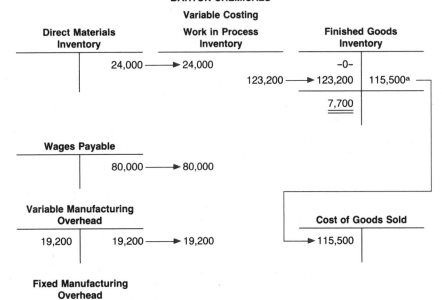

b.

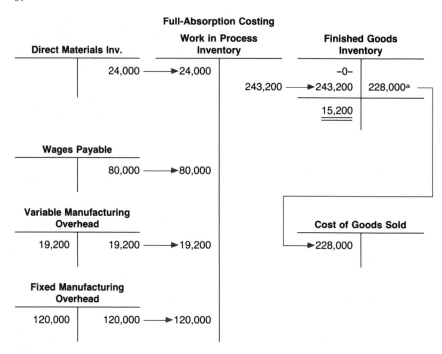

Full-Absorption Costing

| Direct Materials Inv. | Work in Process Inventory | Finished Goods Inventory |

a $115,500 = \left(\frac{7,500}{8,000}\right) \times 123,200$; $228,000 = \left(\frac{7,500}{8,000}\right) \times \$243,200$.

c.

Contribution Margin Approach

Sales revenue	$450,000
Less:	
Variable cost of goods sold	115,500
Variable marketing and administrative costs	24,800
Contribution margin	309,700
Less:	
Fixed manufacturing overhead	120,000
Fixed marketing and administrative costs	110,000
Operating profit	$ 79,700

d.

Traditional Approach

Sales revenue	$450,000
Cost of goods sold	228,000
Gross margin	222,000
Less:	
Variable marketing and administrative costs	24,800
Fixed marketing and administrative costs	110,000
Operating profit	$ 87,200

DIFFERENTIAL COSTS FOR DECISION MAKING

OUTLINE

Cost Estimation

LEARNING OBJECTIVES

After reading this chapter, you should be able to:

1. Use accounting data to estimate fixed and variable costs.
2. Interpret cost data presented in scattergraphs and the results of high-low cost estimates.
3. Estimate costs using regression.
4. Interpret the results of regression estimates.
5. Evaluate the advantages and disadvantages of alternative ways to estimate costs.
6. Explain the effect of learning curves on costs.

*I*n deciding among alternative actions, management needs to know the costs that are likely to be incurred for each alternative. Here are frequently asked questions that require cost estimates:

- University of Illinois administrators ask: "What will happen to total costs if we increase enrollment by 10 percent over the present level?"
- Managers at Andersen Consulting ask: "What bid should we enter on this systems job?"
- Managers of Tower Records ask: "What profit can we expect if we sell the projected number of CDs this period?"

This chapter discusses methods of estimating costs to answer questions like these.

METHODS OF ESTIMATING COSTS

The basic idea in cost estimation is to estimate the relation between costs and the variables affecting costs. In this chapter, we focus on the relation between costs and one important variable that affects costs—activity levels. Activities can be measured by volume (units of output, machine-hours, pages typed, miles driven, for example), by complexity (number of setups, number of different types of products, for example), or by any other cost driver.

You are already familiar with the term *variable costs*, and you know that variable costs are those that change proportionately with activity levels. The formula that we use to estimate costs is the familiar cost equation:

$$TC = F + VX$$

where *TC* refers to total costs, *F* refers to fixed costs that do not vary with activity levels, *V* refers to variable costs per unit of activity, and *X* refers to the volume of activity.

In practice, we usually have data about the total costs incurred at each of various activity levels, but we do not have a breakdown of costs into fixed and variable components. Yet, knowing which costs are fixed and how costs change as the volume of activity changes is important for most financial decisions made in companies.

This chapter discusses four methods of estimating the relation between cost behavior and activity levels that are commonly used in practice:

1. Account analysis.
2. Engineering estimates.
3. Scattergraph and high-low estimates.
4. Statistical methods (usually employing regression analysis).

Results are likely to differ from method to method. Consequently, more than one approach is often applied so that results can be compared. Because line managers bear ultimate responsibility for all cost estimates, they frequently apply their own best judgment as a final step in the estimation process, modifying the estimates submitted by the controller's staff. These methods, therefore, should be seen as ways of helping management to arrive at the best estimates possible. Their weaknesses as well as their strengths require attention.

We discuss each of the four estimation methods in this chapter. The discussion of regression methods centers on practical applications rather than on the underlying statistical theory. A brief overview of the theory and some important considerations for its application are discussed in the appendix to this chapter.

ACCOUNT ANALYSIS

Account Analysis The method of cost estimation that calls for a review of each account making up the total cost being analyzed.

The **account analysis** approach calls for a review of each cost account used to record the costs that are of interest. Each cost is identified as either fixed or variable, depending on the relationship between the cost and some activity.

The relationship between the activity and the cost is extremely important. For example, in estimating the production costs for a specified number of units within the range of present manufacturing capacity, direct materials and direct labor costs would be considered variable, while building occupancy costs would be considered fixed.

ILLUSTRATION

10–1

*Cost Estimation Using
Account Analysis,
Estimators, Inc.*

Account	Costs at 4,600 Units of Output (115 machine-hours)		
	Total	Variable Cost	Fixed Cost
Indirect Labor	$ 321	$ 103	$ 218
Indirect Materials	422	307	115
Building Occupancy	615		615
Property Taxes and Insurance	51	40	11
Power	589	535	54
Equipment Repairs and Maintenance	218	119	99
Data Processing	113	88	25
Quality Inspections	187	187	
Personnel Services	115	47	68
Totals	$2,631	$1,426	$1,205

Illustration 10–1 shows a typical schedule of estimated manufacturing overhead costs prepared for a particular production level by Estimators, Inc. The production process is assumed to produce 40 units per machine-hour. Management has initially considered a production level of 4,600 units. To attain this production level, 115 machine-hours (4,600 units ÷ 40 units per hour) are required. The variable manufacturing overhead may be expressed as a cost per machine-hour or as a cost per unit, depending upon management's preference.

Following this approach, each major class of manufacturing overhead costs is itemized. Each cost is then divided into its estimated variable and fixed components. Management considers building occupany costs, for example, to be entirely fixed and classifies the costs of quality inspections as entirely variable. The other costs are mixed—they have some fixed and some variable elements. The fixed and variable components of each cost item may be determined on the basis of the experience and judgment of accounting or other personnel. Additionally, other cost-estimation methods discussed later in this chapter might be used to divide costs into fixed and variable components.

The total costs for the coming period are the sum of the estimated total variable and total fixed costs. For Estimators, Inc., assume that accounting personnel have relied on judgments of a number of people in the company and estimated fixed costs to be $1,205 and the total variable costs to be $1,426, as shown in Illustration 10–1.

Since the variable costs are directly related to the quantity of expected production, the variable manufacturing overhead per unit may be stated as $.31 ($1,426 ÷ 4,600 units). The general cost equation may be expressed as:

$$TC = F + VX$$

Manufacturing overhead costs = $1,205 per period + $.31 per unit times the
number of units of output

For 4,600 units:

Manufacturing overhead costs = $1,205 + ($.31 × 4,600)
= $1,205 + $1,426
= $2,631

Now, if management wanted to estimate the costs at a production level of 4,800 units, it would substitute that figure for the 4,600 units in the previous equation. This results in:

Manufacturing overhead costs = $1,205 + ($.31 × 4,800)
= $1,205 + $1,488
= $2,693

This is simpler than reestimating all of the manufacturing overhead cost elements listed in Illustration 10–1 for the different activity levels that management might wish to consider. Moreover, management's attention is drawn to the variable cost amount as the cost that changes with each increment in unit volume.

The variable costs could also be expressed in terms of costs per machine-hour. Assume 115 machine-hours are required to produce 4,600 units (at 40 units per hour), the variable cost per machine-hour would be:

$1,426 ÷ 115 hours = $12.40 per machine-hour

Account analysis is a useful way of estimating costs. It makes use of the experience and judgment of managers and accountants who are familiar with company operations and the way costs react to changes in activity levels. Account analysis relies heavily on personal judgment. This may be an advantage or disadvantage depending on the bias of the person making the estimate. Decisions based on cost estimates often have major economic consequences for the people making the estimates. Thus, these individuals may not be entirely objective. More objective methods are often used in conjunction with account analysis so that the advantages of multiple methods are obtained.

Self-Study Question

1 Propylon, the wonder fabric of the 21st century, is the primary product of Propylon Textiles. By the end of its second year of operations, Propylon Textiles had enough data for Natalie Martin, the company's chief financial officer, to do a detailed analysis of its overhead cost behavior. Ms. Martin accumulated monthly data that are summarized below as two-year totals.

Indirect materials	$ 503,000
Indirect labor	630,000
Lease	288,000
Utilities (heat, light, etc.)	206,000
Power to run machines	104,000
Insurance	24,000
Maintenance	200,000
Depreciation	72,000
Research and development	171,000
Total overhead	$2,198,000

Direct labor-hours	815,800 hours
Direct labor-costs	$4,997,400
Machine hours	1,022,700 hours
Units produced	202,500 units

Ms. Martin has asked you to prepare three analyses that, using the account analysis method, calculates the *monthly average* fixed costs and the variable cost rate per:

1. Direct labor-hour.
2. Machine hour.
3. Unit of output.

You discuss operations with production managers who inform you that three costs are variable—indirect labor, indirect materials, and power to run machines. All other costs are fixed.

The solution to this question is at the end of this chapter on page 403.

ENGINEERING ESTIMATES

Engineering Estimates Cost estimates based on measurement and pricing of the work involved in a task.

Engineering estimates of costs are usually made by measuring the work involved in a task. A detailed step-by-step analysis of each phase of each manufacturing process, together with the kinds of work performed and the costs involved, is prepared. (This is sometimes part of a *time-and-motion* study.) The time it should take to perform each step is then estimated. These times are often available from widely published manuals and trade association documents.

The times required for each step in the process are summed to obtain an estimate of the total time involved, including an allowance for unproductive time. This serves as a basis for estimating direct labor costs. Engineering estimates of the materials required for each unit of production are usually obtainable from drawings and specifications sheets.

Other costs are estimated in a similar manner. For example, the size and cost of a building needed to house the manufacturing operation can be estimated based on area construction costs and space requirements. An estimate of the needed number of supervisors and support personnel can be based on an estimate of direct labor time.

One advantage to the engineering approach is that it can detail each step required to perform an operation. This permits comparison with other settings where similar operations are performed. It enables a company to review its manufacturing productivity and identify specific strengths and weaknesses. Another advantage is that it does not require data from prior activities in the organization. Hence, it can be used to estimate costs for totally new activities.

A company that uses engineering estimates can often identify where "slack" exists in its operations. For example, if an engineering estimate indicates that 80,000 square feet of floor area are required for an assembly process but the company has been using 125,000 square feet, the company may find it beneficial to rearrange the plant to make floor space available for other uses.

A difficulty with the engineering approach is that it can be quite expensive to use because each activity is using engineering norms. Another consideration is that engineering estimates are often based on optimal conditions. Therefore, when evaluating performance, bidding on a contract, planning for expected costs, or estimating costs for any other purpose, it is wise to consider that the actual work conditions will be less than optimal.

SCATTERGRAPH AND HIGH-LOW ESTIMATES

One way to overcome some of the shortcomings of account analysis and engineering estimates is to observe past cost behavior in relation to a specified activity measure. If a company's operations have followed a discernible pattern in the past and that pattern is expected to continue in the future, it may be possible to use the relationship between past costs and activity to estimate future costs. Of course, if the relationship changes, it may be necessary to adjust the estimated costs accordingly.

Analysts must be careful when predicting future costs from past data. In many cases, the cost-activity relationship changes. Technological innovation, increased use of robots, more mechanized processes, and the like may make the past cost-activity relationships inappropriate for predictive purposes.

In other cases, the costs themselves change so dramatically that old cost data are almost worthless predictors of future costs. Because of the high variation in prices, manufacturers using copper and silver in recent years have found that past cost data are not very helpful for predicting future costs. While accountants may adjust the data, the resulting cost estimates tend to lose their objectivity as the number of adjustments increases.

Relevant Range of Activity

When attempting to extrapolate from past observations, one must consider the relevance of past activity levels to anticipated future activity levels. Extrapolations beyond the upper and lower bounds of past observations are highly subjective. Suppose, for example, the highest activity level observed in the past was 4,100 units per month and we wished to predict the cost of manufacturing 4,600 units per month. An estimate based on past data may be highly inaccurate, because the past data do not reflect experience with output over 4,100 units.

The limits within which a cost projection may be valid is the *relevant range* for that estimate. The relevant range would include only those activity levels for which the assumed cost relationships used in the estimate are considered to hold. Thus, when past data are used, the relevant range for the projection is usually between the upper and lower limits of the past activity levels for which data are available.

Although the use of past data for future cost estimation has limitations, there are many cases in which it works quite well. In many estimates, past data, even if outside the relevant range, are adequate representations of the cost relationships that are likely to hold in the future. Moreover, reliance on past data is relatively inexpensive. It may be the only readily available, cost-effective basis for estimating costs.

Past data do show the relationships that held in prior periods and, at the least, may be a meaningful starting point for estimating future costs as long as their limitations are recognized. In the following sections, we discuss specific methods of using past data to estimate future costs.

Preparing a Scattergraph

Scattergraph A plot of costs against past activity levels.

Plotting past costs against past activity levels is often a useful way of visually depicting cost-activity relationships. Such a plot, called a **scattergraph,** will also indicate any significant change in the relationship between costs and activity at different activity levels.

To prepare such a plot, we first obtain the relevant data. For example, if estimates of manufacturing overhead costs are to be based on direct labor-hours, we must obtain information about past manufacturing overhead costs and related past direct labor-hours.

Number of Observations

The number of observations to include depends on the availability of the data, the variability within the data, and the relative costs and benefits of obtaining reliable data. A rule of thumb is to use three years of monthly data if the physical processes have not changed significantly within that time. If the company's operations have recently changed significantly, however, data that predate the change may not be useful. If cost and activity levels are highly stable, then a relatively short period (12 months or so) may be adequate.

Data for the past 15 months were collected for Estimators, Inc., to estimate variable and fixed manufacturing overhead. These data are presented and plotted on the scattergraph in Illustration 10–2. Once all the data points were plotted, a line was drawn to fit the points as closely as possible. The line was extended to the vertical axis on the scattergraph.

The slope of the line represents the estimated variable costs, and the intercept with the vertical axis represents an estimate of fixed costs. The slope is referred to as the variable cost per unit because it represents the change in costs that occurs as a result of changes in activity. The intercept is referred to as the fixed cost because it represents the costs that would be incurred at a zero activity level given existing capacity *if the relationship plotted is valid from the data points back to the origin.* Note there are no observations of cost behavior around the zero activity level in this example, so the data do not indicate the costs that would occur when the activity level was zero. Rather, they provide an estimating equation useful within the relevant range. The slope and intercept may be measured using a ruler.

Preparing an estimate on this basis is subject to a good deal of error, especially if the points are scattered widely. Determination of the best fit is often a matter of "eyeball judgment." Consequently, scattergraphs are usually not used as the sole basis for cost estimates. Rather, they are used to illustrate the relationships between costs and activity levels and to point out any past data items that might be significantly out of line.

High-Low Cost Estimation

High-Low Cost Estimation A method of estimating costs based on two cost observations, usually costs at the highest activity level and costs at the lowest activity level.

If the cost relationships can be described by a straight line, any two points on a scattergraph may be used to prepare a cost-estimating equation. Typically, the *highest and the lowest activity points* are chosen—hence the name **high-low cost estimation.** Activity may be defined in terms of units of production, hours of work, or any other measure that makes sense for the problem at hand.

The slope of the total cost line, which estimates the increase of variable costs associated with an increase of one unit of activity, may be estimated by the equation:

ILLUSTRATION

*Data and Scattergraph
for Cost Estimation,
Estimators, Inc.*

Time Period	Overhead Costs	Machine-Hours (MH)
1	$2,107	62
2	2,040	62
3	2,916	120
4	2,322	71
5	1,896	50
6	2,471	95
7	3,105	142
8	2,316	86
9	2,555	112
10	2,780	136
11	2,061	85
12	2,910	103
13	2,835	96
14	2,715	101
15	1,986	53

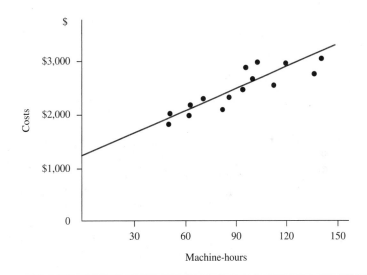

$$\text{Variable cost per unit } (V) = \frac{\text{Cost at highest activity} - \text{Cost at lowest activity}}{\text{Highest activity} - \text{Lowest activity}}$$

The intercept is estimated by taking the total cost at either activity level and subtracting the estimated variable cost for that activity level.

$$\text{Fixed cost } (F) = \frac{\text{Total cost at}}{\text{highest activity}} - (\text{Variable cost} \times \text{Highest activity})$$

or

$$\text{Fixed cost} = \frac{\text{Total cost at}}{\text{lowest activity}} - (\text{Variable cost} \times \text{Lowest activity})$$

Based on the data for Estimators, Inc., in Illustration 10-2, the highest activity level is 142 machine-hours (MH). At this activity level, total manufacturing overhead costs are $3,105. The lowest activity level is 50 hours, with manufacturing overhead costs of $1,896. Substituting these data in the equation for variable cost yields:

$$\text{Variable cost per MH} = \frac{\$3,105 - \$1,896}{142 \text{ MH} - 50 \text{ MH}}$$
$$= \frac{\$1,209}{92 \text{ MH}}$$
$$= \$13.141 \text{ per MH}$$

To obtain the fixed cost estimate, either the highest or lowest activity level and costs may be used. Assuming the highest activity level is used:

$$\text{Fixed cost} = \$3,105 - (\$13.141 \times 142 \text{ MH})$$
$$= \$3,105 - \$1,866$$
$$= \$1,239$$

An estimate for the costs at any given activity level can be computed using the equation:

$$TC = F + VX$$
$$\text{Total cost} = \$1,239 + (\$13.141 \times \text{specified MH})$$

For the 115 hours required to produce 4,600 units, the total cost is:

$$\text{Total cost} = \$1,239 + (\$13.141 \times 115 \text{ MH})$$
$$= \$1,239 + \$1,511$$
$$= \$2,750$$

While the high-low method is easy to apply, care must be taken to assure that the two points used to prepare the estimates are representative of cost and activity relationships over the range of activity for which the prediction is made. The highest and lowest points could, however, represent unusual circumstances. When this happens, one should choose the highest and lowest points within the normal range of activity.

The scattergraph can be used graphically to illustrate cost-activity relationships based on past experience. Whenever costs and activity levels can be plotted in two-dimensional space, the scattergraph is a useful visual display. We recommend using it in conjunction with other cost-estimation methods.

STATISTICAL COST ESTIMATION USING REGRESSION

Regression Statistical procedure to determine the relationship between variables.

Regression techniques are designed to generate a line that best fits a set of data points. Because the regression procedure uses all data points, the resulting estimates have a broader base than estimates based only on high-low points.

In addition, regression techniques generate a number of additional statistics that under certain assumptions enable a manager to determine how well the estimated regression equation describes the relationship between costs and activities. The regression process also permits inclusion of more than one predictor. This latter feature may be useful when more than one activity affects costs. For example, variable manufacturing overhead may be a function of both direct labor-hours and the quantities of direct materials processed.

A comprehensive discussion of regression is not possible within the scope of this text. Many moderately priced hand calculators have regression capabilities. Computer spreadsheets such as Microsoft's Excel® and Lotus 1-2-3® have regression programs. We leave descriptions of the computational details to statistics and computer courses. Instead, we deal with regression from the standpoint of accountants and managers who must interpret and use regression estimates. (The appendix to this chapter discusses some of the more technical considerations that may interest users of such programs.)

Obtaining Regression Estimates

Independent Variables The *X* terms, or predictors, on the right-hand side of a regression equation.

Dependent Variable The *Y* term or the left-hand side of a regression equation.

The most important step in obtaining regression estimates for cost estimation is to establish the existence of a logical relationship between activities that affect costs and the cost to be estimated. These activities are referred to as predictors, *X terms*, **independent variables,** or the *right-hand side (RHS)* of a regression equation. The cost to be estimated may be called the **dependent variable,** the *Y term*, or the *left-hand side (LHS)* of the regression equation.

Although regression programs will accept any data for the *Y* and *X* terms, entering numbers that have no logical relationship may result in misleading estimates. The accountant has the important responsibility of making sure that the activities are logically related to costs.

Assume, for example, that a logical relationship exists between machine-hours and manufacturing overhead costs for Estimators, Inc. Assume that a logical relationship also exists between direct materials costs and overhead costs. This latter assumption would be reasonable if the manufacturing process employed a substantial amount of materials and overhead costs included materials handling and storage. The data on manufacturing overhead costs, machine-hours, and direct materials costs for this process are presented in Illustration 10–3.

Estimators, Inc., first estimates costs using simple regression—only one independent variable—to predict manufacturing overhead costs. They choose machine-hours, so past data on machine-hours would be entered as the *X*, or independent, variable. Past data on manufacturing overhead costs would be entered as the *Y*, or dependent, variable. The computer output giving the estimated relationship between machine-hours and manufacturing overhead for this situation is as follows:

Total manufacturing overhead = \$1,334 + \$12.373 per MH

For cost-estimation purposes, when reading the output of a regression program, the intercept term, \$1,334, is an estimate of fixed costs. Of course, it should be used with caution because the intercept is outside of the relevant range of observations. The coefficient of the *X* term (in this example, \$12.373 per machine-hour) is an estimate of the variable cost per machine-hour. This is the slope of the cost line. The coefficients are often labeled *b* on the program output. Thus, the cost-estimation equation based on the regression results above would be:

ILLUSTRATION

Data for Regression Estimation, Estimators, Inc.

Overhead Costs	Machine- Hours	Direct Materials Costs
$2,107	62	$1,964
2,040	62	1,851
2,916	120	3,615
2,322	71	2,902
1,896	50	1,136
2,471	95	2,315
3,105	142	5,013
2,316	86	2,751
2,555	112	2,816
2,780	136	3,461
2,061	85	1,702
2,910	103	3,819
2,835	96	3,940
2,715	101	3,613
1,986	53	1,741

Total costs = Intercept + b times MH

Substituting 115 MH into the equation yields:

$$\text{Total costs} = \$1,334 + (\$12.373 \times 115 \text{ MH})$$
$$= \$1,334 + \$1,423$$
$$= \underline{\underline{\$2,757}}$$

This estimate of cost behavior is shown graphically in Illustration 10–4.

ILLUSTRATION

Scattergraph with Regression-Estimated Cost Line, Estimators, Inc.

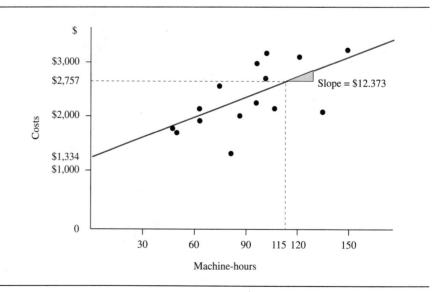

Correlation Coefficient

Correlation Coefficient A measure of the linear relationship between two or more variables, such as cost and some activity measure.

In addition to the cost-estimating equation, the regression program provides other useful statistics. The **correlation coefficient** (R) is a measure of the proximity of the data points to the regression line. The closer R is to 1.0, the closer the data points are to the regression line. Conversely, the closer R is to zero, the poorer the fit of the regression line.

The square of R is called R-square or the coefficient of determination. R-square is interpreted as the proportion of the variation in Y explained by the right-hand side of the regression equation; that is, by the X predictors.

Adjusted R-Square The correlation coefficient squared and adjusted for the number of independent variables used to make the estimate.

The **adjusted R-square** is the correlation coefficient squared and adjusted for the number of independent variables used to make the estimate. This adjustment to R-square recognizes that as the number of independent variables increases, R-square (unadjusted) increases. Statisticians believe that adjusted R-square is a better measure of the association between X and Y than the unadjusted R-square value when there is more than one X predictor.

For Estimators, Inc., the correlation coefficient, R-square, and adjusted R-square are:

Correlation coefficient *(R)* 896
R-square 802
Adjusted R-square 787

Since the R-square is .802, it can be said that 80.2 percent of the changes in overhead costs can be explained by changes in machine-hours. For data drawn from accounting records, an R-square of .802 would be considered a good fit of the regression equation to the data.

The most commonly used regression technique is called *ordinary least squares regression*. With this technique, the regression line is computed so that the sum of the squares of the vertical distances from each point on the scattergraph to the regression line is minimized. Thus, as a practical consideration, it is important to beware of including data points that vary significantly from the usual. Because the regression program seeks to minimize squared differences, the inclusion of these extreme outliers may significantly affect the results. Consequently, organizations often exclude data for periods of such unusual occurrences as strikes, extreme weather conditions, and shutdowns for equipment retooling. A scattergraph often reveals such outliers so they can then be easily identified and omitted.

Self-Study Question

2 The following computer output presents the results of two simple regressions for Propylon Textiles, one using machine hours as the independent variable and the other using units of output as the independent variable. Each regression has 24 data points, one data point per month for two years. Which activity base, units of output or machine hours, do you believe best explains variation in overhead costs?

OUTPUT NO. 1
Dependent variable = Overhead
Independent variable: Mach. hrs.
R-square = .863   Adjusted R-square = .857
24 observations

Variable	Estimated Coefficient	Standard Error	*t*-Statistic
M-hrs.	4.9015	.41645	11.770
Intercept	−117.28	17.796	− 6.5902

OUTPUT NO. 2
Dependent variable = Overhead
Independent variable: Units produced
R-square = .870   Adjusted R-square = .864
24 observations

Variable	Estimated Coefficient	Standard Error	t-Statistic
Units produced	23.799	1.9610	12.136
Intercept	− 109.22	16.597	− 6.5805

The solution to this question is at the end of this chapter on page 404.

Regression with
Multiple Predictors

While the prediction of overhead costs in the previous example, with its adjusted R-square of .787, was considered good, management may wish to see if a better estimate might be obtained using additional predictor variables. In such a case, they examine the nature of the operation to determine which additional predictors might be useful in deriving a cost-estimation equation.

Assume Estimators, Inc., has determined that direct materials costs may also affect manufacturing overhead. The results of using both machine-hours (X_1) and direct materials costs (X_2) as *predictors* of overhead (Y) were obtained using a computer program. The computer output from the program using machine-hours and direct materials costs yields the prediction equation:

$$\text{Manufacturing overhead costs} = \text{Intercept} + b_1X_1 + b_2X_2$$
$$= \$1{,}334 + \$4.359X_1 + .258X_2$$

where X_1 refers to machine-hours and X_2 refers to direct materials costs. (The intercepts in the simple and multiple regressions round to the same whole number by coincidence.) The statistics supplied with the output are:

Correlation coefficient (multiple R) 976
Multiple R-square 952
Adjusted multiple R-square 944

The correlation coefficient (now expressed as *multiple R* because it is related to more than one predictor variable) for this regression is .976, and the adjusted multiple R-square is .944. Both of these are improvements over the results obtained when the regression equation included only machine-hours. Improved results may be expected because some overhead costs may be related to direct materials costs but not to machine-hours (for example, storeroom maintenance).

To prepare a cost estimate using this multiple regression equation requires not only the estimated machine-hours for the coming period but the direct materials costs as well. The additional data requirements for multiple regression models may limit their usefulness in many applications. Of course, in planning for the next period's production activity, companies will usually have already estimated direct materials costs and machine-hours, and in such a situation the added costs of obtaining data may be quite low.

For example, Estimators, Inc., estimates its direct materials cost to be $.80 per output unit based on engineering estimates of materials needed and accounting estimates of direct materials costs. Production is estimated at 4,600 units, so direct materials costs of $3,680 (4,600 units × $.80 per unit) are expected in the coming period.

.Substituting the 115 machine-hours and the $3,680 direct materials costs in the regression equation results in the following overhead estimate:

$$
\begin{aligned}
\text{Overhead} &= \$1,334 + (\$4.359 \times 115) + (.258 \times \$3,680) \\
&= \$1,334 + \$501 + \$949 \\
&= \underline{\underline{\$2,784}}
\end{aligned}
$$

This estimate has the advantage of being based on two factors (machine time and direct materials) that appear to be jointly affecting overhead costs. The correlation coefficient is higher for this equation than for the single predictor equation. An increase in R, alone, should not be the sole criterion for selecting a regression model; however, it is important that the independent variables have a logical relation to the dependent variable.

Using the bs *as Variable Cost Estimates*

When using a simple linear regression, the intercept is often considered analogous to fixed costs and the slope to variable cost. Indeed, in many companies, regression estimates are used for estimating the fixed and variable components of manufacturing overhead for overhead application and analysis. Care should be exercised when doing this, however. For example, it is possible to have negative intercepts in empirical estimates, but it is highly unlikely that a company would have negative fixed costs.

If more than one predictor variable is used, as in Estimators, Inc.'s multiple regression above, the interpretation of the bs as variable costs is somewhat more hazardous. For the multiple regression of Estimators, Inc., the following correlation matrix was part of the computer output. It shows that the machine-hours and direct material dollars are highly correlated with one another (that is, a correlation of .832).

Variable	b	
Machine-hours (MH)	4.359	
Direct materials cost (DMC)	.258	
CORRELATION MATRIX:		
	MH	DMC
MH	1.00	.832
DMC	.832	1.00

Multicollinearity Correlation between two or more independent variables in a multiple regression equation.

This means that there is overlapping explanatory power among the two predictors. This problem is referred to as **multicollinearity**. It does not affect the Y estimate, but it affects the interpretation of the contribution that each of the Xs (that is, direct material dollars and machine-hours) is making to the prediction of Y.

Confidence in the Coefficients of the Independent Variables

In many cases, it may be desirable to determine if the bs (that is, the coefficients of the independent variables) are significantly different from zero. The *t*-statistic is used to test for the significance of bs.

***t*-Statistic** t is the value of b, the coefficient, divided by its standard error

To test whether the computed b is statistically different from zero, a *t*-statistic is computed. This t is simply the value of b divided by its standard error (SE_b). For the data used in the simple regression for Estimators, Inc., the *t*-statistic for the coefficient is:

$$t = \frac{b}{SE_b}$$

$$= \frac{12.373}{1.703}$$

$$= 7.265$$

where the SE_b of 1.703 is given by the computer output. As a rule of thumb, a *t* of 2.0 or better may usually be considered statistically significant. With $t \geq 2$, analysts would generally reject the hypothesis that the regression results are due to chance; and they would reject the hypothesis that the true value of *b* is zero.

To construct a 95 percent confidence interval around *b*, we would take the computed *b* and add or subtract the appropriate *t* value for the 95 percent confidence interval times the standard error of *b*. The confidence interval is:

$$b \pm t \times SE_b$$

The computer output for this example gives $SE_b = 1.703$.

The value of *t* for a 95 percent confidence interval may be obtained from a table of *t* values in a statistics book.

$$t_{SE_b} = 2.160$$

Hence, the confidence intervals are:

$$b \pm 2.160 \times 1.703 = b \pm 3.678$$

With *b* equal to $12.373, the upper limit would be:

$16.051 (that is, $12.373 + $3.678)

while the lower confidence limit would be:

$8.695 (that is, $12.373 − $3.678)

We would be 95 percent confident that the variable cost coefficient is between $8.70 (rounded) and $16.05. These limits are quite wide. To narrow these limits, we need to construct a better-fitting regression.

Practical Implementation Problems

Advances in easy-to-use computer software and hand-held calculators have greatly simplified regression analysis and made it available to more people. Consequently, regression has been increasingly used (and potentially misused). In particular, people may be tempted to enter many variables into a regression model without careful thought to their validity. The results can be disastrous.

Some of the more common problems with using regression estimates include: (1) attempting to fit a linear equation to nonlinear data, (2) failing to exclude outliers, and (3) including predictors with apparent but spurious relationships.

Effect of Nonlinear Relationships
The effect of attempting to fit a linear model to nonlinear data is likely to be seen when a company is operating close to capacity limits. Close to maximum capacity, costs accelerate more rapidly than activity due to shift

ILLUSTRATION

10–5

*Effect of Fitting a Linear
Model to Nonlinear Data*

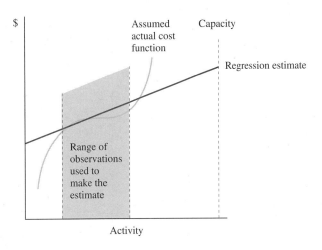

differentials and overtime premiums paid to employees, increased maintenance and repair costs for equipment, and similar factors. The linear cost
estimate understates the slope of the cost line in the ranges close to capacity.
This situation is shown in Illustration 10–5.

One way to overcome the problem would be to define a relevant range of
activity up to, say, 80 percent capacity and use the range for one set of cost-
estimating regression equations. Another equation could be derived for the
81 percent to 100 percent capacity levels.

Another approach is to use nonlinear regression techniques to estimate
the curve directly. However, nonlinear regression does not provide a constant variable cost estimate—the estimate is different at each level.

Effect of Outliers

Because regression seeks to minimize the sum of the squared deviations
from the regression line, observations that lie a significant distance away
from the line may have an overwhelming effect on the regression estimates.
Illustration 10–6 shows a case in which most of the data points lie close to a
straight line, but due to the effect of one significant outlier, the computed
regression line is a significant distance from most of the points.

This kind of problem can easily arise in accounting settings. Suppose a
year's worth of supplies was purchased and expensed entirely in one month,
or a large adjustment was made for underaccruing payroll taxes. The accounting records in such cases are clearly abnormal with respect to the
activity measure. An inspection of a plot of the data can sometimes reveal
this problem.

When an extreme outlier appears in the data set, scrutiny of the output
from the regression equation will rarely identify it. Instead, a plot of the
regression line on the data points is usually needed. If multiple predictors are
used, an outlier will be even more difficult to find. The best way to avoid this
problem is to examine the data in advance and eliminate highly unusual
observations *before* running the regression.

10–6

*Effect of Failure to
Exclude Outliers*

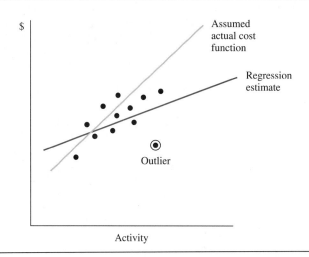

Spurious Relationships

It is sometimes tempting to feed the computer a lot of data and let the regression program "find" relationships among variables. This can lead to spurious relationships. For example, there may appear to be a relationship between Variable 1 and Variable 2, when, in fact, Variable 3, which was left out of the equation, explains the situation. Early medical studies that found an apparent relationship between cholesterol and heart disease were criticized because the relationship may have been spurious. Numerous other variables that may have been correlated with both cholesterol and heart disease, such as age and diet, were left out. Moreover, later studies found there were two types of cholesterol, each with opposite effects on heart disease.

It is important to have a good model for constructing regression equations. A cause-and-effect relation should exist between the predictor variable and the dependent variable. If such a relation does not exist, it is still possible to obtain a good fit and a regression estimate that, on the surface, appears significant. However, there is no assurance that the relation will continue into the future.

For example, there may be a good *statistical* relation between indirect labor costs and energy costs. One might create a regression equation using such a relation and find that the regression explains much of the change in indirect labor costs. However, there is no *logical* relation between the two costs. Both indirect labor and energy costs may, in part, be driven by inflationary factors, but there is no cause-and-effect relationship between them.

*Self-Study
Question*

3 The data from self-study question 1 yields the following computer output: a multiple linear regression with overhead as the dependent variable; and direct labor-hours, direct labor costs, machine-hours, and units of output as independent

variables. Explain the paradox between the high adjusted R^2 value and low *t*-statistics.

Dependent variable = Overhead
Independent variables: DL-hrs., DL cost, Mach.-hrs., units produced
R-square = .894   Adjusted *R*-square = .871
24 observations

Variable		Estimated-	Standard	
Name	No.	Coefficient	Error	*t*-Statistic
DL-hrs.	1	3.1337	2.7705	1.1311
DL cost	2	.30600	.32961	.92839
Mach.-hrs.	3	.79964	2.0756	.38526
Units produced	4	−.09679	12.539	.00772
Intercept		−111.91	17.246	−6.4892

Correlation matrix
of coefficients:

Variable				
1	1.000			
2	.970	1.000		
3	.973	.962	1.000	
4	.982	.970	.980	1.000
	1 DL-hrs.	2 DL cost	3 Mach.-hrs.	4 units produced

The solution to this question is at the end of this chapter on page 404.

Regression Must Be Used with Caution

A regression estimate is still only an estimate. Computerized statistical techniques sometimes have an aura of truth about them that is undeserved. In fact, a regression estimate may be little better than an eyeball estimate based on a scattergraph. Regression has advantages, however. It is objective; it provides a number of statistics not available from other methods; and it may be the only feasible method when more than one predictor is used.

Regression is so accessible that it can be used indiscriminately with unfortunate results. We recommend that users of regression (1) fully understand the methodology and its limitations; (2) specify the model, that is, the hypothesized relationship between costs and cost predictors; (3) know the characteristics of the data being used; and (4) examine a plot of the data.

COMPARISON OF COST ESTIMATES

Each cost-estimation method may yield a different estimate of the costs that are likely to result from a particular management decision. This underscores the advantages of using two or more methods to arrive at a final estimate. The different estimates of manufacturing overhead that resulted from the use of four different estimation methods for Estimators, Inc., are summarized in Illustration 10–7.

The numbers are close, but there are differences. While it is impossible to state which one is best, management may find that having all four alternatives gives the best indication of the likely range within which actual costs will fall. Moreover, by observing the range of cost estimates, management may be better able to determine whether more data need to be gathered. If decisions are the same for all four cost estimates, then management may conclude that further information gathering is not warranted.

ILLUSTRATION

Summary of Cost Estimates, Estimators, Inc.

Method	Total Estimated Costs[a]	Fixed Estimated Costs	Estimated Variable Cost
Account analysis	$2,631	$1,205	$12.40 per MH[b]
High-low	2,750	1,239	13.141 per MH
Simple regression (MH)	2,757	1,334	12.373 per MH
Multiple regression (MH + DMC[c])	2,784	1,334	4.359 per MH + .258 per DMC

a Estimated for activity levels of 115 machine hours (and for $3,680 direct materials for multiple regression).
b MH = Machine-hours.
c DMC = Direct material costs.

USE OF REGRESSION ANALYSIS TO IDENTIFY COST DRIVERS IN ACTIVITY-BASED COSTING

Regression can be particularly helpful in activity-based costing because of the need to identify which of numerous possible cost drivers is related to overhead costs.[1] Use of activity-based costing would require increasing the number of cost drivers beyond the simple one or two independent variables discussed so far. The basic concepts for using regression analysis are the same, nevertheless, whether we have two independent variables (that is, cost drivers) or many independent variables.

As this book goes to press, researchers in universities and analysts in industry are using regression analysis to identify which cost drivers to use in activity-based costing. (See the real world application for this chapter, "Using Regression Analysis to Identify Manufacturing Overhead Cost Drivers and the Effect of Quality on Costs," for an example of the work being done.) Students who graduate with an understanding of regression and cost accounting, and who are able to use computer spreadsheets with regression functions, will have ample opportunities to help organizations understand their costs better. Of course, it is important to remember that statistical analysis merely aids our understanding of the relation between costs and causes of costs; it does not substitute for experience, good sense, and managerial judgment.

Where does one start in identifying possible cost drivers? The answer to that question is simple—start with people who are familiar with the day-to-day operations of the company, such as supervisors and department heads. In addition, we think you will find it helpful to refer to the discussion in Chapter 7 about the hierarchy of product cost analysis (Illustration 7–10). Finally, note that research to date has found overhead costs to be associated with cost drivers reflecting (1) complexity of operations (for example, number of setups, number of different products), (2) volume, and (3) capacity (for example, the value of buildings and equipment).

---

[1] See the article by A. M. Novin, "Applying Overhead: How to Find the Right Bases and Rates," *Management Accounting,* March 1992 for a discussion of the use of the Lotus 1-2-3® regression function to find cost drivers and overhead rates.

REAL WORLD APPLICATION

*Using Regression Analysis to Identify Manufacturing Overhead Cost Drivers and the Effect of Quality on Costs**

Based on a study of 31 manufacturing plants in three industries—electronics, automobile components, and machinery—researchers at the University of Minnesota used regression analysis to identify manufacturing overhead cost drivers. Their approach treated manufacturing overhead cost as the dependent variable, and various possible cost drivers as independent variables. Each plant was a separate data point, so there were 31 observations in total. The researchers' model appeared to fit the data well, with an adjusted R-square of .779; the coefficients on several independent variables (that is, cost drivers) had t-statistics greater than 2.0.

As we have discussed in previous chapters (Chapter 7, in particular), many accountants and managers believe simple volume-based overhead cost drivers, like machine-hours and labor-hours, do not fully capture the causes of overhead costs. They argue that other factors, such as the complexity of the production process, also cause overhead costs, and that activity-based costing is superior to traditional volume-based overhead allocation methods. Others disagree about the need to identify additional cost drivers, claiming that more complicated accounting systems will not solve most business problems.

Despite often intense arguments for and against expanding the set of cost drivers, there has been little empirical work to provide guidance to managers and accountants. One previous study, using regression analysis, found a statistically significant relation between overhead costs and volume-based cost drivers, but only a limited association between overhead costs and cost drivers based on the complexity of the production process.† The University of Minnesota researchers, however, found a strong relation between overhead costs and both complexity-based cost drivers and volume-based cost drivers.

The researchers also found that plants implementing new manufacturing methods, namely, just-in-time production, total quality management, and the use of work teams for problem solving on the shop floor, had lower overhead costs than those that had not implemented these new manufacturing methods, all other things being equal. This result is particularly important in view of questions whether improved quality increases or decreases costs.

---

* Based on the paper by R. J. Banker, G. Potter, and R. G. Schroeder, "An Empirical Analysis of Manufacturing Overhead Cost Drivers." Paper presented at the American Accounting Association Annual Meetings, Washington, D.C., August 1992.
† G. Foster and M. Gupta, "Manufacturing Overhead Cost Driver Analysis," *Journal of Accounting and Economics* 12, no. 1.

LEARNING CURVES

Companies have found a systematic nonlinear cost function when employees gain experience performing a particular task. As their experience increases, their productivity improves and costs per unit decrease. Experience, or learning, obviously affects direct labor costs, but it also affects costs that are related to direct labor, like supervision and many others. In some cases, materials costs may be affected due to reductions in spoilage and waste.

Learning Phenomenon A systematic relationship between the amount of experience in performing a task and the time required to carry out the task.

The **learning phenomenon** often occurs when new production methods are introduced, when new products (either goods or services) are made, and when new employees are hired. For example, the effect of learning on the cost of aircraft manufacturing is well known. Manufacturers of products for the aerospace industry, like Martin Marietta and Grumman, write contracts that recognize the effect of learning by establishing a lower cost for the second item of an order than for the first, a lower cost for the third than for the second, and so forth.

Learning Curve The mathematical or graphic representation of the learning phenomenon.

For example, National Electronics, Inc., makes an electronic navigation guidance system that is used for spacecraft, aircraft, and submarines. The direct labor to make the system is subject to an 80 percent *cumulative* **learning curve.** This means that the unit *average* time required for two units is 80 percent of the time required for one unit; the unit *average* time for four units is 80 percent of the *average* time required per unit for two units; and so forth.

The first unit of a production batch, or run, of guidance systems is estimated to require 1,250 direct labor-hours. If the 80 percent cumulative learning curve is used, then the *average* for two units is estimated to be 1,000 hours (.80 × 1,250 hours), a total of 2,000 hours for both units. Thus, the second unit takes 750 hours to produce (750 = 2,000 − 1,250). Four units would take an average of 800 hours each (.80 × 1,000 hours), or a total of 3,200 hours. This means that a total of 1,200 hours (3,200 − 2,000) must be expended to produce the third and fourth units. As the labor-hours change, so do the costs that are affected by labor-hours.

Mathematically, the learning curve effect can be expressed as:[2]

$$Y = aX^b$$

where

Y = *Average* number of labor-hours required for the first X units
a = Number of labor-hours required for the first unit
X = Cumulative number of units produced
b = Index of learning equal to the log of the learning rate divided by the log of 2; for the example with an 80 percent cumulative learning rate, $b = -.322$

Thus, the number of labor-hours for the National Electronics example could be derived as follows:

X	Average (Y)	Total	Marginal	Computations for Y
	Number of Labor-Hours			
1	1,250	1,250	1,250	
2	1,000 (80% × 1,250)	2,000[a]	750[b]	$Y = 1,250 \times (2^{-.322}) = 1,000$
3	878	2,634[a]	634[b]	$Y = 1,250 \times (3^{-.322}) = 878$
4	800 (80% × 1,000)	3,200	566	$Y = 1,250 \times (4^{-.322}) = 800$
.	.	.	.	.
.	.	.	.	.
.	.	.	.	.
8	640 (80% × 800)	5,120		$Y = 1,250 \times (8^{-.322}) = 640$

[a] 2,000 = 2 units × 1,000 hours, 2,634 = 3 units × 878 hours, and so on.
[b] 750 = 2,000 hours − 1,250 hours, 634 = 2,634 hours − 2,000 hours, and so on.

Illustration 10–8 presents the total and average labor-hours required for National Electronics, Inc. The curvilinear nature of the relationship between activity volume and labor-hours shows that the learning effects are large

---

[2] In performing these calculations, note that many calculations have logarithm (log) and power functions (Y^X or X^Y).

ILLUSTRATION

10–8

*Labor-Hours and
Volume Graphs, National
Electronics, Inc.*

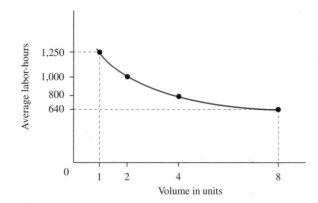

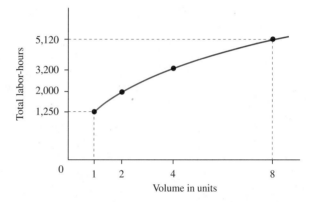

initially but become increasingly smaller as employees learn more about how to make the product.

The function

$$Y = aX^b$$

is curvilinear, as shown in Illustration 10–8. The function is linear when expressed in logs because

$$\log Y = \log a + b \log X$$

The function is linear when plotted on log-log paper as shown in Illustration 10–9. A good approximation of the average labor-hours required for X units can be obtained from a plot on log-log paper.

Assume that National Electronics, Inc., estimates the variable cost of producing each unit as follows:

Direct materials cost . . . . $40,000 per unit

Direct labor . . . . $20 per hour

Variable manufacturing overhead . . . . . . $1,000 per unit plus 60 percent of direct labor costs

10–9

Labor-Hours and Volume—
Log-Log Relationship

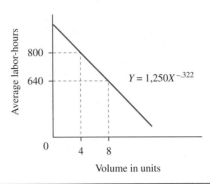

So, the variable manufacturing cost per unit is estimated to be:

Unit No.	Direct Materials	Direct Labor	Variable Manufacturing Overhead	Total Variable Manufacturing Cost of the Unit
1	$40,000	$20 × 1,250 hours = $25,000	$1,000 + (.6 × $25,000) = $16,000	$81,000
2	40,000	$20 × 750 hours = $15,000	$1,000 + (.6 × $15,000) = $10,000	65,000
3	40,000	$20 × 634 hours = $12,680	$1,000 + (.6 × $12,680) = $8,608	61,288
4	40,000	$20 × 566 hours = $11,320	$1,000 + (.6 × $11,320) = $7,792	59,112

Applications of Learning
Curves to Accounting

The learning phenomenon applies to time; thus, it could affect any costs that are a function of time. Hourly labor costs per unit would be affected, while straight piecework pay per unit would not. Any overhead costs that are affected by labor time would also be affected. For example, if indirect labor is a variable cost, reductions in worker time could result in a reduction in indirect labor.

Whenever costs are estimated, the potential impact of learning should be considered. The learning phenomenon can affect costs used in inventory valuation, costs used in decision making, and costs used in performance evaluation. However, learning curves usually apply only to the early phases of production. After the steady state is achieved, costs tend to stabilize.

Inventory Valuation

Failing to recognize learning effects can have some unexpected consequences, as shown in this example. Suppose production of a new product starts in January and continues through the year. The direct materials cost is $10 per unit throughout the year. Because of learning, the labor-hours (cost) per unit drops from 1 hour, at $16 per hour, in January to .25 hour in May. Manufacturing overhead, which is all fixed, is $8,000. The accountants estimate that 1,000 units will be produced in January, requiring 1,000 direct labor-hours, so they apply this overhead to units at the rate of $8 per hour for inventory valuation. This same rate is (mistakenly) used throughout the year. In May of the same year, 1,000 units were produced, requiring only 250 direct labor-hours. Fixed manufacturing overhead was $8,000. As shown in

ILLUSTRATION

10-10

Effect of Learning on Inventory Valuation

	January	May Is	May Should Be
		Unit Inventory Value	
Direct materials	$10	$10	$10
Direct labor	16 (= 1 hour × $16)	4 (= .25 hour × $16)	4
Manufacturing overhead applied	8 (= 1 hour × $8)	2 (= .25 hour × $8)	8
	$34	$16	$22

Illustration 10–10, the overhead was applied at $8 per hour, which turned out to be only $2 per unit. The amount of overhead applied per unit should have been $8 per unit, like it was in January.

Decision Making

AAA Company is considering producing a new product. Fixed costs would be unaffected by the product. The variable cost of making and selling the first unit of the product is $40 per unit, while the selling price is $38. At first glance, the product appears unprofitable because it doesn't even cover variable costs. However, because of learning, the variable cost will drop from $40 to $20 by the end of the first year of production, making it much more profitable.

Performance Evaluation

First National Bank has developed labor time and cost standards for some of its clerical activities. These activities were subject to the learning curve phenomenon. The bank management observed that time spent on these activities systematically exceeded the standard. Upon investigating the problem, management found high personnel turnover, which meant the activities were carried out by inexperienced people. After changes were made in personnel policy, personnel turnover was reduced and the jobs were staffed with more experienced people. Hence, the time spent on clerical activities no longer exceeded standards.

 *Self-Study Question*

4 A company recently recorded the following costs, which are subject to a 75 percent cumulative learning effect.

Cumulative Number of Units Produced	Average Manufacturing Cost Per Unit	Total Manufacturing Costs
1	$1,333	$1,333
2	?	?
4	?	?
8	?	?
16	?	?

Complete the chart by filling in the cost amounts for volumes of 2, 4, 8, and 16 units.

The solutions to this question is at the end of the chapter on page 404.

The solutions to this question is at the end of the chapter on page 404.

SUMMARY

Accurate cost estimation helps management to make informed decisions concerning the incurrence of future costs and how future costs may vary if conditions change. This chapter discusses four methods of cost estimation: (1) account analysis, (2) engineering estimates, (3) scattergraph and high-low estimates, and (4) statistical methods (usually employing regression analysis). Different methods of estimation are likely to produce different estimates of costs. Consequently, it is often desirable to use more than one approach and to permit management to apply its own best estimate to those arrived at by the controller's staff.

Account analysis calls for judgment determination of whether a cost is fixed or variable. The advantages of the method are its relative ease of application and its use of managerial experience and judgment. The disadvantage is that heavy reliance on judgmental decisions may cause estimates to be biased toward the decision makers' personal biases or perceptions.

Engineering estimates involve careful measurement of the actual cost-causing process. Engineers break the process into parts and compare what they observe to standards, specifications, and established scientific relationships. The advantage of the engineering approach is that it can detail each step required to perform an operation. This provides a useful means of reviewing a company's total manufacturing process. Disadvantages are that the engineering approach is often quite expensive and that engineering estimates are often based on particular past conditions that may not occur in the future.

Scattergraphs and high-low estimates are past cost behaviors and their relation to some activity measure to estimate future costs given a specific activity level. This approach (and any other approach that uses past data) is limited to future estimates that are made within the relevant range of past activity levels. The focus of the regression portion of the chapter is on obtaining a basic understanding of the approach. Data are plotted on a scattergraph. Regression forms a mathematically determined line of best fit (minimal variation). We must be careful to find any unrepresentative outliers, and to restrict cost estimates to the relevant range. The correlation coefficient (R) and the adjusted R-square help to indicate the amount of the cost variation that is explained by the predictors (independent variables). Simple regression uses only one predictor, while multiple regression uses more than one predictor to help explain a particular cost.

The systematic relation between labor time and experience is a common nonlinear relationship between costs and activity. This learning curve phenomenon implies that unit costs go down as more and more units are made (up to a point) because labor time per unit decreases. The potential impact of the phenomenon should be considered whenever costs are estimated.

**TERMS
AND CONCEPTS**

The following terms and concepts should be familiar to you after reading this chapter:

Account Analysis, *361*

Adjusted *R*-Square, *371*

Correlation Coefficient, *371*

Dependent Variable, *369*

Engineering Estimates, *364*

High-Low Cost Estimation, *366*

Independent Variable, *369*

Learning Curve, *380*

Learning Phenomenon, *379*

Multicollinearity, *373*

Regression, *368*

Scattergraph, *366*

***t*-Statistic,** *373*

APPENDIX

Technical Notes on Regression

This appendix discusses technical issues that often arise when regression analysis is used.

Confidence Intervals for Cost Estimates

When making predictions about future costs, it is almost impossible to develop an estimate that will be exactly equal to the costs that are finally incurred. While it is not possible to eliminate all estimation error, it is possible to place bounds on an estimate so that a decision maker can know the range of likely costs. These bounds are usually expressed in the form of a *prediction interval*, sometimes called a *confidence interval*.

A prediction interval represents a range within which the actual cost is expected to fall a specified percentage of the time. Thus, a 95 percent prediction interval would represent a range within which the actual costs are expected to fall 95 percent of the time. The boundaries of a prediction interval are based on the assumption that the residuals from a regression are normally distributed. If this assumption holds, then the boundaries are equal to the predicted Y value plus or minus the standard error of the estimate of Y times the t-statistic for the specified prediction level. This may be expressed mathematically as:

$$Y \pm t \times SE_Y$$

The wider the desired prediction interval, the larger the value of t, all other things being equal.

The standard error of estimate (SE_Y) for a simple regression is:

$$SE_Y = SE \sqrt{1 + \frac{1}{n} + \frac{(X' - \overline{X})^2}{\Sigma(X_i - \overline{X})^2}}$$

where

SE = Standard error of the regression, given in the regression output and measuring the variation of errors around the regression line
n = Number of observations
X' = Value of X for which the estimate is desired
$\overline{X}$ = Mean of the X values in the data set
X_i = Value of each X in the data set

The more distant the specified X value is from the mean, the wider the prediction interval.

For example, assume management of Estimators, Inc., had estimated the overhead costs for 115 machine-hours as follows:

$$Y = \$1,334 + \$12.373 \text{ per MH}$$
$$= \$1,334 + \$12.373 \times 115 \text{ MH}$$
$$= \underline{\$2,757}$$

The computer output for the regression indicated a standard error for the regression of \$182. The standard error of estimate for a Y based on 115 machine-hours is \$192, computed as follows:

$$SE_Y = \$182 \times \sqrt{1 + \frac{1}{15} + \frac{(115 - 91.6)^2}{11,455.6}}$$

$$= \$182 \times \sqrt{1 + .06667 + .04780}$$

$$= \$182 \times 1.05568$$

$$= \underline{\$192}$$

The computer would provide the information necessary to construct the prediction interval and, in many cases, would compute the interval itself. In this example, we obtain the following output from the computer (or from a statistics book for the t-statistic):

Standard error of the regression $182
Standard error of estimate (115 hours) $192
t-statistic for 95% confidence interval, $n = 15$; $n - 2 = 13$ . . . 2.160

We compute the prediction interval as:

$$\$2,757 \pm (\$192 \times 2.160) = \$2,757 \pm \$415$$

The upper limit of the prediction interval is:

$$\$3,172 = \$2,757 + \$415$$

and the lower limit is:

$$\$2,342 = \$2,757 - \$415$$

which means that we are 95 percent confident that the overhead will be between \$2,342 and \$3,172 when an activity level of 115 machine-hours is attained.

Assumptions about the Residuals

The differences between the *estimated* Y values (found on the regression line) and the *actual Y*s are called *residuals*. If a residual is random, its expected value is zero for any observation. There are three important assumptions about the residuals: (1) The residuals are independent of each other; (2) the variance of the residuals is constant over the range of independent variables; and (3) the residuals are normally distributed. Violation of these assumptions makes certain inferences about confidence intervals and the significance levels of b estimates questionable.

If the residuals are not normally distributed, the residual for any observation may be statistically related to the residual for another observation. The expected value for the residual is not zero. One such condition in which residuals are related to each other, because observations are related to each other over time, is known as *serial correlation* or *autocorrelation*. When the residuals are related to each other, the correlation coefficients and the presence of autocorrelation may be tested by using the Durbin-Watson statistic, which is usually provided on the output when regression is run on a computer. Another approach is to obtain a plot of the residuals over time from the regression program. If there is a pattern in the plotted residuals, then an autocorrelation problem exists.

The variance in cost data may not be constant over all levels of costs. This condition is known as *heteroscedasticity*.

To determine if heteroscedasticity is present, a plot of the residuals over different values of *Y* is needed. If the scatter of residuals is not constant over these *Y* values, the assumption of constant variance may be rejected. The problem may be cured by transforming the variables (*X*s and *Y*s) to their logarithms or square roots, or by constructing a regression with a new set of variables. Alternatively, one might adjust the confidence intervals at different activity levels.

We mention these assumptions because they are often violated in cost data. Consequently, we should be careful about the inferences that we draw from regressions. You should consult statistics books for more information about how to deal with violations of these assumptions.

QUESTIONS

10-1   Which method of cost estimation is not usually based on company records?

10-2   The following costs are labeled fixed or variable according to a typical designation in accounting. Identify the circumstances under which any of these costs would behave in a manner opposite to that listed:
  a.   Direct labor—variable.
  b.   Equipment depreciation—fixed.
  c.   Utilities (with a minimum charge)—variable.
  d.   Supervisory salaries—fixed.
  e.   Indirect materials purchased in given sizes that become spoiled within a few days—variable.

10-3   What is the connection between the relevant range and the range of observations included in a data set for cost-estimation purposes?

10-4   Why would a long-time executive prefer account analysis to statistical cost-estimation methods?

10-5   If one simply wishes to prepare a cost estimate using regression analysis and enters data into a program to compute regression estimates, what problems might be encountered?

10-6   When preparing cost estimtes for account analysis purposes, should the costs be extracted from the historical accounting records?

10-7   How can one compensate for the effects of price instability when preparing cost estimates using high-low or regression techniques?

10-8   Under what conditions would the engineering estimates technique be preferred to other estimation techniques?

10-9   When using cost-estimation methods based on past data, what are the tradeoffs between gathering more data and gathering less?

10-10   The scattergraph and the regression methods seem to go hand in hand. Why?

10-11   What problems might arise when multiple independent variables are used?

10-12   When using past data to predict a cost that has fixed and variable components, it is possible to have an equation with a negative intercept. Does this mean that at a zero production level the company will make money on its fixed costs? Explain.

10-13   Refer to this chapter's real world application. What did the University of Minnesota researchers find about the relation between complexity-based cost drivers and overhead costs? What about the relation between new manufacturing methods and overhead costs?

10-14   (Appendix) What considerations need to be included when constructing a confidence interval for a specific cost estimate (Y)?

10-15   (Appendix) A decision maker is interested in obtaining a cost estimate based on a regression equation. There are no problems with changes in prices, costs, technology, or relationships between activity and cost. Only one variable is to be used. What caveats might be in order if a regression is prepared for this purpose?

EXERCISES

10-16   Methods of Estimating Costs— Account Analysis
(L.O.1)

The accounting records of a company report the following manufacturing costs for the past year:

Direct materials	$210,000
Direct labor	175,000
Manufacturing overhead	394,000

Production was 70,000 units. Fixed manufacturing overhead was $240,000.

For the coming year, the direct materials costs are expected to increase by 20 percent, excluding any effects of volume changes. Direct labor rates are scheduled to increase by 4 percent. Fixed manufacturing overhead is expected to increase 7.5 percent, and variable manufacturing overhead per unit is expected to remain the same.

Required:

a.   Prepare a cost estimate for an activity level of 80,000 units of product this year.

b.   Determine the costs per unit for last year and for this year.

10-17   Methods of Estimating Costs— Account Analysis
(L.O.1)

The accounting records of a company indicate the following manufacturing costs were incurred in Year 1:

Direct materials	$615,000
Direct labor	479,000
Manufacturing overhead	760,000

These costs were incurred to produce 50,000 units of product. Fixed manufacturing overhead amounts to $475,000.

For Year 2, direct materials costs are expected to increase by 10 percent per unit. Direct labor costs are due to increase by 15 percent per unit. Variable manufacturing costs are expected to remain constant per unit, while fixed manufacturing overhead for Year 2 is expected to increase by 5 percent.

Required:

a. Year 2 production is estimated to be 65,000 units. What are the estimated direct materials, direct labor, variable overhead, and fixed overhead costs for Year 2.

b. Determine the total manufacturing costs per unit for Year 1 and Year 2.

10–18 Methods of Estimating Costs— High-Low
(L.O.2)

The Paradise Cruiselines Company provides you with the following cost data for maintenance work on its fleet of cruiseships:

Hours Operated per Month	Maintenance Cost ($ millions)
5,200	$1.2
6,800	1.4
8,400	1.6

Required:

a. Use the high-low method to estimate the fixed cost per month and the variable cost per hour.

b. What would be Paradise's estimated costs if they operate 8,000 hours this month? 10,000 hours?

10–19 Methods of Estimating Costs— High-Low
(L.O.2)

Yamahonda Motors Company makes motorcycles. Management wants to estimate overhead costs to plan its operations. A recent trade publication revealed that overhead costs tend to vary with machine-hours and/or materials costs. To check this, they collected the following data for the past 12 months:

Month No.	Machine-Hours	Materials Cost	Overhead Costs
1	175	$4,750	$4,500
2	170	4,600	4,225
3	160	4,200	3,780
4	190	5,900	5,250
5	175	4,600	4,800
6	200	5,250	5,100
7	160	4,350	4,450
8	150	4,350	4,200
9	210	6,000	5,475
10	180	4,950	4,760
11	170	4,450	4,325
12	145	3,800	3,975

Required:

a. Use the high-low method to estimate the fixed and variable portions of overhead costs based on machine-hours.

b. If the plant is planning to operate at a level of 190 machine-hours next period, what would be the estimated overhead costs? (Assume no inflation.)

10–20 Methods of Estimating Costs— Scattergraph
(L.O.2)

Prepare a scattergraph based on the overhead and direct machine-hour data in exercise 10–19.

10–21 Methods of Estimating Costs— Scattergraph
(L.O.2)

Prepare a scattergraph based on the overhead and materials cost data in exercise 10–19.

10–22 Estimating Costs— Simple Regression
(L.O.3)

Simple regression results from the data of Yamahonda Motors Company (exercise 10–19) are as follows:

Equation:

Overhead = \$348.17 + (\$24,298 × Machine-hours)

Statistical data:

Correlation coefficient 904

R-square 818

Required:

Prepare an estimate of overhead if the company expects to use 190 machine-hours for the next period and costs are stable.

10–23 Estimating Costs—Simple Regression (L.O.3)

Megolith Co. has developed a regression equation to analyze the behavior of its maintenance costs (Q) as a function of machine-hours (Z). The following equation was developed using 30 monthly observations:

$$Q = \$6,000 + \$5.25Z$$

Required:

If 1,000 machine-hours are worked in one month, the estimate of total maintenance costs would be:

(1) \$11,250.
(2) \$10,125.
(3) \$ 5,250.
(4) \$ 4,725.

(CPA adapted)

10–24 Estimating Costs—Multiple Regression (L.O.3)

Multiple regression results from the data of Yamahonda Motors Company (exercise 10–19) are as follows:

Equation:

Overhead = \$694.24 + (\$9.1840 × Machine-hours) + (.47833 × Materials cost)

Statistical data:

Correlation coefficient 935

R-square .874

Assume that management predicts the materials cost to be \$5,000 and machine-hours to be 190 for the coming period.

Required:

Use the multiple regression results to prepare an estimate of overhead costs for the coming period.

10–25 Interpreting Regression Results—Multiple-Choice (L.O.4)

Horizon Company is making plans for the introduction of a new product that it will sell for \$6 a unit. The following estimates have been made for manufacturing costs on 100,000 units to be produced the first year:

Direct materials \$50,000

Direct labor 40,000 (the labor rate is \$4 an hour × 10,000 hours)

Manufacturing overhead costs have not yet been estimated for the new product, but monthly data on total production and overhead costs for the past 24 months have been analyzed using simple linear regression. The following results were derived from the simple regression and will provide the basis for overhead cost estimates for the new product.

Simple Regression Analysis Results

Dependent variable—Factory overhead costs

Independent variable—Direct labor-hours

Computed values:

Intercept \$55,000

Coefficient of independent variable . . . . \$ 3.20

Coefficient of correlation 953

R^2 908

Required:

a. What percentage of the variation in overhead costs is explained by the independent variable?
   (1) 90.8 percent.
   (2) 42 percent.
   (3) 48.8 percent.
   (4) 95.3 percent.
   (5) Some other amount.

b. The total overhead cost for an estimated activity level of 20,000 direct labor-hours would be:
   (1) $55,000.
   (2) $64,000.
   (3) $82,000.
   (4) $119,000.
   (5) Some other amount.

c. What is the expected contribution margin per *unit* to be earned during the first year on 100,000 units of the new product? (Assume all marketing and administrative costs are fixed.)
   (1) $4.78.
   (2) $4.89.
   (3) $4.14.
   (4) $5.10.
   (5) Some other amount.

d. How much is the variable manufacturing cost per *unit*, using the variable overhead estimated by the regression (and assuming direct materials and direct labor are variable costs)?
   (1) $.90.
   (2) $1.11.
   (3) $1.22.
   (4) $3.
   (5) Some other amount.

e. What is the manufacturing cost equation implied by these results, where *x* refers to *units* produced?
   (1) $TC = \$40,000 + \$1.11x$.
   (2) $TC = \$55,000 + \$1.22x$.
   (3) $TC = \$145,000 + \$3.20x$.
   (4) Some other equation.

(CMA adapted)

10–26 Interpreting Regression Results
(L.O.4)

The advertising manager of the Jarvis Company wants to know if the company's advertising program is successful. The manager used a pocket calculator to estimate the relation between advertising expenditures (the independent variable) and sales dollars. Monthly data for the past two years were entered into the calculator. The regression results indicated the following equation:

Sales dollars = $845,000 − ($520 × Advertising)
Correlation coefficient = −.902

These results might imply that the advertising was reducing sales. The manager was about to conclude that statistical methods were so much nonsense when you walked into the room.

Required:

Help the manager. What might cause the negative relationship between advertising expenditures and sales?

10–27 Interpreting Regression Results— Simple Regression
(L.O.4)

A fast-food restaurant, Burger Bell, is estimating overhead based on food cost. Data were gathered for the past 24 months and entered into a regression program. The following output was obtained:

Equation:

Intercept $37,650

Slope 1.150

Statistical data:

Correlation coefficient 872
R-square 760
Adjusted R-square 731

The company is planning to operate at a level of $28,000 of food costs per month for the coming year.

Required:

a. Use the regression output to write the overhead cost equation.

b. Based on the cost equation, compute the estimated overhead cost per month for the coming year.

10–28 Interpreting Regression Data (L.O.4)

Gillespie Insurance Company needs to forecast its Personnel Department costs. The following output was obtained from a regression program used to estimate Personnel Department costs as a function of the number of employees:

Equation:

Personnel costs = $8,420 + ($492 × Employees)

Statistical data:

Correlation coefficient 923
R-square 852
Adjusted R-square 834
Standard error of slope 34.250
t-statistic for slope 11.912

Monthly data for the past two years were used to construct these estimates. Cost relationships are expected to be the same for the coming period.

Required:

a. What are the estimated personnel costs for 2,800 employees?

b. Construct a 95 percent confidence interval for the slope coefficient. (Use $t = 2.074$.)

10–29 Learning Curves (L.O.6)

Apogee Electronics manufactures high-technology instruments for spacecraft. The company recorded the following costs subject to a 75 percent cumulative learning effect.

Cumulative Number of Units Produced, X	Average Manufacturing Costs per Unit	Total Manufacturing Costs
1	$2,000	$2,000
2	1,500	3,000
4	?	?
8	?	?
16	?	?

Required:

Complete the chart by filling in the cost amounts for volumes of 4, 8, and 16 units.

10–30 Learning Curves (L.O.6)

Holte Manufacturing estimates the variable cost of producing each unit of a product as follows:

Materials . . . . $1,500 per unit

Direct labor . . . . $30 per hour

Variable overhead . . . $200 per unit plus 75% of direct labor costs

The first unit requires 100 hours to make. Labor time is subject to an 80 percent cumulative learning curve; therefore, $Y = aX^{-.322}$.

Required:

Compute the variable costs of making two units and four units.

PROBLEMS

10–31 Methods of Estimating Costs— High-Low, Scattergraph, and Regression

The Franklin Plant of the Ramon Company manufactures electrical components. Plant management has experienced difficulties with fluctuating monthly overhead costs. Management wants to be able to estimate overhead costs accurately to plan its operations and its financial needs. A trade association publication reports that for companies manufacturing electrical components, overhead tends to vary with machine-hours.

A member of the controller's staff proposed that the behavior pattern of these overhead costs be determined to improve cost estimation.

Another staff member suggested that a good starting place for determining cost behavior patterns would be to analyze historical data.

Following this suggestion, monthly data were gathered on machine-hours and overhead costs for the past two years. There were no major changes in operations over this period of time. The raw data are as follows:

Month Number	Machine-Hours	Overhead Costs
1	20,000	$84,000
2	25,000	99,000
3	22,000	89,500
4	23,000	90,000
5	20,000	81,500
6	19,000	75,500
7	14,000	70,500
8	10,000	64,500
9	12,000	69,000
10	17,000	75,000
11	16,000	71,500
12	19,000	78,000
13	21,000	86,000
14	24,000	93,000
15	23,000	93,000
16	22,000	87,000
17	20,000	80,000
18	18,000	76,500
19	12,000	67,500
20	13,000	71,000
21	15,000	73,500
22	17,000	72,500
23	15,000	71,000
24	18,000	75,000

These data were entered into a computer regression program. The following output was obtained:

Coefficient of correlation	.9544
R-square	.9109
Coefficients of the equation:	
Intercept	39,859.000
Independent variable (slope)	2.1549

Required:

a. Use the high-low method to estimate the Franklin Plant overhead costs.

b. Prepare a scattergraph showing the overhead costs plotted against machine-hours.

c. Use the results of the regression analysis to prepare the cost-estimation equation and to prepare a cost estimate for 22,500 machine-hours.

(CMA adapted)

10–32 Methods of Cost Estimation—Account Analysis, Simple and Multiple Regression

Mountain View Outdoor Products Corporation has prepared a schedule of estimated overhead costs for the coming year. This schedule was prepared on the assumption that production would equal 80,000 units. Costs have been classified as fixed or variable according to the judgment of the controller.

The following overhead items and the classification as fixed or variable form the basis for the overhead cost schedule:

Item	Total Cost
Indirect materials	$ 37,500 (all variable)
Indirect labor	194,200 ($171,000 fixed)
Building occupancy	236,420 (all fixed)
Power	27,210 (all variable)
Equipment depreciation	181,000 (all fixed)
Equipment maintenance	24,330 ($8,500 fixed)
Personal property taxes	14,100 ($6,350 fixed)
Data processing	11,220 ($9,470 fixed)
Technical support	16,940 (all fixed)
Total estimated overhead	$742,920

In the past, the overhead costs have been related to production levels. However, price instability has led management to suggest that explicit consideration be given to including an appropriate price index in the cost equation. While management realizes that to estimate future costs using a regression model that includes both production and a price index as independent variables requires predicting a future value not only for production but for the price index as well, at least some recognition would be given to the dramatic price changes that have been experienced in the past few years. For cost-estimation purposes, it is assumed that the next value of the index will be the same as the last period value of the index (that is, 113).

Following management instructions, data were gathered on past costs, production levels, and an appropriate price index. These data are:

Overhead Costs	Production (units)	Price Index
$718,480	62,800	89
735,110	72,800	90
768,310	93,400	93
717,670	56,900	95
715,960	58,800	98
726,880	69,000	100
753,420	87,000	101
777,640	98,000	103
720,410	59,200	103
718,100	62,600	106
736,800	73,100	108
714,220	60,400	113

There have been no significant changes in operations over the period covered by these data nor are there any significant changes expected in the coming period.

When the data above were entered into a regression program using only the production level as the independent variable, the following results were obtained:

Equation:
  Overhead = $626,547 + ($1.504 × Production units)

Statistical data:

  Correlation coefficient 988

  R-square 976

  Adjusted *R*-square 974

When both predictors were entered in the regression program, the following results were obtained:

MULTIPLE REGRESSION RESULTS:

Equation:
  Overhead = $632,640 + ($1.501 × Production) − ($59.067 × Index)

Statistical data:

  Correlation coefficient (multiple *R*)   .988

  R-square   .976

  Adjusted *R*-square   .972

Correlation matrix:

	Production	Index
Production	1.00	− .087
Index	− .087	1.00

Required:

a. Prepare a cost-estimation equation using the account analysis approach.

b. Use the high-low method to prepare a cost estimate for the 80,000 units of activity expected in the coming period.

c. Prepare a cost estimate for 80,000 units using simple linear regression.

d. Use the multiple regression results to prepare an estimate of overhead costs for 80,000 units for the coming period.

e. Comment on which method you think is more appropriate under the circumstances.

10–33 Interpreting Regression Results— Simple Regression (computer optional)

Your company is preparing an estimate of its production costs for the coming period. The controller estimates that direct materials costs are $7.35 per unit and that direct labor costs are $15.40 per hour. Overhead is applied on the basis of direct labor costs. However, estimating total overhead is difficult.

The controller's office estimated overhead costs at $300 for fixed costs and $12 per unit for variable costs. Your nemesis on the staff, Farleigh O. Tuvvit, suggested that the company use the regression approach. Farleigh has already done the analysis on a home computer and reports that the "correct" cost equation is:

Overhead = $883 + $10.70 per unit

Farleigh further reports that the correlation coefficient for the regression is .82 and says, "With 82 percent of the variation in overhead explained by the equation, it certainly should be adopted as the best basis for estimating costs."

When asked for the data used to generate the regression, Farleigh produces the following list:

Month	Overhead	Unit Production
1	$4,762	381
2	5,063	406
3	6,420	522
4	4,701	375
5	6,783	426
6	6,021	491
7	5,321	417
8	6,133	502
9	6,481	515
10	5,004	399
11	5,136	421
12	6,160	510
13	6,104	486

The company controller is somewhat surprised that the cost estimates would be so different. You have, therefore, been given the task of checking out Farleigh's equation.

Required:

Analyze Farleigh's results and state your reasons for supporting or rejecting Farleigh's cost equation.

10–34 Interpreting Regression Results— Multiple Regression

Malibu Products Corporation molds fiberglass into automobile bodies that are replicas of antique cars. A major component of the company's overhead is the cost of handling materials used in the molding process. It was suggested at a recent meeting of the controller and the production vice president that past data be reviewed to see if a relationship could be found between the materials-handling costs and some predictor variable. The production vice president suggested that the quantity of materials be used. The controller suggested that the dollar value of the materials be used since the dollar value would explicitly include the effects of price fluctuations. It was also noted in the discussion that some of the materials-handling costs seem to vary with the number of shipments received in a month.

Data were gathered on materials-handling costs, weight of materials received, dollar value of receipts, and number of shipments. The data were gathered for the past 18 months. Eighteen months ago, the semiautomated materials-handling equipment in use today was installed. Prior to that time, a manual system was in use.

The data appear as follows:

Materials-Handling Costs	Weight of Materials	Dollar Value of Materials	Number of Shipments
$606,000	2,425	$3,031,000	6
491,000	1,790	2,238,000	14
621,000	2,613	3,266,000	21
602,000	2,419	3,084,000	32
561,000	2,110	2,701,000	7
684,000	2,732	3,688,000	9
630,000	2,504	3,305,000	12
681,000	2,915	3,717,000	6
599,000	2,004	2,725,000	15
518,000	1,610	2,222,000	13
539,000	1,824	2,517,000	10

Materials- Handling Costs	Weight of Materials	Dollar Value of Materials	Number of Shipments
$581,000	1,996	$2,730,000	8
611,000	2,103	2,934,000	11
713,000	2,741	3,826,000	7
737,000	2,602	3,851,000	14
622,000	2,191	3,111,000	9
681,000	2,508	3,674,000	12
599,000	1,941	2,788,000	7

Based on these data, the following regressions are obtained:

REGRESSION 1: Materials-handling costs and weight of materials

Equation:
Materials-handling costs = $271,610 + ($150.80 × Weight)

Statistical data:

Correlation coefficient	.863
R-square	.745
Standard error of slope	22.054
t-statistic for slope coefficient	6.838

REGRESSION 2: Materials-handling costs and value of materials

Equation:
Materials-handling costs = $236,790 + (.123 × Value)

Statistical data:

Correlation coefficient	.975
R-square	.950
Standard error of slope	.007
t-statistic for slope coefficient	17.438

REGRESSION 3: Materials-handling costs and shipments

Equation:
Materials-handling costs = $628,680 − ($1,127.8 × Shipments)

Statistical data:

Correlation coefficient	.109
R-square	.012
Standard error of slope	2,578.4
t-statistic for slope coefficient	−.437

After reviewing the above regressions, it was decided that a multiple regression including the dollar value of materials and the weight of materials might be more useful. The results of that regression were:

REGRESSION 4

Equation:
Materials-handling costs = $251,760 + (.176 × Value) − ($78.50 × Weight)

Statistical data:

Correlation coefficient	.987
R-square	.973

Correlation matrix

	Weight	Value
Weight	1.00	.94
Value	.94	1.00

Required:

a. Prepare the cost estimate for handling 2,600 units of weight with a value of $4,005,000, using each relevant regression.

b. Which regression would you recommend, if any? Why?

10–35 Interpreting Regression Results— Multiple-Choice

Armer Company is accumulating data to prepare its annual profit plan for the coming year. The behavior pattern of the maintenance costs must be determined. The accounting staff has suggested that regression be employed to derive an equation in the form of $y = a + bx$ for maintenance costs. Data regarding maintenance-hours and costs for last year and the results of the regression analysis are as follows:

	Hours of Activity	Maintenance Costs
January	480	$ 4,200
February	320	3,000
March	400	3,600
April	300	2,820
May	500	4,350
June	310	2,960
July	320	3,030
August	520	4,470
September	490	4,260
October	470	4,050
November	350	3,300
December	340	3,160
Sum	4,800	43,200
Average	400	3,600

Average cost per hour (43,200 ÷ 4,800) = $9

Intercept	$684.65
b coefficient	$ 7.2884
Standard error of the intercept	$ 49.515
Standard error of the b coefficient	$ .12126
R-square	.99724
t-value; intercept	13.827
t-value; b	60.105

Required:

a. In the standard regression equation of $y = a + bx$, the letter b is best described as the:
   (1) Independent variable.
   (2) Dependent variable.
   (3) Constant coefficient.
   (4) Variable cost coefficient.
   (5) Correlation.

b. The letter y in the standard regression equation is best described as the:
   (1) Independent variable.
   (2) Dependent variable.
   (3) Constant coefficient.
   (4) Variable coefficient.
   (5) Correlation.

c. The letter x in the standard regression equation is best described as the:
   (1) Independent variable.
   (2) Dependent variable.
   (3) Constant coefficient.
   (4) Variable coefficient.
   (5) Correlation.

d. If the Armer Company uses the high-low method of analysis, the equation for the relationship between hours of activity and maintenance cost would be:
   (1) $y = 400 + 9.0x$.
   (2) $y = 570 + 7.5x$.

(3) $y = 3,600 + 400x$.
(4) $y = 570 + 9.0x$.
(5)   Some other equation.

e.   Based upon the data derived from the regression analysis, 420 maintenance-hours in a month would mean the maintenance would be budgeted at:
(1) $3,780.
(2) $3,461.
(3) $3,797.
(4) $3,746.
(5)   Some other amount.

f.   The correlation coefficient for the regression equation for the maintenance activities is:
(1) $34.469 \div 49.515$.
(2) $.99724$.
(3) $\sqrt{.99724}$.
(4) $(.99724)^2$.
(5)   Some other amount.

g.   The percent of the total variance that can be explained by the regression equation is:
(1)   99.724%.
(2)   69.613%.
(3)   80.982%.
(4)   99.862%.
(5)   Some other amount.

(CMA adapted)

10–36   Learning Curves

Kelly Company plans to manufacture a product called Electrocal, which requires a substantial amount of direct labor on each unit. Based on the company's experience with other products that required similar amounts of direct labor, management believes that there is a learning factor in the production process used to manufacture Electrocal.

Each unit of Electrocal requires 50 square feet of direct material at a cost of $30 per square foot, for a total material cost of $1,500. The standard direct labor rate is $25 per direct labor-hour. Variable manufacturing overhead is assigned to products at a rate of $40 per direct labor-hour. The company adds a markup of 30 percent on variable manufacturing costs in determining an initial bid price for all products.

Data on the production of the first two lots (16 units) of Electrocal are as follows:

1.   The first lot of eight units required a total of 3,200 direct labor-hours.

2.   The second lot of eight units required a total of 2,240 direct labor-hours.

Based on prior production experience, Kelly anticipates that there will be no significant improvement in production time after the first 32 units. Therefore, a standard for direct labor-hours will be established on the average hours per unit for units 17–32.

Required:

a.   What is the basic premise of the learning curve?

b.   Based upon the data presented for the first 16 units, what learning rate appears to be applicable to the direct labor required to produce Electrocal? Support your answer with appropriate calculations.

c.   Calculate the standard for direct labor-hours that Kelly Company should establish for each unit of Electrocal.

d.   After the first 32 units have been manufactured, Kelly Company was asked to submit a bid on an additional 96 units. What price should Kelly bid on this order of 96 units? Explain your answer.

e. Knowledge of the learning curve phenomenon can be a valuable management tool. Explain how management can apply the learning curve in the planning and controlling of business operations.

(CMA adapted)

10–37 Learning Curves

Xyon Company has purchased 80,000 pumps annually from Kobec, Inc. The price has increased each year, and it reached $68 per unit last year. Because the purchase price has increased significantly, Xyon management has asked that an estimate be made of the cost to manufacture pumps in its own facilities. Xyon's products consist of stampings and castings. The company has little experience with products requiring assembly.

The engineering, manufacturing, and accounting departments have prepared a report for management that included the estimate shown below for an assembly run of 10,000 units. Additional production employees would be hired to manufacture the subassembly. However, no additional equipment, space, or supervision would be needed.

The report states that total costs for 10,000 units are estimated at $957,000 or $95.70 a unit. The current purchase price is $68 a unit, so the report recommends a continued purchase of the product.

Components (outside purchases)	$120,000
Assembly labor[a]	300,000
Factory overhead[b]	450,000
General and administrative overhead[c]	87,000
Total costs	$957,000

Fixed overhead	50% of direct labor-dollars
Variable overhead	100% of direct labor-dollars
Factory overhead rate	150% of direct labor-dollars

[a] Assembly labor consists of hourly production workers.

[b] Factory overhead is applied to products on a direct labor-dollar basis. Variable overhead costs vary closely with direct labor-dollars.

[c] General and administrative overhead is applied at 10 percent of the total cost of materials (or components), assembly labor, and factory overhead.

Required:

a. Were the analysis prepared by the Engineering, Manufacturing, and Accounting Departments of Xyon Company and the recommendation to continue purchasing the pumps, which followed from the analysis, correct? Explain your answer and include any supportive calculations you consider necessary.

b. Assume Xyon Company could experience labor cost improvements on the pump assembly consistent with an 80 percent learning curve. An assembly run of 10,000 units represents the initial lot or batch for measurement purposes. Should Xyon produce the 80,000 pumps in this situation? Explain your answer.

(CMA adapted)

INTEGRATIVE CASES

10–38 Interpreting Regression Results— Process Costing

(Knowledge of equivalent units is required for this problem.) Management of Waverly Processing, Inc., wants to obtain better cost estimates to evaluate the company's operations more satisfactorily. As a new management trainee, you recall some of the cost-estimation techniques discussed in cost accounting and suggest that these techniques may be useful in this situation.

The following data are given to you for analysis purposes:

Month	Equivalent Production	Overhead
1	1,425	$12,185
2	950	9,875
3	1,130	10,450
4	1,690	15,280
5	1,006	9,915
6	834	9,150
7	982	10,133
8	1,259	11,981
9	1,385	12,045
10	1,420	13,180
11	1,125	11,910
12	980	10,431

Last month, the beginning work in process inventory contained 1,000 units that were 65 percent complete with respect to conversion costs. The Manufacturing Department transferred out 1,500 units last month. There were 1,200 units in ending inventory, and these units were 30 percent complete with respect to conversion costs.

Using the above information, you obtain the following output from your regression output:

Equation:

Intercept $3,709.000

Slope 6.487

Statistical data:

Correlation coefficient (R) 956

Adjusted R-square 904

Required:

a. Use the high-low method to estimate the overhead cost function.

b. Use the regression method to estimate the overhead cost function.

c. Compute the equivalent units of production with respect to conversion costs for last month using FIFO.

d. Use the regression results to estimate the overhead costs for last month.

10–39 Methods of Estimating Costs— Account Analysis and Regression Methods—Bayview Manufacturing Company[3]

(Computer required.) Bayview Manufacturing Company is preparing cost estimates for the coming year. The controller's staff prepared a preliminary income statement for the coming year based on an analysis of the various cost accounts and on a study of orders received. The projected income statement appeared as follows:

Sales revenue		$3,000,000
Cost of sales:		
Direct materials	$1,182,000	
Direct labor	310,000	
Factory overhead	775,000	
Total cost of sales		2,267,000
Gross profit		733,000
Marketing costs		450,000
Projected operating profit . . .		$ 283,000

[3] Adapted from a problem in "Report of the Committee on the Measurement Methods Content of the Accounting Cirriculum," *Supplement to Volume XLVI of The Accounting Review.*

Bayview produces three products: A, B, and C. A profit per unit for each product has been prepared by management and appears as follows:

	A	B	C
Sale price	$20.00	$10.00	$30.00
Less:			
Direct materials	7.00	3.75	16.60
Direct labor	2.00	1.00	3.50
Factory overhead	5.00	2.50	8.75
Marketing	3.00	1.50	4.50
Net unit profit	$ 3.00	$ 1.25	$ (3.35)

On the basis of this information, the company planning committee decided that as few Cs should be produced as possible. Moreover, the committee recommended that the company emphasize the production of A and perhaps start a promotional campaign to increase sales of A.

Before a final recommendation on the plan, the management planning committee asked the controller's office to make certain that these profit numbers were correct.

A review of the controller's recommendations indicated that the controller estimated that 20 percent of the overhead was variable and that 50 percent of the marketing costs were also variable.

Some additional data have been gathered from the accounting records.

First, the units are produced in two departments (Molding and Finishing). The following production rates indicate the times required to produce each unit in each department:

	A	B	C
Molding	2 per hour	4 per hour	3 per hour
Finishing	4 per hour	8 per hour	$4/3$ per hour

Direct labor cost and overhead incurred in each department and for the company as a whole over the past 10 years are as follows:

Direct Labor Cost (in thousands)			Overhead Cost (in thousands)		
Molding	Finishing	Total	Molding	Finishing	Total
$140	$170	$310	$341	$434	$775
135	150	285	340	421	761
140	160	300	342	428	770
130	150	280	339	422	761
130	155	285	338	425	763
125	140	265	337	414	751
120	150	270	335	420	755
115	140	255	334	413	747
120	140	260	336	414	750
115	135	250	335	410	745

Production cost relationships have not changed over this period. Information on marketing costs for the past 10 years and on the sales of products A, B, and C for the same period was obtained also. These data are:

	Sales (in thousands)			Marketing Costs (in thousands)
Product A	Product B	Product C	Total	
$2,000	$400	$600	$3,000	$450
1,940	430	610	2,980	445
1,950	380	630	2,960	445
1,860	460	620	2,940	438
1,820	390	640	2,850	433
1,860	440	580	2,880	437
1,880	420	570	2,870	438
1,850	380	580	2,810	434
1,810	390	580	2,780	430
1,770	290	610	2,670	425

Required:

a. Comment on the use of the per unit profit measures for planning purposes.

b. Use regression estimates to determine if the estimates of fixed and variable overhead are reasonable.

c. Would you recommend the use of plantwide or departmental overhead rates?

d. Prepare regression estimates of the fixed and variable components of marketing costs.

SOLUTIONS TO

Self-Study Questions

1

Indirect materials	$ 503,000
Indirect labor	630,000
Power	104,000
Total variable costs	$1,237,000
Lease	$ 288,000
Utilities	206,000
Insurance	24,000
Maintenance	200,000
Depreciation	72,000
Research and development	171,000
Total fixed costs	$ 961,000

$$\text{Average monthly fixed costs} = \frac{\$961,000}{24} = \$40,042$$

$$\text{Variable cost per DLH} = \frac{\$1,237,000}{815,800} = \$1.516$$

$$\text{Variable cost per machine-hour} = \frac{\$1,237,000}{1,022,700} = \$1.210$$

$$\text{Variable cost per unit produced} = \frac{\$1,237,000}{202,500} = \$6.109$$

2 Selecting either appears appropriate on a purely statistical basis, considering the high adjusted *R*-square values. The choice of an activity base should not be based purely on statistical results, in any case, but should be determined by common sense and good judgment. Statistical results can help, but statistics do not substitute for good sense.

3 The independent variables are correlated to each other, giving rise to the problem of multicollinearity. This causes large standard errors resulting in low *t*-statistics. Nevertheless, most of the variance in the dependent variable is explained by the regression, and hence the high adjusted *R*-square.

4

Cumulative Number of Units Produced	Average Manufacturing Cost per Unit	Total Manufacturing Costs
1	$1,333	$1,333
2	1,000 ($1,333 × 75%)	2,000
4	750 ($1,000 × 75%)	3,000
8	562.50 ($750 × 75%)	4,500
16	421.88 ($562.50 × 75%)	6,750

Cost-Volume-Profit Analysis

LEARNING OBJECTIVES

After reading this chapter, you should be able to:

1. Understand how costs, volume, and profit are related.
2. Use cost-volume-profit (CVP) analysis as a planning and decision-making aid.
3. Apply extensions of the basic CVP model.
4. Apply CVP analysis in multi product situations.
5. Critically evaluate CVP analysis in view of the assumptions underlying CVP.

*T*he local cellular telephone company is advertising two levels of service: level 1 for $50 per month plus $.40 per minute for air time and level 2 for $20 per month plus $.70 per minute for air time. How many minutes of air time justifies moving from level 2 to level 1? (The answer is in the solution to self-study question 1, part g, on page 440 at the end of this chapter.)

A student organization wants to show movies on campus. The organization can rent a particular movie for one weekend for $1,000. Rent for an auditorium, salaries to the ticket takers and other personnel, and other fixed costs would be $800 for the weekend. The organization would sell tickets for $4 per person. In addition, profits from the sale of soft drinks, popcorn, and candy are estimated to be $1 per ticket holder. How many people would have to buy tickets to justify renting the movie? (The answer is in the solution to self-study question 1.)

During one of the many recent crises in the U.S. automobile industry, automobile executives announced a price increase. Several business news reporters expressed surprise that the executives would increase prices in the face of declining sales volume. The executives believed the price increase would increase profits. Does this make sense?

The solution to all of the above problems requires an understanding of the relationship among costs, volume, and profit. This chapter discusses the

Cost-Volume-Profit (CVP) Analysis The study of the interrelationships between costs and volume and how they impact profit.

use of **cost-volume-profit (CVP) analysis** for managerial decision making. Managers must understand the interrelationship of cost, volume, and profit for planning and decision making. They rely on their cost accounting departments to supply the information and analyses that help them anticipate and make sound decisions involving any of these three items.

Regarding the automobile industry example above, the executives needed to understand relationships among selling prices, revenues, volume, and costs. They also needed to understand which costs would vary with changes in volume and which costs would stay the same. Without this kind of analysis, they could not accurately estimate the effect of price, volume, or cost changes on the company's operating profits.

The automobile executives' decision to raise prices in the face of decreasing demand struck some people as odd. However, these executives believed that the increase in price, coupled with an expected decrease in volume, would have little impact on total revenue. But since the total variable costs would be reduced with lower volume, operating profits would be higher.

THE PROFIT EQUATION

Every organization's financial operations can be stated as a simple relation among total revenues (*TR*), total costs (*TC*), and operating profit (π):

$$\text{Operating profit} = \text{Total revenues} - \text{Total costs}$$
$$\pi = TR - TC$$

Profit Equation Operating profit equals total contribution margin less fixed costs.

(If the organization is one that is not-for-profit, then $\pi = 0$.) Both total revenues and total costs are likely to be affected by changes in the quantity of output.[1] A statement of the **profit equation** that takes quantity of output into account adds useful information for examining the effects of revenue, costs, and volume on operating profits. Total revenue (*TR*) equals average selling price per unit (*P*) times the units of output (*X*):

$$TR = PX$$

The total costs (*TC*) may be divided into a fixed component that does not vary with changes in output levels and a variable component that does vary. The fixed component is made up of total fixed costs (*F*) per period, while the variable component is the product of the average variable cost per unit (*V*) times the quantity of output (*X*). Therefore, the cost function is:

$$TC = VX + F$$

Substituting the expanded expressions in the profit equation yields a more useful form, as follows:

$$\text{Operating profit} = \text{Total revenue} - \text{Total costs}$$
$$\pi = TR - TC$$
$$TC = VX + F, \text{ so}$$
$$\pi = PX - (VX + F)$$

Collecting terms gives us:

$$\pi = (P - V)X - F$$

---

[1] Unless otherwise stated, we adopt the simplifying assumption that production volume equals sales volume so that changes in inventories may be ignored.

Contribution Margin The difference between revenues and variable costs.

The **contribution margin**, $(P - V)X$, is the amount units sold *contribute* toward (1) covering fixed costs and (2) providing operating profits. Sometimes, we use the contribution margin, in total, as in the above equation. Other times, we use the contribution margin per unit, which is just $P - V$.

Note that V is the sum of *variable manufacturing costs per unit* and *variable marketing and administrative costs per unit*; F is the sum of total fixed *manufacturing costs*, fixed *marketing costs*, and fixed *administrative costs* for the period; and X refers to the number of units produced and sold during the period.

This model assumes *all* fixed costs are *period* costs; that is, they are not allocated to products and "unitized." Thus, the CVP model is consistent with variable costing but inconsistent with full-absorption costing.

Example Assume Sport Autos is an automobile dealership that carries one line of sports cars. During the month of February, Sport Autos purchased 30 sports cars and sold them at an average price of $30,000 each. The average variable cost of each car was $22,000, computed as follows:

Cost of each automobile to Sport Autos	$21,000
Dealer preparation costs and sales commission	1,000
Average variable cost per car	$22,000

The fixed costs of operating the dealership for a typical month are $200,000. Using the profit equation, the results for February are:

$$
\begin{aligned}
\text{Operating profit} &= \text{Contribution margin} - \text{Fixed costs} \\
\pi &= (P - V)X - F \\
&= (\$30,000 - \$22,000)30 \text{ cars} - \$200,000 \\
&= \underline{\underline{\$40,000}}
\end{aligned}
$$

Although the $40,000 operating profit was derived algebraically, it could also be determined from the company's income statement for the month, as shown in Illustration 11-1.

The profit equation is useful for managers to determine how much volume is required to obtain desired profit levels. Assume, for example, that the manager of Sport Autos is hoping for an improvement in sales in April—the time when many people's thoughts turn to the joys of driving a sports car. Given the data, price (P) = $30,000, variable cost per unit (V) = $22,000 (therefore contribution margin per unit = $8,000), and fixed costs

ILLUSTRATION

11-1

Income Statement

SPORT AUTOS
Income Statement
February

Sales (30 cars at $30,000)	$900,000
Less:	
Variable cost of goods sold (30 × $21,000)	630,000
Variable selling costs (30 × $1,000)	30,000
Contribution margin	240,000
Less: Fixed costs	200,000
Operating profit	$ 40,000

(*F*) for the month of April are estimated to be $200,000, the manager wants answers to two questions: What volume would be required to break even? What volume would be required to make an operating profit of $120,000?

The formulas that follow will enable us to provide answers to the above questions. We start with the answer to the last question, which we call finding a *target volume* for the target profit. Managers may want to know the volume for a target profit expressed either in units or in sales dollars. If the company makes many products, it is often much easier to think of volume in terms of sales dollars; if we are dealing with only one product, it's easier to work with units as the measure of volume.

Formulas to Find a Target Volume

Target Volume in Units

The formula to find a volume expressed in units for a target profit is:

$$\text{Target volume (units)} = \frac{\text{Fixed costs + Target profit}}{\text{Contribution margin per unit}}$$

Using the data from Sport Autos, we find the volume that provides an operating profit of $120,000 as follows:

$$\text{Target volume} = \frac{\text{Fixed costs + Target profit}}{\text{Contribution margin per unit}}$$
$$= \frac{\$200,000 + \$120,000}{\$8,000}$$
$$= 40 \text{ cars}$$

Proof: If Sport Autos sells 40 cars, its operating profit would be:

$$\pi = (P - V)X - F$$
$$= (\$8,000 \times 40 \text{ cars}) - \$200,000$$
$$= \$120,000$$

Also:

$$\pi = TR - TC$$
$$= PX - VX - F$$
$$= (\$30,000 \times 40 \text{ cars}) - (\$22,000 \times 40 \text{ cars}) - \$200,000$$
$$= \$120,000$$

Target Volume in Sales Dollars

Contribution Margin Ratio Contribution margin as a percentage of sales revenue.

To use the formula to find a target volume expressed in sales dollars, we must first define a new term, the contribution margin ratio. The **contribution margin ratio** is the contribution margin as a percentage of sales revenue. For example, for Sport Autos, the contribution margin ratio equals:

$$\frac{\text{Contribution margin per unit}}{\text{Sales price per unit}} = \frac{\$8,000}{\$30,000} = .267 \text{ (rounded)}$$

Also, we can compute the contribution margin ratio for a total volume of activity. Pick, say, 30 units for Sport Autos. Now we compute the contribution margin ratio as follows:

$$\frac{\text{Contribution margin}}{\text{Sales revenue}} = \frac{\$240,000 \ (\$8,000 \times 30 \text{ units})}{\$900,000 \ (\$30,000 \times 30 \text{ units})}$$
$$= .267 \text{ (rounded)}$$

Note the contribution margin ratio is the same whether computed per unit or in total.

Using the contribution margin ratio, the formula to find the target volume for a target profit is as follows:[2]

$$\text{Target volume (sales dollars)} = \frac{\text{Fixed costs} + \text{Target profit}}{\text{Contribution margin ratio}}$$

For Sport Autos, the target volume expressed in sales dollars is:

$$\text{Target volume (sales dollars)} = \frac{\$200,000 + \$120,000}{.267 \text{ (rounded)}}$$
$$= \$1,200,000$$

Note that sales dollars of $1,200,000 translates into 40 automobiles at a price of $30,000 per car. We get the same result whether expressed in units (40 cars) or dollars (sales of 40 cars generates revenue of $1,200,000).

Finding Target Volume for a Target Profit Percent

Suppose instead of a target dollar profit, the manager of Sport Autos wants to find the sales dollars that would provide a 20 percent of sales profit margin. We use the same concept as above, but modify the target operating profit to express it as a percent of sales instead of a target dollar amount, as follows:

$$\text{Target volume (sales dollars)} = \frac{\text{Fixed costs} + \text{Target profit}}{\text{Contribution margin ratio}}$$

$$\text{Target } PX = \frac{\$200,000 + (20\% \times \text{Sales dollars})}{.267}$$

$$\text{Target } PX = \frac{\$200,000 + .2PX}{.267}$$

$$\text{Target } PX = \frac{\$200,000}{.267} + \frac{.2PX}{.267}$$

$$\text{Target } PX = \$750,000 + .75PX$$

$$\text{Target } PX - .75PX = \$750,000$$

$$.25PX = \$750,000$$

$$PX = \$3,000,000$$

That is, Sport Autos must generate sales of $3,000,000 to provide a profit of 20 percent of sales.

---

[2] We can derive the target volume for sales dollars from the original formula for units:

$$X = \frac{F + \pi}{P - V}$$

The modified formula for dollars multiplies both sides of the equation by P:

$$PX = \left(\frac{F + \pi}{P - V}\right) P$$

Since dividing the denominator by P is the same as multiplying the entire term by P, we obtain:

$$PX = \frac{F + \pi}{\dfrac{(P - V)}{P}}$$

The term $\dfrac{P - V}{P}$ is the contribution margin ratio. The result can also be derived from the formula:

$$PX = \frac{F + \pi}{1 - \dfrac{V}{P}}$$

Proof: The total contribution margin equals the contribution margin ratio times total revenue. When total revenue equals $3,000,000, the total contribution margin equals .267 (rounded) × $3,000,000 = $800,000. If fixed costs are $200,000, then operating profit equals $600,000 ($800,000 contribution margin − $200,000 fixed costs). Profit of $600,000 equals 20 percent of sales revenue, as required.

Formulas to Find the Break-Even Point

Break-Even Point The volume level where profits equal zero.

The **break-even point** is the volume level where profits equal zero. Thus, to find the break-even point, we use the target volume formulas, but set profits equal to zero ($\pi = 0$).

Break-Even Point in Units
The formula to find the break-even point in units is:

$$\text{Break-even volume (units)} = \frac{\text{Fixed costs}}{\text{Contribution margin per unit}}$$

Using the data from Sport Autos, we find the volume that provides an operating profit of zero as follows:

$$\text{Break-even volume} = \frac{\text{Fixed costs}}{\text{Contribution margin per unit}}$$
$$= \frac{\$200,000}{\$8,000}$$
$$= 25 \text{ automobiles}$$

Sport Autos must sell 25 cars per month to break even. Each additional car sold would increase operating profits by $8,000.

Break-Even Point in Sales Dollars
To find the break-even point in sales dollars, we use the contribution margin ratio instead of the contribution margin per unit. The formula to find the break-even volume is:

$$\text{Break-even volume (sales dollars)} = \frac{\text{Fixed costs}}{\text{Contribution margin ratio}}$$

For Sport Autos, the break-even volume expressed in sales dollars is:

$$\text{Break-even volume (sales dollars)} = \frac{\$200,000}{.267 \text{ (rounded)}}$$
$$= \$750,000$$

Note that sales dollars of $750,000 translates into 25 automobiles at a price of $30,000 per car. We get the same break-even point whether expressed in units (25 cars) or dollars (sales of 25 cars generates revenue of $750,000).

Illustration 11–2 summarizes the four formulas for finding target and break-even volumes.

Graphic Presentation of Cost-Volume-Profit Relationships

Illustration 11–3 presents the cost-volume-profit (CVP) relationships for Sport Autos graphically. Such a graph is a helpful aid in presenting cost-volume-profit relationships. We may want to project the profits that could be earned from a product or a division or a company using a graph like Illustration 11–3, for example. Or we may want to show various versions of the graph that result if the product's prices, variable costs per unit, and/or

ILLUSTRATION

*Summary of Target Volume
and Break-Even Formulas*

Target Volume:

$$\text{Units: Target volume (units)} = \frac{\text{Fixed costs} + \text{Target profit}}{\text{Contribution margin per unit}}$$

$$\text{Sales dollars: Target volume (sales dollars)} = \frac{\text{Fixed costs} + \text{Target profit}}{\text{Contribution margin ratio}}$$

Break-Even:

$$\text{Units: Break-even volume (units)} = \frac{\text{Fixed costs}}{\text{Contribution margin per unit}}$$

$$\text{Sales dollars: Break-even volume (sales dollars)} = \frac{\text{Fixed costs}}{\text{Contribution margin ratio}}$$

ILLUSTRATION

11-3

CVP Graph, Sport Autos

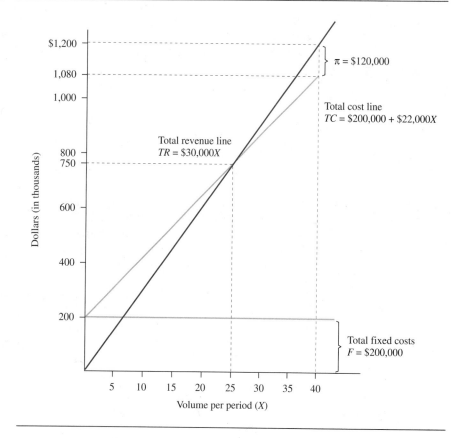

fixed costs per time period change. Next, we discuss specific features of the graph.

The *vertical axis* represents dollars (for example, revenue dollars, cost dollars). The *horizontal axis* represents the volume of activity for a time period (for example, number of cars sold per month, or sales dollars).

The *total revenue (TR)* line relates total revenue to volume (for example, if Sport Autos sells 40 cars in a month, its total revenue would be $1,200,000,

---

REAL WORLD APPLICATION

Breaking Even in the Automobile Industry*

For some companies, the break-even point is a target to achieve for survival. During the 1980s and first half of the 1990s, Chrysler, Ford, and General Motors found themselves, at various times, striving to reach the break-even point.

Chrysler was the first of the "Big Three" automobile companies to reach the brink of disaster when, in the early 1980s, the company substantially reduced fixed costs to cut its break-even point from 2.2 million units in 1979 to 1.2 million units in 1982. In the mid-1980s, Ford found its most successful cars still cost thousands of dollars more to manufacture than comparable cars made by Japanese companies. During the 1980s and early 1990s, Ford suffered losses, but retooled its manufacturing facilities, came out with new, popular designs, improved quality, and developed efficiencies that substantially cut costs.

General Motors was the last of the Big Three to see losses, possibly because its huge size enabled the company to make profits despite its problems. After a top-management shake-up in 1992 that brought in more outside talent, the company increased its focus on improving production methods, improving quality, and reducing costs.

Perhaps because these three companies were so large, all three among the top 10 companies in the United States at one time, their management became complacent about the need to improve quality, provide cars that appealed to younger customers, and reduce costs. Now that the Japanese automobile industry has become a competitive force in the United States, the Big Three have been striving to find ways to break even again.

* Based on the authors' research.

---

according to the graph). The slope of *TR* is the price per unit, *P* (for example, $30,000 per car for Sport Autos.)

The *total cost* (*TC*) line shows the total cost for each volume [for example, the total cost for a volume of 40 cars is $1,080,000 = (40 × $22,000) + $200,000]. The intercept of the total cost line is the fixed cost for the period, *F* (for example, $200,000 for the month), and the slope is the variable cost per unit, *V* (for example, $22,000 per car).

The *break-even point* is the volume at which *TR* = *TC* (that is, the *TR* and *TC* lines intersect). Volumes lower than break-even result in an operating loss because *TR* < *TC*; volumes higher than break-even result in an operating profit because *TR* > *TC*. For Sport Autos, the break-even volume is 25 cars.

The amount of operating profit or loss can be read from the graph by measuring the vertical distance between *TR* and *TC*. For example, the vertical distance between *TR* and *TC* when *X* = 40 indicates π = $120,000.

 *Self-Study Question*

1 Given the following information for Marge and Sara's Ice Cream Company for April:

Sales	$180,000
Fixed manufacturing costs	22,000
Fixed marketing and administrative costs	14,000
Total fixed costs	36,000
Total variable costs	120,000
Unit price	$9
Unit variable manufacturing cost	5
Unit variable marketing cost	1

Compute the following:

a. Operating profit when sales are $180,000 (as above).

b. Break-even quantity in units.

c. Quantity that would produce an operating profit of $30,000.

d. Sales dollars required to generate an operating profit of $20,000.

e. Number of units sold in April.

f. Quantity of units sold that would produce an operating profit of 20 percent of sales dollars.

g. Answer the two questions—cellular phone example and student organization example—posed at the beginning of this chapter.

The solution to this question is at the end of this chapter on page 439.

PROFIT-VOLUME MODEL

Profit-Volume Analysis A version of CVP analysis using a single profit line.

For convenience, the cost and revenue lines are often collapsed into a single profit line. This summary version of CVP analysis is called **profit-volume analysis**.

A graphic comparison of profit-volume and CVP relationships is shown in Illustration 11–4. Note that the slope of the profit-volume line equals the average unit contribution margin. The intercept equals the loss at zero

I L L U S T R A T I O N   *Comparison of CVP and Profit-Volume Graphs, Sport Autos*

11–4

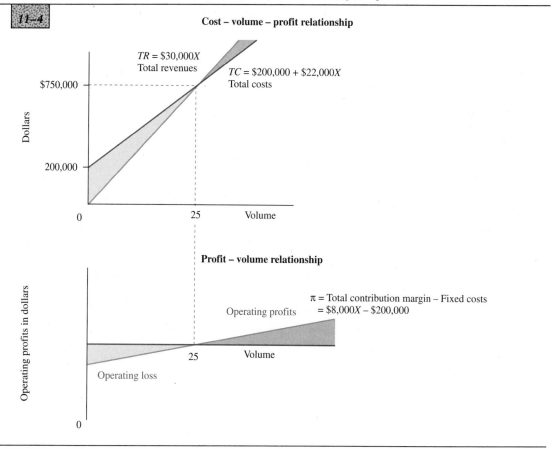

volume, which equals fixed costs. The vertical axis shows the amount of operating profit or loss.

USE OF SPREADSHEETS IN COST-VOLUME-PROFIT ANALYSIS

Computer spreadsheets, like Lotus 1-2-3® and Excel®, provide you with considerable additional power in analyzing costs, volume, and profits. For example, Illustration 11–5 presents a "what-if" analysis prepared using a computer spreadsheet based on data for Sport Autos. Column E shows the operating profit computed by the spreadsheet program for each of 9 different scenarios. Column A shows three different price scenarios, column B shows three different volume scenarios, and column D shows three different fixed cost scenarios. To keep the presentation simple, we did not change the variable cost per unit (column C).

Once you have set up the basic CVP formula, you can see how easy it is to determine the effect if you change the values of prices, costs, and volume. Spreadsheet applications of CVP are particularly helpful in answering what-if questions in planning and decision making. Also, computer spreadsheets make CVP analysis more fun!

SOLVING FOR UNKNOWNS

A major application of the CVP model is solving for unknowns. For example, suppose that after examining the figures just presented, Sport Autos' manager pointed out, "We cannot obtain 40 cars from the manufacturer to sell in April. If we can only get 30 cars to sell, can we still make $120,000 in April?" An answer can be obtained by holding outputs at 30 units and operating profits at $120,000, then solving for each of the other terms in the following profit equation:

$$\$120,000 = (P - V)30 \text{ cars} - F$$

ILLUSTRATION 11–5

Computer Spreadsheet Output

	A Price	B Volume	C Variable Cost per Unit	D Fixed Costs	E Operating Profit
1					
2					
3	$30,000	40	$22,000	$200,000	$120,000
4	31,000	38	22,000	200,000	142,000
5	29,000	42	22,000	200,000	94,000
6	30,000	40	22,000	180,000	140,000
7	31,000	38	22,000	180,000	162,000
8	29,000	42	22,000	180,000	114,000
9	30,000	40	22,000	220,000	100,000
10	31,000	38	22,000	220,000	122,000
11	29,000	42	22,000	220,000	74,000

1. Solve for Contribution Margin

Find the average contribution margin per unit required to cover Sport Autos' $200,000 fixed costs and provide target operating profits of $120,000:

$$\$120,000 = (P - V)30 - \$200,000$$
$$\$320,000 = (P - V)30$$
$$(P - V) = \frac{\$320,000}{30}$$
$$= \underline{\underline{\$10,667}}$$

Thus, the average contribution margin per car must be increased from $8,000 to $10,667 if Sport Autos is to make $120,000. The increase in the contribution margin must come from a price increase, a decrease in variable costs per unit, or a combination of the two.

2. Solve for Fixed Cost

Next, we try holding the contribution margin per unit constant at $8,000 to find the decrease in fixed costs that provides operating profits of $120,000 if 30 cars are sold:

$$\$120,000 = \$8,000 \times 30 \text{ cars} - F$$
$$\$120,000 = \$240,000 - F$$
$$F = \underline{\underline{\$120,000}}$$

For Sport Autos to sell 30 cars while holding the unit contribution margin at $8,000 and to make operating profits of $120,000, a reduction in fixed costs from $200,000 to $120,000 would be required.

Managers can thus use CVP analysis to determine how to achieve profit goals by changing particular variables in the CVP equation, as noted above in discussing computerized spreadsheet analysis.

CVP analysis provides a valuable tool for determining the impact of prices, costs, and volume on operating profits. An important part of management's job is to manage each variable that affects operating profits in order to improve profitability.

MARGIN OF SAFETY

Margin of Safety The excess of projected or actual sales over the break-even volume.

The **margin of safety** is the excess of projected (or actual) sales over the break-even sales level. This tells managers the margin between current sales and the break-even point. In a sense, margin of safety indicates the risk that a company faces of losing money; that is, the margin by which sales can fall before the company is in the loss area. The margin of safety formula is:

Sales volume − Break-even sales volume = Margin of safety

If Sport Autos sells 30 cars and its break-even volume is 25 cars, then its margin of safety is:

Sales − Break-even = 30 − 25
$$= \underline{\underline{5 \text{ cars}}}$$

Sales volume could drop by five cars per month before a loss is incurred, all other things held constant, as shown in Illustration 11–6. In practice, the margin of safety may also be expressed in sales dollars or as a percent of current sales.

Margin of Safety

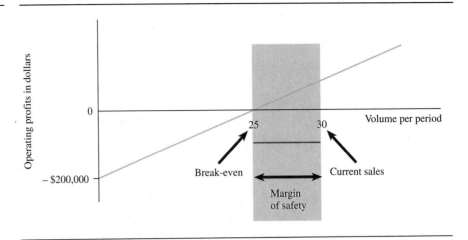

EXTENSIONS OF THE BASIC MODEL

CVP: Cash Flow Analysis

Sometimes decision makers may be more interested in the impact of the volume of activity on cash or working capital than on accrual profits. They often want to know if it is possible to operate at a loss and still generate positive cash flows. This type of analysis may be particularly relevant in adverse economic times or when a company is phasing out part of its operations. So long as there are sufficient cash flows, it may be optimal to continue the operation, even though there is an accounting loss.

Both revenues and costs include noncash items. But the most significant noncash item tends to be depreciation, which is usually included in fixed costs. This classification is common because depreciation generally represents the allocation of the acquisition cost of plant and equipment (capacity) over time based on an estimate of their useful lives.

To see how noncash items can affect CVP analysis, suppose that the fixed costs of Sport Autos include depreciation of equipment and other assets of $40,000 per month and that this is the only noncash revenue or expense.

Illustration 11–7 compares cash flow and accrual profit-volume relationships. By substituting appropriate numbers into the profit equation, you can demonstrate that if Sport Autos operates at an accrual profit break-even volume each month, it will generate monthly net cash flows of $40,000. This is a short-run phenomenon only, of course. When the time comes to replace the depreciable assets, the need for a large cash outflow must be faced.

Depreciation also may be included in *variable costs* if it is based on the *units of production* of some asset and thus related to volume. A common example is the depreciation of a machine based on its usage. Also, oil companies like Exxon and Louisiana Land and Exploration deplete the costs of oil or gas wells over the number of units of oil or gas produced since the economic life is dependent on the number of units of the resource rather than the age of the well.

Income Taxes

Assuming that operating profits before taxes and taxable income are the same, income taxes may be incorporated into the basic model as follows:

I L L U S T R A T I O N

Comparison of Short-Run Cash and Accrual Profit-Volume Relationships for Sport Autos

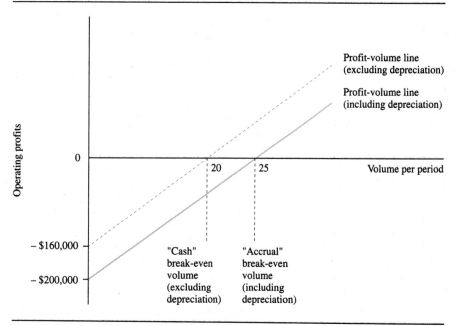

Note: The cash break-even point is found as follows:

$$X = \frac{\text{Fixed cash costs}}{\text{Cash contribution margin per unit}}$$

$$= \frac{\$200,000 - \$40,000 \text{ depreciation}}{\$8,000} = \frac{\$160,000}{\$8,000} = 20 \text{ cars}$$

$$\text{After-tax operating profits} = [(P - V)X - F](1 - t)$$

where t is the tax rate.

Finding a Target Volume

Suppose the manager of Sport Autos wants to find the number of units required to generate after-tax operating profits of $60,000. Recall that $P = \$30,000$, $V = \$22,000$, the contribution margin per unit = $8,000, and $F = \$200,000$. We assume the tax rate $t = .4$; that is, Sport Autos has a 40 percent tax rate.

To find the target volume, we modify our original target volume formula to after-tax amounts, as follows:

$$\text{Target volume} = \frac{\text{After-tax fixed costs} + \text{Target after-tax profits}}{\text{After-tax contribution margin}}$$

Fixed costs are tax deductible. With a 40 percent tax rate, the fixed costs of $200,000 save $80,000 in taxes. Thus, the after-tax fixed costs are $120,000 ($200,000 − $80,000). In general, to compute the after-tax fixed costs, we multiply before-tax fixed costs by 1 − tax rate. In the case of Sport Autos, using this formula:

$$\begin{aligned}\text{After-tax fixed costs} &= \$200,000 \times (1 - .4) \\ &= \$200,000 \times .6 \\ &= \$120,000\end{aligned}$$

Using the same reasoning, the contribution margin per unit adds to taxable income. To compute the after-tax contribution margin per unit, multiply the contribution margin by 1 − tax rate. Recall that for Sport Autos, the before-tax contribution margin per unit was $8,000. Therefore,

$$\text{After-tax contribution margin} = \$8,000 \times (1 - .4)$$
$$= \$8,000 \times .6$$
$$= \$4,800$$

Having found the after-tax fixed costs and contribution margin, we compute the target volume to provide after-tax operating profits of $120,000 as follows:

$$\text{Target volume} = \frac{\text{After-tax fixed costs + Target after-tax profits}}{\text{After-tax contribution margin}}$$
$$= \frac{\$120,000 + \$60,000}{\$4,800}$$
$$= 37.5 \text{ cars}$$

We assume the company cannot sell fractional cars (at least, we hope not), so we arbitrarily choose to round up the number of cars to 38, which would provide somewhat more than the required $60,000 after-tax profits.[3]

What if you want to find the target volume expressed in sales dollars? Simply convert the contribution margin ratio to an after-tax ratio as follows:

$$\text{After-tax contribution margin ratio} = \text{Before-tax ratio} \times (1 - t)$$

For Sport Autos, the before-tax contribution ratio was .267 (rounded), so:

$$\text{After-tax contribution margin ratio} = .267 \times (1 - .4)$$
$$= .267 \times .6$$
$$= .16$$

To find the target volume:

$$\begin{array}{l}\text{Target volume} \\ \text{(sales dollars)}\end{array} = \frac{\text{After-tax fixed costs + Target after-tax profits}}{\text{After-tax contribution margin ratio}}$$
$$= \frac{\$120,000 + \$60,000}{.16}$$
$$= \$1,125,000$$

which works out to be 37.5 cars at $30,000 each.

Semifixed (Step) Costs

It is common for fixed costs to behave in a step fashion as follows:

Step Cost A cost that increases with volume in steps. Also called a semifixed cost.

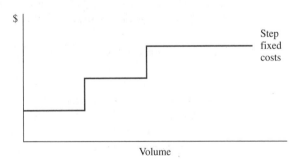

---

[3] Don't be too concerned about rounding fractional products in practice. Simply report the results, fully disclose whether you are rounding up or down, and, if necessary, indicate how much above or below the target profit the company will earn if it sells at the volume you report.

Suppose the managers of a company are considering adding an evening shift. Assume the prices, volumes, and costs would be as follows:

	Monthly Production and Sales	Total Fixed Costs	Variable Cost	Price
Regular shift	0–10,000 units	$200,000	$15 per unit	$40 per unit
Evening shift	10,001–18,000 units	300,000	15 per unit	40 per unit

The CVP lines are shown in Illustration 11–8. The slope of the total cost is $15 ($V$), but the line "steps up" at 10,000 units.

As indicated on the graph, if the company operates only one shift, its capacity is limited to 10,000 units. Adding the second shift increases the capacity to 18,000 units. Profits will increase if enough additional units can be sold.

The company would have two break-even points—one within each level of activity:

$$X = \frac{F}{P - V}$$

$$\text{Break-even volume (regular shift)} = \frac{\$200,000}{\$40 - \$15} = \underline{\underline{8,000 \text{ units}}}$$

$$\text{Break-even volume (regular and evening shifts)} = \frac{\$300,000}{\$40 - \$15} = \underline{\underline{12,000 \text{ units}}}$$

Should the company open the second shift, assuming all other things are the same except for the increase in each period's fixed costs and the increase in volume noted above? From the calculations shown on the next page, and assuming the company can sell everything it makes, it is more profitable to operate with two shifts than with one.

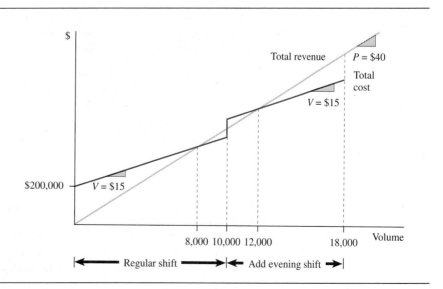

	Regular Shift Only	Two Shifts
Volume in units	10,000	18,000
Sales revenue	$400,000 ($40 × 10,000)	$720,000 ($40 × 18,000)
Variable costs	150,000 ($15 × 10,000)	270,000 ($15 × 18,000)
Total contribution	250,000	450,000
Fixed costs	200,000	300,000
Operating profit	$ 50,000	$150,000

Self-Study
Question

2 Refer to the data for self-study question 1. The following two questions are independent of each other.

   a. Holding everything else constant, what contribution margin per unit is required for the company to make an operating profit of $30,000 if the sales volume was 20,000 units?

   b. Assume a tax rate of 30 percent of before-tax operating profit. What sales volume in dollars is required for the company to earn an after-tax profit of $40,000?

The solution to this question is at the end of this chapter on page 440.

MULTIPRODUCT CVP ANALYSIS

We assumed that Sport Autos buys and sells only one line of sports cars. Many companies, of course, produce and/or sell many products from the same asset base.

Dual Autos sells two car models: Sport and Deluxe. The prices and costs of the two are:

	Sport	Deluxe
Average sales price	$25,000	$35,000
Less average variable costs	20,000	25,000
Average contribution margin per car	$ 5,000	$10,000

Average monthly fixed costs are $300,000.

The profit equation presented earlier must now be expanded to consider the contribution of each product:

Operating profit = (Contribution margin per unit for Sports × Volume of
            Sports) + (Contribution margin per unit for Deluxes
            × Volume of Deluxes) − Fixed costs

Let the subscript s designate the Sport model and subscript d designate the Deluxe model. Thus, the company's profit equation is:

$$\pi = (\$5,000X_s) + (\$10,000X_d) - \$300,000$$

The manager of Dual Autos has been listening to a debate between two of the sales personnel about the break-even point for the company. According to one, they have to sell 60 cars a month to break even. But the other claims that 30 cars a month would be sufficient. Who is right? The claim that 60 cars must be sold to break even is correct if *only* the *Sport* model is sold, while the claim that 30 cars need to be sold to break even is correct if *only*

ILLUSTRATION

Combinations of Break-Even Volumes for Dual Autos

Sport Model		Deluxe Model		Total Contribution for Both Models
Quantity	Total Contribution	Quantity	Total Contribution	
60	$300,000	0	–0–	$300,000
58	290,000	1	$ 10,000	300,000
56	280,000	2	20,000	300,000
. . . .	.	.	.	.
. . . .	.	.	.	.
. . . .	.	.	.	.
4	20,000	28	280,000	300,000
2	10,000	29	290,000	300,000
0	–0–	30	300,000	300,000

the *Deluxe* model is sold. In fact, there are many break-even points. This is evident from Dual Auto's profit equation, which has two unknown variables. Alternative break-even points for Dual Autos are listed in Illustration 11–9.

Illustration 11–10 is a graphic presentation of the possible break-even volumes for Dual Autos. Operating profits are zero for any combination of volumes at any point on that line. (We present a solid line with no breaks although each car actually represents a point on the line.)

The dashed line parallel to the break-even line shows the various combinations of volumes that would provide $10,000 in operating profits. Note in Illustration 11–10 that any combination of products to the right of the break-even line provides profits, while any combination to the left results in losses.

In general, the multiproduct CVP equation for *n* different products is:

$$\pi = (P_1 - V_1)X_1 + (P_2 - V_2)X_2 + \ldots + (P_n - V_n)X_n - F$$

CVP analysis of multiple products is *much* more complex than is analysis of a single product. As indicated in the Dual Autos example, even for a two-product company, the number of possible solutions is large because there are many combinations of product volumes that will yield a given profit. You can imagine the complications when hundreds of products are involved.

Simplifying Multiproduct CVP

To simplify matters, managers often assume a particular product mix and compute break-even or target volumes using either of two methods: fixed product mix or weighted-average contribution margin.

Assume a Fixed Product Mix

Using this method, managers define a "package" of products in the typical product mix, then compute the break-even or target volume for the package.

For example, suppose the manager of Dual Autos would be willing to assume that the Sport and Deluxe models would be sold in a 3:1 ratio; that is, out of every four cars sold, three would be Sport models and one would be a

ILLUSTRATION

11–10

Illustration of Possible Break-Even Volumes for Dual Autos

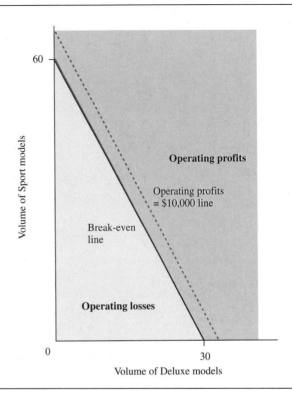

Deluxe model. Defining X as a "package" of three Sports and one Deluxe, the contribution margin from this package is:

Sport: 3 × $ 5,000	=	$15,000
Deluxe: 1 × $10,000	=	$10,000
Contribution margin		$25,000

Now the break-even point is computed as follows:

$$X = \frac{\text{Fixed costs}}{\text{Contribution margin}}$$
$$= \frac{\$300,000}{\$25,000}$$
$$= 12 \text{ packages}$$

where X refers to the break-even number of packages. This means that the sale of 12 packages of three Sports and one Deluxe per package, totaling 36 Sports and 12 Deluxes, would be required to break even.

Assume a Weighted-Average Contribution Margin
This approach also requires an assumed product mix, which we continue to assume is 75 percent Sports and 25 percent Deluxes. The problem can be solved by using a weighted-average contribution margin per unit. When a company assumes a constant product mix, the contribution margin is the **weighted-average contribution margin** of all of its products.

Weighted-Average Contribution Margin The contribution margin of more than one product when a constant product mix is assumed.

For Dual Autos, the weighted-average contribution margin per unit could be computed by multiplying each product's proportion by its contribution margin per unit:

$$(.75 \times \$5,000) + (.25 \times \$10,000) = \underline{\underline{\$6,250}}$$

The multiple-product break-even for Dual Autos can be determined from the break-even formula:

$$X = \frac{\$300,000}{\$6,250}$$
$$= \underline{\underline{48 \text{ cars}}}$$

where X refers to the break-even quantity. The product mix assumption means Dual Autos must sell 36 (.75 × 48) Sport models and 12 (.25 × 48) Deluxe models to break even.

COMMON FIXED COSTS IN CVP ANALYSIS

Suppose that Dual Autos' total fixed costs of $300,000 can be attributed to the two products as follows:

Direct fixed costs:	
Sport model	$ 80,000
Deluxe model	100,000
Common fixed costs	120,000
Total fixed costs	$300,000

What is the break-even quantity for each product and for the company as a whole?

We compute the break-even volume for the Sport model:

$$X_s = \frac{F}{P - V} = \frac{\$80,000}{\$5,000} = \underline{\underline{16 \text{ cars}}}$$

and break-even volume for the Deluxe model:

$$X_d = \frac{F}{P - V} = \frac{\$100,000}{\$10,000} = \underline{\underline{10 \text{ cars}}}$$

If each product line just breaks even, the operating loss for the company as a whole is:

$$\pi = (\$5,000 \times 16) + (\$10,000 \times 10) - \$300,000$$
$$= -\underline{\underline{\$120,000}}$$

Although the sale of 16 Sport models and 10 Deluxe models would make each product appear to break even, the company would lose $120,000.

This demonstrates a common problem in applying CVP analysis. The volume required for a specific product to break even will not cover unassigned common costs.

One way of dealing with the problem is to allocate the common costs to the products. This permits a CVP analysis for each product. Of course, the results depend on the allocation method. In such cases, it is wise to perform sensitivity analysis with various allocation methods to discover any that might affect management decisions.

I L L U S T R A T I O N   *Impact of Common Cost Allocation Methods on Break-Even Volume, Dual Autos*

11–11

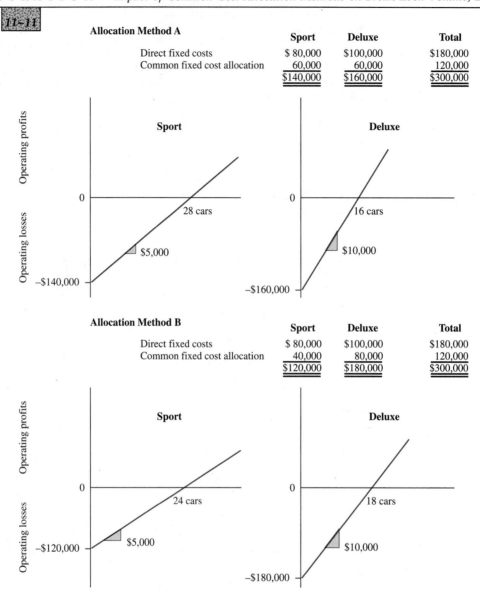

Allocation Method A

	Sport	Deluxe	Total
Direct fixed costs	$ 80,000	$100,000	$180,000
Common fixed cost allocation	60,000	60,000	120,000
	$140,000	$160,000	$300,000

Allocation Method B

	Sport	Deluxe	Total
Direct fixed costs	$ 80,000	$100,000	$180,000
Common fixed cost allocation	40,000	80,000	120,000
	$120,000	$180,000	$300,000

For example, Illustration 11–11 presents profit-volume graphs for Dual Autos. Allocation Method A assumes that the $120,000 in common fixed costs are allocated evenly to the two products. Allocation Method B allocates two thirds of the common fixed costs to the Deluxe model and one third to the Sport model. As you can see, changing the allocation of fixed costs changes the product mix required to break even or to achieve a target level of operating profits for the company as a whole.

The break-even volumes shown in Illustration 11–11 are only two of many possible combinations. Allocating common fixed costs to products

---

REAL WORLD APPLICATION

*Using Break-Even Analysis for Management Education**

The dean of the Graduate School of Management at the University of California at Davis was considering whether to offer a particular seminar for executives. The tuition was $650 per person. Variable costs, which included meals, parking, and materials, were $80 per person. Certain costs of offering the seminar, including advertising the seminar, instructors' fees, room rent, and audiovisual equipment rent, would not be affected by the number of people attending (within a "relevant range"). Such costs, which could be thought of as step costs, amounted to $8,000 for the seminar.

In addition to these costs, a number of staff, including the dean of the school, worked on the program. Although the salaries paid to these staff were not affected by offering the seminar, working on the seminar took these people away from other duties, thus creating an opportunity cost, estimated to be $7,000 for this seminar.

Given this information, the school estimated the break-even point to be ($8,000 + $7,000)/ ($650 − $80) = 26.3 students. If the school wanted to at least break even on this program, it should offer the program only if it expected at least 27 students to attend.

* Based on the authors' research.

---

does not dispense with the product mix problem. Nonetheless, it makes product-line CVP analysis possible, and it ensures that common fixed costs are not ignored. Because the allocation of common fixed costs is often arbitrary, we recommend performing sensitivity analysis on the allocation method before using the information for decision making.

 *Self-Study Question*

3 Multiproduct Company produces these products with the following characteristics:

	Product I	Product II	Product III
Price per unit	$5	$6	$7
Variable cost per unit	3	2	4
Expected sales (units) . . .	100,000	150,000	250,000

Total fixed costs for the company are $1,240,000. Assuming the product mix would be the same at the break-even point, compute the break-even point in:

   a. Units.

   b. Sales dollars.

The solution to this question is at the end of this chapter on page 440.

THE ECONOMIST'S PROFIT-MAXIMIZATION MODEL

The classical economist's profit-maximization model provides the foundation for CVP analysis. It assumes that management's goal is profit maximization, where profits are the difference between total revenues and total costs. Management's job is to determine and take the most profitable actions possible.

In general, accountants accept the classical economist's model, but they make two simplifying assumptions:

1. In economics, *total revenue and total cost curves* are usually assumed to be nonlinear. The linearity simplifications are usually considered valid within some appropriate range of volume, termed the *relevant range*.

2. The opportunity cost of invested equity capital is usually excluded in the accountant's cost measures, while it is included in the economist's model. Thus, in economic terms, the accountant's measurement of total costs is understated.

A comparison of accountants' and economists' assumptions about the behavior of costs and revenue is shown in Illustration 11–12. The solid lines represent accountants' assumptions about cost and revenue behavior, while the dashed lines designate economists' assumptions. Note the difference in assumptions about linearity as well as the systematically higher economists' costs because accounting costs do not include the opportunity cost of capital.

Simplifying Assumptions about Cost and Revenue Behavior
Strictly speaking, neither model is "correct," because both economists and accountants have made simplifying assumptions about cost and revenue behavior. The actual curves would be disjointed and would take into account inconsistencies such as sales discounts for certain customers, costs that are neither strictly fixed nor strictly variable, and so forth. However, a cost-benefit analysis of more "accurate" data about cost and revenue behavior may yield little additional benefit to decision makers.

Limitations and Assumptions

Like any other tool, CVP analysis has limitations that make it more applicable to some decisions than to others. Some of these limitations and the impact they can have on the results of CVP analysis follow. As with any

ILLUSTRATION
11–12

Comparison of Economists' and Accountants' Assumed Cost and Revenue Behavior

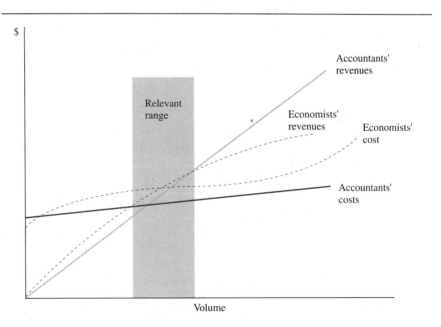

management information, the system is judged in terms of a cost-benefit test. Overcoming some of the listed limitations may not be cost-justified.

Assumed and Actual Cost Behavior

A linear CVP analysis assumes that:

1. Revenues change proportionately with volume.
2. Total variable costs change proportionately with volume.
3. Fixed costs do not change at all with volume.

One useful feature of CVP analysis is its simplicity in showing the impact of sales prices, costs, and volume on operating profits (or cash flows). But the cost of this simplicity is often a lack of realism. Some costs cannot be easily classified. Costs seldom behave in a neat linear fashion. CVP analysis is based on the assumption that within a specific range of activity, the linear expression approximates reality closely enough that the results will not be badly distorted.

Assumed linear relationships are more likely to be valid for short time periods (one year or less) and small changes in volume than for long periods and large changes in volume. Most fixed costs are only fixed in the short run. Over time, management may make decisions that change fixed costs. For example, during a recent downturn in the economy, a steel company announced the closing of two of the four blast furnaces in one of its plants. Many costs that were fixed while all four blast furnaces were operating (for example, supervisory salaries, product inspection costs, some maintenance and utilities costs) were temporarily eliminated.

Also, many nonvolume factors that would affect prices and costs (for example, limited capacity, technological changes, and input factor prices) are more likely to be constant over short time periods.

Assuming a Constant Product Mix

As we saw earlier in the chapter, with multiple products, a change in product mix can affect operating profits. Holding the product mix constant allows the analyst to focus on the impact of prices, costs, and volume on operating profits. Product mix usually changes constantly, in the real world; thus, spreadsheets that show many alternative product mixes are quite helpful.

Recording Costs as Expenses

If the costs used in CVP analysis are not the same ones expensed in the financial statements, the resultant operating profit will not be the same. Discrepancies are usually caused by timing differences in the recognition of expenses.

The most common source of difference is the treatment of fixed manufacturing costs when production volume is not equal to sales volume. As discussed in Chapter 9, generally accepted accounting principles (GAAP) and income tax regulations require use of *full-absorption costing*. For financial statements, fixed manufacturing costs must be treated as product costs and expensed when the goods are sold. However, CVP analysis is like variable costing—*all* fixed costs, including fixed manufacturing costs, are treated as if they will be expensed during the period. Thus, while fixed manufacturing costs are treated as product costs for external financial reporting, they are treated as period costs for CVP analysis.

SUMMARY

CVP analysis examines the impact of prices, costs, and volume on operating profits, as summarized in the profit equation:

$$\pi = (P - V)X - F$$

where

π = Operating profits
P = Average unit selling price
V = Average unit variable costs
X = Quantity of output
F = Total fixed costs

CVP analysis is both a management tool for determining the impact of selling prices, costs, and volume on profits and a conceptual tool, or way of thinking, about managing a company. It helps management focus on the objective of obtaining the best possible combination of prices, volume, variable costs, and fixed costs.

An advantage of the CVP model is its simplicity. However, the price of such simplicity is a set of limiting assumptions that result in some loss of realism. When multiple products are analyzed, a constant product mix must be assumed or common costs must be allocated. Whenever assumptions are made, it is advisable to perform sensitivity analysis to determine whether (and how) the assumption affects decisions.

TERMS AND CONCEPTS

The following terms and concepts should be familiar to you after reading this chapter:

Break-Even Point, *410*

Contribution Margin, *407*

Contribution Margin Ratio, *408*

Cost-Volume-Profit (CVP) Analysis, *406*

Margin of Safety, *415*

Profit Equation, *406*

Profit-Volume Analysis, *413*

Semifixed (Step) Costs, *418*

Weighted-Average Contribution Margin, *422*

QUESTIONS

11–1 Define the profit equation.

11–2 What are the components of total costs in the profit equation?

11–3 What is the meaning of the term *contribution margin*?

11–4 How does the total *contribution margin* differ from the *gross margin* that is often shown on companies' financial statements?

11–5 Compare cost-volume-profit (CVP) analysis with profit-volume analysis. How do they differ?

11–6 Is a company really breaking even if it produces and sells at the break-even point? What costs might not be covered?

11-7   What is usually the difference between CVP analysis on a cash basis and that on an accounting accrual basis? For a company having depreciable assets, would you expect the accrual break-even point to be higher, lower, or the same as the cash break-even point?

11-8   How is the profit equation expanded when multiproduct CVP analysis is used?

11-9   Is it possible to have many break-even points and many alternative ways to achieve a target operating profit when a company has multiple products?

11-10   Why is a constant product mix often assumed in multiproduct CVP analysis?

11-11   Define the contribution margin when a constant product mix is assumed in multiproduct CVP analyses.

11-12   When would the sum of the break-even quantities for each of a company's products not be the break-even point for the company as a whole?

11-13   What is the difference between economic "profit" and accounting "net income" or "operating profit"?

11-14   How can CVP analysis be used for planning and performance evaluation?

11-15   Name three common assumptions of linear CVP analysis.

11-16   Why might there be a difference between the operating profit calculated by CVP analysis and the net income reported in financial statements for external reporting?

11-17   Fixed costs are often defined as "fixed over the short run." Does this mean they are not fixed over the long run? Why or why not?

11-18   Why does the accountant use a linear representation of cost and revenue behavior in CVP analysis? How can this use be justified?

11-19   The following graph implies that profits increase continually as volume increases:

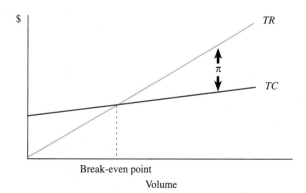

What are some of the factors that might prevent the increasing profits that are indicated when linear CVP analysis is employed?

11-20   Why would fixed costs tend not to be relevant for a typical CVP analysis? Under what circumstances might the fixed costs be relevant in CVP analyses?

11-21   "CVP analysis is an oversimplification of the real-world environment. For this reason, it has little to offer a decision maker." Comment.

11-22   Refer to the first real world application on page 412. If the auto companies cannot raise prices, what must they do to break even?

11-23   Refer to the second real world application on page 425. What costs were "step" costs? Why were they called *step costs*?

EXERCISES

11-24 Profit Equation—Components
(L.O.1)

Identify each of the following profit equation components on the graph that follows:

a. The total cost line.

b. The total revenue line.

c. The total variable costs area.

d. Variable cost per unit.

e. The fixed costs area.

f. The break-even point.

g. The profit area (or volume).

h. The loss area (or volume).

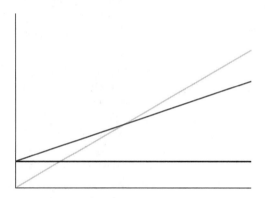

11-25 Profit Equation—Components
(L.O.1)

Identify the profit equation components on the graph (indicated by the letters) below:

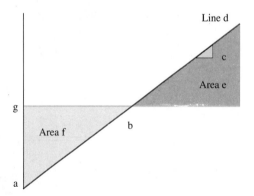

11-26 CVP Analysis—Planning and Decision Making
(L.O.2)

Western Cinema has the following costs and revenues for the year for movie ticket sales:

Total revenues	$7,200,000
Total fixed costs	$1,500,000
Total variable costs	$4,800,000
Total quantity	1,200,000 tickets

Required:

a. What is the average selling price per unit?

b. What is the average variable cost per unit?

c. What is the average contribution margin per unit?

d. What is the break-even point?

e. What quantity of movie ticket sales is required for Western Cinema to make an operating profit of $2 million for the year on ticket sales?

11–27 CVP Analysis— Planning and Decision Making (L.O.2)

Choose the *best* answer for each of the following:

a. If a firm has a negative contribution margin, to reach break-even:
   (1) Sales volume must be increased.
   (2) Sales volume must be decreased.
   (3) Fixed cost must be decreased.
   (4) Fixed cost must be increased.
   (5) Unit selling price must be increased.

b. If total contribution margin is decreased by a given amount, operating profit would:
   (1) Decrease by the same amount.
   (2) Decrease by more than the given amount.
   (3) Increase by the same amount.
   (4) Remain unchanged.
   (5) None of the above.

c. The break-even point would be increased by:
   (1) A decrease in fixed costs.
   (2) An increase in contribution margin ratio.
   (3) An increase in variable costs.
   (4) A decrease in variable costs.
   (5) None of the above.

(CPA adapted)

11–28 CVP Analysis— Planning and Decision Making (L.O.2)

Southwind Corporation has been organized to sell and install wind-powered generator systems in the Southwest. The marketing consultants for the company estimate that at a selling price of $4,000 per unit, the company should be able to sell 10,000 units per year. However, the company's financial advisor believes sales will be 7,000 units per year at the same price.

The company's controller estimates annual fixed costs will equal $12 million regardless of volume and that the variable cost on each unit will be $2,400.

Required:

a. Determine the profit or loss at the 7,000-unit and 10,000-unit activity levels.

b. What is the break-even point?

11–29 CVP Analysis— Planning and Decision Making (L.O.2)

Plume, Inc., is considering introduction of a new water ski with the following price and cost characteristics:

Sales price	$ 200 each
Variable costs	120 each
Fixed costs	300,000 per year

Required:

a. What quantity is required for Plume, Inc., to break even?

b. What quantity is required for Plume, Inc., to make an operating profit of $100,000 for the year?

11–30 CVP Analysis— Planning and Decision Making (L.O.2)

Refer to the data for Plume, Inc., in exercise 11–29. Assume the projected quantity for the year is 8,000 units. Consider *b*, *c*, and *d* independent of each other.

a. What will the operating profit be?

b. What would be the impact on operating profit if the sales price decreases by 10 percent? Increases by 20 percent?

c. What would be the impact on operating profit if variable costs per unit decrease by 10 percent? Increase by 20 percent?

d. Suppose fixed costs for the year are 10 percent lower than projected, while variable costs per unit are 10 percent higher than projected. What impact would these cost changes have on operating profit for the year? (Would profit go up? Down? By how much?)

11–31 CVP Analysis— Planning and Decision Making
(L.O.2)

a. Given the following formulas, which one represents the break-even sales level in units? P = Selling price per unit; F = Total fixed costs; V = Variable cost per unit.

(1) $\dfrac{F}{P - V}$

(2) $\dfrac{P}{F \div V}$

(3) $\dfrac{F}{V \div F}$

(4) $\dfrac{V}{P - F}$

(5) $\dfrac{P}{F - V}$

b. Which of the following assumptions is *not* made in break-even analysis?
   (1) Volume is the only factor affecting cost.
   (2) No change between beginning and ending inventory.
   (3) The sales mix is maintained as volume changes.
   (4) All of the above are assumptions sometimes required in break-even analysis.

c. A company increased the selling price for its products from $1 to $1.10 a unit when total fixed cost increased from $400,000 to $480,000 and variable cost per unit remained the same. How would these changes affect the break-even point?
   (1) The break-even point in units would increase.
   (2) The break-even point in units would decrease.
   (3) The break-even point in units would remain unchanged.
   (4) The effect cannot be determined from the given information.

(CPA adapted)

11–32 Extensions of the Basic Model— Semifixed (Step) Costs
(L.O.3)

Reyes Manufacturing Company manufactures and sells one product. The sales price of $10 remains constant per unit regardless of volume, as does the variable cost of $6 per unit. The company can choose to operate at one of the following three levels of monthly operations:

	Volume Range (Production and Sales)	Total Fixed Costs
Level 1	0–16,000	$ 56,000
Level 2	16,001–28,000	82,000
Level 3	28,001–38,000	108,000

Required:

a. Calculate the break-even point(s).

b. If the company can sell everything it makes, should it operate at level 1, level 2, or level 3? Support your answer.

11–33 Extensions of the Basic Model—Taxes
(L.O.3)

The Pedal-Pro bicycle shop is considering adding a type of helmet to its merchandise products. These helmets have the following prices and costs:

Selling price per helmet . . . . $	40.00
Variable cost per helmet	23.60
Fixed costs per year associated with these helmets	492,000.00
Income tax rate	40%

Required:

a. Pedal-Pro's break-even point in units is:
   (1) 18,000.
   (2) 90,000.
   (3) 30,000.
   (4) 72,000.
   (5) Some other amount.

b. How many units would Pedal-Pro have to sell in order to earn $246,000 after taxes?
   (1) 6,150 units.
   (2) 25,000 units.
   (3) 45,000 units.
   (4) 55,000 units.
   (5) Some other amount.

11–34 Extensions of the Basic Model—Taxes (L.O.3)

Lucky Locks Hair Care Corporation is contemplating introducing a new line of home perm kits. The kits would sell for $12 each. The variable costs associated with each kit amount to $3. If the kits are to be introduced nationwide, the company will have to obtain acceptable profits on a test-market basis. The fixed costs associated with test marketing amount to $324,000 per year.

Required:

a. Compute the break-even point in units for test-market sales.

b. If the desired profit level is $90,000 before tax, compute the sales level in units required to attain that profit level.

c. Assuming the tax rate is 40 percent and the desired profit level is $90,000 after tax, compute the required unit sales level.

11–35 Using CVP Analysis to Measure Volume (L.O.4)

Page's Bookstore estimates its fixed costs to be $28,000 per month.

a. Determine the break-even point in sales dollars if the contribution margin ratio is $1/3$.

b. Determine the break-even point in sales dollars if fixed costs remained at $28,000 per month but the contribution margin ratio was $4/10$.

11–36 CVP Analysis— Multiple Products (L.O.4)

Round Hut Pizza produces two products, 12-inch pizzas and 16-inch pizzas, with the following characteristics:

	12-Inch Pizza	16-Inch Pizza
Selling price per unit	$8	$12
Variable cost per unit	$4	$ 7
Expected sales (units)	10,000	15,000

The total fixed costs for the company are $69,000.

Required:

a. What is the anticipated level of profits for the expected sales volumes?

b. Assuming that the product mix would be the same at the break-even point, compute the break-even point.

c. If the product sales mix were to change to four 12-inch pizzas for each 16-inch pizza, what would be the new break-even volume for each of the products?

11–37 CVP Analysis— Multiple Products (L.O.4)

The Bay Street Submarine Shop sells three types of sandwiches with the following prices and costs:

	Selling Price per Sandwich	Variable Cost per Sandwich	Fixed Cost per Month
Sub #1	$3	$2	—
Sub #2	5	3	—
Sub #3	8	5	—
Entire company	—	—	$40,000

The sales mix is: 50 percent Sub #1, 33⅓ percent Sub #2, and 16⅔ percent Sub #3.

Required:
a. At what sales revenue does the company break even?

b. Draw a cost-volume-profit graph for the company.

PROBLEMS

11–38 CVP and Decisions

Peterson Publishing Corporation is currently selling a line of executive education courses at a price of $90 per course. The company maintains office and publishing facilities at an annual fixed cost of $800,000 for office and administration and $720,000 for publishing operations. The variable costs of each course unit include $15 for promotion, $6 for administration, and $12 for the published materials. At the present time, the company distributes 25,000 course units per year. Management is dissatisfied with the profitability of current operations and wishes to investigate the profit effects of several alternatives. The following questions have been raised by members of management in an attempt to evaluate the alternatives (each alternative should be considered independently).

Required:
a. What is the break-even level in terms of unit sales?

b. The company can hire an educational representative to sell the course materials independently of current sales activity. Current sales would remain the same, but the representative should be able to sell an additional 10,000 units at the $90 price. Promotion costs would amount to $20 per unit, and the representative would receive a commission of 25 percent of the sales price of each course unit. All other costs would remain unchanged. What is the profit effect of hiring the representative?

c. A publishing company has offered to produce the course materials at a price of $40 per course unit regardless of the number of course units. If this alternative is chosen, the fixed and variable costs of the current publishing operation would be eliminated. What is the profit effect of this alternative if sales remain at 25,000 units? If sales increase to 40,000 units?

11–39 CVP Analysis and Price Changes

Hillary's Pharmaceuticals is concerned about the possible effects of inflation on its operations. Presently, the company sells 200,000 units at a unit price of $15. The variable costs of production are $8, and fixed costs amount to $1,120,000. The present profit level is $280,000. Production engineers have advised management that unit labor costs are expected to rise by 10 percent in the coming year and unit materials costs are expected to rise by 15 percent. Of the $8 variable costs, 25 percent are from labor and 50 percent are materials. Variable overhead costs are expected to increase by 5 percent. Sales prices cannot increase more than 8 percent. It is also expected that fixed costs will rise by 2 percent as a result of increased taxes and other miscellaneous fixed charges.

The company wishes to maintain the same level of profit in real-dollar terms. It is expected that to accomplish this objective, profits will have to increase by 6 percent during the year.

Required:
a. Compute the volume in units and the dollar sales level necessary to maintain the present profit level of $280,000, assuming the maximum price increase is implemented.

b. Compute the volume of sales and the dollar sales level necessary to provide the 6 percent increase in profits, assuming the maximum price increase is implemented.

c.   If the volume of sales were to remain at 200,000 units, what price increase would be required to attain the 6 percent increase in profits?

11–40   CVP Analysis

Sunspot Company manufactures and sells sunglasses. Price and cost data are as follows:

Selling price per pair of sunglasses	$25.00
Variable costs per pair of sunglasses:	
Raw materials	$11.00
Direct labor	5.00
Manufacturing overhead	2.50
Selling expenses	1.30
Total variable costs per unit	$19.80
Annual fixed costs:	
Manufacturing overhead	$192,000
Selling and administrative	276,000
Total fixed costs	$468,000
Forecasted annual sales volume (120,000 pairs)	$3,000,000
Income tax rate	40%

Required:

a.   Sunspot Company estimates that its direct labor costs will increase 8 percent next year. How many units will Sunspot have to sell next year to reach break-even?

(1)   97,500 units.
(2)   101,740 units.
(3)   83,572 units.
(4)   86,250 units.
(5)   Some other amount.

b.   If Sunspot Company's direct labor costs do increase 8 percent, what selling price per unit of product must it charge to maintain the same contribution margin ratio?

(1) $25.51.
(2) $27.00.
(3) $25.40.
(4) $26.64.
(5)   Some other amount.

11–41   CVP Analysis with Changes in Cost Structure

Smokey Mountains Picket Fence Company manufactures prefabricated fence sections that sell at $6 per unit. The present facilities use an older model of semiauto-mated equipment. Variable costs are $4.50 per unit, and fixed costs total $300,000 per year.

An alternate semiautomated fence machine can be rented. This alternate machine would increase fixed costs to $550,000 per year, but variable costs would be reduced to $3.25 per unit.

Another fence machine supplier offers a fully automatic machine that would result in annual fixed costs of $800,000. However, the fully automatic machine would reduce the variable costs to $2 per unit.

There are no other costs or cash flows affected by the choice among these three alternatives.

Management is concerned about the break-even point for operations using each of these machines. Moreover, the sales volume for fence sections is quite erratic. Management is interested in the profit or losses that would occur with each type of equipment if the sales volume were 175,000 units and if the sales volume were 250,000 units.

Required:

Prepare a schedule showing the break-even point and the profit or loss obtainable for each equipment alternative at sales volumes of 175,000 and 250,000 units.

11–42 CVP Analysis with Semifixed Costs: Discovery Day Care Center†

Beverly Miller, director and owner of the Discovery Day Care Center, has a master's degree in elementary education. In the seven years she has been running the Discovery Center, her salary has ranged from nothing to $10,000 per year. "The second year," she says, "I made 62 cents an hour."

Her salary is what's left over after all other expenses are met.

Could she run a more profitable center? She thinks perhaps she could if she increased the student-teacher ratio, which is currently five students to one teacher. (Government standards for a center like this set a maximum of 10 students per teacher.) However, she refuses to increase the ratio to more than six to one. "If you increase the ratio to more than 6:1, the children don't get enough attention. In addition, the demands on the teacher are far too great." She does not hire part-time teachers.

Beverly rents the space for her center in the basement of a church for $1,000 per month, including utilities. She estimates that supplies, snacks, and other nonpersonnel costs are $100 per student per month. She charges $400 per month per student. Teachers are paid $1,200 per month, including fringe benefits. There are no other operating costs. At present, there are 30 students and 6 teachers in addition to Ms. Miller, who is not considered a teacher for this analysis.

Required:

a. What is the present operating profit per month of the Discovery Day Care Center before Ms. Miller's salary?

b. What is (are) the break-even point(s) assuming a student-teacher ratio of 6:1?

c. What would be the break-even point(s) if the student-teacher ratio was allowed to increase to 10:1?

d. Ms. Miller has an opportunity to increase the student body by six students. She must take all six or none. Should she accept the six students if she wants to maintain a maximum student-teacher ratio of 6:1?

e. [Continuation of part (d).] Suppose Ms. Miller accepts the six children. Now she has the opportunity to accept one more. What would happen to profit if she did, assuming she has to hire one more teacher?

11–43 Profit Targets: R. A. Ro & Company

R. A. Ro & Company, maker of quality handmade pipes, has experienced a steady growth in sales for the past five years. However, increased competition has led Mr. Ro, the president, to believe that an aggressive advertising campaign will be necessary next year to maintain the company's present growth.

To prepare for next year's advertising campaign, the company's accountant has prepared and presented Mr. Ro with the following data for this year (Year 1):

Cost Schedule

Variable costs:	
Direct labor	$8.00 per pipe
Direct materials	3.25 per pipe
Variable overhead	2.50 per pipe
Total variable costs	$13.75 per pipe
Fixed costs:	
Manufacturing	$ 25,000
Selling	40,000
Administrative	70,000
Total fixed costs	$135,000
Selling price per pipe	$25.00
Expected sales this year (Year 1) (20,000 units) . . .	$500,000
Tax rate: 40%	

---

† © Michael W. Maher, 1993.

Mr. Ro has set the sales target for next year (Year 2) at a level of $550,000 (or 22,000 pipes).

Required:

a. What is the projected after-tax operating profit for this year (Year 1)?

b. What is the break-even point in units for Year 1?

c. Mr. Ro believes an additional selling expense of $11,250 for advertising in Year 2, with all other costs remaining constant, will be necessary to attain the sales target. What will be the after-tax net income for Year 2 if the additional $11,250 is spent?

d. What will be the break-even point in dollar sales for Year 2 if the additional $11,250 is spent for advertising?

e. If the additional $11,250 is spent for advertising in Year 2, what is the required sales level in dollars to equal Year 1 after-tax operating profit?

f. At a sales level of 22,000 units, what is the maximum amount that can be spent on advertising in Year 2 if an after-tax operating profit of $60,000 is desired?

(CMA adapted)

11–44 CVP Analysis with Semifixed Costs and Changing Unit Variable Costs

Torous Company manufactures and sells one product. The sales price, $50 per unit, remains constant regardless of volume. Last year's sales were 12,000 units, and operating profits were −$20,000 (i.e., a loss). "Fixed" costs depended on production levels, as shown below. Variable costs per unit are 20 percent *higher* in level 2 (night shift) than in level 1 (day shift) because of additional labor costs due primarily to higher wages required to employ workers for the night shift.

	Annual Production Range (in units)	Annual Total Fixed Costs
Level 1 (day shift)	0–15,000	$200,000
Level 2 (night shift)	15,001–25,000	264,000

Last year's cost structure and selling price are not expected to change this year. Maximum plant capacity is 25,000 units. The company sells everything it produces.

Required:

a. Compute the contribution margin per unit for last year for each of the two production levels.

b. Compute the break-even points for last year for each of the two production levels.

c. Compute the volume in units that will maximize operating profits. Defend your choice.

INTEGRATIVE CASE

11–45 Converting Full-Absorption Costing Income Statements to CVP Analysis

Pralina Products Company is a regional firm that has three major product lines—cereals, breakfast bars, and dog food. The income statement for the year ended April 30, Year 4, is shown below; the statement was prepared by product line using full-absorption costing.

PRALINA PRODUCTS COMPANY
Income Statement
For the Year Ended April 30, Year 4
(in thousands)

	Cereals	Breakfast Bars	Dog Food	Total
Sales in pounds	2,000	500	500	3,000
Revenue from sales	$1,000	$400	$200	$1,600
Cost of sales:				
Direct materials	330	160	100	590
Direct labor	90	40	20	150
Factory overhead	108	48	24	180
Total cost of sales	528	248	144	920
Gross margin	472	152	56	680
Operating costs:				
Selling costs:				
Advertising	50	30	20	100
Commissions	50	40	20	110
Salaries and related benefits	30	20	10	60
Total selling expenses	130	90	50	270
General and administrative costs:				
Licenses	50	20	15	85
Salaries and related benefits	60	25	15	100
Total general and administrative costs	110	45	30	185
Total operating costs	240	135	80	455
Operating profit before taxes	$ 232	$ 17	$(24)	$ 225

Other data:
1. *Costs of sales.* The company's inventories of direct materials and finished products do not vary significantly from year to year. The inventories at April 30, Year 4, were essentially identical to those at April 30, Year 3.

    Factory overhead was applied to products at 120 percent of direct labor-dollars. The factory overhead costs for the Year 4 fiscal year were as follows:

Variable indirect labor and supplies	$ 15,000
Variable employee benefits on factory labor	30,000
Supervisory salaries and related benefits	35,000
Plant occupancy costs	100,000
	$180,000

    There was no overapplied or underapplied overhead at year-end.
2. *Advertising.* The company has been unable to determine any direct causal relationship between the level of sales volume and the level of advertising expenditures. However, because management believes advertising is necessary, an annual advertising program is implemented for each product line. Each product line is advertised independent of the others.
3. *Commissions.* Sales commissions are paid to the sales force at the rates of 5 percent on the cereals and 10 percent on the breakfast bars and dog food.
4. *Licenses.* Various licenses are required for each product line. These are renewed annually for each product line.

5. *Salaries and related benefits.* Sales, and general administrative personnel devote time and effort to all product lines. Their salaries and wages are allocated on the basis of management's estimates of time spent on each product line.

Required:

a. The controller of Pralina Products Company has recommended that the company do a CVP analysis of its operations. As a first step, the controller has requested that you prepare a revised income statement for Pralina Products Company that employs a product contribution margin format that will be useful in CVP analysis. The statement should show the profit contribution for each product line and the operating profit before taxes for the company as a whole.

b. The controller of Pralina Products Company is going to prepare a report, which he will present to the other members of top management, explaining CVP analysis. Expand on the following points for the report:
   (1) The advantages that CVP analysis can provide to a company.
   (2) The difficulties Pralina Products Company could experience in the calculations involved in CVP analysis.
   (3) The dangers that Pralina Products Company should be aware of in using the information derived from the CVP analysis.

(CMA adapted)

SOLUTIONS TO

Self-Study
Questions

1 *a.* Operating profit:

$$\pi = PX - VX - F$$
$$= \$180,000 - \$120,000 - \$36,000$$
$$= \$24,000$$

b. Break-even point:

$$X = \frac{F}{P - V} = \frac{\$36,000}{\$9 - \$6}$$
$$= 12,000 \text{ units}$$

c. Target volume:

$$X = \frac{F + \text{Target } \pi}{P - V}$$
$$= \frac{\$36,000 + \$30,000}{\$3}$$
$$= 22,000 \text{ units}$$

d. Target volume in sales dollars:

$$\text{Contribution margin ratio} = \frac{\$3}{\$9} = .333 \text{ (rounded)}$$
$$\text{Target volume} = \frac{\$36,000 + \$20,000}{.333}$$
$$= \$168,000$$

e. Units sold in April:

$$X = \frac{\$180,000}{\$9}$$
$$= 20,000 \text{ units}$$

f.

$$\text{Target volume} \atop \text{(sales dollars)} = \frac{\text{Fixed costs} + \text{Target profit}}{\text{Contribution margin ratio}}$$

$$\text{Target } PX = \frac{\$36,000 + .2PX}{.333} = \frac{\$36,000}{.333} + \frac{.2PX}{.333}$$

$$\text{Target } PX = \$108,000 + .6PX$$
$$.4PX = \$108,000$$
$$PX = \$270,000$$
$$X = \frac{\$270,000}{\$9 \text{ per unit}} = 30,000 \text{ units}$$

g. *Solution to cellular phone problem:*

Let X = Minutes of air activity. Set equations for the two levels of service equal to each other to find the indifference point.

Level 1   Level 2

$$\$50 + \$.40X = \$20 + \$.70X$$
$$\$30 = \$.30X$$
$$X = \frac{\$30}{\$.30} = 100 \text{ minutes}$$

Level 1 is cheaper if you use more than 100 minutes per month; level 2 is cheaper if you use less than 100 minutes per month.

Solution to student organization problem:

$$\text{Break-even} \atop \text{volume} = \frac{\$1,000 + \$800}{\$4 + \$1}$$
$$= 360 \text{ ticket holders}$$

2 *a.* To find the required contribution margin per unit:

$$\$30,000 = (P - V)20,000 \text{ units} - \$36,000$$
$$\$66,000 = (P - V)20,000 \text{ units}$$
$$\frac{\$66,000}{20,000} = (P - V) = \$3.30$$

The contribution margin per unit must be \$3.30.

b. To find the target volume expressed in sales dollars:

$$\text{Target volume} = \frac{\text{After-tax fixed costs} + \text{Target after-tax profits}}{\text{After-tax contribution margin ratio}}$$

$$= \frac{\$36,000 \times (1 - .3) + \$40,000}{.333 \times (1 - .3)}$$
$$= \frac{\$25,200 + \$40,000}{.233 \text{ (rounded)}}$$
$$= \$279,429$$

3 *a.* Compute the weighted-average contribution margin:

	I	II	III	Total
Units	100,000	150,000	250,000	500,000
Product mix	20%	30%	50%	100%

Weighted-average contribution margin:

$$.20(\$2) + .30(\$4) + .50(\$3) = \$3.10 \text{ per unit}$$

Or

$$\frac{(100{,}000 \text{ units})(\$2) + (150{,}000 \text{ units})(\$4) + (250{,}000 \text{ units})(\$3)}{500{,}000} = \$3.10$$

$$X = \frac{\$1{,}240{,}000}{\$3.10} = \underline{\underline{400{,}000 \text{ units}}}$$

b. To compute break-even sales dollars, find the weighted-average contribution margin ratio:

$$(.2 \times \$2/\$5) + (.3 \times \$4/\$6) + (.5 \times \$3/\$7) = .492 \text{ (rounded)}$$

$$\text{Break-even } PX = \frac{\$1{,}240{,}000}{.492 \text{ (rounded)}}$$

$$= \underline{\underline{\$2{,}520{,}000}}$$

Differential Cost Analysis

LEARNING OBJECTIVES

After reading this chapter, you should be able to:

1. Apply the concept of differential cost analysis.
2. Explain the effect of short-term special orders on costs.
3. Use cost analysis for pricing decisions.
4. Prepare a cost analysis for make-or-buy decisions.
5. Apply differential analysis when planning to add or drop product lines.

---

*I*n this chapter, we discuss the use of cost analysis in making such short-run operating decisions as pricing, whether to make or buy products, and whether to drop or add a product line. Each decision requires the comparison of one or more proposed alternatives with the status quo. The task is to determine how costs in particular and profits in general will be affected if one alternative is chosen over another. This process is called *differential analysis*. Although decision makers are usually interested in *all* differences between alternatives, including financial and nonfinancial ones, we focus our attention on financial decisions that involve costs and revenues.

Differential Analysis Process of estimating the consequences of the alternative actions that decision makers can take.

Short Run The period of time over which capacity will be unchanged.

Differential analysis is the process of estimating the consequences of alternative actions that decision makers can take. Differential analysis is used for both short-run decisions, like the ones we discuss in this chapter and the next, and for long-run decisions, like those discussed in Chapters 15 and 16. Generally, the term **short run** is applied to decision horizons over which capacity will be unchanged—one year is usually used for convenience.

There is an important distinction between short-run and long-run decisions. Short-run decisions affect cash flow for such a short period of time that the time value of money is immaterial and hence ignored. Thus, the *amount* of cash flows is important for short-run analysis, but their *timing* is assumed to be unimportant. If an action affects cash flows over a longer period of time (usually more than one year), the time value of money is taken into account, as discussed in Chapters 15 and 16.

Decisions by colleges whether to drop their football programs, such as at Santa Clara University and California State University, Long Beach, and decisions by professional sports teams to sign draft picks (for example, Patrick Ewing for the New York Knickerbockers and Michael Jordan for the Chicago Bulls) involve long-term differential analysis. Decisions by airlines to drop prices, such as USAir's decision to cut fares in the Northeast United States, are generally short-run decisions that have long-run implications.

DIFFERENTIAL COSTS VERSUS VARIABLE COSTS

Differential Costs Costs that change in response to a particular course of action.

Differential costs are costs that change in response to alternative courses of action. Both variable costs and fixed costs may be differential costs. Variable costs are differential costs when a decision involves possible changes in volume. For example, a decision to close a plant would usually reduce variable costs and some fixed costs. All of the affected costs would be termed *differential costs*. On the other hand, if a machine replacement does not affect either the volume of output or the variable cost per unit, variable costs would not be differential costs.

As the illustrations in this chapter are presented, you will find that differential analysis requires an examination of the facts for each option that is relevant to the decision to determine which costs will be affected. Differential and variable costs have independent meanings and applications and should not be considered interchangeable.

ARE HISTORICAL COSTS RELEVANT FOR DECISION MAKING?[1]

You have probably seen retailers advertise their products for sale at prices below invoice cost. And you may have wondered how they could stay in business if they sold their products below cost. Of course, they could not stay in business if they consistently sold below cost. Retailers recognize, however, that the original cost of their merchandise is a *sunk cost*—a cost that has already been incurred and is *not differential* when it comes to holding versus selling merchandise.

For example, suppose that a clothing shop has 15 pairs of slacks that each cost the retailer $20. No slacks have been sold at the established price of $39.95, and the retailer believes they can only be sold if the price is reduced. In repricing, the retailer should disregard the original $20 per pair cost. A number of marketing and inventory control issues might be considered, but the historical cost is irrelevant.

Of course, if the slacks are sold for less than $20 per pair, the retailer's financial statement would show a loss. If the slacks were sold for $18 per pair, for example, the statement would be as follows:

Sale of slacks (15 pairs at $18)	$270
Cost of goods sold (15 pairs at $20)	300
Loss on sale	$(30)

---

[1] Many of the concepts presented in this chapter were developed by J. M. Clark in his classic work, *Studies in the Economics of Overhead Costs* (Chicago: University of Chicago Press, 1923). Clark developed the notion that costs that are relevant for one purpose are not necessarily relevant for another. If the term *sacrifice* is used to summarize the various meanings of cost, then it becomes clear that the sacrifices (costs) for one set of actions are not necessarily the same as those for another set of actions.

REAL WORLD APPLICATION

The Great Gretzky Deal: A Good Business Decision?*

When the Los Angeles Kings acquired Wayne Gretzky from the Edmonton Oilers for $15 million and other considerations, many hockey executives and analysts said it was a good deal for both sides. This was true because of the different business climates of the two teams and their effects on the differential cost analyses.

The Edmonton Oilers were an established NHL powerhouse, with a captive sports audience. They were the only game in town. While the initial uproar over the trade of a national hero was, as expected, loud and rancorous, it did not translate to a great loss in attendance.

The benefits for the Oilers were substantial. In addition to the $15 million windfall, the Oilers were able to lay the foundation for the future by acquiring a young star (Jimmy Carson) and three number-one draft picks over the next five years. If the competition for the Edmonton sports dollar became more intense, the Oilers would be able to maintain their fan loyalty by fielding a consistently oustanding team. Finally, the Oilers would be reducing their payroll by the amount of Gretzky's salary. For the Oilers, differential revenues clearly were greater than differential costs.

The differential analysis for the Los Angeles Kings was more complicated. The Kings needed a big draw to compete in a sports market that included two professional football teams (the Rams and the Raiders), two major college football teams (UCLA and USC), two professional basketball teams (the Lakers and the Clippers), and two major college basketball teams (UCLA and USC). The Kings management hoped that Gretzky would provide star quality to a faceless franchise and also be the foundation for a winning team.

Before making the deal, the Kings concluded that they could recoup their investment in three years. In view of Gretzky's subsequent injury problems, this time horizon turned out to be fortuitous. The Kings consulted with the people who contracted for concessions and TV rights and estimated yearly differential revenues. They also estimated additional revenues from ticket sales.

Differential Analysis (dollars in millions)

Increase in Revenue:

Season ticket sales	$ 4.5
Single-game ticket sales	2.0
Sale of cable television rights	1.0
Play-off game	2.0
Concessions	1.0
Total increase in yearly revenues	$10.5

Increase in Costs:

One-time payment to the Oilers	$15.0
Interest on borrowed funds per year	$ 1.5
Payroll increase per year	2.0
Total increase in annual costs	$ 3.5

Three-Year Analysis:

Total differential revenue (3 × $10.5)	$31.5
Total differential costs [$15.0 + (3 × $3.5)]	25.5
Increase in profit	$ 6.0

* Based on J. Mills, "Gretzky: Deal with Dividends," *New York Times*, August 20, 1988, pp. 17, 29.

Decision makers are sometimes tempted to hold merchandise rather than sell it below cost in order to avoid showing a loss on their financial statements. In doing so, they may make a bad decision. If the merchandise is not sold immediately at a loss, it may be sold at a greater loss later, or it may have to be written off entirely if it cannot be sold at all. Under the circumstances, unless there is a possibility of a higher price later, the decision to sell now is the best.

The historical cost of an item is not always irrelevant, however. A decision to purchase an item for resale requires information about both its cost and its probable selling price. Nonetheless, once the merchandise *has been purchased*, the cash outlay (or promise to pay) has already occurred.

The cost is *sunk*, and although it is relevant to income determination, it is irrelevant to subsequent marketing decisions.

 *Self-Study* *uestion*

1 The following is a true story. An executive joined a tennis club and paid a $1,000 yearly membership fee. After two weeks of playing, the executive developed "tennis elbow" but continued to play (in pain), saying, "I don't want to waste the $1,000!" Comment.

The solution to this question is at the end of this chapter on page 478.

DIFFERENTIAL ANALYSIS: AN OVERVIEW

Special Order An order that will not affect other sales and is usually a short-run occurrence.

Which costs are relevant depends on the decision under consideration. A framework for decision making, based on a company that receives a **special order,** is diagrammed in Illustration 12–1. First, each alternative is set forth as a branch of a decision tree. Second, the value of each alternative is determined. Third, the alternative with the highest value is chosen.

For example, Quick-Print uses a modern copy machine to make copies for walk-in customers. The machine is usually idle about two hours each day. On October 15, B. Onst, who is running for political office, asks Quick-Print to produce 10,000 copies of letters, speeches, memoranda, and other campaign materials to be ready on October 22. Quick-Print has idle capacity adequate for this job. The candidate wants to pay only 8 cents per copy, even though the regular price is 10 cents per copy.

In deciding whether to accept the special order, the owner of Quick-Print estimates the following operating data for the week in question:

Sales (100,000 copies at 10¢)	$10,000
Variable costs, including paper, maintenance, and usage payment to machine owner (100,000 copies at 6¢)	6,000
Total contribution margin	4,000
Fixed costs (operators, plus allocated costs of the print shop)	2,500
Operating profit	$ 1,500

I L L U S T R A T I O N

Framework for Decision Making

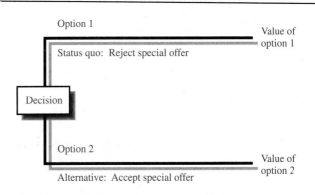

To make the decision, the owner identifies the alternatives, determines the value of each alternative to the company, and selects the alternative with the highest value to the company.

The values of the alternatives are shown in Illustration 12–2. The best economic decision is to accept the order because the company will gain $200 from it. Fixed costs are not affected by the decision because they are not differential in this situation. Therefore, they are not relevant to the decision.

Differential Costs versus Total Costs

Although the chapter focuses on differential costs, the information presented to management can show either the detailed costs that were included for making a decision or it can show just the differences between alternatives. For example, the first two columns in the Quick-Print example in Illustration 12–2 show the total operating profit under the status quo as well as under the special order alternative. This part of the presentation is referred to as the *total format*. The third column shows just the differences. This presentation is called the *differential format*.

Some managers prefer the total format because it enables them to see what their total revenues, costs, and profits will be under each alternative. Others prefer the differential format because it highlights the costs and revenues that are affected by the decision and enables them to focus on those items alone. We have found that in practice, managers will ask for a report that shows both total and differential costs similar to the format used in Illustration 12–2. Managers tell us that the costs of presenting both formats is relatively low. In addition, in complex organizations, decisions must often be approved by more than one person. By including both formats with a recommendation, one need not worry whether every person that must sign off on the report is going to want a total cost or a differential cost format.

I L L U S T R A T I O N

12–2

Analysis of Special Order, Quick-Print

a.   Comparison of Totals

	Status Quo: Reject Special Order	Alternative: Accept Special Order	Difference
Sales revenue	$10,000	$10,800	$800
Variable costs	(6,000)	(6,600)	(600)
Total contribution	4,000	4,200	200
Fixed costs	(2,500)	(2,500)	–0–
Operating profit	$ 1,500	$ 1,700	$200

b.   Alternative Presentation: Differential Analysis

Differential sales, 10,000 at 8¢	$800
Less differential costs, 10,000 at 6¢	600
Differential operating profit (before taxes)	$200

The Full-Cost Fallacy

Full Cost The sum of the fixed and variable costs of manufacturing and selling a unit.

Full-Cost Fallacy The assumption that fixed costs will vary with production.

The terms **full cost** or *full product cost* are used to describe a product's cost that includes both (1) the variable costs of producing and selling the product and (2) a share of the organization's fixed costs. Sometimes decision makers use these full costs, mistakenly thinking they are variable costs.

For example, D. Facto, a Quick-Print employee, claims that accepting B. Onst's special order would be a mistake. "Since our variable costs are $6,000 and our fixed costs are $2,500, our total costs for the week without the special order are $8,500 for 100,000 copies. That works out to be 8½ cents per copy, which is more than 8 cents per copy offered by Onst. We'd be losing a half cent per copy!"

By considering fixed costs in the analysis, D. Facto is including irrelevant information. The fixed costs will be incurred whether the special order is accepted or rejected, so they should not bear on the decision. This is known as the **full-cost fallacy** because it is incorrect to assume that *all* costs are relevant to every decision. This is a common mistake in short-run decisions, in part because full product costs are emphasized and readily available in accounting records. However, even though all costs must be covered in the long run or the company will fail, in the short run, it would be profitable to accept the order. While full product costs serve a wide variety of important purposes, they are not relevant to the kind of short-run operating decision described in the example above.

Differential Fixed Costs

In many short-run operating decisions, fixed costs remain unchanged because they are the costs of providing production capacity and capacity does not change in the short run. When short-run operating decisions do not involve a change in capacity, fixed costs remain unchanged and are therefore not differential.

In long-run decisions, however, fixed costs may be differential costs. For example, the addition of a new plant and new machines often involves differential fixed costs. Therefore, like variable costs, fixed costs must be carefully examined to determine if they are differential.

 **Self-Study Question**

2 Vista Enterprises, Inc., has an annual plant capacity to produce 2,500 units. Its predicted operations for the year are:

> Sales revenue (2,000 units at $40 each) $80,000
> Manufacturing costs:
>   Variable . . . . $24 per unit
>   Fixed $17,000
> Selling and administrative costs:
>   Variable (commissions on sales) . . . . $2.50 per unit
>   Fixed $2,500

Should the company accept a special order for 400 units at a selling price of $32 each, which is subject to half the usual sales commission rate per unit? Assume no effect on regular sales at regular prices. What is the effect of the decision on the company's operating profit?

The solution to this question is at the end of this chapter on page 478.

*COST ANALYSIS
FOR PRICING*

The price-volume trade-off is derived from the market demand for a product. By definition, variable costs change with volume. If a change in price results in a change in volume, variable costs change too. Therefore:

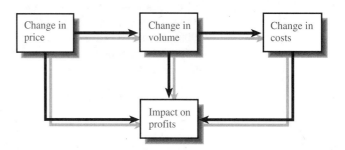

Thus, price-volume changes automatically involve changes in variable costs. The critical consideration for management is whether the joint effect of cost, price, and volume results in an increase or decrease in operating profits.

Cost-Plus Pricing. Some products are so unique, or their market price is unknowable, that costs plus a specified allowance for profits provide a basis for pricing. For construction jobs, defense contracts, most custom orders, and many new products, the cost of the product plays a significant role in determining its price.

An estimate of specific job costs is also an important guide for bidding on a job. If a bid price is too low compared to costs, the contract may be obtained, but the job will be performed at a loss. If a bid is considerably higher than costs, the contract will probably be lost.

*Short-Run and Long-Run
Differential Costs
for Pricing*

Sometimes the only way to sell a product is to cut its price. In such a case, the *minimum price is the differential cost that must be incurred to produce and/or sell the product.*

For example, Advent Manufacturing has a supply of products *on hand* that cost $4 each to manufacture. Selling them would require an additional $2 variable cost per unit. What is the *minimum* price Advent can charge? A quick answer might be $6 (manufacturing costs of $4 plus selling costs of $2). Actually, Advent can drop the price to $2, which is the differential cost to sell the products, and be no worse off than if it held the products unsold. Of course, the $2 is a *minimum* price; Advent's managers would prefer a higher price.

We observe theaters charging lower prices for matinee performances or airlines charging lower prices for certain kinds of passengers. These are examples of price discrimination to sell a product. **Price discrimination** exists when a product or service is sold at two or more prices that do not reflect proportional differences in marginal costs. If a seat would otherwise go unsold, airlines and theaters should be willing to sell it at a lower price, as long as the price exceeds the variable cost of filling the seat and does not decrease normal sales.

Price Discrimination Sale of product or service at different prices that do not reflect differences in marginal costs.

When used in pricing decisions, the differential costs required to sell and/or produce a product provide a floor. In the short-run, differential costs may be very low, as when selling one more seat on an already scheduled airline flight or allowing one more student into an already scheduled course in college.

In the long-run, however, differential costs are much higher. Returning to the airline example, long-run differential costs include the costs of buying and maintaining the aircraft, salaries for the crew, landing fees, and so forth. In the long run, these costs must be covered. To simplify this kind of analysis, the *full product costs* of making and/or selling a product are often used to estimate long-run differential costs. Hence, a common saying in business is: "I can drop my prices to just cover variable costs in the short run, but in the long run, my prices have to cover full product costs."

Use of Costs to Determine Legality of Pricing Practices

The Clayton and Sherman Anti-Trust Acts, the Robinson-Patman Act, and many state and local laws forbid certain pricing practices unless they are cost-justified. For example, predatory pricing to prevent or eliminate competition is illegal. A price that is below differential cost may be considered predatory. Certain kinds of price discrimination among customers are also illegal unless the discrimination is justified by actual differences in the costs of serving different customers. While this is only a brief overview of the highly complex legal issues involved, it serves as a reminder of the necessity to maintain cost records to justify pricing practices.

COST ANALYSIS FOR MAKE-OR-BUY DECISIONS

Make-or-Buy Decision A decision whether to make needed goods internally or purchase them from outside sources.

A **make-or-buy decision** is any decision in which a company decides whether to meet its needs internally or acquire goods or services from external sources. A restaurant that uses its own ingredients in preparing meals "makes," while one that serves meals from frozen entrees "buys." A steel company that mines its own iron ore and coal and processes the ore into pig iron "makes," while one that purchases pig iron for further processing "buys."

The make-or-buy decision is often part of a company's long-run strategy. Some companies choose to integrate vertically to control the activities that lead up to the final product. Other companies prefer to rely on outsiders for some inputs and specialize in only certain steps of the total manufacturing process.

Whether to rely on outsiders for a substantial quantity of materials depends on both differential cost comparisons and other factors that are not easily quantified, such as suppliers' dependability and quality control. Although make-or-buy decisions sometimes appear to be simple one-time choices, they are frequently part of a more strategic analysis in which top management makes a policy decision to move the company toward more or less vertical integration.

For example, the Better Homes Construction Company currently does its own site preparation and foundation work on the houses it builds. This work costs Better Homes $15,000 per house for labor, materials, and variable overhead. Should Better Homes consider buying site preparation and foundation work from an outside supplier? If satisfactory quality work could be subcontracted at anything below $15,000, Better Homes could save some of the money it now spends. The decision to buy would then provide a differential cost saving.

Make-or-Buy Decisions Involving Differential Fixed Costs

Net Minder Manufacturing produces tennis rackets. At the present time, it makes a cover for each racket at the following cost:

	Per Unit	10,000 Units
Costs that can be directly assigned to the product:		
Direct materials	$2.00	$20,000
Direct labor	1.00	10,000
Variable manufacturing overhead	.75	7,500
Fixed manufacturing overhead		2,500
Common costs allocated to this product line		15,000
		$55,000

This year's expected production is 10,000 units, so the full product cost is $5.50 ($55,000 ÷ 10,000 units).

Net Minder has received an offer from an outside supplier to supply any desired volume of covers at a price of $4.10 each. Here is the differential cost analysis that the Accounting Department prepared for management:

1. Differential costs are materials, labor, and variable overhead. These costs will definitely be saved if the covers are bought.
2. The direct fixed manufacturing overhead is the cost of leasing the machine for producing the covers. Although the machine cost is fixed for levels of production ranging from one unit to 20,000 units, it can be eliminated if we stop producing covers. Thus, although the machine cost is a fixed cost of producing covers, it is a *differential* cost if we eliminate the product.
3. No other costs would be affected.

The Accounting Department also prepared cost analyses at volume levels of 5,000 and 10,000 units per year, as shown in Illustration 12–3. At the volume of 10,000 units, it is less costly for Net Minder to make the racket covers. But if the volume of racket covers needed drops to 5,000, Net Minder would save money by buying the racket covers.

This decision is sensitive to volume. To see why, consider only the costs that are affected by the make-or-buy decision: direct materials, direct labor, variable overhead, and fixed overhead. By setting the costs of making equal to the costs of buying, we find there is a unique volume at which Net Minder is indifferent (in terms of costs) between making and buying as shown below:

Make		Buy
Direct Fixed Manufacturing Overhead	Variable Manufacturing Costs	Costs to Purchase Covers
$2,500 +	$3.75X =	$4.10X

where X equals the quantity of racket covers.

Solving for X:

$$\$2,500 + \$3.75X = \$4.10X$$
$$\$2,500 = \$.35X$$
$$\frac{\$2,500}{\$.35} = X$$
$$X = \underline{7,143}$$

12–3		Status Quo: Make Product	Alternative: Buy Product	Difference
Make-or-Buy Analysis, *Net Minder Manufacturing*	**a. 10,000 Units** Direct costs:			
	Direct materials	$20,000	$41,000ᵃ	$21,000 higher
	Labor	10,000	–0–	10,000 lower
	Variable overhead	7,500	–0–	7,500 lower
	Fixed overhead	2,500	–0–	2,500 lower
	Common costs	15,000ᵇ	15,000ᵇ	–0–
	Total costs	$55,000	$56,000	$ 1,000 higher

Differential costs *increase* by $1,000, so *reject* alternative to *buy*.

	b. 5,000 Units Direct costs:			
	Direct materials	$10,000ᶜ	$20,500ᵈ	$10,500 higher
	Labor	5,000ᶜ	–0–	5,000 lower
	Variable overhead	3,750ᶜ	–0–	3,750 lower
	Fixed overhead	2,500	–0–	2,500 lower
	Common costs	15,000ᵇ	15,000ᵇ	–0–
	Total costs	$36,250	$35,500	$ 750 lower

Differential costs *decrease* by $750, so *accept* alternative to *buy*.

ᵃ 10,000 units purchased at $4.10 = $41,000.

ᵇ These common costs remain unchanged for these volumes. Since they do not change, they could be omitted from the analysis.

ᶜ Total variable costs reduced by half because volume was reduced by half.

ᵈ 5,000 units purchased at $4.10 = $20,500.

The result is shown graphically in Illustration 12–4. At a volume greater than 7,143, the preferred alternative is to make; at a volume less than 7,143, the preferred alternative is to buy.

Note the importance of separating fixed and variable costs for this analysis. Although determining which costs are differential usually requires a special analysis, the work can be made simpler if costs have been routinely separated into fixed and variable components in the accounting system. The previous analysis would not have been possible for Net Minder if overhead costs had not been separated into fixed and variable components.

Opportunity Cost

Opportunity Cost The lost benefit from the best forgone alternative use of a resource.

Suppose Net Minder's volume is projected to be 10,000 covers. If volume is expected to be greater than 7,143 covers, the preceding analysis indicates that Net Minder should continue to produce the covers. However, that analysis has not considered the opportunity cost of the facilities being used to make racket covers. **Opportunity costs** are the forgone returns from not employing a resource in its best alternative use. Theoretically, determining opportunity cost requires consideration of every possible use of the resource in question. If Net Minder has no alternative beneficial use for its facilities, the opportunity cost is zero, in which case the previous analysis would stand.

ILLUSTRATION

12–4

Graphical Illustration of Make-or-Buy Analysis

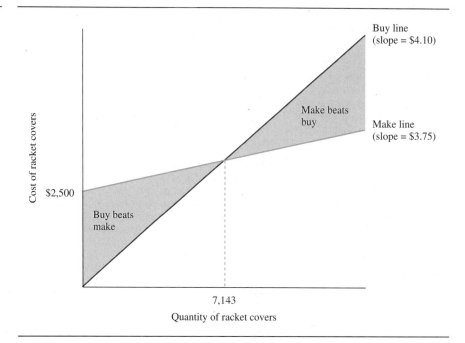

But suppose that the facilities where covers are made could be used to assemble a cheaper version of the racket Net Minder presently produces. This cheaper version would provide a differential contribution of $4,000. If making rackets is the best alternative use of the facility, the opportunity cost of using the facility to make covers is $4,000. In that case, Net Minder would be better off buying the covers and using the facilities to make rackets, as shown by the two alternative ways to analyze the problem in Illustration 12–5.

Almost without exception, determining opportunity cost is very difficult and involves considerable subjectivity. Opportunity costs are not routinely collected with other accounting cost data because they are not the result of completed transactions. They are possibilities only and must be estimated for each individual decision.

Some opportunity costs may be estimated in monetary terms, like the possible wages from the best job forgone; others may not be so readily quantified, like the status that accompanies certain occupations. Furthermore, if a benefit is forgone—and therefore never concretely existed—it is difficult to attach a realistic value to it.

Because they are so nebulous, opportunity costs are often omitted from decision-making analysis. It is easy to neglect them because they are not paid for and recorded in the accounts. Consequently, it is an accountant's responsibility to assist decision makers by reminding them that such costs exist. In general, opportunity costs occur whenever a scarce resource has multiple uses. Plants, equipment, money, time, and managerial talent all usually have opportunity costs. When a resource is not scarce or when a scarce resource can only be used in one way, opportunity costs are zero.

ILLUSTRATION

Make-or-Buy Analysis with Opportunity Cost of Facilities, Net Minder Manufacturing

	Status Quo: Make Product	Alternative: Buy Product	Difference
a. Method 1:			
Total costs of 10,000 covers from Illustration 12–3	$55,000	$56,000	$1,000 higher[a]
Opportunity cost of using facilities to make covers	4,000	–0–	4,000 lower[a]
Total costs, including opportunity cost	$59,000	$56,000	$3,000 lower[a]

Differential costs *decrease* by $3,000, so *accept* alternative to *buy*.

	Status Quo: Make Product	Alternative: Buy Product, Use Facility to Make Rackets	Difference
b. Method 2:			
Total costs of 10,000 covers from Illustration 12–3	$55,000	$56,000	$1,000 higher[a]
Less margin from use of facilities for making rackets	–0–	– 4,000	4,000 lower[a]
Net cost	$55,000	$52,000	$3,000 lower[a]

Although the presentation is different, the result is still a $3,000 cost *decrease* if the alternative is accepted.

[a] These indicate whether the alternative is higher or lower than the status quo.

Whether such costs should be measured precisely or only approximately depends on the costs and benefits of the resulting information.

Q Self-Study uestion

3 Electronics, Inc., produces an electronic part used in guidance and navigation systems. The cost of the electronic part at the company's normal volume of 4,000 units per month is shown in Exhibit A. Unless otherwise stated, a regular selling price of $940 per unit should be assumed.

   a. *Special order with opportunity costs.* On March 1, a contract offer is made to Electronics, Inc., by the federal government to supply 1,000 units to the Air Force for delivery by March 31. Electronics, Inc., plans to produce and sell 5,000 units during March, which will use all available capacity. If the government order is accepted, 1,000 units normally sold to their regular customers would be lost to a competitor for this month only. The contract given by the government would reimburse the government's share of March variable manufacturing costs, plus pay a fixed fee of $140,000. There would be no variable nonmanufacturing costs incurred on the government's units. What impact would accepting the government contract have on March profits?

   b. *Special order without opportunity costs.* How would your answer to (*a*) change if Electronics, Inc., had planned to produce and sell only 3,000 units in March; hence, they would not have lost sales to a competitor?

The solution to this question is at the end of this chapter on page 478.

EXHIBIT

Unit manufacturing costs:	
Variable manufacturing costs $400	
Fixed overhead (based on 4,000 units) . . . . <u>120</u>	
Total unit manufacturing costs	$520
Unit nonmanufacturing costs:	
Variable 150	
Fixed (based on 4,000 units) . . . . <u>140</u>	
Total unit nonmanufacturing costs	<u>290</u>
Total unit costs	<u>$810</u>

ADDING AND DROPPING PRODUCT LINES

Campus Bookstore hired a new general manager, a recent business school graduate, to improve its profit performance. As could be expected, the new manager asked to see the store's financial statements for the past year. The statements were prepared by product line for each of the store's three product categories: books, supplies, and general merchandise.

The statement that the manager received is presented in Illustration 12–6. It shows that the General Merchandise Department lost money during the third quarter of last year. "We could have increased operating profits from $6,000 to $13,000 for the quarter if we had dropped general merchandise," claimed the manager of the Supplies Department. "That department sold $120,000 worth of merchandise but cost us $127,000 to operate."

Although the economics of dropping the general merchandise line appeared favorable, the new manager asked an accountant to investigate which costs would be differential (that is, avoidable in this case) if that product line were dropped. According to the accountant:

1. *All* variable costs of goods sold for that line could be avoided.
2. *All* salaries presently charged to general merchandise, $14,000, could be avoided.
3. *None* of the rent could be avoided.
4. Marketing and administrative costs of $6,000 could be saved.

The accountant prepared the differential cost and revenue analysis shown in Illustration 12–7 and observed the following:

1. Assuming the sales of the other product lines would be unaffected, sales would decrease by $120,000 from dropping the general merchandise line.
2. Variable cost of goods sold of $95,000 would be saved by dropping the product line.
3. Fixed costs of $20,000 ($14,000 in salaries and $6,000 in marketing and administrative expenses) would be saved.
4. In total, the lost revenue of $120,000 exceeds the total differential cost saving by $5,000. Thus, Campus Bookstore's net income for the third quarter would have been $5,000 *lower* if general merchandise had been dropped.

ILLUSTRATION

CAMPUS BOOKSTORE
Third-Quarter Product-Line Financial Statement
(in thousands)

	Total	Books	Supplies	General Merchandise
Sales revenue	$400	$200	$80	$120
Cost of goods sold (all variable)	300	160	45	95
Gross margin	100	40	35	25
Less fixed costs:				
Rent	18	6	6	6
Salaries	40	16	10	14
Marketing and administrative	36	12	12	12
Operating profit (loss)	$ 6	$ 6	$ 7	$ (7)

ILLUSTRATION

CAMPUS BOOKSTORE
Differential Analysis
(in thousands)

		Status Quo: Keep General Merchandise	Alternative: Drop General Merchandise	Differential: Increase (or Decrease) in Operating Profits
1.	Sales revenue	$400	$280	$120 decrease
2.	Cost of goods sold (all variable)	300	205	95 decrease
	Contribution margin	100	75	25 decrease
3.	Less fixed costs:			
	Rent	18	18	–0–
	Salaries	40	26	14 decrease
	Marketing and administrative	36	30	6 decrease
4.	Operating profits	$ 6	$ 1	$ 5 decrease

The discrepancy between the supplies manager's claim that operating profits would have *increased* by $7,000 and the accountant's finding that operating profits would have *decreased* by $5,000 stems from their basic assumptions. The supplies manager assumed that the entire $32,000 in fixed costs allocated to general merchandise were differential and would be saved if the product line were dropped. The accountant's closer examination revealed that only $20,000 of the fixed costs would be saved—thus, the $12,000 discrepancy.

This example demonstrates the fallacy of assuming that all costs presented on financial statements are differential. The financial statement presented in Illustration 12–6 was designed to calculate department profits, not to identify the differential costs for this decision. Thus, using operating profit calculated after all cost allocations, including some that were not differential to this decision, incorrectly indicated the product line should be dropped. Financial statements prepared in accordance with generally accepted accounting principals do not routinely provide differential cost information. Differential cost estimates depend on unique information that usually requires separate analysis.

The bookstore statement, which was prepared on a contribution margin basis, clearly reveals the revenues and variable costs that are differential to this decision. But a separate analysis was required to determine which fixed costs are differential. It is, of course, possible to prepare division reports that reflect the division's contribution to companywide costs and profits. This *segment margin* would include division revenues less all direct costs of the division. Allocated costs would be excluded. These issues are addressed more fully in Chapter 22, "Decentralization and Performance Evaluation."

The Opportunity Cost of a Product Line

Keeping the General Merchandise Department may have an opportunity cost that we have not yet considered. Assume that the shelf space currently occupied by general merchandise could be used to increase the sale of books. The opportunity cost of retaining general merchandise is then measured by the probable forgone differential profits from the increased book sales. The accountant estimated the following figures to describe the substitution of increased book sales for general merchandise:

Drop general merchandise (from Illustration 12–7):	
Lost revenue	$120,000
Cost savings	115,000
Differential lost profit	$ 5,000
Add additional book sales:	
Additional book sales	$155,000
Less additional cost of books sold (all variable)	120,000
Contribution margin	35,000
Less additional fixed costs:	
Salaries	14,000
Marketing and administrative	4,000
Profit gained from additional book sales	$ 17,000

The analysis presented in Illustration 12–7 indicated that Campus Bookstore would lose $5,000 by eliminating general merchandise. However, given this additional information, an opportunity loss of $17,000 is incurred if the bookstore retains general merchandise and forgoes the opportunity to increase book sales. Based on these facts, Campus Bookstore is $12,000 ($17,000 gained from additional book sales − $5,000 lost from dropping general merchandise) better off to drop the General Merchandise Department and increase book sales. Illustration 12–8 presents a summary analysis for all three options: status quo, eliminate general merchandise, and eliminate general merchandise and increase book sales.

ILLUSTRATION

12–8

CAMPUS BOOKSTORE
Comparison of Three Alternatives
(in thousands)

	Status Quo: Keep General Merchandise[a]	Alternative 1: Drop General Merchandise[a]	Alternative 2: Drop General Merchandise, Increase Book Sales
Sales revenue	$400	$280	$435 ($280 + $155[b])
Cost of goods sold (all variable)	300	205	325 ($205 + $120[b])
Contribution margin	100	75	110
Less fixed costs:			
Rent	18	18	18
Salaries	40	26	40 ($26 + $14[b])
Marketing and administrative	36	30	34 ($30 + $4[b])
Operating profit	$ 6	$ 1	$ 18
		Worst	Best

[a] These columns are taken directly from Illustration 12–7.

[b] These amounts are the increase in revenue and costs taken from the discussion in the text.

APPLYING DIFFERENTIAL ANALYSIS TO QUALITY

The issue of quality is critical to a company's success in today's internationally competitive markets. We can use differential analysis to help us make choices among quality alternatives.

Consider Wafco, Inc., which purchases silicon wafers and then etches and plates them with copper so that they can be used to make specialized chips. Their purchase order specifications require that the chips be 15 mm in diameter with a thickness of .45 mm to .47 mm and not warped. Current purchasing specifications allow one reject for each 10,000 wafers purchased. Each wafer costs $1.00 to purchase. Wafco uses 6 million wafers a year and currently inspects all incoming wafers.

The inspection station currently identifies only 75 percent of all incoming wafers that do not meet Wafco's standards. However, 25 percent of the wafers that do not meet Wafco's specifications pass through and are processed until they reach the plating stage. Here the poor-quality wafers are detected because they cause the plating equipment to malfunction. The estimated cost of each interruption in production due to poor-quality wafers is $15,600. The annual costs of operating the incoming inspection station are $250,000.

Wafco is considering tightening its purchasing requirements from one reject per 10,000 wafers to only one reject per 1,000,000 wafers. If this can be achieved, Wafco will eliminate its incoming inspection station. Wafco's supplier of silicon wafers has agreed to the more stringent purchasing requirements, but at a new cost of $1.25 per wafer. Should Wafco accept this price or continue to operate as it has in the past? What other aspects should be considered when building quality into the process?

Under the current structure there are 600 bad incoming wafers per year (usage of 6,000,000 and 1 bad wafer per 10,000). Of these 600, 75 percent are caught by incoming inspection, but 25 percent slip by.

These 150 (25% × 600) will eventually cause the plating machines to malfunction at an estimated cost of $2,340,000 (150 × $15,600). If you add to that the cost of the inspection station, $250,000, and the cost of the wafers ($6,000,000), then you have the total costs incurred by Wafco when the quality of its incoming wafers is 1 bad wafer per 10,000. This totals $8,590,000, as shown in the status quo column in Illustration 12–9.

If the quality of its incoming wafers is improved to only one reject per million, then the number of rejects that will cause the plating equipment to malfunction will only be six. Remember Wafco no longer has an incoming inspection station. The calculations for this alternative are shown in Illustration 12–9.

These six malfunctions will cost Wafco an estimated $93,600 (6 × $15,600). Of course, the wafers cost more to purchase. The cost of the wafers is now $7,500,000 ($1.25 × 6,000,000). If we add this $7,500,000 to the $93,600, we get $7,593,600, which is the cost incurred by Wafco when the quality of its incoming wafers is 1 bad wafer per 1,000,000 wafers purchased.

Illustration 12–9 shows that Wafco's costs are lower if it purchases the wafers when the rejection rate is only 1 bad wafer per 1,000,000. By switching to this alternative, Wafco will save $996,400 per year ($8,590,000 − $7,593,600). This example is relatively straightforward because it assumes that all out-of-specification wafers are caught either at incoming inspection, or at the plating process. We simply choose the solution with the least cost.

Quality and Customers

Quality decisions, however, are not always this straightforward. In many cases, the defective product does not get detected until it reaches the consumer. Then, the consumer may not return the product, but simply purchase a competitor's product. In that case, the company loses market share and may even go out of business.

The major inroads by Honda, Toyota, and Sony in the U.S. market during the 1970s and 1980s came about because the Japanese products were higher quality. They were not cheaper, nor necessarily better styled, but they were higher quality, on average, than the products of their U.S. competitors. The good news for a company that suffers from a reputation for poor-quality products is that such a reputation can be changed. Many of us forget that, at one time, "made in Japan" implied *poor* quality, not good

ILLUSTRATION

12–9

	Status Quo	Alternative	Difference	
Cost of wafers	$6,000,000	$7,500,000	$ 1,500,000	higher
Cost of malfunction	2,340,000	93,600	(2,246,400)	lower
Cost of inspection	250,000	–0–	(250,000)	lower
Total	$8,590,000	$7,593,600	$ (996,400)	lower

---

quality. With dedication to continuous improvement in quality, Japanese manufacturers have completely changed their reputation from poor quality to high quality.

Is There a Trade-Off between Cost and Quality?

The impact of poor-quality products on your customer and on your company's reputation must be considered in any analysis of quality, even though such an impact is probably not accurately quantifiable. Many people have assumed there is a trade-off between cost and quality—higher quality comes only at a higher cost. In many situations, higher quality results in lower costs, if all costs are considered. For example, suppose a poor-quality part is inserted at the early stages in making a cellular telephone. All of the subsequent work done on that product until the defect is found is wasted. If the defect is not found until the product goes to the customer, the company incurs additional costs of dealing with customer returns and loss of reputation.

A total quality management approach would require quality from the outset. The small additional costs of purchasing higher-quality parts, inspecting at early stages, and requiring the work force to find ways to improve quality are usually justified by the waste that is avoided because labor and materials are not spent on a defective product and by the benefits of customer goodwill.

An added benefit of total quality management is employee morale. In general, employees want to work on quality products. Can you imagine how frustrating it would be to spend a significant amount of your workdays producing poor-quality products? Further, employees who participate in helping improve quality generally develop a strong sense of ownership and pride in their work.

Accounting systems are only partially able to measure the costs of quality. For example, Texas Instruments attempts to identify the following four categories of quality costs:[2]

---

[2] "Texas Instruments: Cost of Quality (A)" (Boston: Harvard Business School, Case 9-189-029).

1. *Prevention.* Costs of preventing poor quality products.
2. *Appraisal.* Costs of detecting poor quality products.
3. *Internal failure.* Costs of poor quality detected *before* products are shipped to customers.
4. *External failure.* Costs of poor quality *after* products are shipped to customers.

The accounting system can measure costs of prevention and appraisal (for example, inspection), but is not good at measuring the cost of external failure after a product gets to the customer.

Decisions involving trade-offs between costs and quality require top-management involvement, as exemplified in the Exxon plants in the real world application, "Costs and Quality." In general, only top management is in a position to evaluate the impact of quality on production, purchasing, *and* customers.

SUMMARY

This chapter discusses *differential analysis*. Differential analysis determines *what* would differ and by *how much* if alternative actions are taken. Differential analysis is performed by comparing alternatives to the *status quo*, using the following model:

Status Quo	Alternative	Difference
Revenue	Revenue	Change in revenue
less	less	less
Variable costs	Variable costs	Change in variable costs
equals	equals	equals
Total contribution	Total contribution	Change in total contribution
less	less	less
Fixed costs	Fixed costs	Change in fixed costs
equals	equals	equals
Status quo's profit	Alternative's profit	Change in profits

This chapter has focused on identifying and measuring differential costs, which are the costs that are different under different alternatives. Costs that are different under alternative actions are also known as relevant costs. Costs that do *not* differ are not relevant for determining the financial consequences of alternatives.

TERMS AND CONCEPTS

The following terms and concepts should be familiar to you after reading this chapter:

Differential Analysis, *442*

Differential Costs, *443*

Full Cost, *447*

Full-Cost Fallacy, *447*

Make-or-Buy Decision, *449*

Opportunity Costs, *451*

Price Discrimination, *448*

Short Run, *442*

Special Order, *445*

Sunk Cost, *443*

QUESTIONS

12–1   One of your acquaintances notes: "This whole subject of differential costing is easy—variable costs are the only costs that are relevant." How would you respond?

12–2   When, if ever, are fixed costs differential?

12–3   What is the difference between a sunk cost and a differential cost?

12–4   Are sunk costs ever differential costs?

12–5   A manager in your organization just received a special order at a price that is "below cost." The manager points to the document and says: "These are the kinds of orders that will get you in trouble. Every sale must bear its share of the full costs of running the business. If we sell below our full cost, we'll be out of business in no time." Respond to this remark.

12–6   What factors should a company consider when deciding whether to close a division that shows an operating loss?

12–7   Why are opportunity costs often excluded from differential cost analyses?

12–8   Should opportunity costs be excluded from differential cost analyses? Why or why not?

12–9   If you are considering driving to a weekend resort for a quick break from school, what are the differential costs of operating your car for that drive?

12–10   If you are considering buying a second car, what are the differential costs of that decision? Are the differential costs in this question the same as in question 12–9? Why or why not?

12–11   Multiple-choice. Choose the best answer.

    a.   In a make-or-buy decision:
        (1)   Only direct materials costs are relevant.
        (2)   Fixed costs that can be avoided in the future are relevant to the decision.
        (3)   Fixed costs that will not change regardless of the decision are relevant.
        (4)   Only conversion costs are relevant.

    b.   In deciding whether to manufacture a part or buy it from an outside vendor, a cost that is irrelevant to the short-run decision is:
        (1)   Direct labor.
        (2)   Variable overhead.
        (3)   Fixed overhead that will be avoided if the part is bought from an outside vendor.
        (4)   Fixed overhead that will continue even if the part is bought from an outside vendor.

    c.   Production of a special order will increase operating profit when the additional revenue from the special order is greater than:
        (1)   The conversion costs incurred in producing the order.
        (2)   The direct material costs in producing the order.
        (3)   The fixed costs incurred in producing the order.
        (4)   The indirect costs of producing the order.
        (5)   The differential costs of producing the order.

    d.   In considering a special-order situation that will enable a company to make use of presently idle capacity, which of the following costs would probably not be differential?
        (1)   Materials.
        (2)   Depreciation of buildings.

(3)   Direct labor.

(4)   Variable overhead.

(CPA adapted)

12-12   Refer to the real world application about Gretzky. For a sports star that was recently traded, or signed as a rookie, what analysis do you think the hiring team used?

12-13   Refer to the real world application, "Costs and Quality." Why might the manager of the maintenance staff not already have hired the maintenance people needed to prevent the compressor breakdowns?

EXERCISES

Note: Income taxes should be ignored unless explicitly required in the exercise, problem, or case.

12-14   Using Differential Analysis
(L.O.1)

Memory Corporation has a batch of obsolete DRAMS, which are carried in inventory at a cost of $20,000. If the DRAMS are remachined for $5,000, they could be sold for $9,000. If the DRAMS are scrapped, they could be sold for $3,000.

Required:

What is the optimal alternative? What costs are differential?

(CPA adapted)

12-15   Special Orders
(L.O.2)

Halotech Company makes car headlights. Data from the forecasted income statement for the year before any special orders are as follows:

	Amount	Per Unit
Sales revenue	$ 4,000,000	$10.00
Manufacturing costs	3,200,000	8.00
Gross profit	800,000	2.00
Marketing costs	300,000	.75
Operating profit	$ 500,000	$ 1.25

Fixed costs included in the above forecasted income statement are $1,400,000 in manufacturing costs and $100,000 in marketing costs. These costs would not be affected by the following order.

A special order offering to buy 50,000 headlights for $6.50 each was made to Halotech. Halotech has enough idle capacity to process this order.

Required:

What impact would acceptance of the special order have on operating profit?

(CPA adapted)

12-16   Special Orders
(L.O.2)

Burnett Manufacturing, Inc., is presently operating at 50 percent of practical capacity and producing about 50,000 units annually of a patented electronic component. Burnett recently received an offer from a company in Yokohama, Japan, to purchase 30,000 components at $6 per unit. No other orders are foreseen. Burnett has not previously sold components in Japan. Budgeted production costs for 50,000 and 80,000 units of output follow:

Units	50,000	80,000
Costs:		
Direct materials	$75,000	$120,000
Direct labor	75,000	120,000
Factory overhead	200,000	248,000
Total costs	$350,000	$488,000
Cost per unit	$7.00	$6.10

The sales manager thinks the order should be accepted, even if it results in a loss, because she feels the sales may build up future markets. The production manager does not wish to have the order accepted, primarily because the order would show a loss of $.10 per unit when computed on the new average unit cost.

Required:

a. Explain what caused the drop in cost from $7 per unit to $6.10 per unit when budgeted production increased from 50,000 to 80,000 units. Show supporting computations.

b. Should the order from the company in Yokohama be accepted?

(CPA adapted)

12–17 Pricing Decisions
(L.O.3)

The following data relate to a year's budgeted activity (100,000 units) for Classic Corporation, a single-product company:

	Per Unit
Selling price	$5.00
Variable manufacturing costs	1.00
Variable marketing costs	2.00
Fixed manufacturing costs (based on 100,000 units)	.25
Fixed marketing costs (based on 100,000 units)	.65

Total fixed costs remain unchanged between 25,000 units and total capacity of 160,000 units.

An order is received for 10,000 units to be used in an unrelated market. The sale would require production of 10,000 extra units.

Required:

What price per unit should be charged on the special order to increase operating profit by $15,000?

(CPA adapted)

12–18 Pricing Decisions
(L.O.3)

Penguin's sells ice cream for $3.00 per quart. The cost of each quart is as follows:

Materials	$1.00
Labor	.50
Variable overhead	.25
Fixed overhead ($20,000 per month, 20,000 quarts per month)	1.00
Total cost per quart	$2.75

One of Penguin's regular customers asked the company to fill a special order of 800 quarts at a selling price of $2.25 per quart for a special picnic. The order could be filled with Penguin's capacity without affecting total fixed costs for the month.

Penguin's general manager was concerned about selling the ice cream below the cost of $2.75 per quart and has asked for your advice.

Required:

a. Prepare a schedule to show the impact on Penguin's profits of providing 800 quarts of ice cream in addition to the regular production and sales of 20,000 quarts per month.

b. Based solely on the data given, what is the lowest price per quart at which the ice cream in the special order could be sold without reducing Penguin's profits?

12–19 Cost Analysis for Pricing Decisions
(L.O.3)

Sound Safe, Inc., has operated a violin case manufacturing business since 1920. The regular price of violin cases is $50 each. Sound Safe's controller has prepared cost data on these cases based on a normal selling volume of 20,000 cases per year:

Direct materials	$ 7.50
Direct labor	10.00
Overhead	8.00 (75% fixed)
Marketing and administrative	4.00 (all fixed)
Total cost	$29.50

This week, the Ness Corporation moved into Sound Safe's market area. Ness instituted a media campaign designed to lure Sound Safe's customers away. Indeed, Ness offered violin cases at one half of Sound Safe's selling price.

Sound Safe estimates that if it meets the Ness Corporation price, its volume will increase to 25,000 cases because people who previously were buying elsewhere would be induced to buy locally. However, if it does not meet Ness's price, Sound Safe's volume will fall to 5,000 cases per year.

Required:

a. Prepare a schedule that compares the "status quo" (price = $50; quantity = 5,000) with the alternative (price = $25; quantity = 25,000).

b. What should Sound Safe do?

12–20 Make-or-Buy Decisions (L.O.4)

Quiksilver makes bicycles. For years it has made the rear wheel assembly for its bicycles. Recently, Weeler Company offered to sell these rear wheel assemblies to Quiksilver. If Quiksilver makes the assembly, its cost per rear wheel assembly is as follows:

Direct materials	$ 7
Direct labor	30
Variable overhead	12
Fixed overhead applied	16
	$65

These costs are based on annual production of 20,000 units.

Weeler offered to sell the assembly to Quiksilver for $60 each. The total order would amount to 20,000 rear wheel assemblies per year. Quiksilver's management will buy these assemblies instead of making them if Quiksilver can save at least $25,000 per year. If Quiksilver accepts Weeler's offer, annual fixed overhead of $200,000 would be eliminated.

Required:

Should Quiksilver make rear wheel assemblies or buy them from Weeler? Prepare a schedule that shows the differential costs per rear wheel assembly.

12–21 Make-or-Buy Decisions (L.O.4)

Yaver, Inc., has been manufacturing 5,000 units per month of part 10541, which is used in the manufacture of one of its products. At this level of production, the cost per unit of manufacturing part 10541 is as follows:

Direct materials	$ 3
Direct labor	11
Variable overhead	4
Fixed overhead applied	6
Total	$24

Brown Company has offered to sell Yaver 5,000 units of part 10541 for $22 a unit. Yaver has determined that it could use the facilities presently used to manufacture part 10541 to manufacture product RAC, which would generate an additional contribution margin per month of $15,000. Yaver has also determined that one third of the fixed overhead applied will be saved even if part 10541 is purchased from Brown and product RAC is made.

Required:

Prepare a schedule to show the effect of purchasing part 10541 from Brown at $22 a unit. Assume Yaver would take the opportunity to make product RAC.

(CPA adapted)

12–22 Make-or-Buy Decisions
(L.O.4)

Snead Company needs 20,000 units of a certain part to use in its production cycle. Snead estimates the costs to make the part as follows:

Direct materials	$ 6
Direct labor	21
Variable overhead	8
Fixed overhead applied	10
Total	$45

The cost to buy the part from the Palmer Company is $42. Sixty percent of the fixed overhead applied to this product will continue regardless of what decision is made. What are the differential costs of the make-or-buy decision?

(CPA adapted)

12–23 Make-or-Buy Decisions
(L.O.4)

Sailsport purchases sails and produces sailboats. It currently produces 1,500 sailboats a year, operating at 70 percent of capacity. Currently, Sailsport purchases sails for $280 each, but the company is considering making sails instead. Sailsport can manufacture sails for $90 per sail for materials, $80 per sail for direct labor, and $130 per sail for overhead. Sails could be made without increasing Sailsport's capacity.

Sam Sport, the president of Sailsport, has come to you for advice. "It would cost me $300 to make the sails," he said, "but only $280 to buy. Should I continue buying them?" He added, "Materials and labor are variable costs, but variable overhead would be only $60 per sail." (Sam uses one sail per boat.)

Required:

What should Sam do? Prepare a schedule to show the differential costs.

12–24 Make or Buy with Opportunity Costs
(L.O.4)

Refer to the facts in exercise 12–23. If Sam suddenly finds an opportunity to rent out the unused capacity of his factory for $80,000 per year, would your answer in exercise 12–23 change? Why or why not?

12–25 Dropping Product Lines
(L.O.5)

Refer to the data for Campus Bookstores that appear in Illustration 12–8. Assume that all facts are the same as presented in Illustration 12–8 except the following:

1. Salaries listed under fixed costs are $40,000 under all three alternatives (that is, there is no reduction in fixed cost salaries under alternative 1).

2. Under alternative 2, rent increases to $32,000.

Required:

Prepare a new comparison of the three choices; namely, status quo, alternative 1, and alternative 2.

12–26 Dropping Product Lines
(L.O.5)

Bonzai Ski Company is presently operating at 75 percent of capacity. Worried about the company's performance, the president is considering dropping the company's line of cross-country skis. If the cross-country skis are dropped, the revenue associated with cross-country skis would be lost and the related variable costs would be saved. In addition, fixed costs for the company would be reduced by 15 percent of the total fixed costs.

Segmented income statements appear as follows:

	Product		
	Downhill Racing Skis	Cross-Country Skis	Regular Downhill Skis
Sales	$32,600	$ 42,800	$ 51,200
Variable costs	22,000	38,600	40,100
Contribution margin	10,600	4,200	11,100
Fixed costs allocated to each product line	4,700	6,000	7,100
Operating profit (loss)	$ 5,900	$ (1,800)	$ 4,000

Required:

Prepare a differential cost schedule like the one in Illustration 12–7 to indicate whether Bonzai Ski Company should drop the cross-country ski product line.

12–27 Dropping Product Lines
(L.O.5)

Anderhouse & Watersen is a public accounting firm that offers three types of services: audit, tax, and consulting. The firm is concerned about the profitability of its consulting business and is considering dropping that line. If the consulting business is dropped, more tax work would be done. If consulting is dropped, all consulting revenues would be lost, all of the variable costs associated with consulting would be saved, and 50 percent of the fixed costs associated with consulting would be saved. Tax revenues are expected to increase by 45 percent, the variable costs associated with tax would increase by 45 percent, and the fixed costs associated with tax would increase by 20 percent. Revenues and costs associated with auditing would not be affected.

Segmented income statements for these three product lines appear as follows:

	Product		
	Consulting	Tax	Auditing
Revenue	$300,000	$400,000	$500,000
Variable costs	250,000	300,000	350,000
Contribution margin	50,000	100,000	150,000
Fixed costs	50,000	60,000	80,000
Operating profit	$ -0-	$ 40,000	$ 70,000

Required:

Prepare a differential cost schedule like the one in Illustration 12–8 to indicate whether Anderhouse & Watersen should (1) drop the consulting line without increasing tax, or (2) drop consulting and increase tax work.

PROBLEMS

12–28 Special-Order Costs

Brike Company, which manufactures robes, has enough idle capacity available to accept a special order of 10,000 robes at $8 a robe. A predicted income statement for the year without this special order is as follows:

	Per Unit	Total
Sales revenue	$12.50	$1,250,000
Manufacturing costs:		
Variable	6.25	625,000
Fixed	1.75	175,000
Total manufacturing costs	8.00	800,000
Gross profit	4.50	450,000
Marketing costs:		
Variable	1.80	180,000
Fixed	1.45	145,000
Total marketing costs	3.25	325,000
Operating profit	$ 1.25	$ 125,000

If the order is accepted, variable marketing costs on the special order would be reduced by 25 percent because all of the robes would be packed and shipped in one lot. However, if the offer is accepted, management estimates that it will lose the sale of 2,000 robes at regular prices.

Required:

What is the net gain or loss from the special order?

(CPA adapted)

12-29 **New Product Introduction— CVP Considerations**

Servo Gimmicks, Ltd., produces and sells new and unusual household products. The company recently received a proposal to manufacture a left-handed bottle opener. The Product Engineering Department estimates variable manufacturing costs for each unit of:

Materials	$ .25
Labor	.50
Overhead	.30
Total	$1.05

Variable selling costs include $.55 for packaging and shipping. In addition, Servo allocates $.10 of common fixed costs to each unit sold. If Servo decides to sell the product, they will launch a media campaign on late-night television. The media campaign will cost $450,000. Of course, Servo has a number of products, and if they don't produce the left-handed bottle opener, they will manufacture some other item. Servo estimates that any product they sell must contribute at least $500,000 to after-tax profits.

The Marketing Department estimates that the optimal selling price for the product is $3.99.

Required:

If Servo's tax rate is 45 percent, how many left-handed bottle openers must be sold to meet the profit target? Show computations in good form.

12-30 **Pricing Based on Costs—Multiple Choice**

E. Berg and Sons build custom-made pleasure boats, which range in price from $10,000 to $250,000. For the past 30 years, Mr. Berg, Sr., has determined the selling price of each boat by estimating the costs of material, labor, a prorated portion of overhead, and adding 20 percent to these estimated costs.

For example, a recent price quotation for boat A was determined as follows:

Direct materials	$ 5,000
Direct labor	8,000
Overhead	2,000
	$15,000
Plus 20 percent	3,000
Selling price	$18,000

The overhead figure was determined by estimating total overhead costs for the year and allocating them at 25 percent of direct labor costs.

If a customer rejected the price and business was slack, Mr. Berg, Sr., would often be willing to reduce his markup to as little as 5 percent over estimated costs. Thus, average markup for the year is estimated at 15 percent.

Mr. Ed Berg, Jr., has just completed a course on pricing and believes the firm could use some of the techniques discussed in the course. The course emphasized the contribution margin approach to pricing, and Mr. Berg, Jr., feels such an approach would be helpful in determining the selling prices of their custom-made boats.

Total manufacturing overhead for the year has been estimated at $150,000, of which $90,000 is fixed and the remainder varies in direct proportion to direct labor.

Required:

a. What is the proportion of variable overhead to total overhead used by E. Berg and Sons?
(1) 60 percent.
(2) 40 percent.
(3) 25 percent.
(4) 30 percent.

b. What is the variable overhead rate as a percent of direct labor-dollars?
(1) 25 percent.
(2) 30 percent.

(3) 10 percent.

(4) 15 percent.

c. If E. Berg and Sons accepts a customer's offer of $15,000 for boat A, what is the effect on profit (loss)?

(1) ($8,000).

(2) $1,200.

(3) $800.

(4) ($1,500).

d. What is the minimum price that E. Berg and Sons should accept for boat A, assuming no markup over cost?

(1) $18,000.

(2) $15,750.

(3) $15,000.

(4) $13,800.

(CMA adapted)

12–31 Special Order

George Jackson operates a small machine shop. He manufactures one standard product, which is available from many other similar businesses, and he also manufactures products to customer order. His accountant prepared the annual income statement shown below:

	Custom Sales	Standard Sales	Total
Sales revenue	$50,000	$25,000	$75,000
Materials	10,000	8,000	18,000
Labor	20,000	9,000	29,000
Depreciation	6,300	3,600	9,900
Power	700	400	1,100
Rent	6,000	1,000	7,000
Heat and light	600	100	700
Other	400	900	1,300
Total costs	44,000	23,000	67,000
Operating profit	$ 6,000	$ 2,000	$ 8,000

The depreciation charges are for machines (based on time) used in the respective product lines. The power charge is apportioned on the estimate of power consumed. The rent is for the building space, which has been leased for 10 years at $7,000 per year. The rent and heat and light are apportioned to the product lines based on amount of floor space occupied. All other costs are current expenses identified with the product line causing them.

A valued custom parts customer has asked Mr. Jackson if he would manufacture 5,000 special units for him. Mr. Jackson is working at capacity and would have to give up some other business in order to take this business. He can't renege on custom orders already agreed to, but he could reduce the output of his standard product by about one half for one year while producing the specially requested custom part. The customer is willing to pay $7 for each part. The material cost will be about $2 per unit, and the labor will be $3.60 per unit. Mr. Jackson will have to spend $2,000 for a special device, which will be discarded when the job is done.

Required:

Should Mr. Jackson take the order? Explain your answer.

(CMA adapted)

12–32 Costs of Health-Care Quality

Research Corners Hospital performs 7,400 major surgical procedures per year. To prevent postoperative infections, surgeons order the administration of antibiotics two hours before each major procedure. If the antibiotics are not administered at the proper time, or if they are not administered at all, the risk of postoperative infection is significant. At present, the hospital experiences 20 infections per thousand procedures, which is equivalent to the national average rate. The cost of an average postoperative infection is $14,000, which is borne by the hospital.

Patient Monitoring Systems, Inc., offers a computerized system that is placed at the patient's bedside and will notify the nurses' station when antibiotics should be administered to a surgery patient. The monitoring device will also note if and when the antibiotics are administered. Hospitals using the system discovered that the rate of postoperative infections fell to three per thousand when this monitoring system was used. Research Corners Hospital estimates it will require 50 of these monitoring units for all of its surgical procedures. The annual cost of each unit is $2,700.

Required: Should Research Corners Hospital acquire the monitoring units?

12-33 Quality and Costs Rupee Imports, Ltd., purchases and processes cloth. The cloth is cut by laser and assembled using a computerized system that handles all stages of processing. The cloth must be processed in its entirety, that is, in bolts. (It is not feasible to inspect the cloth, cut out defects, and still process the bolt.) Ten percent of the cloth received contains defects in weave that are severe enough to cause the cutting operation to shut down.

Engineers estimate that because of these defects, Rupee Imports must rent a laser cutting machine to prevent bottlenecks in the production. The cost of renting this machine is $8,500 per month. Incremental power, repairs, and other machine-related costs for the rental machine are $3,650 per month. The rental machine must be operated by one person whose wages and fringe benefits equal $2,500 per month. An estimated $4,100 of materials are lost each month due to weave defects.

Other defects such as dye irregularities are noted at final inspection prior to shipment to customers. Three thousand units per month are found to be defective at this stage.

Cost estimates to process each unit of cloth are as follows:

Cloth	$17.45
Trim, thread	6.20
Power	.90
Direct labor	1.40
Other variable overhead	7.30
Packing and marketing	2.80
Inspection costs	1.85
Allocated fixed costs	9.15
Total unit costs	$47.05

All of these unit costs are variable, except the allocated fixed costs. These unit costs do not include any provision for reworked or scrapped goods, nor do these estimates include costs associated with an additional cutting machine. Merchandise that is found to be defective at the inspection station is shredded and disposed at an additional cost of $0.75 per unit.

Rupee Imports' production limits are determined by market conditions and not by constraints on its capacity. Rupee manufactures and sells 20,000 units of good output per month. Fixed costs are allocated on the number of units of good output. The selling price per unit of good output is $100.00.

Rupee is considering purchasing cloth from an alternative supplier. The supplier will provide a higher-quality cloth with weaving defects that do not exceed 1 percent of the cloth area. If weave defects are this low, then Rupee can avoid renting an extra cutting machine. The engineers estimate that costs caused by weave defect shut-downs will total $2,750 per month plus material losses due to weave defects totaling $1,265 per month. Because the quality of the cloth is superior, Rupee estimates that final inspection rejects will total only 800 units per month. Of course, the higher-quality cloth will cost more. The price per unit is $22.35 instead of the $17.45 currently incurred.

Required:

What are the costs and benefits of each plan—that is, (1) rent the laser cutting machine to avoid bottlenecks and buy from the current supplier or (2) buy from the supplier of the higher-quality cloth? What other factors should be considered before making the final decision on the supplier?

12–34 Costs of Process Quality

Regent Chain Co. manufactures link chain for industrial use. Since a length of chain is only as strong as its weakest link, and since the industrial applications of Regent's customers require chain that will handle specific loads, quality control for Regent's output is extremely important. No defects are permitted in the output.

Under the current processing system, 1/2,000 links is defective because the welding of the link is not strong enough to meet output specs. Regent's monthly output is 1 million links. Regent maintains an inspection facility that tests every link for ability to bear the specified load. The testing facility costs $86,200 per month to operate. This facility will identify any link that is defective.

Defective links must be reprocessed by hand. The steps involved include removing the link from the chain, placing a new link in the chain, and hand-welding it. The reprocessed link must also be tested to make sure that it meets specifications. The cost to reprocess a link by hand is $11.83 per link. Testing facility costs are estimated at $28,000 fixed plus $116.40 every time the inspection process must be stopped to remove defective chain and send it for reprocessing.

Regent's management is considering a proposal to acquire a new welding machine and to use new welding rods. The new machine would cost $2,900 per month to rent and operate. The new rods would cost $.05 more per link than the present rods. With the new machine and rods, the rate of defective links would fall to 1/100,000.

Required:

Prepare a cost analysis to indicate whether Regent Chain Co. should adopt the proposal.

12–35 Cost of Quality

Cyberdene Robotics, Inc., manufactures robot arms used in automated manufacturing. Specifications for the robot arm include a requirement that the arm function for 2,000 hours without malfunctioning. Cyberdene finds that this level of reliability can be obtained only if the alloy used to construct the arm joints is cast so that there are no void spaces in the alloy greater than one micron in total volume. Cyberdene buys the arm joints (model X50) from an outside supplier. Cyberdene tests the alloy in the model X50 joints it receives using computer assisted tomography (CAT) scans. Rental of the scanning equipment and maintaining the scanning operation result in differential costs of $1,970,000 per year.

It has been Cyberdene's experience that 1/10,000 joints contains void spaces greater than one micron in total volume. The CAT scan process is able to identify 92 percent of the cast joints with this defect. These joints are returned to the supplier for credit. The remaining 8 percent enter the production process. Seven eighths of these defective joints are discovered after they have been installed on a robot arm and the assembled arm is inspected. These arms must be reworked to remove the defective joint and replace it with a good joint. The reworking costs are an average of $8,175 per defective joint discovered. The remaining one eighth of the defective joints escape detection and are shipped to customers. Many of these defective arms still meet the 2,000-hour requirement. However, 75 percent of them will fail before completing 2,000 hours of operation. When this happens, Cyberdene must replace the arm. This requires sending a repair crew by private aircraft to perform the replacement. Cyberdene estimates that the cost of sending a repair crew to replace an arm is $85,000 per arm replaced, including the cost of the replacement arm. All defective units installed at customer sites that fail within the 2,000 hours do so within one year of shipment.

Cyberdene manufactures 115,000 arms per year. Each arm requires 42 joints. For analysis purposes, assume that no more than one defective joint ever gets included in any one robotic arm. The current cost of the joints is $18.00 each. Cyberdene's supplier has offered to redesign the joint and make changes to the alloy. These efforts would result in a model X200 joint with a defect rate of 1/200,000 but would increase the price to $18.40 per joint. The detection rates during processing and at customer's sites would not change.

Required:

Prepare a cost analysis to indicate which model joint would be economically optimal for Cyberdene to purchase. Consider the following alternatives: (1) buy model X50, using the CAT scanning equipment, and (2) buy model X200, without using the CAT scanning equipment.

12–36 Comprehensive Differential Costing Problem

Hospital Supply, Inc., produces hydraulic hoists that are used by hospitals to move bedridden patients. The costs of manufacturing and marketing hydraulic hoists at the company's normal volume of 3,000 units per month are shown in Exhibit 12–36A.

Unless otherwise stated, assume there is no connection between the situations described in the questions; each is to be treated independently. Unless otherwise stated, a regular selling price of $740 per unit should be assumed. Ignore income taxes and other costs that are not mentioned in Exhibit 12–36A or in a question itself.

a. What is the break-even volume in units? In sales-dollars?

b. Market research estimates that volume could be increased to 3,500 units, which is well within hoist production capacity limitations, if the price were cut from $740 to $650 per unit. Assuming the cost behavior patterns implied by the data in Exhibit 12–36A are correct, would you recommend that this action be taken? What would be the impact on monthly sales, costs, and income?

c. On March 1, a contract offer is made to Hospital Supply by the federal government to supply 500 units to Veterans Administration hospitals for delivery by March 31. Because of an unusually large number of rush orders from their regular customers, Hospital Supply plans to produce 4,000 units during March, which will use all available capacity. If the government order is accepted, 500 units normally sold to regular customers would be lost to a competitor. The contract given by the government would reimburse the government's "share of March manufacturing costs," plus pay a fixed fee (profit) of $50,000. (There would be no variable marketing costs incurred on the government's units.) What

---

EXHIBIT

Costs per Unit for Hydraulic Hoists

Unit manufacturing costs:		
Variable materials	$100	
Variable labor	150	
Variable overhead	50	
Fixed overhead	120	
Total unit manufacturing costs		$420
Unit marketing costs:		
Variable	50	
Fixed	140	
Total unit marketing costs		190
Total unit costs		$610

impact would accepting the government contract have on March income? (Part of your problem is to figure out the meaning of "share of March manufacturing costs.")

d. Hospital Supply has an opportunity to enter a foreign market in which price competition is keen. An attraction of the foreign market is that demand there is greatest when demand in the domestic market is quite low; thus idle production facilities could be used without affecting domestic business.

An order for 1,000 units is being sought at a below-normal price in order to enter this market. Shipping costs for this order will amount to $75 per unit, while total costs of obtaining the contract (marketing costs) will be $4,000. No other variable marketing costs would be required on this order. Domestic business would be unaffected by this order. What is the minimum unit price Hospital Supply should consider for this order of 1,000 units?

e. An inventory of 230 units of an obsolete model of the hoist remains in the stockroom. These must be sold through regular channels (thus incurring variable marketing costs) at reduced prices, or the inventory will soon be valueless. What is the minimum price that would be acceptable in selling these units?

f. A proposal is received from an outside contractor who will make and ship 1,000 hydraulic hoist units per month directly to Hospital Supply's customers as orders are received from Hospital Supply's sales force. Hospital Supply's fixed marketing costs would be unaffected, but its variable marketing costs would be cut by 20 percent for these 1,000 units produced by the contractor. Hospital Supply's plant would operate at two thirds of its normal level, and total fixed manufacturing costs would be cut by 30 percent. What in-house unit cost should be used to compare with the quotation received from the supplier? Should the proposal be accepted for a price (that is, payment to the contractor) of $425 per unit?

g. Assume the same facts as above in requirement (f) except that the idle facilities would be used to produce 800 modified hydraulic hoists per month for use in hospital operating rooms. These modified hoists could be sold for $900 each, while the costs of production would be $550 per unit variable manufacturing expense. Variable marketing costs would be $100 per unit. Fixed marketing and manufacturing costs would be unchanged whether the original 3,000 regular hoists were manufactured or the mix of 2,000 regular hoists plus 800 modified hoists were produced. What is the maximum purchase price per unit that Hospital Supply should be willing to pay the outside contractor? Should the proposal be accepted for a price of $425 per unit to the contractor?

12–37 Analyze Alternative Products

Ocean Company manufactures and sells three different products: Ex, Why, and Zee. Projected income statements by product line for the year are presented below:

	Ex	Why	Zee	Total
Unit sales	10,000	500,000	125,000	635,000
Sales revenue	$925,000	$1,000,000	$575,000	$2,500,000
Variable cost of units sold	285,000	350,000	150,000	785,000
Fixed cost of units sold	304,200	289,000	166,800	760,000
Gross margin	335,800	361,000	258,200	955,000
Variable nonmanufacturing costs	270,000	200,000	80,000	550,000
Fixed nonmanufacturing costs	125,800	136,000	78,200	340,000
Operating profit	$ (60,000)	$ 25,000	$100,000	$ 65,000

Production costs are similar for all three products. Fixed nonmanufacturing costs are allocated to products in proportion to revenues. The fixed cost of units sold is allocated to products by various allocation bases, such as square feet for factory rent and machine-hours for repairs.

Ocean management is concerned about the loss on product Ex and is considering two alternative courses of corrective action.

Alternative A. Ocean would lease some new machinery for the production of product Ex. Management expects that the new machinery would reduce variable production costs so that total variable costs (cost of units sold and nonmanufacturing costs) for product Ex would be 52 percent of product Ex revenues. The new machinery would increase total fixed costs allocated to product Ex from $430,000 to $480,000 per year. No additional fixed costs would be allocated to products Why or Zee.

Alternative B. Ocean would discontinue the manufacture of product Ex. Selling prices of products Why and Zee would remain constant. Management expects that product Zee production and revenues would increase by 50 percent. The machinery devoted to product Ex could be sold at scrap value that equals its removal costs. Removal of this machinery would reduce fixed costs allocated to product Ex by $30,000 per year. The remaining fixed costs allocated to product Ex include $155,000 of rent expense per year. The space previously used for product Ex can be rented to an outside organization for $157,500 per year.

Required:

Prepare a schedule analyzing the effect of alternative A and alternative B on projected total operating profit.

(CPA adapted)

12–38   Differential Costs of Alternative Marketing Strategies

Calco Corporation has been a major producer and distributor of plastic products for industrial use. The Product Engineering Department has recently presented a proposal to produce a new product designed for the consumer market. The product is very well suited for the company's manufacturing process. No modification of machinery or molds would be required nor would operations in the Assembly Department have to be changed in any way. In addition, there is an adequate amount of manufacturing capacity available.

Management is considering two alternatives for marketing the product. The first is to add this responsibility to Calco's current Marketing Department. The other alternative is to acquire a small, new company named Jasco, Inc. Jasco was started by some former employees of a firm that specialized in marketing plastic products for the consumer market when they lost their jobs as a result of a merger. The only requirements of the Jasco people are that Calco hire the Jasco employees and take over a lease for office space.

The product would be manufactured by Calco, and the manufacturing costs would be the same for either marketing alternative. The Product Engineering Department has prepared the following estimates of the unit manufacturing costs for the new product:

Direct materials	$14.00
Direct labor	3.50
Manufacturing overhead	10.00
Total	$27.50

Twenty-five percent of the total overhead rate is for variable costs like supplies, employee benefits, power, and so forth; and 75 percent for fixed costs like supervision, depreciation, insurance, and taxes.

Calco's Marketing Department has developed a proposal for the distribution of the new consumer product. The Marketing Department's forecast of the annual financial results for its proposal to market the new product is as follows:

Sales revenue (100,000 units at $45)	$4,500,000
Costs:	
Cost of units sold (100,000 units at $27.50)	2,750,000
Marketing costs:	
Additional people hired	600,000
Sales commission (5% of sales)	225,000
Advertising program	400,000
Promotion program	200,000
Share of current Marketing Department's management costs	100,000
Total costs	4,275,000
Operating profit	$ 225,000

The Jasco people also prepared a forecast of the annual financial results. The forecast presented below was based on the assumption that Jasco would become part of Calco and be responsible for marketing the new product in the consumer market.

Sales revenue (120,000 units at $50)	$6,000,000
Costs:	
Cost of units sold (120,000 units at $27.50)	3,300,000
Marketing costs:	
Personnel—sales	660,000
Personnel—sales management	200,000
Commissions (10%)	600,000
Advertising program	800,000
Promotion program	200,000
Office rental (the annual rental of a long-term lease already signed by Jasco)	50,000
Total costs	5,810,000
Operating profit	$ 190,000

Calco's management believes profits will be $35,000 higher ($225,000 − $190,000) if the marketing is done by Calco's Marketing Department, but they have turned to you for help.

Required:

Prepare a schedule of differential costs and revenues to assist management in deciding whether to enter the consumer market.

(CMA adapted)

12–39   Analyze Auto Rental versus Reimbursement Policy

G & H Real Estate Agency requires all of its agents to travel throughout the entire area to list and sell property. The company has a reimbursement policy of $.25 per mile for all business-connected travel. The agents are responsible for all costs associated with the operation of their own automobiles. Last year, the average mileage claimed by an agent was 50,000 miles. G & H offices are open 300 days a year.

Jack Golden, the president, senses that some of the agents may have been claiming excess miles during the year. Golden is convinced that the annual mileage use would drop to 42,000 miles per year if the agents were not using their own cars. Therefore, he is considering providing automobiles to the agents.

Golden asked both International Car Rental and a local automobile dealer, Aron Motor, to present proposals. The proposals are described below:

International Car Rental's Proposal

International presented a lease arrangement with the following requirements:

1. G & H would rent 20 automobiles for an entire year at $66 per week per automobile and $.14 per mile.

2. When one of the 20 automobiles is in for service, International would provide a replacement at $7 per day and $.20 per mile. International would absorb all repair and maintenance costs. Normally, an automobile would be out of service only one day at a time, and each automobile can be expected to be out of service 12 days per year.

3. Cost of insurance is included in the weekly rental rate.

4. G & H would be required to purchase the gasoline for the automobiles at an average cost of $1.50 per gallon. International estimates that G & H should expect to get 21 miles per gallon.

Aron Motor's Proposal

Aron offered a purchase-buy-back arrangement with the following requirements:

1. G & H would buy 20 automobiles at $12,000 each. Aron would buy the automobiles back after one year at $7,000 each.

2. G & H would have to bring each automobile in once every two months for preventive maintenance and service. The cost to G & H for each visit would be $50. Aron would provide a loaner automobile at no additional cost. Aron would accept responsibility for any additional repair and maintenance charges.

3. G & H would have to purchase insurance at an annual cost of $200 for each automobile.

4. G & H would purchase one new set of tires each year at $400 per set.

5. G & H would be responsible for the purchase of gasoline at an average cost of $1.50 per gallon. The automobiles will average 28 miles per gallon.

Golden has asked your help in comparing the alternatives.

Required:

Calculate an annual before-tax cost to G & H for:

a.   The current reimbursement practice.

b.   The proposal of International Car Rental.

c.   The proposal of Aron Motor.

Based on these data, which alternative would you recommend that Golden accept?

(CMA adapted)

INTEGRATIVE CASES

12–40   **Sell or Process Further**

The management of Bay Company is considering a proposal to install a third production department within its existing factory building. With the company's present production setup, 200,000 pounds per year of direct materials are passed through Department I to produce materials A and B in equal proportions. Material A is then passed through Department II to yield 100,000 pounds of product C. One hundred thousand pounds of material B are presently being sold as is at a price of $20.25 per pound.

The costs for the Bay Company are as follows:

	Department I (Materials A and B)[a]	Department II (Product C)[a]	(Material B)[a]
Prior department costs	—	$33.25	$33.25
Direct materials	$20.00	—	—
Direct labor	7.00	12.00	—
Variable overhead	3.00	5.00	—
Fixed overhead:			
Direct (Total = $675,000)	2.25	2.25	—
Allocated (²⁄₃, ¹⁄₃)	1.00	1.00	—
	$33.25	$53.50	$33.25

[a] Cost per pound.

The fixed costs were developed using the production volume of 200,000 pounds of direct materials as the volume. Common fixed overhead costs of $300,000 are allocated to the two producing departments on the basis of the space used by the departments.

The proposed Department III would process material B into product D. One pound of material B yields one pound of product D. Any quantity of product D can be sold for $30 per pound. Costs under this proposal are as follows:

	Department I (Materials A and B)	Department II (Product C)	Department III (Product D)
Prior department costs	—	$33.00	$33.00
Direct materials	$20.00	—	—
Direct labor	7.00	12.00	5.50
Variable overhead	3.00	5.00	2.00
Fixed overhead:			
Direct (Total = $850,000)	2.25	2.25	1.75
Allocated (¹⁄₂, ¹⁄₄, ¹⁄₄)	.75	.75	.75
	$33.00	$53.00	$43.00

Required:

If sales and production levels are expected to remain constant in the foreseeable future, these cost estimates are expected to be true, and there are no foreseeable alternative uses for the available factory space, should Bay Company produce product D? Show calculations to support your answer.

(CMA adapted)

12–41   Differential Costs and CVP Analysis

You have been asked to assist the management of Arcadia Corporation in arriving at certain decisions. Arcadia has its home office in Ohio and leases factory buildings in Texas, Montana, and Maine, all of which produce the same product. The management of Arcadia provided you with a projection of operations for next year, as follows:

	Total	Texas	Montana	Maine
Sales revenue	$4,400,000	$2,200,000	$1,400,000	$800,000
Fixed costs:				
Factory	1,100,000	560,000	280,000	260,000
Administration	350,000	210,000	110,000	30,000
Variable costs	1,450,000	665,000	425,000	360,000
Allocated home office costs	500,000	225,000	175,000	100,000
Total	3,400,000	1,660,000	990,000	750,000
Operating profit	$1,000,000	$ 540,000	$ 410,000	$ 50,000

The sales price per unit is $25.

Due to the marginal results of operations of the factory in Maine, Arcadia has decided to cease operations and sell that factory's machinery and equipment by the end of this year. Arcadia expects that the proceeds from the sale of these assets would be greater than their book value and would cover all termination costs.

Arcadia, however, would like to continue serving its customers in that area if it is economically feasible and is considering one of the following three alternatives:

1. Expand the operations of the Montana factory by using space presently idle. This move would result in the following changes in that factory's operations:

	Increase over Factory's Current Operations
Sales revenue	50%
Fixed costs:	
Factory	20
Administration	10

   Under this proposal, variable costs would be $8 per unit sold.

2. Enter into a long-term contract with a competitor who will serve that area's customers. This competitor would pay Arcadia a royalty of $4 per unit based on an estimate of 30,000 units being sold.

3. Close the Maine factory and not expand the operations of the Montana factory.

   Total home office costs of $500,000 will remain the same under each situation.

Required:

To assist the management of Arcadia Corporation, prepare a schedule computing Arcadia's estimated operating profit from each of the following options:

a. Expansion of the Montana factory.

b. Negotiation of long-term contract on a royalty basis.

c. Shutdown of Maine operations with no expansion at other locations.

(CPA adapted)

SOLUTIONS TO

Self-Study
Questions

1   The $1,000 is a sunk cost and should be irrelevant to the executive. The executive should consider only the advantages and disadvantages of playing henceforth, including the pain, but the $1,000 should be ignored. (The executive later quit playing until the tennis elbow healed.)

2   The special order should be accepted, as shown by the following two alternative analyses:

	Status Quo	Alternative	Difference
Sales revenues	$80,000	$92,800	$12,800
Variable costs	(53,000)	(63,100)	(10,100)
Contribution	27,000	29,700	2,700
Fixed costs	(19,500)	(19,500)	–0–
Operating profit	$ 7,500	$10,200	$ 2,700
Special-order sales (400 × $32)			$12,800
Less variable costs:			
Manufacturing (400 × $24)		$ 9,600	
Sales commission (400 × $1.25)		500	10,100
Addition to company profit			$ 2,700

3   *a.*   Accepting the special order would reduce profits by $250,000.

	Status Quo	Alternative			Difference
		Regular	Government	Total	
Volume	5,000 regular	4,000	1,000	5,000	
Sales revenue	$4,700,000	$3,760,000	$540,000	$4,300,000	$400,000 lower
Variable costs	2,750,000	2,200,000	400,000	2,600,000	150,000 lower
Contribution	1,950,000	1,560,000	140,000	1,700,000	250,000 lower
Fixed costs	1,040,000			1,040,000	–0–
Profit	$ 910,000			$ 660,000	$250,000 lower

b.   Accepting the order would increase profits by $140,000—the amount of the fee.

Multiple-Product Decisions

LEARNING OBJECTIVES

After reading this chapter, you should be able to:

1. Use accounting data to choose among alternative products.
2. Use linear programming for cost-based decisions.
3. Understand the sensitivity of linear programming solutions to the cost data entered into the program.

This chapter continues the discussion of differential cost analysis by explaining how differential costing is used to choose among multiple products.

PRODUCT-CHOICE DECISIONS

Choosing which products to manufacture and sell is a common managerial decision. Most companies are capable of producing a great variety of goods and services but may be limited in the short run by the capacity they have available. Campus Bookstore, in Chapter 12, had to decide whether to use its limited space to sell general merchandise or to increase book sales. Due to a shortage of personnel, a small CPA firm may have to choose between performing work for client A or for client B. Students have to choose how to allocate their study time among their courses. Chrysler Corporation's Grand Cherokee plant will have to choose among production of Laredo and other models.

We usually think of product choices as short-run decisions because we have adopted the definition that in the short run, capacity is fixed, while in the long run, capacity can be changed. Thus, McDonnell–Douglas and Boeing may be able to produce both jumbo and narrow-body models in the *long run* by increasing capacity, and the CPA firm may be able to serve both client A and client B in the *long run* by hiring more professional staff. Nonetheless, in the short run, capacity limitations require choices.

For example, Glover Manufacturing makes two kinds of baseballs— hardballs and softballs. For now, assume that the company can sell all the baseballs it produces. Glover's cost and revenue information is presented in Illustration 13–1.

Revenue and Cost Information, Glover Manufacturing

	Hardballs	Softballs
Sales revenue per unit	$10.00	$9.00
Less variable costs per unit:		
Materials	4.00	2.50
Labor	1.50	2.00
Variable overhead	.50	.50
Contribution margin per unit	$ 4.00	$4.00

Fixed manufacturing costs: $800,000 per month.
Marketing and administrative costs (all fixed): $200,000 per month.

ILLUSTRATION

13–2

Profit-Volume Relationship Assuming Hardballs and Softballs Use Equal Scarce Resources, Glover Manufacturing

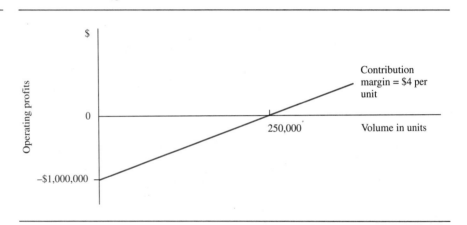

The profit-volume relationship for Glover's products is shown in Illustration 13–2. For instance, Glover Manufacturing can sell 250,000 hardballs or 250,000 softballs or any combination of hardballs and softballs totaling 250,000 to break even. The contribution margin of each product is the same, so the profit-volume relationship is the same regardless of the mix of products produced and sold.

PRODUCT CONTRIBUTION MARGIN WITH A SINGLE CONSTRAINED RESOURCE

Recall that Glover Manufacturing can sell all of the baseballs it can produce. Glover's objective is to maximize the contribution from its sales of hardballs and softballs. But should it produce hardballs or softballs? Without knowing either Glover's maximum production capacity or the amount of that capacity that is used by producing one product or the other, we might say that it doesn't matter because both products are equally profitable. But because capacity is limited, that answer would be incorrect if Glover uses up its capacity at a different rate for each product.

Suppose that Glover's capacity is limited to 7,200 machine-hours per month. This limitation is known as a **constraint.** Further, assume that machines may be used to produce either 30 hardballs per machine-hour or 50 softballs per machine-hour.

Constraints Activities, resources, or policies that limit or bound the attainment of an objective.

Contribution Margin per Unit of Scarce Resource Contribution margin per unit of a particular input with limited availability.

With a constrained resource, the important measure of profitability is the **contribution margin per unit of scarce resource** used, *not* contribution margin per unit of product. In this case, softballs are more profitable than hardballs because softballs contribute $200 per machine-hour ($4 per softball × 50 softballs per hour), while hardballs contribute only $120 per machine-hour ($4 per hardball × 30 hardballs per machine-hour). The hours required to produce one ball times the contribution per hour equals the contribution per ball.

For the month, Glover could produce 360,000 softballs (50 per hour × 7,200 hours) or 216,000 hardballs (30 per hour × 7,200 hours). If only softballs are produced, Glover's operating profit would be $440,000 (360,000 softballs times a contribution of $4 each minus fixed costs of $1 million). If only hardballs are produced, Glover's net *loss* would be $136,000 (216,000 hardballs times a contribution margin of $4 each minus $1 million). By concentrating on the product that yields the greater contribution per unit of scarce resource, Glover can maximize its profit.

Mathematical Representation of the Problem

The relationship between the usage of machine-hours to produce hardballs and softballs may be expressed as:

$$\left(\frac{1}{30}\right)H + \left(\frac{1}{50}\right)S \leq 7,200 \text{ machine-hours}$$

(To be precise, there are two more constraints that prevent negative production of either product. These are $H \geq 0$ and $S \geq 0$, but these are ignored in our discussion because negative production is not possible.)

The first term in the production expression reflects the fact that a hardball uses $1/30$ hour of machine time. The second term indicates that each softball uses $1/50$ hour of machine time. The third term or right-hand side constrains production time to 7,200 hours or less. Although it is possible to use fewer than 7,200 hours, that would indicate idle capacity. Hence, Glover is better off to use as many hours as possible. This point may also be shown mathematically, but we leave that to operations researchers.

In short, the relationship between the product contribution margins and the constraints for Glover would be written as follows:

Objective function:

Maximize: $4H + $4S

Constraints:

Subject to: $\left(\frac{1}{30}\right)H + \left(\frac{1}{50}\right)S \leq 7,200 \text{ hours}$

The objective function states that the objective is to select the product mix that maximizes total contribution, given the unit contribution of hardballs is $4 and of softballs is $4. The constraint states that each hardball uses $1/30$ of a machine-hour, each softball uses $1/50$ of a machine-hour, and in total, no more than 7,200 hours are available.

Graphic Solution

Illustration 13–3 shows that relationship between production of each product and the amount of the scarce resources available. Glover Manufacturing can produce at any point along the line labeled "machine capacity constraint,"

ILLUSTRATION

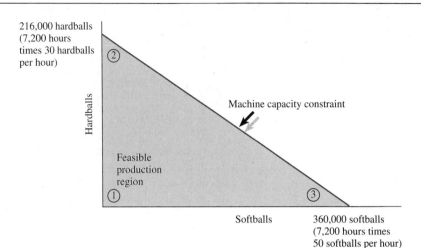

Corner Point	Produce and Sell		Total Contribution Margin	Fixed Costs	Operating Profits (loss)
	Hardballs	**Softballs**			
1	-0-	-0-	-0-	$1,000,000	$(1,000,000)
2	216,000	-0-	216,000 × $4 = $864,000	1,000,000	(136,000)
3	-0-	360,000	360,000 × $4 = $1,440,000	1,000,000	440,000

Feasible Production Region The area in a graph of production opportunities bounded by the limits on production.

Corner Point A corner of the feasible production region in linear programming.

or at any interior point in the **feasible production region.** The feasible production region is the area in the graph bounded by the constraints on operating activities. In this case, production is bounded by zero on the low side and by 7,200 machine-hours on the high side.

Because Glover can sell all it produces at a positive contribution margin for each product, it would prefer to produce as much as possible, which is at some point on the machine capacity line. Analysis of each **corner point** (that is, each corner of the feasible region) shows that it is optimal for Glover to produce and sell 360,000 softballs and no hardballs at corner point 3.

Why Will the Optimal Solution Always Be at a Corner Point?
If point 3 is better than point 2, then it must also be better than any place on the *straight line* between points 2 and 3.[1] By knowing that there can be no solution better than the solution at the optimal corner enables us to limit our search for the maximum profit combination to the corner points in the feasible region. The following example shows what happens if we move from corner point 3.

---

[1] Of course, if two corner points have the same total contribution, any point on a straight line between those two corners would have the same total contribution as either corner point.

Glover's total contribution, and therefore total operating profit, is reduced if it moves toward corner point 2 from corner point 3. For example, the total contribution with production of 360,000 softballs is $1,440,000. Moving from corner point 3 towards corner point 2 by producing one hardball requires giving up $5/3$ softballs, calculated as follows:

1. Start with the following constraint:

$$\left(\frac{1}{30}\right)H + \left(\frac{1}{50}\right)S \le 7,200 \text{ machine-hours}$$

2. The choice requires no change in total machine-hours; 7,200 machine-hours are still used. There is only a substitution of hardballs for softballs, so set $1/30H + 1/50)S = 0$.

3. Now, find the number of softballs given up for each hardball produced (the symbol Δ refers to change):

$$\left(\frac{1}{50}\right)\Delta S = -\left(\frac{1}{30}\right)\Delta H$$

$$\Delta S = -\frac{\left(\frac{1}{30}\right)}{\left(\frac{1}{50}\right)}\Delta H = -\frac{.03333}{.02000}\Delta H$$

$$\Delta S = -\left(\frac{5}{3}\right)\Delta H$$

4. If you substitute 1 for ΔH, then $\Delta S = -5/3$. Thus, every hardball produced requires giving up $5/3$ softballs.

5. The net effect on total contribution is:

Contribution gained (1 hardball $\times$ \$4)	\$4.00
Contribution lost ($5/3$ softballs $\times$ \$4)	6.67
Net contribution lost per hardball produced	\$2.67

This loss occurs as we move from corner point 3 toward corner point 2. Moving from corner point 3 toward corner point 1 is obviously inferior to producing at corner point 3 because we give up production of some softballs as we move toward corner point 1.

What Is Really Sold?

In working with production constraints, it is often useful to think in terms of selling the service of the productive resources rather than selling units of product. For example, we can think of Glover as selling machine-hours, with each machine-hour contributing $200 if used to make softballs, $120 if used to make hardballs, and $0 if not used at all.

CONTRIBUTION MARGIN VERSUS GROSS MARGIN

Notice that Glover Manufacturing's costs were divided into fixed and variable portions. By definition, the variable costs are differential with volume changes. In some companies, variable costs are not separated from fixed costs. This can lead to serious product mix errors if fixed costs allocated to each unit of product are included when comparing the profitability of products. This error would result from treating fixed costs as differential costs.

ILLUSTRATION

13-4

*Full Costs of the Product,
Glover Manufacturing*

	Hardballs	Softballs
Sales revenue per unit	$10.00	$9.00
Less full absorption costs per unit:		
Materials	4.00	2.50
Labor	1.50	2.00
Overhead (applied at a rate of 200% of labor)[a]	3.00	4.00
Gross margin per unit	$ 1.50	$ .50

Marketing and administrative costs (all fixed): $200,000 per month.

[a] Any under- or overapplied overhead is written off as an expense of the period.

For example, suppose that before any attempt was made to determine the optimal product mix for Glover Manufacturing, the Accounting Department had prepared the report in Illustration 13–4. As you can see, fixed and variable overhead costs are not separated. By applying overhead at 200 percent of labor, overhead *appears to vary with labor*, whereas we know that a substantial amount of the overhead is fixed. Based on this presentation, hardballs *appear* to be more profitable per unit of scarce resource than softballs, but in fact, the opposite is true.

Accounting information is sometimes sent to personnel in operations and engineering who are unaware of the important but subtle distinction between *gross margin* and *contribution margin* that we have emphasized in this book. For example, suppose that the gross margin per unit from Illustration 13–4 is used instead of the contribution margin per unit from Illustration 13–1. Illustration 13–3 shows that there are two extreme production possibilities: 216,000 hardballs or 360,000 softballs. Using the gross margins from Illustration 13–4, production of 216,000 hardballs at $1.50 (total gross margin = $324,000) *appears* economically superior to production of 360,000 softballs at $.50 (total gross margin = $180,000).

Of course, we know that is wrong. As shown in Illustration 13–5, producing 216,000 hardballs and no softballs would result in a net loss of $136,000, while the correct product mix of 360,000 softballs and no hardballs provides operating profit of $440,000.

Thus, a common mistake in product mix decisions stems from the failure to recognize which costs are differential. Fixed costs for different product mixes often do not differ in the short run. For purposes of valuing inventory for external reporting, however, fixed manufacturing overhead is assigned to units produced, thereby making fixed costs appear variable to the unsophisticated user of cost information. As in the other differential cost problems we have seen, it is important to determine which costs are *really differential* for decision making.

This is another example of a common problem in accounting. Costs that were assigned to units for one purpose (inventory valuation, in this case) could be inappropriately used for another purpose (product mix decisions, in this case).

ILLUSTRATION

*Comparison of
Product Mix Analyses,
Glover Manufacturing*

	Gross Margin Method, Wrong Decision: Produce All Hardballs	Contribution Margin Method, Right Decision: Produce All Softballs
Sales revenue:		
Hardballs (216,000 × $10)	$2,160,000	
Softballs (360,000 × $9)		$3,240,000
Less variable manufacturing costs:		
Hardballs (216,000 × $6)	1,296,000	
Softballs (360,000 × $5)		1,800,000
Total contribution margin	864,000	1,440,000
Less fixed costs:		
Manufacturing	800,000	800,000
Marketing and administrative	200,000	200,000
Operating profit (loss)	$ (136,000)	$ 440,000

OPPORTUNITY COST OF RESOURCES

In the multiproduct setting, machine capacity, or any other constraint, may have an opportunity cost. Computing the opportunity cost is facilitated with the type of analysis presented in this chapter. For example, what is the opportunity cost to Glover Manufacturing of not having one more hour of machine capacity? First, assume that the increase in machine time would change neither fixed manufacturing nor fixed selling costs. With one more hour of machine time, Glover could produce 50 more softballs, as shown below:

Before: $\frac{1}{30}H + \frac{1}{50}S \leq 7,200$ machine-hours. If only softballs are produced:

$$\left(\frac{1}{50}\right) S = 7,200$$

$$S = \frac{7,200}{\left(\frac{1}{50}\right)}$$

$$= \underline{360,000 \text{ softballs}}$$

With one additional machine-hour and producing only softballs:

$$\left(\frac{1}{50}\right) S = 7,201$$

$$S = \frac{7,201}{\left(\frac{1}{50}\right)}$$

$$= \underline{360,050 \text{ softballs}}$$

With a unit contribution margin of $4, production of 50 more softballs would add $200 to profits. Thus, the opportunity cost of one hour of machine time is $200. This opportunity cost is also known as a **shadow price**.

Shadow Price Opportunity cost of an additional unit.

With this information, Glover's management can decide whether it is worthwhile to add machine time. If additional machine time can be leased for any amount less than $200 per hour, for example, doing so would increase operating profits.

MULTIPLE CONSTRAINTS

With one constraint, it is easy to see that Glover could maximize contribution by producing only softballs. But the situation becomes more complex when there are multiple constraints. Suppose that the sale of softballs is temporarily restricted so that only 200,000 can be sold during the next production period. Further, suppose that Glover cannot hold baseballs in inventory so everything produced must be sold in the same period. Now the constraints are:

(1) $\left(\dfrac{1}{30}\right)H + \left(\dfrac{1}{50}\right)S \le 7{,}200$ machine-hours

(2) $S \le 200{,}000$

These relationships are shown graphically in Illustration 13–6. Now, to determine the optimal product mix, we find the monthly operating profit at each of the four corner points labeled. The solution for corner point 3 is found by simultaneously solving for the machine and sales constraints. The

ILLUSTRATION

13–6

Product Choice with Multiple Constraints, Glover Manufacturing

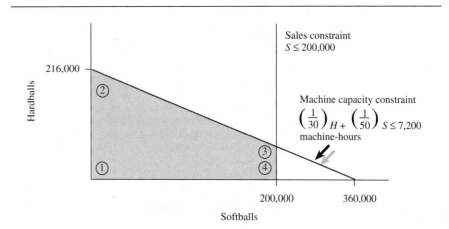

Corner Point	Produce and Sell		Total Contribution Margin	Fixed Costs	Operating Profit (Loss)
	Hardballs	Softballs			
1	-0-	-0-	-0-	$1,000,000	$(1,000,000)
2	216,000	-0-	216,000 × $4 = $864,000	1,000,000	(136,000)
3	96,000	200,000	(96,000 × $4) + (200,000 × $4) = $1,184,000	1,000,000	184,000
4	-0-	200,000	200,000 × $4 = $800,000	1,000,000	(200,000)

calculations are as follows:

$$\left(\frac{1}{30}\right)H + \left(\frac{1}{50}\right)S = 7,200 \text{ machine-hours}$$
$$S = \underline{200,000}$$

so

$$\left(\frac{1}{30}\right)H + \left(\frac{1}{50}\right)(200,000) = 7,200$$
$$\left(\frac{1}{30}\right)H + 4,000 = 7,200$$
$$\left(\frac{1}{30}\right)H = 3,200$$
$$H = \underline{96,000}$$

This optimal solution is to produce as many softballs as can be sold, 200,000, and use the remaining capacity to produce 96,000 hardballs.

As more constraints and products are added, solving for product mixes becomes more complex. Although it is possible to solve these problems by hand, they are typically solved by computer (see the following section). Nevertheless, a simple graph can be a quite effective means to present your results.

Self-Study Question

1 Pacperson, Inc., manufactures two series of computer hardware: Twopack and Threepack. Data concerning selling prices and costs for each unit are as follows:

	Twopack	Threepack
Selling price	$1,000	$1,700
Materials	350	370
Direct labor	210	230
Overhead (80% fixed)	150	200
Gross margin	290	900
Marketing costs (variable)	80	240
Administrative costs (fixed)	60	80
Profit	$ 150	$ 580

Management decided that at least 500 units of Twopack must be manufactured and sold each month. Likewise, at least 150 Threepack models must be manufactured and sold each month.

The company's production facilities are limited by machine capacity in the assembly control section. Each Twopack model requires one fourth of an hour in the assembly control section. Each Threepack model, however, requires three fourths of an hour in the assembly area. There is a total of 250 available hours per month in the assembly control section. There are no other relevant constraints on production.

a. What is the appropriate objective function for these two products if management's objective is to maximize profits?

b. What equations would represent the constraints on the profitability from these two products?

c. Given the information in the problem, which product would management prefer to produce to maximize profits?

d. What is the optimal production schedule and the optimal contribution margin at that schedule?

e. What is the maximum price management would be willing to pay for one more hour of assembly control section capacity?

The solution to this question is at the end of this chapter on page 515.

LINEAR PROGRAMMING

Graphic Method Graphic solution of a linear programming problem by selecting the best corner solution visually.

Simplex Method Solution of a linear programming problem using a mathematical technique.

The product-choice problem is often much more complex than the two-product, two-constraint problems just presented for Glover Manufacturing. Companies often have many constraints and many choices. The method we used to find the optimal product mix for Glover Manufacturing is called the **graphic method.** The graphic method is a useful way to see how linear programming works, but it is impractical for complex problems with many choices and constraints.

A mathematical technique, known as the **simplex method,** has been developed for solving complex product mix problems. This technique solves for corner solutions much as we did earlier in this chapter using graphs. Many computer software packages include the simplex method, or a variation of it, for solving product mix problems.

For the rest of this chapter, we assume product mix decisions are solved on the computer. Our focus will be on setting up the problems so they can be entered into the computer and on interpreting the output, not on the mathematical procedures used to derive solutions.[2]

COMPREHENSIVE LINEAR PROGRAMMING EXAMPLE

This section presents an example that we solved using the computer. We discuss how to set up the problem to enter it into the computer and how to interpret the results.

Assume that Hixon Company manufactures and sells three wood products—armchairs, labeled A; bookshelves, labeled B; and cabinets, labeled C. Each product must be processed through two departments—Cutting, and Assembly and Finishing—before it is sold.

Illustration 13–7 presents data about product selling prices, costs, and the rate at which each product uses scarce resources. In addition to the information provided in Illustration 13–7, we learn that only 2,000 board-feet of direct material can be obtained per week. The Cutting Department has 180 hours of labor available each week, and the Assembly and Finishing Department has 240 hours of labor available each week. No overtime is allowed.

Hixon Company's contract commitments require it to make at least 100 armchairs per week. Also, due to keen competition, no more than 100 bookshelves can be sold each week.

---

[2] More details on the mathematics of linear programming are available from books on operations research and quantitative methods. For example, see H. Bierman, C. Bonini, and W. Hausman, *Quantitative Analysis for Business Decisions*, 8th ed. (Homewood, Ill.: Richard D. Irwin, 1991).

ILLUSTRATION

13–7

Hixon Company Facts

	Armchairs per Unit	Bookshelves per Unit	Cabinets per Unit
Selling price	$14.00	$18.00	$24.00
Direct labor cost	6.00	7.20	10.80
Direct material cost	.80	1.40	2.00
Variable overhead	1.52	2.00	2.96
Contribution margins	5.68	7.40	8.24
Fixed manufacturing overhead	5.00	5.00	5.00
Gross margins	$ .68	$ 2.40	$ 3.24
Material requirements in board-feet per unit of output	4	7	10
Labor requirements in hours per unit of output:			
Cutting Department	.30	.30	.40
Assembly and Finishing Department	.20	.30	.50

Fixed manufacturing overhead costs are estimated to be $1,500 per week. They are arbitrarily allocated to each unit at the rate of $5 per unit. Fixed manufacturing costs are unaffected by the product mix. Nonmanufacturing costs of $1,000 per week are fixed and unaffected by the product mix decision.

Problem Formulation

Hixon Company's product mix decision problem can be solved using linear programming. The constrained optimization problem is formulated as follows:

ⓐ Maximize total contribution margin:
$5.68A + $7.40B + $8.24C

ⓑ Subject to the following constraints:

4A	+	7B	+	10C ≤ 2,000 board-feet	Direct material
.30A	+	.30B	+	.40C ≤ 180 labor-hours	Cutting
.20A	+	.30B	+	.50C ≤ 240 labor-hours	Assembly and Finishing
A				≥ 100 units sold	Product A's sales
		B		≤ 100 units sold	Product B's sales

Using a linear programming computer package, we can obtain a solution for the above model. Illustration 13–8 shows how this problem was entered into the computer using a particular software package. The circled letters are there to help you trace the steps in the computer input back to the formulation above.

The initial table in Illustration 13–8 is from the printout of the linear programming problem formulation. Illustration 13–9 shows the output. Most software packages present the output like that in Illustration 13–9.

Solution

The "Summary of Problem" in Illlustration 13–9 lists the linear programming (LP) solution to the optimization problem. The total contribution margin is maximized if Hixon Company produces 500 armchairs and no

ILLUSTRATION

Linear Programming Input,[a]
Hixon Company

:
(a & b)   MAX $5.68A + $7.40B + $8.24C
?
SUBJECT TO
?
(DIRECT MATERIAL) 4A + 7B + 10C < 2000
?
(CUTTING) .3A + .3B + .4C < 180
?
(ASSEMBLY AND FINISHING) .2A + .3B + .5C < 240
?
(PROD A SALES) A > 100
?
(PROD B SALES) B < 100
?
END

A = Armchairs
B = Bookshelves
C = Cabinets

Note: Circled letters cross-reference to the problem formulation in the text.
[a] Based on the linear programming package called LINDO.

ILLUSTRATION

Linear Programming Output,
Hixon Company

Summary of Problem

OBJECTIVE FUNCTION VALUE $2,840 ©

VARIABLE	VALUE	REDUCED VALUE
Armchairs	500.00	0.0
Bookshelves	0.0	2.54
Cabinets	0.0	5.96

CONSTRAINTS	TYPE	VALUE	SHADOW PRICE
Direct material	Slack	0.0	ⓓ $1.42
Cutting	Slack	30.00	0.0
Assembly and finishing	Slack	140.00	0.0
Armchair sales	Surplus	400.00	0.0
Bookshelf sales	Slack	100.00	0.0

Objective Function Coefficient Ranges

VARIABLE	CURRENT COEF	ALLOWABLE INCREASE	ALLOWABLE DECREASE
Armchairs	5.68	Infinity	1.45
Bookshelves	7.40	2.54	Infinity
Cabinets	8.24	5.96	Infinity

Right-Hand-Side Ranges

CONSTRAINTS	CURRENT RHS	ALLOWABLE INCREASE	ALLOWABLE DECREASE
Direct material	2000.00	400.00	1600.00
Cutting	180.00	Infinity	30.00
Assembly and finishing	240.00	Infinity	140.00
Armchair sales	100.00	400.00	Infinity
Bookshelf sales	100.00	Infinity	100.00

bookshelves or cabinets. The maximum total contribution obtainable under the present resource constraints is approximately \$2,840 (see ©). Hence the operating profit realized from this production mix is \$340 (\$2,840 − \$1,500 fixed manufacturing costs − \$1,000 fixed nonmanufacturing costs).

Opportunity Costs

Of the five constraints, only the direct material constraint has an opportunity cost attached to it. This opportunity cost figure, which is reflected on the output as a shadow price, shows us how total contribution margin changes as a result of a per unit change in the constraint. Thus, if we increase the direct material constraint from 2,000 board-feet to 2,001 board-feet, Hixon's contribution margin will increase by approximately \$1.42 (see ⓓ in Illustration 13–9).

Effects of Forcing Nonsolution Products into the Solution

The optimal solution *excludes* bookshelves and cabinets. What happens if we *force* one bookshelf or cabinet into the solution? That is, we require there to be one unit produced that would not be produced with the optimal solution. You would predict that the value of the optimal solution (the \$2,840 in Illustration 13–9) would go down—but, by how much?

The column in Illustration 13–9 that is titled "Reduced Value" answers the following question: How much will the value of the solution (that is, Hixon's contribution margin) go down if Hixon produces one unit of a product that is not produced in the optimal solution? Bookshelves and cabinets have values of \$2.54 and \$5.96, respectively, as shown in Illustration 13–9. This means, if we force Hixon to produce one bookshelf, for example, total contribution margin to the firm will be reduced by \$2.54. This is because some production of the more profitable armchairs will have to be given up to produce a bookshelf. Similarly, the production of an additional cabinet would lower the contribution margin by \$5.96.

Nonbinding Constraints

Four of the constraints each have a nonzero value. This means that these constraints are not binding. The amounts shown under the "Value" heading in Illustration 13–9 are the amounts of the scarce resources, or constraints, still available. For example, 30 labor-hours are still available in the Cutting Department; only 150 hours of the available 180 labor-hours were used. This unused scarce resource is sometimes known as *slack*. In the Assembly and Finishing Department, 140 labor-hours are still available. For bookshelf *sales*, an additional 100 units could be produced and sold before the market constraint becomes binding. (Recall that no more than 100 bookshelves could be sold per week. The optimal solution is to sell no bookshelves.) Finally, for armchairs, the solution value shows that optimal production of armchairs exceeds the specified minimum by 400 units; that is, there is a "surplus" over the specified minimum.

Whereas binding constraints have an opportunity cost (for example, \$1.42 per unit for direct materials), no shadow price, or opportunity cost, is shown in the solution for the constraints that are not binding. For example, there is no shadow price for labor-hours in the Cutting Department because there is no value for having one additional hour, nor a loss for having one less hour.

Sensitivity Analysis

The parameters specified in this linear programming (LP) model are subject to some degree of estimation error. Decision makers need to know how much error can be tolerated before making a difference in the decision.

Under the heading "Objective Function Coefficient Ranges" in Illustration 13–9, we are given the ranges within which the contribution margins of each product can change without changing the optimal mix of products, all other things equal. For example, the contribution margin of an armchair is $5.68. This contribution margin could increase by an infinite amount without changing the fact that the optimal product mix includes 500 armchairs.

Bookshelves presently have a value of zero in the optimal solution. If their contribution margin was increased (by raising the selling price, for example) by more than $2.54 from its present level of $7.40, then bookshelves would become part of the optimal solution with a value greater than zero. In general, the optimal solution for Hixon Company is to produce 500 armchairs and none of the other two products within the objective function ranges shown, all other things equal.

The bottom panel in Illustration 13–9 has the heading "Right-Hand-Side Ranges." These ranges give the allowable increase or decrease for values of the constraints before a binding constraint becomes nonbinding, or a nonbinding constraint becomes binding, all other things equal.

For example, the direct material constraint, which is presently a binding constraint, could increase by 400 or decrease by 1,600 board-feet before it would become nonbinding, all other things held constant. Suppose the number of board-feet dropped by more than 1,600 to less than 400 available (that is, current level of 2,000 minus 1,600 leaves 400 board-feet). Then the company could not satisfy its constraint to make at least 100 armchairs because each armchair requires 4 board feet.

Labor-hours in the Cutting Department are not binding in the solution in Illustration 13–9. In fact, there are 30 available hours for this constraint. The "Right-Hand-Side Ranges" panel tells us that this constraint could decrease as much as 30 hours before it becomes binding.

Misspecifying the Objective Function

Suppose Hixon Company incorrectly specified its objective function—using gross margins in the objective function instead of contribution margins. Based on the gross margins given in Illustration 13–7, this would result in the following formulation of the problem:

Maximize total gross margin:

$$\$.68A + \$2.40B + \$3.24C$$

Subject to the following constraints:

Material	$4A + 7B + 10C \leq$	2,000 board-feet
Cutting	$.30A + .30B + .40C \leq$	180 hours
Assembly and Finishing	$.20A + .30B + .50C \leq$	240 hours
Armchairs	$A \qquad\qquad\quad \geq$	100 units
Bookshelves	$B \quad\quad \leq$	100 units

The constraints are the same as those previously formulated.

The computer solution to this LP problem is given in Illustration 13–10. It is interesting to note that as a result of misspecifying the values of the

Linear Programming Output Incorrectly Using Gross Margins instead of Contribution Margins, Hixon Company

Linear Programming Input

MAX $0.68 A + $2.4 B + $3.24 C
SUBJECT TO

Direct material	4 A + 7 B + 10 C ≤ 2000
Cutting	0.3 A + 0.3 B + 0.4 C ≤ 180
Assembly and finishing	0.2 A + 0.3 B + 0.5 C ≤ 240
Armchair sales	A ≥ 100
Bookshelf sales	B ≤ 100

Summary of Problem

OBJECTIVE FUNCTION VALUE $599.60[a]

VARIABLE	VALUE	REDUCED VALUE
Armchairs	100.00	0.0
Bookshelves	100.00	0.0
Cabinets	90.00	0.0

CONSTRAINT	TYPE	VALUE	SHADOW PRICE
Direct material	Slack	0.0	0.32
Cutting	Slack	84.00	0.0
Assembly and finishing	Slack	145.00	0.0
Armchair sales	Surplus	− 0.0	−0.62
Bookshelf sales	Slack	0.0	0.13

[a] This is not the correct contribution because of the data errors noted in the text.

objective function, Hixon Company will make a suboptimal production decision of manufacturing 100 armchairs, 100 bookshelves, and 90 cabinets. Now, we compare this solution with the prior optimal solution in which contribution margins were used in the objective function.

	Gross Margin Method: Wrong Decision		Contribution Margin Method: Right Decision	
	Number of Units	Unit Contribution Margin	Number of Units	Unit Contribution Margin
Total contribution:				
Armchairs 100	×	$5.68 = $ 568.00	500 ×	$5.68 = $2,840
Bookshelves 100	×	7.40 = 740.00		–0–
Cabinets 90	×	8.24 = 741.60		–0–
Total		$2,049.60		$2,840
Less fixed costs:				
Manufacturing		1,500.00		1,500
Nonmanufacturing		1,000.00		1,000
Operating profit (loss) ...		$ (450.40)		$ 340

The optimal value of the solution reported in the output of Illustration 13–10, $599.60, is an incorrect number because the analysis incorrectly treats fixed manufacturing costs as variable costs. If you compare this solution in Illustration 13–10 with the correct solution in Illustration 13–9, you will find numerous errors in Illustration 13–10. This demonstrates the

I L L U S T R A T I O N

13–11

*Removal of a Binding
Constraint, Problem
Formulation,
Hixon Company*

Linear Programming Input

MAX $5.68A + $7.40B + $8.24C
SUBJECT TO

Cutting	.30A +	.30B +	.40C	≤	180
Assembly and Finishing	.20A +	.30B +	.50C	≤	240
Armchair sales	A			≥	100
Bookshelf sales		B		≤	100

Summary of Problem

OBJECTIVE FUNCTION VALUE $3,780

VARIABLE	VALUE	REDUCED VALUE
Armchairs	100.00	0.0
Bookshelves	100.00	0.0
Cabinets	300.00	0.0

CONSTRAINT	TYPE	VALUE	SHADOW PRICE
Cutting	Slack	0.0	$20.60
Assembly and Finishing	Slack	40.00	0.0
Armchair sales	Surplus	0.0	1.22
Bookshelf sales	Slack	0.0	0.50

importance of using contribution margins, not gross margins, in linear programming problems.

*Removing a
Binding Constraint*

Suppose Hixon Company has access to an unlimited supply of direct material. The optimal production mix for Hixon can be found using the LP formulation in Illustration 13–11. Without a materials constraint, the solution to the production decision problem is to produce 100 armchairs, 100 bookshelves, and 300 cabinets. Armchairs, which use the least amount of material, are not as attractive as they were before because the supply of material is no longer a binding constraint.

This new optimum production point has a total contribution margin of $3,780. This is $940 ($3,780 − $2,840) greater than the optimum obtained in Illustration 13–9 where availability of direct material was a binding constraint. The constraints that are now binding are the availability of labor in the Cutting Department, the size of the market for bookshelves, and the minimum required sales for armchairs.

Note that the opportunity costs associated with the binding constraints on this new optimum are different from those presented in Illustration 13–9. The Cutting Department, which had an excess of 30 labor-hours before, now has an opportunity cost of $20.60 per unit of the scarce resource, labor-hours.

*Introducing an
Additional Constraint*

Now, suppose that Hixon's contract commmitments also require it to produce a minimum of 100 cabinets each week. Assume also that Hixon is once again facing a limited availability of direct material. The effect of an additional constraint on Hixon's optimal production decision can be seen in Illustration 13–12.

ILLUSTRATION

13–12

Introducing an Additional Constraint, Problem Formulation, Hixon Company

Linear Programming Input

MAX $5.68A + $7.40B + $8.24C
SUBJECT TO

Direct material	4 A + 7 B + 10 C ≤ 2000
Cutting	0.3 A + 0.3 B + 0.4 C ≤ 180
Assembly and finishing	0.2 A + 0.3 B + 0.5 C ≤ 240
Armchair sales	A ≥ 100
Bookshelf sales	B ≤ 100
Cabinet sales	C ≥ 100

Summary of Problem

OBJECTIVE FUNCTION VALUE $2,244

VARIABLE	VALUE	REDUCED VALUE
Armchairs	250.00	0.0
Bookshelves	0.0	$2.54
Cabinets	100.00	0.0

CONSTRAINTS	TYPE	VALUE	SHADOW PRICE
Direct material	Slack	0.0	$1.42
Cutting	Slack	65.00	0.0
Assembly and finishing	Slack	140.00	0.0
Armchair sales	Surplus	150.00	0.0
Bookshelf sales	Slack	100.0	0.0
Cabinet sales	Slack	0.0	5.96

The "Summary of Problem" shows that Hixon's optimal product decision is to produce 250 armchairs and 100 cabinets. The total contribution margin now drops from $2,840 to $2,244.

One of the benefits of linear programming is to examine the effects of introducing additional constraints. Is the optimal solution affected? Does the solution value change when additional constraints are added? Managers frequently do not know the answers to these questions without using linear programming. For example, managers frequently ask what-if questions like: What if at least 40 percent of the material in our hot dogs is beef (or chicken or turkey)? What if class enrollments are limited to 50 students per class? Linear programming can often be used to help answer questions like these, making it a useful short-run planning tool.

Self-Study Question

2[3] Yakima, Inc., a rapidly expanding company, manufactures three lines of skis— Alpine, Nordic, and Racer. Currently faced with labor and machine capacity constraints, the company wants to select the optimal product mix in order to maximize operating profits. The following linear programming model of the problem was formulated and run on the computer:

Maximize:

Total contribution margin = $30X_1 + 23X_2 + 29X_3$

---

[3] Prepared by Jean M. Lim under the supervision of Michael W. Maher.

Subject to:

Labor-hours $= 12X_1 + 10X_2 + 6X_3 \leq 40,000$
Machine-hours $= 8X_1 + 4X_2 + 10X_3 \leq 10,000$

where

$X_1 =$ Alpine model
$X_2 =$ Nordic model
$X_3 =$ Racer model

Using the computer output in Exhibit A, answer the questions below. Assume that all things are held constant in each case.

a. What is the optimal production level of the Nordic model? The Racer model? The Alpine model?

b. What would happen to the optimal value if the available capacity of the labor constraint was decreased to 30,000 hours? If the machine-hours constraint was increased to 15,000 hours?

c. How much of the labor-hours resource is unused? How much of the machine-hours resource is unused?

d. The Racer model shows a *reduced value* of $28.50. Explain the meaning of this value.

e. Show how the optimal value of $57,500 was computed. Show how the *shadow price* of $5.75 for the machine-hours constraint was computed.

f. Suppose an error in the data exists and $23 is not the correct contribution margin of the Nordic model. What is the optimal production level of the Nordic model if the correct unit contribution margin is $18? If it is $12? (Indicate if unknown, given the available information.)

The solution to this question is at the end of this chapter on page 516.

EXHIBIT

Solution, Yakima, Inc.

Summary of Problem

OBJECTIVE FUNCTION VALUE $57,500

VARIABLE	VALUE	REDUCED VALUE
Alpine	0.0	$16.0
Nordic	$2,500.00	0.0
Racer	0.0	28.50

CONSTRAINTS	TYPE	VALUE	SHADOW PRICE
Labor-hours	Slack	15,000	$0.0
Machine-hours	Slack	0.0	5.75

Objective Function Coefficient Ranges

VARIABLE	CURRENT COEF	ALLOWABLE INCREASE	ALLOWABLE DECREASE
Alpine	$30	$16.00	Infinity
Nordic	23	Infinity	$8.00
Racer	29	28.50	Infinity

Right-Hand-Side Ranges

	CURRENT RHS	ALLOWABLE INCREASE	ALLOWABLE DECREASE
Labor-hours	40,000	Infinity	15,000
Machine-hours	10,000	6,000	10,000

SUMMARY

This chapter presents the use of differential costing and linear programming models in making product-choice decisions. The problem arises when there are limited amounts of resources that are being fully used and must be assigned to multiple products. The problem is to choose the optimal product mix within the constraints of limited resources.

The objective of product-choice decisions is to maximize the contribution margin per unit of scarce resource used. For example, if the scarce resource is the limited number of hours a machine can operate per month and the machine can make either of two products, the objective is to maximize the contribution per hour (or other unit of time) that each of the two products makes, and then produce the product with the higher contribution margin per hour of machine time used.

Short-run product-choice decisions assume fixed costs do not change regardless of product mix. It is important that product margins being optimized assume only variable costs change. Hence, product-choice decisions use contribution margins, not gross margins.

Computerized linear programming models are widely used to derive the optimal product mix. Data are input to these models using objective functions that specify the contribution margin of each product and constraints that indicate the amount of scarce resource each product uses. Provided the right data have been entered, the linear programming model then computes the contribution margin per unit of scarce resource for all products and all constraints (that is, scarce resources). The output indicates the mix of products and the quantity of each product to produce and sell that maximizes total contribution.

TERMS
AND CONCEPTS

The following terms and concepts should be familiar to you after reading this chapter:

Constraints, *480*

Contribution Margin per Unit of Scarce Resource, *481*

Corner Point, *482*

Feasible Production Region, *482*

Graphic Method, *488*

Shadow Price, *485*

Simplex Method, *488*

QUESTIONS

13–1   If we want to maximize profit, why do we use unit contribution margins in our analysis instead of unit gross margins?

13–2   Management notes that the contribution from one product is greater than the contribution from a second product. Hence, they conclude that the company should concentrate on production of the first product. Under what, if any, conditions will this approach result in maximum profits?

13–3   A company has learned that a particular input product required for its production is in limited supply. What approach should management take to maximize profits in the presence of this constraint?

13-4   What is the feasible production region?

13-5   Why are corner points on the feasible production region important for profitability analysis?

13-6   What do we mean by the opportunity cost of a constraint?

13-7   Under what circumstances would fixed costs be relevant when management is making decisions in a multiproduct setting?

13-8   Describe how to compute the maximum price that a company would be willing to pay to obtain additional capacity for a scarce resource.

13-9   At what point does the opportunity cost of a constraint change?

13-10 What is the role of the accountant in the management decision process that uses linear programming models (or other mathematical programming techniques)?

EXERCISES

13-11   The Role of Accounting Data
(L.O.1)

Ontario, Inc., manufactures three products labeled A, B, and C. Data concerning the three products are as follows:

	A	B	C
Selling price	$30	$40	$50
Manufacturing costs:			
Materials	5	6	7
Direct labor	7	7	11
Overhead:			
Variable	3	3	6
Fixed	2	2	4

Variable marketing costs equal 15 percent of the sales price of each product. Variable administrative costs are estimated at $1 per unit of product. Fixed administrative costs are allocated to each unit produced as follows: product A, $3; product B, $4; and product C, $5.

Required:

What is the equation representing the objective function for the product mix decision?

13-12   The Role of Accounting Data
(L.O.1)

Management of Eurostyle Corporation has been reviewing its profitability and attempting to improve performance through better planning. The company manufactures three products in its jewelry line: necklaces, bracelets, and rings. Selected data on these items are:

	Necklaces	Bracelets	Rings
Selling price	$100	$75	$50
Contribution margin	$ 40	$30	$20
Machining time required	.5 hour	.25 hour	.30 hour

The machining time is limited to 120 hours per month. Demand for each product far exceeds the company's ability to meet the demand. There are no other relevant production constraints.

At the present time, management produces equal quantities of each product. The production vice president has urged the company to concentrate on necklace production because that has the greatest margin. No bracelets or rings would be produced if this recommendation were followed.

Required:

a. If fixed costs are $5,000 per month, what profit will be obtained by following the production vice president's recommendation?

b. What is the maximum profit obtainable and what product or product combination must be sold to obtain that maximum?

13–13 The Role of Accounting Data (L.O.1)

Lemus Company has formulated the following profit function:

$$\text{Profit} = \$12R + \$25S - \$20,000$$

where R and S are products and the $20,000 is the fixed costs for the company.

Production is limited by capacity in the quality control section. The constraint for that section is formulated as:

$$2R + 4S \leq 2,500$$

A subcontractor has offered to perform additional quality control services, which would increase quality control capacity, at a cost of $3 per quality control unit.

Required:

Should the company utilize the services of the subcontractor? Show supporting calculations.

13–14 Linear Programming (L.O.2)

Bianchi Corporation manufactures two models—small and large. Each model is processed as follows:

	Machining	Polishing
Small (S)	1 hour	2 hours
Large (L)	4 hours	3 hours

The time available for processing the two models is 100 hours per week in machining and 90 hours per week in polishing. The contribution margin is $6 for the small model and $8 for the large model.

Required:

Formulate the equations necessary to solve this product mix problem.

(CPA adapted)

13–15 Linear Programming (L.O.2)

The Epsilon Company manufactures two products, Zeta and Beta. Each product must pass through two processing operations. All materials are introduced at the start of Process No. 1. There are no work in process inventories. Epsilon may produce either one product exclusively or various combinations of both products subject to the following constraints:

	Process Number 1	Process Number 2	Contribution Margin per Unit
Hours required to produce one unit of:			
Zeta	2 hours	1 hour	$4.00
Beta	1 hour	3 hours	5.25
Total capacity in hours per day	1,000 hours	1,275 hours	

A shortage of technical labor has limited Beta production to 400 units per day. There are *no* constraints on the production of Zeta other than the hour constraints in the above schedule. Assume that all relationships between capacity and production are linear.

Required:

a. Given the objective to maximize total contribution margin, what is the production constraint for Process No. 1?
  (1) 2 Zeta + Beta ≤ 1,000.
  (2) Zeta + Beta ≤ 1,000.
  (3) 2 Zeta + Beta ≥ 1,000.
  (4) Zeta + Beta ≥ 1,000.

b. Given the objective to maximize total contribution margin, what is the labor constraint for production of Beta?
  (1) Beta ≤ 400.
  (2) Beta ≥ 400.
  (3) Beta ≤ 425.
  (4) Beta ≥ 425.

c. What is the objective function of the data presented? Max:
  (1) 2 Zeta + 1 Beta
  (2) $4.00 Zeta + 3($5.25) Beta
  (3) $4.00 Zeta + $5.25 Beta
  (4) 2($4.00) Zeta + 3($5.25) Beta

(CPA adapted)

13–16 Linear Programming
(L.O.2)

Marquez Industries manufactures two products, X and Y. Each product must be processed in each of two departments: Assembling and Finishing. The hours needed to produce one unit of product per department and the maximum possible hours per department follow:

Department	Production Hours per Unit		Maximum Capacity in Hours
	X	Y	
Assembling	2	2	500
Finishing	2	3	600
Other restrictions:			
X ≥ 50			
Y ≥ 50			

The estimated gross margin on each product is $7 for *X* and $5 for *Y*. These gross margins include estimated fixed costs of $3 per unit. The total fixed costs are estimated at $320.

Required:

What is the optimal mix of output and what is the profit that would be obtained if the optimal mix were produced and sold? (You may find it helpful to use a graph to find the corner points.)

13–17 Applying Linear Programming Techniques: The Graphic Method
(L.O.2)

The Taggart Company manufactures product A and product B, each of which requires two processes, polishing and grinding. The contribution margin is $3 for product A and $4 for product B. The graph shows the maximum number of units of each product that may be processed in the two departments.

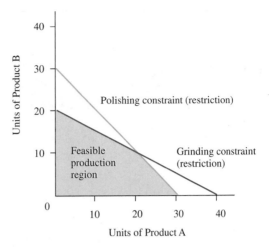

Required:

Considering the constraints on processing, which combination of product A and product B maximizes the total contribution?

(CPA adapted)

13–18 Sensitivity of Data
(L.O.3)

Use the data in exercise 13–17 to answer each of the independent questions that follow.

Required:

a. How much contribution is given up if a minimum production of 25 units of A is required?

b. How much contribution is given up if a minimum production of 15 units of B is required?

c. What would be the increased contribution margin from relaxing the polishing constraint to allow production of 40 units of A, or 40 units of B, or some combination along a straight line that would connect those two production points?

d. What would be the increased contribution from relaxing the grinding constraint so that the company could produce 50 units of A or 25 units of B or some combination along a straight line that would connect those two production points?

13–19 Sensitivity of Cost Data
(L.O.3)

Tower Company produces two types of gloves, G1 and G2. The cost and production data concerning these two products are as follows:

	G1	G2
Selling price	$12.00	$14.00
Manufacturing costs:		
Materials	4.00	1.50
Labor	3.00	6.00
Fixed overhead	2.50	5.00
Gross margin per unit	$ 2.50	$ 1.50
Required production time/unit	2 hours	2 hours

Total production time available is 2,500 hours per month. Since production time is limited and gross margin per unit for G1 is higher than G2, Tower Company management decided to produce and sell G1 exclusively.

Required:

Did Tower Company management make the correct decision?

PROBLEMS

13-20 Product Mix— Graphic Analysis

The graph shows the constraints (all ≤) of a chair manufacturing company. Each kitchen chair contributes $8 per chair; each office chair contributes $5 per chair. Only 3,000 kitchen chairs can be produced.

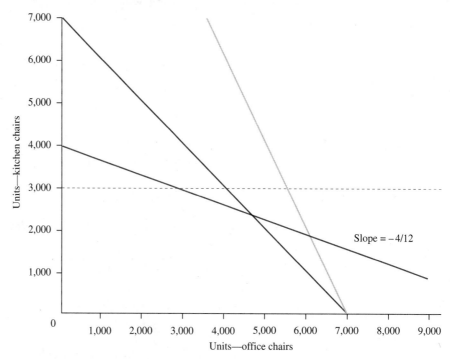

Required:

What mix of chairs maximizes profits?

13-21 Determining Optimum Product Mix

Farside Enterprises makes and sells three types of stuffed toys. Management is trying to determine the most profitable mix. Sales prices, demand, and use of manufacturing inputs are as follows:

	Bears	Cows	Dogs
Sales price	$15	$32	$95
Annual demand	20,000 units	10,000 units	30,000 units
Input requirements per unit:			
Direct material	.5 yards	.3 yards	.6 yards
Direct labor	.7 hours	2 hours	7 hours
Costs:			
Variable costs:			
Materials	$10 per yard		
Direct labor	8 per hour		
Factory overhead . . .	2 per direct labor-hour		
Marketing	10% of sales price		
Fixed Costs 1:[a]			
Manufacturing	$18,000 per year		
Marketing	4,000 per year		
Administration	15,000 per year		

[a] Fixed costs are allocated using direct labor-hours.

Not only does the company face limits on the volume of stuffed toys that it can sell, the layout of the plant is such that the company cannot have more than 30,000 direct labor-hours per year during normal shift hours.

Required: Show supporting data in good form.

a.   How much operating profit could the company earn if it were able to satisfy the annual demand?

b.   Which of the three product lines makes the most profitable use of the constrained resource, direct labor?

c.   Given the information in the problem so far, what product mix do you recommend?

d.   What amount of operating profit should your recommended product mix generate?

e.   Suppose the company could expand its labor capacity by running an extra shift. The extra shift could provide up to 10,000 more hours, but the cost would increase from $8 per hour to $9.50 per hour. What additional product(s) would Farside manufacture and what additional profit would be expected with the use of the added shift?

13–22   Interpreting Computer Output— One Constraint

Computer output for problem 13–22 is as follows:

Summary of Problem

OBJECTIVE FUNCTION VALUE $30,000

VARIABLE	VALUE	REDUCED VALUE
Product X	600.00	0.0
Product Y	0.0	$1.67
Product Z	0.0	0.0

CONSTRAINT	TYPE	VALUE	SHADOW PRICE
Machining time	Slack	0.0	$166.67

Objective Function Coefficient Ranges

VARIABLE	CURRENT COEFFICIENT	ALLOWABLE INCREASE	ALLOWABLE DECREASE
Product X	$50.00	Infinity	$0.0
Product Y	40.00	$1.67	Infinity
Product Z	25.00	0.0	Infinity

Right-Hand-Side Ranges

	CURRENT RHS	ALLOWABLE INCREASE	ALLOWABLE DECREASE
Machining time	180.00	Infinity	180.00

Required: Interpret the computer output for this problem by answering the following questions:

a.   Formulate the objective function for this problem.

b.   What is the optimal production level of product X?

c.   What is the total contribution at the optimal production level? How was it computed?

d.   How much would the company be willing to pay for an additional hour of machining capacity?

e. Product Y shows a reduced value of $1.67. Explain the meaning of this value.

f. Suppose that an error was made in figuring out the contribution margin for product Y. The contribution margin for product Y is supposed to be $41 instead of $40. What is the optimal production level for Y?

13–23 Interpreting Computer Output— Multiple Constraints

Computer output for problem 13–23 is as follows:

Linear Programming Input

MAX   41.5 P1 + 35.5 P2
SUBJECT TO
Machining   2 P1 + 1.5 P2 ≤ 2000
Assembly   3 P1 + 3 P2 ≤ 3000
Demand for P2   P2 ≥ 500

Summary of Problem

OBJECTIVE FUNCTION VALUE $38,500

VARIABLE	VALUE	REDUCED VALUE
P1	500.00	0.0
P2	500.00	0.0

CONSTRAINT	TYPE	VALUE	SHADOW PRICE
Machining	Slack	250.0	0.0
Assembly	Slack	0.0	13.83
Demand for P2	Surplus	0.0	−6.00

Required:

Answer the following questions using the computer output.

a. What is the optimal production level for P1? For P2?

b. What is the total contribution margin obtained at the optimal production level and how was it computed?

c. How much of the machine-hours resource is unused? How much of the assembly-hours resource is unused?

d. How much would the company be willing to pay for an additional hour of machining time? For an additional hour of assembly time?

13–24 Product Mix Choice

Leastan Company manufactures a line of carpeting that includes a commercial carpet and a residential carpet. Two grades of fiber—heavy-duty and regular—are used in manufacturing both types of carpeting. The mix of the two grades of fiber differs in each type of carpeting, with the commercial grade using a greater amount of heavy-duty fiber.

Leastan will introduce a new line of carpeting in two months to replace the current line. The present fiber in stock will not be used in the new line. Management wants to exhaust the present stock of regular and heavy-duty fiber during the last month of production.

Data regarding the current line of commercial and residential carpeting are as follows:

	Commercial	Residential
Selling price per roll	$1,000	$800
Production specifications per roll of carpet:		
Heavy-duty fiber	80 pounds	40 pounds
Regular fiber	20 pounds	40 pounds
Direct labor-hours	15 hours	15 hours
Standard cost per roll of carpet:		
Heavy-duty fiber ($3 per lb.)	$240	$120
Regular fiber ($2 per lb.)	40	80
Direct labor ($10 per DLH)	150	150
Variable manufacturing overhead (60% of direct labor cost)	90	90
Fixed manufacturing overhead (120% of direct labor cost)	180	180
Total standard cost per roll	$700	$620

Lestan has 42,000 pounds of heavy-duty fiber and 24,000 pounds of regular fiber in stock. All fiber not used in the manufacture of the present types of carpeting during the last month of production can be sold as scrap at $.25 a pound.

There are a maximum of 10,500 direct labor-hours available during the month. The labor force can work on either type of carpeting.

Sufficient demand exists for the present line of carpeting so that all quantities produced can be sold.

Required:

a. Calculate the number of rolls of commercial carpet and residential carpet Leastan Company must manufacture during the last month of production to exhaust completely the heavy-duty and regular fiber still in stock.

b. Can Leastan Company manufacture these quantities of commercial and residential carpeting during the last month of production? Explain your answer.

(CMA adapted)

13–25 Product Mix Choice

Excelsion Corporation manufactures and sells two kinds of containers—paperboard and plastic. The company produced and sold 100,000 paperboard containers and 75,000 plastic containers during the month of April. A total of 4,000 and 6,000 direct labor-hours were used in producing the paperboard and plastic containers, respectively.

The company has not been able to maintain an inventory of either product due to the high demand; this situation is expected to continue in the future. Workers can be shifted from the production of paperboard to plastic containers and vice versa, but additional labor is not available in the community. In addition, there will be a shortage of plastic material used in the manufacture of the plastic container in the coming months due to a labor strike at the facilities of a key supplier. Management has estimated there will be only enough direct material to produce 60,000 plastic containers during June.

The income statement for Excelsion Corporation for the month of April is shown below. The costs presented in the statement are representative of prior periods and are expected to continue at the same rates or levels in the future.

EXCELSION CORPORATION
Income Statement
For the Month Ended April 30

	Paperboard Containers	Plastic Containers
Sales revenue	$220,800	$222,900
Less:		
Returns and allowances	6,360	7,200
Discounts	2,440	3,450
Total	8,800	10,650
Net sales	212,000	212,250
Cost of sales:		
Direct material cost	123,000	120,750
Direct labor	26,000	28,500
Indirect labor (variable with direct labor-hours)	4,000	4,500
Depreciation—machinery	14,000	12,250
Depreciation—building	10,000	10,000
Cost of sales	177,000	176,000
Gross profit	35,000	36,250
Nonmanufacturing expenses:		
Variable	8,000	7,500
Fixed	1,000	1,000
Commissions—variable	11,000	15,750
Total operating expenses	20,000	24,250
Income before tax	15,000	12,000
Income taxes (40%)	6,000	4,800
Net income	$ 9,000	$ 7,200

Required:

What is the optimal product mix, given the constraints in the problem?

(CMA adapted)

13–26 Multiple-Choice

A company markets two products, Alpha and Gamma. The contribution margins per gallon are $5 for Alpha and $4 for Gamma. Both products consist of two ingredients, D and K. Alpha contains 80 percent D and 20 percent K, while the proportions of the same ingredients in Gamma are 40 percent and 60 percent, respectively. The current inventory is 16,000 gallons of D and 6,000 gallons of K. The only company producing D and K is on strike and will neither deliver nor produce them in the foreseeable future. The company wishes to know the numbers of gallons of Alpha and Gamma that it should produce with its present stock of raw materials in order to maximize its total profit. Let X_1 refer to Alpha and X_2 refer to Gamma.

Required:

a. The objective function for this problem could be expressed as:
   (1) Max $0X_1 + 0X_2$.
   (2) Min $5X_1 + 4X_2$.
   (3) Max $5X_1 + 4X_2$.
   (4) Max $X_1 + X_2$.
   (5) Max $4X_1 + 5X_2$.

b. The constraint imposed by the quantity of D on hand could be expressed as:
   (1) $X_1 + X_2 \geq 16,000$.
   (2) $X_1 + X_2 \leq 16,000$.
   (3) $.4X_1 + .6X_2 \leq 16,000$.

(4) $.8X_1 + .4X_2 \geq 16,000.$
(5) $.8X_1 + .4X_2 \leq 16,000.$

c. The constraint imposed by the quantity of K on hand could be expressed as:
  (1) $X_1 + X_2 \geq 6,000.$
  (2) $X_1 + X_2 \leq 6,000.$
  (3) $.8X_1 + .2X_2 \leq 6,000.$
  (4) $.8X_1 + .2X_2 \geq 6,000.$
  (5) $.2X_1 + .6X_2 \leq 6,000.$

d. To maximize total profit, the company should produce and market:
  (1) 106,000 gallons of Alpha only.
  (2) 90,000 gallons of Alpha and 16,000 gallons of Gamma.
  (3) 16,000 gallons of Alpha and 90,000 gallons of Gamma.
  (4) 18,000 gallons of Alpha and 4,000 gallons of Gamma.
  (5) 4,000 gallons of Alpha and 18,000 gallons of Gamma.

e. Assuming that the marginal contributions per gallon are $7 for Alpha and $9 for Gamma, the company should produce and market:
  (1) 106,000 gallons of Alpha only.
  (2) 90,000 gallons of Alpha and 16,000 gallons of Gamma.
  (3) 16,000 gallons of Alpha and 90,000 gallons of Gamma.
  (4) 18,000 gallons of Alpha and 4,000 gallons of Gamma.
  (5) 4,000 gallons of Alpha and 18,000 gallons of Gamma.

(CPA adapted)

13–27 Formulate Objective Function and Constraints

The Witchell Corporation manufactures and sells three grades, A, B, and C, of a single wood product. Each grade must be processed through three phases—cutting, fitting, and finishing—before they are sold.

The following information is provided:

	A	B	C
Selling price	$10.00	$15.00	$20.00
Direct labor	5.00	6.00	9.00
Direct material	.70	.70	1.00
Variable overhead	1.00	1.20	1.80
Fixed overhead	.60	.72	1.08
Materials requirements in board-feet	7	7	10
Labor requirements in hours:			
Cutting	$3/6$	$3/6$	$4/6$
Fitting	$1/6$	$1/6$	$2/6$
Finishing	$1/6$	$2/6$	$3/6$

Only 5,000 board-feet per week can be obtained.

The Cutting Department has 180 hours of labor available each week. The Fitting and Finishing Departments each have 120 hours of labor available each week. No overtime is allowed.

Contract commitments require the company to make 100 units of A per week. In addition, company policy is to produce at least 50 units of B and 50 units of C each week. Product C is constrained to a maximum of 130 units per week.

Required:

Formulate the objective function and constraints.

13–28 Analyze Costs in a Multiproduct Setting

Bright Tubes, Inc., manufactures projection devices for large television screens. The devices come in two models, 48X and 60X, designed for screens with diagonal measurements of 48 and 60 inches, respectively. Data on sales prices and costs for each model are:

	48X	60X
Selling price	$140	$220
Variable costs:		
Materials	45	60
Other	40	45
Allocated fixed costs	20	50
Profit per unit	$ 35	$ 65

Allocated fixed costs are based on total monthly fixed costs of $140,000.

The only production limitation is on the availability of titanium oxide extruders (abbreviated TOEs), which are required for each projection tube. The 48X model requires one TOE, while the 60X model requires two TOEs. There are 4,000 TOEs available per month. Management has decided that it must sell at least 1,000 of each model per month to maintain a full product line.

Last month the company used a linear programming package with the profit function:

$$\text{Maximize profit} = \$35X + \$65Y$$

where X represented the 48-inch model and Y represented the 60-inch model. Product outputs, unit revenues and unit variable costs, and total fixed costs were exactly as planned.

Nonetheless, profit performance for last month was disappointing. You have been called in to help management analyze the cause for the poor performance last month and to help improve performance in the future.

Required:

a. What profit was earned last month?

b. What product mix would you recommend this month, and what profit would be expected with your recommended product mix? Show supporting calculations.

13–29 Analyze Alternative Actions with Multiple Products

Rienz Corporation manufactures two models: Average and Deluxe. The following data are derived from company accounting records for the two products for the past month:

	Average	Deluxe
Sales volume	1,000 units	800 units
Sales revenue	$135,000	$160,000
Manufacturing costs:		
Variable	25,000	40,000
Fixed	45,000	50,000
Marketing costs (all variable)	27,000	32,000
Administrative costs (all fixed)	20,000	25,000
Total costs	117,000	147,000
Division profit	$ 18,000	$ 13,000

Production is constrained by the availability of certain materials. Each Average model takes 10 kg of these materials, while each Deluxe model uses 15 kg. There are 22,000 kg of materials available each month. Marketing constraints limit the number of Average models to 1,800 per month. Deluxe models are similarly limited to 1,200 per month.

The fixed manufacturing costs for each product would be eliminated if the product was no longer manufactured. However, administrative costs will not change with the elimination of either product.

Required:	What is the optimal product mix and what is the profit that would be earned at that product mix? Show computations.
13–30 Analyze Alternative Products with Differential Fixed Costs	Siberian Ski Company recently expanded its manufacturing capacity, which will allow it to produce up to 15,000 pairs of cross-country skis of the Mountaineering model or the Touring model. The Sales Department assures management that it can sell between 9,000 and 13,000 of either product this year. Because the models are very similar, Siberian Ski will produce only one of the two models. The following information was compiled by the Accounting Department.

	Model	
	Mountaineering	**Touring**
Selling price per unit	$88.00	$80.00
Variable costs per unit	52.80	52.80

Fixed costs will total $369,600 if the Mountaineering model is produced but will be only $316,800 if the Touring model is produced.

Required:

a. If Siberian could be assured of selling 12,000 of either model, which model would it sell? How much operating profit would be earned with sales of that product?

b. At what sales level, in units, would Siberian be indifferent regardless of the model it chooses to produce?

c. If Siberian faces a limitation on labor so that a maximum of 6,000 Mountaineering models or a maximum of 12,000 Touring models or some combination of models that would fall along that constraint can be produced, what is the optimal production schedule?

(CMA adapted)

13–31 Formulate and Solve Linear Program

The Elon Company manufactures two industrial products—X-10, which sells for $90 a unit, and Y-12, which sells for $85 a unit. Each product is processed through both of the company's manufacturing departments. The limited availability of labor, material, and equipment capacity has restricted the ability of the firm to meet the demand for its products. The Production Department believes that linear programming can be used to routinize the production schedule for the two products.

The following data are available to the Production Department:

	Amount Required per Unit	
	X-10	**Y-12**
Direct material: Weekly supply is limited to 1,800 pounds at $12 per pound	4 pounds	2 pounds
Direct labor:		
Department 1—weekly supply limited to 10 people at 40 hours each at an hourly cost of $6	$2/3$ hour	1 hour
Direct labor:		
Department 2—weekly supply limited to 15 people at 40 hours each at an hourly rate of $8	$1^1/_4$ hours	1 hour
Machine time:		
Department 1—weekly capacity limited to 250 hours	$1/2$ hour	$1/2$ hour
Department 2—weekly capacity limited to 300 hours	0 hours	1 hour

The overhead costs for Elon are accumulated on a plantwide basis. The overhead is assigned to products on the basis of the number of direct labor-hours required to manufacture the product. This base is appropriate for overhead assignment because most of the variable overhead costs vary as a function of labor time. The estimated overhead cost per direct labor-hour is:

Variable overhead cost	$ 6
Fixed overhead cost	6
Total overhead cost per direct labor-hour	$12

The Production Department formulated the following equations for the linear programming statement of the problem.

A = Number of units of X-10 to be produced
B = Number of units of Y-12 to be produced

Objective function to minimize costs:

Minimize $85A + 62B$

Constraints:
Material:

$$4A + 2B \leq 1,800 \text{ pounds}$$

Department 1 labor:

$$\tfrac{2}{3}A + 1B \leq 400 \text{ hours}$$

Department 2 labor:

$$1\tfrac{1}{4}A + 1B \leq 600 \text{ hours}$$

Nonnegativity:

$$A \geq 0, B \geq 0$$

Required:

a. The formulation of the linear programming equations as prepared by Elon Company's Production Department is incorrect. Explain what errors have been made in the formulation prepared by the Production Department.

b. Formulate and label the proper equations for the linear programming statement of Elon Company's production problem.

c. (Computer required). Solve the linear program and determine the increase in the price of direct materials that would be required to change the product mix from that obtained in the optimal solution.

(CMA adapted)

13–32 Multiple-Product Choice

Girth, Inc., makes two kinds of men's suede leather belts. Belt A is a high-quality belt, while belt B is of somewhat lower quality. The company earns a contribution margin of $7 for each unit of belt A that is sold and $2 for each unit sold of belt B. Each unit (belt) of type A requires twice as much manufacturing time as is required for a unit of type B. Further, if only belt B is made, Girth has the capacity to manufacture 1,000 units per day. Suede leather is purchased by Girth under a long-term contract that makes available to Girth enough leather to make 800 belts per day (A and B combined). Each belt uses the same amount of suede leather. Belt A requires a fancy buckle, of which only 400 per day are available. Belt B requires a different (plain) buckle, of which 700 per day are available. The demand for the suede leather belts (A or B) is such that Girth can sell all that it produces.

Required:

a. Construct a graph to determine how many units of belt A and belt B should be produced to maximize daily profits.

b. Assume the same facts as above except that the sole supplier of buckles for belt A informs Girth, Inc., that it will be unable to supply more than 100 fancy buckles per day. How many units of each of the two belts should be produced each day to maximize profits?

c. Assume the same facts as in requirement (*b*) except that Texas Buckles, Inc., could supply Girth, Inc., with the additional fancy buckles it needs. The price would be $3.50 more than Girth, Inc., is paying for such buckles. How many, if any, fancy buckles should Girth, Inc., buy from Texas Buckles, Inc.? Explain how you determined your answer.

(CMA adapted)

INTEGRATIVE CASES

13–33   Solve Linear Programming Problem

(Computer required.) Golden Company management wants to maximize profits on its three products. Ooh, Ahh, and Wow. The following information is available from the company accounting records:

	Ooh	Ahh	Wow
Sales price	$9	$8	$12
Manufacturing costs:			
Direct materials	2	1	3
Direct labor	3	2	2
Overhead	2	3	3
Selling and administrative costs	1	1	1
Profit per unit	$1	$1	$ 3

Analysis of selling and administrative costs indicates that 50 percent of those costs vary with sales. The remaining amount is fixed at $90,000.

Manufacturing overhead costs are based on machine-hours. A regression equation was computed based on the past 30 months of cost data. The equation was:

$$OVH = \$285{,}000 + \$.35MHR$$

where

$$OVH = \text{Overhead}$$
$$MHR = \text{Machine-hours}$$

The regression equation had an overall R-square of .85. Each Ooh requires .8 machine-hour. Each Ahh and Wow requires 1.2 machine-hours.

Each product requires usage of limited facilities. These time requirements in hours for each unit are:

	Ooh	Ahh	Wow
Preparation	.2	.1	.4
Molding	.1	.3	.5
Finishing	.3	.2	.1

There are 125,000 hours available in Preparation; 85,000 hours available in Molding; and 70,000 hours available in Finishing.

Required:

a. Formulate the above as a linear programming problem.

b. Solve the problem and compute the profit at the optimal product mix.

13–34   **Bayview Manufacturing Company (Linear Programming and Cost Estimation)[4]**

(Computer required.) In November 1994, the Bayview Manufacturing Company was in the process of preparing its budget for 1995. As the first step, it prepared a pro forma income statement for 1994 based on the first 10 months' operations and revised plans for the last two months. This income statement, in condensed form, was as follows:

Sales revenue		$3,000,000
Materials	$1,182,000	
Labor	310,000	
Factory overhead	775,000	
Selling and administrative	450,000	2,717,000
Net income before taxes		$ 283,000

These results were better than expected and operations were close to capacity, but Bayview's management was not convinced that demand would remain at present levels and hence had not planned any increase in plant capacity. Its equipment was specialized and made to its order; over a year's lead time was necessary on all plant additions.

Bayview produces three products; sales have been broken down by product, as follows:

100,000 of product A at $20	$2,000,000
40,000 of product B at $10	400,000
20,000 of product C at $30	600,000
	$3,000,000

Management has ordered a profit analysis for each product and has available the following information:

	A	B	C
Material	$ 7.00	$ 3.75	$16.60
Labor	2.00	1.00	3.50
Factory overhead	5.00	2.50	8.75
Selling and administrataive costs	3.00	1.50	4.50
Total costs	17.00	8.75	33.35
Selling price	20.00	10.00	30.00
Profit	$ 3.00	$ 1.25	$ (3.35)

Factory overhead has been applied on the basis of direct labor costs at a rate of 250 percent, and management asserts that approximately 20 percent of the overhead is variable and does vary with labor costs. Selling and administrative costs have been allocated on the basis of sales at the rate of 15 percent; approximately one half of this is variable and does vary with sales in dollars. All of the labor expense is considered to be variable.

As the first step in the planning process, the Sales Department has been asked to make estimates of what it could sell; these estimates have been reviewed by the firm's consulting economist and by top management. They are as follows:

A	130,000 units
B	50,000 units
C	50,000 units

---

[4] Based on "Report of the Committee on the Measurement Methods Content of the Accounting Curriculum," *Supplement to Volume XLVI of The Accounting Review*, pp. 229–36. The original version of this problem was developed by Professor Carl Nelson.

Production of these quantities was immediately recognized as being impossible. Estimated cost data for the three products, each of which requires activity of both departments, were based on the following production rates:

	Product		
	A	B	C
Department 1 (molding)	2 per hour	4 per hour	3 per hour
Department 2 (finishing)	4 per hour	8 per hour	$4/3$ per hour

Practical capacity in Department 1 is 67,000 hours and in Department 2, 63,000 hours; and the Industrial Engineering Department has concluded that this cannot be increased without the purchase of additional equipment. Thus, while last year Department 1 operated at 99 percent of its capacity and Department 2 at 71 percent of capacity, anticipated sales would require operating both Departments 1 and 2 at more than 100 percent capacity.

These solutions to the limited production problem have been rejected: (1) subcontracting the production out to other firms is considered to be unprofitable because of problems of maintaining quality; (2) operating a second shift is impossible because of a shortage of labor; and (3) operating overtime would create problems because a large number of employees are "moonlighting" and would therefore refuse to work more than the normal 40-hour week. Price increases have been rejected; although they would result in higher profits this year, the long-run competitive position of the firm would be weakened, resulting in lower profits in the future.

The treasurer then suggested that product C has been carried at a loss too long and that now was the time to eliminate it from the product line. If all facilities are used to produce A and B, profits would increase.

The sales manager objected to this solution because of the need to carry a full line. In addition, he maintains that there is a group of loyal customers whose needs must be met. He provided a list of these customers and their estimated purchases (in units), which total as follows:

A   80,000
B   32,000
C   12,000

These contentions appeared to be reasonable and served to narrow the bounds of the problem, so the president concurred.

The treasurer reluctantly acquiesced but maintained that the remaining capacity should be used to produce A and B. Because A produced 2.4 times as much profit as B, he suggested that the production of A (in excess of the 80,000 minimum set by the sales manager) be 2.4 times that of B (in excess of the 32,000 minimum set by the sales manager).

The production manager made some quick calculations and said the budgeted production and sales would be about:

A 104,828
B   42,344
C   12,000

The treasurer then made a calculation of profits as follows:

A	104,828 at $3.00	$314,484
B	42,344 at $1.25	52,930
C	12,000 at ($3.35)	(40,200)
		$327,214

As this would represent an increase of almost 15 percent over the current year, there was a general feeling of self-satisfaction. Before final approval was given, however, the president said that he would like to have his new assistant check over the figures. Somewhat piqued, the treasurer agreed, and at that point the group adjourned.

The next day the above information was submitted to you as your first assignment in your new job as the president's assistant.

Required:

Prepare an analysis showing the president what he should do.

Exhibits 13–34A and 13–34B contain information that you are able to obtain from the accounting system, which may help you to estimate an overhead cost breakdown into fixed and variable components different from that given in the case.

EXHIBIT

13–34A

Cost Data for Last Ten Years

Direct Labor Cost by Department (in thousands)			Overhead Cost by Department (in thousands)		
1	2	Total	1	2	Total
$140	$170	$310	$341	$434	$775
135	150	285	340	421	761
140	160	300	342	428	770
130	150	280	339	422	761
130	155	285	338	425	763
125	140	265	337	414	751
120	150	270	335	420	755
115	140	255	334	413	747
120	140	260	336	414	750
115	135	250	335	410	745

EXHIBIT

13–34B

Data for Last Ten Years

Sales (in thousands)				Marketing and Administrative Costs (in thousands)
Product A	Product B	Product C	Total	
$2,000	$400	$600	$3,000	$450
1,940	430	610	2,980	445
1,950	380	630	2,960	445
1,860	460	620	2,940	438
1,820	390	640	2,850	433
1,860	440	580	2,880	437
1,880	420	570	2,870	438
1,850	380	580	2,810	434
1,810	390	580	2,780	430
1,770	290	610	2,670	425

SOLUTIONS TO

 *Self-Study*
Questions

1 *a.* Determine the contributions for each product:

	Twopack	Threepack
Selling price	$1,000	$1,700
Variable costs:		
Materials	350	370
Direct labor	210	230
Variable overhead (20%)	30	40
Variable marketing	80	240
Total variable costs	670	880
Contribution margin	$ 330	$ 820

Maximize profit = $330 (Twopack) + $820 (Threepack)

b. Constraints:

$$\text{Twopack} \geq 500$$
$$\text{Threepack} \geq 150$$
$$\tfrac{1}{4} \text{ (Twopack)} + \tfrac{3}{4} \text{ (Threepack)} \leq 250$$

c. Contribution per assembly control–hour:

Twopack $330/.25 = $1,320
Threepack $820/.75 = $1,093

The Twopack is preferred because it gives a greater contribution per assembly control–hour.

d.

Produce and Sell		Total Contribution
Twopacks	Threepacks	Margin
500	150	$330(500) + $820(150) = $288,000
500	167[a]	$330(500) + $820(167) = $301,940
550[b]	150	$330(550) + $820(150) = $304,500

---

[a] $\tfrac{1}{4}(500) + \tfrac{3}{4}$ Threepack = 250, from assembly control constraint

$$\text{Threepack} = \frac{250 - \tfrac{1}{4}(500)}{3/4}$$

$$= 167$$

[b] $\tfrac{1}{4}$ Twopack + $\tfrac{3}{4}(150)$ = 250, from assembly control constraint

$$\text{Twopack} = \frac{250 - \tfrac{3}{4}(150)}{1/4}$$

$$= 550$$

e. $1,320 plus the cost of assembly control time included in the objective function.

2   *a.*   Optimal production level for:
         (1) Nordic model = 2,500 units.
         (2) Racer model = 0 units.
         (3) Alpine model = 0 units.

   b.   *Labor constraint:* Total contribution remains the same since only 25,000 labor-hours are currently used.
         Machine constraint: Total contribution increases by:

   $$\$28,750 = \$5.75 \ (15,000 - 10,000)$$

   c.   Fifteen thousand labor-hours unused. Zero machine-hours unused.

   d.   If a decision to produce one unit of the Racer model is made, total contribution margin will decrease by $28.50. Producing a unit of the Racer model means that 2½ units of the Nordic model are forgone (see the relation between the Nordic and Racer models for the machine constraint, which is binding).

   e. $57,500 = $23 × 2,500 units of the Nordic model. Each additional machine-hour allows production of .25 units of the Nordic model. Since the Nordic model has a unit contribution margin of $23, the value of one more unit of the scarce machine-hour resource is $5.75.

   f.   If the contribution margin drops by $5 to $18, then 2,500 units of the Nordic model will be produced, since the objective function coefficient is still within the range of allowable increase or decrease according to the objective function coefficient ranges. If the contribution margin drops by $11 to $12, the optimal production level of the Nordic model will be unknown, since the value of the objective function coefficient lies outside the allowable range of decrease.

Inventory Management Costs

LEARNING OBJECTIVES

After reading this chapter, you should be able to:

1. Derive the economic order quantity (EOQ) for purchasing and production.
2. Apply the EOQ model to cases having order size restrictions or quantity discounts.
3. Find the optimal safety stock of inventory.
4. Identify the differential costs of a particular inventory policy.

*I*n this chapter we discuss how cost data are used in inventory management. Inventory *management* costs should be distinguished from the cost of *producing* inventory. The cost of manufacturing products is made up of the materials, labor, and manufacturing overhead required to make the product. The inventory management costs discussed in this chapter are costs of keeping products in inventory.

Inventory management techniques are applicable in all types of organizations that have inventories, even those in which the only inventory is an inventory of office supplies. Merchandise organizations, such as Macy's, Blockbuster Video, Toys "R" Us, Nordstrom's, and Wal-Mart, are particularly concerned about inventory management. Too much inventory results in unnecessary costs of carrying inventory. Too little inventory results in lost sales if customers buy the product elsewhere.

Most companies use complex computer models to manage their inventories. But these models are all based on the fundamental models we introduce here. We present the classical economic order quantity (EOQ) model and the costs it should include. We examine the problem of stockouts and how to use cost data to determine the optimal safety-stock policy. Finally, we discuss recent innovations, such as *just-in-time* inventory models and *flexible manufacturing*, which are having an exciting impact on inventory management.

INVENTORY MANAGEMENT

Inventory management activities can range from ensuring that there is an adequate selection of different sizes of clothing available in a retail store to stocking necessary replacement parts for commercial aircraft. The underlying principles are similar in both situations. The primary objective is to minimize the total costs of maintaining inventory.

Inventory-related costs include the costs of carrying inventory, the costs of replenishing goods that have been sold or used, and the costs of running out of inventory. As we shall see, inventory management involves finding the minimum annual total of these three kinds of costs.

Inventory control models have been in use for some time. Operations research techniques and the advancement of computer systems resulted in the development of highly sophisticated inventory models. These models can monitor demand, forecast usage, calculate the most economic quantity to order, indicate when to order, and determine the optimal levels of inventory to keep on hand.[1]

Engineers and operations research specialists depend upon accountants for information about the costs that are relevant for use in these models. In cost accounting, we discuss issues in formulating the cost data necessary to use these techniques.

INVENTORY MANAGEMENT COSTS

Carrying Costs Those costs that increase with the number of units of inventory.

Ordering Costs Costs that increase with the number of orders placed for inventory.

The goal in controlling inventory costs is to minimize total costs while maintaining the quantities of inventories needed for smooth operation. Some costs increase with the quantities of inventory on hand, while other costs decrease.

Carrying costs increase with the quantity of inventory on hand. There are two classes of carrying costs: (1) *out-of-pocket costs* and (2) *cost of capital*. Out-of-pocket costs include the cost of such items as insurance on the value of the inventory, inventory taxes, annual inspections, and obsolescence. The *cost of capital* is the opportunity cost of having funds in inventory rather than in other earning assets.

Ordering costs increase with the number of orders and decrease with the quantity of inventory on hand. Ordering costs include people's time to place the order and costs of telephoning or placing an order by fax machine.

Given a constant usage rate, the greater the inventory on hand, the less frequently one must order, thus, the lower the ordering costs. An optimal inventory policy minimizes the sum of carrying costs and ordering costs.

Inventory costs can be represented graphically as in Illustration 14–1.

THE ECONOMIC ORDER QUANTITY (EOQ) MODEL

For analytical purposes, we divide inventory into two categories: (1) *working inventory*, which represents the units that are used in the normal course of operations, and (2) *safety stock,* which is the units that are kept on hand to protect against running out of inventory due to late deliveries, a speed-up in production rates, and other similar factors.

The cost-management problems for inventory are determining the optimal quantity to order and deciding when to place an order. These two

---

[1] These models and their mathematical derivation are presented in operations research texts such as T. E. Vollman, W. Barry, and D. C. Whybark, *Manufacturing, Planning and Control*, 2nd ed. (Homewood, Ill.: Richard D. Irwin, 1988).

ILLUSTRATION

*Economic Lot Size
Cost Behavior*

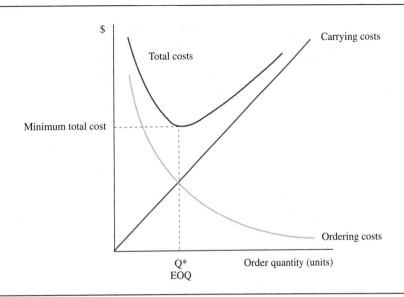

decisions should be based on the carrying cost of the inventory and the cost to place an order. The inventory manager wants to know the point at which the total of these costs is minimized. We will see next how these costs are represented in the basic inventory models.

*Carrying Costs and
Ordering Costs*

Carrying costs are usually expressed in terms of the average number of units in the inventory. That is, in a given year, one would expect to incur carrying costs of:

$$\frac{Q}{2} \times S$$

where S is the cost to carry one unit in the inventory for one year and is composed of out-of-pocket costs as well as cost of capital. The average inventory is presumed to be the average of the Q units that arrive at the start of the inventory cycle and the zero units that are left at the end. That is, $(Q + 0)/2 = Q/2$.

Ordering costs are expressed as the product of the number of orders placed in a year times the cost to place one order. This function is:

$$\frac{A}{Q} \times P$$

where A is the annual usage of the inventory item, and P is the cost of placing one order. The term A/Q is the number of orders placed per year. As the quantity per order increases, the number of orders required per year decreases. Thus, the ordering cost function decreases as Q increases, as shown in Illustration 14–1.

The total inventory carrying and ordering cost is:

$$TC = \frac{QS}{2} + \frac{AP}{Q}$$

Note from the graph in Illustration 14–1 that the minimum total cost occurs at the point where the two cost functions are equal. This coincidence occurs in the most basic EOQ problem but may not be generalized to more complex problems. For this problem, the optimal Q (labeled Q^*) is referred to as the **economic order quantity (EOQ)**. It may be found by the equation:

Economic Order Quantity (EOQ)
The order size that minimizes the total of carrying and ordering costs.

$$Q^* = \sqrt{\frac{2AP}{S}}$$

If Q^* units are ordered each time and inventory usage and costs continue as planned, the inventory carrying and ordering costs will be at a minimum. Note how carrying costs increase with the quantity of inventory on hand, while ordering costs decrease with the quantity on hand. Inventory management seeks to minimize total costs and to identify the point Q^*. The total cost to maintain a given inventory level decreases in the range of zero to Q^* and then increases from Q^* to the maximum possible inventory level. To find Q^*, it is necessary both to construct the mathematical relationship for the cost functions and to identify the elements of cost that should be included in each function. The first task is handled by operations research specialists; the second is the responsibility of cost accountants.

For example, Tri-Ply Company uses 25,000 units of material Z per year in the manufacture of a specialty line of plywood laminates. Out-of-pocket costs for carrying material Z are $2.50 per unit. Each unit costs $80, and the company's cost of capital is 25 percent. Thus, carrying costs are $22.50 per unit [$2.50 + ($80 × 25%)]. The cost to place an order for material Z is $648. What is the optimal order size?

In this example, A = 25,000 units; P = $648; and S = $2.50 + ($80 × 25%) = $22.50. The optimal order size is:

$$Q^* = \sqrt{\frac{2 \times 25,000 \times \$648}{\$22.50}}$$

$$= \sqrt{1,440,000}$$

$$= \underline{1,200 \text{ units}}$$

Now, if Tri-Ply management follows the policy and orders 1,200 units each time, the annual costs of the inventory policy will be:

Carrying costs:

$$\frac{QS}{2} = \frac{1,200 \times \$22.50}{2} = \underline{\underline{\$13,500}}$$

Ordering costs:

$$\frac{AP}{Q} = \frac{25,000 \times \$648}{1,200} = \underline{\underline{\$13,500}}$$

so that costs amount to $27,000 (that is, the $13,500 carrying costs plus $13,500 ordering costs). This is the minimum cost. In this case, the total carrying costs equal total ordering costs, which is consistent with Illustration 14–1.

Applications

The EOQ model can also be used to compute the optimal (least-cost) length of a production run. The costs to set up a production run are analogous to the ordering costs in the basic EOQ model. Carrying costs are the same as for a basic model.

For example, if the differential cost of setting up a production line to produce a specific type of item is $2,500, the demand for the item is 720,000 per year, and the cost to carry each item in inventory is $1, then the *economic production run* size is:

$$Q^* = \sqrt{\frac{2 \times 720,000 \times \$2,500}{\$1}}$$

which equals 60,000 units.

While the EOQ model discussed here sets forth the principles for inventory management models, actual applications are usually much more complex. Quite often the demand (or usage) variable changes from one order period to the next. In addition, rarely does a company order only one product from a given supplier. When multiple products are procured from one supplier, it may be possible to obtain ordering cost savings by ordering several items at one time. Inventory management models are so complex that they are almost always computerized. A computer model can simultaneously consider the various products ordered from a vendor and estimate the optimal time to place an order for one or more of them.

Although more complex models will be encountered, the basic model contains the elements that a cost accountant must consider in developing an optimal inventory policy.

EXTENSIONS OF THE BASIC EOQ MODEL

The classical EOQ model may be extended to include other costs and considerations. The following examples show how inventory management costs may be incorporated in some more complex settings.

Orders in Round Lots

Many companies will accept orders only for round lots such as even dozens, hundreds, tons, and the like. These restrictions are often related to assembly-line or packaging requirements. When there are restrictions on order size, computation of Q^* using the basic EOQ model will not necessarily provide an acceptable order quantity. If Q^* is not equal to one of the allowed order quantities, it is necessary to determine the total annual cost of ordering the two allowed quantities on either side of Q^*. In such cases, the optimal order size will be either Q^*, if allowed, or the allowed quantity closest to Q^*, whether greater than or less than. Drawing lines on a cost graph to show order size restrictions as shown in Illustration 14–2 demonstrates why the optimal alternative is limited to the choices mentioned.

For example, suppose that the supplier of material Z accepts orders only in round lots of 500 units. An order for 1,200 units would not be acceptable, but Tri-Ply could order 500, 1,000, or 1,500 units. The two order sizes, 1,000 units and 1,500 units, comprise the set from which the optimal order size is obtained. To determine which order size is optimal, the total annual costs for each alternative are examined.

If 1,000 units are ordered, then the annual inventory costs are $27,450. This is the sum of the carrying costs computed as:

$$\frac{QS}{2} = \frac{1,000 \times \$22.50}{2} = \$11,250$$

EOQ with Order Size
Restrictions

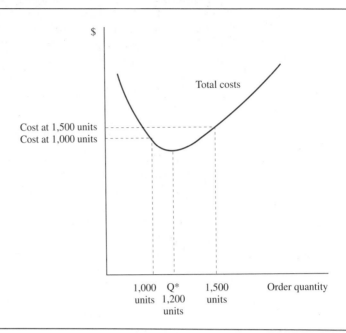

and the ordering costs:

$$\frac{AP}{Q} = \frac{25,000 \times \$648}{1,000} = \underline{\$16,200}$$

Total $\underline{\underline{\$27,450}}$

If 1,500 units are ordered at a time, then the annual costs are \$27,675, which is the sum of the carrying costs:

$$\frac{QS}{2} = \frac{1,500 \times \$22.50}{2} = \$16,875$$

and the ordering costs:

$$\frac{AP}{Q} = \frac{25,000 \times \$648}{1,500} = \underline{\$10,800}$$

Total $\underline{\underline{\$27,675}}$

Therefore, the optimal policy, given the restrictions on order size, is to order 1,000 units each time.

Note that the difference in total costs between the two order sizes is relatively small (\$225). If the actual order quantity is significantly different, however, the cost changes can be substantial. For example, at an order size of 500 units, the total costs increase to \$38,025. [Carrying costs of \$22.50 per unit times 250 units = \$5,625, and ordering costs for 50 orders (25,000/500) at \$648 = \$32,400.] This computation highlights how the total costs change at different activity levels. Typically, they change very little for values close to Q^*; but as order size decreases, the total inventory management costs increase rather rapidly. However, we highlight the point that the optimal inventory quantity will be at one of the two feasible order quantities adjacent to the initial Q^*.

ILLUSTRATION

*EOQ with Order Size
Constraints*

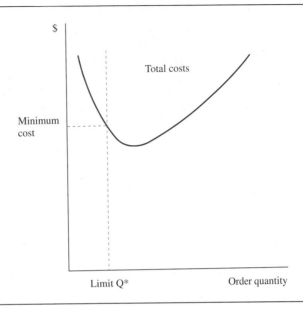

Order Size Constraints

In today's just-in-time business environment, inventory levels are kept deliberately low. Management sets maximum order sizes to avoid obsolescence or to keep carrying costs low.

If there are order size constraints on the maximum number of units that may be stored and the computed value of Q^* is greater than the constraint, then the appropriate order size is the value of the constraint. This may be confirmed by inspecting the cost function graph in Illustration 14–1 and drawing a constraint line anywhere between zero and Q^*. The minimum total cost is at the constraint. This may be seen from Illustration 14–3, which shows the constraint imposed on the inventory cost function.

When there are storage constraints, management may ask whether it is economically justifiable to relax the constraint. Suppose that Tri-Ply has a capacity constraint of 750 units. It could obtain additional warehouse space for $6,000 per year that would enable it to store the additional 450 units indicated by the economic lot size model. Should the company obtain the additional space?

To decide, they must look at the differential cost of the alternatives. If 750 units were ordered at a time (since this is the best that can be done with the constraint), the costs are:

Carrying costs:

$$\frac{QS}{2} = \frac{750 \times \$22.50}{2} = \$\ 8,437.50$$

Ordering costs:

$$\frac{AP}{Q} = \frac{25,000 \times \$648}{750} = \underline{\$21,600.00}$$

Total $\underline{\underline{\$30,037.50}}$

From the initial example, we know that the optimal inventory costs without the constraint are $27,000. The expected savings from the additional warehouse space are $3,037.50 (the difference between $30,037.50 and $27,000). Since the rental cost exceeds the expected savings, it is better to forgo the rental and order in lots of 750 units.

This may also be formulated in the same manner as other differential cost problems. A comparison of the costs under the alternatives "Maintain Present Storage" and "Rent Space" appears as:

Cost Item	Maintain Present Storage	Rent Space	Differential Costs
Carrying costs (excluding space rentals)	$ 8,437.50	$13,500.00	$5,062.50 higher
Ordering costs	21,600.00	13,500.00	8,100.00 lower
Space rental	–0–	6,000.00	6,000.00 higher
Total costs	$30,037.50	$33,000.00	$2,962.50 higher

This analysis yields the same results, namely, that the differential costs of renting exceed the savings.

Quantity Discounts

Quantity Discounts Price reductions offered for bulk purchases.

Suppliers often offer **quantity discounts** on purchases of materials, or shipping charges may be lower for bulk shipments. In such situations, the savings from ordering in large lots may more than offset the incremental carrying costs. As a general rule, when quantity price breaks are available, the minimum EOQ will be the amount determined by the computation of Q^* without regard to price-break considerations. It may, however, be less costly to order a large quantity to obtain the price break.

Assume the supplier of material Z offers the following price breaks:

Number Ordered	Discount
0–999	None
1,000–1,999	$1.00 per unit
2,000–4,999	1.50
5,000–9,999	1.75
10,000 and over	1.80

The optimal order quantity for Tri-Ply would be either 1,200 units—the optimal quantity ignoring the price breaks—or 2,000, 5,000, or 10,000 units. No other quantity is more economic than one of those four.

Tri-Ply management can analyze which of the four quantities is least costly if the price breaks are considered as *opportunity costs*. Forgoing the maximum available discount results in an opportunity cost equal to the difference between that maximum and the discount that Tri-Ply could obtain with its selected order policy. For example, if Tri-Ply orders in lots of 1,200 units, they obtain a discount of $1 per unit but forgo the opportunity to obtain a $1.80 discount. If they order 1,200 units at a time, there is a *forgone discount cost* of $.80 on each unit ordered. Over the year, discounts of $20,000 would be lost. That is based on the 25,000 units ordered per year times the $.80 in lost discounts per unit.

In addition, the dollar cost of capital per unit of inventory is reduced if they obtain a discount. The greater the discount, the greater the reduction.

ILLUSTRATION

*Optimal Order Quantity
with Price Breaks*

Panel A

Order Size	Carrying Costs	Ordering Costs	Forgone Discount	Total Costs
1,200	$ 13,500[a]	$13,500[b]	$20,000[c]	$ 47,000
2,000	22,375[d]	8,100[e]	7,500[f]	37,975 (optimal)
5,000	55,781[g]	3,240[h]	1,250[i]	60,271
10,000	111,500[j]	1,620[k]	–0–	113,120

Panel B

Computations:

[a] $13,500 = \dfrac{1,200 \times (\$2.50 + 25\% \times \$80.00)}{2}$, assuming the $80 price is net of the discount at this level. (Recall that $2.50 equals out-of-pocket carrying costs and 25% is the cost of capital expressed as a percent.)

[b] $13,500 = \dfrac{25,000}{1,200} \times \$648$. (Recall that the annual quantity ordered equals 25,000 and the cost to place an order is $648.)

[c] $20,000 = 25,000 \times (\$1.80 - \$1.00)$, where $1.80 is the maximum price break available.

[d] $22,375 = \dfrac{2,000 \times (\$2.50 + 25\% \times \$79.50)}{2}$, where $79.50 is $80 less the incremental $.50 discount.

[e] $8,100 = \dfrac{25,000}{2,000} \times \$648$.

[f] $7,500 = 25,000 \times (\$1.80 - \$1.50)$.

[g] $55,781$ (rounded) $= \dfrac{5,000 \times (\$2.50 + 25\% \times \$79.25)}{2}$, where $79.25 = $80.00 less the $.75 incremental discount.

[h] $3,240 = \dfrac{25,000}{5,000} \times \$648$.

[i] $1,250 = 25,000 \times (\$1.80 - \$1.75)$.

[j] $111,500 = \dfrac{10,000 \times (\$2.50 + 25\% \times \$79.20)}{2}$, where $79.20 is $80 less the $.80 incremental discount.

[k] $1,620 = \dfrac{25,000}{10,000} \times \$648$.

The reduction in cost equals the percent cost of capital times the dollar amount of discount. For example, if Tri-Ply orders 1,200 units, the discount is $1.00 per unit. If its cost of capital is 25 percent, then the reduction in cost of capital per unit is $.25 (25 percent × $1.00).

One way to analyze the EOQ when price breaks are available is to consider the total carrying cost, ordering cost, and forgone discount for the initial Q^* and the minimum quantities required to earn each additional price break. Such an analysis for Tri-Ply's purchases of material Z is presented in Illustration 14–4.

The optimal order quantity, then, is the one with the lowest total cost, in this case, 2,000 units. Note the behavior of the carrying costs and ordering costs with changes in quantities, and compare them to the patterns in Illustration 14–1.

INVENTORY MANAGEMENT UNDER UNCERTAIN CONDITIONS

Lead Time The time between order placement and order arrival.

Stockout Running out of inventory.

So far we have considered only working inventory in our cost analyses. If usage rates and **lead time** (the time between order placement and order arrival) are known for certain, inventory management is simplified. Usage rates may vary due to unforeseen circumstances, and lead times may vary due to events beyond management's control. If an inventory item is used faster than anticipated or if lead time is longer than expected, a **stockout** may occur.

Using just-in-time methods, where inventory replenishment is expected just as needed for production or sale, stockouts are expected. Analyzing these costs may help minimize the costs of a just-in-time system.

Two kinds of stockouts are diagrammed in Illustration 14–5. In case A, an order was placed at Time T, but the rate of use increased. As a result, the inventory on hand was used up before the new shipment arrived. In case B, the usage rate remained constant, but the new shipment did not arrive on time.

Stockouts Can Be Costly

Depending on the nature of the product, a stockout may require a special trip to pick up extra materials, or the shutting down of operations until new materials can be obtained, resulting in lost sales and customer ill will. Such added costs can be minimized by obtaining an optimal amount of *safety*

ILLUSTRATION

Inventory Flows under Uncertainty

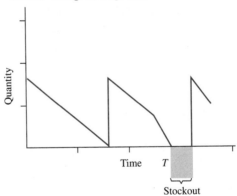

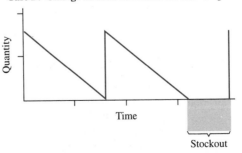

stock. Had the company in the previous example maintained sufficient safety stock, then no stockout would have occurred.

By contrast, the costs to carry additional inventory may be so great that it is economical to incur stockouts. The situations from Illustration 14–5 are reproduced in Illustration 14–6 with the addition of safety stock. Now, in case A, the increased usage is satisfied from the safety stock, and the new order replenishes both the safety stock and the working inventory. In case B, the safety stock is used while awaiting the delayed arrival of the inventory order. Safety stock is replenished with subsequent orders.

Cost Considerations for Safety Stock

Two costs must be considered in establishing an optimal safety-stock policy: (1) the *cost to carry safety stock* and (2) the *cost of a stockout*.

The cost of carrying safety stock is the same as the cost of carrying working inventory. The full quantity of safety stock is the same as the average inventory of safety stock. Because the safety stock on hand at the start of the period should equal the safety stock on hand at the end of the

ILLUSTRATION

Inventory Flows with Safety Stock

Case A: Change in Usage Rate

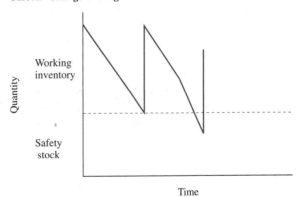

Case B: Change in Time of Arrival for New Shipment

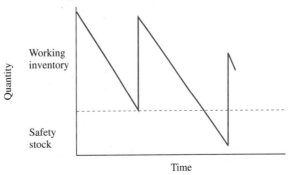

period, the average of these two numbers is the full quantity of safety stock. Although safety stock may decrease from time to time as events require its use, these decreases are usually ignored.

Stockout costs require separate consideration. In the first place, the cost of one stockout is usually expressed in terms of the costs of alternative sources of supply or shutting down operations over the stockout period. Stockouts also cause customer ill will, as you know if you have placed an order with Lands' End, Eddie Bauer, or any other company only to be told the item is "out of stock." Second, the number of stockouts is an expected value. The *expected annual stockout cost* is the product of the cost of one stockout times the number of orders placed per year times the probability of a stockout on any one order.

Returning to the original example for Tri-Ply Company's inventory of material Z, let us consider that the company has a choice of alternative safety-stock levels, each of which will yield a different probability of a stockout. The staff determined that there is a .5 probability of a stockout if no safety stock is maintained. A safety stock of 100 units would reduce the stockout probability to .3. If the safety stock is maintained at 250 units of material Z, then there is a .05 probability of a stockout. Finally, a .01 probability of a stockout would be expected if the safety-stock level were 500 units. If the costs of one stockout are estimated at $3,200, the best choice of these four safety-stock levels is 250 units, as shown by the analysis in Illustration 14–7. (Recall the annual usage is 25,000 and the optimal order size is 1,200.)

Even with the optimal safety-stock level, there is a .05 probability of a stockout. Given that the company orders about 21 times a year (25,000 ÷ 1,200 ≈ 20.8), Tri-Ply can expect one stockout a year for material Z (21 × .05 ≈ 1). But it is more economical to incur this stockout cost than to maintain the additional safety stock. Inventory management seeks to find the least-cost policy with respect to safety-stock levels and stockouts.

ILLUSTRATION

14–7

Cost Analysis of Safety-Stock Policies

Safety Stock	Carrying Costs	Expected Stockout Costs	Total Costs
0 . . . . . 0 × $22.50		$\frac{25,000^a}{1,200}$ × .5 × $3,200	
	= $0	= $33,333	$33,333
100 . . . . . 100 × $22.50		$\frac{25,000}{1,200}$ × .3 × $3,200	
	= $2,250	= $20,000	22,250
250 . . . . . 250 × $22.50		$\frac{25,000}{1,200}$ × .05 × $3,200	
	= $5,625	= $3,333	8,958 (optimal)
500 . . . . . 500 × $22.50		$\frac{25,000}{1,200}$ × .01 × $3,200	
	= $11,250	= $667	11,917

[a] The ratio 25,000/1,200 is the number of orders per year, and therefore the number of possible stockouts.

Similar cost analyses can be prepared if, for example, there are different stockout costs depending on the size of the stockout. The shortage of a few items that can be obtained by alternative transportation may result in incurring only the cost of the incremental transport charges, but one that involves several hundred large items may not be so easily, or inexpensively, resolved.

Stockout Costs as Ordering Costs

Expected annual stockout costs vary directly with the number of orders placed in a year, so stockout costs are an ordering cost. The problem in including these costs in the EOQ and safety-stock models is that the two models are interdependent. The cost per order used in the EOQ model depends on the optimal stockout probability. Discussion of some of the more complex problems in inventory management such as the joint solution to this problem is beyond the scope of this text. Our intention is to familiarize you with the nature of the problem and its implications for cost accounting.

Reorder Point

Goods should be reordered when the quantity of inventory on hand has fallen to the sum of the usage over the lead time plus the safety stock. If an order is placed when the inventory has reached that level, the new shipment is expected to arrive when the total number of units on hand is equal to the safety stock—that is, the working inventory has fallen to zero.

For example, a safety stock of 250 has been chosen for material Z. The lead time is six working days, and the annual usage is 25,000 units. Assuming 220 working days per year, the *reorder point* for material Z is 932 units. This is computed as follows:

$$\left(\frac{25,000}{220 \text{ days}} \times 6\right) + 250 = (113.64 \times 6) + 250$$
$$= 682 + 250 = 932$$

When inventory falls to 932 units, an order should be placed for the optimal number of units (Q^* in the unconstrained problem or other cost-effective Q values in the presence of constraints). During the six days between order placement and order arrival, units are used at the rate of 113.64 per day. After six days, if all goes as planned, there will be approximately 250 units in inventory (the 932 units at reorder time less the 6×113.64 used during the lead time) when the new shipment of Q units arrives. This is diagrammed in Illustration 14–8. The reorder point is noted R. If an order is placed at that point in time, then 682 units will be used between the reorder time and the time when the new order arrives.

DIFFERENTIAL COSTS OF INVENTORY POLICY

Selecting the costs that are relevant to the EOQ is an application of *differential costing*. When preparing cost data for inventory models, we look at each cost and ask whether it will change with the number of:

1. Units carried in inventory.
2. Units purchased.
3. Orders placed in a year.

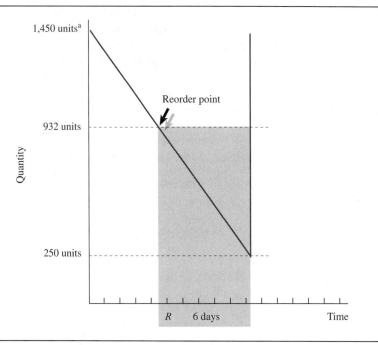

ª 1,450 units = *Q** + Safety stock = 1,200 units + 250 units.

For example, let's consider the costs obtained from Tri-Ply Company's records on a different inventory item. These costs are related to a specific inventory item:

Purchase price . . . . $	6.50 per unit
Transportation-in per unit	.50
Telephone call for order	11.00
Cost to unload a shipment	25.00 + $.15 per unit
Inventory taxes	.60 per unit per year
Costs to arrange for shipment of the material to the company	125.00
Salary of receiving dock supervisor (per month)	1,800.00
Insurance on inventory	.10 per unit per year
Warehouse rental	12,000.00 per month
Average spoilage costs	1.30 per unit per year
Cost of capital	20% per year
Orders handled per month	600

Which of these items should be included in the EOQ computation? Using the three cost categories mentioned earlier, let's classify each item.

1. Costs that vary with the average number of units carried in inventory:

Inventory taxes	$ .60 per unit
Insurance on inventory	.10
Average spoilage costs	1.30
Total	$2.00

2. Costs that vary with the number of units purchased:

Purchase price	$6.50 per unit
Transportation-in	.50
Costs to unload	.15
Total	$7.15

Total annual *carrying costs per unit* is the sum of the carrying costs from category 1, above, plus the cost of capital rate times the investment cost in category 2:

$$\$.60 + \$.10 + \$1.30 + (20\% \times \$7.15) = \$2.00 + (20\% \times \$7.15)$$
$$= \$3.43$$

3. Costs to place an order:

Costs of placing the order	$ 11.00 per order
Unloading the shipment	25.00
Arranging for the shipment	125.00
	$161.00

The total *ordering cost* is $161 per order.

The other costs (warehouse rental and supervisor's salary) usually do not vary with the number of units in inventory, the number of units purchased, or the number of orders during the inventory planning horizon. Those costs are, therefore, irrelevant for this decision (although they may be important for long-range decision making).

Self-Study Question

Main Mart Discount Electronics is a customer of your bank. The president of the company was in your office earlier in the day to apply for an additional line of credit. Trying to help your client, you note that there is a substantial sum of money tied up in inventory. When you pointed this out to the company president, the response was:

"We can't afford to run out of stock. Therefore, our policy is to order as infrequently as possible and to keep as much safety stock on hand as can be stored in our warehouse."

As part of your analysis of the company's loan requirements, you call up the controller of the company for some further information. From the conversation, it appears that the company has a substantial quantity of one particular product in its warehouse. The controller relates the following information on this product:

Invoice cost	$ 120.00
Shipping charges	2.50 per unit
Inventory insurance	1.00 per unit per year
Annual costs to audit and inspect inventory	2.60 per unit
Warehouse utilities	980.00 per month

Warehouse rental	$1,500.00 per month
Unloading costs for units received (paid to shipper)	.80 per unit
Receiving supervisor salary . . .	1,760.00 per month
Processing invoices and other purchase documents	16.00 per order
Allowable order quantity: 250 or multiples thereof	

The company policy is to keep a safety stock of 3,000 units and to order 5,000 units at a time. Annual demand for the product is 45,000 units. The lead time for an order is 10 working days, and there are 250 working days per year for the purposes of purchasing this product. The controller indicated that if there is a stockout, it would be necessary to obtain the products by special air courier at an additional cost of $8,100 per stockout. The probabilities of a stockout with various safety-stock levels are given below:

Safety Stock	Probability of Stockout
500	.25
1,000	.08
1,500	.02
2,000	.01

You estimated that the company's cost of capital is approximately 30 percent. You also know that the state has an inventory tax equal to 1 percent of the cost of items in inventory, which the state defines as the sum of the invoice price, shipping cost per unit, and the unloading costs. You assume for analysis purposes that a stockout probability of .02 would be reasonable for order cost determination in an optimal inventory policy.

    a. What is the annual cost of the company's present inventory policy? Assume 5,000 units are ordered each time an order is placed.

    b. How many units should the company order at a time? (Note the allowable order quantity is in multiples of 250 units.)

    c. What is the optimal safety-stock level?

    d. What is the annual cost of the optimal inventory policy identified in (*b*) and (*c*) (including expected stockout costs)?

    e. What is the reorder point?

The solution to this self-study question is at the end of this chapter on page 544.

JUST-IN-TIME INVENTORY PRODUCTION AND PURCHASING

Just-in-Time A system designed to obtain goods just in time for production (in manufacturing) or sale (in merchandising).

Recent innovations in inventory management and manufacturing methods have the potential to revolutionize both inventory management and the way accounting is done in manufacturing companies. One of these is the **just-in-time** philosophy, discussed in detail in Chapter 5. The objective of the just-in-time (JIT) philosophy is to obtain materials just in time for production and to provide finished goods just in time for sale and other inventory items just when needed. This reduces, or potentially eliminates, inventory carrying costs.

Just-in-time production also requires that processes or people making defective units be corrected immediately because there is no inventory where defective units can be sent to await reworking or scrapping. Manufacturing managers find that eliminating inventories can prevent production problems from being hidden.

In theory, a JIT system eliminates the needs for inventories because no production takes place until it is known that the item will be sold. As a practical matter, companies using this system will normally have a backlog of orders so they can keep their production operations going. The benefits of the JIT system would be lost if a company had to shut down its operations for lengthy periods of time while awaiting receipt of a new order.

Users of this system claim that it minimizes the need to carry inventories. Moreover, by producing only enough to fill orders, better control is initiated over goods lost or spoiled in production, because the entire production line is set up to produce just enough units to fill the order received. If there are spoiled or lost units, a supplemental order is required. The supplemental order serves to notify management of the spoilage or lost goods.

REDUCING SETUP TIME

Companies that make several types of a product in a single operation are experimenting with flexible manufacturing methods to reduce *both inventory levels and the cost of setups*. An automobile manufacturer that we studied made fenders for several models of cars using one manufacturing operation. When it was time to make left-side fenders instead of right-side fenders, or when it was time to stop making fenders for car model A and start making them for car model B, the production line was stopped while workers changed the machines to make the new fenders. It traditionally took from 4 to 16 hours to make this changeover and start producing new fenders without defects.

Companies are finding ways to reduce the length of these changeovers. This reduces the costs of setups because workers are not spending as much time making these changeovers and the company has less idle production

---

REAL WORLD APPLICATION

*When JIT by the Manufacturer Creates a Disaster for the Distributor**

A Japanese parent company that we will call J Company produces a product for sale in Japan, the United States, and more than 50 other countries around the world. The U.S. market makes up a significant portion of J Company's sales.

At one time, J Company manufactured products using the just-in-time (JIT) philosophy, shipping products to its U.S. subsidiary and other distributors virtually as soon as the products were manufactured. As long as demand for the product in the U.S. market was strong, the U.S. subsidiary had reasonable levels of inventory—about a three months' supply, on average.

After demand for J Company's product in the United States dropped, the U.S. subsidiary was in trouble. J Company continued producing at the old levels, thus keeping its work force employed and maintaining its production at an optimal level for manufacturing purposes. By continuing to ship products to the United States at the previous rate, J Company was able to minimize its inventory levels. However, the U.S. subsidiary watched its inventories increase from a three-month supply to more than a year's supply. The U.S. subsidiary incurred huge losses because of additional inventory carrying costs, increased advertising and promotion costs, and price discounting to sell the excess inventory.

* Based on the authors' research.

time. Flexible manufacturing techniques allow companies to make quick changeovers using automated equipment and sophisticated computer software. These methods enable the companies to make products just in time for use because of the flexibility in changing from making one product to another. Using flexible manufacturing, companies can *both maintain low inventories and have low setup costs.*

These methods provide an opportunity for exciting advances in the way products are made and for reducing inventory management costs. These methods are still at an experimental stage in many companies, however, so their advantages and disadvantages remain to be learned. It is important for accountants to be involved in the development of these production methods because it affects an important cost: that of managing inventory. Future cost accountants may spend relatively little time determining inventory costs and more time helping managers plan and control production activities.

SUMMARY

Adopting an inventory management policy can be a source of significant cost savings to many organizations. The models are designed to determine the most economic order quantity (EOQ) under both constrained and unconstrained situations, the optimal level of safety stock, and the reorder point. Computer software packages have been developed to monitor inventories. These models rely on a significant amount of data from the accountant in order to find the minimum cost of alternative inventory management decisions. The costs that are relevant for these inventory management decisions are those costs that will change with the decision. Thus, for example, in an EOQ decision, the accountant estimates the costs that will change with the number of units ordered. These include ordering costs and carrying costs. In a decision concerning safety-stock levels, the differential costs include the costs to carry the safety stock and the stockout costs. The accountant performs a significant role in these decisions.

TERMS AND CONCEPTS

The following terms and concepts should be familiar to you after reading this chapter:

Carrying Costs, *518*	**Ordering Costs,** *518*
Economic Order Quantity (EOQ), *520*	**Quantity Discounts,** *524*
Just-in-Time, *532*	**Stockout,** *526*
Lead Time, *526*	

QUESTIONS

14–1 Since the operations research specialists develop and maintain inventory models, why does the accountant become concerned with inventory policy decisions?

14–2 Why is the cost of capital included as a carrying cost of inventory?

14–3 In determining economic order quantities, the carrying cost per unit is divided by two. Why?

14–4 A staff accountant for Percolators, Inc., noted that the annual carrying cost for a specific inventory item is estimated at $28,500, while the annual order cost is estimated at $14,150. Does this information tell you anything about the relationship of the actual order quantity to the optimal order quantity? Explain.

14–5 In terms of the specifics of the costs associated with inventory policy, how does the concept of differential costs apply to the problem of inventory policy?

14–6 For each of the following costs, indicate whether the cost would be an out-of-pocket carrying cost (*C*) or a cost of placing an order (*P*). If the item does not qualify for either of these categories, note it as none of the above (*N*). Assume that wages vary with the level of work while salaries are fixed for a monthly or longer time period.

   a. Hourly fee for inventory audit.

   b. Salary of purchasing supervisor.

   c. Costs to audit purchase orders and invoices on a per order basis.

   d. Taxes on inventory.

   e. Stockout costs.

   f. Storage costs charged per unit in inventory.

   g. Fire insurance on inventory.

   h. Fire insurance on warehouse.

   i. Obsolescence costs on inventory.

   j. Shipping costs per shipment.

14–7 When constraints appear in an inventory problem, why is the optimal decision either Q^* or one of the alternatives adjacent to Q^*?

14–8 The following is a diagram of the quantities of an inventory item on hand over a recent time period. Supply labels for the lettered items in the diagram.

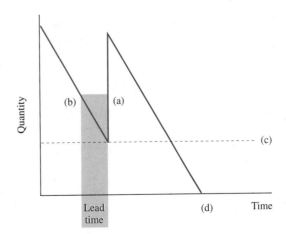

14–9 A company estimates that the lead time for a particular material is five days but that the demand over lead time is uncertain. The distribution of demand over lead time is best approximated by the normal distribution (that is, a symmetric, bell-shaped curve). If there is a great number of possible values for the demand over lead time and if no safety stock is maintained, how frequently would a stockout be expected?

14-10 "Our company orders 5,000 units at a time just to make sure we don't experience a stockout." Comment on this statement.

14-11 Phenerome Corporation is a diversified company that has acquired a number of subsidiaries through mergers. The company is instituting an inventory control system that would incorporate economic inventory policy considerations. One of the company officers has noted that some subsidiaries use last-in, first-out (LIFO) for financial reporting and others use first-in, first-out (FIFO). The officer asks you: "These different inventory methods make it very difficult for us to prepare the corporate financials and our tax return. How will they affect operation of an inventory system since the inventory costs will be different for the same item in a different subsidiary?"

14-12 How does a just-in-time philosophy result in better control over goods spoiled or lost in production?

14-13 How does flexible manufacturing work to support the just-in-time philosophy?

14-14 Refer to the real world application in this chapter. How did the just-in-time philosophy at the Japanese parent company affect the U.S. subsidiary?

EXERCISES

14-15 Compute EOQ
(L.O.1)

One of the inventory items at a company has a purchase price of $40. The annual demand for the item is 40,000 units. It costs $240 to place an order for the material, and out-of-pocket storage costs amount to $4.80 per unit. The company cost of capital is 18 percent.

Required: Determine the EOQ.

14-16 Compute EOQ
(L.O.1)

Coloma Software, Inc., uses 155,000 cartons of computer disks each year. Order costs amount to $620 each time an order is placed. Carrying costs are $125 per carton.

Required: Compute the economic order quantity.

14-17 Find Missing Data for EOQ
(L.O.1)

Olivas Corporation manufactures Errantos, a consumer product, in optimal production runs of 3,500 units 20 times per year. It is estimated that the setup costs (including nonproductive labor) amount to $612.50 for each batch. The company's cost of capital is 20 percent, and the out-of-pocket cost to store an Erranto for one year is $1.60.

Required: Solve the unknown inventory cost of an Erranto.

14-18 EOQ—Multiple-Choice
(L.O.1)

a. The following information relates to Fong Industries:

Units required per year 60,000
Cost of placing an order $300
Unit carrying cost per year $400

Assuming that the units will be required evenly throughout the year, what is the EOQ?
(1) 200.
(2) 300.
(3) 400.
(4) 500.

b. Pierce Incorporated has to manufacture 48,000 blades for its electric lawn mower division. The blades will be used evenly throughout the year. The setup cost every time a production run is made is $100, and the cost to carry a blade in inventory for the year is $.60. Pierce's objective is to produce the blades at the lowest cost possible. Assuming that each production run will be for the same number of blades, how many production runs should Pierce make?

(1) 12.

(2) 10.

(3) 8.

(4) 4.

c. The Aron Company requires 40,000 units of product Q for the year. The units will be required evenly throughout the year. It costs $54 to place an order. It costs $12 to carry a unit in inventory for the year. What is the EOQ?

(1) 200.

(2) 400.

(3) 600.

(4) 1,600.

(CPA adapted)

14–19 Orders in Round Lots
(L.O.2)

Medina Corporation uses a direct material, Zelda, in its production processes. The company uses 86,000 units of Zelda a year. The carrying costs of Zelda amount to $25.00 per unit, while order costs are $325 per order. The manufacturer of Zelda will only accept orders in lots of even thousands.

Required:

What is the optimal order quantity and the annual inventory costs, given the restriction on order sizes?

14–20 Impact of Quantity Discounts on Order Quantity
(L.O.2)

Rollins Company uses 1,620 tankloads a year of a specific input material. The tankloads are delivered by rail to a siding on the company property. The supplier is offering a special discount for buyers of large quantities. The schedule is as follows:

Quantity Ordered (tankloads)	Discount
1–19	–0–
20–79	2%
80–149	5
150 and over	6

Ordering costs amount to $500, and carrying costs are $450 per tankload and are not affected by the discounts. Each tankload costs $1,500.

Required:

Compute the optimal order quantity. (Round to the nearest whole number.)

14–21 Impact of Constraints on Optimal Order
(L.O.2)

Considering the situation in exercise 14–20, suppose that the maximum storage capacity for the company is 100 tankloads. What would the optimal order be? Demonstrate why.

14–22 Evaluate Safety-Stock Policy
(L.O.3)

Agri-chem Corporation manufactures commercial fertilizer. The manufacturing process requires several inputs including a nitrogen fixer, NFX. The company uses 39,000 units of NFX per year and makes 15 orders per year in economic lot sizes of 2,600 units. The cost to carry a unit of NFX is $32.00. If there is a stockout, a carload of NFX must be purchased at retail from a local supplier. The retail price is $1,650 per order greater than the price from the regular supplier.

Looking at the past order records, it appears that certain safety-stock levels would result in stockouts according to the following schedule:

Safety-Stock Quantity	Probability of Stockout
0	.60
100	.20
175	.08
250	.04

Required:

**14–23 Safety-Stock—
Multiple-Choice
(L.O.3)**

What level of safety stock would result in the least cost to the company?

a.   McNeely Company wishes to determine the amount of safety stock that they should maintain for product No. 135 that will result in the lowest cost. Each stockout will cost $150, and the carrying cost of each unit of safety stock will be $1. Product No. 135 will be ordered five times a year. Which of the following will produce the lowest cost?

(1)   A safety stock of 10 units that is associated with a 40 percent probability of running out of stock during an order period.

(2)   A safety stock of 20 units that is associated with a 20 percent probability of running out of stock during an order period.

(3)   A safety stock of 40 units that is associated with a 10 percent probability of running out of stock during an order period.

(4)   A safety stock of 80 units that is associated with a 5 percent probability of running out of stock during an order period.

b.   Eaton Company wishes to determine the amount of safety stock that it should maintain for product D that will result in the lowest costs.

The following information is available:

Stockout cost	$60 per occurrence
Carrying cost of safety stock	$ 4 per unit
Number of purchase orders	5 per year

The options available to Eaton are as follows:

Units of Safety Stock	Probability of Running Out of Safety Stock
10	50%
20	40
30	30
40	20
50	10
55	5

The number of units of safety stock that will result in the lowest cost is:

(1)   10.

(2)   30.

(3)   40.

(4)   55.

(CPA adapted)

**14–24 Differential Costs of
Inventory Policy
(L.O.4)**

A review of the inventories of Audio Technologies, Inc., indicates the following cost data for speaker cabinets:

Invoice price	$ 97.50 per unit
Cost to arrange for the shipment	$ 27.60 per order
Permit fees for shipping	$201.65 per truckload

Inventory tax . . . . 2% of the invoice price

Insurance on shipments . . . . $ 1.50 per unit

Insurance on inventory . . . . $ 2.80 per unit

Warehouse rental . . . . $985.00 per month

Stockout costs . . . . $122.00 per order

Cost of capital 25%

Unloading—per order . . . . $ 80.20 per order

Required:

Show the differential costs that would be included in an EOQ model.

14–25   Differential Costs of Inventory Policy (L.O.4)

A company uses 2,700 units of Zeron per year. Each unit has an invoice cost of $317, including shipping costs. Because of the volatile nature of Zeron, it costs $860 for liability insurance on each shipment. The costs of carrying the inventory amount to $75 per unit per year exclusive of a 20 percent cost of capital. Other order costs amount to $18 per order.

At present, the company orders 250 units at a time.

Required:

a.   What is the annual cost of the company's current order policy?

b.   What is the annual cost of the optimal economic order policy?

PROBLEMS

14–26   Determine Optimal Safety-Stock Levels

Wildridge Products, Inc., has expressed concern over the erratic delivery times for a critical product, Westovers. The company orders 3,000 at a time and has maintained a safety stock of 200 Westovers but has been experiencing frequent stockouts and production delays. The plant operates 270 days per year. The company estimates that the lead time for Westovers is five days, over which time 500 units will be used in production. The cost of storing a unit is $22 per year including capital costs. A stockout is estimated to cost $4,200 for each day that the company must wait for shipment. Any time a stockout occurs, the company must wait until its sole supplier delivers these units.

Over the past several years, the lead times have been as follows:

Lead Time (days)	Probability of Lead Time
9	.05
8	.15
6	.20
5	.40
4	.20

Other lead times have not occurred and may be ignored.

Required:

Determine the most economic safety-stock level.

14–27   Inventory Policy Cost Evaluation

Astatic, Inc., is a wholesaler of Protoxid for industrial clients. Demand for Protoxid is stable at 350,000 units per year. Astatic orders the product from its supplier four times a year. An order is placed when the total Protoxid on hand amounts to 25,000 units. This represents a nine-day working supply plus safety stock. The company works 300 days per year. Recently, management of Astatic has expressed concern over the costs of carrying inventory and is seeking to evaluate the present inventory order and safety-stock policies.

As a part of the study, the following costs were identified with respect to Protoxid:

Invoice price	$ 32.92
Weight per unit	1.5 kg
Shipping charges	$ 1.05 per unit + $640 per truck + $.40 per kg
Tax on each unit	1.80
Special packaging per unit	3.65 ($1 is refunded on return of the shipping container)
Insurance on shipment	1.76 per unit—casualty insurance
	415.00 per shipment—liability bond
Processing order documents	183.00
Unloading operations	.82 per unit + $1,800 per week
Inspect and count for annual inventory . .	2.63 per unit
Rental of unloading equipment . . . . (1-day minimum rental— 200,000-unit daily capacity)	222.00 per day
Estimated obsolescence costs	1.35 per unit
Inventory record maintenance	.92 per unit + $2,200 per week
Inventory tax	3% of invoice price
Inventory insurance	15% of invoice price + $4,100 per month

The company estimates its cost of capital is 22 percent. In addition, a study was conducted on the costs of a stockout. The average stockout costs $5,400 due to the need to request special shipments from alternate suppliers. With various safety-stock levels, the probabilities of a stockout decrease as follows:

Safety Stock	Probability of Stockout
0	.5
7,000	.1
14,000	.02
21,000	.01

For determining order quantity, a stockout probability per order of .02 may be assumed. Order sizes are restricted to round lots of 5,000. The company has the capacity to store 90,000 units.

Required:

a. What are the differential costs for inventory policy making?

b. What are the annual costs under the present order and safety-stock system?

c. What are the annual costs under the optimal order and safety-stock system?

d. What is the reorder point under the optimal order and safety-stock system?

14–28 Sensitivity of EOQ Computations to Changes in Cost Estimates

Retem & Company is instituting an economic order policy for its inventory. The following data are presented for one item in the inventory:

Annual usage	160,000 units
Storage costs	$7 per unit (out of pocket)
Cost of capital	30% of $275 purchase price per unit
Order costs	$808

Required:

a. What is the EOQ, given these data?

b. What is the annual cost of following the order policy in requirement (*a*) if the cost of capital were 15 percent?

c. What is the EOQ and total annual costs if the cost of capital were 20 percent?

14–29 Inventory Cycle Analysis— Multiple-Choice

Thoran Electronics Company began producing pacemakers last year. At that time, the company forecasted the need for 10,000 integrated circuits annually. During the first year, the company placed orders when the inventory dropped to 600 units so that it would have enough to produce pacemakers continuously during a three-week lead time. Unfortunately, the company ran out of this component on several occasions, causing costly production delays. Careful study of last year's experience resulted in the following expectations for the coming year:

Weekly Usage	Related Probability of Usage	Lead Time	Related Probability of Lead Time
280 units	.2	3 weeks	.1
180 units	.8	2 weeks	.9
	1.0		1.0

The study also suggested that usage during a given week was statistically independent of usage during any other week, and usage was also statistically independent of lead time.

Required:

a. The expected average usage during a regular production week is:
  (1) 180 units.
  (2) 200 units.
  (3) 280 units.
  (4) 460 units.
  (5) Some usage other than those given above.

b. The expected usage during lead time is:
  (1) 840 units.
  (2) 400 units.
  (3) 360 units.
  (4) 420 units.
  (5) Some usage other than those given above.

(CMA adapted)

14–30 Alternative Order Policy Costs

The Committee for Human Improvement (CHI) is planning a fund-raising benefit. As part of the publicity and as a means of raising money, the committee plans to sell T-shirts with the CHI logo and a design commemorating the benefit event. However, since the committee has never held one of these benefits previously, there is no experience about the quantity of T-shirts to order.

You've been asked to volunteer your knowledge of cost accounting and provide the committee with some information on the cost of alternatives. The committee expects it can sell 500 shirts at a minimum, but it will probably sell five times that amount. However, these numbers are very "soft." Since the committee is operating with limited funds, there is a desire to avoid undue risk in this T-shirt adventure.

After contacting several T-shirt manufacturers, you conclude that the best price structure is as follows:

Design logo and shirt	$75.00
Setup each production run	50.00
Cost per shirt:	
Order of 1–99	5.00
100–499	3.00
500–749	2.50
750–999	2.25
1,000–1,999	2.00
2,000–2,999	1.90
3,000 and over	1.80

The shirts are expected to sell for $5 each. There are no costs to store the shirts since one of the committee members has volunteered storage space. However, unsold shirts are valueless.

Required:

Prepare an analysis of the costs of alternative T-shirt order policies for the committee. Since the sales volume is unknown, your report will have to focus on possible volumes. Use those suggested by the committee. Indicate to the committee the costs of each alternative and the differential or opportunity cost of selecting a less risky order size.

14–31 Determine Optimal Safety-Stock Levels

The Starr Company manufactures several products. One of its main products requires an electric motor. The management of Starr Company uses the EOQ model to determine the optimum number of motors to order. Management now wants to determine how much safety stock to keep on hand.

The company uses 30,000 motors annually at the rate of 100 per working day. The motors regularly cost $60 each. The lead time for an order is five days. The cost to carry a motor in stock is $10. The cost to place an order is $1,500. If a stockout occurs, management must purchase motors at retail from an alternate supplier. The alternate supplier charges $80 per motor.

Starr Company has analyzed the usage during the past reorder periods by examining inventory records. The records indicate the following usage patterns during past reorder periods:

Usage during Lead Time	Number of Times Quantity Was Used
440	6
460	12
480	16
500	130
520	20
540	10
560	6
	200

Required:

Determine the least-cost safety-stock level and the total differential costs at that level, ignoring the cost of capital. (The optimal order size must also be derived.)

(CMA adapted)

14–32 Determine Optimal Order Quantity with Price Breaks and Constraints

Weldone Supply offers discounts for quantity orders according to the following schedule:

Quantity	Discount
1–999	None
1,000–1,999	$1.00
2,000–4,999	1.50
5,000–9,999	2.00
10,000–19,999	4.00
20,000 and over	6.50

To decide whether to take advantage of the price-break system, you review your records and find that the order cost for this product is $400 and the carrying costs are $4. Usage amounts to 20,000 units per year. Your company has space to store up to 15,000 units. The cost of capital effect of the discount may be ignored.

Required:

Prepare a schedule showing the optimal order quantity.

INTEGRATIVE CASE

14–33   Overhead Application and Inventory Management Costs

Pointer Furniture Company manufactures and sells several brands of office furniture. The manufacturing operation is organized by the item produced rather than by the furniture line. Thus, the desks for all brands are manufactured on the same production line. The desks are manufactured in batches. For example, 10 high-quality desks might be manufactured during the first two weeks in October and 50 units of a lower-quality desk during the last two weeks. Because each model has its own unique manufacturing requirement, the change from one model to another requires the factory's equipment to be adjusted.

Management of Pointer wants to determine the most economical production run for each of the items in its product lines. One of the costs that must be estimated is the setup cost incurred when there is a change to a different furniture model. The Accounting Department has been asked to determine the setup cost for the desk model JE 40 as an example.

The Equipment Maintenance Department is responsible for all of the changeover adjustments on production lines in addition to the preventive and regular maintenance of all the production equipment. The equipment maintenance staff has a 40-hour workweek; the size of the staff is changed only if there is a change in the workload that is expected to persist for an extended period of time. The Equipment Maintenance Department had 10 employees last year, and they each averaged 2,000 hours for the year. They are paid $10.80 an hour. The other departmental costs, which include such items as supervision, depreciation, and insurance, total $50,000 per year.

Two workers from the Equipment Maintenance Department are required to make the change on the desk line for model JE 40. They spend an estimated five hours in setting up the equipment. The desk production line on which model JE 40 is manufactured is operated by five workers. During the changeover, these workers assist the maintenance workers when needed and operate the line during the one-hour test run. However, they are idle for approximately 40 percent of the time required for the changeover.

The production workers are paid a basic wage rate of $7.50 an hour. Two overhead bases are used to apply the overhead costs of this production line because some of the costs vary in proportion to direct labor-hours while others vary with machine-hours. The overhead rates applicable for the current year are as follows:

	Based on Direct Labor-Hours	Based on Machine-Hours
Variable	$2.75	$ 5.00
Fixed	2.25	15.00
	$5.00	$20.00

These department overhead rates are based on an expected activity of 10,000 direct labor-hours and 1,500 machine-hours for the current year. This department is not scheduled to operate at full capacity because production capability currently exceeds sales potential.

The estimated cost of the direct materials used in the test run totals $200. Salvage material from the test run should total $50. Pointer's cost of capital is 20 percent.

Required:

a. Prepare an estimate of Pointer Furniture Company's setup cost for desk model JE 40 for use in the economic production run model. For each cost item identified in the problem, justify the amount and the reason for including the cost item in your estimate. Explain the reason for excluding any cost item from your estimate.

b.   Identify the cost items that would be included in an estimate of Pointer Furniture Company's cost of carrying the desks in inventory.

(CMA adapted)

SOLUTION TO

 *Self-Study Question*

a.

1.   Investment costs:

Invoice cost	$120.00
Shipping cost	2.50
Unloading	.80
Total investment costs	$123.30

2.   Carrying costs:

Cost of capital	$ 36.99 ($123.30 × 30%)
Insurance	1.00
Inventory tax	1.23 (1% × $123.30)
Audit and inspection	2.60
Total carrying costs	$ 41.82

Carrying costs per year:

Working inventory	5,000 units × ½ × $41.82 =	$104,550
Safety stock	3,000 units × $41.82 =	125,460
Total carrying costs		$230,010

Order costs:

Shipping	$175
Record processing	16
Total	$191

Annual order costs:

$$\frac{45,000}{5,000 \text{ per order}} \times \$191 = \$1,719$$

Total annual costs of the present inventory policy:
$231,729, which is $230,010 + $1,719

b.   Economic order quantity (EOQ):
First determine Q^*, ignoring the order size restrictions:
Carrying costs (S), $41.82 [per requirement (*a*)].
Order costs (P), $353.00 ($191 + .02 × $8,100).

$$Q^* = \sqrt{\frac{2 \times 45,000 \times \$353}{\$41.82}}$$

$$= \sqrt{759,684.36}$$

$$= \underline{872 \text{ units}}$$

Next, determine the annual costs at the next higher and lower allowable order quantity:

Quantity	Carrying Costs	Order Costs	Total Costs
750	$\frac{750}{2} \times \$41.82$	$\frac{45,000}{750} \times \$353.00$	
	= $15,682.50	= $21,180.00	$36,862.50
1,000	$\frac{1,000}{2} \times \$41.82$	$\frac{45,000}{1,000} \times \$353.00$	
	= $20,910.00	= $15,885.00	$36,795.00

The optimal order quantity given the restrictions on order size is 1,000 units.

c. Optimal safety-stock level:

Prepare a schedule showing the expected annual costs of each alternative safety-stock quantity:

Safety-Stock Quantity	Carrying Costs	Expected Stockout Costs	Total Costs
500	500 × $41.82	$\frac{45,000}{1,000} \times \$8,100 \times .25$	
	= $20,910	= $91,125	$112,035
1,000	1,000 × $41.82	$\frac{45,000}{1,000} \times \$8,100 \times .08$	
	= $41,820	= $29,160	$ 70,980
1,500	1,500 × $41.82	$\frac{45,000}{1,000} \times \$8,100 \times .02$	
	= $62,730	= $7,290	$ 70,020 (optimal)
2,000	2,000 × $41.82	$\frac{45,000}{1,000} \times \$8,100 \times .01$	
	= $83,640	= $3,645	$ 87,285

Therefore, the most economic safety-stock level would be 1,500 units with a total expected stockout and carrying cost of $70,020.

d. The total annual cost of the optimal inventory policy is computed as follows:

Costs of working inventory [per requirement (*b*)] . $ 36,795
Costs of safety stock 70,020
$106,815

e. The reorder point is:

$$\text{Usage over lead time} + \text{Safety stock} = \left(\frac{45,000}{250} \times 10\right) + 1,500$$
$$= 1,800 + 1,500$$
$$= \underline{3,300 \text{ units}}$$

Capital Investment Cash Flows

LEARNING OBJECTIVES

After reading this chapter, you should be able to:

1. Explain the concept of present value.
2. Compute the present value of cash flows.
3. Incorporate the effects of taxes in present value computations.
4. Incorporate the effects of inflation in present value analysis.
5. Identify problems in justifying investment in new technology.
6. Apply present value analysis to investment decisions in nonprofit organizations.

*C*apital investment decisions are very important because they commit companies to a particular course of action for years, sometimes for decades. General Motors' decision to invest in the Saturn Company committed the company to the technology and concepts involved in making the Saturn for the foreseeable future. By deciding to expand outside of its home base in Arkansas, Wal-Mart committed itself to change from a small, regional company to become a large, national company. When United Airlines purchased Hertz, it committed itself to be in the travelers' services business, not just the airline business. By investing in the Skoda automobile in the Czech Republic, Volkswagen AG committed itself to become a major player in the Eastern European automobile industry.

Capital investments often involve large sums of money and considerable risk. Specific investments over a certain dollar amount, often in the $100,000 to $500,000 range (or less in small companies), require approval by the board of directors in many companies. The investment should not only be wise, economically, but it should also be consistent with the company's strategic plan. In each of the companies listed in the previous paragraph, the investment was consistent with each company's long-term strategy for success.

While the final decision about asset acquisition is the responsibility of management, capital investment models have been developed by accountants, economists, and other financial experts to help managers make those decisions. Accountants have the particularly important role of estimating the *amount* and *timing* of the cash flows used in capital investment decision models.

In this chapter, we discuss the process of estimating future cash flows from capital investment projects. In Chapter 16, we discuss additional models used to evaluate the cash flows.

ANALYZING CASH FLOWS

Capital investment models are based on the future cash flows expected from a particular asset investment opportunity. The amount and timing of the cash flows from an investment project determine the economic value of capital investment projects. The timing of those flows is important because cash received earlier in time has greater economic value than cash received later. As soon as cash is received, it can be reinvested in an alternative profit-making opportunity. Thus, there is an opportunity cost for cash committed to any particular investment project. Because the horizon of capital investment decisions extends over many years, the **time value of money** is often a significant factor.

Time Value of Money The concept that cash received earlier is worth more than cash received later.

To recognize the time value of money, the future cash flows associated with a project are adjusted to their **present value** using a predetermined discount rate. Summing the discounted values of the future cash flows and subtracting the initial investment yields the **net present value** of a project. This net present value represents the economic value of the project to the company at a given point in time. The decision models used for capital investments attempt to optimize the economic value to the firm by optimizing the net present value of future cash flows.

Net Present Value The economic value of a project at a point in time.

For example, suppose an investor must choose between two very similar projects. Each project requires an immediate cash outlay of $10,000. Project 1 will return $14,000 at the end of two years, while Project 2 will return $14,000 at the end of three years. Clearly, the investor would prefer Project 1 over Project 2 because Project 1 will return the $14,000 one year earlier, and that amount would be available for reinvestment. Consequently, Project 1 has a higher net present value than Project 2.

Of course, the net present value alone does not indicate whether either project is worth the investment. The final decision involves a number of other factors.

Will either project fit within the present organization? Will the project help the firm keep up with changing markets and technology? Does management have the expertise to operate the new business? What are the social and legal implications of the project? Is the project risk acceptable? While all of these questions are important, to simplify our examples, we assume that the projects we are comparing all meet these criteria equally. This allows us to focus on the analysis of cash flows from projects and how that analysis affects net present values and decision making.

Hurdle Rate The discount rate required by the company before it will invest in a project.

Discount Rate An interest rate used to compute net present values.

Returning to the question of whether to invest in Project 1 or Project 2, we must determine if the net present value of the project is positive. If the net present value is positive, the project will earn a rate of return greater than its discount rate. This rate is often referred to as the **hurdle rate** or **discount rate.** If the project can earn a rate of return greater than its hurdle rate, then it has passed the hurdle of the net present value criterion for investment decisions. Projects whose rate of return does not meet the hurdle rate are rejected because the funds that would be invested in such projects can earn a higher rate of return in some other investment.

Distinguishing between Revenues, Costs, and Cash Flows

There is often a *timing difference* between revenue recognition and cash inflow, on the one hand, and the incurrence of a cost and the related cash outflow, on the other hand. When this occurs, it is important to *distinguish cash flows from revenues and costs*. Note that capital investment analysis often *uses cash flows, not revenues and costs*. For example, revenue from a sale is often recognized on one date but not collected until later. In such cases, the cash is not available for other investment or consumption purposes until it is collected.

NET PRESENT VALUE

Present Value The amounts of future cash flows discounted to their equivalent worth today.

The **present value** of cash flows is the amount of future cash flows discounted to their equivalent worth today. The *net present value* of a project can be computed by using the equation:

$$NPV = \sum_{n=0}^{N} C_n \times (1 + d)^{-n}$$

where

C_n = Cash to be received or disbursed at the end of time period n
d = Appropriate *discount rate* for the future cash flows
n = Time period when the cash flow occurs
N = Life of the investment, in years

Use of the equation with a calculator or computer spreadsheet is the most efficient approach to computing net present values. Tables of present value factors are in Appendix B to this chapter and may also be used to find present values. We use the equation in all chapter illustrations, computations, and discussions and round all printed factors to three decimals. Therefore, if we want to discount $20,000, to be received in two years, at 10 percent, we find the value of $(1.10)^{-2}$ by a power function in the calculator. In the calculator, the result of this computation is .826446281, which, multiplied by $20,000, yields the present value of $16,529. We show such computations as:

$$\$20,000 \times (1 + .10)^{-2} = \$20,000 \times .826$$
$$= \underline{\underline{\$16,529}}$$

We abbreviate the present value factor because it is simply an intermediate result. If you use the abbreviated factor or the factors from the present value tables, your answer will differ due to rounding. This should not cause alarm. Capital investment decisions are yes or no decisions that are rarely (if ever) affected by rounding.

If you use the tables in Appendix B, simply look up the factor by referring to the appropriate year and discount rate. For a discount rate of 10 percent and a cash flow at the end of two years, Illustration 15–9 in Appendix B shows the present value factor to be .826.

Applying Present Value Analysis

Now, let's look at how present value analysis is used for capital investment decisions. As an example, consider the two projects mentioned earlier in the chapter. If the appropriate discount rate is 15 percent, then the net present value of each project may be computed as follows:

Project 1:

Cash inflow	$14,000 \times (1 + .15)^{-2}$	
	$= \$14,000 \times .756$	$= \$ \ 10,586$
Cash outflow		$= -10,000$
Net present value . . .		$\$ \ \ \ \ 586$

Project 2:

Cash inflow	$14,000 \times (1 + .15)^{-3}$	
	$= \$14,000 \times .658$	$= \$ \ \ 9,205$
Cash outflow		$= -10,000$
Net present value . . .		$\$ \ \ (795)$

The starting time for capital investment projects is assumed to be Time 0. Therefore, any cash outlays required at the start of the project are not discounted. We enter them at their full amount.

At a discount rate of 15 percent, Project 1 is acceptable and Project 2 is not. Project 1 will earn more than the required 15 percent return, while Project 2 will earn less.

You should check for yourself to see that at a 20 percent discount rate, the present values of both projects are negative. Therefore, if our required rate were 20 percent, neither project would meet the investment criterion. Alternatively, at 10 percent, both projects have positive net present values and would be acceptable.

Of course, the cash flows in most business investment opportunities are considerably more complex than our simplified examples, but the method for computing net present values remains the same.

Consider, for example, the cash flow pattern in Illustration 15–1. The cash flows can be either positive or negative in any year. This cash flow

ILLUSTRATION

15–1

Example of Net Present Value Calculations

Period	Net Cash Inflow or (Outflow)	PV Factor $(1 + d)^{-n}$ $d = 20$ Percent	Present Value[a]
0	$(80,000)	1.000	$(80,000)
1	(9,000)	.833	(7,500)
2	31,200	.694	21,667
3	14,800	.579	8,565
4	(42,100)	.482	(20,303)
5	76,800	.402	30,864
6	79,600	.335	26,658
7	74,500	.279	20,792
8	61,100	.233	14,210
9	43,600	.194	8,450
10	(39,700)	.162	(6,412)
Net present value			$ 16,991

[a] Cash flow times factor does not equal present value because factor is rounded to three places.

pattern is characteristic of a project that will begin with a pilot operation. If the pilot operation proves successful, full-scale facilities will be installed in Year 4. Operations will continue until Year 10, at which time costs will be incurred to dismantle the operation. Once the cash flows are determined, computation of the present value is a mechanical operation. The critical problem for the accountant, however, is to estimate the amount and timing of the expected future cash flows.

CATEGORIES OF PROJECT CASH FLOWS

This section of the chapter outlines a method for estimating cash flows for investment projects. This is an important part of the accountant's job in making investment decisions. We start by setting up four major categories of cash flows for a project:

1. Investment cash flows.
2. Periodic operating cash flows.
3. Cash flows from the depreciation tax shield.
4. Disinvestment cash flows.

Each category of cash flows requires a separate treatment.

Investment Flows

There are three types of investment flows:

1. Asset acquisition, which includes:
   a. New equipment costs, including installation (outflow).
   b. Proceeds of existing assets sold, net of taxes (inflow).
   c. Tax effects arising from a loss or gain (inflow or outflow).
2. Working capital commitments.
3. Investment tax credit.

Asset Acquisition

Asset Acquisition Costs involved in the purchase and installation of an investment or inventory. May involve the disposal of old assets, resulting in a gain or a loss.

Asset acquisition involves not only the cost of purchasing and installing new assets but also the cash inflows that may result from the proceeds, net of taxes, of selling replaced equipment. Additionally, there may be a loss or gain to consider, arising from the difference between the sale proceeds and the tax basis of the equipment being replaced.

The primary outflow for most capital investments is the acquisition cost of the asset. Acquisition costs may be incurred in Time 0 and in later years. In some cases, they are incurred over periods of 10 to 20 years. All acquisition costs are listed as cash outflows in the years in which they occur. Installation costs are considered a cash outflow.

If the depreciation tax basis of the replaced equipment is not equal to the proceeds received from the sale of the replaced equipment, a gain or loss will occur and will affect the tax payment. The tax effect will be considered a cash inflow (for a loss) or a cash outflow (with a gain).

For example, Kwik Press, a publishing company, commissioned a team of business students to conduct a customer satisfaction survey. The results of the survey showed the number-one complaint by customers was the time it took Kwik Press to complete desktop publishing jobs. Kwik Press was working at capacity and losing customers to the local competition. Management decided to consider replacing slower machines with fast, state-of-the-art machines.

The new machines would cost $280,000 in two payments: $130,000 immediately (Time 0) and $150,000 in Year 1. The depreciation that would be allowed for tax purposes would be $80,000 in Years 1 and 2, and $40,000 in Years 3–5. A tax rate of 40 percent is used.

The existing machines had been purchased several years ago. The tax basis of the existing machines is $52,500, and they would have been depreciated for tax purposes at the rate of $26,250 in Year 1 and $26,250 in Year 2. The estimated current salvage value is $45,000 which is the estimated cash inflow from the sale of the existing machines. The difference between the tax basis of $52,500 and the salvage value of $45,000 results in a tax loss of $7,500. These cash flows for asset acquisition appear in Illustration 15–2.

Working Capital Commitments

Working Capital Cash, accounts receivable, and other short-term assets required to maintain an activity.

In addition to the cash for purchase of long-term assets, many projects require additional funds for **working capital** needs; for example, a retail establishment needs to have cash available in a bank account because future cash payments will often precede cash receipts. The working capital committed to the project normally remains constant over the life of the project, although it is sometimes increased because of inflation. Kwik Press plans to commit an additional $50,000 in working capital at Time 0 to maintain a cash balance in a bank account to cover future cash transactions.

Outlays for working capital items are shown when those outflows occur. The projected investment cash flows of Kwik Press are summarized in Illustration 15–2.

Investment Tax Credit (ITC)

Investment Tax Credit A reduction in federal income taxes arising from the purchase of certain assets.

The **investment tax credit** allows a credit against the federal income tax liability based on the cost of an acquired asset. This credit effectively reduces the cost of making investments by giving companies a credit against their corporate income taxes equal to, say, 10 percent of the purchase price. The investment tax credit has been in effect at various times since the early 1960s. Our examples in the text, and in the exercises and problems, will tell you if the investment tax credit is to be considered.

ILLUSTRATION

15–2

Scheduling Investment Flows, Kwik Press

	Time 0	Year 1
Investment cash flows:		
New equipment and installation	($130,000)	($150,000)
Proceeds, existing equipment	45,000	
Tax benefit from loss on equipment	3,000	
Working capital	(50,000)	
Total cash flows	($132,000)	($150,000)

Tax benefit from loss on existing equipment:
($52,500 tax basis − $45,000 salvage value) × 40% tax rate
= $7,500 loss for tax purposes × 40% tax rate
= $3,000 tax benefit from loss

For example, we assume Kwik Press would not receive an investment tax credit under current tax laws. If the tax laws were to change to allow a 10 percent ITC, then Kwik Press would receive a tax credit of $13,000 (.10 × $130,000) in Year 1 and $15,000 (.10 × $150,000) in Year 2. These amounts would be considered cash inflows in the present value analysis in each of Years 1 and 2.

Periodic Operating Flows

The primary reason for acquiring long-term assets is usually to generate positive *periodic operating cash flows*. These positive flows may result from such *revenue-generating* activities as new products, or they may stem from *cost-saving* programs. In either case, actual cash inflows and outflows from operating the asset are usually determinable in a straightforward manner. The most important task is to identify and measure the cash flows that will differ because of the investment. *If the revenues and costs are differential cash items, then they are relevant for the capital investment decision.*
Periodic operating flows include:

1. Period cash inflows (+) and outflows (−) before taxes.
2. Income tax effects of inflows (−) and outflows (+).

Kwik Press has determined that the revenues and costs will differ because of the investment and should therefore be included as differential cash flow items. The differential revenues, net of taxes, would be cash inflows. The differential costs, net of taxes, would be considered cash outflows. The projected differential costs and revenues are presented in Illustration 15–3 and explained below.

The schedule in Illustration 15–3 has been divided into two columns to separate all accounting costs that will arise due to the project from the differential cash flows that would be considered for purposes of the present value analysis. The left column shows all costs that would be allocated to the project if the investment were made, including depreciation for financial accounting purposes and other costs, such as reallocated fixed costs that would be allocated to the new project. We show the two separate columns to emphasize that all periodic costs allocated to a project are not necessarily differential cash flows that would be considered in the analysis.

The operating revenues and costs that represent differential cash flows are included in the differential cash flow column. Costs that do not involve cash (depreciation, depletion, and amortization) are excluded from the differential cash flow column. (For example, see line 6 in Illustration 15–3.)

If there are cash costs in other departments that change as a result of the project, then those other department costs should be included in the differential cash flow schedule. For this reason, $1,500 of allocated Service Department costs are included in the differential cash flow column. For example, assume that $3,500 of Service Department costs (repairs and maintenance) would be allocated to this project if the investment is made; however, only $1,500 of that amount would actually increase *because* of the project. (That is, only $1,500 are differential costs.) The remaining $2,000 ($3,500 − $1,500) would merely be reallocated from other parts of the company. In this case, only the $1,500 would be shown as a *differential cash cost*. (See line 5 in Illustration 15–3.) Just because costs are allocated to a project does not mean they are necessarily differential costs.

*Schedule of Project
Revenues and Costs
(Years 1–5), Kwik Press*

Differential Flows		Amount	Differential Cash Flow	Remarks
(1)	Project revenues	$210,285	$210,285	All cash
(2)	Direct materials and direct labor	(62,342)	(62,342)	All cash
	Manufacturing overhead:			
(3)	Indirect labor	(1,800)	(1,800)	All cash
(4)	Supplies	(6,500)	(6,500)	All cash
(5)	Allocated Service Department costs	(3,500)	(1,500)	2,000 is an allocation of costs that would not change with this decision
(6)	Accounting depreciation	(70,000)	–0–	Depreciation is not a cash flow
(7)	Other overhead	(6,076)	(6,076)	All cash
(8)	Selling commissions	(1,985)	(1,985)	All cash
	Administration:			
(9)	Direct	(3,700)	(3,700)	All cash
(10)	Indirect	(2,500)	–0–	Allocation of fixed costs
(11)	Tax and insurance on equipment and inventory	(18,200)	(18,200)	All cash
	Subtotals	$ 33,682	108,182	
(12)	Income tax on differential cash flows		43,273	Based on analysis of tax regulations
	Net operating cash flows for Years 1–5		$ 64,909	

For another example of allocated costs that are not differential, note that indirect administrative costs of $2,500 have been allocated to the project but are not differential (line 10). *Total indirect administrative costs* for the company are not affected in this example; they would just be allocated differently if the investment were made.

Financing costs such as interest costs on loans, principal repayments, and payments under financing leases are typically excluded under the assumption that the financing decision is separate from the asset-acquisition decision. Under this assumption, the decision to acquire the asset is made first. If the asset-acquisition decision is favorable, then a decision will be made to select the best financing.

For purposes of analysis, asset acquisitions are typically recorded in the full amount when the cash purchase payments are made, regardless of how that cash was acquired.

Tax Effects of Periodic Cash Flows

The income tax effects of the periodic cash flows from the project are also computed and considered in the present value analysis. (For this example, we assume the marginal tax rate to be applied to these cash flows is 40 percent.) Note that for purposes of calculating the net present value, only the tax effects related to differential project cash flows are considered. It is the *differential effect on our tax liability* we include in the present value analysis.

The income tax effect of depreciation is different than the depreciation used for financial or internal reporting purposes, which is not considered a differential cash flow. Therefore, any reductions in tax payments arising from depreciation of these assets are considered differential cash flows and treated separately.

The steps carried out to compute the net operating cash flows for the project are repeated for each year in the project life. In some cases, the computations can be simplified, by use of an annuity factor, if the project is expected to yield identical cash flows for more than one year.

Depreciation Tax Shield

Tax Shield The reduction in tax payment because of depreciation deducted for tax purposes.

To measure the income of an organization or one of its subunits, depreciation is used to allocate the cost of long-term assets over their useful lives. These depreciation charges are not cash costs and thus do not directly affect the net present values of capital investments. However, tax regulations permit depreciation write-offs that reduce the required tax payment. The reduction in the tax payment is referred to as a **tax shield.** *The depreciation deduction computed for this tax shield is not necessarily the same amount as the depreciation computed for financial reporting purposes.* The predominant depreciation method for financial reporting has been the *straight-line method.* With this method, the cost of the asset, less any salvage value, is allocated equally to each year of the expected life of the asset. For income tax purposes, faster depreciation write-offs are allowed.

The tax allowance for depreciation is one of the primary incentives used by tax policy makers to promote investment in long-term assets. The faster an asset's cost can be written off for tax purposes, the sooner the tax reductions are realized and, hence, the greater the net present value of the tax shield. In recent years, tax depreciation has been accelerated to allow write-offs over very short time periods regardless of an asset's expected life. To maximize present value, it is usually best to claim depreciation as rapidly as possible.

There are two effects of the depreciation tax shield:

1. Depreciation tax shield on assets acquired.
2. Forgone depreciation tax shield on assets disposed.

Consider the tax depreciation schedule of the new machines Kwik Press is considering. The machines have a depreciation tax basis of $280,000 over five years. The annual depreciation tax shield and the present value of the tax shield are computed in columns 2–5 in Illustration 15–4, using the 40 percent tax rate and a 15 percent discount rate. (All amounts given in this text are for illustrative purposes only. They do not necessarily reflect the amount of depreciation allowed by the tax regulations, which varies by type of asset and often changes as Congress passes new "tax reforms.") No salvage value has been assumed. Present value factors appear in Appendix B to this chapter.

Kwik Press also forgoes depreciation of $26,250 in each of Years 1 and 2 because it would dispose of assets having a depreciable tax base. The

ILLUSTRATION

Present Value of Depreciation Tax Shield—Kwik Press

Tax rate: 40%   Depreciation basis: $280,000

(1) Year	*(2)* Depreciation Deducted on the Tax Return	*(3)* Tax Shield (40% × Depreciation Deduction)	*(4)* PV Factor (15%)[a]	*(5)* Present Value (Tax Shield × PV Factor)[a]
1	$ 80,000	$ 32,000	.870	$27,826
2	80,000	32,000	.756	24,197
3	40,000	16,000	.658	10,520
4	40,000	16,000	.572	9,148
5	40,000	16,000	.497	7,955
Totals	$280,000	$112,000		$79,646

[a] PV factor is rounded to three places. The present value amounts in column (5) are derived from unrounded PV computations.

ILLUSTRATION

Forgone Depreciation Tax Shield—Kwik Press

Tax rate: 40%   Depreciation basis: $52,500

(1) Year	*(2)* Forgone Depreciation	*(3)* Forgone Tax Shield (40% × Column 2)
1	$26,250	$10,500
2	26,250	10,500
Totals	$52,500	$21,000

forgone depreciation and forgone tax shield of $10,500 each year, assuming a 40 percent tax rate, appear in Illustration 15–5. The amounts in column 3 of Illustration 15–4 and column 3 of Illustration 15–5 will then be transferred to the cash flow schedule, as seen later in Illustration 15–6.

To review the basic relationships, a portion of the $280,000 is deducted each year on the tax return as shown in column 2 of Illustration 15–4. The tax shield in column 3 is the tax rate times the depreciation deduction. This is the cash flow resulting from a reduction in the annual tax liability, which is generated by the tax shield.

Disinvestment Flows

The end of a project's life will usually result in some or all of the following cash flows:

1. Cash freed from working capital commitments (now as cash inflow).
2. Salvage of the long-term assets (usually a cash inflow, unless there are disposal costs).
3. Tax consequences for differences between salvage proceeds and the remaining depreciation tax basis of the property.
4. Other cash flows, such as employee severance payments and restoration costs.

Disinvestment Flows   Cash flows that take place at the termination of a capital project.

The cash flows at the end of the life of the project are referred to as **disinvestment flows.**

Return of Working Capital

When a project ends, there are usually some leftover inventory, cash, and other working capital items that were used to support operations. These working capital items are then freed for use elsewhere or liquidated for cash. Therefore, at the end of a project's life, the return of these working capital items is shown as a cash inflow. In the Kwik Press example, Kwik Press will have $50,000 in working capital available for other uses, which is the money it put in the bank to facilitate cash transactions.

It is important not to double-count these items. Suppose that cash collected from a customer was already recorded as a cash inflow to the company, but it was left in the project's bank account until the end of the project's life. It should not be counted again as a cash inflow at the end of the project.

The return of working capital is recorded as an inflow whenever it is freed for use in other organizational activities. If that does not occur until the end of the project's life, the cash inflow is included as part of disinvestment flows.

Salvage of Long-Term Assets

Ending a project will usually require disposal of its assets. These are usually sold in secondhand markets. In some cases, more money is spent in disassembling the assets and disposing of them than is gained from their sale. Any net outflows from disposal of a project's assets become tax deductions in the year of disposal. The *net salvage value* (sometimes negative) of an asset is listed as a cash inflow or outflow at the time it is expected to be realized (or incurred), regardless of the book value or **tax basis** of the asset. The difference between the book value (tax basis) and the net salvage value may result in a taxable gain or loss.

Tax Basis   Remaining tax-depreciable "book value" of an asset for tax purposes.

For an asset replacement decision, we must also consider the forgone salvage value (and related tax effects) from the old asset. For example, assume "Asset New" replaced "Asset Old" for the next five years. Asset Old could be sold for $2,000 at the end of five years; Asset New could be sold for $10,000 at the end of five years. If Asset New replaces Asset Old, then the *incremental* salvage of $8,000 should be the disinvestment cash flow for the analysis. Any additional taxes paid (or tax payments reduced) because we are salvaging Asset New instead of Asset Old should be included in the analysis, too.

Tax Consequences of Disposal

Any difference between the tax basis of a project's assets (generally, the undepreciated balance) and the amount realized from project disposal results in a tax gain or loss. Therefore, a company's tax liability will be affected in the year of disposal. Tax laws on asset dispositions are complex, so tax advice should be sought well in advance of the proposed disposal date. In this chapter, we assume that any gains or losses on disposal are treated as ordinary taxable income or losses.

Suppose that an asset is carried in the financial accounting records at a net book value of $80,000 and is salvaged for $30,000 cash. The tax basis of the asset is $10,000, and the tax rate is 40 percent. What are the cash flows from disposal of this asset?

First, the company receives the $30,000 as a cash inflow. Second, the company reports a taxable gain of $20,000, which is the difference between the $30,000 cash inflow and the $10,000 tax basis. This $20,000 gain is taxed at 40 percent, resulting in a cash outflow of $8,000. The net-of-tax cash inflow on disposal is $22,000, the net of the $30,000 inflow and the $8,000 cash outflow, as shown below:

Cash inflow	$30,000
Tax payment:	
($30,000 cash inflow − $10,000 tax basis) × 40% tax rate	(8,000)
Net-of-tax cash inflow	$22,000

Consider the tax consequences of the new machines at Kwik Press upon disposal in Year 5. The machines will have a remaining net book value in the accounting records of $70,000, which is irrelevant for the present value analysis. The assets will have been fully depreciated for tax purposes and are salvaged for $105,000 cash. (Assume the old assets would have no salvage value in Year 5, so all of the salvage value of the new machines are incremental.) The tax rate is 40 percent. What are the cash flows from disposal of this asset?

First, the company receives the $105,000 as a cash inflow. They report a taxable gain of $105,000, since the asset is fully depreciated for tax purposes. This $105,000 gain is taxed at 40 percent, which results in a cash outflow of $42,000, which is Kwik Press's additional tax liability arising from the gain. The net cash inflow on disposal of the machines is $63,000, which equals $105,000 from the sale minus 40 percent times the $105,000 gain, or $105,000 − $42,000.

Other Disinvestment Flows

The end of project operations may result in a number of costs that are not directly related to the sale of assets. It may be necessary to make severance payments to employees. Sometimes payments are required to restore the project area to its original condition. Some projects may incur regulatory costs when they are closed down. A cost analyst must inquire about the consequences of disposal to determine the costs that should be included in the disinvestment flows for a project.

PREPARING THE NET PRESENT VALUE ANALYSIS

Once the cash flow data have been gathered, they are assembled into a schedule that shows the cash flows for each year of the project's life. These flows may be classified into the four categories we just discussed:

1. Investment flows.
2. Periodic operating flows.
3. Depreciation tax shield.
4. Disinvestment flows.

A summary schedule that shows the total of the annual cash flows and the net present value of the project is prepared. This summary may be supported by as much detail as management deems necessary for making the investment decision.

For example, consider the data collected thus far and summarized in Illustration 15–6 for the investment proposal for Kwik Press. The project is expected to earn higher than the 15 percent used to discount the cash flows because the net present value of the project is greater than zero. (If the net present value of the project had been less than zero, the project would have been expected to earn less than the 15 percent used to discount the cash flows.)

Depreciation is deducted for tax purposes as follows: Year 1, $80,000; Year 2, $80,000; and $40,000 per year in each of Years 3–5. Project costs include the equipment outlays in Time 0 and Year 1. The working capital requirements are shown as outflows in Time 0.

Annual cash flows are computed using the schedule of revenues and costs shown under computations in Illustration 15–6 and adjusted for the costs that are not differential (allocated Service Department costs and allocated administrative costs) or that are not cash costs (depreciation). The net cash inflow of $108,182 is then reduced by the tax liability that is expected to arise from taxing this inflow at the 40 percent marginal tax rate. The after-tax cash inflow of $64,909 is shown for each year of the project's life.

In the last year of the project, the disinvestment flows are given. These include the return of working capital and the proceeds from disposal of the asset. In addition, the tax consequences from selling the equipment for more than the zero tax basis are considered, and the related $42,000 tax liability is included in the cash flow computations.

The net present value of the project is computed as the sum of the present values of each year's cash flow. The positive net present value of $73,908 indicates that the project is expected to earn better than the 15 percent used to discount the cash flows.

The schedule in Illustration 15–6 indicates the net cash flows in each year, thus assisting management in preparing its cash budgets for the life of the project. The net present value of each year's cash flow is presented for computational purposes and may not be required for management.

Self-Study Question

1 Melwood Corporation is considering the purchase of a new computer to further automate its accounting system. Management has been considering several alternative systems including a model labeled the P–25. The supplier of the P–25 has submitted a quote to the company of $7,500 for the equipment plus $8,400 for software. Assume the equipment can be depreciated for tax over three years as follows: Year 1, $2,500; Year 2, $2,500; Year 3, $2,500. The software may be written off immediately for tax purposes. The company expects to use the new machine for four years and to use straight-line depreciation for financial reporting purposes. The market for used computer systems is such that Melwood would realize $1,000 for the equipment at the end of four years. The software would have no salvage value at that time.

Melwood management believes that introduction of the computer system will enable the company to dispose of its existing accounting equipment. The existing equipment is fully depreciated for tax purposes and can be sold for an estimated $100, but would have no salvage value in four years.

Management believes that it will realize improvements in operations and benefits from the computer system that will be worth $8,000 per year before taxes.

I L L U S T R A T I O N   *Cash Flow Schedule with Present Value Computations, Kwik Press*

15–6

	Time 0	Year 1	Year 2	Year 3	Year 4	Year 5
Investment flows:						
Equipment cost and installation	($130,000)	($150,000)				
Proceeds of assets sold, net of tax	45,000					
Tax benefit on loss[a]	3,000					
Working capital	(50,000)					
Periodic operating flows, net of tax[b]		64,909	$64,909	$64,909	$64,909	$64,909
Depreciation tax shield:						
Tax shield from depreciation[c]		32,000	32,000	16,000	16,000	16,000
Forgone tax shield[d]		(10,500)	(10,500)			
Disinvestment flows:						
Return of working capital						50,000
Proceeds on disposal						105,000
Tax on gain[e]						(42,000)
Total cash flows	(132,000)	(63,591)	86,409	80,909	80,909	193,909
PV factor at 15%	1.000	.870	.756	.658	.572	.497
Present values[f]	($132,000)	($ 55,296)	$65,338	$53,199	$46,260	$ 96,407
Net present value of project	$ 73,908					

Computations:
[a] $3,000 = ($52,500 − $45,000) × 40%.
[b] Net operating cash flow (after tax):

Revenues		$210,285
Differential cash outflows:		
Direct materials and direct labor	($62,342)	
Taxes and insurance on equipment and inventory	(18,200)	
Manufacturing overhead	(15,876)	
Selling commission	(1,985)	
Direct administrative costs	(3,700)	(102,103)
Revenues net of differential cash costs (before tax)		108,182
Income taxes on differential net cash flows (40%)		43,273
Differential cash flows (after taxes)		$ 64,909

[c] Depreciation computations:

Year	Depreciation	Tax Shield (at 40%)
1	$ 80,000	$ 32,000
2	80,000	32,000
3	40,000	16,000
4	40,000	16,000
5	40,000	16,000
Totals	$280,000	$112,000

[d] Forgone depreciation:

Year	Forgone Depreciation	Forgone Tax Shield
1	$26,250	$10,500
2	26,250	10,500

[e] Gain is equal to salvage since the asset is fully depreciated for tax purposes. The tax is 40 percent of the gain, or 40% × $105,000 = $42,000.
[f] PV factor shown is rounded to three places. Present values are derived from unrounded PV computations. Present value factors are shown in Appendix B to this chapter.

Melwood uses a 15 percent discount rate for this investment and has a marginal income tax rate of 45 percent after considering both state and federal taxes.

a. Prepare a schedule showing the relevant cash flows for the project.

b. Indicate whether the equipment purchase meets Melwood's hurdle rate.

The solution to this question is at the end of this chapter on page 588.

INFLATION CONSIDERATIONS IN CAPITAL BUDGETING

Nominal Dollars Actual numerical count of money exchanged.

When prices and costs are expected to change significantly over a project's life, it is important to consider the effects of those changes on project cash flows. In many cases, the cash flows will not change uniformly over the life of the project. Therefore, a careful analysis of each cost item may be necessary. Cash flows that will be received in the future will have a different real value than dollars received today due to changes in the purchasing power of those dollars. The actual dollars to be received are called **nominal dollars.**

Nominal Discount Rate A rate of interest that includes compensation for inflation.

The schedule of project cash flows can be adjusted to consider the nominal cash flows. The resulting nominal net cash flows are then discounted at a rate that recognizes inflation. This is the **nominal discount rate.** These adjustments compensate the company for the effects of inflation as well as for a return on capital.

Adjusting the Discount Rate

It is commonly accepted that the interest rate that the market demands includes elements of a return on capital as well as an adjustment for the effects of inflation. The discounting equation can be expanded to include the inflation element as a specific component:

$$[(1 + r)(1 + i)]^{-n}$$

where

r = Real return on capital required from now to period n
i = Expected inflation rate between now and period n
n = Number of the period in the future when the cash is to be received

Real Return Return on capital after adjustment for the effects of inflation.

The **real return** is the return on capital after adjustment for the effects of inflation. This equation may be used with a constant value of i, or the value of i may be changed from one period to the next. In general, though, a constant inflation rate is assumed.

The terms within the brackets may be multiplied before the exponentiation operation. Subtracting 1 from the result of this multiplication gives the nominal discount rate for the project:

$$\text{Nominal rate} = (1 + r)(1 + i) - 1$$

In practice, the nominal discount rate implicitly considers the need to compensate for inflation.

For example, a company has concluded that its projects should earn a real return of 15 percent and that the expected inflation rate over the project's life will be 6 percent per year. To find the nominal discount rate, d, for present value, the following calculation is performed:

$$(1 + r)(1 + i) - 1 = (1.15)(1.06) - 1$$
$$= .219 \text{ or } 21.9\%$$

Management will discount the future cash flows using a 21.9 percent rate in the discounting equation:

$$(1 + d)^{-n} = (1.219)^{-n}$$

Adjusting Future Cash Flows

The effects of inflation may be considered in the same four categories as the cash flows for capital investment projects. When considering inflation, the future cash flows are also adjusted for inflation by the factor $(1 + i)^n$.

Investment Outflows

Cash requirements for the initial investment may need to be adjusted if costs are likely to change over the investment period. This is particularly common with projects that require several years to construct.

Working capital requirements often increase with the increased volume of nominal dollars. That is, more dollars are required to support the same level of activity. The investment in inventory generally will not change. The initial costs were incurred to procure a given quantity of inventory. Inventory may cost more to replace, but the replacement costs are included in period cash outflows.

For initial investment outlays, then, the inflation adjustment simply requires revising any outlays that are expected to change as a result of increasing costs. Any increases in working capital levels (other than inventory) are scheduled when they are required.

For example, consider the cash flows for Kwik Press in Illustration 15–6. Those flows ignored the effects of inflation. Now, let's consider the impact of inflation on these flows. Suppose the equipment costs that were originally $130,000 in Time 0 and $150,000 in Year 1 are not expected to increase with inflation. The $50,000 in working capital requirements must increase with the rate of inflation. How will an inflation rate of 6 percent per year affect the investment cash outflows?

1. Equipment cost: The Time 0 cost of $130,000 is unaffected. The Year 1 cost of $150,000 is not changed in this example but could increase with inflation in other cases.

2. The initial cash outflow for working capital remains $50,000 in Time 0. However, in Year 1, working capital must be increased to $53,000 to keep up with the effects of inflation on nominal dollars ($50,000 × 1.06). Therefore, in Year 1 there will be an additional $3,000 cash outflow to working capital to account for inflation.

In Year 2, an additional $3,180 will be added to working capital to bring the balance to $56,180 (that is $53,000 × 1.06 = $56,180). In Year 3, working capital will need to be increased by an additional $3,371; and in Year 4, the increase will be $3,573, for a total balance of $63,124. There is no increase in Year 5 because that is the end of the project's life, and the working capital for noninventory items is returned at that time.

Periodic Operating Flows

The operating cash flows for each year are adjusted by multiplying the original amounts by $(1 + i)^n$. This restates the original cash inflow to the nominal dollar amount to be received in Year n. In this case, the adjusted amounts are $64,909 × 1.06 = $68,804 for Year 1; $64,909 × (1.06)^2 = $72,932 for Year 2, and so forth. (We assume that Year 1 operating flows increase by 6 percent over Time 0.)

These net nominal cash flows are entered into the appropriate columns of the cash flow schedule in Illustration 15–7 in place of the original unadjusted cash flows.

Tax Shield

Depreciation is based on the original cost of an asset. Hence, the tax shield from depreciation is only changed if the original investment costs change. Under inflation, the real value of the tax shield from depreciation declines relative to the other cash flows from the project. Note that the discount rate recognizes inflation, but the tax shield does not increase with inflation. Consequently, the higher the inflation rate, the lower the net present value of the depreciation tax shield.

Disinvestment Flows

Under conditions of inflation, disinvestment flows become more complex. The return of working capital will include all nominal cash and accounts receivable committed to the project. Therefore, the periodic cash outflows for working capital are summed and the total listed as a recovery at the end of the project's life.

ILLUSTRATION   *Cash Flow Schedule Adjusted for Inflation with Present Value Computations*

15–7

	Time 0	Year 1	2	3	4	5
Investment outflows:						
Equipment cost	($130,000)	($150,000)				
Proceeds of assets sold, net of tax	45,000					
Tax benefit on loss	3,000					
Working capital	(50,000)	(3,000)	($ 3,180)	($ 3,371)	($ 3,573)	
Periodic operating flows, net of tax[a]		68,804	72,932	77,308	81,946	$86,863
Depreciation tax shield:						
Tax shield from depreciation		32,000	32,000	16,000	16,000	16,000
Forgone tax shield		(10,500)	(10,500)			
Disinvestment flows:						
Return of working capital[b]						63,124
Proceeds on disposal						147,268
Tax on gain						(58,907)
Total cash flows	(132,000)	(62,696)	91,252	89,937	94,373	254,348
PV factor at 21.9%	1.000	.820	.673	.552	.453	.372
Present values[c]	($132,000)	($51,432)	$61,409	$49,651	$42,740	$94,495
Net present value of project	$64,863					

Nominal rate = 1.15 × 1.06 − 1 = .219 = 21.9%

---

[a] Operating cash flows = $64,909 (1.06)^n, n = 1, . . . , 5.

[b] $63,124 = Sum of cash released from working capital requirements = $50,000 + $3,000 + $3,180 + $3,371 + $3,573.

[c] Cash flow times PV factor does not equal present values because PV factors are rounded.

The working capital returned in Year 5 includes the $50,000 initial outlay plus the outlays in Years 1 through 4 for a total return of $63,124 (which is $50,000 + $3,000 + $3,180 + $3,371 + $3,573).

The proceeds from disposal of the long-term assets and their tax impact are also included in the disinvestment computation. Any difference between the proceeds on disposal as adjusted for inflation and the tax basis of the property is taxed.

For Kwik Press, we assume that the market for used equipment similar to that used in the project is increasing at the rate of 7 percent per year. As a result, the proceeds from disposal are estimated as:

$$\$105,000 \times (1.07)^5 = \underline{\$147,268}$$

Since the asset has been fully depreciated for tax purposes, this entire amount is a gain, taxable at ordinary rates. The tax liability from the gain is:

$$40\% \times \$147,268 = \underline{\$58,907}$$

This amount is shown as an outflow in Year 5.

Summarizing the Cash Flows

The adjusted cash flows for Kwik Press under inflation are summarized in the cash flow schedule in Illustration 15–7 as they were in Illustration 15–6 with no inflation considered. That is, all cash flows are scheduled and summed for each year of the project's life. In this case, however, yearly cash flows represent the amounts expected to be realized under certain inflation conditions.

The cash flows for the project are discounted using the 21.9 percent rate computed earlier, and the present values are shown for each year of the project's life. The net present value of the project is then computed. For this project, the net present value is $64,863.

Analysts sometimes incorrectly ignore the effect of inflation on cash flows but increase the discount rate to reflect the market rates of interest. These market interest rates include inflationary expectations. On some projects, discounting the unadjusted cash flows with an inflation-adjusted interest rate can yield the opposite answer from what is optimal. In short, analysts should consider inflation in both the cash flows and the discount rate.

Self-Study Question

2 Refer to the data in self-study question 1. Inflation has affected cash flows as follows: Operating cash flows are the same as in self-study question 1 for Time 0 and Year 1. Operating cash flows increase 10 percent in Year 2 over the Year 1 level, and another 10 percent in Year 3 over the Year 2 level, and another 10 percent in Year 4. The salvage value of the new equipment will increase to $1,330, at the end of Year 4. All other facts about cash flows and taxes remain the same as in self-study question 1. Assume a discount rate of 26.5 percent for this question.

a. Prepare a schedule showing the relevant cash flows for the project.

b. Indicate whether the equipment purchase meets Melwood's hurdle rate.

The solution to this question is at the end of this chapter on page 589.

INVESTING IN IMPROVED TECHNOLOGY

When companies invest in new technology, they often find high-tech investments do not show a positive net present value. High-tech investments usually have a high investment outlay and considerable delay before the benefits are realized as cash inflows or cash savings. It is common for computer assisted manufacturing equipment to take several years to reach their potential benefits. If a company has a high discount rate, cash flows received several years in the future have a low present value.

For example, Yamazaki Machinery Company's plant in Kentucky obtained substantial cost savings from its investment in flexible manufacturing equipment, but the savings came in the long run, not in the short run. If the company had used a discount rate of 15 or 20 percent, it would likely have rejected this investment. We have seen discount rates of 30 percent or more. Using a discount rate of 30 percent, one dollar received at the end of five years has a present value of only 27 cents. Consequently, companies using high discount rates have trouble justifying investment in new technology when payoff is several years into the future. See the real world application, "Investing in Improved Technology," for an example of a company struggling to justify investing in new innovative equipment despite negative net present value computations.

Companies have much to learn, by definition, from investing in new technology. Naturally, analysts often have trouble measuring the benefits of new technology before the investment has been made. Simmonds Precision Products, which makes aerospace products, found its computerized manu-

---

REAL WORLD APPLICATION

Investing in Improved Technology*

Investments in improved technology frequently do not show a positive net present value when investment analysis is performed. Technological innovations usually have a high investment outlay and a long time period before cash flows are returned from the project. It is not unusual for an investment in automated equipment to take two or three years (or more) before it is fully operational. In companies with high discount rates, cash flows received, or cash savings, several years in the future have low present values. Furthermore, technological improvements frequently provide benefits that are not easily quantified, so cash benefits are often omitted from the analysis.

We observed the capital-budgeting process at work for technological improvements in one of the U.S. automobile companies. This company was considering investing in new equipment that would make the manufacturing operation more flexible. With this equipment, the company could change quickly from making one part to another; reduce setup costs, inventory levels, and production down-

time; and introduce other potential savings. In addition to these cost savings, the engineers and production managers who supported this project saw it as a way of learning more about flexible manufacturing, which *could* provide major benefits to the company in the future. These benefits were not quantifiable, however, so no *explicit* weight was given to them in the discounted cash flow analysis.

Using a high discount rate (after-tax rate greater than 25 percent), the company initially rejected the project. The president of the company was subsequently convinced that the project had additional benefits beyond those explicitly considered in the discounted cash flow analysis. These additional benefits, which included learning about improved production methods that could have a major impact on the way the company does business, were believed to justify the project. The project was then accepted, and the investment was made.

* Based on the authors' research.

facturing methods allowed it to increase creativity in product design, an intangible benefit that is difficult to quantify. If such benefit cannot be measured and quantified, then it is often omitted in the net present value analysis—yet another strike against investing in new technology. Companies that are serious about investing in new ideas, whether the new ideas involve technology, new products, or quality improvement, must recognize that many benefits of new ideas cannot be accurately quantified or measured.

Companies should recognize that many things cannot be reduced to simple cash flow estimates. The consequences of new ideas should at least be stated qualitatively, if they cannot be quantified. One manager explained his approach as follows, "If we omit the benefit of an investment from net present value analysis, then we are saying its value is zero. We may not know the exact amount of the benefit, but we know it's not zero. It is better to be approximately right with an imprecise estimate of the benefit than to be precisely wrong by omitting the benefit altogether."

CAPITAL BUDGETING IN NONPROFIT ORGANIZATIONS

Not-for-profit organizations, including governmental agencies, are subject to limitations on the availability of capital for investment purposes. They, too, make use of capital investment analysis to allocate cash efficiently. Since not-for-profit organizations are exempt from income taxation, there are no tax effects on the operating cash flows nor on disinvestment flows. Likewise, there is no tax shield from depreciation. These features result in a somewhat simplified analysis.

For example, assume that the U.S. Postal Service is considering a purchase of advanced automated sorting equipment for its Urbana station. The equipment will cost $600,000 and has a useful life of five years. Salvage value is estimated at $10,000. Installation of the equipment will cost $8,000.

ILLUSTRATION   *Capital Budgeting in Nonprofit Organizations*

15-8

Item	Time 0	Year 1	Year 2	Year 3	Year 4	Year 5
Investment flows:						
New equipment	($600,000)					
Other investment costs	(8,000)					
Annual operating flows		$160,000[a]	$160,000	$160,000	$160,000	$160,000
Disinvestment flows:						
Salvage value						10,000
Total cash flows	(608,000)	160,000	160,000	160,000	160,000	170,000
Discount factor	1.000	0.909	0.826	0.751	0.683	0.621
Present value	($608,000)	$145,455	$132,231	$120,210	$109,282	$105,557
Net present value	$4,735					

[a] $160,000 = $40,000 + ($30,000 × 4).

The old equipment can be shipped to a post office that is using semiauto-mated equipment. It is assumed that the costs to dismantle and ship the old equipment will exactly offset the benefits received at the other post office.

Use of the new equipment will reduce non labor costs by $40,000 per year. One operator will be able to handle the volume of letters that five operators handled in the past. The average pay for each operator is $30,000 including fringe benefits. The postal service uses a discount rate of 10 percent. What are the cash flows from the project and the net present value?

The results are shown in Illustration 15–8. As you may note, this is very similar to Illustration 15–6, which was used for a taxable organization.

ETHICAL ISSUES IN CAPITAL INVESTMENT DECISIONS

The people who request additional capital investment in a project often have a strong interest in assuring that the net present value of the project is positive. In a company that we studied, a group of engineers wanted the company to purchase new equipment with the latest technology. Because they were so interested in getting the new equipment, the engineers omitted some of the costs of installing the equipment in the data they submitted with the project proposal. By omitting these installation costs, the engineers reduced the initial investment outflow in the discounted cash flow analysis, which increased the chance that the net present value of the project would be positive.

If the company's top managers had known about the installation costs, they would have rejected the proposal to buy the new equipment. Based on the false data, the company subsequently purchased the equipment. The company's total investment in the equipment was considerably higher than originally projected because the costs of installing the equipment had been omitted from the discounted cash flow analysis.

During your career, you may be pressured to omit certain data from capital investment proposals or to make inaccurate projections. Don't. In the case just described, the engineers got their equipment, but they paid a price. Top management learned about the omitted installation costs after reviewing monthly divisional income statements. Some of the engineers were dismissed. The credibility of the remaining engineers was substantially undermined.

POST-AUDIT OF CAPITAL INVESTMENT PROJECTS

Because capital investment projects are so important, companies commonly compare the cash flows that are actually realized from a project with the estimated flows in the original capital investment proposal. In that way, they hope to learn if the estimation process can be improved.

Some projects may improve reported accounting profits in the short run but result in suboptimal net present values. When this occurs, it is necessary to identify the reasons for choosing a project that improves accounting profits rather than net present value. There may be rational explanations for such decisions, but management should critically evaluate those reasons.

A capital investment control program must consider more than initial project estimates. It must also determine if the capital investment decision-making process is operating well.

SUMMARY

Capital investment planning involves a number of managerial and financial considerations. The accountant's role is to determine the amount and timing of relevant cash flows from the project. These cash flows are discounted back to the present to determine if the proposed project meets the established hurdle rate.

The net present value of a project is computed using the following equation:

$$NPV = \sum_{n=0}^{N} C_n \times (1 + d)^{-n}$$

where

C_n = Cash flows at the end of time period n
d = Discount rate
n = Time period when the cash flow occurs
N = Total number of time periods in the project's life

The accountant's primary task is to estimate cash flows used in the net present value equation. These cash flows and their effects are:

1. Investment:
    a. Acquisition cost ($-$).
    b. Investment tax credit ($+$).
    c. Working capital commitments ($-$).
    d. Proceeds of assets sold ($+$).
    e. Tax effects from a loss or gain on sale of old assets ($+/-$).
2. Periodic operating flows, including:
    a. Period cash inflows ($+$) and outflows ($-$) before taxes.
    b. Income tax effects of inflows ($-$) and outflows ($+$).
3. Depreciation tax shield:
    a. Tax shield benefits ($+$).
    b. Forgone tax shield benefits ($-$).
4. Disinvestment flows:
    a. Cash freed from working capital commitments ($+$).
    b. Incremental salvage value of long-term assets (usually $+$ unless there are disposal costs).
    c. Tax consequences of gain or loss on disposal ($-$ or $+$, respectively).
    d. Other cash flows, such as severance or relocation payments to employees, restoration costs, and similar costs (usually $-$).

Income taxes are an extremely important consideration, particularly due to regulations designed to encourage investment. The accountant may be the only analyst on the management team who understands the income tax effects. Improper treatment of tax effects may lead to suboptimal decisions.

Under conditions of inflation, the discount rate is usually adjusted to compensate for changes in price levels.

TERMS AND CONCEPTS

The following terms and concepts should be familiar to you after reading this chapter:

Asset Acquisition, *550*	Nominal Dollars, *560*
Discount Rate, *547*	Present Value, *548*
Disinvestment Flows, *556*	Real Return, *560*
Hurdle Rate, *547*	Tax Basis, *556*
Investment Tax Credit, *551*	Tax Shield, *554*
Net Present Value, *547*	Time Value of Money, *547*
Nominal Discount Rate, *560*	Working Capital, *551*

APPENDIX A

Computing Net Present Values for Annuities

When periodic cash flows are expected to be equal over a period of time, a shortcut method may be used to compute the net present value of those cash flows. A series of level periodic payments is referred to as an *annuity*. The *present value of an annuity* may be obtained using the equation:

$$\text{Present value} = C \times \frac{1 - (1 + d)^{-n}}{d}$$

where

d = Discount rate
n = Number of periods over which the periodic payment (C) will be received

For example, the present value of a series of six payments of $40,000 each at a discount rate of 25 percent is:

$$PV = \$40,000 \times \frac{1 - (1 + .25)^{-6}}{.25}$$
$$= \$40,000 \times 2.951424$$
$$= \$118,057$$

This amount may also be computed the long way by taking the present value of each year's cash flow as follows:

Year	Cash Flow	PV Factor	Present Value
1	$40,000	.800	$ 32,000
2	40,000	.640	25,600
3	40,000	.512	20,480
4	40,000	.410	16,384
5	40,000	.328	13,107
6	40,000	.262	10,486
		2.952	$118,057

The sum of the present value factors for the six periods is the same with rounding as the computed factor for the six-year annuity. The present values computed under either method are the same. As with other present value calculations, the use of a calculator will be more efficient and will give more accurate answers than will use of the tables. A set of tables is given in Appendix B to this chapter.

| APPENDIX B |

Present Value Tables

The present value of $1 shown in Illustration 15–9 gives the present value of an amount received n periods in the future. It is computed using the equation $(1 + d)^{-n}$ as discussed in the chapter.

For example, to find the present value of $20,000 received 11 years from now at a discount of 16 percent, look over the 11-year row to the 16 percent column and find the relevant factor, .195. Multiply the $20,000 by this factor to obtain the present value of $3,900.

If you perform this same computation with a calculator, you will obtain the somewhat more precise answer of $3,908. The difference is due to rounding.

The present value of an annuity is the value of a series of equal periodic payments discounted at a stated rate. Illustration 15–10 gives a set of factors for present values of an annuity.

For example, to find the present value of a series of nine annual payments of $5,000 each at a discount rate of 18 percent, look across the nine-year row to the 18 percent column and find the factor, 4.303. Multiply the $5,000 by the 4.303 to obtain the present value of those future payments, $21,515.

Illustration 15–11 provides the net present values for the text problems that are based on the recognition of inflation in the cash flow analysis.

I L L U S T R A T I O N   *Present Value of $1*

15–9

Year	8%	10%	12%	14%	15%	16%	18%	20%	22%	24%
1	.926	.909	.893	.877	.870	.862	.847	.833	.820	.806
2	.857	.826	.797	.769	.756	.743	.718	.694	.672	.650
3	.794	.751	.712	.675	.658	.641	.609	.579	.551	.524
4	.735	.683	.636	.592	.572	.552	.516	.482	.451	.423
5	.681	.621	.567	.519	.497	.476	.437	.402	.370	.341
6	.630	.564	.507	.456	.432	.410	.370	.335	.303	.275
7	.583	.513	.452	.400	.376	.354	.314	.279	.249	.222
8	.540	.467	.404	.351	.327	.305	.266	.233	.204	.179
9	.500	.424	.361	.308	.284	.263	.225	.194	.167	.144
10	.463	.386	.322	.270	.247	.227	.191	.162	.137	.116
11	.429	.350	.287	.237	.215	.195	.162	.135	.112	.094
12	.397	.319	.257	.208	.187	.168	.137	.112	.092	.076
13	.368	.290	.229	.182	.163	.145	.116	.093	.075	.061
14	.340	.263	.205	.160	.141	.125	.099	.078	.062	.049
15	.315	.239	.183	.140	.123	.108	.084	.065	.051	.040

Year	25%	26%	28%	30%	32%	34%	35%	36%	38%	40%
1	.800	.794	.781	.769	.758	.746	.741	.735	.725	.714
2	.640	.630	.610	.592	.574	.557	.549	.541	.525	.510
3	.512	.500	.477	.455	.435	.416	.406	.398	.381	.364
4	.410	.397	.373	.350	.329	.310	.301	.292	.276	.260
5	.328	.315	.291	.269	.250	.231	.223	.215	.200	.186
6	.262	.250	.227	.207	.189	.173	.165	.158	.145	.133
7	.210	.198	.178	.159	.143	.129	.122	.116	.105	.095
8	.168	.157	.139	.123	.108	.096	.091	.085	.076	.068
9	.134	.125	.108	.094	.082	.072	.067	.063	.055	.048
10	.107	.099	.085	.073	.062	.054	.050	.046	.040	.035
11	.086	.079	.066	.056	.047	.040	.037	.034	.029	.025
12	.069	.062	.052	.043	.036	.030	.027	.025	.021	.018
13	.055	.050	.040	.033	.027	.022	.020	.018	.015	.013
14	.044	.039	.032	.025	.021	.017	.015	.014	.011	.009
15	.035	.031	.025	.020	.016	.012	.011	.010	.008	.007

ILLUSTRATION   *Present Value of an Annuity*

15–10

Year	8%	10%	12%	14%	15%	16%	18%	20%	22%	24%
1	.926	.909	.893	.877	.870	.862	.847	.833	.820	.806
2	1.783	1.736	1.690	1.647	1.626	1.605	1.566	1.528	1.492	1.457
3	2.577	2.487	2.402	2.322	2.283	2.246	2.174	2.106	2.042	1.981
4	3.312	3.170	3.037	2.914	2.855	2.798	2.690	2.589	2.494	2.404
5	3.993	3.791	3.605	3.433	3.352	3.274	3.127	2.991	2.864	2.745
6	4.623	4.355	4.111	3.889	3.784	3.685	3.498	3.326	3.167	3.020
7	5.206	4.868	4.564	4.288	4.160	4.039	3.812	3.605	3.416	3.242
8	5.747	5.335	4.968	4.639	4.487	4.344	4.078	3.837	3.619	3.421
9	6.247	5.759	5.328	4.946	4.772	4.607	4.303	4.031	3.786	3.566
10	6.710	6.145	5.650	5.216	5.019	4.833	4.494	4.192	3.923	3.682
11	7.139	6.495	5.938	5.453	5.234	5.029	4.656	4.327	4.035	3.776
12	7.536	6.814	6.194	5.660	5.421	5.197	4.793	4.439	4.127	3.851
13	7.904	7.103	6.424	5.842	5.583	5.342	4.910	4.533	4.203	3.912
14	8.244	7.367	6.628	6.002	5.724	5.468	5.008	4.611	4.265	3.962
15	8.559	7.606	6.811	6.142	5.847	5.575	5.092	4.675	4.315	4.001

Year	25%	26%	28%	30%	32%	34%	35%	36%	38%	40%
1	.800	.794	.781	.769	.758	.746	.741	.735	.725	.714
2	1.440	1.424	1.392	1.361	1.331	1.303	1.289	1.276	1.250	1.224
3	1.952	1.923	1.868	1.816	1.766	1.719	1.696	1.673	1.630	1.589
4	2.362	2.320	2.241	2.166	2.096	2.029	1.997	1.966	1.906	1.849
5	2.689	2.635	2.532	2.436	2.345	2.260	2.220	2.181	2.106	2.035
6	2.951	2.885	2.759	2.643	2.534	2.433	2.385	2.339	2.251	2.168
7	3.161	3.083	2.937	2.802	2.677	2.562	2.508	2.455	2.355	2.263
8	3.329	3.241	3.076	2.925	2.786	2.658	2.598	2.540	2.432	2.331
9	3.463	3.366	3.184	3.019	2.868	2.730	2.665	2.603	2.487	2.379
10	3.571	3.465	3.269	3.092	2.930	2.784	2.715	2.649	2.527	2.414
11	3.656	3.543	3.335	3.147	2.978	2.824	2.752	2.683	2.555	2.438
12	3.725	3.606	3.387	3.190	3.013	2.853	2.779	2.708	2.576	2.456
13	3.780	3.656	3.427	3.223	3.040	2.876	2.799	2.727	2.592	2.469
14	3.824	3.695	3.459	3.249	3.061	2.892	2.814	2.740	2.603	2.478
15	3.859	3.726	3.483	3.268	3.076	2.905	2.825	2.750	2.611	2.484

ILLUSTRATION

15-11

*Present Value Table for
Inflation Problems*

Year	18.80%	20.96%	21.90%	23.20%	26.50%	28.80%	31.76%	39.08%
1	.842	.827	.820	.812	.791	.776	.759	.719
2	.709	.683	.673	.659	.625	.603	.576	.517
3	.596	.565	.552	.535	.494	.468	.437	.372
4	.502	.467	.453	.434	.391	.363	.332	.267
5	.423	.386	.372	.352	.309	.282	.252	.192
6	.356	.319	.305	.286	.244	.219	.191	.138
7	.299	.264	.250	.232	.193	.170	.145	.099
8	.252	.218	.205	.188	.153	.132	.110	.071
9	.212	.180	.168	.153	.121	.103	.084	.051
10	.179	.149	.138	.124	.095	.080	.063	.037
11	.150	.123	.113	.101	.075	.062	.048	.027
12	.127	.102	.093	.082	.060	.048	.037	.019
13	.107	.084	.076	.066	.047	.037	.028	.014
14	.090	.070	.062	.054	.037	.029	.021	.010
15	.075	.058	.051	.044	.029	.022	.016	.008

QUESTIONS

15-1   What are the two most important factors the accountant must estimate in the capital investment decision?

15-2   What is meant by the *time value of money?*

15-3   Given two projects with equal cash flows but different timings, how can we determine which (if either) project should be selected for investment.

15-4   What are the four types of cash flows related to a capital investment and why do we consider them separately?

15-5   Refer to the real world application in this chapter. Engineers and production managers often complain that discounted cash flow analysis is biased against investing in new technology. Why might they make such a statement?

15-6   Fatigue Corporation has a division operating at a $200,000 cash loss per year. The company cannot dispose of the division due to certain contractual arrangements it has made that require continued operation of the division. However, Fatigue has just received a proposal to invest in some new equipment with an estimated operating life of 10 years for the division at a cost of $150,000. If the equipment is purchased, the division will operate at a $40,000 cash loss per year. Should Fatigue Corp. consider acquisition of the equipment? Why or why not?

15-7   How do tax policies provide an incentive for capital investment?

15-8   Is depreciation included in the computation of net present value? Explain.

15-9   "Every project should bear its fair share of all of the costs of the company. To do otherwise would make present operations subsidize new projects." Comment.

15-10   "The total tax deduction for depreciation is the same over the life of the project regardless of depreciation method. Why then would one be con-

cerned about the depreciation method for capital investment analysis?"
Comment.

15–11   How can we express the relationship of the desired real return to capital (*r*)
and the inflation rate (*i*) that is used to discount nominal project cash flows
under conditions of inflation?

15–12   Why might inflation be a disincentive to investment? What impact might
inflation have on the present value of future cash flows and the future tax
shield from the original investment?

15–13   Why could the investment in working capital increase over a project's life
under conditions of inflation while inventory values (under LIFO) would
not?

EXERCISES

**15–14   Present Value of
Cash Flows[1]**
(L.O.2)

A city government is considering investing in street reconstruction that will require
outlays as follows:

Year	Item	Amount
0	Engineering studies	$ 50,000
1	Project initiation	200,000
2	Project construction	900,000

Required:

Compute the net present value of these cash outlays if the appropriate discount rate
is 10 percent.

**15–15   Present Value of
Cash Flows**
(L.O.2)

Clinton City is considering investment in an addition to the community center that is
expected to return the following cash flows:

Year	Net Cash Flow
1	$10,000
2	25,000
3	40,000
4	40,000
5	50,000

This schedule includes all cash flows from the project. The project will require an
immediate cash outlay of $100,000. The city is tax exempt, therefore no taxes need be
considered.

Required:

a.   What is the net present value of the project if the appropriate discount rate is 20
percent?

b.   What is the net present value of the project if the appropriate discount rate is 12
percent?

15–16   Effects of Inflation
(L.O.4)

Refer to the data in exercise 15–15.

a.   What is the net present value of the project if the inflation rate is 10 percent and
the discount rate under no inflation is 12 percent? (Hint: Inflation affects both

---

[1] Refer to Appendix B of this chapter for present value tables.

cash flows and the nominal rate of interest; and the cash flows for Year 1 are $11,000, 10 percent higher than in exercise 15–15.)

b. Compare your answer in (a) to the result you got in part (b) of exercise 15–15. Explain why these two answers are the same (or different).

15–17   Present Value of Cash Flows
(L.O.2)

KPIV Television is considering investment in a new show that is expected to return the following cash flows from syndication:

Year	Net Cash Flow (in thousands)
1	$1,500
2	1,700
3	2,400
4	2,000
5	1,200

This schedule includes all cash flows from the project. The project will require an immediate cash outlay at Time 0 of $5 million. KPIV is tax exempt.

Required:

a. Complete the following schedule to determine the net present value of the project if the appropriate discount rate is 20 percent.

	Time 0	Year 1	2	3	4	5
Investment flows:						
Investment						
Operating flows:						
Net cash flows						
Total cash flows						
PV factor: 20%						
Present values						
Net PV of project:						

b. Complete the following net present value schedule for the project if the appropriate discount rate is 15 percent.

	Time 0	Year 1	2	3	4	5
Investment flows:						
Investment						
Operating flows:						
Net cash flows						
Total cash flows						
PV factor: 15%						
Present values						
Net PV of project:						

15–18   Effects of Inflation on Cash Flows
(L.O.4)

Refer to the cash flow data in exercise 15–17 and adjust as indicated below. Complete the following schedule to determine the net present value of the project if the inflation rate is 6 percent and the *no-inflation* discount rate is 15 percent. (Hint: Inflation affects both cash flows and the nominal rate of interest and the Year 1 cash flows are $1,590, six percent higher than in exercise 15–17.)

KPIV TELEVISION

	Time	Year				
	0	1	2	3	4	5
Investment flows:						
Investment						
Operating flows:						
Net cash flows						
Total cash flows						
PV factor						
Present values						
Net PV of project:						
Calculations:						
Nominal rate = ____						

15–19 Effects of Inflation on Cash Flows
(L.O.4)

Refer to exercise 15–18. Would your answer be different if you had used real (no-inflation) cash flows and discount rate instead of the nominal amounts in 15–18?

E X H I B I T

A

Schedule for Depreciation Tax Shield Calculations (for exercises 15–20 to 15–24)

Year	Depreciation	Tax Shield at _%	Present Value Factor	Present Value
1				
2				
3				
4				
5				
Totals				

Net present value of tax shield: _____

Refer to Exhibit A to compute the present value of depreciation tax shields.

15–20 Compute Present Value of Tax Shield
(L.O.3)

The Chill Factor Ski Corporation plans to acquire production equipment at a cost of $200,000 that will be depreciated for tax purposes as follows: Year 1, $40,000; Year 2, $70,000; and $30,000 per year in each of Years 3–5. An 18 percent discount rate is appropriate for this asset, and the company's tax rate is 40 percent.

Required:

a. Compute the present value of the tax shield resulting from depreciation. Refer to Exhibit A for format.

b. Compute the present value of the tax shield from depreciation assuming straight-line depreciation ($40,000 per year). Refer to Exhibit A for format.

15–21 Present Value of Depreciation Tax Shield under Inflation
(L.O.3, L.O.4)

Refer to the data in exercise 15–20.

a. Using the accelerated tax depreciation deductions in exercise 15–20, what is the present value of the tax shield if the inflation rate is 8 percent and the no-inflation discount rate is 22 percent?

b. What is the present value of the tax shield if the inflation rate is 14 percent and the no-inflation discount rate is 22 percent?

	c. What happens to the net present value of the tax shield as the inflation rate increases?
15–22 Present Value of Tax Shield (L.O.3)	The Metz Company plans to acquire an asset at a cost of $800,000 that will be depreciated for tax purposes as follows: Year 1, $230,000; Year 2, $300,000; and $90,000 per year in each of Years 3–5. A 15 percent discount rate is appropriate for this asset, and the company's tax rate is 35 percent.
Required:	Compute the present value of the tax shield. Refer to Exhibit A for format.
15–23 Present Value of Tax Shield (L.O.3)	Refer to the data in exercise 15–22. Compute the present value of the tax shield from depreciation assuming the asset qualifies for straight-line depreciation ($160,000 per year). Refer to Exhibit A for format.
15–24 Present Value of Tax Shield under Inflation (L.O.3, L.O.4)	Refer to the data in exercise 15–22. The no-inflation discount rate is 15 percent. Using the tax depreciation deductions in exercise 15–22, what is the present value of the tax shield if the inflation rate is 6 percent. Refer to Exhibit A for format.
15–25 Present Value of Cash Flows under Inflation (L.O.4)	Driscoll Corporation has concluded that its cost of capital is 8 percent in real terms. The company is considering an investment in a project having annual cash flows (before taxes and inflation) of $36,000 per year for five years. At disinvestment, the costs of disposal will equal any liquidation value of the project. No additional working capital is required for the project. The project costs $120,000 and will be depreciated for tax purposes over five years as follows: Year 1, 15 percent of the cost; Year 2, 22 percent; and 21 percent per year in each of Years 3–5. The company's marginal tax rate is 40 percent.
Required:	a. Assuming no inflation, complete the table below to compute the net present value of this project.

	Time	Year				
	0	1	2	3	4	5
Investment flows:						
New equipment	(a)					
Operating flows:						
Cash flows		b	b	b	b	b
Tax shield:						
Depreciation		c	d	e	e	e
Total cash flows						
PV factor (8%)						
Present values						
Net PV of project:						

b.   If inflation is expected to be 12 percent, what is the present value of the project? Refer to Illustration 15–11 for present value table under inflation. (Hint: Inflation affects both cash flows and the nominal rate of interest.)

15–26 Present Value Analysis in Nonprofit Organizations (L.O.6)	The Oakland Naval Shipyard bought machine 1 on March 5, Year 1, for $5,000 cash. The estimated salvage was $0, and the estimated life was 11 years. On March 5, Year 2, the shipyard learned that it could purchase a different machine for $6,000 cash. The new machine would save the shipyard an estimated $300 per year compared to machine 1. The new machine would have no estimated salvage value and an estimated life of 10 years. The shipyard could get $3,000 for machine 1 on March 5, Year 2. As a government agency, the shipyard pays no taxes.
Required:	a. Which of the following calculations would best assist the shipyard in deciding whether to purchase the new machine?

(1)   Present value of $300 savings per year + $3,000 − $6,000.
(2)   Present value of $300 savings per year − $6,000.
(3)   Present value of $300 savings per year + $3,000 − $6,000 − $5,000.
(4) $3,000 − $6,000

b.   Calculate the net present value of the purchase of the new machine using differential costs. Assume a 12 percent discount rate. (Refer to Illustration 15–10, Appendix B, for annuity factors.)

c.   Should the Oakland Naval Shipyard invest in the new machine?

15–27   Present Value Analysis in Nonprofit Organizations
(L.O.6)

The Complete Cure Hospital is considering buying laboratory equipment with an estimated life of seven years, so they will not have to use outsiders' laboratories for certain types of laboratory work. All of the cash flows affected by the decision are listed below. (The hospital is a nonprofit organization that does not pay taxes.)

Investment outflows at Time 0	$2,000,000
Periodic operating flows:	
Annual cash savings because outside laboratories are not used	700,000
Additional cash outflow for people and supplies to operate the equipment	100,000
Disinvestment flows:	
Salvage value after seven years, which is the estimated life of this project	200,000
Discount rate	12%

Required:

Calculate the net present value of this decision using the following schedule. Should the hospital buy the equipment?

	Time 0	Year 1	Year 2	. . .	Year 7
Investment flows					
Periodic operating flows:					
Annual cash savings					
Additional cash outflow					
Disinvestment flows	_____	_____	_____	. . .	_____
Net annual cash flow					
Present value factor (12%)	_____	_____	_____	. . .	_____
Present values	_____	_____	_____	. . .	_____
Net present value	_____				

15–28   Impact of Inflation on Net Present Value in Nonprofit Organizations
(L.O.4, L.O.6)

Refer to the data in exercise 15–27. Complete the following schedule to calculate the net present value if the real interest rate is 12 percent and inflation is expected to be 8 percent per year. Refer to Illustration 15–11 for present value table under inflation. (Hint: Inflation affects both the nominal rate of interest and cash flows, and the cash flows for Year 1 will be 8 percent higher than the amounts indicated in exercise 15–27.)

	Time 0	Year 1	Year 2	. . .	Year 7
Net annual cash flow					
Present value factor	_____	_____	_____	. . .	_____
Present values	_____	_____	_____	. . .	_____
Net present value	_____				

PROBLEMS

15–29 New Machine Decision

Pretty Good Yogurt (PGY), Inc., is considering the purchase of a newer, more efficient yogurt-making machine. If purchased, the new machine would be acquired on January 2, Year 1. PGY expects to sell 300,000 gallons of yogurt in each of the next five years. The selling price of the yogurt is expected to average $2.00 per gallon.

PGY, Inc., has two options: (1) continue to operate the old machine purchased four years ago or (2) sell the old machine and purchase the new machine. The following information has been prepared to help decide which option is more desirable:

	Old Machine	New Machine
Original cost of machine at acquisition	$800,000	$1,000,000
Useful life from date of acquisition	7 years	5 years
Expected annual cash operating expenses:		
Variable cost per gallon	$1.20	$1.00
Total fixed cash costs	$200,000	$80,000

Depreciation:

Age of Equipment (Years)	Tax Depreciation (Percent)
1	15%
2	25
3	20
4	20
5	20

Estimated cash value of machines:

	Old Machine	New Machine
January 2, Year 1	$200,000	$1,000,000
December 31, Year 3	$100,000	$ 500,000

PGY, Inc., is subject to an income tax rate of 40 percent on all income. Assume tax depreciation is calculated without regard to salvage value. Use a three-year time horizon for the analysis.

Required:

Use the net present value method to determine whether PGY, Inc., should retain the old machine or acquire the new machine. You should assume there is no inflation. Use an after-tax discount rate of 10 percent.

15–30 Ethical Issues

Instant Dinners, Inc. (IDI), is in the business of manufacturing microwavable frozen foods. However, recent competition from the "vacuum packed, store it on the shelf" food manufacturers has necessitated a look at all of IDI's divisions. West Division is in a little financial trouble much to the dismay of Jackie Johnson, IDI's chief financial officer. Jackie has many friends at West, and is anxious to save the division. She assigns Bob Furlow, a member of the planning and analysis staff, to investigate the possibility of installing a conveyor belt automation system to replace the forklift and their operators. She has provided Bob with estimates of costs, increased sales revenue, and so on. Bob uses these figures and determines that the project has a very positive net present value. Jackie is quite pleased with the results and Bob's work. Bob, however, decides to investigate the equipment for himself. His research reveals that Jackie had overestimated the useful life of the conveyor belt automation system, as well as its residual value. Bob recomputed his NPV analysis and presented his results to Jackie. Jackie ordered him not to discuss this revised NPV analysis with anyone at IDI, especially those on the board who will vote on the proposal.

Required:

a. How should Bob Furlow evaluate Jackie Johnson's order to repress the revised NPV analysis? Is it ethical?

b. How should Bob resolve this issue?

(CMA adapted)

15-31 Ethical Issues

Evans Company is considering expanding its manufacturing operations. It can either convert a warehouse it currently owns in the suburbs, or it can expand its current manufacturing plant downtown. After the board of directors approved the expansion, George Watson, the controller, set about to determine which proposal had the higher net present value. He assigned this task to Helen Dodge, the assistant controller. Dodge completed her task and discovered that the warehouse proposal had a negative net present value, while the downtown expansion proposal was slightly positive. Watson was displeased with Dodge's report on the warehouse proposal. He returned it to her stating that, "You must have made an error. This proposal should look better." Helen Dodge suspected that Watson wanted the warehouse proposal to succeed so that he could avoid his daily commute to the city. Dodge checked her figures and found nothing wrong. She made some slight revisions, however, to her report, changing her estimates from those that were probable to those that were remotely possible.

Watson was quite angry and demanded a second revision. He told her to start with a positive net present value of $100,000 and work backwards to compute supporting estimates and projections. Dodge is quite upset and unsure what she should do!

Required:

a. Was Helen Dodge's first revision on the proposal for the warehouse conversion unethical?

b. Was George Watson's conduct unethical when he gave Helen specific instructions on preparing the second revision?

c. How should Helen Dodge attempt to resolve this issue? Should she discuss this issue with those outside of the organization?

(CMA adapted)

15-32 Investment Decision in a Nonprofit Organization

Edmonton Machine Shop, a government vehicle repair shop, purchased a special purpose machine on January 1, Year 0. On December 31, Year 0, the company can purchase a more modern machine for $800,000. The new machine would be able to increase production by 25,000 service units per year. Shop management estimates the additional 25,000 service units can be utilized and will *not* affect the current charge of $8 per service unit. Edmonton pays no taxes. Other information related to the two machines is as follows:

	Old Machine	New Machine
Remaining useful life	5 years	5 years
Book value on December 31, Year 0	$250,000	$800,000
Salvage value on December 31, Year 0	200,000	
Salvage value on December 31, Year 5	–0–	100,000
Annual straight-line depreciation	50,000	140,000
Revenue per service unit	8.00	8.00
Variable cost per unit	4.00	4.75
Fixed cost per year (does not include depreciation on machine)	70,000	70,000
Cost to install new machine		8,000
Expected service units performed per year	75,000	100,000

Required:

a. Complete the following schedule of differential costs associated with the potential purchase of the new machine.

	Time	Year				
	0	1	2	3	4	5
Investment:						
New equipment	(a)					
Installation costs	(b)					
Old equipment salvage	c					
Periodic operating flows:						
Differential contribution from additional units		d	d	d	d	d
Differential costs from existing units		(e)	(e)	(e)	(e)	(e)
Disinvestment flows:						
New equipment salvage						f
Total cash flows	(g)	h	h	h	h	i
PV factor at 20%	1.000	.833	.694	.579	.482	.402
Present values	(j)	k	l	m	n	o

Net present value of project: p

Calculations:

Differential contribution from additional units:

Differential costs from existing units:

b. Based on a discount rate of 20 percent, recommend whether or not to purchase the new machine.

15–33 Compute Net Present Value

Essen Manufacturing Company is evaluating a proposal to purchase a new drill press as a replacement for a less efficient machine presently in use. The cost of the new equipment in Time 0, including delivery and installation, is $200,000. If the equipment is purchased, Essen will incur costs of $5,000 to remove the present equipment and revamp its facilities. This $5,000 is tax deductible at Time 0.

Depreciation for tax purposes will be allowed as follows: Year 1, $40,000; Year 2, $70,000; and $30,000 per year in each of Years 3–5. The existing equipment has a book and tax value of $100,000 and a remaining useful life of 10 years. However, the existing equipment could be sold for only $40,000. The existing equipment is being depreciated for book and tax purposes using the straight-line method over its actual life.

Management has provided you with the following comparative manufacturing cost data:

	Present Equipment	New Equipment
Annual capacity	400,000 units	400,000 units
Annual costs:		
Labor	$30,000	$25,000
Depreciation	10,000	14,000
Other (all cash)	48,000	20,000
Total annual costs	$88,000	$59,000

The existing equipment is expected to have salvage value equal to its removal costs at the end of 10 years. The new equipment is expected to have a salvage value of $60,000 at the end of 10 years, which will be taxable, and no removal costs. No changes in working capital are required with the purchase of the new equipment. The sales force does not expect any changes in volume of sales over the next 10 years. The company's cost of capital is 15 percent, and its tax rate is 45 percent.

Required:

a. Calculate the equipment removal costs net of tax effects.

b. Compute the depreciation tax shield.

c. Compute the forgone tax benefits of the old equipment.

d. Calculate the cash inflow, net of taxes, from the sale of new equipment in Year 10.

e. Calculate the tax benefit arising from the loss on the old equipment.

f. Compute the annual differential cash flows arising from the investment in Years 1–10.

g. Complete the following schedule and compute the net present value of the project.

	Time 0	Year 1	2	...	9	10
Investment flows:						
Equipment						
Removal						
Salvage of old equipment						
Tax benefit of loss on old equipment						
Periodic operating flows						
Tax shield:						
New equipment:						
Year 1: 40,000 × .45						
Year 2: 70,000 × .45						
Years 3, 4, 5: 30,000 × .45						
Old equipment (forgone if sold)						
Disinvestment:						
Proceeds of disposal						
Tax on gain						
Cash flows						
15% PV factor		.870	.756	...	.284	.247
Present values				...		
Net present value						

15–34 Impact of Inflation on Net Present Value

Management of Essen Manufacturing Company (problem 15–33) received your report on the estimated net present value of the new equipment. (All numbers in 15–33 assumed no inflation.) However, management is disturbed about their economist's report, which indicates an expected inflation rate of 6 percent over the next 10 years.

Required:

a. Calculate the new nominal interest rate.

b. Prepare a schedule showing how inflation would affect annual operating flows, assuming Year 1 operating flows are 6 percent higher than the annual savings computed in problem 15–33.

c. Prepare a report indicating how this expectation would affect your computed net present values. Assume the new equipment could be sold for $100,000 after 10 years. Show supporting computations in good form.

15–35 Assess Net Present Value of Training Costs

MacDonald & Company operates a diversified company with several operating divisions. Division M has consistently shown losses. Management is considering a proposal to obtain training for Division M employees that is designed to reduce labor and other operating costs.

The latest division income statement appears as follows (all dollar amounts in this problem are in thousands):

Revenues		$ 4,500
Costs:		
Direct materials	$1,250	
Direct labor	1,400	
Factory overhead:		
Indirect materials	200	
Indirect labor	350	
Utilities, taxes, etc.	600	
Depreciation	890	
Miscellaneous	120	
Division selling costs	450	
Division administrative costs	380	
Total costs		5,640
Division contribution		$(1,140)

The costs are expected to continue in the future unless the training is obtained.

With the training, direct labor is expected to be reduced by 55 percent, and other costs are expected to be reduced by $275 per year. These cost savings will continue for 10 years. The training will cost $5,000 and can be deducted for tax purposes in the year it is obtained.

Required: If the company's cost of capital is 12 percent and its marginal tax rate is 40 percent, determine whether the new training should be purchased. Show supporting computations.

15–36   Make-or-Buy Decision

Company Z has contracted to supply a governmental agency with 50,000 units of a product each year for the next five years. A certain component of this product can either be manufactured by Company Z or purchased from X Corporation, which will enter into a subcontract for 50,000 units of the component each year for five years at a price of $1.50 per unit. These alternative methods of procurement are regarded as equally desirable, except for costs.

If Company Z decides to manufacture the component, it expects the following to occur: (No tax rate is needed to solve this problem because all cash flows are subject to the same tax rate.)

1. A special-purchase machine costing $30,000 per year for five years will be rented. No other equipment or working capital will be required. (These payments are deducted in the year paid, for tax purposes.)

2. The manufacturing operation will require 1,000 square feet of productive floor space. This space is available in a building owned by Company Z and will not be needed for any other purpose in the foreseeable future. The costs of maintaining this building (including repairs, utilities, taxes, and depreciation) amount to $2 per square foot of productive floor space per year.

3. Variable manufacturing costs—materials, direct labor, and so forth—are estimated to be 50 cents a unit.

4. Fixed factory costs other than those mentioned in 1 and 2—such as supervision and so forth—are estimated at $20,000 a year.

5. Company Z uses an after-tax discount rate of 20 percent.

Required: Should Company Z make the component or buy it from X Corporation? (Ignore taxes because all cash flows are subject to the same rate.)

15–37 Estimate Relevant Cash Flows

Mariposa Recreational Products Corporation produces skateboards for street use. As a result of recent promotion of the sport, the company is considering expanding its facilities to increase production and sales by 35,000 units per year. The expansion will require an immediate outlay of $740,000 for the specialized equipment required for skateboard assembly. The company estimates the useful life of the project will be seven years. The company uses straight-line depreciation for book purposes but will depreciate for tax purposes as follows: Year 1, $140,000; Year 2, $240,000; and Years 3–5, $120,000 per year. Once the equipment is installed, it has no salvage value.

The project requires an estimated cash and accounts receivable balance of $10,000. The project will also require $17,000 in working inventory. All $27,000 working capital will be liquidated at the end of the last year of the project life.

The assembled skateboards sell for $29 each wholesale. The cost of materials for unassembled skateboards is $17 per kit, including shipping. In addition to the $17 cost of the unassembled parts, there is a cost of $6.50 per kit for assembly labor, power, and other variable overhead. All variable overhead is included in the $6.50 charge, and all such variable overhead requires current cash outlays.

The existing fixed overhead of the factory and equipment amounts to $162,857, including the book depreciation, for financial reporting purposes, on the new equipment. Except for the equipment depreciation, all of these fixed overhead items require current cash outlays. All fixed overhead is included in this amount.

A 12 percent rate is applicable for investment evaluation purposes. The tax rate applicable to the project income is 40 percent.

Required:

Prepare a schedule showing the net present value for the project with supporting details.

15–38 Estimate Relevant Cash Flows

Wyle Company is considering a proposal to acquire new manufacturing equipment. The new equipment has the same capacity as the current equipment but will provide operating efficiencies in direct and indirect labor, direct material usage, indirect supplies, and power. Consequently, the savings in operating costs are estimated at $150,000 annually. Only 60 percent of the estimated annual savings can be obtained in the first year.

The new equipment will cost $300,000. Wyle will incur a one-time cost of $30,000 to transfer the production activities from the old equipment to the new equipment. These costs will be deductible for tax purposes at Time 0.

The current equipment has been fully depreciated for book and tax purposes. Wyle Company could receive $5,000 net of removal costs if it elected to buy the new equipment and dispose of its current equipment at this time.

Wyle currently leases its manufacturing plant. The annual lease payments are $60,000. The lease, which will have five years remaining when the equipment installation would begin, is not renewable. Wyle Company would be required to remove any equipment in the plant at the end of the lease. The cost of equipment removal in five years is expected to equal the salvage value of either the old or new equipment at the time of removal.

The asset must be depreciated for tax purposes as follows: Year 1, $60,000; Year 2, $120,000; Years 3–5, $40,000 per year. Any gain or loss on disposal is taxed at ordinary income tax rates.

The company is subject to a 40 percent income tax rate and requires an after-tax return of at least 12 percent on any investment.

Required:

a. Calculate the differential after-tax cash flows for Wyle Company's proposal to acquire the new manufacturing equipment.

b. Calculate the net present value of Wyle Company's proposal to acquire the new manufacturing equipment.

(CMA adapted)

15–39 Compute After-Tax Net Present Value

World of Chocolate, Inc., is considering the purchase of a newer, more efficient cookie-making machine. If purchased, the new machine would be acquired on

January 2, Year 1. World of Chocolate expects to sell 300,000 dozen cookies in each of the next five years. The selling price of the cookies is expected to average $0.50 per dozen.

World of Chocolate, Inc., has two options: (1) continue to operate the old machine purchased two years ago or (2) sell the old machine and purchase the new machine. The following information has been assembled to help decide which option is more desirable:

	Old Machine	New Machine
Original cost of machine at acquisition	$80,000	$120,000
Useful life from date of acquisition	7 years	5 years
Expected annual cash operating expenses:		
Variable cost per dozen	$0.20	$0.14
Total fixed costs	15,000	14,000

Depreciation:

Age of Equipment (Years)	Tax Depreciation (Percent)
1	15%
2	25
3	20
4	20
5	20

Estimated cash value of machines:

January 2, Year 1	40,000	120,000
December 31, Year 5	7,000	20,000

World of Chocolates, Inc., is subject to an income tax rate of 40 percent on all income.

Required:

Use the net present value method to determine whether World of Chocolate, Inc., should retain the old machine or acquire the new machine. World of Chocolate, Inc., requires an after-tax return of 16 percent.

15–40   Capital Investment Analysis under Inflation

Management of Excello Retail Corporation is considering the purchase of energy-saving equipment costing $250,000.

The equipment has an expected useful life of seven years, at which time it will have no salvage value. The equipment will be depreciated for tax purposes over five years as follows: Year 1, $50,000; Year 2, $80,000; Years 3–5, $40,000 per year.

Present energy costs for the activities related to this equipment are $120,000 per year before taxes. The equipment will save 60 percent of these costs.

Working capital will be reduced by an estimated 5 percent of the initial year's after-tax cash energy cost savings. The working capital reduction will be an additional 5 percent each year with inflation in future years until Year 7, when it is assumed that the company will have to restore the entire working capital savings.

The expected inflation rate is 5 percent per year. The company's marginal tax rate is 40 percent, and its nominal cost of capital is 18.80 percent, after considering expected inflation of 5 percent per year.

Required:

Compute the net present value of the project.

15–41   Capital Investment Analysis under Inflation with Investment Tax Credit

Each division of Catix Company has the authority to make capital expenditures up to $200,000 without approval of the corporate headquarters. The corporate controller has determined that the cost of capital for Catix Corporation is 12 percent. This rate does not include an allowance for inflation, which is expected to occur at an average rate of 8 percent each year. Catix pays income taxes at the rate of 40 percent.

The Electronic Division of Catix is considering the purchase of automated machinery for manufacture of its printed-circuit boards. The divisional controller estimates that if the machine is purchased, two positions will be eliminated, yielding a cost savings for wages and employee benefits. However, the machine would require additional supplies and more power. The cost savings and additional costs in beginning-of-Year-1 prices are as follows:

Wages and employee benefits of the two positions eliminated ($25,000 each) $50,000
Cost of additional supplies 3,000
Cost of additional power 10,000

The new machine would be purchased and installed at the beginning of Year 1 at a net cost of $80,000. If purchased, the machine would be depreciated for tax purposes as follows: Year 1, $16,000; Year 2, $28,000; Years 3–5, $12,000 each year. It would qualify for an investment tax credit of $8,000 in Year 1. The machine will become technologically obsolete in eight years and will have no salvage value at that time.

The Electronics Division compensates for inflation in capital expenditure analyses by adjusting the above cash flows for inflation, starting with end-of-Year-1 cash flows. The adjusted after-tax cash flows are then discounted using the appropriate discount rate. No changes are expected in working capital.

Required:

Prepare a schedule showing the expected future cash flows in nominal dollars. Also show the net present value of the project. (See Illustration 15–11 for present value factors under inflation.)

(CMA adapted)

15–42 Capital Investment Cash Flows with Research Credits

Microhard Development Corp. is working on a new spreadsheet program that can take a manager's ideas and convert them into cash flow analyses without the need to enter numerical data. The initial development costs of the project are estimated at $2.5 million. Marketing costs are estimated at $3.2 million. Ten percent of all development costs are subject to a research and development tax credit, which is an immediate reduction in a company's income taxes.

Microhard expects that the project will return cash flows of $2.5 million in each of Years 1 and 2; $1.5 million in Year 3; $900,000 in Year 4; $700,000 in Year 5; and $200,000 in Year 6.

Microhard can forestall the decline in cash flows by developing an enhancement to the program. Development costs of the enhancement would be $900,000 in each of Years 1 through 3. Marketing costs of $2 million would be required in Year 3 to promote the enhancement. If Microhard develops the enhancement, cash flows in Years 1 and 2 would be the same. Year 3 cash flows would decline to $1.1 million because customers would wait for the enhancement. Cash flows in Years 4 and 5 would be $2.7 million each year, and $1,650,000 would be obtained in Year 6.

Microhard's marginal tax rate is 39 percent, and it uses a 20 percent discount rate. Development costs and marketing expenses are deductible when incurred.

Required:

Would the net present value of the spreadsheet program be greater with the enhancement?

INTEGRATIVE CASES

15–43 Equipment Purchase and Maximum Price Decision

Transcontinental Oil Company has some oil properties that are now at the point where further production is not worthwhile without better equipment. Even with the better equipment, the properties would be economically productive for only six more years.

If Transcontinental Oil Company decides to buy the equipment, it will enter into a contract at Time 0 to purchase the equipment. The supplier of the equipment has made an initial offer of a contract that calls for a payment of $2 million. The company's management believes it can reduce this price by negotiating with the supplier. For tax purposes, 40 percent of the cost of the equipment could be deducted at the end of Year 1. This is true whether the amount paid is $2 million or some other amount. The remaining 60 percent would be depreciated on a straight-line basis over five years (Years 2–6).

The equipment purchase contract also has a provision that calls for the manufacturer of the equipment to do additional work at the end of Year 2. The contract specifies a payment of $1 million to be made at that time for this service. All of this Year 2 payment would be deductible for tax purposes at the end of Year 2.

Production expectations, prices of crude oil per barrel, and variable costs of production are as follows:

Year	Expected Production (barrels)	Per Barrel	
		Price	Variable Costs
1 40,000		$18	$3
2 70,000		18	3
3 60,000		18	3
4 50,000		18	3
5 40,000		18	3
6 30,000		18	3

Both the prices per barrel of crude oil and variable costs are based on Time 0 prices. It is expected that the value of the properties at the end of Year 6 will be zero. The tax rate for the company is 40 percent.

Required:

a. Ignoring the effects of inflation and assuming a desired after-tax rate of return of 15 percent, should Transcontinental buy the equipment for $2 million?

b. What is the amount that Transcontinental would be willing to pay for the equipment to make the NPV of the project equal to zero?

15–44   Make-or-Buy—
Liquid Chemical Co.[2]

Liquid Chemical Company manufactures products that require careful packing. The company has a special patented container lining made from a material known as GHL, and the firm operates a department especially to maintain its containers in good condition and to make new ones as needed.

Mr. Walsh, the general manager, believed the firm might save money and get equal service by buying its containers from an outside source. He approached Packages, Inc., and asked for a quotation from it. He also asked Mr. Dyer, his chief accountant, for a statement of the cost of operating the Container Department.

Packages, Inc.'s quotation specified it would supply 3,000 new containers for $1,250,000 a year, the contract to run for a guaranteed term of five years and renewable from year to year thereafter. If the required quantity increased, the contract price would be increased proportionally. Additionally, and irrespective of whether the above contract was concluded or not, Packages, Inc., offered to perform routine maintenance on containers for $375,000 a year, on the same contract terms.

---

[2] Adapted from a case by Professor David Solomons, Wharton School, University of Pennsylvania.

Mr. Walsh compared these figures with Mr. Dyer's cost figures for one year's Container Department operations. Those figures are as follows:

Materials		$ 700,000
Labor:		
Supervisor		50,000
Workers		450,000
Department overheads:		
Manager's salary	$ 80,000	
Rent on Container Department	45,000	
Depreciation of machinery	150,000	
Maintenance of machinery	36,000	
Other expenses	157,500	
		468,500
		1,668,500
Proportion of general administrative overheads		225,000
Total cost of department for year		$1,893,500

Walsh concluded that closing the department and entering into the contract offered by Packages, Inc., was optimal. However, he gave the manager of the department, Mr. Duffy, an opportunity to question this conclusion before he acted on it. Even if his department were closed, Duffy's own position was not in jeopardy. There are no net cash consequences for the firm of transferring Duffy to another position.

Mr. Duffy thought the matter over. The next morning he spoke to Mr. Walsh and said he thought there were a number of factors to consider before his department was closed. "For instance," he said, "what will you do with the machinery? It cost $1,200,000 four years ago, but you'd be lucky if you got $200,000 for it now, even though it's good for another five years. And then there's the stock of GHL that cost us $1 million. At the rate we're using it now, it'll last us another four years. Dyer's figure of $700,000 for materials includes $200,000 for GHL. We bought it for $5,000 a ton one year ago. Today's purchase price is $6,000. But you wouldn't have more than $4,000 a ton left if you sold it because of handling expenses."

Walsh called Dyer in and put Duffy's points to him. Dyer said, "I think my figures are pretty conclusive. We're paying $85,000 a year in rent for a warehouse for other corporate purposes. If we closed Duffy's department, we'd have all the warehouse space we need without renting."

"That's a good point," said Walsh, "Moreover, I don't think we can find room for any of the workers elsewhere in the firm. I'd feel bound to give two of them a pension—$15,000 a year each for five years, say."

Duffy added, "What about this $225,000 for general administrative overheads? You surely don't expect to sack anyone in the general office if I'm closed, do you?"

"Probably not," said Dyer, "but someone has to pay for these costs. We can't ignore them when we look at an individual department, because if we do that with each department in turn, we shall finish up by convincing ourselves that directors, accountants, typists, stationery, and the like don't have to be paid for."

"Well, I think we've thrashed this out pretty fully," said Walsh, "but I've been considering the possibility of perhaps keeping on the maintenance work ourselves. What are your views on that, Duffy?"

"I don't know," said Duffy, "but it's worth looking into. We shouldn't need any machinery for that, and I could hand the supervision over to the current supervisor, who earns $50,000 a year. You'd only need about one fifth of the workers, but you could avoid the pension costs. You wouldn't save any space, so I suppose the rent would be the same. I shouldn't think the other expenses would be more than $65,000 a year."

"What about materials?" asked Walsh.

"We use 10 percent of the total on maintenance," Duffy replied.

"Well, I've told Packages, Inc., that I'd let them know my decision within a week," said Walsh. "I'll let you know what I decide to do before I write to them."

Assume the company has an after-tax cost of capital of 10 percent per year and uses an income tax rate of 40 percent for decisions like these. Depreciation for book and tax purposes is straight-line over 8 years. The machinery has a tax basis of $600,000. Any gain or loss on the sale of machinery or the GHL sales is taxed at 40 percent. Any GHL needed for Year 5 is purchased in Year 5.

Required:

a. What are the four alternatives implied in the case?

b. What action should be taken? Support your conclusion with a net present value analysis of all the mutually exclusive alternatives (assume a five-year time horizon).

c. What, if any, additional information do you think is necessary for a sound decision? Why?

SOLUTIONS TO

 Self-Study Questions

1   *a.*

MELWOOD CORPORATION

	Time 0	Year 1	Year 2	Year 3	Year 4
Investment:					
Equipment	$ (7,500)				
Software ($8,400 × 55%)ᵃ	(4,620)				
Old equipment ($100 × 55%) . . .	55				
Annual operating flows:					
($8,000 × 55%)		$4,400	$4,400	$4,400	$4,400
Tax shieldᵇ		1,125	1,125	1,125	
Disinvestment ($1,000 × 55%)					550
Cash flows	(12,065)	5,525	5,525	5,525	4,950
Discount factors at 15%		.870	.756	.658	.572
Present values	$(12,065)	$4,804	$4,178	$3,633	$2,830
Net present value	$ 3,380				

Additional computations:
ᵃ 55% = 1 − 45% tax rate, which converts before-tax cash flows to after-tax cash flows.
ᵇ Tax shield: (continued on page 589)

Year	Depreciation	Tax Shield
1	$2,500	$1,125
2	2,500	1,125
3	2,500	1,125
	$7,500	$3,375

b. With a positive net present value cash flow of $3,380, the equipment meets the hurdle rate. The cost savings justify purchase of the equipment.

2 a.

MELWOOD CORPORATION
With Inflation

	Time 0	Year 1	Year 2	Year 3	Year 4
Investment:					
Equipment	$ (7,500)				
Software ($8,400 × 55%)	(4,620)				
Old equipment ($100 × 55%)	55				
Annual operating flows		$4,400	$4,840[a]	$5,324[b]	$5,856[c]
Tax shield		1,125	1,125	1,125	
Disinvestment ($1,330 × 55%)					732
Cash flows	(12,065)	5,525	5,965	6,449	6,588
Discount factors at .265		.791	.625	.494	.391
Present values	$(12,065)	$4,368	$3,728	$3,186	$2,573
Net present value	$ 1,790				

Additional computations:
[a] $8,000 × 1.10 × .55 = $8,800 × .55 = $4,840.
[b] $8,800 × 1.10 × .55 = $9,680 × .55 = $5,324.
[c] $9,680 × 1.10 × .55 = $10,648 × .55 = $5,856.

b. With a positive net present value of $1,790, the project meets the hurdle rate. The cost savings justify purchase of the equipment.

Capital Investment Models

LEARNING OBJECTIVES

After reading this chapter, you should be able to:

1. Rank investment alternatives using the net present value index.
2. Identify how portfolio considerations and the effect of a project on reported net income could affect managers' investment decisions.
3. Analyze investment alternatives using the internal rate of return method.
4. Analyze investment alternatives using nondiscounting methods—payback and accounting rate of return.
5. Explain the importance of sensitivity analysis in capital investment decisions.
6. Analyze the difference between leasing and borrowing-to-buy (Appendix).

*T*his chapter expands our discussion of capital budgeting to cover additional methods for evaluating projects. This chapter discusses the following topics:

1. The effects of capital budget constraints, which show ways of ranking projects that all have positive net present values but cannot all be accepted.
2. How the effect of the project on company risk and accounting earnings plays a role in making investment decisions.
3. How companies evaluate investments in highly risky projects.
4. Comparison of leasing and borrow-to-buy financing alternatives (Appendix).
5. The alternatives to net present value that companies use in making investment decisions.

We now examine alternative ways that management uses to select the projects it will undertake. Let's consider a set of five investment projects with net cash flows as indicated in Illustration 16–1.

16-1

*Cash Flow Schedules
for Alternative Projects
(in thousands)*

Year	Project				
	A	B	C	D	E
0	$(425)	$(135)	$ (80)	$(170)	$ (90)
1	25	0	0	60	10
2	50	90	0	60	20
3	75	80	0	60	40
4	100	70	0	60	40
5	150	50	0	60	40
6	300	20	200	60	30
7	380	10	100	60	20
Totals	$ 655	$ 185	$220	$ 250	$110
Net present value (at 15%)[a]	$ 88	$ 63	$ 44	$ 80	$ 23

Additional computations:

[a] $88 = -\$425 + (\$25 \times 1.15^{-1}) + (\$50 \times 1.15^{-2}) + (\$75 \times 1.15^{-3}) + (\$100 \times 1.15^{-4}) + (\$150 \times 1.15^{-5}) + (\$300 \times 1.15^{-6}) + (\$380 \times 1.15^{-7})$;
$63 = -\$135 + (\$90 \times 1.15^{-2}) + (\$80 \times 1.15^{-3}) + (\$70 \times 1.15^{-4}) + (\$50 \times 1.15^{-5}) + (\$20 \times 1.15^{-6}) + (\$10 \times 1.15^{-7})$; and so forth.

EFFECT OF CONSTRAINTS ON CAPITAL INVESTMENT DECISIONS

Using a 15 percent discount rate, each project has a positive net present value. Therefore, if funds were available and if investment in one project did not exclude the possibility of investing in another project, all five projects would be chosen. However, there are often constraints on management's choice of projects.

For example, suppose management wanted to invest no more than $450,000 in these projects because of a shortage of managerial people to manage more than $450,000 of these investments. Which projects, if any, would it select? Or suppose that if Project B is selected, then Project C cannot be selected. Which project should then be chosen?

When the amount to be invested in capital investment projects is limited, management usually considers the total net present values of all selected investments rather than the net present value of each investment alone. Although all of these projects have positive net present values, they must be ranked to decide which is more desirable if there are constraints on the amount that can be invested.

Net Present Value Index Method

Net Present Value Index Ratio of the net present value of a project to the funds invested in the project.

The **net present value index** is often used to rank projects. The net present value index relates the net present value of a project to the dollars invested in it. The index is computed by dividing the net present value of a project by the initial investment. In equation form, we have:

$$\text{Net present value index} = \frac{\text{Project net present value}}{\text{Initial investment}}$$

For Project A in Illustration 16–1, the net present value index is:

$$\frac{\$88}{\$425} = \underline{\underline{.21}}$$

The net present value indexes for the other projects are:

> Project B .47 = $63 ÷ $135
> Project C .55 = $44 ÷ $80
> Project D .47 = $80 ÷ $170
> Project E .26 = $23 ÷ $90

For investment choice purposes, projects are ranked by the amount of their net present value index. The higher the index, the more desirable the investment. Thus, Project C is the most desirable according to the net present value index method.

The net present value index is useful for ranking investments of different sizes. Net present value analysis will tend to favor large projects over small projects if we rank projects in order of the size of their net present values. The net present value index is a means of correcting for this bias that favors large projects.

Partial Projects

If it is possible to fund each project in part rather than acquire the entire project, such as through partnership or joint venture arrangements, then by taking the projects in rank order, the maximum net present value could be obtained. Partial investments are common in real estate and natural resource projects. They are less common in manufacturing or other projects. Hence, the possibility of a partial investment may depend on the nature of the project.

In the example, the $450,000 is apportioned first to Project C, which costs $80,000 and has the greatest net present value index. Next selected are Project D, costing $170,000, and Project B, costing $135,000.

After making these three investments, $65,000 (that is, $450,000 − $80,000 − $135,000 − $170,000) is left for other projects. If we can fund a partial investment, we will invest the remaining $65,000 in Project E and obtain a 72.22 percent (that is, $65,000/$90,000) share in that project.

With this investment strategy, the net present value of the $450,000 investment is $203,611, which is the sum of the present values on Projects B through D plus 72.22 percent of the present value of Project E. No alternative strategy yields a higher net present value.

As a counterexample, suppose we were to invest $425,000 in Project A and use the remaining $25,000 to acquire a 31.25 percent (that is, $25,000/$80,000) investment in Project C. The net present value from this combination is:

	Percent Acquired	Net Present Value
Project A	100.00%	$ 88,000
Project C	31.25	13,750 (that is, 31.25% × $44,000)
Total net present value		$101,750

This alternative offers a lower net present value than the one obtained using the present value index ranking method.

Indivisible Investments

Of course, it may not be possible to acquire a partial interest in Project E. If the projects cannot be subdivided, their appropriate ranking becomes more complex. It may not be possible to invest the full $450,000. Any funds not invested in these projects would be expected to earn the cost of capital rate and, hence, have no positive net present value. The optimal solution to the project rank ordering could no longer be based entirely on the net present value index. Rather, we would have to consider the total present value of all selected projects, however chosen.

For the data in Illustration 16–1, the optimal ranking is to select Projects B, C, and D, which cost a total of $385,000 (total of $135,000 + $80,000 + $170,000). These three projects provide a combined net present value of $187,000 (which is the sum of $63,000 + $44,000 + $80,000). The uninvested funds of $65,000 (the net of $450,000 − $385,000) will earn a net present value of zero because they are presumed to earn the cost of capital and no more. No other combination of projects costing an aggregate of $450,000 or less will provide a greater net present value for the company when partial investment in projects is not possible. In this example, the ranking is identical to the net present value index ranking, but this will not always be the case.

Mutually Exclusive A situation where selection of one project precludes the selection of another.

In many cases, projects are **mutually exclusive.** That is, selecting one project precludes selecting another project. You can use an IBM personal computer or a MacIntosh, but you may not need both, for example.

When investment funds are limited, net present value cannot be the sole basis of choice because selection of one project reduces the capital available for investment in other projects. The opportunity cost of the mutually exclusive project is, in part, the return that could be earned on the excluded project rather than the cost of capital for the company as a whole.

For example, if Projects B and C from Illustration 16–1 are mutually exclusive and if investment funds are not limited, then the company prefers Project B. Investing in Project B results in a net present value of $63,000, whereas Project C yields a net present value of only $44,000. The critical assumption here is that the company has no better alternatives for the differential funds required for Project B. A comparison of differential investment and differential net present values shows the following:

	Project C	Project B	Differential
Initial cost	$80,000	$135,000	$55,000
Net present value	$44,000	$ 63,000	$19,000

The differential investment in Project B yields a differential net present value of $19,000. Now, if the differential $55,000 could be invested in another project (for example, a new Project F) with a net present value greater than $19,000, the company would be better off selecting both Project C and the new Project F.

For example, if Project F costs $55,000 and has a net present value of $22,000, by investing in Projects C and F the company obtains a net present value of $66,000 (which is the $44,000 from Project C plus $22,000 from Project F). This net present value is greater than the $63,000 from Project B. The increased present value is obtained with the same $135,000 investment.

Thus, when a company has limited capital and is unable to fund partial projects, the optimal set of projects is determined by considering the total net present value of all projects selected rather than the individual project net present values.

Self-Study Question

1 Assume an investment of $11,615 at Time 0 has after-tax cash inflows as follows: $5,525 per year in Years 1–3, and $4,950 in Year 4. Compute the net present value index, using a 15 percent discount rate.

The solution to this question is at the end of this chapter on page 618.

OTHER EVALUATION CONSIDERATIONS

Management considers factors other than net present values when making capital investment decisions. We note differences in the *riskiness* of projects, how well the project fits with other company projects, and the impact of projects on accounting income because these factors are frequently encountered by accountants.

Differences in Project Risk

There is often a correlation between the amount of risk a project entails and the return that can be earned from that project. If management uses net present values without adjustment for risk, high-risk projects with high expected returns may be the most commonly accepted. This outcome may be contrary to management intentions. Indeed, if management continues to accept riskier projects, overall company risk may increase. Its cost of capital will then increase to compensate lenders and investors for the greater risks. This will result in an increased hurdle rate.

Risk Premium Additional interest or other compensation required for risks in investments.

To avoid this problem, management may require a higher rate of return from riskier projects. This **risk premium** is determined by analyzing the characteristics of a specific project and relating them to the company's other assets.[1] Management must be aware of the trade-offs between risk and return and select projects that meet predetermined objectives for overall company risk.

Portfolio Considerations

Investing in capital assets requires consideration of how they will fit with a company's existing *portfolio of assets*. The ways in which a specific investment can enhance a company's overall asset structure is another aspect of the capital investment decision. For example, in recent years companies that are significant energy users have acquired energy companies to assure themselves of a reliable energy supply. Brokerage firms have been merged with other kinds of financial institutions, such as credit card companies and retail stores, to expand the services they can offer to their customers. These considerations extend beyond the accountant's domain, but they are significant for evaluating whether capital investment projects meet management's objectives, or fail to meet them, as discussed in the real world application on page 595.

Effects on Income

Management considers accounting measures of income to evaluate organization performance and to measure compliance with contracts. For example, restrictive covenants in a loan agreement may require that a company maintain certain levels of working capital and retained earnings. Manage-

---

[1] See, for example, S. Ross, R. Westerfield, and J. Jaffee, *Corporate Finance* (Homewood, Ill.: Richard D. Irwin, 1993).

ment will rarely select projects that have such an adverse effect on the working capital or other accounting numbers if, by so doing, the company no longer complies with contractual arrangements.

Management may also prefer to see growth in the income reported in the financial statements. In such cases, they will prefer projects that provide long-term growth over projects that show declining or level income trends.

For example, in Illustration 16–1, Project C has no net cash inflows for the first five years of its life. (Perhaps Project C is a new, genetically altered product that will take five years to develop.) When depreciation is deducted from this zero cash flow to obtain net income for financial reporting, Project C shows net losses for its first five years. Management may decide to exclude Project C from consideration on this basis alone.

To extend the Project C example, a schedule of accounting income from each project is shown in Illustration 16–2. These accounting income data would be developed from sources other than those discussed in this chapter. As expected, Project C shows losses for the first five years.

Management may decide to select Project C in spite of the accounting losses because it yields a positive net present value, as shown in Illustration 16–1. But management would be unlikely to place all of its capital invest-

ILLUSTRATION

16–2

Accounting Income from Projects A through E (in thousands)

Year	A	B	C	D	E
1	($65)	($10)	($10)	$ 20	$ 0
2	5	80	(10)	30	10
3	45	70	(10)	40	10
4	70	40	(10)	50	20
5	150	20	(10)	50	30
6	330	10	220	40	30
7	120	(25)	50	20	10
Totals	$655	$185	$220	$250	$110

ment funds in ventures like Project C unless the company had other sources of income, was particularly adventurous, or management had incentives to maximize long-run payoffs instead of short-run accounting income.

If the company had loan agreements or other contracts that required it to maintain certain net income levels, the early accounting losses from Project C could cause the company to default on its loan agreements and thus preclude it from staying in business long enough to earn the later rewards from Project C.

Externally required accounting income considerations for project investments may be considered a constraint by management on the company's investment program. In some cases, managers require that projects have both a positive net present value and increase earnings by a specified amount.

ALTERNATE CAPITAL INVESTMENT MODELS

Due to the complexity of the capital investment decision, one model of analysis is sometimes considered insufficient for evaluating investment proposals.[2] The most common models for assessing capital investment projects are:

1. Net present value.
2. Internal rate of return.
3. Payback.
4. Accounting rate of return.

We will discuss each of these alternative models in turn. Each model has its own advantages and may be encountered in certain decision settings. In a complex capital investment decision, it is likely that several alternative measures will be employed by management.

Net Present Value

As noted in the previous chapter, a project's net present value is computed by discounting its future cash flows to their equivalent value today. A discount rate must be selected for this computation. Quite often companies adjust the rate to reflect inflationary effects. As noted in Chapter 15, the cash flows should also be adjusted for the effects of price-level changes. Some companies vary the rate to account for the differences in risk characteristics of different projects. Other companies use a rate that is determined as management's judgment of what a capital investment should earn. Whatever method is used for determining the discount rate, the end result is directed toward the objective of making the net present value an estimate of the economic value of the asset to the company.

Since the details of net present value calculations have been presented in Chapter 15, we will not repeat them here. Other alternative methods that we will discuss in more detail include internal rate of return, payback, and accounting rate of return.

---

[2] See T. Klammer, B. Koch, and N. Wilner, "Capital Budgeting Practices—A survey of Corporate Use," *Journal of Management Accounting Research* 3, pp. 113–30, for a survey of practices.

Internal Rate of Return

Internal Rate of Return (IRR)
The interest rate that equates the present value of inflows and outflows from an investment project.

The **internal rate of return** or **IRR** is the rate of interest that a project is expected to earn over its life. If the internal rate of return (also known as the *time-adjusted rate of return*) were used as the cost of capital for discounting project cash flows, the net present value of the project would be exactly equal to zero. Thus, the IRR is that rate that makes the present value of project cash outflows equal to the present value of project cash inflows. This contrasts with the net present value method, which employs a predetermined discount rate.

For example, consider Project A from Illustration 16–1. We know that the IRR from that project is in excess of 15 percent because the net present value is greater than zero. The IRR is the discount rate that equates the present value of Project A's cash inflows and outflows.

To compute the IRR, it is usually necessary to use a calculator, a computer program, or an iterative trial-and-error technique. For Project A, a computer program gives an IRR of 19.4 percent.[3]

Internal Rate of Return with Constant Cash Flows

When the cash flows from a project are constant, it is possible to use the tables for present value of an annuity (Appendix B to Chapter 15) to find the approximate rate of return. Dividing the required investment by the annual net cash flow gives the factor for a project with a life equal to that of the project and an interest rate equal to the internal rate of return. All we need do is look across the row for number of periods until we come to the factor closest to our computed factor. The interest rate for the column of the table related to that factor is the approximate internal rate of return.

For Project D in Illustration 16–1, the factor is:

$$\frac{\text{Required investment}}{\text{Annual net cash flow}} = \frac{\$170,000}{\$60,000} = \underline{\underline{2.83}}$$

which, for a seven-year project, is closest to the factor 2.802 in the column headed by an interest rate of 30 percent. Therefore, we estimate the IRR on this project to be 30 percent.

---

[3] The IRR can also be found by trial and error. For Project A, we know the rate is greater than 15 percent. Is it 20 percent? To find out, we discount the Project A cash flows using a 20 percent discount rate. This results in a net present value of $(11,014). Since this value is negative, the internal rate of return must be less than 20 percent. We then interpolate between the two interest rates based on the spread between the net present values as follows:

$$\text{Lower rate} + \left[\frac{\begin{array}{c}\text{Present value} \\ \text{at lower} \\ \text{rate}\end{array} - \begin{array}{c}\text{Actual} \\ \text{present} \\ \text{value}\end{array}}{\begin{array}{c}\text{Present value} \\ \text{at lower} \\ \text{rate}\end{array} - \begin{array}{c}\text{Present value} \\ \text{at higher} \\ \text{rate}\end{array}}\right] \times \left(\begin{array}{c}\text{Higher} \\ \text{rate}\end{array} - \begin{array}{c}\text{Lower} \\ \text{rate}\end{array}\right)$$

$$= 15\% + \left[\frac{\$88,166 - \$0}{\$88,166 - (\$11,014)}\right] \times (20\% - 15\%) = 15\% + \left[\frac{\$88,166}{\$99,180} \times 5\%\right]$$

$$= 15\% + 4.4\% = 19.4\%$$

Some Questions about IRR

While the internal rate of return is widely used for project evaluations, it is sometimes considered inferior to net present value. Its primary disadvantage is its built-in assumption that net cash inflows are reinvested at the project's internal rate of return. By contrast, the net present value method assumes that the net cash inflows are invested at the cost of capital rate. If funds will be reinvested at the cost of capital, the IRR method will make a project whose rate of return is greater than the cost of capital appear more attractive than a similar project using the net present value approach.

In some cases, the differences between the assumptions in the IRR method and the present value method result in differences in the rankings of projects using each method. The present value index ranking may differ from the IRR ranking. The choice that management makes in such a situation will depend on management's objectives and evaluation of the assumptions underlying the two methods.

Self-Study Question

2 Refer to the information in self-study question 1. Compute the project's internal rate of return to the nearest percent.

The solution to this question is at the end of this chapter on page 618.

Payback

Payback One method of assessing capital investment projects using the rationale that there is a positive relationship between the speed of payback and the rate of return.

Payback Period The time required to recoup an investment from the cash flows from the project.

It is generally assumed that the longer a company's funds are tied up in an investment, the greater the risk to the company. In addition, there is a relationship between the speed of **payback** and the rate of return on a typical investment. For these reasons, companies often consider the length of time it takes to obtain a return of the investment in the project as a measure for project evaluation. The **payback period** is the number of years that will elapse before the original investment is repaid. As with most other capital investment models, cash flow data are used for this computation. With level annual cash flows, the payback formula is:

$$\frac{\text{Payback}}{\text{period}} = \frac{\text{Investment}}{\text{Annual cash flow}}$$

With different annual cash flows, the analysis is more complex. For example, using the data from Illustration 16–1, the payback period for Project B appears in Illustration 16–3. A running balance of the net cash flow for the investment is maintained until the balance turns positive. For this

---

ILLUSTRATION

Payback Method, Project B

Year	Net Cash Flow	Cash Flow Balance
0	$(135,000)	$(135,000)
1	–0–	(135,000)
2	90,000	(45,000)
3	80,000	35,000

project, the balance turns positive during the third year. The fraction of that third year that was required before the investment achieved payback is usually estimated by dividing the absolute value of the last negative balance in the balance column by the total cash flow in the payback year:

$$\frac{\text{Balance, end of Year 2}}{\text{Net cash flow, Year 3}}$$

or

$$\frac{\$45,000}{\$80,000} = \underline{\underline{.5625}}$$

Project payback would then be stated as 2.5625 years, or approximately 2 years and 7 months. The fraction-of-a-year computation is based on the assumption that the cash flows are received evenly throughout the payback year.

Shortcut Payback Computation

If a project has level cash flows throughout its life, the payback computation is simplified. The payback period may be computed in this case by dividing the project cost by the annual cash flow. For Project D from Illustration 16–1, the payback period is:

$$\frac{\$170,000}{\$60,000} = \underline{\underline{2.83 \text{ years}}}$$

Payback Reciprocal

Payback Reciprocal One divided by the payback period in years.

When a project's life is at least twice the payback period and the annual cash flows are approximately equal, the **payback reciprocal** may be used to estimate the rate of return for the project.

Thus, for Project D from Illustration 16–1, the payback reciprocal is:

$$\frac{1}{2.83} = \underline{\underline{.35}}, \text{ or } \underline{\underline{35\%}}$$

Programmed functions in calculators and computers are generally used to compute the rate of return directly. Therefore, use of the payback reciprocal approach is simply a rough, first-cut approximation.

Discounted Payback

Discounted Payback Method A method of assessing investment projects that recognizes the time value of money in a payback context.

A method that recognizes the time value of money in a payback context is the **discounted payback method.** This method is used to compute the payback in terms of discounted cash flows received in the future. That is, the periodic cash flows are discounted using an appropriate cost of capital rate. The payback period is computed using the discounted cash flow values rather than the actual cash flows. If the discounted payback method was used for Project D from Illustration 16–1 and a 15 percent cost of capital rate was employed, the discounted payback period would be as shown in Illustration 16–4, which is a discounted payback period of four years.

Evaluation of Payback Methods

Payback approaches are generally easy to compute and, to the extent that long payback implies high risk, give some measure of a company's risk exposure from a project. However, the payback period tells nothing about

Year	Cash Flow	Discount Factor[a]	Discounted Cash Flow	Balance
0	$(170)	—	$(170)	$(170)
1	60	.870	52	(118)
2	60	.756	45	(73)
3	60	.658	39	(34)
4	60	.572	34	–0–

[a] Discount factors rounded to three places.

profitability. Thus, a project that returns the entire investment in Year 1 but results in no further cash flows appears better using the payback criterion than does a project that returns 50 percent of the investment cost per year for three years. With an investment of $100,000 and a cost of capital of 15 percent, a comparison of the net present value and payback period for these two projects is shown in Illustration 16–5. Clearly, Project 2 is the better choice when discounting all cash flows. The payback method gives a misleading signal about the relative desirability of the two projects.

Thus, when using payback, it is important to consider what will happen after the payback period is over. Managers often use payback as a screening device because it is easy (and therefore inexpensive) to use. The choice of the investment analysis model should be based on its costs and benefits compared to the alternative models. If decisions are sensitive to the decision model, then more care and expense is warranted than when decisions are the same regardless of the model used.

Accounting Rate of Return

Accounting Rate of Return A measure of project returns using accounting concepts of income.

The **accounting rate of return** measures a project's rate of return in terms of accounting income, however defined by management, rather than in terms of cash flows. It relates the average accounting income from a project to the investment in the project and is computed using the following equation:

$$\text{Accounting rate of return} = \frac{\text{Average accounting income}}{\text{Investment}}$$

The accounting income for this computation is approximately equal to the sum of the average incremental cash flow from the project less the average book depreciation. Investment may be based either on the *initial investment* or on the *average investment*. Average investment is usually assumed to equal one half of the sum of initial investment and salvage value. Incremental cash flows are usually approximated using revenues minus costs other than depreciation.

For example, consider Project D in Illustration 16–1. The project has an annual cash flow of $60,000 and an initial cost of $170,000 and no salvage value. Assume that $154,000 of the investment cost is depreciable using a straight-line rate over the seven-year project life. This basis was determined by management's internal accounting procedures. Book depreciation is $22,000 per year (computed as $154,000/7 years). Average investment in the

ILLUSTRATION

16–5

Comparison of Net Present Value and Payback Periods

	Project 1	Project 2
Investment cost	$100,000	$100,000
Annual cash flows:		
Year 1	$100,000	$ 50,000
Year 2	–0–	50,000
Year 3	–0–	50,000
Years 4 and after	–0–	–0–
Payback	1 year[a]	2 years[b]
Net present value at 15%	$ (13,043)[c]	$ 14,161[d]

Additional computations:
[a] One year = $100,000 investment/$100,000 annual cash flow.
[b] Two years = $100,000 investment/$50,000 annual cash flow.
[c] $-13,043 = $-100,000 + $100,000 \times 1.15^{-1}$.
[d] $14,161 = $-100,000 + $50,000 \times 1.15^{-1} + $50,000 \times 1.15^{-2} + $50,000 \times 1.15^{-3}$.

project is $85,000, which is one half of the original investment cost of $170,000.

$$R = \frac{C - D}{\frac{1}{2} \times I}$$

or

$$\frac{\$60,000 - \$22,000}{\$85,000} = \underline{\underline{44.7\%}}$$

where

> C = Average annual cash flow from the investment
> D = Accounting depreciation
> I = Initial investment

The accounting rate of return may also be computed using the initial investment rather than the average investment. This estimate of the accounting rate of return is:

$$R = \frac{C - D}{I}$$

or

$$\frac{\$60,000 - \$22,000}{\$170,000} = \underline{\underline{22.4\%}}$$

The accounting rate of return averages the cash flows to be received from a project and averages the depreciation. The accounting rate of return also ignores the time value of money. Thus, the accounting rate of return method is rarely suitable for investment decision-making purposes.

Sometimes management will constrain the investment decision to include only those projects that exceed a particular accounting rate of return in order to maintain particular financial accounting ratios. However, such managers will not be maximizing the long-run wealth of the organization.

REAL WORLD APPLICATION

Capital Budgeting Methods

In the 1950s, the payback method was the most popular method for capital investment analysis, according to surveys of practice. Since then, discounted cash flow techniques (net present value and internal rate of return) have been used by more and more companies.

Most companies appear to use more than one method of capital investment analyses. A recent survey of practice indicated that "Over 86 percent of the respondents use IRR or NPV or both, but only 16 percent use one or both without also using [payback] or [accounting rate of return]."* Another survey found that more than 80 percent of the

companies surveyed used net present value or internal rate of return methods for decisions about expanding operations.†

Payback and accounting rate of return are apparently used as supplements to discounted cash flow methods in most companies because of their familiarity and ease of use.

* L. Schall, G. Sundem, and W. Geijabeck, Jr., "Survey and Analysis of Capital Budgeting Methods," *The Journal of Finance* 33, no. 1, p. 282.

† T. Klammer, B. Koch, and N. Wilner, "Capital Budgeting Practices—A Survey of Corporate Use," *Journal of Management Accounting Research* 3, p. 118.

Comments on Alternative Methods

Capital investment decisions are among the most important decisions made by managers because they are long-run commitments. Consequently, managers typically use as much information as possible in making decisions. Although the net present value method discussed in Chapter 15 is the most theoretically defensible model, managers often use the alternative models discussed in this chapter as ways of getting a different picture of the project, as indicated in the real world application "Capital Budgeting Methods." If the information has already been collected to do a net present value analysis, then the additional cost to the company of using these additional models is typically low.

A summary of the four main models discussed in Chapters 15 and 16 is presented in the chapter summary.

Self-Study Question

3 Refer to the information in self-study question 1. Compute:

    a. The payback period.

    b. Discounted payback, using the 15 percent cost of capital rate.

The solution to this question is at the end of this chapter on page 620.

INVESTMENTS IN HIGH TECHNOLOGY AND HIGHLY UNCERTAIN PROJECTS

Sensitivity Analysis The study of the effect of changes in assumptions on the results of a decison model.

To be competitive, companies must continue to invest in new technology or projects with highly uncertain payoffs. Because estimation of cash flows from these projects is difficult, some have suggested that companies make these decisions without considering the usual capital investment criteria such as NPV. In practice, though, companies do consider potential cash flows and net present values from such projects. **Sensitivity analysis** is usually performed to examine the effect of the widely different possible outcomes from the investment. Management can then consider not just one net present value but a range of present values when making an investment

ILLUSTRATION

16–6

*Alternative NPV and
IRR Scenarios
(in thousands)*

Year	Cash Flows		
	Best Case	Expected	Worst Case
0	($80)	($80)	($80)
1	0	0	0
2	0	0	0
3	0	0	0
4	0	0	0
5	0	0	0
6	400	200	50
7	300	100	25
Net present value @ 15%	$206	$ 44	($49)
Internal rate of return	40%	23%	(1%)

decision. Management then decides whether to invest in a given project based on a combination of the expected net present value and other performance measures as well as the range of the performance measures and the impact of the project on the future of the company.[4]

For example, Project C from Illustration 16–1 offers high cash returns late in the life of the investment. It is quite difficult to predict cash flows very far in the future. Management might, therefore, analyze the alternative possibilities for this project to obtain some idea of the risk of the investment. Let's assume that there is a chance that the project will only return 25 percent of the estimated cash flows in Years 6 and 7, but there is also the possibility that the cash flows could be $400,000 in Year 6 and $300,000 in Year 7. These are the "worst case" and "best case" scenarios. The cash flow schedule in Illustration 16–1 is the "expected" outcome. Net present value and IRR analyses would be conducted under all three outcomes. A summary of the alternatives in Illustration 16–6 could be presented to management for its evaluation.

SUMMARY

When capital investment opportunities with positive net present values exceed capital budget constraints, the net present value index may be used

[4] See R. Kaplan, "Must CIM Be Justified on Faith Alone," *Harvard Business Review*, March–April 1986, pp. 87–95.

REAL WORLD APPLICATION

*NPV Analysis in Oil Exploration**

When exploring for oil on the North Slope of Alaska, oil companies such as Exxon and British Petroleum invested $12 million in research on the oil field and in exploratory drilling. At that time, it was uncertain whether there was any recoverable oil in the ground. Moreover, if there was oil in the ground, it was unknown whether or how it could be transported to consuming markets. Many what-if studies were conducted to analyze the combinations of possible discovery sizes, methods of transportation, and related costs as well as future price scenarios.

Cash outlays occurred over a 10-year period prior to the start of production from the field. How-ever, the major portion of the cash outlays did not occur until most of the questions concerning volumes of crude oil and costs of the transportation system had been settled. Studies of the net present value of the project were conducted at all stages of the project life. Clearly, at the start, this was a project with highly uncertain costs and returns. Nonetheless, cash flow and net present value analyses were used to monitor the investment decision through all stages of the project.

* Based on the authors' research.

---

to rank the projects. This index is calculated as follows:

$$\text{Net present value index} = \frac{\text{Project net present value}}{\text{Investment in the project}}$$

When partial investments are not possible, a ranking by net present value index may not indicate the optimal set of projects because there may be leftover, uninvested funds that have a positive net present value. Consequently, various combinations of projects must be evaluated to find the set of projects with the highest net present value.

Projects with high returns are not necessarily better than those with lower returns. If a high-return project entails greater risk, management will often use a higher discount rate. In addition, when investing in capital assets, management must consider how the new investment will fit with the company's portfolio of assets and its overall strategy. Sometimes projects with lower returns are accepted because they are more compatible with the company's long-range plans.

Management may use more than one evaluation method for assessing capital investment projects. Several alternatives are summarized in Illustration 16–7. Internal rate of return expresses a project's return as an interest rate rather than as a net present value. Payback indicates how long a project will take to earn back its initial investment. Discounted payback indicates how long it will take to earn back the initial investment after discounting the cash flows. Accounting rate of return shows a project's effect on accounting income. Each of these alternatives to net present value is frequently criticized as a primary means of investment analysis. But given the importance of capital investment decisions to most organizations, use of more than one method may provide additional useful insights.

When investments are made in a high-risk project, companies will often prepare a sensitivity analysis using several alternate cash flow scenarios.

ILLUSTRATION

16–7

Summary of Alternative Capital Investment Models

Net Present Value: Find the net present value of a project using the following formula:

$$NPV = \sum_{n=0}^{N} C_n \times (1 + d)^{-n}$$

See Chapter 15 for details.

Internal Rate of Return: Find the project rate of return that makes the project net present value equal to zero. This rate is compared to a hurdle rate. If it exceeds the hurdle rate, then the project is acceptable.

Payback: Find the number of years it will take for the project to "pay back" the investment. The shorter the payback period, the better, according to this decision criterion. This method ignores the time value of money and gives no explicit weight to cash flows after the payback period.

Accounting Rate of Return: The accounting rate of return for a project is computed as follows:

$$\frac{\text{Average accounting income}}{\text{Investment}}$$

This method ignores the time value of money.

TERMS AND CONCEPTS

The following terms and concepts should be familiar to you after reading this chapter.

Accounting Rate of Return, *600*

Discounted Payback Method, *599*

Internal Rate of Return (IRR), *597*

Lease versus Borrow-to-Buy (Appendix), *605*

Mutually Exclusive, *593*

Net Present Value Index, *591*

Payback, *598*

Payback Period, *599*

Payback Reciprocal, *599*

Risk Premium, *593*

Sensitivity Analysis, *602*

APPENDIX

Lease versus Borrow-to-Buy

Lease versus Borrow-to-Buy Choice of financing the investment in an asset through either a lease or a purchase using borrowed funds.

Once a project has been evaluated and found to have met all of the criteria for investment, a decision must be made about how to finance it. There are numerous variations in project financing that are designed to meet the specific needs of both borrower and lender. As has been well established in the finance literature, investment and financing decisons are normally separated. Some special financing opportunities may be linked to a specific capital investment, however. One such example is leasing instead of borrowing and buying. This appendix provides a general guideline for evaluating **lease versus borrow-to-buy,** a common financing alternative.

It is important to recognize that the type of leases we are discussing here are forms of debt financing. The literature in finance considers these leases to be perfect substitutes for debt. Consequently, decisions about leasing assets should not be made by simply computing the net present value of lease payments and the other cash flows associated with the investment. Instead, the analysis has two steps:

Step 1. First, determine whether the investment should be made if the asset was purchased. This analysis would be done like the other investment analyses discussed in Chapters 15 and 16. If the decision is made to reject the investment, then there is no reason to go on to step 2. (There is no reason to analyze financing alternatives if the investment is not going to be made.)

Step 2. Second, determine the best financing alternative. If the company has an opportunity to lease the asset, then an alternative is to borrow the money to buy the asset. This comparison is made by finding the lowest-cost financing alternative. The following example demonstrates how this comparison can be made.

Uni-Queue Company has decided to acquire an asset. They can either lease the asset for $15,000 per year during its five-year life or pay $70,000 for the asset and take out a loan for that amount. The loan is repayable at the rate of $14,000 per year on principal plus interest at 20 percent on each year's beginning loan balance. Both the lease and the loan are linked to the asset acquisition.

Under the proposed lease agreement, Uni-Queue is simply a lessee. They would not obtain the benefits of the tax shield. At the end of the five years, the asset is returned to the lessor. On the other hand, if Uni-Queue Company purchases the asset, they obtain the benefit of the tax shield.

At the end of five years, management estimates that they could sell the asset for $15,000. All income taxes are at the company's ordinary tax rate of 40 percent. We assume the risk to the company is the same whether the asset is acquired through lease or borrow-to-buy. Should management lease or borrow-to-buy?

To analyze this problem, we prepare a schedule of the differential cash flows for each financing alternative. We assume the periodic operating cash inflows generated by the project are the same whether the asset is leased or acquired through buying and borrowing. Hence, we ignore the operating cash inflows under both alternatives. The lease requires an annual outlay of $15,000, which is deductible for tax purposes, thus resulting in an after-tax cash outflow of $9,000 (computed as the $15,000 times 60 percent).

The present value of this outflow is computed by taking the present value of the $9,000 per year for five years, using the *after-tax interest rate that the firm would pay on an equivalent loan,* which would (in this case) be 12 percent [20 percent before tax $\times$ (1 − .40)]. (Note that this is *not* the discount rate used for investment decisions.)

The present value of the lease payments may be found by using the shortcut equation for a series of equal payments:

$$C \times \frac{1 - (1 + d)^{-n}}{d}$$

or by using the present value of an annuity table in Appendix B at the end of Chapter 15. The computation is:

$$\$(9,000) \times \frac{1 - (1.12)^{-5}}{.12} = \$(9,000) \times 3.605 = \underline{\underline{\$(32,443)}}$$

This present value of leasing cash outlays is compared to the present value from borrowing to buy the asset.

The present value from buying the asset and borrowing the purchase amount requires consideration of four types of differential cash flows:

1. Investment flows.
2. Periodic cash flows (only those related to financing in this case).
3. Tax shield.
4. Disinvestment flows.

These are the same four categories used to analyze cash flows when deciding whether to acquire the asset in the first place. The analysis for the data in this example is provided in Illustration 16–8. The investment flows include the $70,000 outlay for the asset less the $70,000 in proceeds from the bank loan for a net of zero. Depreciation for tax purposes is assumed to be as follows: Year 1, $15,000; Year 2, $25,000; Years 3–5, $10,000 per year.

The periodic cash flows represent the repayment of principal at $14,000 per year, based on $70,000 repaid equally over the five years. Interest is computed on the loan balance. Since interest is deductible for tax purposes, the amount shown for interest is equal to 60 percent (which is one minus the 40 percent tax rate) of the gross interest payment.

For Year 1, then, the net interest payment is:

$$\$70,000 \times 20\% \times 60\% = \underline{\underline{\$8,400}}$$

For Year 2:

$$\$(70,000 - \$14,000) \times 20\% \times 60\% = \underline{\underline{\$6,720}}$$

And so forth for Years 3 through 5. These calculations are detailed in Illustration 16–8.

The disinvestment flows include the $15,000 salvage value. The asset will be fully depreciated at the time of salvage, so there is a taxable gain on the full amount of the disposal proceeds. The tax on the gain is equal to the tax rate times the salvage value. This comes to $6,000, which is $15,000 times 40 percent.

The cash flows in each year are summed, and the net present value is computed by discounting the flows back to the present using the 12 percent after-tax borrowing rate. The result is a present value for borrowing of ($43,906). This amount indicates that the present value cost of borrowing is greater than the ($32,443) present value cost from leasing, so the preferred alternative is to lease. Of course, the net present value of the entire project must be greater than or equal to zero or no investment will take place. In this situation, we first assumed that the project has a positive net present value and then analyzed the financing alternatives. This two-step process is the one managers usually follow when financing and investment decisions are independent.

Leasing and financing arrangements arise because of differences in the financial, risk, and tax situations of companies and investors. Leases and loan agreements therefore differ. This example should be viewed as a gen-

ILLUSTRATION   *Cash Flow Analysis for Borrowing-to-Buy Schedule of After-Tax Cash Flows*

	Year					
	0	1	2	3	4	5
Investment flows:						
Asset purchase	$(70,000)					
Loan	70,000					
Depreciation tax shield[a]		$ 6,000	$ 10,000	$ 4,000	$ 4,000	$ 4,000
Periodic flows:						
Loan repayment		(14,000)	(14,000)	(14,000)	(14,000)	(14,000)
Interest after tax[b]		(8,400)	(6,720)	(5,040)	(3,360)	(1,680)
Disinvestment flows:						
Salvage value						15,000
Tax on gain or loss on disposal[c]						(6,000)
Total cash flows	–0–	$(16,400)	$(10,720)	$(15,040)	$(13,360)	$(2,680)
Present value factor (12%)		.893	.797	.712	.636	.567
Present values[d]	$ –0–	$(14,643)	$(8,546)	$(10,705)	$(8,491)	$(1,521)
Net present value	$(43,906)					

Additional computations:

[a] Depreciation schedule:

Year	Depreciation	Tax Effect (40 percent)
1	$15,000	$ 6,000
2	25,000	10,000
3	10,000	4,000
4	10,000	4,000
5	10,000	4,000
Totals ...	$70,000	$28,000

[b] Interest calculation:

Year	Loan Balance	Interest at 20 Percent	Interest after Tax (1 − .40)
1	$70,000	$14,000	$8,400
2	56,000	11,200	6,720
3	42,000	8,400	5,040
4	28,000	5,600	3,360
5	14,000	2,800	1,680

[c] Salvage value $15,000
Tax rate for this gain 40%
Tax on gain .... $ 6,000

[d] Cash flow times present value factor does not equal present value because the present value factors shown here have been rounded to three places, while the present value is computed using the formula $(1 + d)^{-n}$, $n = 1, \ldots 5$.

eral guide to the approach that can be taken to evaluate alternatives in terms of the impact on cash flows and, hence, on present values.

QUESTIONS

16–1 If there are no budget constraints, why would we invest in all projects with a positive net present value?

16–2 In the presence of budget constraints, what method is suggested for evaluating capital investment projects? Why?

16–3 When there are both budget constraints and investment indivisibilities, what method should be used for capital investment analysis? Why?

16–4 What is the appropriate method for choosing from among mutually exclusive projects? Why is the method appropriate?

16–5 There is a danger in relying entirely on net present value evaluations for projects. What is the danger?

16–6 Management must consider a number of factors in making a capital investment decision. What are some of the factors in addition to net present value?

16–7 Management often has a choice of financing alternatives for certain projects. How should the financing decision be handled?

16–8 What is the benefit of the use of payback for evaluating capital investment projects?

16–9 How can the payback method be improved to account for the effect of the time value of money?

16–10 Why would management use capital investment evaluation methods that are often criticized as inferior to net present value?

16–11 Some authors suggest that when investment outcomes are highly uncertain, more extensive capital investment analysis techniques are appropriate. Comment on this suggestion.

16–12 The real world application in this chapter about the Alaska North Slope oil field ("NPV Analysis in Oil Exploration") described a project with a long time between initial investment and project returns. What are some of the factors that may have made the use of capital investment techniques helpful for analyzing this project?

EXERCISES

16–13 Net Present Value Index
(L.O.1)

A company with limited investment funds and a cost of capital of 20 percent must choose from among three competing capital investment projects with the following cash flow patterns (in thousands):

	Project		
Year	A	B	C
0	$(200)	$(350)	$(300)
1	50	80	70
2	90	190	125
3	100	250	170
4	100	120	200

The company has $600,000 available for investment.

Required:

How can the company optimally invest its $600,000 among the three projects, assuming no other constraints on investment and partial investments in projects can be made?

16–14 Effect of Constraints
(L.O.1)

Use the same data as in exercise 16–13 and assume that the projects are indivisible (that is, you must buy 100 percent of any project or else none of that project). Determine the optimal investment policy for the company.

16–15 Effect of Constraints
. (L.O.1)

Use the same data as in exercise 16–13 and assume that Projects A and B are mutually exclusive and that the projects are indivisible. Determine the optimal investment policy for the company.

16–16 Net Present Value Index
(L.O.1)

Morris and Associates, a medical partnership, has $1.5 million available for investment in venture capital projects. The cost of capital is 15 percent. As a partnership, Morris pays no income taxes. The following opportunity ventures are available. Each has an estimated seven-year life.

A. Software Designs, an innovative software development company, has requested $900,000. The firm estimates no returns until Year 5. Years 5 through 7 should return $1 million per year.

B. Sunset Mall, a new shopping center development, will cost Morris $550,000. The project will return $65,000 per year for each of Years 1–3 and $250,000 per year in Years 4–7.

C. Nutri-care, a health food chain, requires an investment of $650,000 to open a new store. This project will return $260,000 in each of Years 1–3 and $60,000 per year in Years 4–7.

D. Marvin Gardens, a housing development, would require $850,000 and return $250,000 in each of Years 1–7.

Required:

Complete the following schedule (dollars in thousands) to:

a. Calculate the net present value index for each investment.

			Year		
Project	0	1	. . .	6	7
A: Amounts	($)	$		$	$
PV factor					
Present values	($ ___)	$___		$___	$___
Net present value	___				
Net present value index	% = $	/$			
.					
.					
.					
D: Amounts	($)	$		$	$
PV factor					
Present values	($ ___)	$___		$___	$___
Net present value	$___				
Net present value index	% = $	/$			

b. Determine how the company can optimally invest its venture capital funds. Assume no other constraints on investment.

16–17 Effect of Constraints
(L.O.1)

Refer to the data in exercise 16–16. Assume that the projects available to Morris and Associates are indivisible. Determine the optimal investment policy for the partnership. Show supporting calculations.

16–18 Effect of Constraints
(L.O.1)

If Morris and Associates (exercise 16–16) can invest in either Software Designs or the Sunset Mall, but not both, and the projects are indivisible, what is the optimal investment policy for the company? Show supporting calculations.

16–19 Alternative Project Evaluation Measures
(L.O.3., L.O.4)

Farm Fresh Corporation is considering whether to invest in a pasteurizing machine that costs $300,000 and will return $80,000 after tax for each of the next seven years. After that the asset will have no value.

Required:

Compute the following items for this project:

a. Payback.

b. Internal rate of return (using a calculator, computer, or trial and error and interpolation).

c. Internal rate of return if the life is 12 years rather than 7.

16–20 Alternative Project Evaluation Measures
(L.O.3, L.O.4)

Diamondback, Inc., is a manufacturer of western hats. The company has an opportunity to expand production by purchasing a new automatic hat bander. The bander costs $200,000 and is fully depreciable for tax purposes using the straight-line method over a four-year life. The machine will have no salvage value. No additional working capital is required. The bander will result in cost savings of $90,000 per year. The company has a tax rate of 40 percent.

Required:

Compute the following investment evaluation measures for the bander:

a. Payback period.

b. Internal rate of return (using a calculator, computer, or trial and error and interpolation).

c. Accounting rate of return on the initial investment.

16–21 Alternative Project Evaluation Measures, No Discounting
(L.O.4)

Quintana Company plans to replace an old piece of equipment that has no book value for tax purposes and no salvage value. The replacement equipment will provide annual cash savings of $8,000 before income taxes. The equipment costs $20,000 and will have no salvage value at the end of its five-year life. Quintana uses straight-line depreciation for both book and tax purposes. The company incurs a 40 percent marginal tax rate, and its after-tax cost of capital is 14 percent.

Required:

Compute the following performance measures for Quintana's proposed investment:

a. Payback period.

b. Payback reciprocal.

c. Accounting rate of return on average investment.

(CMA adapted)

16–22 Alternative Project Evaluation Measures with Discounting
(L.O.1, L.O.3, L.O.4)

Using the data for Quintana Company in exercise 16–21, compute the following investment performance measures:

a. Net present value.

b. Present value index.

c. Internal rate of return (using a calculator, computer, or trial and error and interpolation).

d. Discounted payback.

16–23 Alternative Project Evaluation Measures
(L.O.3, L.O.4)

Hazel Ridge Company is considering a capital investment proposal with an initial cost of $72,000. The asset is depreciated over a six-year period on the straight-line basis for both book and tax purposes. No salvage value is expected at the end of the asset life. The before-tax cash inflow for the project is $27,000 per year. The income tax rate is 40 percent, and the company's after-tax cost of capital is 15 percent.

Required: Compute the following:

a. Accounting rate of return on average investment.

b. Payback reciprocal.

c. Internal rate of return (using a calculator, computer, or trial and error and interpolation).

16–24   Alternative Project Evaluation Methods (L.O.3, L.O.4)

Choose the best answer for each of the following separate cases. All analyses are before tax.

Multiple-choice:

a. Bartos, Inc., is planning to purchase a new machine for $40,000. The payback period is expected to be five years. The new machine is expected to produce cash flow from operations of $9,000 a year in each of the next three years and $7,000 in the fourth year. Book depreciation of $5,000 a year will be charged against revenue for each of the five years of the payback period. What is the amount of cash flow from operations that the new machine is expected to produce in the last (fifth) year of the payback period?

   (1) $1,000.
   (2) $3,500.
   (3) $6,000.
   (4) $8,500.

b. The Fudge Company is planning to purchase a new machine, which it will depreciate on a straight-line basis over a 10-year period with no salvage value and a full year's depreciation taken in the year of acquisition. The new machine is expected to produce cash flow from operations of $77,000 a year in each of the next 10 years. The accounting (book value) rate of return on the initial investment is expected to be 12 percent. How much will the new machine cost?

   (1) $300,000.
   (2) $350,000.
   (3) $660,000.
   (4) Some other amount.

c. McGraw Company invested in a two-year project with an internal rate of return of 10 percent. The present value of $1 for one period at 10 percent is .909, and the present value of $1 for two periods at 10 percent is .826. The project is expected to produce cash flow from operations of $40,000 in the first year and $60,000 in the second year. How much will the project cost? (Use these rounded PV factors.)

   (1) $74,340.
   (2) $77,660.
   (3) $85,920.
   (4) Some other amount.

(CPA adapted)

16–25   Sensitivity Analysis in Capital Investment Decisions (L.O.5)

Andron Corporation is considering investing in a robotics manufacturing line. If the line is installed, it will cost an estimated $1.5 million. This amount must be paid immediately even though construction will take three years to complete (Years 0, 1, and 2). Year 3 will be spent testing the production line and, hence, will not yield any positive cash flows. If the operation is very successful, the company expects after-tax cash savings of $1 million per year in each of Years 4 through 7. After reviewing the use of these systems with managements of other companies, the controller of Andron concluded that the operation will most probably result in annual savings of $700,000 per year for each of Years 4 through 7. Further, it is entirely possible that the savings could be as low as $300,000 per year for each of Years 4 through 7.

Required:

Complete the following schedule to determine the IRR and NPV at 16 percent under the three scenarios.

Year	Best Case	Expected	Worst Case
0	($)	($)	($)
1			
2			
3			
4			
5			
6			
7			
Net present value at 16 percent	$____	$____	$____
Internal rate of return	____ %	____ %	____ %

16–26 Sensitivity Analysis in Capital Investment Decisions (L.O.5)

Octagon Corporation is a large marketing company. Management is considering whether to expand operations by opening a new chain of specialty stores. If the company embarks on this program, cash outlays for inventories, lease rentals, working capital, and other costs are expected to amount to $3.5 million in Year 0. The company expects break-even cash flows in each of Years 1 and 2. Cash flows are expected to increase to $1 million in each of Years 3 and 4, $2 million in Year 5, and $3 million in each of Years 6 and 7.

Management is aware that this is a risky venture because the economy can change over the next few years and consumer tastes could also change. For these reasons, data were obtained on worst-case and best-case scenarios. In the worst case, cash flows in each of Years 1 and 2 will be minus $500,000. In each of Years 3 through 7, cash flows may only equal $1 million. By contrast, the best case scenario projects positive cash flows of $500,000 in Years 1 and 2, $1.5 million in each of Years 3 and 4, and $3 million in each of Years 5 through 7.

The company's after-tax cost of capital is 20 percent. All cash flows are net of tax.

Required:

Complete the following schedule to show the net present values and internal rates of return for this venture for the expected, worst-case, and best-case scenarios.

Year	Best Case	Expected	Worst Case
0			
1			
2			
3			
4			
5			
6			
7			
Net present value at 20 percent	$____	$____	$____
Internal rate of return	____ %	____ %	____ %

16–27 Sensitivity Analysis in Capital Investment Decisions: Research Organization
(L.O.5)

Freeport University is considering establishing a computer technology research center. The research center will require the university to invest $1 million in equipment and facilities. During each of the first two years of operations, the university will incur net cash outflows of $150,000 for faculty and staff support. During this period, institute staff will conduct some research and write grants to obtain financial support. If the institute is moderately successful, it will obtain sufficient grant monies to break even in Year 3. After that, the institute expects to operate in such a manner that its cash inflows from grants will exceed its costs by $500,000 per year for Years 4 through 8.

Operation of a research institute is quite risky. It is possible that the annual net cash outflows of $150,000 will continue through Year 4. If the institute gets off to this slow a start, it is likely that the positive cash flows will only equal $400,000 in each of Years 5 through 8. On the other hand, university administrators estimate that the institute could break even as early as Year 2 and could receive enough grant money so that cash inflows exceed outflows by $600,000 per year for Years 3 through 8.

The university considers that its opportunity cost of funds is 10 percent. As a tax-exempt organization, it incurs no income tax liability.

Required:

Complete the following schedule to show the net present values and internal rates of return for this venture for the expected, worst-case, and best-case scenarios.

Year	Best Case	Expected	Worst Case
0			
1			
2			
3			
4			
5			
6			
7			
8			
Net present value at 10 percent	$	$	$
Internal rate of return	%	%	$ %

16–28 Present Value of Lease versus Buy (Appendix)
(L.O.6)

The owner of Ruggles Company, a sole proprietorship, decided she should acquire some new labor-saving equipment. If the equipment is acquired, it may either be leased or a special nonrecourse loan obtained for the total amount of the equipment purchase.

The lease calls for payments of $12,500 per year for eight years, whereas the loan calls for eight annual principal payments of $10,000 each plus 15 percent interest on the balance outstanding at the start of each year. Under the lease, the lessor obtains all tax benefits from equipment ownership.

The equipment, which cost $80,000, is depreciable for tax purposes as follows: Year 1, $16,000; Year 2, $28,000; Years 3–5, $12,000 per year. The equipment will have no value at the end of the project life (eight years).

Ruggles has a tax rate of 40 percent and uses an after-tax borrowing rate of 9 percent to discount all cash flows.

Required:

Complete the schedule to determine whether Ruggles should lease or borrow and buy the asset. (Assume Ruggles has already decided to make the investment, but has not yet decided whether to lease or borrow.)

	Year				
Item	1	2	. . .	7	8
Buying:					
Periodic flows:					
Loan principal	$_____	_____		_____	_____
Interest (after tax)					
Tax shield	_____	_____		_____	_____
Cash flows	_____	_____		_____	_____
Discount factor (9%)	_____	_____		_____	_____
Present value	$_____	_____		_____	_____
Net present value	$_____				

Leasing:

Net present value = (Annuity factor) × (After-tax series of payments)

= $ _____

16–29 Effect of Tax Rates on the Lease-versus-Buy Decision (Appendix)
(L.O.6)

If the marginal tax rate for Ruggles (exercise 16–28) was 60 percent and the after-tax borrowing rate was 6 percent, would your decision in exercise 16–28 remain the same? Show supporting data.

16–30 Present Value of Lease versus Buy (Appendix)
(L.O.6)

Mush Paper Company placed an order to purchase a new paper roller. The cost of the equipment is $490,000. Mush Paper has two alternatives for financing this acquisition. Mush can take out a nonrecourse loan for $490,000 at an annual interest rate of 12 percent on the beginning-of-year balance. The loan would extend for seven years and require equal principal payments over that period.

The seller of the paper roller offered Mush a 15 percent discount on the purchase price if Mush leases the roller. The lease payments are $75,000 per year for six years. At the end of Year 7, Mush would make a payment of $190,000.

The equipment is depreciable as follows: Year 1, $95,000; Year 2, $140,000; Year 3, $140,000; Year 4, $50,000; Year 5, $50,000. The equipment has no value at the end of the seven years.

Mush Paper's tax rate is 35 percent, and the company uses an after-tax borrowing rate of 10 percent to discount all cash flows.

Required:

Complete the following schedule to show whether Mush Paper should lease the roller or borrow to buy.

	Year				
	1	2	. . .	6	7
Lease payments					
PV factor	_____	_____		_____	_____
Present values	$_____	$_____		$_____	$_____
Net present value	$_____				
Loan principal					
Interest					
Tax shield					
Annual cash outflow					
PV factor	_____	_____		_____	_____
Present values	$_____	$_____		$_____	$_____
Net present value	$_____				

16–31	**Present Value of Lease versus Buy (Appendix)** (L.O.6)	Refer to the information for Mush Paper Company (exercise 16–30). If the relevant tax rate is 45 percent and the annual lease payments are $95,000 for Years 1–6 and $200,000 in Year 7, would your decision in exercise 16–30 remain the same? Show supporting data.

PROBLEMS

16–32	**Choosing from Alternative Investment Possibilities**	Oakla Realty Partners has $1.4 million available for investment in real estate ventures. The partnership's cost of capital is 18 percent. As a partnership, Oakla pays no income taxes. The company has the following ventures available to it, all of which have seven-year lives:

1. Tulsa Shopping Center, which will cost $500,000. This project will return $50,000 per year for each of the first three years and $250,000 per year in each of the remaining four years.

2. Wichita Falls Mixed-Use Development, which will cost $900,000. This project will return nothing in each of the first four years and $1 million in each of the last three years.

3. Baton Rouge Apartment Complex, which will cost $800,000 and return $230,000 per year for each of the seven years.

4. Shreveport Technical Centre, which will cost $600,000. This project will return $250,000 per year for each of the first three years and $50,000 per year for each of the remaining four years.

	Required:	How can the company optimally invest its $1.4 million assuming no other constraints on investment? (Partial investments can be made.) Show supporting data.
16–33	**Effect of Constraints on Project Selection**	Assume that the projects available to Oakla Realty Partners (problem 16–32) are indivisible. Determine the optimal investment policy for the partnership. Show supporting data.
16–34	**Effect of Mutually Exclusive Projects**	If Oakla Realty Partners (problem 16–32) can invest in either the Wichita Falls Mixed-Use Development or the Tulsa Shopping Center but not both, and the other projects are divisible, what is the optimal investment policy for the company? Show supporting data.
16–35	**Assess Impact of Tax Policy**	Assume that a provision of the Federal Tax Code permits a taxpayer to write off 75 percent of the first $10,000 in outlays for new capital equipment. However, if the taxpayer chooses to take the immediate write-off, the taxpayer loses the depreciation tax shield on the full $10,000.
		Assume your company acquired $10,000 in new capital equipment and now must decide whether to take the immediate write-off or depreciate the asset over a five-year life as follows: Year 1, $1,200; Year 2, $2,500; Years 3–5, $2,100 per year. Your company has an after-tax cost of capital of 20 percent and a marginal tax rate of 40 percent.
	Required:	Prepare an analysis to show the following items for each alternative:

a. Net present value.

b. Internal rate of return.

c. Payback period.

d. Optimal decision for the company.

16–36	**Assess Asset Write-Off versus Capitalization**	HighPotential Corporation made a $5,000 investment in equipment that qualifies for a three-year straight-line tax depreciation write-off. The financial manager of High Potential indicated that there is a tax policy that allows the company to write off 90

percent of this investment against current period income rather than take the depreciation. Your recommendation will be followed by the company. The company has a marginal tax rate of 40 percent and an after-tax cost of capital of 20 percent.

Required:

a. Compute the internal rate of return for the write-off.

b. Make your recommendation and offer supporting comments.

16–37 Assess Capital Investment Project with Alternative Measures

Baxter Company manufactures toys and other short-lived products. The Research and Development Department came up with a product that would be a good promotional gift for office equipment dealers. Efforts by Baxter's sales personnel resulted in commitments for this product for the next three years. It is expected that the product's value will be exhausted by that time.

To produce the quantity demanded, Baxter will need to buy additional machinery and rent additional space. About 25,000 square feet will be needed; 12,500 square feet of presently unused space is available now. This space would not be used for the next three years. Baxter's present lease with 10 years to run costs $3 a foot, including the 12,500 feet of unused space. There are another 12,500 square feet adjoining the Baxter facility which Baxter can rent for three years at $4 per square foot per year if it decides to make this product.

The equipment will be purchased for about $900,000 and will have a salvage value of about $180,000 at the end of the third year.

The following estimates of revenues and costs for this product for the three years have been developed:

	Year 1	Year 2	Year 3
Sales	$1,000,000	$1,600,000	$800,000
Material, labor, and variable overhead	400,000	750,000	350,000
Allocated fixed general overhead[a]	40,000	75,000	35,000
Rent	87,500	87,500	87,500
Depreciation	300,000	300,000	300,000
	827,500	1,212,500	772,500
Income before tax	172,500	387,500	27,500
Income tax (40%)	69,000	155,000	11,000
	$ 103,500	$ 232,500	$ 16,500

[a] Total fixed overhead will not be affected by this product. Each product is allocated some general overhead, however.

Required:

a. Prepare a schedule to show the differential after-tax cash flows for this project. Assume equipment must be depreciated on a three-year, straight-line basis, assuming no salvage value, for tax purposes.

b. If the company requires a two-year payback period for its investment, would it undertake this project?

c. Calculate the after-tax accounting rate of return for the project (based on the average investment).

d. If the company sets a required discount rate of 20 percent after taxes, will this project be accepted?

(CMA adapted)

16–38 Capital Investment Measures with Constraints

The Los Alamos Atoms have the option to purchase a contract of the leading national quarterback at a price of $4 million. The contract is good for five years. If the Atoms purchase the contract, they estimate that revenues from television franchises and from ticket sales will increase by the amounts shown in column 1 of Exhibit 16–38A.

Franchise and other fees will increase by 10 percent of the amount of the increases in gross revenues. (These are cash outflows.)

The Atoms also have an opportunity to purchase a contract for a world-class wide receiver. This contract also runs for five years and costs $2.5 million. The expected revenue increases for this person are shown in the second column of Exhibit 16–38A.

Finally, for $1 million the Atoms can pick up the rights to the "Rookie of the Year" under a five-year contract. The expected cash flows are shown in column 3 of Exhibit 16–38A.

Although the Atoms would like to take all three, their budget is limited to $4 million. The Atom's cost of capital is 10 percent. Ignore taxes.

Required:

a. Determine the NPV index for each player.

b. To maximize net present value, how should the Atoms allocate their resources among the available contracts?

EXHIBIT

16–38A

Revenue Increase

	(1) Quarterback	(2) Receiver	(3) Rookie
Year 1	$1,500,000	$1,000,000	0
Year 2	1,500,000	1,000,000	$ 100,000
Year 3	1,500,000	1,000,000	100,000
Year 4	1,000,000	600,000	300,000
Year 5	800,000	300,000	1,500,000

16–39 Sensitivity Analysis in Capital Budgeting

Management of Savannah Export Co. is considering whether to install warehouse and terminal facilities to expand its business. If it can obtain the appropriate licenses in all countries involved, the company can earn after-tax cash flows of $1 million per year for Years 2 through 10. However, the problem is the costs that will be incurred to obtain licenses and permits. The company engaged an engineering firm that estimated that the cost to build the warehouse facilities would be $2.2 million. These costs include $200,000 for domestic permits and licenses. Based on prior experience, Savannah management expects to incur an additional $1.8 million in international permit and license fees from other governmental agencies. In addition, the company expects a net cash outflow of $150,000 in Year 1 due to meeting various regulatory requirements.

Legal advisors indicated to Savannah's management that in their experience with a similar operation, total international licensing costs could run as high as $2.8 million in Year 0. Moreover, during the first year of operations, net cash outflows could be as high as $600,000. On the other hand, recent efforts to expand international trade suggest that international licensing and related costs could be as low as $300,000 in Year 0, and that the company could break even in Year 1.

The company's cost of capital is 15 percent after tax.

Required:

a. What is the net present value and internal rate of return under the three scenarios?

b. Should the company make this investment?

16–40 Lease versus Buy with Constraints (Appendix)

Provo Airport Authority has $45 million in its airport capital funds account that is available for the acquisition of capital equipment for the airport. The following projects, with the cost of each project, need to be constructed at the airport (dollars in millions):

Project	Cost	Annual Lease
Neutron security scanners	$19	$6
Control tower radar	34	9
Doppler radar	15	4
New runway lighting system	11	3
Jetways for new wing	18	5

The total cost of these projects is $97 million. None of the projects is divisible. However, each of the projects can be leased by making the annual lease payment shown above for a period of seven years. At the end of the lease period, the project becomes the property of the airport. The airport authority determined that it must acquire all of these projects. Those that cannot be acquired with the funds in the capital account must be leased.

Analysis of alternative investment opportunities shows that there is an annual opportunity benefit of $.10 for each $1 unused in the capital funds account. For example, if the total cost of projects purchased from the capital funds account is $35 million, the opportunity benefit from the $10 million in idle funds is $1 million per year over the seven-year lease period. The authority uses a 7.5 percent discount rate and is tax exempt. This discount rate is used regardless of the opportunity benefit noted above.

Required:

Which project should Provo Airport Authority purchase with the $45 million in the capital funds account? Show computational support for your choices.

INTEGRATIVE CASE

16–41   Sell or Process Further; Cash Flow Evaluation; Internal Rate of Return

Algonquin River Products Corporation extracts ores from an open-pit mine. Each year, 400,000 tons of ore are extracted. If the products from the extraction process are sold immediately after removal of dirt, rocks, and other impurities, a price of $65 per ton of ore can be obtained. The company estimates that extraction costs are 75 percent of the net realizable value of the ore.

Rather than sell all of the ore at the $65 price, 20 percent of it could be processed further.

To perform the additional processing, the company would install equipment costing $1,300,000. This equipment would qualify for tax depreciation as follows: Year 1, $300,000; Year 2, $400,000; Years 3–5, $200,000 per year. At the end of the six-year project life, the equipment could be salvaged and the company would obtain $50,000 salvage proceeds.

Further processing would cost $6 per ton in addition to the first processing costs. The processed ore would yield two products in equal proportion: A and B. Product A would sell for $44 per one-half ton, while product B would sell for $34 per one-half ton.

Average inventory required would increase by 5,000 tons of ore. In addition, a cash balance of $45,000 would be needed to operate the additional process.

The company estimates its cost of capital at 20 percent and its marginal tax rate at 40 percent.

Required:

a.   Prepare a schedule of the cash flows from the investment and indicate the net present value of the project.

b.   What is the internal rate of return from the project?

SOLUTIONS TO

Self-Study
Questions

1 Present value index:

$$\frac{\text{Net present value}}{\text{Initial investment}} = \frac{\$3,830^a}{\$11,615} = \underline{.33}$$

a $3,830 = ($5,525 × 1.15^{-1}) + ($5,525 × 1.15^{-2}) + ($5,525 × 1.15^{-3}) + ($4,950 × 1.15^{-4}) − $11,615.

2 Internal rate of return:

Because the net present value is positive at the 15 percent discount rate, we know the IRR must be greater than 15 percent. Trying several rates, we obtain:

		Rates	
Year	Cash Flow	30 Percent	31 Percent
0	$(11,615)	$(11,615)	$(11,615)
1	5,525	4,250	4,218
2	5,525	3,269	3,220
3	5,525	2,515	2,458
4	4,950	1,733	1,681
		$ 152	$ (38)

So, the IRR is a little less than 31 percent.

3 *a.* Payback:

Year	Cash Flow
0	$(11,615)
1	5,525
2	5,525
3	5,525

$$\text{Payback} = \frac{\$11,615}{\$5,525} = \underline{2.10 \text{ years}}$$

b. Discounted payback:

Year	Cash Flow	Balance
0	($11,615)	($11,615)
1	4,804	(6,811)
2	4,178	(2,633)
3	3,633	—

$$2 + \frac{\$2,633}{\$3,633} \text{ years} = \underline{2.72 \text{ years}}$$

COST DATA FOR PERFORMANCE EVALUATION

The Master Budget

LEARNING OBJECTIVES

After reading this chapter, you should be able to:

1. Understand the role of budgets in overall organization plans.
2. Estimate sales.
3. Develop production and cost budgets.
4. Estimate cash flows.
5. Develop budgeted financial statements.
6. Explain why ethical issues arise in budgeting.

Budget A financial plan of the resources needed to carry out tasks and meet financial goals.

The use of budgeting in organizations was well stated by a controller who explained: ''At our company, we view our master **budget** as a blueprint for operations, much like an architect's blueprint for the construction of a building. Like the architect's blueprint, our master budget helps us plan and coordinate activities, determine the means for achieving our goals, and establish some norms against which we can measure our performance. We consider our budget to be a comprehensive plan through which all levels of management formally indicate what they expect the future to hold. It expresses, in dollars, our plans for achieving company goals.''

Master Budget The financial plan for the coming year or other planning period.

This chapter shows how a **master budget** is developed and how it fits into the overall plan for achieving organizational goals.

THE OVERALL PLAN

A master budget is part of an overall organizational plan made up of three components:

1. Organizational goals.
2. The strategic long-range profit plan.
3. The master budget (tactical short-range profit plan).[1]

Organizational Goals

Organizational Goals Set of broad objectives established by management that company employees work to achieve.

Organizational goals are the set of broad objectives established by management that company employees work to achieve. For example, the following quote is taken from internal documents of a manufacturing company in the paper industry: "Our organizational goal is to increase earnings steadily while maintaining our current share of market sales and maintain profitability within the top one third of our industry. We plan to achieve this goal while providing our customers with high-quality products and meeting our social responsibilities to our employees and the communities in which they live."

Such broad goals provide a philosophical statement that the company is expected to follow in its operations. Many companies include statements of their goals in published codes of conduct and annual reports to stockholders.

Strategic Long-Range Profit Plan

Strategic Long-Range Plan Statement detailing steps to be taken in achieving a company's organization goals.

While a statement of goals is necessary to guide an organization, it is important to detail the specific steps that will be taken to achieve them.[2] These steps are expressed in a **strategic long-range plan.** Because the long-range plans look into the intermediate and distant future, they are usually stated in rather broad terms. Strategic plans discuss the major capital investments required to maintain present facilities, increase capacity, diversify products and/or processes, and develop particular markets. For example, the previously mentioned paper company's strategies, as stated in their policy manual, included:

1. *Cost control.* Optimize contribution from existing product lines by holding product cost increases to less than the general rate of inflation. This will involve acquiring new machinery proposed in the capital budget as well as replacing our five least efficient plants over the next five years.
2. *Market share.* Maintain our market share by providing a level of service and quality comparable to our top competitors. This requires improving our quality control so that customer complaints and returned merchandise are reduced from a current level of 4 percent to 1 percent within two years.

Each strategy statement was supported by projected activity levels (sales volumes, aggregate costs, and cash flow projections) for each of the next five years. At this stage, the plans were not laid out in too much detail, but they were well thought out. Hence, the plans provided a general framework for guiding management's operating decisions.

---

[1] For a more detailed description of these phases, see G. Welsch, R. Hilton, and P. Gordon, *Budgeting: Profit Planning and Control,* 5th ed. (Englewood Cliffs, N.J.: Prentice Hall, 1988).

[2] A classic discussion of organization goal setting is provided by J. March and H. Simon in *Organizations* (New York: John Wiley & Sons, 1958).

The Master Budget (Tactical Short-Range Profit Plan)

Profit Plan The income statement portion of the master budget.

Long-range plans are achieved in year-by-year steps. The guidance is more specific for the coming year than it is for more distant years. The plan for the coming year is called the *master budget.* The master budget is also known as the *static budget*, the *budget plan*, or the *planning budget*. The income statement portion of the master budget is often called the **profit plan.** The master budget indicates the sales levels, production and cost levels, income, and cash flows that are anticipated for the coming year. In addition, these budget data are used to construct a budgeted statement of financial position (balance sheet).

Budgeting is a dynamic process that ties together goals, plans, decision making, and employee performance evaluation. The master budget and its relationship to other plans, accounting reports, and management decision-making processes is diagrammed in Illustration 17–1. On the left side are the organization goals, strategies, and objectives that set the long-term plan for the company. The master budget is derived from the long-range plan in consideration of conditions that are expected during the coming period. Such plans are subject to change as the events of the year unfold. Recently, the long-range plan for a U.S. automobile manufacturer called for development of several new product lines, but unfavorable short-run economic conditions required their postponement.

The Human Element in Budgeting

The conditions anticipated for the coming year are based in part on managers' near-term projections. The individual's relationship to the budget is diagrammed on the right side of Illustration 17–1. Managers' beliefs about the coming period are affected by a number of factors, including their

---

I L L U S T R A T I O N   *Organizational and Individual Interaction in Developing the Master Budget*

17–1

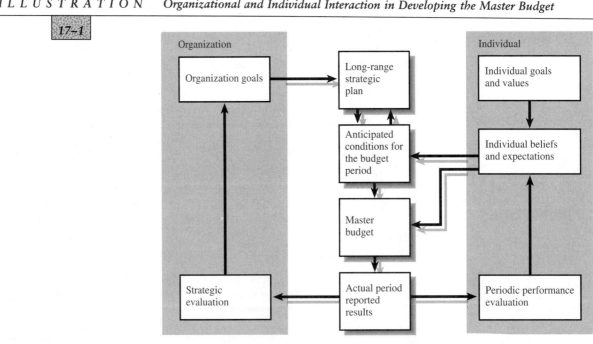

personal goals and values. Although budgets are often viewed in purely quantitative, technical terms, the importance of this human factor cannot be overemphasized.

Budget preparation rests on human estimates of an unknown future. People's forecasts are likely to be greatly influenced by their experiences with various segments of the company. For example, district sales managers are in an excellent position to project customer orders over the next several months, while market researchers are usually better able to identify long-run market trends and make macro forecasts of sales. One challenge of budgeting is to identify who in the organization is best able to provide the best information about particular topics.

Participative Budgeting

Participative Budgeting The use of input from lower- and middle-management employees, also called *grass roots budgeting*.

The use of input from lower- and middle-management employees is often called **participative budgeting** or *grass roots budgeting*. The use of lower and middle managers in budgeting has an obvious cost—it is time-consuming. But it also has some benefits. It enhances employee motivation and acceptance of goals; it provides information that enables employees to associate rewards and penalties with performance.[3] Participative budgeting can yield information that employees know but managers do not.

A number of studies have shown that employees often provide inaccurate data when asked to give budget estimates. They may request more money than they need because they expect their request to be cut. And employees who believe the budget will be used as a norm for evaluating their performance may provide an estimate that will not be too hard to achieve.

Thus, managers usually view the technical steps required to construct a comprehensive tactical budget plan in the context of the effect that people have on the budget and the effect that the budget will have on people. Ideally, the budget will motivate people and facilitate their activities so that organizational goals can be achieved.

DEVELOPING THE MASTER BUDGET

While each organization is unique in the way it puts together its budget, all budgeting processes share some common elements. After organization goals, strategies, and long-range plans have been developed, work begins on the master budget. This is a detailed budget for the coming fiscal year, with some less-detailed figures for subsequent years. While budgeting is an ongoing process in most companies, the bulk of the work is usually done in the six months immediately preceding the beginning of the coming fiscal year. Final budget approvals by the chief executive and board of directors are made a month to six weeks before the beginning of the fiscal year.

To envision the master budgeting process, picture the financial statements most commonly prepared by companies: the income statement, the balance sheet, and the cash flow statement. Then imagine preparing these statements *before* the fiscal period.

We begin with a forecast of revenues for the budget period.

---

[3] General discussion of behavioral aspects of budgeting are available in A. Hopwood, *Accounting and Human Behavior* (Englewood Cliffs, N.J.: Prentice Hall, 1974); R. Swieringa and R. Moncur, *Some Effects of Participative Budgeting on Managerial Behavior* (New York: National Association of Accountants, 1975); and G. Hofstede, *The Game of Budget Control* (New York: Van Nostrand Reinhold, 1967).

Sales Forecasts

Forecasting sales is perhaps the most difficult aspect of budgeting because it involves considerable subjectivity. To reduce subjectivity and simultaneously gather as much information as possible, management often uses a number of different methods to obtain forecasts from a number of different sources.

Sales Staff

Salespeople are in the unique position of being close to the customers, and they may possess the best information in the company about customers' immediate and near-term needs. As previously indicated, however, they may be tempted to bias their sales forecasts if such forecasts are used as the norm for performance evaluation.

For example, Peter Jones is a district sales manager for Shasta Design, Inc. Shasta Design manufactures tents for backpacking. The company purchases fabric, makes tents, and sells to companies that add frames. For the coming budget year, he expects his district's sales to be $1 million, although they could drop as low as $800,000 or run as high as $1.2 million. His bonus at the end of next year will be 1 percent of the excess of actual sales over the sales budget. So, if the budget is $1 million and actual sales are also $1 million, he will receive no bonus.

However, if Peter provides a sales forecast that is too low, he will not be able to justify retaining his current number of employees. Further, if his sales forecasts are consistently much below the actual sales results or below what management thinks his district should be doing, he will lose credibility. Thus, Peter decides on a conservative but reasonable sales forecast of $900,000, which, he believes, will give him a high probability of getting a bonus and a low risk of losing his other objectives.

Of course, if Peter's performance were compared against a different set of norms, he would have different incentive. If, for instance, his bonus was a fixed percent of sales, he would have incentive to maximize sales. Then he would be motivated to make an optimistic sales forecast to justify obtaining a larger sales staff. Also, the high sales forecast would be used to estimate the amount of production capacity needed, thus ensuring that adequate inventory would be available to satisfy any and all customer needs. Of course, the managers and staff who receive forecasts usually recognize the subjectivity of the situation. As Peter's superior put it, "We've received sales forecasts from him for several years, and they're always a bit conservative. We don't ask him to revise his estimates. We simply take his conservatism into account when we put together the overall sales forecast."

Market Research

To provide a check on forecasts from local sales personnel, management often turns to market researchers. This group probably does not have the same incentives that sales personnel have to bias the budget. Furthermore, researchers have a different perspective on the market. While they may know little about customers' immediate needs, they can predict long-term trends in attitudes and the effects of social and economic changes on the company's sales, potential markets, and products.

Delphi Technique Forecasting method where individual forecasts of group members are submitted anonymously and evaluated by the group as a whole.

The Delphi Technique

The **Delphi technique** is another method that is employed to enhance forecasting and reduce bias in estimates. With this method, members of the forecasting group prepare individual forecasts and submit them anonymously. Each group member obtains a copy of all forecasts but is unaware of their sources. The group then discusses the results. In this way, differences between individual forecasts can be addressed and reconciled without involving the personality or position of individual forecasters. After the differences are discussed, each group member prepares a new forecast and distributes it anonymously to the others. These forecasts are then discussed in the same manner as before. The process is repeated until the forecasts converge on a single best estimate of the coming year's sales level.

Trend Analysis

Trend Analysis Method of forecasting that ranges from simple visual extrapolation of points on a graph to highly sophisticated computerized time series analysis.

Trend analysis, which can range from a simple visual extrapolation of points on a graph to a highly sophisticated computerized time series analysis, may also be helpful in preparing sales forecasts.

Time series techniques use only past observations of the data series to be forecasted. No other data are included. This methodology is justified on the grounds that since all factors that affect the data series are reflected in the actual past observations, the past data are the best reflection of available information. This approach is also relatively economical because only a list of past sales figures is needed. No other data have to be gathered.

Forecasting techniques based on trend analysis often require long series of past data to derive a suitable solution. Generally, when these models are used in accounting applications, monthly data are required so that an adequate number of observations can be obtained.

Econometric Models

Another forecasting approach is to enter past sales data into a regression model to obtain a statistical estimate of factors affecting sales. For example, the predicted sales for the coming period may be related to such factors as economic indicators, consumer-confidence indexes, back-order volume, and other internal and external factors that the company deems relevant.

Econometric Models Statistical method of forecasting economic data using regression models.

Advocates of these **econometric models** contend that many relevant predictors can be included and that by manipulating the assumed values of the predictors, it is possible to examine a variety of hypothetical conditions and relate them to the sales forecast. This is particularly useful for performing sensitivity analysis, which we discuss later in this chapter.

Sophisticated analytical models for forecasting are now widely available. Most companies' computers have software packages that allow economical use of these models. Nonetheless, it is important to remember that no model removes the uncertainty surrounding sales forecasts. Management has often found that the intuition of local sales personnel is a better predictor than sophisticated analysis and models. As in any management decision, cost-benefit tests should be used to determine which methods are most appropriate.

Comprehensive Illustration

To make our discussion of the budgeting process more concrete, we'll develop the budget for Shasta Design, Inc. We use a manufacturing example because it is the most comprehensive. The methods we discuss are also applicable to nonmanufacturing organizations.

Assume that Shasta Design's management went through the steps discussed above and arrived at the following sales budget for the next budget year:

	Units	Price per Unit	Total Sales Revenues
Estimated sales	6,400	$800	$5,120,000

THE PRODUCTION BUDGET

Production Budget Production plan of resources needed to meet current sales demand and ensure inventory levels are sufficient for future sales.

The **production budget** plans the resources needed to meet current sales demand and ensure that inventory levels are sufficient for expected activity levels. It is necessary, therefore, to determine the required inventory level for the beginning and end of the budget period. The production level may be computed from the basic cost flow equation (also known as the basic inventory formula):

Beginning balance + Transfers-in = Transfers-out + Ending balance
$$BB \quad + \quad TI \quad = \quad TO \quad + \quad EB$$

Adapting that equation to inventories, production, and sales, we have:

Units in   Required   Budgeted   Units in
beginning + production = sales units + ending
inventory   units   for the period   inventory

Rearranging terms to solve for *required production*:

Required   Budgeted   Units in   Units in
production = sales units + ending − beginning
units   for the period   inventory   inventory

This equation states that production is equal to the sales demand plus or minus an inventory adjustment. Production and inventory are assumed to be stated in equivalent finished units.

From the sales budget above, Shasta Design, Inc., has projected sales of 6,400 units. Management estimates that there will be 900 units in the beginning inventory of finished goods. Based on management's analysis, the required ending inventory is estimated to be 1,000 units. We assume for simplicity that there is no beginning or ending work in process inventory. With this information, the budgeted level of production is computed as follows:

Required   = 6,400 units +   1,000 units   −   900 units
production   (sales)   (ending inventory)   (beginning inventory)

= 6,500 units

Illustration 17–2 presents the production budget for Shasta Design. The production budget is reviewed with the management of the production facilities to ascertain whether the budgeted level of production can be reached with the capacity available. If not, management may revise the sales forecast or consider ways of increasing capacity. If it appears that production capacity will exceed requirements, management may want to consider other opportunities for the use of the capacity.

One benefit of the budgeting process is that it facilitates the coordination of activities. It is far better to learn about discrepancies between the sales

ILLUSTRATION

SHASTA DESIGN, INC.
Production Budget
For the Budget Year Ended December 31
(in units)

Expected sales . . . . 6,400 units

Add: Desired ending inventory of
finished goods 1,000

Total needs 7,400

Less: Beginning inventory of
finished goods 900

Units to be produced 6,500

---

forecast and production capacity in advance so that remedial action can be taken. Lost sales opportunities due to inadequate production capacity or unnecessary idle capacity can thus be avoided.

BUDGETED COST OF GOODS MANUFACTURED AND SOLD

Once the sales and production budgets have been developed and the efforts of the sales and production groups are coordinated, the budgeted cost of goods manufactured and sold can be prepared. The primary job is to estimate costs of direct materials, direct labor, and manufacturing overhead at budgeted levels of production.

Direct Materials

Direct materials purchases needed for the budget period are derived from the equation:

$$\begin{matrix} \text{Required} \\ \text{materials} \\ \text{purchases} \end{matrix} = \begin{matrix} \text{Materials to} \\ \text{be used in} \\ \text{production} \end{matrix} + \begin{matrix} \text{Estimated} \\ \text{ending} \\ \text{materials} \\ \text{inventory} \end{matrix} - \begin{matrix} \text{Estimated} \\ \text{beginning} \\ \text{materials} \\ \text{inventory} \end{matrix}$$

The beginning and ending levels of materials inventory for the budget period are estimated, often with the help of an inventory control model, while the materials to be used in production are based on production requirements.

Production at Shasta Design, Inc., for the coming period will require two kinds of materials: material R and material S. For each unit of output, three yards of R and five yards of S are required. The beginning materials inventory is estimated to consist of 2,200 yards of R and 4,000 yards of S. The estimated ending inventory has been determined to equal 1,300 yards of R and 4,600 yards of S. The estimated cost for each yard of R is $10, and the estimated cost of each yard of S is $30. These costs are expected to remain constant during the coming budget period. Required production for the production budget is 6,500 units.

Computation of the required materials purchases in units of each material would be as follows:

$$R = (6,500 \times 3) + 1,300 - 2,200$$
$$= \underline{\underline{18,600 \text{ yards}}}$$

$$S = (6,500 \times 5) + 4,600 - 4,000$$
$$= \underline{\underline{33,100 \text{ yards}}}$$

ILLUSTRATION

SHASTA DESIGN, INC.
Direct Materials Budget
For the Budget Year Ended December 31
(in units)

	Material R	Material S
Units to be produced (from the production budget in Illustration 17–2) 6,500		
Direct materials needed per unit	3 yards	5 yards
Total production needs (amount per unit times 6,500 units)	19,500	32,500
Add: Desired ending inventory	1,300	4,600
Total direct materials needs	20,800	37,100
Less: Beginning inventory of materials	2,200	4,000
Direct materials to be purchased	18,600 yards	33,100 yards
Cost of materials, per yard	$10	$30
Total cost of direct materials to be purchased	$186,000	$ 993,000
Sum of materials R and S to be purchased ($186,000 + $993,000)		$1,179,000

In dollar terms, this would amount to estimated purchases of $186,000 for R (18,600 × $10) and $993,000 for S (33,100 × $30).

The direct materials budget, Illustration 17–3, shows the materials required for production.

Direct Labor

Estimates of direct labor costs are often obtained from engineering and production management. For Shasta Design, Inc., the direct labor costs are estimated at 7.3 hours per unit at $20 per hour (or $146 per output unit produced). Thus, for the budget year, the budgeted direct labor cost of production of 6,500 units is $949,000, as computed and shown in Illustration 17–4.

Overhead

Unlike direct materials and direct labor, which can often be determined from an engineer's specifications for a product, overhead is composed of many different kinds of costs with varying cost behaviors. Some overhead costs vary in direct proportion to production (variable overhead); some costs vary with production, but in a step fashion (for example, supervisory labor); and other costs are fixed and will remain the same unless capacity or long-range policies are changed. Other costs do not necessarily vary with production, but they may be changed at management's discretion (some maintenance costs may be in this category).

Budgeting overhead requires an estimate based on production levels, management discretion, long-range capacity and other corporate policies, and external factors such as increases in property taxes. Due to the complexity and diversity of overhead costs, cost-estimation methods such as those described in Chapter 10 are frequently used. To simplify the budgeting

ILLUSTRATION

17-4

SHASTA DESIGN, INC.
Direct Labor Budget
For the Budget Year Ended December 31

Units to be produced (from Illustration 17–2)	6,500 units
Direct labor time per unit	7.3 hours
Total direct labor-hours needed	47,450 hours
Direct labor cost per hour	$20
Total direct labor cost	$949,000

ILLUSTRATION

17-5

SHASTA DESIGN, INC.
Schedule of Budgeted Manufacturing Overhead
For the Budget Year Ended December 31

Variable overhead needed to produce 6,500 units:		
Indirect materials and supplies	$ 38,000	
Materials handling	59,000	
Other indirect labor	33,000	$ 130,000
Fixed manufacturing overhead:		
Supervisory labor	175,000	
Maintenance and repairs	85,000	
Plant administration	173,000	
Utilities	87,000	
Depreciation	280,000	
Insurance	43,000	
Property taxes	117,000	
Other	41,000	1,001,000
Total manufacturing overhead		$1,131,000

process, costs are usually divided into fixed and variable components, with discretionary and semifixed costs treated as fixed costs within the relevant range.

The schedule of budgeted manufacturing overhead for Shasta Design, Inc., is presented in Illustration 17–5. For convenience, after consultation with department management, the budget staff has divided all overhead into fixed and variable costs. Shasta Design can now determine the budgeted total manufacturing costs by adding the three components—materials, labor, and overhead. This total is $3,250,000, as shown in Illustration 17–6.

Completing the Budgeted Costs of Goods Manufactured and Sold

We need only to include the estimated beginning and ending work in process and finished goods inventories to determine the required number of units produced—6,500. As previously indicated, there are no work in process

ILLUSTRATION

SHASTA DESIGN, INC.
Budgeted Statement of Cost of Goods Manufactured and Sold
For the Budget Year Ended December 31

Beginning work in process inventory		–0–
Manufacturing costs:		
Direct materials:		
Beginning inventory (2,200 R @ $10 + 4,000 S @ $30) . . . . . . $ 142,000		
Purchases (from Illustration 17–3) 1,179,000		
Materials available for manufacturing 1,321,000		
Less: Ending inventory (1,300 R @ $10 + 4,600 S @ $30) . . . . (151,000)		
Total direct materials costs	$1,170,000	
Direct labor (from Illustration 17–4)	949,000	
Manufacturing overhead (from Illustration 17–5)	1,131,000	
Total manufacturing costs		$ 3,250,000
Deduct: Ending work in process inventory		–0–
Cost of goods manufactured		3,250,000
Add: Beginning finished goods inventory (900 units)ᵃ		450,000
Deduct: Ending finished goods inventory (1,000 units)ᵃ		(500,000)
Cost of goods sold		$ 3,200,000

ᵃ Finished goods are valued at $500 per unit $\left(\frac{\$3,250,000}{6,500 \text{ units produced}}\right)$ assuming FIFO. Hence, beginning finished goods inventory is estimated to be $450,000 (900 units × $500), and ending finished goods inventory is estimated to be $500,000 (1,000 units × $500).

inventories.[4] Finished goods inventories are as follows, assuming the cost per unit is estimated to be $500 in both beginning and ending inventory:

	Units	Dollars
Beginning finished goods inventory	900	$450,000
Ending finished goods inventory	1,000	500,000

Adding the estimated beginning finished goods inventory to the estimated cost of goods manufactured, then deducting the ending finished goods inventory yields a cost of goods manufactured and sold of $3,200,000, as shown in Illustration 17–6.

This completes the second major step in the budgeting process: determining budgeted production requirements and the cost of goods manufactured and sold. Obviously, this part of the budgeting effort can be extremely complex in manufacturing companies. It can be very difficult to coordinate production schedules among numerous plants, some using other plants'

---

[4] If the company has beginning and ending work in process inventories, units are usually expressed as equivalent finished units and treated the way we have treated finished goods inventories. In most companies, estimates of work in process inventories are omitted from the budget because they have a minimal impact on the budget.

products as their direct materials. It is also difficult to coordinate production schedules with sales forecasts. New estimates of material availability, labor shortages, strikes, availability of energy, and production capacity often require reworking the entire budget.

Revising the Initial Budget

At this point in the budget cycle, a first-draft budget has been prepared. There is usually a good deal of coordinating and revising before the budget is considered final. For example, projected production figures may call for revised estimates of direct materials purchases and direct labor costs. Bottlenecks may be discovered in production that will hamper the company's ability to deliver a particular product and thus affect the sales forecast. The revision process may be repeated several times until a coordinated, feasible master budget evolves. No part of the budget is really formally adopted until the master budget is finally approved by the board of directors.

*Self-Study
Question*

1 The self-study questions in this chapter provide a comprehensive budgeting problem based on data from the example in the chapter.

Refer to the problem for Shasta Design, Inc., in the chapter example. Assume the sales forecast was increased to 7,000 units with no change in price. The new target ending inventories are:

> Finished goods . . . . 1,200 units
>
> Material R . . . . 1,500 yards
>
> Material S . . . . 4,900 yards

Expected production = 7,300 units.

Prepare a budgeted cost of goods manufactured and sold statement and budgeted overhead statement with these new data.

The solution to this question is at the end of this chapter on page 662.

MARKETING AND ADMINISTRATIVE BUDGET

Budgeting marketing and administrative costs is very difficult because managers have a lot of discretion about how much money is spent and the timing of expenditures. For example, a company hired a new marketing executive who was famous for cost-cutting skills. The executive ordered an immediate 50 percent cut in the company's advertising budget, a freeze on hiring, and a 50 percent cut in the travel budget. The result—costs fell, and there was little immediate impact on sales. A year later, looking for new challenges, the executive moved on to another company. Soon afterward, the executive's former employers noticed that sales were down because the company had lost market share to some aggressive competitors. Were the marketing executive's cost-cutting actions really in the best interest of the company? To this day, nobody can give a documented answer to that question because it is difficult to prove a causal link between the cost cutting and the subsequent decrease in sales.

In another case, a company's president was the only one who used the corporate jet—and he used it only rarely. So the internal audit staff recommended selling it. The company president rejected the idea, saying, "One of the reasons I put up with the pressures and responsibilities of this job is because I enjoy some of its perquisites, including the corporate jet." Some costs that appear unnecessary, especially perquisites, are really part of the total compensation package and may, therefore, be necessary costs.

The budgeting objective here is to estimate the amount of marketing and administrative costs required to operate the company at its projected level of sales and production and to achieve long-term company goals. For example, the budgeted sales figures may be based on a new product promotion campaign. If production and sales are projected to increase, it is likely that an increase in support services—data processing, accounting, personnel, and so forth—will be needed to operate the company at the higher projected levels.

An easy way to deal with the problem is to start with a previous period's actual or budgeted amounts and make adjustments for inflation, changes in operations, and similar changes between periods. This method has been criticized and may be viewed as very simplistic, but it does have one advantage—it is relatively easy and inexpensive. As always, the benefits of improving budgeting methods must justify their increased costs.

At Shasta Design, each level of management submits a budget request for marketing and administrative costs to the next higher level, which reviews it and, usually after some adjustments, approves it. The budget is passed up through the ranks until it reaches top management. As shown in Illustration 17–7, the schedule of marketing and administrative costs is

ILLUSTRATION

17–7

SHASTA DESIGN, INC.
Schedule of Budgeted Marketing and Administrative Costs
For the Budget Year Ended December 31

Variable marketing costs:		
Sales commissions	$260,000	
Other marketing	104,000	
Total variable marketing costs		$ 364,000
Fixed marketing costs:		
Sales salaries	100,000	
Advertising	193,000	
Other	78,000	
Total fixed marketing costs		371,000
Total marketing costs		735,000
Administrative costs (all fixed):		
Administrative salaries	254,000	
Legal and accounting staff	141,000	
Data processing services	103,000	
Outside professional services	39,000	
Depreciation—building, furniture, and equipment	94,000	
Other, including interest	26,000	
Taxes—other than income	160,000	
Total administrative costs		817,000
Total budgeted marketing and administrative costs		$1,552,000

ILLUSTRATION

17–8

SHASTA DESIGN, INC.
Budgeted Income Statement
For the Budget Year Ended December 31

Budgeted revenues:

Sales (6,400 units at $800)		$5,120,000

Costs:

Cost of goods manufactured and sold (from Illustration 17–6)	$3,200,000	
Marketing and administrative costs (from Illustration 17–7)	1,552,000	
Total budgeted costs		4,752,000
Operating profit		368,000
Federal and other income taxes[a]		128,000
Operating profit after taxes		$ 240,000

[a] Computed by the company's tax staff.

divided into variable and fixed components. In this case, variable marketing costs are those that vary with *sales* (not production). Fixed marketing costs are usually those that can be changed at management's discretion—for example, advertising.

BUDGETED INCOME STATEMENT

According to the controller at Shasta Design, "At this point, we're able to put together the entire budgeted income statement for the period (Illustration 17–8), so we can determine our projected operating profits. By making whatever adjustments are required to satisfy generally accepted accounting principles (GAAP) for external reporting, we can project net income after income taxes and earnings per share. If we don't like the results, we go back to the budgeted income statement and, starting at the top, go through each step to see if we can increase sales revenues or cut costs. We usually find some plant overhead, marketing, or administrative costs that can be cut or postponed without doing too much damage to the company's operations."

Shasta Design's board of directors approved the sales, production, and marketing and administrative budgets and budgeted income statements as submitted. Note that the budgeted income statement also includes estimated federal and other income taxes, which were obtained from the tax staff. We will not detail the tax-estimation process because it is a highly technical area separate from cost accounting.

 *Self-Study Question*

2 Refer to self-study question 1. Recall that for the self-study question, Shasta Design, Inc., has a sales forecast of 7,000 units and new target ending inventories of:

Finished goods . . . . 1,200 units

Material R . . . . 1,500 yards

Material S . . . . 4,900 yards

In addition, you learn that income tax expense is $214,547. Variable marketing costs increase proportionately with volume (that is, the amount now is 7,000/6,400 times the amount in the text example).

Prepare a budgeted schedule of marketing and administrative costs and a budgeted income statement.

The solution to this question is at the end of this chapter on page 664.

CASH BUDGET

Cash Budget A statement of cash on hand at the start, expected cash receipts, expected cash disbursements, and the resulting cash balance at the end of the budget period.

Although the budgeted income statement is an important tool for planning operations, a company also requires cash to operate. Cash budgeting is important to assure company solvency, maximize interest earned on cash balances, and determine whether the company is generating enough cash for present and future operations.

Preparing a **cash budget** requires that all revenues, costs, and other transactions be examined in terms of their effects on cash. The budgeted cash receipts are computed from the collections from accounts receivable, cash sales, sale of assets, borrowing, issuing stock, and other cash-generating activities. Disbursements are computed by counting the cash required to pay for materials purchases, manufacturing and other operations, federal income taxes, and stockholder dividends. In addition, the cash disbursements necessary to repay debt and acquire new assets must also be incorporated into the cash budget.

Shasta Design's cash budget is shown in Illustration 17–9. The source of each item is indicated.

ILLUSTRATION

17–9

SHASTA DESIGN, INC.
Cash Budget
For the Budget Year Ended December 31

Cash balance beginning of period[a]		$ 150,000
Receipts:		
Collections on accounts[a]	$5,185,000	
Sales of assets[a]	25,000	
Total receipts		5,210,000
Less disbursements:		
Payments for accounts payable[a]	1,164,000	
Direct labor (from Illustration 17–4)	949,000	
Manufacturing overhead requiring cash less noncash depreciation charges (from Illustration 17–5)	851,000	
Marketing and administrative costs less noncash charges (from Illustration 17–7)	1,458,000	
Payments for federal income taxes (per discussion with the tax staff)	252,000	
Dividends[a]	140,000	
Reduction in long-term debts[a]	83,000	
Acquisition of new assets[b]	320,000	
Total disbursements		5,217,000
Budgeted ending cash balance (ties to Illustration 17–10)		$ 143,000

[a] Estimated by the treasurer's office.
[b] Estimated by the treasurer's office, per the capital budget.

Self-Study
Question

3 This question is based on the previous self-study questions in this chapter and on the Shasta Design example in the text. Prepare a cash budget given the revised figures for Shasta Design provided in the previous two self-study questions. Compared to the text example, assume cash collections will increase proportionately to the increase in sales, except the ending accounts receivable level will increase by another $40,000. Additional payments for purchases of materials will be required, but ending accounts payable will also increase by $2,000. Payments for income taxes will increase to $282,390.

The solution to this question is at the end of the chapter on page 665.

KEY RELATIONSHIPS: THE SALES CYCLE

Assembling the master budget demonstrates some key relations among sales, accounts receivable, and cash flows in the sales cycle. Advantages of understanding these relationships include the ability to solve for amounts that are unknown and to audit the master budget to ensure that the basic accounting equation has been correctly applied.

At Shasta Design, for example, the relationships among budgeted sales, accounts receivable, and cash receipts were as follows:

Sales		Accounts Receivble		Cash (Illustration 17-9)	
		BB 220,000		BB 150,000	
Illustrations 17-8 and 17-10		Illustrations 17-9 and 17-10			
5,120,000 ⟶	5,120,000	5,185,000 ⟶	5,185,000	5,185,000	
				25,000	5,217,000
	EB 155,000		EB 143,000	EB 143,000	

Sales are assumed to be on account. Note that the cash account and the cash budget in Illustration 17-9 are identical.

If an amount in the sales cycle is unknown, the basic accounting equation can be used to find the unknown amount. For example, suppose all of the amounts in the above diagram are known except ending cash balance and sales. Using the basic cost flow equation,

$$BB + TI = TO + EB$$

find sales from the Accounts Receivable account:

$$\$220,000 + TI \text{ (sales)} = \$5,185,000 + \$155,000$$
$$TI = \$5,185,000 + \$155,000 - \$220,000$$
$$= \underline{\$5,120,000}$$

Find ending cash balance from the Cash account:

$$\$150,000 + (\$5,185,000 + \$25,000) = \$5,217,000 + EB$$
$$\$150,000 + \$5,185,000 + \$25,000 - \$5,217,000 = EB$$
$$EB = \underline{\$143,000}$$

BUDGETED BALANCE SHEETS

Budgeted balance sheets, or statements of financial position, combine an estimate of financial position at the beginning of the budget period with the estimated results of operations for the period (from the income statements) and estimated changes in assets and liabilities. The latter results from man-

ILLUSTRATION

17–10

SHASTA DESIGN, INC.
Budgeted Balance Sheets
For the Budget Year Ended December 31
(in thousands)

	Balance (January 1)	Budget Year Additions	Budget Year Subtractions	Balance (December 31)
Assets				
Current assets:				
Cash	$ 150[a]	$ 5,210[a]	$ 5,217[a]	$ 143[a]
Accounts receivable	220[b]	5,120[c]	5,185[a]	155[b]
Inventories	592[d]	3,259[e]	3,200[f]	651[g]
Other current assets	23[b]	100[b]	100[b]	23[b]
Total current assets	985	13,689	13,702	972
Long-term assets:				
Property, plant, and equipment	2,475[b]	320[a]	300[b]	2,495[b]
Less: Accumulated depreciation	(850)[b]	(374)[h]	(275)[b]	(949)[b]
Total assets	$2,610	$13,635	$13,727	$2,518
Liabilities and Shareholders' Equity				
Current liabilities:				
Accounts payable	$ 140[b]	$ 1,179[i]	$ 1,164[a]	$ 155[b]
Taxes payable	156[b]	128[b]	252[a]	32[b]
Current portion of long-term debt	83[b]	–0–[b]	83[a]	–0–[b]
Total current liabilities	379	1,307	1,499	187
Long-term liabilities	576[b]	–0–[b]	–0–[b]	576[b]
Total liabilities	955	1,307	1,499	763
Shareholders' equity:				
Common stock	350[b]	–0–[b]	–0–[b]	350[b]
Retained earnings	1,305[b]	240[j]	140[a]	1,405[b]
Total shareholders' equity	1,655	240	140	1,755
Total liabilities and shareholders' equity	$2,610	$ 1,547	$ 1,639	$2,518

[a] From cash budget (Illustration 17–9).

[b] Estimated by personnel in the company's accounting department.

[c] From budgeted income statement (Illustration 17–8). Assumes all sales are on account.

[d] From budgeted statement of cost of goods manufactured and sold (Illustration 17–6), sum of beginning direct materials, work in process, and finished goods inventories ($142 + 0 + $450 = $592).

[e] From budgeted statement of costs of goods manufactured and sold (Illustration 17–6), sum of materials purchases, direct labor, and manufacturing overhead ($1,179 + $949 + $1,131 = $3,259).

[f] From budgeted statement of cost of goods manufactured and sold (Illustration 17–6).

[g] From budgeted statement of cost of goods manufactured and sold (Illustration 17–6), sum of ending direct materials, work in process, and finished goods inventories ($151 + 0 + $500 = $651).

[h] Depreciation of $280 from schedule of budgeted manufacturing overhead (Illustration 17–5) plus depreciation of $94 from the schedule of budgeted marketing and administrative costs (Illustration 17–7) equals $374 increase in accumulated depreciation.

[i] From budgeted statement of cost of goods manufactured and sold (Illustration 17–6). Accounts payable increases are assumed to be for materials purchases only.

[j] From budgeted income statement (Illustration 17–8), operating profit after taxes.

Budgeted Balance Sheets Statements of financial position that combine estimates of financial position at the beginning and end of the budget period with the estimated results of operations for the period and estimated changes in assets and liabilities.

agement's decisions about optimal levels of capital investment in long-term assets (the capital budget), investment in working capital, and financing decisions. Decision making in these areas is, for the most part, the treasurer's function. We shall assume these decisions have been made and incorporate their results in the budgeted balance sheets. Illustration 17–10 presents Shasta Design's budgeted balance sheets at the beginning and end of the budget year.

MASTER BUDGET DEVELOPMENT IN REVIEW

We have completed the development of a comprehensive budget for Shasta Design. A model of the budgeting process is presented in Illustration 17–11. Although we have simplified the presentation, you can still see that assembling a master budget is a complex process that requires careful coordination of many different organization segments.

MULTIPERIOD CASH FLOW ANALYSIS

Cash flows are often analyzed in more detail than shown in the Shasta Design example. For example, assume the Near-Cash Wholesale Co. has the following information available about its monthly collection experience for sales or credit:

Cash collected from current month's sales	50%
Cash collected from last month's sales	45
Cash discounts taken (percent of gross sales)	2
Written off as a bad debt	3
	100%

ILLUSTRATION

17–11

Assembling the Master Budget: Manufacturing Organization

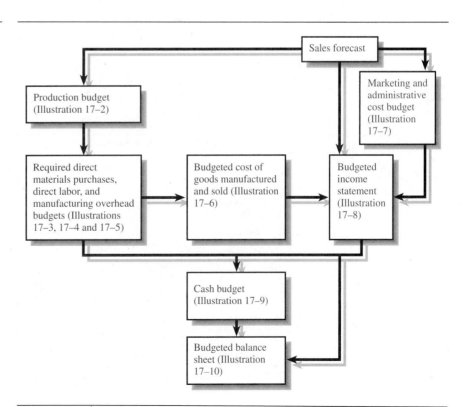

This means that if July's sales on credit are $200,000, then $100,000 is expected to be collected in July and $90,000 is expected to be collected in August; $4,000 is not expected to be collected because the customers paid early enough to get a discount; and $6,000 is not expected to be collected because these accounts will be written off as bad debts.

Illustration 17–12 shows a multiperiod schedule of cash collections for the three months of the quarter ending September 30 for Near-Cash Whole-sale. Assume the beginning accounts receivable balance on July 1 is expected to be $100,000, all of which is expected to be collected during July. The sales for the three months are expected to be:

July sales	$200,000
August sales	300,000
September sales	200,000

The same approach would be used for cash disbursements. Illustration 17–13 shows the cash disbursements for Near-Cash Wholesale Co. Near-Cash Wholesale pays 70 percent of its purchases in the month of purchase, 28 percent in the following month, and takes a 2 percent discount for paying on time. Following is a list of purchases for the three months July through September:

July	$100,000
August	150,000
September	80,000

In addition, all other cash payments for the month are expected to be $70,000 per month. Near-Cash had accounts payable of $40,000 on July 1, all of which were paid in July.

ILLUSTRATION

17–12

NEAR-CASH WHOLESALE CO.
Multiperiod Schedule of Cash Collections
For the Quarter Ended September 30

	Month			Total for
	July	August	September	Quarter
Beginning accounts receivable, July 1, $100,000	$100,000			$100,000
July sales, $200,000[a]	100,000	$ 90,000		190,000
August sales, $300,000[b]		150,000	$135,000	285,000
September sales, $200,000			100,000	100,000
Total cash collections	$200,000	$240,000	$235,000	$675,000

Note: Assumptions for the budget: 50 percent of a month's sales are collected in cash during the month; 45 percent are collected in the next month; 2 percent are taken as a cash discount for early payments; and 3 percent will not be collected because they are written off as a bad debt.

[a] 50 percent collected in July, 45 percent collected in August, and 5 percent not collected according to the assumption above.

[b] 50 percent collected in August, 45 percent collected in September, and 5 percent not collected according to the assumption above.

ILLUSTRATION

NEAR-CASH WHOLESALE CO.
Multiperiod Schedule of Cash Disbursements
For the Quarter Ended September 30

	Month			Total for Quarter
	July	August	September	
Beginning accounts payable, July 1, $40,000	$ 40,000			$ 40,000
July purchases, $100,000[a]	70,000	$ 28,000		98,000
August purchases, $150,000[b]		105,000	$ 42,000	147,000
September purchases, $80,000			56,000	56,000
Additional cash payments	70,000	70,000	70,000	210,000
Total cash disbursements	$180,000	$203,000	$168,000	$551,000

Note: Assumptions for the budget: 70 percent of a month's purchases are paid in cash during the month; 28 percent are paid in the next month; and 2 percent are taken as a cash discount for early payments and not paid.

[a] 70 percent paid in July, 28 percent paid in August, and 2 percent not paid according to the assumption above.

[b] 70 percent paid in August, 28 percent paid in September, and 2 percent not paid according to the assumption above.

BUDGETING IN MERCHANDISING OPERATIONS

While a manufacturing operation provides a good comprehensive example, budgeting is extensively used in other environments as well, as discussed in this and the following sections.

As in manufacturing, the sales budget in merchandising drives the rest of the budgeted income statement. A merchandiser has no production budget. Instead, there is a merchandise purchases budget, which is much like the direct materials purchases budget in manufacturing. For example, managers at Fashions, Inc., prepared the following purchases budget for a line of women's suits:

Estimated sales	100 units
Estimated ending inventory	10
Estimated beginning inventory	15
Estimated cost per unit	$200

Illustration 17–14 (p. 642), presents the merchandise purchases budget for Fashions, Inc.

As you can see, this budget requires extensive coordination between the managers responsible for sales and those in charge of buying. Because of the critical importance of timing and seasonality in merchandising, special attention is usually given to short-term budgets (for example, spring, summer, Christmas season budgets). The budget helps formalize an ongoing process of coordinating buying and selling. This coordination is critical to the success of merchandising enterprises.

BUDGETING IN SERVICE ENTERPRISES

A key difference in the master budget of a service enterprise is the absence of product or material inventories. Consequently, there is no need for a production budget, as in manufacturing, or a merchandise purchases budget, as in merchandising. Instead, service businesses need to carefully coordi-

FASHIONS, INC.
Merchandise Purchases Budget
For the Year Ended December 31
(in units)

Estimated sales	100 units
Add: Estimated ending inventory	10
Total merchandise needs	110
Less: Beginning inventory	15
Merchandise to be purchased	95 units
Estimated cost per unit	$ 200
Total estimated cost of merchandise . .	$19,000

nate sales (that is, services rendered) with the necessary labor. Managers must ensure that personnel with the right skills are available at the right times.

The budget at David & Sons Company, a regional accounting firm, is developed around the three major services offered: audit, tax, and consulting. Projections of revenue are based on estimates of the number and kinds of clients the firm would service in the budget year and the amount of services requested. The forecasts stem primarily from services provided in previous years with adjustments for new clients, new services to existing clients, loss of clients, and changes in the rates charged for services.

Once the quantity of services (expressed in labor-hours) is forecast, the firm develops its budget for personnel. Staffing to meet client needs is a very important part of the budgeting process. As a partner of the firm put it, "If we overestimate the amount of services we'll provide, we may lose money because we have overstaffed. Our labor costs will be too high compared to our revenues. If we underestimate, we may lose business because we can't provide the services our clients need."

BUDGETING IN NONPROFIT ORGANIZATIONS

The master budget has added importance in nonprofit organizations because it is used to authorize the expenditure of funds. In many governmental units, *the approved budget is a legal authorization for expenditure*, and the penalties for exceeding the authorized expenditures in the budget could be severe. This partially explains why a balanced budget takes on added importance in nonprofit organizations.

State, provincial, and local governments are generally required to have a balanced budget; that is, a budget in which expenditures do not exceed revenues. During its recent budget crisis, the State of California installed an 800 hot line for citizens to call with suggestions to help balance the budget. (While many suggestions were implemented, one idea that was not adopted was to abolish the legislature.)[5]

---

[5] For further discussion of budgeting in government and other nonprofit organizations, see K. Ramanathan, *Management Control in Nonprofit Organizations* (New York: John Wiley & Sons, 1982); and R. Anthony and D. Young, *Management Control in Nonprofit Organizations*, 5th ed. (Homewood, Ill.: Richard D. Irwin, 1993).

ETHICAL ISSUES IN BUDGETING

Budgeting creates serious ethical issues for many people. Much of the information for the budget is provided by managers and employees whose performance is then compared with the budget they helped develop. For example, as a manager, suppose you believed that, while it was possible to achieve a 10 percent increase in your department's sales, a 2 percent increase would be almost certain. If you tell upper management that a 10 percent increase is an appropriate budget, but you fall short of 10 percent, you will lose opportunities for merit pay increases and a promotion. Management may assume the reason you fell short of 10 percent was not because of market circumstances beyond your control, but because you did not perform well in making sales. On the other hand, if you report that only a 2 percent increase is possible, the company will not provide for enough production capacity to fill the sales orders if the 10 percent increase comes through. Should you do what is in your best interest or give your best estimate of reality?

People in companies face these dilemmas all the time. We hope companies provide incentives for people to report truthfully, which means the company must reward both for honest estimates and good performance. But reality is that many companies put considerable pressure on employees to achieve increasingly difficult targets. Fraudulent financial reporting at the division level, such as that experienced at PepsiCo and Datapoint, occurred because managers could not meet difficult targets. This chapter's real world application describes General Electric's attempts to instruct employees on ways to deal with conflicts between high standards of ethical conduct and the demands of their jobs.

BUDGETING UNDER UNCERTAINTY

Any projection of the future is uncertain. Recognizing this, managers often perform sensitivity analysis on their projections. This analysis is based on hypothetical questions, such as: What if labor costs are 10 percent higher (or lower) than projected? What if new health and safety regulations are passed that increase our costs of operations? What if our major supplier of direct materials goes bankrupt? By asking and answering such questions during the planning phase, management can discover the riskiness of various phases of its operations and can develop contingency plans.

As part of the budget plan at Shasta Design, for example, local managers were asked to provide three forecasts: their best estimate, an optimistic estimate (defined as "a 10 percent or less chance that conditions would be better than the optimistic estimate"), and a pessimistic estimate (defined as the situation where there is "a 10 percent or less chance that conditions would be worse"). The optimistic and pessimistic forecasts were not nearly so detailed as the best estimates, but they did highlight some potential problems and risks. From this analysis, top management learned that a major supplier to a distant plant was on the verge of bankruptcy. As a result, management developed relationships with other suppliers, increased the stockpiles of direct materials in the plant, and worked with the supplier to improve its financial position.

Top management at Shasta Design also learned that if all costs were as expected and the pessimistic forecast of sales came true, the company would suffer an operating loss. The primary reason for this would be a worsening of general economic conditions that would decrease demand for the company's products. This was important information to consider in making financial analyses. Further, management put an "early warning" system in place in which it carefully monitored such key economic variables as unemployment, consumer spending, gross national product, and the like. If these indicators signaled a downturn in the economy, management's contingency plan was to reduce production gradually so excess inventories would not build up and to reduce discretionary spending on overhead, marketing, and administrative costs.

Illustration 17–15 provides an overview of sensitivity analysis and contingency planning. For each hypothesis in the sensitivity analysis, there is a choice of steps that can be taken. The procedure can be as simple as a diagram and a few notes on a piece of paper or as complex as a mathematical model incorporated into computerized formal planning models.[6] Of course,

---

[6] Chapter 26 discusses the use of mathematical models to deal with uncertainty.

ILLUSTRATION

17-15

Sensitivity Analysis and Contingency Planning

Sensitivity analysis	Contingency planning
"What if?"	"If, then"
	Status quo
Optimistic (Economic conditions	Increase discretionary costs
and sales better than expected)	Increase production
Expected sales	Status quo
	Status quo
Pessimistic (Economic conditions	Reduce discretionary costs
and sales worse than expected)	Curtail production

decisions about these models' degree of sophistication should be subject to cost-benefit analysis.

The incorporation of uncertainty into budget estimates can be quite useful. A major benefit of formal planning models is to explore many alternatives and options in the planning process. While it is beyond the scope of this book to go into details of formal corporate planning models, we think you can see how the budget plan can be integrated with formal planning models that set forth mathematical relationships among the operating and financial activities of an organization. The use of computer-based simulation models facilitates the asking of numerous what-if questions, which become too difficult to deal with by hand as their number grows.

BUDGETING AND SPREADSHEETS

Spreadsheets are extremely helpful in preparing budgets. Budgeting requires considerable what-if thinking. Spreadsheets help link the various what-if scenarios to changes in financial variables and to financial consequences.

For example, the simple spreadsheet in Illustration 17–16 shows three scenarios of estimated sales prices and sales quantities. Each of the three scenarios is associated with estimated changes in cost of goods sold and changes in marketing and administrative costs. (Row 4 presents the budget used in the text; assume the other scenarios were worked out by management and presented to us.) Note that operating profits before tax would vary considerably between the worst scenario in row 6 and the best scenario shown in row 5. This analysis alerts management that Shasta Designs will incur losses under the scenario shown in row 6 unless management finds ways to cut costs or takes other actions.

These are only some of numerous scenarios that management could develop. Further, managers could develop alternative scenarios for any of the budgets that we have discussed. Large companies usually develop complex financial models to deal with the numerous interactions of the budget.

ILLUSTRATION 17–16

Spreadsheet Analysis of Alternative Budgets, Shasta Designs, Inc.

	A Sales Price	B Sales Quantity	C Cost of Goods Sold	D Marketing and Administrative Costs	E Operating Profits before Tax
1					
2					
3					
4	$800	6,400	$3,200,000	$1,552,000	$368,000
5	$900	6,000	$3,000,000	$1,400,000	$1,000,000
6	$700	6,750	$3,350,000	$1,650,000	($275,000)
7	$850	6,300	$3,170,000	$1,515,000	$670,000
8	$750	6,620	$3,290,000	$1,590,000	$85,000
9	$800	6,400	$3,300,000	$1,560,000	$260,000
10	$800	6,400	$3,100,000	$1,540,000	$480,000

SUMMARY

This chapter has discussed and illustrated the budget process. The budget is part of the overall plan for achieving an organization's objectives. The master budget is usually a one-year plan that encompasses budgeted sales and production, budgeted income statement, balance sheet, and cash flow statement, as well as supporting schedules.

The key to the budget is a good sales forecast because so many other parts of the budget depend on the sales forecast. The sales forecast is usually derived from multiple sources of data, including data provided by sales personnel, by market researchers, and from statistical analyses. Illustration 17–11 shows how the rest of the master budget relates to the sales forecast.

Merchandising budgets are similar to manufacturing, except they have no production budget. Service organizations are similar, except they have no inventories. The budget is not only a planning tool but also a legal authorization for expenditure in governmental units.

Budgeting under uncertainty involves making many forecasts, each representing a different possible set of circumstances. Sensitivity analysis ("what if") and contingency planning ("if, then") are used to derive a set of plans for each possible set of circumstances.

TERMS AND CONCEPTS

The following terms and concepts should be familiar to you after reading this chapter:

Budget, *622*	**Organizational Goals,** *623*
Budgeted Balance Sheets, *639*	**Participative Budgeting,** *624*
Cash Budget, *636*	**Production Budget,** *628*
Delphi Technique, *626*	**Profit Plan,** *624*
Econometric Models, *627*	**Strategic Long-Range Plan,** *623*
Master Budget, *622*	**Trend Analysis,** *627*

QUESTIONS

17–1 Explain the difference between strategic plans and the budget plan.

17–2 Why would more detail be included in a budget for the coming period than appears in a longer-range forecast?

17–3 The chief executive officer of Rigid Plastics Corporation remarked to a colleague, "I don't understand why other companies waste so much time in the budgeting process. I set our company goals, and everyone strives to meet them. What's wrong with that approach?" Comment on the executive's remarks.

17–4 If a company prepares budgeted income statements and balance sheets, why is there a need to prepare a cash budget?

17–5 List four methods used to estimate sales for budgeting purposes.

17–6   How would the use of a just-in-time inventory system affect a company's budget plans?

17–7   For governmental agencies, a budget is also a legal limitation on expenditures. If governmental employees are asked about their agencies' needs for the coming fiscal period, what types of biases are they likely to incorporate in their estimates? Why?

17–8   What are the relationships between organization goals, strategic plans, and a master budget for the coming period?

17–9   What is the danger in relying entirely on middle-management estimates of sales, costs, and other data used in budget planning?

17–10   Multigoal Corporation has established a bonus plan for its employees. An employee receives a bonus if the employee's subunit meets the cost levels specified in the annual budget plan. If the subunit's costs exceed the budget, no bonus is earned by employees of that subunit. What problems might arise with this bonus plan?

17–11   What issue is General Electric dealing with in this chapter's real world application?

17–12   How can budgeting aid in the coordination of corporate activities?

17–13   Surveying the accounts payable records, a clerk in the controller's office noted that expenses appeared to rise significantly within a month of the close of the budget period. The organization did not have a seasonal product or service to explain this behavior. Do you have a suggested explanation?

17–14   Budgets in not-for-profit organizations have an additional purpose beyond those in for-profit organizations. What is that purpose?

17–15   Which of the following budgets is most important from management's perspective: the budgeted balance sheet or the budgeted income statement? Why?

EXERCISES

17–16   Estimate Sales Revenues
(L.O.2)

Davidson Bros. is a large securities dealer. Last year, the company made 60,000 trades with an average commission of $225 per trade. Smaller investors are abandoning the market, which is expected to reduce marketwide volume by 16 percent for the coming year. Davidson expects that its volume generally changes with the market. However, in addition to market factors, Davidson expects an additional 10 percent decline in the number of trades due to unfavorable publicity.

Offsetting these factors is the observation that the average commission per trade is likely to increase by 21 percent because trades are expected to be large in the coming year.

Required: Estimate the commission revenues for the coming year.

17–17   Estimate Sales Revenues
(L.O.2)

Security Atlantic Bank (SAB) has $40 million in commercial loans with an average interest rate of 11.5 percent. The bank also has $30 million in consumer loans with an average interest rate of 15 percent. Finally, the bank owns $8 million in securities with an average rate of 9 percent.

SAB estimates that next year its commercial loan portfolio will fall to $38 million, and the rate will fall to 11 percent. Its consumer loans will expand to $33 million with an average interest rate of 16 percent, and its government securities portfolio will increase to $10 million with an average rate of 8 percent.

Required: Prepare an estimate of Security Atlantic's revenues for the coming year.

17-18 Estimate Sales Revenues
(L.O.2)

Wright Company manufactures ballpoint pens. Last year, the company sold 450,000 type A pens at a price of $2 per unit. The company estimates that this volume represents a 20 percent share of the current type A pens market. The market is expected to increase by 5 percent. Marketing specialists have determined that as a result of a new advertising campaign and packaging, the company will increase its share of this larger market to 24 percent. Due to changes in prices, the new price for the type A pens will be $2.10 per unit. This new price is expected to be in line with the competition and have no effect on the volume estimates.

Required: Estimate the sales revenues for the coming year.

17-19 Estimate Production Levels
(L.O.3)

Limbo Corporation has just made its sales forecasts for the coming period. The Marketing Department estimates that the company will sell 480,000 units during the coming year. In the past, management has found that inventories of finished goods should be maintained at approximately two months' sales. The inventory at the start of the budget period is 32,000 units. Sales take place evenly throughout the year.

Required: Estimate the production level required for the coming year to meet these objectives.

17-20 Estimate Production and Materials Requirements
(L.O.3)

Graphix, Inc., makes a special line of graphic tubing items. For each of the next two years, Years 5 and 6, the company expects to sell 160,000 units. The beginning finished goods inventory, at the start of Year 5, has 40,000 units. However, the target ending finished goods inventory for each year is 20,000 units.

Each unit requires five feet of plastic tubing. At the beginning of Year 5, there are 100,000 feet of plastic tubing in inventory. Management has set a target of tubing materials on hand equal to three months' production requirements. Sales and production take place evenly throughout the year.

Required: Compute the total targeted production of the finished product for Year 5. Compute the required purchases of tubing materials for Year 5. (Note that production in Year 6 should be 160,000 units of the finished product.)

17-21 Estimate Purchases and Cash Disbursements
(L.O.3, L.O.4)

Inflated Ego Company buys plain mylar balloons and prints different designs on them for various occasions. The plain balloons are imported from Taiwan, so a stock equal to the balloons needed for two months' sales should be kept on hand at all times. Plain balloons cost $1.35 each and must be paid for in cash. There are 14,000 plain balloons in the company's stock. Sales estimates, based on contracts received, are as follows for the next six months:

January	6,200
February	8,900
March	6,600
April	7,100
May	4,800
June	3,600

Required:
a. Estimate purchases (in units) for January, February, and March.

b. Estimate cash required to make purchases in January, February, and March.

17-22 Estimate Purchases and Cash Disbursements
(L.O.3, L.O.4)

Kentron Products wishes to purchase goods in one month for sale in the next. On March 31, the company has 4,000 digital tape players in stock, although sales for the next month (April) are estimated to total 4,300 players. Sales for May are expected to equal 3,500 players, and June sales are expected to total 3,700 players.

Tape players are purchased at a wholesale price of $290. The supplier has a financing arrangement whereby Kentron pays 60 percent of the purchase price in the month when the players are delivered and 40 percent in the following month. Five thousand players were purchased in March.

Required:
a. Estimate purchases (in units) for April and May.

b. Estimate cash required to make purchases in April and May.

17–23 Estimate Cash Disbursements
(L.O.4)

Herald Company is preparing its cash budget for the month of April. The following information is available concerning its inventories:

Inventories at beginning of April .... $ 90,000
Estimated purchases for April 440,000
Estimated cost of goods sold for April 450,000
Estimated payments in April for purchases in March 110,000
Estimated payments in April for purchases prior to March 20,000
Estimated payments in April for purchases in April 70%

Required:

What are the estimated cash disbursements in April?

17–24 Estimate Cash Collections
(L.O.4)

Ishima Corporation is preparing its cash budget for the month of May. The following information is available concerning its accounts receivable:

Estimated credit sales for May $200,000
Actual credit sales for April 150,000
Estimated collections in May for credit sales in May 25%
Estimated collections in May for credit sales in April 70%
Estimated collections in May for credit sales prior to April ...... $ 16,000
Estimated write-offs in May for uncollectible credit sales 8,000
Estimated provision for bad debts in May for credit sales in May . 7,000

Required:

What are the estimated cash receipts from accounts receivable collections in May?
(1) $156,000.
(2) $163,000.
(3) $164,000.
(4) $171,000.

(CPA adapted)

17–25 Estimate Cash Collections
(L.O.4)

Brewer's Supply Company is preparing a cash budget for the month of May. The following information on accounts receivable collections is available from past collection experience:

Percent of current month's sales collected this month 28%
Percent of prior month's sales collected this month 60
Percent of sales two months prior to current month collected this month ... 6
Percent of sales three months prior to current month collected this month .. 3
The remaining 3 percent are not collected and are written off as bad debts.

Credit sales to date are as follows:

May—estimated $100,000
April 90,000
March 80,000
February 95,000

Required:

What are the estimated cash receipts from accounts receivable collections in May?
(1) $83,000.
(2) $89,650.
(3) $92,450.
(4) $100,000.

(CPA adapted)

17–26 Estimate Cash Receipts
(L.O.4)

Kathy's Bridal Designs is a custom clothing shop that specializes in wedding attire. The average price of each of Kathy's wedding ensembles is $3,200. For each wedding, Kathy's receives a 20 percent deposit two months before the wedding, 50 percent the month before, and the remainder on the day when the goods are delivered. Based on information at hand, Kathy's expects to prepare outfits for the following number of weddings during the coming months:

January	10
February	6
March	4
April	8
May	10
June	22

Required:

a. What are the expected revenues for Kathy's Bridal Designs for each month, January through June? Revenues are recorded in the month of the wedding.

b. What are the expected cash receipts for each month, January through April?

17–27 Estimate Cash Receipts (L.O.4)

Deep Six Pool Service manages neighborhood pools in Oceanside. The company attempts to make service calls at least once a month to all homes that subscribe to Deep Six's service. More frequent calls are made during the summer. The number of subscribers also varies with the season. The following table shows the number of subscribers and the average number of calls to each subscriber for the months of interest here:

	Subscribers	Service Calls
March	50	.5
April	60	1.0
May	130	1.8
June	150	2.2
July	150	2.0
August	140	1.7

The average price charged for a service call is $50. 20 percent of the service calls are paid in the month when the service is rendered; 60 percent in the month after the service is rendered; and 18 percent in the second month after. The remaining 2 percent are uncollectible.

Required:

What are Deep Six's expected cash receipts for May, June, July, and August?

17–28 Prepare Budgeted Financial Statements (L.O.5)

Refer to the data in exercise 17–27.

Deep Six estimates the number of subscribers in September should fall 10 percent below August levels, and the number of service calls should decrease by an estimated 20 percent. The following information is available for costs incurred in August. All costs except depreciation are paid in cash.

Service costs:	
Variable costs	$2,360
Maintenance and repair	2,100
Depreciation (fixed)	1,100
Total	5,560
Marketing and administrative costs:	
Marketing (variable)	1,250
Administrative (fixed)	1,150
Total	2,400
Total costs	$7,960

Variable cash costs and variable marketing costs will change with volume. Fixed depreciation will remain the same, while fixed administrative costs will increase by 5 percent beginning September 1. Maintenance and repair are provided by contract, which calls for a 1 percent increase in September.

Required:

Prepare a budgeted income statement for September.

17–29   Prepare Budgeted Financial Statements
(L.O.5)

Finn, Inc., is a fast growing start-up firm that manufactures surfboards. The following income statement is available for Year 1.

Revenues (100 units @ $250/unit)	$25,000
Less:	
Manufacturing costs:	
Materials	1,450
Other variable costs	1,140
Fixed costs	2,285
Depreciation (fixed)	8,590
Total manufacturing costs	13,465
Gross profit margin	11,535
Less:	
Marketing:	
Variable costs	3,640
Depreciation (fixed)	1,314
Administrative:	
Fixed costs (cash)	4,390
Depreciation (fixed)	649
Total marketing and administrative	9,993
Operating profits	$ 1,542

Sales volume is expected to increase by 20 percent in Year 2, while the sales price is expected to fall 10 percent. Materials prices are expected to increase 4 percent. Other variable manufacturing costs are expected to increase by 3 percent per unit in Year 2. Fixed manufacturing costs are expected to increase 5 percent. In addition to these cost changes, variable manufacturing and variable marketing costs will also change with sales volume. Administrative cash costs are expected to increase by 10 percent.

Finn operates on a cash basis and maintains no inventories. Depreciation is fixed and should remain unchanged over the next three years.

Required:

Prepare a budgeted income statement for Year 2.

17–30   Ethics and Budgeting
(L.O.6)

Norton Company manufactures infant furniture and carriages. The accounting staff is currently preparing next year's budget. Michelle Jackson is new to the firm and is interested in learning how this process occurs. She has lunch with Maria, the sales manager, and Barry, the production manager, to discuss the planning process. Over the course of lunch Michelle discovers that Maria lowers sales projections 5 to 10 percent before submitting her figures, while Barry increases cost estimates by 10 percent before submitting his figures. When Michelle inquires as to why this is done, the response is simply that everyone around here does it.

Required:

a.   What do Maria and Barry hope to accomplish by their methods?

b.   How might this backfire and work against them?

c.   Are the actions of Maria and Barry unethical?

(CMA adapted)

PROBLEMS

17–31 Prepare Budgeted Financial Statements

The following information is available for Year 1 for Digital Electronics:

Revenues (100,000 units)	$725,000
Manufacturing costs:	
Materials	42,000
Variable cash costs	35,600
Fixed cash costs	81,900
Depreciation (fixed)	249,750
Marketing and administrative costs:	
Marketing (variable, cash)	105,600
Marketing depreciation	37,400
Administrative (fixed, cash)	127,300
Administrative depreciation	18,700
Total costs	698,250
Operating profits	$ 26,750

Depreciation charges are all fixed and are expected to remain the same for Year 2. Sales volume is expected to increase by 18 percent, but prices are expected to fall by 5 percent. Materials costs are expected to decrease by 8 percent. Variable manufacturing costs are expected to decrease by 2 percent per unit. Fixed manufacturing costs are expected to increase by 5 percent.

Variable marketing costs will change with volume. Administrative cash costs are expected to increase by 10 percent. Inventories are kept at zero.

Required:

Prepare a budgeted income statement for Year 2.

17–32 Estimate Cash Receipts

Refer to the data in problem 17–31. Estimate the cash from operations expected in Year 2.

17–33 Prepare Budgeted Financial Statements

Monumental Designs has the following data from Year 1 operations, which are to be used for developing Year 2 budget estimates:

Revenues (100,000)	$746,000
Manufacturing costs:	
Materials	133,000
Variable cash costs	180,900
Fixed cash costs	72,000
Depreciation (fixed)	89,000
Marketing and administrative costs:	
Marketing (variable, cash)	95,000
Marketing depreciation	22,600
Administrative (fixed, cash)	90,110
Administrative depreciation	8,400
Total costs	691,010
Operating profits	$ 54,990

Depreciation charges are all fixed. Old manufacturing equipment with an annual depreciation charge of $9,700 will be replaced in Year 2 with new equipment that will incur an annual depreciation charge of $14,000. Sales volume is expected to increase by 12 percent, and prices are expected to increase by 6 percent. Materials costs are expected to increase by 10 percent for each unit produced. Variable manufacturing costs are expected to decrease by 4 percent on a per unit basis. Fixed manufacturing costs are expected to decrease by 7 percent.

Variable marketing costs will change with volume. Administrative cash costs are expected to increase by 8 percent. Inventories are kept at close to zero.

Required: Prepare a budgeted income statement for Year 2.

17–34 Estimate Cash Receipts

Refer to the data in problem 17–33. Estimate the cash from operations expected in Year 2.

17–35 Prepare a Production Budget

Eastern Forest Products Corporation manufactures floral containers. The controller is preparing a budget for the coming year and asked for your assistance. The following costs and other data apply to container production:

Direct materials per container:

1 pound Z-A styrene at $.40 per pound

2 pounds Vasa finish at $.80 per pound

Direct labor per container:
1/4 hour at $8.60 per hour

Overhead per container:

Indirect labor	$.12
Indirect materials	.03
Power	.07
Equipment costs	.36
Building occupancy	.19
Total overhead per unit	$.77

You learn that equipment costs and building occupancy are fixed costs; these unit costs are based on a normal production of 20,000 units per year. Other overhead costs are variable. Plant capacity is sufficient to produce 25,000 units per year.

Labor costs per hour are not expected to change during the year. However, the supplier of the Vasa finish has informed the company that a 10 percent price increase will be imposed at the start of the coming budget period. No other costs are expected to change.

During the coming budget period, the company expects to sell 18,000 units. Finished goods inventory is targeted to increase from 4,000 units to 7,000 units to get ready for an expected sales increase the year after next. Production will take place evenly throughout the year. Inventory levels for Vasa finish and Z-A styrene are expected to remain unchanged throughout the year. There is no work in process inventory.

Required: Prepare a production budget and estimate the materials, labor, and overhead costs for the coming year.

17–36 Sales Expense Budget

Compuware Corporation has just received its sales expense report for January. The report is reproduced below.

Item	Amount
Sales commissions	$135,000
Sales staff salaries	32,000
Telephone and mailing	16,200
Building lease payment	20,000
Heat, light, and water	4,100
Packaging and delivery	27,400
Depreciation	12,500
Marketing consultants	19,700

You have been asked to develop budgeted costs for the coming year. Since this month is typical, you decide to prepare an estimated budget for a typical month in the coming year.

You uncover the following additional data:

1. Sales volume is expected to increase by 5 percent.
2. Sales prices are expected to increase by 10 percent.
3. Commissions are based on a percentage of selling price.
4. Sales staff salaries will increase 4 percent next year regardless of sales volume.
5. Building rent is based on a five-year lease that expires in three years.
6. Telephone and mailing expenses are scheduled to increase by 8 percent even with no change in sales volume. However, these costs are variable with the number of units sold, as are packaging and delivery costs.
7. Heat, light, and water are scheduled to increase by 12 percent regardless of sales volume.
8. Depreciation includes furniture and fixtures used by the sales staff. The company has just acquired an additional $19,000 in furniture that will be received at the start of next year and will be depreciated over a 10-year life using the straight-line method.
9. Marketing consultant expenses were for a special advertising campaign. The company runs these campaigns from time to time. During the coming year, the costs are expected to average $35,000 per month.

Required:

Prepare a budget for sales expenses for a typical month in the coming year.

17–37 Budgeted Purchases and Cash Flows— Multiple-Choice

D. Tomlinson Retail seeks your assistance to develop cash and other budget information for May, June, and July. At April 30, the company had cash of $5,500; accounts receivable of $437,000; inventories of $309,400; and accounts payable of $133,055. The budget is to be based on the following assumptions:

Sales:

Each month's sales are billed on the last day of the month.

Customers are allowed a 3 percent discount if payment is made within 10 days after the billing date. Receivables are recorded in the accounts at their gross amounts (*not* net of discounts).

Sixty percent of the billings are collected within the discount period; 25 percent are collected by the end of the month; 9 percent are collected by the end of the second month; and 6 percent turn out to be uncollectible.

Purchases:

Fifty-four percent of all purchases of merchandise and selling, general, and administrative expenses are paid in the month purchased and the remainder in the following month. The number of units in each month's ending inventory is equal to 130 percent of the next month's units of sales.

The cost of each unit of inventory is $20.

Selling, general, and administrative expenses, of which $2,000 is depreciation, are equal to 15 percent of the current month's sales.

Actual and projected sales are as shown below:

	Dollars	Units
March	$354,000	11,800
April	363,000	12,100
May	357,000	11,900
June	342,000	11,400
July	360,000	12,000
August	366,000	12,200

Required: Choose the best answer or indicate none of the above.

a. Budgeted purchases in dollars for May are:
   (1) $244,800.
   (2) $225,000.
   (3) $238,000.
   (4) $357,000.

b. Budgeted purchases in dollars for June are:
   (1) $243,600.
   (2) $228,000.
   (3) $292,000.
   (4) $242,000.

c. Budgeted cash collections during the month of May are:
   (1) $333,876.
   (2) $355,116.
   (3) $340,410.
   (4) $355,656.

d. Budgeted cash disbursements during the month of June are:
   (1) $292,900.
   (2) $287,379.
   (3) $294,900.
   (4) $285,379.

e. The budgeted number of units of inventory to be purchased during July is:
   (1) 15,860.
   (2) 12,260.
   (3) 12,000.
   (4) 15,600.

(CPA adapted)

17–38 Comprehensive Budget Plan

No-Spills, Inc., a manufacturer of coffee cups, decided in October 19X0 that it needed cash to continue operations. The corporation began negotiating for a one-month bank loan of $100,000 starting November 1, 19X0. The bank would charge interest at the rate of 1 percent per month and require the company to repay interest and principal on November 30, 19X0. In considering the loan, the bank requested a projected income statement and cash budget for the month of November.
   The following information is available:

1. The company budgeted sales at 120,000 units per month in October 19X0, December 19X0, and January 19X1, and at 90,000 units in November 19X0. The selling price is $2 per unit.

2. The inventory of finished goods on October 1 was 24,000 units. The finished goods inventory at the end of each month is to equal 20 percent of sales anticipated for the following month. There is no work in process.

3. The inventory of raw materials on October 1 was 22,800 pounds. At the end of each month, the raw materials inventory is to equal not less than 40 percent of production requirements for the following month. The company purchases materials as needed in minimum quantities of 25,000 pounds per shipment.

4. Selling expenses are 10 percent of gross sales. Administrative expenses, which include depreciation of $500 per month on office furniture and fixtures, total $33,000 per month.

5. The manufacturing budget for coffee cups, based on normal production of 100,000 units per month, follows:

Materials (½ pound per cup, 50,000 pounds, $2.00 per pound)	$ 50,000
Labor	40,000
Variable overhead	20,000
Fixed overhead (includes depreciation of $4,000)	10,000
Total	$120,000

Required:

a. Prepare schedules computing inventory budgets by months for
   (1)   Production in units for October, November, and December.
   (2)   Raw material purchases in pounds for October and November.

b. Prepare a projected income statement for the month of November. Cost of goods sold should equal the variable manufacturing cost per unit times the number of units sold plus the total fixed manufacturing cost budgeted for the period.

(CPA adapted)

17–39   Comprehensive Budget Plan

C. L. Corporation appeared to be experiencing a good year. Sales in the first quarter were one third ahead of last year, and the Sales Department predicted that this rate would continue throughout the entire year. Ruth Keenan, assistant controller, was asked to prepare a new forecast for the year and to analyze the differences from last year's results. The forecast was to be based on actual results obtained in the first quarter plus the expected costs of programs to be carried out in the remainder of the year. She worked with various department heads (Production, Sales, and so on) to get the necessary information. The results of these efforts are presented below:

C. L. CORPORATION
Expected Account Balances for December 31, This Year
(in thousands)

Cash	$ 1,200	
Accounts Receivable	80,000	
Inventory (January 1, next year)	48,000	
Plant and Equipment	130,000	
Accumulated Depreciation		$ 41,000
Accounts Payable		45,000
Notes Payable (due within one year)		50,000
Accrued Payables		23,250
Common Stock		70,000
Retained Earnings		108,200
Sales		600,000
Other Income		9,000
Manufacturing costs:		
Materials	213,000	
Direct Labor	218,000	
Variable Overhead	130,000	
Depreciation	5,000	
Other Fixed Overhead	7,750	
Marketing:		
Commissions	20,000	
Salaries	16,000	
Promotion and Advertising	45,000	
Administrative:		
Salaries	16,000	
Travel	2,500	
Office Costs	9,000	
Income Taxes	—	
Dividends	5,000	
	$946,450	$946,450

Adjustments for the change in inventory and for income taxes have not been made. The scheduled production for this year is 450 million units, and planned sales volume is 400 million units. Sales and production volume was 300 million units last year. A full-absorption costing, FIFO inventory system is used. The company is subject to a

40 percent income tax rate. The actual income statement for last year is presented below:

C. L. CORPORATION
Statement of Income and Retained Earnings
For the Year Ended December 31, Last Year
(in thousands)

Revenue:			
Sales		$450,000	
Other income		15,000	$465,000
Expenses:			
Cost of goods manufactured and sold:			
Materials	$132,000		
Direct labor	135,000		
Variable overhead	81,000		
Fixed overhead	12,000		
	360,000		
Beginning inventory	48,000		
	408,000		
Ending inventory	48,000	360,000	
Selling:			
Salaries	13,500		
Commissions	15,000		
Promotion and advertising	31,500	60,000	
General and administrative:			
Salaries	14,000		
Travel	2,000		
Office costs	8,000	24,000	
Income taxes		8,400	452,400
Operating profit			12,600
Beginning retained earnings			100,600
Subtotal			113,200
Less: Dividends			5,000
Ending retained earnings			$108,200

Required: Prepare a budgeted income statement and balance sheet.

(CMA adapted)

INTEGRATIVE CASES

17–40   Prepare Cash Budget for Service Organization

The Triple-F Health Club (Family, Fitness, and Fun) is a nonprofit health club. The club's board of directors is developing plans to acquire more equipment and expand club facilities. The board plans to purchase about $25,000 of new equipment each year and wants to begin a fund to purchase an adjoining property in four or five years when the expansion will need the space. The adjoining property has a market value of about $300,000.

The club manager is concerned that the board has unrealistic goals in light of its recent financial performance. She sought the help of a club member with an accounting background to assist her in preparing the club's records, including the cash basis income statements presented below. The review and discussions with the manager disclosed the additional information that follows the statement.

TRIPLE-F HEALTH CLUB
Statement of Income (Cash Basis)
For the Year Ended October 31
(in thousands)

	19X7	19X6
Cash revenues:		
Annual membership fees	$355.0	$300.0
Lesson and class fees	234.0	180.0
Miscellaneous	2.0	1.5
Total cash received	591.0	481.5
Cash costs:		
Manager's salary and benefits	36.0	36.0
Regular employees' wages and benefits	190.0	190.0
Lesson and class employee wages and benefits	195.0	150.0
Towels and supplies	16.0	15.5
Utilities (heat and light)	22.0	15.0
Mortgage interest	35.1	37.8
Miscellaneous	2.0	1.5
Total cash costs	496.1	445.8
Cash income	$ 94.9	$ 35.7

Additional information:

1. Other financial information as of October 31, 19X7:
   a. Cash in checking account, $7,000.
   b. Petty cash, $300.
   c. Outstanding mortgage balance, $360,000.
   d. Accounts payable for supplies and utilities that are unpaid as of October 31, 19X7, and due in November 19X7, $2,500.
2. The club purchased $25,000 worth of exercise equipment during the current fiscal year. Cash of $10,000 was paid on delivery, and the balance was due on October 1 but has not yet been paid as of October 31, 19X7.
3. The club began operations in 19X1 in rental quarters. In October 19X3, it purchased its current property (land and building) for $600,000, paying $120,000 down and agreeing to pay $30,000 plus 9 percent interest annually on the unpaid loan balance each November 1, starting November 1, 19X4.
4. Membership rose 3 percent during 19X7. This is approximately the same annual rate of increase the club has experienced since it opened and is expected to continue in the future.
5. Membership fees were increased by 15 percent in 19X7. The board has tentative plans to increase the fees by 10 percent in 19X8.
6. Lesson and class fees have not been increased for three years. The board policy is to encourage classes and lessons by keeping the fees low. The members have taken advantage of this policy and the number of classes and

lessons have grown significantly each year. The club expects the percentage growth experienced in 19X7 to be repeated in 19X8.

7. Miscellaneous revenues are expected to grow in 19X8 (over 19X7) at the same percentage as experienced in 19X7 (over 19X6).

8. Lesson and class employees' wages and benefits will increase to $291,525. The wages and benefits of regular employees and the manager will increase 15 percent. Towels and supplies, utilities, and miscellaneous expenses are expected to increase 25 percent.

Required:

a. Construct a cash budget for 19X8 for the Triple-F Health Club.

b. Identify any operating problem(s) that this budget discloses for the Triple-F Health Club. Explain your answer.

c. Is the manager's concern that the board's goals are unrealistic justified? Explain your answer.

(CMA adapted)

17–41 Estimate Cash Receipts for a City

Early in March, the Jackson City administrator presented a budget to the city council. This is four months prior to the start of the new fiscal year, which begins July 1. Most of the important amounts are estimated because the final budget data (1) will not be available until much closer to the end of the year or (2) are based upon estimates of events that occur in the next year.

City revenues are a good example of the data requirement problem. The city obtains its cash revenues from four sources: property taxes, city income tax, parking fees and fines, and other revenues. Property taxes are based on the assessed valuation of all the property in the city. The final assessment values for the fiscal year are not available until late May. Income tax receipts depend upon the income earned next year by the residents of the city. The parking fees and fines depend, to a large extent, on the size of the population.

The city administrator added an estimate of monthly cash receipts and disbursements for next year to the budget material he presented to the council. Cash receipts were estimated using a cash forecasting model developed in the controller's department. The model was the result of statistical analysis of prior years' results and is presented below:

$$C_i = mr_i A_t + \frac{(1 + I)T_{t-1}}{12} + \frac{(1 + G)P_{t-1}}{12} + \frac{(1 + G)R_{t-1}}{12}$$

where

C_i = Cash collected for the ith month (July = 1)

m = Property tax rate per $1,000 of assessed valuation

r_i = Percent of property tax collected in the ith month (July = 1)

A_t = Assessed valuation of property in Year t (t = budget year) in thousands of dollars

I = Inflation rate (decimal)

T = Income taxes withheld from taxpayers

G = Population growth (decimal)

P = Parking fees and fines collections

R = Other revenues collections

The assessed valuation in thousands of dollars, A_t, was estimated from the regression equation:

$$A_t = \$50,000 + 1.05A_{t-1} + \$3S$$

where

S = Thousands of square feet of new construction since the last assessment

The numerical data shown below were available at the end of February when the budget for this fiscal year was constructed. The data for last fiscal year represent either actual figures or data projected for the entire year based on the first eight months of the last fiscal year. The data for the new fiscal year represent either rates or amounts that were actually experienced or estimates of what is expected to be experienced.

Fiscal Year		
Last	Population (actual)	100,000 people
New	Population growth rate (estimated)	8%
Last	Assessed valuation (actual)	$600,000,000
Last	Square feet of new construction since last assessment (projected)	30,000,000 sq. ft.
New	Property tax rate per $1,000 of assessed valuation (actual)	$25
Last	Income taxes withheld (projected)	$4,000,000
Last	Collections of parking fees and fines (projected)	$1,000,000
Last	Other revenues collections (projected)	$500,000
New	Inflation rate (estimated)	11% per year

The collection pattern for property taxes that has been experienced the past three years is shown below. City officials expected this pattern to persist in this fiscal year.

July	20%	January	1%
August	60	February	1
September	10	March	1
October	5	April	—
November	1	May	—
December	1	June	—

Required:

Estimate the cash receipts for the month of August that the Jackson City administrator included in the budget material presented to the city council in March. Use the cash forecasting model developed by the controller's department and the data available in February.

(CMA adapted)

SHASTA DESIGN, INC.
Schedule of Budgeted Manufacturing Overhead
For the Budget Year Ended December 31
(compare to Illustration 17–5)

Variable (based on production of 7,300 units):[a]

Indirect materials and supplies	$ 42,677	
Materials handling	66,261.5	
Other indirect labor	37,061.5	$ 146,000

Fixed (same as for production of 6,500 units):

Supervisory labor	175,000	
Maintenance and repairs	85,000	
Plant administration	173,000	
Utilities	87,000	
Depreciation	280,000	
Insurance	43,000	
Property taxes	117,000	
Other	41,000	1,001,000
Total manufacturing overhead		$1,147,000

[a] Additional computations:

$$\text{Indirect materials:} \quad \$38,000 \times \frac{7,300}{6,500} = \$42,677$$

$$\text{Materials handling:} \quad \$59,000 \times \frac{7,300}{6,500} = \$66,261.5$$

$$\text{Other indirect labor:} \quad \$33,000 \times \frac{7,300}{6,500} = \$37,061.5$$

EXHIBIT

B

1 (concluded)

SHASTA DESIGN, INC.
Budgeted Statement of Cost of Goods Manufactured and Sold
for the Budget Year Ended December 31
(compare to Illustration 17–6)

Beginning work in process inventory			–0–
Manufacturing costs:			
Direct materials:			
Beginning inventory (Illustration 17–6) . . . . . $	142,000		
Purchases^a (21,200 R @ $10 + 37,400 S @ $30)	1,334,000		
Materials available for manufacturing	1,476,000		
Less: Ending inventory (1,500 R @ $10 + 4,900 S @ $30)	(162,000)		
Total direct materials costs		$1,314,000	
Direct labor $\left(\$949{,}000 \times \dfrac{7{,}300}{6{,}500}\right)$		1,065,800	
Manufacturing overhead (Exhibit A)		1,147,000	
Total manufacturing costs			$3,526,800
Deduct: Ending work in process inventory			–0–
Cost of goods manufactured			3,526,800
Add: Beginning finished goods inventory			450,000
Deduct: Ending finished goods inventory^a			(579,748)
Cost of goods sold			$3,397,052

^a Additional computations:

Required production:

$$
\begin{array}{lllll}
BB & + \text{Production} & = \text{Sales} & + EB \\
900 & + \quad P & = 7{,}000 & + 1{,}200 \\
 & \quad\; P & = \underline{7{,}300} \\
\end{array}
$$

Materials requirements:

$$
\begin{array}{lll}
\text{R: } BB & + \text{Purchases} & = \text{Production} + EB \\
2{,}200 + & P & = (7{,}300 \times 3) + 1{,}500 \\
 & P & = \underline{21{,}200} \\
\end{array}
$$

$$
\begin{array}{lll}
\text{S: } BB & + \text{Purchases} & = \text{Production} + EB \\
4{,}000 + & P & = (7{,}300 \times 5) + 4{,}900 \\
 & P & = \underline{37{,}400} \\
\end{array}
$$

Ending finished goods inventory (assuming FIFO):

$$
\frac{\text{Ending units}}{\text{Units produced}} \times \text{Cost of goods manufactured} = \frac{1{,}200}{7{,}300} \times \$3{,}526{,}800
$$

$$
= \underline{\$579{,}748}
$$

EXHIBIT

C

2

SHASTA DESIGN, INC.
Schedule of Budgeted Marketing and Administrative Costs
For the Budget Year Ended December 31
(compare to Illustration 17–7)

Variable marketing costs:[a]

Sales commissions	$284,375	
Other marketing	113,750	
Total variable marketing costs		$ 398,125

Fixed marketing costs:

Sales salaries	100,000	
Advertising	193,000	
Other	78,000	
Total fixed marketing costs		371,000
Total marketing costs		769,125

Administrative costs (all fixed):

Administrative salaries	254,000	
Legal and accounting staff	141,000	
Data processing services	103,000	
Outside professional services	39,000	
Depreciation—building, furniture, and equipment	94,000	
Insurance	26,000	
Taxes—other than income	160,000	
Total administrative costs		817,000
Total budgeted marketing and administrative costs		$1,586,125

[a] Additional computations:

$$\text{Sales commissions: } \$284,375 = \$260,000 \times \frac{7,000 \text{ units}}{6,400 \text{ units}}$$

$$\text{Other marketing: } \quad \$113,750 = \$104,000 \times \frac{7,000 \text{ units}}{6,400 \text{ units}}$$

2

SHASTA DESIGN, INC.
Budgeted Income Statement
For the Budget Year Ended December 31
(compare to Illustration 17–8)

Budgeted revenues:

Sales (7,000 units at $800)		$5,600,000

Budgeted expenses:

Cost of goods manufactured and sold (see solution to self-study question 1, Exhibit B)	$3,397,052	
Marketing and administrative costs (Exhibit C)	1,586,125	
Total budgeted costs		4,983,177
Budgeted operating profits		616,823
Federal and other income taxes (given in question)		214,547
Budgeted operating profits after taxes		$ 402,276

EXHIBIT

E

3

SHASTA DESIGN, INC.
Cash Budget
For the Budget Year Ended December 31
(compare to Illustration 17–9)

Cash balance beginning of period		$ 150,000
Receipts:		
Collections on accounts[a]	$5,625,000	
Sales of assets (per management)	25,000	
Total receipts		5,650,000
Less disbursements:		
Payments for accounts payable[b]	1,317,000	
Direct labor[c]	1,065,800	
Manufacturing overhead requiring cash less noncash depreciation charges[c]	867,000	
Marketing and administrative costs less noncash charges[d]	1,492,125	
Required payments for federal income taxes (given)	282,390	
Dividends and other distributions to shareholders	140,000	
Reduction in long-term debt	83,000	
Acquisition of new assets	320,000	
Total disbursements		5,567,315
Budgeted ending cash balance		$ 232,685

Additional computations:

[a] Collections on account per Illustration 17–9	$5,185,000
Additional sales ($5,600,000 − $5,120,000) (from Exhibit D and Illustration 17–8)	480,000
Less increase in receivables	(40,000)
	$5,625,000
[b] Payments on account per Illustration 17–9	$1,164,000
Additional materials purchases—per Exhibit B and Illustration 17–6 ($1,334,000 − $1,179,000)	155,000
Less increase in payables	(2,000)
	$1,317,000

[c] See solution to self-study question 1.

[d] See solution to self-study question 2.

Using the Budget for Performance Evaluation and Control

LEARNING OBJECTIVES

After reading this chapter, you should be able to:

1. Use budgets for performance evaluation.
2. Develop and use flexible budgets.
3. Compute and interpret the sales activity variance.
4. Prepare and use a profit variance analysis.
5. Explain how responsibility centers are used.
6. Identify how ethical problems arise when budgets are used for performance evaluation.

*I*n Chapter 17, we described the development of the master budget as a first step in the budgetary planning and control cycle. This chapter carries the process a step further to use the budget as a tool for performance evaluation and control. The master budget can be thought of as a blueprint for achieving the company's goals. The control process assures that the blueprint is followed or, if changes are required, that the best alternative is chosen.

The master budget includes **operating budgets** (for example, the budgeted income statement, the production budget, the budgeted cost of goods sold) and **financial budgets** (for example, the cash budget, the budgeted balance sheet). When management uses the master budget for control purposes, it focuses on the key items that must be controlled to ensure company success. Most such items are in the operating budgets, although some also appear in the financial budgets. In this chapter, we focus on the income statement because it is the most important financial statement used by managers to control operations.

When reported income statements are compared to budgeted income statements, there are nearly always **variances** or differences between the budgeted and reported amounts. Managers spend considerable time and effort understanding causes of these variances, interpreting them, and taking corrective action. Later chapters discuss these variances in detail; this

Operating Budgets Refers to the budgeted income statement, the production budget, the budgeted cost of goods sold, and supporting budgets.

Financial Budgets Refers to budgets of financial resources; for example, the cash budget and the budgeted balance sheet.

Variances Differences between planned results and actual outcomes.

chapter presents the "big-picture" comparison of budgeted to reported profits. Understanding this big picture will help you understand where the details discussed in later chapters fit.

FLEXIBLE BUDGETING

Static Budget A budget for a single activity level—usually the master budget.

Flexible Budget A budget that indicates revenues, costs, and profits for different levels of activity.

Flexible Budget Line The expected monthly costs at different levels of output.

A master budget presents a comprehensive view of anticipated operations. Such a budget is typically a **static budget**; that is, it is developed in detail for one level of anticipated activity. A **flexible budget,** by contrast, indicates budgeted revenues, costs, and profits for virtually all feasible levels of activities. Since variable costs and revenues change with changes in activity levels, these amounts are budgeted to be different at each activity level in the flexible budget.

For example, studies of past cost behavior of labor costs of the surgical nurses in the operating rooms of Sierra Memorial Outpatient Center indicate that the Surgical Nursing Department expects to incur fixed costs of $500,000 per year and variable costs of $50 per operating room–hour. This cost function is graphed in Illustration 18–1. This is the same type of cost line that is used for cost-volume-profit (CVP) analysis as discussed in Chapter 11. The expected activity level for the period is budgeted at 100,000 hours. From the **flexible budget line** in Illustration 18–1, we find the budgeted costs at a planned activity of 100,000 operating room–hours to be $5.5 million [$500,000 + ($50 × 100,000 hours)].

Suppose that actual costs are only $5 million. At first glance, one might assume that a good job of cost control was done because costs were $500,000 lower than the budget plan. But in fact, only 80,000 operating room–hours were actually incurred instead of the 100,000 hours originally planned. According to the flexible budget concept, the master budget must be ad-

---

I L L U S T R A T I O N

18–1

Comparison of Master and Flexible Budget, Surgical Nursing Department, Sierra Memorial Outpatient Center

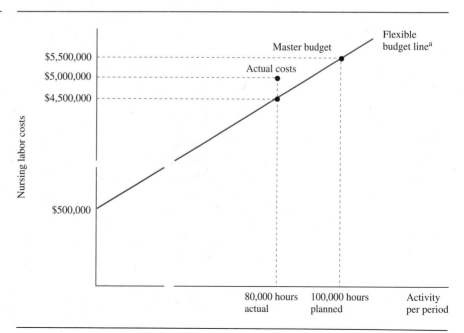

a This is the cost line from cost-volume-profit analysis.

justed for this change in activity. The adjusted budgeted costs for control and performance evaluation purposes would be $4.5 million [$500,000 + ($50 × 80,000 hours)]. Now it is clear that while costs are lower than planned, they are $500,000 higher than they should be after *taking into account the level of activity in the department.*

The estimated cost-volume line in Illustration 18–1 is known as the *flexible budget line* because it shows the budgeted costs allowed for each level of activity. For example, if activity would increase to 120,000 operating room–hours, budgeted costs would be $6.5 million [$500,000 + ($50 × 120,000 hours)]. If activity drops to 50,000 operating room–hours, budgeted costs would drop to $3 milliion [$500,000 + ($50 × 50,000 operating room–hours)]. Whatever level of activity occurred during the period is entered into the flexible budget equation:

$$TC = F + VX$$

where

TC = Total budgeted costs for the period
F = Fixed costs for the period
V = Variable costs per unit
X = Activity expressed as quantity of units

For the Surgical Nursing Department at Sierra Memorial Outpatient Center:

$$TC = \$500,000 + \$50X$$

You can compare the master budget with the flexible budget by thinking of the master budget as an ex ante (before-the-fact) prediction of X (activity), while the flexible budget is based on ex post (after-the-fact) knowledge of the actual X.

COMPARING BUDGETS AND RESULTS

A comparison of the master budget with the flexible budget and with actual results forms the basis for analyzing differences between plans and actual performance. The following example is used in this and subsequent chapters to illustrate the comparison of plans with actual performance.

The Evergreen Company makes wooden crates for shipping fruits. Its master budget income statement is presented in Illustration 18–2. The format is consistent with variable costing, not full-absorption costing. We use this variable costing format for analyzing differences between actual and planned results because it separates fixed and variable costs. This separation is important for managerial estimates of cost behavior and profits.

The flexible budget, presented in Illustration 18–3, is based on *actual* activity. In May, 10,000 crates were actually produced and sold. The difference between operating profits in the master budget and operating profits in the flexible budget is called an **activity variance.** The $22,000 variance is due to the 2,000-unit difference between actual sales and planned sales. This difference can also be seen on the flexible budget profit-volume line in Illustration 18–4.

Activity Variance Effect of changes in sales or production activity on profits.

Favorable versus Unfavorable Variances

Note the use of F for favorable and U for unfavorable beside each of the variances in Illustration 18–3. These terms describe the impact of the variance on the budgeted operating profits. A *favorable variance increases*

Master Budget,
Evergreen Company

	Master Budget (based on 8,000 units planned)
Sales revenue (8,000 units at $20)	$160,000
Less:	
Variable manufacturing costs	64,000[a]
Variable marketing and administrative costs	8,000[b]
Contribution margin	88,000
Less:	
Fixed manufacturing costs	36,000
Fixed marketing and administrative costs	40,000
Operating profit	$ 12,000

The following estimates are used by Evergreen Company to prepare the master budget:

Sales price	$20 per crate
Sales volume	8,000 crates
Production volume	8,000 crates
Variable manufacturing costs	$8 per crate
Variable marketing and administrative costs	1 per crate
Fixed manufacturing costs	36,000
Fixed marketing and administrative costs	40,000

[a] 8,000 budgeted units at $8 per unit.
[b] 8,000 budgeted units at $1 per unit.

operating profits, holding all other things constant. An *unfavorable variance decreases* operating profits, holding all other things constant. These terms are not intended to be used in a normative sense; thus, a **favorable variance** is *not necessarily good,* and an **unfavorable variance** is *not necessarily bad.*

Favorable Variance Variance that, taken alone, results in an addition to operating profit.

Unfavorable Variance Variance that, taken alone, reduces operating profit.

An excellent case in point is the sales activity or volume variance in Illustration 18–3. Holding everything else constant, the 2,000-unit increase in sales creates a favorable variance. Is this really good? Perhaps not. Economic conditions may have been better than planned, which increased the volume demanded by the market. Hence, perhaps, the 2,000-unit increase in sales volume should have been even greater taking everything into account.

Note that the variable cost variances are both labeled unfavorable. But this doesn't mean that they are bad for the company. Variable costs are expected to increase when volume is greater than planned.

Sales Activity Variance

The information in Illustration 18–3 has a number of uses. First, it isolates the increase in operating profits caused by the increase in activity from the master budget. Further, the resulting flexible budget shows budgeted sales, costs, and operating profits *after* taking into account the activity increase but *before* considering differences in *unit* selling prices, variable costs, and

18–3

Flexible and Master Budget,
Evergreen Company (May)

	Flexible Budget[a] (based on actual activity of 10,000 units)	Sales Activity Variance (based on variance in sales volume)	Master Budget (based on 8,000 units planned)
Sales revenue	$200,000	$40,000 F	$160,000
Less:			
Variable manufacturing costs[b] (at $8 per unit)	80,000	16,000 U	64,000
Variable marketing and administrative costs (at $1 per unit)	10,000	2,000 U	8,000
Contribution margin	110,000	22,000 F	88,000
Less:			
Fixed manufacturing costs	36,000	—	36,000
Fixed marketing and administrative costs	40,000	—	40,000
Operating profits	$ 34,000	$22,000 F	$ 12,000

[a] Calculations for flexible budget:
   $200,000 = 10,000/8,000 × $160,000.
   $ 80,000 = 10,000/8,000 × $ 64,000.
   $ 10,000 = 10,000/8,000 × $ 8,000.
   Fixed costs are not expected to change between 8,000 and 10,000 units.
[b] This can be thought of as variable cost of goods sold.
   U = Unfavorable variance.
   F = Favorable variance.

Sales Activity Variance Difference between operating profit in master budget and operating profit in flexible budget. Variance arises because the actual quantity of units sold is different than the budgeted quantity.

fixed costs from the master budget. As noted before, we refer to this change from the master budget plan as the **sales activity variance.** The sales activity variance is also known as a *sales volume variance.*

Some writers suggest that variance analysis is unnecessary when there are differences between planned and actual activity levels. Rather, they suggest that tabulating the difference in volume alone is sufficient. For example, rather than point out that Evergreen Company had a favorable sales activity variance of $22,000, they would report that Evergreen Company sold 2,000 more units than planned. In practice, managers prefer variance data because it provides information about the impact of differences between plans and actual results on profit amounts.

Note the makeup of the $22,000 sales activity variance in Illustration 18–3. First, the difference between the master budget sales of $160,000 and the flexible budget sales of $200,000 (which is the estimated $20 unit sales price times the 10,000 units actually sold) is $40,000. This is based on the 2,000-unit increase in sales volume times the estimated $20 unit sales price. We use the *estimated* unit sales price instead of the *actual* price because we want to isolate the impact of the activity increase from changes in the sales price. We want to focus on the effects of volume alone. Thus, the sales amount in the flexible budget is *not the actual revenue* (actual price times actual volume) but the *estimated unit sales price times the actual number of*

ILLUSTRATION

Flexible Budget Line,
Evergreen Company

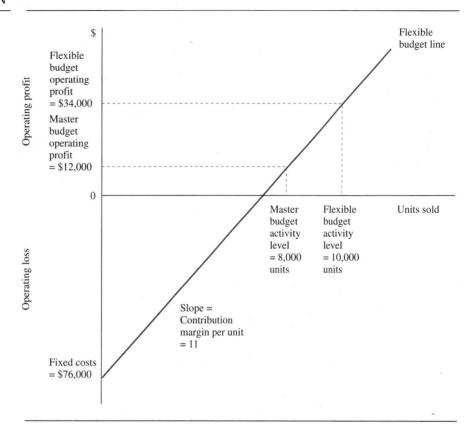

units sold. Second, variable costs are *expected* to increase by $18,000, giving a favorable contribution margin of $22,000 ($40,000 − 18,000), which is the favorable sales activity variance.

 *Self-Study*
Question

1 Prepare a flexible budget for Evergreen Company for May with the same master budget as in Illustration 18–3 but assuming 7,000 units were actually sold.

The solution to this question is at the end of this chapter on page 696.

COMPARING ACTUAL
TO THE FLEXIBLE
BUDGET

Assume the actual results for May are shown in the following table.

	Actual
Sales price	$21 per crate
Sales volume	10,000 crates
Variable manufacturing costs . . .	$85,440
Variable marketing and administrative costs	11,000
Fixed manufacturing costs	37,000 for May
Fixed manufacturing and administrative costs	44,000 for May

Profit Variance Analysis Analysis of the causes of differences between budgeted profits and the actual profits earned.

The **profit variance analysis** shows the cause of differences between the budgeted profits and the actual profits earned. Now the actual results can be compared with both the flexible budget and the master budget in a profit variance analysis, as shown in Illustration 18–5. Columns 5, 6, and 7 are carried forward from Illustration 18–3.

Column 1 is the reported income statement based on the facts presented above. Column 2 summarizes manufacturing variances (which are discussed in more detail in Chapter 19), and column 3 shows marketing and administrative variances (which are discussed in more detail in Chapter 21). Costs have been divided into fixed and variable portions here and would be presented in more detail to the managers of centers having responsibility for them.

Cost variances result from deviations in costs and efficiencies in operating the company. They are important for measuring productivity and helping to control costs.

Sales Price Variance

The sales price variance, column 4, is derived from the *difference between the actual and budgeted selling price times the actual number of units sold* [$10,000 = ($21 − $20) × 10,000 units].

Variable Manufacturing Cost Variances

Be careful (in Illustration 18–5) to distinguish the variable cost variances in columns 2 and 3, which are input variances, from the variable cost variances in column 6, which are part of the sales activity variance. Management *expects* the latter costs to be higher in this case because the sales volume is higher than planned.

Looking at column 5, we see that variable manufacturing costs *should have been* $80,000 for a production and sales volume of 10,000 units, not $64,000 as expressed in the master budget in column 7. We see from column 1 that the actual variable manufacturing costs *were* $85,440, some $21,440 higher than the master budget, but only $5,440 higher than the flexible budget. Which number should be used to evaluate manufacturing cost control—the $21,440 variance from the master budget or the $5,440 variance from the flexible budget?

The number that should be used to evaluate manufacturing performance is the $5,440 variance from the flexible budget. This points out a benefit of flexible budgeting. A superficial comparison of the master budget plan with the actual results would have indicated the variance to be $21,440. But, in fact, manufacturing is responsible for only $5,440, which is caused by deviation from production norms. We discuss the source of this $5,440 in more detail in Chapter 19.

Fixed Manufacturing Cost Variance

The fixed manufacturing cost variance is simply the difference between actual and budgeted costs. Fixed costs are treated as period costs; they are not expected to be affected by activity levels within a relevant range. Hence, the flexible budget fixed costs equal the master budget fixed costs.

Marketing and Administrative Costs

Marketing and administrative costs are treated like manufacturing costs. Variable costs are expected to change as activity changes; hence, variable costs were expected to increase by $2,000 between the flexible and master budgets, as shown in Illustration 18–5, because volume increased by 2,000

ILLUSTRATION 18-5 Profit Variance Analysis, Evergreen Company (May)

	(1) Actual (based on actual activity of 10,000 units sold)	(2) Manufacturing Variances	(3) Marketing and Administrative Variances	(4) Sales Price Variance	(5) Flexible Budget (based on actual activity of 10,000 units sold)	(6) Sales Activity Variance	(7) Master Budget (based on 8,000 units planned)
Sales revenue	$210,000	—	—	$10,000 F	$200,000	$40,000 F	$160,000
Less:							
Variable manufacturing costs	85,440	$5,440 U [a]	—	—	80,000	16,000 U	64,000
Variable marketing and administrative costs	11,000	—	$1,000 U	—	10,000	2,000 U	8,000
Contribution margin	113,560	5,440 U	1,000 U	10,000 F	110,000	22,000 F	88,000
Less:							
Fixed manufacturing costs	37,000	1,000 U	—	—	36,000	—	36,000
Fixed marketing and administrative costs	44,000	—	4,000 U	—	40,000	—	40,000
Operating profits	$ 32,560	$6,440 U	$5,000 U	$10,000 F	$ 34,000	$22,000 F	$ 12,000

→ Total variance from flexible budget = $1,440 U

→ Total variance from master budget = $20,560 F

[a] Highlighted to make this amount easier for reference throughout this chapter and in Chapter 19.

673

units. Comparing actual with the flexible budget reveals $1,000 U variance for marketing and administrative costs. Fixed marketing and administrative costs do not change as volume changes; hence, the flexible and master budget amounts are the same.

Self-Study Question

2 In August, Containers, Inc., produced and sold 50,000 "notebook computer" cases at a sales price of $10 each. Budgeted sales were 45,000 units at $10.15.

Budget:

Standard variable costs per unit
(that is, per case) ....$ 4.00

Fixed manufacturing overhead cost:

   Monthly budget   80,000

Marketing and administrative:

   Variable ....   1.00 per case

   Fixed   100,000

Actual:

Actual manufacturing costs:

   Variable costs per unit 4.88

   Fixed overhead   83,000

Actual marketing and administrative:

   Variable (50,000 @ $1.04)   52,000

   Fixed   96,000

Using variable costing, prepare a profit variance analysis comparing actual results with the flexible and master budgets for August. Include variances.

The solution to this question is at the end of this chapter on page 697.

UNITS PRODUCED VERSUS UNITS SOLD

In the previous example, production volume and sales volume were equal. But the analysis becomes more complicated when the units sold are not equal to the units produced.

Suppose that 12,000 units were produced in May, but only 10,000 units were sold. Also, assume there was no beginning inventory. This has no effect on the sales activity variance because the master budget and flexible budget are based on *sales* volume. Thus, columns 5, 6, and 7 of Illustration 18–5 remain unchanged. In addition, the sales price variance is based on units sold, so column 4 remains the same. Generally, marketing and administrative costs are not affected by *producing* 12,000 instead of 10,000 units, so we assume they do not change. This allows us to focus on columns 1 and 2, which would change.

Assume that actual variable manufacturing costs are $8.544 *per unit* and fixed manufacturing costs are $37,000 *for the period*. This leaves the fixed manufacturing cost variance of $1,000 U unchanged. However, the variable manufacturing cost variance changes. In the month units are produced, the following variable manufacturing cost variances are computed:

Units produced × (Actual variable cost − Estimated variable cost) = Variance

ILLUSTRATION 18-6   *Profit Variance Analysis when Units Produced Do Not Equal Units Sold, Evergreen Company (May)*

	(1) Actual (based on 10,000 units)[a]	(2) Manufacturing Variances	(3) Marketing and Administrative Variances	(4) Sales Price Variance	(5) Flexible Budget (based on 10,000 units)	(6) Sales Activity (volume) Variance	(7) Master Budget (based on 8,000 units planned)
Sales revenue	$210,000	—	—	$10,000 F	$200,000	$40,000 F	$160,000
Less:							
Variable manufacturing costs	86,528	$6,528 U			80,000	16,000 U	64,000
Variable marketing and administrative costs	11,000	—	$1,000 U	—	10,000	2,000 U	8,000
Contribution margin	112,472	6,528 U	1,000 U	10,000 F	110,000	22,000 F	88,000
Less:							
Fixed manufacturing costs	37,000	1,000 U			36,000	—	36,000
Fixed marketing and administrative costs	44,000	—	4,000 U	—	40,000	—	40,000
Operating profits	$ 31,472	$7,528 U	$5,000 U	$10,000 F	$ 34,000	$22,000 F	$ 12,000

Total variance from flexible budget = $2,528 U

Total variance from master budget = $19,472 F

[a] Based on 10,000 units sold and 12,000 units produced.

675

Previous example for *10,000 units produced* (Illustration 18–5):

$$10,000 \times (\$8.544 - \$8.00) = \$5,440 \text{ U}$$

Present example for *12,000 units produced* (Illustration 18–6):

$$12,000 \times (\$8.544 - \$8.00) = \$6,528 \text{ U}$$

The entire variable manufacturing cost variance for units *produced* in May is $6,528. This amount may be treated as a period cost and expensed in May, or it may be prorated to units sold and to units still in inventory. If prorated, $2/12 \times \$6,528$ would be charged to inventory in this case because 2,000 of the 12,000 units produced in May are still in inventory at the end of May. In most companies, the $6,528 variance due to May's production is written off as a period expense in May. The $6,528 would appear as a variance, as shown in Illustration 18–6.

Note that the actual variable manufacturing costs of $86,528 in Illustration 18–6 are really a hybrid—$80,000 in flexible budget costs (based on 10,000 units sold this period times $8 estimated cost per unit) plus the $6,528 variable manufacturing cost variance from the 12,000 units produced this period.

RECONCILING FULL-ABSORPTION AND VARIABLE COSTING

Assume that Evergreen Company produced 12,000 units and sold 10,000 units in May. There was no beginning inventory on May 1, so the ending inventory on May 31 was 2,000 units. Using variable costing, the entire *fixed manufacturing cost* of $37,000 would be expensed, as shown in Illustrations 18–3 through 18–6. Such would not be the case, however, when full-absorption costing is used and production and sales volume are not the same.

Using full-absorption costing, a portion of the fixed manufacturing costs would be allocated to the 2,000 units in ending inventory:

$$\frac{2,000 \text{ units}}{12,000 \text{ units}} \times \$37,000 = \underline{\underline{\$6,167}}$$

Or $\dfrac{\$37,000}{12,000 \text{ units}} = \$3.08^{1}/_{3}$ fixed manufacturing cost per unit. 2,000 units are in ending inventory from current period production, so $6,167 (2,000 units $\times$ 3.08^{1}/_{3}$) fixed manufacturing costs are allocated to ending inventory.

Thus only $30,833 ($37,000 − $6,167) of the actual fixed manufacturing costs are expensed in May using full-absorption costing. In this case, full-absorption operating profit would be $37,639 in May, or $6,167 higher than variable costing operating profit.[1] This $6,167 difference in profits is due to the accounting system and not to managerial efficiencies. Care should be taken to identify the cause of such profit differences so those due to accounting method are not misinterpreted as being caused by operating activities.

The budget planning and control methods presented in this book are based on the variable costing approach to product costing unless otherwise stated. Illustration 18–7 shows how the reported income statement under full-absorption would be reconciled with that using variable costing. The

---

[1] Of course, as discussed in Chapter 9, if units sold exceed units produced, we expect the reverse to be true; that is, full-absorption operating profit would be lower than variable costing operating profit.

ILLUSTRATION

18-7

Reconciling Actual Income Using Full-Absorption Costing and Variable Costing

	(1a)	(1b) (Inventory Adjustment) Fixed Manufacturing Costs Going into Inventory Using Full-Absorption	(1c)
	Actual Using Full-Absorption		Actual Using Variable Costing
Sales revenue	$210,000		$210,000
Less:			
Variable manufacturing costs	86,528		86,528
Variable marketing and administrative costs	11,000		11,000
Contribution margin	112,472		112,472
Less:			
Fixed manufacturing costs	30,833	$6,167[a]	37,000
Fixed marketing and administrative costs	44,000		44,000
Operating profits	$ 37,639	$6,167	$ 31,472

[a] 2,000 units put into inventory times $3.083 $\left(= \dfrac{\$37,000}{12,000\ \text{units}} \right)$ fixed manufacturing cost per unit.

comparison of budget to actual results presented in Illustration 18–6 would still be used; however, additional columns (1a and 1b) would be added to reconcile actual results using variable costing to those using full-absorption costing.

SERVICE AND MERCHANDISING ACTIVITIES

The comparison of the master budget, the flexible budget, and actual results can also be used in service and merchandising organizations. The basic framework in Illustration 18–5 would be retained. Output would usually be defined as sales units in merchandising, but other measures are used in service organizations. For example:

Organization	Units of Activity
Public accounting, legal, and consulting firms	Professional staff hours
Laundry	Weight or pieces of clothing
Hospital	Patient-days

Merchandising and service organizations focus on marketing and administrative costs to measure efficiency and to control costs. The key items to control are labor costs, particularly in service organizations, and occupancy costs per sales-dollar, particularly in merchandising organizations.

RESPONSIBILITY CENTERS

Budgets for performance evaluation and cost control are typically organized into **responsibility centers.** Responsibility centers are organizational units for which someone has responsibility. For example, a business school within a

Responsibility Centers Organizational units for which someone has responsibility.

university is often a responsibility center. The dean of the business school has a budgeted level of resources to work with and is responsible to university officials for the way those resources are used to achieve the university's goals. Other examples are:

Responsibility Center	Person in Charge	Responsible for
Company	Chief executive officer	All assets, equities, revenues, and costs of the company
Division	Division vice president	Divisional assets, equities, revenues, and costs
Plant	Plant manager	Plant production and costs
Department store	Store manager	Store's revenues and costs
Secretarial pool	Secretarial pool supervisor	Costs and secretarial production

For example, the assignment of responsibilities for Electronics, Inc., is shown in Illustration 18–8. Each of the three vice presidents—administrative, production, and marketing—is responsible for part of the organization.

ILLUSTRATION

18–8

Responsibility Centers, Electronics, Inc.

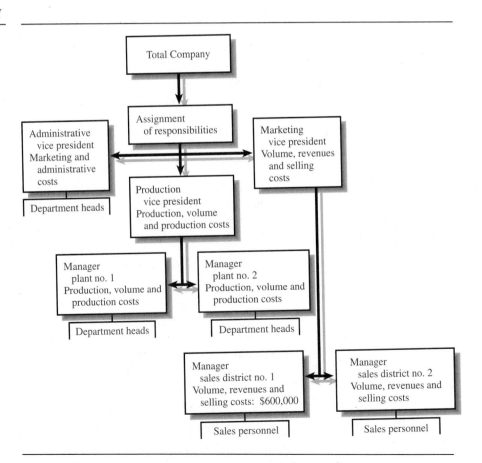

The administrative responsibility center is subdivided into departments (Data Processing, Accounting, Personnel). The production responsibility center is further divided among plant managers, who assign responsibility to department heads (Assembly, Processing, Quality Control, Warehousing). The marketing vice president assigns marketing responsibility to the district sales managers.

Profit and Cost Centers

Cost Center Organizational unit responsible for costs.

Profit Center Organizational unit responsible for profits. Profit center is usually responsible for revenues, costs, production volume, and sales volume.

We discuss various types of responsibility centers in considerable depth later in this book. For now, we want you to know the two basic types of responsibility centers that organizations use with a profit variance analysis. The first is a **cost center,** in which managers of organizational units are responsible for costs. Of course, managers are also responsible for quality and quantity of output, employee morale, and other things, too. However, managers of cost centers are not responsible for revenues. For example, the department heads of the production plants are probably in charge of cost centers.

Profit center managers are responsible for both revenue and costs. The manager of the bank where you keep your accounts, the manager of the service station or auto repair shop where you have your car repaired, and the manager of your favorite restaurant are likely to be profit center managers. Profit center managers use a profit variance analysis to plan and control their operations. A cost center manager would use the cost portion of a profit variance analysis to manage activities. Both profit and cost center managers require more detailed information about expected and actual costs than the detail presented in a profit variance analysis. Chapter 19 discusses additional cost analyses for managers to use.

PRESSURE TO PERFORM AND PERSONAL CHOICES

Comparing budget and actual results can lead to considerable pressure to perform well, so much pressure that people sometimes play games with revenue recognition. For example, how would you deal with the following situation? You have just made a large sale on December 31, the last day of your company's fiscal year. The paperwork cannot be processed until January 2 of next year, meaning the sale will be recorded next year. Your department's sales performance has not been good this year, so you face the prospect of being fired. Recording the sale this year would considerably help your prospects of being kept on the job. You learn from a friend in accounting that you could backdate the paperwork from January 2 to December 31, as long as no other sales have yet been recorded for next year. What would you do?

Employees constantly face situations like this. Most companies have a policy that allows employees a reasonable period of time to take care of necessary paperwork. In addition, by explaining the circumstances to your supervisors, you would probably be given some credit for the sale even if it were not recorded until next year. Nevertheless, many people in organizations face considerable pressure to recognize revenue ''early,'' which means the sale is recorded before it has been finalized.

For example, Comserv Corporation was a computer software company that installed specialized software for manufacturing companies. Comserv would record a portion of the revenue from a contract at the time the contract was signed, and record the remaining revenue when the software

---

MiniScribe Corporation, a manufacturer of computer disk drives, had reported record earnings for several quarters. Its stock had increased fivefold over an 18-month period, but fabricated financial results lay behind the company's reported excellent financial performance. A subsequent court suit revealed evidence that $16 million of sales made on the day after the fiscal year-end were backdated to the previous year. The company had shipped disk drives to customers who had not ordered them. The company booked revenue for 432 disk-drives that it shipped to its own warehouse instead of to customers. Two years after the fraud, the company restated its originally reported profits of $22.7 million to $12.2 million.

* Based on Lee Berton, "How MiniScribe Got Its Auditor's Blessing on Questionable Sales," *The Wall Street Journal,* May 14, 1992, pp. A1 and A5.

---

was installed. (A similar case involved MiniScribe Corporation, as described in this chapter's real world application.) Comserv's management felt the pressure to report substantial profits so the company would keep up with its competitors in the computer software industry. The Securities and Exchange Commission subsequently learned that salespeople had been backdating contracts and writing contracts based only on oral confirmation from customers.[2]

At a plant in Ronson Corporation's Aerospace Division, employees claimed large jobs had been completed and sold when in fact the jobs were hidden from the auditors in buildings the auditors did not inspect. In both the Comserv and Ronson cases, the Securities and Exchange Commission filed formal charges against corporate employees alleging they had committed financial fraud.[3]

Whatever your career choice, whether in a large business or in a one-person operation, whether public accounting, private industry, or the public sector, you will face pressure to perform that can lead to difficult personal choices. We hope you are able to recognize situations that could compromise your ethical standards. A key signal is the "tone at the top." Top managers who emphasize results at all costs create an environment in which it may be difficult to perform well professionally while maintaining high ethical standards. Also, watch for situations where people are desperate to perform well, perhaps because of financial difficulties.

BEHAVIORAL ISSUES IN BUDGETING

"You should hold employees responsible for those things they can control" is sometimes claimed to be an important behavioral factor in designing accounting systems. This appeals to a sense of fairness that "the manager of the Assembly Department should not be charged with inefficiencies caused by the Cutting Department." Perhaps of more significance in an economic sense, is the idea that holding employees responsible for the things they can control focuses managers' attention on the things they can influence and

---

[2] Michael Maher, "Case Studies in Financial Fraud" (University of California, Davis, 1992).

[3] Ibid.

reduces their risk. Flexible budgets can reduce risk to a worker, as demonstrated by the following example.

Assume that the manager of the Repairs Department has a budget of $100,000 for December. It turns out that machine time is low in December, and repairs can be easily scheduled without overtime. As a result, the manager spends only $90,000 of the budget. However, suppose production increases during the month of January, and department personnel are working overtime to make the necessary repairs. Expenditures for the Repairs Department are $110,000 in January.

The manager of the Repairs Department believes performance is evaluated according to the budget and that his bonus, raises, promotions, and job could depend on meeting the budget. A risk-averse manager will prefer a system that adjusts the budget down to $90,000 in December and up to $110,000 in January to reflect the changing levels of production, even though the average results for the two months are the same.

The idea that ''employees should be held accountable for what they control'' does not mean factors outside of their control should be ignored in evaluating performance. For example, information about an employee's peers may be useful in evaluating how well the employee is performing. This is analogous to ''grading on the curve,'' where knowing how well a student did relative to the rest of the class is usually more informative about student exam performance than just knowing the student's own exam score. Few employers will ignore information about factors outside an employee's control that nevertheless affect the employee's performance.

How "Tight" Should Budget Levels Be?

Research indicates that budgets that are very difficult to achieve or those that are easily achievable may not lead to the best employee performance. The motivational problems of employees are similar to those of students. For example, if it is virtually impossible to improve your grade by studying hard for a test, you may not be as motivated to study as hard as you would if you believed there was a good chance that studying would improve your grade. On the other hand, if you believe that you will get a good grade with minimal studying, you may not be inclined to study beyond that minimal level.

In general, the budget levels that seem to motivate best are moderately tight yet are perceived by employees as reasonable and attainable. This generalization may vary from situation to situation, of course.

ZERO-BASE BUDGETING

Zero-Base Budgeting A system of establishing financial plans beginning with an assumption of no activity and justifying each program or activity level.

Many organizations have attempted to manage discretionary costs through a budgeting method called **zero-base budgeting.** Numerous companies (including Texas Instruments, Xerox, and Control Data) and governmental units (including some agencies of the federal government) have implemented zero-base budgeting at one time or another. One reason the approach has attracted considerable popularity in public sector organizations is that it is seen as a means of managing expenditures in a setting where the benefits of the expenditures cannot be traced to the costs as easily as they can in manufacturing.

The novel part of zero-base budgeting is the requirement that the budgeting process start at zero, with all expenditures to be completely justified. This contrasts with the usual approach, in which a certain level of expenditures is allowed as a starting point, and the budgeting process focuses on requests for incremental expenditures. However, a strict zero-base approach has been found to be generally impracticable because of the massive amount of time required for implementation. Thus, many organizations that use zero-base budgeting in fact allow a floor that does not have to be justified in as much detail. In many organizations, this has been set at around 80 percent of the current level of expenditures. This floor is the lowest amount of money that would enable a responsibility center to continue its operations at a minimal level. Proposed increments of activity above this level are evaluated one by one in terms of costs and benefits.

SUMMARY

This chapter discussed and illustrated the use of the budgeted income statement for performance evaluation and control. The master budget income statement was compared with actual results. Differences, or variances, between actual results and the master budget were analyzed to determine why budgeted results did not occur.

The master budget is typically static: that is, it is developed in detail for one level of activity. A flexible budget recognizes that variable costs and revenues are expected to differ from the budget if the actual activity (for example, actual sales volume) differs from what was budgeted. A flexible budget can be thought of as the costs and revenues that would have been budgeted if the activity level had been correctly estimated in the master budget. The general relationship between the actual, the flexible budget, and the master budget is shown below:

Actual	**Flexible Budget**	**Master Budget**
Actual costs and revenues based on actual activity	Costs and revenues that would have been budgeted if actual activity had been budgeted	Budgeted costs and revenues based on budgeted activity

Differences or variances between actual results and the flexible budget are differences between actual results and the budget that would have been prepared if activity had been accurately estimated. These variances include the sales price variance, manufacturing cost variances, and nonmanufacturing cost variances. Differences between the flexible and master budget results are due to the impact on revenues and costs of the differences between actual and budgeted volume.

When units produced and sold are not the same, a decision has to be made whether to prorate variances to units sold and those in inventory or to write off the variance as a period cost.

TERMS AND CONCEPTS

The following terms and concepts should be familiar to you after reading this chapter:

QUESTIONS

18–1 What is a responsibility center?

18–2 Could some responsibility centers differ in the types of budget items they are accountable for? That is, might some responsibility centers be responsible only for costs, some only for revenues, and some for both? Give examples.

18–3 Does a line worker avoid responsibility because he or she is not included formally in the responsibility reporting system? How can management keep control of the line worker's activities in the absence of formal budget control?

18–4 Budgets for governmental units are usually prepared one year in advance of the budget period. Expenditures are limited to the budgeted amount. At the end of the period, performance is evaluated by comparing budget authorizations with actual receipts and outlays. What management control problems are likely to arise from such a system?

18–5 "I don't understand why you accountants want to prepare a budget for a period that is already over. We know the actual results by then—all that flexible budgeting does is increase the controller's staff and add to our overhead." Comment on this remark.

18–6 Why is a contribution margin format based on variable costing more useful for performance evaluation purposes than the traditional format based on full-absorption costing?

18–7 "All costs 'flex' with activity." True or false? Why or why not?

18–8 How will the performance measurement system differ when a company is using the LIFO inventory system from when a company is using the FIFO system?

18–9 What is zero-base budgeting, and how does it differ from other budgeting practices?

18–10 The basic difference between a master budget and a flexible budget is that:

(1) A flexible budget considers only variable costs, but a master budget considers all costs.

(2) A flexible budget allows management latitude in meeting goals, whereas a master budget is based on a fixed standard.

(3) A master budget is for an entire production facility, but a flexible budget is applicable to single departments only.

(4) A master budget is based on a predicted level of activity, and a flexible budget is based on the actual level of activity.

(CPA adapted)

18–11 A flexible budget is:

(1) Appropriate for control of factory overhead but not for control of direct materials and direct labor.

(2) Appropriate for control of direct materials and direct labor but not for control of factory overhead.

(3) Not appropriate when costs and expenses are affected by fluctuations in volume.

(4) Appropriate for any level of activity.

(CPA adapted)

18–12 Refer to the real world application for this chapter. Why would managers at MiniScribe ship disk drives to customers who had not ordered them and backdate invoices to the previous fiscal year?

18–13 How does the concept of flexible budgeting reinforce the notion that employees should be held responsible for what they can control?

EXERCISES

18–14 Flexible Budgeting
(L.O.2)

Orcutt Corporation prepared a budget last period that called for sales of 9,000 units at a price of $12 each. The costs were estimated to be $5 variable per unit and $27,000 fixed. During the period, actual production and actual sales were 9,200 units. The selling price was $12.15 per unit. Variable costs were $5.90 per unit. Actual fixed costs were $27,000.

Required:

Prepare a flexible budget for Orcutt.

18–15 Sales Activity Variance
(L.O.3)

Refer to the data in exercise 18–14 for Orcutt Corporation. Prepare a sales activity variance analysis like the one in Illustration 18–3.

18–16 Profit Variance Analysis
(L.O.4)

Refer to the data in exercises 18–14 and 18–15. Prepare a profit variance analysis like the one in Illustration 18–5.

18–17 Flexible Budgeting, Service Organization
(L.O.2)

Ortega & Reiser (OR) is a CPA firm that gets a large portion of its revenue from tax services. Last year, OR's billable tax hours were higher than expected; but as shown by the following data, profits from the Tax Department were lower than anticipated.

	Reported Income Statement	Master Budget
Billable hours[a]	46,000 hours	40,000 hours
Revenue	$3,300,000	$3,000,000
Professional salaries (all variable)	1,850,000	1,500,000
Other variable costs (e.g., supplies, certain computer services)	425,000	400,000
Fixed costs	580,000	600,000
Tax Department profit	$ 445,000	$ 500,000

[a] These are hours billed to clients. They are less than the hours worked because there is nonbillable time (e.g., slack periods, time in training sessions) and because some time worked for clients is not charged to them.

Required:

Prepare a flexible budget for Ortega & Reiser. Use billable hours as the measure of output (that is, "units produced").

18–18 Sales Activity Variance, Service Organization
(L.O.3)

Refer to the data in exercise 18–17 for Ortega & Reiser. Prepare a sales activity variance analysis like the one in Illustration 18–3.

18–19 **Profit Variance Analysis, Service Organization** (L.O.4)

Refer to the data in exercise in 18–17 for Ortega & Reiser. Prepare a profit variance analysis like the one in Illustration 18–5 for Ortega & Reiser.

18–20 **Flexible Budget** (L.O.2)

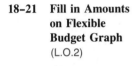

Required:

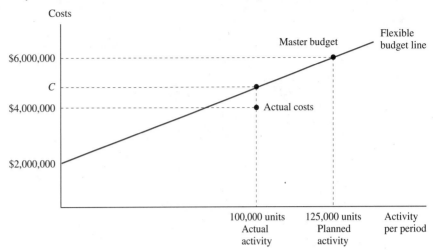

Given the data shown in the graph, what are the following:

a. The budgeted fixed cost per period?

b. The budgeted variable cost per unit?

c. The value of *C* (that is, the flexible budget for an activity level of 100,000 units)?

d. If the actual activity had been 200,000 units, what would be the flexible budget cost amount?

18–21 **Fill in Amounts on Flexible Budget Graph** (L.O.2)

Fill in the missing amounts for (*a*) and (*b*).

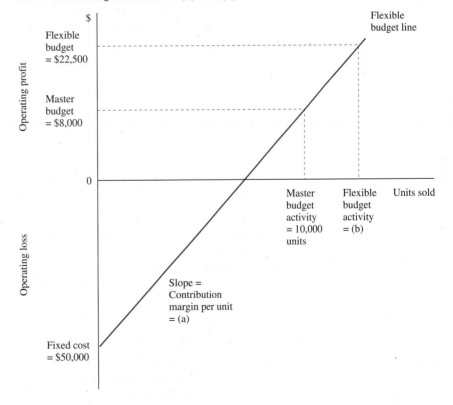

18–22   Flexible Budget
(L.O.2)

Label (*a*) and (*b*) in the graph and give the number of units sold for each.

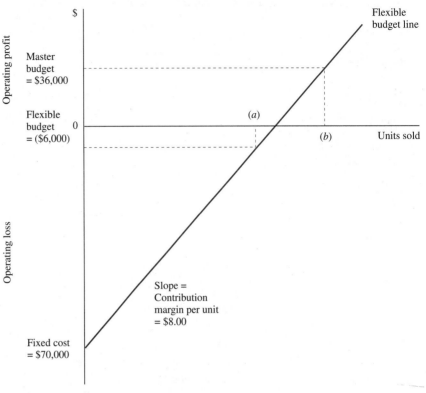

18–23   Prepare Flexible Budget
(L.O.2)

Visions, Inc., manufactures and sells compact disks for a variety of New Age groups. The company only produces when orders are received and, therefore, has no inventories. The following information is available for the current month:

	Actual (based on actual of 425,000 units)	Master Budget (based on budgeted 400,000 units)
Sales revenue	$1,930,000	$2,000,000
Less:		
Variable costs:		
Blank disks	600,000	600,000
Direct labor	165,000	140,000
Variable overhead	239,000	260,000
Variable marketing and administrative	205,000	200,000
Total variable costs	1,209,000	1,200,000
Contribution margin	721,000	800,000
Less:		
Fixed costs:		
Manufacturing overhead	388,000	400,000
Marketing	120,000	120,000
Administrative	65,000	75,000
Total fixed costs	573,000	595,000
Operating profits	$ 148,000	$ 205,000

Required:		Prepare a flexible budget for Visions.
18–24	**Sales Activity Variance** (L.O.3)	Refer to the data in exercise 18–23 for Visions, Inc. Prepare a sales activity variance analysis like the one in Illustration 18–3.
18–25	**Profit Variance Analysis** (L.O.4)	Use the information for Visions, Inc. (exercise 18–23). Prepare a profit variance analysis like the one in Illustration 18–5.
18–26	**Assigning Responsibility** (L.O.5)	Taxes 'R Us public accountants perform both audit and tax work for clients. The Tax Department relies on the Audit Department's work to prepare tax returns. On a recent job, the audit team goofed. Consequently, the tax people prepared the tax return improperly.

Now, the client is being audited by the Internal Revenue Service. The audit is requiring a great deal of time and effort by the Tax Department with no compensation from the client. The manager of the Tax Department argues that the Audit Department should bear some of the cost of the tax audit. The Audit Department manager says the Tax Department should have checked the numbers before using them.

Required:		As the manager of the accounting firm, how would you assign responsibility?
18–27	**Assigning Responsibility** (L.O.5)	The manager of the soldering area in a company that manufactures computer circuit boards asked the manager of the start station to shut down production for a few hours for emergency maintenance work on the soldering machines. The start station manager refused saying, "My job requires me to keep the production line going." Consequently, the production line kept running, and the quality reject rate for products coming out of the soldering operation increased from virtually zero to nearly 50 percent.

Management learned about the quality problem, and ordered the production line to be stopped. The product rejects cost the company about $50,000.

Required:	As top management, to whom would you assign the responsibility for the $50,000 cost of product rejects?

PROBLEMS

18–28	**Solve for Master Budget Given Actual Results**	Oleander Enterprises lost the only copy of the master budget for this period. Management wants to evaluate this period's performance but needs the master budget to do so. Actual results for the period were:

Sales volume	120,000 units
Sales revenue	$672,000
Variable costs:	
Manufacturing	147,200
Marketing and administrative	61,400
Contribution margin	463,400
Fixed costs:	
Manufacturing	205,000
Marketing and administrative	113,200
Operating profit	$145,200

The company planned to produce and sell 108,000 units at a price of $5 each. At that volume, the contribution margin would have been $380,000. Variable marketing and administrative costs are budgeted at 10 percent of sales revenue. Manufacturing fixed costs are estimated at $2 per unit at the normal volume of 108,000 units. Management notes: "We budget an operating profit of $1 per unit at the normal volume."

Required:

a. Construct the master budget for the period.

b. Prepare a profit variance analysis like the one in Illustration 18–5.

18–29 Find Missing Data for Profit Variance Analysis

	Reported Income Statement (750 units)	Manu-facturing Variances	Marketing and Administrative Variance	Sales Price Variance	Flexible Budget (a)	Sales Activity Variance	Master Budget (800 units)
Sales revenue	$1,950			(b)	$2,025	(c)	(d)
Variable manufacturing costs	(e)	$60 F			(f)	$38 F	(g)
Variable marketing and administrative costs	(h)		(i)		(j)	(k)	$240
Contribution margin	$1,240	(l)	(m)	(n)	(o)	(p)	(q)

Required:

Find the values of the missing items (*a*) through (*q*). Assume that the actual sales volume equals actual production volume. (There are no inventory level changes.)

18–30 Find Data for Profit Variance Analysis

Refer to Exhibit 18–30A. Find the values of the missing items (*a*) through (*x*). Assume that actual sales volume equals actual production volume. (There are no inventory level changes).

18–31 Ethical Issues in Managing Reported Profits

Pittsburgh Walsh Company is a manufacturing company that produces lighting fixtures and electronic timers. Midyear, the CEO suffered a heart attack and retired. The new CEO did a little reorganization including discontinuing the Lighting Fixtures Division's midrange product line. The new CEO, relying on market research, wanted to focus production on the remaining two product lines produced by the Lighting Fixtures Division. (The Electronic Timers Division was unaffected by the change in top management.)

Market studies had proven correct, and, by the end of the year, the Lighting Fixtures Division had exceeded budgeted profits by 15 percent. The controller, Mary Chan, knew that her annual bonus was dependent on exceeding budgeted profit and that it would plateau at 10 percent above budgeted profit. Mary expected next year's profit plan to be similar, but that next year's budget would take into account the changes in the product lines. Mary discovered that she could accrue some of next year's expenses and defer some of this year's revenue, while still exceeding budgeted profit by 10 percent.

Required:

Why would Mary Chan, the controller of Pittsburgh Walsh Company, want to defer revenue but accrue expenses? Is this ethical?

(CMA adapted)

EXHIBIT

18–30A

	Reported Income Statement (based on actual sales volume)	Manufacturing Variance	Marketing and Administrative Variance	Sales Price Variances	Flexible Budget (based on actual sales volume)	Sales Activity Variance	Master Budget (based on budgeted sales volume)
Units	(a)				(b)	2,000 F	10,000
Sales revenue	(g)			$18,000 F	(h)	(i)	$150,000
Less:							
Variable manufacturing costs	(n)	(o)			$96,000	(j)	80,000
Variable marketing and administrative costs	$21,600		(p)		24,000	$4,000 U	(c)
Contribution margin	(q)	$9,000 U	(s)	(x)	60,000	(k)	50,000
Less:							
Fixed manufacturing costs	(r)	2,000 F			(m)		(d)
Fixed marketing and administrative costs	18,000		(v)		15,000	(l)	(e)
Operating profits	(t)	(u)	(w)	$18,000 F	$20,000		(f)

18–32   Prepare Flexible
Budget

The following information is provided concerning the operations of the 47th Street Company for the current period:

	Actual (based on actual of 90 units)	Master Budget (based on budgeted 100 units)
Sales revenue	$9,200	$10,000
Less:		
Manufacturing costs:		
Direct labor	1,420	1,500
Materials	1,200	1,400
Variable overhead	820	1,000
Marketing	530	600
Administrative	500	500
Total variable costs	4,470	5,000
Contribution margin	4,730	5,000
Less:		
Fixed costs:		
Manufacturing	485	500
Marketing	1,040	1,000
Administrative	995	1,000
Total fixed costs	2,520	2,500
Operating profits	$2,210	$ 2,500

There are no inventories.

Required:

Prepare a flexible budget for the 47th Street Company.

18–33   Sales Activity
Variance

Refer to the data in problem 18–32 for the 47th Street Company. Prepare a sales activity variance analysis like the one in Illustration 18–3.

18–34   Profit Variance
Analysis

Use the information for the 47th Street Company in problem 18–32 to prepare a profit variance analysis like the one in Illustration 18–5.

18–35   Derive Amounts
for Profit
Variance Analysis

Orange Taxi Company operates a limousine and taxicab service. They want to compare this month's results with last month's, which management felt was a typical "base period." The following information is provided:

	Last Month	This Month
Number of trips	14,000	16,100
Revenues	$151,000	$152,000
Variable costs	38,200	43,500
Contribution margin	$112,800	$108,500

Required:

Compute the flexible budget, sales activity variance, and a profit variance analysis (like the one in Illustration 18–5) in as much detail as possible. (Hint: Use last month as the master budget and this month as the "actual.") What impact did the changes in number of trips and average revenues (i.e., sales price) have on Orange Taxi's contribution margin?

**18–36 Flexible Budget—
Multiple-Choice**

The University of Burns operates a motor pool with 20 vehicles. The motor pool furnishes gasoline, oil, and other supplies for the cars and hires one mechanic who does routine maintenance and minor repairs. Major repairs are done at a nearby commercial garage. A supervisor manages the operations.

Each year, the supervisor prepares a master budget for the motor pool. Depreciation on the automobiles is recorded in the budget to determine the costs per mile.

The schedule below presents the master budget for the year and for the month of March.

The annual budget was based on the following assumptions:

1. 20 automobiles in the pool.
2. 30,000 miles per year per automobile.
3. 20 miles per gallon per automobile.
4. $1.20 per gallon of gas.
5. $0.006 per mile for oil, minor repairs, parts, and supplies.
6. $135 per automobile per year in outside repairs.

The supervisor is unhappy with the monthly report. He claims it unfairly presents his performance for March. His previous employer used flexible budgeting to compare actual costs to budgeted amounts.

UNIVERSITY MOTOR POOL
Budget Report for March

	Annual Master Budget	One-Month Master Budget	March Actual	Over or (Under) Budget
Gasoline	$ 36,000	$ 3,000	$ 3,800	$800
Oil, minor repairs, parts, and supplies	3,600	300	380	80
Outside repairs	2,700	225	50	(175)
Insurance	6,000	500	525	25
Salaries and benefits	30,000	2,500	2,500	—
Depreciation	26,400	2,200	2,310	110
	$104,700	$ 8,725	$ 9,565	$840
Total miles	600,000	50,000	63,000	
Cost per mile	$0.1745	$0.1745	$0.1518	
Number of automobiles	20	20	21	

Required:

a. What are the gasoline monthly flexible budget and the resulting over or under budget? (Use miles as the activity base.)

	Flexible Budget	Over (Under) Budget
(1)	$3,000	$800
(2)	3,520	280
(3)	3,800	-0-
(4)	3,780	20

b. What are the oil, minor repairs, parts, and supplies monthly flexible budget and over or under budget? (Use miles as the activity base.)

	Flexible Budget	Over (Under) Budget
(1)	$400	$(20)
(2)	300	80
(3)	378	2
(4)	300	-0-

c. What are the salaries and benefits monthly flexible budget and the resulting over or under budget?

	Flexible Budget	Over (Under) Budget
(1)	$2,625	$125
(2)	2,500	(125)
(3)	2,625	-0-
(4)	2,500	-0-

d. What is the *major* reason for the cost per mile to decrease from $0.1745 budgeted to $0.1518 actual?
(1) Decreased *unit* fixed costs.
(2) Decreased *unit* variable costs.
(3) Increased *unit* fixed cost and decreased *unit* variable cost.
(4) Neither variable nor fixed *unit* costs decreased.

(CMA adapted)

18–37 Analyze Performance for a Restaurant

Persons Deli is planning to expand operations and, hence, is concerned that its reporting system may need improvement. The master budget income statement for its Akron Persons Deli, which contains a delicatessen and restaurant operation, is (in thousands):

	Delicatessen	Restaurant	Total
Gross sales	$1,000	$2,500	$3,500
Purchases	600	1,000	1,600
Hourly wages	50	875	925
Franchise fee	30	75	105
Advertising	100	200	300
Utilities	70	125	195
Depreciation	50	75	125
Lease cost	30	50	80
Salaries	30	50	80
Total costs	960	2,450	3,410
Operating profit	$ 40	$ 50	$ 90

The performance report that the company uses for management evaluation is as follows:

PERSONS RESTAURANT-DELI
Akron, Ohio
Net Income for the Year
(in thousands)

	Actual Results				Over (Under) Budget
	Delicatessen	Restaurant	Total	Budget	
Gross sales	$1,200	$2,000	$3,200	$3,500	$(300)[a]
Purchases[b]	780	800	1,580	1,600	(20)
Hourly wages[b]	60	700	760	925	(165)
Franchise fee[b]	36	60	96	105	(9)
Advertising	100	200	300	300	—
Utilities[b]	76	100	176	195	(19)
Depreciation	50	75	125	125	—
Lease cost	30	50	80	80	—
Salaries	30	50	80	80	—
Total costs	1,162	2,035	3,197	3,410	(213)
Operating profit	$ 38	$ (35)	$ 3	$ 90	(87)

[a] There is no sales price variance.

[b] Variable costs. All other costs are fixed.

Required:

Prepare a profit variance analysis for the delicatessen segment. (Hint: Use gross sales as your measure of volume.)

(CMA adapted)

INTEGRATIVE CASES

18–38   Analyze Budget Planning Process: Behavioral Issues

RV Industries manufactures and sells recreation vehicles. The company has eight divisions strategically located near major markets. Each division has a sales force and two to four manufacturing plants. These divisions operate as autonomous profit centers responsible for purchasing, operations, and sales.

The corporate controller, T. Collins, describes the divisional performance measurement system as follows: "We allow the divisions to control the entire operation from the purchase of direct materials to the sale of the product. We at corporate headquarters only get involved in strategic decisions such as developing new product lines. Each division is responsible for meeting its market needs by providing the right products at a low cost on a timely basis. Frankly, the divisions need to focus on cost control, delivery, and services to customers to become more profitable. However, being as close as they are to their markets, they are best qualified to determine how to do this.

"We give the divisions considerable autonomy, but we watch their monthly income statements very closely. Each month's actual performance is compared with the budget in considerable detail. If the actual sales or contribution margin is more than 4 or 5 percent below budget, we demand an immediate report from the division people. I might add that we don't have much trouble getting their attention. All of the management people at the plant and division level can add appreciably to their annual salaries with bonuses if actual net income is considerably greater than budget."

The budgeting process begins in August when division sales managers consult with their sales personnel to estimate sales for the next calendar year. These estimates are sent to plant managers, who use the sales forecasts to prepare production estimates. At the plants, production statistics, including direct material quantities, labor-hours, production schedules, and output quantities, are developed by operating personnel. Using the statistics prepared by the operating personnel, the plant accounting staff determines costs and estimates the plant's budgeted variable cost of goods sold and other plant expenses for each month of the coming calendar year.

In October, each division's accounting staff combines plant budgets with sales estimates and adds additional division expenses. "After the divisional management is satisfied with the budget," said Collins, "I visit each division to review their budget and make sure it is in line with corporate strategy and projections. I really emphasize sales forecasts because of the volatility in the demand for our product. For many years, we lost sales to our competitors because we projected production and sales too low and couldn't meet market demand. More recently, we were caught with large excess inventory when the bottom dropped out of the market for recreational vehicles.

"I generally visit all eight divisions during the first two weeks in November. After that the division budgets are combined and reconciled by my staff, and they are ready for approval by the board of directors in early December. The board seldom questions the budget.

"One complaint we've had from plant and division management is that they are penalized for circumstances beyond their control. For example, they failed to predict the recent sales decline. As a result, they didn't make their budget targets and, of course, they received no bonuses. However, I point out that they are well rewarded when they exceed their budget. Furthermore, they provide most of the information for the budget, so it's their own fault if the budget is too optimistic. Indeed, they should have been the first to see the coming sales decline."

Required:

a. Identify and explain the biases the corporate management of RV Industries should expect in the communication of budget estimates by its division and plant personnel.

b. What sources of information can the top management of RV Industries use to monitor the budget estimates prepared by its divisions and plants?

c. What services could top management of RV Industries offer the divisions to help them in their budget development, without appearing to interfere with the division budget decisions?

d. The top management of RV Industries is attempting to decide whether it should get more involved in the budget process. Identify and explain what management needs to consider in reaching its decision.

(CMA adapted)

18–39 Adapt Budget Control Concepts to Research Organization

Argo Company has a well-organized research program. Each project is broken down into phases. Completion times and the cost of each phase are estimated. Project description and related estimates are used to develop the annual Research Department budget.

The schedule below presents the costs for the research activities budgeted for last year. Actual costs incurred by projects or overhead category are compared to estimates for each activity, and the variances are noted on this same schedule.

The director of research prepared a narrative statement of research performance for the year to accompany the schedule. The director's statement follows the schedule.

ARGO COMPANY
Profit Variance Analysis of Research Costs
(in thousands)

	Approved Activity for the Year	Actual Costs for the Year	(Over) Under Budget
Total research costs:			
Projects in progress:			
4–1	$ 23.2	$ 46.8	$(23.6)
5–3	464.0	514.8	(50.8)
New projects:			
8–1	348.0	351.0	(3.0)
8–2	232.0	257.4	(25.4)
8–3	92.8	—	92.8
Total research costs, including the indirect costs listed below	$1,160.0	$1,170.0	$(10.0)
Indirect research costs (allocated to projects in proportion to their direct costs):			
Administration	50.0	52.0	(2.0)
Laboratory facilities	110.0	118.0	(8.0)
Total	$ 160.0	$ 170.0	$(10.0)

"The year has been most successful. The two projects, 4–1 and 8–1, scheduled for completion in this year were finished. Project 8–2 is progressing satisfactorily and should be completed next year as scheduled. The fourth phase of project 5–3, with estimated direct research costs of $100,000, and the first phase of project 8–3, both included in the approved activity for the year, could not be started because the principal researcher left our employment. They were resubmitted for approval in next year's activity plan."

Required:

From the information given, prepare an alternative schedule that will provide Argo Company management with better information to evaluate research cost performance for the year.

(CMA adapted)

18–40 Analyze Activity Variances—FIFO Process Costing

Fellite, Inc., manufactures foam padding for medical uses. The padding is produced in a continuous process. The company uses the FIFO process costing system for internal recordkeeping purposes. Since materials and conversion costs are added evenly throughout the process, it is not necessary to maintain separate accounts of materials and conversion costs for equivalent unit computations.

The master budget and actual results for the current period are reproduced as follows:

	Actual	Master Budget
Physical count of units:		
Beginning work in process inventory	1,000 units (80% complete)	1,000 units (50% complete)
Transferred to next department	2,500 units	3,200 units
Ending inventory	800 units ($^5/_8$ complete)	600 units ($^2/_3$ complete)
Current period costs:		
Direct materials	$30,000	$32,500
Direct labor	24,600	27,000
Manufacturing overhead:		
Variable	16,200	14,500
Fixed	24,100	26,000

Required:

a. Compute the equivalent units of production this period. (Note: Equivalent unit computations are discussed in Chapter 4.)

b. Prepare a profit variance analysis like the one in Illustration 18–5.

SOLUTIONS TO

 Self-Study
Questions

1   Flexible budget for Evergreen Company based on actual sales of 7,000 units:

Sales	$140,000
Variable manufacturing costs	56,000
Variable marketing and administrative	7,000
Contribution margin	77,000
Fixed manufacturing costs	36,000
Fixed marketing and administrative	40,000
Operating profits	$ 1,000

Note: Sales and variable costs are $^7/_8$ (7,000 units/8,000 units) of the amounts in the master budget. Fixed costs are unchanged from the master budget.

2 Profit Variance Analysis, Containers, Inc. (August)

	Actual (based on 50,000 units)	Manufacturing Variances	Marketing and Administrative Variances	Sales Price Variances	Flexible Budget (based on 50,000 units)	Sales Activity (Volume) Variance	Master Budget (based on 45,000 units planned)
Sales revenue	$500,000	—	—	$7,500 U	$507,500	$50,750 F	$456,750
Less:							
Variable manufacturing costs	244,000	$44,000 U	—	—	200,000	20,000 U	180,000
Variable marketing and administrative costs	52,000	—	$2,000[a] U	—	50,000	5,000 U	45,000
Contribution margins	204,000	44,000 U	2,000 U	7,500 U	257,500	25,750 F	231,750
Less:							
Fixed manufacturing costs	83,000	3,000 U	—	—	80,000	—	80,000
Fixed marketing and administrative costs	96,000	—	4,000 F	—	100,000	—	100,000
Operating profits	$ 25,000	$47,000 U	$2,000 F	$7,500 U	$ 77,500	$25,750 F	$ 51,750

Total variance from flexible budget = $52,500 U

Total variance from master budget = $26,750 U

[a] $2,000 = $.04 × 50,000 = ($1.04 − $1.00) 50,000 units.

697

Production Cost Variances

LEARNING OBJECTIVES

After reading this chapter, you should be able to:

1. Compute and use variable cost variances.
2. Compute and use variances from activity-based costs.
3. Compute and use fixed cost variances.
4. Develop the comprehensive cost variance analysis.
5. Identify and use nonfinancial performance measures in performance evaluation.
6. Compare the two-way, three-way, and four-way analyses of overhead variances (Appendix).

Variance Difference between planned results and actual outcome.

*I*n management accounting, any deviation from a predetermined benchmark is a **variance.** In Chapter 17, we developed the master budget and, in Chapter 18, the flexible budget. We saw how the difference between the flexible budget and the master budget creates an activity variance and how differences between actual results and the flexible budget create a number of other variances. In this chapter, we examine in detail how a specific group of variances—cost variances—are developed, interpreted, and used.

Although we shall use a manufacturing company example in this chapter because it is the most comprehensive application we can find, the variances that we describe are also used in nonmanufacturing organizations. Service organizations in particular can use the labor and overhead variances to assess efficiency and control costs. Labor standards and variances are used in many financial institutions such as banks to assess transaction and check-processing efficiency. Labor standards are also used in fast-food restaurants to assess efficiency in preparing and serving food.

STANDARD COSTS

Standard Cost The anticipated cost of producing and/or selling a unit of output.

A *standard* is a benchmark or norm. There are, for example, standards for admittance to school, standards for passing a course, standards for product safety. In accounting, the term *standard* is used in a similar fashion. A **standard cost** is the anticipated cost of producing and/or selling a unit of output; it is a predetermined cost assigned to goods produced.

Some Clarifications

Standards versus Budgets

A standard cost is a *predetermined unit cost*, while a budget is a *financial plan*. Standard costs are often used to make up the financial plan. While in practice these terms are sometimes used interchangeably, standards usually refer to *per unit amounts*, while budgets usually refer to *total amounts*.

In many companies, standards, like budgets, are developed and maintained "off the books." That is, they are not part of the formal accounting system. So, when we discuss standard costs in this chapter, we are referring to standards developed to facilitate control of personnel and operations. Whether they are entered into the records to value inventory is another issue.

Sources of Standard Costs

The following description of the way standard costs are set is based on an interview with a controller in a manufacturing company. It is representative of the standard-setting process in most companies.

Manufacturing Costs

Materials A standard cost for evey direct material used is computed by (1) examining current purchase prices and adjusting them for expected changes and (2) estimating the quantity of each direct material required to make each final product. The Purchasing Department helps us estimate how material prices will change. Our operations managers and industrial engineers help determine the quantities of materials needed to make our product.

Labor Industrial engineers and operating managers often estimate the number of direct labor-hours (or fractions of hours) required for each step of production by timing employees while they perform their duties. Employees themselves set standards in many cases. (See the discussion about the Toyota–GM joint venture in this chapter's real world application.) These hours are costed by accountants based on expected wage rates and fringe benefits during the period.

Variable overhead Variable overhead includes things like energy to run machines, indirect materials, and supplies. Several years ago we began using regression analysis to estimate variable overhead rates. We ran actual variable overhead as the dependent variable and actual machine-hours as the independent variable or cost driver for each production department. Each year we adjust the unit variable overhead rate based on feedback from production managers and accountants about changes in cost. In the future, we expect to use activity-based costing and increase the number of cost drivers.

Budgeted fixed overhead Production department managers and our accountants estimate the amount of fixed overhead that will be incurred in each production department, including service department costs (for example, maintenance) that have been allocated to the production department.

Review All of these estimates are reviewed on a sample basis for reasonableness by our accounting staff and by our internal auditors. They are adjusted once a year to reflect changes.

Approvals All standards are approved once a year by top management.

Despite the use of statistical techniques and industrial engineering methods for cost estimation, setting cost standards is more an art than a science.

SETTING STANDARDS: AN ILLUSTRATION

We now illustrate how standard variable manufacturing cost variances are developed for the Evergreen Company example that was introduced in Chapter 18. The standard variable manufacturing cost, which we called the *estimated cost* in Chapter 18, was $8 per crate.

Direct Materials

Here is how the Evergreen Company determines the standard price of the lumber it uses to make crates. The standard price reflects the price of the product delivered to Evergreen Company, net of purchase discounts.

Direct Materials: Standard Price (per board-foot)

Purchase price of lumber	$ .23
Shipping costs	.04
Less purchase discounts	(.02)
Standard price per board-foot	$ .25

Note: A board-foot is a quantity measure equal to the volume in a piece of lumber 12 by 12 inches and 1 inch thick.

Direct materials are purchased by the board-foot, so the purchase price standard is expressed per *foot*, not per *crate*.

Direct material quantity standards are based on the quantity of direct material that should be used to make one unit under normal operating conditions. Each crate requires nine board-feet of lumber. One additional board-foot of lumber is the allowance for waste in cutting the lumber to the proper size and constructing the crate.

Direct Materials: Standard Quantity (board-feet)

Requirements per crate	9
Allowance for waste	1
Standard quantity per crate	10

The standard direct material cost per *crate* is then computed:

$.25 per board-foot × 10 board-feet per crate = $2.50 per crate

Direct Labor

Direct labor standards are based on a standard labor rate for the work performed and the standard labor-hours required. The standard labor rate includes not only wages earned but also fringe benefits, such as medical insurance and pension plan contributions, and taxes paid by the employer (for example, unemployment taxes and the employer's share of an employee's social security taxes).

Direct Labor: Standard Rate (price per hour)

Wage rate	$ 8.00
Employer's payroll taxes and fringe benefits	2.00
Standard rate	$10.00

Most companies develop one standard for each category of labor. We assume Evergreen Company has only one category of labor.

Standard direct labor time is based on an estimate of the time required to perform each operation. For example, at Evergreen Company, the amount of time required to make each crate—to cut the lumber to size, to assemble the crate, and to finish and inspect it—is estimated by timing each step and adding some time for personal needs and breaks. Sometimes a crate is assembled but later rejected when inspected, so an allowance is made for time spent on crates that will later be rejected. These estimates for each crate are as follows:

Direct Labor: Standard Time (hours)

Cutting Department:	
Cutting	.04
Personal time	.01
Allowance for rejects	.01
Total Cutting Department	.06
Assembly Department:	
Assembly	.18
Personal time	.02
Total Assembly Department	.20
Finishing and Inspection Department:	
Finishing and inspection	.03
Personal time	.01
Total Finishing and Inspection Department	.04
Standard time per good crate completed	.30

For each good crate that is completed, the standard labor cost is:

$10 per hour $\times$ .30 hours per crate = $\underline{\$3 \text{ per crate}}$

Variable Manufacturing Overhead

The first step in setting variable overhead standards is to find an activity measure that relates the cost to the product, that is, to determine x in the formula:

$$Y = a + bx$$

where

Y = Estimated total overhead (the dependent variable)
a = Estimated fixed overhead
b = Estimated variable overhead rate per unit
x = Independent variable (a cost driver)

For example, Evergreen Company could develop a variable overhead rate per crate, which would be using crates as an activity measure, and apply that rate to each crate produced. Companies that use activity-based costing will have multiple *b*s and *x*s.

Selecting Activity Measures for Applying Overhead

Output Measures versus Input Measures of Activity

Output measures of activity (for example, number of crates produced at Evergreen Company or number of automobiles produced in an automobile factory) sometimes work well as a basis for applying overhead—especially when a single product is completely produced in a single work operation. However, it becomes difficult to measure departmental activity in terms of output when the department works on multiple products and only a portion of the product is completed in each department. Hence, most companies find input measures, like direct labor-hours or machine-hours, more practical.

If an input measure is used, a company should consider the following issues in its selection:

1. *Causal relationship between the activity measure and variable overhead costs.* An increase in the activity measure should result in an increase in variable overhead costs. If an operation is labor-intensive, labor-hours would probably be causally related to variable overhead, where variable overhead is made up of support staff, supervisors, and other indirect labor. On the other hand, for a capital-intensive operation, machine-hours could be the cause of variable overhead. As a product moves through several departments in a manufacturing operation, different activity bases may be used, as shown in the following diagram (the arrows refer to the movement of the product through various departments until it is finished):

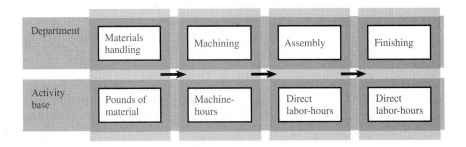

There is usually more than one cause of variable overhead, but to simplify matters, one independent variable is usually selected for a particular manufacturing department or work station.

2. *Physical units versus dollars.* Physical units are often used for the activity base instead of dollars. If labor-dollars are used, a contract settlement or other wage change could affect labor costs, but that does not necessarily mean that variable overhead costs would change.

3. *Cost-benefit constraints.* A model that specifies the relationship between variable overhead costs and their causes in so much detail that measures are precise could be quite costly. The benefits of such

a complete model rarely justify its costs. Thus, a simplified model is usually preferred. For example, a simple regression model with one independent variable is often used in place of a multiple regression model, even though multiple regression may explain more variation in variable overhead. When examining variances between actual and standard costs, managers recognize that some variance is due purely to the infeasibility of setting perfect standards.

Evergreen Company uses a simple variable overhead basis, direct labor-hours, to determine its variable overhead standards. Management reviewed prior period activitites and costs, estimated how costs will change in the future, and did a regression analysis in which overhead cost was the dependent variable and labor-hours the independent variable. After analyzing these estimates, the accountants decided to use 8.33^1/3$ per standard labor-hour as the variable manufacturing overhead rate for each department because variable overhead averaged about 8.33^1/3$ per standard direct labor-hour.

In practice, different departments may have different rates. Activity-based costing acknowledges that each activity center will have a different rate. At times, different departments will have different rates, and multiple bases are used.

Variable manufacturing cost standards are summarized in a standard cost computer record or file. Illustration 19–1 presents the contents of such a file for Evergreen Company.

I L L U S T R A T I O N   *Summary of Costs, Evergreen Company*

19–1

	Standard Costs		
	(1) **Standard Input Quantity**	*(2)* **Standard Input Price or Rate**	*(1) × (2)* **Standard Cost per Crate**
Direct materials (all charged to Cutting Department)	10 feet	$ .25 per foot	$2.50
Direct labor	.30 hour	10.00 per hour	3.00
Variable manufacturing overhead	.30 hour	8.33¹/₃ per hour	2.50
Total standard variable cost per crate			$8.00

	Actual Costs		
	(1) **Actual Input Quantity**	*(2)* **Actual Input Price or Rate**	*(1) × (2)* **Actual Cost per Crate**
Direct materials (all charged to Cutting Department)	11 feet	$ .264 per foot	$2.904
Direct labor	.32 hour	9.35 per hour	2.992
Variable manufacturing overhead	.32 hour	8.275 per hour	2.648
Total actual variable cost per crate			$8.544

How Workers Develop Their Own Standards at the Toyota–GM Joint Venture*

The Toyota–General Motors joint venture in Fremont, California, known as New United Motor Manufacturing, Inc. (NUMMI), has succeeded in allowing employees to set their own work standards. The NUMMI plant, which makes Toyota Corollas, Geo Prizms, and certain Toyota truck models, used to be a General Motors plant that was notorious for poor quality, low productivity, and morale problems. One worker said he used to be ashamed of the products turned out by the Fremont GM plant, but after he had seen one of the plant's cars parked at the Monterey Aquarium, he left a business card under the windshield wiper with a note that said, "I helped build this one."†

At the old Fremont GM plant, industrial engineers who had little if any work experience making cars would shut themselves in a room and ponder how to set standards. The industrial engineers ignored the workers, who in turn ignored the standards. The worker "did the job however he or she was able—except of course when one (supervisor or industrial engineer) was looking. If an industrial engineer was actually 'observing'—stopwatch and clipboard in hand—standard practice was to slow down and make the work look harder."‡

Now, at NUMMI, workers themselves hold the stopwatches and set the standards. Worker team members time each other, looking for the most efficient and safest way to do the work. They standardize each task so everyone in the team will do it the same way. The workers compare the standards across shifts and for different tasks, and prepare detailed written specifications for each task. The workers are both more informed about how to do the work right than industrial engineers, and more motivated to meet the standards they set, instead of those set by industrial engineers working in an ivory tower.

Involving the workers has had benefits in addition to improved motivation and standards. These include improved safety, higher quality, easier job rotation because tasks are standardized, and more flexibility because workers are both assembly-line workers and industrial engineers. For example, if orders for the product increase or decrease, NUMMI can change the speed of the assembly line to respond. At the old Fremont plant, the assembly line ran at one speed, and responses to changes in orders occurred in inventory or consisted of adding or dropping entire shifts.

* Based on the article by P. Adler, "Time-and-Motion Regained," *Harvard Business Review*, January–February 1993, pp. 97–108.
† Ibid. p. 106.
‡ Ibid. p. 103.

ANALYSIS OF COST VARIANCES

General Model

Cost Variance Analysis Comparison of actual input quantities and prices with standard input quantities and prices.

Price Variance Difference between actual costs and budgeted costs arising from changes in the cost of inputs to a production process or other activity.

Efficiency Variance Difference between budgeted and actual results arising from differences between the inputs that were budgeted per unit of output and the inputs actually used.

The conceptual **cost variance analysis** model compares actual input quantities and prices with standard input quantities and prices. *Both these actual and standard input quantities are for the actual output attained.* As shown in Illustration 19–2, a **price variance** and an **efficiency variance** can be computed for each variable manufacturing input. The actual costs incurred (column 1) for the time period are compared with the standard allowed per unit times the number of good units of output produced (column 3). This comparison provides the **total variance** for the cost or input.

In some companies, only the total variance is computed. In other companies, a more detailed breakdown into price and efficiency variances is made.

Managers who are responsible for price variances may not be responsible for efficiency variances and vice versa. For example, purchasing department managers are usually held responsible for direct materials price variances while manufacturing department managers are usually held responsible for using the direct materials efficiently.

This breakdown of the total variance into price and efficiency components is facilitated by the middle term, column 2, in Illustration 19–2. In going from column 1 to column 2, we go from *actual prices* (AP) times *actual quantity* (AQ) of input to *standard price* (SP) times *actual quantity* (AQ) of

ILLUSTRATION

*General Model for Cost
Variance Analysis*

Actual	Actual Inputs at Standard Price	Flexible Production Budget
Actual input price (*AP*) times *actual* quantity (*AQ*) of input	*Standard* input price (*SP*) times *actual* quantity (*AQ*) of input	*Standard* input price (*SP*) times *standard* quantity (*SQ*) of input allowed for actual good output
(1) $(AP \times AQ)$	*(2)* $(SP \times AQ)$	*(3)* $(SP \times SQ)$

Price variance[a]
(1) minus (2)

Efficiency variance[a]
(2) minus (3)

Total variance
(1) minus (3)

[a] The terms *price* and *efficiency* variances are general categories. While terminology varies from company to company, the following specific variance titles are frequently used:

Input	Price Variance Category	Efficiency Category
Direct materials	Price (or purchase price) variance	Usage or quantity variance
Direct labor	Rate variance	Efficiency variance
Variable overhead	Spending variance	Efficiency variance

We shall avoid unnecessary complications by simply referring to these variances as either a *price* or *efficiency* variance.

Total Variance Difference between total actual costs for the time period and the standard allowed per unit times the number of good units produced.

input. Thus, the variance is calculated as:

$$\text{Price variance} = (AP \times AQ) - (SP \times AQ)$$
$$= (AP - SP)AQ$$

The efficiency variance is derived by comparing column 2, standard price times actual quantity of input, with column 3, standard price times standard quantity of input. Thus, the efficiency variance is calculated as:

$$\text{Efficiency variance} = (SP \times AQ) - (SP \times SQ)$$
$$= SP(AQ - SQ)$$

This general model may seem rather abstract at this point, but as we work examples, it will become more concrete and intuitive to you.

As the general model outlined in Illustration 19–2 is applied to each variable and fixed cost incurred, a more comprehensive cost variance analysis will result. The general model of the comprehensive cost variance analysis will be applied to Evergreen Company's manufacturing costs. The comprehensive cost variance analysis will ultimately explain, in detail, the unfavorable variable manufacturing variance of $5,440 that we showed in Chapter 18, column 2 of Illustration 18–5.

As we proceed through the variance analysis for each manufacturing cost input—direct materials, direct labor, variable manufacturing overhead, and fixed manufacturing costs—you will notice some minor modifications from the general model presented in Illustration 19–2. It is important to recognize that these are *modifications of one general approach* rather than a number of independent approaches to variance analysis. In variance analysis, a few basic methods can be applied with minor modifications to numerous business and nonbusiness situations.

Direct Materials

Information about Evergreen Company's use of direct materials for the month of May is presented below:

Standard costs: 10 board-feet per crate @ $.25 per board-foot = $2.50 per crate

Crates produced in May: 10,000

Actual materials purchased and used: 110,000 board-feet @ .264 per board-foot = $29,040

These relationships are shown graphically as:

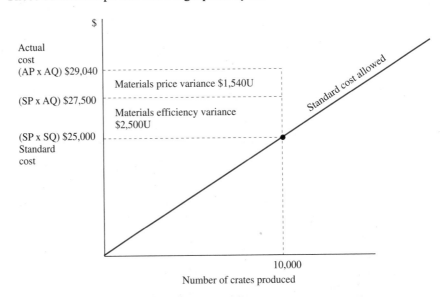

Based on these data, the direct materials price and efficiency variances were calculated as shown in Illustration 19–3. Note that with a standard of 10 board-feet per crate and 10,000 crates actually produced in May, Evergreen Company expects to use 100,000 board-feet to produce the 10,000 crates. Since each board-foot has a standard cost of $.25, the standard materials cost allowed to make 10,000 crates is:

Standard cost allowed to produce
10,000 crates

$$= SP \times SQ$$
$$= \$.25 \times (10 \text{ board-feet} \times 10,000 \text{ crates})$$
$$= \underline{\$25,000}$$

Flexible Production Budget
Standard input price times standard quantity of input allowed for actual good output.

Note that column 3 of Illustration 19–3 is called the **flexible production budget.** The flexible budget concept can be applied to production as well as to sales. The flexible budget in Chapter 18 was based on actual *sales* volume (that is, crates *sold*). The flexible budget in Illustration 19–3 is based on actual production volume (that is, crates *produced*).

Responsibility for Direct Materials Variances
The direct materials price variance shows that in May the prices paid for direct materials exceeded the standards allowed, thus creating an unfavor-

ILLUSTRATION

19-3

Direct Materials Variances,
Evergreen Company (May)
(10,000 crates)

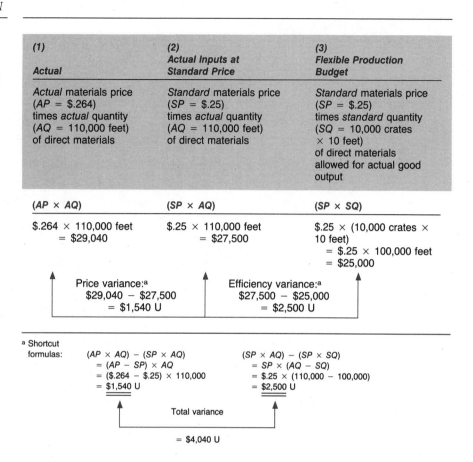

able variance of $1,540. Responsibility for this variance is usually assigned to the Purchasing Department. Reports to management would include an explanation of the variance—for example, failure to take purchase discounts, transportation costs were higher than expected, different grade of direct material purchased, or changes in the market price of direct materials.

The explanation for the variance at Evergreen Company was that home construction in the economy has increased significantly, thus driving the price of lumber higher than expected. Further, prices were expected to continue climbing during the year. Based on this information, management began market research to determine if they should increase sales prices for their crates.

Direct materials efficiency variances are typically the responsibility of production departments. In setting standards, an allowance is usually made for defects in direct materials, inexperienced workers, poor supervision, and the like. If actual materials usage is less than these standards, there is a favorable variance. If usage is in excess of standards, there is an unfavorable variance.

At Evergreen Company, the unfavorable materials efficiency variance was attributed to the recent hiring of some inexperienced laborers who, in an effort to keep up with the production schedule, improperly measured and cut lumber to the wrong lengths. The Cutting Department manager claimed this was a one-time occurrence and foresaw no similar problems in the future.

ILLUSTRATION   *Direct Labor Variances, Evergreen Company (May)*

19–4

(1) Actual	(2) Actual Inputs at Standard Price	(3) Flexible Production Budget
Actual labor price (AP = $9.35) times *actual* quantity (AQ = 3,200 hours) of direct labor-hours used	*Standard* labor price (SP = $10) times *actual* quantity (AQ = 3,200 hours) of direct labor-hours used	*Standard* labor price (SP = $10) times *standard* quantity SQ = (10,000 crates × .3 hour) of direct labor-hours allowed for actual good output
$(AP \times AQ)$	$(SP \times AQ)$	$(SP \times SQ)$
$9.35 × 3,200 hours = $29,920	$10 × 3,200 hours = $32,000	$10 × (10,000 crates × .3 hour) = $10 × 3,000 hours = $30,000

Price variance:
$29,920 − $32,000
= $2,080 F

Efficiency variance:
$32,000 − $30,000
= $2,000 U

Total variance

= $80 F

Direct Labor

To illustrate the computations of direct labor variances, assume for Evergreen Company:

Standard costs: .30 hour per crate @ $10 per hour = $3 per crate

Crates produced in May: 10,000

Actual direct labor costs: Actual hours worked were 3,200, while the total actual labor cost was $29,920. Hence, the average cost per hour was $9.35 ($29,920 ÷ 3,200 hours).

The computation of the direct labor price and efficiency variances is shown in Illustration 19–4.

Direct Labor Price Variance

The direct labor price variance is caused by the difference between actual and standard labor costs per hour. Evergreen Company's direct labor costs were less than the standard allowed, creating a favorable labor price variance of $2,080. The explanation given for Evergreen Company's favorable labor price variance is that many inexperienced workers were hired in May. These inexperienced workers were paid a wage less than standard, thus reducing the *average* wage rate for all workers to $9.35.

In many companies, wage rates are set by union contract. If the wage rates used in setting standards are the same as those in the union contract, labor price variances will be nonexistent.

Labor Efficiency Variance

The labor efficiency variance is a measure of labor productivity. It is one of the most closely watched variances because it is usually controllable by production managers. A financial vice president of a manufacturing company told us: "Direct materials are 57 percent of our product cost, while direct labor is only 22 percent. We give direct materials price variances only a passing glance. But we carry out the labor efficiency variance to the penny; and we break it down by product line, by department, and sometimes by specific operation. Why? Because there's not much we can do about materials price changes, but there's a lot we can do to keep our labor efficiency in line."

Unfavorable labor efficiency variances have many causes. The workers themselves may be the cause. Poorly motivated or poorly trained workers will be less productive, whereas highly motivated and well-trained workers are more likely to generate favorable efficiency variances. Sometimes poor materials or faulty equipment can cause productivity problems. And poor supervision and scheduling can lead to unnecessary idle time.

Production department managers are usually responsible for direct labor efficiency variances. Scheduling problems may stem from other production departments that have delayed production. The Personnel Department may be responsible if the variance occurs because they provided the wrong kind of worker. The $2,000 unfavorable direct labor efficiency variance at Evergreen Company was attributed to the inexperienced workers previously mentioned. Note that one event, such as hiring inexperienced workers, can affect more than one variance.

Variable Manufacturing Overhead

To illustrate the computation of variable manufacturing overhead variances, assume for Evergreen Company:

> Standard costs: .30 direct labor-hour per crate @ 8.33\frac{1}{3}$ per hour (variable manufacturing overhead rate) = $2.50 per crate
>
> Crates produced in May: 10,000
>
> Actual variable overhead costs in May: $26,480

The computation of the variable manufacturing overhead price and efficiency variances is shown in Illustration 19–5.

Variable Manufacturing Overhead Price Variances

The variable overhead standard rate was derived from a two-stage estimation: (1) an estimate of costs at various levels of activity and (2) an estimate of the relationship between those estimated costs and the basis, which is direct labor-hours at Evergreen Company. The price variance could have occurred because (1) actual costs—for example, machine power, materials handling, supplies, some direct labor—were different from those expected. Also, (2) the price variance could occur because the relationship between variable manufacturing overhead costs and direct labor-hours is not perfect.

The variable overhead price variance actually contains some efficiency items as well as price items. For example, suppose utilities costs are higher than expected. One reason could be that utility rates are higher than expected; but an additional reason could be that kilowatt-hours (kwh) per labor-hour are higher than expected (for example, if workers do not turn off power switches when machines are not being used). Both would be part of

ILLUSTRATION

Variable Overhead Variances, Evergreen Company (May)
(10,000 crates)

19–5

(1) Actual	(2) Actual Inputs at Standard Price	(3) Flexible Production Budget
Sum of actual variable manufacturing overhead costs[a]	Standard variable overhead price (SP = $8.33⅓) (rate) times *actual* quantity (AQ = 3,200 hours) of the overhead base	Standard variable overhead price (SP = $8.33⅓) times *standard* quantity (SQ = 3,000 hours) of the overhead base (direct labor-hours in this example) allowed for actual good output
(AP × AQ)	(SP × AQ)	(SP × SQ)
$26,480	$8.33⅓ × 3,200 hours = $26,667	$8.33⅓ × 3,000 hours = $25,000

Price variance:
$26,480 − $26,667
= $187 F

Efficiency variance:
$26,667 − $25,000
= $1,667 U

Total variance

= $1,480 U

[a] Total actual variable overhead costs also can be thought of as actual price (AP) times actual quantity (AQ). Divide the total actual variable overhead costs by the actual quantity of the variable overhead base:

AP = $26,480 ÷ AQ
    = $26,480 ÷ 3,200 direct labor-hours
    = $8.275

the price variance because jointly they cause utility costs to be higher than expected. In some companies, these components of the variable overhead price variance are separated. This is commonly done for energy costs in heavy manufacturing companies, for example.

At Evergreen Company, the unfavorable price variance for May was attributed to waste in using supplies and recent increases in rates charged for power to run the saws in the Cutting Department.

Variable Overhead Efficiency Variance
The variable overhead efficiency variance must be interpreted carefully. It is related to efficiency in using the base on which variable overhead is applied.

For example, at Evergreen Company, variable overhead is applied on the basis of direct labor-hours. Thus, if there is an unfavorable direct labor efficiency variance because actual direct labor-hours were greater than the standard allowed, there will be a corresponding unfavorable variable overhead efficiency variance. Evergreen Company used 200 direct labor-hours more than the standard allowed, resulting in the direct labor and variable overhead efficiency variances shown on the following page.

Direct labor efficiency: $10 × 200 hours = $2,000 U (Illustration 19–4)

Variable overhead efficiency: $8.33¹/₃ × 200 hours = $1,667 U (Illustration 19–5)

Total direct labor and variable overhead efficiency variances: $18.33¹/₃ × 200 hours = $3,667 U

Variable overhead is assumed to vary directly with direct labor-hours, which is the base on which variable overhead is applied.

Thus, inefficiency in using the base (for example, direct labor-hours, machine-hours, units of output) is assumed to cause an increase in variable overhead. This emphasizes the importance of selecting the proper base for applying variable overhead. Managers who are responsible for controlling the base will probably be held responsible for the variable overhead efficiency variance as well. Whoever is responsible for the $2,000 unfavorable direct labor efficiency variance at Evergreen Company will probably be held responsible for the unfavorable variable overhead efficiency variance, too.

Graphic Presentation of Variable Manufacturing Cost Variances

The variable manufacturing cost variances are summarized in Illustration 19–6. Note that the total variable manufacturing cost variance is the same as that derived in Chapter 18. The analysis of cost variances in this chapter is just a more detailed analysis of the variable manufacturing cost variance that was derived in Chapter 18.

A summary of this kind is useful for reporting variances to high-level managers. It provides both an overview of variances and their sources. When used for reporting, the computations shown at the right of Illustration 19–6 are usually replaced with a brief explanation of the cause of the variance.

Management may want more detailed information about some of the variances. This can be provided by extending each variance branch in

ILLUSTRATION   *Variable Manufacturing Cost Variance Summary, Evergreen Company (May)*

19–6

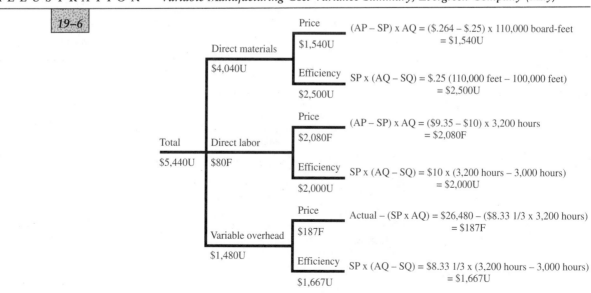

Illustration 19–6 to show variances by product line, by department, or by other breakdowns.

ACTIVITY-BASED COSTING: STANDARDS AND VARIANCES

Activity-based costing is commonly used with standard costing. Hewlett-Packard, a pioneer in the development of activity-based costing, used activity-based costing to develop standard costs. Using activity-based costing, a company has multiple activity bases, or cost drivers, one for each activity center. Each activity center would have an overhead cost pool that would be charged to the center's activities, then to the product based on the activities required to make the product.

For example, assume Evergreen Company used activity-based costing to set standard costs for its variable costs. Assume the company has the three activity centers shown in the top panel of Illustration 19–7. (In practice, companies typically have more than three activity centers, but we want to keep the example simple while still demonstrating how to use activity-based costing.) Managers and accountants determine a cost driver for each activity center and a rate per cost driver unit.

For example, as shown in Illustration 19–7, the cost driver for activity center number 2 is machine-minutes because the more machine-minutes, the more energy is required to run the machines. The rate per cost driver unit is $.02 per machine-minute. This rate could be determined by relating energy costs to machine time from the records or by getting input from energy experts. The rate could be determined by running a regression of machine time on overhead costs from data for past periods, and using the coefficient, b, from the regression equation. In fact, all of the rates for the cost drivers could be derived from a multiple regression in which the cost drivers are

ILLUSTRATION

19–7

Using Activity-Based Costing to Develop Standard Costs

Activity Center	Cost Driver	Standard Rate per Cost Driver
1. Indirect materials	Number of board-feet	$.05 per board-foot
2. Energy	Machine-minutes	.02 per machine-minute
3. Quality testing and repair	Number of minutes in testing	.50 per minute in testing

	Standard Rate per Cost Driver (from top panel)	Standard Number of Cost Driver Units Required to Make One Crate	Standard Cost per Crate
1. Indirect materials	$.05 per board-foot	10 board-feet	$ .50 per crate
2. Energy	.02 per machine-minute	25 minutes	.50 per crate
3. Quality testing and repair	.50 per test minute	3 minutes	1.50 per crate
Total variable overhead			$2.50 per crate

independent variables. However derived, whether by simple common sense or sophisticated analyses, management must determine the standard rate per cost driver unit, which appears in the top panel of Illustration 19–7.

Next we compute the standard cost per crate produced based on the number of cost driver units required to make one crate. These calculations appear in the bottom panel of Illustration 19–7. The standard cost driver units per crate, for example, the number of minutes of machine time required to make a crate, would require information from engineering and production people. (Developing good standards requires a lot of teamwork between production people, engineers, accountants, and managers.)

Note the total variable cost per crate, $2.50, is assumed to be the same as calculated earlier in this chapter using the simple traditional approach for Evergreen Company. In the real world, different costing methods will usually give different product costs, however.

Variance Analysis for Activity-Based Costing

We use the same approach to variance analysis for activity-based costing as for traditional costing. The price variance is the difference between standard prices and actual prices for the actual quantity of input used for each cost driver. The efficiency variance measures the difference between the actual amount of input, or cost driver units used, and the standard allowed to make the output, with this difference multiplied by the standard price per cost driver unit.

To make this idea concrete, assume the following data for Evergreen Company for the three activities in Illustration 19–7:

	Standard Price per Unit (from Illustration 19–7)	Standard Quantity per Crate (from Illustration 19–7)	Actual Cost	Actual Quantity of Input Used
Indirect materials	$.05 per board-foot	10 board-feet	$ 5,180	110,000 board-feet
Energy	$.02 per machine-minute	25 minutes	5,300	240,000 machine-minutes
Quality testing and repair	$.50 per test minute	3 minutes	16,000	34,000 test minutes

Recall that the company produced 10,000 crates, so the total standard quantity of input allowed is 10,000 times the standard quantity per crate. Related to the quality testing and repair, for example, the standard per crate is three minutes in testing and repair, so the total allowed for 10,000 crates is 30,000 minutes. Using the same reasoning, the total standard board-feet allowed are 100,000 and the total machine-minutes allowed are 250,000 minutes.

Illustration 19–8 shows the results of the variance analysis. In effect, we have taken the principle underlying variance computations shown throughout this chapter and applied it to a situation having three activity centers. If a company had 50 activity centers, the computations would look like Illustration 19–8, but with 50 computations of price and efficiency variances instead of only 3.

ILLUSTRATION   Activity-Based Costing Variances

19–8

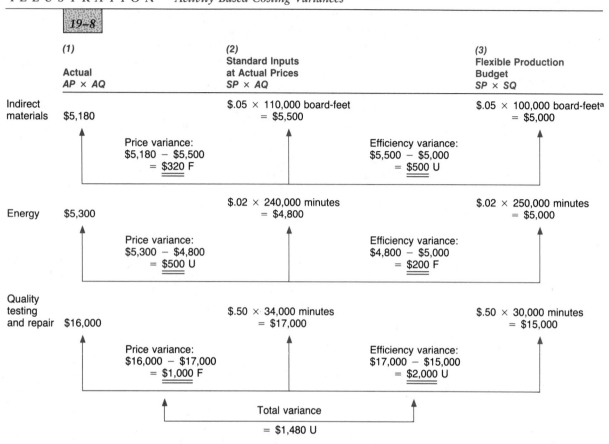

	(1) Actual $AP \times AQ$	(2) Standard Inputs at Actual Prices $SP \times AQ$	(3) Flexible Production Budget $SP \times SQ$
Indirect materials	$5,180	$.05 × 110,000 board-feet = $5,500	$.05 × 100,000 board-feet[a] = $5,000

Price variance:
$5,180 − $5,500
= $320 F

Efficiency variance:
$5,500 − $5,000
= $500 U

Energy	$5,300	$.02 × 240,000 minutes = $4,800	$.02 × 250,000 minutes = $5,000

Price variance:
$5,300 − $4,800
= $500 U

Efficiency variance:
$4,800 − $5,000
= $200 F

Quality testing and repair	$16,000	$.50 × 34,000 minutes = $17,000	$.50 × 30,000 minutes = $15,000

Price variance:
$16,000 − $17,000
= $1,000 F

Efficiency variance:
$17,000 − $15,000
= $2,000 U

Total variance
= $1,480 U

[a] See computation of direct materials variance: 10,000 crates at 10 board-feet per crate = 100,000 board-feet.

Even with just three activity drivers, we think you can see the potential for managers to get a lot more information from activity-based costing than from the traditional costing approach. Compare Illustration 19–8 and Illustration 19–5. Illustration 19–5 contains almost no information about the causes of variable overhead cost variances, except that the total variance equals $1,480 unfavorable. We have purposely constructed the example so the total variance would still be $1,480 unfavorable using activity-based costing, but note in Illustration 19–8 that the manager has more information about the cause of the variance.[1] For example, time in quality testing and repair was 34,000 minutes instead of the 30,000 minutes allowed. Does this "inefficiency" reflect poorer quality materials or production than expected? Does it represent extra concern about putting out a quality product? Is the standard, three minutes per crate, too low? In short, Illustration 19–8 raises numerous specific questions that managers can address to improve quality and productivity.

---

[1] We have not constructed the example to make the total price (or efficiency) variance in Illustration 19–8 equal the price (or efficiency) variance in Illustration 19–5 because the input used to break the total variance into price and efficiency components in Illustration 19–5 is unrelated to the input used in Illustration 19–8.

FIXED MANUFACTURING COSTS—PRICE (SPENDING) VARIANCE

Spending Variance A price variance for fixed overhead.

Budget Variance A price variance for fixed overhead.

Comparison of Actual to Flexible Production Budget to Master Production Budget

Activity Variance Variance due to changes in volume of sales or production.

In variance analysis, fixed manufacturing costs are treated differently from variable manufacturing costs. For illustrative purposes, we assume these fixed manufacturing costs are all overhead. Other manufacturing costs also may be fixed; if so, they can be treated the same way that we treat fixed manufacturing overhead. It is usually assumed that fixed costs are unchanged when volume changes, so the amount budgeted for fixed overhead is the same in both the master and flexible budgets. This is consistent with the variable costing method of product costing.

There are no input-output relationships for fixed overhead. Thus, there is no efficiency variance. The difference between the flexible budget and the actual fixed overhead is entirely due to changes in the costs that make up fixed overhead (for example, insurance premiums on the factory are higher than expected). Hence, the variance falls under the category of a price variance. (It is also called a **spending** or a **budget variance.**)

The fixed manufacturing overhead in both the flexible and master budgets in Chapter 18 was $36,000. Assume the actual cost is $37,000. The variance analysis is shown in Illustration 19–9. Note that there is no calculation of the efficiency with which inputs are used.

A comparison of actual results with the flexible and master budget was presented in Chapter 18 for *sales volume.* A similar comparison can be made for *production volume,* as shown in Illustration 19–10. This difference between the master production budget and the flexible production budget is the production **activity variance.**

Now that the actual production costs, flexible budget amounts, and variances have been presented (see columns 1, 2, 3, and 4 of Illustration 19–10), we can make the final comparison of budget to actual results. The master budget, which is shown in column 6, is based on a projected or budgeted production of 8,000 crates, based on the information given in Chapter 18. The flexible production budget (column 4) tells us the standard variable costs allowed when the *actual production output* is 10,000 crates (total = $80,000). The actual costs (column 1) tell us the actual amounts spent for each cost.

Comparing Illustration 19–10 with Illustration 18–5 (in Chapter 18) will help you to relate these detailed price and efficiency variances with the big-

ILLUSTRATION 19–9

Fixed Overhead Variances, Evergreen Company (May)

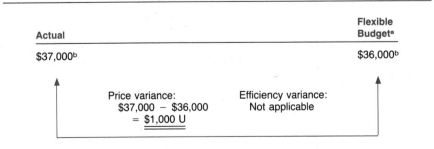

a For fixed costs, there is no difference between the flexible and master (or static) budget within the relevant range.

b These amounts tie to Illustration 18–5, which presents an overview of the use of budgets for performance evaluation at Evergreen Company.

ILLUSTRATION   *Cost Variance Analysis, Evergreen Company*

19-10

	(1) Actual (based on production of 10,000 crates)	(2) Price Variance	(3) Efficiency Variance	(4) Flexible Budget (based on actual production of 10,000 crates)	(5) Production Activity Variance	(6) Master Budget (based on estimated production of 8,000 crates)
Variable manufacturing costs:						
Direct materials	$29,040	$1,540 U	$2,500 U	$25,000	$ 5,000 U	$20,000
Direct labor	29,920	2,080 F	2,000 U	30,000	6,000 U	24,000
Variable overhead	26,480	187 F	1,667 U	25,000	5,000 U	20,000
Subtotal	$85,440ᵃ	$ 727 F	$6,167 U	$80,000ᵃ	$16,000 U	$64,000

Total
= 5,440 Uᵃ

ᵃ Numbers tie to Illustration 18–5, Chapter 18.

picture overview presented in Chapter 18. All we have done here is to break down the variable cost variances from Chapter 18 into more detail. Note that the $5,440 unfavorable variable cost variance from column 2 of Illustration 18–5 has been explained in more detail because of our analysis in this chapter.

This completes the basic variance analysis process. We next consider two extensions.

MATERIALS VARIANCES WHEN QUANTITY PURCHASED DOES NOT EQUAL QUANTITY USED

So far we have assumed that the amount of materials used equals the amount of materials purchased. Now we show how to calculate variances when the quantities purchased and used are not the same.

Recall the following facts from the Evergreen Company example:

Standard costs: 10 board-feet per crate @ $.25 per board-foot = $2.50 per crate

Crates produced in May: 10,000

Actual materials used: 110,000 board-feet @ $.264 per board-foot = $29,040

Now, let's assume that 250,000 board-feet were purchased in May at $.264 per board-foot, 110,000 board-feet were used, and there was no inventory on May 1.

The variance calculations are shown in Illustration 19–11. Note that the **purchase price variance** is different from the earlier example in the chapter because *it is based on the materials purchased.* The efficiency variance is the same as in the previous example because it is based on materials used, which has not changed.

Purchase Price Variance The price variance based on the quantity of materials purchased.

Self-Study Question

1 Last month, the following events took place at Containers, Inc.:

    1. Produced 50,000 plastic "notebook computer" cases.

    2. Standard variable costs per unit (that is, per case):

ILLUSTRATION

Direct Materials Variances when Quantities Purchased and Used Are Not Equal, Evergreen Company (May)

19–11

(1) **Actual**	(2) **Inputs at Standard Price**	(3) **Flexible Production Budget**
Actual materials price (*AP* = \$.264) times *actual* quantity of direct materials purchased (*AQ* = 250,000 feet purchased)		*Standard* materials price (*SP* = \$.25) times *standard* quantity of direct materials allowed for actual good output (*SQ* = 100,000 feet)
(AP × AQ)	**(SP × AQ)**	**(SP × SQ)**

Purchase
Computations

$.264 × 250,000 feet purchased = $66,000

$.25 × 250,000 feet purchased = $62,500

Price variance:
$66,000 − $62,500

= $3,500 U

Usage
Computations

$.25 × 110,000 feet used = $27,500

$.25 × 100,000 feet used = $25,000

Efficiency variance:
$27,500 − $25,000

= $2,500 U

Direct materials: 2 pounds at \$1 . . . . \$2.00

Direct labor: .10 labor-hour at \$15 . . . . 1.50

Variable manufacturing overhead: .10 machine-hour at \$5 50

\$4.00 per case

3. Actual production costs:

Direct materials purchased: 200,000 pounds at \$1.20 . . . . \$240,000

Direct materials used: 110,000 pounds at \$1.20 132,000

Direct labor: 6,000 labor-hours at \$14 84,000

Variable overhead 28,000

Compute the direct materials, labor, and variable manufacturing overhead price and efficiency variances.

The solution to this question is at the end of this chapter on page 745.

FIXED MANUFACTURING COSTS—PRODUCTION VOLUME VARIANCE

So far, we have assumed that fixed manufacturing costs are treated as period costs, which is consistent with variable costing. If fixed manufacturing costs are unitized and treated as product costs, then another variance is computed. *This occurs when companies use full-absorption, standard costing.*

Developing the Standard Unit Cost for Fixed Manufacturing Costs

Like other standard costs, the fixed manufacturing standard cost is determined before the start of the production period. Unlike standard variable manufacturing costs, fixed costs are period costs by nature. To convert them to product costs requires an estimation of both the period cost and the production volume for the period. The formula is:

$$\frac{\text{Standard (or predetermined)}}{\text{fixed manufacturing overhead cost}} = \frac{\text{Budgeted fixed manufacturing cost}}{\text{Budgeted activity level}}$$

Assume that the estimated annual fixed manufacturing overhead at Evergreen Company was $432,000 and the estimated annual production volume was estimated to be 96,000 crates (or 28,800 direct labor-hours at .30 hour per crate). Thus Evergreen Company would determine its standard fixed manufacturing cost per crate as follows:

$$\begin{aligned} \frac{\text{Standard cost}}{\text{per crate}} &= \frac{\$432,000 \text{ (budgeted fixed manufacturing cost)}}{96,000 \text{ crates (budgeted activity level for the year)}} \\ &= \underline{\$4.50 \text{ per crate}} \end{aligned}$$

Or the rate could be computed per direct labor-hour, as follows:

$$\frac{\text{Standard rate per}}{\text{direct labor-hour}} = \frac{\$432,000}{28,800 \text{ hours}} = \underline{\$15 \text{ per direct labor-hour}}$$

Each crate is expected to require .3 direct labor-hour $\left(\frac{28,800 \text{ hours}}{96,000 \text{ crates}}\right)$, so the standard cost per crate would still be $4.50 ($15 per hour × .3 hour per crate).

If 10,000 units are actually produced during the month, then $45,000 of fixed overhead costs is applied to these units produced.

Production Volume Variance A variance that arises because the quantity used to apply overhead differs from the estimated quantity used to estimate fixed costs per unit.

The **production volume variance** is the difference between the $45,000 applied fixed overhead and the $36,000 budgeted fixed overhead as shown in Illustration 19-12. Hence, in this situation there would be a $9,000 favorable production volume variance. The variance is favorable because more overhead was applied than was budgeted—production was greater than the average monthly estimate. This variance is a result of the full-absorption costing system; it does not occur in variable costing.

This $45,000 applied equals $4.50 per crate times 10,000 units *actually produced*. (See Illustration 19–13.) If the $15.00 rate per direct labor-hour had been used, then the amount applied to the 10,000 units produced would still be $45,000, computed as follows: $15.00 per hour times .3 standard direct labor-hour per crate times 10,000 crates actually produced ($15 × .3 × 10,000 = $45,000).

A variance will arise if the number of units actually produced differs from the number of units used to estimate the fixed cost per unit. This variance is commonly referred to as a *production volume variance*. (It is also called a *capacity variance*, an *idle capacity variance*, or a *denominator variance*.)

In our example, there is a production volume variance because the 10,000 crates actually produced during the month are not equal to the 8,000 $\left(\frac{96,000}{12 \text{ months}}\right)$ estimated for the month. Consequently, production is charged with $45,000 (point A in Illustration 19–13) instead of $36,000 (point B in Illustration 19–13). The $9,000 difference is the production volume variance

ILLUSTRATION

19–12

Fixed Overhead Variances

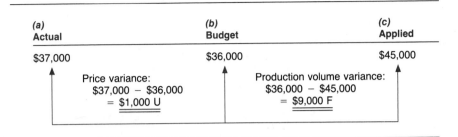

ILLUSTRATION   *Fixed Overhead Variances: Graphic Presentation*

19–13

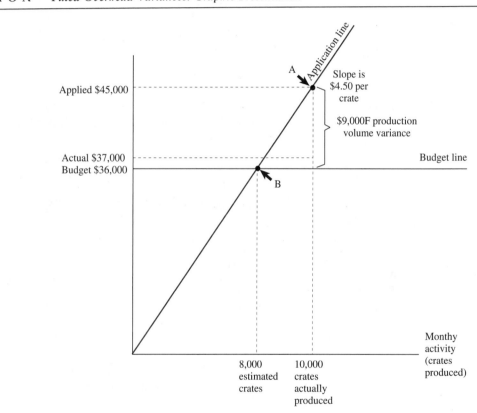

because it is caused by a deviation in production volume level (number of crates produced) from that estimated to arrive at the standard cost.

If Evergreen Company had estimated 10,000 crates per month instead of 8,000 crates, then the standard cost would have been $3.60 per crate $\left(\dfrac{\$36,000}{10,000 \text{ crates}}\right)$. Thus, $36,000 ($3.60 × 10,000 crates) would have been applied to units produced, and there would have been no production volume variance.

The production volume variance applies only to fixed costs and emerges because we are allocating a fixed period cost to units on a predetermined basis. It does not represent resources spent or saved. It is unique to full-absorption costing. The benefits of calculating the variance for control purposes are questionable. While the production volume variance signals a difference between expected and actual production levels, so does a simple production report of actual versus expected production quantities.

Compare with the Fixed Manufacturing Cost Price Variance
The fixed manufacturing cost price variance is the difference between actual and budgeted fixed manufacturing costs. Unlike the production volume variance, the price variance is commonly used for control purposes because it is a measure of differences between actual and budgeted period costs.

Illustrations 19–12 and 19–13 should help you see the relationship between *actual*, *budget*, and *applied* fixed manufacturing costs and to summarize the computation of the fixed manufacturing *price* (spending) and *production volume* variances.

SUMMARY OF OVERHEAD VARIANCES

Illustration 19–14 summarizes the four-way analysis of variable and fixed overhead variances, based on facts given in the chapter. Appendix A to this chapter shows two-way and three-way methods that are alternatives to the four-way method.

I L L U S T R A T I O N   *Summary of Overhead Variances: Four-Way Analysis*

19–14

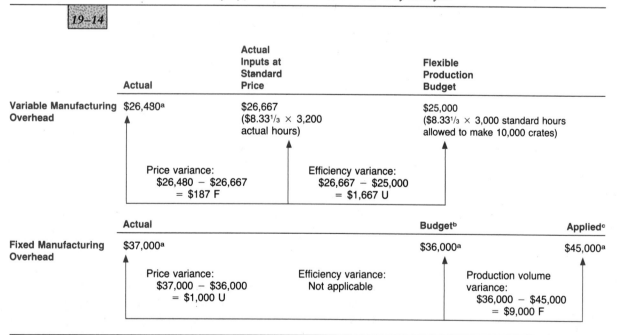

	Actual	Actual Inputs at Standard Price	Flexible Production Budget
Variable Manufacturing Overhead	$26,480[a]	$26,667 ($8.33⅓ × 3,200 actual hours)	$25,000 ($8.33⅓ × 3,000 standard hours allowed to make 10,000 crates)

Price variance: $26,480 − $26,667 = $187 F

Efficiency variance: $26,667 − $25,000 = $1,667 U

	Actual		Budget[b]	Applied[c]
Fixed Manufacturing Overhead	$37,000[a]		$36,000[a]	$45,000[a]

Price variance: $37,000 − $36,000 = $1,000 U

Efficiency variance: Not applicable

Production volume variance: $36,000 − $45,000 = $9,000 F

[a] Amount given in chapter.
[b] This amount appears in both the master budget and the flexible budget.
[c] This is the amount of fixed manufacturing overhead applied to units produced under full-absorption costing.

Key Points   There are several key points to keep in mind regarding overhead variances.

1. The variable overhead efficiency variance measures the efficiency in using the base (for example, direct labor-hours).
2. The production volume variance only occurs when fixed manufacturing cost is unitized (for example, when using full-absorption costing). Further, the budgeted fixed overhead is not the amount applied to units produced.
3. There is no efficiency variance for fixed manufacturing costs. (Do not confuse production volume variance with an efficiency variance.)

Self-Study Question

2 This question follows up self-study question 1. Assume the fixed manufacturing cost budget was $80,000 for the month, and actual fixed manufacturing overhead costs were $83,000. The estimated monthly production was 40,000 cases (or 4,000 standard labor-hours).

Compute the fixed manufacturing overhead price variance and the fixed manufacturing overhead production volume variance.

The solution to this question is at the end of this chapter on page 746.

VARIANCE ANALYSIS IN NONMANUFACTURING SETTINGS

The analysis of price and efficiency variances in nonmanufacturing settings for nonmanufacturing costs is increasing. We find banks, fast-food outlets, hospitals, consulting firms, retail stores, and many others applying the variance analysis techniques discussed in this chapter to their labor and overhead costs.

Efficiency Measures

In some cases, an efficiency variance can be used to analyze variable nonmanufacturing costs. This efficiency computation requires a reliable measure of output activity. Ideally, this requires some quantitative input that can be linked to output.

For example, the personnel in the Accounts Receivable Department of a retail merchandiser are expected to contact 10 delinquent customers per hour. The standard labor cost is $12 per hour including benefits. During July, 7,000 hours were worked, 65,000 contacts were made, and the average wage rate was $13 per hour. For 65,000 contacts, the standard labor-hours allowed were 6,500 (65,000 contacts ÷ 10 contacts per hour). Unfavorable price and efficiency variances were computed as shown below:

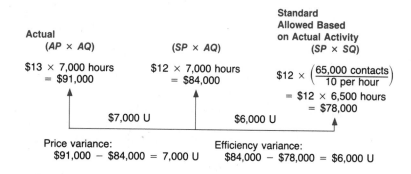

These calculations are similar to the ones used for labor variances in manufacturing.

Computing these efficiency variances requires some assumed relationship between input and output activity. Some examples are:

Department	Input	Output
Mailing	Labor-hours worked	Number of pieces mailed
Personnel	Labor-hours worked	Number of personnel changes processed
Food service	Hours worked	Number of meals served
Consulting	Billable hours worked	Customer revenues
Nursing	Labor-hours worked	Patients (of a particular care level) served
Check processing	Computer-hours worked	Checks processed

In general, jobs with routine tasks lend themselves to efficiency measures, while jobs with nonroutine tasks—like most administrative positions—do not.

Attempts to measure efficiency sometimes lead to employee resentment. In other cases, the measurement results in both better performance and better morale. Often, employee participation in the measurement process helps improve morale, while a top-down imposed measurement system provokes employee resentment.

HOW MANY VARIANCES TO CALCULATE?

We noted at the beginning of this chapter that every organization has its own approach to variance analysis although virtually all are based on the fundamental model presented here. Because of the unique circumstances in each organization, we cannot generalize very much about which variances should be calculated. Managers and accountants in each organization should perform their own cost-benefit analysis to ascertain which calculations are justified.

In deciding how many variances to calculate, it is important to note the **impact** and **controllability** of each variance. When considering *impact*, we ask: "Does this variance matter? Is it so small that the best efforts to improve efficiency or control costs would have very little impact even if the efforts were successful?" If so, it's probably not worth the trouble to calculate and analyze. Hence, detailed variance calculations for small overhead items may not be worthwhile.

Impact The monetary effect that is likely from an activity (such as a variance).

Controllability The extent to which an item can be managed.

When considering the controllability of a variance, we ask: "Can we do something about it?" No matter how great the impact of the variance, if nothing can be done about the variance, then it is hard to justify spending resources to compute and analyze it. For example, materials purchase price variances are often high-impact items. They are hard to control, however, because materials prices fluctuate due to market conditions that are outside the control of managers.

In general, high-impact, highly controllable variances should get the most attention, while low-impact, uncontrollable variances should get the least attention, as shown below:

Impact

	Low	High
Controllability		
Low	Variances get the least attention	
High		Variances get the most attention

Labor and materials efficiency variances are often highly controllable. With sufficient attention to scheduling, quality of employees, motivation, and incentives, these variances can often be dealt with effectively. An example of a high-impact, but hard-to-control, item for many companies has been the cost of energy. Many organizations, from airlines to taxicab companies to steel mills, have been able to do little about rising energy costs in the short run. Over time, of course, actions could be taken to reduce energy usage through acquisition of energy-efficient equipment. In general, the longer the time interval, the greater the ability to control an item.

MANAGEMENT BY EXCEPTION AND VARIANCE INVESTIGATION

Management by Exception An approach to management requiring that reports emphasize the deviation from an accepted basing point, such as a standard, a budget, an industry average, or a prior-period experience.

After variances have been computed, managers and accountants must decide which variances should be investigated. Illustration 19–15 shows one such investigation where, apparently, Joe's efficiency idea has not worked out very well.

Because a manager's time is a scarce resource, some priorities must be set. This can be done through cost-benefit analysis. Only the variances for which the benefits of correction exceed the costs of follow-up should be pursued. In general, this is consistent with the **management by exception** philosophy, which says, in effect, "Don't worry about what is going according to plan; worry about the exceptions."

But this is easier said than done. It may be almost impossible to predict either costs or benefits of investigating variances. So, while the principle is straightforward, it is difficult to apply. In this section, we identify some characteristics that are important for determining which variances to investigate. In Chapter 25, we discuss statistical models for investigating variances.

Some problems are easily corrected as soon as they are discovered. When a machine is improperly set or a worker needs minor instruction, the investigation cost is low and benefits are very likely to exceed costs. This is often a usage or efficiency variance and is reported frequently—often daily—so immediate corrective action can be taken.

Some variances are not controllable in the short run. Labor price variances due to changes in union contracts and overhead spending variances due to unplanned utility and property tax rate changes may require little or no follow-up in the short run. Such variances sometimes prompt long-run action, such as moving a plant to a locale with lower wage rates and lower utility and property tax rates. In such cases, the short-run benefits of variance investigation are low, but the long-run benefits may be higher.

Many variances occur because of errors in recording, bookkeeping adjustments, or timing problems. A variance-reporting system (and the Accounting Department) can lose credibility if it contains bookkeeping errors and adjustments. For this reason, the accounting staff must carefully check variance reports before sending them to operating managers.

UPDATING STANDARDS

Standards are estimates. As such, they may not reflect the conditions that actually occur. This is especially likely to happen when standards are not updated and revised to reflect current conditions. If prices and operating methods are frequently changed, standards may be constantly out of date.

In many companies, standards are revised once a year. Thus, variances will occur because conditions change during the year but standards don't. When conditions change, but are known to be temporary, some companies develop a **planned variance.** For example, an unexpected series of snowstorms curtailed activities to much below normal in a steel plant in the Midwest. This affected the workers' productivity and created large unfavorable labor efficiency variances. In response, the accounting staff developed planned variances for a number of costs based on expected differences between actual costs and standard costs due to the snowstorms. For example, the January labor report for a particular department was as follows:

Planned Variance A variance that is expected to arise if certain conditions affect operations.

Item	Total Efficiency Variance	Planned Efficiency Variance	Unplanned Efficiency Variance
Direct labor—department xx	$11,242 U	$9,100 U	$2,142 U

The department manager was not held responsible for the entire $11,242 U variance, but only the $2,142 U unplanned efficiency variance.

NONFINANCIAL PERFORMANCE MEASURES

Although variances provide important measures of performance, nonfinancial performance measures are also important. Nonfinancial performance measures are particularly important for evaluating quality and customer service. For example, Illustration 19–16 presents five nonfinancial performance measures managers use to evaluate performance in customer service and production.

Quality Control Performance Measures

The first set of measures appearing in Illustration 19–16 reflects quality control. Quality can be measured by the number and type of customer complaints or by the number of product defects. If we reduce the number of product defects, we will likely reduce the number of customer complaints. The objective is to increase customer satisfaction with our product, reduce costs of dealing with customer complaints, and reduce costs of repairing products or providing a new service.

Quality-oriented organizations continually monitor the quality of their products and solicit feedback from customers to assess customer satisfaction with goods and services. J. Peterman and Company, a merchandising company, tells its customers to "please hassle us" if customers are not completely satisfied. Nordstrom's, Southwest Airlines, and Toyota are among the companies that have built a reputation based on the notion of "hassle us" if you are not completely satisfied. If you visit a manufacturing plant, such as the Nissan plant near Nashville, Tennessee, you will see some of the previous day's production of cars and trucks in the lobby of the plant together with charts showing how many defects were found in the previous day's production. This display of the product and performance report gives workers a sense of pride in their work and an incentive to reduce defects.

Delivery Performance Measure

The second type of nonfinancial measure in Illustration 19–16 deals with delivery time. For some companies, like American Airlines, Amtrak, Chicago's Metra, and other metropolitan transit systems, Federal Express, United Parcel Service, and other delivery services, delivery performance is critical to success. The success of companies that sell through catalogs, such

ILLUSTRATION 19–16

Nonfinancial Performance Measures

	Objective
1. Quality control:	
Number of customer complaints	Customer satisfaction
Number of defects	Quality product
2. Delivery performance:	
Percentage of on-time deliveries	Increase on-time deliveries
3. Materials waste:	
Scrap and waste as a percentage of total materials used	Decrease scrap and waste
4. Inventory:	
Inventory levels	Reduce inventory levels
Number of different inventoried items	Decrease number of different items
5. Machine downtime:	
Percentage of machine downtime	Decrease downtime

as Lands' End, L. L. Bean, and The Territory Ahead, is dependent on quick delivery of their merchandise. Bottlers of soft drinks like Pepsi-Cola and canneries like Campbell Soup require the timing of the delivery of cans and bottles to be precise for their production needs; ideally, the truck or railroad carload of containers is ready to unload right onto the production line.

Materials Waste
Performance Measure

Reducing materials waste, the third type of nonfinancial measure, can be accomplished by improving the quality of raw materials so there is less waste from defective materials, increasing employee training so workers make fewer mistakes, and improving the production process. Materials waste may show up in the materials efficiency variance. However, standards often allow for some waste, so an unfavorable variance would only be for the excess waste over that allowed in the standard. Workers are generally motivated to find ways to reduce waste if companies keep track of materials waste on the basis of the quantity (for example, board-feet in construction of wood products) every day, with immediate feedback to workers the next day, often in the form of large charts. While the report of variances from standard costs is important to department heads and plant managers, workers are more likely to be motivated by immediate feedback in nonfinancial language.

Inventory Performance
Measures

The fourth type of nonfinancial performance measure shown in Illustration 19–16 deals with inventory levels. Companies try to reduce both the inventory levels of each item and the number of different items in inventory. A food wholesaler found its inventory contained hundreds of items that were rarely ordered by the convenience stores that were its customers. Instead of keeping those rare items in inventory, the wholesaler simply ordered them from its supplier when needed by the convenience stores. As a result, the wholesaler reduced its inventory by nearly one third.

Machine Downtime
Performance Measure

The fifth type of nonfinancial measure, machine downtime, is very important in all types of companies. At the NUMMI plant, a joint venture of General Motors and Toyota, assembly-line workers have the authority to stop the assembly line when they see something wrong. It should come as no surprise that such an action brings a lot of attention to the problem from many people in the plant. Stopping production causes a loss of output while people wait for the machine to start up. Machine downtime also can cause customer dissatisfaction and loss of sales, as you may have experienced when you go to the bank and are told you cannot be served because "the computer is down," or when your airline flight has been cancelled because of an airplane's maintenance problems.

SUMMARY

This chapter discusses the computation and analysis of manufacturing cost variances. A variance is the difference between a predetermined standard and an actual result.

The model used for calculating variable manufacturing cost variances is based on the following diagram, which divides the total variance between actual and standard into price and efficiency components:

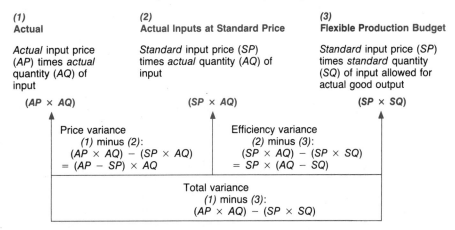

(1)	**(2)**	**(3)**
Actual	**Actual Inputs at Standard Price**	**Flexible Production Budget**
Actual input price (*AP*) times *actual* quantity (*AQ*) of input	*Standard* input price (*SP*) times *actual* quantity (*AQ*) of input	*Standard* input price (*SP*) times *standard* quantity (*SQ*) of input allowed for actual good output
(*AP* × *AQ*)	(*SP* × *AQ*)	(*SP* × *SQ*)

Price variance
(1) minus (2):
(*AP* × *AQ*) − (*SP* × *AQ*)
= (*AP* − *SP*) × *AQ*

Efficiency variance
(2) minus (3):
(*SP* × *AQ*) − (*SP* × *SQ*)
= *SP* × (*AQ* − *SQ*)

Total variance
(1) minus (3):
(*AP* × *AQ*) − (*SP* × *SQ*)

Fixed manufacturing costs have no efficiency variance. The price variance is the difference between actual fixed costs and the fixed costs in the flexible budget. If fixed costs are unitized and assigned to units produced, then a production volume variance can also arise. The production volume variance is the difference between the budgeted fixed costs and the amount applied to production.

A key managerial question is: How many variances should be calculated and investigated? The answer depends on the impact and controllability of variances. In general, the greater the impact of a variance on profits and the more controllable it is, the easier it is to justify analysis of the variance.

TERMS AND CONCEPTS

The following terms and concepts should be familiar to you after reading this chapter:

Activity Variance, *715*	**Planned Variance,** *724*
Budget Variance, *715*	**Price Variance,** *704*
Controllability, *722*	**Production Volume Variance,** *718*
Cost Variance Analysis, *704*	**Purchase Price Variance,** *716*
Efficiency Variance, *704*	**Spending Variance,** *715*
Flexible Production Budget, *706*	**Standard Cost,** *699*
Impact, *722*	**Total Variance,** *705*
Management by Exception, *723*	**Variance,** *698*

APPENDIX A

Two-Way and Three-Way Analysis of Overhead Variance

The method of computing overhead variances described in this chapter is known as the four-way analysis of overhead variances because the following four variances are computed:

	Price	Efficiency	Production Volume
Variable Costs	$ 187 F	$1,667 U	Not applicable
Fixed Costs	1,000 U	Not applicable	$9,000 F

Companies also prepare alternative two-way or three-way analyses of manufacturing overhead variances.

Two-Way Analysis

The two-way analysis of overhead variances has just two variances: a *production volume variance*, computed like the production volume variance in the four-way analysis above, and a *spending*, or *budget variance*, which is the difference between the actual and budgeted overhead. Think of the spending variance as including all three of the overhead variances computed in the four-way analysis besides the production volume variance. The spending variance is useful for management control purposes, but the production volume variance is not.

If Evergreen Company does not break down its variances into fixed and variable components, then the actual overhead costs would be $63,480 ($26,480 variable plus $37,000 fixed, as shown in Illustration 19–14), and the budgeted overhead would total $61,000 ($25,000 variable plus $36,000 fixed, as shown in Illustration 19–14).

The following diagram shows how to compute the two overhead variances.

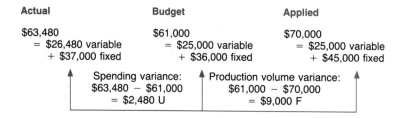

Actual	Budget	Applied
$63,480	$61,000	$70,000
= $26,480 variable	= $25,000 variable	= $25,000 variable
+ $37,000 fixed	+ $36,000 fixed	+ $45,000 fixed

Spending variance:
$63,480 − $61,000
= $2,480 U

Production volume variance:
$61,000 − $70,000
= $9,000 F

The amount of variable overhead applied to units produced ($25,000) is the standard allowed for the flexible production budget, so "applied equals budget" for variable overhead. This is not true for fixed overhead if there is a production volume variance.

Three-Way Analysis

The three-way analysis is like the four-way analysis except the two fixed and variable price variances are combined into one overhead price variance. The three-way analysis is done in companies that do not separate costs into fixed and variable components.

The three variances computed in the three-way analysis are (1) the overhead price variance, (2) the variable overhead efficiency variance, and (3) the fixed overhead production volume variance. These are computed for Evergreen Company as follows:

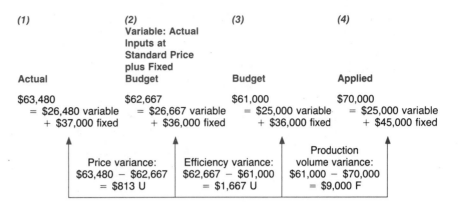

The new term in column 2 is made up of:

Variable:	$26,667	actual inputs at standard price (see Illustration 19–14)
Fixed:	36,000	budgeted fixed overhead
Total	$62,667	

The budget (column 3) and applied (column 4) overhead for the three-way analysis are the same as for the two-way analysis.

In deciding whether to use two-way analysis or three-way analysis, managers should weigh the costs of computing and interpreting the variable ovehead efficiency variance against the benefits of obtaining the data from that variance.

Illustration 19–17 summarizes the two-way, three-way, and four-way analyses of overhead variance. We start with the four-way analysis at the top and show how the numbers in the two-way and three-way analyses fit into the four-way analysis. Note that there could also be a one-way analysis, which is the total under/overapplied overhead; that is, the $6,520 F difference between actual overhead ($63,480 in this example) and the amount applied to production ($70,000 in this example).

APPENDIX B

Alternative Division of Total Variance into Price and Efficiency Components

In this chapter, we calculated each price variance based on actual quantity. That is:

$$(AP \times AQ) \qquad (SP \times AQ) \qquad (SP \times SQ)$$

Price variance: $(AP - SP) \times AQ$ Efficiency variance: $SP \times (AQ - SQ)$

But suppose that the order was reversed so that the efficiency variance was calculated first and based on actual prices:

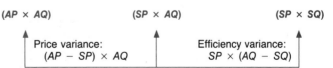

ILLUSTRATION   *Alternative Ways of Computing Overhead Variances*

19–17

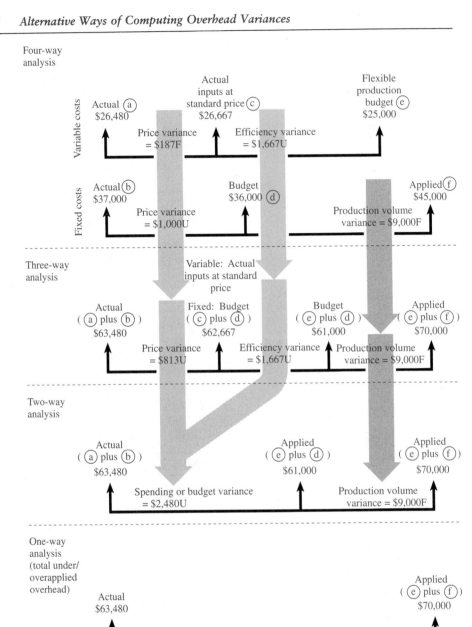

Note that the two endpoints are the same, but the middle point is different.

The effect on variance calculations can be seen from the following if the direct materials data from Evergreen Company are used:

Standard costs: 10 board-feet @ \$.25 per board-foot = \$2.50 per crate

Crates produced in May: 10,000

Actual materials used: 110,000 board-feet @ \$.264 per board-foot = \$29,040

For this example, assume the quantity of board-feet purchased equals the quantity used.

The calculation in the chapter was as follows:

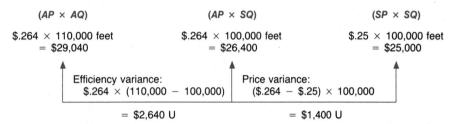

(*AP* × *AQ*)	(*SP* × *AQ*)	(*SP* × *SQ*)
$.264 × 110,000 feet = $29,040	$.25 × 110,000 feet = $27,500	$.25 × 100,000 feet = $25,000

Price variance:
($.264 − $.25) × 110,000
= $1,540 U

Efficiency variance:
$.25 × (110,000 − 100,000)
= $2,500 U

The alternative calculation is as follows:

(*AP* × *AQ*)	(*AP* × *SQ*)	(*SP* × *SQ*)
$.264 × 110,000 feet = $29,040	$.264 × 100,000 feet = $26,400	$.25 × 100,000 feet = $25,000

Efficiency variance:
$.264 × (110,000 − 100,000)

Price variance:
($.264 − $.25) × 100,000

= $2,640 U   = $1,400 U

Note that the *total* variance is the same in both cases—$4,040 U. However, that partition into price and efficiency (quantity) variances is different. There are really three variances: a pure price variance ($1,400 in this case), a pure efficiency variance ($2,500), and a joint variance ($140 in this case). The joint variance is part of the price variance in the first calculation and part of the efficiency variance in the second. The graph in Illustration 19–18 shows these relationships.

By isolating the joint variance, we may be able to resolve disputes between purchasing people and production people. Purchasing argues that it should not be accountable for the joint variance because production controls quantities. Production says they manage quantities not prices. Illustration 19–18 shows that a piece of the variance is, in fact, a joint responsibility.

ILLUSTRATION

19–18

Graphic Analysis of Variance, Direct Materials, Evergreen Company

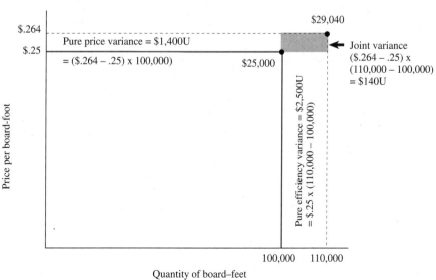

Note: The area inside the solid line represents the total standard costs allowed to make 10,000 crates. The area inside the dashed line represents the total actual costs incurred.

QUESTIONS

19–1   Why should management want to divide manufacturing cost variances into price and efficiency variances?

19–2   What is the difference between a standard and a budget?

19–3   What is the difference between a flexible budget and inputs priced at standard?

19–4   The manager of the Production Department has just received a responsibility report that shows a substantial unfavorable variance for overtime premium. The manager objects to the inclusion of this variance because the overtime was due to the acceptance of a large rush order by the Sales Department. To whom should this variance be charged?

19–5   Many companies set wage rates through negotiations with unions. Under these circumstances, how would a labor price variance arise that would be the responsibility of a line manager?

19–6   One of the principles espoused by management is the idea that one should manage by exception. How can responsibility reporting systems and/or analysis of variances assist in that process?

19–7   What are the three primary sources of variances for variable costs?

19–8   Why are the variances for fixed costs different from the variances computed for variable costs?

19–9   Would the production volume variance represent a difference in the cash outflows for the company when compared to budgeted cash outflows?

19–10   Why might management decision making be enhanced if materials price variances are recognized at the time of purchase rather than at the time of use?

19–11   In a service environment where there are no inventories, would variance analysis be useful? Why or why not?

19–12   Refer to the real world application for this chapter. What were the benefits of worker involvement in setting standards at NUMMI?

19–13   What nonfinancial performance measures could be used to encourage better product quality? Better customer service?

19–14   What nonfinancial performance measures would encourage reduced inventories?

EXERCISES

19–15   Variable Cost Variances
(L.O.1)

The standard direct labor cost per reservation for the Elegance Inns Reservation System is $1.30 ($13 per hour divided by 10 reservations per hour). Actual direct labor costs during the period totaled $89,000; 6,800 labor-hours were worked during the period; and 72,000 reservations were made.

Required:

Compute the direct labor price and efficiency variances for the period. (Refer to Illustration 19–4 for format.)

19–16   Variable Cost Variances
(L.O.1)

The standard direct labor cost per unit for a company was $20 ($10 per hour times two hours per unit). Actual direct labor costs during the period amounted to $37,600, 3,900 labor-hours were worked during the period, and 1,900 units were produced.

Required:

Compute the direct labor price and efficiency variances for the period. (Refer to Illustration 19–4 for format.)

19–17   Variable Cost Variances
(L.O.1)

The data below reflect the current month's activity of Pelnar, Inc.:

Actual total direct labor	$44,200
Actual hours worked	14,000
Standard labor-hours allowed for actual output (flexible budget)	15,000
Direct labor price variance	$ 800 U
Actual variable overhead	$22,100
Standard variable overhead rate per standard direct labor-hour	$1.70

Variable overhead is applied based on standard direct labor hours allowed.

Required: Compute the labor and variable overhead price and efficiency variances.

19–18   Variable Cost Variances
(L.O.1)

Information on Ventura Corporation's direct materials costs is as follows:

Actual quantities of direct materials used	20,000
Actual costs of direct materials used	$43,800
Standard price per unit of direct materials	$2.10
Flexible budget for direct materials	$39,900

Ventura Corporation has no materials inventories.

Required: What were Ventura Corporation's direct materials price and efficiency variances?

19–19   Variances from Activity-Based Costs
(L.O.2)

Analysis of the variable overhead costs for Jordan Shoe Company reveals three cost drivers with the following standard and actual amounts:

Activity Center	Cost Driver	Standard Rate per Cost Driver Unit	Standard Input per Unit of Output	Actual Costs	Actual Number of Inputs Used
Quality testing	Test minutes	$ .50	2 test minutes	$ 5,000	10,000 test minutes
Energy	Machine-hours	1.00	2 machine-hours	10,000	10,500 machine-hours
Indirect labor	Direct labor-hours	.50	3 hours	7,100	14,000 hours

Assume 5,000 units of output were actually produced.

Required: Prepare an analysis of variances.

19–20   Variable Cost Variances
(L.O.1)

Information on Hobart Chemical's direct materials costs is as follows:

Quantities of palladium purchased and used	1,200 ounces
Actual cost of palladium used	$206,000
Standard price per unit of palladium	$180
Standard quantity of palladium allowed	1,100 ounces

Required: What were Hobart Chemical's direct materials price and efficiency variances?

19–21   Variable Cost Variances where Materials Purchased and Materials Used Are Not Equal
(L.O.1)

Dal Porto Company reported the following information concerning its direct materials:

Direct materials purchased (actual)	$406,852
Standard cost of materials purchased	407,391
Standard price times actual quantity of materials used	74,193
Actual production	28,000 units
Standard direct materials costs per unit produced	$ 2.62

Required: Compute the direct materials cost variances. Prepare an analysis like the one in Illustration 19–11.

19–22   Fixed Cost Variances   Information on Styler Company's fixed overhead costs is as follows:
(L.O.3)

Overhead applied	$120,000
Actual overhead	127,000
Budgeted overhead	123,000

Required: What are the fixed overhead price and production volume variances? (Refer to Illustration 19–12 for format.)

19–23   Fixed Cost Variances   Refer to the data in exercise 19–22. Prepare graphs like those shown in Illustration 19–13.
(L.O.3)

19–24   Fixed Cost Variances   Garza Corporation applies overhead at the rate of $4.40 per unit. Budgeted fixed overhead was $67,860. 16,000 units were produced this month, and actual overhead was $65,110.
(L.O.3)

Required: What are the fixed overhead price and production volume variances for Garza?

19–25   Comprehensive Cost Variance Analysis (L.O.4)   Dura-tread, Inc., manufactures construction equipment and farm machinery tires. The following information is available for June, Year 1.

1. Dura-tread produced and sold 4,600 tires at a price of $1,000 each. Budgeted production was 5,000 tires.

2. Standard variable costs per tire were as follows:

Direct materials: 100 lbs. at $2.00	$200
Direct labor: 20 hours at $9.00	180
Variable manufacturing overhead: 4.5 machine-hours at $10.00 per hour	45
Total variable costs	$425

3. Fixed manufacturing overhead costs:

Monthly budget $1,900,000

4. Fixed overhead is applied at the rate of $380 per tire.

5. Actual production costs:

Direct materials purchased and used: 480,000 pounds at $1.80	$ 864,000
Direct labor: 88,000 hours at $9.20	809,600
Variable overhead: 21,600 machine-hours at $10.20 per hour	220,320
Fixed overhead	2,000,000

6. Machine-hours: 21,600.

Required: *a.* Prepare a cost variance analysis for each variable cost for Dura-tread.

b. Prepare a fixed overhead cost variance analysis.

19–26   Comprehensive Cost Variance Analysis (L.O.4)   Optique, Inc., is a fast growing chain of operations that specializes in optical care and contact lenses. The following data are available for last year's eye care exam services:

1. Optique performed 50,000 eye exams last year. Budgeted exams were 45,000 exams, averaging 40 minutes per exam.

2. Standard variable costs per exam were as follows:

Direct optometrist services: 40 minutes at $36.00 per hour $24.00

Variable support staff and overhead: 1.1 labor-hours at
$15.00 per hour 16.50

3. Fixed overhead costs:

Annual budget $180,000

4. Fixed overhead is applied at the rate of $4 per exam.

5. Actual eye exam costs:

Direct optometrist services: 50,000 exams averaging
45 minutes at $39.00 .... $1,462,500

Variable support staff and overhead: 1.2 labor-hours at
$14.00 per hour × 50,000 exams 840,000

Fixed overhead 187,000

Required:

a. Prepare a cost variance analysis for each variable cost for last year.

b. Prepare a fixed overhead cost variance analysis like the one in Illustration 19–12.

19–27 Variances from Activity-Based Costs (L.O.2)

Eyes 'R Us offers optical care. Management has asked you to analyze its variable overhead. Analysis of the variable overhead costs reveals three cost drivers with the following standard and actual amounts:

Activity Center	Cost Driver	Standard Rate per Cost Driver Unit	Standard Input per Unit of Output (exam)	Actual Costs	Actual Number of Inputs Used
Purchasing	Number of purchases	$4.00 per purchase	1 purchase per exam	$200,000	46,000 purchases
Support staff labor	Number of fittings	8.00 per fitting	1.2 fittings per exam	440,000	52,000 fittings
Special contact lenses	Pairs of contacts sold	7.00 per pair	0.6 pairs per exam	200,000	31,000 pairs of contact lenses

Last year, the number of units of output, that is, exams, was 50,000.

Required:

Prepare a cost variance analysis.

19–28 Two-Way and Three-Way Overhead Variances (Appendix A) (L.O.6)

Using the data in exercise 19–26, compute the following (assume full-absorption costing is used to apply overhead to units produced):

a. Total over/underapplied overhead.

b. Two-way analysis of overhead variances.

c. Three-way analysis of overhead variances.

19–29 Overhead Variances (L.O.1, L.O.3)

MPC Corporation shows the following overhead information for the current period:

Actual overhead incurred ...... $12,600, of which $3,500 is fixed and $9,100 is variable

Budgeted fixed overhead ...... $3,600 (3,000 direct labor-hours budgeted)

Standard variable overhead rate per direct labor-hour $3

Standard hours allowed for actual production .... 3,500 hours

Actual labor-hours used .... 3,300 hours

Required:	What are the variable overhead price and efficiency variances and the fixed overhead price variance?
19–30 Two-Way and Three-Way Overhead Variances (Appendix A) (L.O.6)	Using the data in exercise 19–29, compute the following (assume full-absorption costing is used to apply overhead to units produced). *a.* Total over/underapplied overhead. *b.* Two-way analysis of overhed variances. *c.* Three-way analysis of overhead variances.
19–31 Two-Way and Three-Way Overhead Variances (Appendix A) (L.O.6)	Moffett Company incurred total overhead costs of $178,360 during the month when 4,100 hours were worked. The normal workload for the company is 4,000 hours. The flexible budget for the output attained this period indicates that 4,300 hours were allowed. Standard costs per hour are as follows:

Variable overhead $13.75

Fixed overhead 27.70

Fixed overhead cost $2,170 more than budgeted.

Required: Compute the following:

a. Total over/underapplied overhead, assuming full-absorption costing is used.

b. Two-way analysis of overhead variances.

c. Three-way analysis of overhead variances.

PROBLEMS

19–32 Nonmanufacturing Cost Variances	Home Loan Company originates mortgage loans for residential housing. The company charges a service fee for processing loan applications. This fee is set twice a year based on the cost of processing a loan application. For the first half of this year, Home Loan estimated that it would process 75 loans. Correspondence, credit reports, supplies, and other materials that vary with each loan are estimated to cost $45 per loan. The company hires a loan processor at an estimated cost of $27,000 per year and an assistant at an estimated cost of $20,000 per year. The cost to lease office space and pay utilities and other related costs are estimated at $58,000 per year.
	      During the first six months of this year, Home Loan processed 79 loans. Cost of materials, credit reports, and other items related to loan processing were 8 percent greater than expected for the volume of loans processed.
	      The loan processor and her assistant cost $23,800 for the six months. Leasing and related office costs were $28,100.

Required:	Prepare an analysis of the variances for Home Loan Corp. (Hint: Loans are the output.)
19–33 Direct Materials	Information about Pons Platinum Company's direct materials cost is as follows:

Standard price per materials ounce $345

Actual quantity used . . . . 420 ounces

Standard quantity allowed for production . . . . . 435 ounces

Price variance . . . . $2,950 F

Required: What was the actual purchase price per ounce, rounded to the nearest cent?

19–34 Solve for Direct Labor-Hours   Santa Barbara Company reports the following direct labor information for product CER for the month of October:

Standard rate . . . . $7.00 per hour

Actual rate paid . . . . $7.20 per hour

Standard hours allowed for actual production . . . . 1,400 hours

Labor efficiency variance . . . . $500 U

Required:

Based on these data, what were the actual hours worked and what was the labor price variance?

19–35 Overhead Variances

Space, Inc., shows the following overhead information for the current period:

Actual overhead incurred . . . . $14,700, of which $9,800 is variable

Budgeted fixed overhead $4,320

Standard variable overhead rate per direct labor-hour $3

Standard hours allowed for actual production . . . . 3,500 hours

Actual labor-hours used . . . . 3,300 hours

Required:

What are the variable overhead price and efficiency variances and fixed overhead price variance?

19–36 Manufacturing Variances

Biograde Company prepares its budgets on the basis of standard costs. A responsibility report is prepared monthly showing the differences between master budget and actual. Variances are analyzed and reported separately. Materials price variances are computed at the time of purchase.

The following information relates to the current period:

Standard costs (per unit of output):

Direct materials, 1 kilogram @ $1 per kilogram . . . . $ 1

Direct labor, 2 hours @ $4 per hour 8

Factory overhead:

Variable (25% of direct labor cost) 2

Total standard cost per unit $11

Actual costs for the month:

Materials purchased . . . . 3,000 kilograms at $.90 per kilogram

Output . . . . 1,900 units using 2,100 kilograms of materials

Actual labor costs . . . . 3,200 hours at $5 per hour

Actual variable overhead $4,500

Required:

Prepare a variance analysis for the variable costs.

19–37 Alternative Variance Calculations (Appendix B)

Refer to the labor and variable overhead data given in problem 19–36. Compute the labor and overhead variances using the method set forth in Appendix B.

19–38 Overhead Cost and Variance Relationships

Navajo Company reported a $50 unfavorable price variance for variable overhead and a $500 unfavorable price variance for fixed overhead. The flexible budget had $32,100 variable overhead based on 10,700 direct labor-hours; only 10,600 hours were worked. Total actual overhead was $54,350. Estimated hours for computing the fixed overhead application rate were 11,000 hours.

Required:

a. Prepare a variable overhead analysis like the one in Illustration 19–5.

b. Prepare a fixed overhead analysis like the one in Illustration 19–12.

19–39 Analysis of Cost Reports

Marcia is the production manager of the Bridgton Plant, a division of the larger corporation, Dartmoor, Inc. Marcia has complained several times to the corporate office that the cost reports used to evaluate her plant are misleading. Marcia states, "I know how to get good quality product out. Over a number of years, I've even cut raw materials used to do it. The cost reports don't show any of this; they're always negative, no matter what I do. There's no way you can win with accounting or the people at headquarters who use these reports."

A copy of the latest report is shown below.

BRIDGTON PLANT
Cost Report
Month of November 1992
(in thousands)

	Master Budget	Actual Cost	Excess Cost
Raw material	$ 400	$ 437	$ 37
Direct labor	560	540	(20)
Overhead	100	134	34
Total	$1,060	$1,111	$ 51

Required: Identify and explain at least three changes to the report that would make the cost information more meaningful and less threatening to the production managers.

(CMA adapted)

19-40   Change of Policy to Improve Productivity

Brock Toy Company has been experiencing declining profit margins and has been looking for ways to increase operating income. It cannot raise selling prices for fear of losing business to its competitors. It must either cut costs or improve productivity.

Brock uses a standard cost system to evaluate the performance of the Assembly Department. All negative variances at the end of the month are investigated. The Assembly Department rarely completes the operations in less time than the standard allows (which would result in a positive variance). Most months the variance is zero or slightly negative. Reasoning that the application of lower standard costs to the products manufactured will result in improved profit margins, the production manager has recommended that all standard times for assembly operations be drastically reduced. The production manager has informed the assembly personnel that she expects the Assembly Department to meet these new standards.

Required: Will the lowering of the standard costs (by reducing the time of the assembly operations) result in improved profit margins and increased productivity?

(CMA adapted)

19-41   Behavioral Impact of Implementing Standard Cost System

Windsor Healthcare, Inc., a manufacturer of custom-designed home health-care equipment, has been in business for 15 years. Last year, in an effort to better control the costs of their products, the controller implemented a standard cost system. Reports are issued monthly for tracking performance and any negative variances are further investigated.

The production manager complained that the standards are unrealistic, stifle motivation by concentrating only on negative variances, and are out of date too quickly. He noted that his recent switch to titanium for the wheelchairs has resulted in higher materials costs but decreased labor-hours. The net result was no increase in the total cost of producing the wheelchair. The monthly reports continue to show a negative materials variance and a positive labor variance, despite the fact that there are indications that the workers are slowing down.

A standard cost system can have a strong impact on both costs and employees.

Required: *a.*   Describe several ways that a standard cost system strengthens management cost control.

b.   Give at least two reasons why a standard cost system may negatively impact the motivation of production employees.

(CMA adapted)

19-42   Ethics and Standard Costs

Quincy Farms is a producer of items made from local farm products that are distributed to supermarkets. Because over the years price competition has become increasingly important, Doug Gilbert, the company's controller, is planning to implement a standard cost system for Quincy Farms. He asked his cost accountant, Joe Adams, to gather cost information on the production of strawberry jam (Quincy Farms' most popular product). Joe reported that strawberries cost $.80 per quart, the price he intends to pay to his good friend who has been operating a strawberry farm in the red for the last couple of years. Due to an oversupply in the market, the prices for strawberries have dropped to $.50 per quart. Joe is sure that the $.80 price will be enough to pull his friend's strawberry farm out of the red and into the black.

Required:

Is Joe Adam's behavior regarding the cost information he provided to Doug Gilbert unethical? Explain your answer.

(CMA adapted)

19–43 Comprehensive Variance Problem

Minneapolis Manufacturing Company manufactures one product, with a standard cost detailed as follows:

Direct materials, 20 meters at $.90 per meter $18

Direct labor, 4 hours at $6 per hour 24

Factory overhead applied at five-sixths of direct labor
(Variable costs = $15; Fixed costs = $5) 20

Variable selling and administrative 12

Fixed selling and administrative   7

Total unit costs $81

Standards have been computed based on a master budget activity level of 2,400 direct labor-hours per month.

Actual activity for the past month was as follows:

Materials purchased . . . . 18,000 meters at $.92 per meter

Materials used . . . .   9,500 meters

Direct labor . . . . 2,100 hours at $6.10 per hour

Total factory overhead $11,100

Production . . . .   500 units

Required:

Prepare variance analyses for the variable and fixed costs. Indicate which variances cannot be computed.

(CPA adapted)

19–44 Find Actual and Budget Amounts from Variances

Assume that IBM manufactures a new electronic game. The current standard costs per game are as follows:

Direct materials, 6 kilograms at $1 per kilogram . . . . . . $ 6 per game

Direct labor, 1 hour at $4 per hour . . . .   4 per game

Overhead . . . .   3 per game

Total costs . . . . $13 per game

Assume the following data appeared in IBM's records at the end of the past month:

Actual production . . . . 4,000 units

Actual sales . . . . 2,500 units

Purchases (26,000 kilograms) $27,300

Materials price variance . . . . 1,300 U

Materials efficiency variance . . . . 1,000 U

Direct labor price variance . . . .   760 U

Direct labor efficiency variance . . . .   800 F

Underapplied overhead (total) . . . .   500 U

The materials price variance is computed at the time of purchase.

Required: *a.* Prepare a variance analysis for direct materials and direct labor.

b. Assume that all manufacturing overhead is fixed, and the $500 underapplied is the only overhead variance that can be computed. What are the actual and applied overhead amounts?   *(CPA adapted)*

19–45 Variance Computations with Missing Data

The following information is provided to assist you in evaluating the performance of the manufacturing operations of the Madison Company:

Units produced (actual)   21,000

Master production budget:
    Direct materials $165,000
    Direct labor   140,000
    Overhead   199,000

Standard costs per unit:
    Direct materials . . . . $1.65 × 5 pounds per unit of output
    Direct labor . . . . $14 per hour × ½ hour per unit
    Variable overhead . . . . $11.90 per direct labor-hour

Actual costs:
    Direct materials purchased
    and used . . . . $188,700 (102,000 pounds)
    Direct labor . . . .   140,000 (10,700 hours)
    Overhead . . . .   204,000 (61% is variable)

Variable overhead is applied on the basis of direct labor-hours.

Required: Prepare a table to show all variable manufacturing cost price and efficiency variances and fixed manufacturing cost price and production volume variances.

19–46 Comprehensive Variance Problem

Indianapolis Company manufactures two products, Florimene and Glyoxide, used in the plastics industry. The company prepares its master budget on the basis of standard costs. The following data are for the month of August:

	Florimene	Glyoxide
Standards:		
Direct materials	3 kilograms at $1 per kilogram	4 kilograms at $1.10 per kilogram
Direct labor	5 hours at $4 per hour	6 hours at $5 per hour
Variable overhead (per direct labor-hour)	$3.20	$3.50
Fixed overhead (per month)	$22,356	$26,520
Expected activity (direct labor-hours)	5,750	7,800
Actual data:		
Direct material	3,100 kilograms at $.90 per kilogram	4,700 kilograms at $1.15 per kilogram
Direct labor	4,900 hours at $4.05 per hour	7,400 hours at $5.10 per hour
Variable overhead	$16,170	$25,234
Fixed overhead	$20,930	$26,400
Units produced (actual)	1,000 units	1,200 units

Required: *a.* Prepare a variance analysis for each variable cost for each product.

b. Prepare a fixed overhead variance analysis like the one in Illustration 19–12 for each product.

19–47 Two-Way, Three-Way, and Four-Way Overhead Variances (Appendix A)

Refer to the data in problem 19–46. Assume the fixed overhead costs are applied to units produced using the following standard rate per labor-hour:

$$\text{Florimeme: \$3.888 per hour} = \frac{\$22,356}{5,750 \text{ expected labor-hours}}$$

$$\text{Glyoxide: \$3.40 per hour} = \frac{\$26,520}{7,800 \text{ expected labor-hours}}$$

Required:

Prepare two-way, three-way, and four-way analyses of overhead variances for each product.

19–48 Performance Evaluation in Service Industries

Rock City Insurance Company estimates that its overhead costs for policy administration should cost $72 for each new policy obtained and $2 per year for each $1,000 face amount of insurance outstanding. The company set a budget of selling 5,000 new policies during the coming period. In addition, the company estimated that the total face amount of insurance outstanding for the period would equal $10,800,000.

During the period, actual costs related to new policies amounted to $358,400. A total of 4,800 new policies were sold.

The cost of maintaining existing policies was $23,200. Had these costs been incurred at the same prices as were in effect when the budget was prepared, the costs would have been $22,900; however, some costs changed. Also, there was $12,100,000 in policies outstanding during the period.

Required:

Prepare a schedule to show the differences between master budget and actual costs for this question.

19–49 Comprehensive Review of Variances with Missing Data

Merriweather Company makes oil for whale oil lamps. One product, Interno, is manufactured as a blend of three chemicals: Alpha-28, Beta-32, and Gamma-07 (A, B, and G, for short). This solvent is very active and must be shipped in special containers, one container per unit of output. In addition to the materials, the blending process requires three direct labor-hours per liter of solvent. Factory overhead is applied at the rate of 150 percent of direct labor costs.

You have been working for Merriweather Company as a new management trainee in the controller's office. Today you had an opportunity to talk to the controller and advise him on the merits of your background and your education. The controller handed you some information on last month's production of industrial solvents and asked you to analyze the variances for the product Interno. Confident in your abilities, you carried the computer printout with you as you left the office. Unfortunately, on the way home a gust of wind blew some of your papers away. You were able to retrieve some of the information, but a good deal of it was torn or shredded.

At home, you have pieced together the following fragments from the computer printouts:

d cost per un		
.500 1 Alpha	28 @	5.00/1
.200 1 Beta	32 @	10.00
.400 1 Gamma	07 @	
tal		$ 8.30 lit

Expect
12,000 direct la
$80,000 fixed over
$71,500 variable ove
$4,000 container costs

ual costs		
2,200 1 Alpha	28 @	5.0
800 1 Beta	32 @	$11.20/1
1,000 1 Gamma	07 @	$ 9.10/1
4,010 containers	@	$ .95
Total materials		$32,979.50
direct labor		97,200.
variable ovh		61,700.
fixed overhead		80,960.

Varia
$927 Fav. Eff

You recall the $927 favorable efficiency variance applies to chemicals but not to containers. You also recall a discussion concerning the new direct labor rate of $9 per hour and how that rate had caused the Production Planning Department to recommend a reevaluation of the product line since certain products may not be profitable at this rate.

Required:

Defend your reputation with the controller and compute as many variances as possible. (Hint: Separating the chemical inputs from the containers will make the solution more manageable.) If any variances cannot be computed, state why.

INTEGRATIVE CASES

19–50   Process Costing Variances; Equivalent Units

Cherry Pink, Inc., produces a single product known as Apple Blossom White. Cherry Pink uses the FIFO process costing method.

To analyze production performance, actual results are compared to the flexible budget, and any variances are computed. The standard costs that form the basis for the budget are as follows:

Direct materials	1 kilogram at $10 per kilogram
Direct labor	2 hours at $4 per hour
Variable overhead	2 hours at $1.25 per hour

Data for the month are presented below:

1. Beginning inventory consisted of 2,500 units that were 100 percent complete with respect to direct materials and 40 percent complete with respect to conversion costs.

2. Ten thousand units were started during the month.

3. Ending inventory consisted of 2,000 units that were 100 percent complete with respect to direct materials and 40 percent complete with respect to conversion costs.

4. Costs applicable to the current period production are as follows:

	Actual Costs	Flexible Budget
Direct materials (11,000 kilograms)	$123,750	$100,000
Direct labor (25,000 hours)	105,575	82,400
Variable overhead	30,350	25,750

Required:

Compute variances. Materials are added at the beginning of the process; conversion costs are added evenly throughout.

19–51   Racketeer, Inc.* (Comprehensive Overview of Budgets and Variance)

"I just don't understand these financial statements at all!" exclaimed Mr. Elmo Knapp. Mr. Knapp explained that he had turned over management of Racketeer, Inc., a division of American Recreation Equipment, Inc., to his son, Otto, the previous month. Racketeer, Inc., manufactures tennis rackets.

"I was really proud of Otto," he beamed. "He was showing us all the tricks he learned in business school, and if I say so myself, I think he was doing a rather good job for us. For example, he put together this budget for Racketeer, which makes it very easy to see how much profit we'll make at any sales volume (Exhibit 19–51A). As best as I can figure it, in March we expected to have a volume of 8,000 units and a

---

* © Michael W. Maher, 1993.

EXHIBIT

19-51A

*Profit Graph,
Racketeer, Inc.*

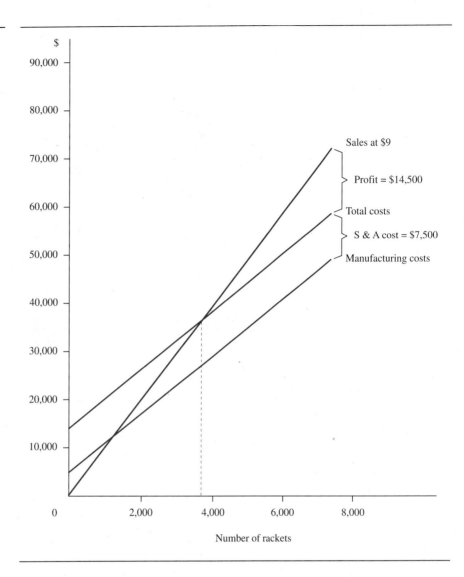

profit of $14,500 on our rackets. But we did much better than that! We sold 10,000 rackets, so we should have made almost $21,000 on them."

"Another one of Otto's innovations is this standard cost system." said Mr. Knapp proudly. "He sat down with our production people and came up with a standard production cost per unit (see Exhibit 19–51B). He tells me this will tell us how well our production people are performing. Also, he claims it will cut down on our clerical work."

Mr. Knapp continued, "But one thing puzzles me. My calculations show that we should have earned profit of nearly $21,000 in March. However, our accountants came up with less than $19,000 in the monthly income statement (Exhibit 19–51C). This bothers me a great deal. Now, I'm sure our accountants are doing their job properly. But still, it appears to me that they're about $2,200 short."

"As you can probably guess," Mr. Knapp concluded, "we are one big happy family around here. I just wish I knew what those accountants are up to . . . coming in with a low net income like that."

EXHIBIT

19–51B

Standard Costs,[a]
Racketeer, Inc.

		Per Racket
Raw material:		
Frame (one frame per racket)	$3.15	
Stringing materials: 20 feet at 3¢ per foot	.60	
Direct labor:		
Skilled: 1/8 hour at $9.60 per hour	1.20	
Unskilled: 1/8 hour at $5.60 per hour	.70	
Plant overhead:		
Indirect labor	.10	
Power	.03	
Supervision	.12[b]	
Depreciation	.20[b]	
Other	.15[b]	
Total standard cost per frame	$6.25	

[a] Standard costs are calculated for an estimated production volume of 8,000 units each month.
[b] Fixed costs.

EXHIBIT

19–51C

RACKETEER, INC.
Income Statement for March
Actual

Sales:		
10,000 rackets at $9		$90,000
Standard cost of goods sold:		
10,000 rackets at $6.25		62,500
Gross profit after standard costs		27,500
Variances:		
Materials variance	(490)	
Labor variance	(392)	
Overhead variance	(660)	
Gross profit		25,958
Selling and administrative expense		7,200
Operating profit		$18,758

Required:

Prepare a report for Mr. Elmo Knapp and Mr. Otto Knapp that reconciles the profit graph with the actual results for March (see Exhibit 19–51D). Show the source of each variance from the original plan (8,000 rackets) in as much detail as you can and evaluate Racketeer's performance in March. Recommend improvements in Racketeer's profit planning and control methods.

EXHIBIT

Actual Production Data for March, Racketeer, Inc.

Direct materials purchased and used:

Stringing materials . . . . 175,000 feet at 2.5¢ per foot

Frames (note: some frames were ruined
during production) . . . . 7,100 at $3.15 per frame

Labor:

Skilled ($9.80 per hour) . . . . 900 hours

Unskilled ($5.80 per hour) . . . . 840 hours

Overhead:

Indirect labor . . . . $ 800

Power   250

Depreciation 1,600

Supervision   960

Other 1,250

Production . . . . 7,000 rackets

SOLUTIONS TO

Q *Self-Study* *uestions*

1 Variable cost variances:

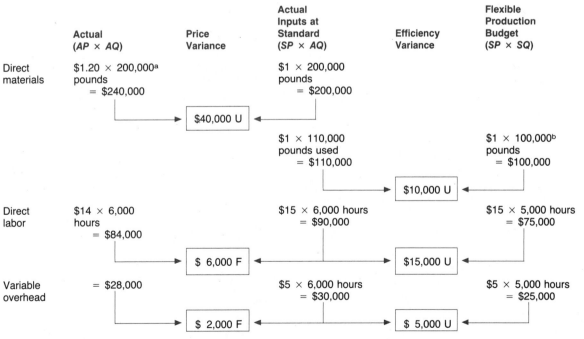

a Direct materials pounds purchased.

b Standard direct materials pounds used in production per unit times units produced (2 pounds × 50,000 units).

2   Fixed overhead variances:

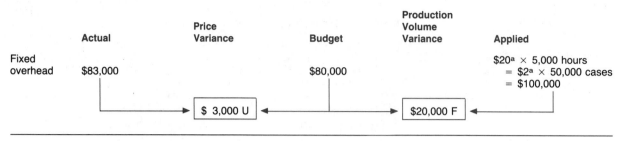

	Actual	Price Variance	Budget	Production Volume Variance	Applied
Fixed overhead	$83,000		$80,000		$20[a] × 5,000 hours = $2[a] × 50,000 cases = $100,000
		$ 3,000 U		$20,000 F	

[a] Fixed overhead rate = $\dfrac{\$80,000}{40,000 \text{ cases}}$ = $2 per case, or $\dfrac{\$80,000}{4,000 \text{ hours}}$ = $20 per standard labor-hour.

Standard Costing

After reading this chapter, you should be able to:

1. Identify the advantages of standard costing.
2. Demonstrate how standard costs flow through accounts.
3. Explain when and how to prorate variances to inventories and cost of goods sold.
4. Compare standard costing in a just-in-time environment to standard costing in a traditional environment.
5. Contrast product costs under variable costing to product costs under full-absorption costing. Contrast product costs under actual costing, normal costing, and standard costing.

Virtually all companies, including banks, fast-food restaurants, and manufacturers, use standards for evaluating performance. In addition, some companies record product costs in the accounting records using standard costs. If Chrysler Corporation uses standard costs to record product costs, for example, then every Dodge Viper would be carried on the books at its standard cost, not at its actual cost.

ADVANTAGES OF STANDARD COSTING

Standard Costing A method of accounting whereby costs are assigned to cost objects at predetermined amounts.

The use of standard costs instead of actual costs in the accounting records means that standard costs can be used for product costing as well as for performance evaluation. The use of standards instead of actual costs can greatly reduce the complexity of product costing for inventory valuation.

Under **standard costing,** the value of inventory is the number of units times the standard cost per unit. Cost flow assumptions such as FIFO and LIFO are unnecessary for all units that have the same standard costs. This reduces the clerical work needed to value inventories because records of the actual cost per unit are not kept. Every time a unit is produced, its standard cost is entered in the accounting records. At the end of the period, differences between the standard costs charged to production for all units and the actual costs of production are computed and analyzed.

For example, a sailboat manufacturer makes five models of small fiberglass sailboats. When the company used actual costs in the accounting system, recordkeeping was very detailed. According to the controller, ''We kept track of the amount of direct materials and direct labor that went into each sailboat. Every worker had to keep track of the amount of time spent on *each sailboat.* We added a predetermined rate for variable and fixed overhead to give us the cost of each unit. We make about 50,000 sailboats each year, so you can imagine how much time was required by both operating people and accounting staff.

''We were already using standard manufacturing costs for budgeting and performance evaluation, so it was relatively easy to convert from an actual system to a standard system for product costing. Now we keep track of costs by department, by kind of input (direct material, direct labor, variable overhead, fixed overhead), and by product line. And we've saved a lot of time in keeping and checking records. We lost some data because we no longer know how much *each* sailboat costs. But we found that level of detail wasn't useful for management purposes and wasn't needed to value inventory.''

The costs and benefits of using standard costing rather than actual costing varies from company to company. The benefits of standard costing increase with the amount of difficulty a company has in assigning costs to individual units of product. Thus, standard costing is often found in companies that use mass-production methods, particularly in conjunction with process costing. While standard costing may also be used in companies that make relatively large, heterogeneous units, it is relatively rare in that setting.

STANDARD COST FLOWS

When using standard costing, costs are transferred through the production process at their standard costs. This means the entry debiting Work in Process Inventory at standard cost could be made before actual costs are known. In process costing, units transferred between departments are valued at standard cost, while in job costing, standard costs are used to charge the job for its components. Actual costs are accumulated in accounts like Accounts Payable and Factory Payroll. Actual costs are compared with the *standard costs allowed for the output produced.* The difference between the actual costs assigned to a department and the standard cost of the work done is the variance for the department.

Use of standards in the accounting system can facilitate the recording and transfer of costs from one department to another. Standard costs can be

*Overview of Standard
Costing*

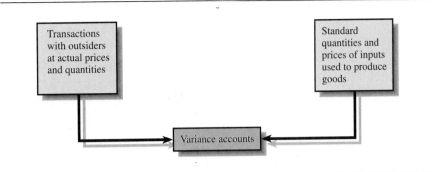

transferred with the physical flow of product—there is no need to wait until the actual cost data about the particular units become known.

For example, automobile repair shops charge customers for services at a predetermined (standard) hourly rate. In addition, these shops often use standard times for each task included on a repair order. If a shop is using this standard cost system and you take your car in for a tune-up, you will be billed the standard hours for that task times the standard hourly rate. This happens regardless of the actual time it takes to perform the tune-up and the actual cost of the labor used.

Illustration 20–1 shows an overview of cost flows using standard costs. Note the transactions with employees, outside suppliers of materials, and other vendors are at actual. (Vendors like to be paid for the *actual* price they charge.) The goods are produced at standard costs.

In the following sections, we discuss the flow of costs in a standard cost system, compare the actual and standard costs of work, and demonstrate how the variances are isolated in the accounting system. The variances are based on the calculations introduced in Chapter 19. Standard cost systems vary somewhat from company to company, so in reality, the method presented here may be modified a bit to meet a company's particular needs.

The example in this chapter continues the Evergreen Company example started in Chapter 18 and carried through Chapter 19. Illustration 20–2 summarizes the facts for Evergreen Company. The variances shown in the following journal entries were previously computed in Chapter 19 and are summarized in Illustration 20–2. (We use the example from Chapter 19 in which direct materials purchases do not equal usage.)

Direct Materials

Direct materials are purchased at their actual cost, but in a standard cost system they are often carried in direct materials inventory at the standard price per unit.[1] We assume that 250,000 feet are purchased and that 110,000 feet are used. We assume the price variance is recorded at the time materials

---

[1] An alternative treatment is to carry materials at actual cost and then to charge materials into production at a standard price per unit.

ILLUSTRATION 20-2   Cost Data, Evergreen Company (facts taken from example in Chapter 19)

Actual production output in May: 10,000 crates

Variable manufacturing cost data:

	Actuals	Variances		Standards
		Price	Efficiency	
Direct materials	250,000 board-feet purchased @ \$.264 per board-foot = \$66,000 110,000 board-feet used @ \$.264 per board-foot = \$29,040	250,000 feet × (\$.264 − .25) = \$3,500 U	(110,000 − 100,000 feet) × \$.25 = \$2,500 U	100,000 board-feet allowed @ \$.25 per board-foot = \$25,000
Direct labor	3,200 hours @ \$9.35 = \$29,920	3,200 hours × (\$10.00 − \$9.35) = \$2,080 F	(3,200 − 3,000 hours) × \$10.00 = \$2,000 U	3,000 hours @ \$10 per hour = \$30,000
Variable manufacturing overhead (applied at \$8.33⅓ per standard direct labor-hour)	\$26,480	\$26,480 − (\$8.33⅓ × 3,200 hours) = \$187 F	(3,200 − 3,000 hours) × \$8.33⅓ = \$1,667 U	3,000 hours @ \$8.33⅓ = \$25,000

Fixed Manufacturing Cost Data:

	Actual	Price Variance	Budget	Production Volume Variance	Applied
	\$37,000	\$37,000 − \$36,000 = \$1,000 U	\$36,000	\$36,000 − \$45,000 = \$9,000 F	\$4.50 × 10,000 crates = \$15.00 × 3,000 standard hours = \$45,000

are purchased. Therefore, materials inventory will be carried at standard prices. The purchasing entry is:

Direct Materials Inventory	62,500	
Materials Price Variance	3,500	
Accounts Payable		66,000

To record the purchase of 250,000 board-feet at the actual cost of 26.4 cents per foot, the transfer to Direct Materials Inventory at the standard cost per foot of 25 cents, and the materials purchase price variance for the difference.

We refer to the cost of direct materials inventory as a standard cost because 25 cents per foot is the standard allowed per unit of *input* (board-feet), *not* the standard cost per unit of *output* (crates).

When materials are placed in production, Work in Process Inventory is debited for the standard quantity of input used at the standard cost per unit. The Cutting Department is allowed a standard of 100,000 board-feet of lumber to make 10,000 crates at 25 cents per foot, but they actually used 110,000 board-feet. The entry charging production for the standard cost of direct materials is:

Work in Process Inventory	25,000	
Materials Efficiency Variance	2,500	
Direct Materials Inventory		27,500

To record the requisition of 110,000 actual board-feet at the standard cost per foot of 25 cents, the charge to Work in Process Inventory at $2.50 per crate times 10,000 crates (or 25 cents per foot times 100,000 board-feet allowed for 10,000 crates), and the materials efficiency variance for the difference.

The materials price variance is usually the responsibility of the Purchasing Department, whereas the efficiency variance is usually the responsibility of the production departments.

Direct Labor

Direct labor is credited to payroll liability accounts, such as Accrued Payroll or Payroll Payable, for the actual cost (including accruals for fringe benefits and payroll taxes) and charged to Work in Process Inventory at standard. The following entry is based on the facts about the standard costs allowed for Evergreen Company as described in Chapter 19 and in Illustration 20–2:

Work in Process Inventory	30,000	
Labor Efficiency Variance	2,000	
Labor Price Variance		2,080
Payroll Payable Accounts		29,920

To charge the production departments for the standard cost of direct labor at $10 per hour times 3,000 hours (10,000 crates times .30 hour allowed), to record the actual cost of $29,920, and to record the labor efficiency variance and the labor price variance.

This completes our presentation of standard cost journal entries for materials and labor. These journal entries are summarized in Illustration 20–3.

I L L U S T R A T I O N   *Standard Cost Flows—Materials and Labor (Evergreen Company)*

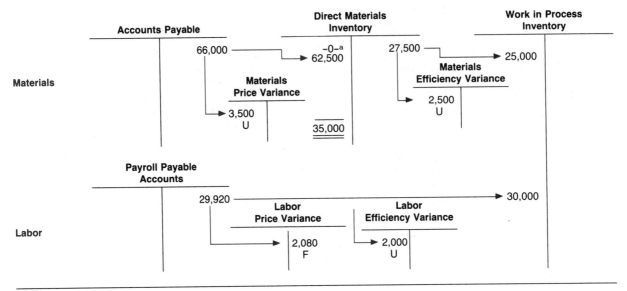

ᵃ Assume no beginning materials inventory balance.

Variable Manufacturing Overhead

Standard overhead costs are charged to production based on standard direct labor-hours per unit of output produced at Evergreen Company. Overhead costs are often charged to production before the actual costs are known. This is demonstrated by the following sequence of entries:

1. Standard overhead costs are charged to production during the period. The credit entry is to an overhead applied account.
2. Actual costs are recorded in various accounts and transferred to an overhead summary account. This accounting procedure is completed after the end of the period.
3. Variances are computed as the difference between the standard costs charged to production (overhead applied) and the actual costs.

This procedure is similar to that used to charge overhead to production using predetermined rates in normal costing.

Based on the data from Chapter 19 and Illustration 20–2, variable overhead is charged to production as follows:

Work in Process Inventory 25,000
    Variable Overhead Applied   25,000

Note that overhead is applied to Work in Process Inventory on the basis of standard labor-hours *allowed*. As we shall see shortly, over- or underapplied overhead will represent a combination of the variable overhead price and efficiency variances.

Actual variable overhead costs are recorded in various accounts and transferred to each department's variable manufacturing overhead account as follows:

Variable Overhead (Actual) 26,480		
Supplies Inventory		
Accrued Payroll—Indirect Labor		
Accounts Payable—Power		26,480
Maintenance Department		
Etc. (other accounts and service departments)		

Variable overhead variances were computed in Chapter 19: price, $187 F, and efficiency, $1,667 U. These variable overhead variances are recorded by closing the applied and actual accounts as follows:

Variable Overhead Applied 25,000	
Variable Overhead Efficiency Variance 1,667	
Variable Overhead Price Variance	187
Variable Overhead (Actual)	26,480

These entries are shown in T-accounts in Illustration 20-4.

Fixed Manufacturing Overhead

For the purposes of this example, we assume Evergreen uses full-absorption costing because the amounts recorded will ultimately be used to prepare statements for external financial reporting. Fixed manufacturing costs are charged to units at $4.50 per crate ($15 per *standard* direct labor-hour) using full-absorption costing. The company produced 10,000 crates in May, for which 3,000 standard direct labor-hours are allowed at the rate of .3 hour per crate. Hence, the total fixed manufacturing overhead costs applied to production (that is, debited to Work in Process Inventory) amounted to $45,000 ($4.50 × 10,000 crates or $15 × 3,000 hours), as shown in the following entry:

Work in Process Inventory 45,000	
Fixed Overhead Applied	45,000

Actual fixed overhead costs are recorded in various accounts and transferred to each department's fixed overhead account as follows:

Fixed Overhead (Actual) 37,000		
Accumulated Depreciation—Building		
Accrued Payroll—Indirect Labor		
Accounts Payable—Heat		37,000
Plant Administration		
Etc. (other accounts and allocations from service departments)		

Recall that the price variance ($1,000 U) is the difference between actual ($37,000) and budgeted ($36,000) fixed manufacturing costs. The production volume variance ($9,000 F) is the difference between budgeted ($36,000) and applied ($45,000) fixed manufacturing costs. Fixed overhead variances are recorded by closing the applied overhead and actual overhead accounts as follows:

Fixed Overhead Applied	45,000	
Fixed Overhead Price Variance	1,000	
Fixed Overhead Production Volume Variance		9,000
Fixed Overhead (Actual)		37,000

The above entry shows a favorable fixed overhead production volume variance. This production volume variance occurred because Evergreen produced 10,000 crates when it had estimated only 8,000 crates. Recall from Chapter 19 that this production volume variance results from attempting to compute unit costs under full-absorption costing. It has no meaning for planning and control purposes.

These entries are summarized in Illustration 20–4.

Contrast with Variable Costing

Using variable costing, the entire *actual* fixed manufacturing overhead of $37,000 would be expensed in the period. Using full-absorption costing, fixed manufacturing overhead of $45,000 is applied to Work in Process Inventory, as shown in Illustration 20–4.

Transfer to Finished Goods Inventory and to Cost of Goods Sold

When all production work has been completed, units are transferred to Finished Goods Inventory and to Cost of Goods Sold at standard cost.

Finished Goods Inventory

This month 10,000 crates were finished and transferred to Finished Goods Inventory. After the crates have been finished and inspected, they are transferred to a finished goods storage area and recorded by the following entry (full-absorption, standard costing):

Finished Goods Inventory	125,000	
Work in Process Inventory		125,000

To record the transfer of 10,000 completed crates at $12.50 per unit ($8.00 variable plus $4.50 fixed) times 10,000 crates.

Cost of Goods Sold

For this example, assume the company sold 9,000 of the crates it produced for $21 per crate. This was recorded by the following entries:

Accounts Receivable	189,000	
Sales Revenue		189,000
Cost of Goods Sold	112,500	
Finished Goods Inventory		112,500

To record the sale of 9,000 crates at a price of $21 and a standard cost of $12.50 per crate.

Self-Study Question

1 (This is a continuation of the Containers, Inc., self-study questions 1 and 2 from Chapter 19.)

    1. Containers, Inc., produced 50,000 and sold 40,000 plastic "notebook computer" cases at a sales price of $10 each. Budgeted sales were 45,000 units at $10.15 each.

ILLUSTRATION *Standard Cost Flows—Overhead (Evergreen Company)*

20-4

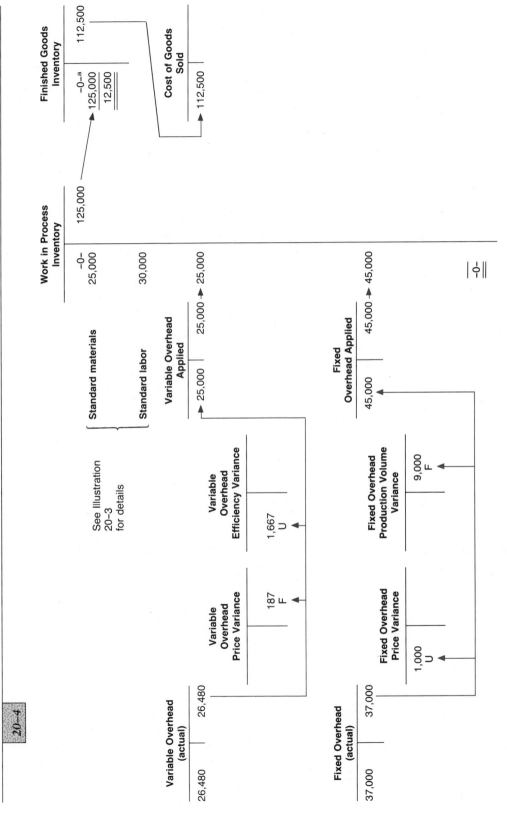

2. Standard variable costs per unit (that is, per case):

Direct materials: 2 pounds at $1 .... $2.00

Direct labor: .10 hour at $15 .... 1.50

Variable manufacturing overhead: .10 hour at $5 .... .50

$4.00 per case

3. Fixed manufacturing overhead:

Monthly budget $80,000

Estimated monthly production .... 40,000 cases or
4,000 hours

Fixed overhead application rate .... ?

4. Actual production costs:

Direct materials purchased: 200,000 pounds
at $1.20 .... $240,000

Direct materials used: 110,000 pounds at $1.20 132,000

Direct labor: 6,000 hours at $14 84,000

Variable overhead 28,000

Fixed overhead 83,000

Use a full-absorption, standard costing system to

   a. Record the transactions using journal entries.

   b. Show the flow of transactions thorugh T-accounts.

The solution to this question is at the end of this chapter on page 780.

PRORATING STANDARD COST VARIANCES

Prorating Variances Assigning portions of variances to the inventory and Cost of Goods Sold accounts to which the variances are related.

If the inventory values must be adjusted to actual costs for contract settlements, taxes, and financial reporting purposes, this will usually require **prorating the variances** to each account that has been debited or credited with the standard cost that is now being adjusted to actual. When proration is complete, the balances in the inventory accounts closely approximate actual costs, and the variance accounts have no balances.

To illustrate the proration of variances, we use the Evergreen Company example. The variances are prorated in the following sequence:

1. Materials price variance.
2. Materials efficiency variance.
3. Labor and overhead variances.

Materials Variances

Materials Price Variance

First, the materials price variance is prorated *to all accounts that contain standard materials costs purchased in the current period;* namely, Direct Materials Inventory, Materials Efficiency Variance, Work in Process Inventory, Finished Goods Inventory, and Cost of Goods Sold. Standard direct materials costs are 20 percent ($25,000 direct materials debit to Work in

Process ÷ $125,000 total debit to Work in Process) of the total standard cost per crate. The amounts for direct materials at standard prices in each of these accounts are:

Ending Direct Materials Inventory (from Illustration 20–3)		Materials Efficiency Variance (from Illustration 20–3)		Ending Work in Process Inventory (see Illustration 20–4)		Ending Finished Goods Inventory (20% × $12,500 finished goods ending inventory is direct materials cost)		Cost of Goods Sold (20% of the $112,500 Cost of Goods Sold is direct materials cost)		Total Materials Purchased This Period, at Standard Prices (see debit to Materials Inventory in Illustration 20–3)
$35,000	+	$2,500	+	$0	+	$2,500	+	$22,500	=	$62,500

These balances add up to the total materials costs purchased at standard prices. The materials price variance of $3,500 U is prorated to each account in proportion to the account balance's percentage of the total materials costs at standard prices. The proration of the $3,500 U appears in Illustration 20–5.

The journal entry to assign the prorated variance to accounts is as follows (amounts are from Illustration 20–5):

Direct Materials Inventory	1,960	
Materials Efficiency Variance	140	
Finished Goods Inventory	140	
Cost of Goods Sold	1,260	
Materials Price Variance		3,500

The variance account is closed when this journal entry is made.

Materials Efficiency Variance

Second, the materials efficiency variance to be prorated is now $2,640—that is, the original $2,500 (from Illustration 20–3) plus the $140 (from Illustration 20–5) that has been prorated from the Materials Price Variance account. The materials efficiency variance is prorated to the materials in ending Work in Process Inventory and Finished Goods Inventory and the materials in Cost

---

ILLUSTRATION

20–5

Prorating Materials Price Variance

Account	(1) Materials at Standard Price in the Account	(2) Amount as a Percent of Total Materials Costs at Standard Price	Variance to Be Prorated (column 2 × $3,500)
Materials Inventory	$35,000	56%[a]	$1,960
Efficiency Variance	2,500	4	140
Work in Process Inventory	–0–	0	0
Finished Goods Inventory	2,500	4	140
Cost of Goods Sold	22,500	36	1,260
Total	$62,500	100%	$3,500

[a] 56.0% = $35,000 ÷ $62,500, etc.

of Goods Sold. These amounts are as follows, after adjusting for the proration of the materials price variance:

Account	Materials in Account before Proration	Materials Price Variance Prorated in Illustration 20–5	Total
Work in Process Inventory	–0–	–0–	–0–
Finished Goods Inventory	$ 2,500	$ 140	$ 2,640
Cost of Goods Sold	22,500	1,260	23,760

The materials efficiency variance is prorated, using the amounts computed above:

Account	(1) Materials Cost in the Account	(2) As a Percent of Total	Variance to Be Prorated (column 2 × $2,640)
Work in Process Inventory	–0–	0%	–0–
Finished Goods Inventory	$ 2,640	10	$ 264
Cost of Goods Sold	23,760	90	2,376
Total	$26,400	100%	$2,640

The journal entry to prorate the variance is:

Finished Goods Inventory	264	
Cost of Goods Sold	2,376	
Materials Efficiency Variance		2,640

Instead of using the materials costs in each account after prorating the price variance, we could obtain the same prorating of the materials efficiency variance if we used percentages (column 2 above) based on the original materials balances before prorating the materials price variance ($2,500 in Finished Goods Inventory and $22,500 in Cost of Goods Sold). This shortcut is often used in practice.

Labor and Overhead Variances

After prorating the materials price and efficiency variances, labor and overhead variances are prorated based on the standard cost of labor and overhead from the current period's production in ending Work in Process and Finished Goods Inventories and in Cost of Goods Sold.

To prorate these variances, first find the percent of labor and overhead in the current period's product cost by examining the debits to Work in Process Inventory this period. The calculation for Evergreen Company is as follows:

	(1) Debit to Work in Process Inventory for Each Cost (see Illustration 20–4)	(2) Total Debits to Work in Process Inventory This Period	(3) Percent of Cost in Total Product Cost (1) ÷ (2)
Labor	$30,000	$125,000	24%
Variable overhead	25,000	125,000	20
Fixed overhead	45,000	125,000	36

Next, find the amount of standard labor and overhead costs in Work in Process and Finished Goods Inventories, and in Cost of Goods Sold. Since there is no ending Work in Process Inventory, we need to deal only with Finished Goods and Cost of Goods Sold, as shown below:

	(1) Total Standard Cost in Account (see Illustration 20–4)	*(2)* Proportion (from calculation above)	*(3)* Particular Cost in Each Account *(1)* × *(2)*
Ending Finished Goods Inventory:			
Labor	$ 12,500	24%	$ 3,000
Variable overhead	12,500	20	2,500
Fixed overhead	12,500	36	4,500
Cost of Goods Sold:			
Labor	112,500	24	27,000
Variable overhead	112,500	20	22,500
Fixed overhead	112,500	36	40,500

Evergreen Company's labor and overhead variances for the period are:

Labor:
 Price . . . . $2,080 F
 Efficiency . . . . 2,000 U
  Total . . . . $ 80 F

Variable overhead:
 Price . . . .   187 F
 Efficiency . . . . 1,667 U
  Total . . . .   1,480 U

Fixed overhead:
 Price . . . . 1,000 U
 Production volume . . . . . . 9,000 F
  Total . . . .   8,000 F

Each of these variances is prorated to Finished Goods and Cost of Goods Sold based on the appropriate standard cost in each account. For example, 10 percent of the labor variance is allocated to Finished Goods Inventory because 10 percent of the standard labor cost for the period is in Finished Goods Inventory, as shown below:

	(1) Labor Cost in the Account	*(2)* As a Percent of Total	*(3)* Variance to Be Prorated (column 2 × $80 F)
Finished Goods Inventory	$ 3,000	10%	$ 8
Cost of Goods Sold	27,000	90	72
Total	$30,000	100%	$80

The journal entry to prorate the labor variance is:

Labor Price Variance 2,080		
Labor Efficiency Variance		2,000
Finished Goods Inventory		8
Cost of Goods Sold		72

Overhead variances are allocated the same way:

	(1) Overhead Cost in the Account	(2) As a Percent of Total	(3) Variance to Be Prorated (column 2 × variance)
For variable overhead:			
Finished Goods Inventory	$ 2,500	10%	$ 148 (10% × $1,480)
Cost of Goods Sold	22,500	90	1,332
	$25,000	100%	$1,480
For fixed overhead:			
Finished Goods Inventory	$ 4,500	10%	$ 800 (10% × $8,000)
Cost of Goods Sold	40,500	90	7,200
	$45,000	100%	$8,000

Entries to close the variance accounts to Finished Goods Inventory and Cost of Goods Sold would be made like the labor variance entry.

The Finished Goods Inventory account and Cost of Goods Sold account now reflect an approximation of the actual cost of each inventory item. The variance accounts are closed.

Alternative Treatment
for Variances

If the variances are immaterial, it may make little difference whether they are prorated or expensed as a period cost or as a write-off to Cost of Goods Sold. Under the alternative treatment, all variances are closed, and the net variance is debited or credited to Cost of Goods Sold or to Variance Summary expense. For managerial purposes, we assume variances are closed to Variance Summary, and variances are not prorated unless otherwise stated.

Self-Study
Question

2 Refer to the data for self-study question 1. Assume all inventory accounts have no beginning balances. Assume Work in Process Inventory has no ending balance.

Prorate the variances to ending Materials Inventory, ending Finished Goods Inventory, and Cost of Goods Sold. Use the basis for proration shown in the chapter example. Namely, prorate the efficiency variance for materials based on the standard cost of materials in ending Materials Inventory, the standard cost of materials in Finished Goods Inventory, and the standard cost of materials in Cost of Goods Sold; prorate the labor variances based on the standard cost of labor in ending Finished Goods Inventory and the standard cost of labor in Cost of Goods Sold; and so forth for the materials price variance and the overhead variances.

The solution to this question is at the end of this chapter on page 782.

*STANDARD COSTING
IN A JUST-IN-TIME
ENVIRONMENT*

In just-in-time manufacturing settings with demand-pull of products through manufacturing, inventories are minimized. As a result, the accounting system is simplified because all costs are charged directly to Cost of Goods Sold. If there are inventories at the end of the period, then a portion of the current period costs originally charged to Cost of Goods Sold is credited to Cost of Goods Sold and debited to the respective inventory account as an end-of-period adjustment. This method of accounting is known as *backflush* costing.

Using backflush standard costing, costs are charged to Cost of Goods Sold at standard. Variances are charged to a separate account. If there are no inventories at the end of the period, the variance account is expensed or combined with Cost of Goods Sold at standard. The latter result is Cost of Goods Sold at actual.

If there are inventories at the end of the period and if the difference between the standard cost of inventories and actual cost is immaterial, the inventories may be stated at standard cost. In this situation, variances need not be prorated.

If, however, prorating variances would make a material difference in the financial statements or is required by contract, the variance is prorated *from* the variance account *to* the respective inventory accounts based on the proportions of the current period costs in each of the inventory and Cost of Goods Sold accounts, as described in the discussion on variance proration above. The results should be the same as if one had accounted for the variances in the traditional manner discussed earlier in this chapter.

For example, if a company were using demand-pull accounting, assume the Cost of Goods Sold and related variance account would appear as follows before adjustment:

Cost of Goods Sold (Standard Costs)

Materials	60,000
Labor	30,000
Overhead	70,000

Cost Variances

Materials price	3,500		
Materials efficiency	2,500		
		Labor and overhead	6,600

Debits to Cost of Goods Sold are standard price (SP) $\times$ standard quantity of input per unit of output (SQ) times actual units produced. If inventories were minimal, the balance in the variance account would be expensed.

If the company has substantial ending inventories, the costs in Cost of Goods Sold are transferred to the inventory accounts. Assume no beginning inventories. Assume that $42,000 of the $60,000 standard cost of materials is traced to the inventory accounts:

Materials Inventory	$35,000
Work in Process	5,000
Finished Goods	2,000
Total	$42,000

The total amount is credited to Standard Cost of Goods Sold with debits to each inventory account, as shown in Illustration 20–6.

A similar adjustment is made for labor and overhead. Assume that 20 percent of the labor and overhead amounts are still in Work in Process and 8 percent are in Finished Goods. The dollar amounts to be transferred from Cost of Goods Sold to the inventory accounts are as follows:

	Labor	Overhead
Work in Process	$6,000	$14,000
Finished Goods	2,400	5,600
Total	$8,400	$19,600

The resulting inventory and Cost of Goods Sold accounts appear in Illustration 20–6 after adjustments.

COMPARISON OF PRODUCT (INVENTORY) VALUES UNDER ALTERNATIVE COSTING METHODS

We have now completed the discussion of six alternative methods of valuing products (and inventory) in this book. These six methods and the major chapters in which they were primarily discussed are as follows:

	Actual costing	Normal costing	Standard costing
Variable costing	Chapter 9	Chapter 9	Chapters 19 and 20
Full-absorption costing	Chapter 3	Chapter 3	Chapters 19 and 20

Illustration 20–7 shows the difference between variable and full-absorption costing. Full-absorption includes a share of fixed manufacturing costs in the unit cost, while variable costing does not, as seen from comparing rows 4 and 8.

The difference between actual and normal costing is in the treatment of overhead. **Normal costing** uses predetermined overhead rates times an actual base, while actual costing uses actual costs, as seen from comparing columns A and B. Under standard costing, all manufacturing costs assigned to a unit are predetermined, as shown in column C.

Illustration 20–8 presents a numerical comparison of the differences in product costs under various costing systems using data from Evergreen Company.

Normal Costing A system of accounting whereby direct materials and direct labor are charged to cost objects at actual, and manufacturing overhead is applied using a predetermined rate.

ILLUSTRATION *Backflush Standard Costing*

20-6

Materials Inventory

-0-	
35,000	

Work in Process

-0-	
Materials	5,000
Labor	6,000
Overhead	14,000
Balance	25,000

Finished Goods

-0-	
Materials	2,000
Labor	2,400
Overhead	5,600
Balance	10,000

Cost of Goods Sold (Standard Costs)

Materials	60,000		42,000
Labor	30,000		8,400
Overhead	70,000		19,600

Variances

Materials price	3,500	Labor and overhead	6,600
Materials efficiency	2,500		

ILLUSTRATION

20-7

Product (Inventory) Values under Alternative Costing Methods

	A Actual Costing	B Normal Costing	C Standard Costing
Variable Costing:			
1. Direct materials	Actual	Actual	Standard
2. Direct labor	Actual	Actual	Standard
3. Variable manufacturing overhead	Actual	Predetermined rate × Actual inputs or output	Standard rate × Standard inputs allowed for actual output
4. Fixed manufacturing overhead[a]	—	—	—
Full-Absorption Costing:			
5. Direct materials	Actual	Actual	Standard
6. Direct labor	Actual	Actual	Standard
7. Variable manufacturing overhead	Actual	Predetermined rate × Actual inputs or output	Standard rate × Standard inputs allowed for actual output
8. Fixed manufacturing overhead	Actual	Predetermined rate × Actual inputs or output	Standard rate × Standard inputs allowed for actual output

[a] Treated as a period cost in variable costing; not part of inventory.

SUMMARY

This chapter describes cost flows using standard cost systems. In standard cost systems, the standard costs are part of the accounting system; they replace actual costs in recording transactions between work in process production departments and in recording transactions between Work in Process Inventory and Finished Goods Inventory.

A major advantage of a standard system is that it reduces recordkeeping. Records of actual costs per unit are not kept. Instead, unit costs are standard costs. Many companies that manufacture with processes (for example, chemicals and petroleum) use standard cost systems because there is little benefit and great cost to record actual cost of each unit produced.

An overview of the standard cost system model is presented in Illustration 20-1. The basic idea is that costs are accumulated at actual cost in Accounts Payable, Accrued Payroll, and similar accounts. Costs are debited to Work in Process Inventory at standard cost. Standard costs are used to reflect the transfer of units between work in process departments, and from Work in Process Inventory to Finished Goods Inventory, and from Finished Goods Inventory to Cost of Goods Sold.

Manufacturing cost variances for a period are sometimes prorated among inventories and Cost of Goods Sold. This has the effect of restating Cost of Goods Sold and ending inventories to actual cost.

A summary of the variance proration process is shown in Illustration 20-9. Note how the Materials Price Variance is first allocated to the Materials Efficiency Variance, inventory balances, and Cost of Goods Sold. Then

Facts:

1. Actual production costs:

Direct materials: 110,000 board-feet at $.264	$ 29,040
Direct labor: 3,200 hours at $9.35	29,920
Variable manufacturing overhead	26,480
Fixed manufacturing overhead	37,000
Total costs	$122,440

2. Predetermined overhead rates:

Variable overhead: 8.33\frac{1}{3}$ per direct labor-hour

Fixed overhead rate per direct labor-hour

$$= \frac{\text{Estimated annual fixed manufacturing costs}}{\text{Estimated standard direct labor-hours worked based on estimated number of crates produced}}$$

$$= \frac{\$432,000}{28,800 \text{ hours}^a} = \$15.00 \text{ per direct labor-hour}$$

3. Standard variable manufacturing costs:

Direct materials: 10 board-feet per crate at $.25	$	2.50 per crate
Direct labor: .3 hour per crate at $10		3.00
Variable manufacturing overhead: .3 hour at 8.33\frac{1}{3}$		2.50
Total standard variable manufacturing costs	$	8.00

4. Standard fixed manufacturing cost:

.3 hour per crate times $15 per hour = $4.50 per crate

Comparison of costing methods:

	Actual Costing (10,000 units)		Normal Costing (10,000 units)		Standard Costing (10,000 units)	
	Total[b]	Unit[c]	Total[b]	Unit[c]	Total[b]	Unit[c]
Variable Costing:						
Direct materials	$ 29,040	$ 2.904	$ 29,040	$ 2.904	$ 25,000	$ 2.50
Direct labor	29,920	2.992	29,920	2.992	30,000	3.00
Variable manufacturing overhead	26,480	2.648	26,667[d]	2.667	25,000	2.50
Total	$ 85,440	$ 8.544	$ 85,627	$ 8.563	$ 80,000	$ 8.00
Full-Absorption Costing:						
Direct materials	$ 29,040	$ 2.904	$ 29,040	$ 2.904	$ 25,000	$ 2.50
Direct labor	29,920	2.992	29,920	2.992	30,000	3.00
Variable manufacturing overhead	26,480	2.648	26,667[d]	2.667	25,000	2.50
Fixed manufacturing overhead	37,000	3.700	48,000[e]	4.800	45,000	4.50
Total	$122,440	$12.244	$133,627	$13.363	$125,000	$12.50

Calculations:

[a] Assumes annual production of 96,000 crates:

96,000 crates × .3 standard direct labor-hour allowed per crate = 28,800 standard direct labor-hours

[b] Amount that would be charged to Work in Process Inventory in the month under each alternative costing method.

[c] Total divided by 10,000 crates produced in May.

[d] 8.33\frac{1}{3}$ per direct labor-hour times 3,200 direct labor-hours actually worked.

[e] $15 × 3,200 direct labor-hours actually used.

ILLUSTRATION   *Summary of Variance Proration*

20-9

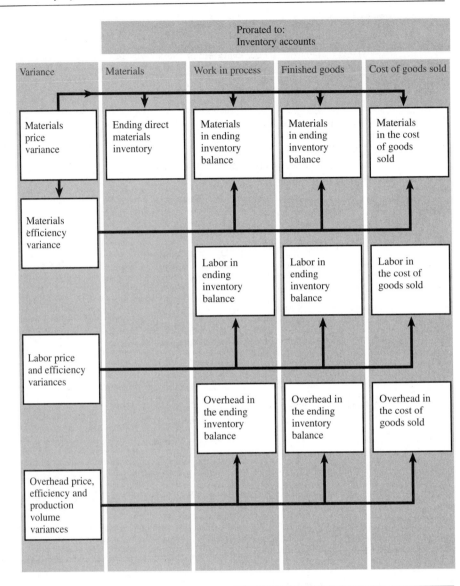

the remaining variances are allocated to inventory balances and Cost of Goods Sold.

In this text we have presented the following six different methods of placing cost value on products:

	Actual costing	Normal costing
Variable costing	X	X
Full-absorption costing	X	X

TERMS AND CONCEPTS

The following terms and concepts should be familiar to you after reading this chapter:

Normal Costing, *762*

Prorating Variances, *756*

Standard Costing, *748*

QUESTIONS

20–1   What are the advantages of a standard cost system?

20–2   How do you distinguish between a standard cost and an actual cost?

20–3   One manager was heard to remark, "We don't believe in using artificial numbers in our accounting system. Standard costing systems just make the readers fool themselves. We use normal costing instead—that gives us the true costs." Is the manager right? Comment.

20–4   Standard costing eliminates the need to compute equivalent units since all costs are transferred out at a standard amount per completed unit. Do you agree? Why or why not?

20–5   What is the difference in the way labor and material costs are accounted for versus the way overhead costs are accounted for in a standard costing system?

20–6   How are variable overhead costs treated differently in a standard costing system from their treatment in a normal costing system?

20–7   How should variances be disposed of at the end of the year?

20–8   Why is it difficult to relate fixed costs to outputs from a production process?

20–9   "Just like price and efficiency variances, the production volume variance indicates whether a company has spent more or less than called for in the budget." Comment on this quote.

20–10   How is the use of a standard cost system simplified in an automated environment?

EXERCISES[2]

**20–11 Standard Costing—
Journal Entries**
(L.O.2)

Ullrich Company purchased 26,000 units of material A at a price of $1.30 per pound. The standard price of material A is $1.40 per pound. During the month, 14,000 units of material A were used, which was 1,500 pounds more than the standard allowed. Prepare journal entries to record these transactions.

**20–12 Standard Costing—
T-Accounts**
(L.O.2)

Refer to the data in exercise 20–11. Prepare T-accounts to show the flow of costs for these transactions.

---

[2] Do *not* use the backflush method described in the section titled "Standard Costing in a Just-in-Time Environment" unless explicitly required.

20–13   Standard Costing—
Service Organization
(L.O.2)

Drawem & Bildem, P.A., is an architectural firm that uses standard cost analysis to help control the costs of its professional staff. On a recent project, Drawem & Bildem prepared the following estimates for Mega Towers using standard costs:

	Totals
Drafting: 440 hours @ $37.50	$16,500
Architectural: 120 hours @ $45.00	5,400
Engineering: 60 hours @ $125	7,500
	$29,400

When the job was complete, actual total costs were significantly greater than expected. The hours and total costs for each type of staff cost were as follows:

	Totals
Drafting: 420 hours	$15,200
Architectural: 200 hours	9,400
Engineering: 90 hours	13,300
	$37,900

Required:

Prepare journal entries for each cost category; namely, drafting, architectural, and engineering. Debit Work in Process for the standard costs, and credit Payroll Payable for actual costs.

20–14   Standard Labor Costs
(L.O.2)

Monroe Products has a standard labor cost of $60 per unit of output. During the past month, 3,000 output units were manufactured. The total labor-hours allowed for this output were 22,500 hours. The actual labor costs were $176,240. Actual labor-hours were 22,600.

Required:

Prepare journal entries to record these transactions.

20–15   T-Accounts for
Standard Labor Costs
(L.O.2)

Refer to the data in exercise 20–14. Prepare T-accounts to show the flow of costs through accounts.

20–16   Standard
Overhead Costs
(L.O.2)

Standard Company developed standard overhead costs based on a monthly capacity of 90,000 machine-hours as follows:

Standard costs per unit:	
Variable portion: 1 hour at $7	$ 7
Fixed portion: 1 hour at $10	10
	$17

During April, 84,000 units were scheduled for production; however, only 80,000 units were actually produced. The following data relate to April:

1. Actual machine-hours totaled 82,000.
2. Actual overhead incurred totaled $1,378,000—$518,000 variable and $860,000 fixed.
3. There was no work in process inventory and no beginning finished goods inventory. All inventories are carried at standard cost.

Required:

Prepare journal entries to record these transactions and set up overhead variances.

20–17   T-Accounts
for Standard
Overhead Costs
(L.O.2)

Refer to the data in exercise 20–16. Show the flow of costs through T-accounts.

20–18 Prorate Variances
(L.O.3)

Refer to the variance calculations for exercise 20–16. Assume 75 percent of the units produced were sold. Prorate the variances to ending Finished Goods Inventory (25%) and Cost of Goods Sold (75%).

20–19 Standard Overhead Costs
(L.O.2)

Philadelphia Company uses a standard cost accounting system. The following overhead costs and production data are available for August:

Standard fixed overhead rate per direct labor-hour . . . . $	1.00
Standard variable overhead rate per direct labor-hour . . . . $	4.00
Budgeted monthly direct labor-hours	40,000
Actual direct labor-hours worked	39,000
Standard direct labor-hours allowed for actual production	38,000
Overall overhead variance—favorable . . . . $	2,000
Actual variable overhead	$158,200

Required:

Compute overhead variances, then prepare journal entries for these transactions.

(CPA adapted)

20–20 Standard Overhead Costs—T-Accounts
(L.O.2)

Use the data in exercise 20–19 to show the flow of these overhead costs through T-accounts.

20–21 Standard Overhead Costs
(L.O.2)

The following information appeared in the accounts of the Rapid Cities Corporation:

Actual manufacturing overhead:		$490,000
Fixed portion $215,000		
Variable portion 275,000		
Overhead applied at standard:		465,836
Fixed portion 215,900		
Variable portion 249,936		

Fixed overhead was applied at the rate of $4.25 per direct labor-hour, and 50,000 hours were budgeted for the period. The company uses a standard costing system. The 100,000 units produced during the period required 49,500 actual direct labor-hours.

Required:

Prepare journal entries for these transactions, including overhead variances. Units sold were 80,000. There were no beginning or ending work in process inventories, and no beginning finished goods inventory.

20–22 T-Accounts for Standard Overhead Costs
(L.O.2)

Use the data in exercise 20–21 to show the flow of costs through T-accounts.

20–23 Prorate Variances
(L.O.3)

Use the variance calculations in exercise 20–21. Prorate the variations to ending Finished Goods Inventory (20%) and Cost of Goods Sold (80%).

20–24 Standard Materials Costs
(L.O.2)

Armadillo Corporation acquired 50,000 units of direct materials for $70,000 last year. The standard price paid for the materials was $1.30 per unit. During last year, 45,000 units of materials were used in the production process. Materials are entered into production at the beginning of the process. The standard allowed was 48,000 units for the amount of output that was actually produced. Eighty percent of the units that used these materials were completed and transferred to Finished Goods Inventory. Sixty percent of these units that had been transferred to Finished Goods Inventory were sold this period. There were no beginning inventories.

Required:

Prepare journal entries and show the flow of costs through T-accounts.

20–25	**Prorate Materials Variances** (L.O.3)	Refer to the variances calculated for exercise 20–24. Prorate the materials price variance to the Materials Efficiency Variance, ending inventories, and Cost of Goods Sold; and prorate the efficiency variance to ending inventories and the Cost of Goods Sold.
20–26	**Standard Costing in a Just-in-Time Environment** (L.O.4)	During the current period, Otter Co. paid $38,000 for 30,000 units of material. All of these materials were immediately put into process. During the period, 14,800 units of output were produced, and 14,500 units were sold. Three hundred units remain in Finished Goods Inventory. Each unit of output requires two units of material, which has a standard cost of $1.35 per unit of material. Standard variable overhead is $69,600 for 15,000 units of production. The variable overhead efficiency variance was $1,800 U, and actual variable overhead was $69,341.

Fixed overhead, which includes all labor costs, is budgeted at $146,000. Actual fixed overhead for the period was $143,200. Fixed overhead is applied to production at $10 per unit of output. All variances are expensed.

Required:

a. Show the flow of these costs if the company initially charges all manufacturing costs to Cost of Goods Sold at standard (that is, backflush standard costing).

b. Show the adjustment that would be made to reflect the ending inventory balances.

20–27	**Standard Costing in a Just-in-Time Environment** (L.O.4)	Refer to the data for the Armadillo Corporation, exercise 20–24, above. If Armadillo Corp. were operating in a just-in-time environment and charging its standard costs directly to Standard Cost of Goods Sold, show the flow of costs through T-accounts that would be required to adjust the Standard Cost of Goods Sold account to reflect end-of-period inventories. Variances are expensed.

PROBLEMS

20–28	**Standard Costs and Prorating Variances— Multiple-Choice**	A Company used a traditional standard cost system in accounting for the cost of production of its only product, product A. The standards for the production of one unit of product A are as follows:

Direct materials: 10 feet of item 1 at $.75 per foot and 3 feet of item 2 at $1.00 per foot

Direct labor: 4 hours at $15.00 per hour

Manufacturing overhead: Applied at 150 percent of standard direct labor costs

There were no inventories on hand on July 1. Following is a summary of costs and related data for the production of product A during the month ended July 31:

100,000 feet of item 1 were purchased at $.78 per foot.

30,000 feet of item 2 were purchased at $.90 per foot.

8,000 units of product A were produced, which required 78,000 feet of item 1; 26,000 feet of item 2; and 31,000 hours of direct labor at $16.00 per hour.

6,000 units of product A were sold.

On July 31, there are 22,000 feet of item 1; 4,000 feet of item 2; and 2,000 completed units of product A on hand. All direct materials purchases and transfers are debited at standard.

Required:

Choose the best answers (or indicate "none of the above"):

a. For the month ended July 31, the total debits to the Direct Materials Inventory account for the purchase of item 1 would be:

(1) $75,000.

(2) $78,000.

    (3) $58,500.

    (4) $60,000.

b. For the month ended July 31, the total debits to the Work in Process account for direct labor would be:

    (1) $496,000.

    (2) $465,000.

    (3) $480,000.

    (4) $512,000.

c. Before prorating variances, the balance in the Materials Efficiency Variance account for item 2 was:

    (1) $1,000 credit.

    (2) $2,600 debit.

    (3) $600 debit.

    (4) $2,000 debit.

d. If all variances were prorated to inventories and Cost of Goods Sold, the amount of materials efficiency variance for item 2 to be prorated to Raw Materials Inventory would be:

    (1) $0.

    (2) $333 credit.

    (3) $333 debit.

    (4) $500 debit.

e. If all variances were prorated to inventories and Cost of Goods Sold, the amount of materials price variance for item 1 to be prorated to Raw Materials Inventory would be:

    (1) $0.

    (2) $647 debit.

    (3) $600 debit.

    (4) $660 debit.

(CMA adapted)

20–29 Standard Costs: Journal Entries and T-Accounts

Armando Corporation manufactures a product with the following standard costs:

Direct materials: 20 yards at $1.35 per yard $27

Direct labor: 4 hours at $9 per hour 36

Factory overhead—applied at five sixths of direct labor:

  Ratio of variable costs to fixed costs: 2 to 1 . . . . <u>30</u>

  Total standard cost per unit of output . . . . <u>$93</u>

Standards are based on normal monthly production involving 2,400 direct labor-hours (600 units of output).

Following are actual costs for the month of July:

Direct materials purchased: 18,000 yards at $1.38 per yard $24,840

Direct materials used: 9,500 yards

Direct labor: 2,100 hours at $9.15 per hour 19,215

Actual factory overhead 16,650

Five hundred units of the product were actually produced in July and transferred to Finished Goods Inventory.

Required:

a. Prepare journal entries to record the above transactions for a traditional standard cost system.

b. Show the flow of these costs using T-accounts.

(CPA adapted)

20–30 Compute Variances and Use T-Accounts to Show Standard Cost Flows

Juneau Company manufactures a line of clothing. At the beginning of the period, there were 1,000 units in stock at a variable cost of $400 per unit. The full-absorption cost of these units is $450 each.

Plans for the period call for the following standards and activity:

Units produced and sold 2,000

Standard cost per unit:

Direct materials $175

Direct labor   200

Overhead . . . .   100 (60% variable)

Total $475

During the period, 2,200 units were produced and 1,800 were sold. The following costs were incurred:

Direct materials $360,000

Direct labor 412,000

Overhead:

Variable   135,000

Fixed   81,000

Direct materials price variances are recorded at the time of purchase. No materials were purchased this period. Actual direct labor costs were 5 percent less per hour of labor than the standard allowed. Overhead costs are applied to production as a percent of standard direct labor costs. A standard costing system is used.

Required:

a. Compute variable manufacturing price and efficiency variances. Compute fixed manufacturing cost, price, and production volume variances.

b. Use T-accounts to show the flow of costs through the system, assuming a traditional FIFO system.

20–31 Prorate Variances

Refer to the data for the Juneau Company in problem 20–30. Prorate variances for the Juneau Company. Show the proration with journal entries and T-accounts.

20–32 Comprehensive Standard Cost Problem

The following information is provided to assist you in evaluating the performance of the manufacturing operations at the Ashwood Company:

Units of output produced   21,000

Standard costs per unit:

Direct materials: $1.65 × 5 pounds per unit of output

Direct labor: $14.00 per labor-hour × .5 hour per unit

Variable overhead: $11.90 per labor-hour × .5 hour per unit

Actual costs:

Direct materials purchased and used . . . . $188,700 (102,000 pounds)

Direct labor . . . . 140,000 (10,700 hours)

Overhead . . . . 204,000 (61% is variable)

Variable overhead is applied on the basis of the direct labor-hours allowed. There were $440 F price and $4,000 F production volume variances for fixed overhead.

Required:

a. Prepare journal entries to show the transactions, using traditional standard, full-absorption costing in as much detail as possible.

b. Use T-accounts to show the flow of costs.

20–33 Comprehensive Prorating of Variances

Refer to the data for the Ashwood Company (problem 20–32). Use T-accounts to show how the variances would be prorated at the end of the period. Assume 100 percent of the production had been transferred to Finished Goods Inventory, and 90 percent of the completed production had been sold.

20–34 Standard Costing in a Just-in-Time Environment

Refer to the data for the Ashwood Company (problems 20–32 and 20–33 above). For this problem, assume that Ashwood charges all standard costs directly to Cost of Goods Sold and maintains a separate account for variances. At the end of the period, adjustments are made to reflect inventories and to prorate variances.

Required:

Use T-accounts to show the cost flows under this scenario.

20–35 Standard Costing in a Just-in-Time Environment

Ell-A Fear manufactures sport shoes. The company produces goods as orders are received. Hence, inventories are maintained at very low levels. An order was received for 5,000 pairs of the Shootout Running model. Standard costs for these shoes are:

Direct materials	$4.20
Direct labor (.25 hour)	1.35
Overhead (.5 machine-hour)	6.46

Direct materials costs are based on expected usage of precut materials that are available in a complete package for each pair of shoes. That is, for each package of materials, expected good output is one pair of shoes.

While producing this order, Ell-A Fear had to purchase materials for $4.27. The extra cost was incurred to obtain the raw materials sooner than was expected. Due to an equipment malfunction, 50 packages of materials were destroyed. These 50 packages were replaced at a cost of $4.27 per package.

Direct labor costs were $7,200, and the rate was $5.20 per direct labor-hour. Actual overhead costs exceeded the planned rate by 8 cents per machine-hour. A total of 2,750 machine-hours were required. The extra machine-hours were primarily caused by the equipment malfunction.

Ell-A Fear charges all costs directly to Cost of Goods Sold at standard. Variances are identified and charged to a separate account: Manufacturing Variances Expensed.

Not all of the Shootout Running model shoes ordered had been shipped at the end of the period. Fifty pairs were still on hand in the shipping area at the end of the period.

Required:

Use T-accounts to show the cost flows for these events.

20–36 Prorate Variances

SmurfKind-Merc Pharmaceuticals purchased 80,000 grams of deuterial oxide at a cost of $124,000 and 40,000 grams of milaidium chloride at a cost of $89,600. Standard costs for this quantity of deuterial oxide is $120,000, and the milaidium chloride was expected to cost $92,000. These chemicals are the ingredients in its accounting knowledge booster pill: Mind-Warp. During the period, 280,000 Mind-Warp pills were manufactured, of which 30,000 remain in finished goods.

Production of 280,000 Mind-Warps is expected to require 70,000 grams of deuterial oxide and 30,000 grams of milaidium chloride. Actual use was 71,000 grams of deuterial oxide and 29,500 grams of milaidium chloride.

SmurfKind-Merc includes labor costs with its variable overhead for cost analysis purposes. The standard variable overhead cost for each Mind-Warp pill is 75 cents. During the period, actual variable overhead was $217,300. Variable overhead is applied to production based on machine-hours. The machine-hour standard for 280,000 pills is 3,500 hours. Actual machine-hour use during the month was 3,360 hours.

Fixed costs are charged to period expense as incurred, and may be ignored in your analysis. There is no Work in Process Inventory.

Required:

a. Show the standard costs for each inventory account and Cost of Goods Sold in T-accounts.

b. Prorate the variances to the appropriate accounts.

20–37 Prorate Variances

Thai Imports acquires clothing from Bangkok and completes the clothing in a *maquilladora* plant in Juarez. The company uses a traditional standard costing system so it can evaluate variances. During the fall season, Thai Imports received materials for 50,000 men's shirts at its Juarez plant. Forty-eight thousand unfinished shirts were started in production. Work was completed on 41,500 shirts, and 39,800 were sold. The shirts still in process were 50 percent complete at the end of the period. Certain information about standards and actual results are as follows:

	Standard (per shirt)	Actual (per shirt)
Unfinished shirts	$6.00	$6.10
Finishing materials	.75	.80
Total finishing overhead	.60	.73
Labor costs	.30	.34

The company expected to complete 50,000 shirts during the period and purchased sufficient finishing materials for the expected output. Labor is paid on a piecework basis based on production volume. Overhead and labor costs are incurred equally throughout the finishing process so that the 6,500 shirts still in process at the end of the period are equivalent to 3,250 completed shirts for the purposes of evaluating standard costs for finishing materials, labor, and overhead. Overhead is applied based on the 44,750 (41,500 + 3,250) equivalent number of shirts produced.

Budgeted fixed overhead is equal to 30 percent of the total finishing overhead. Actual fixed overhead for the period, which is included in the 73-cent cost, above, was $4,400.

There were no beginning inventories.

Required:

Prepare the journal entries to prorate the variances for the period. A single entry may be used for all overhead variances.

20–38 Prorate Labor Variances

Nanron Company has a traditional process standard cost system for all its products. All inventories are carried at standard during the year. The inventories and Cost of Goods Sold are adjusted for all variances considered material in amount for financial statement purposes. All products are considered to flow through the manufacturing process to finished goods and ultimate sale in a FIFO pattern.

The standard cost of one of Nanron's products manufactured in the Dixon Plant, unchanged from the prior year, is shown below:

Direct materials	$2
Direct labor (.5 direct labor-hour at $8)	4
Manufacturing overhead	3
Total standard cost	$9

There is no work in process inventory of this product due to the nature of the product and the manufacturing process.

The schedule below reports the manufacturing and sales activity measured at standard cost for the current fiscal year.

	Units	Dollars
Product manufactured	95,000	$855,000
Beginning finished goods inventory	15,000	135,000
Goods available for sale	110,000	990,000
Ending finished goods inventory	19,000	171,000
Cost of goods sold	91,000	$819,000

Manufacturing performance relative to standard costs both this year and last year was not good. The balance of the Finished Goods Inventory, $140,800, reported on the balance sheet at the beginning of the year included a $5,800 proration adjustment for unfavorable variances from standard cost. The unfavorable standard cost variances for labor for the current fiscal year consisted of a wage rate variance of $32,000 and a labor efficiency variance of $20,000 (2,500 hours at $8). There were no other variances from standard cost for this year.

Required:

Adjust the inventories and Cost of Goods Sold to reflect actual costs.

(CMA adapted)

20–39   Revisions of Standards

Lenco Company employs a traditional standard cost system as part of its cost control program. The standard cost per unit is established at the beginning of each year. Any revisions in standards are deferred until the beginning of the next fiscal year. However, to recognize changes in standards in the current year, the company includes "planned" variances in the monthly budgets prepared after such changes have been introduced.

The following labor standard was set for one of Lenco's products effective July 1, the beginning of the fiscal year:

Class I labor: 4 hours at $6	$24.00
Class II labor: 3 hours at $7.50	22.50
Class V labor: 1 hour at $11.50	11.50
Standard labor cost per 100 units	$58.00

The standard was based on the quality of material used in prior years and that expected for the current fiscal year. Labor activity is performed by a team consisting of four persons with Class I skills, three persons with Class II skills, and one person with Class V skills. This is the most economical combination.

Manufacturing operations occured as expected during the first five months of the year. However, the company received a significant increase in orders for delivery in the spring. There was an inadequate number of skilled workers available to meet the increased production. As a result, the production teams, beginning in January, were made up of more Class I labor and less Class II labor than the standard specified. The teams would consist of six Class I persons, two Class II persons, and one Class V person. This labor team is less efficient than the normal team. As a result, only 90 units are produced in the same time period that 100 units would normally be produced. No changes in direct materials used per unit of output will occur because of the change in the labor mix.

Lenco was notified by its materials supplier that a lower quality material would be supplied after January 1. One unit of direct material normally is required for each good unit produced. Lenco and its supplier estimate that 5 percent of the units manufactured would be rejected upon final inspection due to the lower quality material. Normally, no units are lost due to defective material.

Required:

a. How much of the lower quality material must be entered into production to produce 42,750 units of good production in January with the new labor teams? Show your calculations.

b. How many hours of each class of labor will be needed to produce 42,750 good units from the material input? Show your calculations.

c. What amount should be included in the January budget for the planned labor variance due to the labor team and material changes? What amount of this planned labor variance can be associated with the (1) material change and (2) the team change? Show your calculations.

(CMA adapted)

INTEGRATIVE CASES

20–40 Comprehensive Review of Variances and Standard Cost Flows with Proration

In its plant near Guadalajara, Longhorn Manufacturing Corporation produces only one product, Bevo, and accounts for the production of Bevo using a traditional standard cost system.

At the end of each year, Longhorn prorates all variances among the various inventories and cost of sales. Because Longhorn prices its inventories on the FIFO basis and all the beginning inventories are used during the year, the variances that had been allocated to the ending inventories are immediately charged to cost of sales at the beginning of the following year. This allows only the current year's variances to be recorded in the variance accounts in any given year.

Following are the standards for the production of one unit of Bevo: 3 units of item A at $1 per unit, 1 unit of item B at $.50 per unit, 4 units of item C at $.30 per unit, and 20 minutes of direct labor at $4.50 per hour. Separate variance accounts are maintained for each type of direct material and for direct labor. Direct materials are recorded at standard prices when purchased. Manufacturing overhead is applied at $9 per actual direct labor-hour and is not related to the standard cost system. There was no overapplied or underapplied manufacturing overhead at December 31, Year 1. After proration of the variances, the various inventories at December 31, Year 1, were costed as follows:

Direct materials:

Item	Number of Units	Unit Cost	Amount
A	15,000	$1.10	$16,500
B	4,000	.52	2,080
C	20,000	.32	6,400
			$24,980

Work in Process:

Nine thousand units of Bevo were 100 percent complete as to items A and B, 50 percent complete as to item C, and 30 percent complete as to labor. The composition and cost of the inventory follows:

Item	Amount
A	$28,600
B	4,940
C	6,240
Direct labor	6,175
	45,955
Overhead	11,700
	$57,655

Finished goods:

Forty-eight hundred units of Bevo were costed as follows:

Item	Amount
A	$15,180
B	2,704
C	6,368
Direct labor	8,540
	32,792
Overhead	16,200
	$48,992

Following is a schedule of direct materials purchased and direct labor incurred for the year ended December 31, Year 2. Unit cost of each item of direct material and direct labor cost per hour remained constant throughout the year.

Purchases:

Item	Number of Units or Hours	Unit Cost	Amount
A	290,000	$1.15	$333,500
B	101,000	.55	55,550
C	367,000	.35	128,450
Direct labor	34,100	4.60	156,860

During the year ended December 31, Year 2, Longhorn sold 90,000 units of Bevo and had ending physical inventories as follows:

Direct materials:

Item	Number of Units
A	28,300
B	2,100
C	28,900

Work in process:

Seventy-five hundred units of Bevo were 100 percent complete as to items A and B, 50 percent complete as to item C, and 20 percent complete as to labor, as follows:

Item	Number of Units or Hours
A	22,900
B	8,300
C	15,800
Direct labor	800

Finished goods:

Fifty-one hundred units of Bevo, as follows:

Item	Number of Units or Hours
A	15,600
B	6,300
C	21,700
Direct labor	2,050

There was no overapplied or underapplied manufacturing overhead at December 31, Year 2.

Required:

a. Prepare a schedule showing all materials and direct labor variances arising from activity in Year 2.

b. Use T-accounts to show the flow of materials and direct labor costs under the standard costing system in use.

(CPA adapted)

20–41 Racketeer: Comprehensive Cost Flow Problem

Refer to the data presented in Chapter 19, problem 19–51, on Racketeer. Using traditional standard, full-absorption costing for Racketeer, present the flow of costs through accounts, using journal entries and T-accounts.

20–42 Woodside Products, Inc.* (Profit Variance Analysis)

Phil Brooks, president of Woodside Products, Inc., called Marilyn Mynar into his office one morning in early July. Ms. Mynar was a business major in college and was employed by Woodside during her college summer vacation.

"Marilyn," Brooks began, "I've just received the preliminary financial statements for our current fiscal year, which ended June 30. Both our board of directors and our shareholders will want, and deserve, an explanation of why our pretax income was virtually unchanged even though revenues were up by more than $175,000. The accountant is tied up working with our outside CPA on the annual audit, so I thought you could do the necessary analysis. What I'd like is as much of a detailed explanation of the $1,950 profit increase as you can glean from these data (Exhibit 20–42A). Also, draft a statement for the next board meeting that explains the same $1,950 profit increase. Since the board of directors understands variable costing, I recommend that you convert everything to variable costing for the variance computations, then reconcile your variable costing numbers with the amounts shown in Exhibit 20–42A, if necessary."

Required:

Prepare the detailed analysis of the $1,950 profit increase from last fiscal year to the current fiscal year and draft an explanation for Woodside's board of directors, as requested by Phil Brooks. (Hint: Let last year's amounts be budgets or standards.) Assume that finished goods inventory was valued at $24 per unit (using full-absorption costing) at the end of this year.

---

* Copyright © Osceola Institute, 1979.

EXHIBIT

WOODSIDE PRODUCTS, INC.
Operating Results
For the Years Ended June 30

	Last Year	Current Year
Sales revenues	$3,525,000	$3,701,250
Cost of goods sold	2,115,000	2,310,450
Gross margin	1,410,000	1,390,800
Selling and administrative	902,400	881,250
Income before taxes	$ 507,600	$ 509,550

Other Data for Last Year

1. Sales = 88,125 units @ $40.

2. Cost of goods sold = 88,125 units @ $24.

3. Selling and administrative costs were $1.84 per unit variable selling cost plus $740,250 fixed S&A.

4. Production volume and sales volume were equal.

5. Production costs per unit were:

Materials	$ 9.60 (8 pounds at $1.20)
Direct labor	4.80 (.75 hour at $6.40)
Variable overhead	1.60 (per unit)
Fixed overhead	8.00 (based on estimated production volume of 88,125 units)
	$24.00

Other Current Year Data

1. Sales = 78,750 units @ $47.

2. Cost of goods sold includes the current year's production cost variances.

3. Selling and administrative costs were $2 per unit variable selling cost plus $723,750 fixed S&A.

4. Actual production volume was 81,100 units; estimated volume was 88,125 units.

5. 626,200 pounds of material at $1.40 were consumed by production.

6. 64,860 direct labor-hours were worked at $6.90.

7. Actual variable overhead costs were $152,000.

SOLUTIONS TO

Self-Study
uestions

1 *a.* **Journal entries:**

(1) Direct Materials Inventory 200,000
    Materials Price Variance 40,000
        Accounts Payable   240,000
    To record the purchase of 200,000 pounds of materials
    at an actual cost of $1.20 per pound and to record the
    transfer to Direct Materials Inventory at the standard
    cost of $1 per pound.

(2) Work in Process Inventory 100,000
    Materials Efficiency Variance 10,000
        Direct Materials Inventory   110,000
    To record the requisition of 110,000 pounds of materials
    at the standard cost of $1 per pound and to charge
    Work in Process Inventory with the standard usage
    of 100,000 pounds of materials at the standard price.

(3) Work In Process Inventory 75,000
    Labor Efficiency Variance 15,000
        Labor Price Variance   6,000
        Accrued Payroll   84,000
    To charge Work in Process Inventory for the standard
    cost of direct labor at $15 per hour times 5,000 stan-
    dard hours allowed and to record the actual cost of $14
    per hour times the 6,000 hours actually worked.

(4) Work in Process Inventory 25,000
        Variable Overhead Applied   25,000
    To apply overhead to production at $5 per standard
    direct labor-hour times the 5,000 hours allowed.

(5) Variable Overhead (Actual) 28,000
        Miscellaneous accounts (Cash, Accounts Payable,
        etc.)   28,000
    To record actual variable overhead.

(6) Variable Overhead Applied 25,000
    Variable Overhead Efficiency Variance 5,000
        Variable Overhead Price Variance   2,000
        Variable Overhead (Actual)   28,000
    To record variable overhead variances and to close the
    Variable Overhead Applied and Variable Overhead
    (Actual) accounts.

(7) Work in Process Inventory 100,000
        Fixed Overhead Applied   100,000
    To record fixed overhead at a standard cost of $20 per
    direct labor-hour times 5,000 standard hours

$$\left(\frac{\$80,000}{4,000 \text{ hours}} = \$20 \text{ per hour}\right).$$

(8) Fixed Overhead (Actual)   83,000

      Miscellaneous accounts (Cash, Accounts Payable,
      etc.)   83,000

      To record actual fixed overhead.

(9) Fixed Overhead Applied   100,000

      Fixed Overhead Price Variance   3,000

          Fixed Overhead Production Volume Variance   20,000

          Fixed Overhead (Actual)   83,000

      To record fixed overhead variances and to close the
      Fixed Overhead accounts.

(10) Finished Goods Inventory   300,000

      Work in Process Inventory   300,000

      To record the transfer of 50,000 units of finished goods
      at the standard cost of $6 per unit.

(11) Cost of Goods Sold   240,000

      Finished Goods Inventory   240,000

      To record the sale of 40,000 units at a standard cost of
      $6 per unit.

b. **Cost flows through T-accounts:**

2   Prorate variances:

Materials Price Variance:

Account	(1) Cost in Account	(2) Percent of Total Cost	Variance to Be Prorated (column 2 × $40,000)
Direct Materials Inventory	$ 90,000	45	$18,000
Materials Efficiency Variance	10,000	5	2,000
Finished Goods Inventory	20,000	10	4,000
Cost of Goods Sold	80,000	40	16,000
	$200,000	100	$40,000

Materials efficiency variance:

Account	(1) Cost in Account	(2) Percent of Total Cost	Variance to Be Prorated (column 2 × $12,000[a])
Finished Goods Inventory	$ 24,000	20	$ 2,400
Cost of Goods Sold	96,000	80	9,600
	$120,000	100	$12,000

Labor and Overhead Variances:

Labor price variance	$ 6,000 F
Labor efficiency variance	15,000 U
Variable overhead price variance	2,000 F
Variable overhead efficiency variance	5,000 U
Fixed overhead price variance	3,000 U
Fixed overhead production volume variance	20,000 F
Net total	$ 5,000 F

Account	(1) Cost in Account	(2) Percent of Total Cost	Variance to Be Prorated (column 2 × $5,000)
Finished Goods Inventory	$ 15,000	20	$ 1,000
Cost of Goods Sold	60,000	80	4,000
	$ 75,000	100	$ 5,000

[a] $12,000 equals $10,000 variance before proration plus $2,000 materials price variance prorated to Materials Efficiency Variance.

CHAPTER

21

Mix, Yield, and Revenue Variances

LEARNING OBJECTIVES

After reading this chapter, you should be able to:

1. Understand how to compute and use gross margin and contribution margin variances.
2. Use market share variances to evaluate marketing performance.
3. Use sales mix variances to evaluate marketing performance.
4. Evaluate production performance using production mix and yield variances.

*I*n this chapter, we discuss variances for revenues and nonmanufacturing costs, and how managers use these variances to evaluate marketing and administrative performance. The basic principles are the same as those presented in Chapters 18 through 20.

A variance is the difference between a predetermined norm and the actual results for a period. To illustrate the development of revenue and nonmanufacturing cost variances, we continue the Evergreen Company example discussed in Chapters 18 through 20. The basic facts about the Evergreen Company example are reviewed in Illustration 21–1.

ILLUSTRATION

Evergreen Company

	Actual	Master Budget
Sales price	$21 per crate	$20 per crate
Sales volume	10,000 crates	8,000 crates
Variable manufacturing costs	$8.544 per crate	$8 per crate
Variable marketing and administrative costs	$1.10 per crate	$1 per crate
Fixed manufacturing costs	$37,000	$36,000
Fixed marketing and administrative costs	$44,000	$40,000

REPORTING ON MARKETING PERFORMANCE

Like manufacturing managers, marketing managers usually are evaluated on the basis of planned results versus actual outcomes. Marketing performance analysis looks at how well the company has done in terms of revenues and marketing costs compared to the plans that are reflected in the master budget.

Using Sales Price and Activity Variances to Evaluate Marketing Performance

Sales Price Variance Variance arising from changes in the price of goods sold.

Sales Activity Variance Variance due to changes in volume of sales. (Also known as the *Sales Volume Variance*.)

The **sales price** and **sales activity variances** are often used to evaluate marketing performance. Sales price and activity variances would be computed as follows:

$$\text{Price variance} = (\text{Actual sales price} - \text{Budgeted sales price}) \times \text{Actual sales volume}$$

For Evergreen Company:

$$\left(\begin{array}{c}\text{Actual} \\ \text{price}\end{array} - \begin{array}{c}\text{Budgeted} \\ \text{price}\end{array}\right) \times \text{Actual sales volume}$$

$$(\$21 \quad - \quad \$20) \quad \times \; 10,000 \text{ units} = \underline{\$10,000} \text{ F}$$

$$\text{Sales activity variance} = \text{Budgeted contribution margin} \times (\text{Actual sales volume} - \text{Master budget sales volume})$$

For Evergreen Company:

$$\begin{array}{c}\text{Budgeted} \\ \text{contribution} \\ \text{margin}\end{array} \times \left(\begin{array}{c}\text{Actual} \\ \text{sales} \\ \text{volume}\end{array} - \begin{array}{c}\text{Master} \\ \text{budget} \\ \text{sales} \\ \text{volume}\end{array}\right)$$

$$(\$20 - \$9) \quad \times \; (10,000 - 8,000)$$
$$= \$11 \qquad \times \; 2,000 \text{ crates}$$
$$= \underline{\$22,000} \text{ F}$$

The budgeted contribution margin equals the budgeted unit sales price (SP) of $20 minus the budgeted (or standard) variable cost (SV), which is $9 (sum of $8 variable manufacturing and $1 variable marketing and administrative). Consequently, the *budgeted contribution margin per unit* is:

$$\$20 - (\$8 + \$1) = \$20 - \$9$$
$$= \underline{\$11}$$

Illustration 21–2 presents a general model for computing these variances and applies it to the Evergreen Company example. Note that the method is similar to that used to compute cost variances in Chapter 19. To compare with the profit variance analysis in Chapter 18, we also show the actual contribution and the variable cost variances in Illustration 21–2. The actual variable cost (AV) equals $9.644 based on the data given for Evergreen Company in Chapter 18. (The $9.644 is the sum of the actual variable manufacturing cost and the variable marketing and administrative cost.)

Contribution Margin versus Gross Margin

Contribution Margin Variance Variance from changes in revenues and variable costs.

When the contribution margin is used to compute the variances, the variances are called **contribution margin variances.** An alternative is to compute the variances using a budgeted gross margin instead of a budgeted contribution margin. When this method of computing the variances is used, the

ILLUSTRATION   *Contribution Margin Variances, Evergreen Company*

21–2

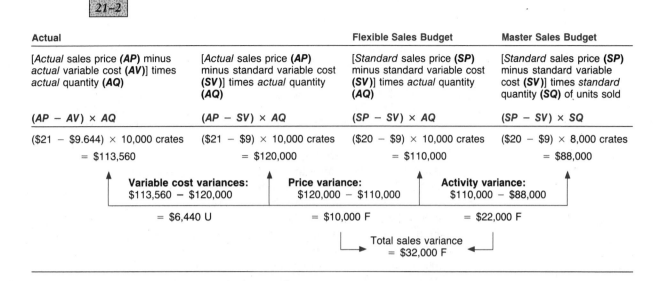

Actual		Flexible Sales Budget	Master Sales Budget
[*Actual* sales price (**AP**) minus *actual* variable cost (**AV**)] times *actual* quantity (**AQ**)	[*Actual* sales price (**AP**) minus standard variable cost (**SV**)] times *actual* quantity (**AQ**)	[*Standard* sales price (**SP**) minus standard variable cost (**SV**)] times *actual* quantity (**AQ**)	[*Standard* sales price (**SP**) minus standard variable cost (**SV**)] times *standard* quantity (**SQ**) of units sold
(**AP** − **AV**) × **AQ**	(**AP** − **SV**) × **AQ**	(**SP** − **SV**) × **AQ**	(**SP** − **SV**) × **SQ**
($21 − $9.644) × 10,000 crates = $113,560	($21 − $9) × 10,000 crates = $120,000	($20 − $9) × 10,000 crates = $110,000	($20 − $9) × 8,000 crates = $88,000

Variable cost variances:
$113,560 − $120,000
= $6,440 U

Price variance:
$120,000 − $110,000
= $10,000 F

Activity variance:
$110,000 − $88,000
= $22,000 F

Total sales variance
= $32,000 F

Gross Margin Variance Variance from changes in revenues and cost of goods sold.

variance is known as the **gross margin variance.** The basic approach is the same as for contribution margin variances except that the calculation is based on a unit gross margin instead of a unit contribution margin.

Calculation of the contribution margin variance requires that accountants know which costs are fixed and which are variable. If this information is not available, the gross margin variance is sometimes calculated in place of the contribution margin variance. (Note that computation of the sales price variance is independent of the choice between the gross margin and contribution margin methods of computing sales activity variances.)

Incentive Effects of Commissions Based on Revenue versus Contribution Margins

Sales personnel are often given commissions or bonuses based on sales revenue. Suppose a salesperson has an opportunity to sell *one* of the following two products to a customer, *but not both:*

	Revenue	Standard Variable Cost	Contribution Margin
Product A	$100,000	$90,000	$10,000
Product B	50,000	30,000	20,000

If the salesperson's commission is 2 percent of sales, he or she would clearly prefer to sell product A, even though product B provides a greater contribution to profits.

An alternative incentive plan would give the salesperson a commission based on contribution margin. If the salesperson's commission were 10 percent of contribution margin, *both* the salesperson and the company would benefit from the sale of product B.

In general, it is best to tie employee incentives as closely to organizational goals as possible. If the organizational goal is to maximize current sales, a commission based on revenue makes sense. If the goal is current profit maximization, a commission based on contribution margins may be more appropriate.

Summary

If you recall from previous chapters, the bottom-line objective in variance analysis is to compare the reported income statement amounts with the master budget. To keep in touch with the big picture, in Illustration 21–3 we present the profit variance analysis that compares the master budget to the reported income statement that was first presented in Chapter 18. The sales price and activity variances, which are relevant for our discussion in this chapter, are shown in columns 4 and 6 of Illustration 21–3.

Illustration 21–3 shows that actual revenue exceeds budgeted revenue by $50,000 ($10,000 favorable price variance plus $40,000 difference between the flexible budget revenue and the master budget revenue). It would be incorrect to say that favorable sales results have increased profits by $50,000, however, because the favorable increase in sales volume is partly offset by the variable costs of the additional 2,000 crates produced and sold. Therefore, we say the favorable sales results have increased profits by $32,000 ($10,000 F sales price variance + $22,000 F sales activity variance).

We next discuss further analysis of these sales variances.

ILLUSTRATION   *Comparison of Actual to Master Budget, Evergreen Company*

21–3

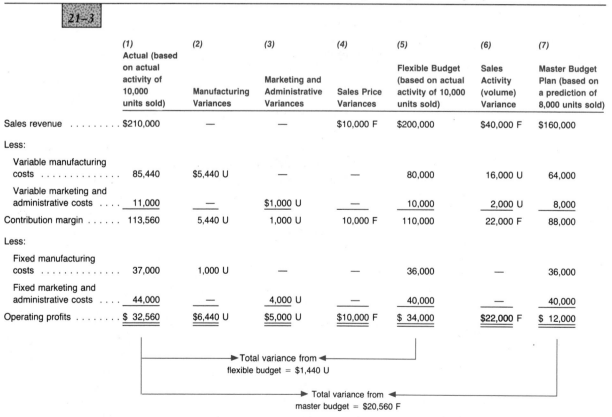

	(1) Actual (based on actual activity of 10,000 units sold)	(2) Manufacturing Variances	(3) Marketing and Administrative Variances	(4) Sales Price Variances	(5) Flexible Budget (based on actual activity of 10,000 units sold)	(6) Sales Activity (volume) Variance	(7) Master Budget Plan (based on a prediction of 8,000 units sold)
Sales revenue	$210,000	—	—	$10,000 F	$200,000	$40,000 F	$160,000
Less:							
Variable manufacturing costs	85,440	$5,440 U	—	—	80,000	16,000 U	64,000
Variable marketing and administrative costs	11,000	—	$1,000 U	—	10,000	2,000 U	8,000
Contribution margin	113,560	5,440 U	1,000 U	10,000 F	110,000	22,000 F	88,000
Less:							
Fixed manufacturing costs	37,000	1,000 U	—	—	36,000	—	36,000
Fixed marketing and administrative costs	44,000	—	4,000 U	—	40,000	—	40,000
Operating profits	$ 32,560	$6,440 U	$5,000 U	$10,000 F	$ 34,000	$22,000 F	$ 12,000

Total variance from flexible budget = $1,440 U

Total variance from master budget = $20,560 F

Market Share Variance and Industry Volume Variance

Managers frequently wonder *whether the sales activity variance is due to general market conditions or to a change in the company's market share.* For example, if sales at The Limited go down, is the decrease due to general market conditions? Or has The Limited's share of the market gone down? The cause may be significant because of promotional strategies and/or pricing policies. At Evergreen Company, for example, the marketing vice president wondered about the cause of the favorable activity variance of 2,000 units: "Our estimated share of the market was 20 percent. We projected industry sales of 40,000 crates, of which we would sell 8,000. We actually sold 10,000 crates. Was that because our share of the market went up from 20 percent to 25 percent (25% × 40,000 crates = 10,000 crates)? Or did we just hold our own at 20 percent, while the market increased to 50,000 crates (20% × 50,000 crates = 10,000 crates)?"

You can find numerous sources of data about industry volume (for example, trade journals, government census data). When these data are available, the activity variance could be divided into an industry volume variance and a market share variance. The **industry volume variance** tells how much of the sales activity variance is due to changes in industry volume. The **market share variance** tells how much of the activity is due to changes in market share. The market share variance is usually more controllable by the Marketing Department and is a measure of their performance.

Industry Volume Variance The portion of the sales activity variance due to changes in industry volume.

Market Share Variance The portion of the activity variance due to change in the company's proportion of sales in the markets in which the company operates.

The marketing vice president at Evergreen Company learned that the favorable sales activity resulted from an improvement in both industry volume and market share. Industry volume went up from 40,000 units to 41,667, while market share went up from 20 percent to 24 percent. Hence, the 2,000-unit favorable activity variance can be broken down into an industry effect and a market share effect, as shown in Illustration 21–4. Of the 2,000-unit increase in company volume, 333 crates, which is 20 percent of 1,667 units, is due to the increase in industry volume (holding market share constant), while 1,667 crates, which is 4 percent of 41,667 units, is due to an increased share of the market. Multiplying each figure by the *standard contribution margin* gives the impact of these variances on operating profits (amounts are rounded):

Industry volume: ($20 − $9) ×   333 crates = $ 3,663 F
Market share: ($20 − $9) × 1,667 crates = $18,337 F
Total activity: ($20 − $9) × 2,000 crates = $22,000 F

ILLUSTRATION

21–4

Industry Volume and Market Share Variances

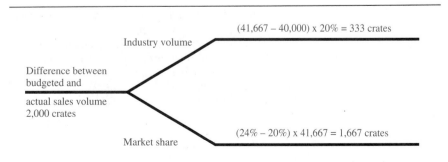

ILLUSTRATION

*Breakdown of Sales Activity Variance into Industry Volume
and Market Share Variances, Evergreen Company*

21–5

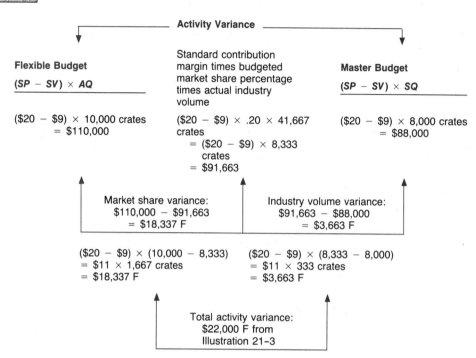

Calculation of these variances is also shown in Illustration 21–5.

Use of the industry volume and market share variances enables management to separate that portion of the activity variance that coincides with changes in the overall industry from that which is specific to the company. Favorable market share variances indicate that the company is achieving better than industry average volume changes. This can be very important information to marketing managers who are constantly concerned about their products' market share.

 Self-Study
Question

1 Insta-Pour Concrete, Inc., produces precast beams for highway and other bridge construction. The company's master budget called for sales of 20,000 beams, which would have been 16 percent of the market in their market area. The contribution margin on each beam is $215. During the year, 21,000 beams were sold. The company's market share had increased to 22 percent of the total market, but the total market was only 95,455 units.

Compute the industry volume and market share variances.

The solution to this question is at the end of this chapter on page 805.

EVALUATING PRODUCT MIX

Sales Mix Variance Variance arising from the relative proportion of different products sold.

A **sales mix variance** provides useful information when a company sells multiple products, and the products are substitutes. For example, an automobile dealer sells two kinds of cars: Super and Standard. For October, the estimated sales for the company were 1,000 cars: 500 Super models and 500 Standard models. The Super models were expected to have a contribution margin of $3,000 per car, while the Standard models were expected to have a contribution margin of $1,000 per car. Thus, the budgeted total contribution for October was:

```
Super: 500 at $3,000  . . . . . . . . $1,500,000
Standard: 500 at $1,000  . . . . . . .   500,000
            Total contribution . . . . . . . $2,000,000
```

When the results for October were tabulated, the company had sold 1,000 cars, and each model had provided the predicted contribution margin per unit. But the total contribution was a disappointing $1,400,000 because instead of the predicted 50–50 mix of cars sold, the mix was 20 percent Super and 80 percent Standard, with the following results:

```
Super: 200 at $3,000  . . . . . . . $  600,000
Standard: 800 at $1,000  . . . . . .   800,000
            Total contribution  . . . . . $1,400,000
```

The $600,000 decrease from the budgeted contribution margin is the *sales mix variance*. In this case, it occurred because 300 fewer Super models were sold (for a loss of 300 × $3,000 = $900,000), while 300 more Standard models were sold (for a gain of 300 × $1,000 = $300,000). The net effect is a loss of $2,000 in contribution margin for each Standard model that was sold instead of a Super model. (This emphasizes the importance of the substitutability assumption. If a store sells, among other things, jewelry and garden tractors, the mix variance would probably not be as useful as when comparing two products that are close substitutes.)

Sales Mix Variances

Assume Electron Company makes and sells two electronic games: Spacetrack and Earth Evaders. The estimated and actual results for the first quarter of the year were as follows:

	Spacetrack	Earth Evaders	Total
Standard sales price per unit	$20	$10	—
Actual sales price per unit	22	9	—
Standard variable cost per unit	10	5	—
Actual variable cost per unit	11	4.50	—
Estimated sales volume	120,000	80,000	200,000
Estimated sales activity percentage	60%	40%	100%
Actual sales volume	140,000	140,000	280,000
Actual sales activity percentage	50%	50%	100%

An analysis of contribution margin variances is shown in Illustration 21–6. This is the analysis that would be presented if the sales mix variance were ignored.

ILLUSTRATION   *Contribution Margin Variances, Electron Company (First Quarter)*

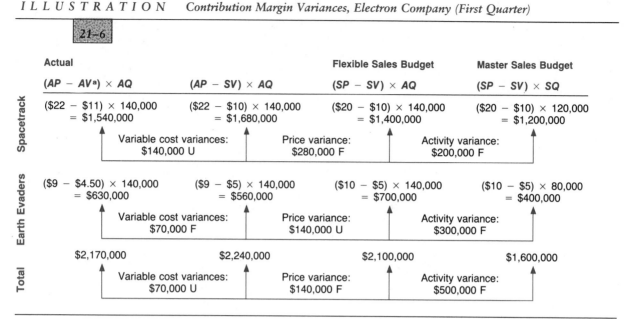

21–6

^a *AV* refers to actual variable cost.

There are many ways to calculate sales mix variances. Each starts with the same total variance between actual and master budget but then breaks it down in a different manner.

Our computation of the sales mix variances allows us to break down the sales activity variance into two components: sales mix and sales quantity. The *sales mix variance measures the impact of substitution* (it appears Earth Evaders has been substituted for Spacetrack), while the **sales quantity variance** *measures the variance in sales quantity, holding the sales mix constant.*

Calculations for this example are presented in Illustration 21–7. The sales price variance is unaffected by our analysis, while the sales activity variance is broken down into the mix and quantity variances.

Sales Quantity Variances In multiproduct companies, a variance arising from the change in volume of sales, independent of any change in mix.

Source of the Sales Mix Variance

While we have calculated each product mix variance to show exact sources, the *total* mix variance ($140,000 U) is most frequently used. In this example, the unfavorable mix variance is caused by the substitution of the lower-contribution Earth Evaders for the higher-contribution Spacetrack. To be precise, the substitutions are:

Decrease in Spacetrack	28,000 @ $10 =	$280,000 U
Increase in Earth Evaders	28,000 @ $ 5 =	140,000 F
Net effect in units	–0–	
Net effect in dollars		$140,000 U

The quantity variance results from the sale of 80,000 more units than expected. More precisely:

Spacetrack:	(168,000 − 120,000) × $10 =	$480,000 F
Earth Evaders:	(112,000 − 80,000) × $ 5 =	160,000 F
Total quantity variance:	80,000 units	$640,000 F

ILLUSTRATION

Sales Mix and Quantity Variances, Electron Company (First Quarter)

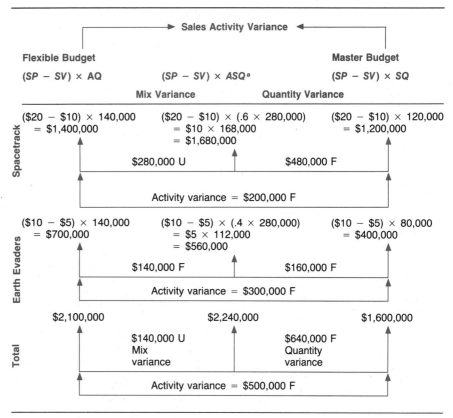

ᵃ *ASQ* = Quantity of units that would have been sold at the standard mix.

By separating the activity variance into its mix and quantity components, we have isolated the pure mix effect by holding constant the quantity effects, and we have isolated the pure quantity effect by holding constant the mix effect.

Self-Study Question

2 Assume that the master budget has sales of 1,200 units of product A and 800 units of product B. Actual sales volumes were 1,320 of product A and 780 of product B. The expected contribution per unit of product A was $1 ($4 price − $3 standard variable cost), and the expected contribution of product B was $3.50 ($6.50 price − $3 standard variable cost).

Compute the sales activity variances and further break them down into sales mix and quantity components.

The solution to this question is at the end of this chapter on page 806.

PRODUCTION MIX AND YIELD VARIANCES

Our analysis of mix and quantity variances for sales can also be applied to production. Often a mix of inputs is used in production. Chemicals, steel, fabrics, plastics, and many other products require a mix of direct materials, some of which can be substituted for each other without greatly affecting product quality.

Mix and Yield Variances in Service Organizations

Companies substitute different types of labor, too. Ernst and Young might substitute partner time for staff time on a particular audit job, for example.

Consider a consulting firm that has bid a job for 1,000 hours—300 hours of partner time at a cost of $60 per hour and 700 hours of staff time at a cost of $20 per hour. Due to scheduling problems, the partner spends 500 hours and the staff member spends 500 hours. If the actual costs are $60 and $20 for partner and staff time, respectively, then there is no labor price variance. But even though the 1,000 hours required were exactly what was bid, the job cost is $8,000 over budget, as shown below:

$$\text{Actual cost} = (500 \text{ hours} \times \$60) + (500 \text{ hours} \times \$20)$$
$$= \$30,000 + \$10,000$$
$$= \underline{\$40,000}$$

$$\text{Budgeted cost} = (300 \text{ hours} \times \$60) + (700 \text{ hours} \times \$20)$$
$$= \$18,000 + \$14,000$$
$$= \underline{\$32,000}$$

Production Mix Variance A variance that arises from a change in the relative proportion of inputs (a materials or labor mix variance).

The $8,000 over budget results from the substitution of 200 hours of partner time at $60 per hour for 200 hours of staff time at $20 per hour. The **production mix variance** is the difference in labor costs per hour ($60 − $20 = $40) times the number of hours substituted (200): $40 × 200 hours = $8,000.

Two factors are important when considering mix variances. First, there is an assumed *substitutability of inputs,* just as there was an assumed substitutability of sales products to make the sales mix variance meaningful. While partner time may have been substitutable for staff time, the reverse may not have been true. Second, the input costs must be different for a mix variance to exist. If the hourly costs of both partners and staff were the same, the substitution of hours would have no effect on the total cost of the job.

Mix and Yield Variances in Manufacturing

With the general concept in mind, we proceed with another example, using direct materials, which is a common application of mix variances in a production setting.

The Clean Chemical Company makes a product—XZ—that is made up of two direct materials. The standard costs and quantities are:

Direct Material	Standard Price per Pound	Standard Number of Pounds per Unit of Finished Product
X	$4	5
Z	8	5
		10

The standard cost per unit of finished product is:

X: 5 pounds @ $4 =	$20
Z: 5 pounds @ $8 =	40
Total	$60

During June, Clean Chemical had the following results:

Units produced . . . .   1,000 units of finished product

Materials purchased and used:

   Material X . . . .   4,400 pounds at $5

   Material Z . . . .   5,800 pounds at $8

                                                 10,200 pounds

Production Yield Variance Difference betweeen expected output from a given level of inputs and the actual output obtained from those inputs.

Our computation of the mix variance breaks down the direct materials efficiency variance into two components: mix and yield. The mix variance for costs is conceptually the same as the mix variance for sales, and the yield variance is conceptually the same as the sales quantity variance. The mix variance measures the impact of substitution (material Z appears to have been substituted for material X), while the **production yield variance** measures the input-output relationship holding the standard mix inputs constant. Standards called for 10,000 pounds of materials to produce 1,000 units of output; however, 10,200 pounds of input were actually used. The overuse of 200 pounds is a physical measure of the yield variance.

To derive mix and yield variances, we use the term *ASQ. ASQ is the actual amount of input used at the standard mix.*

Calculations for the three variances (price, mix, yield) for Clean Chemical are shown in Illustration 21–8. Note that the sum of the mix and yield variances equals the materials efficiency variance, which was discussed in Chapter 19. In examining these calculations, recall that the standard proportions (mix) of direct materials are X = 50 percent and Z = 50 percent, while 10,200 pounds were used in total. Thus, *ASQ* for each material is:

X : .5 × 10,200 pounds =   5,100 pounds

Z : .5 × 10,200 pounds =   5,100

                                   10,200

We have calculated the mix variance for each direct material to demonstrate its exact source. However, it is the *total* mix variance ($2,800 U) that is frequently used. In this example, the unfavorable mix is caused by a substitution of the more expensive direct material Z for the less expensive direct material X. To be precise, the substitutions are:

Decrease in X . . . .   700 pounds @ $4 = $2,800 decrease

Increase in Z . . . .   700 pounds @ $8 = $5,600 increase

Net effect in pounds . . . . . .   –0–

Net effect in dollars . . . . $2,800 increase

As previously indicated, the yield variance results from the overuse of 200 pounds. More precisely:

Material X: 100 pounds @ $4 = $ 400 U

Material Z: 100 pounds @ $8 =   800 U

      Totals 200 pounds $1,200 U

ILLUSTRATION   *Mix and Yield Variances, Clean Chemical*

21–8

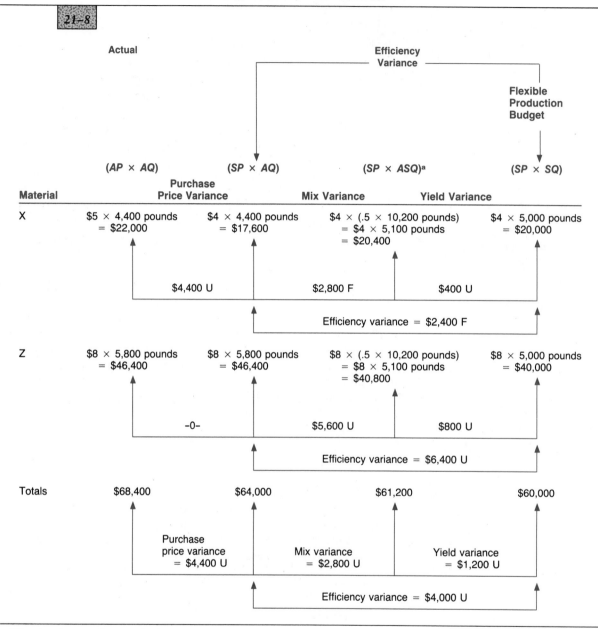

^a *ASQ* = Actual amount of input used at the standard mix.

By separating the efficiency variance into its mix and yield components, we have isolated the pure mix effect by holding constant the yield effect, and we have isolated the pure yield effect by holding constant the mix effect.

Self-Study
Question

3 Alexis Company makes a product, AL, from two materials: ST and EE. The standard prices and quantities are as follows:

	ST	EE
Price per pound	$2	$3
Pounds per unit of AL	10 pounds	5 pounds

In May, 7,000 units of AL were produced by Alexis Company, with the following actual prices and quantities of materials used:

	ST	EE
Price per pound	$1.90	$2.80
Pounds used	72,000	38,000

a. Compute materials price and efficiency variances.
b. Compute materials mix and yield variances.

The solution to this question is at the end of this chapter on page 806.

The solution to this question is at the end of this chapter on page 806.

SUMMARY

Contribution margin variances explain the impact of differences between budgeted and actual sales activity and price. Sales activity variances may be further analyzed as to the effects of changes in market share or industrywide volume factors. If several products are sold, the sales activity variance may be subdivided into quantity and sales mix variances.

Mix and yield variances can also be prepared for production costs where multiple inputs are used. In these cases, the efficiency variance is divided into mix and yield variances.

TERMS AND CONCEPTS

The following terms and concepts should be familiar to you after reading this chapter:

Contribution Margin Variance, *784*
Gross Margin Variance, *785*
Industry Volume Variance, *787*
Market Share Variance, *787*
Production Mix Variance, *792*
Production Yield Variance, *793*
Sales Activity Variance, *784*
Sales Mix Variance, *789*
Sales Price Variance, *784*
Sales Quantity Variance, *790*

QUESTIONS

21–1   We normally deduct standard costs from the actual revenues when analyzing revenue variances. Why not use actual costs and actual revenues?

21–2   Why is there no efficiency variance for revenues?

21–3   The marketing manager of a company noted: "We had a favorable revenue variance of $425,000, yet company profits only went up by $114,000. Some part of the organization has dropped the ball—let's find out where the problem is and straighten it out." Comment on this remark.

21-4   A production manager was debating with company management because production had been charged with a large unfavorable production volume variance. The production manager explained: "After all, if marketing had lined up sales for these units we would not have been forced to cut production. Marketing should be charged with the production volume variance, not production." Do you agree with the production manager? Why or why not?

21-5   What information does the computation of an industry volume variance provide?

21-6   If the activity variance is zero, could there be any reason to compute a mix variance?

21-7   How could a CPA firm use the mix variance to analyze its revenues?

21-8 . How could a CPA firm use the mix variances to analyze salary costs regarding audit services?

21-9   A company has three products that must be purchased in a single package. Is there any benefit to computing a sales mix variance under these circumstances?

21-10   Give examples of companies that probably use materials mix and yield variances.

EXERCISES

21-11   Sales Price and Activity Variances
(L.O.1)

Wavesport, Inc., manufactures and sells beach towels. The business is very competitive. The master budget for the last year called for sales of 200,000 units at $9 each. However, as the summer season approached, management realized that they could not sell 200,000 units at the $9 price. Rather, they would have to offer price concessions. Budgeted variable cost is $3.65 per unit. Actual results showed sales of 190,000 units at an average price of $8.50 each.

Required:
Compute sales price and activity variances for Wavesport.

21-12   Sales Price and Activity Variances
(L.O.1)

Wavesport is trying to decide what to do in the coming year, given the events that transpired last year (see exercise 21-11). Management conducted a marketing survey, which indicated that the company had two sales alternatives:

1.   Sell 220,000 units at $8 each.

2.   Sell 185,000 units at $9 each.

The company has actual and standard variable costs of $3.95 per unit.

Required:
Compare the two alternatives and show the effect of activity and price differences between the two alternatives. Treat alternative 2 as "master budget" and the other as "actual."

21-13   Sales Price and Activity Variances
(L.O.1)

Flavor-Rite, Inc., makes bulk artificial seasonings for use in processed foods. A seasoning was budgeted to sell in 20-liter drums at a price of $48 per drum. The company expected to sell 150,000 drums. Budgeted variable costs are $10 per drum.
    During the year, 125,000 drums were sold at a price of $47.

Required:
Compute sales price and activity variances.

21-14   Industry Volume and Market Share Variances
(L.O.2)

Refer to the data in exercise 21-13. Assume that the budgeted sales volume was based on an expected 10 percent of a total market volume of 1.5 million drums, but the actual results were based on a 12.5 percent share of a total market of 1 million drums.

Required: Compute market share and industry volume variances.

21–15 Industry Volume and Market Share Variances (L.O.2)

Sakata Products budgeted sales of 20,000 units of product B, assuming the company would have 20 percent of 100,000 units sold in a particular market. The actual results were 18,000 units, based on a 15 percent share of a total market of 120,000 units. The budgeted contribution margin is $3 per unit.

Required: Compute the sales activity variance and break it down into market share and industry volume.

21–16 Industry Volume and Market Share Variances— Missing Data (L.O.2)

The following graph is like the one presented in Illustration 21–4 in the chapter. Actual sales volume for the firm exceeds its estimated sales volume.

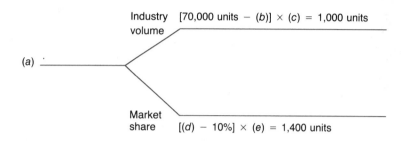

Industry volume   [70,000 units − (b)] × (c) = 1,000 units

(a)

Market share   [(d) − 10%] × (e) = 1,400 units

Required: Find the missing amounts:

a. Budgeted minus actual sales volume.

b. Estimated industry volume.

c. Estimated market share percent.

d. Actual market share percent.

e. Actual industry volume.

21–17 Sales Price and Activity Variances (L.O.1)

Dutton, Harbaugh & Smith operate a law firm with partners and staff members. Each billable hour of partner time has a budgeted price of $275 and budgeted variable cost of $130. Each billable hour of staff time has a budgeted price of $65 and budgeted variable cost of $35. This month, the partnership budget called for 8,500 billable partner-hours and 34,650 staff-hours. Actual results were as follows:

Partner revenue: . . . . . . $2,150,000   8,000 hours

Staff revenue: 2,225,000   34,000 hours

Required: Compute the sales price and activity variances for these data.

21–18 Sales Mix and Quantity Variances (L.O.3)

Refer to the data in exercise 21–17. Compute the sales mix and quantity variances.

21–19 Sales Mix and Quantity Variances (L.O.3)

Sure-grip Corporation sells two models of golfing gloves. The Basic model has a price of $10.95 per unit, while the Ultra model has a price of $24.95 per unit. The master budget called for sales of 400,000 Basics and 180,000 Ultras during the current year. Actual results showed sales of 300,000 Basics, with a price of $11.29 per unit, and 200,000 Ultras, with a price of $25.39 per unit. The standard variable cost is $5 per unit for a Basic and $10 per unit for Ultras.

Required: a. Compute the activity variance for these data.

b. Break down the activity variance into mix and quantity parts.

21–20 Materials Mix and Yield Variances (L.O.4)

Allentown Alloys had the following direct materials data for its product:

Standard costs for one unit of output:

Material A, 10 units of input at $100

Material B, 20 units of input at $150

During August, the company had the following results:

Units of output produced . . . .   2,000 units

Materials purchased and used:
    Material A . . . . 22,000 units at $94
    Material B . . . . 38,000 units at $152

Required:

a. Compute materials price and efficiency variances.

b. Compute materials mix and yield variances.

21–21   Labor Mix and Yield Variances
(L.O.4)

Taco Time has two categories of direct labor: unskilled, which costs $6.50 per hour, and skilled, which costs $10.30 per hour. Management has established standards per "equivalent meal," which has been defined as a typical meal consisting of a taco, a drink, and a side order. Standards have been set as follows:

Skilled labor . . . .   4 minutes per equivalent meal
Unskilled labor . . . . . . 10 minutes per equivalent meal

During May, Taco Time sold 30,000 equivalent meals and incurred the following labor costs:

Skilled labor . . . . 1,800 hours $17,500
Unskilled labor . . . . . . 4,600 hours   33,000

Required:

a. Compute labor price and efficiency variances.

b. Compute labor mix and yield variances.

PROBLEMS

21–22   Sales Price, Industry Volume, and Mix Variances

Oversea Airlines plans its budget and subsequently evaluates sales performance based on passenger-miles. A passenger-mile is one paying passenger flying one mile. For this month, the company estimated its contribution margin would amount to 20 cents per passenger-mile and that 40 million passenger-miles would be flown.

As a result of improvement in the economy, 43 million passenger-miles were flown this month. The price per passenger-mile averaged 30.3 cents. The budgeted variable cost per mile was 10 cents. Subsequent analysis by management indicated that the industry flew 7 percent more passenger-miles this month than expected.

Required:

Compute the price, industry volume, and market share effects on company revenues for the month.

21–23   Revenue Analysis Using Industry Data and Multiple Product Lines

Arsco Company makes three grades of indoor-outdoor carpets. Sales volume for the annual budget is determined by estimating the total market volume for indoor-outdoor carpet and then applying the company's prior year market share, adjusted for planned changes due to company programs for the coming year. Volume is apportioned between the three grades based upon the prior year's product mix, again adjusted for planned changes due to company programs for the coming year.

Given below are the company budget and the results of operations for March.

Budget	Grade 1	Grade 2	Grade 3	Total
Sales—units (in thousands)	1,000 rolls	1,000 rolls	2,000 rolls	4,000 rolls
Sales—dollars (in thousands)	$1,000	$2,000	$3,000	$6,000
Variable costs	700	1,600	2,300	4,600
Contribution margin	300	400	700	1,400
Manufacturing fixed cost	200	200	300	700
Product margin	$ 100	$ 200	$ 400	700
Marketing and administrative costs (all fixed)				250
Operating profit				$ 450

Actual	Grade 1	Grade 2	Grade 3	Total
Sales—units (in thousands)	800 rolls	1,000 rolls	2,100 rolls	3,900 rolls
Sales—dollars (in thousands)	$ 810	$2,000	$3,000	$5,810
Variable costs	560	1,610	2,320	4,490
Contribution margin	250	390	680	1,320
Manufacturing fixed cost	210	220	315	745
Product margin	$ 40	$ 170	$ 365	575
Marketing and administrative costs (all fixed)				275
Operating profit				$ 300

Industry volume was estimated at 40,000 rolls for budgeting purposes. Actual industry volume for March was 38,000 rolls.

Required:

a. Prepare an analysis to show the effects of the sales price and sales activity variances.

b. Break down the sales activity variance into the parts caused by industry volume and market share.

(CMA adapted)

21–24 Sales Mix and Quantity Variances

Refer to the data for the Arsco Company (problem 21–23). Break down the total activity variance into sales mix and quantity parts.

21–25 Contribution Margin Variances

Markley Division of Rosette Industries manufactures and sells patio chairs. The chairs are manufactured in two versions—a metal model and a plastic model of a lower quality. The company uses its own marketing force to sell the chairs.

The chairs are manufactured on two different assembly lines located in adjoining buildings. Division management and the Marketing Department occupy the third building on the property. Division management includes a division controller responsible for divisional financial activities and preparation of variance reports. The controller structures these reports such that the marketing activities are distinguished from cost factors so that each can be analyzed separately.

The operating results and the related master budget for the first three months of the fiscal year follow. The budget for the current year assumes Markley Division will maintain its present market share of the estimated total patio chair market (plastic and metal combined). A status report was sent to corporate management toward the end of the second month indicating that divisional operating profit for the first quarter would probably be about 45 percent below budget; this estimate was just about on target. The division's operating income was below budget even though industry volume for patio chairs increased by 10 percent more than was expected when the budget was developed.

	Actual	Budget	Favorable (Unfavorable) Relative to the Budget
Sales in units:			
Plastic model	60,000	50,000	10,000
Metal model	20,000	25,000	(5,000)
Sales revenue:			
Plastic model	$630,000	$500,000	$130,000
Metal model	300,000	375,000	(75,000)
Total sales	930,000	875,000	55,000
Less variable costs:			
Manufacturing (at standard):			
Plastic model	480,000	400,000	(80,000)
Metal model	200,000	250,000	50,000
Marketing:			
Commissions	46,500	43,750	(2,750)
Bad debt allowance	9,300	8,750	(550)
Total variable costs (except variable manufacturing variances)	735,800	702,500	(33,300)
Contribution margin (except variable manufacturing variances)	194,200	172,500	21,700
Less other costs:			
Variable manufacturing cost variances from standards	49,600	—	(49,600)
Fixed manufacturing costs	49,200	48,000	(1,200)
Fixed marketing administrative costs	38,500	36,000	(2,500)
Corporation offices allocation	18,500	17,500	(1,000)
Total other costs	155,800	101,500	(54,300)
Divisional operating profit	$ 38,400	$ 71,000	$(32,600)

During the quarter, the company produced 55,000 plastic chairs and 22,500 metal chairs. The costs incurred by each manufacturing unit are presented below.

	Quantity	Price	Plastic Model	Metal Model
Direct materials (stated in equivalent finished chairs):				
Purchases:				
Plastic	60,000	$5.65	$339,000	
Metal	30,000	6.00		$180,000
Usage:				
Plastic	56,000	5.00	280,000	
Metal	23,000	6.00		138,000

	Quantity	Price	Plastic Model	Metal Model
Direct labor:				
9,300 hours at $6 per hour			$ 55,800	
5,600 hours at $8 per hour				$ 44,800
Manufacturing overhead:				
Variable:				
Supplies			43,000	18,000
Power			50,000	15,000
Employee benefits			19,000	12,000
Fixed:				
Supervision			14,000	11,000
Depreciation			12,000	9,000
Property taxes and other items . . .			1,900	1,300

Standard variable manufacturing costs per unit and budgeted monthly fixed manufacturing costs for the current year are presented below.

	Plastic Model	Metal Model
Direct material	$ 5.00	$ 6.00
Direct labor:		
$1/6$ hour at $6 per direct labor-hour	1.00	
$1/4$ hour at $8 per direct labor-hour		2.00
Variable overhead:		
$1/6$ hour at $12 per direct labor-hour	2.00	
$1/4$ hour at $8 per direct labor-hour		2.00
Standard variable manufacturing cost per unit	$ 8.00	$10.00
Budgeted fixed costs per month:		
Supervision	$4,500	$3,500
Depreciation	4,000	3,000
Property taxes and other items	600	400
Total budgeted fixed costs for month	$9,100	$6,900

Variable marketing costs are budgeted to be 6 percent of sales-dollars.

Required: Compute Markley Division's sales price, mix, and quantity variances.

(CMA adapted)

21–26 Analyze Industry Effects on Contribution Margins   Refer to the data for the Markley Division (problem 21–25). Analyze the extent to which the activity variance can be explained in terms of industry and market share effects.

21–27 Sales Price, Mix, and Quantity Variances

The following information has been prepared by a member of the controller's staff of Duo, Inc.:

DUO, INC.
Income Statement
For the Year Ended December 31,
(in thousands)

	Product AR-10		Product ZR-7		Total	
	Budget	Actual	Budget	Actual	Budget	Actual
Unit sales	2,000	2,800	6,000	5,600	8,000	8,400
Sales	$6,000	$7,560	$12,000	$11,760	$18,000	$19,320
Variable costs	2,400	2,800	6,000	5,880	8,400	8,680
Fixed costs	1,800	1,900	2,400	2,400	4,200	4,300
Total costs	4,200	4,700	8,400	8,280	12,600	12,980
Operating profit	$1,800	$2,860	$ 3,600	$ 3,480	$ 5,400	$ 6,340

Required:

Analyze the above data to show the impact of price, quantity, and sales mix variances on operating profit.

(CMA adapted)

21–28 Materials Mix and Yield Variances

LAR Chemical Company manufactures a wide variety of chemical compounds and liquids for industrial uses. The standard mix for producing a single batch of 500 gallons of one liquid is as follows:

Liquid Chemical	Quantity (in gallons)	Cost (per gallon)	Total Cost
Maxan	100	$2.00	$200
Salex	300	.75	225
Cralyn	225	1.00	225
	625		$650

There is a 20 percent loss in liquid volume during processing due to evaporation. The finished liquid is put into 10-gallon bottles for sale. Thus, the standard material cost for a 10-gallon bottle is $13.

The actual quantities of direct materials and the cost of the materials placed in production during November were as follows (materials are purchased and used at the same time):

Liquid Chemical	Quantity (in gallons)	Total Cost
Maxan	8,480	$17,384
Salex	25,200	17,640
Cralyn	18,540	16,686
	52,220	$51,710

A total of 4,000 bottles (40,000 gallons) were produced during November.

Required:

Calculate the total direct material variance for the liquid product for the month of November and then further analyze the total variance into:

a. Materials price and efficiency variances.

b. Materials mix and yield variances.

21–29 Labor Mix and Yield Variances

Piece O' Rock Insurance Company compares actual results with a flexible budget. The standard direct labor rates used in the flexible budget are established each year at the time the annual plan is formulated and held constant for the entire year.

The standard direct labor rates in effect for the current fiscal year and the standard hours allowed for the actual output of insurance claims for the month of April in a claims department are shown in the schedule below:

	Standard Direct Labor Rate per Hour	Standard Direct Labor-Hours Allowed for Output
Labor class III	$8	500
Labor class II	7	500
Labor class I	5	500

The wage rates for each labor class increased under the terms of a new contract. The standard wage rates were not revised to reflect the new contract.

The actual direct labor-hours worked and the actual direct labor rates per hour experienced for the month of April were as follows:

	Actual Direct Labor Rate per Hour	Actual Direct Labor-Hours
Labor class III	$8.50	550
Labor class II	7.50	650
Labor class I	5.40	375

Required:

Calculate the dollar amount of the total direct labor variance for the month of April for Piece O' Rock Insurance Company and break down the total variance into the following components:

a. Direct labor price and efficiency variances.

b. Direct labor mix and yield variances.

(CMA adapted)

INTEGRATIVE CASES

21–30 Comprehensive Review of Variances, Mix Variances, Analysis of Differences between Budget and Actual

Sip-Fizz Bottling Company prepared a sales and production budget for the 48-ounce bottle, 12-ounce can, and 10-ounce bottle units that the company produces and sells. Unit variable costs per case of soda are calculated as follows:

	Per Case Costs		
Ingredient	48 Ounce	12 Ounce	10 Ounce
Syrup	$1.45	$1.00	$ .80
CO_2 gas	.02	.01	.01
Crown	.04	—	.04
Bottle	1.40		.30
Can		1.64	
Label	.07		
Total manufacturing cost	2.98	2.65	1.15
Sales commission	.08	.14	.09
Advertising allowance	.08	.08	.08
Unit variable cost	$3.14	$2.87	$1.32

The advertising allowance is based on the number of cases sold. The selling price for the 48-ounce case is $5.40; for the 12-ounce case, $4.35; and for the 10-ounce case, $2.80. Sales for the month of November were forecasted at 70,000 cases of the 48-ounce bottles, 60,000 cases of 12-ounce cans, and 110,000 cases of 10-ounce bottles. Fixed costs were estimated at $175,000.

During November, actual sales amounted to 80,000 cases of 48-ounce bottles, 50,000 cases of 12-ounce cans, and 120,000 cases of 10-ounce bottles. Actual and budgeted selling prices were equal. Syrup costs were 10 percent greater than expected, but all other costs were at the same per unit amounts as indicated above. Total fixed costs, which are all other costs not explicitly identified above, amounted to $182,000.

The company uses variable costing for internal reporting purposes. There were no beginning and ending inventories.

Required:

a. Determine the budgeted and actual operating profits.

b. Explain the difference between the budgeted and actual net operating profits in as much detail as possible.

21–31 Dallas Consulting Group (Relate Activity Changes to Industry Effects)[1]

"I just don't understand why you're worried about analyzing our profit variance," said Dave Lundberg to his partner, Adam Dixon. Both Lundberg and Dixon were partners in the Dallas Consulting Group (DCG). "Look, we made $40,000 more profit than we expected (see Exhibit 21–31A). That's great as far as I am concerned," continued Lundberg. Adam Dixon agreed to come up with data that will help sort out the causes of DCG's $40,000 profit variance.

DCG was a professional services partnership of three established consultants who specialize in cost reduction through the use of time-motion studies and through the streamlining of production operations by optimizing physical layout, labor, and so on. In both of these areas, DCG consultants spend a great deal of time studying customers' operations.

The three partners each received fixed salaries that represented the largest portion of operating expenses. Each partner had an independent office and accounted for office costs separately. DCG itself had only a post office box. All other DCG employees were also paid fixed salaries. No other significant operating costs were incurred by the partnership.

Revenues consisted solely of professional fees charged to customers for the two different types of services. Charges were based on the number of hours actually worked on a job. Thus, an increase in the actual number of hours worked on a job caused a corresponding increase in revenue. Since all salaries are fixed, however, DCG's total operating expenses do not change.

[1] Adapted from R. Anthony, G. Welsch, and J. Reece, *Fundamentals of Management Accounting,* 4th ed. (Homewood, Ill.: Richard D. Irwin, 1985).

E X H I B I T

21-31A

Budget and Actual Results

	Budget	Actual	Variance
Sales revenues	$630,000	$670,000	$40,000
Expenses:			
Salaries	460,000	460,000	—
Income	$170,000	$210,000	$40,000

EXHIBIT

21–31B

Detail of Revenue Calculations

Service[a]	Hours	Rate	Amount
Budget:			
A	6,000	$30	$180,000
B	9,000	50	450,000
	15,000		$630,000
Actual:			
A	2,000	$35	$ 70,000
B	12,000	50	600,000
	14,000		$670,000

[a] Service A = Time-motion studies. Service B = Consulting for production operations.

Following the conversation with Lundberg, Dixon gathered the data summarized in Exhibit 21–31B . He took the data with him to Lundberg's office and said, "I think I can identify several reasons for our increased profits. First of all, we raised the price for time-motion studies to $35 per hour. Also, if you remember, we originally estimated that the 10 consulting firms in the Dallas area would probably average about 15,000 hours of work each this year, so the total industry volume in Dallas would be 150,000 hours. However, a check with all of the local consulting firms indicates that the actual total consulting market must have been around 112,000 hours."

"This is indeed interesting, Adam," replied Lundberg. "These new data lead me to believe that there are several causes for our increased profits, some of which may have been negative. . . . Do you think you could quantify the effects of these factors in terms of dollars?"

Required:

Use your knowledge of profit variance analysis to quantify this year's performance of DCG and explain the significance of each variance to Mr. Lundberg.

SOLUTIONS TO

Self-Study Question

1

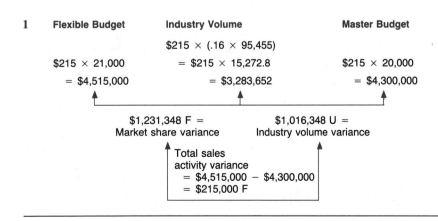

Flexible Budget	Industry Volume	Master Budget
	$215 × (.16 × 95,455)	
$215 × 21,000	= $215 × 15,272.8	$215 × 20,000
= $4,515,000	= $3,283,652	= $4,300,000

$1,231,348 F =
Market share variance

$1,016,348 U =
Industry volume variance

Total sales
activity variance
= $4,515,000 − $4,300,000
= $215,000 F

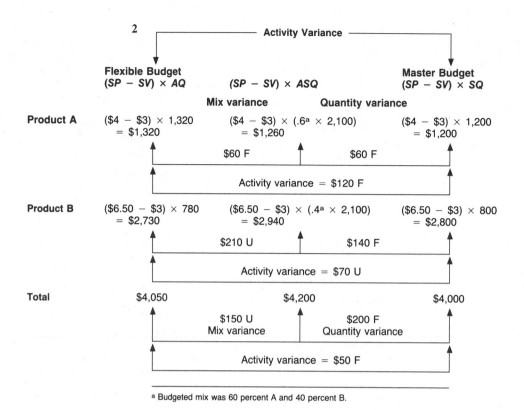

a Budgeted mix was 60 percent A and 40 percent B.

3   *a.*   Price and efficiency variances:

	Actual (*AP* × *AQ*)	Inputs at Standard Prices (*SP* × *AQ*)	Flexible Production Budget (*SP* × *SQ*)
ST	($1.90 × 72,000)	($2 × 72,000)	($2 × 70,000a)
EE	+ ($2.80 × 38,000)	+ ($3 × 38,000)	+ ($3 × 35,000b)
Total	= $243,200	= $258,000	= $245,000

Price variance: Efficiency variance:
$14,800 F $13,000 U

a 70,000 pounds = 7,000 units × 10 pounds per unit.
b 35,000 pounds = 7,000 units × 5 pounds per unit.

b. Mix and yield variances:

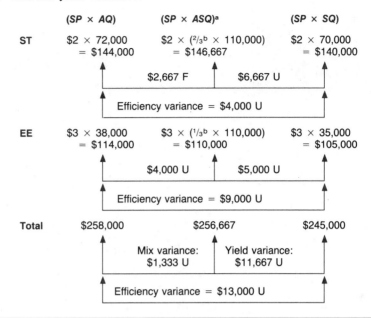

	(SP × AQ)	**(SP × ASQ)[a]**	**(SP × SQ)**
ST	$2 × 72,000 = $144,000	$2 × (²/₃[b] × 110,000) = $146,667	$2 × 70,000 = $140,000
		$2,667 F $6,667 U	
		Efficiency variance = $4,000 U	
EE	$3 × 38,000 = $114,000	$3 × (¹/₃[b] × 110,000) = $110,000	$3 × 35,000 = $105,000
		$4,000 U $5,000 U	
		Efficiency variance = $9,000 U	
Total	$258,000	$256,667	$245,000
		Mix variance: $1,333 U Yield variance: $11,667 U	
		Efficiency variance = $13,000 U	

[a] *ASQ* = Actual amount of the input used at the standard mix.

[b] Mix percentage ratio of ST pounds to total and EE pounds to total. For ST, $\frac{10}{10+5} = \frac{2}{3}$. For EE, $\frac{5}{10+5} = \frac{1}{3}$.

Decentralization and Performance Evaluation

LEARNING OBJECTIVES

After reading this chapter, you should be able to:

1. Explain the role of accounting in measuring performance in decentralized organizations.
2. Identify the advantages and disadvantages of decentralization.
3. Explain the relation between organizational structure and responsibility centers.
4. Interpret and use return on investment (ROI) and residual income (RI).
5. Explain how historical cost and net book value–based accounting measures can be misleading in evaluating performance.
6. Compare return on investment (ROI) measures using current values to ROI measures using historical costs.
7. Explain how decisions using discounted cash flow criteria may not appear to perform well in the short run using accounting measures.

*T*he manager's task grows increasingly difficult as organizations become large and complex. A common rule of thumb is that one supervisor can usually manage about 10 subordinates. Consequently, managerial duties are delegated in all but very small organizations.

Accounting plays an important role in evaluating the performance of those who have been delegated responsibility. The use of accounting for performance evaluation is often called **responsibility accounting.**

Responsibility Accounting A system of reporting tailored to an organizational structure so that costs and revenues are reported at the level having the related responsibility within the organization.

Budgeting and variance analysis, as discussed in Chapters 17 through 21, are part of the responsibility accounting process. In this and the next chapter, we discuss the costs and benefits of decentralization, the structure of organizational units, and the accounting measures used to evaluate the performance of organizational units and their managers.

CONCEPTUAL FRAMEWORK

Principal-Agent Relationship
The relationship between a superior referred to as the *principal,* and a subordinate, called the *agent.*

When authority is decentralized, a superior, whom we call a *principal,* delegates duties to a subordinate, whom we call an *agent.* We find **principal-agent relationships** in many settings, including:

Principals	Agents
Stockholders of General Motors	Top management of General Motors
Corporate (top) managers of General Motors	Divisional managers of the Oldsmobile Division, Saturn Division, etc.
Yellow Cab Company manager	Taxicab drivers
Macy's retail store manager	Department managers of the Children's Clothing Department, Women's Shoes, etc.

Many aspects of both financial and managerial accounting have been developed to measure agents' (that is, subordinates') performance. There is a common saying in business: "What gets noticed is what gets measured." This saying means if employers want their employees to focus on profits, then profits must be measured, and reported for the employees' work. Accounting information is used in employment contracts. Employee commissions and bonuses are often based on accounting performance measures.

Goal Congruence

Goal Congruence When all members of a group hold a common set of objectives.

Total **goal congruence** exists when all members of an organization have incentives to perform in the common interest. This occurs when the group acts as a team in pursuit of a mutually agreed upon objective. Individual goal congruence occurs when an individual's personal goals are congruent with organizational goals.

While total congruence is rare, there are cases in which a strong team spirit suppresses individual desires to act differently. Examples include some military units and some athletic teams. Many companies attempt to achieve this esprit de corps. Japanese companies have worked particularly hard to create a strong team orientation among workers that has resulted in considerable goal congruence.

In most business settings, however, personal goals and organizational goals differ. Performance evaluation and incentive systems are designed to encourage employees to *behave* as if their goals were congruent with organizational goals. This results in **behavioral congruence:** that is, an individual *behaves* in the best interests of the organization, regardless of his or her own goals.

Behavioral Congruence When individuals behave in the best interest of the organization regardless of their own goals.

You have experienced behavioral congruence in your education. Examinations, homework, and the entire grading process are parts of a performance evaluation and incentive system that encourages students to behave in a certain manner. Sometimes the system appears to encourage the wrong kind of behavior, however. For example, if the goal of education is to encourage students to learn, they might be better off taking very difficult courses. But if students' grades suffer when they take difficult courses, they may have an incentive to take easier courses. As a result, some students take difficult courses and learn more, while others take easier courses in an attempt to maximize their grade point averages.

Problems of this kind occur in all organizations. Consider the case of a plant manager who believes that a promotion and bonus will result from high plant operating profits. Short-run profits will be lowered if the production line is closed for much-needed maintenance, but the company may be better off in the long run. The manager must decide between doing what makes the manager look good in the short run and doing what is in the best interest of the company.

Although such conflicts cannot be totally removed, if they are recognized, they can be minimized. To deal with the problem described above, some companies budget maintenance separately. Others encourage employees to take a long-run interest in the company through stock-option and pension plans that are tied to long-run performance. Still others retain employees in a position long enough that any short-term counterproductive actions will catch up with them.

Moral

Managers must address two basic questions when thinking about their performance evaluation systems:

1. What behavior *does* the system motivate?
2. What behavior *should* the system motivate?

As we go about daily life, we see many instances where the performance evaluation system does not create the right incentives because managers have not satisfactorily addressed these two questions. We also see many cases where people work hard and make the right decisions despite the lack of explicit rewards. Ideally, organizational managers will design performance evaluation systems so people are rewarded when they do the right thing. At least, managers should design systems so people are not *punished* when they do the right thing.

ORGANIZATIONAL STRUCTURE

Centralized Refers to those organizations where decisions are made by a relatively few individuals in the high ranks of the organization.

Decentralized Refers to those organizations where decisions are spread among relatively many divisional and departmental managers.

Some organizations are very **centralized**: decisions are handed down from the top, and subordinates carry them out. The military is a good example of centralized authority. At the other extreme are highly **decentralized** companies in which decisions are made at divisional and departmental levels. In many conglomerates, operating decisions are made in the field, while corporate headquarters is, in effect, a holding company.

The majority of companies fall between these two extremes. At General Motors, for example, operating units are decentralized, while the research and development and finance functions are centralized.

Many companies begin with a centralized structure but become more and more decentralized as they grow. Consider the following example of a fast-food franchise that started with one hamburger stand.[1]

> We had a counter and 10 stools when we started. When winter came, we had to take out two stools to put in a heating furnace and almost went broke from the loss of revenue! But during the following year, I obtained the statewide franchise for a nationally known barbecue chain, and I expanded my menu.
>
> At first, I did a little of everything—cooking, serving, bookkeeping, and advertising. I hired one full-time employee. There was little need for any formal management control system—I made all important decisions, and they were carried out. Soon we had eight outlets. I was still trying to manage everything personally. Decisions were delayed. A particular outlet would receive food shipments, but no one was authorized to accept delivery. If an outlet ran out of

---

[1] This example is based on the actual experience of a small company.

supplies or change, its employees had to wait until I arrived to authorize whatever needed to be done. With only one outlet, I was able to spend a reasonable amount of time on what I call high-level decision making—planning for expansion, arranging financing, developing new marketing strategies, and so forth. But with eight outlets, all of my time was consumed with day-to-day operating decisions.

Finally, I realized that the company had grown too big for me to manage alone. So, I decentralized, setting up each outlet just like it was an independent operation. Now each outlet manager takes care of day-to-day operating decisions. Not only has this freed my time for more high-level decision making, but it also provides a better opportunity for the managers to learn about management, and it gives me a chance to evaluate their performance for promotion to higher management positions, which I intend to create soon.

Advantages of Decentralization

The larger and more complex an organization is, the greater the advantages of decentralization are. Some advantages of decentralization include:

1. *Faster response*. As described by the owner-manager of the fast-food chain, local managers can react to a changing environment more quickly than can top management. With centralized decision making, delays occur while information is transmitted to decision makers, and further delays occur while instructions are communicated to local managers.

2. *Wiser use of management's time*. The owner-manager of the fast-food chain complained that there was too little time for high-level decision making. Top management usually has a comparative advantage over middle management in this area. If their time is consumed by day-to-day operating decisions, they will be forced to ignore important strategic decisions. Furthermore, local managers may be able to make better operating decisions because of their technical expertise and knowledge about local conditions.

3. *Reduction of problems to manageable size*. There are limits to the complexity of problems that humans can solve. Even with the aid of computers, some problems are too complex to be solved by central management. By dividing large problems into smaller, more manageable parts, decentralization reduces the complexity of problems.

4. *Training, evaluation, and motivation of local managers*. By decentralizing, managers receive on-the-job training in decision making. Top management can observe the outcome of local managers' decisions and evaluate their potential for advancement. By practicing with small decisions, managers learn how to make big decisions. Finally, ambitious managers are likely to be frustrated if they only implement the decisions of others and never have the satisfaction of making their own decisions and carrying them out. This satisfaction can be an important motivational reward for managers.

Disadvantages of Decentralization

While there are many advantages of decentralization, there are also disadvantages. The major disadvantage is that local managers may make decisions that are not congruent with the preferences of top management and constituents of the organization (such as stockholders). Thus, decentralized companies incur the cost of monitoring and controlling the activities of local managers. They incur the costs that result when local managers make decisions and take actions that are not in the best interest of the organization and are missed by the monitoring system.

A company must weigh the costs and benefits and decide on an economically optimal level of decentralization. One can assume that for organizations that are highly centralized, the disadvantages of decentralization outweigh the advantages, while the reverse is true for companies that are decentralized.

ORGANIZATION OF DECENTRALIZED UNITS

There are five basic kinds of decentralized units: cost centers, discretionary cost centers, revenue centers, profit centers, and investment centers. (A *center* is just a responsibility unit in an organization, such as a department in a store or a division of a company.)

Cost Centers

Cost Centers Organization subunits responsible only for costs.

In **cost centers,** managers are responsible for the cost of an activity for which there is a well-defined relationship between inputs and outputs. Cost centers are often found in manufacturing operations where inputs, such as direct materials and direct labor, can be specified for each output. The production departments of manufacturing plants are examples of cost centers. But the concept has been applied in nonmanufacturing settings too. In banks, for example, standards can be established for check processing, so check-processing departments might be cost centers. In hospitals, food services departments, laundries, and laboratories are often set up as cost centers.

Managers of cost centers are held responsible for the costs and volumes of inputs used to produce an output. Often these costs and volumes will be determined by someone other than the cost center manager, such as the marketplace, top management, or the Marketing Department. A plant manager is often given a production schedule to meet as efficiently as possible. If the plant is operated as a cost center, manufacturing cost variances like those discussed in Chapter 19 are typically used to help measure performance. (Illustration 22–1 shows how the cost center typically appears on the organization chart.)

Standard Cost Center An organization subunit where managers are held responsible for costs and where the relationship between costs and output is well defined.

If the relationship between costs and outputs can be specified, the unit is called a **standard cost center.**

Discretionary Cost Centers

Discretionary Cost Center An organization subunit where managers are held responsible for costs, but the relationship between costs and outputs is not well established.

The cost centers described above require a well-specified relationship between inputs and outputs for performance evaluation. When managers are held responsible for costs, but the input-output relationship is not well specified, a **discretionary cost center** is established. Legal, Accounting, Research and Development, Advertising, and many other administrative and marketing departments are usually discretionary cost centers (for example, see Illustration 22–1). Discretionary cost centers are also common in government and other nonprofit organizations where budgets are used as a ceiling on expenditures. Managers are usually evaluated on bases other than costs. However, there are usually penalties for exceeding the budget ceiling.

Revenue Centers

Revenue Center An organization subunit responsible for revenues and, typically, also for marketing costs.

Managers of **revenue centers** are typically responsible for marketing a product. Consequently, the manager is held responsible for revenue or contribution margin variances (see Chapters 18 and 21 for definitions of these variances). An example of a revenue center is the Sportswear Department of a large department store in which the manager is held responsible for merchandise sales.

*Organization Structure and
Responsibility Centers*

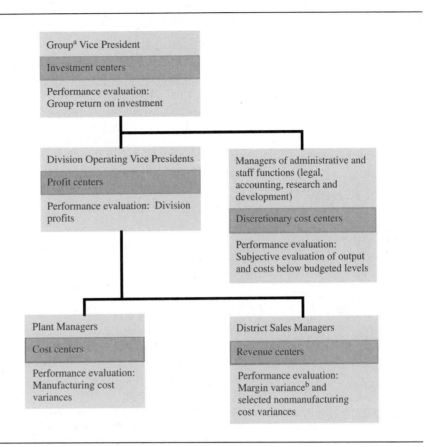

a *Group* refers to a group of divisions.

b Margin variances are based on the contribution margin (price minus variable cost) of the products sold.

Profit Centers

Profit Center An organization subunit responsible for profits; also, usually responsible for revenues, costs, production, and sales volumes.

Managers of **profit centers** are held accountable for profits. They manage both revenues and costs (as shown in Illustration 22–1). For example, a Kentucky Fried Chicken franchise may operate its warehouses as cost centers but its restaurants as profit centers. Managers of profit centers have more autonomy than do managers of cost or revenue centers; thus, they sometimes have more status.

Investment Centers

Investment Center Organization subunit responsible for profits and for investment in assets.

Managers of **investment centers** have responsibility for profits and investment in assets. These managers have relatively large amounts of money with which to make capital budgeting decisions. For instance, in one company, the manager of a cost center cannot acquire assets that cost more than $5,000 without approval from a superior, but an investment center manager can make acquisitions costing up to $500,000 without higher approval. Investment centers are evaluated using some measure of profits related to the invested assets in the center.

Responsibility Centers

As Illustration 22–1 shows, the type of responsibility center is closely related to its position in the organizational structure. For the company shown, plant managers run cost centers, and district sales managers operate revenue centers. Moving up the organizational chart, we find that division managers who are in charge of both plant managers and district sales managers have responsibility for profits.

Of course every company is organized uniquely (in some highly decentralized companies, manufacturing plants are profit centers, for example). However, it is generally true that a broader scope of authority and responsibility, hence profit or investment centers, is found at higher levels in an organization.

PERFORMANCE MEASUREMENT IN DISCRETIONARY COST CENTERS AND PROFIT CENTERS

We discussed the use of variances for evaluating performance in Chapters 18 through 21. Here we look at additional performance measures in discretionary cost centers and profit centers.

Performance Measurement in Discretionary Cost Centers

Discretionary Costs Costs that are difficult to relate to outputs.

Discretionary costs, which may include research and development, accounting systems, and similar costs, are difficult to manage because it is hard to tie costs to output. For the same reason, it is difficult to evaluate the performance of a discretionary cost center manager. Companies have tried numerous methods of determining appropriate relationships between discretionary costs and activity levels and comparison with other firms. But relating costs to activity levels remains primarily a matter of management judgment or discretion. Consequently, managers of discretionary cost centers are typically given a budget and instructed not to exceed it without higher-level authorization. In most governmental units, it is against the law to exceed the budget without obtaining authorization from a legislative body (Congress, the state legislature, the city council).

Such a situation can invite suboptimal behavior. Managers have incentives to spend all of their budgets, even if some savings could be achieved, to support their request for the same or higher budgets in the following year. Furthermore, there is often no well-specified relationship between the quality of services and costs. (Would the quality of research and development go down 10 percent with a 10 percent cut in funds? Would crime increase 10 percent if Police Department funds were cut 10 percent?)

Ideally, we want to measure performance in a well-specified way, as we do when comparing actual inputs to standard inputs in a cost center. But it is very difficult and costly to measure the performance of the manager and workers in a discretionary cost center. Thus, it is also hard to provide incentives for employees to perform at the levels that best achieve organizational goals.

Consequently, the budgets of discretionary cost centers are often based on negotiation and agreement between the cost center manager and top management. The budget then becomes a constraint on cost center operations. Cost center management is expected to perform as well as possible within the budget constraint. Top management often finds it pays to carefully pick discretionary cost center managers who are loyal to the organization and committed to helping achieve its objectives. These managers can be given considerable freedom with a high probability that they will not intentionally suboptimize.

Cost Cutting

Discretionary cost centers are prime targets for short-run cost cutting. It is easy to observe an immediate 10 percent cost savings, while the consequences may not be observed until the distant future, if ever. Therefore, when top management decides to cut costs, discretionary cost centers are often the first to be affected. On the other hand, when times are good, discretionary cost centers may receive a surplus of funds because of overoptimism about future prospects. As a result, managers of discretionary cost centers may try to build in some slack so that when funds are cut they can continue to provide at least minimal services. The manager of an Accounting Department put it this way: "When times are good, we spend a lot on employee training and recruiting, and we stock up on supplies and equipment. In tough times, we can cut out the frills and use up the excess supplies and equipment. This carries us through without drastically hurting our level of services." Whether this is the best way to manage remains open to discussion.

Performance Measurement in Profit Centers

Decentralized organizations depend heavily on profit measures to evaluate the performance of decentralized units and their managers. Due to the difficulties of measuring profits, many companies have tried to use multiple measures of performance. In the early 1950s, General Electric proposed an extensive and innovative performance measurement system that evaluated market position, productivity, product leadership, personnel development, employee attitudes, public responsibility, and balance between short-range and long-range goals in addition to profitability. But even when a company uses a broad range of performance measures, accounting results continue to play an important role in performance evaluation. A commonly heard adage is that "hard" measures of performance tend to drive out "soft" measures. Nevertheless, no accounting measure can fully measure the performance of an organizational unit or its manager.

In profit centers, we encounter the usual problems related to measuring profits for the company as a whole plus an important additional one: How are the company's revenues and costs allocated to each profit center? A profit center that is totally separate from all other parts of the company operates like an autonomous company. The profits of that kind of center can be uniquely identified with it.

But a completely independent profit center is a highly unusual case. Most profit centers have costs (and perhaps revenues) in common with other units. The profit center may share facilities with other units or use headquarters' staff services, for example. If so, the company faces a cost allocation problem (see Chapter 6).

A related problem involves the transfer of goods between a profit center and other parts of the organization. Such goods must be priced so that the profit center manager has incentives to trade with other units when it is in the best interests of the organization. Chapter 23 discusses this transfer pricing problem in more detail.

There are no easy ways to determine how to measure performance in a profit center. Much is left to managerial judgment. Whatever the process chosen, its objectives should be straightforward: measure employees' performance in ways that motivate them to work in the best interest of their employers and compare that performance to standards or budget plans.

PERFORMANCE MEASUREMENT IN INVESTMENT CENTERS

Return on Investment (ROI) The ratio of profits to investment in the asset that generates those profits.

Managers of investment centers are responsible for profits and investment in assets. They are evaluated on their ability to generate a sufficiently high **return on investment (ROI)** to justify the investment in the division.

This return on investment (ROI) is computed as follows:

$$ROI = \frac{Operating\ profits}{Investment\ center\ assets}$$

It is often divided into *profit margin* and *asset turnover* parts, as follows:

$$ROI = Profit\ margin \times Asset\ turnover$$

$$= \frac{Operating\ profit}{Sales} \times \frac{Sales}{Investment\ center\ assets}$$

$$= \frac{Operating\ profit}{Investment\ center\ assets}$$

The profit margin is a measure of the investment center's ability to control its costs for a given level of revenues. The lower the costs required to generate a dollar of revenue, the higher the profit margin.

The asset turnover ratio is a measure of the investment center's ability to generate sales for each dollar of assets invested in the center.

Relating profits to capital investment is an intuitively appealing concept. Capital is a scarce resource. If one unit of a company shows a low return, the capital may be better employed in another unit where the return is higher, or invested elsewhere or paid to stockholders.

Relating profits to investment also provides a scale for measuring performance. For example, investment A generated $200,000 in operating profits, while investment B generated $2 million. But investment A required a capital investment of $500,000, while investment B required an investment of $20 million. As you can see from the following calculation, return on investment (ROI) provides a different picture from operating profits.

	Investment	
	A	**B**
1. Operating profits	$200,000	$ 2,000,000
2. Investment	500,000	20,000,000
3. Return on investment (1) ÷ (2)	40%	10%

Although ROI is a commonly used performance measure, it has its limitations. The many difficulties of measuring profits affect the numerator, while problems in measuring the investment base affect the denominator. Consequently, it is difficult to make precise comparisons among investment centers.

Measuring Investment Center Assets and Profits

Each company is likely to measure an investment center's operating profits and assets in somewhat different ways. For example, Reece and Cool found that 40 percent of the companies that had investment centers defined investment center profits consistently with the way net income is calculated for shareholder reporting. However, many companies did not assess income taxes, allocate corporate administrative costs, or allocate interest on corporate debt to investment centers.

Companies also differ in the assets that they assign to an investment center. Reece and Cool asked which assets were included in the calculation of an investment center's asset base and found the following assets were included by the indicated percentage of companies.[2]

Asset	Percentage Included
Cash	63%
Receivables	94
Inventories	95
Land and buildings used solely by the investment center	94
Allocated share of corporate headquarters' assets	16

Most companies define an asset base that is easily understandable and approximates the assets that the investment center manager is accountable for. Including assets in the base encourages managers to manage those assets.

Choice of Measure: ROI versus Residual Income

ROI evaluation is widely used in companies. However, the method has some drawbacks. Some contend that if managers are encouraged to maximize ROI, they may turn down investment opportunities that are above the minimum acceptable rate for the corporation but below the rate their center is currently earning. For example, suppose that a corporation has a cost of capital of 15 percent. A division has an opportunity to make an additional investment that will return $400,000 per year for a $2 million investment. The ROI for this project is 20 percent (which is $400,000 ÷ $2,000,000), so the project qualified at the corporate level in meeting ROI targets. Assuming the project meets all other corporate requirements, it should be accepted. However, the manager of the division in which the investment would take place may reject the investment if the division's ROI is greater than 20 percent. For example, suppose that the center currently earns:

$$\text{ROI} = \frac{\$1,000,000}{\$4,000,000} = 25 \text{ percent}$$

With the new investment, ROI would be:

$$\text{ROI} = \frac{\$1,000,000 + \$400,000}{\$4,000,000 + \$2,000,000} = 23.3 \text{ percent}$$

Because a comparison of the old and new returns would imply that performance had worsened, the center's manager might hesitate to make such an investment, even though the investment would have a positive benefit for the company as a whole.

Residual Income (RI) The excess of actual profit over the profit targeted for an organization subunit.

An alternative is to measure **residual income (RI)**. Residual income is defined as:

$$\begin{array}{l}\text{Investment center} \\ \text{operating profits}\end{array} - (\text{Capital charge} \times \text{Investment center assets})$$

---

[2] J. Reece and W. Cool, "Measuring Investment Center Performance," *Harvard Business Review,* May–June 1978, pp. 28 ff.

where the capital charge is the minimum acceptable rate of return.

Using the numbers from the previous example, we can see the impact of the investment in additional capacity on residual income. Before the investment:

$$RI = \$1,000,000 - (.15 \times \$4,000,000)$$
$$= \$1,000,000 - \$600,000$$
$$= \underline{\underline{\$400,000}}$$

The residual income from the additional investment in plant capacity is:

$$RI = \$400,000 - (.15 \times \$2,000,000)$$
$$= \$400,000 - \$300,000$$
$$= \underline{\underline{\$100,000}}$$

Hence, after the additional investment, the residual income of the division will increase to:

$$RI = (\$1,000,000 + \$400,000) - [.15 \times (\$4,000,000 + \$2,000,000)]$$
$$= \$1,400,000 - (.15 \times \$6,000,000)$$
$$= \$1,400,000 - \$900,000$$
$$= \underline{\underline{\$500,000}}$$

The additional investment in plant capacity *increases* residual income, appropriately improving the measure of performance.

Most managers recognize the weakness of ROI and take it into account when ROI is lowered by a new investment. This may partially explain why residual income does not dominate ROI as a performance measure. Moreover, residual income is not the net income reported to shareholders. Thus, it may be a less familiar concept for managers than operating profits or divisional net income. In addition, ROI is expressed as a percentage that can be compared with related percentages—like the cost of capital, the prime interest rate, and the Treasury bill rate. In practice, few companies use residual income as the only performance measure, but many companies use both ROI and residual income.

For the remainder of this section, we use ROI for illustrative purposes, but the issues we discuss apply equally to ROI and residual income.

Self-Study Question

1 The Mars Division of Hyperspace Company has assets of $1.4 billion, operating profits of $.35 billion, and a cost of capital of 30 percent.
Compute ROI and residual income.

The solution to this question is at the end of this chapter on page 840.

MEASURING THE INVESTMENT BASE

Three issues are frequently raised in measuring investment bases: (1) Should *gross* book value be used? (2) Should investment in assets be valued at historical cost or current value? and (3) Should investment be measured at the beginning or at the end of the year? While no method is inherently right

The Impact of Net Book Value versus Gross Book Value Methods on ROI (in thousands)

Facts: Operating profits before depreciation (all in cash flows at end of year):
Year 1, $100; Year 2, $100; and Year 3, $100.
Asset cost at *beginning* of Year 1, $500. The only asset is depreciable, with a 10-year life and no salvage value. Straight-line depreciation is used. The straight-line rate is 10% per year. The denominator in the ROI calculations is based on *end*-of-year asset values.

Year	Net Book Value	Gross Book Value
1	$\text{ROI} = \dfrac{\$100^a - (.1 \times \$500)^b}{\$500^c - (.1 \times \$500)^d}$	$\text{ROI} = \dfrac{\$50^e}{\$500}$
	$= \dfrac{\$50}{\$450} = \underline{\underline{11.1\%}}$	$= \underline{\underline{10\%}}$
2	$\text{ROI} = \dfrac{\$100 - (.1 \times \$500)}{\$450 - (.1 \times \$500)}$	$\text{ROI} = \dfrac{\$50}{\$500}$
	$= \dfrac{\$50}{\$400} = \underline{\underline{12.5\%}}$	$= \underline{\underline{10\%}}$
3	$\text{ROI} = \dfrac{\$100 - (.1 \times \$500)}{\$400 - (.1 \times \$500)}$	$\text{ROI} = \dfrac{\$50}{\$500}$
	$= \dfrac{\$50}{\$350} = \underline{\underline{14.3\%}}$	$= \underline{\underline{10\%}}$

[a] The first term in the numerator is the annual cash operating profit.
[b] The second term in the numerator is depreciation for the year.
[c] The first term in the denominator is the beginning-of-the-year value of the assets used in the investment base.
[d] The second term in the denominator reduces the beginning-of-year value of the asset by the amount of current year's depreciation.
[e] Net income = $50 = $100 − ($500 × .1). Companies sometimes use only cash flows in the numerator.

or wrong, some may have advantages over others. Further, it is important to understand how the measure of the investment base will affect ROI.

Gross Book Value versus Net Book Value

Suppose that a company uses straight-line depreciation for a physical asset with a 10-year life and no salvage value.

The cost of the asset does not change; it is the same in Year 3 as in Year 1. Illustration 22–2 compares ROI under net book value and gross book value for the first three years. For simplicity, all operating profits before depreciation in the computation are assumed to take place at the end of the year, and ROI is based on year-end value of the investment.

Note that the ROI increases each year under the net book value method even though no operating changes take place. This occurs because the numerator remains constant, while the denominator decreases each year as depreciation accumulates.

Critics contend that if these ROI numbers are used naively, investment center managers have incentives to postpone replacing assets longer than economically wise because their ROI will go down on replacement. In addition, the net book value method makes a center with old assets look better than a comparable center with new assets. As one manager told us: "The secret is to get into a center just after assets have been bought and run until it's time to replace them. ROI is at a peak then because there is very little investment base. Then transfer to another center that has new assets. Of course, the poor fellow that follows you has to replace assets and watch ROI plummet." While such a strategy may work, we suspect the opportunities for such game playing are relatively few. Moreover, if top management is observant, a manager playing such a strategy should be detected after relatively few moves.

Historical Cost versus Current Cost

Current Cost Cost to replace or rebuild an existing asset.

The previous example assumed no inflation. Working with the same facts, assume that the current replacement cost of the asset increases about 20 percent per year, as do operating cash flows. Illustration 22–3 compares ROI under historical cost and **current cost.**

Note that ROI increases each year under the historical cost methods even though no operating changes take place. This occurs because the numerator is measured in current dollars to reflect current cash transactions, while the denominator and depreciation charges are based on historical cost. The current cost methods reduce the effect by adjusting both the depreciation in the numerator and the investment base in the denominator to reflect price changes. Measuring current costs can be a difficult and expensive task, however, so there is a trade-off in the choice of performance measures.

We derived a level ROI in the current cost, gross book value method because the asset and all other prices increased at the same rate. If inflation affecting cash flows in the numerator increases faster than the current cost of the asset in the denominator, then ROI will increase over the years until asset replacement, under the current cost method. Of course, ROI will decrease over the years until asset replacement if the denominator increases faster than the numerator.

Although current cost may seem to be a superior measure of ROI, recall that there is no single right or wrong measure. Surveys of corporate practice show the vast majority of companies with investment centers used historical cost net book value. In many cases, many assets in the denominator are current assets that are not subject to distortions from changes in prices.

In general, how a performance measure is used is more important than how it is calculated. All of the measures we have presented can offer useful information. As long as the measurement method is understood, it can enhance performance evaluation.

Beginning, Ending, or Average Balance

An additional problem arises in measuring the investment base for performance evaluation. Should the base be the beginning, ending, or average balance? Using the beginning balance may encourage asset acquisitions early in the year to increase income for the entire year. Asset dispositions would be encouraged at the end of the year to reduce the investment base for next year. If end-of-year balances are used, similiar incentives exist to manipulate purchases and dispositions. Average investments would tend to minimize this problem although it may be more difficult to compute. In choosing an investment base, management must balance the costs of the additional computations required for average investment against the potential negative consequences of using the beginning or ending balances.

ILLUSTRATION

Historical Cost versus Current Cost Methods on ROI (in thousands)

Facts: Operating profits before depreciation (all in cash flows at end of year):
Year 1, $100; Year 2, $120; and Year 3, $144.
Annual rate of price changes is 20 percent.
Asset cost at *beginning* of Year 1 is $500. At the *end* of Year 1 the asset would cost $600; at the end of Year 2 it would cost $720; and at the end of Year 3 it would cost $864. The only asset is depreciable with a 10-year life and no salvage value. Straight-line depreciation is used; the straight-line rate is 10 percent per year. The denominator in the ROI computation is based on *end*-of-year asset value for this illustration.

	(1) Historical Cost Net Book Value	(2) Current Cost Net Book Value
Year		

Year 1

$$\text{ROI} = \frac{\$100^a - (.1 \times \$500)^b}{\$500^c - (.1^d \times \$500)} \qquad \text{ROI} = \frac{\$100 - (.1 \times \$600)}{\$600 - (.1^d \times \$600)}$$

$$= \frac{\$50}{\$450} = \underline{11.1\%} \qquad = \frac{\$100 - \$60}{\$600 - \$60} = \frac{\$40}{\$540} = \underline{7.4\%}$$

Year 2

$$\text{ROI} = \frac{\$120 - (.1 \times \$500)}{\$500 - (.2^d \times \$500)} \qquad \text{ROI} = \frac{\$120 - (.1 \times \$720)}{\$720 - (.2^d \times \$720)}$$

$$= \frac{\$70}{\$400} = \underline{17.5\%} \qquad = \frac{\$120 - \$72}{\$720 - \$144} = \frac{\$48}{\$576} = \underline{8.3\%}$$

Year 3

$$\text{ROI} = \frac{\$144 - (.1 \times \$500)}{\$500 - (.3^d \times \$500)} \qquad \text{ROI} = \frac{\$144 - (.1 \times \$864)}{\$864 - (.3^d \times \$864}$$

$$= \frac{\$94}{\$350} = \underline{26.9\%} \qquad = \frac{\$144 - \$86.4}{\$864 - \$259.2} = \frac{\$57.6}{\$604.8} = \underline{9.5\%}$$

	(3) Historical Cost Gross Book Value	(4) Current Cost Gross Book Value

Year 1

$$\text{ROI} = \frac{\$100 - \$50}{\$500} \qquad \text{ROI} = \frac{\$100 - \$60}{\$600}$$

$$= \frac{\$50}{\$500} = \underline{10\%} \qquad = \frac{\$40}{\$600} = \underline{6.7\%}$$

Year 2

$$\text{ROI} = \frac{\$120 - \$50}{\$500} \qquad \text{ROI} = \frac{\$120 - \$72}{\$720}$$

$$= \frac{\$70}{\$500} = \underline{14\%} \qquad = \frac{\$48}{\$720} = \underline{6.7\%}$$

Year 3

$$\text{ROI} = \frac{\$144 - \$50}{\$500} \qquad \text{ROI} = \frac{\$144 - \$86.4}{\$864}$$

$$= \frac{\$94}{\$500} = \underline{18.8\%} \qquad = \frac{\$57.6}{\$864} = \underline{6.7\%}$$

[a] The first term in the numerator is the annual operating profit before depreciation.

[b] The second term in the numerator is depreciation for the year.

[c] The first term in the denominator is the beginning-of-the-first-year value of the assets used in the investment base.

[d] The second term in the denominator reduces the beginning-of-year value of the asset by the amount of accumulated depreciation: By 10 percent for accumulated depreciation at the end of Year 1, by 20 percent at the end of Year 2, and by 30 percent at the end of Year 3.

2 The E. Division of E. T. Enterprises acquired depreciable assets costing $2 million. The cash flows from these assets for three years were as follows:

Year	Cash Flow
1	$500,000
2	600,000
3	710,000

Depreciation of these assets was 10 percent per year; the assets have no salvage value after 10 years. The denominator in the ROI calculation is based on *end-of-year asset values*. If these assets were replaced with identical assets that were new, the assets would cost $2,500,000 at the end of Year 1, $3,125,000 at the end of Year 2, and $3,900,000 at the end of Year 3.

Compute the ROI for each year under each of the following methods:

a. Historical cost, net book value.

b. Historical cost, gross book value.

c. Current cost, net book value.

d. Current cost, gross book value.

The solution to this question is at the end of this chapter on page 840.

MANAGERIAL ISSUES

Comparing the Performance of Investment Centers

A company is often tempted to compare the performance of its investment centers and even to encourage competition among them. The problems inherent in ROI measurement complicate such comparisons. In addition, investment centers may be in very different businesses. It is very difficult to compare the performance of a manufacturing center with the performance of a center that provides consulting service and has a relatively small investment base. Differences in the riskiness of investment centers should also be taken into account. We recommend that when comparing the performance of investment centers these systematic differences should be considered.

When there are diverse investment centers, management will frequently establish target ROIs for the individual investment centers. The investment center will be evaluated by comparing the actual ROI with the target ROI. Such a comparison procedure is similar to the budget versus actual comparisons that are made for cost centers, revenue centers, and profit centers. It sometimes makes more sense to compare the ROI of an investment center with a company in the same industry than to compare it with other investment centers in its company.

Evaluating Managers versus Evaluating Centers

The evaluation of a manager is not necessarily identical to the evaluation of the cost, profit, or investment center. As a general rule, managers are evaluated based on a comparison of actual results to targets. A manager who is asked to take over a marginal operation and turn it around may be given a minimal ROI target, consistent with the past performance of the division. If the manager meets or exceeds that target, the manager would be rewarded. However, it may be that even with the best management, a division cannot be turned around. Thus, it is entirely possible that the center would be disbanded even though the manager had received a highly positive evaluation. In addition, top management would like to reward the manager that performs well in an adverse situation but, conversely, should be willing to bail out of a bad operation if a better use can be made of company resources. Today, the **controllability concept** is widely used as a basis for managerial performance.

Controllability Concept The idea that managers should be held responsible for costs or profits over which they have decision-making authority.

An interesting problem arises in implementing this concept in an ongoing division. How does one evaluate the performance of a manager who takes over an existing division where the assets, operating structure, and markets are established prior to the manager's arrival at the helm? The new manager cannot control the fact that certain assets are on hand, nor can the new manager control the markets in which the division operates at the time the manager takes over. However, in time, the new manager can change all of these factors.

As a general rule, evaluating the manager on the basis of performance targets, as suggested earlier in this chapter, overcomes this problem. The new manager establishes a plan for operating the division and works with top management to set targets for the future. Those targets are compared to actual results as the plan is enacted, and the manager is evaluated based on those results. In short, the longer the manager is at the division, the more responsibility the manager takes for its success.

Performance Measures and Capital Investment Criteria

Neither return on investment nor residual income take into account the *timing* of the cash flows for a project. If two projects cost the same and yield the same cash flows, their ROI and RIs will be the same regardless of the time lag between the time of investment and start-up of the project. This problem is particularly acute in high-technology enterprises, which often require substantial early investment and long time lags before operations commence.

The Tie Division Story

Sixties Corp. has two divisions: Tie Division and Dye Division. The Tie Division invested $700 million in a pharmaceutical venture in 1987. This venture did not begin earning income until 1993. Cash flows (before tax) were $165 million per year, depreciation was $58 million per year ($700 million investment in depreciable assets ÷ 12 years), and profits were $107 million per year. The cash flows and profits are expected to continue for 12 years.

Given Sixties Corp. before-tax cost of capital of 10 percent, Tie Division's project had a net present value of negative $2 million, using discounted cash flows (see Chapter 15). However, Tie Division's ROI for 1993 was 15.3 percent ($107 million profits ÷ $700 million investment). Further, its residual income from the project was $37 million [$107 million profits − (10% capital charge × $700 million investment)].

The Dye Division Story

Dye Division invested $1 billion in 1992 to acquire a developed and licensed pharmaceutical operation. The acquisition is expected to yield cash flows (before tax) of $165 million per year for 12 years. When Dye Division management presented the investment proposal to Sixties Corp.'s top management, they indicated the project would have a net present value of $124 million using the 10 percent discount rate.

Dye Division's profits for 1993 were $82 million, which equals the cash flows of $165 million minus depreciation of $83 million per year ($83 million = $1 billion investment ÷ 12 years). Dye Division's ROI for this project was only 8.2 percent ($82 million profit ÷ $1 billion investment). Since the 8.2 percent ROI was less than Sixties Corp.'s 10 percent cost of capital, Dye Division management received an unpleasant call from Sixties Corp.'s management, who wondered what had gone wrong with the project.

The problem is the ROI and residual income measures do not take into account how long it takes for the returns to come in. Even though Dye Division's project has a greater net present value, the ROI and residual income are lower because the project was acquired at a higher price. The fact that Dye Division's project was acquired in 1992 whereas Tie Division's project was acquired in 1987 does not enter into the ROI or RI calculations. In this case, the performance measures give different signals than the net present value calculations.

Nonfinancial
Performance Measures

Financial performance measures such as return on investment and residual income are usually insufficient measures of performance when taken alone. Recent studies identified the short-term focus of management as a detrimental factor in the decline of the competitiveness of U.S. industry. ROI and RI are short-term performance measures. In addition, financial statistics do not tell the whole story about a division's operations. For these reasons, many companies have developed nonfinancial performance measures to encourage division managers to take actions consistent with other corporate goals.

In highly automated manufacturing environments, quality control is extremely important. Defective goods can generate costly damage to sensitive equipment as well as result in customer dissatisfaction. Incorporating rejection, rework, and defective goods rates into the performance profile tends to minimize the incidence of defects and serves to encourage managers to meet quality control requirements at the risk of lowering division returns in the short run.

A company can tailor a performance measurement system to include nonfinancial as well as financial measures into its profile of divisional activ-

---

REAL WORLD APPLICATION

Encouraging Innovative Ideas

To encourage innovation and long-term growth, 3M Company requires that at least 25 percent of each division's sales come from products developed within the past five years. This encourages managers to invest in longer-term projects and take risks to invest in projects that may have an adverse impact on short-term performance indicators but will enable the company to stay competitive in the long run.

3M also provides incentives for innovation including allowing all employees to spend 15 percent of their time on innovative projects, encouraging employee feedback on any aspect of company performance, sharing technology across divisions, and providing "seed" grants for employees to develop new products.

3M's program and corporate culture result in the company having a worldwide reputation for innovation. Many other companies are studying 3M's approach and implementing similar programs.

ities. By covering all significant aspects of company goals in the performance system, a company can advance corporate goals beyond the short-term focus that ROI and RI measures encourage.

SUMMARY

Performance evaluation is usually based on a responsibility accounting system. The key factor in establishing a performance evaluation system is to encourage all segments of an organization to act to attain common organization goals. The evaluation system must be cost-effective. There is a great diversity in organization structures, ranging from highly centralized to highly decentralized organizations. We presume the degree of centralization is established to optimize the balance between the costs of decentralization and the benefits.

Organization subunits may be organized as cost centers, discretionary cost centers, revenue centers, profit centers, or investment centers. The basis for evaluation of each type of center is designed to capture the activities that are under the control of the center manager. Cost centers, revenue centers, and profit centers are usually evaluated based on a comparison of actual performance with budgeted goals. Investment centers are evaluated on the basis of the efficiency with which the assets employed in the center are used to generate profits. The usual form of measurement for investment centers is return on investment (ROI).

Managers are typically evaluated by comparing established performance targets with actual results. Centers are evaluated using an opportunity cost approach. Hence, a manager can excel in the management of a mediocre center, and conversely, a manager could receive a poor evaluation in a highly profitable center. In general, top managers match the performance measurement system with the factors that are under the control of the center or of the manager of the center. This promotes evaluation based on the factors that the manager or center can use to impact results.

TERMS AND CONCEPTS

The following terms and concepts should be familiar to you after reading this chapter:

Behavioral Congruence, *809*	**Investment Center,** *813*
Centralized, *810*	**Principal-Agent Relationship,** *809*
Controllability Concept, *823*	**Profit Center,** *813*
Cost Centers, *812*	**Residual Income (RI),** *817*
Current Cost, *820*	**Responsibility Accounting,** *808*
Decentralized, *810*	**Return on Investment (ROI),** *816*
Discretionary Cost Centers, *812*	**Revenue Center,** *812*
Discretionary Costs, *814*	**Standard Cost Center,** *812*
Goal Congruence, *809*	

QUESTIONS

22–1   Accounting is supposed to be a neutral, relevant, and objective measure of performance. Why would problems arise when applying accounting measures to performance evaluation contexts?

22–2   A company prepares the master budget by taking each division manager's estimate of revenues and costs for the coming period and entering the data into the budget without adjustment. At the end of the year, division managers are given a bonus if their division profit is greater than the budget. Do you see any problems with this system?

22–3   Is top management ever an agent in a principal-agent relationship as discussed in the chapter?

22–4   Is middle management ever a principal in a principal-agent relationship as discussed in the chapter?

22–5   Sales managers in a company were paid on an incentive system based on the number of units sold to ultimate buyers (that is, the units were not likely to be returned except if defective). How might that incentive system lead to dysfunctional consequences?

22–6   XYZ Division of Multitudenous Enterprises, Inc., produces and sells blank video disks. The division is evaluated based on income targets. The company uses the same measure of income for division performance evaluation as for external reporting. What problems, if any, can you envision in this performance evaluation system?

22–7   You overhear the comment, ''This whole problem of measuring performance for segment managers using accounting numbers is so much hogwash. We pay our managers a good salary and expect them to do the best possible job. At least with our system there is no incentive to play with the accounting data.'' Does the comment make sense?

22–8   What are the advantages of using an ROI–type measure rather than the absolute value of division profits as a performance evaluation technique?

22–9   Under what conditions would the use of ROI measures inhibit goal-congruent decision making by a division manager?

22–10   The chapter suggested there might be some problems in the use of residual income. Can you suggest what some of those problems might be?

22–11   Using historical costs of assets in the ROI denominator is a mismatch with current revenues and costs in the numerator. This problem may be corrected by using current costs in the denominator. No changes need be made to the numerator. How do you feel about this suggestion?

22–12   Central management of Holdum, Inc., evaluated divisional performance using residual income measures. The division managers were ranked according to the residual income in each division. A bonus was paid to all division managers with residual income in the upper half of the ranking. The bonus amount was in proportion to the residual income amount. No bonus was paid to managers in the lower half of the ranking. What biases might arise in this system?

22–13   Parsed Phrases Corporation entered into a loan agreement that contained the provision that Parsed Phrases would be required to make additional interest payments if its net income fell below a certain dollar amount. Immediately after the agreement was signed, the FASB instituted a new accounting requirement that caused Parsed's income to fall below the requirements. Absent the accounting change, Parsed would have met the income requirement.

a. Should the prechange or postchange income number be used to determine if Parsed should pay the additional interest charge? Why or why not?

b. Would your answer in (a) change if Parsed had entered into a management contract that provided that the new manager would be paid a bonus based on achieving certain income levels (but, after his taking office, the accounting rules changed so that the manager could never achieve those agreed-upon income levels)?

22–14   Management of Division A is evaluated based on residual income measures. The division can either rent or buy a certain asset. Might the performance evaluation technique have an impact on the rent-or-buy decision? Why or why not?

22–15   What impact does the use of gross book value or net book value in the investment base have on the computation of ROI?

22–16   "Every one of our company's divisions has a return on investment that is in excess of our cost of capital. Our company must be a blockbuster." Comment on this statement.

22–17   Bleak Prospects, Inc., found that its market share was slipping. Division managers were encouraged to maximize return on investment and made decisions consistent with that goal. Nonetheless, there were frequent customer complaints, with resulting loss of business. Moreover, Bleak depended on an established product line and was unable to find new products for expansion, while its competitors seemed to be able to generate new products almost yearly. What would you suggest Bleak Products' management do to improve its situation?

EXERCISES

22–18 Compute Residual Income and ROI
(L.O.4)

The Austin Division of the Lone Star Corporation has assets of $1.2 million. During the past year, the division had profits of $300,000. Lone Star Corporation has a cost of capital of 14 percent.

Required:

a. Compute the division ROI.

b. Compute the division residual income.

22–19 ROI versus Residual Income
(L.O.4)

A division is considering acquisition of a new asset. The asset will cost $180,000 and have a cash flow of $70,000 per year for each of the five years of its life. Depreciation is computed on a straight-line basis with no salvage value.

Required:

a. What is the ROI for each year of the asset's life if the division uses beginning-of-year asset balances, net book value for the computation?

b. What is the residual income each year if the cost of capital is 25 percent?

22–20 Compare Alternative Measures of Division Performance
(L.O.4)

The following data are available for two divisions in your company:

	East Division	West Division
Division operating profit	$ 70,000	$ 390,000
Division investment	200,000	1,500,000

The cost of capital for the company is 20 percent.

Required:

a. Which division had the better performance? Why?

b. Would your evaluation change if the company's cost of capital was 25 percent?

22–21	**Impact of New Project on Performance Measures** (L.O.4)	A division manager is considering the acquisition of a new asset that will add to profit. The division already earns $780,000 on assets of $2.6 million. The company's cost of capital is 20 percent. The new investment has a cost of $450,000 and will have a yearly cash flow of $167,000. The asset will be depreciated using the straight-line method over a six-year life and is expected to have no salvage value. The new asset meets the company's discounted cash flow investment criteria. Division performance is measured using ROI with beginning-of-year net book values in the denominator.

Required:

a. What is the division ROI before acquisition of the new asset?

b. What is the division ROI in the first year after acquisition of the new asset?

22–22	**Impact of Leasing on Performance Measures** (L.O.4)	The division manager in exercise 22–21 has the option of leasing the asset on a year-to-year lease. The lease payment would be $145,000 per year, and all depreciation and other tax benefits would accrue to the lessor. What is the division ROI if the asset is leased?

22–23	**Residual Income Measures and New Project Consideration** (L.O.4)	Consider the investment project detailed in exercises 22–21 and 22–22.

a. What is the division's residual income before considering the project?

b. What is the division's residual income if the asset is purchased?

c. What is the division's residual income if the asset is leased?

22–24	**Compare Historical Cost, Net Book Value to Gross Book Value** (L.O.5)	The Delphi Division of Oracle Corporation just started operations. It purchased depreciable assets costing $1 million and having an expected life of four years, after which the assets can be salvaged for $200,000. In addition, the division has $1 million in assets that are not depreciable. After four years, the division will have $1 million available from these nondepreciable assets. In short, the division has invested $2 million in assets that will last four years, after which it will salvage $1.2 million, so annual depreciation is $200,000. Annual cash operating flows are $500,000. In computing ROI, this division uses *end-of-year* asset values in the denominator. Depreciation is computed on a straight-line basis, recognizing the salvage values noted above.

Required:

a. Compute ROI, using net book value for each year.

b. Compute ROI, using gross book value for each year.

22–25	**Compare ROI Using Net Book and Gross Book Values** (L.O.5)	Assume the same data as in exercise 22–24, except the division uses *beginning-of-year* asset values in the denominator for computing ROI.

a. Compute ROI, using net book value.

b. Compute ROI, using gross book value.

c. If you worked exercise 22–24, compare these results with those from 22–24. How different is the ROI computed using end-of-year asset values, as in 22–24, from the ROI using beginning-of-year values, as in this exercise?

22–26	**Compare Current Cost to Historical Cost** (L.O.6)	Assume the same data as in exercise 22–24, except all cash flows increase 10 percent at the end of the year. This has the following effect on the assets' replacement cost and annual cash flows:

End of Year	Replacement Cost	Annual Cash Flow
1	$2,000,000 × 1.1 = $2,200,000	$500,000 × 1.1 = $550,000
2	$2,200,000 × 1.1 = $2,420,000	$550,000 × 1.1 = $605,000
⋮	Etc.	Etc.

Depreciation is as follows:

	For the Year	"Accumulated"	
1	$220,000	$ 220,000	(= 10% × $2,200,000)
2	242,000	484,000	(= 20% × 2,420,000)
3	266,200	798,600	etc.
4	292,800	1,171,280	

Note that "accumulated" depreciation is 10 percent of the gross book value of depreciable assets after one year, 20 percent after two years, and so forth.

Required:

a. Compute ROI, using historical cost, gross book value.

b. Compute ROI, using historical cost, net book value.

c. Compute ROI, using current cost, gross book value.

d. Compute ROI, using current cost, net book value.

22–27   Effects of Current Cost on Performance Measurements
(L.O.6)

The Inn Division of Inntell Company acquired an asset with a cost of $200,000 and a life of four years. The cash flows from the asset, considering the effects of inflation, were scheduled as:

Year	Cash Flow
1	$60,000
2	68,000
3	76,000
4	80,000

The current cost of the asset is expected to increase at a rate of 10 percent per year, compounded each year. Performance measures are based on beginning-of-year gross book values for the investment base.

Required:

a. What is the ROI for each year of the asset's life, using a historical cost approach?

b. What is the ROI for each year of the asset's life if both the investment base and depreciation are based on the current cost of the asset at the start of each year?

22–28   ROI, Residual Income, and Net Present Value
(L.O.7)

Pyramid Co. invested $1 billion in an asset in 1985 to develop a patented laser measurement process. Pyramid Co. established its Sphere Division to operate the laser operation. Delays caused by patent infringement litigation prevented the start-up of operations until the beginning of 1991. Before-tax cash flows that year equalled $600 million. This cash flow is expected to continue annually through the end of 1995. At the end of the project life, the asset will have no value. The $1 billion asset is depreciated using the straight-line method over a five-year life starting in 1991.

In 1990, Pyramid Co. established its Cubic Division. The Cubic Division was off to a fast start in a low-technology plastics operation. Cubic invested $1.5 billion in a plastics molding plant. Before-tax cash flows from the plant total $600 million per year and are expected to continue annually for each of the five years beginning in 1991. The $1.5 billion asset is depreciated using the straight-line method over five years starting in 1991. It will have no value at the end of five years.

Pyramid Co. uses the straight-line method for depreciation. The company has a before-tax cost of capital of 15 percent and evaluates divisions based on return on investment and residual income. The company evaluates divisions on the basis of return on *initial* investment (that is, annual before-tax net income divided by $1 billion for Sphere and by $1.5 billion for Cubic).

<table>
<tr><td>Required:</td><td>a.</td><td>Which division's project has the greater net present value?</td></tr>
<tr><td></td><td>b.</td><td>Which division has the greater ROI and RI for 1991?</td></tr>
<tr><td></td><td>c.</td><td>If the rankings differ, how is this explained?</td></tr>
</table>

22–29 ROI, Residual Income, and Net Present Value
(L.O.7)

Sound Enterprises is a conglomerate located on the shore of the Gulf of Siam. Sound invested $850,000 in Container Shipping in 1984. Due to a glut in the availability of ships, Container Shipping had no positive cash flows until 1990. At that time, Container obtained a five-year charter for its entire fleet. The charter provides Container with annual before-tax cash flows of $450,000. Since Container believes that the ships will have no value after that date, Container is depreciating the $850,000 over the five years using the straight-line method starting in 1990 with no salvage value.

Sound Enterprises became impatient with the problems at its shipping subsidiary. In 1988, it formed Herring Fisheries, S.A., and invested $1.2 million to acquire fishing rights and to charter ships. Herring Fisheries began operations in 1990. Cash flows are $450,000 per year and are expected to continue for five years. At the end of five years, the fishing rights and charters will expire. Hence, the investment cost of $1.2 million is being depreciated straight-line over a five-year period starting in 1990. The company evaluates divisions on the basis of return on initial investment (that is, annual before-tax net income divided by $850,000 for Container Shipping and $1.2 million for Herring). The cost of capital (before tax) is 15 percent.

Required:

   a. Which subsidiary's project has the greater net present value?

   b. Which subsidiary has the greater ROI and RI for 1990?

   c. If the rankings differ, how is this explained?

PROBLEMS

22–30 Equipment Replacement and Performance Measures

You have been appointed manager of an operating division of HI-TECH, Inc., a manufacturer of products using the latest microprocessor technology. Your division has $800,000 in assets and manufactures a special chip assembly. On January 2 of the current year, you invested $1 million in automated equipment for chip assembly. At that time, your expected income statement was:

Sales revenue	$3,200,000
Operating costs:	
Variable	400,000
Fixed (all cash)	1,500,000
Depreciation:	
New equipment	300,000
Other	250,000
Division operating profit	$ 750,000

On October 25 you were approached by a sales representative from Mammoth Machine Company. Mammoth offers a new assembly machine at a cost of $1.3 million that offers significant improvements over the equipment you bought on January 2. The new equipment would expand department output by 10 percent while reducing cash fixed costs by 5 percent. The new equipment would be depreciated for accounting purposes over a three-year life. Depreciation would be net of the $100,000 salvage value of the new machine. The new equipment meets your company's 20 percent cost of capital criterion. If you purchase the new machine, it must be installed prior to the end of the year. For practical purposes, though, you can ignore depreciation on the new machine because it will not go into operation until the start of the next year.

The old machine must be disposed of to make room for the new machine. The old machine has no salvage value.

Your company has a performance evaluation and bonus plan based on ROI. The return includes any losses on disposals of equipment. Investment is computed based on the end-of-year balance of assets, net book value.

Required:	*a.* What is your division's ROI if the new machine is not acquired?
	b. What is your division's ROI this year if the new machine is acquired?
	c. If the new machine is acquired and operates according to specifications, what ROI would be expected for next year?

22–31 Evaluate Trade-Offs in Return Measurement

As a division manager of HI-TECH, Inc. (problem 22–30), you are still assessing the problem of whether to acquire the Mammoth Machine Company's machine. You learn that the new machine could be acquired next year. However, if you wait until next year, the new machine will cost 15 percent more than this year's price. The salvage value would still be $100,000. Other costs or revenue estimates would be apportioned on a month-by-month basis for the time each machine is in use. Fractions of months may be ignored.

Required:
a. When would you want to purchase the new machine if you wait until next year?

b. What are the costs that must be considered in making this decision?

22–32 Analyze Performance Report for Decentralized Organization

Bio-grade Products manufactures animal feeds and feed supplements. The need for a widely based manufacturing and distribution system has led to a highly decentralized management structure. Each divisional manager is responsible for production and distribution of corporate products in one of eight geographical areas of the country.

Residual income is used to evaluate divisional managers. The residual income for each division equals each division's contribution to corporate profits before taxes less a 20 percent investment charge on a division's investment base. The investment base of each division is the sum of its year-end balances of accounts receivable, inventories, and net plant fixed assets (cost less accumulated depreciation). Corporate policies dictate that divisions minimize their investments in receivables and inventories. Investments in plant fixed assets are a joint division/corporate decision based on proposals made by divisional plant managers, available corporate funds, and general corporate policy.

Alex Williams, divisional manager for the Southeastern Sector, prepared the Year 2 and preliminary Year 3 budgets for his division late in Year 1. Final approval of the Year 3 budget took place in late Year 2, after adjustments for trends and other information developed during Year 2. Preliminary work on the Year 4 budget also took place at that time. In early October of Year 3, Williams asked the divisional controller to prepare a report that presents performance for the first nine months of Year 3. The report is reproduced in Exhibit 22–32A.

Required:
a. Evaluate the performance of Alex Williams for the nine months ending September Year 3. Support your evaluation with pertinent facts from the problem.

b. Identify the features of Bio-grade Products' divisional performance measurement reporting and evaluating system that need to be revised if it is to effectively reflect the responsibilities of the divisional managers.

(CMA adapted)

22–33 ROI and Management Behavior

Notewon Corporation is a highly diversified and decentralized company. Each division is responsible for its own sales, pricing, production, costs of operations, and the management of accounts receivable, inventories, accounts payable, and use of existing facilities. Cash is managed by corporate headquarters.

Divisional executives are responsible for presenting investment proposals to corporate management. Proposals are analyzed and documented at corporate head-

EXHIBIT

BIO-GRADE PRODUCTS—SOUTHEASTERN SECTOR
(in thousands)

	Year 3			Year 2	
	Annual Budget	Nine-Month Budget[a]	Nine-Month Actual	Annual Budget	Actual Results
Sales	$2,800	$2,100	$2,200	$2,500	$2,430
Divisional costs and expenses:					
Direct materials and labor	1,064	798	995	900	890
Supplies	44	33	35	35	43
Maintenance and repairs	200	150	60	175	160
Plant depreciation	120	90	90	110	110
Administration	120	90	90	90	100
Total divisional costs and expenses	1,548	1,161	1,270	1,310	1,303
Divisional margin	1,252	939	930	1,190	1,127
Allocated corporate fixed costs	360	270	240	340	320
Divisional profits	$ 892	$ 669	$ 690	$ 850	$ 807
	Budgeted Balance 12/31/Year 3	Budgeted Balance 9/30/Year 3	Actual Balance 9/30/Year 3	Budgeted Balance 12/31/Year 2	Actual Balance 12/31/Year 2
Divisional investment:					
Accounts receivable	$ 280	$ 290	$ 250	$ 250	$ 250
Inventories	500	500	650	450	475
Plant fixed assets (net)	1,320	1,350	1,100	1,150	1,100
Total	$2,100	$2,140	$2,000	$1,850	$1,825

[a] Bio-grade's sales occur uniformly throughout the year.

quarters. The final decision to commit funds for investment purposes rests with corporate management.

The corporation evaluates division executive performance by the ROI measure. The asset base is composed of fixed assets employed plus working capital exclusive of cash. The ROI performance of a division executive is the most important appraisal factor for salary changes. In addition, each executive's annual performance bonus is based on ROI results, with increases in ROI having a significant impact on the amount of the bonus.

Notewon Corporation adopted the ROI performance measure and related compensation procedures about 10 years ago. The corporation seems to have benefited from the program. The ROI for the corporation as a whole increased during the first years of the program. Although the ROI continued to grow in each division, corporate ROI has declined in recent years. The corporation has accumulated a sizable amount of short-term marketable securities in the past three years.

Corporate management is concerned about the increase in the short-term marketable securities. A recent article in a financial publication suggested that the use of ROI was overemphasized by some companies, with results similar to those experienced by Notewon.

Required:

a. Describe the specific actions division managers might have taken to cause the ROI to grow in each division but decline for the corporation. Illustrate your explanation with appropriate examples.

b. Explain, using the concepts of goal congruence and motivation of divisional executives, how Notewon Corporation's overemphasis on the use of the ROI measure might result in the recent decline in the corporation's return on investment and the increase in cash and short-term marketable securities.

c. What changes could be made in Notewon Corporation's compensation policy to avoid this problem? Explain your answer.

(CMA adapted)

22–34 Impact of Decisions to Capitalize or Expense on Performance Measurement

Oil and gas companies inevitably incur costs on exploration ventures that are unsuccessful. These ventures are called dry holes. There is a continuing debate over whether those costs should be written off as period expense or whether they should be capitalized as part of the full cost of finding profitable oil and gas ventures. PMX Drilling Company has been writing these costs off to expense as incurred. However, this year a new management team was hired to improve the profit picture of PMX's Oil and Gas Exploration Division. The new management team was hired with the provision that they would receive a bonus equal to 10 percent of any profits in excess of base-year profits of the division. However, no bonus would be paid if profits were less than 20 percent of end-of-year investment. The following information was included in the performance report for the division:

	This Year	Base Year	Increase over Base Year
Sales revenues	$4,100,000	$4,000,000	
Costs incurred:			
Dry holes	–0–	800,000	
Depreciation and other amortization	780,000	750,000	
Other costs	1,600,000	1,550,000	
Division profit	$1,720,000	$ 900,000	$820,000
End-of-year investment	$8,100,000ᵃ	$6,900,000	

ᵃ Includes other investments not at issue here.

During the year, the new team spent $1 million on exploratory activities, but $900,000 was spent on ventures that were unsuccessful. The new management team has included the $900,000 in the current end-of-year investment base because, they state, "You can't find the good ones without hitting a few bad ones."

Required:

a. What is the ROI for the base year and the current year?

b. What is the amount of the bonus that the new management team is likely to claim?

c. If you were on the board of directors of PMX, how would you respond to the new management's claim for the bonus?

22–35 Evaluate Performance Evaluation System: Behavioral Issues

ATCO Company purchased Dexter Company three years ago. Prior to the acquisition, Dexter manufactured and sold electronic products to third-party customers. Since becoming a division of ATCO, Dexter now manufactures electronic components only for products made by ATCO's Macon Division.

ATCO's corporate management gives the Dexter Division management considerable latitude in running the division's operations. However, corporate management retains authority for decisions regarding capital investments, product pricing, and production quantities.

ATCO has a formal performance evaluation program for all division managements. The evaluation program relies substantially on each division's return on investment. The income statement of Dexter Division provides the basis for the evaluation of Dexter's divisional management. (See income statement below.)

Division financial statements are prepared by the corporate accounting staff. Corporate general services costs are allocated on the basis of sales-dollars, and the Computer Department's actual costs are apportioned among the divisions on the basis of use. The net division investment includes division fixed assets at net book value (cost less depreciation), division inventory, and corporate working capital apportioned to the divisions on the basis of sales-dollars.

ATCO COMPANY
Dexter Division
Income Statement
For the Year Ended October 31
(in thousands)

Sales revenue			$4,000
Costs and expenses:			
Product costs:			
Direct materials		$ 500	
Direct labor		1,100	
Factory overhead		1,300	
Total		2,900	
Less: Increase in inventory		350	2,550
Engineering and research			120
Shipping and receiving			240
Division administration:			
Manager's office		210	
Cost accounting		40	
Personnel		82	332
Corporate costs:			
General services		230	
Computer		48	278
Total costs and expenses			3,520
Divisional operating profit			$ 480
Net plant investment			$1,600
Return on investment			30%

Required:

a. Discuss the financial reporting and performance evaluation program of ATCO Company as it relates to the responsibilities of the Dexter Division.

b. Based on your response to requirement (a), recommend appropriate revisions of the financial information and reports used to evaluate the performance of Dexter's divisional management. If revisions are not necessary, explain why revisions are not needed.

(CMA adapted)

22–36 Divisional Performance Measurement: Behavioral Issues

Division managers of SIU Incorporated have been expressing growing dissatisfaction with SIU's methods used to measure divisional performance. Divisional operations are evaluated every quarter by comparison with the master budget prepared during the prior year. Division managers claim that many factors are completely out of their control but are included in this comparison. This results in an unfair and misleading performance evaluation.

The managers have been particularly critical of the process used to establish standards and budgets. The annual budget, stated by quarters, is prepared six months prior to the beginning of the operating year. Pressure by top management to reflect increased earnings has often caused divisional managers to overstate revenues and/or understate expenses. In addition, once the budget is established, divisions must "live with the budget." Frequently, external factors such as the state of the economy, changes in consumer preferences, and actions of competitors have not been recognized in the budgets that top management supplied to the divisions. The credibility of the performance review is curtailed when the budget cannot be adjusted to incorporate these changes.

Top management, recognizing these problems, agreed to establish a committee to review the situation and to make recommendations for a new performance evaluation system. The committee consists of each division manager, the corporate controller, and the executive vice president. At the first meeting, one division manager outlined an Achievement of Objectives System (AOS). In this performance evaluation system, divisional managers are evaluated according to three criteria:

1. Doing better than last year. Various measures are compared to the same measures of the prior year.
2. Planning realistically. Actual performance for the current year is compared to realistic plans and/or goals.
3. Managing current assets. Various measures are used to evaluate the divisional management's achievements and reactions to changing business and economic conditions.

One division manager believed this system would overcome many of the inconsistencies of the current system because divisions could be evaluated from three different viewpoints. In addition, managers would have the opportunity to show how they would react and account for changes in uncontrollable external factors.

Another manager cautioned that the success of a new performance evaluation system would be limited unless it had the complete support of top management.

Required:

a. Explain whether the proposed AOS would be an improvement over the measure of divisional performance now used by SIU Incorporated.

b. Develop specific performance measures for each of the three criteria in the proposed AOS that could be used to evaluate divisional managers.

c. Discuss the motivational and behavioral aspects of the proposed performance system. Also, recommend specific programs that could be instituted to promote morale and give incentives to divisional management.

(CMA adapted)

22–37 ROI, Residual Income, Different Asset Bases

The manager of the Spears Department Store in Evanston is evaluated using return on investment. Spears headquarters requires that a return on investment of 10 percent of assets be employed. For the coming year, the manager estimates that revenues will equal $260,000. Cost of merchandise sold will equal $163,000. Operating expenses for this level of sales are expected to equal $26,000. Investment in the store assets throughout the year is $187,500 before considering the following proposal.

The manager was approached by a representative of Sly Trading Company about carrying Sly's line of sporting goods. This line is expected to generate $75,000 in sales in the coming year at the Spears store with a merchandise cost of $57,000. Operating expenses for this additional line of merchandise are $8,500 per year. To carry the line of goods, an inventory investment of $55,000 throughout the year is required. Sly is willing to floor plan the merchandise so that the Spears store will not have to invest in any inventory. The cost of floor planning would be $6,750 per year. Spears' marginal cost of capital is 10 percent.

Required:	*a.*	What is the Evanston Spears store's expected ROI for the coming year if the Sly sporting goods are not carried in the store?
	b.	What is the store's expected ROI if the manager invests in the Sly inventory and carries the sporting goods merchandise?
	c.	What would the store's expected ROI be if the manager elected to take the floor plan option?
	d.	Would the manager prefer *(a)*, *(b)*, or *(c)*, above? Why?

INTEGRATIVE CASES

22–38 Evaluate Investment Choice and Its Impact on Performance Measures, with Joint Costs

Amberina, Inc., operates several different semiautonomous divisions. A problem arose with respect to two divisions that process and sell plastics products. The Plastics Blending Division obtains materials that it blends and, as a result of a joint process, splits into Phyrene and Extrene. The Plastics Blending Division processes the Phyrene further and sells the resulting product to the outside. The Extrene is sold to the Tools Division, where it is molded into tool handles and sold.

In a typical year, $240,000 of costs are incurred in the blending of the feedstock. Phyrene is processed further at a cost of $80,000 and is then sold to the outside at a price of $325,000. Extrene is sold to the Tools Division at "cost plus 20 percent," where cost is determined on the basis of net realizable value at the split-off point. The Tools Division incurs an additional cost of $60,000 to mold the plastic and sells the resulting tool handles for $175,000.

The company's cost of capital is 15 percent. The Plastics Blending Division has assets of $240,000, while the Tools Division has assets of $120,000.

The Tools Division learned that it could purchase the company that it is selling the handles to and, thus, obtain the ability to manufacture complete tools. The additional processing costs would amount to $61,000 per year, and revenues would amount to $360,000. In addition, depreciation expenses would be incurred based on the amount spent to purchase the tool manufacturing company. The manufacturing company is asking $265,000 for its assets. These assets would be depreciated on a straight-line basis for internal reporting purposes.

The assets are expected to last five years and have no salvage value. Tax depreciation would be as follows: Year 1, $35,000; Year 2, $80,000; Years 3–5, $50,000 per year. In addition, $50,000 in working capital would be required to operate the tool manufacturing plant. Income taxes are 40 percent of net income before taxes.

Required:

The head of the Tools Division wants your assessment of the feasibility of the investment in terms of *(a)* net present value of the project and *(b)* the impact of the project on the Tools Division return on investment. You may assume that if the tool manufacturing plant is acquired, there is no alternative market for the tool handles.

22–39 Capital Investment Analysis and Decentralized Performance Measurement*

The following exchange occurred just after a capital investment proposal was rejected at Diversified Electronics.

Ralph Browning (Product Development): I just don't understand why you rejected my proposal. This new investment is going to be a sure money maker for the Residential Products Division. We can expect to make $230,000 on it annually before tax.

Sue Gold (Finance): I am sorry that you are upset with our decision, but this product proposal just does not meet our short-term ROI target of 15 percent after tax.

---

* J. Lim, M. Maher, and J. Reece, copyright © 1991.

Ralph Browning: I'm not so sure about the ROI target, but it goes a long way toward increasing our earnings per share.

Phil Carlson (executive vice president): Ralph, you are right, of course, about the importance of earnings per share. However, we view our three divisions as investment centers. Proposals like yours must meet our ROI targets. It is not enough that you show an earnings-per-share increase.

Sue Gold: We believe that our company should increase its return on investment, especially given the interest rates we have had to pay recently. This is why we have targeted 15 percent as the appropriate minimum ROI for each division to earn next year.

Phil Carlson: If it were not for the high interest rates and poor current economic outlook, Ralph, we would not be taking such a conservative position in evaluating new projects. This past year has been particularly rough for our industry. Our two major competitors had ROIs of 10.8 and 12.3 percent. Though our ROI of 10.9 percent after tax was reasonable (see Exhibit 22–39C), performance varied from division to division. Professional Services did very well with 15 percent ROI, while the Residential Products Division managed just 11 percent. The performance of the Aerospace Products Division was especially dismal, with an ROI of only 7 percent. We expect divisions in the future to carry their share of the load.

Chris McGregor (Aerospace Products): My division would be showing much higher ROI if we had a lot of old equipment like the Residential Products or relied heavily on human labor like Professional Services.

Phil Carlson: I don't really see the point you are trying to make, Chris.

Diversified Electronics was a growing company in the electronics industry. (See Exhibits 22–39A, 22–39B, and 22–39C for financial data.) Diversified Electronics has three divisions—Residential Products, Aerospace Products, and Professional Services—each of which accounts for about one third of Diversified Electronics' sales. Residential Products, the oldest division, produces furnace thermostats and similar products. The Aerospace Products Division is a large "job shop" that builds electronic devices to customer specifications. A typical job or batch takes several months to complete. About one half of Aerospace Products' sales are to the U.S. Defense

---

EXHIBIT

DIVERSIFIED ELECTRONICS
Statement of Operating Profits
For 19A and 19B
(in thousands)

| | Year Ended December 31 | |
	19A	19B
Sales	$141,462	$148,220
Cost of goods sold	108,118	113,115
Gross margin	33,344	35,105
Selling and general	13,014	13,692
Profit before taxes and interest	20,330	21,413
Interest expense	1,190	1,952
Operating profit before taxes	19,140	19,461
Income tax expense	7,886	7,454
Operating profit after taxes	$ 11,254	$ 12,007

EXHIBIT

22–39B

DIVERSIFIED ELECTRONICS
Balance Sheets
For 19A and 19B
(in thousands)

	December 31	
	19A	19B
Assets		
Cash and temporary investments	$ 1,404	$ 1,469
Accounts receivable	13,688	15,607
Inventories	42,162	45,467
Total current assets	57,254	62,543
Plant and equipment:		
Original cost	107,326	115,736
Accumulated depreciation	42,691	45,979
Net plant and equipment	64,635	69,757
Investments and other assets	3,143	3,119
Total assets	$125,032	$135,419
Liabilities and Owner's Equity		
Accounts payable	$ 10,720	$ 12,286
Taxes payable	1,210	1,045
Current portion of long-term debt	—	1,634
Total current liabilities	11,930	14,965
Deferred income taxes	559	985
Long-term debt	12,622	15,448
Total liabilities	25,111	31,398
Common stock	47,368	47,368
Retained earnings	52,553	56,653
Total owner's equity	99,921	104,021
Total liabilities and owner's equity	$125,032	$135,419

EXHIBIT

22–39C

DIVERSIFIED ELECTRONICS
Ratio Analysis
For 19A and 19B

19A	19B

$$\text{Average tax rate} = \frac{\$7,886}{\$19,140}$$
$$= .412$$

$$\text{ROI} = \frac{\$20,330\,(1 - 0.412)}{\$12,622 + \$99,921}$$
$$= \frac{\$11,954}{\$112,543}$$
$$= 10.6 \text{ percent}$$

$$\text{Average tax rate} = \frac{\$7,454}{\$19,461}$$
$$= .383$$

$$\text{ROI} = \frac{\$21,413\,(1 - 0.383)}{\$1,634 + \$15,448 + \$104,021}$$
$$= \frac{\$13,212}{\$121,103}$$
$$= 10.9 \text{ percent}$$

Department. The newest of the three divisions, Professional Services, provides consulting engineering services. This division has shown tremendous growth since its acquisition by Diversified Electronics four years ago.

Each division operates independently of the others and is treated essentially as a separate entity. Many of the operating decisions are made at the division level. Corporate management coordinates the activities of the various divisions, which includes review of all investment proposals over $400,000.

Diversified Electronic's measure of return on investment is defined as the division's operating profit before taxes and interest times one minus the income tax rate divided by investment. The investment is defined as interest-bearing debt plus owners' equity. (Calculations of ROI for the company are shown in Exhibit 22–39C.) Each division's expenses include a portion of corporate administrative expenses allocated on the basis of divisional revenues.

The details of Ralph Browning's rejected product proposal are shown in Exhibit 22–39D.

Required:

a. Why did corporate headquarters reject Ralph Browning's product proposal? Was their decision the right one? Would they have rejected the proposal if they had used the net present value (NPV) method? The company uses a 15 percent cost of capital (that is, hurdle rate) in evaluating projects such as these.

b. Evaluate the manner in which Diversified Electronics implemented the investment center concept. What pitfalls did they apparently not anticipate? What, if anything, should be done with regard to the investment center approach and the use of ROI as a measure of performance?

c. What conflicting incentives for managers can occur between the use of a yearly ROI performance measure and NPV for capital budgeting?

E X H I B I T

Financial Data for New Product Proposal— Diversified Electronics

1. Projected asset investment[a]

Cash	$200,000
Plant and equipment[b]	800,000
Total	$1,000,000

2. Cost data, before taxes (first year):

Variable cost per unit	$3.00
Differential fixed costs[c]	170,000

3. Price/market estimate (first year):

Unit price	$7.00
Sales	100,000 units

4. Taxes: The company assumes a 40 percent tax rate for investment analyses. Assume that depreciation of plant and equipment for tax purposes will be taken as follows: Year 1, $80,000; Year 2, $240,000; Years 3–5; $160,000 per year. Taxes are paid for taxable income in Year 1 at the end of Year 1; taxes for Year 2, at the end of Year 2; and so on.

5. Inflation is assumed to be 10 percent per year and applies to revenues and all costs except depreciation. A 10 percent increase in cash investment is needed at the end of each year.

---

[a] Assumes sales of 100,000 units.

[b] Annual capacity of 120,000 units.

[c] Includes straight-line depreciation on new plant and equipment. Plant and equipment are expected to last eight years and to have no net salvage value at the end of eight years.

SOLUTIONS TO

Self-Study
Questions

1 $\text{ROI} = \dfrac{\$.35 \text{ billion}}{\$1.4 \text{ billion}} = 25\%$

$\text{RI} = \$.35 \text{ billion} - (.30 \times \$1.4 \text{ billion})$
$= \$.35 \text{ billion} - \$.42 \text{ billion}$
$= -\$.07 \text{ billion (that is, a residual ''loss'' of \$70 million)}$

2 *(a)* and *(b)* historical cost:

Year	Net Book Value[a]	Gross Book Value[b]
1 . . . . ROI =	$\dfrac{\$500,000 - (.10 \times \$2,000,000)}{\$2,000,000 - (.10^c \times \$2,000,000)}$	ROI = $\dfrac{\$300,000}{\$2,000,000}$
	$= \dfrac{\$300,000}{\$1,800,000} = 16.7\%$	$= 15\%$
2 . . . . ROI =	$\dfrac{\$600,000 - (.10 \times \$2,000,000)}{\$2,000,000 - (.20^c \times \$2,000,000)}$	ROI = $\dfrac{\$400,000}{\$2,000,000}$
	$= \dfrac{\$400,000}{\$1,600,000} = 25\%$	$= 20\%$
3 . . . . ROI =	$\dfrac{\$710,000 - (.10 \times \$2,000,000)}{\$2,000,000 - (.30^c \times \$2,000,000)}$	ROI = $\dfrac{\$510,000}{\$2,000,000}$
	$= \dfrac{\$510,000}{\$1,400,000} = 36.4\%$	$= 25.5\%$

[a] The first term in the numerator is the annual cash flow. The second term is the annual depreciation. The first term in the denominator is the gross book value of the assets before accumulated depreciation. The second term is the accumulated depreciation.

[b] The numerator is the annual net income. The denominator is the gross book value of the assets.

[c] This amount is the percent accumulated depreciation: 10 percent of the gross book value after one year, 20 percent after two years, and 30 percent after three years.

(c) and *(d)* current cost:

Year	Net Book Value[a]	Gross Book Value[b]
1 . . . . ROI =	$\dfrac{\$500,000 - (.10 \times \$2,500,000)}{\$2,500,000 - (.10^c \times \$2,500,000)}$	ROI = $\dfrac{\$250,000}{\$2,500,000}$
	$= \dfrac{\$500,000 - \$250,000}{\$2,500,000 - \$250,000} = 11.1\%$	$= 10\%$
2 . . . . ROI =	$\dfrac{\$600,000 - (.10 \times \$3,125,000)}{\$3,125,000 - (.20^c \times \$3,125,000)}$	ROI = $\dfrac{\$287,500}{\$3,125,000}$
	$= \dfrac{\$600,000 - \$312,500}{\$3,125,000 - \$625,000} = 11.5\%$	$= 9.2\%$
3 . . . . ROI =	$\dfrac{\$710,000 - (.10 \times \$3,900,000)}{\$3,900,000 - (.30^c \times \$3,900,000)}$	ROI = $\dfrac{\$320,000}{\$3,900,000}$
	$= \dfrac{\$710,000 - \$390,000}{\$3,900,000 - \$1,170,000}$	$= 8.2\%$
	$= \dfrac{\$320,000}{\$2,730,000} = 11.7\%$	

[a] The first term in the numerator is the annual cash flow. The second term is the annual depreciation. The first term in the denominator is the gross book value of the assets before accumulated depreciation. The second term is the accumulated depreciation.

[b] The numerator is the annual net income. The denominator is the gross book value of the assets.

[c] This amount is the percent accumulated depreciation: 10 percent of the gross book value after one year, 20 percent after two years, and 30 percent after three years.

Transfer Pricing

LEARNING OBJECTIVES

After reading this chapter, you should be able to:

1. Describe the journal entries used to record transfers of goods and services across divisions.
2. Explain the economic transfer pricing rule.
3. Identify the behavioral issues and incentive effects of: negotiated transfer prices, cost-based transfer prices, and market-based transfer prices.
4. Explain economic consequences of multinational transfer prices.
5. Describe the role of transfer prices in segment reporting.

When goods or services are transferred from one unit of an organization to another, the transaction is recorded in the accounting records. The value assigned to the transaction is called the *transfer price*. Considerable discretion can be used in putting a value on the transaction because this exchange takes place inside the organization. Transfer prices are widely used for decision making, product costing, and performance evaluation; hence, it is important to consider alternative transfer pricing methods and their advantages and disadvantages.

TRANSFER PRICING IN DECENTRALIZED ORGANIZATIONS

Responsibility centers in decentralized organizations often exchange products. At General Motors, for example, it is common for one division to buy direct materials from a number of suppliers, including other divisions of General Motors. In effect, responsibility centers buy/sell from/to each other. Companies like Sega of America and Nintendo, which buy video games from their Japanese parents, and Kawasaki, which buys motorcycles from its Japanese parent, provide examples of international transfers.

Transfer Price The price at which goods or services are traded between organization subunits.

The **transfer price** *is the price (or cost) assigned to the goods or services transferred*. It becomes a cost to the buyer division and revenue to the seller division.

If the divisions are evaluated based on some measure of profitability, such as return on investment, then the transfer price can have an impact on the performance of each division. For example, the higher the transfer price, the more profitable the selling division (from higher revenues) and the less profitable the buying division, all other things equal.

Recording a Transfer

Division A of Shockless Power Company makes a motor that is purchased by Division B, which manufactures refrigerators. When the motors are sold or transferred, their cost becomes a part of the cost of goods sold for Division A. Assume that Division A can sell the motors or transfer them to Division B at a price of $50 per motor. The inventoriable cost of the motors to Division A is $40 each. The transfer of 1,000 motors from Division A to Division B would be recorded on Division A's books as:

Receivable from Division B	50,000	
Sales Revenue		50,000
Cost of Goods Sold	40,000	
Finished Goods Inventory		40,000

On Division B's books, the purchase of 1,000 motors from Division A would be recorded as:

Direct Materials Inventory	50,000	
Payable to Division A		50,000

In evaluating the performance of each division, top management of Shockless Power would consider these costs and revenues in computing division profits. However, for external financial-reporting purposes, any interdivisional profits are eliminated to avoid double counting in the financial statements.

Recording the transfer of goods and services is a straightforward accounting procedure. The more difficult problem is determining the appropriate transfer price, as discussed next.

SETTING TRANSFER PRICES

The value placed on transfer goods and services is used to *make it possible to transfer goods and services between divisions while allowing them to retain their autonomy*.[1] The transfer price can be a device *to motivate managers to act in the best interest of the company*.

---

[1] The transfer pricing issue usually occurs at the division level, so we frequently refer to *divisions* or *division managers* instead of the longer *responsibility centers* or *responsibility center managers*.

Aligning Division Managers' Incentives with Those of the Company

As might be expected, a conflict can arise between the company's interests and an individual manager's interests when transfer price–based performance measures are used. The following example demonstrates such a conflict.

The Production Division of Ace Electronics Company was operating below capacity. The Assembly Division of the same company received a contract to assemble 10,000 units of a final product, XX-1. Each unit of XX-1 required one part, A-16, which was made by the Production Division. Both divisions are decentralized, autonomous investment centers and are evaluated based on operating profits and return on investment.

The vice president of the Assembly Division called the vice president of the Production Division and made a proposal:

Meg (Assembly VP): Look, Joe, I know you're running below capacity out there in your department. I'd like to buy 10,000 units of A-16 at $30 per unit. That will enable you to keep up your production lines.

Joe (Production VP): Are you kidding, Meg? I happen to know that it would cost you a lot more if you had to buy A-16s from an outside supplier. We refuse to accept less than $40 per unit, which gives us our usual markup and covers our costs.

Meg: Joe, we both know that your variable costs per unit are only $22. I realize I'd be getting a good deal at $30, but so would you. You should treat this as a special order. Anything over your differential costs on the order is pure profit. Look, Joe, if you can't do better than $40, I'll have to go elsewhere. I have to keep my costs down, too, you know.

Joe: The $40 per unit is firm. Take it or leave it!

The Assembly Division subsequently sought bids on the part and was able to obtain its requirements from an outside supplier for $40 per unit. The Production Division continued to operate below capacity. The actions of the two divisions cost the company $180,000. This amount is the difference between the price paid for the part from the outside supplier ($40) and the differential costs of producing in the Assembly Division ($22) times the 10,000 units in the order.

How can a decentralized organization avoid this type of cost? Although there is no easy solution to this type of problem, there are three general approaches to the problem:

1. Direct intervention by top management.
2. Centrally established transfer price policies.
3. Negotiated transfer prices.

Each of these approaches has advantages and disadvantages. Each may be appropriate under different circumstances. We discuss these alternatives in the next sections.

DIRECT INTERVENTION BY TOP MANAGEMENT

Ace Electronics' top management could have directly intervened in this pricing dispute and ordered the Production Division to produce the A-16s and transfer them to the Assembly Division at a management-specified transfer price. If this were an extraordinarily large order, or if internal product transfers were rare, direct intervention may be the best solution to the problem.

The disadvantage of direct intervention is that top management may become swamped with pricing disputes, and individual division managers will lose the flexibility and other advantages of autonomous decision making. Thus, direct intervention promotes short-run profits by minimizing the type of uneconomic behavior demonstrated in the Ace Electronics case, but the benefits from decentralization are reduced.

As long as the transfer pricing problems are infrequent, the benefits of direct intervention may outweigh the costs. However, if transfer transactions are common, direct intervention can be costly by requiring substantial top-management involvement in decisions that should be made at the divisional level.

CENTRALLY ESTABLISHED TRANSFER PRICE POLICIES

A transfer pricing policy should allow divisional autonomy yet encourage managers to pursue corporate goals consistent with their own personal goals. Additionally, the use of transfer prices to determine the selling division's revenue and the buying division's cost should be compatible with the company's performance evaluation system. The two bases for transfer price policies are: (1) market prices and (2) cost. We discuss these approaches and their advantages and disadantages in the following sections.

Transfer Prices Based on Market Price

Externally based market prices are generally considered the best basis for transfer pricing when there is a competitive market for the product and market prices are readily available. An advantage of market prices is that both the buying and selling divisions can buy and sell as many units as they want at the market price. Managers of both buying and selling divisions are indifferent between trading with each other or with outsiders. From the company's perspective, this is fine as long as the supplying unit is operating at capacity.

However, situations are rare in which such markets exist. Usually there are differences between products produced internally compared to those that can be purchased from outsiders, such as costs, quality, or product characteristics. The very existence of two divisions that trade with one another in one company tends to indicate that there may be advantages to dealing internally instead of with outside markets.

For example, when the Chevrolet Division of General Motors buys parts from other General Motors' divisions, it may be easier to assure quality control and reliability of delivery. Furthermore, costs of negotiating transactions can be reduced or eliminated when dealing internally.

When such advantages exist, it is in the company's interest to create incentives for internal transfer. Top management may establish policies that direct two responsibility centers to trade internally unless they can show good reason why external trades are more advantageous. A common variation on this approach is to establish a policy that provides the buying division a discount for items purchased internally.

Establishing a Market Price Policy

Market Price–Based Transfer Pricing Transfer pricing policy where the transfer price is set at the market price or at a small discount from the market price.

To encourage transfers that are in the interest of the company, management may set a transfer pricing policy based on the use of market prices for the intermediate product, such as part A-16. As a general rule, a **market price–based transfer pricing** policy contains the following guidelines:

1. The transfer price is usually set at a discount from the cost to acquire the item on the open market.
2. The selling division may elect to transfer or to continue to sell to the outside.

Imperfect Markets

Transfer pricing becomes more complex when selling and buying divisions cannot sell and buy all they want in perfectly competitive markets. In some cases, there may be no outside market at all. The transfer pricing problem can become quite complex when there are imperfect markets, and companies often find that not all transactions between divisions occur as top management would prefer. In extreme cases, the transfer pricing problem is so complex that the company is reorganized so that buying and selling divisions report to one manager who oversees the transfers. In effect, a manager is substituted for a transfer pricing policy.

Cost Basis for
Transfer Pricing

General Rule: Differential Outlay Cost plus Opportunity Cost
The **economic transfer pricing rule** for making transfers to maximize a company's profits in either perfect or imperfect markets is:

> Transfer at the differential outlay cost to the selling division plus the opportunity cost to the company of making the internal transfers.

Using the Ace Electronics example to demonstrate this rule, recall that the seller (the Production Division) could sell in outside markets for $40 and had a variable cost of $22, which we shall assume is its differential cost.

Now consider two cases. (1) The seller (Production Division) operates below capacity, in which case there is probably no opportunity cost of the internal transfer because no outside sale is forgone. (2) The seller operates at capacity and would have to give up one unit of outside sales for every unit transferred internally.

In case 2, the opportunity cost of transferring the product to a division inside the company is the forgone contribution of selling the unit in an outside market. Consequently, the optimal transfer price for Ace Electronics would be $22 for the below-capacity case or $40 for the at-capacity case, as shown in Illustration 23–1.

If the seller is operating at capacity, then the seller is indifferent between selling in the outside market for $40 or transferring internally at $40. Note that this is the same solution as the market price rule for competitive

---

23–1

Application of General
Transfer Pricing Rule—
Ace Electronics

	Differential Outlay Cost	+	Opportunity Cost of Transferring Internally	=	Transfer Price
If the seller (that is, Production Division) has idle capacity	$22	+	–0– (probably)	=	$22
If the seller has no idle capacity	22	+	$18 ($40 selling price – $22 variable cost)	=	40

markets (ignoring the wholesaler's markup), because sellers can sell everything they produce at the market price. Consequently, as a rule of thumb, the economic transfer pricing rule can be implemented as follows:

1. If the seller is operating *below* capacity, the seller should transfer at the differential cost of production.
2. If the seller is operating *at* capacity, the seller should transfer at market price.

If the seller is operating below capacity, then the seller is indifferent between providing the product and receiving a transfer price equal to the seller's differential outlay cost or not providing the product at all. For example, if the production division received a price of $22 for the product, then it would be indifferent between selling it or not. In both the below-capacity and at-capacity cases, the selling division is no worse off if the internal transfer is made.

The selling division does not earn a contribution on the transaction in the below-capacity case, however. It earns only the same contribution for the internal transfer as it would for a sale to the outside market in the at-capacity case. The general rule stated above is optimal for the company but does not benefit the selling division for an internal transfer. (For practical purposes, we assume that the selling division will transfer internally if it is indifferent between an internal transfer and an external sale.)

Alternative Cost Measures

Full-absorption cost-based transfers Although the rule "transfer at differential outlay cost to the selling division plus the opportunity cost to the company of making the internal transfer" assumes the company has a measure of differential or variable cost, this is not always the case. Consequently, full-absorption costs are sometimes used in manufacturing firms.

If measures of market prices are not available, then it is impossible to compute the opportunity cost contribution margin required by the general rule. Consequently, companies will frequently use full-absorption costs, which are higher than variable costs but probably less than the market price.

The use of full-absorption costs will not necessarily lead to the profit-maximizing solution for the company; however, it has some advantages. First, these costs are available in the company's records. Second, they provide the selling division with a contribution equal to the excess of full-absorption costs over variable costs, which gives the selling division an incentive to transfer internally. Third, the full-absorption cost may sometimes be a better measure of the differential costs of transferring internally than the variable costs. For example, the transferred product may require engineering and design work that is buried in fixed overhead. In these cases, the full-absorption cost may be a reasonable measure of the differential costs, including the unknown engineering and design costs.

Activity-based costing Many companies are implementing activity-based costing to improve the accuracy of costs in cost-based transfer pricing. One of the primary motives for Deere and Co. to develop activity-based costing, for example, was to improve the accuracy of cost numbers in its internal transfers of parts.

Cost-Plus Transfer Pricing
Transfer pricing policy based on full costing or variable costing and actual cost or standard cost plus an allowance for profit.

Cost-plus transfers We also find companies using **cost-plus transfer pricing** based on either variable costs or full-absorption costs. These methods generally apply a normal markup to costs as a surrogate for market prices when intermediate market prices are not available.

Standard costs or actual costs If actual costs are used as a basis for the transfer, any variances or inefficiencies in the selling division are passed along to the buying division. The problems of isolating the variances that have been transferred to subsequent buyer divisions becomes extremely complex. To promote responsibility in the selling division and to isolate variances within divisions, standard costs are usually used as a basis for transfer pricing in cost-based systems.

For example, suppose Ace Electronics transferred based on variable costs for part A-16. The standard variable cost of producing the part is $22, but the actual cost of producing the part turns out to be $29 because of inefficiencies in the Production Division. Should this inefficiency be passed on to the buying division? The answer is usually no to give the Production Division incentives to be efficient. In these cases, companies will use standard costs for the transfer price. If standards are out of date or otherwise do not reflect reasonable estimates of costs, then the actual cost may be a better measure to use in the transfer price.

Other Motivational Aspects of Transfer Pricing Policies

When the transfer pricing rule does not give the supplier a profit on the transaction, motivational problems can arise. For example, if transfers are made at differential cost, the supplier earns no contribution toward profits on the transferred goods. Then, the transfer price policy does not motivate the supplier to transfer internally because there is no likely profit from internal transfers. This situation can be remedied in several ways.

A supplier whose transfers are almost all internal is usually organized as a cost center. The center manager is normally held responsible for costs, not for revenues. Hence, the transfer price does not affect the manager's performance measures. In companies where such a supplier is a profit center, the artificial nature of the transfer price should be taken into consideration when evaluating the results of that center's operations.

A supplying center that does business with both internal and external customers could be set up as a profit center for external business when the manager has price-setting power, and as a cost center for internal transfers when the manager does not have price-setting power. Performance on external business could be measured as if the center were a profit center, while performance on internal business could be measured as if the center were a cost center.

Dual Transfer Pricing Transfer pricing system where the buying division is charged with costs only, and the selling division is credited with cost plus some profit allowance.

Dual transfer prices A **dual transfer pricing** system could be installed to provide the selling division with a profit but charge the buying division with costs only. That is, the buyer could be charged the cost of the unit, however cost might be determined, and the selling division could be credited with cost plus some profit allowance. The difference could be accounted for by a special centralized account. This system would preserve cost data for subsequent buyer divisions, and it would encourage internal transfers by providing a profit on such transfers for the selling divisions.

We have seen a few companies using dual transfer prices to encourage internal transfers. However, there are other ways to encourage internal transfers. For example, many companies recognize internal transfers and incorporate them explicitly in their reward systems. Other companies base part of a supplying manager's bonus on the purchasing center's profits. There are ways of creating incentives for managers to transfer internally in organizational settings where profit-based transfer prices would be disadvantageous. Management can choose from the cost-based pricing rules when such a policy would be beneficial.

NEGOTIATED PRICES

Negotiated Transfer Pricing System whereby the transfer prices are arrived at through negotiation between managers of buying and selling divisions.

An alternative to a centrally administered transfer pricing policy is to permit managers to negotiate the price for internally transferred goods and services. Under this system, the managers involved act much the same as the managers of independent companies. The major advantage to **negotiated transfer pricing** is it preserves the autonomy of the division managers. However, the two primary disadvantages are that a great deal of management effort may be consumed in the negotiating process, and the final price and its implications for performance measurement may depend more on the manager's ability to negotiate than on what's best for the company.

In the Ace Electronics case, the two managers have room to negotiate the price between $22 and $40. The two managers may choose to "split the difference" or develop some other negotiating strategy.

Self-Study Question

1 The Nykee shoe company has two divisions: Production and Marketing. Production manufactures Nykee shoes, which it sells to both the Marketing Division and to other retailers (the latter under a different brand name). Marketing operates several small shoe stores in shopping centers. Marketing sells both Nykee and other brands.

   Relevant facts for production are as follows:

   Production is operating far below its capacity.

Sales price to outsiders	$ 28.50 per pair
Variable cost to produce	18.00 per pair
Fixed costs	100,000 per month

   The following data pertain to the sale of Nykee shoes by Marketing:

   Marketing is operating far below its capacity.

Sales price	$40 per pair
Variable marketing costs	$ 1 per pair

   The company's variable manufacturing and marketing costs are differential to this decision, while *fixed* manufacturing and marketing costs are not.

   a. What is the minimum price that can be charged by the Marketing Division for the shoes and still cover the company's differential manufacturing and marketing costs?

   b. What is the appropriate transfer price for this decision?

   c. If the transfer price was set at $28.50, what effect would this have on the minimum price set by the Marketing manager?

   d. How would your answer to *b* change if the Production Division was operating at full capacity?

   The solution to this question is at the end of this chapter on page 867.

Method Used	United States[a]	Canada[b]	Japan[c]
Cost based	45%	47%	47%
Market based	33	35	34
Negotiated transfer prices	22	18	19
Total	100%	100%	100%

Note: Companies using other methods were omitted from this illustration. These companies were 2 percent or less of the total.

[a] Source: S. Borkowski, "Environmental and Organizational Factors Affecting Transfer Pricing: A Survey," *Journal of Management Accounting Research,* Fall 1990.

[b] Source: R. Tang, "Canadian Transfer Pricing Practices," *CA Magazine,* March 1980.

[c] Source: R. Tang, C. Walter, and R. Raymond, "Transfer Pricing—Japanese vs. American Style," *Management Accounting,* January 1979.

CURRENT PRACTICES IN THE UNITED STATES, CANADA, AND JAPAN

In a survey of corporate practices, shown in Illustration 23–2, the author reported that nearly half of the U.S. companies surveyed used a cost-based transfer pricing system. Thirty-three percent used a market price–based system, and 22 percent used a negotiated system. Similar results have been found for companies in Canada and Japan, as reported in Illustration 23–2.

Generally, we find that when negotiated prices are used, the prices negotiated are between the market price at the upper limit and some measure of cost at the lower limit.[2]

Is there an optimal transfer pricing policy that dominates all others? The answer is no. An established policy will, most likely, be imperfect in the sense that it will not always work to induce the economically optimal outcome. However, as with other management decisions, the cost of any system must be weighed against the benefits of the system. Improving a transfer pricing policy beyond some point (say, to obtain better measures of variable costs and market prices) will result in the costs of the system exceeding the benefits. As a result, management tends to settle for a system that seems to work reasonably well rather than devise a "textbook" perfect system.

MULTINATIONAL TRANSFER PRICING

In international transactions, transfer prices may affect tax liabilities, royalties, and other payments because of different laws in different countries (or states). Since tax rates are different in different countries, companies have incentives to set transfer prices that will increase revenues (and profits) in low-tax countries and increase costs (thereby reducing profits) in high-tax countries.

Tax avoidance by foreign companies using inflated transfer prices was a major issue in Bill Clinton's 1992 presidential campaign. Foreign companies who sell goods to their U.S. subsidiaries at inflated transfer prices artifically reduce the profit of the U.S. subsidiaries. According to Clinton advisors, the United States could collect as much as $9 billion to $13 billion per year in

---

[2] See R. Benke and J. Edwards, *Transfer Pricing: Techniques and Uses* (New York: National Association of Accountants, 1980).

additional taxes if transfer pricing was calculated according to U.S. tax laws. (Many foreign companies dispute this claim.)

To understand the effects of transfer pricing on taxes, consider the case of the Nehru Jacket Corp. The Nehru Jacket Corp.'s facility in Country N imports materials from the company's Country I facility. The tax rate in Country N is 70 percent, while the tax rate in Country I is 40 percent.

During the current year, Nehru incurred production costs of $2 million in Country I. Costs incurred in Country N, aside from the cost of the jackets, amounted to $6 million. Sales revenues in Country N were $24 million. Similar goods imported by other companies in Country N would have cost an equivalent of $3 million. However, Nehru Jacket Co. points out that because of its special control over its operations in Country I and the special approach it uses to manufacture its goods, the appropriate transfer price is $10 million. What would Nehru Jacket Co.'s total tax liability in both jurisdictions be if it used the $3 million transfer price? What would the liability be if it used the $10 million transfer price?

Assuming the $3 million transfer price, the tax liabilities are computed as follows:

	Country I	Country N
Revenues	$3,000,000	$24,000,000
Third-party costs	2,000,000	6,000,000
Transferred goods costs		3,000,000
Taxable income	1,000,000	15,000,000
Tax rate	40%	70%
Tax liability	$ 400,000	$10,500,000
Total tax liability	$10,900,000	

Assuming the $10 million transfer price, the liabilities are computed as follows:

	Country I	Country N
Revenues	$10,000,000	$24,000,000
Third-party costs	2,000,000	6,000,000
Transferred goods costs		10,000,000
Taxable income	8,000,000	8,000,000
Tax rate	40%	70%
Tax liability	$ 3,200,000	$ 5,600,000
Total tax liability	$8,800,000	

Nehru Jacket Corp. can save $2,100,000 in taxes simply by changing its transfer price!

To say the least, international taxing authorities look closely at transfer prices when examining the tax returns of companies engaged in related-party transactions that cross national boundaries. Companies must frequently have adequate support for the use of the transfer price that they have chosen for such a situation, as discussed in this chapter's real world application. (Transfer pricing disputes also occur at the State and Province level because of different tax rates. Problem 23–34 describes a transfer pricing problem that arose between the North Slope oil producer Atlantic Richfield Co. and the State of Alaska, which taxes crude oil.)

*Just-in-Time Production in Japan and the
Internal Revenue Service in the United States*

This is a story about a Japanese manufacturer that uses just-in-time production for its manufacturing facility in Japan. Its U.S. subsidiary is a distribution company that sells to dealers in the United States. Both the Japanese manufacturing facility and the U.S. distribution subidiary were profitable as long as demand for the product in the United States remained high.

During a recent period, demand in the United States for this product dropped. The U.S. subsidiary found itself with lots of inventory, so much that it had more than a year's supply of the product on hand. Meanwhile, the Japanese manufacturing plant was reluctant to reduce production below its efficient operating level, and, because it followed the just-in-time philosophy, did not stockpile finished goods inventory in Japan.

As inventories grew at the U.S. subsidiary, so did expenses to store and sell the mounting inventory of products. The U.S. subsidiary showed declining profits and eventually incurred losses. The U.S. Internal Revenue Service claimed the low profits and losses were the result of the transfer price set by the Japanese manufacturer (which was based on full-absorption manufacturing costs), and the fact that the Japanese manufacturer continued to ship products that the U.S. subsidiary had difficulty selling.

According to the IRS, the Japanese manufacturer should bear some of the costs of the U.S. subsidiary's high inventory levels. The Japanese manufacturer disagrees. This case is still in dispute as this book goes to print.

* Based on the authors' research.

 *Self-Study Question*

2 Refer to the information on Nehru Jacket Corp. in the text. Assume the tax rate for both Country I and Country N is 40 percent. What would the tax liability be for Nehru Jacket Corp. if the transfer were set at $3 million? At $10 million?

The solution to this question is at the end of this chapter on page 867.

SEGMENT REPORTING

Companies engaged in different lines of business are required by the FASB to report certain information about segments that meet the FASB's technical requirements.[3] This reporting requirement is intended to provide a measure of the performance of those segments of a business that are significant to the company as a whole.

The principal items that must be disclosed about each segment are:

1. Segment revenue.
2. Segment operating profits or loss.
3. Identifiable segment assets.
4. Depreciation and amortization.
5. Capital expenditures.
6. Certain specialized items.

---

[3] The requirements, which are too detailed to cover here, are specified in FASB, *Statement of Financial Accounting Standards No. 14,* "Financial Reporting for Segments of a Business Enterprise" (Stamford, Conn., 1976).

In addition, if a company has significant foreign operations, it must disclose revenues, operating profits or losses, and identifiable assets by geographic region.

Negotiated transfer prices, which may be useful for internal purposes, are not generally acceptable for external segment reporting. In general, the accounting profession has indicated a preference for market-based transfer prices.[4] This preference arises because the purpose of the segment disclosure is to enable an investor to evaluate a company's divisions as though they were free-standing enterprises. Presumably, sales would be based on market transactions and not on the ability of managers to negotiate prices.

Although the conceptual basis for market-based transfer prices is sound in this setting, the practical application may be difficult. Frequently, the segments are really interdependent, so market prices may not really reflect the same risk in an intracompany sale that they do in third-party sales.

In addition, in many situations, market prices are either not readily available, or they may exist for only some products. When these problems arise, management will usually attempt to estimate the market by obtaining market prices for similar goods and adjusting the price to reflect the characteristics of the goods transferred within the company. An alternative is to take the cost of the item transferred and add an allowance to represent the normal profit for the item.

SUMMARY

When companies transfer goods or services between divisions, a price is assigned to that transaction. This transfer price becomes a part of the recorded revenues and costs in the divisions involved in the transfer. As a result, the dollar value assigned to the transfer can have significant implications in measuring divisional performance. Transfer pricing systems may be based on direct intervention, market prices, costs, or negotiation among the division managers. The appropriate method depends on the markets in which the company operates and management's goals. Top management usually tries to choose the appropriate method to promote corporate goals without destroying the autonomy of division managers.

TERMS AND CONCEPTS

The following terms and concepts should be familiar to you after reading this chapter:

Cost-Plus Transfer Pricing, *847*

Dual Transfer Pricing, *847*

Economic Transfer Pricing Rule, *845*

Market Price–Based Transfer Pricing, *844*

Negotiated Transfer Pricing, *848*

Transfer Price, *842*

---

[4] See, for example, FASB, *Statement of Financial Accounting Standards No. 69,* which specifies the use of market-based transfer prices when calculating the results of operations for an oil and gas exploration and production operation.

QUESTIONS

23–1   What are some of the bases for establishing a transfer price?

23–2   Why do transfer prices exist even in highly centralized organizations?

23–3   What are some goals of a transfer pricing system in a decentralized organization?

23–4   Why are market-based transfer prices considered optimal under many circumstances?

23–5   What are the limitations to market-based transfer prices?

23–6   What are the advantages of direct intervention? What are the disadvantages of such a practice?

23–7   Why do companies often use prices other than market prices for interdivisional transfers?

23–8   Division A has no external markets. It produces monofilament that is used by Division B. Division B cannot purchase this particular type of monofilament from any other source. What transfer pricing system would you recommend for the interdivisional sale of monofilament? Why?

23–9   What is the basis for choosing between actual and standard costs for cost-based transfer pricing?

23–10   Some have suggested that managers should negotiate transfer prices. What are the disadvantages of a negotiated transfer price system?

23–11   Describe the economic basis for transfer pricing systems.

23–12   How does the choice of a transfer price affect the operating profits of both segments involved in an intracompany transfer?

23–13   Refer to this chapter's real world application. Why did the Internal Revenue Service dispute the U.S. subsidiary's reported profits and losses?

23–14   When setting a transfer price for goods that are sold across international boundaries, what factors should management take into account?

EXERCISES

23–15 Recording Transfers
(L.O.1)

Aguilar Construction Company has two operating divisions. The Precast Concrete Division manufactures building parts out of concrete. These parts are shipped to building sites and assembled on the site. The company also has a Site Construction Division that constructs buildings from the precast concrete parts. The Precast Concrete Division transferred units that cost $800,000 to a construction site operated by the Site Construction Division. The units were transferred at a price of $950,000.

Required:

What journal entries would be required to record the transfer of the parts on the books of each division?

23–16 Recording Transfers
(L.O.1)

Sky High Realty owns and manages a high-rise building. The company leased one floor of the building for its Sky High Realty Management Division. The lease calls for a monthly rental of $75,000.

Required:

What journal entries are required to record the lease payments on the books of each division?

23–17 Apply Economic Transfer Pricing Rule
(L.O.2)

Dunhill Enterprises is a real estate company with a Leasing Division that rents and manages properties for others and a Maintenance Division that performs services such as carpentry, painting, plumbing, and electrical work. The Maintenance Division has an estimated variable cost of $18 per labor-hour. The Maintenance Division works both for Dunhill Enterprises and for other companies. It could spend 100 percent of its time working for outsiders. The Maintenance Division charges $35 per hour for labor performed for outsiders. This rate is the same as the rates charged by other maintenance companies. The Leasing Division complained that it could hire its own maintenance staff at an estimated variable cost of $20 per hour.

Required:

a. What is the minimum transfer price that the Maintenance Division should obtain for its services, assuming it is operating at capacity?

b. What is the maximum price that the Leasing Division should pay?

c. Would your answers in *a* or *b* change if the Maintenance Division had idle capacity? If so, which answer would change, and what would the new amount be?

23–18   Evaluate Transfer Pricing System
(L.O.3)

Hamilton Corporation has two decentralized divisions, X and Y. Division X has always purchased certain units from Division Y at $75 per unit. Because Division Y plans to raise the price to $100 per unit, Division X desires to purchase these units from outside suppliers for $75 per unit. Division Y's costs follow:

Y's variable costs per unit	$ 70
Y's annual fixed costs	15,000
Y's annual production of these units for X	1,000 units

Required:

If Division X buys from an outside supplier, the facilities Division Y uses to manufacture these units would remain idle. What would be the result if Hamilton enforces a transfer price of $100 per unit between Divisions X and Y?

(CPA adapted)

23–19   Evaluate Transfer Pricing System
(L.O.2, L.O.3)

A company permits its decentralized units to "lease" space to one another. Division X has leased some idle warehouse space to Division Y at a price of $1 per square foot per month. Recently, Division X obtained a new five-year contract, which will increase its production sufficiently so that the warehouse space would be more valuable to them. Division X has notified Division Y that the new rental price will be $3.50 per square foot per month. Division Y can lease space at $2 per square foot in another warehouse from an outside company but prefers to stay in the shared facilities. Division Y's management states that it would prefer not to move. If Division X cannot use the space now being leased to division Y, then Division X will have to rent other space for $3 per square foot per month. (The difference in rental prices occurs because Division X requires a more substantial warehouse building than Division Y.)

Required:

Recommend a transfer price and explain your reasons for choosing that price.

23–20   Evaluate Transfer Pricing System
(L.O.3)

Selling Division offers its product to outside markets at a price of $300. Selling incurs variable costs of $110 per unit and fixed costs of $75,000 per month based on monthly production of 1,000 units.

Buying Division can acquire the product from an alternate supplier at a cost of $315 per unit. Buying Division can also acquire the product from Selling Division for $300, but it must pay $20 per unit in transportation costs in addition to the transfer price charged by Selling Division.

Required:

a. What are the costs and benefits of the alternatives available to Selling and Buying Divisions with respect to the transfer of the Selling Division's product? Assume that Selling can market all that it can produce.

b. How would your answer change if Selling had idle capacity sufficient to cover all of Buying's needs?

23–21   Evaluate Transfer Pricing System
(L.O.3)

Vancouver Transit, Ltd. (of Canada), operates a local mass transit system. The transit authority is a governmental agency and is related to the provincial government. Vancouver Transit has an agreement with the provincial government whereby it will provide rides to senior citizens at a fare of 10 cents per trip. The government will reimburse Vancouver Transit for the "cost" of each trip taken by a senior citizen.

The regular fare is $1.00 per trip. After conducting an analysis of its costs, Vancouver Transit figured that with its operating deficit, the full cost of each ride on the transit system is $2.50. Routes, capacity, and operating costs are unaffected by the number of senior citizens on any route.

Required:

a. What are the alternative prices that could be used for determining the governmental reimbursement to Vancouver Transit?

b. Which price would Vancouver Transit prefer? Why?

c. Which price would the provincial government prefer? Why?

d. If Vancouver Transit provides an average of 200,000 trips for senior citizens in a given month, what is the monthly value of the difference between the prices in *b* and *c,* above?

23–22 Evaluate Transfer Pricing System
(L.O.3)

New Sweden Plant Perfections grows specimen plants for landscape contractors. The wholesale price of each plant is $30. During the past year, New Sweden Plant Perfections sold 5,000 specimen plants. New Sweden Plant Perfections is owned 60 percent by Mr. New and 40 percent by Ms. Sweden.

Of the plants sold last year, 1,000 were sold to Fayette Landscape Co. Mr. New has a 20 percent interest in Fayette Landscape Co., and Ms. Sweden has a 60 percent interest in Fayette Landscape Co. At the end of the year, Ms. Sweden noted that Fayette was the largest buyer of New Sweden plants. She suggested that the plant company give Fayette Landscape a 10 percent reduction in prices for the coming year in recognition of their position as a preferred customer.

Required:

Assuming that Fayette Landscape purchases the same number of plants at the same prices in the coming year, what effect would the price reduction have on the operating profits that accrue to Mr. New and to Ms. Sweden for the coming year?

23–23 International Transfer Prices
(L.O.4)

Elsinor Lumber Corp. has two operating divisions. The company has a logging operation in Canada. The logs are milled and shipped to the United States where they are used by the company's Building Supplies Division. Operating expenses in Canada amount to $4 million. Operating expenses in the United States amount to $12 million exclusive of the costs of any goods transferred from Canada. Revenues in the United States are $30 million.

If the lumber were purchased from one of the company's U.S. lumber divisions, the costs would be $6 million. However, if the lumber had been purchased from an independent Canadian supplier, the cost would be $8 million. The marginal income tax rate in Canada is 60 percent, while the U.S. tax rate is 40 percent.

Required:

What is the company's total tax liability to both jurisdictions for each of the two alternative transfer pricing scenarios ($6 million or $8 million)?

23–24 Segment Reporting
(L.O.5)

Cracker Box Builders, Inc., has a Building Division and a Financing Division. The Building Division oversees construction of single-family homes in "economically efficient" subdivisions. The Financing Division takes loan applications and packages mortgages into pools and sells them in the loan markets. The Financing Division also services the mortgages. Both divisions meet the requirements for segment disclosures under accounting rules.

The Building Division had $34 million in sales last year. Costs, other than costs charged by the Finance Division, totaled $26 million. The Financing Division obtained revenues of $8 million from servicing mortgages and incurred outside costs of $7 million. In addition, the Financing Division charged the Building Division $4 million for loan-related fees. The manager of the Building Division complained to the CEO of Cracker Box stating that the Financing Division was charging twice the commercial rate for loan-related fees and that the Building Division would be better off sending its buyers to an outside lender.

The Financing Division manager stated that although commercial rates might be lower, it was more difficult to service Cracker Box mortgages, and therefore, the higher fees were justified.

Required:

a. What are the reported segment operating profits for each division ignoring income taxes, using the $4 million transfer price for the loan-related fees?

b. What are the reported segment operating profits for each division ignoring income taxes, using a $2 million commercial rate as the transfer price for the loan-related fees?

23–25   Segment Reporting
(L.O.5)

Sidney Corporation has two operating divisions: (1) an amusement park and (2) a hotel. The two divisions meet the requirements for segment disclosures. Before considering transactions between the two divisions, revenues and costs were as follows (dollars in thousands):

	Amusement Park	Hotel
Revenues	$5,600	$3,700
Costs	3,100	2,500

The amusement park and the hotel had a joint marketing arrangement whereby the hotel gave out free passes to the amusement park and the amusement park gave out discount coupons good for stays at the hotel. The value of the free passes to the amusement park redeemed during the past year totaled $800,000. The discount coupons redeemed at the hotel resulted in a decrease in hotel revenues of $300,000. As of the end of the year, all of the coupons for the current year have expired.

Required:

What are the operating profits for each division considering the effects of the costs arising from the joint marketing agreement?

PROBLEMS

23–26   Transfer Pricing with Imperfect Markets— ROI Evaluation, Normal Costing

Division S of S&T Enterprises has an investment base of $600,000. Division S produces and sells 90,000 units of a product at a market price of $10 per unit. Its variable costs total $3 per unit. The division also charges each unit with a share of fixed costs based on capacity production of 100,000 units per year. The fixed cost "burden" is computed at $5 per unit. Any production volume variance is written off to expense at the end of the period.

Division T wants to purchase 20,000 units from Division S. However, Division T is willing to pay only $6.20 per unit. The reason Division T can pay only the lower amount is that Division T has an opportunity to accept a special order at a reduced price. The order is economically justifiable only if Division T can acquire the Division S output at a reduced price.

Required:

a. What is the ROI for Division S without the transfer to Division T?

b. What is Division S's ROI if it transfers 20,000 units to Division T at $6.20 each?

c. What is the minimum transfer price for the 20,000-unit order that Division S would accept if Division S were willing to maintain the same ROI with the transfer as they would accept by selling their 90,000 units to the outside market?

23–27   Evaluate Profit Impact of Alternative Transfer Decisions

A. R. Oma, Inc., manufactures a line of men's colognes. The manufacturing process entails mixing and the addition of aromatic and coloring ingredients; the finished product is packaged in a company-produced glass bottle and packed in cases containing six bottles each.

Since sales volume is heavily influenced by the appearance of the bottle, the company developed unique bottle production processes.

All bottle production is used by the cologne manufacturing plant. Each division is considered a separate profit center and evaluated as such. As the new corporate controller, you are responsible for the definition of a proper transfer price to use for the bottles produced for the Cologne Division.

At your request, the Bottle Division general manager asked other bottle manufacturers to quote a price for the quantity and sizes demanded by the Cologne Division. These competitive prices are:

Volume	Total Price	Price per Case
2,000,000 equivalent cases[a]	$ 4,000,000	$2.00
4,000,000	7,000,000	1.75
6,000,000	10,000,000	1.67

[a] An equivalent case represents six bottles.

A cost analysis of the Bottle Division indicates that they can produce bottles at these costs:

Volume	Total Cost	Cost per Case
2,000,000 equivalent cases	$3,200,000	$1.60
4,000,000	5,200,000	1.30
6,000,000	7,200,000	1.20

These costs include fixed costs of $1.2 million and variable costs of $1 per equivalent case. These data have caused considerable corporate discussion as to the proper price to use in the transfer of bottles to the Cologne Division. This interest is heightened because a significant portion of a division manager's income is an incentive bonus based on profit center results.

The Cologne Division has the following costs in addition to the bottle costs:

Volume	Total Cost	Cost per Case
2,000,000 cases	$16,400,000	$8.20
4,000,000	32,400,000	8.10
6,000,000	48,400,000	8.07

The Marketing Department furnished the following price-demand relationship for the finished product:

Sales Volume	Total Sales Revenue	Sales Price per Case
2,000,000 cases	$25,000,000	$12.50
4,000,000	45,600,000	11.40
6,000,000	63,900,000	10.65

Required:

a. A. R. Oma, Inc., has used market price transfer prices in the past. Using the current market prices and costs, and assuming a volume of 6 million cases, calculate operating profits for:

(1) The Bottle Division.
(2) The Cologne Division.
(3) The corporation.

b.   Is this production and sales level the most profitable volume for:
(1)   The Bottle Division?
(2)   The Cologne Division?
(3)   The corporation?

Explain your answers.

(CMA adapted)

23–28   International Transfer Prices

Merchant Marine Corp. (MMC) operates a fleet of container ships in international trade between Great Britain and Thailand. All of the shipping income (that is, that related to MMC's ships) is deemed as earned in Great Britain. MMC also owns a dock facility in Thailand. This facility services MMC's fleet. Income from the dock facility is, however, deemed earned in Thailand. MMC income that is deemed attributable to Great Britain is taxed at a 75 percent rate. MMC income attributable to Thailand is taxed at a 20 percent rate. Last year, the dock facility in Thailand had operating revenues of $4 million, excluding services performed for MMC's ships. MMC's shipping revenues for last year were $26 million.

Operating costs of the dock facility were $5 million last year, and operating costs of the shipping operation, before deduction of dock facility costs, were $17 million. There are no similar dock facilities in Thailand that would be available to MMC.

However, there is a facility in Malaysia that would have charged MMC an estimated $3 million for the services that MMC's Thailand dock provided to MMC's ships. MMC management noted that if the services had been provided in Great Britain, the costs for the year would have totaled $8 million. MMC argued to the British tax officials that the appropriate transfer price is the price that would have been charged in Great Britain. British tax officials suggest that the Malaysian price is the appropriate one.

Required:

What is the difference in tax costs to MMC between the alternate transfer prices for dock services: price in Great Britain versus price in Malaysia?

23–29   Analyze Transfer Pricing Data

MultiProduct Enterprises, Inc., is a decentralized organization that evaluates division management based on measures of division contribution margin. Divisions A and B operate in similar product markets. Division A produces a solid-state electronic assembly that may be sold to the outside market at a price of $16 per unit. The outside market can absorb up to 140,000 units per year. These units require two direct labor-hours each.

If A modifies the units with an additional one-half hour of labor time, the units can be sold to Division B at a price of $18 per unit. Division B will accept up to 120,000 of these units per year.

If Division B does not obtain 120,000 units from A, then B will purchase the needed units for $18.50 from the outside. Division B incurs $8 of additional labor and other out-of-pocket costs to convert the assemblies into a home digital eletronic radio, calculator, telephone monitor, and clock unit. The unit can be sold to the outside market at a price of $45 each.

Division A estimates its total costs are $925,000 for fixed costs and $6 per direct labor-hour. Capacity in Division A is limited to 400,000 direct labor-hours per year.

Required:

Determine the following:

a.   Total contribution margin to A if it sells 140,000 units to the outside.

b.   Total contribution margin to A if it sells 120,000 units to B.

c.   The costs to be considered in determining the optimal company policy for sales by Division A.

d.   The annual contributions and costs for Divisions A and B under the optimal policy.

23–30   Selecting a Transfer Price

Lorax Electric Company manufactures components for the electronics industry. The firm is organized into several divisions, with division managers given the authority to make virtually all operating decisions. Management control over divisional operations is maintained by a system of divisional profit and return-on-investment measures that are reviewed regularly by top management.

The Devices Division manufactures solid-state devices and is operating at capacity. The Systems Division asked the Devices Division to supply a large quantity of integrated circuits IC378. The Devices Division currently is selling this component to its regular customers at $40 per hundred.

The Systems Division, which is operating at about 60 percent capacity, wants this particular component for a digital clock system. It has an opportunity to supply large quantities of these digital clock systems to Centonic Electric, which offered to pay $7.50 per clock system. Each clock requires five units of IC378.

The Systems Division prepared an analysis of the costs to produce the clock systems. The amount that could be paid to the Devices Division for the integrated circuits was determined by working backward from the selling price. The cost estimates employed by the division reflected the highest per unit cost the Systems Division could incur for each cost component and still leave a sufficient margin so that the division's income statement could show reasonable improvement. The cost estimates are:

Proposed selling price		$7.50
Costs excluding required integrated circuits (IC378):		
Components purchased from outside suppliers	$2.75	
Circuit board etching—labor and variable overhead	0.40	
Assembly, testing, packaging—labor and variable overhead	1.35	
Fixed overhead allocations	1.50	
Profit margin	0.50	6.50
Amount that can be paid for integrated circuits IC378 (5 @ $20 per hundred)		$1.00

As a result of this analysis, the Systems Division offered the Devices Division a price of $20 per hundred for the integrated circuit. This bid was refused by the manager of the Devices Division because he felt the Systems Division should at least meet the price of $40 per hundred that regular customers pay. When the Systems Division found that it could not obtain a comparable integrated circuit from outside vendors, the situation was brought to an arbitration committee that had been set up to review such problems.

The arbitration committee prepared an analysis that showed that 15 cents would cover variable costs of producing the integrated circuit, 28 cents would cover the full cost including fixed overhead, and 35 cents would provide a gross margin equal to the average gross margin on all of the products sold by the Devices Division. The manager of the Systems Division reacted by stating, "They could sell us that integrated circuit for 20 cents and still earn a positive contribution toward profit. In fact, they should be required to sell at their variable cost—15 cents—and not be allowed to take advantage of us."

The manager of Devices countered by stating, "It doesn't make sense to sell to the Systems Division at $20 per hundred when we can get $40 per hundred outside on all we can produce. In fact, Systems could pay us more than $50 per hundred, and they would still have a positive contribution margin."

The recommendation of the committee, to set the price at 35 cents per unit ($35 per hundred), so that Devices could earn a fair gross margin, was rejected by both division managers. Consequently, the problem was brought to the attention of the vice president of operations.

Required:

a. What is the immediate economic effect on the Lorax Electric Company as a whole if the Devices Division were required to supply IC378 to the Systems Division at 35 cents per unit—the price recommended by the arbitration committee? Explain your answer. Discuss the advisability of intervention by top management as a solution to transfer pricing disputes between division managers such as the one experienced by Lorax Electric Company.

b. Suppose that Lorax adopted a policy of requiring that the price to be paid in all internal transfers by the buying division be equal to the variable costs per unit of the selling division for that product and that the supplying division be required to sell if the buying division decided to buy the item. Discuss the consequences of adopting such a policy as a way of avoiding the need for the arbitration committee or for intervention by the vice president.

c. Suggest an alternative transfer price that would overcome some of the problems mentioned. Show how it would result in goal congruence.

(CMA adapted)

23–31 Transfer Pricing— Performance Evaluation Issues

The Ajax Division of Gunnco Corporation, operating at capacity, has been asked by the Defco Division of Gunnco to supply it with electrical fitting no. 1726. Ajax sells this part to its regular customers for $7.50 each. Defco, which is operating at 50 percent capacity, is willing to pay $5 each for the fitting. Defco will put the fitting into a brake unit that it is manufacturing on a cost-plus basis for a commercial airplane manufacturer.

Ajax has a variable cost of producing fitting no. 1726 of $4.25. The cost of the brake unit as built by Defco is as follows:

Purchased parts—outside vendors	$22.50
Ajax fitting—1726	5.00
Other variable costs	14.00
Fixed overhead and administration	8.00
	$49.50

Defco believes the price concession is necessary to get the job.

The company uses ROI and dollar profits in the measurement of division and division manager performance.

Required:

a. If you were the division controller of Ajax, would you recommend that Ajax supply fitting 1726 to Defco? (Ignore any income tax issues.) Why or why not?

b. Would it be to the short-run economic advantage of the Gunnco Corporation for the Ajax Division to supply the Defco Division with fitting 1726 at $5 each? (Ignore any income tax issues.) Explain your answer.

c. Discuss the organizational and manager behavior difficulties, if any, inherent in this situation. As the Gunnco controller, what would you advise the Gunnco Corporation president to do in this situation?

(CMA adapted)

23–32 Evaluate Transfer Price System

MBR, Inc., consists of three divisions: Boston Corporation, Raleigh Company, and Memphis Company. The three divisions operate as if they were independent companies. Each division has its own sales force and production facilities. Each division management is responsible for sales, cost of operations, acquisition and financing of divisional assets, and working capital management. MBR corporate management evaluates the performance of the divisions and division managements on the basis of ROI.

Memphis Company has just been awarded a contract for a product that uses a component manufactured by outside suppliers as well as by the Raleigh Company, which is operating well below capacity. Memphis used a cost figure of $3.80 for the component manufactured by Raleigh in preparing its bid for the new product. This cost figure was supplied by Raleigh in response to Memphis's request for the average variable cost of the component and represents the standard variable manufacturing cost and variable marketing costs.

Raleigh's regular selling price for the component Memphis needs for the new product is $6.50. Raleigh management indicated that it could supply Memphis with the required quantities of the component at the regular selling price less variable selling and distribution expenses. Memphis management responded by offering to pay standard variable manufacturing cost plus 20 percent.

The two divisions have been unable to agree on a transfer price. Corporate management has never established a transfer price policy. The corporate vice president of finance suggested a price equal to the standard full manufacturing cost (that is, no selling and distribution expenses) plus a 15 percent markup. This price has been rejected by the two division managers because each considered it grossly unfair.

The unit cost structure for the Raleigh component and the suggested prices are shown below.

Costs:

Standard variable manufacturing cost	$3.20
Standard fixed manufacturing cost	1.20
Variable selling and distribution expenses	.60
	$5.00

Prices:

Regular selling price	$6.50
Regular selling price less variable selling and distribution expenses ($6.50 − .60)	$5.90
Variable manufacturing plus 20% ($3.20 × 1.20)	$3.84
Standard full manufacturing cost plus 15% ($4.40 × 1.15)	$5.06

Required:

a. Discuss the effect each of the proposed prices might have on the Raleigh Company management's attitude toward intracompany business.

b. Is the negotiation of a price between the Memphis and Raleigh divisions a satisfactory method to solve the transfer price problem? Explain your answer.

c. Should the corporate management of MBR, Inc., become involved in this transfer price controversy? Explain your answer.

(CMA adapted)

23–33   Transfer Prices and Tax Regulations

ExIm, Inc., has two operating divisions in a semiautonomous organization structure. Division Ex is located in the United States. It produces a part labeled XZ-1, which is an input to Division Im, which is located in the south of France. Division Ex has idle capacity that it used to produce XZ-1. The market price of XZ-1 domestically is $60. The variable costs are $25 per unit. The company's U.S. tax rate is 40 percent of income.

After paying the transfer price for each XZ-1 received from Division Ex, Division Im also pays a shipping fee of $15 per unit. Part XZ-1 becomes a part of Division Im's output product. The output product costs an additional $10 to produce and sells for an equivalent $115. Division Im could purchase part XZ-1 from a Paris supplier at a cost of $50 per unit. The company's French tax rate is 70 percent of income. Assume French tax laws permit transferring at either variable cost or market price. Assume the U.S. division's income is taxed at 40 percent.

Required:

What transfer price is economically optimal for ExIm, Inc.? Show computations.

**23–34 Transfer Pricing—
Third-Party
Consequences**

Arco owns a substantial interest in oil production in the northern part of Alaska. The North Alaska market for crude oil cannot absorb all of the production from the area. Hence, nearly all of the oil must be shipped through the Trans Alaska Pipeline System to the southern part of Alaska for delivery to tankers that then deliver the crude to the U.S. West Coast where all of Arco's Alaska crude oil is refined and marketed. The U.S. West Coast market faces an oversupply of crude oil. Some Alaska producers, therefore, ship their oil though the Panama Canal to the U.S. Gulf Coast where their crude oil is then refined and marketed. Arco's share of Alaska production is approximately 150 million barrels of crude oil per year. Production quantities are fixed by the capacity of the pipeline system to carry the crude oil across Alaska.

Oil production is subject to a severance tax due the state based on the value of the crude oil at the point of production and a royalty that is an amount paid to the landowner for the rights to produce. Severance taxes in Alaska equal 12 percent of the value of production. The royalty amount is effectively equal to 12.5 percent of the value of each barrel of oil produced. In the early 1980s, the federal government levied a windfall profit tax which, for our purposes, is equivalent to 15 percent of the value of oil and gas produced. These three cost items (severance taxes, royalty, windfall profit taxes) are based on a percentage of the value of production before the oil enters the pipeline system. However, value cannot be determined directly at that point because virtually no oil is sold at that point. It is necessary to determine a transfer price at the point where the crude oil leaves the producing field and enters the pipeline system. The greater the transfer price, the greater the royalty and taxes and vice versa. The transfer price is calculated by taking the "market value" of the crude oil where there is a market and deducting the costs to ship the crude oil through the pipeline system (known as a tariff) and the costs of transporting the crude oil from the pipeline to the market. None of the pipeline operating costs are affected by the amount of the tariff. Other operating costs are estimated at $2.50 per barrel regardless of the method used for transfer pricing.

In recent years, the selling price for crude oil on the U.S. West Coast has been $19 per barrel. Costs to ship from the southern coast of Alaska to the U.S. West Coast approximate 75 cents per barrel. The selling price for crude oil on the U.S. Gulf Coast averages $20 per barrel. However, shipping costs from Alaska to the U.S. Gulf Coast average $3.70 per barrel. Arco argues that although it sells no oil on the U.S. Gulf Coast, that is the appropriate market because the U.S. West Coast is so flooded with Alaska crude oil that it is not an appropriate market for valuation purposes. Regardless of the basis for the transfer price, Arco will dispose of its crude oil on the U.S. West Coast and incur the costs to ship it to that destination.

Arco owns a proportional interest in the Trans Alaska Pipeline Company equivalent to its interest in production from northern Alaska. Unlike crude oil production, pipeline earnings are not subject to royalty, severance taxes, or windfall profit taxes. Arco argues that the cost to ship the crude oil through the pipeline system (the tariff) is $6 per barrel, based primarily on the assumption that the pipeline should be depreciated over one half of its useful life and that the cost of building the pipeline should be based on the assumption that Arco used 100 percent equity rather than leveraged the costs of pipeline construction. The state of Alaska and others argue that the pipeline shipping cost is closer to $3 per barrel based on straight-line depreciation over the expected useful life of the pipeline and based on recognition of the fact that 90 percent of the pipeline costs were financed with debt at less than prime lending rates. The value of the pipeline service cannot be determined through open market transactions because those who ship through the pipeline are the same companies as those who produce the crude oil.

Required:

a. What are the four possible combinations of valuation techniques for Northern Alaska crude oil?

b. Prepare a schedule showing the annual severance taxes, royalty, windfall profit taxes, and operating profits to Arco from each of the four valuation methods.

c. Assuming there were no tax or royalty considerations, if you wanted to establish a market price for Arco's North Alaska crude oil, would you use the U.S. West Coast price or the U.S. Gulf Coast price as a starting point in the valuation exercise? Support the price you choose.

23–35   Segment Reporting

Allegiance Corp. has four operating divisions: (1) Airline; (2) Hotel; (3) Auto Rental; and (4) Travel Services. Each division is a separate segment for financial-reporting purposes. Revenues and costs related to outside transactions were as follows for the past year (dollars in millions):

	Airline	Hotel	Auto Rental	Travel Services
Revenues	$245	$106	$89	$32
Costs	157	71	66	30

The airline participated in a frequent stayer program with the hotel chain. During the past year, the airline reported that it traded hotel award coupons for travel that had a retail value of $26 million, assuming that the travel was redeemed at full airline fares. The Auto Rental Division offered 20 percent discounts to Allegiance's airline passengers and hotel guests. These discounts to airline passengers were estimated to have a retail value of $7 million. Allegiance hotel guests redeemed $3 million in auto rental discount coupons. Allegiance hotels provided rooms for flight crews on Allegiance's airline. The value of the rooms for the year was $13 million.

The Travel Services Division booked flights on Allegiance's airline. This service was valued at $4 million for the year. This service for intracompany hotel bookings was valued at $2 million and for intracompany auto rentals at $1 million.

While preparing all of these data for financial statement presentation, the Hotel Division's controller stated that the value of the airline coupons should be based on the differential and opportunity costs of the travel awards, not on the full fare for the tickets issued. This argument was suppported because award travel is usually allocated to seats that would otherwise be empty or contains restrictions similar to those on discount tickets. If the differential and opportunity costs were used for this transfer price, the value would be $5 million instead of $26 million. The airline controller made a similar argument concerning the auto rental discount coupons. If the differential cost basis were used for the auto rental coupons, the transfer price would be $1 million instead of the $7 million above.

Allegiance reports assets in each segment as follows:

Airline	$955 million
Hotel	385 million
Car Rental	321 million
Travel Services	65 million

Required:

a. Using the retail values for transfer pricing for segment reporting purposes, what are the operating profits for each division of Allegiance Corp.?

b. What are the operating profits for each division of Allegiance Corp. using the differential cost basis for pricing transfers?

c. Rank each division by return on investment using the transfer pricing method in *a,* above, as well as using the transfer pricing method in *b,* above. What difference does the transfer pricing system have on the rankings?

INTEGRATIVE CASES

23–36   Decentralization and Transfer Pricing: Calvin's Auto

Calvin's Auto was divided into three departments: New-Car Sales, Used-Car Sales, and Service. Department managers were told to run their departments as if they were independent businesses. To give department managers an incentive, most of their remuneration was to be calculated as a straight percentage of their department's operating profit.

A customer wanted to trade in his old car as part of the purchase price of a new one with a list price of $16,000. Before closing the sale, the new-car manager had to decide on the amount he would offer the customer for the trade-in value of the old car. He knew that if no trade-in were involved, he would deduct about 10 percent from the list price of this model new car to be competitive with other dealers in the area. He also wanted to make sure that he did not lose the sale by offering too low a trade-in allowance.

To establish the trade-in value of the car, the used-car manager accompanied the new-car manager and the customer out to the parking lot to examine the car. In the course of his appraisal, the used-car manager estimated that the car would require reconditioning work costing about $1,000, after which the car would retail for about $3,500. The used-car manager estimated that he could get about $2,100 for the car "as is" (that is, without any work being done to it) at a weekly auction at which dealers regularly buy and sell used cars.

The New-Car Sales Department manager had the right to take any trade-in at any price he thought appropriate, but then it was his responsibility to dispose of the car. He had the alternative of either trying to persuade the used-car manager to take over the car and accepting the used-car manager's appraisal price, or he himself could sell the car at the auction.

The new-car manager decided he would allow $4,000 for the used car, provided the customer agreed to pay the list price of $16,000 for the new car. After some discussion, the $4,000 allowance and $16,000 list price were agreed upon.

The company's accountant set about recording the sale in the accounting records of the business. She saw the new car had been purchased from the manufacturer for $13,000; she was uncertain about the value she should place on the trade-in car. The new car's list price was $16,000 and it had cost $13,000, so she reasoned the gross margin on the new-car sale was $3,000. Yet the new-car manager had allowed $4,000 for the old car, which needed $1,000 in repairs, after which it could be sold retail for $3,500. Uncertain about the value she should place on the used car for inventory valuation purposes, the accountant decided that she would temporarily put down a value of $4,000, and await instructions from her superiors.

When the manager of the Used-Car Sales Department found out what the accountant had done, he went to the New-Car Sales Deparment manager's office and stated forcefully that he would not accept $4,000 as the value of the used car. He stated:

> I never would have allowed the customer $4,000 for that car. My department has to make a profit too, you know. My own income is dependent on the profit I show on the sale of used cars, and I will not stand for having my income hurt because you are too generous.

The service manager arrived with Calvin Cline, the company president, and stated:

> There is something bothering me about this accounting system we've been using. I can't charge as much on an internal job as I would for the same job performed for an outside customer. If I did work costing $1,000 for an outside customer, I would be able to charge about $1,600 for the job. I figure that I

should be able to make the same charge for repairing a trade-in as I would get for an outside repair job.

Required:

a. Suppose the new-car deal is consummated, with the repaired used car being retailed for $3,500 and the variable cost of the repairs being $1,000. Assume that all sales personnel are on salary (no commissions), and that department and company costs not explicitly mentioned in the case are fixed and not affected by this transaction. What is the dealership contribution on the total transaction (that is, new and repaired used cars sold)?

b. Assume each department (New-Car Sales, Used-Car Sales, Service) is treated as a profit center, as described in the case.
  (1) At what value should this trade-in (unrepaired) be transferred from the New-Car Sales Department to the Used-Car Sales Department? Why?
  (2) How much should the Service Department be able to charge the Used-Car Sales Department for the repairs on this trade-in car if the Service Department operates below capacity? Why?
  (3) How much should the Service Department be able to charge if it operates at capacity? Why?

c. Given your responses to *b*, what will be each of the three departments' contributions on this transaction, assuming:
  (1) The Service Department is operating below capacity.
  (2) The Service Department is operating at capacity.

d. If the Service Department was operating at capacity, would the dealership be better off to repair and retail the used car or sell it as is?

e. Do you feel the three-profit-center approach is appropriate for the auto dealership? If so, explain why, including an explanation of how this is better than other specific alternatives. If not, propose a better alternative and explain why it is better than the three-profit-center approach and any other alternatives you have considered.

23–37 Birch Paper Company (Evaluate Transfer Pricing Policy and Use of Responsibility Centers)*

"If I were to price these boxes any lower than $480 a thousand," said James Brunner, manager of Birch Paper Company's Thompson Division, "I'd be countermanding my order for last month for our sales force to stop shaving their bids and to bid full-cost quotations. If I turn around now and accept this for something less than $480, I'll be tearing down my own orders. The division can't very well show a profit by putting in bids that don't even cover a fair share of overhead costs, let alone give us a profit."

Birch Paper Company was a medium-sized, partly integrated paper company, producing white and kraft papers and paperboard. A portion of its paperboard output was converted into corrugated boxes by the Thompson Division, which also printed the outside surface of the boxes. Including Thompson, the company had four producing divisions and a Timberland Division, which supplied part of the company's pulp requirements.

For several years, each division had been judged independently on the basis of its profit and ROI. Top management had been working to gain effective results from a policy of decentralizing responsibility and authority for all decisions except those relating to overall company policy. The company's top officials felt that in the past few years the concept of decentralization had been successfully applied and that the company's profits and competitive position had definitely improved.

* Copyright © 1957 by the President and Fellows of Harvard College. Harvard Business School case 158-001. This case was prepared by William Rotch under the direction of Neil E. Harlan as a basis for class discussion rather than to illustrate either effective or ineffective handling of an administrative situation. Reprinted by permission of the Harvard Business School.

Early in the year, the Northern Division designed a special display box for one of its papers in conjunction with the Thompson Division, which was equipped to make the box. Thompson's package design and development staff spent several months perfecting the design, production methods, and materials that were to be used; because of the unusual color and shape, these were far from standard. According to an agreement between the two divisions, the Thompson Division was reimbursed by the Northern Division for the out-of-pocket cost of its design and development work.

When the specifications were all prepared, the Northern Division asked for bids on the box from the Thompson Division and from two outside companies, West Paper Company and Erie Papers, Inc. Each division manager normally was free to buy from whichever supplier he wished, and even on sales within the company, divisions were expected to meet the going market price if they wanted the business.

At this time, the profit margins of converters such as the Thompson Division were being squeezed. Thompson, as did many other similar converters, bought its board, liner, or paper; and its function was to print, cut, and shape it into boxes. Though it bought most of its materials from other Birch divisions, most of Thompson's sales were to outside customers. If Thompson got the order from Northern, it probably would buy its linerboard and corrugating medium from the Southern Division of Birch. The walls of a corrugated box consist of outside and inside sheets of linerboard sandwiching the corrugating medium.

About 70 percent of Thompson's variable cost of $400 a thousand for the order represented the cost of linerboard and corrugating medium. Though Southern Division had been running below capacity and had excess inventory, it quoted the market price, which had not noticeably weakened as a result of the oversupply. Its variable costs on liner and corrugating medium were about 60 percent of selling price.

The Northern Division received bids on the boxes of $480 a thousand from the Thompson Division, $430 a thousand from West Paper, and $432 a thousand from Erie Papers. Erie offered to buy from Birch the outside linerboard and corrugating medium. The outside liner would be supplied by the Southern Division at a price equivalent to $90 a thousand boxes and would be printed for $30 a thousand by the Thompson Division. Of the $30, about $25 would be variable costs.

Since this situation appeared to be a little unusual, William Kenton, manager of the Northern Division, discussed the wide discrepancy of bids with Birch's commercial vice president. He told the commercial vice president, "We sell in a very competitive market, where higher costs cannot be passed on. How can we be expected to show a decent profit and return on investment if we have to buy our supplies at more than 10 percent over the going market?"

Knowing that Brunner had on occasion in the past few months been unable to operate the Thompson Division at capacity, the commercial vice president thought it odd that Brunner would add the full 20 percent overhead and profit charge to his variable costs. When he asked Brunner about this over the telephone, his answer was the statement that appears at the beginning of the case. Brunner went on to say that having done the developmental work on the box, and having received no profit on that, he felt entitled to a normal markup on the production of the box itself.

The vice president explored further the costs of the various divisions. He remembered a comment the controller had made to the effect that costs that for one division were variable could be largely fixed for the company as a whole. He knew that in the absence of specific orders from top management, Kenton would accept the lowest bid; namely, that of West Paper for $430. However, it would be possible for top management to order the acceptance of another bid if the situation warranted such action. And though the volume represented by the transactions in question was less than 5 percent of the volume of any of the divisions involved, other transactions could conceivably raise similar problems later.

Required: Does the system motivate Mr. Brunner in such a way that actions he takes in the best interests of the Thompson Division are also in the best interests of the Birch Paper

Company? If your answer is no, give some specific instances related as closely as possible to the type of situation described in the case. Would the managers of other divisions be correctly motivated? What should the vice president do?

SOLUTIONS TO

Q Self-Study Question

1 *a.* From a company's perspective, the minimum price would be the variable cost of producing and marketing the goods, $19. If the company was centralized, we would expect this information would be conveyed to the manager of Marketing, who would be instructed not to set a price below $19.

    b. The transfer price that correctly informs the Marketing manager about the differential costs of manufacturing is $18.

    c. If the Production manager set the price at $28.50, the Marketing manager would set the minimum price at $29.50 ($28.50 + $1.00). So, the Marketing manager sets the price in excess of $29.50 per pair. In fact, prices of $28, $25, or anything greater than $19 would have generated a positive contribution margin from the production and sale of shoes.

    d. If the Production Division had been operating at capacity, there would have been an implicit opportunity cost of internal transfers. The implicit opportunity cost to the company is the lost contribution margin ($28.50 − $19 = $9.50) from not selling in the wholesale market.

The transfer price should have been:

$$\text{Differential cost of production} + \text{Implicit opportunity cost to company if goods are transferred internally}$$

$$= \$19 + \$9.50$$

$$= \$28.50$$

Marketing would have appropriately treated the $28.50 as part of its differential cost of buying and selling the shoes.

2 For the $3 million transfer, the total tax is (40% × $1,000,000) + (40% × $15,000,000) = $6,400,000. For $10 million, the total tax is (40% × $8,000,000) + (40% × $8,000,000) = $6,400,000. With equal tax rates, there is no advantage to inflating the transfer price.

SPECIAL TOPICS

Management Ethics and Financial Fraud

LEARNING OBJECTIVES

After reading this chapter, you should be able to:

1. Explain the nature of fraudulent financial reporting.
2. Describe common types of fraudulent financial reporting, such as early revenue recognition and overstating inventory, and explain how they affect reported profits.
3. Recognize motives and opportunities that create conditions conducive to financial fraud.
4. Explain why the "tone at the top" of companies is important in preventing fraudulent financial reporting.
5. Explain how separation of duties helps prevent fraudulent financial reporting.
6. Describe actual case studies of fraudulent financial reporting.
7. Explain how the combination of autonomy and pressure to achieve short-term financial results is conducive to fraudulent financial reporting.

*T*his chapter deals with ethical issues in financial reporting. We focus on motives and opportunities for committing fraud by managers and employees in companies.

We have added this chapter to the book because an increasing number of former students have come to us stressing the importance of discussing real ethical dilemmas that people face on the job. This discussion should take place in a variety of classes, they say, and not be limited to classes on ethics. We agree. Although we have included discussions on ethical issues in numerous chapters in this book, we believe an entire chapter should be devoted to the problems associated with fraudulent financial reporting.

Former students and our own research indicate that many managers and other employees are often placed under enormous pressure to meet high performance standards. Performance is often measured by short-term financial results, like profits and return on investment. Because of this pressure to meet short-term financial targets, managers and other employees may be tempted to "cook the books" by carrying obsolete inventory on the books, overstating revenues, understating costs, or other methods.

Many of you will find yourselves in situations where there is a great deal of pressure to fudge the numbers. Some of you will help companies design control systems to prevent unethical behavior. Still others will be auditors or examiners who will attempt to detect fraudulent reporting. Some of you will work in the growing field of forensic accounting in which you might assist attorneys in litigation, often as expert witnesses or as consultants. Forensic accountants also get involved in computing damages due to lost profits, finding problems in auditing procedures, and finding fraud in business records. All of you will benefit from an understanding of the conditions conducive to fraudulent financial reporting.

The purpose of this chapter is to help you recognize conditions that are conducive to fraudulent financial reporting. After discussing these conditions, we present three actual cases of fraudulent divisional financial reports—Doughtie's Foods, Ronson Corporation, and PepsiCo. These are not cases in which "bad people" committed criminal acts. These are not like certain highly publicized cases involving grand schemes designed to obtain funds illegally through insider trading or by establishing fictitious companies. Instead, these are cases where managers and accountants in companies found themselves under a great deal of pressure to perform well, and they succumbed to the pressure. While these people did not go to prison, the consequences of their actions were serious, nevertheless. They all lost their jobs. In some cases, they were involved in lengthy litigation.

Before continuing, we want to emphasize that, in our view, the vast majority of people in business organizations behave ethically. However, even people who behave ethically find that they or people they know are sometimes in situations where they are pressured to behave unethically.

FRAUDULENT FINANCIAL REPORTING

Fraudulent Financial Reporting Intentional or reckless conduct that results in materially misleading financial statements.

Materiality Magnitude of financial misstatement such that it is likely to affect the judgment of a reasonable person relying on the information.

Fraudulent financial reporting is conduct that is intended to produce materially misleading financial statements. Not writing off obsolete inventory and recognizing revenue before the sale has been made are common examples of fraudulent financial reporting. Embezzlement or theft of assets and unintentional errors in preparing financial statements do not constitute fraud.

The two key concepts in the definition of fraudulent financial reporting are (1) the conduct must be intentional or reckless, and (2) the misstatement must be material to the financial statements. **Materiality,** in this setting, refers to the magnitude of the misstatement. To be material, the magnitude of the misstatement must be large enough that it would likely affect the judgment of a reasonable person relying on the information. Simply stated, the misstatement must be important.

Intent to commit fraud or reckless conduct is difficult to prove in financial fraud cases. Consequently, when the Securities and Exchange Commission (SEC) charges someone with fraud under the provisions of the securities laws, the accused often signs a document consenting to certain restrictions without admitting to or denying the charges. In some cases, such as Barry Minkow and his company ZZZZ Best, the fraud is so extensive that criminal charges are brought.[1] The cases we discuss are the more common variety in which people reported inaccurate financial numbers, but authorities would find it difficult or even impossible to *prove* fraud. When we refer to cases of financial fraud, keep in mind that financial fraud has generally not been proven; therefore, the cases we discuss actually represent *alleged* fraud cases.

Who Commits Fraud?   Employees at all levels in the organization could be involved in fraudulent financial reporting, from top management to low-level employees. A company's external auditors may also be held responsible for their client's fraudulent financial reporting.

Department and division managers may commit fraud in financial reports to their superiors. For example, managers at certain PepsiCo bottling plants misled their superiors at corporate headquarters in Purchase, New York, by failing to write off obsolete or unusable bottle inventories. Fraudulent reporting inside a company misleads top management and the board of directors, as well as stockholders and other outsiders who rely on the company's financial information. In a recent fraud case involving the women's apparel manufacturer Leslie Fay, the chief executive expressed disappointment in the actions of the controller and other employees who had covered up financial problems by making false financial entries in the company's records. The chief executive said, "Had the false entries not been made and the senior management been furnished with accurate financial information during the year, we could have taken steps to improve the situation."[2]

Top managers may be involved in attempts to mislead outsiders. Most cases that are reported by the media involve top management. Many cases that occur inside the company are either too small to be considered material to the numbers in the external financial statements, or the frauds are detected and the numbers corrected before the frauds would have affected published annual reports and filings with the Securities and Exchange Commission. In many cases, people started out bending the rules a little, only to find themselves in deep trouble after bending the rules a little for a long time.

Self-Study Question

1 An accounting clerk leaves work early on December 31, Year 1, to attend a New Year's Eve party. The clerk calls in sick every day for the first week of Year 2, so management hires a temporary clerk. The temporary clerk records revenues from a stack of sales documents left on the sick clerk's desk. The sales documents were not dated, but since they had been left on the desk from December 31, Year 1, the temporary clerk assumed they represented Year 1 sales. In fact, the sales documents actually related to Year 2 sales that took place on January 2—the documents had been left undated because the sale had not taken place as of December 31. The temporary clerk recorded these sales in Year 1. The error was never found.

---

[1] "Do You Know Me? I Stole Millions and Here's How," *The Wall Street Journal*, April 1, 1991, pp. A1, A6.

[2] "Leslie Fay Now Expects to Post '92 Loss of $13.7 Million, Will Restate '91 Results," *The Wall Street Journal*, March 1, 1993, p. A5.

Is this an example of fraudulent financial reporting? Would your answer change if you knew the amount of the sales was material?

The solution to this question is at the end of this chapter on page 906.

TYPES OF FRAUD

The different types of financial fraud are too numerous to list. These include omitting liabilities from financial statements, overstating assets on the balance sheet, and preparing false appraisals and other documents to support loans, as was done in many of the savings and loan companies that failed in the 1980s. Many cases of fraud directly affect the income statement by understating costs, such as capitalizing items that should be expensed, or overstating revenues. In our research, we have found the two most common types of fraud involve improper revenue recognition and overstating inventory.

Improper Revenue Recognition

Improper revenue recognition often results from backdating sales to report revenue on December 30, Year 1, when the sales legitimately should have been reported in January of Year 2. Thus, the company shows both the revenue and the cost of goods sold in Year 1 instead of Year 2. Assuming revenue equals $100 and cost of goods sold equals $60, the journal entry recorded in Year 1 would be as follows:

Accounts Receivable	100	
Sales		100
Cost of Goods Sold	60	
Inventory		60

Of course, this entry *should* be made in Year 2, not in Year 1. Therefore, the timing change overstates Accounts Receivable at the end of Year 1 by $100 and understates Inventory at the end of Year 1 by $60. After the sale is properly made in Year 2, the Accounts Receivable and Inventory accounts are correct, but until then the two asset accounts are incorrect. Recording the sale in Year 1 would overstate operating profits in Year 1 by $40 and understate operating profits in Year 2 by $40, assuming no other expenses were affected by the fraudulent entry. Computing the effect on the corporate "bottom line" net income requires taking the effect of taxes into account. This entry also increases the taxes paid in Year 1 and decreases taxes in Year 2.

We can find plenty of examples of early revenue recognition. In the case of MiniScribe, a Denver-based computer disk drive manufacturer, invoices for sales made on the first day of the year were backdated to the last day of the previous year.[3] Among other activities, the company had shipped bricks to distributors and booked them as sales of disk drives. In other cases, companies have shipped products to company-owned warehouses but claimed the shipments were sales.

Early revenue recognition, resulting from backdating invoices or prematurely recording a sale, has only a temporary effect on reported revenues

---

[3] "How MiniScribe Got Its Auditor's Blessing on Questionable Sales," *The Wall Street Journal*, May 14, 1992, p. A5.

and profits. Pulling a sale out of Period 2 and reporting it in Period 1 improves profits for Period 1, but results in the loss of a legitimate sale in Period 2. Now Period 2 does not look as good as it should legitimately, so perhaps a sale from Period 3 will be moved back to Period 2 to cover for the sale previously moved from Period 2 to Period 1.

Overstating Inventory

An example of overstating inventory occurs when managers or accountants fail to write down obsolete inventory. Department or division managers may not want to "take a hit" on the financial reports now, postponing the write-off until a later period. In other cases, people falsify the ending inventory numbers during physical inventory counts or on audit papers. For example, investigators of the MiniScribe case said that senior company officials "apparently broke into locked trunks containing the auditors' workpapers" during the audit and inflated inventory values by approximately $1 million. In addition, employees created a computer program called "Cook Book" to inflate inventory figures.[4]

Overstating ending inventory increases reported profits in the period of overstatement, but it has the opposite effect in the following period. For

_____

[4] "Coopers & Lybrand Agrees to Payment of $95 Million in the MiniScribe Case," *The Wall Street Journal*, October 30, 1992, p. A2.

ILLUSTRATION

24–1

The Effects of Overstating Ending Inventory

Panel A: Period 1

	(1) Correct	(2) Fraudulent
Sales	$1,500	$1,500[a]
Beginning inventory	100	100[a]
Add purchases	900	900[a]
Subtract ending inventory	100	200
Equals cost of goods sold	900	800
Administrative and marketing expenses	450	450[a]
Operating profits	$ 150	$ 250

Panel B: Period 2

	(1) Correct	(2) Fraudulent	(3) Fraudulent
Sales	$1,500	$1,500[a]	$1,500[a]
Beginning inventory	100[b]	200[b]	200[b]
Add purchases	900	900[a]	900[a]
Subtract ending inventory	100	200	300
Equals cost of goods sold	900	900	800
Administrative and marketing expenses	450	450[a]	450[a]
Operating profits	$ 150	$ 150	$ 250

[a] Correct amount, not a fraudulent number.

[b] From Period 1 ending inventory.

example, assume the top panel of Illustration 24–1 shows both correct and fraudulent numbers for Period 1. Assume sales are $1,500 and administrative and marketing expenses are $450 in both Period 1 and Period 2, for both the correct and fraudulent cases.

As shown in column 2 of Panel A, the operating profit is $100 higher because ending inventory was fraudulently overstated by $100. Next period, the $200 beginning inventory, which should only have been $100, works in the opposite direction. As shown in column 2 of Panel B, one must continue to overstate ending inventory to $200 just to stay even with the correct bottom line shown in column 1. As shown in column 3, if the perpetrators of the fraud want to appear as successful in Period 2 as they did when they committed fraud in Period 1, then they must overstate ending inventory to $300. In short, to continue to appear successful, the perpetrators of the fraud have to continually overstate ending inventory, sometimes in increasing amounts.

Effect on Taxes

If fraudulent financial reporting also overstates taxable income, then the present value of a company's tax payments are likely to increase. Overstating taxable income in one period will often be offset by understating taxable income in some subsequent period. Thus, the fraud might not affect the total tax paid, but would affect the timing of tax payments and therefore the present value of tax payments.

Q

2 Refer to the facts in Illustration 24–1. Assume the perpetrator of the fraud decides to "come clean" at the end of Period 2 and report the correct ending inventory numbers. What would be the profit for Period 2, in this case?

The solution to this case is at the end of this chapter on page 906.

HOW SMALL "EARNINGS MANAGEMENT" LEADS TO BIG-TIME FRAUD

Most fraud that leads to big trouble starts small. For example, suppose you take an exciting job as the financial analyst in a department of a well-known, highly successful company. After a few years of continually improving performance, your boss, the department manager, becomes worried that the department will not live up to top management's expectations that year. Because of his concern that the department will not achieve its profit target for Year 1, your boss requests that you backdate some sales from January of Year 2 to December of Year 1. These are real sales, but they are not made until January, Year 2. Your boss asks that you simply date the invoices that will be sent to the customers with a December date, instead of the January date when the sales are actually made. You are uncomfortable with this practice, but your boss points out that as a team player, you should cooperate. "Besides," your boss says, "what we are doing is just a little 'earnings management.'"

In the real world, some people do call this practice *managing earnings*. Others, however, call it *fraud*.

Early in Year 2, top management gives your boss a good bonus based on meeting the department's profit target for Year 1, and indicates your boss is in line for a promotion. Recognizing how well your department appeared to perform in Year 1, top management increases the profit target for Year 2. Now your boss has a problem. Year 2 has already lost legitimate sales to Year 1. Also, top management expects continually improved performance. At the end of Year 2, your boss wants to backdate *even more* sales from Year 3 to Year 2—some backdated sales to make up for the sales backdated from Year 2 to Year 1 and additional sales backdated to meet the higher profit targets! If this situation continues, what started as a small timing adjustment to manage earnings compounds into massive fraud.

Now we assume that, as the financial analyst, you did not "blow the whistle" on your boss or otherwise prevent the fraud because you wanted to keep your job and you consider yourself to be a team player. After a few years of managing earnings, you find you are involved in a major fraud. If the fraud comes to light, your boss may even blame you for "cooking the books" because you are the financial expert. In the real world, you might hear your boss say something like, "Sure, I wanted the department to perform well, but I never wanted anyone to do anything unethical! My job is to manage the department; I leave the numbers to (insert your name here). If there is a problem with the books, you should talk to (insert your name here)."

Consider a different scenario. Your boss gets promoted to division vice president at the beginning of Year 4, and you are promoted to department head. Now you have a difficult choice. If you stop backdating sales, Year 4 will look bad because legitimate Year 4 sales have been moved back to Year 3. How do you explain the department's poor performance in Year 4, just after you took over? If you report the fraud, you are obviously implicated because you were involved in Years 1, 2, and 3. If you continue the fraud, you will get in deeper and deeper. If you resign, your successor will reveal the fraud and implicate you.

Our point is that small earnings management often ends in big trouble with no easy way out. Difficult as it may be to refuse to participate in a fraud or blow the whistle at the early stages, it is far better to do so than to face the consequences of extricating yourself from the problem at a later time.

If you find yourself involved in a possible fraud, you should tell *someone*. If your superior is involved, you should go to someone higher in the organization, if possible. Boards of directors, particularly the audit committee, internal auditors and external auditors are groups outside the normal hierarchy that you can inform. Many companies have an ombudsman whose job is to deal with unethical behavior. The Institute of Management Accountants offers an 800-number service for its members to call and discuss ethical dilemmas.

At minimum, put your concerns in writing and send them to people who can investigate the situation. If necessary, be prepared to resign. Otherwise, you may find yourself in the middle of a messy situation at work, and even get involved as a defendant in legal actions.

The next sections in the chapter focus on situations that are likely to lead to fraud.

CAUSES OF FINANCIAL FRAUD

Short-Term Orientation

Returning to the example of your boss who wanted you to backdate sales, why would managers inside companies report fraudulent numbers? The primary reason is to make themselves look good. Accounting numbers are often the "grades" of managers. Bonuses, merit pay increases, and promotions often depend on how well the numbers turn out.

You may ask why a manager would have incentives to backdate sales from one year to an earlier year? This practice merely shifts profits; it does not create profits. There are several reasons why managers may want to manage earnings this way. Managers may have a short-run perspective. In some companies, top management makes it clear to department and division managers that they may not be in their jobs next year if they do not meet the company's profit or return on investment (ROI) targets this year. Department and division managers may believe they have an opportunity to be promoted to a new position, or transferred to another part of the company, if they perform well in the current year. If this is the case, they have strong incentives to look good in their current jobs in the current year.

In some companies, rewards are based on achieving a performance threshold. Managers who achieve the threshold receive substantially greater rewards than if they do not. For example, a company may offer a bonus of 50 percent of salary if the manager's division achieves its target ROI, 25 percent of the manager's salary if the division achieves 90 percent of the target ROI, and no bonus if the division's ROI is less than 90 percent of the target. A manager who scores just below the threshold, say just under 90 percent of the target ROI, has a tremendous incentive to make the 90 percent level. The manager may believe that the benefit this year of moving some sales back from next year will outweigh the negative consequences of such action on next year's sales.

Do Performance Evaluation Systems Create Incentives to Commit Fraud?

There are two fundamental questions that management should address in evaluating how well the company's performance evaluation system works:

What behavior *does* the system motivate?
What behavior *should* the system motivate?

Management may find their employees are highly motivated by high-pressure performance evaluation systems. In that case, management must also realize that pressuring people to perform well is also an incentive to commit fraud. The pressure to perform is not limited to middle managers and employees. Top executives in a company often feel considerable pressure to perform because of the demands of stockholders, the expectations of financial analysts, or, simply, their own egos.

In 1987, the Treadway Commission reported the results of its study of financial fraud involving top management and fraudulent reporting to stockholders. The commission concluded that fraudulent financial reporting occurred because of a combination of pressures, incentives, opportunities, and environment. According to the commission, the forces that seemed to give rise to financial fraud "are present to some degree in all companies. If the right combustible mixture of forces and opportunities is present, fraudulent financial reporting may occur."[5]

The commission went on to say that a frequent incentive for fraud in financial reporting was the desire to improve a company's financial appearance to obtain a higher stock price or escape penalty for poor performance.

---

[5] Treadway Commission, *Report of the National Commission on Fraudulent Financial Reporting* (Washington, D.C.: National Commission on Fraudulent Financial Reporting, 1987), p. 23.

The commission listed examples of pressures that may lead to financial fraud, including:

> Unrealistic budget pressures, particularly for short-term results. These pressures occur when headquarters arbitrarily determines profit objectives and budgets without taking actual conditions into account.
>
> Financial pressure resulting from bonus plans that depend on short-term economic performance. This pressure is particularly acute when the bonus is a significant component of the individual's total compensation.[6]

It is particularly important to note the Treadway Commission's reference to companies' emphasis on *short-term* performance. As we noted above, most cases of financial fraud involve a timing adjustment. Management is willing to take a chance on the future to make the current period look good. Why? Because companies emphasize short-term results for top managers and everyone else in the organization. One department manager told us, "Of course I'm more concerned about the short run than the long run. If I don't look good now, I won't be around in the long run!"

The Treadway Commission also noted that unrealistic profit objectives in budgets have been a cause of financial fraud. It is difficult for top management in large and widely dispersed companies to know what is realistic to expect in their far-flung divisions. One of the fraud cases that we discuss later involved the Mexico and Philippines operations of PepsiCo, which is headquartered in Purchase, New York. It would be surprising if top management at corporate headquarters knew enough about every local operation to set profit targets that are both realistic and challenging each and every year for every division. The fact that companies decentralize their operations reflects the reality that top management of large companies with dispersed divisions cannot be involved in the details of local operations. Consequently, top management may mistakenly expect unrealistically good performance.

Companies can mitigate the problem of unrealistic performance targets by using participative budgeting, as discussed in Chapter 17. Using participative budgeting, lower-level managers and employees provide input into the budgeting process that provides top management with information about local conditions. Participative budgeting should help top management understand local conditions and, therefore, set more realistic performance targets.

The MiniScribe case provides a clear example of extreme pressure from top management. According to investigators of the fraud at MiniScribe, MiniScribe's chief executive's "unrealistic sales targets and abusive management style created a pressure cooker that drove managers to cook the books or perish. And cook they did—booking shipments as sales, manipulating reserves, and simply fabricating figures—to maintain the illusion of unbounded growth even after the industry was hit by a severe slump."[7] The chief executive's style included inviting employees to an intensive retreat at which he would berate authors of business plans and budgets, showering the

---

[6] Ibid., p. 24.

[7] "How Pressure to Raise Sales Led MiniScribe to Falsify Numbers," *The Wall Street Journal*, September 11, 1989, p. A1.

group with ripped-up copies of the reports he didn't like. At one meeting, the chief executive asked two controllers to stand, and then he fired them saying, "That's just to show everyone that I'm in control of the company."[8]

ENVIRONMENTAL CONDITIONS THAT SET THE STAGE FOR FRAUD

Perhaps the most important factor in fraudulent financial reporting is known as *the tone at the top*. The *tone at the top* refers to the tone that top management sets in dealing with ethical issues. No matter how extensive the list of rules, no matter whether employees are expected to read and sign a code of conduct, top management sends a signal about how things are really done through its behavior. Just looking the other way when subordinates act unethically can set a tone that encourages fraudulent reporting.

During the 1970s, many companies operating in foreign countries paid bribes to top-government officials to get business. Lockheed Aircraft Corporation, for example, bribed Japanese prime minister Tanaka in order to sell airplanes to the government-owned Japanese Airlines (JAL). The prime minister subsequently resigned. Grumman Corporation, Textron's Bell Helicopter division, and Rockwell International paid bribes to top Iranian government officials to sell aircraft to Iran.[9]

Many top executives of the companies paying bribes to foreign government officials claimed they knew nothing of the bribes, and the bribes had been paid without their authorization. In many cases, however, top management expected their employees to get the business by doing whatever was required. Since the local custom in many of these countries was to pay bribes to government officials (for example, in the form of political contributions), the employees of the U.S. companies felt they had to pay bribes to compete. From the employees' viewpoint, top management had said, in effect, "Do whatever you have to do to get the business; we don't want to know about any bribes."

As a result of both the bribery and the tone at the top in many companies that had paid bribes, Congress passed a two-part law entitled the Foreign Corrupt Practices Act of 1977. The first part of this law made it illegal to bribe foreign government officials. The second part of the law required companies to maintain adequate internal controls and keep accurate accounting records so that, as Senator Proxmire stated, top management will know if a bribe is paid by someone in the company.[10]

During your careers, you will almost certainly get a sense of the tone at the top in companies that you work with or for. If top management exhibits a "look the other way" attitude toward unethical behavior, the chances are greater that people will commit financial fraud than if top managers set firm guidelines and follow those guidelines themselves. (Note: Problems 24–32 and 24–33 also describe "tone at the top" problems that have occurred at Leslie Fay and NBC.)

---

[8] Ibid.

[9] M. Clinard, et al., *Illegal Corporate Behavior* (Washington, D.C.: Department of Justice, National Institute of Law Enforcement and Criminal Justice, October 1979), pp. 196–98.

[10] M. Maher, "The Impact of Regulation on Controls: Firms' Response to the Foreign Corrupt Practices Act," *The Accounting Review* 56, no. 4, p. 754.

CONTROLS TO PREVENT FRAUD

Internal Controls Policies and procedures designed to provide top management with reasonable assurances that organizational goals will be met.

Collusion The cooperative effort of employees to commit fraud or another unethical act against a company.

In general, it is almost impossible to prevent fraud if enough clever people work together to commit it. Companies have established internal controls to help prevent fraud, however. **Internal controls** are policies and procedures designed to provide top management with reasonable assurances that organizational goals will be met. Internal controls help assure top management that the data it relies on for decision making have not resulted from fraudulent reports by lower-level managers and employees. However, internal controls do not necessarily assure stockholders and other readers of companies' financial statements that top management is reporting accurately because top management can override internal controls.

An example of an internal control to prevent fraud is the separation of duties. For example, separation of duties in a department store would require the duties of the person who makes a sale in the store to be separate from the accountant who records the sale in the financial records. For the sale to be fraudulently reported, the accountant and the salesperson would have to work together, or collude. **Collusion** is the cooperative effort of employees to commit fraud or another unethical act against a company.

Internal controls that separate duties make it difficult for people to commit fraud unless there is collusion. If enough people are willing to collude to commit a fraud, however, fraudulent financial reporting is almost impossible to prevent. Where there is separation of duties, fraud can only be committed if there is collusion between people, perhaps among several people. As the number of people involved increases, so does the chance of whistle blowing to higher authorities, auditors, the Securities and Exchange Commission, the media, or others.

Internal Auditing

Internal auditors are employed to audit on behalf of management and/or the board of directors. They often report to the audit committee of a company's board of directors. Internal auditors can both deter and detect fraud.

They can deter fraud by reviewing and testing internal controls and assuring controls are in place and working well. For example, in a large insurance company in Connecticut that we studied, internal auditors spent weeks trying to break the secret codes set up by the information systems department to protect computer files.

Internal auditors check to see if duties that are supposed to be separated are really separated. Internal auditors also deter fraud simply by their presence. The fact that the auditors make periodic visits, often unannounced, may deter fraud. In some companies, internal auditors are the people you turn to if you think fraud is occurring or if you feel pressured by others to commit fraud.

Internal auditors also detect fraud. Many companies now have specialized fraud examiners or investigators whose job is to identify fraud and build a case against the perpetrators of the fraud. Fraud examiners sometimes work with law enforcement officials to bring legal action against people who commit fraud.

Independent Auditors

The primary purpose of independent audits by outside audit firms is to express an opinion on published financial statements, not to detect or deter fraud. Nevertheless, the presence of the independent auditors (also called *external auditors*) and their role in reviewing a company's internal controls may help prevent fraud and sometimes detect it. The board of directors, management, or stockholders can also hire independent auditors to do special examinations for fraud. Many people, including managers, mistakenly believe there is no fraud if the independent auditors have issued an unqualified audit report on a company. That is simply not true. Independent auditors will not necessarily uncover fraud in performing a routine audit designed to express an opinion whether the published financial statements comply with generally accepted accounting principles.

Public accounting firms are increasingly held accountable for fraudulent financial reports, nonetheless. In some cases, people who relied on financial statements, such as stockholders or bondholders, see the public accounting firms as one of the few places where they can collect for damages, particularly if the auditee went bankrupt. For example, after MiniScribe Corp. sought protection in bankruptcy court, its bondholders filed a large lawsuit against MiniScribe's investment banking firm and its auditors; the lawsuit was settled before going to trial.

All of the large public accounting firms in the United States have been sued by people who claimed to rely on the financial statements in making investment decisions. Some of these cases are filed not because the independent auditors have failed to follow appropriate auditing procedures, but because the auditing firm is a potential source of funds. In other cases, the auditors have allegedly failed to follow generally accepted auditing standards, which are the general professional guidelines that aid auditors in fulfilling their professional responsibilities in auditing financial statements. According to the Treadway Commission's study of fraud cases, auditors who were charged by the Securities and Exchange Commission with failure to follow generally accepted auditing standards had generally failed to recognize or investigate possible problems with weak internal controls. "In many cases, although indications of possible improprieties, or 'red flags' existed, independent public accountants failed to recognize or pursue them with skepticism."[11]

 *Self-Study Question*

3 Your Uncle Harry recently inherited $300,000 that he wants to invest. He has a modest but steady retirement income that covers his living costs, so he claims that he does not really need the income from the $300,000. He tells you that he wants to invest it wisely because he would feel bad if he were to lose the $300,000 (and he points out that you may come in for a share of whatever amount he can accumulate with the $300,000). Uncle Harry is considering investing in a chain of coffee shops in your college community. He has no reason to suspect the integrity of the coffee shop's managers, but after reading the coffee shop's financial statements, he asks you how he can be sure the numbers are right. He asks for your advice, saying: "Suppose I ask the coffee shop managers to have their books audited, then can I rest assured that the financial numbers are correct? The company's stock is not publicly traded, and the books have not been audited before, but the managers have assured me they would be willing to have the books audited by an independent public accounting firm."

[11] Treadway Commission, *Report of the National Commission on Fraudulent Financial Reporting*, p. 26.

Remarking how clever Uncle Harry is to think about the audit, and pondering the future of the $300,000, you tell him you'll get back to him with some good advice.

Can Uncle Harry rest assured the financial numbers are correct if the financial statements are audited?

The solution to this question is at the end of this chapter on page 906.

THREE CASES OF FINANCIAL FRAUD

The next three sections describe three financial fraud cases. As you read these cases, keep the following factors in mind:

- What were the incentives to commit fraud?
- What was the tone at the top of the organization?
- What controls or audit steps to prevent fraud were lacking?

Our objective in describing these cases is to provide you with a sense of conditions conducive to fraudulent financial reporting inside companies in the real world. These are real cases involving real people caught up in the daily rush of doing their jobs. These people did not have a record of criminal activities.

DOUGHTIE'S AND THE FICTITIOUS FROZEN FOODS

Doughtie's Foods was a food processor and distributor that operated in the southeastern United States.[12] The fraud occurred in a food distribution division of the company that supplied food to schools and government agencies. Illustration 24–2 shows the company's organization chart.

During the years of the fraud, the company had been experiencing lower profit margins than others in the industry—less than 2 percent of sales compared to an industry average of approximately 7 percent. Other than low profit margins, the company's financial statements did not show signs of financial distress.

Mark Hanley had advanced rapidly through the ranks of Doughtie's Foods, starting as a salesperson and rising to manager of a large food distribution division.[13] After several years as division manager, top management began singling him out for criticism at corporate planning meetings because his division was not performing well. After one particularly unpleasant session, another division manager gave Hanley the idea that he could boost his division's reported profits by overstating end-of-period inventory.

If Hanley could find a way to overstate ending inventory, then he could understate cost of goods sold. (Recall from the basic cost flow model that Cost of goods sold = Beginning inventory + Purchases − Ending inventory.) By understating the cost of goods sold, Hanley could increase gross margin and profits.

According to Hanley, his associate said, "Man, if a guy's calling you from 200 miles away and asking what your (inventory) number is, you're a

---

[12] The description of this case is based on the following documents: Doughtie's Foods Form 8-K filed with the Securities and Exchange Commission, October 12, 1982; Securities and Exchange Commission, *Docket* 27, no. 11 (March 28, 1983), pp. 716–17; Securities and Exchange Commission, *Docket* 30, no. 11 (May 21, 1984), pp. 711–14; and *The Wall Street Journal*, June 2, 1983, pp. 1, 19.

[13] We have changed the name of the division manager to protect his privacy.

*Doughtie's Foods:
Organization Chart*

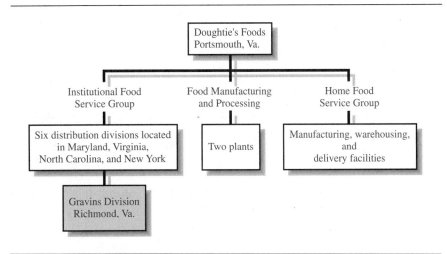

Note: The colored box is the site of the alleged financial fraud.

fool if you (give numbers showing you) lose money." Hanley said that he tried reporting honestly, but one day his superiors came up with some ridiculous figure showing poor results for his division. "I thought they were hosing me," he said.[14]

Although overstating ending inventories would increase the profits of Hanley's division, it would work against him in the next period, as previously discussed in this chapter. Hanley testified during the subsequent investigation by the Securities and Exchange Commission he thought his division would eventually make enough profits to justify the false numbers. The economy went into a recession, however, and the anticipated profit recovery did not happen.

*Description of the
Fraudulent Activities*

At month-end, Hanley and his employees would count the inventory. Hanley would compile the data and report the figures to corporate headquarters. Since headquarters required no documentation for monthly inventories, he simply added a fictitious number to the inventory on hand. One method he used was to change the unit of measure when compiling inventory. For example, he changed one entry from "13 boxes of crab cakes" to "13 cases of crab cakes."

Year-end amounts were more difficult to fudge because the independent auditors performed a physical observation of the inventories. Hanley noted that the auditors did not like to spend much time in the freezers, so he was able to add fictitious items to frozen foods that the auditors did not question. One year, after the auditors had finished their inventory observation and left, Hanley sent three fictitious inventory count sheets to the auditors, claiming the auditors had overlooked the sheets and left them behind. The auditors were satisfied with Hanley's explanations and added the amounts from the fictitious count sheets to ending inventory. The inventory on these

---

[14] *The Wall Street Journal*, June 2, 1983, p. 19.

three count sheets totaled $140,000, which was 18.4 percent of the division's reported ending inventory for that year.

Discovering the Fraud

The fraud was discovered after an executive at corporate headquarters became curious about the high inventory levels at Hanley's division. Inventory turnover, defined as Cost of Goods Sold divided by Inventory, was lower at Hanley's division than at comparable divisions in the company, implying unusually high levels of inventory. The curious executive went to Hanley to get an explanation for the high inventory levels.

Recall that Hanley felt considerable pressure when he started overstating the numbers, so you can imagine how much stress he felt when the executive from corporate headquarters showed up asking questions. Hanley immediately told the executive what he had been doing, handed over a notebook in which he had kept track of the inventory overstatements, and resigned.

Epilog

Realizing the fraudulent numbers from Hanley's division had been included in the companies external financial statements, corporate officials at Doughtie's Foods informed the Securities and Exchange Commission (SEC). After an investigation by the company and Price Waterhouse, the company's new independent auditors who replaced the original audit firm, the SEC filed a formal complaint against Hanley for violating securities laws.

The SEC also filed charges against two members of the audit firm charging the independent auditors had violated generally accepted auditing standards in conducting the audit. According to the SEC, the audit firm took inadequate steps in view of the importance of inventory as an asset and the weak internal controls. For example, there was no separation of duties in accounting for inventory. Hanley had sole control over the entire process from counting the inventory, to compiling the data, to reporting the numbers. The auditors did not check Hanley's excuses when they found irregularities, according to the SEC investigation. On one occasion, the auditors could not tie 22 of 99 count sheets to other data, so they wrote to Hanley to ask for an explanation. He did not reply, and the auditors did not pursue the discrepancy.

RONSON CORPORATION AND THE DISAPPEARING JOBS

Ronson Corporation is perhaps best known for such consumer products as lighters and butane gas appliances. Fraudulent financial reporting occurred in Ronson's aerospace division, however, at a plant in Duarte, California.[15] See Illustration 24–3 for the company's organization chart.

Although not on the verge of bankruptcy, Ronson faced serious financial difficulties at the time of the fraud. Ronson was continually renegotiating with its creditors to restructure debt and extend dates when principal payments were due. The aerospace division in which the fraud occurred appeared to be successful, however. Ronson pointed with pride to the success

---

[15] The description of this case is based on the following documents: Ronson Corporation Form 8-K filed with the Securities and Exchange Commission, November 2, 1982; Securities and Exchange Commission *Docket*, Release no. 19212, vol. 26, no. 10 (November 4, 1982), pp. 735–40; and Ronson Corporation Form 10-K filed with the Securities and Exchange Commission, December 31, 1981.

*Ronson Corporation:
Organization Chart*

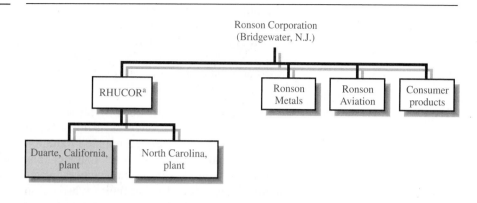

Note: The colored box is where the alleged financial fraud occurred.

[a] Ronson Hydraulic Units Corp. (wholly owned subsidiary of Ronson).

of its aerospace division in annual reports while putting on the pressure to perform well. The Duarte plant had pretax profit margin requirements of 9 to 12 percent of sales, although the company as a whole was barely breaking even in the best of years, and showed more losses than profits in the years surrounding the fraud.

Nature of the Fraud

The Duarte plant management would meet shortly before year-end to determine which jobs were near completion and would presumably be shipped within a few weeks after the start of the year. Those jobs were recognized as sales in the current year and removed from inventory with an entry like the following (XX refers to the amount of the sale and YY refers to the cost of the product):

Accounts Receivable	XX	
Sales		XX
Cost of Goods Sold	YY	
Inventory		YY

Although these jobs were recognized as sales in the financial records, they were physically unfinished and still in the production work area at the end of the year. This presented a dilemma. If the jobs were not removed from the production area, during their year-end inventory observation the independent auditors would notice a discrepancy between the financial records and the physical inventory. The jobs that were sold according to the books were actually still being produced. To hide these jobs from the independent auditors, plant personnel moved them from the production area to buildings that were not inspected by the auditors.

Meanwhile, plant personnel prepared false shipping documents so it would appear the jobs had been shipped to customers. These false shipping documents included invoices that were dated earlier than the date of the actual shipment. Now the plant was literally keeping two sets of books. According to the subsequent SEC investigation: "A clerk was assigned to keep a file of all invoices relating to products recognized as sales but not shipped. The accounting manager was assigned to review the file on a weekly basis and accumulate the 'value of unshipped goods.' The aged accounts receivable ledger was also reviewed weekly and annotated with a series of legend tickmarks to indicate the status of the receivables."[16]

At one point, the jobs recorded as sales but not yet shipped exceeded $3 million on division sales of $28 million and the value of unshipped inventory was approximately 20 to 25 percent of the plant's total year-end inventory.

Epilog

As you can imagine, it became increasingly difficult to keep the fraud a secret, and after a few years, Ronson's top management learned of the fraud. At that point, the company's independent auditors, Touche Ross & Co. (now part of Deloitte and Touche), Ronson's audit committee of its board of directors, senior management, and the SEC conducted an investigation of the fraud. During their investigation of the fraud, the independent auditors withdrew their certification of the previously published financial statements at which point the New York Stock Exchange temporarily halted trading in Ronson common stock.

In view of how extensive the activities were to commit the fraud and cover it up, numerous people at the plant may have colluded to commit the fraud. However, the SEC charged only the plant manager, plant controller, and a clerk. The SEC did not file a complaint against the independent auditors.

Meanwhile, Ronson announced that no funds were missing and there were no material adverse effects from using incorrect accounting procedures. A year later, the Duarte plant's assets were sold to the Boeing Company at a substantial gain.

PEPSICO AND OLD BOTTLES

The PepsiCo case is particularly interesting because the company's management style was so attractive to aggressive, highly motivated management-level employees. Yet the very factors that made PepsiCo an attractive place to work contributed, in part, to the fraud. During the period in which the fraud was committed, PepsiCo portrayed itself as an aggressive, high-performance company.[17] Its annual report stated, "It is widely recognized that PepsiCo is a highly results-oriented company. This characteristic of our operating environment is frequently commented on by the press, and is supported by all our management programs and processes."[18] The annual report went on to say that the company rewarded outstanding results with high pay.

PepsiCo was known for giving its division managers a great deal of autonomy in their operations and supporting a wide range of management styles. According to its annual report, "Developing key managers is a top priority for us; whenever possible, we fill managerial vacancies by promoting from within. Besides ensuring a continuity of management, this is one of the ways we live up to our commitment to foster a climate of personal

---

[16] Securities and Exchange Commission, *Docket* 26, no. 10 (November 4, 1982), p. 738.

[17] The description of this case is based on the following documents: PepsiCo annual reports for the years ending 1979, 1980, 1981, and 1982; PepsiCo 8-K Form filed with the Securities and Exchange Commission; Securities and Exchange Commission, *Docket*, Release no. 10807, July 1, 1985, pp. 1005–7.

[18] PepsiCo 1980 Annual Report, p. 4.

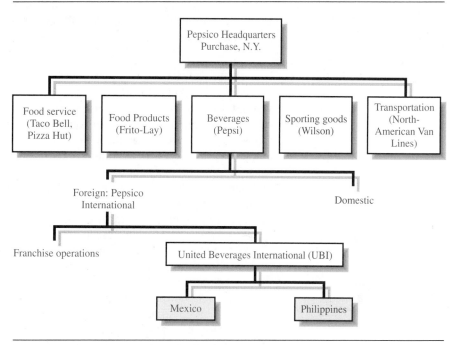

Note: The colored boxes were the sites of the alleged financial fraud.

growth. . . . We value entrepreneurship, so we encourage risk-taking in strategy, programs, and people decisions.''[19]

Nature of the Fraud

PepsiCo had five main groups of divisions: food products, including Frito-Lay, Inc.; transportation, including North American Van Lines, Inc.; sporting goods, including Wilson Sporting Goods Co.; food service, including Pizza Hut, Inc., and Taco Bell; and its primary business, beverages. (See Illustration 24–4 for the company's organization chart.) The beverage group included a company called United Beverages International (UBI), which bottled soft drinks in 11 foreign countries.

The fraud was committed by employees in the UBI subsidiary in two countries: Mexico and the Philippines. These employees used numerous techniques to falsify income, including keeping inventories of broken or unusable bottles on the books, failing to write off uncollectible accounts receivable, writing up the value of bottles inventory above cost, and falsifying expense accounts. According to a company statement, these activities required extensive collusion. In the Philippines, employees kept more than $45 million of obsolete bottles on the books to satisfy the country's debt-equity requirements. (Writing off the bottle inventory would have reduced both assets and equity, thus creating a problem with the country's debt-equity requirements.)

---

[19] Ibid., p. 5.

PepsiCo's net income was overstated by a total of approximately $92 million over a five-year period from these fraudulent activities. In the highest year, the overstatement was $36 million, which was 12 percent of PepsiCo's net income from all five of its main groups.

Internal Auditing

Consistent with its management style of granting considerable autonomy to division managers, PepsiCo's Internal Audit Department acted less like watchdogs and more like management consultants. For example, at PepsiCo, the Internal Audit Department did not conduct surprise audits, but would notify division managers in advance of its visit to ensure that key employees were present. Many companies use internal auditors as consultants because internal auditors gain broad experience with many parts of the company. Using their experience, internal auditors can assist managers all over the company. Using internal auditors as consultants has the advantage of improving operations and of making the Internal Audit Department an excellent place to develop managers.

In general, if companies use internal auditors more as consultants than as watchdogs, then internal auditors are less likely to deter or detect financial fraud. Despite their role as consultants, PepsiCo's internal auditors uncovered the fraudulent activities at PepsiCo's Mexico and Philippines operations. After discovering the fraud, the Internal Audit Department at PepsiCo became less consulting-oriented and started conducting surprise audits. Some people in the company believe the reorientation of internal audit away from consulting was a major negative repercussion of the fraud.

Epilog

Prior to the fraud, PepsiCo prided itself on its morale and sense of community in the company. PepsiCo's management style and structure, which included giving autonomy to division managers and using internal auditors more as consultants than as watchdogs, and its policy of decentralization supported the notion that the company had aggressive, hard-working, and trustworthy employees. After the fraud was discovered, the distressed PepsiCo chairman referred to the fraud perpetrators as a "conspiracy of trusted employees."[20]

In all, the SEC filed formal complaints against 12 employees in the two countries. PepsiCo terminated the people involved, plus the U.S.–based manager of the bottling unit of UBI. The SEC did not file a complaint against PepsiCo's independent auditors, Arthur Young & Co. (now part of Ernst & Young).

WHY WAS THE FRAUD COMMITTED?

We have described these three cases to provide you with some insights into the conditions that are conducive to fraud. All three cases involved considerable pressure to perform, autonomy from corporate headquarters, and either a failure to perform proper audit practices or extensive collusion.

Pressure to Perform

All three companies had put significant pressure on the division managers to perform well. At Doughtie's Foods, the division manager felt considerable

---

[20] *The Wall Street Journal*, July 29, 1983, pp. 1, 12.

personal pressure from the top. Further, he felt singled out for criticism. Ronson was suffering from financial problems and looked to the aerospace division to bail out the rest of the company. PepsiCo's well-intentioned method of rewarding outstanding results, promoting aggressiveness, and encouraging risk-taking created an environment in which some managers overreacted to these incentives.

We should note that pressure to meet demanding standards was very likely felt by all managers in these companies, yet only a few committed fraud. Although many companies place a great deal of pressure on employees, to our knowledge, the vast majority do not commit fraud. Nevertheless, fraud cases can often be traced to intensive pressure to achieve short-term financial results.

Autonomy

The division managers at PepsiCo and Ronson had considerable autonomy. At PepsiCo, the company had a corporate structure and culture that encouraged autonomy. In addition, the geographical distance and language differences between corporate headquarters in Purchase, New York, and the divisions in Mexico and the Philippines made it difficult for top managers to know what was going on at these divisions. At Ronson, the California plant at which the fraud occurred was geographically distant from corporate headquarters in New Jersey and produced a product that was not in the company's mainstream product line. Divisional autonomy was not as evident at Doughtie's Foods, but here too, the division manager had sole control over inventory.

Granting autonomy to a manager does not mean the manager is likely to commit fraud. Most managers operate with considerable autonomy, yet reported cases of fraud are rare. Granting autonomy does increase the risk of fraud, because autonomy creates an opportunity to commit fraud. Thus, most fraud cases inside organizations are committed by autonomous managers, but granting managers autonomy by no means implies they will commit fraud.

Controls, Auditing, and Collusion

Earlier in this chapter, we noted that effective internal controls such as separation of duties make it difficult to commit fraud unless people collude. The fraud at PepsiCo and Ronson required the involvement of several people who colluded to commit the fraud. Doughtie's Foods demonstrates an example in which the lack of separation of duties in inventory counting, compiling, and reporting made it possible for the division manager to report fraudulent inventory numbers. Since the division manager had sole control, he was able to falsify the numbers without collusion. In view of Doughtie's Foods' weak internal controls in Hanley's division, Doughtie's Foods' independent auditors should have performed additional audit steps.

Collusion often occurs because of an attitude that those out in the field are fighting together against corporate headquarters. Problem 24–34 describes such an "us versus them" situation that developed at H. J. Heinz.

In general, it is very difficult for independent auditors to discover a fraud if management or a group of employees really wants to hide it. At Ronson, for example, the employees physically hid the jobs that they claimed had been shipped.

Compensating Factors

We noted earlier that financial fraud is usually the result of a combustible mixture of motives and opportunities. While no one factor would lead to fraud, the right combination of factors creates conditions conducive to fraud. If a company has an incentive system that pressures employees to achieve short-term financial results, then it should offset this motive to commit fraud by reducing opportunities to commit fraud. The company could provide assurances that internal controls and internal auditing are effective, for example, and it could exhibit an ethical tone at the top.

If a company wants to give managers considerable autonomy, as at PepsiCo, then it might compensate for this high opportunity to commit fraud in the following ways:

1. By having a high degree of the watchdog variety of auditing, thus reducing the opportunity to commit fraud.
2. By reducing pressure on division managers to achieve short-run financial results, thus reducing the motive to commit fraud.
3. By top management's portrayal of an ethical tone at the top that encourages excellence in ethics.

The ethical tone at the top reduces the motive to commit fraud because it reduces the tolerance for unethical behavior. It also decreases the opportunity for fraud because it signals support for antifraud devices such as strong internal controls. Also, it encourages people who are inclined to behave ethically to stay with the company and discourages people who are otherwise inclined.

Characteristics of People Who Commit Fraud

We have noted before that the combination of pressure to achieve short-term financial results, weak internal controls and auditing, an opportunity to commit fraud through autonomy, and a tone at the top that looks the other way at unethical employee behavior is a combustible mixture of forces conducive to fraud. One might liken this mixture of motives and opportunities to a mixture of dry fuel and oxygen on a hot summer afternoon in a forest. Just as a forest will not burn without a spark, fraud will not occur without a person committing the act. (A famous fraud examiner calls these people *fraudsters*.)

Many top executives in companies have observed that, in their view, fraud is the work of a few "bad apples." If top management or the boards of directors knew who these bad apples were, then fraud could be eliminated.

While we have focused on management and organizational issues, rather than on the personality characteristics of people who commit fraud, we acknowledge that certain people may be more inclined to commit fraud than others. Although little is known about the personality types of people who commit fraud, we may learn from the advice of a perpetrator of one of the biggest frauds in recent years. Barry Minkow, who formerly ran the ZZZZ Best carpet cleaning company and a fictitious restoration company, is presently serving a 25-year prison sentence for fraud. According to Minkow, we should "watch out for that guy with the big ego. . . .Watch that guy that has no respect for anyone but himself."[21]

---

[21] "Do You Know Me? I Stole Millions—And Here's How," *The Wall Street Journal,* April 1, 1991, p. A6.

SUMMARY

Fraudulent financial reporting is intentional conduct that results in materially misleading financial statements. The two key concepts in the definition of fraudulent financial reporting are (1) the conduct must be intentional or reckless, and (2) the misrepresentation must be material to the financial statements. Common examples of fraudulent financial reporting are failure to write down obsolete inventory and recognition of revenue before the sale has been made.

The objective of this chapter is to help you understand conditions conducive to fraudulent financial reporting. There generally must be a motive and an opportunity for financial fraud to occur. Motives include pressure to achieve short-run financial targets. Opportunities include autonomy, weak internal controls, and the lack of "watchdog" auditing. Effective internal controls, such as separation of duties, make it difficult to commit fraud unless people collude.

A tone at the top of the company that promotes ethical behavior is particularly important to eliminate tolerance for unethical behavior. It also reduces the opportunity for fraud by signaling support for antifraud devices such as strong internal controls. In the final analysis, financial fraud usually results from a combustible mixture of motives and opportunities. While no one factor would necessarily lead to fraud, the right combination of motives and opportunities creates conditions conducive to fraud.

TERMS AND CONCEPTS

The following terms and concepts should be familiar to you after reading this chapter:

Collusion, *880*

Fraudulent Financial Reporting, *871*

Internal Controls, *880*

Materiality, *871*

QUESTIONS

24–1   What is fraudulent financial reporting? What are the two key concepts in the definition of fraudulent financial reporting?

24–2   What is meant by materiality? Why is materiality difficult to define in practice?

24–3   What are common types of fraudulent financial reporting?

24–4   An employee has been stealing some of the company's parts and selling them. Is this behavior financial fraud?

24–5   Suppose the employee in question 24–4 covers up the theft by accounting for it as spoilage. Would accounting for the stolen items as spoilage be financial fraud?

24–6   Suppose an accounting clerk who knows nothing about the theft in question 24–4 erroneously records the "lost" parts as spoilage. Would that be fraudulent financial reporting?

24–7   Suppose an accounting clerk fails to write off $5 million of obsolete inventory at a large department store. The amount is material. Suppose the Securities and Exchange Commission filed a charge against the clerk alleging financial fraud. Do you believe the clerk's failure to write off the inventory, which resulted in misstated financial statements, could be considered unintentional? Explain your answer.

24–8   Why are the three cases discussed in the chapter—Doughtie's Foods, Ronson, and PepsiCo—actually cases of *alleged* financial fraud?

24–9   An automobile dealership sells an automobile on January 2, Year 2, but records it as being sold on December 31, Year 1. Accounts Receivable are credited for the amount of the sale on January 2, Year 2, when the customer pays for the car in cash. The sales commission payable to the salesperson was recorded on January 2, Year 2. What items on the dealership's financial statements are in error for Year 1, including the balance sheet at December 31, Year 1? What accounts are in error for Year 2, including the balance sheet at December 31, Year 2?

24–10   A friend says, "I don't see what's the big deal about early revenue recognition. It's just a matter of recording sales in the right time period. It's not like making up a fictitious sale. And after a few years everything is correct again." How would you respond?

24–11   In both the Doughtie's Foods and Ronson Corporation cases, people kept track of the amount of the fraud in separate records. In effect, they were keeping two sets of books. Why keep both sets of records? Why not simply keep the fraudulent records?

24–12   A friend was hired by a large company. She confides in you about a problem with her boss. Her boss is asking customers to sign a sales agreement just before the end of the year that indicates a sale has been made. Her boss then tells these customers that he will give them 30 days, which is well into next year, to change their minds. If they do not change their minds, then he sends the merchandise to them. If they change their minds, her boss agrees to cancel the orders, take back the merchandise, and cancel the invoices. Her boss gives the sales agreements to the Accounting Department, which prepares an invoice and records the sale. One of the accounting people keeps the invoices and shipping documents for these customers in a desk drawer until the customers either change their minds, in which case the sale is canceled, or until the merchandise is sent at the end of the 30-day waiting period.

Your friend likes the company very much, and she wants to keep her job. What would you advise her to do?

24–13   Why does small earnings management often result in major fraud after a time?

24–14   A manager says, "We avoid financial fraud by just paying workers a cost-of-living increase each year and promoting them based on the number of years they have been in their position. That way we avoid putting pressure on people and we avoid the problems of financial fraud." Comment on this incentive approach. What behavior will this approach motivate?

24–15   The Treadway Commission commented that the forces leading to financial fraud were present in all companies to some extent, but fraudulent financial reporting resulted from the right combustible mixture of forces and opportunities to commit fraud. Give examples of the combustible mixture the Treadway Commission mentioned.

24–16   The Treadway Commission commented that a factor giving rise to fraud is the existence of pressures on division managers to achieve unrealistic profit objectives. Why might top management set profit targets that are unrealistic?

24–17   The Treadway Commission indicated that bonus plans based on achieving short-run financial results have been a factor in financial frauds, particularly when the bonus is a large component of an individual's compensation. Why are these bonus plans a factor affecting fraud?

24–18   International Telephone and Telegraph (ITT) historically put a great deal of pressure on its employees to achieve short-term profit targets. At the same time, ITT provided its division managers a lot of autonomy. What compensating factors should be present to reduce the likelihood of fraudulent financial reporting?

24–19   How was MiniScribe's top management's behavior, as described in the chapter, potentially a factor in the fraud at MiniScribe?

24–20   What is meant by the tone at the top? Why is the tone at the top an important factor in preventing financial fraud?

24–21   The title of the Foreign Corrupt Practices Act implies that it deals with foreign corrupt practices. The law not only prohibits bribing foreign government officials, but it also regulates companies' internal controls. Why were the internal control regulations included in this law?

24–22   How does the separation of duties help prevent financial fraud?

24–23   How do internal auditors deter or detect financial fraud?

24–24   Why are public accounting firms increasingly held accountable for their clients' fraudulent financial reporting?

24–25   According to Barry Minkow, who was a perpetrator of a major fraud, "Watch out for the guy with the big ego." Why do you think Minkow said to watch out for the guy with the big ego?

PROBLEMS[22]

24–26   Explain Early Revenue Recognition

You have been asked to advise a manufacturing company how to detect fraudulent financial reporting. Management does not understand how early revenue recognition by backdating invoices from next year to this year would affect financial statements. Further, management wants to know which accounts could be audited for evidence of fraud in the case of early revenue recognition.

Required:

a.   Using your own numbers, make up an example to show management the effect of early revenue recognition.

b.   Prepare a short report to management explaining what accounts would be affected by early revenue recognition. Suggest some ways management could find errors in those accounts.

24–27   Explain Inventory Overstatement

You have been asked to advise a merchandising company how to detect fraudulent financial reporting. Management wants your help in detecting inventory overstatement. Further, management wants to know how to find evidence of inventory overstatement.

Required:

a.   Using your own numbers, make up an example to show management the effect of overstating inventory. Show how inventory overstatement at the end of Year 1 carries through to Year 2 beginning inventory overstatement.

b.   Prepare a short report to management explaining how inventory might be overstated, including examples, and discuss how inventory overstatement might be

---

[22] We have not included exercises in this chapter because of the nature of the material.

detected. For your examples, it might be helpful to review the Doughtie's Foods and PepsiCo cases, as well as the other examples discussed in the chapter.

24–28 Causes of Fraudulent Financial Reporting: Doughtie's Foods

Refer to the Doughtie's Foods case described in the chapter, starting at page 882.

a. What were the incentives to commit fraud?

b. What was the tone at the top of the organization?

c. What controls to prevent fraud were lacking?

d. How did the independent auditors contribute to the fraud?

24–29 Causes of Fraudulent Financial Reporting: Ronson Corporation

Refer to the Ronson Corporation case described in the chapter, starting on page 884.

a. What were the incentives to commit fraud?

b. Could the fraud have been committed without collusion?

c. What controls to prevent fraud were lacking?

d. Did the independent auditors have responsibility for the fraud? Why or why not?

24–30 Causes of Fraudulent Financial Reporting: PepsiCo

Refer to the PepsiCo case described in the chapter, starting on page 886.

a. What were the incentives to commit fraud?

b. What was the tone at the top of the organization?

c. What controls to prevent fraud were lacking?

d. How might the role of internal auditors as consultants be a factor in financial fraud in companies like PepsiCo?

24–31 Effect of Bonus Plan on Financial Fraud

An article in *The Wall Street Journal* indicated the dressmaker, Leslie Fay, backdated invoices so the revenue would be recorded in the quarter before sales were actually made. "As long as sales remained strong, the practice could go undetected. But as the recession hit retailers in 1991, revenue sagged and it became more difficult to cover one quarter's shortfall with anticipated revenue from the next."[23]

Leslie Fay had a bonus plan in which the chief operating officer and the chief financial officer received bonuses if the company's net income reached $16 million (approximately 2 percent of sales), but no bonuses if net income was below $16 million. The company reported a net income of $23 million, and the two executives received bonuses.

The fraud occurred away from corporate headquarters in New York at the company's Wilkes-Barre, Pennsylvania, office where the company's financial affairs are handled. Leslie Fay's chief financial officer "was establishing something of an autocratic rule in Wilkes-Barre. What the growing operation lacked in organization, he evidently tried to make up through frenzied effort. Employees say they were sometimes pushed to work 16-hour days, including many weekends and holidays, and were sometimes reprimanded for arriving as little as two minutes late to work."[24]

The chairman and chief executive officer of the company, who was paid $3.6 million, mostly bonus, "says he is bewildered by the accounting scandal. 'We just don't know why they would do it,' he says of the midlevel employees whose scheme concealed Leslie Fay's sliding fortunes."[25]

Required:

a. Describe how the invoice backdating could have affected reported profits? Would those profits have been overstated permanently or just for a period?

b. What effect might the bonus plan for the chief operating officer and chief financial officer have had on the fraud, if any?

c. How might the location of financial operations in Wilkes-Barre, Pennsylvania, instead of at corporate headquarters in New York have made it easier for someone to commit fraud?

---

[23] "Loose Threads: Dressmaker Leslie Fay Is an Old-Style Firm That's in a Modern Fix," *The Wall Street Journal*, February 23, 1993, p. A20.

[24] Ibid.

[25] Ibid, p. A1.

24–32   Top-Management Awareness of Fraud

The chief executive of Leslie Fay, the dressmaking company charged with committing financial fraud, was dismayed that the controller and other employees had committed fraud, saying the company could have taken steps to improve the situation if senior management had been informed of poor financial results. Financial analysts who follow the company had noted, however, that the company had marked down its clothing line in sales to retail stores such as May Department Stores and Federated Department Stores.

After the company cut prices 20 percent across the board, retail executives who were customers of Leslie Fay wondered how Leslie Fay could continue to be profitable. " 'When you cut 20 percent out, you must get dramatically large orders to make up for it,' says one. 'We were wondering how they could continue to make a profit.' "[26]

One analyst wondered how top management could not have known about the company's financial difficulties in view of the 20 percent markdown.

For your information, top management is located in New York City, and the fraud occurred at the financial offices in Wilkes-Barre, Pennsylvania. The line of reporting was as follows: The controller reported to the chief financial officer and the chief financial officer reported to the chief executive of the company. Both the controller and the chief financial officer work in Wilkes-Barre. The chief financial officer reportedly has considerable autonomy.

Required:

Write a short report indicating whether you think top management of the company is responsible for the fraud and why (or why not).

24–33   Top Management's Responsibility for Fraud

In a "Dateline" news story, NBC employees allegedly rigged a General Motors truck to explode on impact to demonstrate that GM had improperly placed gas tanks on the trucks. Although this case does not involve fraudulent financial reporting, it involves a different type of fraud that is similar in many respects to fraudulent financial reporting. Of particular interest is the response of NBC News chief executive—he resigned after NBC News issued an apology to General Motors.

The executive "was apparently enough out of touch with his troops that he didn't know all of GM's complaints until he saw them broadcast—along with thousands of other people—at a live GM news conference."[27]

Meanwhile, the NBC News executive's superior, the president of NBC, "told employees that the problem with the 'Dateline' incident wasn't so much that it happened, but that NBC got caught."[28]

Required:

Comment on the apparent tone at the top at NBC. Should the NBC News executive have resigned? Why (or why not)?

24–34   Motives and Opportunities for Fraud

A report on "income transferal" activities at the H. J. Heinz Company made the following statements.[29] First, decentralized authority is the central principle of the company's operations. Second, the company expected its divisions to generate an annual growth in profits of approximately 10 to 12 percent per year. Third, it was not unusual nor undesirable for management to put pressure on the division managers and employees to produce improved results.

The report noted that putting pressure on the divisions to produce improved results coupled with the company's philosophy of autonomy, which it extended to financial and accounting controls, provided both an incentive and an opportunity for division managers to misstate financial results. The report further stated, "The

---

[26] Ibid., p. A20.

[27] "NBC News President, Burned by Staged Fire and GM, Will Resign," *The Wall Street Journal*, March 2, 1993, p. A1.

[28] Ibid., p. A8.

[29] This problem is based on the "Report of Audit Committee to the Board of Directors, Income Transferal and Other Practices," H. J. Heinz Company, May 6, 1980.

autonomous nature of the (divisions) combined with the relatively small World Headquarters financial staff permitted the conception of what at best can be described as a communications gap. . . . In its simplest form, there seems to have been a tendency to issue an order or set a standard with respect to achieving a financial result without regard to whether complete attainment was possible."[30] "In the managements of certain of the (divisions), there was a feeling of 'us versus them' towards World Headquarters."[31]

The report indicated there was an effort in certain divisions to transfer income from one fiscal period to another to provide a "financial cushion" for achieving the goal for the succeeding year. For example, divisions would overpay expenses so they could get a credit or refund in a subsequent year. Or they would pay an expense such as insurance or advertising early, but instead of charging the amount to a prepaid expense account, they would charge the amount to expense. In good years, this practice would keep profits down and provide a cushion to meet the company's target for constantly increasing profits.

Required:

a.   Using your own numbers, make up an example to demonstrate the kind of income transferal that was done at H. J. Heinz.

b.   What was the motive to transfer income from one period to the other? What were the opportunities to transfer income?

c.   Comment on how the communications gap and the us-versus-them attitude contributed to the fraud.

d.   Refer to requirement c. Have you seen communications gaps in organizations that have resulted in an us-versus-them attitude on the part of employees? If so, briefly describe the circumstances and the cause of the us-versus-them attitude. What could have been done (or be done) to change the "us versus them" attitude in your example?

24–35   Taking Action in the Face of Fraud

Refer to the example in the text in which we hypothetically put you in the position of the financial analyst for a department manager who wanted you to backdate sales. (See pages 875 to 876 in the chapter.) Assume you have a close friend who is the financial analyst in the example. It is now Year 4. Your friend's boss has been promoted, and your friend has been offered the job of department head.

Your friend comes to you for advice. Recall that your friend has been involved in the fraud for three years.

Required:

What would you tell your friend to do?

INTEGRATIVE CASES

24–36   Case Study in Fraudulent Financial Reporting: Disctech— Part I*

On a gray February day in 1994, Mr. William Winslow, the newly appointed president of Disctech, Inc., sat at his desk contemplating the future of the company. Disctech had been the rising star of the computer disk memory industry. After going public in 1987, sales had grown at a compound rate of 33 percent and earnings had

---

[30] Ibid., p. 9.

[31] Ibid., p. 14.

* All parts of this case are copyright © 1986 by the President and Fellows of Harvard College. Harvard Business School case 187-066. Joseph P. Mulloy prepared this case under the direction of Kenneth A. Merchant as the basis for class discussion rather than to illustrate either effective or ineffective handling of an administrative situation. Reprinted by permission of the Harvard Business School. This case was produced by Harvard Business School as a single case.

grown at 47 percent. Earnings per share (EPS) had risen every quarter, and the stock price had increased from $3.00 a share in 1987 to $67.50 a share in December 1993. (See Exhibits 24–36A and 24–36B for financial data.)

In just the last week the entire fortune of the company had changed for the worse as reports of fraudulent sales, inflated inventory values, and possible insider stock trading rocked the company. The board of directors had stepped in and asked the chief executive officer (CEO), chief financial officer (CFO), and executive vice president for Sales and Marketing to take leave without pay until the board completed their investigation of the matter, and they abruptly resigned. The board also selected a new president/CEO, Mr. Winslow, and retained an outside law firm to conduct an investigation of possible improprieties.

Bill Winslow viewed his job for the next few months as reorganizing the firm to get it through this difficult period. Reorganization required identifying and relieving the stresses that generated this crisis and restoring employee, consumer, and investor confidence in the company.

The Hard Disk Industry

Disctech manufactured and sold disk drives. Disks are circular platters covered with magnetic material that record data in concentric circles. Disks access data more slowly than true random access devices like semiconductors or magnetic cores but faster than magnetic tape. Since the mid-1960s, disks had dominated the rapid access portion of the data storage market.

Although disk technology was well established, the market was fast growing and dynamic. Data capacity doubled every three years, and market experts expected this trend to continue. Market positions changed rapidly, and disk-drive manufacturers had to keep up with technological advances in order to survive.

The market for disk drives has two distinct submarkets: one for disks installed as part of large computer systems and one for those installed as part of minicomputer systems. IBM dominated the market for large computer disk drives, although other

EXHIBIT

24–36A

DISCTECH, INC.
Income Statements for Fiscal Years Ending December 31
(all dollar amounts in thousands, except per share amounts)

	1989	1990	1991	1992	1993
Revenue	$59,646	$81,119	$107,076	$134,916	$164,598
Cost of sales	41,752	55,161	72,812	91,743	111,927
Gross margin	17,984	25,958	34,264	43,173	52,671
R&D expense	3,772	4,056	4,283	4,722	4,938
Selling, general, and administrative expense	6,561	10,545	13,920	17,539	21,398
Operating profit	7,561	11,357	16,061	20,912	26,335
Interest income	119	162	214	(104)	(541)
Profit before tax	7,680	11,519	16,275	20,808	25,794
Income tax	3,533	5,299	7,487	9,572	11,866
Net income	$ 4,147	$ 6,220	$ 8,788	$ 11,236	$ 13,928
Earnings per share	$0.60	$0.90	$1.27	$1.61	$1.99

EXHIBIT

24–36B

DISCTECH, INC.
Consolidated Balance Sheets at December 31
(all dollar amounts in thousands)

	1989	1990	1991	1992	1993
Assets					
Cash and marketable securities	$ 3,778	$ 3,273	$ 2,947	$ 2,808	$ 3,920
Accounts receivable (net)	11,921	15,508	22,091	30,843	39,300
Inventories (net)	11,241	15,122	22,046	27,557	36,682
Prepaid expenses	525	746	730	750	809
Total current assets	27,465	34,649	47,814	61,958	80,711
Property, plant, and equipment (net)	9,661	13,719	18,657	24,628	31,031
Other	169	239	284	321	364
Total assets	$37,295	$48,607	$66,755	$86,907	$112,106
Liabilities					
Accounts payable	$ 5,041	$ 9,158	$12,734	$16,849	$ 23,190
Accrued liabilities	2,100	2,982	4,056	5,354	6,746
Total current liabilities	7,141	12,140	16,790	22,203	29,936
Bank debt	–0–	–0–	–0–	2,000	–0–
Capital leases	6,820	8,917	12,127	16,008	18,170
Bonds	–0–	–0–	4,000	4,000	10,000
Owner's Equity					
Common stock	3,703	3,729	3,755	3,782	3,807
Other capital	21,062	21,104	21,146	21,188	21,231
Retained earnings	(1,431)	2,717	8,937	17,726	28,962
Total liabilities and equities	$37,295	$48,607	$66,755	86,907	$112,106

large mainframe manufacturers such as Control Data also made disk drives for their own use. Independent disk-drive manufacturers served this market by supplying IBM plug–compatible systems directly to end users. Independent disk-drive manufacturers concentrated on replacing IBM drives because the sales volume for non-IBM models was considered too small. Market experts expected the mainframe disk-drive market to grow about 5 percent per year.

The market for minicomputer disk drives, in which Disctech participated, was highly competitive. Some leading minicomputer manufacturers made some of their own disk drives, but most minicomputer manufacturers were part of the original equipment manufacturer (OEM) market that a large number of small independent disk-drive manufacturers serviced. Market experts expected this market to grow 25 to 30 percent per year.

Disctech

Mr. John Garvey, a former executive of a large manufacturer of minicomputers and computer disk memories, founded Disctech in 1980. John had trained as an electrical engineer, but was better known for his organizational skills. The staid corporate

I L L U S T R A T I O N   *Disctech, Inc.—Organizational Chart*

24–36C

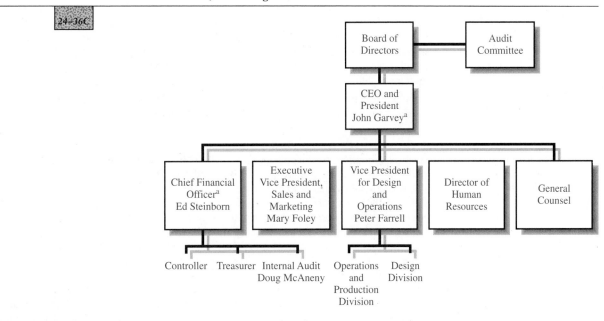

a Member of the board of directors.

environment had constrained John and he wanted to venture out on his own. He thought that with a good product, good marketing, and the right pitch to the capital markets a "killing could be made." Three other talented executives left the large company to join John in his new endeavor: Ed Steinborn (controller for the large manufacturer) became Disctech's chief financial officer, Peter Farrell (director of manufacturing) became the vice president for Design and Operations, and Mary Foley (manager of Minicomputer Marketing) became the executive vice president for Sales and Marketing. (See Exhibit 24–36C for an organization chart.)

The team of executives spent the period from 1980 to 1982 organizing the corporation and building prototypes of the advanced disk drives that the company would market. Early in 1987 the corporation went public with 3.3 million shares offered at $3.00 a share. At a large party for shareholders and analysts, John announced that the corporation already had significant amounts of guaranteed sales for its new drives and that he expected Disctech products to become an industry standard. John also stated that the company expected to increase revenues and earnings per share (EPS) by a minimum of 30 percent per year.

Since the inception of the company, the planning cycle had been a very simple, top-down process. During the summer of each year, John met with Mary and Ed and set sales growth for the next year. They would then roll this sales figure to the bottom line using expected margins and estimates of fixed expenses to get a net income figure and a tentative EPS. Prior to the beginning of the fiscal year in October, they would pass down these goals for net income and EPS through the Finance and Marketing organizations where they became "law." The Design and Operations Division planned production from the expected revenue and gross margin figures, while John and Peter negotiated the R&D budget separately.

John, Ed, Mary, and the senior people of the marketing and sales staff conceived and implemented strategies to reach the annual plan at regularly scheduled "revenue meetings." These meetings primarily sought the means of identifying and generating potential revenues.

Disctech derived revenues from the sale and service of the company's equipment. The firm recorded revenues at the time of shipment of products or performance of services. Disctech initiated customer orders on receipt of an equipment order form (EOF); either the customer completed the order or Disctech personnel prepared it pursuant to a master sales agreement signed by the customer. The EOF included a description of the equipment, the price of the equipment, and the earliest equipment delivery date acceptable to the customer.

Required:

Comment on the environment and the nature of Disctech's business. Do you see anything that could be conducive to fraudulent financial reporting?

24–37 Disctech—Part II: The Auditors and the Audit Committee

Board of Directors and Audit Committee

Since the company's inception, Disctech's board of directors comprised seven members: two inside directors (the CEO and the CFO) and five outside directors. The board usually met four times a year to review the corporation's progress and plans for the future. The meetings were generally short and standardized, with John in control of the agenda. The company's performance and the dedication the top officers displayed impressed all of the outside directors.

The Audit Committee of the board comprised three outside directors. The members of the Audit Committee served three-year terms on a rotating basis, although the chair of the committee usually served for a longer period. The Audit Committee generally met twice a year, before and after the annual audit.

A number of changes came about in 1990 after the firm named Richard (Rich) O'Donnell, an outside director, as chairman of the Audit Committee. Rich firmly believed that an audit committee "could not be effective without being active." He increased the committee's schedule to at least four meetings a year and set up private meetings between the committee and the outside auditors. Rich tried to get the committee to look at the company's exposures and to question discretionary items in the financial statements. He suggested that the inside and outside auditors make some unannounced inspections and audits, and he wanted to strengthen the internal audit function through training and improving hiring practices.

Rich admitted in 1991 that he had some concerns about serving on a board of directors and, particularly, on an Audit Committee.

A member of an Audit Committee is always a potential victim of management and the outside auditors since you depend on them so much. To a great extent you have to trust them. However, I try to set a tone of watchfulness by asking a lot of questions at all of our meetings; but I need to get other board members to do it or I will just look like an old crank.

I may be too cautious, however, because the top officers have talent, and John Garvey is dedicated. He wants to make good disk drives and sell a lot of them.

Internal and External Audit

The Internal Audit Division, consisting of the head auditor, Doug McAneny, and two staff members, reported to Ed Steinborn (CFO). Internal Audit primarily ensured that the firm followed corporate accounting policies and that safeguards existed to protect the company's assets. Internal Audit was also alert to opportunities for cost cutting and efficiency.

At the request of Rich O'Donnell, Doug McAneny had attended some meetings of the Audit Committee. Rich tried to establish a rapport with Doug and assured him that any misgivings that he had about anything, or anyone, in the company would be brought to the attention of the Audit Committee.

Disctech's external audit firm was Touche, Young, and Andersen (TYA), a Big Six firm. Each year in July, the auditors met with top management and the Audit Committee to lay out the schedule of the annual audit and to review changes in the company since the previous year.

Required:

How effective do you think Internal Audit and the Audit Committee of the board would be at detecting or deterring financial fraud?

24–38 Disctech—Part III: The Early-Shipment Policy

Early Years

The early years were exciting at Disctech; sales revenues grew at a compound rate of 39 percent. Every quarter the company announced record earnings, and the stock market reacted as John predicted, with the trading price continually reaching new highs. John made regular announcements about the company, stating how earnings would continue to grow at above-industry rates. The total market six years ago for minicomputer disk memories at original equipment manufacturer (OEM) prices was $2.1 billion, so Disctech had plenty of room to grow.

Disctech continued to make modest R&D expenditures, but by the middle of 1990 its once "head of the pack" products began to fall behind the latest technology. In response, John applied pressure to the Product Design Division to come out with new products, even if they improved only slightly on existing products.

1991

The sales pattern in 1991 proved to be a little erratic. John Garvey and Mary Foley (executive vice president, Sales and Marketing) agreed that quarterly sales (and earnings) must continue to grow to keep the glowing image of Disctech alive. To maintain this growth record, they sometimes found it necessary to work the Shipping Department round-the-clock during the last few days of each quarter in order to push as many orders as possible out the door to recognize the revenue for those transactions.

Mary also decided to take advantage of the way some OEMs ordered disk drives. Many OEMs would place a large order for 100 to 200 disks, get a discount, and then ask for delivery at a date 2 to 3 months in the future. This procedure assured them of a supply of the disks and a delivery date that supported their computer construction and shipment schedules. Many times the firm would schedule an order placed in one quarter for delivery in the next quarter. To recognize these sales in the present period, Mary directed that as many orders as possible receive early shipment to the OEM, with the understanding that the OEMs would not be liable for payment until the previously agreed-upon delivery dates.

The auditors from TYA questioned this early-shipment program but Ed Steinborn convinced them that the sales met the requirement of "sales" as defined under generally accepted accounting principles: Title to the disks did transfer to the OEM upon shipment; under the contract the OEM was obliged to pay Disctech for the disks; and Disctech did contact the OEM prior to shipment to get their authorization. Some of these authorizations were, however, verbal; the salesperson responsible for an account would get the authorization and call it back to the home office.

This early-shipment policy suited some OEMs, but many other OEMs did not have extra storage room and would not accept early delivery. The salespeople were told to "use their imaginations" and either find storage at the local Disctech distributor or another convenient location. The company needed the sales and the salespeople were told to "get as many authorizations as possible."

These two policies resulted in end of 1991 revenues that had grown from $81.1 million to $107.1 million, but $5.9 million of the 1991 sales were for disks originally scheduled for delivery in 1992. (Of the $5.9 million, the firm shipped $3.7 million without a valid authorization.)

1992

The only major change Disctech made in 1992 was in marketing policy. John Garvey had long thought that the minicomputer memory industry would slowly evolve to become more like the mainframe business, with fewer sales to computer manufacturers and more sales directly to end users. This evolution accelerated as the economy slowed, as many companies held onto the systems they already had installed. John believed that a truism of computers—"information to be stored quickly grows to fill all available memory"—would save Disctech. The firm hired more salespeople and directed the sales force to start approaching all current users of minicomputers compatible with Disctech disk memories to generate sales in this potentially large market.

After the firm announced the results of the second quarter (another record high), John called Mary, Ed, and Peter together for a private meeting. John indicated that he was proud of their results and that he knew they would continue to outperform the industry. He pointed out, however, that each quarter's goals were more difficult to reach, and that delays in the completion of new disk designs and prototype construction and the growing obsolescence of their inventory might level or even decrease the company's short-term earnings.

John went on to say that with his children nearing college age, he needed a lot of money set aside, not tied up in risky investments. As a result he had begun quietly to sell some of his Disctech stock, which had appreciated so much. He told them he was still optimistic about the company's future but they might be wise to examine their own financial needs. If they were to sell stock, he reminded them that they must inform the Securities and Exchange Commission of the sales, but he urged them to go about the sales discreetly in all other ways.

The marketing shift toward memory end users was a big success and significantly contributed to another record year, and early shipments continued to increase as the Marketing Department pressured OEMs and salespeople for early authorization. Total sales for the year were $134.9 million. Early-shipment revenues were $12.4 million, of which the firm shipped $9.8 million without a valid authorization.

Required:

a. Describe each of the early-shipment practices.

b. What was the purpose of the early-shipment policy?

c. Were the early-shipment practices ethical? Explain your answer for each of the early-shipment practices.

d. Were the insider stock sales ethical? Explain your answer.

24–39   Disctech—Part IV: Inventory Control and Allowances for Obsolescence

Disctech broke down its inventory into three categories: raw materials, work in progress (WIP), and finished goods inventory (FGI). In 1989, over 85 percent of total inventory consisted of FGI, and this percentage increased in later years. This unusual inventory mix resulted from a general shortage of raw materials in the industry, and Disctech and other manufacturers responded by sending raw materials directly to the production line. In addition, Disctech wanted as little work in process inventory as possible because partially assembled disk drives were highly susceptible to damage; even the slightest dirt or dent rendered the disk or its drive unit inoperable.

The firm tested and then stored assembled units until sale and shipment. The company's first-year production capacity was limited, so the firm shipped out units as soon as they were assembled. Efforts to improve efficiency and cleanliness raised production yields, and by 1988 production began to produce drives for inventory.

In 1990 the Design Division began to improve the disk drives to ensure that the product remained competitive. These improvements affected inventory levels. Disassembling the finished disk drive often caused complete disk failure, and therefore, very little rework on FGI drives resulted. Instead, the firm would modify new drives in production and then assemble them. Thus each change or alteration created another layer of FGI slightly different from the last.

Disctech's policy for creating allowances for obsolescence of inventory follows:

Any equipment over two years old would have an allowance at 5 percent per quarter for five years so that at the end of seven years the allowance would be at 100 percent.

Any equipment declared unmarketable would have a 100 percent allowance taken against it.

These rules resulted in small allowances. Little technically obsolete equipment was actually sold. Moreover, Disctech had no corporate standards or guidelines for ascertaining when disk drives became unmarketable. The corporate attitude that Disctech equipment was not subject to obsolescence intensified the problem.

At the end of 1990 a production controller forwarded a memo via Peter Farrell to the CFO and the executive vice president for Sales and Marketing that summarized a study he had done on the growing inventory problem. It listed three recommendations:

1. A study to produce a new allowance policy, since it appeared that the product life cycle was far shorter than five years.
2. An intensive effort by the Marketing Department to sell the older inventory as soon as possible.
3. An increase in the allowance for obsolescence from $800,000 to $1.4 million.

The senior corporate officers discussed this memo. They all believed that the problem was not serious; they were unwilling to increase the allowance by any amount. Marketing, however, attempted to stimulate sales of the older disk drives with various specials, discounts, and promotions. The CFO also stated that he would "watch the inventory problem."

In 1991 the amount of obsolete inventory grew faster than the increase in allowances, and by the end of the fiscal year the production controller estimated the deficit to be almost $2.4 million. The outside auditors did not see the total extent of the problem but they did question the obsolescence allowance policy in their management letter.

> Top management should continually monitor Disctech's allowance policy and should implement procedures to develop historical experience to measure the propriety of the formula adopted. Management should also extend the policy to recognize sooner obsolescence of products no longer in production.

Disctech's management acknowledged the auditors' report but also informed the Audit Committee that they already had done an internal study in 1990 and were working actively to fix all problems with inventory control.

During 1992, Disctech management was aware that the exposure for FGI obsolescence was increasing, but did little other than continuing the marketing promotions and taking allowances as the formula calculated. Disctech's management maintained that allowing for or writing off inventory made it less likely that the firm would sell it. They stressed that they were obligated to the stockholders to find uses for the inventory rather than write it off.

By the time of the 1992 year-end audit, the inventory situation (in addition to the aggressive revenue recognition practices) agitated the auditors who sought written assurance from Disctech's management that a formal program existed to "significantly affect the obsolescence exposure." The CFO, Ed Steinborn, wrote to the auditors:

> We respond to the problems in the inventory area by outlining the programs we have underway to reduce inventory levels. We will agree to study policy alternatives in the area of providing allowances for excess equipment; however, affordability considerations really preclude our ability to make any meaningful change in this area this year.

Management informed the board and the Audit Committee that a problem with inventory control still existed and that they were making ongoing efforts to rectify the situation. They also informed the board and Audit Committee that "they might have to increase reserves for obsolescence next year as the product life cycle for disk memories shortens." They did not show the board and the committee the 1992 auditors' management letter containing the following sentence:

This policy results in full valuation of excess inventory, overstates inventory, and may lead to serious future financial adjustments.

They did not tell the board that the exposure on inventory had grown to an estimated $3.9 million.

The Audit Committee asked questions about inventory valuation, but John and Ed gave quick answers and were confident that they would soon have the inventory situation under control. Nevertheless, the Audit Committee in a private session with the outside auditors admitted that some things, including inventory obsolescence, worried them. They also told the engagement partner that they intended to meet more often in 1993 and they wanted a senior representative from the outside auditors and Doug McAneny, the head of internal auditing, at their meetings.

Required:

a. Could Disctech's allowance for inventory obsolescence policy be a problem for the company? Explain your answer.

b. Should management have kept the board better informed about the inventory problem? If they had, what steps would the board have taken?

c. Did Disctech's allowance for inventory obsolescence represent fraudulent financial reporting? Explain your answer.

24-40 Disctech—Part V: The Board Gets Involved

1993

The year 1993 was difficult for Disctech, and the firm placed tremendous pressure on the sales force to achieve the planned sales goal. A combination of a soft market and unexpected delays in production of the popular products made sales difficult.

Some salespeople came up with some ingenious ideas to stimulate sales that were often designed to take advantage of the company's aggressive revenue policies. For example, one such scheme could occur when a customer filled out an equipment order form (EOF) with a delivery date far in the future and submitted it to Disctech for processing. Within a week or two the responsible salesperson would contact the Marketing Department and inform them that he or she had convinced the customer to accept an early delivery in the current quarter—with the understanding that payment would not be due until the date on the EOF. From the salesperson's view this made everyone happy: Disctech booked a sale, the salesperson got a commission, and the customer received a disk memory at a reasonable price with delayed payments and no finance charges.

At the same time sales were becoming more difficult, the firm had a growing problem with order cancellations. As Disctech's competitors came out with new products, many original equipment manufacturers (OEMs) switched disk memory suppliers; new products also affected direct end-user sales because people wanted more memory and shorter access time for their dollars.

Near the end of the first quarter of 1993, the Marketing Department met to discuss the order cancellation problem. Mary chose this opportunity to announce a new policy: The firm would ship any order cancelled within six weeks of expected delivery and record the revenue. Her staff told her that most customers would just refuse to accept delivery. She responded that on each of these deliveries the responsible salesperson would go along and ensure that "the sale stuck." All of these problems caused a lot of consternation in the sales force but they all knew better than to argue with Mary when she made up her mind.

A Midyear Meeting

At midyear John Garvey called a meeting of the top officers to review some pressing problems. The first problem was financing. As receivables grew, cash grew short. Consequently the firm would issue $10 million in bonds for public sale early in the fourth quarter; the firm would use $4 million of the cash raised to retire the bonds currently outstanding, and the rest of the proceeds would go to operations.

Second, inventory problems were getting worse. An internally generated estimate of the current obsolescence exposure was $6.8 million, and the firm expected this figure to grow to over $8 million by the end of the year. The outside auditors worried about the obsolescence exposure, but John explained he had placated them by informing them that the company was internally studying obsolescence policies and that he expected a write-down probably as early as the first quarter of 1994.

Third, the new disk memory designs still had development problems, but John expected them to be available before the end of the calendar year. Finally, the problem of returned equipment continued to grow. This problem would probably cause a significant reversal in revenues in future periods.

John admitted that all of these factors together would probably break the record string of growth and profits. John wanted the company to take all its "lumps" in the first quarter of 1994, and he wanted to take the inventory write-down at the same time as the new product announcement. He also stated that strong quarterly and annual results in 1993 would help the bond issue and would likely mitigate the impact of a loss in the first quarter of 1994. Everyone came away from the meeting clearly understanding that they had to make the 1993 budget—no matter what they had to do.

Despite heroic efforts by the sales force, fourth-quarter predictions indicated that without further action Disctech would come up short of the 1993 budget. The Marketing Department worked out a plan to make a large shipment to a warehouse Disctech rented under another name; the firm booked this shipment (for $4.2 million) as revenue in 1993. The firm planned to use the equipment to help fill early 1994 orders.

In the end, the firm achieved the 1993 goal of $162 million in sales; annual sales totaled $164.6 million. (See Exhibit 24–36A in Disctech—Part I.) Early-shipment revenues totaled $15.8 million, of which the firm shipped $10.6 million of equipment without authorization. This $15.8 million did not include the $4.2 million shipped to the new warehouse.

1994

The board of directors met in January 1994 to review the results of 1993. John first went over the high points of the year and the records achieved. He next turned to the inventory problem and gave a quick summary of the events of the last few years. John then told them that to bring inventory back in line, a one-time write-down of $8.2 million would be required in 1994.

Unfortunately for John, this write-down did not surprise the outside directors. Prompted by knowledge of a large number of customer complaints, increasing levels of returned equipment, and the possible inventory obsolescence problem, they had asked the external and internal auditors to conduct some additional investigations in the last two quarters. The outside directors proceeded to ask John some difficult questions about the company's policies and practices and also questioned him on his personal finances and his recent stock dealings.

Receiving nothing but evasive answers, they told John they were retaining an outside law firm to conduct an investigation to be reported directly to the Audit Committee. The board also informed John that it would be best if he, Ed, and Mary went on leave until the investigation was complete.

With feelings of anger and humiliation, all three resigned immediately rather than accept the forced leave of absence. Disctech hired an interim president, Bill Winslow, and informed the Securities and Exchange Commission that the company was conducting an internal investigation that could affect their reported financial statements for the last three years.

Required: Prepare a report for Bill Winslow that addresses each of the following questions:

a.   What was the financial fraud that occurred at Disctech? Be specific, and indicate whether the activities that you describe are definitely fraudulent or all in a gray area where they may be considered fraud in some situations but not in others.

b.   Why did the fraud occur? What factors gave management an incentive to commit fraud?

c.   How could the fraud have been prevented?

SOLUTIONS TO

Self-Study Questions

1   It is unlikely that the temporary clerk either committed a reckless act or intended to commit fraud. The clerk's supervisor could be faulted for failing to provide adequate instructions, however. If the amounts are immaterial, this example would probably fall into the category of accounting errors. If the amounts are material, failure to supervise and instruct the temporary clerk could fall under the category of reckless conduct.

2   The "coming clean" results would be only $50 profit, computed as follows:

Sales	$1,500
Beginning inventory	200[a]
Add purchases	900
Subtract ending inventory	100[b]
Equals cost of goods sold	1,000
Administrative and marketing expenses . .	450
Operating profits	$ 50

---

[a] From Period 1 ending inventory.
[b] Correct amount, not a fraudulent number.

Moral: It's painful to come clean after one has committed a fraud.

3   An external audit will indicate whether the financial statements are in compliance with generally accepted accounting principles, but it's no guarantee that the numbers are "right." It would be possible for the managers to mislead the auditors. If this is a small business, as it appears, then it is difficult to have sufficient separation of duties to assure internal controls are adequate. Uncle Harry could get additional assurance by requesting a regular audit for compliance with generally accepted accounting principles and a special examination for fraud. A fraud examination implies suspicion of fraud, and may sour the relationship between Uncle Harry and the managers of the coffee shops, however. The final word is that Harry will take some risk if he makes the investment; he has to decide whether the expected return on the investment justifies that risk.

Quality Control and Variance Investigation

LEARNING OBJECTIVES

After reading this chapter, you should be able to:

1. Explain the importance of variance investigation in quality control.
2. Analyze the costs and benefits from investigating variances.
3. Estimate critical probabilities at which it pays to investigate variances.
4. Describe the cost-to-investigate model that underlies the variance investigation decision.
5. Explain how to use statistical control techniques to assess variances and improve quality.

*T*he notion of total quality management requires finding ways to control production processes. Variances represent differences between planned results and actual performance. A variance may be caused by a change in output activity, a change in the efficiency with which inputs are used, or a change in the unit cost of an input. Variance analysis is important for performance evaluation and control, as we discussed in Chapters 18 to 21.

A substantial number of variances are usually included in any set of internal management reports, and managers don't have the time to investigate all of them. So, some method must be found to investigate only those variances that are expected to produce a benefit in excess of investigation costs. This methodology is generally referred to as **variance investigation.**

Variance Investigation The steps taken if managers judge that the expected benefits of correction exceed the costs of follow-up.

In this chapter, we discuss how to determine which variances should be investigated. The chapter also provides an overview of statistical quality control, an engineering approach to determining which variances should be investigated. The application of the concepts of these variance investigation models in a real-world setting is also discussed.

THE INVESTIGATION SETTING

Imagine that you manage the employee benefits section of the Great Plains Corporation. The employee benefits section is a cost center in the company's organization. Your compensation and your future with the company will be evaluated on the basis of the cost center's performance. The monthly report on your cost center has just arrived. It appears as follows:

GREAT PLAINS CORPORATION
Employee Benefits Section
Responsibility Report
(in thousands)

Cost Item	Budget	Actual	Variance
Staff salaries	$155	$156	$ 1 U
Operator wages	137	151	14 U
Other wages	41	39	2 F
Communications	12	9	3 F
Utilities	39	48	9 U
Supplies	16	11	5 F
Maintenance and repairs	24	8	16 F
All other	80	85	5 U
Totals	$504	$507	$ 3 U

How do you decide which variances to investigate? To make the decision, consider the costs associated with your decision alternatives. These alternatives may be restricted to:

1. Investigate the variance.
2. Do not investigate.

You might also wait until you receive next month's report before investigating. Or you might decide to conduct a very brief pilot study before deciding to carry on a full-fledged investigation. To minimize the complexity of our discussion, we will limit our consideration to the first two alternatives. Adding other choices makes the mathematics more complex, but the underlying approach is the same.

Essentially, you must consider the trade-offs between the costs of investigating and the costs of allowing the process to continue without investigation. You must determine the differential costs and a method for assessing the trade-offs.

If management needs to make a decision whether to investigate a variance, it is necessary that there be costs associated with the investigation and that there be potential benefits received as a result of making an investigation. As with all other areas of cost-based decision making, the relevant costs are those that are differential with respect to the decision. All of the costs discussed here are differential.

Investigation Decision Costs

The costs that need to be considered are: (1) the costs to conduct an investigation, (2) the costs to correct an out-of-control process, and (3) the costs of allowing an out-of-control process to continue out of control. The first two costs can usually be specified based on the nature of the operation subject to the investigation. Some typical investigation costs include:

1. Opportunity costs of the time spent tracking down the cause of a variance.

2. Opportunity costs of the time spent in the investigation.
3. Costs to test equipment that may be out of adjustment.
4. Costs to shut down an operation while testing equipment.
5. Costs to restart or rearrange activities to increase efficiency.
6. Consulting fees of outside experts hired to examine operations.

For example, the costs to investigate the unfavorable variance in utilities costs may require an inspection tour of the operating area to check that lights and equipment are shut off when not in use. A more elaborate investigation might involve hiring a consulting firm to study utilities usage and suggest a conservation program.

It is important to note that some variances are so large that correction is indicated without conducting an investigation. For example, if your car normally obtains 20 miles per gallon and suddenly obtains only 5 miles per gallon, no investigation is necessary for you to take the car to the repair shop and have the problem fixed. In these situations, no investigation costs are incurred.

The costs of allowing a process to remain out of control depend on several factors. These costs are related to the inefficiencies caused by an out-of-control operation as well as the time before the operation is corrected. An operation may be self-correcting or may require intervention. It is generally agreed that the longer a process remains out of control, the greater the costs of allowing it to continue out of control. Sooner or later, however, out-of-control processes are corrected.

Some examples of the costs of allowing a process to remain out of control include:

1. Costs of continued inefficient operations, including inefficient use of labor, materials, and energy.
2. Costs of improperly adjusted equipment, including failure to meet product specifications, damaged or defective goods, and hazardous operating conditions.
3. Customer ill-will if defective product gets sold.

Texas Instruments, in its cost of quality program, included the following items: costs of hiring additional people, cost of technical services to deal with customers' complaints, additional inventory carrying costs, and costs to rework product produced by an out-of-control production process.[1]

Random Event An occurrence that is beyond the control of the decision maker or manager.

The purpose of investigating a variance is to save future costs. But costs can be saved only if an investigation uncovers a factor that can be adjusted. This does not always occur. Sometimes, a variance is just a **random event.** If the variance is a random event, investigating it will yield no benefits to offset investigation costs. For example, there would be no benefit in discovering that a variance stemmed from an error in reading the utility meter that is offset in subsequent periods. If a variance is due to an increase in utility rates, then there is probably little management can do except adjust future budgets. Additional, but less direct, actions might include taking steps to reduce future energy use.

Estimating the costs of an out-of-control process is illustrated by the following example.

[1] "Texas Instruments (B)" (Boston: Harvard University, Harvard Business School case 189–111).

Rosebud Industries runs an automated diode manufacturing operation. The diode manufacturing equipment is set to certain tolerances. With use, the machine settings can go out of control. The longer the machine is out of control, the greater the cost of allowing it to continue out of control. A corollary to this is that the greater the manufacturing costs, the higher the unfavorable variances, and the more likely management is to check the machines and correct the settings.

Assume the machines *are* out of control, but that management does not know this for certain. Costs related to the time that the machine is out of control and the related probabilities that the machine will be checked out and reset are presented in the following table:

Additional Time out of Control	Present Value of Out-of-Control Costs This Period	Probability of Investigation and Correction
1	$ 4,000	.10
2	9,000	.25
3	15,000	.60
4	30,000	.90
5	65,000	1.00

If the machine is out of control and remains out of control for just Period 1, the expected cost is computed as follows:

$$\$4,000 \times (1 - .10) = \$3,600$$

If the machine is left out of control for Period 1 and Period 2, the expected cost is:

$$\$3,600 + [\$9,000 \times .9 \times (1 - .25)] = \$3,600 + \$6,075$$
$$= \$9,675$$

So for each period that the machine is out of control, the cost increases by the accumulated costs of leaving the machine out of control times the probability that the machine will be left out of control until that period times the probability that the machine will remain out of control that period. The out-of-control costs are a cumulative function of time. Thus, the expected costs through Period 3 are:

$$\$9,675 + [\$15,000 \times .9 \times .75 \times (1 - .6)] = \$9,675 + \$4,050$$
$$= \$13,725$$

and the expected costs through Period 4 are:

$$\$13,725 + [\$30,000 \times .9 \times .75 \times .4 \times (1 - .9)] = \$13,725 + \$810$$
$$= \$14,535$$

There are no costs for Period 5 because the machine would be checked and reset that period.

Hence, if the variance is not investigated now, the expected costs are $14,535, which is the sum of the costs of being out of control for each period before correction is assured times the probability that the machine will remain out of control through that period. This is the basic approach to determining the cost of allowing a process to remain out of control.

CONCEPTUAL BASIS
FOR INVESTIGATION
DECISIONS

In deciding whether a variance investigation is likely to yield net benefits, a manager focuses on two important issues:

1. The importance or materiality of the variance.
2. The ability to control the causes of the variance.

Variances that are quite small are typically not investigated. Small cost variances usually do not indicate large benefits from investigating and correcting the cause of the variance.

Guidance about which types of variances are worth investigating comes from considering the sources of variances.

Causes of Variances

Just because a variance appears in a report does not necessarily mean that management can take action that will prevent the variance from recurring. The reason is that variances may be due to a number of different causes. These causes may be broken into three categories, each of which has its own implications for the managerial action that may be the optimal reaction to the variance.

Information System Variances

Information system variances are those that arise because the data used either to establish standards or to report variances are in error. If budgets or standards are set in such a way that they do not reflect expectations, a variance will be reported. In this situation, management may be better off adjusting the standards or budget, since investigating the variance will not result in an improvement in operations. For example, if management had based its cost estimates for a trucking company on fuel costs that were out of date, a variance would probably be reported. However, there is nothing management can do in the short run about the costs of fuel, so the benefits from investigating such a variance would be zero.

The management reporting system may also contain errors as a result of incorrect data entry, coding, or other problems in the system. Investigating such variances will not change the underlying events. The benefits will arise through a more accurate report about operations, but operations themselves will not be affected.

Random Variances

Random variances are those that arise beyond the control of management. Machinery is normally subject to some changes in operating characteristics over time. Prices of goods and services acquired in open markets vary with market conditions. Although variance reports will capture differences between expected costs and those actually realized due to these random events, management usually cannot benefit from investigating these variances.

Controllable Operating Variances

Controllable operating variances are the variances that arise from some change in operations that can be corrected by management action. Excessive use of materials due to equipment malfunctions, work delays due to scheduling errors, and high reject or rework rates due to labor or equipment failures are examples of controllable operating variances. Identifying and correcting the cause of these types of variances usually provide benefits to management.

Take the Texas Eastman division of the Eastman Chemicals Company for example, which separated variances into controllable and noncontrollable components. Controllable variances were those under the control of department managers, and included efficiency variances. Price variances for materials and labor were considered to be noncontrollable by department managers, however.[2]

As a manager, you need to know which variances fall into the controllable operating variance class. This can be a complex task. Consider the situation of airline schedules. To keep an airline system operating smoothly, planes must depart and arrive relatively close to schedule. If planes are late, flights are delayed, connections missed, crew schedules upset, and other costs incurred. Similarly, if planes arrive too early, they usually must wait on the ground until gate space becomes available. This causes congestion on the ground and passenger irritation.

At one point, for competitive reasons, airlines published schedules that shortened the reported time between destinations. This created havoc because planes were chronically late. The lateness caused by unrealistic schedules was an *information system variance*. However, weather can also delay flights. These delays are due to *random variance*.

Finally, flights may be delayed due to mechanical problems and similar factors. These are *controllable operating variances* that management likes to focus on to improve operations. The issue for the airlines is: Given daily reports on thousands of flights, even if only 5 percent of them are not on schedule, how does an airline determine which schedule variances to investigate? The approach discussed here provides guidance in this effort.

Decision Approach

In deciding whether to investigate a variance, managers will use subjective judgment based on their experience and records about past production results. The decision model for the variance investigation decision may be diagrammed as:

		Managerial Alternatives	
State of the Production Process		Investigate	Do Not Investigate
	In control	I	0
	Out of control	$C + I$	L

The two columns represent the alternative management actions (Investigate, Do not investigate), and the two rows represent the unknown state of the process (In control, Out of control). Each cell represents a pairing of a decision alternative and a state of the process. The symbols in the cells represent the costs of each pairing.

---

[2] "Texas Eastman Company" (Boston: Harvard University, Harvard Business School case 190–039).

For example, if we investigate the utilities cost variance, we incur an investigation cost *(I)* if the process is in control. Hence, the first cell in the matrix shows that *I* is the cost from the paired event "Investigate, In control." If the process is out of control and we investigate, our cost is the cost to correct *(C)* and the investigation cost *(I)*. Thus, the cost in the first column of the second row of the matrix is *C + I.*

If we don't investigate and the process is in control, we incur zero costs. The zero is entered in the first row of the second column.

Finally, if we do not investigate and the process is out of control, we incur the cost (or loss) of letting the process stay out of control. This loss is labeled *L* and entered in the appropriate cell. Generally, variance investigation decisions are made on a periodic basis and are reviewed as each new report is issued. Therefore, if the process is out of control, subsequent variance reports will tend to signal this. The value of *L,* therefore, must be stated in terms of the costs that will be incurred until management intervenes and corrects the process. Some out-of-control processes may remain out of control only until the next report. Others can remain out of control for months or years. Computing *L,* then, involves considering these future management actions.

Since we don't know the state of the process until after we make the investigation decision, the costs of each alternative are conditional on the probability that the alternative reflects the actual situation. The cost of each alternative, then, is an expected value. The manager chooses the alternative whose cost has the lowest expected value.

Suppose the costs to investigate the variance in utilities expense is $500. The cost to correct an out-of-control process is $1,000, and the cost of allowing the utilities to remain out of control for another period is $4,000. (Assume this is a short-term problem. If this were a long-term problem, the procedure would be the same but the amounts would be present values of future costs.) We enter each cost in the appropriate cell in the decision model and derive a cost for each cell, as follows:

		Managerial Alternatives	
State of the Production Process		Investigate	Do Not Investigate
	In control	$ 500	$ 0
	Out of control	1,500	4,000

Role of Probabilities

In-Control Probability The likelihood that a process is operating within specifications.

Out-of-Control Probability The probability that a process is not operating according to specifications.

Once the costs of each state are known, we apply the probabilities that the state has occurred, to obtain an expected cost of each alternative decision (Investigate or Do not investigate). The important probabilities are (1) **in-control probability,** which is the likelihood that the process is functioning properly given the variance information received, and (2) **out-of-control probability,** which is the likelihood that the process is not operating properly given the variance information received. These probabilities are conditional upon receipt of a specific variance report. Presumably, the greater the variance, the higher the out-of-control probability. The probabilities can then be used to compute an expected cost of each alternative action.

If the out-of-control probability is .3, which is the less costly alternative for the utilities cost variance investigation decision? To answer the question, we must compute the expected value of each alternative. If we investigate, the probability is .3 that we will obtain the benefits of correcting the out-of-control process and .7 that we will find nothing wrong. The value .7 is the in-control probability. The expected cost of the investigation alternative is, therefore:

$$.7 \times \$500 + .3 \times \$1,500 = \$350 + \$450$$
$$= \underline{\underline{\$800}}$$

The expected value of the alternative "Do not investigate" is computed similarly. Since the cost of the pair "Do not investigate, In control" is zero, that term will equal zero and is ignored. The expected cost of not investigating is the product of the out-of-control probability times the cost of being out of control. For this example:

$$.3 \times \$4,000 = \underline{\underline{\$1,200}}$$

Since the expected cost of an investigation is less than the expected cost of not investigating, the results suggest that the variance should be investigated.

Finding the Critical Probability Where It Pays to Investigate

Critical Probability (p*) The probability of different outcomes that equalizes the value of the outcomes.

If we assume that the greater the variance, the greater the out-of-control probability, an investigation policy can be established that relates the variance amount to an out-of-control probability. At some probability, management is indifferent to whether an investigation is conducted. If the actual out-of-control probability (as indicated by the dollar amount of the variance) is greater than implied by our **critical probability** (p*), it pays to investigate. Otherwise, the expected value of not investigating is greater. This critical probability is, in essence, a break-even point between two cost functions.

The expected costs of an out-of-control process (L) increase as the out-of-control probability increases. We can express the cost function for the out-of-control situation as *Lp*, where *p* is the out-of-control probability.

Likewise, the expected cost to correct an out-of-control process increases as the out-of-control probability increases. That is, if we investigate, as the value of *p* increases, so does the chance that we will discover and correct the out-of-control process. Hence, the cost of investigating is equal to *I* plus *Cp*.

If we diagram the relationship between the expected costs of investigating and not investigating, the point where the two cost functions are equal represents the value of *p**, the critical probability. This diagram is shown in Illustration 25–1. Illustration 25–1 shows that as the probability of the process being out of control increases, the loss, *Lp*, increases.

To find *p**, we set the expected cost of investigating equal to the expected cost of not investigating and solve for the unknown *p**. We then must relate the variance data in the responsibility report to the out-of-control probability. If, as indicated by the variance report, that probability is greater than *p**, we initiate an investigation. Otherwise we do not.

ILLUSTRATION

*Cost Functions for
Variance Investigation*

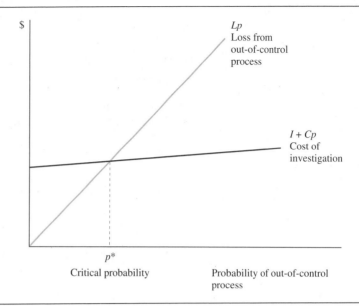

To find the critical probability, p^*, set the equations for the cost of investigating and the cost of not investigating equal to each other. The cost of investigating is:

$I + Cp$

The cost of not investigating is:

Lp

Setting the cost functions equal to each other and solving for p^* gives:

$$I + Cp^* = Lp^*$$
$$I = Lp^* - Cp^*$$
$$I = (L - C)p^*$$
$$p^* = \frac{I}{(L - C)}$$

Using this formula for the data given for our utility cost investigation problem, we obtain a critical probability of:

$$p^* = \frac{\$500}{\$4,000 - \$1,000}$$
$$= .16^2/_3$$

Therefore, as long as the out-of-control probability is greater than $.16^2/_3$, the expected investigation costs will be less than the expected costs of allowing the process to continue without investigation.

To check, should we investigate if the out-of-control probability is .15? By knowing the critical probability, we can immediately answer no. The following computations support this:

The expected cost of the investigation is:

$$(1 - .15) \times \$500 + .15 \times (\$1,000 + \$500) = \$425 + \$225$$
$$= \$650$$

The expected cost of not investigating is:

$$.15 \times \$4,000 = \$600$$

Hence, the model indicates that with an out-of-control probability of .15, the better alternative is not to investigate.

Self-Study Question

1   Wild and Crazy Lens Corporation has been experiencing problems in controlling costs. A recent responsibility report for one of the company's divisions indicated the following (in thousands):

Item	Budget	Actual	Variance
Direct materials	$ 45	$ 39	$6 F
Direct labor	40	48	8 U
Overhead:			
Utilities	10	9	1 F
Property taxes	6	5	1 F
Supervision	8	6	2 F
Equipment repairs	7	10	3 U
Totals	$116	$117	$1 U

The division manager stated that there was no problem since the overall variance was less than 1 percent of total costs, and that was close enough.

As a member of the controller's staff, you learn that the cost to investigate each variance is $1,250. If the process is out of control, it costs an estimated $1,000 to correct. Correction would eliminate an unfavorable variance. However, if the process is out of control and stays out of control, the variance in next month's report is expected to be the same as this month's variance. If the variance appears next month, the process will be investigated and controlled. Hence, the only loss of delay is one month's variance.

a.   What is the critical probability for investigating the direct labor variance?

b.   Given the stated costs from the problem, which other variances would you investigate and correct if they are out of control?

c.   Can you suggest some possible causes for the variances that appear in this report?

The solution to this question is at the end of this chapter on page 928.

QUALITY CONTROL CHARTS

In situations where there are a large number of units produced by a process, production engineering developed a method for sampling some of the units produced and comparing the samples to product specifications. If the sample fell within certain tolerances, the production process was considered in control and no further investigation was conducted. However, if the sample was beyond some tolerance limit, an investigation was conducted to see if the process was out of control. The procedure is referred to as **statistical**

Statistical Quality Control A method for evaluating a repetitive process to determine if the process is out of control.

quality control, and is commonly used in Japanese manufacturing companies.

A familiar example of this method is testing the weight of cereal in a box of cereal. To make certain that the machines that fill the boxes are operating properly, several filled cereal boxes are pulled from the production line and weighed. If the weight of the cereal in the box is within certain limits, it is assumed that the machines filling the boxes are operating properly.

Accounting data may be analyzed using statistical quality control methods to help management approach the variance investigation decision. With this method, the process that generates a cost variance is considered to have a mean of zero. If we know the **standard deviation** of the process that generates variances, we can set tolerance limits for variances. Those that fall within the tolerance limits are assumed to come from an in-control process; otherwise, the variance is investigated.

Standard Deviation A measure of risk. It is computed as the square root of the sum of the squared differences between actual observations and the mean of the data series divided by one less than the number of observations.

We usually assume that the in-control process is normally distributed, although other assumptions are possible. Assuming a zero mean, in the statistical quality control method, the variance is divided by the standard deviation for the variance. The result is a z value. If the z value is greater than 1.96, the probability that the variance came from an in-control process is less than .025 (that is, 2.5 percent). If the z value is 2.56 or more, the probability that it came from an in-control process is no greater than .005.

For example, the variance in utilities costs for the employee benefits section of Great Plains was \$9,000. If the standard deviation for that variance is \$4,500, then the z value is 2. That z value is close enough to 1.96 for us to state that the probability of its coming from an in-control process is about .025.

When there are frequent observations of variances, it may be helpful to diagram the variances by their relationship to the in-control process. This may be done using statistical quality control charts. An example is reproduced in Illustration 25–2.

The chart is constructed by drawing a horizontal time line for the mean of the process. The vertical scale gives the values for the observations. For cereal weights, the scale would be grams. For accounting variances, the

ILLUSTRATION

25–2

Quality Control Chart

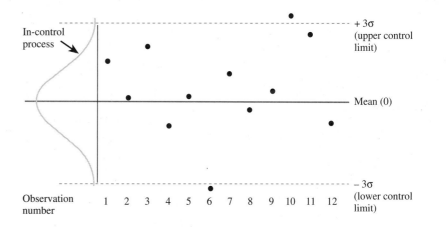

scale would be monetary amounts. The vertical scale could also be converted to *z* values since any observed number when divided by its standard deviation gives a *z* value. The specific scaling would be specified by the managers using the charts.

An **upper** and **lower control limit** is drawn on the chart at the observation values that are considered critical by management. An observation that falls within the control limits is considered acceptable; one that falls without is not. If the observation falls outside the control limits, the process is investigated. In the United States, the control limits are often set at three standard deviations. Statisticians use the Greek letter **sigma** (σ) for denoting the standard deviation of a population. Hence, control charts are frequently referred to as three-sigma or two-sigma control charts, depending on how many standard deviations are used to set the control limits.

Using the observations in Illustration 25–2, we note that observations 6 and 10 fall outside the control limits. These observations would be investigated.

Upper Control Limit The maximum value of some observation that still indicates that a process is in control.

Lower Control Limit The minimum value of some observation that still indicates that the process is in control.

Sigma (σ) Standard deviation.

Control Charts and Variance Investigation

The statistical quality control chart is based on engineering observations of repetitive processes. As a conceptual model, it is useful because if we can relate *p** to the in-control process, and if we set the upper and lower control limits in terms of *p**, it is possible to construct control charts that illustrate observations that may need investigation. They provide a visual effect not possible from a numerical report. If we use the control chart to plot variances in a specific account over time, it may be possible to detect trends or other patterns in variances that would signal the need to investigate even if the control limits were not exceeded. For example, if a cost was relatively stable for several months and then began to show successively greater unfavorable variances, as in Illustration 25–3, a manager might decide to investigate the variance even though it falls within the control limits.

 Self-Study Question

2 Shag O'Nile was recently appointed controller for a new firm in the Southeast. His first assignment is to investigate whether material usage within the plant is under control. He recalls studying statistical quality control techniques in a management

---

ILLUSTRATION

Highlighting Trends in Variances with a Statistical Quality Control Chart

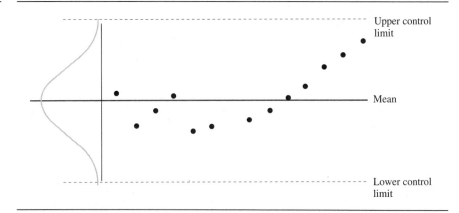

education course and decided to apply it to his investigation. He took the following two samples:

Sample Number	Cost of Each Item			
1	$945	$876	$852	$941
2	822	943	949	782

The control limits specified are $880 ± $60.

    a. Prepare a control chart using the designated control limits.

    b. Comment on the results.

The solution to this question is at the end of this chapter on page 929.

MANAGEMENT INVESTIGATION POLICIES

So far, we have assumed that a variance should be investigated only if the expected benefits from investigation outweigh the costs. This approach focuses on finding a critical probability of being out of control and relating the variance report data to that critical probability. As a practical matter, management usually sets an investigation policy based on some threshold dollar or percentage limitation for variances. For example, management may set a policy that says:

> Investigate all variances that exceed $7,000 or are greater than 20 percent of the flexible budget amount for the specific cost item.

Such a policy is easy to implement, does not require extensive statistical analysis every period, and can be cost-effective if its limits actually do approximate the amounts that would be obtained by a formal analysis of out-of-control probabilities.

    If this policy was in effect for the employee benefits section of Great Plains, the following costs would be investigated based on the responsibility report earlier in the chapter:

Cost	Reason to Investigate
Operator wages	Exceeds $7,000
Communications	Exceeds 20%
Utilities	Exceeds both limits
Supplies	Exceeds 20%
Maintenance and repairs	Exceeds both limits

Assuming that the limits have been established to approximate the investigations that would be conducted using the p^*-based minimum-cost approach, your investigations would be cost-effective.

SUMMARY

The decision to investigate variances is an important management decision because the investigation requires the use of scarce management resources, while letting a process continue out of control may result in waste. *All* variances should rarely be investigated. Many are caused by random processes. Conceptually, a variance may be a signal that a process is out of control. If the signal indicates that the out-of-control probability exceeds the critical point where it is more cost-effective to investigate than not to investigate, management should conduct an investigation.

An alternative approach is to use statistical quality control charts to monitor variances over time. Managers usually establish an investigation rule based on the absolute amount of the variance or on the amount as a percentage of the flexible budget. Such ad hoc rules are usually relatively easy to implement, and are probably cost-effective in many companies.

TERMS AND CONCEPTS

The following terms and concepts should be familiar to you after reading this chapter:

Critical Probability *(p*)*, *914*

In-Control Probability, *913*

Lower Control Limit, *918*

Out-of-Control Probability, *913*

Random Event, *909*

Sigma (σ), *918*

Standard Deviation, *917*

Statistical Quality Control, *917*

Upper Control Limit, *918*

Variance Investigation, *907*

QUESTIONS

25–1   Why doesn't management just investigate all unfavorable variances and forget about complex investigation rules?

25–2   What is the basic decision that management must make when considering whether to investigate a variance?

25–3   The larger a variance, the more likely management is to investigate it. What is the rationale for this?

25–4   Should favorable variances be investigated? Why or why not?

25–5   Nuts N' Bolts runs a highly automated process. The company monitors its equipment on a daily basis. Over each of the past three days, the company noted that the out-of-control probability for a boltmaker was .3, .45, and .7, respectively. The manager of the boltmaker operation suggested that the company initiate an investigation to determine whether the equipment was out of control. Past experience suggests that there is less than a .01 probability that an in-control process would show three consecutive increases in the out-of-control probability. The costs of leaving the process out of control are approximately twice the costs of an investigation. Would you recommend conducting an investigation? Why or why not? If you require additional information, specify the information needed.

25–6   If processes sooner or later go out of control, and if eventually it is so obvious that a process is out of control that management will repair the process without an investigation, why would one be interested in knowing investigation costs?

25–7   What is the role of the out-of-control probability in the variance investigation decision?

25–8   Under what conditions would statistical quality control charts be useful in a responsibility-reporting setting?

25–9   Management usually sets a variance investigation policy such as "Investigate all variances greater than $10,000 or 20 percent of the budgeted amount for the item." Why would management use such a rule when statistical rules give a more precise answer?

25–10   Why do we study statistical rules for variance investigation if they are not widely used by managers?

25–11   Alpha Corporation has implemented the use of statistical quality control charts for analyzing variances. The company has set upper and lower control limits equal to two standard deviations. Assuming there are no out-of-control situations anywhere in the company, what proportion of variances are expected to be outside the control limits?

EXERCISES

25–12 Costs of Variance Investigation
(L.O.2)

Ceylon Industries, Inc., observed an unfavorable variance of $25,000 in its direct materials usage. They estimate this variance indicates there is a .60 probability that the manufacturing process is out of control. To investigate this variance, an $8,000 cost of shutting down operations will be incurred. If the process is out of control, repairs will cost $15,000. In addition, the production line will stay closed during the repair process, which will cost an additional $26,000.

   If the process is out of control and is left out of control, the company will use $45,000 in excess materials between now and the time when the next variance report comes out. At that time, the variance would indicate a 1.0 probability that the process was out of control.

Required:

a. What are the expected costs of:
   (1) Investigating the variance?
   (2) Not investigating?

b. Should the variance be investigated?

25–13 Costs of Variance Investigation
(L.O.2)

A production manager of Northwind, Inc., notes there is an unfavorable direct labor efficiency variance of $30,000. He estimates that this variance indicates that there is a .70 probability that the manufacturing process is out of control. The cost to investigate this variance will be $7,500. If the process is found to be out of control, it will cost $35,000 to correct. If the process is not investigated and is out of control, the company expects that $50,000 in excess labor will be used until the next variance report, which would indicate a 1.0 probability that the process was out of control.

Required:

What are the expected costs of:

a. Investigating the variance?

b. Not investigating?

25–14 Determine Which Variances to Investigate
(L.O.2)

The manager of the Sport Shoe Manufacturing Division of Stylite Products received the following report of variances in the manufacturing operation for the past month:

Item	Actual Cost	Variance	
Direct materials:			
Top fabric	$211,500	$14,029	F
Soles	141,620	4,312	U
Packing	37,980	2,260	U

Item	Actual Cost	Variance	
Conversion costs:			
Labor	$ 65,119	$ 2,107	F
Machine rental	218,732	5,328	U
Property taxes	17,143	12	F
Insurance	10,422	279	U
Power, utilities	18,309	766	U
Maintenance	31,596	1,478	F

Stylite Products conducted a statistical evaluation of its costs and variances and determined that all variances that exceeded 5 percent of actual cost or $5,000 (whichever is less) should be investigated.

Required:

For each of the costs listed in the variance report, indicate which costs would be investigated under the company's rule. Also indicate why the cost should be investigated.

25–15   Estimate Critical Probabilities
(L.O.3)

The cost of an investigation is $3,000. If the process is out of control, it will cost $9,000 to correct. However, if the process stays out of control, the company expects it will cost $15,000 until the process is corrected.

Required:

What is the critical probability?

25–16   Estimate Critical Probabilities
(L.O.3)

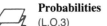

At Hawes Company, the cost of an investigation is $13,000. If the process is out of control, it will cost $15,000 to correct. However, if the process stays out of control, the company will lose $35,000 until it is corrected.

Required:

What is the critical probability?

25–17   Estimate Critical Probabilities
(L.O.3)

At the Elverta Corporation, the cost of an investigation is $4,000. If the process is out of control, it will cost $10,000 to correct. However, if the process stays out of control, the company will lose $20,000 until the process is corrected.

Required:

What is the critical probability?

25–18   Investigating a Process
(L.O.3, L.O.4)

A production manager of Brausch, Inc., is trying to determine if a production process is in control. The cost of investigation is $7,000, and if the process is out of control, it will cost the company $14,000 to correct the error. By correcting the error, the present value of the cost savings until the next scheduled investigation will be $42,000. The in-control probability is .80, and the out-of-control probability is .20.

Required:

a. Should the process be investigated? Why or why not?

b. At what out-of-control probability level would the manager be indifferent about whether to investigate?

25–19   Investigating a Process
(L.O.3, L.O.4)

A production manager is considering whether to investigate a manufacturing process. The cost of investigation is $6,000, and if the process is out of control, the cost of correcting it will be $18,000. If they correct it, the present value of cost savings until the next scheduled inspection will be $50,000. The in-control probability is .70 and the out-of-control probability is .30.

Required:

a. Should the process be investigated? Why or why not?

b. At what out-of-control probability would the manager be indifferent about whether to investigate?

25–20   Investigating a Process
(L.O.3, L.O.4)

Cordova Company's production manager is considering whether to investigate a production process. The cost of investigation is $7,000. If the process is found to be out of control, the cost of correcting it is $26,000. If the process is out of control and they correct it, they will have cost savings of $42,000 until the next scheduled investigation. The in-control probability is .65, and the out-of-control probability is .35.

Required:

a. Should the process be investigated? Why or why not?

b. At what out-of-control probability would the manager be indifferent about whether to investigate?

25-21 Investigating a Process
(L.O.3, L.O.4)

An unfavorable variance of $20,000 was reported for a manufacturing process. If no investigation is conducted and the process is out of control, the present value of avoidable excess production costs is $10,00⸍ The cost of conducting an investigation is $2,000. If the process was actually out of control, the cost of correction would be an additional $3,000. There is a .25 probability that the $20,000 variance indicates the process is out of control.

Required:

a. Should the process be investigated?

b. At what out-of-control probability does the expected cost of investigating equal the expected cost of not investigating?

25-22 Statistical Quality Control
(L.O.5)

Wick Industries has a process with a standard deviation of $125 for each batch of candles produced and an expected cost of $1,430 per batch. Six batches of candles were produced in the current week. The costs for each batch are as follows:

Batch	Cost
A	$1,365
B	1,115
C	1,478
D	1,622
E	1,522
F	1,708

Wick uses a two–standard deviation quality control limit.

Required:

Which of the six batches should be investigated? For each batch that should be investigated, state the reason for the investigation.

25-23 Statistical Quality Control
(L.O.5)

Refer to the information for Wick Industries in problem 25–22, above. Prepare a statistical quality control chart to reflect the upper and lower control limits as well as the costs for each of the six batches.

25-24 Statistical Quality Control
(L.O.5)

The expected cost to produce a batch of compact discs at Global Records is $17,200. The standard deviation for the cost is $420 per batch. Eight batches of compact discs were produced in the current week. The cost for each batch is as follows:

Batch	Cost
Rock	$16,810
Rap	17,918
Classical	16,444
Country	18,283
Oldies	17,391
Heavy metal	16,984
Punk	15,899
New age	18,305

Global uses a two–standard deviation quality control limit.

Required:

Which of the eight batches should be investigated? For each batch that should be investigated, state the reason for the investigation.

25-25 Statistical Quality Control
(L.O.5)

Refer to the information for Global Records in problem 25–24, above. Prepare a statistical quality control chart to reflect the upper and lower control limits as well as the costs for each of the eight batches.

PROBLEMS

25–26   Variance Investigation Costs and Benefits

Micro Parts, Inc., manufactures silicon wafers used in semiconductor chip assemblies. The company operates under a contract with Mega Mainframes. Part of the contract requires that the silicon wafers meet certain tolerances. If the silicon wafers do not meet these specifications, Micro Parts could lose its contract. Since Micro Parts operates a highly automated system, there is always a chance that its system will go out of control. If the system goes out of control for a short period of time, the costs of the out-of-control process are relatively low. However, if the process is out of control for a long enough period, the costs escalate rapidly. The following table shows the costs related to the time the silicon wafer process is out of control and the probability of investigation for each period:

Additional Time Out-of-Control	Out-of-Control Costs This Period	Probability of Investigation
1	$ 18,000	.20
2	49,000	.45
3	177,000	.85
4	350,000	.95
5	1,900,000	1.00

Required:

a. What is the expected cost of having the process remain out of control assuming that the process has just gone out of control?

b. What is the potential savings in costs of allowing its process to remain out of control if Micro Parts, Inc., were to change its investigation rules such that the probability of investigation in Period 1 increased from .20 to .60 and the probability of investigation increased from .45 to .75 in Period 2?

25–27   Variance Investigation Costs and Benefits

Hurst Cartoon Products Corp. manufactures T-shirts, buttons, stuffed toys, and other goods using the motif of cartoon characters. If a process is out of control, costs are relatively low since a lot of goods can be sold as "seconds" at a slight markdown from the regular price. The following table shows the costs related to the time the stuffed-toy process is out of control and the probability of investigation for each period:

Additional Time Out-of-Control	Out-of-Control Costs This Period	Probability of Investigation
1	$ 4,000	.10
2	7,000	.25
3	15,000	.35
4	37,000	.55
5	78,000	.70
6	122,000	1.00

Required:

a. What is the expected cost of having the stuffed-toy process remain out of control assuming that the process has just gone out of control?

b. What is the potential savings in costs of allowing its process to remain out of control if Hurst were to change its investigation rules such that the probability of investigation in Period 1 increased from .10 to .20 and the probability of investigation in all other periods remained the same?

26–28   Costs of Investigation

Texas Oil Company currently sells three grades of gasoline: regular, unleaded, and unleaded plus, which is a mixture of unleaded and an octane enhancer. Unleaded plus is advertised as being "at least 10 percent higher octane than unleaded." Although any mixture containing 10 percent or more premium gas could be sold as unleaded plus, it is less costly to increase the octane by exactly 10 percent. The amount of octane enhancer in the mixture is determined by a valve in the blending machine. If the valve is properly adjusted, the machine provides a mixture that yields the 10 percent higher octane. If the valve is out of adjustment, the machine provides a mixture that yields 20 percent higher octane.

Once the machine is started, it must continue until 100,000 gallons of unleaded plus have been mixed.

Cost data available:

Cost per gallon—unleaded	70¢
Cost per gallon—regular	65¢
Cost of checking the valve	$1,000
Cost of adjusting the valve	$ 500

The octane enhancer costs 5 cents per gallon to make unleaded plus at 10 percent higher octane than unleaded. If the 20 percent higher octane is produced, the octane enhancer costs 12¼ cents per gallon.

The probabilities of the valve's condition are estimated to be:

Event	Probability
In adjustment	.7
Out of adjustment	.3

Required:

a. Should Texas investigate the valve?

b. At what probability would Texas be indifferent about whether to investigate?

(CMA adapted)

25–29 Issues in Variance Investigation— Multiple Choice

The Folding Department supervisor must decide each week whether the department will operate normally the following week. Corrective action is ordered only if the Folding Department will operate inefficiently. The supervisor receives a weekly Folding Department efficiency variance report from the Accounting Department. A week in which the Folding Department operates inefficiently is usually preceded by a large efficiency variance. The graph below gives the probability that the Folding Department will operate normally in the following week as a function of the magnitude of the current week's variance reported to the supervisor:

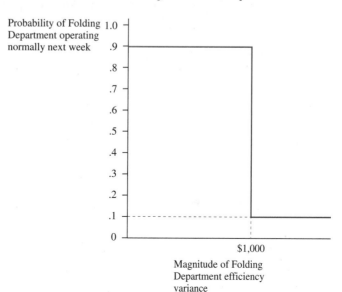

Required:

a. An efficiency variance of $1,500 this week means the probability of operating normally the following week is:
(1) 0 percent.
(2) 10 percent.
(3) 90 percent.
(4) 100 percent.

b. What are the possible relationships between the current efficiency variance and next week's operations?
(1) Large variance followed by normal operation, large variance followed by inefficient operation, small variance followed by normal operation, and small variance followed by inefficient operation.
(2) Large variance followed by normal operation, small variance followed by inefficient operation, and small variance followed by normal operation.
(3) Large variance followed by inefficient operation, small variance followed by normal operation, and small variance followed by inefficient operation.
(4) Large variance followed by 90 percent of normal operation, small variance followed by 10 percent of normal operation, large variance followed by inefficient operation, and small variance followed by inefficient operation.

c. If the supervisor can determine for certain whether the Folding Department will operate normally next week, and the cost of corrective action is less than the extra cost of operating the Folding Department inefficiently, then the best decision rule for the supervisor to follow is:
(1) If normal operations are predicted, do not take corrective action; if inefficient operations are predicted, take corrective action.
(2) Regardless of the current variance, do not take corrective action.
(3) If normal operations are predicted, take corrective action; if inefficient operations are predicted, do not take corrective action.
(4) Regardless of the current variance, take corrective action.

d. The following cost information is relevant to the Folding Department supervisor in deciding whether corrective action is warranted:

> $500 = Cost of corrective action that will assure normal operation of Folding Department for the following week
> $3,000 = Excess cost of operating Folding Department inefficiently for one week

The supervisor receives a report that the Folding Department efficiency variance is $600. The expected cost of not taking corrective action is:
(1) $0.
(2) $300.
(3) $2,700.
(4) $3,000.

(CPA adapted)

25–30   Control Charts

An engineer for Jordan Valley Tool Company specified that the diameter of a particular part should have tolerance limits of .352 and .356. An assistant to the controller asked production personnel to sample these parts. A random sample of 20 parts had the diameters shown in Exhibit 25–30A.

EXHIBIT

25-30A

Number	Diameter
1	.351
2	.350
3	.353
4	.352
5	.359
6	.360
7	.362
8	.351
9	.353
10	.358
11	.355
12	.350
13	.353
14	.354
15	.353
16	.354
17	.355
18	.355
19	.356
20	.354

The mean and standard deviation of the diameter for this type of part have been established as .354 and .003, respectively. Jordan Valley Tool management established a policy that variances outside of the two-sigma limit should be investigated. By contrast, engineering and production personnel believe a process is in control as long as variances are within three standard deviations from the mean.

Required:

a. Construct a control chart and plot the sample on it.

b. Are the engineer's tolerance limits currently attainable? If not, what alternatives are open to the company?

25–31 Statistical Quality Control

Star Ferry Products, Ltd., manufactures a line of microcomputer motherboards. The company manufactures these boards in two divisions: Hong Kong Division and Kowloon Division. Company specifications indicate that each board should cost $460 and that for a day's production of boards at each division, the standard deviation for the average cost is $36. Exhibit 25–31A shows the average unit cost for production for the first 17 days of the month.

EXHIBIT

Day	Hong Kong Division Unit Cost	Kowloon Division Unit Cost
1	$445	$485
2	469	471
3	427	427
4	439	439
5	421	445
6	429	321
7	449	449
8	455	455
9	461	433
10	448	571
11	452	452
12	466	446
13	475	459
14	468	468
15	473	473
16	520	501
17	555	456

The company uses a three–standard deviation control limit for variance investigation purposes.

Required:

a. Which variances would you investigate? Why?

b. Prepare a statistical quality control chart for each of the two divisions.

SOLUTIONS TO

Q *Self-Study Questions*

1 *a.* If L is equal to the $8,000 variance, then the cost functions may be set up as:

$$Lp^* = I + Cp^*$$
$$\$8,000p^* = \$1,250 + \$1,000p^*$$
$$\$7,000p^* = \$1,250$$
$$p^* = \underline{\underline{.179}}$$

The critical probability, p^*, is .179.

b. The only other costs that would be investigated are those with unfavorable variances greater than $2,250 ($1,250 cost to investigate + $1,000 cost to correct). The only cost meeting this criterion is equipment repairs.

c. It appears there is a significant drop in materials costs, which suggests the possibility that substandard materials may have been purchased. If so, this may explain why labor costs have such a high variance and why equipment repair costs are substantially greater than budget. This section of the problem is designed to illustrate how management judgment enters the variance investigation decision process. Management's experience would override any statistical analysis of the data.

2   *a.*

	Sample 1	Sample 2

```
         Sample 1          Sample 2
          X           X        X   X
$940 __X_____ UCL
$880      X   X                             X̄
$820 _____X_____ LCL
                              X
```

b.   The apparently wide dispersion of costs may reflect unusual activities in production or unusual cost-recording behavior. If it reflects neither of these, then management should consider widening the control limits. If nearly all data points outside of the control limits are investigated, then it is likely that the costs of investigation exceed the benefits.

Decision Making under Uncertainty and Information Economics

LEARNING OBJECTIVES

After reading this chapter, you should be able to:

1. Describe the six steps in decision making under uncertainty.
2. Compute expected values.
3. Explain how simulation can be used to analyze cost-volume-profit decisions under uncertainty.
4. Compute the expected value of perfect information.
5. Determine the expected value of imperfect information.
6. Determine the cost of making prediction errors.

*I*n earlier chapters, we assumed managers could predict with certainty. The real world, however, is characterized by uncertainty. Decisions must be made and actions taken without definite knowledge of the results.

For example, suppose that HyperMedical Engineering Company has developed a new device for modifying viral cells. Demand for the product exceeds the company's present manufacturing capacity. HyperMedical Engineering's management could build a new plant, in which case the capital budgeting techniques discussed in Chapters 15 and 16 would be employed.

But building a plant takes several years; moreover, competitors in the biomedical engineering field may develop a similar product and, hence, cut into HyperMedical's market. To meet the immediate demand, management is considering obtaining a new plant under a short-term lease. The fixed lease payments for a new plant will result in a step increase in costs similar to that diagrammed in Illustration 26–1. Point *A* on the volume axis represents the current level of activity, which is also the full capacity of the old plant.

Management expects that volume will increase to the level represented by point *B*. If this happens, then the profits at *B* will be large enough to warrant leasing the new plant. However, the costs of operating the new plant result in a step increase in the fixed costs. If management is certain that the number of units represented by point *B* on the volume axis will be sold with

Effect of Leased Plant on CVP Relationships

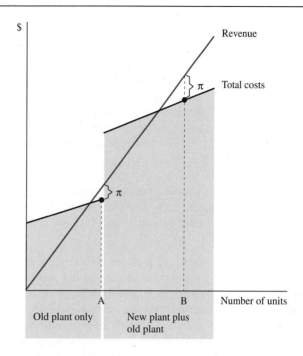

Note: *A* is the capacity of the old plant.

the new plant, then the lease would be justified. Unfortunately, demand is rarely known with certainty.

Suppose management expected profit from a demand increase to point *B* and went ahead with the lease. Management would be unpleasantly surprised if actual demand was less than expected.

Knowledge of the extent of uncertainty and the impact of that uncertainty on decision outcomes is important information for decision making in an uncertain world. In this chapter, we introduce the concepts used to deal with uncertainty and discuss the economic value of information in making decisions under uncertainty.

DEALING WITH UNCERTAINTY

We suggest that you follow six steps when dealing with decisions under uncertainty:

1. Establish a set of mathematically quantified objectives.
2. Determine the set of actions that can be taken.
3. Estimate the various outcomes that are likely to occur after the decision.
4. Assign probabilities to those outcomes.
5. Compute the payoffs that are likely under each paired set of actions and outcomes.
6. Choose the action that is best in achieving objectives.

Use of this approach does not assure profitable operations, but it does provide a rational basis for decision making. In the long run, following this method can be expected to result in decisions that achieve established objectives.

Step 1: Establishing Objectives

Company management usually establishes objectives. In addition to maximizing profit, management may seek to avoid excessive risk, attain certain market shares, or introduce new products. Once the qualitative objectives are determined, they must be expressed in mathematical terms. This mathematical statement of management goals is called an objective function. An example of an objective function is the expression:

Maximize profit (π), where

$$\pi = (P - V)X - F$$

This is the profit equation from Chapter 11. The term X represents the quantity sold per period, P is the price per unit, V represents the variable cost per unit, and F is the fixed costs per period.

Step 2: Determining the Action Set

Action Set The alternatives available to managers in a given decision setting.

Once objectives have been established, management must consider the alternative actions in the action set that may be taken to attain them. In our example, there may be several ways to meet the increased demand. As we noted, management might construct a new plant. Or it might subcontract for a certain amount of production. It might also purchase another company that is in the same business. Each action has different profits and risks.

Management considers each alternative as a possible way to meet its established objectives. Other alternatives may also be considered. For example, management could ignore the increased demand and continue to produce at the same level as before. To simplify the discussion, we will assume that the only alternative actions are to lease a new plant or to subcontract for the added demand.

Step 3: Estimating Outcomes

Exogenous Factors Outside events that can influence an outcome.

The outcome that will occur after the decision has been made is unknown and usually beyond the control of management. The external influences that affect the outcome are called exogenous factors. For example, in the Hyper-Medical example, management may expect that future demand for the product will continue to increase. But the level of future demand is affected by such factors as the state of the economy, competition, and technological change. When management makes its expansion decisions, it cannot know the exact level of future demand because it cannot perfectly predict these exogenous factors.

Outcomes Possible results of a given action.

Nevertheless, management can estimate the possibilities of specific outcomes. While HyperMedical's management may expect future demand to increase by 5,000 units next year, they may estimate that demand could increase by as much as 40,000 units. The 5,000-unit increase is considered much more likely than the 40,000 increase, but both are possibilities.

A set of mutually exclusive and collectively exhaustive outcomes is constructed to represent the possible future outcomes. As a practical matter, a small representative set of possibilities is usually chosen. In our example, the set of possible demand increases is limited to 1,000, 2,000, 5,000, 10,000, and 40,000 units. In reality, demand increases *might* be 1,386 units or 61,903 units or any other number; but to avoid excessive computations, the limited set is usually sufficient.

Step 4: Assigning Probabilities to Outcomes

Payoff The value of each outcome.

Probabilities Likelihoods that given outcomes will, in fact, occur.

Now that we have the set of five estimated future demand levels, the next task is to think about each outcome, estimate how likely it is to occur, and evaluate the payoffs. In the decision literature, the term **payoff** is used to indicate the value of each outcome.

The probability of each demand level's occurrence is estimated statistically or by other means. Marketing studies may be conducted to evaluate future demand levels and the related **probabilities** that those levels will, in fact, occur. Past trends may be used when there is reason to believe the trends will continue in the future. Management may use its own judgment based on knowledge of contract negotiations with potential buyers or other factors.

Assessing these probabilities is always a subjective process even though mathematical models may yield results that are precise to the last unit of production. Because the future is uncertain, probability statements about the future are also uncertain.[1] Nonetheless, management uses such probability assessments when their benefits exceed the cost of obtaining them.

Based on quantified data about future demand levels, HyperMedical's management assesses the future increases in demand and, based on experience and judgment, estimates the following set of probabilities, which are presented as follows:

Increased Future Demand (units)	Probability
1,000	.10
2,000	.20
5,000	.50
10,000	.15
40,000	.05
Total	1.00

The set of probabilities may contain as few or as many demand levels as needed to obtain the desired degree of precision. The desired precision in the results will depend on the reliability of the data and the trade-off between the costs and benefits of gathering additional information. The probabilities must always sum to one, as they do here. It is generally assumed that probabilities associated with the demand are independent of the decision. In our example, whether HyperMedical leases a new plant or subcontracts, the set of probabilities for future demand levels will be the same.

Step 5: Computing Payoffs

The accountant must often compute the payoffs for each alternative and for each outcome. To do this, the costs that are likely for each level of activity

---

[1] See R. Libby, *Accounting and Human Information Processing* (Englewood Cliffs, N.J.: Prentice Hall, 1981), for a discussion of behavioral probability estimation and revision.

and for each alternative action choice must be considered. This is a direct application of the concepts of differential costing introduced earlier in this book. For example, assume that HyperMedical's management could subcontract any number of units at any time and obtain the profit function:

$$\pi = (\$8 - \$7)X_s$$

where

π = Operating profit from subcontracting
X_s = Quantity subcontracted and sold

This equation indicates a $1 net profit per unit.

Or management could lease a new plant capable of producing 10,000 units with a profit function of:

$$\pi' = (\$8 - \$2)X_p - \$20,000$$

where

π' = Operating profit from leasing
X_p = Quantity produced and sold
$20,000 is the fixed cost.

The payoffs for each outcome under each alternative action are computed and shown in the following **payoff table**:

Payoff Table A schedule showing the alternate outcomes from a decision.

Future Demand (units)	Payoffs	
	Subcontract	Lease Plant
1,000	$ 1,000	$ − 14,000[a]
2,000	2,000	− 8,000
5,000	5,000	10,000
10,000	10,000	40,000
40,000	40,000	70,000[b]

Additional computations:

[a] $ − 14,000 = 1,000($8 − $2) − $20,000; $ − 8,000 = 2,000($8 − $2) − $20,000; etc.
[b] See following paragraph for computations at the 40,000-unit level.

At the 40,000-unit level, both manufacturing and subcontracting would be required since the plant can produce only 10,000 units. Manufacturing 10,000 at a profit of $40,000 plus subcontracting 30,000 (that is, 40,000 − 10,000) at a profit of $30,000 are necessary to obtain the $70,000 total.

To make its decision, HyperMedical's management computes the expected payoffs under each considered alternative action. The expected payoff for each action is the sum of the payoffs for each outcome times the probability associated with that outcome. For subcontracting, the expected payoff is:

Outcome	Probability	Payoff at This Level		Expected Payoff
1,000	.10	× $ 1,000	=	$ 100
2,000	.20	× 2,000	=	400
5,000	.50	× 5,000	=	2,500
10,000	.15	× 10,000	=	1,500
40,000	.05	× 40,000	=	2,000
Expected payoff for subcontracting				$6,500

For the alternative to lease a new plant, the expected payoff is computed using the same method:

Outcome	Probability	Payoff at This Level		Expected Payoff
1,000	.10	× $− 14,000	=	$− 1,400
2,000	.20	× − 8,000	=	− 1,600
5,000	.50	× 10,000	=	5,000
10,000	.15	× 40,000	=	6,000
40,000	.05	× 70,000	=	3,500
Expected payoff for leasing				$ 11,500

Step 6: Making the Decision

The expected payoff levels are compared, and the alternative with the higher expected payoff is selected under the decision criterion established in step 1. Since the expected payoff from leasing a new plant ($11,500) is greater than the expected payoff from subcontracting ($6,500), the data suggest that management should lease the new plant. However, this is only a suggestion. The final decision is the responsibility of management, and management may elect to use other decision criteria.

Self-Study Question

1 Thunder Manufacturing Company produces a volatile chemical, Vapo, that must be sold in the month produced or else discarded. Thunder can manufacture Vapo itself at a variable cost of $40 per unit, or they can purchase it from an outside supplier at a cost of $70 per unit. Thunder can sell Vapo at $80 per unit. Production levels must be set at the start of the period and cannot be changed during the period.

The production process is such that at least 9,000 units must be produced during the period. Thus, Thunder must incur costs of at least $360,000 (9,000 × $40) even if demand is less than 9,000 units. Thunder management must decide whether to produce Vapo or whether to purchase it from the outside supplier.

The possible sales of Vapo and their probabilities are:

Demand (units)	Probability
4,000	.4
7,000	.5
11,000	.1

Determine the following:

a. Expected demand.

b. Expected profit from purchasing Vapo from an outside supplier and selling it.

c. Expected profit from manufacturing Vapo internally and selling it.

The solution to this question is at the end of this chapter on page 958.

CVP UNDER UNCERTAINTIES IN PRICES AND COSTS

Accountants also consider the impact of uncertainty on CVP analysis. Up to this point, we have assumed that the only uncertainty in CVP analysis was the expected value of X, the quantity of units produced and sold. But in reality, any of the inputs to the profit equation are uncertain. Indeed, the probability of obtaining profit numbers that are equal to plans is very small. When all the variables in the CVP equation are uncertain, the same approach that was used for uncertainties in X is extended to the other variables.

Since the number of computations rapidly increases as the number of uncertain variables increases, computer assistance is usually required. A technique known as **Monte Carlo simulation** is used to sample from the distributions of each variable and to compute the profit for each sampled combination of selling price, variable cost, unit volume, and fixed costs, labeled P, V, X, and F, respectively. The resulting expected profit and standard deviation can be used in exactly the same manner as when only X was uncertain.

To use Monte Carlo simulation, we must specify the distributions for each variable in the profit function. If we focus on the profit from leasing a new plant, we need to specify distributions for P, V, and F. The distribution for X that was obtained earlier will be used.

Let us assume the following distributions for the variables:

Monte Carlo Simulation A method of sampling from an assumed distribution function to obtain simulated observations of costs or other variables.

	Value	Probability
For P:	$7	.3
	8	.4
	9	.3
For V:	$1.50	.3
	1.75	.2
	2.00	.1
	2.50	.1
	3.00	.3
For F:	$18,000	.4
	20,000	.2
	22,000	.4

These data are entered into a computer program that uses random numbers to sample from the distributions and compute an expected profit as well as the standard deviation for that profit. In addition, the program may be designed to plot the different outcomes and their frequencies.

The plotted outcomes from this program are shown in Illustration 26–2. Note the concentration of outcomes at profit levels of $-15,000$ to $15,000$. Overall, it appears that the probable outcome would be a modest profit in the range of zero to $45,000. There is some risk of a loss and the very high profits occur infrequently. Further analysis of these higher profits and their likelihood might be conducted if management were risk seeking.

The advantage of using computer simulation is that the distribution of payoffs may be observed even with very complex interrelationships. Indeed, the Monte Carlo method could be extended to include prices, costs, and quantities for multiple products as well as interrelationships between the products. For example, if the price of one output increases more than 20 percent, consumers may switch to another alternative output. A computer simulation could be designed to include the switch when the specific round of the simulation indicated a 20 percent increase in price for the first output.

ILLUSTRATION   *Monte Carlo Simulation Results for CVP Analysis (in thousands of dollars)*

26–2

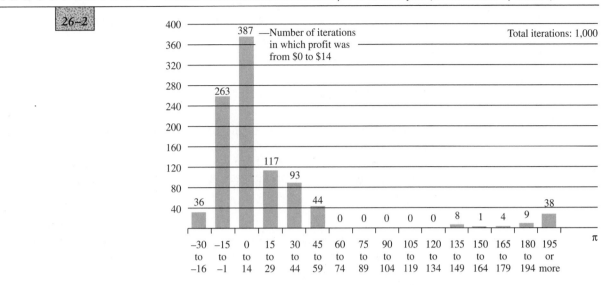

COST DATA AND INFORMATION ECONOMICS

Information Cost Cost of obtaining information.

Value of Information Value placed on information one could possibly obtain in a decision-making context.

Information Economics A formal system for evaluating whether the cost-benefit test has been met for information.

Decisions about how much information to acquire are a part of management's process. This section focuses on information-related aspects of management decision making under uncertainty. To decide whether to acquire information, management must evaluate the **information cost** and compare that to the **value of the information.** The conceptual basis for determining how much information to request is found in the field of **information economics.**

Consider the decision-making problem facing the management of Biohealth Corporation. They must decide whether or not to harvest a rare plant that grows in a distant country. The seed of this plant will enable Biohealth to produce and sell a new vaccine if the seed produces the right extract.

To harvest the seed, Biohealth will have to purchase an export license from the local government. The export license will cost Biohealth $7 million, payable in advance.

Assume, for simplicity, that there are only two possible outcomes from management's decision:

1. The seeds will produce the right extract and future cash flows to the company will be worth a net present value of $20 million. This is a "success" outcome.

2. The seeds do not produce the right extract, and the total investment of the cost of the export license ($7 million) is lost. This is a "failure" outcome.

Biohealth management faces a possible gain (or payoff) of $20 million from the investment. Against this they run the risk of losing the $7 million investment. Before investing in such a risky project, they would at least want to assess the relative probabilities of making $20 million versus losing $7 million. Assume the probability of making the $20 million is equal to .60;

then we can compute the expected value of the project as follows:

Payoff (millions)	Probability	Expected Value (millions)
$20	.60	$12.0
(7)	.40	(2.8)
Project expected value		$ 9.2

Since the expected value of the project is positive, we will assume that the project is acceptable to the manager from the standpoint of maximizing company values. However, there is a significant, .40, probability that the company will suffer a $7 million loss. Can management do anything to avoid that loss?

THE OPPORTUNITY LOSS CONCEPT

Opportunity Loss Loss from an unfavorable outcome.

Perfect Information Information that predicts with complete accuracy the outcome that will occur from a decision.

By making a decision to accept the project, there is a .4 chance that a loss will be incurred. The $7 million loss from the unfavorable outcome is referred to as an **opportunity loss**. The loss may never actually be realized, but there is a .4 chance that it will occur.

Now, let's assume that management could acquire information that would make a perfect prediction of the project's success. Such information would be called **perfect information**. This information would provide management with perfect knowledge about the future. If management had such perfect knowledge, the project would be accepted only when the positive outcome was assured. This would occur with a .6 probability. Otherwise, management would avoid the project and, at least, avoid the loss. Hence, with perfect knowledge, the outcome with the highest payoff for each known state would be selected. The expected value of the project would be the sum of the expected values for each outcome and its related best action:

Outcome (millions)	Best Action	Probability	Expected Value (millions)
$20	Invest	.60	$12
-0-	Avoid	.40	-0-
Expected value of project with perfect information			$12

EXPECTED VALUE OF INFORMATION

With perfect knowledge about the future, management would be able to identify when the harvest would be successful. Under such circumstances, management would invest in the project.

Expected Value of Perfect Information

The expected value of perfect information is the amount that could be saved with perfect knowledge about the future. That amount is also the difference between the $12 million expected value of the project with perfect information and the $9.2 million expected value of the project without perfect information. If management could obtain perfect information, the information would be worth up to $2.8 million. (Note that this value of perfect information equals .40 times the avoided opportunity loss of $7 million.) If the information cost is less than this, management's expected value would increase if the information were obtained.

Suppose a research company could be hired to conduct a field study to determine whether the seeds produce the desired extract. As a result of this study, management will have perfect information about the outcome of this project. The total cost of the field study is $1 million. This $1 million is an information cost. Should management pay for the study?

The study will indicate with certainty whether the seeds will produce the desired extract. Therefore, with probability .6, Biohealth will obtain the $20 million payoff less the $1 million spent on the study.

On the other hand, with probability .4, the study will indicate that the harvest will not be successful. When this occurs, Biohealth will lose the $1 million cost of the study, but no more.

The expected value of this decision with costly perfect information is:

Payoff (millions)	Probability	Expected Value (millions)
$19	.6	$11.4
(1)	.4	(.4)
Project expected value		$11.0

The payoffs are $1 million less than the expected value of the project with costless perfect information.

PERFECT VERSUS IMPERFECT INFORMATION

Imperfect Information Information that is not 100 percent accurate, but may be used to revise the probabilities of certain decision outcomes.

So far we have discussed the value of information that provides a perfect prediction. However, information about the future will probably be imperfect.

Imperfect information does not allow certain prediction of the outcome that will occur, but it allows us to revise our probabilities about the outcomes of a decision. The value of imperfect information is the increase in the expected value of the decision that arises from the ability to revise the probabilities. The value of imperfect information can be estimated using the technique called *Bayesian statistics*.

Now, let's extend the example. We now assume that the study will provide *imperfect* information. The report can have two possible outcomes: a "good" report indicating that the harvest will be successful or a "bad" report showing that the harvest will fail. Since the study is an imperfect information source, a good report can occur even if the harvest will fail. Likewise, a bad report can occur even though the harvest will succeed. Nonetheless, use of the report may enable us to revise our initial probabilities and make a better decision. The initial probabilities are called **prior probabilities** or **priors.**

Prior Probabilities (Priors) Initial probability estimates.

Revising Prior Probabilities with Information

In deciding to conduct the study, the relevant criterion is whether the expected value of the project will increase sufficiently to cover the cost of the study. Biohealth management must know how reliable the report will be. That is, if they receive a good report, what is the probability that the harvest will actually be successful?

The following discussion describes the process, which is summarized in Illustration 26–3. To conduct this analysis, some statistical notation is help-

ILLUSTRATION

Table of Probabilities

Step 1: Set up the table and enter the prior probabilities of success *(S)* and failure *(F)* as the row totals.

	Report Good (G)	Report Bad (B)	Totals
Harvest Succeeds (S)			.60
Harvest Fails (F)			.40
Totals			1.00[a]

[a] Probabilities must sum to 1.0.

Step 2: Compute the joint probabilities in each cell by multiplying the conditional probabilities [for example, $p(G/S)$] times the prior probabilities of success or failure [for example, $p(S) = .60$]. Recall that $p(G/S) = .85$; $p(B/S) = .15$; $p(G/F) = .20$; and $p(B/F) = .80$.

	Report Good (G)	Report Bad (B)	Totals
Harvest Succeeds (S)	$.85 \times .60$ $= .51$	$.15 \times .60$ $= .09$	.60
Harvest Fails (F)	$.20 \times .40$ $= .08$	$.80 \times .40$ $= .32$	.40
Totals			1.00

Step 3: Compute the column totals, which are the probabilities of receiving a good report or a bad report.

	Report Good (G)	Report Bad (B)	Totals
Harvest Succeeds (S)	.51	.09	.60
Harvest Fails (F)	.08	.32	.40
Totals	.59	.41	1.00

ful. Using the symbol *S* to indicate a successful harvest and the symbol *F* to indicate a failure, we note that the prior probabilities are:

$$p(S) = .6$$
$$p(F) = .4$$

as discussed before and as entered in step 1 in Illustration 26–3.

The second step is to find out the probabilities of obtaining a good report *(G)* or a bad report *(B)* given that the harvest will be successful. These are called **conditional probabilities** because they depend on the actual, unknown outcome. This information must be obtained from other sources, perhaps

Conditional Probabilities
Those likelihoods that depend on a specific result.

from the field research company or from management's judgment about similar past projects. For the example, we assume these probabilities are:

$$p(G|S) = .85$$
$$p(B|S) = \underline{.15}$$
$$1.00$$

This means that the probability of a good report given a successful harvest is .85, and so forth. From similar sources, we must also obtain the probabilities of each report given that the harvest will fail. We assume these are:

$$p(G|F) = .20$$
$$p(B|F) = \underline{.80}$$
$$1.00$$

This information is used to compute the probabilities of getting a good or bad report before the study is ordered. If the probabilities of each report type are known, the expected value of the project with the imperfect information can be computed. This information is used to help decide whether to order the study. The difference in the value with the imperfect information and the value of the project without any information is the maximum price we would be willing to pay for the imperfect information, using the expected value criterion.

Joint Probability The probability of two or more events occurring.

To obtain the probabilities of getting each kind of report, we add the probabilities of obtaining that report under each possible outcome. The probability of getting both a certain kind of report and a certain outcome is called a joint probability. (See step 2 in Illustration 26–3.) In our example, the probability of getting a good report is equal to the sum of the joint probability of a good report when the outcome is success plus the probability of a good report when the outcome is failure.

Thus, we multiply the probability of success times the probability of getting a good report when the outcome will be success ($.6 \times .85 = .51$). Then we multiply the probability of failure times the probability of getting a good report when the outcome will be failure ($.4 \times .2 = .08$). Then we add the results of these two multiplications:

$$p(G) = [p(S) \times p(G|S)] + [p(F) \times p(G|F)]$$

which, for the example data, yields:

$$p(G) = (.6 \times .85) + (.4 \times .2)$$
$$= .51 + .08$$
$$= \underline{\underline{.59}}$$

We therefore have a .59 probability of getting a good report before contracting for the field study, as shown in step 3 of Illustration 26–3.

The probability of getting a bad report is equal to $1 - .59$, or .41. This probability may be verified by computing the probabilities of a bad report conditioned on both possible outcomes just as was done for the good report. The calculations are:

$$p(B) = [p(S) \times p(B|S)] + [p(F) \times p(B|F)]$$
$$= (.6 \times .15) + (.4 \times .8)$$
$$= .09 + .32$$
$$= \underline{\underline{.41}}$$

These calculations are also shown in steps 2 and 3 in Illustration 26–3.

Now, before we incur the cost of acquiring the report, we know the probability that we will obtain a good report or a bad report. This information is important because if the report is to have any impact on our decision, the different type of report must result in a change in our decision. That is, in this limited situation, if the report is good, then the investment meets the expected value criterion. If the report is bad, then the investment would not meet the criterion and, presumably, would be avoided. If we will take one action or the other regardless of the type of report, then the report has no value. Why spend resources on information that has no potential to change a decision?

Regardless of which report we receive, the project can still succeed or fail. Hence, after receiving the report we must make a decision whether to embark on the project. At this point, it is helpful to diagram the possible outcomes. A decision tree is useful for this purpose, as shown in Illustration 26–4.

The first decision is whether to conduct the study. These are the two main branches of the decision tree. If we decide to conduct the study and, hence, acquire the report, we must make the investment decision after receipt of the report. The decision will be based on the expected payoff from each outcome. To make the decision, we must know the probabilities of success or failure after receiving each kind of report. These probabilities are called **posterior probabilities.**

Posterior Probabilities The probabilities obtained as a result of revising prior probabilities with additional conditional probability data.

ILLUSTRATION

26–4

Decision Tree for Information Evaluation

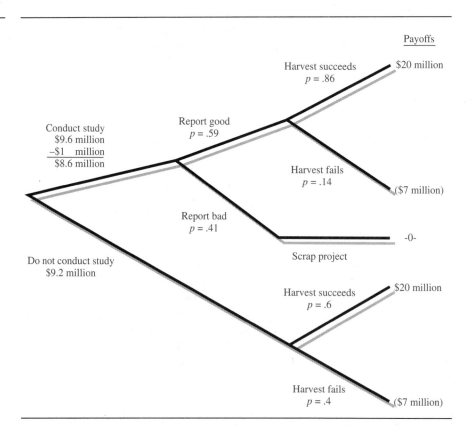

Prior to receiving the report, we were given the probability of project success as .6 and the probability of failure as .4. The expected value of the project without the report is the lower main branch in Illustration 26–4: $9.2 million. Now we want to see if the expected value of the project is greater with the information in the report.

Revising Probabilities Using Bayes' Theorem

The objective of this analysis is to find out how the report will revise the prior probabilities (.6 for success and .4 for failure). This process of revising probabilities requires knowledge of the probabilities of success and failure given each type of report. These probabilities, known as posterior probabilities, may be found using Bayes' Theorem as follows. If the report is good *(G)*, the probability of success *(S)* is estimated as:

$$p(S|G) = \frac{p(G|S) \times p(S)}{p(G)}$$

$$= \frac{.85 \times .6}{.59} = \underline{\underline{.86}} \text{ (rounded)}$$

The posterior probability of failure *(F)* given a good report *(G)* is the complement of this amount, or .14, and is computed as follows:

$$p(F|G) = \frac{p(G|F) \times p(F)}{p(G)}$$

$$= \frac{.20 \times .40}{.59} = \underline{\underline{.14}} \text{ (rounded)}$$

The posterior probabilities when a bad report is received are computed in the same manner. For success, the probability is:

$$p(S|B) = \frac{p(B|S) \times p(S)}{p(B)}$$

$$= \frac{.15 \times .6}{.41} = \underline{\underline{.22}} \text{ (rounded)}$$

The probability of failure *(F)* given the bad report *(B)* is then .78, which is the complement of the probability of success.

These posterior probabilities have been entered on the decision tree in Illustration 26–4 and are used to compute the expected value of the project with imperfect information.

Computing the Value of Imperfect Information

The expected value of the decision to harvest the plant with imperfect information is obtained by computing the expected value of the project given each report. This is referred to as the *conditional value of the decision* given a certain report. That is, if we get a good report, we compute an expected value for the project conditioned on the good report, as follows:

Outcome (millions)	Posterior Probability	Expected Value (millions)
$20	.86	$17.2
(7)	.14	(1.0)
Expected value given a good report		$16.2

If the report is good, Biohealth would invest in the harvest because the expected $16.2 million payoff is positive. Before we order the field study, we have a .59 probability that the report will be favorable. Therefore, before ordering the study, we expect that the value of the joint outcome of a good report and the decision to go ahead with the harvest will be $9.6 million (.59 probability of a good report × $16.2 million).

Next, we find the expected value of going ahead with the harvest in the face of a bad report:

Outcome (millions)	Posterior Probability	Expected Value (millions)
$20	.22	$ 4.4
(7)	.78	(5.5)
Expected value of project after a bad report		$(1.1)

Since the expected value of the project would be negative after receiving a bad report, management of Biohealth would not proceed with the harvest if a bad report was received. Hence, the expected payoff would be zero.

The value of the decision to proceed with imperfect information is, then, the sum of the values of the decision for each report outcome. That is, $9.6 million plus zero, or $9.6 million, before considering the cost of the information.

The value with imperfect information is compared to the value with no information. The increase represents the maximum that we would be willing to pay for the imperfect information. In this case, the difference is $.4 million ($9.6 million − $9.2 million).

If the cost of the field study was $1 million, the decision would be not to commission the study. Its cost exceeds the $.4 million benefit that can be expected from it.

Self-Study Question

2 After several years of supplying tofu to several supermarket chains, the Soong family decided that it was time to diversify operations. Laura Soong, a recent biochemistry graduate, then suggested that they exploit the growing diet and health food market by introducing soybean ice cream. "It tastes almost like the real thing!" She then provided her estimates of costs for the project.

Based on Laura's figures, David Soong, the family accountant, estimates that if sales are high, the total contribution margin from the product will be $300,000. If sales are low, the total contribution margin earned by the Soongs will be $50,000. Fixed costs for the project will be $150,000. David is uncertain as to what the probability of sales would be. Hence, he assigns a prior probability of .5 for high sales and .5 for low sales.

The Soong family can conduct a survey of various health food outlets to determine the demand for the new product. The reliability of the survey is such that it will signal high sales 70 percent of the time when actual sales will be high, and signal low sales 90 percent of the time when actual sales will be low. The costs of such a survey are $20,000.

Assuming that the Soong family bases its decisions on expected value:

a.   What action will they take without the survey?

b.   Should the Soong family conduct the survey? What should their decision be?

The solution to this question is at the end of this chapter on page 959.

OTHER CONSIDERATIONS IN INFORMATION EVALUATION

Before analyzing information value, a manager will ask the following questions:

1. Will the information make a difference?

2. How costly would the error be if the action was taken without the information?

The first question asks if the information will possibly change the decision. The second asks about the cost of "prediction error." Unless the information can be expected to make a difference and unless the value of the difference exceeds the cost of the information, the information should not be obtained.

CHANGING A DECISION WITH INFORMATION

In the Biohealth example, the imperfect field study had value because the decision involved a choice. If a bad report was received, management would not harvest the plant and, hence, avoid the related loss. But if the receipt of a bad report would not deter the harvest, the study would have no value in this context. That is, regardless of the outcome of the study, the decision would not change. In such a case, there would be no economic reason to conduct the study. We invest in the harvest, period. No formal analysis of information value is needed.

Why would management proceed with a project when the outcome of a test study is negative? Several possibilities exist. In some cases, management may be required to proceed with the project due to legal requirements, contract obligations, or other imperatives. In this situation, the set of outcomes has been misspecified—any outcome that is based on avoiding the project is not possible. In other cases, the information may be so unreliable that a bad report would not dissuade management from proceeding with the project.

COST OF PREDICTION ERROR

Cost of Prediction Error The difference between the actual cost incurred based on incorrect information and the cost that would have been incurred with correct information.

There is always the question of how much difference information makes in the decision-making process. We have seen that information enables a manager to avoid certain losses. This may be expanded into the concept of the **cost of prediction error**. The cost of prediction error is the difference between the actual cost incurred based on the incorrect information and the cost that would be incurred with the correct information.

The cost of prediction error is the opportunity cost from making an economically suboptimal decision based on information that later appeared to be in error. For example, assume that Mean Green Company receives a special order for a product. The special order price is $7.00 per unit; 5,000 units are ordered. Mean Green has excess capacity and estimates the unit costs for the product as follows:

Variable $4.50
Fixed 5.00

Based on this estimate, Mean Green figures that operating profits will increase by $2.50 (the $7.00 price less the $4.50 variable cost) for each unit in the special order. After accepting the order, Mean Green learns that its unit costs are actually:

Variable $7.50
Fixed 2.00

Mean Green lost $2,500 on the special order (5,000 units times $7.00 revenue less $7.50 variable costs). Assuming there was no other use for the capacity, the cost of prediction error is the $2,500 since the company would not have accepted the order if it had known that the order price was less than its variable costs.

Capital budgeting decisions are also subject to this type of analysis. In these situations, the cost of prediction error is usually considered as equal to the opportunity cost of capital invested in the project.

For example, Peaches, Inc., has an after-tax cost of capital of 12 percent. Peaches invested $80,000 in a tricycle manufacturing project with the following expected cash inflows:

Year	Amount
1	$30,000
2	35,000
3	30,000
4	20,000
5	10,000

The net present value of the project was $14,425. The project did not turn out as well as expected. Actual cash inflows were as follows:

Year	Amount
1	$30,000
2	25,000
3	20,000
4	5,000
5	-0-

and the net present value was ($15,870). In this situation, the cost of prediction error is $15,870 since the company would not have invested in the project had the actual cash flows been known. The funds tied up in the project carried an opportunity cost of 12 percent. A project that earns exactly 12 percent would have a net present value of zero.

Cost of prediction error analysis should be limited to those situations where it is possible to improve a model or to obtain better data. If an event occurs that is totally unexpected, and that event results in a loss to the company, the costs of that loss should be assigned to the unexpected event, not to prediction error.

3 Opus' Designs imports formal wear and wholesales it to major retailing companies. Opus' Designs must order more suits than it expects to sell because a substantial number of ordered goods are defective and must be scrapped. When placing an order, Opus requests a total number of suits that, after eliminating the rejects, yields 1,000 good suits. If a given order does not yield 1,000 suits, the difference between 1,000 suits and the number of good suits received must be made up by purchasing from a local subcontractor at a price of $100 per suit, none of which will be defective.

   The company had two alternative sources of supply for its most recent order. It could purchase suits from Afgha at a cost of $50 each (regardless of whether they were defective). Suits ordered from Afgha have an expected reject rate of 25 percent, which means that Opus' Designs needs to order 1,333 suits. Alternatively, the suits could be ordered from Amer at a cost of $65 each. The reject rate for Amer source suits is expected to be 10 percent, so Opus needs to order 1,111 suits from Amer. Based on this information, Opus decided to order from the source in Afgha at a total cost of $66,650 versus a total cost of $72,215 for the suits from Amer. After receiving the order, 40 percent of the suits were found to be defective.

   What is the cost of the prediction error? (Round numbers of suits to the nearest whole number.)

The solution to this question is at the end of this chapter on page 960.

MANAGEMENT USES OF INFORMATION ECONOMICS

It is unlikely that management would *routinely* go through the formal analytical process described here to decide whether to gather information. However, in general, managers give at least informal consideration to the economic usefulness of information. Otherwise, the demand for information would be unlimited!

   When very large investments are incurred, and when there is sufficient information to permit specification of the probabilities, managers may perform formal analysis. Indeed, petroleum exploration companies make wide use of the techniques described here. In their operations, they gather information in a given location. The costs to drill and install production facilities are so high that the benefits of gathering information exceed the costs. Moreover, there have been so many deposits explored that a sufficient data base exists to estimate probabilities. Pharmaceutical manufacturers also evaluate information from drug trials to assess whether to go forward with development of a drug or whether to abandon the potential product.

   As financial experts, we (the readers, teachers, authors, and practitioners) need to understand that the commodity supplied (information) will only be purchased if required or if the user perceives it is economical. Understanding how information has value should enable the user of information to relate information costs and benefits. The mathematics of information economics becomes very complex when the number of choices increases and when the decision includes other factors characteristic of a real-world setting. However, the concepts are based on the information economics model presented here. Presumably, accountants are hired because someone decides that accounting information has economic value.

REAL WORLD APPLICATION

Dealing with Uncertainty in the Airline Industry*

The airline industry has continually faced a problem of accepting reservations and holding seats for passengers only to have the passenger not show up for the flight. Frequently, the airline could have sold the seat to another paying passenger. When this occurs, the empty seat is an opportunity cost.

To solve the problem, airlines routinely overbook by accepting more reservations than the number of seats available on the flight. The possibility exists, of course, that more passengers with reservations will appear for a flight than there are seats available. In these situations, airlines offer monetary incentives to passengers willing to give up their reservations and take another flight. The airlines balance the costs of nonshowing passengers with the costs of overbooking.

To strike the optimal balance, airlines have a yield management section that gathers information about the relative number of no-shows on a given flight on a given day of the week. In addition, airlines found that passengers with nonrefundable tickets are more likely to show up for a flight than

passengers with no-penalty tickets. Hence, the probability of a no-show is determined based on past history of the flight plus the number of passengers booked with various types of penalty and non-penalty tickets.

In addition, airlines ask their local employees to advise the yield management section about special events such as football games, spring break, and local festivals because that information affects the no-show rate. When all of this information is entered into a computer model, an airline will know the optimal number of seats by which it can overbook a flight.

Gathering all of this information is costly. The airlines have found that the benefits exceed the costs, however. They can minimize the sum of the opportunity costs from empty seats and the monetary incentives for passengers to voluntarily give up reserved seats by obtaining this information.

* Based on the authors' research.

SUMMARY

In the uncertainty that characterizes the real world, decision makers must consider the possibility that the outcome they expect from a decision may not be the outcome that actually occurs. The role of the accountant is to provide information to help managers make decisions and reduce uncertainty.

Information is a product that may have value just as any other product. Management must make decisions concerning whether to gather information for decision making and other purposes. Information economics is the field of study that established the concepts used to formalize management's decisions about gathering information.

On a hindsight basis, it is sometimes possible to compare the profit that could have been attained with correct information to that with the information actually used to set policy. The difference is referred to as the cost of prediction error.

The concepts behind information economics models serve as general guidelines to management for decisions about the acquisition of information. After all, accountants are information producers and command a pecuniary reward for their services. If information had no value, what would become of accountants?

TERMS AND CONCEPTS

The following terms and concepts should be familiar to you after reading this chapter:

Action Set, *932*	**Opportunity Loss,** *938*
Conditional Probabilities, *940*	**Outcomes,** *932*
Cost of Prediction Error, *945*	**Payoff,** *933*
Exogenous Factors, *932*	**Payoff Table,** *934*
Imperfect Information, *939*	**Perfect Information,** *938*
Information Cost, *937*	**Posterior Probabilities,** *942*
Information Economics, *937*	**Prior Probabilities (Priors),** *939*
Joint Probability, *941*	**Probabilities,** *933*
Monte Carlo Simulation, *936*	**Value of Information,** *937*

QUESTIONS

26–1 What are the steps in decision making under uncertainty?

26–2 What is the role of the accountant in decision making under uncertainty?

26–3 The comment, ''Since we can't know the future, there's not much point in doing all this elaborate analysis,'' is frequently heard. Respond to this comment.

26–4 Why do we limit the possible outcomes to discrete numbers such as 3,000 units or $500,000 in revenues when the actual numbers might be 3,129 units, $486,313 in revenue, or some other odd number?

26–5 Why would management give up a project with a lucrative payoff in exchange for a different project with a smaller payoff, which has little or no risk of loss?

26–6 What are the problems in applying simulation analysis to the assessment of risk?

26–7 A manager was overheard saying, ''I want all the information before I make a decision. Get me all the information!'' Comment on this quote.

26–8 Does information reduce the risk in a manager's decision?

26–9 Since no one can supply perfect information, why do we even consider the perfect information case?

26–10 ''Imperfect information is worthless since it cannot predict the future with certainty.'' Comment on this quote.

26–11 Management has invested $8 million in a project. The payoffs from the project will either be zero or a present value of $20 million. Either event is equally likely. The original investment cost will be deducted in computing the profit from the project. Now management learns that it can obtain perfect information about the outcome from the project. What is the maximum value of that information for this investment project?

26–12 What are the limitations on the use of the information economics approach by management?

26–13 Management knows that if it purchases a report there is a good chance the results of the report will affect its decision. Should management purchase the report or should they consider something in addition?

26–14   Miracle Pharmaceuticals has discovered a cure for heart disease. Miracle conducted tests that showed that its product completely eliminated heart disease in a sample of 1,000 people at high risk for the disease. The results were very impressive. Under the present economic circumstances, Miracle expects the project will have a positive net present value assuming a price of $200 per year for the product. Miracle's forecast assumes that the Food and Drug Administration will approve the product in one year. If approval is delayed five years, the project attains the same net present value as the one-year approval if the price is increased to $350 per year. Demand would be unaffected by the two prices considered. Miracle could invest $7 million in an expanded test that would assure approval in one year. *From a purely economic perspective,* should Miracle conduct the expanded test?

26–15   What is the difference between the value of information and the cost of prediction error?

26–16   When does a cost of prediction error arise?

26–17   Refer to the real world application about the airline industry. Assume Northern Airlines has a yield management model that determined that Northern could overbook Flight 1313 on June 20 by 30 seats, which it did. Southern Airlines, which competes with Northern on this route, went bankrupt without any preliminary warning on June 19. As a result, Northern had 24 more passengers show up for Flight 1313 than there were seats available. Northern had to give 24 passengers $500 each in compensation to get them to take a later flight. What was the cost of prediction error?

EXERCISES

26–18
Formulate
Objective Function
(L.O.1)

Speedy Delivery Company provides courier services. The company can deliver packages with its own equipment or subcontract. Revenues from any delivery average $10 per item regardless of how the package was delivered. The company's fixed costs are $20,000 per month, which gives them the capacity to deliver 18,000 packages. Variable costs are $1.70 per package delivered using the company's own equipment. If Speedy subcontracts additional packages, the costs to deliver a package total $7.40.

Required: State, in mathematical form, Speedy Company's objective function.

26–19
Compute
Expected Values
(L.O.2)

Lynch Company is considering a make-or-buy alternative. An outside supplier has agreed to sell the materials at a price of $40 per unit. If they produced the unit themselves, the costs of the materials would be as follows:

Cost per Unit	Probability
$30	.15
35	.25
40	.30
45	.20
50	.10

Required: What is the expected cost per unit if they produce the unit themselves?

26–20
Outcomes, Expected
Values, and
Information Value
(L.O.2, L.O.4)

GMG Studios, Inc., is considering producing a new action movie. Production and distribution costs are estimated at $15 million. GMG estimates the following probabilities for cash inflows from the movie:

Probability

$50 million	.4
3 million	.6

Required:

a. What is the expected value of the movie?

b. What are the possible outcomes if GMG Studios decides to produce and distribute the movie?

c. How much would GMG be willing to pay to find out for certain if the movie was going to be a blockbuster or a dud?

26–21 Outcomes, Expected Values, and Information Value
(L.O.2, L.O.4)

Sue & Em Esquires, P.A., specializes in contract liability litigation. The firm believes that law is a matter of economics. The firm's motto is: "If the expected value of the verdict exceeds our fee, then SUE!" One of the firm's partners was presenting details of a case to Three Initial Corp. (TIC), a prospective client. The partner stated that the costs of the litigation would be $10 million. The partner stated that there was a 10 percent probability that the court would award a $170 million judgment in TIC's favor.

Required:

a. What is the expected value of the lawsuit?

b. What are the possible outcomes if TIC pursues the litigation?

c. How much would TIC be willing to pay to find out for certain if the court was going to award it the $170 million?

26–22 Information Value
(L.O.4, L.O.5)

Daytona Corp. is evaluating whether to obtain an oil change franchise. The costs of the franchise and other investments total $10 million. If the franchise is successful, Daytona will have a project with a present value of future cash flows of $100 million (that is, before deducting the initial investment cost). The probability of success is .4. If the franchise is not successful, the present value of the future cash inflows will be $15 million. Manny, Moe & Jack Marketing Corp. offered to conduct a survey for Daytona that could inform them more precisely whether the franchise would be successful.

Manny, Moe & Jack provide the following probabilities for their reports:

$$p(G) = .5$$
$$p(S|G) = .7$$
$$p(S|B) = .1$$

where

G = Good report
B = Bad report
S = Successful franchise

(Note: No probability revisions are required.)

Required:

a. What is the maximum price, if anything, Daytona would be willing to pay Manny, Moe & Jack to conduct the marketing study?

b. If the unsuccessful outcome were to have a negative present value of $20 million, which does include loss of the initial investment, what is the maximum price Daytona would be willing to pay Manny, Moe & Jack to conduct the marketing study?

c. If the answers to part a and part b differ, explain why.

26–23 Information Value
(L.O.4, L.O.5)

Hanabar, Inc., is evaluating whether to construct and operate a new amusement park. The cost of the project is $200 million. If the park is successful, Hanabar will have a project with a present value of future cash flows of $400 million (that is, before deducting the initial investment cost). If the park is not successful, the present value of the future cash inflows will be $80 million. There is a .55 probability that the project will be successful. Squiggley Marketing Corp. offered to conduct a survey for Hanabar that could inform them more precisely whether the park would be successful.

Squiggley provided the following probabilities for their reports:

$$p(G) = .7$$
$$p(S|G) = .8$$
$$p(S|B) = .1$$

where

> G = Good report
> B = Bad report
> S = Successful park

(Note: No probability revisions are required.)

Required:

a. What is the maximum price Hanabar would be willing to pay Squiggley to conduct the marketing study?

b. If the probability of a successful project given a good report is .6, what is the maximum price Hanabar would be willing to pay Squiggley to conduct the marketing study?

c. If the answers to part a and part b differ, explain why.

26–24 Value of Perfect Information (L.O.4)

Suppose an oil driller is faced with the following options:

State of Nature	Probability	Payoff	
		Drill	Don't Drill
No oil	.75	− $ 80,000	–0–
Oil	.25	+ 150,000	–0–

The driller can obtain information from seismic tests that perfectly predict whether oil will be found if drilling commences.

Required:

a. What action would the driller take without any information?

b. What action would the driller take with the perfect information?

c. What is the value of the perfect information?

26–25 Value of Perfect Information (L.O.4)

A treasure hunter, who searches for treasure in sunken ships, is faced with the following options on a particular treasure hunt:

State of Nature	Probability	Payoff
No treasure	.90	− $ 200,000
Treasure	.10	+ 1,600,000

Assume the treasure hunter can obtain information from an old seaman who knows exactly where the ship was sunk.

Required:

a. What is the expected value of the action with no information?

b. What is the expected value of the action with the perfect information?

c. What is the value of the perfect information?

26–26 Value of Perfect Information (L.O.4)

A manager is trying to decide whether to accept a special order. If the order is accepted, the increased revenue to the company will be $1 million. The costs of making the products for the special order are either $800,000 or $1.2 million, depending on how much time is needed for its manufacture. Hence, acceptance of the order would result in a net gain of $200,000 *or* a net loss of $200,000, while rejection will produce neither gain nor loss.

The manager regards the two production cost events as having the following probabilities: (1) there is a .7 probability that production costs will be low, hence, a $200,000 profit would be made on the order; (2) there is a .3 probability that production costs will be high, hence, a $200,000 *loss* would be incurred if the order is accepted.

Before deciding whether to accept or reject the order, the manager can analyze a set of special orders already in production, thereby gaining information. The cost of setting up the records and analyzing the data is $30,000.

Required:

a. If the manager wants to maximize expected value, what is the best decision for the manager before considering the information?

b. Assuming the information is perfect, what is the value of that information to the manager? Should the information be obtained?

26–27 Value of Imperfect Information— Revising Probabilities Not Required
(L.O.5)

Refer to exercise 26–26. Suppose the information that the manager can obtain is not perfect. Past experience for similar information indicates that when the information predicts low production costs, production costs turn out to be low 80 percent of the time and high 20 percent of the time. When the information predicts high production costs, production costs turn out to be high 80 percent of the time and low 20 percent of the time. There is a 70 percent chance the information will predict low costs. This relationship between high and low costs and the related information are summarized as follows:

$$p(low\ costs|\text{information } predicts\ low\ costs) = .80$$
$$p(high\ costs|\text{information } predicts\ low\ costs) = .20$$
$$p(low\ costs|\text{information } predicts\ high\ costs) = .20$$
$$p(high\ costs|\text{information } predicts\ high\ costs) = .80$$

Note that probabilities do not have to be revised using Bayes' Theorem.

Required:

a. What action would the manager take if the imperfect information was obtained?

b. What is the value of the imperfect information?

26–28 Improving the Accuracy of Information
(L.O.5)

Refer to exercise 26–27. Suppose the accuracy of the imperfect information could be improved. For an additional cost of $15,000, the accuracy of the information could be improved from 80 percent to 90 percent.

Required:

Is it worthwhile to obtain the more accurate information?

26–29 Revising Probabilities Using Bayes' Theorem
(L.O.5)

Refer to exercise 26–26. Suppose the manager receives information in the following form: p(information signal|event), which requires using Bayes' Theorem to revise probabilities. The manager believes that the information would correctly identify high costs 60 percent of the time and correctly identify low costs 40 percent of the time. The cost of this information is $40,000.

Required:

Should this information be obtained? What is its value?

26–30 Cost of Prediction Error—Capital Investments
(L.O.6)

Fast Buck, Inc., invests in high-technology, short useful life projects. Two years ago, the company evaluated a product with an investment cost of $1.5 million and expected cash flows of $1 million per year for three years. The company's cost of capital is 18 percent. The product did not perform as well as expected. The company knows that the cash flows in Years 1 and 2 were $800,000 and the expected cash flow in Year 3 is $400,000.

Required:

What is the cost of prediction error?

26–31 Cost of Prediction Error—Differential Costs
(L.O.6)

Indigo Company estimates the following costs, prices, and volume for its single product:

Selling price . . . . $	225	per unit
Variable cost	170	per unit
Fixed costs	1,000,000	per period
Sales volume	40,000	units

The company then produced 40,000 units. Prices and costs were as expected, except sales were only 37,000 units. Due to the nature of the product, 3,000 units were scrapped for a net-of-salvage-cost revenue of $20,000.

Required: Compute the cost of prediction error.

PROBLEMS

26–32 Payoff Table

Jon Co. agreed to supply Arom Chemical, Inc., with a substance critical to Arom's manufacturing process. Due to the critical nature of the substance, Jon Co. has agreed to pay Arom $1,000 for any shipment that is not received by Arom on the day it is required.

Arom establishes a production schedule that enables it to notify Jon Co. of the necessary quantity 15 days in advance of the required date. Jon can produce the substance in five days. However, capacity is not always readily available, which means that Jon may not be able to produce the substance for several days. Therefore, there may be occasions when there are only one or two days available to deliver the substance. When the substance is completed by Jon Co.'s Manufacturing Department and released to its Shipping Department, the number of days remaining before Arom Chemical, Inc., needs the substance will be known.

Jon Co. has undertaken a review of delivery reliability and costs of alternative shipping methods. The results are presented in the following table:

Shipping Method	Cost per Shipment	Probability that the Shipment Will Take ___ Days					
		1	2	3	4	5	6
Motor freight	$100	—	—	.10	.20	.40	.30
Air freight	200	—	.30	.60	.10	—	—
Air express	400	.80	.20	—	—	—	—

Required: Prepare a payoff table for Jon Co.'s shipping clerk to decide which shipping alternative to select if there is: (1) one day before delivery is required; (2) two days before delivery is required; and so forth, up to seven days before delivery is required.

(CMA adapted)

26–33 Expected Value of Sales

Jackson, Inc., manufactures and distributes a line of toys. The company neglected to keep its doll house line current. As a result, sales have decreased to approximately 10,000 units per year from a previous high of 50,000 units. The doll house was recently redesigned and is considered by company officials to be comparable to its competitors' models. Joan Blocke, the sales manager, is not sure how many units can be sold next year, but she is willing to place probabilities on her estimates. Blocke's estimates of the number of units that can be sold during the next year and the related probabilities are as follows:

Estimated Sales in Units	Probability
20,000	.10
30,000	.40
40,000	.30
50,000	.20

The units will sell for $20 each.

The entire year's sales must be manufactured in one production run. If demand is greater than the number of units manufactured, sales will be lost. If demand is below supply, the extra units cannot be carried over to the next season and must be discarded. Production and distribution cost estimates are listed below.

	Units Manufactured			
	20,000	30,000	40,000	50,000
Variable costs	$180,000	$270,000	$360,000	$450,000
Fixed (step) costs	140,000	140,000	160,000	160,000
Total costs	$320,000	$410,000	$520,000	$610,000

The company must decide on the optimal size of the production run.

Required:

Prepare a payoff table for the different sizes of production runs required to meet the four sales estimates prepared by Joan Blocke. If Jackson, Inc., relied solely on the expected monetary value approach to make decisions, what size of production run would be selected?

(CMA adapted)

26–34 CVP Analysis under Uncertainty

Wing Manufacturing Corporation produces a chemical compound, product X, which deteriorates and must be discarded if it is not sold by the end of the month during which it is produced. The total variable cost of the manufactured compound, product X, is $50 per unit, and its selling price is $80 per unit. Wing can purchase the same compound from a competing company at $80 per unit plus $10 transportation per unit. Management estimates that failure to fill orders would result in the loss of 80 percent of customers placing orders for the compound. Wing has manufactured and sold product X for the past 20 months. Demand for the product has been irregular, with no consistent sales trend. During this period, monthly sales have been as follows:

Units Sold per Month	Probabilities
8,000	.25
9,000	.60
10,000	.15

To produce product X, Wing uses a primary ingredient, K-1, which it purchases for $24 per unit of compound. There is a 70 percent chance that the supplier of K-1 may be unable to deliver the ingredient for an indefinite period. A substitute ingredient, K-2, is available at $36 per unit of compound, but a firm purchase contract for either material must be made now for production next month. If an order was placed for K-1, but it was unavailable, then management would have to purchase product X from a competitor and sell it at a loss. (Otherwise, it would permanently lose important customers.) Assume that 9,000 units are to be manufactured and all sales orders are to be filled.

Required:

a. Compute the monthly contribution margin from sales of 8,000; 9,000; and 10,000 units if the substitute ingredient, K-2, is ordered. What is the expected contribution if K-2 is ordered?

b. Prepare a schedule computing the expected monthly contribution margin if the primary ingredient, K-1, is ordered, given the chance of nondelivery. For this requirement, assume that the expected average monthly contribution margin from manufacturing is $130,000 using K-1 and the expected average monthly loss from purchasing product X from the competitor is $45,000.

(CPA adapted)

26–35   **Value of Perfect Information**

Vendo Company operated the concession stands at the university football stadium. Records of past sales indicate that there are basically four kinds of football weather, that sales of hot dogs depend on the weather, and that the percentage of football games played in each kind of weather is as follows:

Weather	Percentage of Game Days	Hot Dogs Sold
Snow 10%		10,000
Rain 20		20,000
Clear/warm 40		30,000
Clear/cold 30		40,000

Hot dogs cost Vendo Company 60 cents each and are sold for $1.00. Hot dogs unsold at the end of each game are worthless. Ignore income taxes.

Required:

a. Prepare a table with four rows and four columns showing the contribution margin from each of the four purchasing strategies of buying 10,000, 20,000, 30,000, or 40,000 hot dogs and the four weather conditions (snow, rain, clear/warm, and clear/cold).

b. Assuming that the chances of snow, rain, clear/warm, and clear/cold are 10 percent, 20 percent, 40 percent, and 30 percent, respectively, compute the expected contribution margin from each of the following purchasing strategies:
    (1)   Buy 10,000 hot dogs.
    (2)   Buy 20,000 hot dogs.
    (3)   Buy 30,000 hot dogs.
    (4)   Buy 40,000 hot dogs.

c. What is the optimal purchasing strategy in the absence of a weather forecast, and what is the expected contribution margin from following this strategy? (This answer will be the largest of the four expected payoffs computed in b.)

d. If Vendo had a perfect weather forecast for each game, it would buy 10,000 hot dogs when snow is predicted; 20,000 when rain is predicted; 30,000 when clear/warm is predicted; and 40,000 when clear/cold is predicted. What is the expected average contribution margin per football game, assuming the availability of a perfect weather forecast and that the four kinds of weather will occur in the frequencies 10, 20, 40, and 30 percent?

e. What is the expected dollar value to Vendo Company of a perfect weather forecast per football game? That is, what is the expected dollar value of the information from a perfect weather forecast?

(CMA adapted)

26–36   **Value of Imperfect Information**

Rosetta Stone Exploration Co. has obtained information that suggests that an unusual formation of malachite might be found in the Sonora Desert. The deposit will cost $15 million for rights, permits, and development. There is a 40 percent probability that the deposit will provide a present value of future cash inflows of $75 million before deducting the cost of the investment. On the other hand, there is a 60 percent probability that the deposit will provide no future cash inflows and that the company will have to pay an additional $2 million (present value) to restore the site to its original condition before Rosetta Stone began its development project.

There are two approaches that can be taken to investigate this deposit further. Rosetta Stone can pay $3 million to conduct a detailed geologic study of the area. If Rosetta Stone decides to perform this study, past experience indicates that if the deposit will have a good outcome, the report will indicate that the deposit is valuable 90 percent of the time. If the deposit is not economically feasible, the report will indicate this 80 percent of the time.

The second approach is to conduct a reconnaissance survey at a cost of $500,000. These surveys are less accurate. If the deposit is valuable, the reconnaissance survey will provide a good report with a .7 probability. If the deposit is not valuable, the reconnaissance survey will provide a bad report with a .7 probability.

Required:

Which report, if either, should Rosetta Stone Exploration Co. acquire to assist it in evaluating the malachite deposit? Prepare a decision tree for this information that will help management assess the alternatives.

26–37   Value of Alternate Imperfect Information Sources

Laser Biomedical Corp. is developing a new drug for the treatment of high cholesterol. Based on the data gathered to date, Laser Biomedical estimates that there is a .65 probability that the drug is effective. To obtain approval to market the drug, the company needs to conduct a trial that will show that the product is effective. If the product is successful, the drug will have a net present value of $30 million before consideration of the testing costs.

The company can carry out two tests in its attempt to prove effectiveness of the drug. The final test requires the use of 1,500 patients. Half of the patients would receive a placebo (sugar pill), and the other half would receive the drug. A comparison of cholesterol levels between the two groups would indicate whether the drug was effective. This test will cost $2 million. If the drug is effective, this test will indicate effectiveness an estimated .7 of the time. If the drug is not effective, this test will indicate effectiveness an estimated .05 of the time. If this test does not indicate that the drug is effective, Laser Biomedical will repeat the test using 4,000 patients. The repeat will cost $6 million. If the drug is effective, the repeat test will indicate this with probability .95. If the drug is not effective, the repeat test will indicate this with probability 1.0. If the repeat test indicates that the product is not effective, all $6 million testing costs will be lost.

An alternative is to conduct the trials using 5,000 patients. This test will cost $3 million. If the drug is effective, this test will indicate effectiveness .9 of the time. If the drug is not effective, this test will never indicate that the drug is effective. If this test indicates that the drug is not effective, the project will be abandoned and the test costs will be lost.

Required:

Which drug trial should Laser Biomedical conduct? It is suggested that you draw a decision tree to show the alternatives and their respective payoffs.

26–38   Cost of Prediction Error—Make-or-Buy Decision

Hersh Optical Corp. was considering whether to manufacture their own lenses or to purchase them from a subcontractor. Hersh Optical had an offer from a subcontractor to manufacture lenses at $14 each in lots of 5,000. Lenses received from a subcontractor would have to be inspected by Hersh Optical at a cost of 25 cents each. The subcontractor required a commitment from Hersh to purchase a minimum of 50,000 lenses per year.

Hersh considered the cost of manufacturing the lenses in its own facilities. The company prepared a cost estimate for a lot of 5,000 lenses with the following details:

Materials	$31,250
Labor	17,450
Equipment rental	13,150
Inspection costs	4,200
Other overhead	3,500

The equipment rental is based on an annual cost of $157,800. The equipment is leased on a year-to-year basis, with no requirement that the equipment lease be renewed for a subsequent year. All other costs vary with units produced. When preparing this cost data, the staff accountant estimated that the company would manufacture and sell 60,000 lenses per year. Hersh Optical made its decision whether to make or buy on the basis that 60,000 lenses would be required in a year. The lower-cost alternative was chosen.

Required:

    a. Did Hersh make or buy? Show computations.

    b. If actual demand was 50,000 units, what was the cost of prediction error?

26–39 Cost of Prediction Error—Capital Investment Analysis

Asahi Heavy Equipment Corp. was considering investing in a project with an initial investment cost of $70 million. After studying the market for the product, Asahi estimated that future cash flows would equal $20 million per year for five years. Using a 10 percent discount rate, Asahi concluded that the project met its net present value criteria and signed contracts under which it was committed to go forward with the project.

After spending $15 million, Asahi learned that government approvals would delay marketing the product for one full year. If marketing were delayed for a year, the future cash inflows would amount to $20 million per year for only four years instead of the planned five years.

If Asahi decides to complete the project, the company will spend the remaining $55 million in Year 0, but the cash inflows will not begin until Year 2. The contract has a clause that will permit Asahi to end the contract. In this case, Asahi will not be liable for any additional payments, but the contractor will obtain title to the project and Asahi will not be reimbursed for any part of the $15 million already spent.

Required:

    a. What are the net present values of the alternatives available to Asahi at this time?

    b. If Asahi had reason to believe it was possible that the project could have been delayed, what is the cost of prediction error?

    c. Would the cost of prediction error be different if Asahi had spent $10 million on the project so far and had to spend the remaining $60 million in Year 0 to obtain the reduced cash flows? Why or why not?

SOLUTIONS TO

Self-Study Questions

1 *a.* Expected demand is 6,200 units, computed as:

Demand (units)	Probability	Expected Demand (units)
4,000	.4	1,600
7,000	.5	3,500
11,000	.1	1,100
Expected demand		6,200

    b. The expected profit from purchasing and selling would be equal to the unit contribution times the expected quantity or

$$(\$80 - \$70) \times 6{,}200 \text{ units} = \underline{\underline{\$62{,}000}}$$

    c. Even though the production cost is stated as a variable cost, since a minimum of 9,000 units must be produced, the cost is really fixed up to that point because of minimum production constraints. Units produced in excess of the

9,000 minimum would carry the variable cost of $40 each. The expected profit from manufacturing is:

Demand (units)	Probability	Manufacturing Cost	Profit	Expected Profit
4,000	.4	$360,000	$ (40,000)	$ (16,000)
7,000	.5	360,000	200,000	100,000
11,000	.1	440,000	440,000	44,000
Expected profit				$128,000

2 *a*.

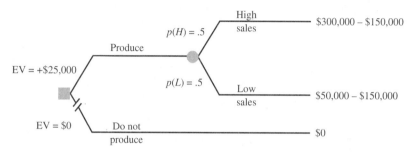

Decision without survey: Accept project.

b. Let:

H = Actual high-sales state
L = Actual low-sales state
Y_H = Survey signal for high-sales state
Y_L = Survey signal for low-sales state
p = Probability

$$p(Y_H|H) = .7$$
$$\therefore p(Y_L|H) = .3$$
$$\therefore p(Y_L|L) = .9$$
$$p(Y_H|L) = .1$$
$$p(Y_H) = p(Y_H|L)p(L) + p(Y_H|H)p(H)$$
$$= .1(.5) + .7(.5)$$
$$= .4$$
$$p(Y_L) = p(Y_L|L)p(L) + p(Y_L|H)p(H)$$
$$= .9(.5) + .3(.5)$$
$$= .6$$
$$p(H|Y_H) = \frac{p(Y_H|H)p(H)}{p(Y_H)}$$
$$= \frac{.7(.5)}{.4}$$
$$= .875$$
$$\therefore p(L|Y_H) = .125$$
$$p(H|Y_L) = \frac{p(Y_L|H)p(H)}{p(Y_L)}$$
$$= \frac{.3(.5)}{.6}$$
$$= .25$$
$$\therefore p(L|Y_L) = .75$$

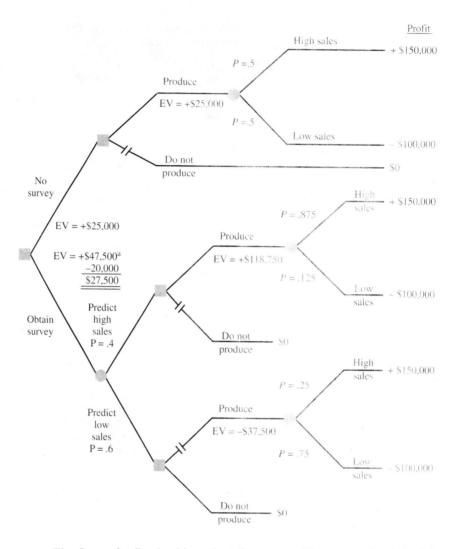

The Soong family should conduct the survey. The expected value of the project, less the cost of the survey, is:

$$\$47,500 \; - \; \$20,000 \; = \; \underline{\underline{\$27,500}}$$

Without the survey, the expected value of the project is:

$$\underline{\underline{\$25,000}}$$

3 For its $66,650, Opus' Designs received 800 good suits (1,333 ordered − 40% × 1,333 defective suits). Opus then had to purchase 200 suits to make up the shortfall. The price of the 200 suits was $20,000, which is 200 suits at $100 each. The total cost of the order from the source in Afgha is $86,650 ($66,650 + $20,000). The alternative cost was $72,215. The cost of prediction error is $14,435—the difference between the two costs.

Here is a list of articles and books that supplement the textbook. These readings include both academic articles, like those published in *The Accounting Review,* and applied articles, like those published in *Management Accounting* and the *Journal of Cost Management.* We have divided the list into the following categories of readings:

1. Activity-based costing.

2. Just-in-time, quality, and the new production environment.

3. International applications.

4. Implementing cost systems.

5. Managerial decision making.

6. Managerial planning and performance evaluation.

7. Other readings.

Many of you will use this list to do research for a class project; others will find these readings helpful for developing and implementing new managerial accounting methods. For either use, please note that these are representative readings, not an exhaustive list. The list of readings that we initially developed was several hundred pages long, which should give you some idea about how extensive is the literature on managerial accounting.

1. Activity-Based Costing

Albright, Thomas L., and James M. Reeve, "A Case Study on the Impact of Material Yield Related Cost Drivers on Economics Improvement," *Journal of Management Accounting Research* 4 (Fall 1992), pp. 20–43.

Banker, Rajiv, and Gordon Potter, "Economic Implications of Single Cost Driver Systems," *Journal of Management Accounting Research* 5 (Fall 1993).

Beaujon, George J., and Vinod R. Singhal, "Understanding the Activity Costs in Activity-Based Costing Systems," *Journal of Cost Management* 4, no. 1 (Spring 1990), pp. 51–72.

Berlant, Debbie, Reese Browning, and George Foster, "How Hewlett-Packard Gets Numbers It Can Trust," *Harvard Business Review,* January–February 1990, pp.178–83.

Bonsack, Robert A., "Does Activity-Based Costing Replace Standard Costing?" *Journal of Cost Management* 4, no. 4 (Winter 1991), pp. 46–47.

Borden, James P., "Review of Literature of Activity-Based Costing," *Journal of Cost Management* 4, no. 1 (Spring 1990), pp. 5–13.

Cooper, Robin, "Cost Classification in Unit-Based and Activity-Based Manufacturing Cost Systems," *Journal of Cost Management* 4, no. 3 (Fall 1990), pp. 4–14.

Cooper, Robin, and Robert S. Kaplan, "Profit Priorities from Activity-Based Costing," *Harvard Business Review,* May–June 1991, pp. 130–35.

_____, "Activity-Based Systems: Measuring the Costs of Resource Usage," *Accounting Horizons* 6, no. 3 (September 1992), pp. 1–14.

Foster, George, and Mahendra Gupta, "Manufacturing Overhead Cost Driver Analysis," *Journal of Accounting and Economics* 12, no. 1–3 (1990), pp. 309–37.

Greenwood, Thomas G., and James M. Reeve, "Activity-Based Cost Management for Continuous Improvement: A Process Design Framework," *Journal of Cost Management* 5, no. 4 (Winter 1992), pp. 22–40.

Harr, David J., "How Activity Accounting Works in Government," *Management Accounting,* September 1990, pp. 36–40.

Johnson, Thomas H., T. P. Vance, and R. S. Player, "Pitfalls in Using ABC Cost-Driver Information to Manage Operating Cost," *Corporate Controller,* January–February 1991, pp. 26–32.

Kaplan, Robert S., "In Defense of Activity-Based Cost Management," *Management Accounting* 74, no. 5 (November 1992), pp. 58–63.

Lee, John Y., "Activity-Based Costing at CAL Electronic Circuits," *Management Accounting,* October 1990, pp. 36–38.

Noreen, Eric, "Conditions under Which Activity-Based Cost Systems Provide Relevant Costs," *Journal of Management Accounting Research* 3 (Fall 1991), pp. 159–68.

Novin, Adel M. "Applying Overhead: How to Find the Right Bases and Rates," *Management Accounting* 73, no. 9 (March 1992), pp. 40–43.

Raffish, Norm, and Peter B. B. Turney, "Glossary of Activity-Based Management Terms," *Journal of Cost Management* 5, no. 3 (Fall 1991), pp. 53–63.

Rotch, William, "Activity-Based Costing in Service Industries," *Journal of Cost Management* 4, no. 2 (Summer 1990), pp. 4–14.

Roth, Harold, and A. Faye Borthick, "Getting Closer to Real Product Costs," *Management Accounting,* May 1989, pp. 28–33.

Scott, Peter, and Mike Morow, "Activity-Based Costing and Make-or-Buy Decisions," *Journal of Cost Management* 4, no. 4 (Winter 1991), pp. 48–51.

Sharman, Paul, "A Practical Look at Activity-Based Costing," *CMA Magazine* (Canada), February 1990, pp. 8–12.

Srinidhi, Bin, "The Hidden Costs of Specialty Products," *Journal of Management Accounting Research* 4 (Fall 1992), pp. 198–208.

Troxel, Richard B., and Milan G. Weber, "Evolution of Activity-Based Costing," *Journal of Cost Management* 4, no. 1 (Spring 1990), pp. 14–22.

Turney, Peter B. B., "How Activity-Based Costing Helps Reduce Cost," *Journal of Cost Management* 4, no. 4 (Winter 1991), pp. 29–35.

Turney, Peter B. B., and Bruce Anderson, "Accounting for Continuous Improvement," *Sloan Management Review,* Winter 1989, pp. 37–47.

Turney, Peter B. B., and James M. Reeve, "The Impact of Continuous Improvement on the Design of Activity-Based Cost Systems," *Journal of Cost Management* 4, no. 2 (Summer 1990), pp. 43–50.

Turney, Peter B. B., and Alan J. Stratton, "Using ABC to Support Continuous Improvement," *Management Accounting,* September 1992, pp. 46–50.

Woods, Michael D., "Completing the Picture: Economic Choices with ABC," *Management Accounting,* December 1992, pp. 53–57.

2. Just-in-Time, Quality, and the New Production Environment

Brinker, Barry J., ed., *Emerging Practices in Cost Management* (Boston: Warren, Gorham & Lamont, 1991).

Dhavale, Dileep G., "Product Costing in Flexible Manufacturing Systems," *Journal of Management Accounting Research* 1 (Fall 1989), pp. 66–88.

Dolinsky, Larry R., and Thomas E. Vollmann, "Transaction-Based Overhead Considerations for Product Design," *Journal of Cost Management* 5, no. 2 (Summer 1991), pp. 7–19.

Drucker, Peter F., "The Emerging Theory of Manufacturing," *Harvard Business Review,* May–June 1990, pp. 94–102.

Edmonds, Thomas P., Bor-Yi Tsay, and Wen-Wei Lin, "Analyzing Quality Costs," *Management Accounting,* November 1989, pp. 25–29.

Griffin, Lynn, and Adrian Harrell, "An Empirical Examination of Managers' Motivation to Implement Just-in-Time Procedures," *Journal of Management Accounting Research* 3 (Fall 1991), pp. 98–112.

Hall, Robert W., H. Thomas Johnson, and Peter B. B. Turney, *Measuring Up: Charting Pathways to Manufacturing Excellence* (Homewood, Ill.: Business One Irwin, 1991).

Hansen, Don R., Maryanne M. Mowen, and Lawrence H. Hammer, "Profit-Linked Productivity Measurement," *Journal of Management Accounting Research* 4 (Fall 1992), pp. 79–98.

Harrell, Horace W., "Materials Variance Analysis and JIT: A New Approach," *Management Accounting,* May 1992, pp. 33–38.

Hayes, Robert D., and James A. Millar, "Measuring Production Efficiency in a Not-for-Profit Setting," *The Accounting Review* 65, no. 3 (July 1990), pp. 505–19.

———, "A Rejoinder to 'Measuring Production Efficiency in a Not-for-Profit Setting: An Extension,'" *The Accounting Review* 68, no. 1 (January 1993), pp. 89–92.

Heagy, Cynthia D., "Determining Optimal Quality Costs by Considering Cost of Lost Sales," *Journal of Cost Management* 5, no. 3 (Fall 1991), pp. 64–72.

Kaplan, Robert S., "Measures for Manufacturing Excellence: A Summary," *Journal of Cost Management* 4, no. 3 (Fall 1990), pp. 22–29.

Lessner, John, "Performance Measurement in a Just-in-Time Environment: Can Traditional Performance Measurements Still Be Used?" *Journal of Cost Management,* Fall 1989, pp. 22–28.

Mensah, Yaw M., and Shu-Hsing Li, "Measuring Production Efficiency in a Not-for-Profit Setting: An Extension," *The Accounting Review* 68, no. 1 (January 1993), pp. 66–88.

Ostrenga, Michael R., "Return on Investment Through the Cost of Quality," *Journal of Cost Management* 5, no. 2 (Summer 1991), pp. 37–44.

Pasewark, William R., "The Evolution of Quality Control Costs in American Manufacturing," *Journal of Cost Management* 5, no. 1 (Spring 1991), pp. 46–52.

Polakoff, Joel C., "Computer Integrated Manufacturing: A New Look at Cost Justifications," *Journal of Accountancy,* March 1990, pp. 24–29.

Ponemon, Lawrence A., "Accounting for Quality Costs," *Journal of Cost Management* 4, no. 3 (Fall 1990), pp. 44–48.

Troxler, Joel, "Estimating the Cost Impact of Flexible Manufacturing," *Journal of Cost Management* 4, no. 2 (Summer 1990), pp. 26–32.

Turk, William T., "Management Accounting Revitalized: The Harley-Davidson Experience," *Journal of Cost Management,* Winter 1990, pp. 28–39.

3. Internationl Applications

Bailey, Derek, "Accounting in the Shadow of Stalinism," *Accounting, Organizations and Society* 15, no. 6 (1990), pp. 513–25.

Daniel, Shirley J., and Wolf D. Reitsperger, "Linking Quality Strategy with Management Control Systems: Empirical Evidence from Japanese Industry," *Accounting, Organizations and Society* 16, no. 7 (1991), pp. 601–18.

Enthoven, Adolf J. H., "Accounting in Russia: From Perestroika to Profits," *Management Accounting,* October 1992, pp. 27–31.

Frucot, Veronique, and Winston T. Shearon, "Budgetary Participation, Locus of Control, and Mexican Managerial Performance and Job Satisfaction," *The Accounting Review* 66, no. 1 (January 1991), pp. 80–99.

Hiromoto, Toshiro, "Restoring the Relevance of Management Accounting," *Journal of Management Accounting Research* 3 (Fall 1991), pp. 1–15.

Jacobs, Fred A., and Ernest R. Larkins, "Management Control of a Foreign Sales Corporation: Some Special Considerations," *Journal of Management Accounting Research* 4 (Fall 1992), pp. 99–115.

Monden, Yasuhiro, and Kazuki Hamada, "Target Costing and Kaizen Costing in Japanese Automobile Companies," *Journal of Management Accounting Research* 3 (Fall 1991), pp. 16–34.

Wardell, Mark, and Leslie W. Weisenfeld, "Management Accounting and the Workplace in the United States and Great Britain," *Accounting, Organizations and Society* 16, no. 7 (1991), pp. 655–70.

Yoshikawa, Takeo, John Innes, and Falconer Mitchell, "Cost Tables: A Foundation of Japanese Cost Management," *Journal of Cost Management* 4, no. 3 (Fall 1990), pp. 30–36.

4. Implementing Cost Systems

Anthony, Robert N., "Reminiscences about Management Accounting," *Journal of Management Accounting Research* 1 (Fall 1989), pp. 1–20.

Brausch, John M., "Selling ABC," *Management Accounting,* February 1992, pp. 42–46.

Cooper, Robin, "You Need a New Cost System When . . . ," *Harvard Business Review,* January–February 1989, pp. 77–82.

————, "Implementing an Activity-Based Cost System," *Journal of Cost Management* 4, no. 1 (Spring 1990), pp. 33–42.

Cooper, Robin, Robert S. Kaplan, Lawrence S. Maisel, Eileen Morrissey, and Ronald M. Oehm, "From ABC to ABM," *Management Accounting* 74, no. 5 (November 1992), pp. 54–57.

Eiler, Robert G., and John P. Campi, "Implementing Activity-Based Costing at a Process Company," *Journal of Cost Management* 4, no. 1 (Spring 1990), pp. 43–50.

Emore, James R., and Joseph A. Ness, "The Slow Pace of Meaningful Change in Cost Systems," *Journal of Cost Management* 4, no. 4 (Winter 1991), pp. 36–45.

Ferrara, William L. "The New Cost/Management Accounting—More Questions Than Answers," *Management Accounting,* October 1990, pp. 48–52.

Frank, Gary B., Steven A. Fisher, and Allen R. Wilkie, "Linking Cost to Price and Profit," *Management Accounting,* June 1989, pp. 22–26.

Horngren, Charles T., "Cost and Management Accounting: Yesterday and Today," *Journal of Management Accounting Research* 1 (Fall 1989), pp. 21–32.

Shank, John K., and Vijay Govindarajan, *Strategic Cost Analysis: The Evolution from Managerial to Strategic Accounting* (Homewood, Ill.: Richard D. Irwin, 1989).

Shields, Michael P., and S. Mark Young, "A Behavioral Model for Implementing Cost Management Systems," *Journal of Cost Management,* Winter 1989, pp. 17–27.

Shillinglaw, Gordon, "Managerial Cost Accounting: Present and Future," *Journal of Management Accounting Research* 1, (Fall 1989), pp. 33–46.

Solomons, David, "Accounting and Social Change: A Neutralist View," *Accounting, Organizations and Society* 16, no. 3 (1991), pp. 287–95.

Walker, K. B., and T. Zinsli, "The Coors Shenandoah Experience." *Management Accounting,* March 1993, pp. 37–41.

5. Managerial Decision Making

Balakrishnan, Ramji, "Information Acquisition and Resource Allocation Decisions," *The Accounting Review* 66, no. 1 (January 1991), pp. 120–39.

Banker, Rajiv D., Srikant M. Datar, and Sunder Kekre, "Relevant Costs, Congestion and Stochasticity in Production Environments," *Journal of Accounting and Economics* 10, no. 3 pp. 171–97.

Carter, William K., "To Invest in New Technology or Not? New Tools for Making the Decision," *Journal of Accountancy,* May 1992, pp. 58–64.

Cheng, C. S. Agnes, and Rene P. Manes, "The Marginal Approach to Joint Cost Allocation: A Model for Practical Application," *Journal of Management Accounting Research* 4 (Fall 1992), pp. 44–63.

Fellingham, John C., and Richard A. Young, "The Value of Self-Reported Costs in Repeated Investment Decisions,'' *The Accounting Review* 65, no. 4 (October 1990), pp. 837–56.

Gordon, Lawrence A., and Kimberly J. Smith, ''Postauditing Capital Expenditures and Firm Performance: The Role of Asymmetric Information,'' *Accounting, Organizations and Society* 17, no. 8 (1992), pp. 741–57.

Klammer, Thomas, Bruce Koch, and Neil Wilner, ''Capital Budgeting Practices—A Survey of Corporate Use,'' *Journal of Management Accounting Research* 3 (Fall 1991), pp. 113–30.

Schwan, Edward S., and William A. Remaley, ''Marginal Return on Invested Capital versus Internal Rate of Return,'' *Journal of Cost Management,* Summer 1991, pp. 55–58.

Turner, Leslie D., ''Improve Measures of Manufacturing Maintenance in a Capital Budgeting Context: An Application of Data Envelopment Analysis Efficiency Measures,'' *Journal of Management Accounting Research* 2 (Fall 1990), pp. 127–33.

Turner, Martha J., and Ronald W. Hilton, ''Use of Accounting Product-Costing Systems in Making Production Decisions,'' *Journal of Accounting Research* 27, no. 2 (Autumn 1989), pp. 297–312.

6. *Managerial Planning and Performance Evaluation*

Abernethy, Margaret A., and Johannes U. Stoelwinder, ''Budget Use, Task Uncertainty, System Goal Orientation and Subunit Performance: A Test of the 'Fit' Hypothesis in Not-for-Profit Hospitals,'' *Accounting, Organizations and Society* 16, no. 2 (1991), pp. 105–20.

Amershi, Amin H., Rajiv D. Banker, and Srikant M. Datar, ''Economic Sufficiency and Statistical Sufficiency in the Aggregation of Accounting Signals,'' *The Accounting Review* 65, no. 1 (January 1990), pp. 113–30.

Aranoff, Gerald, ''Transfer Pricing for Short-Run Profit Maximization in Manufacturing,'' *Journal of Cost Management* 4, no. 3 (Fall 1990), pp. 37–43.

Aranya, Nissim, ''Budget Instrumentality, Participation and Organizational Effectiveness,'' *Journal of Management Accounting Research* 2 (Fall 1990), pp. 67–77.

Argyris, Chris, ''The Dilemma of Implementing Controls: The Case of Managerial Accounting,'' *Accounting, Organizations and Society* 15, no. 6 (1990), pp. 503–11.

Awasthi, Vidya, and Jamie Pratt, ''The Effects of Monetary Incentives on Effort and Decision Performance: The Role of Cognitive Characteristics,'' *The Accounting Review* 65, no. 4 (October 1990), pp. 797–811.

Baiman, Stanley, ''Agency Research in Managerial Accounting: A Second Look,'' *Accounting, Organizations and Society* 15, no. 4 (1990), pp. 341–71.

Baiman, Stanley, and Konduru Sivaramakrishnan, ''The Value of Private Pre-Decision Information in a Principal-Agent,'' *The Accounting Review* 66, no. 4 (October 1991), pp. 747–66.

Banker, Rajiv D., Srikant M. Datar, and Robert S. Kaplan, ''Productivity Measurement and Management Accounting,'' *Journal of Accounting, Auditing and Finance* 4, no. 4 pp. 528–54.

Borkowski, Susan C., ''Environmental and Organizational Factors Affecting Transfer Pricing: A Survey,'' *Journal of Management Accounting Research* 2 (Fall 1990), pp. 78–99.

Briers, Michael, and Mark Hirst, ''The Role of Budgetary Information in Performance Evaluation,'' *Accounting, Organizations and Society* 15, no. 4 (1990), pp. 373–98.

Brown, Robert M., ''An Investigation of Organizational-Professional Conflict in Management Accounting,'' *Journal of Management Accounting Research* 1 (Fall 1989), pp. 104–18.

Brownell, Peter, and Alan S. Dunk, ''Task Uncertainty and Its Interaction with Budgetary Participation and Budget Emphasis: Some Methodological Issues and Empirical Investigation,'' *Accounting, Organizations and Society* 16, no. 8 (1991), pp. 693–703.

Campbell, Robert J., Michael Janson, and James Bush, ''Developing Strategic Cost Standards in a Machine-Paced Environment,'' *Journal of Cost Management* 4, no. 4 (Winter 1991).

Chalos, Peter, and Susan Haka, ''Transfer Pricing under Bilateral Bargaining,'' *The Accounting Review* 65, no. 3 pp. 624–41.

Chan, Yee-Ching Lilian, and Bernadette Eleanor Lynn, ''Performance Evaluation and the Analytic Hierarchy Process,'' *Journal of Management Accounting Research* 3 (Fall 1991), pp. 57–87.

Cheatham, Carole, ''Updating Standard Cost Systems,'' *Journal of Accountancy,* December 1990, pp. 57–60.

Chow, Chee W., Jean C. Cooper, and Kamal Haddad, ''The Effects of Pay Schemes and Ratchets on Budgetary Slack and Performance: A Multiperiod Experiment,'' *Accounting, Organizations and Society* 16, no. 1 (1991), pp. 47–60.

Chow, Chee W., Michael D. Shields, and Yoke Kai Chan, ''The Effects of Management Controls and National Culture on Manufacturing Performance: An Experimental Investigation,'' *Accounting, Organizations and Society* 16, no. 3 (1991), pp. 209–26.

Dempsey, Stephen J., ''Predisclosure Information Search Incentives, Analyst Following, and Earnings

Announcement Price Response," *The Accounting Review* 4 (October 1989), pp. 748–57.

Dermer, Jerry, "The Strategic Agenda: Accounting for Issues and Support," *Accounting, Organizations and Society* 15, no. 1/2 (1990), pp. 67–76.

Dunk, Alan S., "Reliance on Budgetary Control, Manufacturing Process Automation and Production Subunit Performance: A Research Note," *Accounting, Organizations and Society* 17, no. 3/4 (1992), pp. 195–203.

Frederickson, James R., "Relative Performance Information: The Effects of Common Uncertainty and Contract Type on Agent Effort," *The Accounting Review* 67, no. 4 (October 1992), pp. 647–69.

Gribbin, Donald W., and Amy Hing-Ling Lau, "Some Empirical Evidence on the Non-Normality of Cost Variances," *Journal of Management Accounting Research* 3 (Fall 1991), pp. 88–97.

Jaworski, Bernard J., and S. Mark Young, "Dysfunctional Behavior and Management Control: An Empirical Study of Marketing Managers, *Accounting, Organizations and Society* 17, no. 1 (1992), pp. 17–35.

Kaplan, Steven E., and James T. Mackey, "An Examination of the Association between Organizational Design Factors and the Use of Accounting Information for Managerial Performance Evaluation," *Journal of Management Accounting Research* 4 (Fall 1992), pp. 116–30.

Kren, Leslie, "Budgetary Participation and Managerial Performance: The Impact of Information and Environmental Volatility," *The Accounting Review* 67, no. 3 (July 1992), pp. 511–26.

MacIntosh, Norman B., and Robert W. Scapens, "Management Accounting and Control Systems: A Structuration Theory Analysis," *Journal of Management Accounting Research* 3 (Fall 1991), pp. 131–58.

McInnes, Morris, and Ram T. S. Ramakrishnan, "A Decision-Theory Model of Motivation and Its Usefulness in the Diagnosis of Management Control Systems," *Accounting, Organizations and Society* 16, no. 2 (1991), pp. 167–84.

McNair, C. J. "Do Financial and Nonfinancial Performance Measures Have to Agree?" *Management Accounting,* November 1990, pp. 28–36.

Melumad, N., D. Mookherjee, and S. Reichelstein, "A Theory of Responsibility Centers," *Journal of Accounting and Economics* 15, no. 4 (1992), pp. 445–84.

Merchant, K. A., *Rewarding Results; Motivating Profit Center Managers* (Boston: Harvard Business School Press, 1989).

Merchant, K. A., and J. Manzoni, "The Achievability of Budget Targets in Profit Centers: A Field Study," *The Accounting Review* 64, no. 3 (1989), pp. 539–58.

Mia, Lokman, "The Impact of Participation in Budgeting and Job Difficulty on Managerial Performance and Work Motivation: A Research Note," *Accounting, Organizations and Society* 14, no. 4 (1989), pp. 347–57.

Newman, Harry A., "Selection of Short-Term Accounting-Based Bonus Plans," *The Accounting Review* 4 (October 1989), pp. 758–72.

Pasewark, William R., and Robert B. Welker, "A Vroom-Yetton Evaluation of Subordinate Participation in Budgetary Decision Making," *Journal of Management Accounting Research* 2 (Fall 1990), pp. 113–26.

Penno, Mark, "Accounting Systems, Participation in Budgeting, and Performance Evaluation," *The Accounting Review* 65, no. 2 (April 1990), pp. 303–14.

⸻, "Auditing for Performance Evaluation," *The Accounting Review* 65, no. 3 (July 1990), pp. 520–36.

Pierce, Bethane Jo, and Jeffrey J. Tsay, "A Study of the Post-Completion Audit Practices of Large American Corporations: Experience from 1978 and 1988," *Journal of Management Accounting Research* 4 (Fall 1992), pp. 131–55.

Poe, C. Douglas, Winston T. Shearon, Jr., and Robert H. Strawser, "Accounting Evaluative Styles and the Contagion Effect in Middle-Managers: An Empirical Study," *Journal of Management Accounting Research* 3 (Fall 1991), pp. 169–93.

Preston, Alistair M., David J. Cooper, and Rod W. Coombs, "Fabricating Budgets: A Study of the Production of Management Budgeting in the National Health Service," *Accounting, Organizations and Society* 17, no. 6 (1992), pp. 561–93.

Rajan, Madhav V., "Cost Allocation in Multiagent Settings," *The Accounting Review* 67, no. 3 (1992), pp. 527–45.

⸻, "Management Control Systems and the Implementation of Strategies," *Journal of Accounting Research* 30, no. 2 (Autumn 1992), pp. 227–48.

Reichelstein, Stefan, "Constructing Incentive Schemes for Government Contracts: An Application of Agency Theory," *The Accounting Review* 67, no. 4 (October 1992), pp. 712–31.

Schroeder, Douglas A., "A Heuristic for Determining Budget-Based Contracts in Multi-Period Settings," *Journal of Management Accounting Research* 4 (Fall 1992), pp. 156–78.

Simons, Robert, "The Role of Management Control Systems in Creating Competitive Advantage: New Perspectives," *Accounting, Organizations and Society* 15, no. 1/2 (1990), pp. 127–43.

Suh, Yoon, "Noncontrollable Costs and Optimal Performance Measurement," *Journal of Management Accounting Research* 1 (Fall 1989), pp. 144–48.

Thomas, Michael F., "An Application of Socio-Technical Systems Analysis to Accounting Variance Control Theory," *Journal of Management Accounting Research* 1, (Fall 1989). pp. 149–56.

Walker, Kenton B., and Craig E. Bain, "Sales Volume Forecasting: A Comparison of Management, Statistical, and Combined Approaches," *Journal of Management Accounting Research* 1 (Fall 1989), pp. 119–35.

Waller, William S., and Rachel A. Bishop, "An Experimental Study of Incentive Pay Schemes, Communication, and Intrafirm Resource Allocation," *The Accounting Review* 65, no. 4 (October 1990), pp. 812–36.

Weisenfeld, Leslie W., and Larry N. Killough, "A Review and Extension of Using Performance Reports: A Field Study Based on Path-Goal Theory," *Journal of Management Accounting Research* 4 (Fall 1992), pp. 209–25.

Williams, John J., Norman B. MacIntosh, and John C. Moore, "Budget-Related Behavior in Public Sector Organizations: Some Empirical Evidence," *Accounting, Organizations and Society* 15, no. 3 (1990), pp. 221–46.

7. Other Readings

Birnberg, Jacob G., Michael D. Shields, and S. Mark Young, "The Case for Multiple Methods in Empirical Management Accounting Research," *Journal of Management Accounting Research* 2 (Fall 1990), pp. 33–66.

Fleischman, Richard K., and Lee D. Parker, "British Entrepreneurs and Pre-Industrial Revolution Evidence of Cost Management," *The Accounting Review* 66, no. 2 (April 1991), pp. 361–75.

Frank, Werner G., " 'Back to the Future:' A Retrospective View of J. Maurice Clark's Studies in the Economics of Overhead Costs," *Journal of Management Accounting Research* 2 (Fall 1990), pp. 155–66.

Luckett, Peter F., and Ian R. C. Eggleton, "Feedback and Management Accounting: A Review of Research into Behavioral Consequences," *Accounting, Organizations and Society* 16, no. 4 (1991), pp. 371–94.

Rogerson, William P., "Overhead Allocation and Incentives for Cost Minimization in Defense," *The Accounting Review* 67, no. 4 (1992), pp. 671–90.

Shank, John K., "Strategic Cost Management: New Wine, or Just New Bottles?" *Journal of Management Accounting Research* 1 (Fall 1989), pp. 47–65.

Shank, John K., and Vijay Govindarajan, "Strategic Cost Management and the Value Chain," *Journal of Cost Management* 5, no. 4 (Winter 1992), pp. 5–21.

Thomas, Jacob K., and Samuel Tung, "Cost Manipulation Incentives under Cost Reimbursement: Pension Costs for Defense Contracts," *The Accounting Review* 67, no. 4 (October 1992), pp. 691–711.

GLOSSARY

The numbers in parentheses after each definition are the chapters in which the term or concept is most extensively discussed.

Abnormal Spoilage Spoilage due to reasons other than the usual course of operations of a process. This may include goods spoiled as a result of error or as a result of casualty losses. (5)

Absorption Costing See *Full-Absorption Costing*.

Account Analysis The method of cost estimation that reviews each account making up the total cost being analyzed, and classifies it as fixed or variable. (10)

Accounting Rate of Return A measure of project returns using accounting concepts of income. (16)

Acquisition Cost Cost to purchase an investment or inventory item and to get it in place and in condition for use. (15)

Action Set The alternatives available to managers in a given decision-making setting. (26)

Activity Center A unit of the organization that performs some activity. (7)

Activity Variance Effect of difference between budgeted and actual sales or production activity levels on profits. (18, 19, 21)

Activity-Based Costing A costing method that assigns indirect costs to activities, then computes product cost as the sum of the costs of the activities needed to make the product. (1, 7, 10, 19)

Actual Costing A system of accounting whereby overhead is assigned to products based on actual overhead incurred. (3)

Actual Costs Amounts determined on the basis of actual (historical) costs incurred. See *Actual Costing*.

Adjusted R-Square The correlation coefficient in regression squared and adjusted for the number of independent variables used to make the estimate. (10)

Administrative Costs Costs required to manage the organization and provide staff support for organization activities. (2)

Allocation Base A measure related to two or more cost objects used to allocate indirect or common costs shared by two or more cost objects. For example, direct labor-hours may be related to each unit produced. If direct labor-hours are used to assign manufacturing overhead costs to products, then the direct labor-hours are called the *allocation base*. (6)

Applied Overhead Overhead assigned to a job or other cost object using a predetermined overhead rate. (3)

Asset Acquisition Costs involved in purchasing and installing an asset. May involve the disposal of assets currently owned and any gain or loss. (15)

Autocorrelation See *Serial Correlation*.

Backflush Costing A costing method that works backword from output to assign costs to inventories. (5)

Basic Cost Flow Model (Also known as the *basic inventory formula*.) Beginning balance plus transfers-in equals transfers-out plus ending balance. (3)

Batch Orders consisting of identical units that go through the exact same production process. (5)

Batch Production Manufacturing process characterized by the production of product groups that are varied enough to require frequent production line changes. (5)

Behavioral Congruence When individuals behave in the best interest of the organization regardless of their own goals. (22)

Break-Even Point The volume level where profits equal zero. (11)

Budget A financial plan of the resources needed to carry out tasks and meet financial goals. (1, 17)

Budget Plan See *Master Budget*.

Budget Variance See *Spending Variance*.

Budgeted Balance Sheets Statements of financial position that combine estimates of financial position at the beginning and end of the budget period with the estimated results of operations for the period and estimated changes in assets and liabilities. (17)

Budgeting under Uncertainty Making many forecasts, each representing a different possible set of circumstances. (17)

By-Products Outputs of joint production processes that are relatively minor in quantity and/or value. (8)

Carrying Costs Costs that increase with the size of inventory. (14)

Cash Budget Statement of cash on hand at the start of a budget period; expected cash receipts classified by source; expected cash disbursements classified by function, responsibility, and form; and the resulting cash balance at the end of the budget period. (17)

Centralized Refers to those organizations where decisions are made by relatively few individuals at the highest ranks of the organization. (22)

Certified Management Accountant Program A program established to recognize educational achievement and professional competence in management accounting. (1)

CMA Acronym for the certificate issued for the Certified Management Accountant Program. Someone who has received the CMA. (1)

Collusion The cooperative effort of employees to commit fraud or some other unethical act. (24)

Common Costs A synonym for indirect costs. Costs of shared facilities, products, or services. (6)

Conditional Probabilities Those likelihoods that depend on a specific result. (26)

Constraints Activities, resources, or policies that limit or bound the attainment of an objective. (13)

Continuous-Flow Processing Systems that generally mass-produce a single, homogeneous output in a continuing process. (4)

Contribution Margin The difference between revenues and variable costs. (2, 9, 11)

Contribution Margin Format A financial statement that shows the contribution margin as an intermediate step in computing operating profits or income (9, 11)

Contribution Margin per Unit of Scarce Resource Contribution margin per unit of a particular input with limited availability. (13)

Contribution Margin Ratio Contribution margin as a ratio of sales revenue. (11)

Contribution Margin Variance Variance from changes in revenues minus variable costs. (21)

Controllability Concept The idea that managers should be held responsible for costs or profits over which they have decision-making authority. (22)

Controllability of Variance The extent that a variance can be managed. One rationale used in deciding whether a variance should be calculated, analyzed, or investigated. (19)

Controllable Cost A cost that can be affected by a manager in the short run.

Controller The chief accounting officer in most corporations. (1)

Conversion Costs The sum of direct labor and manufacturing overhead. (2, 4, 5)

Corner Point A corner of the feasible production region in linear programming. (13)

Correlation Coefficient A measure of the linear relationship between two or more variables, such as cost and some activity measure. (10)

Cost A sacrifice of resources. (2)

Cost Accounting The field of accounting that records, measures, and reports information about costs. (1)

Cost Accounting Standards Board The federal government body set up to establish methods of accounting for costs by government defense contractors. (1)

Cost Accumulation The process of adding costs to a cost object, such as a job, department, or inventory account. (3, 4, 5)

Cost Allocation The process of assigning indirect costs to cost objects. (6, 7, 8)

Cost-Benefit Requirement The criterion that an alternative will be chosen if and only if the benefits from it exceed the costs. This criterion is one basis for evaluating cost systems. (1, 26)

Cost Centers Organizational units responsible for costs. (18, 22)

Cost Driver A factor that causes or drives an activity's costs. (7, 10, 19)

Cost Object Any end to which a cost is assigned. Examples include a product, a department, or a product line. (2, 6, 7, 8)

Cost of Goods Finished See *Cost of Goods Manufactured.*

Cost of Goods Manufactured The cost of goods completed and transferred to the finished goods storage area. (2, 3)

Cost of Goods Manufactured and Sold Statement Statement that incorporates and summarizes the information from the direct materials costs schedule, the cost of goods manufactured schedule, and the cost of goods sold schedule. (2, 3)

Cost of Goods Sold The cost assigned to products sold during the period. (2, 3, 9, 20)

Cost of Prediction Error The difference between the actual cost incurred based on incorrect information and the cost that would have been incurred with the correct information. (26)

Cost-Plus Transfer Pricing Transfer pricing policy based on full costing or variable costing plus an allowance for profit. (23)

Cost Pool A grouping of individual costs. (7)

Costs for Decision Making Costs that are included in financial analysis by managers. See *Differential Costs.* (1)

Costs for Performance Evaluation Costs that are used in planning and performance evaluation analysis by managers. (1)

Cost Variance Analysis Comparison of actual input quantities and prices with standard input quantities and prices. (19)

Cost-Volume-Profit (CVP) Analysis Study of the interrelationships among costs and volume and how they impact profit. (11)

Critical Probability The probability of different outcomes that equalizes the value of the outcomes. (25)

Cross-Department Monitoring A reason for allocating costs where it is hoped that managers of user departments have incentives to monitor the service department's costs. (6)

Current Costs Costs to replace or rebuild an existing asset. (22)

CVP Cost-volume-profit. (11)

CVP under Uncertainty Consideration of the extent of uncertainty and the impact of that uncertainty on decision inputs and outcomes in cost-volume-profit decision analysis. (26)

Decentralized Refers to those organizations where decisions are spread out among relatively many divisional and departmental managers. (22)

Decremental Costs Costs that decrease with a particular course of action. See *Differential Costs.*

Delphi Technique Forecasting method where individual forecasts of group members are submitted anonymously and evaluated by the group as a whole. (17)

Denominator Reason Overhead variance caused by differences between actual activity and the estimated activity used in the denominator of the formula used to compute the predetermined overhead rate. See *Production Volume Variance.* (3, 19, 20)

Department Allocation Method Using this method, companies have a separate overhead cost pool for each department. Each department has its own overhead allocation rate or set of rates. (7)

Dependent Variable In a cost-estimation context, the costs to be estimated from an equation. Also called the *Y-term* or the *left-hand side (LHS)* in regression. (10)

Differential Analysis Process of estimating the consequences of alternative actions that decision makers can take. (12)

Differential Costs Costs that change in response to a particular course of action. (1, 2, 12)

Direct Costing A synonym for variable costing. (9)

Direct Labor The cost of workers who transform the materials into a finished product at some stage of the production process. (2)

Direct Materials Those materials that can be feasibly identified with the product. (2)

Direct Method A method of cost allocation that charges costs of service departments to user departments and ignores any services used by other service departments. (6)

Discount Rate An interest rate used to compute net present values. (15)

Discounted Payback Method A method of assessing investment projects that recognizes the time value of money in a payback context. (16)

Discretionary Cost Center An organization unit where managers are held responsible for costs, but the relationship between costs and outputs is not well established. (22)

Discretionary Costs Costs that are difficult to relate to outputs. Examples include research and development costs, information systems costs, and some advertising costs. (22)

Disinvestment Flows Cash flows that take place at the termination of a capital project. (15)

Dual Rates A method of cost allocation that separates a common cost into fixed and variable components and then allocates each component using a different allocation base. (6)

Dual Transfer Pricing Transfer pricing system where the buying department is charged with costs only, and the selling department is credited with the cost plus some profit allowance. (23)

Econometric Models Statistical method of forecasting economic data using regression models. (17)

Economic Order Quantity (EOQ) The number of units to order at one time to minimize total expected annual costs of an inventory system. (14)

Efficiency Variance Difference between the inputs that were expected per unit of output and the inputs that were actually used. (19, 20, 21)

Engineering Estimates Cost estimates based on measurement and pricing of the work involved in a task. (10)

EOQ Abbreviation for economic order quantity. (14)

Equivalent Unit The amount of work actually performed on products with varying degrees of completion, translated to that work required to complete an equal number of whole units. (4)

Error Term The unexplained difference between predicted and actual outcomes. Sometimes called *random error.* (25)

Estimate A considered judgment about future events that takes into account past experience and probable changes in circumstances and conditions. (10)

Estimated Net Realizable Value Sales price of final product minus estimated additional processing costs from split-off point necessary to prepare a product for sale. (8)

Exogenous Factors Outside events that can influence an outcome. (26)

Expected Opportunity Loss A loss that may occur if certain unfavorable outcomes result after a decision has been implemented. (26)

Expected Value The weighted average of all of the outcomes of a decision process. (26)

Expense A cost that is charged against revenue in an accounting period. (2)

Factory Burden See *Manufacturing Overhead.*

Factory Overhead See *Manufacturing Overhead.*

Favorable Variances Variances that, taken alone, result in an addition to operating profit. (18)

Feasible Production Region The area in a graph of production opportunities bounded by the limits on production. (13)

Final Cost Center A cost center, such as a production or marketing department, from which costs are not allocated to another cost center. (6)

Financial Accounting The preparation of financial statements and data for outsiders, primarily stockholders and creditors. (1)

Financial Budget Refers to the budget of financial resources; for example, the cash budget and the budgeted balance sheet. (18)

Finished Goods Product that has been completed and is in inventory awaiting sale. (2)

First-in, First-out (FIFO) Costing The first-in, first-out inventory method whereby the first goods received are the first charged out when sold or transferred. (4)

Fixed Costs Costs that are unchanged as volume changes within the relevant range of activity. (2, 10, 11)

Flexible Budget A budget that indicates revenues, costs, and profits for different levels of activity. (18)

Flexible Manufacturing A computer-based manufacturing system that allows companies to make a variety of products with minimal setup time. (5)

Fraudulent Financial Reporting Intentional or reckless conduct that results in materially misleading financial statements. (24)

Freight-in An alternative term for transportation-in.

Full-Absorption Cost The cost used to compute a product's inventory value under generally accepted accounting principles. Variable manufacturing costs plus each unit's share of fixed manufacturing costs. (2)

Full-Absorption Costing A system of accounting for costs in which both fixed and variable manufacturing costs are considered product costs. (2, 9)

Full Cost The sum of the fixed and variable costs of manufacturing and selling a unit of product. (2)

GAAP Acronym for generally accepted accounting principles. (2)

Generally Accepted Accounting Principles (GAAP) The rules, standards, and conventions that guide the preparation of financial accounting statements. (1, 2)

Goal Congruence When all members of a group hold a common set of objectives. (22)

Good Output Units that are expected to be completed and suitable for further processing or for sale at the end of a production process. (5)

Graphic Method Graphic solution of a linear programming problem by selecting the best corner solution visually. (13)

Gross Margin The difference between sales revenues and manufacturing costs as an intermediate step in the computation of operating profits or net income. (2)

Gross Margin Variance Variance from change in revenues minus cost of goods sold. (21)

Heteroscedasticity In regression analysis, the condition in which the errors are correlated with the magnitude of values of the independent variables. (10)

High-Low Cost Estimation A method of estimating costs based on two cost observations, usually costs at the highest activity level and costs at the lowest activity level. (10)

Hurdle Rate The discount rate required by a company before it will invest in a project. (15)

Hybrid A costing system that incorporates both job and process costing concepts. See *Operation Costing.*

Impact of a Variance The likely effect of a variance. One rationale used in deciding whether a variance is important enough to compute, analyze, and investigate. (19)

Imperfect Information Information that is not 100 percent accurate but may be used to revise the probabilities of certain decision outcomes. (26)

In-Control Probability The likelihood that a process is operating within specifications. (25)

Incremental Costs Costs that increase in response to a particular course of action. These are a subset of differential costs. See *Differential Costs.*

Independent Variables The X-terms, or predictors, on the right-hand side of a regression equation. In cost accounting, they are cost drivers expected to affect costs. (10)

Industry Volume Variance The portion of the sales activity variance that is due to changes in industry volume. (21)

Information Cost Cost of obtaining information. (26)

Information Economics A formal system for evaluating whether the cost-benefit test has been met for information. (26)

Information Overload A characteristic of too much data. The intended user is overwhelmed by the quantity of data supplied.

Intercept The point where a line crosses the vertical axis. In regression, this line is the regression line and the intercept is the constant term on the right-hand side of the equation. In cost estimation, the intercept is sometimes used as the fixed cost estimate. (10)

Intermediate Cost Center A cost center whose costs are charged to other departments in the organization. Intermediate cost centers are frequently service departments. (6)

Internal Controls Policies and procedures designed to provide top management with reasonable assurances that organizational goals will be met. (24)

Internal Rate of Return (IRR) The interest rate that equates the inflows and outflows from an investment project. (16)

Inventoriable Costs Costs of a product regarded as an asset (inventory). (2)

Investment Centers Organizational units responsible for profits and for investment in assets. (22)

Investment Tax Credit A reduction in federal income taxes arising from the purchase of long-term assets. Usually treated as a reduction in investment cost for analytical purposes. (15)

IRR Abbreviation for internal rate of return. (16)

Isoprofit Lines Family of constant profit lines where operating profits are the same for any combination of product volumes on any one line.

Job Cost Record The source document for entering costs under job costing. This is sometimes referred to as a *job cost sheet, job cost file,* or *job card.* (3)

Job Costing An accounting system that traces costs to individual units for output or specific contracts, batches of goods, or jobs. (3)

Jobs Units that are easily distinguishable from other units. (3)

Joint Cost A cost of a manufacturing process in which two or more outputs come from the process. (8)

Joint Probability The probability of two or more events occurring. (26)

Joint Products Outputs from a common input and common production process. (8)

Just-in-Time Method of production or purchasing designed to obtain goods just in time for use. (1, 5, 20)

Last-in, First-out (LIFO) Costing The last-in, first-out inventory method whereby the last goods received are charged out first when transferred or sold. See *First-in, First-out.*

Lead Time The time between order placement and order arrival. (14)

Learning Curve The mathematical or graphic representation of the learning phenomenon. (10)

Learning Phenomenon A systematic relationship between the amount of experience in performing a task and the time required to carry out the task. (10)

Lease versus Borrow-to-Buy Choice of financing the investment in an asset through either a lease or a purchase using borrowed funds. (16)

Linear Programming—Graphic Method Graphic solution of a linear programming problem by selecting the best corner solution. (13)

Lost Units Goods that evaporate or otherwise disappear during a production process. (5)

Lower Control Limit The minimum value of some obser-

vation that still indicates that the process is in control. (25)

Make-or-Buy Decision A decision whether to acquire needed goods internally or to purchase them from outside sources. (12)

Management by Exception An approach to management requiring that reports emphasize the deviation from an accepted basing point, such as a standard, a budget, an industry average, or a prior-period experience. (18, 19)

Managerial Accounting The preparation of cost and related data for managers to use in performance evaluation or decision making. (1)

Manufacturing Department Production departments in organizations that produce goods. (6)

Manufacturing Organization An organization characterized by the conversion of raw inputs into some other output products. (3)

Manufacturing Overhead All manufacturing costs except direct materials and direct labor. (2)

Manufacturing Overhead Variance The difference between applied and actual overhead. (3)

Margin of Safety The excess of projected or actual sales over the break-even volume. (11)

Market-Based Transfer Pricing Transfer pricing policy where the transfer price is set at the market price, or at a small discount from the market price. (23)

Market Share Variance The portion of the sales activity variance due to change in the company's proportion of sales in the markets in which the company operates. (21)

Marketing Costs Costs to obtain customer orders and provide customers with the finished product. (2)

Master Budget The financial plan for the coming year or other planning period. (17)

Materiality Magnitude of financial misstatement such that it is likely to affect the judgment of a reasonable person relying on the information. (24)

Materials Requisition A form used to obtain materials from a storeroom. It is the source document for recording the transfer of materials to production. (3)

Merchandise Inventory In a merchandising organization, the cost of goods acquired but not yet sold. (3)

Merchandising Organization An organization characterized by marketing goods or services rather than converting raw inputs into outputs. (3)

Mix Variance A variance that arises from a change in the relative proportion of outputs (a sales mix variance) or inputs (a materials or labor mix variance). (21)

Mixed Cost A cost that has both fixed and variable components. (2)

Monte Carlo Simulation A method of sampling from the assumed distribution function to obtain simulated observations of costs or other variables. (26)

Multicollinearity Correlation between two or more independent variables in a multiple regression equation. (10)

Multiple-Factor Formula An allocation formula that uses multiple bases for an allocation base when allocating costs. (6)

Multiple Rates of Return Problem arising when computing the internal rate of return for cash flows that change signs more than once in the project's life. It is possible, then, for such a project to have more than one internal rate of return. (16)

Mutually Exclusive Term used in capital investment decisions to describe a situation where selection of one project precludes the selection of another. (16)

Negotiated Transfer Price System whereby the transfer prices are arrived at through negotiation between managers of buying and selling departments. (23)

Net Income Operating profit adjusted for interest, income taxes, extraordinary items, and other items required to comply with GAAP and other regulations. (2)

Net Present Value Difference between the discounted future cash flows from a project and the value of the discounted cash outflows to acquire the project. (15)

Net Present Value Index Ratio of the net present value of a project to the funds invested in the project. (16)

Net Realizable Value Method Joint cost allocation based on the proportional values of the joint products at the split-off point. (8)

Nominal Discount Rate A rate of interest that includes compensation for inflation. (15)

Nominal Dollars Actual numerical count of money exchanged without adjusting for inflation. (15)

Noncontrollable Cost A cost that cannot be changed or influenced by a given manager.

Nonmanufacturing Costs Administrative and marketing costs. (2)

Normal Costing A system of accounting whereby direct materials and direct labor are charged to cost objects at actual, and manufacturing overhead is applied. (3, 9)

Normal Costs Product cost amounts where actual direct materials and direct labor costs are assigned to products, but where manufacturing overhead is applied using a predetermined rate. (3, 9)

Normal Spoilage Spoiled goods that are a result of the regular operation of the production process. (5)

Numerator Reason A difference between actual and applied overhead caused by differences between estimated overhead costs and actual overhead costs for the period. (3)

Objective Function Mathematical statement of an objective to be maximized or minimized. (13, 26)

Operating Budgets Refers to the budgeted income statement, the production budget, the budgeted cost of goods sold, and supporting budgets. (18)

Operating Profit The excess of operating revenues over the operating costs to generate those revenues. (2)

Operation A standardized method or technique that is repetitively performed. (3, 5)

Operation Costing A costing system often used in manufacturing goods that have some common characteristics plus some individual characteristics. Typically, the production methods are standardized, but materials are different in each product or batch. (3, 5)

Opportunity Cost The lost benefit that an alternative course of action could provide. (2, 12)

Opportunity Loss Loss from an unfavorable outcome. (26)

Ordering Costs Costs that increase with the number of orders placed for inventory. (14)

Ordinary Least Squares Regression A regression method that minimizes the sum of the squared distances of each observation from the regression line. (10)

Organizational Goals Set of broad objectives established by management that company employees work to achieve. (17)

Outcomes Possible results of a given action. (26)

Outlay Cost A past, present, or future cash outflow. (2)

Outliers Observations of costs of different activity levels (or similar phenomena) that are significantly different from other observations in the data series. (10)

Out-of-Control Probability The probability that a process is not operating according to specifications. (25)

Overapplied Overhead The excess of applied overhead over actual overhead incurred during a period. (3)

Overhead See *Manufacturing Overhead* (Chapter 2). It is an ambiguous term when unmodified. Lay people often refer to everything but direct materials and direct labor as overhead (including administrative costs).

Overhead Variance The difference between actual and applied overhead. (3)

Participative Budgeting The use of input from lower- and middle-management employees; also called *grass roots budgeting*. (17)

Payback One method of assessing capital investment projects using the rationale that there is a positive relationship between the speed of payback and the rate of return. (16)

Payback Period The time required to recoup an investment from the cash flows from the project. (16)

Payback Reciprocal One divided by the payback period in years. (16)

Payoff The value of each outcome. (26)

Perfect Information Information that predicts with complete accuracy the outcome that will occur from a decision. (26)

Period Costs Costs that can be attributed to time intervals. (2, 9)

Periodic Inventory A method of inventory accounting whereby inventory balances are determined on specific dates (such as quarterly) by physical count rather than on a continuous basis. (3)

Perpetual Inventory A method of accounting whereby inventory records are maintained on a continuously updated basis. (3)

Physical Quantities Method Joint cost allocation based on measurement of the volume, weight, or other physical measure of the joint products at the split-off point. (8)

Planned Variance Variances that are expected to arise if certain conditions affect operations. (19)

Planning Budget Another term for master budget. (17, 18)

Plantwide Allocation Method This method uses one cost pool for the entire plant, and a single allocation rate or set of rates for the entire plant. Contrast this method with *Department Allocation Method*. (7)

Posterior Probabilities The probabilities obtained as a result of revising prior probabilities with additional conditional probability data. (26)

Predetermined Overhead Rate An amount obtained by dividing total estimated overhead for the coming period by the total overhead allocation base for the coming period. It is used for applying overhead to cost objects in normal or standard cost systems. (3, 9)

Predictors The variables on the right-hand side of a regression equation (the X-terms) used to predict costs or a similar dependent variable. They are cost drivers that are expected to affect costs. (10)

Present Value The amount of future cash flows discounted to their equivalent worth today. (15)

Price Discrimination Sale of products or services at different prices when the different prices do not reflect differences in marginal costs. (12)

Price Variance Difference between actual and budgeted or standard prices. See *Sales Price Variance* when the price variance applies to sales. (18, 19)

Prime Cost The sum of direct materials and direct labor. (2)

Principal-Agent Relationships The relationship between a superior, referred to as the *principal,* and a subordinate, called the *agent*. (22)

Prior Department Costs Costs incurred in an upstream department and charged to a subsequent department in the production process. (4)

Prior Probabilities (Priors) Initial probability estimates. (26)

Probabilities Likelihoods that given outcomes will, in fact, occur. (26)

Process Costing An accounting system that is used when identical units are produced through an ongoing series of uniform production steps. Used in continuous processing production settings. (4)

Product-Choice Decisions The product-choice problem arises when there are limited amounts of resources that are being fully used and must be allocated to multiple products. The decision is to choose the optimal product mix. (13)

Product Costs Those costs that can be attributed to products; costs that are part of inventory. For a manufacturer, they include direct materials, direct labor, and manufacturing overhead. The fixed manufacturing costs attributed to products differ under the variable costing and the full-absorption costing systems. (2, 9)

Product Mix A combination of outputs to be produced within the resource constraints of an entity. (11, 13)

Production Budget Production plan of resources needed to meet current sales demand and ensure inventory levels are sufficient for future sales. (17)

Production Cost Report A report that summarizes production and cost results for a period. This report is generally used by managers to monitor production and cost flows. (4)

Production Departments Departments in service, merchandising, or manufacturing organizations that generate goods or services that are ultimately sold to outsiders. (6)

Production Mix Variance A variance arising from a change in the relative proportion of inputs (a materials or labor mix variance). (21)

Production Volume Variance A fixed cost variance caused by a difference between the actual and estimated volume used to estimate unit fixed costs. (3, 19, 20)

Production Yield Variance Difference between expected and actual inputs required to produce a given level of output. (21)

Profit Center An organizational unit responsible for profits; usually responsible for revenues, costs, production, and sales volumes. (18, 22)

Profit Equation Operating profits equal total contribution margin less fixed costs. (11)

Profit Plan The income statement portion of the master budget. (17)

Profit Variance Analysis Analysis of the causes of differences between budgeted profits and the actual profits earned. (18)

Profit-Volume Analysis A version of CVP analysis where the cost and revenue lines are collapsed into a single profit line. See *Cost-Volume-Profit Analysis*. (11)

Project A complex job that often takes months or years to complete and requires the work of many different departments, divisions, or subcontractors. (3)

Prorated Overhead Variance Assigning portions of overapplied or underapplied manufacturing overhead to goods in inventory and goods sold. (3)

Prorating Variances Assigning portions of variances to the inventory and cost of goods sold accounts to which the variances are related. (3, 20)

Purchase Price Variance The price variance based on the quantity of materials purchased. (19)

Quantity Discounts Price reductions offered for bulk purchases. (14)

Random Event An occurrence that is beyond the control of the decision maker or manager. (25)

Raw Materials An alternative term for direct materials. (2, 3)

Real Discount Rate The discount rate that compensates only for the use of money, not for inflation. (15)

Real Dollars Monetary measures that are adjusted for the effects of inflation so they have the same purchasing power over time. (15)

Real Return Return on capital after adjustment for the effects of inflation. (15)

Reciprocal Allocation The method of allocating service department costs that recognizes services provided to and from other service departments. (6)

Regression Statistical procedure to determine the relationship between variables. (10)

Relative Sales Value Method See *Net Realizable Method.* (8)

Relevant Costs Costs that are different under alternative actions. (12)

Relevant Range The activity levels within which a given fixed cost will be unchanged even though volume changes. (2, 11)

Reorder Point The quantity of inventory on hand that triggers the need to order more inventory. (14)

Repetitive Manufacturing Production process characterized by long production runs, few products, and infrequent production line changes.

Replacement Method Joint cost allocation based on the change in cost arising from a change in the mix of outputs. (8)

Residual Income Investment center profit minus (capital charge times investment center assets). (22)

Responsibility Accounting Reporting financial results for each responsibility center (for example, profits for a profit center, costs for a cost center). (22)

Responsibility Center An organizational unit assigned to a manager who is held accountable for its operations and resources. (1, 18, 22)

Return on Investment (ROI) The ratio of profits to investment in the assets that generate those profits. (22)

Revenue Center An organizational unit responsible for revenues and, typically, also for marketing costs. (22)

Revenue Variances Variances in prices and activity that affect sales or other revenues. (21)

Risk Premium Additional interest or other compensation required for risks in investments. (15, 16)

Safety Stock Inventory carried to protect against delays in delivery, increased demand, or other similar factors. (14)

Sales Activity Variance Variance due to difference between budgeted and actual volume of sales. (18, 21)

Sales Forecasts Estimates of future sales. (17)

Sales Mix Variance Variance arising from the relative proportion of different products sold. (21)

Sales Price Variance Difference between budgeted and actual sales price. (18)

Sales Quantity Variance In multiproduct companies, a variance arising from the change in volume of sales, independent of any change in mix. (21)

Sales Volume Variance See *Sales Activity Variance.*

Scattergraph A plot of costs against past activity levels; sometimes used as a rough guide for cost estimation. (10)

Sensitivity Analysis The study of the effect of changes in assumptions on the results of a decision model. (17)

Serial Correlation In regression, the condition of a systematic relationship between the residuals in the equation. Sometimes referred to as *autocorrelation.* (10)

Service Department An organizational unit whose main job is to provide services to other units in the organization. (6)

Service Organizations Organizations whose output product is a result of the performance of some activity rather than some physical product.

Shadow Price Opportunity cost of an additional unit in a constrained multiple product setting. (13)

Short Run Period of time over which capacity will be unchanged. (12)

Sigma Standard deviation. (25)

Simplex Method Solution of a linear programming problem using a mathematical technique. (13)

Simulation See *Monte Carlo Simulation.*

Simultaneous Solution Method See *Reciprocal Allocation.*

Slope of Cost Line The angle of a line to the horizontal axis. In cost estimation, the slope is usually considered the variable cost estimate. (10)

Source Document A basic record in accounting that initiates the entry of an activity in the accounting system. (3)

Special Order An order that will not affect other sales and is usually a short-run occurrence. (12)

Spending Variance Difference between actual and standard or budgeted overhead costs. (3, 19)

Split-Off Point Stage of processing where two or more products are separated. (8)

Spoilage Goods that are damaged, do not meet specifications, or are otherwise not suitable for further processing or sale as good output. (5)

Staff A corporate group or employee with specialized technical skills, such as accounting or legal staff.

Standard Cost The anticipated cost of producing and/or selling a unit of output. (19, 20)

Standard Cost Center An organizational unit where managers are held responsible for costs and where the relationship between costs and output is well defined. See *Cost Center*. (22)

Standard Cost System An accounting system in which products are costed using standard costs instead of actual costs. (20)

Standard Costing A method of accounting whereby costs are assigned to cost objects at predetermined amounts. (20)

Standard Deviation A measure of risk based on dispersion. It is computed as the square root of the sum of the squared differences between actual observations and the mean of the data series divided by one less than the number of observations. (25)

Static Budget Budget for a single activity level. Usually the master budget. (18)

Statistical Quality Control A method for evaluating a repetitive process to determine if the process is out of control. (25)

Step Method The method of service department cost allocation that recognizes some interservice department services. (6)

Stockout Running out of inventory. (14)

Strategic Long-Range Plan Statement detailing specific steps to be taken in achieving a company's organizational goals. (17)

Sunk Cost An expenditure made in the past that cannot be changed by present or future decisions. (2, 12)

t-Statistic t is equal to the coefficient b divided by its standard error. (10)

Tax Basis Remaining tax-depreciable "book value" of an asset for tax purposes. (15)

Tax Credit Recapture Recapture of investment tax credit taken on an asset if the asset is taken out of service before the time required to earn the investment tax credit.

Tax Shield The reduction in tax payment because of depreciation deducted for tax purposes. (15)

Time Value of Money The concept that cash received earlier is worth more than cash received later. (15)

Total Cost Variance Difference between total actual costs for the time period and the standard allowed per unit times the number of good units produced. (19)

Total Manufacturing Costs Total costs charged to work in process in a given period. (3)

Total Quality Management A method of management

such that the organization is managed to excel on all dimensions and customers ultimately define quality. (1)

Transfer Price The price at which goods or services are traded between organizational units. (23)

Transferred-in Costs An alternative term for prior department costs. (4)

Transportation-in Costs The costs incurred by the buyer of goods to ship those goods from the place of sale to the place where the buyer can use the goods.

Treasurer The corporate officer responsible for cash management and financing corporate activities. (1)

Trend Analysis Method of forecasting that ranges from simple visual extrapolation of points on a graph to highly sophisticated computerized time series analysis. (17)

Underapplied Overhead The excess of actual overhead over applied overhead in a period. (3)

Unfavorable Variances Variances that, taken alone, reduce the operating profit or net income. (18)

Upper Control Limit The maximum value that may be observed and still assume that a process is in control. (25)

Usage Variance An alternative term for efficiency variance, usually related to materials used. (19)

User Department A department that uses the services of service departments. (6)

Value of Information Value placed on information one could obtain in a decision-making context. (26)

Variable Cost Ratio Variable costs as a percentage of sales-dollars. (11)

Variable Costing A system of accounting for costs that assigns products with only the variable costs of manufacturing. (2, 9)

Variable Costs Costs that change with a change in volume of activity. (2, 9, 10, 11, 12, 18, 19)

Variance Investigation The expected step taken if managers judge that the benefits of correction exceed the costs of follow-up. (19, 25)

Variances Differences between planned results and actual outcomes. (3, 18, 19, 20, 21)

Weighted-Average Contribution Margin The contribution margin of more than one product when a constant product mix is assumed. (11)

Weighted-Average Costing The inventory method that combines costs and equivalent units of a period with the costs and equivalent units in beginning inventory for product-costing purposes. (4)

Work in Process Uncompleted work on the production line. (3)

Working Capital Cash, accounts receivable, and other short-term assets required to maintain an activity. (15)

X-Terms The terms on the right-hand side of a regression